# OURSELVES
# AMONG OTHERS

*Cross-Cultural Readings
for Writers*

# OURSELVES AMONG OTHERS

*Cross-Cultural Readings for Writers*

Third Edition

BY

Carol J. Verburg

Bedford Books *of* St. Martin's Press · Boston

*Dedicated to the memory of my parents,*
*Robert M. and Jane H. Verburg*

**For Bedford Books**
*Publisher:* Charles H. Christensen
*Associate Publisher/General Manager:* Joan E. Feinberg
*Managing Editor:* Elizabeth M. Schaaf
*Developmental Editor:* Karen S. Henry
*Production Editor:* Michelle McSweeney
*Text Design:* Anna Post-George
*Cover Design:* Hannus Design Associates
*Cover Art:* Jacob Lawrence, *Bumbershoot*, 1976. Photograph courtesy of the Seattle
Arts Commission through the cooperation of the Francine Seders Gallery.
*Map Design:* Richard D. Pusey

Library of Congress Catalog Card Number: 92–85307

Manufactured in the United States of America.
8   7   6   5   4
f   e   d   c   b   a

*For information, write:* St. Martin's Press, Inc.
175 Fifth Avenue, New York, NY 10010

*Editorial Offices:* Bedford Books *of* St. Martin's Press
29 Winchester Street, Boston, MA 02116

ISBN: 0–312–08677–6

## ACKNOWLEDGMENTS

David Abram, "Making Magic," *Parabola*, August 1982. Reprinted by permission of the author.
Chinua Achebe, "Civil Peace" from *Girls at War and Other Stories* by Chinua Achebe. Copyright
   © 1972, 1973 by Chinua Achebe. Used by permission of Doubleday, a division of Bantam
   Doubleday Dell Publishing Group, Inc.

*Acknowledgments and copyrights are continued at the back of the book on pages 725–730, which*
*constitute an extension of the copyright page.*

# PREFACE
# FOR INSTRUCTORS

Every daily paper and nightly newscast reminds us how interdependent we in the United States are with our worldwide neighbors. Look at recent debates over our country's responsibility in relation to Bosnia, Somalia, the Middle East, or South Africa and you see urgent reasons for encouraging college students to become better informed about our "global village." Yet most freshmen arrive on campus with alarmingly little knowledge about foreign politics, geography, culture, or literature.

Many teachers believe (as I do) that much of the best writing today is being done outside the United States. When I started work on the first edition of *Ourselves Among Others* nearly a decade ago, some teachers already had made the same connection I had: We can kill two birds with one stone — broaden students' horizons and their familiarity with outstanding writing — by giving the freshman composition course a global focus. This idea has worked so well that *Ourselves Among Others* is now in its third edition, and several publishers have commissioned books in a similar vein.

The goals of *Ourselves Among Others* include supplying readers in this country with information they can use in writing about (and thus better understanding) the larger world; encouraging them to think, read, and write critically; and introducing them to the craft, imagination, and social consciousness of the best current foreign writers. Yet even to say "foreign" is to recall that many students have roots, experience, or both outside the United States. For them, *Ourselves Among Others* offers recognition, a chance to utilize knowledge that is too often undervalued or ignored. This recognition is reinforced by "Looking at Ourselves," sets of short comments and essays by diverse writers within this country that provide multicultural introductions to Parts 2 through 7.

*Ourselves Among Others* consists of seven thematic parts comprising fifty-one essays from all rhetorical categories and fourteen pieces of short fiction. (For an overview of each part's theme and contents, see the introduction on its opening page.) The book emphasizes insider accounts: selections that depict a culture from within, rather than from the "objective" viewpoint of a Western commentator. The authors are of both literary and political importance: Václav Havel, Nadine Gordimer, Nelson Mandela, Isabel Allende, Günter Grass, Gabriel García Márquez. Each part also includes at least one selection from and about the United States, by writers representing a range of subcultures: Ishmael Reed, Leslie Marmon Silko, Neil Postman, Amy Tan. These full-length pieces augment "Looking at Ourselves," which opens each part with shorter observations on the topic by U.S. writers.

The third edition has two completely new features and three noteworthy changes from the second edition. The first new feature is a brief introduction for students discussing the connection between cross-cultural reading and critical thinking (p. xix). The second is a set of critical thinking questions after each "Looking at Ourselves" section. Users of previous editions of this book know that its pedagogical apparatus always has emphasized the importance of reading, writing, and thinking critically; the new features make this focus more explicit. The third edition also contains more than 50 percent new selections, a change that reflects not only the political and geographical upheavals since the second edition but also an increase in the literature available in English translation. Examples include Eduard Shevardnadze's "Life with the Party," in which the former Soviet foreign minister (now president of Georgia) recalls his climb up the Communist career ladder, and Ken Bugul's "The Artist's Life in Brussels," which chronicles a young rural Senegalese woman's adventures in urban Europe. The "Looking at Ourselves" sections have been expanded in this edition, with more than 70 percent new contents and a number of longer passages to strengthen the book's representation of experience within the United States, particularly multicultural experience. For instance, Malcolm X and Joyce Carol Oates hail the power of reading (Part 3); Haunani-Kay Trask, Toni Morrison, and Jim Whitewolf look at tension between contrasting U.S. subcultures (Part 6); Joan Didion, George Will, and an anonymous looter comment on urban violence (Part 7). The titles of Parts 6 and 7 have been changed to reflect political shifts since the second edition. Thanks partly to the end of the Cold War, Part 6 now focuses less on ideology and more on the ground-level relationship between individuals and institutions. Part 7 considers not only war but all violence, including the internal forms that currently plague the United States.

To help students and instructors place each selection in context, extensive headnotes provide geographic, political, and historical background, as well as a biographical introduction to the author. (Some headnotes contain titles of foreign works with English translations in parentheses. When the translation is simply a literal one, the title is set in quotation marks. If the work has been published in an English translation, the title of the English publication is given in italic type.) A world map on the book's endpapers provides students with additional geographic assistance. As indicated, critical thinking questions called "Reflections" follow each "Looking at Ourselves" section. Three other kinds of questions follow each main selection: "Explorations," which focus on content, strategy, and craft; "Connections," which link this essay or story to others in the book; and "Elaborations," which guide students' writing in response to the selection. A note on translations (p. xxiii) compares three different renderings of the opening paragraph of Gholam-Hossein Sa'edi's story "The Game Is Over" from Farsi into English, demonstrating some of the obstacles to cross-cultural comprehension. An appendix (p. 723) provides supplementary information on the European Community and NATO.

The comprehensive instructor's manual has been prepared by two veteran composition instructors and users of previous editions of *Ourselves Among Others*, Alice Adams of Miami University (Ohio) and David Londow of Miami-Dade Community College. Thanks to both of them for their fine work, boosted by the efforts in past editions of Kathleen Shine Cain of Merrimack College and Marilyn Rye of Rutgers University. *Resources for Teaching Ourselves Among Others* offers practical advice on launching the course, sample syllabi, suggestions for teaching selections, suggested answers for the Explorations and Connections questions in the text, a rhetorical index to the selections, a chart listing rhetorical writing assignments, an index to headnote information, and a list of audiovisual resources.

## Acknowledgments

My thanks to the following instructors, who answered a detailed questionnaire about the second edition of the book, for their help in shaping this third edition: Randy Accetta, Humboldt State University; Dianne Armstrong, University of Southern California; Beverly Lynne Aronowitz, J. Sargent Reynolds Community College; Janice Aslanian, Kalamazoo Valley Community College; R. A. Beckham, Germanna Community College; Robert Boon, Columbia College; Phyllis N. Braxton, American University; Elizabeth Breau, Vanderbilt University; Vicki Collins, University of South Carolina; Angelo Costanzo, Shippensburg University; Karin Costello, Santa Monica College; Richard Courage, Westchester Community College; Norma Cruz-Gonzales, San Antonio College; Dr. Carmen

M. Decker, Cypress College; Virginia Denham, Missouri Southern State College; Steve Dennis, Northern Arizona University; Patricia A. D'itri, Michigan State University; Marci Douglas, Gavilan College; Jane Dresser, Portland State University; Marie Eichler, University of California, Irvine; Toni Empringham, El Camino College; Sheela S. Eswara, Maryville University; Joanne Ferreira, State University of New York College at New Paltz; Michael Fukuchi, Barton College; Donald Gilzinger, Suffolk Community College; Jack Giordano, Bronx Community College; Irma Goldknopf, State University of New York College at New Paltz; Sally Griffith, Atlantic College; Sheila Gullickson, Moorehead State University; Jared Haynes, University of California, Davis; Marjorie Holcombe, Cabrillo College; Joan Holle, Bloomfield College; Shawn Holliday, Marshall University; Patricia Honda, Boston University; Carolina Hospital, Miami-Dade Community College; Susan Hoyne, Centralia College; Robert Jacklosky, Rutgers University, New Brunswick Campus; Fred Rue Jacobs, Bakersfield College; Beth Kalikoff, University of Puget Sound; Dr. William Keough, Fitchburg State College; Alice Trower Kirk, Western Oregon State College; Jan Luton, Teikyo Marycrest University; Dr. Phoebe A. Mainster, Wayne State University; Virginia Melton, College of St. Benedict; Elizabeth Miller, Wayne State University; Randa Minter, University of Louisville; Thomas Palakeel, University of North Dakota; Dr. Vera Piper, Erie Community College; Hazel Retzlaff, Moorehead State University; Michael Karl Ritchie, Arkansas Tech University; Anca Rosu, Rutgers University, New Brunswick Campus; Wendy Ryden, Montclair State College; Mary Margaret Salewic, George Washington University; Barbara Saunier, Grand Rapids Community College; Jan Z. Schmidt, State University of New York College at New Paltz; Scott E. Sciortino, Brandeis University; Sydney Sims, Moorpark College; Ken Smith, Rutgers University, New Brunswick Campus; Joan Spangler, California State University, Fullerton; John D. Stahl, Virginia Polytechnic Institute and State University; David Strong, Indiana University at Bloomington; Priscilla Underwood, Quinsigamond Community College; Bryan Willis, Centralia College; Steve Wilson, Southwest Texas State University; Diana Wolf, Clark University; Gary Wood, Portland State University.

Essential to the creation of *Ourselves Among Others*, Third Edition, were the staff of Bedford Books. Publisher Chuck Christensen continues to be a strong supporter of useful and innovative textbooks. My editor, Karen S. Henry, also a writer, supplied endless patience and imagination to this revision as to the previous one. Laura McCready, Beth Chapman, and Kim Chabot responded with creative thinking and hours of work to diverse obstacles along the way. Production editor Michelle McSweeney managed to get married without losing a beat during the production process, and to identify both problems and solutions with equal élan. Thanks also to production assistant Heidi Hood and permissions editor Jonathan Burns, and to my friend and favorite librarian, Noël Yount, for her free-lance help with headnote research.

Thanks most of all to the worldwide writers represented in *Ourselves Among Others*, many of whom make their creative contributions under harsher conditions than most of us in the United States can appreciate.

# CONTENTS

# INTRODUCTION FOR STUDENTS

## *Cross-Cultural Reading and Critical Thinking*

What will you gain from using this book?

If you make the effort to read these selections carefully and critically, you will come away with two useful assets: knowledge of a variety of people and situations you are likely to encounter in and out of college and ability to communicate effectively.

Both these accomplishments hinge on critical thinking. That is, as a reader, you play an active role: You evaluate what you read, and you respond to it. You do not take someone else's printed words at face value; rather, you examine the assumptions and biases behind those statements, the evidence on which assertions are based, the process by which conclusions are drawn, and the rhetorical and stylistic techniques used to make a case.

This book has several features designed to encourage critical thinking. First, as the term *cross-cultural* in the subtitle suggests, its contents come from countries beyond the United States. *Ourselves Among Others* is also *multicultural*, meaning that it includes writing from the diverse ethnic and social groups within the United States. The book consists of seven parts. The main selections in each part are essays and stories whose settings range from Argentina to Zimbabwe. Parts 2 through 7 open with a section called "Looking at Ourselves," which comprises shorter pieces by U.S. authors. These writers' ancestry may be European, African, Asian, American Indian, or some combination, and their religious, political, and personal orientations vary as well.

Cross-cultural and multicultural reading can strengthen your skills as a critical thinker by sharpening your awareness of the many perspectives in the world that contradict and complement your own. For instance: If you pass a woman on the street who is veiled in black from head to foot so that only her eyes are visible, what is your reaction? Do you speculate about her religious affiliation? Her devoutness? Her sexuality? Her views on female and male social roles? In "The Veil Does Not Prevent Women from Working" (p. 372), Miriam Cooke examines the contrasting assumptions made by Westerners and Arabs of different periods and nationalities about veiled Islamic women. In reading this work you can confront and clarify your own assumptions about the role of women in Islamic society and develop those assumptions into knowledge grounded in facts, not stereotypes.

The first part of *Ourselves Among Others* specifically compares our habits of thought in the United States with those of other cultures. In "The West and the World," writers from France, Mexico, South Africa, and elsewhere consider the question posed here at home by Ishmael Reed: "What's American about America?" These authors also discuss what qualities differentiate Western from non-Western culture and what impact the United States and the West have had on the rest of the world. If you listen closely to their voices and views, you may be surprised by the ideas we in this country take for granted that are not shared beyond our borders. You may even find yourself questioning some of the voices and views you have heard around you all your life.

The other six parts of this book center on themes such as the family, work, and violence. Each part opens with "Looking at Ourselves," comments by writers from various subcultures within the United States. Some names will be familiar to you: Malcolm X, John Updike, Joyce Carol Oates, Vladimir Nabokov, Toni Morrison. Others probably are unfamiliar: Jim Whitewolf, Haunani-Kay Trask, Bernard Cooper, Rose Weitz. These authors present their distinctive ideas on the topic at hand; many of them also dispute ideas held by other Americans. Compare, for instance, Whitewolf's description of a Kiowa Apache peyote ceremony with Richard Rodriguez's memories of a Roman Catholic mass. Again, as you evaluate what these writers have to say, you may discover unexpected assumptions behind your own point of view.

To help you sharpen your critical thinking skills, questions at the end of each section of the book encourage you to examine, analyze, and evaluate what you have read. "Reflections" focus on views from the United States expressed in "Looking at Ourselves." "Explorations," after each main selection, ask you to look closely at the writer's arguments, biases, hidden assumptions, supporting evidence, stylistic techniques, and other tools and tactics. "Connections" relate an essay or a story to others in the book with similar or contrasting elements. For example, by comparing what Ishmael Reed has to say about the United States as a "cultural bouillabaisse" with Paul Harrison's concern that the world has become a melting pot, you can gain a new appreciation of the facts — and the complexity — behind popular concepts such as *multiculturalism* and *diversity*. "Elaborations" suggest ways you can use the readings as a basis or starting point for writing an essay of your own. The questions also ask you to think critically about your process of reaching an answer: How do you know? On what evidence do you base your conclusions?

The prospect of pushing your mind in this way may seem daunting at first — like learning a new language or navigating in a strange city. The rewards are worth the work. Once you master the foreign vocabulary and constructions for Spanish or Japanese, you can converse with a whole new assortment of people. Once you know your way around the Paris Métro or the streets of Hong Kong, you can find restaurants, museums, shops, and parks. Critical thinking, too, is a mental challenge that takes effort at the beginning but opens up a world of new experiences and insights once you develop the habit.

# A NOTE
# ON TRANSLATIONS

The three excerpts that follow come from different English translations of the same Iranian short story, originally written in Farsi. As you compare them, keep an eye out for differences and also for unexpected similarities. What do you learn from these passages about the choices a translator must make?

## 1

Hasani himself told me. He said, "Let's go over to my place tonight." I'd never been to their place, nor had he to mine; that is, I'd always been too afraid of what my father would do to ask him over, and he, he too, feared his father. But that night being unlike other nights, I couldn't get out of it; Hasani was mad at me, he imagined I no longer liked him, I wasn't his friend — so I went; it was the first time I had set foot in his place. We always ran into each other outdoors; mornings I would go by his little shanty and would whistle loud like a bulbul,[1] with a pretty bulbul's whistle that he himself had taught me. And so, it was as if I had whistled, "Come on, Hasani, it's time to get going." Hasani would pick up a can and come out. Instead of saying Hi, we would box with each other a bit, with firm, respectable punches that hurt. So had we arranged — whenever we would see each other, whenever we would part, we would box. Unless we were angry with one another, or we had cheated each other.

> – "The Game Is Over"
> Gholamhosein Saedi
> Translated by Robert A. Campbell (1978)

---

[1] A Persian songbird, probably a nightingale, frequently mentioned in poetry. — ED.

# 2

Hasani himself asked me. He asked me to go to their hut that evening. I had never gone to their hut. He had never come to ours. I'd never asked him to, because I was scared of my pa. He was scared of his pa, too — a lot more than I was of mine. But that evening was different. I had to go. Hasani would feel hurt and get angry at me if I didn't. He would think I didn't like him anymore and wasn't his friend. That's why I went. That was the first time I set foot in their hut. We always met outside. Our huts were in a cluster of squatters' huts. I'd stop by their hut in the morning and whistle — a pretty whistle he had taught me. This was our signal. It was like saying, "Come Hasani! Time to go to work." Hasani would pick up his bucket and come out of the hut. Instead of saying hello, we would fistfight for a spell — nice, hard blows that hurt really good. We fistfought when we met, and we fistfought when we parted — except when we were mad at each other for some reason.

> – "The Game Is Up"
> Ghulamhusayn Sa'idi
> Translated by Minoo S. Southgate (1980)

# 3

Hasani said it to me himself: "Let's go over to my place tonight." I'd never been to their place. He'd never been to mine. What I'm getting at is, we were always too afraid of our fathers. He was a lot more afraid than I was. But that night it was different: Hasani was mad at me. He imagined that I didn't like him anymore, that I wasn't his friend. So we went. Usually we just met each other outside. In the morning I would go to their little shack and give a long-drawn-out whistle that Hasani had taught me. When I whistled, Hasani would grab a can and come out. Instead of saying "Hi," we would fight a little. We would hit each other hard so it hurt. That's how we'd decided to behave, and whenever we met, or whenever we left each other, we would fight like that — unless we were either angry or had tricked each other.

> – "The Game Is Over"
> Gholam-Hossein Sa'edi
> Translated by Robert Campbell (1981)

What structural differences do you notice in these three translations?

What contrasts in emphasis can you identify? What ideas are condensed in one version and spelled out in another?

Which passages in each one do you think are more successful than in the other two? Which translation do you like best and why?

# OURSELVES
# AMONG OTHERS

*Cross-Cultural Readings
for Writers*

# PART ONE

# THE WEST
# AND THE WORLD

◇◇◇◇◇

Ishmael Reed, *What's American About America?*
(UNITED STATES)

Raymonde Carroll, *Money and Seduction*
(FRANCE/UNITED STATES)

Octavio Paz, *Hygiene and Repression* (MEXICO/UNITED STATES)

Gish Jen, *Helen in America* (CHINA/UNITED STATES)

Margaret Atwood, *A View from Canada*
(CANADA/UNITED STATES)

Es'kia Mphahlele, *Tradition and the African Writer*
(SOUTH AFRICA/THE WEST)

Paul Harrison, *The Westernization of the World*

V. S. Naipaul, *Entering the New World*
(IVORY COAST/THE WEST)

Patrick Smith, *Nippon Challenge* (UNITED STATES/JAPAN)

"OH, EAST IS EAST, AND WEST IS WEST, AND NEVER THE TWAIN SHALL meet," wrote Rudyard Kipling in 1889. *East* for Kipling and his fellow Britons meant colonies such as India, Egypt, and Hong Kong. *West* was home — Europe, England, the hub of civilization.

Now, most European colonies are independent nations. Indeed, one former colony — the United States — epitomizes the West. As expanding political, economic, technological, and even recreational networks shrink the globe, Westerners can no longer cling to the old fantasy that we define civilization. Instead, we are discovering that every culture has something to teach us. Yet our first response to foreign customs and ideas may not be appreciation but alienation. Like us, the people we meet take their superiority for granted. To most of the world's inhabitants, we, not they, are the foreigners.

Part One looks at the West in general and the United States in particular, first from the inside and then from various viewpoints around the globe. In "What's American About America?" Ishmael Reed holds up a mirror: Is the United States a melting pot, where diverse traditions blend into one, or a "cultural bouillabaisse," in which each ingredient contributes a distinct flavor? Raymonde Carroll's "Money and Seduction" contrasts taboos in the United States and France. Octavio Paz turns food into a social and political metaphor, casting an ironic eye northward from Mexico in "Hygiene and Repression." Gish Jen's short story "Helen in America" shows us New York City and its inhabitants as seen by the Changs, immigrants from China. In "A View from Canada," Margaret Atwood comments on the unequal relationship between her country and its southern neighbor. The South African writer Es'kia Mphahlele looks inward at the tension created by contrasting cultural pressures in "Tradition and the African Writer." An overall assessment of the West's impact on other countries is offered by Paul Harrison in "The Westernization of the World." V. S. Naipaul, a native of Trinidad, watches the balance tilt between the Ivory Coast's African heritage and its French colonial legacy in "Entering the New World." Finally, Patrick Smith follows a Japanese sailing syndicate trying to enter the new world of America's Cup racing in "Nippon Challenge." ◈

# ISHMAEL REED

## *What's American About America?*

The African-American novelist, poet, editor, and essayist Ishmael Reed was born in 1938 in Chattanooga, Tennessee. Known for his satiric wit, Reed abolishes time and rearranges history in his novels to create and revive a special kind of black folklore that includes magic and voodoo. With the aesthetic he calls "Neo-HooDoo" he has parodied genre fiction such as westerns and mysteries. *Flight to Canada* (1976) is a farcical treatment of slavery; *Japanese by Spring* (1993) satirizes academic posturing over multiculturalism, among other issues. Besides editing and publishing several volumes of poetry and essays, Reed has produced a video soap opera and founded a publishing company devoted to the work of unknown ethnic artists. He is currently a senior lecturer at the University of California, Berkeley. "What's American About America?" is reprinted from the March-April 1989 *Utne Reader*. A longer version originally appeared in Reed's *Writin' Is Fightin'* (1983).

As Reed suggests in this essay, the United States is not the WASP (white Anglo-Saxon Protestant) society of Norman Rockwell paintings. Indeed, white Americans may become a minority in the twenty-first century. Census statistics show that already one out of four Americans is nonwhite or Hispanic. Immigration and birth rates indicate that by the year 2000, the collective population of Hispanics, Asians, and blacks will have doubled, while the white population will have increased by only a few percent. In some parts of the country — California schools, for example — a nonwhite majority is already a reality. As more and more Americans recognize the diversity of our population and heritage, questions such as What language do we speak? What holidays do we observe? and Who are our heroes? challenge the Anglo-Saxon bias in our culture.

An item from the *New York Times*, June 23, 1983: "At the annual Lower East Side Jewish Festival yesterday, a Chinese woman ate a pizza slice in front of Ty Thuan Duc's Vietnamese grocery store. Beside her a Spanish-speaking family patronized a cart with two signs: 'Italian Ices' and 'Kosher by Rabbi Alper.' And after the pastrami ran out, everybody ate knishes."

On the day before Memorial Day, 1983, a poet called me to describe a city he had just visited. He said that one section included mosques, built by the Islamic people who dwelled there. Attending his reading, he said, were large numbers of Hispanic people, 40,000 of whom lived in the same city. He was not talking about a fabled city located in some mysterious region of the world. The city he'd visited was Detroit.

A few months before, as I was visiting Texas, I heard the taped voice used to guide passengers to their connections at the Dallas Airport announcing items in both Spanish and English. This trend is likely to continue; after all, for some southwestern states like Texas, where the largest minority is now Mexican-American, Spanish was the first written language and the Spanish style lives on in the western way of life.

Shortly after my Texas trip, I sat in a campus auditorium at the University of Wisconsin at Milwaukee as a Yale professor — whose original work on the influence of African cultures upon those of the Americas has led to his ostracism from some intellectual circles — walked up and down the aisle like an old-time Southern evangelist, dancing and drumming the top of the lectern, illustrating his points before some Afro-American intellectuals and artists who cheered and applauded his performance. The professor was "white." After his lecture, he conversed with a group of Milwaukeeans — all of whom spoke Yoruban, though only the professor had ever traveled to Africa.

One of the artists there told me that his paintings, which included   5
African and Afro-American mythological symbols and imagery, were hanging in the local McDonald's restaurant. The next day I went to McDonald's and snapped pictures of smiling youngsters eating hamburgers below paintings that could grace the walls of any of the country's leading museums. The manager of the local McDonald's said, "I don't know what you boys are doing, but I like it," as he commissioned the local painters to exhibit in his restaurant.

Such blurring of cultural styles occurs in everyday life in the United States to a greater extent than anyone can imagine. The result is what the above-mentioned Yale professor, Robert Thompson, referred to as a cultural bouillabaisse. Yet members of the nation's present educational and cultural elect still cling to the notion that the United States belongs to some vaguely defined entity they refer to as "Western civilization," by which they mean, presumably, a civilization created by people of Europe, as if Europe can even be viewed in monolithic terms. Is Beethoven's Ninth Symphony, which includes Turkish marches, a part of Western civilization? Or the late-nineteenth- and twentieth-century French paintings, whose creators were influenced by Japanese art? And what of the cubists, through whom the influence of African art changed modern painting? Or the surrealists, who were so impressed with the art of the Pacific Northwest Indians that, in their map of North America, Alaska dwarfs the lower forty-eight states in size?

Are the Russians, who are often criticized for their adoption of "Western" ways by Tsarist dissidents in exile, members of Western civilization? And what of the millions of Europeans who have black African and Asian ancestry, black Africans having occupied several European countries for hundreds of years? Are these "Europeans" a part of Western civilization? Or the Hungarians, who originated across the Urals in a place called Greater Hungary? Or the Irish, who came from the Iberian Peninsula?

Even the notion that North America is part of Western civilization because our "system of government" is derived from Europe is being challenged by Native American historians who say that the founding fathers, Benjamin Franklin especially, were actually influenced by the system of government that had been adopted by the Iroquois hundreds of years prior to the arrival of Europeans.

Western civilization, then, becomes another confusing category — like Third World, or Judeo-Christian culture — as humanity attempts to impose its small-screen view of political and cultural reality upon a complex world. Our most publicized novelist recently said that Western civilization was the greatest achievement of mankind — an attitude that flourishes on the street level as scribbles in public restrooms: "White Power," "Niggers and Spics Suck," or "Hitler was a prophet." Where did such an attitude, which has caused so much misery and depression in our national life, which has tainted even our noblest achievements, begin? An attitude that caused the incarceration of Japanese-American citizens during World War II, the persecution of Chicanos and Chinese Americans, the near-extermination of the Indians, and the murder and lynchings of thousands of Afro-Americans.

The Puritans of New England are idealized in our schoolbooks as the     10 first Americans, "a hardy band" of no-nonsense patriarchs whose discipline razed the forest and brought order to the New World (a term that annoys Native American historians). Industrious, responsible, it was their "Yankee ingenuity" and practicality that created the work ethic.

The Puritans, however, had a mean streak. They hated the theater and banned Christmas. They punished people in a cruel and inhuman manner. They killed children who disobeyed their parents. They exterminated the Indians, who had taught them how to survive in a world unknown to them. And their encounter with calypso culture, in the form of a servant from Barbados working in a Salem minister's household, resulted in the witchcraft hysteria.

The Puritan legacy of hard work and meticulous accounting led to the establishment of a great industrial society, but there was the other side — the strange and paranoid attitudes of that society toward those different from the elect.

The cultural attitudes of that early elect continue to be voiced in everyday life in the United States: the president of a distinguished university, writing a letter to the *Times*, belittling the study of African civilizations; the television network that promoted its show on Vatican art with the boast that this art represented "the finest achievements of the human spirit."

When I heard a schoolteacher warn the other night about the invasion of the American educational system by foreign curricula, I wanted to yell at the television set, "Lady, they're already here." It has already begun because the world is here. The world has been arriving at these shores for at least 10,000 years from Europe, Africa, and Asia. In the late nineteenth and early twentieth centuries, large numbers of Europeans arrived, adding their cultures to those of the European, African, and Asian settlers who were already here, and recently millions have been entering the country from South America and the Caribbean, making Robert Thompson's bouillabaisse richer and thicker.

North America deserves a more exciting destiny than as a repository    15
of "Western civilization." We can become a place where the cultures of the world crisscross. This is possible because the United States and Canada are unique in the world: The world is here.

## EXPLORATIONS

1. What are the defining qualities of a "cultural bouillabaisse" (para. 6)? How does this image of the United States differ from the frequently cited "melting pot"?

2. What reasons does Ishmael Reed give for disputing "the notion that the United States belongs to . . . 'Western civilization'" (para. 6)? What evidence does he give that "the nation's present educational and cultural elect still cling" to that notion? Do you think he needs more evidence for that accusation? Why or why not?

3. What is the thesis of Reed's essay? What recommendations does he make, and to whom?

## CONNECTIONS

1. Look at Paul Harrison's "The Westernization of the World" (p. 41). Harrison describes Western culture as spreading around the world and overwhelming traditional local customs and values. How does Harrison's concept of Western culture differ from Reed's? On what points do you think these two writers would agree?

2. On page 513, Toni Morrison writes in *Looking at Ourselves* about the influence of African-Americans on American literature. What are the similarities and differences between Morrison's views and Ishmael Reed's?

## ELABORATIONS

1. Write an essay comparing and contrasting these two concepts of the United States: a melting pot and a cultural bouillabaisse. In your opinion, which concept more accurately describes our culture, and why? Which one should we work to bring about, and why?

2. Using Reed's essay as a starting point, list as many elements or qualities as you can think of that (1) European, (2) African, (3) Asian, and (4) Native American civilizations have contributed to our contemporary culture. Which contributions have stayed mostly within the original group? Which ones have spread? Write an essay defining "American culture" as it exists in the United States today, or classifying the elements that make it up.

# RAYMONDE CARROLL

## *Money and Seduction*

"When I meet someone from another culture, I behave in the way that is natural to me, while the other behaves in the way that is natural to him or her," writes Raymonde Carroll. "The only problem is that our natural ways do not coincide." Born in Tunisia, Carroll was educated in France and the United States. Her work as an anthropologist has taken her, among other places, to the Pacific atoll of Nukuoro, where she lived for three years and published *Nukuoro Stories* (1980). On her return, Carroll interviewed a wide variety of subjects in France and the United States for her book *Évidences Invisibles* (1987). "Money and Seduction," translated from the French by Carol Volk, comes from the conclusion of the American edition of this book, *Cultural Misunderstandings: The French-American Experience* (1988). A United States citizen, Carroll currently teaches at Oberlin College in Ohio, where she lives with her American husband.

Although France was settled by the Parisii in the third century B.C., the French celebrated their bicentennial in 1989. Bastille Day, July 14, marks the date in 1789 when outraged citizens stormed Paris's notorious Bastille prison and launched the Revolution, which ended nearly a thousand years of monarchy. King Louis XVI was beheaded by the guillotine in 1793, followed by his queen, the extravagant and unpopular Marie Antoinette. After a two-year orgy of executions and a short-lived republic, Napoleon Bonaparte ruled as emperor from 1804 to 1815. After him came a series of republics and the brief Second Empire, culminating in the Fifth Republic, which holds power today. During World War II, France was occupied by Germany. Having accumulated worldwide colonies during the centuries of European expansion, France withdrew in the 1950s from Indochina, Morocco, and Tunisia, and subsequently from most of its other African territories. France also withdrew most of its troops in 1966 from the North Atlantic Treaty Organization (NATO). A founding member of the European Community (see Appendix, p. 723), France continues to play a significant political, economic, and cultural role in Europe and the world.

Money. For a French person, the face of an American could easily be replaced by a dollar sign. A sign of "incurable materialism," of arrogance, of power, of "vulgar," unrefined pleasure . . . the list goes on. I have never read a book about Americans, including those written with sympathy, which did not speak of the "almighty dollar"; I have never had or heard a conversation about Americans which did not mention money.

Foreigners often discover with "horror" or "repulsion" that "everything in the United States is a matter of money." Indeed, one need only read the newspapers to find constant references to the price of things. Thus, a fire is not a news item but an entity (natural or criminal), the dimensions of which are calculated by what it has destroyed — for example, ". . . a house worth two hundred *thousand* dollars . . ." In fact, if it is at all possible to attach a price to something, as approximate as it may be, that price will surely be mentioned. Thus, a French woman became indignant toward her American brother-in-law: "He showed us the engagement ring he had just bought, and he just had to give us all the details about the deal he got in buying the diamond. . . . Talk about romantic!" I cannot even count the number of informants who had similar stories to tell ("I was admiring the magnificent antique pieces in his living room, and do you know what he did? He gave me the price of each piece, with all kinds of details I hadn't asked for. I felt truly uncomfortable . . . really . . ."). Many French informants claimed to be shocked by the "constant showing off," the "lack of taste typical of nouveaux riches" and added, some not in so many words, "As for me, you know, I am truly repulsed by money."

On the other side, many Americans expressed surprise at the frequency with which French people spoke about money, only to say that "they weren't interested in it" ("so why talk about it?"), or at the frequency with which they say "it's too expensive" about all types of things. Some find the French to be "cheap" ("They always let you pay") or "hypocritical" ("Why, then, do the French sell arms to just anyone?"), too respectful of money to trifle with it, or too petty to take risks. The list of adjectives hurled from either side on this topic seems particularly long.

Yet a brief examination of certain ethnographic details left me puzzled. For instance, what is the American article, about the forest fire that destroyed the row of two-hundred-thousand-dollar homes in California, really saying? Living in the United States, I know that a house worth two hundred thousand dollars in California is far from a palace; on the contrary. Thus, if I took the price quoted literally, I would misinterpret the article as meaning that the fire had destroyed a row of quite ordinary houses — in which case the mention of the "price" is uninformative, uninteresting, and useless. Therefore, what this article conveys, by talking about hundreds of thousands of dollars, is the fact that the fire destroyed very valuable homes. This meaning is also conveyed by the use of the word "homes," which connotes individuality and uniqueness, rather than "houses," which suggests plain buildings. The mention of the price, therefore, carries meaning of a different nature: I think that this "price" serves only as a common point of reference; it does not represent the true monetary values but a symbolic value which can be grasped immediately by anyone reading this article. A French equivalent would be a reference to the period ("from the seventeenth century") with no mention of the state of the building.

Similarly, it is difficult to take the example of the engagement ring                5 literally ("I'm a tightwad"; "I'm not romantic"); it is more comprehensible if we interpret it as a message with a different meaning. For the American in question, having obtained a discount in no way altered the true value of the diamond or the symbolic value of the gesture; this "feat" probably made the gesture even more significant because of the time and attention devoted to it (the worst gift is the one that demands no effort) and probably earned him the admiration and appreciation of his fiancée.

The study of cases in which money is mentioned would require an entire book. . . . I will content myself merely with raising the question here and will indicate the general orientation of my interpretation.

The striking thing is that money is charged with a multiplicity of meanings in American culture, that it has attained a level of abstraction difficult to imagine elsewhere. Money represents both good and bad, dependence and independence, idealism and materialism, and the list of opposites can go on indefinitely, depending on whom one speaks to. It is power, it is weakness, seduction, oppression, liberation, a pure gamble, a high-risk sport; a sign of intelligence, a sign of love, a sign of scorn; able to be tamed, more dangerous than fire; it brings people together, it separates them, it is constructive, it is destructive; it is reassuring, it is anxiety-producing; it is enchanting, dazzling, frightening; it accumulates slowly or comes in a windfall; it is displayed, it is invisible; it is solid, it evaporates. It is everything and nothing, it is sheer magic, it exists and does not exist at the same time; it is a mystery. The subject provokes hatred, scorn, or impassioned defense from Americans themselves, who are constantly questioning themselves on the topic.

I believe that one association remains incontestable, no matter how much resentment it provokes. Money symbolizes success. It is not enough to have money to be admired, but quite the contrary; there is no excuse for the playboy who squanders an inherited fortune. To earn money, a lot of money, and to spend it, is to give the most concrete, the most visible sign that one has been able to realize one's potential, that one has not wasted the "opportunities" offered by one's parents or by society, and that one always seeks to move on, not to stagnate, to take up the challenge presented in the premises shaping the education of children. . . .

As a result, money has become a common denominator. It is supposed to be accessible to all, independent of one's origins. And if it creates classes, it also allows free access to those classes to whoever wants to enter. (Let's not forget that we are talking here about "local verities," about cultural premises, and not about social realities.) Money is therefore the great equalizer, in the sense that the highest social class is, in principle, open to everyone, and that while those who are born into this social class have definite advantages, they must nonetheless deserve to remain there, must "prove themselves." And the newspapers are filled with enough stories of poor people turned millionaires to reinforce this conviction.

From this perspective, it is understandable that one does not hide one's success but displays it, shows it off. By making my humble origins known, by displaying my success, I am not trying to humiliate others (although it is possible that I, personally, am a real "stinker"), but I am showing others that it is possible, I am encouraging emulation through example, I am reaffirming a cultural truth: "if I can do it, you can do it." Hence the constant copresence of dreams and success, that is to say, the constant reaffirmation that the impossible is possible, and that attaining the dream depends solely on me. The logical, and ironic, conclusion to all this is the essentially idealistic significance of money in American culture, which does not exclude its "materialistic" utilization.

I do not believe that the misunderstanding between the French and Americans concerning money can be resolved by performing a parallel analysis of the meaning of money in French culture, not because money is not a concern for the French, but because I believe that what Americans express through money is expressed by the French in another domain.

From this brief analysis, I will reiterate three points. The first is that money in America serves as a common point of reference, a shortcut for communication, a means of defining a context that is recognizable by all and comprehensible no matter what one's financial situation may be. The second is that it is not in bad taste to recount one's triumphs, one's success in this domain, whether it is a matter of having obtained a half-price diamond or of having accumulated a veritable fortune, insofar as this in no way implies that I wish to put down others, that I am conceited, and so on, characteristics which depend not on money but on my personality. And the third is that money is accessible to all, makes possible upward mobility, that is to say, access to any class.

To the extent that these three points I just made are not "true" for French culture — and that they might in fact provoke "real repulsion" — one must look in a realm other than that of money for what carries the same message. . . .

The repulsion with which many French people react to the "bad taste" of Americans who "brag about their wealth," "show off their money," and so on closely resembles the disgust with which many Americans speak of the "bad taste," the "vulgarity" of French people who "brag about their sexual exploits," "are proud of their sexual successes," which is a subject reserved by Americans for the "uncivilized" world of locker rooms, for the special and forced intimacy of these dressing rooms for athletes. (Although the expression "locker-room talk" traditionally evokes male conversation, it is just as applicable today to female locker-room talk.) The repugnance on the part of "tasteful" Americans to speak in public about their successes with men or women or their sexual "conquests" is interpreted, among the French, as additional proof of American "puritanism," whereas the French "modesty" concerning public conversations about money would tend to be interpreted by Americans as a type of French "puritanism."

This reciprocal accusation of "bad taste" led me to wonder if what was true for financial successes and conquests in American culture was not true for seduction, for amorous conquests, for sexual successes in French culture.

While it is not looked on favorably, in France, to show off one's money or titles, one may speak of one's amorous conquests without shocking anyone (unless one does it to belittle others with one's superiority, to insult them, etc., in which case it is not the subject that is important but the manner in which a particular person makes use of it). We have, in France, a great deal of indulgence and admiration for the "irresistible" man or woman, for "charmers" large and small of both cases. Seduction is an art which is learned and perfected.

Like money for Americans, amorous seduction is charged with a multiplicity of contradictory meanings for the French, depending on the person to whom one is speaking and the moment one raises the topic. Nonetheless, if a (French) newspaper article defines a particular person as *séduisante*, the term does not refer to indisputable characteristics but to a category recognizable by all, to a common point of reference, to a comprehensible descriptive shortcut. (It is interesting to note that the American translation of *séduisante* would be "attractive," a word which, as opposed to the French, evokes identifiable and predictable characteristics. The word *seductive* — not an adequate translation — evokes manipulation and the negative connotations attached to taking advantage of naiveté.)

Seduction, as I have said, is an art for the French. It is not enough to be handsome or beautiful to seduce; a certain intelligence and expertise are necessary, which can only be acquired through a long apprenticeship,

15

even if this apprenticeship begins in the most tender infancy. (Thus, an ad for baby clothing, a double spread in the French version of the magazine *Parents*, shows the perfect outfit for the "heartbreak girl" and for the "playboy"; this is an indication of the extent to which this quality is desirable, since I assume the ad is geared toward the parents who provide for and teach these babies, and not toward the babies themselves.) It is therefore "normal" for me to be proud of my successes, for me to continually take up the challenge of new conquests, for me never to rest on my laurels, for me not to waste my talent. It is therefore not in "bad taste" to talk about it (bad taste and seduction are, in a sense, mutually exclusive in French). What is more, I can "freely" share my secrets and my "reflections" on the subject of men or women — a topic I have thoroughly mastered.

Like money for Americans, seduction for the French may be the only true class equalizer. In fact, one of the greatest powers of amorous seduction is precisely the fact that it permits the transgression of class divisions. The French myths of the "kept woman," of the attractiveness of the *midinette* (a big-city shopgirl or office clerk, who is supposed to be very sentimental), of the seductive powers of "P'tit Louis" (a "hunk," a good dancer, from the working class), and the innumerable seducers of both sexes in French novels, songs, and films are sufficient proof.

The interest of a parallel such as the one I have just established is that    20
it shows how astonishingly similar meanings can be expressed in areas which seem to be completely unrelated. Yet the greatest attraction of cultural analysis, for me, is the possibility of replacing a dull exchange of invectives with an exploration that is, at the very least, fascinating — a true feast to which I hereby invite you.


## EXPLORATIONS

1. What is the thesis of Raymonde Carroll's essay? What are her main sources of information on American attitudes toward money? On French attitudes toward seduction? Is her evidence convincing? Why or why not?

2. In her last paragraph, what course of action or change of attitude or both is Carroll recommending? What is the effect of her phrasing her recommendations as an invitation?

3. Carroll uses the word *playboy* in paragraphs 8 and 18. What kind of person is the American playboy? The French playboy? On the basis of Carroll's essay, what would you expect a French and an American playboy to think of each other?

# CONNECTIONS

1. In paragraphs 7–10, Carroll describes the symbolic role of money in the United States. In what way(s) does her description suggest that all Americans are alike (the "melting pot" view)? In what way(s) does her description reflect the diversity noted by Ishmael Reed in "What's American About America?" (p. 3) (the "cultural bouillabaisse" view)?

2. In paragraph 19 Carroll writes: "Like money for Americans, seduction for the French may be the only true class equalizer." According to Ishmael Reed, what other differences besides class divide Americans into subgroups? The vast majority of French people are native-born white Roman Catholic French-speakers whose ancestors have lived there for centuries. How do you think historic and demographic factors may have influenced the contrasting roles of money and seduction in these two countries?

# ELABORATIONS

1. Carroll notes in paragraph 9 that her comments on money as "the great equalizer" refer to "cultural premises, and not . . . social realities." What does she mean by this? Write an essay defining or classifying the social role(s) of money in the United States. You may focus on the equalizing role that our culture wishes for money to play (its ideal role), or the limits on money's equalizing power (its real role), or both.

2. According to Carroll, money is openly discussed and used as a class equalizer in the United States, while seduction is a taboo topic. Do you agree? Why or why not? Write an essay stating and supporting your own view of the roles played in this country by money and seduction.

# OCTAVIO PAZ

## *Hygiene and Repression*

Although Octavio Paz is represented here by an essay, he is also known for his fiction, his art criticism, and most of all for his poetry. "Poetic activity is revolutionary by nature," he has written, "a means of interior liberation." Paz was born in Mexico City in 1914. Educated at a Roman Catholic school and the National University of Mexico, he founded an avant-garde literary journal at age seventeen; at nineteen he published his first book of poems. Four years later he went to Europe, where he supported the Republican side in the Spanish Civil War, established himself as a writer with another book of poems, and met prominent Surrealist poets in Paris. Back in Mexico Paz founded and edited several literary reviews, including the journal *Vuelta* ("Return"), which he started in 1976 and still publishes. In 1950 he produced his famous study of Mexican character and culture, *El laberinto de la soledad* (*The Labyrinth of Solitude*, 1961). After working for the Mexican embassies in Paris and Japan, Paz served as Mexico's ambassador to India from 1962 to 1968, resigning over Mexico's brutal treatment of student radicals. He has also lived in England, France, and the United States, where he taught at Harvard University and at the University of Texas. "Hygiene and Repression" comes from "At Table and in Bed," which he wrote at Harvard in 1971. Translated from the Spanish by Helen R. Lane, the essay appears in Paz's 1987 collection *Convergences: Essays on Art and Literature.* In 1990 Paz won the Nobel Prize for literature.

The United States' neighbor to the south has been populated since around 21,000 B.C. The great Olmec, Toltec, Mayan, and Aztec civilizations arose between A.D. 100 and A.D. 900. When Hernán Cortés and other explorers arrived from Spain in the 1500s, they conquered the ruling Aztecs and made Mexico a heavily exploited colony until a series of rebellions achieved independence in 1821. A republic was declared in 1823, followed by two emperors, several dictators, and a series of presidents. Although democracy has persisted, reform has progressed haltingly. "Mexico is a bureaucratic state halfway between capitalism and socialism," Octavio Paz has observed; "it is between democracy and dictatorship with a constitutional transfer of power, but also a president with absolute power and one-party rule." After an oil boom in the 1970s, Mexico's economy declined severely in the mid-1980s. Recently it has been improving, after years of stagnation, as wages, job opportunities, and exports increase; however, most of the rural and much of the urban population remains poor, so many workers seek jobs across the northern border. In the early 1990s, controversy arose over the North American

Free Trade Agreement, aimed at lifting economic barriers between Mexico, Canada, and the United States. Meanwhile, Mexico's folk art and fine art have both burgeoned: Writers such as Paz and Carlos Fuentes (see p. 303) are internationally regarded, as are a number of Mexican painters, composers, and other artists.

Traditional American cooking is a cuisine without mystery: simple, nourishing, scantily seasoned foods. No tricks: a carrot is a homely, honest carrot, a potato is not ashamed of its humble condition, and a steak is a big, bloody hunk of meat. This is a transubstantiation[1] of the democratic virtues of the Founding Fathers: a plain meal, one dish following another like the sensible, unaffected sentences of a virtuous discourse. Like the conversation among those at table, the relation between substances and flavors is direct: sauces that mask tastes, garnishes that entice the eye, condiments that confuse the taste buds are taboo. The separation of one food from another is analogous to the reserve that characterizes the relations between sexes, races, and classes. In our countries food is communion, not only between those together at table but between ingredients; Yankee food, impregnated with Puritanism, is based on exclusions. The maniacal preoccupation with the purity and origin of food products has its counterpart in racism and exclusivism. The American contradiction — a democratic universalism based on ethnic, cultural, religious, and sexual exclusions — is reflected in its cuisine. In this culinary tradition our fondness for dark, passionate stews such as moles, for thick and sumptuous red, green, and yellow sauces, would be scandalous, as would be the choice place at our table of *huitlacoche*, which not only is made from diseased young maize but is black in color. Likewise our love for hot peppers, ranging from parakeet green to ecclesiastical purple, and for ears of Indian corn, their grains varying from golden yellow to midnight blue. Colors as violent as their tastes. Americans adore fresh, delicate colors and flavors. Their cuisine is like watercolor painting or pastels.

American cooking shuns spices as it shuns the devil, but it wallows in slews of cream and butter. Orgies of sugar. Complementary opposites: the almost apostolic simplicity and soberness of lunch, in stark contrast to the suspiciously innocent, pregenital pleasures of ice cream and milkshakes. Two poles: the glass of milk and the glass of whiskey. The first affirms the primacy of home and mother. The virtues of the glass of milk are twofold: It is a wholesome food and it takes us back to childhood. . . . As for whiskey and gin, they are drinks for loners and introverts. For

---

[1]A change in form; usually refers to the Roman Catholic Eucharist's conversion of bread and wine into the body and blood of Christ. — ED.

Fourier,[2] Gastrosophy was the science of combining not only foods but guests at table: Matching the variety of dishes is the variety of persons sharing the meal. Wines, spirits, and liqueurs are the complement of a meal, hence their object is to stimulate the relations and unions consolidated round a table. Unlike wine, pulque, champagne, beer, and vodka, neither whiskey nor gin accompanies meals. Nor are they apéritifs or digestifs.[3] They are drinks that accentuate uncommunicativeness and unsociability. In a gastrosophic age they would not enjoy much of a reputation. The universal favor accorded them reveals the situation of our societies, ever wavering between promiscuous association and solitude.

Ambiguity and ambivalence are resources unknown to American cooking. Here, as in so many other things, it is the diametrical opposite of the extremely delicate French cuisine, based on nuances, variations, and modulations — transitions from one substance to another, from one flavor to another. In a sort of profane Eucharist, even a glass of water is transfigured into an erotic chalice:

> Ta lèvre contre le cristal
> Gorgée à gorgée y compose
> Le souvenir pourpre et vital
> De la moins éphémère rose.[4]

It is the contrary as well of Mexican and Hindu cuisine, whose secret is the shock of tastes: cool and piquant, salt and sweet, hot and tart, pungent and delicate. Desire is the active agent, the secret producer of changes, whether it be the transition from one flavor to another or the contrast between several. In gastronomy as in the erotic, it's desire that sets substances, bodies, and sensations in motion; this is the power that rules their conjunction, commingling, and transmutation. A reasonable cuisine, in which each substance is what it is and in which both variations and contrasts are avoided, is a cuisine that has excluded desire.

Pleasure is a notion (a sensation) absent from traditional Yankee cuisine. Not pleasure but health, not correspondence between savors but the satisfaction of a need — these are its two values. One is physical and the other moral; both are associated with the idea of the body as work. Work in turn is a concept at once economic and spiritual: production and redemption. We are condemned to labor, and food restores the body after the pain and punishment of work. It is a real *reparation*, in both the

---

[2]Charles Fourier (1772–1837), French philosopher and social theorist. — ED.
[3]Drinks served before or after a meal to whet the appetite or to aid digestion. — ED.
[4]Your lip against the crystal / Sip by sip forms therein / The vital deep crimson memory / Of the least ephemeral rose. — Stéphane Mallarmé, "Verre d'eau." (My translation — TRANS.)

physical and the moral sense. Through work the body pays its debt; by earning its physical sustenance, it also earns its spiritual recompense. Work redeems us and the sign of this redemption is food. An active sign in the spiritual economy of humanity, food restores the health of body and soul. If what we eat gives us physical and spiritual health, the exclusion of spices for moral and hygienic reasons is justified: They are the signs of desire, and they are difficult to digest.

Health is the condition of two activities of the body, work and sports.     5 In the first, the body is an agent that produces and at the same time redeems; in the second, the sign changes: Sports are a wasteful expenditure of energy. This is a contradiction in appearance only, since what we have here in reality is a system of communicating vessels. Sports are a physical expenditure that is precisely the contrary of what happens in sexual pleasure, since sports in the end become productive — an expenditure that produces health. Work in turn is an expenditure of energy that produces goods and thereby transforms biological life into social, economic, and moral life. There is, moreover, another connection between work and sports: Both take place within a context of rivalry; both are competition and emulation. . . . Sports possess the rigor and gravity of work, and work possesses the gratuity and levity of sports. The play element of work is one of the few features of American society that might have earned Fourier's praise, though doubtless he would have been horrified at the commercialization of sports. The preeminence of work and sports, activities necessarily excluding sexual pleasure, has the same significance as the exclusion of spices in cuisine. If gastronomy and eroticism are unions and conjunctions of substances and tastes or of bodies and sensations, it is evident that neither has been a central preoccupation of American society — as ideas and social values, I repeat, not as more or less secret realities. In the American tradition the body is not a source of pleasure but of health and work, in the material and the moral sense.

The cult of health manifests itself as an "ethic of hygiene." I use the word *ethic* because its prescriptions are at once physiological and moral. A despotic ethic: sexuality, work, sports, and even cuisine are its domains. Again, there is a dual concept: Hygiene governs both the corporeal and the moral life. Following the precepts of hygiene means obeying not only rules concerning physiology but also ethical principles: temperance, moderation, reserve. The morality of separation gives rise to the rules of hygiene, just as the aesthetics of fusion inspires the combinations of gastronomy and erotics. In India I frequently witnessed the obsession of Americans with hygiene. Their dread of contagion seemed to know no bounds; anything and everything might be laden with germs: food, drink, objects, people, the very air. These preoccupations are the precise counterpart of the ritual preoccupations of Brahmans fearing contact with certain foods and impure things, not to mention people belonging to a caste different from their own. Many will say that the concerns of the American are justified, whereas those of the Brahman are superstitions. Everything depends on the point of view: For the Brahman the bacteria that the American fears are illusory, while the moral stains produced by contact with alien people are real. These stains are stigmas that isolate him: No member of his caste would dare touch him until he had performed long and complicated rites of purification. The fear of social isolation is no less intense than that of illness. The hygienic taboo of the American and the ritual taboo of the Brahman have a common basis: the concern for purity. This basis is religious even though, in the case of hygiene, it is masked by the authority of science.

In the last analysis, the cult of hygiene is merely another expression of the principle underlying attitudes toward sports, work, cuisine, sex, and races. The other name of purity is separation. Although hygiene is a social morality based explicitly on science, its unconscious root is religious. Nonetheless, the form in which it expresses itself, and the justifications for it, are rational. In American society, unlike in ours, science from the very beginning has occupied a privileged place in the system of beliefs and values. The quarrel between faith and reason never took on the intensity that it assumed among Hispanic peoples. Ever since their birth as a nation, Americans have been modern; for them it is natural to believe in science, whereas for us this belief implies a negation of our past. The prestige of science in American public opinion is such that even political disputes frequently take on the form of scientific polemics. . . . Two recent examples are the racial question and the feminist movement: Are intellectual differences between races and sexes genetic in origin or a historico-cultural phenomenon?

The universality of science (or what passes for science) justifies the development and imposition of collective patterns of normality. Obviating[5] the necessity for direct coercion, the overlapping of science and Puritan morality permits the imposition of rules that condemn peculiarities, exceptions, and deviations in a manner no less categorical and implacable than religious anathemas. Against the excommunications of science, the individual has neither the religious recourse of abjuration nor the legal one of *habeas corpus*.[6] Although they masquerade as hygiene

---

[5]Removing, dispensing with. — ED.

[6]Paz is again using Roman Catholic imagery. Anathemas: taboos. Excommunication: expulsion from the Church. Abjuration: renouncing one's sin. *Habeas corpus* (Latin: "have the body"): a legal means of requiring that an imprisoned person be charged and tried for a crime. — ED.

and science, these patterns of normality have the same function in the realm of eroticism as "healthful" cuisine in the sphere of gastronomy: the extirpation or the separation of what is alien, different, ambiguous, impure. One and the same condemnation applies to blacks, Chicanos, sodomites, and spices.

## EXPLORATIONS

1. What does Octavio Paz mean by *hygiene*? Reread paragraphs 5–7. What examples can you give, besides those noted here, of "the obsession of Americans with hygiene"?

2. Does Paz regard the United States as a melting pot or a "cultural bouillabaisse"? What is his opinion of American cooking and culture? What specific words, similes, and metaphors reveal this opinion?

3. What terms with religious connotations does Paz use in this essay? What is the impact of his use of such terms?

4. Do you think Paz's assessment of American culture is fair? Exaggerated? Meant to be taken seriously? At what points does he use humor, and with what effect? Which of his tactics aim at his readers' emotions rather than their reason?

## CONNECTIONS

1. What comments in Raymonde Carroll's "Money and Seduction" (p. 8) suggest that she would agree with Paz's view of American puritanism? What similarities can you find in the Latin attitude toward Americans described by Paz and in the French attitude described by Carroll?

2. What statements by Ishmael Reed in "What's American About America?" (p. 3) contradict Paz's observations about American food? About American culture?

3. What words and statements in "Hygiene and Repression" and in Reed's "What's American About America?" paint a similar portrait of the early European settlers in the United States?

# ELABORATIONS

1. Does American (U.S.) cooking indeed hint at hygiene and repression, or is the diversity of our culture reflected in our cuisine? Write an essay classifying, defining, or describing the foods that you or your family eat, or that your school cafeteria or local restaurants serve, identifying the national origins of various dishes or ingredients.

2. Having read Paz's "Hygiene and Repression" and Carroll's "Money and Seduction," write an essay comparing and contrasting the social functions in American culture of money, sex, and food.

# GISH JEN

## *Helen in America*

Gish Jen's original first name was Lillian; an affinity with movie star Lillian Gish led to the switch. Born in 1955, she grew up in one of the few Asian-American families in Yonkers and then Scarsdale, New York. Although Jen was not much daunted by racism at the time, she later observed: "If you are a minority, you never know when the rug is going to be pulled out from under you — whether or not you have education, dignity, or accomplishment." Jen started writing as a Harvard University undergraduate. At her parents' urging she went on to study business at Stanford University, but she took off a year and a half to work at Doubleday Publishing Company and never returned to finish her degree. Instead she taught English in China, then earned her M.F.A. in the writing program at the University of Iowa. She has taught and lectured at Tufts University and the University of Massachusetts and now lives in Cambridge, Massachusetts. Jen's novel *Typical American*, from which "Helen in America" is excerpted, was published in 1991. In it, Jen uses italicized English for characters' conversations in Chinese.

The characters in "Helen in America" fled China after Communists led by Mao Zedong took control in 1949. Japan's defeat in World War II had ended its long effort to wrest China away from Nationalist forces led by General Chiang Kai-shek. Civil war followed between Chiang's Kuomintang government, backed by the United States, and Mao's Communist rebels, backed by the Soviet Union. The victorious Maoists forced the Kuomintang into exile on Taiwan and began restructuring China's economy on the Soviet model: Private property was turned over to collectives, and central planning replaced markets. In 1966 the decade-long Cultural Revolution began, glorifying workers, peasants, and soldiers and purging "bourgeois" intellectuals and officials — including Deng Xiaoping, who would become Mao's successor after his death in 1976. Today tight Communist political control continues: In the Spring of 1989, student demonstrations in Tiananmen Square for faster-paced and wider-ranging governmental reforms were dispersed by the army, and hundreds — perhaps thousands — of unarmed protesters were killed. Deng's government has fended off reprisal from the United States by continuing to loosen economic restrictions on free enterprise and trade with the West.

For more background on China, see page 97.

Helen's life in China had been in every way perfect. Though a girl, she had been preceded by a twin sister who had died, so that her own touch-and-go start was cheered breath by halting breath; and in later life, she'd been blessed by just enough lingering, sometimes serious illness, to win her much fuss. Well — maybe some of the fuss she could have done without, for instance the sort that involved her grandfather firing doctors; her mother was always hiding with embarrassment, or else whispering at the edge of Helen's bed, in a voice so low that Helen felt the words more than she heard them. They were a sensation, a stirring, something she could not have sworn came from outside herself.

Still she was content, so sweet-natured that her two sisters and three brothers, who might have resented her, instead vied in their efforts to please. They carried her up and down the stairs, sang her songs. She was a family pastime. Her life ambition was to stay home forever. The way Americans in general like to move around, the Chinese love to hold still; removal is a fall and an exile. And for Helen, the general was particularly true. The one gnarl of her childhood was the knowledge that, if she did not die of one of her diseases, she would eventually have to marry and go live with in-laws. And then she'd probably wish she *had* died. How faint she felt, just listening to the stories other girls told — about a neighbor's daughter, for example, who walked all the way home from Hangzhou, only to be sent back. That was extreme, of course, but how about her friend's cousin who, married away into the countryside, was made to take baths in a big copper vat? Over a pit fire, as though she were a pork joint, in water that had already been used by her father-in-law, her husband, her husband's seven brothers, and her mother-in-law. *Don't worry*, Helen's parents reassured her, *we'll find you someone nice, someone you like too. No one's going to beat you.* But at best, Helen knew, she would be sent to scratch out some new, poor spot for herself, at the edge of a strange world, separated from everyone she loved as though by a violent, black ocean.

Now, America. For the first few months, she could hardly sit without thinking how she might be wearing out her irreplaceable clothes. How careful she had to be! Theresa could traipse all over, searching out that elusive brother of hers; Helen walked as little and as lightly as she could, sparing her shoes, that they might last until the Nationalists saved the country and she could go home again. She studied the way she walked too, lightly — why should she struggle with English? She wrote her parents during class, every day hoping for an answer that never came. She went to Chinatown three times a week, thinking of it as one more foreign quarter of Shanghai, like the British concession, or the French. She learned to cook, so that she'd have Chinese food to eat. When she could not have Chinese food, she did not eat. Theresa (who would eat anything, even cheese and salad) of course thought her silly. *"In Shanghai you ate foreign food,"* Theresa said (*da cai,* she called it — big vegetables). *"Why shouldn't you eat it here?"* Still, for a long time, Helen would not, which they both thought would make her sick.

She was not at home enough, though, even to fall ill.

This could not go on forever. Eventually, faith faltering, Helen studied    5
harder, walked more, bought new clothes, wrote her parents less. She did continue to spend whole afternoons simply sitting still, staring, as though hoping to be visited by ghosts, or by a truly wasting disease; but she also developed a liking for American magazines, American newspapers. American radio — she kept her Philco in the corner of the living room nearest the bedroom, so she could listen nonstop. She sang along: "The corn is as high as an el-e-phant's eyyye . . ." She did not insist on folding all her clothes, but used the closet too. She began to say "red, white, and blue" instead of "blue, white, and red" and to distinguish "interest" from "interested" from "interesting." She caught a few colds. And she married Ralph, officially accepting what seemed already true — that she had indeed crossed a violent, black ocean; and that it was time to make herself as at home in her exile as she could.

Not that Helen would ever be at home anywhere but her real home. And yet sometimes she couldn't help but be infected with a bit of Ralph and Theresa's enormous enthusiasm for their new arrangement. How right it all did seem! That Ralph should marry her, friend of Theresa — it was just as their parents would have had it.

*"Don't you think she's just like our little sister?"* Ralph asked Theresa once.

*"There's a resemblance,"* said Theresa.

Helen blushed.

*"Such a coincidence,"* said Ralph. *"You know, someone at school was*    10 *talking the other day about a person who took his house apart, and moved it, and then rebuilt it, just the way it was."*

*"That's like us, and our family,"* Theresa agreed.

*"The odd thing was that that house had a leak. So why did the man move it, if it had a leak? That's the question. Also, he had always hated the inside of it. Too small."*

*"Well,"* said Theresa, *"leaks or no leaks, maybe he was used to it."*

*"I guess,"* said Ralph, uncertainly.

Helen sighed. At home, room had always been made for her in the    15 conversation; people paused before going on, and looked at her. Here, she had to launch herself into the talking, for instance during a lull, as now.

"*You know that saying about a wife's ankle?*" she put in softly.

"*What?*" said Ralph.

"*Don't interrupt,*" said Theresa. "*She's talking.*"

"*I can't hear her.*"

"*That saying,*" Helen said louder. "*Do you know that saying, about a*   20
*wife's ankle? Being tied to her husband's?*"

"*Of course,*" encouraged Theresa. "*With a long red string. From the*
*time she's born.*"

"*Well, I think maybe my ankle was tied to my husband's and sister-in-*
*law's both.*"

"*Ah no! To both? To my ankle too?*" Theresa protested, laughing. Then,
in English, "Are you trying to pull my leg?"

They all laughed. "*Good joke!*" cried Ralph.

"*Good one!*" Helen agreed.   25

Weren't they happy, though? At least until it was time for them to move
to a run-down walk-up north of 125th Street, whose air smelled of mildew
and dog. It was the kind of place where the poorest of students lived,
where the differences in housekeeping between the halls and the rooms
were as dramatic as the occupants could manage. An economy. Ralph
and Helen and Theresa had agreed on it. Yet they were belatedly shocked.
So many Negroes! Years later, they would shake their heads and call
themselves prejudiced, but at the time they were profoundly disconcerted.
And what kind of an apartment was this? This apartment sagged. Theresa
poked a finger in a soft spot of plaster, occasioning a moist avalanche.
"*We're not the kind of people who live like this,*" she said.

But their super, it seemed, thought they were. That Pete! He expected
them to stand endlessly in his doorway, his half German shepherd jumping up on them as he rambled on about the boiler. As for their situation — Was it an "urgency"? he'd ask. Only, yes or no, to not be
coming — not to see about their plumbing problems, not to see about
their ceiling problems, not to see about the crack in the back bedroom
wall that seemed quite definitely to be widening.

"Leaks," said Ralph, batting the dog away. "Paint come down. Big
crack." Politely at first. Then, with more vigor, "You do nothing! This
building falling down!" The result was that Pete once said he'd "swing by
sometime," once explained that his boss, the owner, had some months
ago done a bit of work on the roof.

"So?"

"Well now, I don't know that ever'thing a body says has got to have a   30
*point,*" he said.

*Fan tong,* Ralph called him — rice barrel. Helen and Theresa
laughed. And here was the most irritating thing: fly open, feet up on his
legless desk, dog at the door, he'd often be thumbing through course

catalogs, exchanging one for another, sometimes working through two at once. Should he be a lawyer? A doctor? An engineer? As if he could be an engineer! As if he could get a Ph.D.!

A man, Pete said, was what he made up his mind to be.

*"That man is fooling himself!"* Ralph shook his head.

Helen, meanwhile, hired a plumber, scraped the loose paint so it wouldn't hang, walked Ralph's file cabinet into the back bedroom to hide the crack. Could this place ever be a home? Next to the file cabinet she put a tall bookcase, and straddling them, a small, wide one that only just cleared the ceiling.

*"Smart,"* admired Ralph.                                                            35

*"I saw it in a magazine,"* she told him. *"This is called* wall unit."

"Wall-unit," repeated Ralph. And later he observed that it was exactly in solutions like hers that a person could see how well the Changs were going to do in their new life.

*"Not like that Pete,"* he said. *"He's fooling himself."*

Entertainment: Ralph took to imitating Pete's walk. He'd slump, a finger cleaning his ear, only to have Theresa gamely cry out, *"No, no like this,"* and add a shuffle, turning out her knees as Helen laughed. They studied the way Pete blew his nose, that they might get it right; they studied his sneeze, his laugh, the self-important way he flipped through his calendar. "Well, now, let me have some look-see," growled Theresa. "Typical Pete!" Ralph roared in approval. "Typical, typical Pete!" Ralph even mimicked Boyboy, Pete's mutt — strutting around, barking showily, calling himself "Ralph-Ralph." He paced back and forth, guarding the door with wide swishes of a brush tail; he jumped up on Helen and Theresa as they tried to dodge by with grocery bags. And pretty soon, no one knew quite how, "typical Pete" turned "typical American" turned typical American this, typical American that. "Typical American no-good," Ralph would say; Theresa, "typical American don't-know-how-to-get-along"; and Helen, wistfully, "typical American just-want-to-be-the-center-of-things." They were sure, of course, that they wouldn't "become wild" here in America, where there was "no one to control them." Yet they were more sure still as they shook their heads over a clerk who short-changed them ("typical American no-morals!"). Over a neighbor who snapped his key in his door lock ("typical American use-brute-force!"). Or what about that other neighbor's kid, who claimed the opposite of a Democrat to be a pelican? ("Peckin?" said Ralph. "A kind of bird," explained Theresa; then he laughed too. "Typical American just-dumb!") They discovered stories everywhere. A boy who stole his father's only pair of pants. A mother who kept her daughter on a leash. An animal trainer who, in a fit of anger, bit his wife's ear off.

*"With his mouth?"* Ralph couldn't believe it.                                    40

But it was true. Helen had read it in the American newspaper, which was honest enough to admit, one day, that they were right. Americans had degenerated since the War. As for why, that was complicated. Sitting in the green room that was the living room and Theresa's bedroom both, she read the whole article aloud. Ralph and Theresa listened carefully.

*"That's what we were saying,"* Ralph commented finally. He looked to Theresa, who nodded.

*"Americans want to loosen up now, have a good time,"* she said. *"They're sick of rationing."*

*"Would you read it again?"*

Helen would — glad, she supposed, to have in the family at least this    45
one rickety seat. And sure enough, there it was once more, evidence of how smart they were. Imagine that — that they could see, in a foreign country, what was what! Above them, the ceiling light dropped haloes in their hair as they listened on. Everything, they heard, was going to be okay.

## EXPLORATIONS

1. Name at least three qualities of Helen's life in China that made it "perfect" (para. 1). What tactics does Helen use to find or recreate these qualities in her life in America? Where does she succeed and where does she fail?

2. In paragraphs 10–14, Ralph and his sister Theresa compare their family with a man who moved his house. What points is Gish Jen implying about the Changs by using this comparison?

3. Look at the "typical American" characteristics cited by Helen, Theresa, and Ralph in paragraph 39. Which ones also describe themselves? Give the evidence for your answers.

4. From what sources do the Changs get their information about American life and behavior? Which of these sources are most and least reliable?

## CONNECTIONS

1. Which of the "typical American" qualities (if any) listed by the Changs in paragraph 39 are also cited by Octavio Paz in "Hygiene and Repression" (p. 15)? What types of behavior are of most interest to the Changs? What types of behavior are of most interest to Paz?

2. How do you think Ralph, Theresa, and Helen Chang would respond to the American openness about money described by Raymonde Carroll in "Money

and Seduction" (p. 8)? How do you think they would respond to the French openness about seduction? What can you infer from "Helen in America" about Chinese attitudes toward money and seduction?

3. In "What's American About America?" (p. 3), Ishmael Reed cites influences from around the world on life in the United States. In what ways does this American eclecticism help the Changs to feel at home in New York?

## ELABORATIONS

1. Which of the "typical American" flaws mentioned by Jen's characters in paragraph 39 do you agree are typically American? Use "Helen in America" as your starting point for an essay describing typical American behavior as a new immigrant might perceive it, or as you perceive it yourself.

2. How do the Changs solve the problems they encounter in America, and particularly in their apartment? In a country where so many people move around, what sources of information have developed to help Americans solve such problems? Write an essay classifying the sources of information someone might use who is setting up housekeeping in a new place; or compare and contrast the problems of setting up housekeeping in a new place with those of moving into a familiar neighborhood full of family members and friends.

# MARGARET ATWOOD

## A View from Canada

Margaret Atwood is one of Canada's most distinguished novelists, poets, and critics. Born in Ottawa, Ontario, in 1939, she was educated at Victoria College, University of Toronto, Radcliffe College, and Harvard University. She has taught at colleges and universities in Canada and the United States and has received more than a dozen literary awards and fellowships. Since her earliest poems and her first novel, *The Edible Woman* (1969), Atwood has been noted for her themes of distance and defenses and for her poignant characterizations, particularly of women. Her virtuosity with language ranges from wildly passionate (*Surfacing*, 1972) to coldly controlled (*Life Before Man*, 1979). Her ironic futuristic novel *The Handmaid's Tale* (1986) was made into a motion picture. The author of several volumes of short stories, as well as occasional plays and children's books, Atwood currently lives in Toronto. "A View from Canada" comes from a speech given at Harvard University in 1981 and reprinted in *Second Words* (1982).

Canada, the world's second-largest country (after Russia), extends from the Atlantic to the Pacific Ocean and from the North Pole to the U.S. border. The French explorer Jacques Cartier claimed it for France in 1534. Settlers followed, starting in Acadia (now Nova Scotia) and moving into Quebec. As the English colonies to the south became more established, conflicts arose over hunting, trapping, and fishing rights. In the early 1700s the English took over Newfoundland, Hudson Bay, and Acadia. Many of the evicted French speakers migrated south to Louisiana, where "Acadians" became slurred to "Cajuns." Various British colonies united in 1867 as the Dominion of Canada, which stayed subject to British rule until 1982. Although today Canada's head of government is an elected prime minister, its head of state is still the British monarch. Ottawa, the nation's capital, lies in a narrow section of Ontario between New York State and Quebec, a province where French remains the predominant language. Tension continues between Canadians of English and French heritage, with Quebec periodically threatening to secede. In 1990 the Meech Lake accord, which would have given Quebec the protection of distinct constitutional status, failed to win national approval.

I spent a large part of my childhood in northern Quebec, surrounded by many trees and few people. My attitude toward Americans was formed by this environment. Alas, the Americans we encountered were usually

29

pictures of ineptitude. We once met two of them dragging a heaving metal boat, plus the motor, across a portage from one lake to another because they did not want to paddle. Typically American, we thought, as they ricocheted off yet another tree. Americans hooked other people when they tried to cast, got lost in the woods, and didn't burn their garbage. Of course, many Canadians behaved this way too; but somehow not *as* many. And there were some Americans, friends of my father, who could shoot a rapids without splintering their canoe and who could chop down a tree without taking off a foot in the process. But these were not classed as Americans, not *real* Americans. They were from Upper Michigan State or Maine or places like that, and were classed, I blush to admit, not as Americans but as honorary Canadians. I recognize that particular cross-filing system, that particular way of approving of people you as a rule don't approve of, every time a man tells me I think like a man; a sentence I've always felt had an invisible comma after the word *think*. I've since recognized that it's no compliment to be told you are not who you are, but as children we generalized, cheerfully and shamelessly. The truth, from our limited experience, was clear: Americans were wimps who had a lot of money but did not know what they were doing.

That was the rural part of my experience. The urban part was somewhat different. In the city I went to school, and in the early years at any rate the schools I went to were still bastions of the British Empire. In school we learned the Kings of England and how to draw the Union Jack and sing "Rule Britannia," and poems with refrains like, "Little Indian, Sioux or Cree, Don't you wish that you were me?" Our imaginations were still haunted by the war, a war that we pictured as having been fought between us, that is, the British, and the Germans. There wasn't much room in our minds for the Americans and the Japanese. Winston Churchill was a familiar figure to us; Franklin D. Roosevelt was not.

In public school we did not learn much about Americans, or Canadians either, for that matter. Canadian history was the explorers and was mostly brown and green, for all those trees. British history was kings and queens, and much more exciting, since you could use the silver and gold colored pencils for it.

That era of Canadian colonialism was rapidly disappearing, however. One explanation for the reason it practically vanished during the postwar decade — 1946 to 1957, say, the year I graduated from high school — is an economic one. The Canadians, so the theory goes, overextended themselves so severely through the war effort that they created a capital vacuum in Canada. Nature and entrepreneurs hate a vacuum, so money flowed up from the United States to fill it, and when Canadians woke up in the sixties and started to take stock, they discovered they'd sold their birthright for a mess. This revelation was an even greater shock for me; not only was my country owned, but it was owned by the kind of people who carried tin boats across portages and didn't burn their garbage. One doubted their competence.

Looking back on this decade, I can see that the changeover from British cultural colony to American cultural colony was symbolized by what happened after school as opposed to in it. I know it's hard to believe in view of my youthful appearance, but when I was a child there was no television. There were, however, comic books, and these were monolithically American. We didn't much notice, except when we got to the ads at the back, where Popsicle Pete reigned supreme. Popsicle Pete would give you the earth in exchange for a few sticky wrappers, but his promises always had a little asterisk attached: "Offer good only in the United States." International world cynics may be forgiven for thinking that the same little asterisk is present invisibly in the Constitution and the Declaration of Independence and the Bill of Rights, not to mention the public statements of prominent Americans on such subjects as democracy, human dignity and freedom, and civil liberties. Maybe it all goes back to Popsicle Pete. We may all be in this together, but some of us are asterisked.

Such thoughts did not trouble our heads a great deal. When you were finished with Donald Duck and Mickey Mouse (and Walt Disney was, by the way, a closet Canadian), you could always go on to Superman (whose creator was also one of ours). After that it would be time for Sunday night radio, with Jack Benny and Our Miss Brooks. We knew they talked funny, but we didn't mind. Then of course there were movies, none of which were Canadian, but we didn't mind that either. Everyone knew that was what the world was like. Nobody knew there had once been a Canadian film industry.

After that I went to high school, where people listened to American pop music after school instead of reading comic books. During school hours we studied, among other things, history and literature. Literature was still the British tradition: Shakespeare, Eliot, Austen, Thomas Hardy, Keats and Wordsworth and Shelley and Byron; not experiences anyone should miss, but it did tend to give the impression that all literature was written by dead Englishmen, and — this is important — by dead Englishwomen. By this time I wanted to be a writer, and you can see it would be a dilemma: Being female was no hindrance, but how could one be a writer and somehow manage to avoid having to become British and dead? . . .

In history it was much the same story. We started with ancient Egypt and worked our way through Greece, Rome, and medieval Europe, then

5

the Renaissance and the birth of the modern era, the invention of the steam engine, the American revolution, the French revolution, the Civil War, and other stirring events, every single one of which had taken place outside Canada.

Finally, in the very last year, by which time many future citizens had dropped out anyway, we got a blue book called *Canada in the World Today*. It was about who grew the wheat, how happy the French were, how well the parliamentary system worked for everybody, and how nice it was that the Indians had given us all their land in exchange for the amenities of civilization. The country we lived in was presented to us in our schools as colorless, dull, and without much historical conflict to speak of, except for a few massacres, and nobody did *that* any more. Even the British war of conquest was a dud, since both of the generals died. It was like a hockey game in which both teams lost.

As for Canada in the World Today, its role, we were assured, was an    10 important one. It was the upper northwest corner of a triangle consisting of Canada, the United States, and Britain, and its position was not one to be sneezed at: Canada, having somehow become an expert at compromise, was the mediator. It was not to be parochial and inward-looking any more but was to be international in outlook. Although in retrospect the role of mediator may shrink somewhat — one cannot quite dispel the image of Canada trotting back and forth across the Atlantic with sealed envelopes, like a glorified errand boy — there's a little truth to be squeezed from this lemon. Canadians, oddly enough, *are* more international in outlook than Americans are; not through any virtue on their part but because they've had to be. If you're a Canadian traveling in the United States, one of the first things you notice is the relative absence of international news coverage. In Canada, one of the most popular news programs ever devised has two radio commentators phoning up just about anyone they can get on the line, anywhere in the world. Canadians live in a small house, which may be why they have their noses so firmly pressed to the windows, looking out.

I remember *Canada in the World Today* with modified loathing — "Canada comes of age," it trumpeted, not bothering to mention that what happened to you when you came of age was that you got pimples or a job or both — and still not a year passes without some politician announcing that Canada has finally grown up. Still, the title is significant. Canada sees itself as part of the world; a small sinking *Titanic* squashed between two icebergs, perhaps, but still inevitably a part. The States, on the other hand, has always had a little trouble with games like chess. Situational strategy is difficult if all you can see is your own borders, and beyond that some wispy brownish fuzz that is barely worth considering.

The Canadian experience was a circumference with no center, the American one a center which was mistaken for the whole thing.

A few years ago I was in India and had occasion to visit both the Canadian and American enclaves in New Delhi. The Canadian there lived in a house decorated with Indian things and served us a meal of Indian food and told us all about India. One reason for going into the foreign service, in Canada anyway, is to get out of Canada, and Canadians are good at fitting in, partly because they can't afford to do otherwise. They could not afford, for instance, to have the kind of walled compound the Americans had. We were let in to do some shopping at the supermarket there, and once the gate had closed you were in Syracuse, New York. Hot dogs, hamburgers, cokes, and rock music surrounded you. Americans enter the outside world the way they landed on the moon, with their own oxygen tanks of American air strapped to their backs and their protective spacesuits firmly in place. If they can't stay in America they take it with them. Not for them the fish-in-the-water techniques of the modern urban guerrilla. Those draft dodgers of the sixties who made it as far as Canada nearly died of culture shock: They thought it was going to be like home.

It's not their fault, though. It's merely that they've been oddly educated. Canadians and Americans may look alike, but the contents of their heads are quite different. Americans experience themselves, individually, as small toads in the biggest and most powerful puddle in the world. Their sense of power comes from identifying with the puddle. Canadians as individuals may have more power within the puddle, since there are fewer toads in it; it's the puddle that's seen as powerless. One of our politicians recently gave a speech entitled, "In the Footsteps of the Giant." The United States of course was the giant and Canada was in its footsteps, though some joker wondered whether Canada was in the footstep just before or just after the foot had descended. One of Canada's problems is that it's always comparing itself to the wrong thing. If you stand beside a giant, of course you tend to feel a little stunted. When we stand beside Australia, say, or the ex-British West Indies, we feel more normal. I had lunch recently with two publishers from Poland. "Do Canadians realize," they said, "that they live in one of the most peaceful, happy, and prosperous countries on earth?" "No," I said. . . .

Americans and Canadians are not the same; they are the products of two very different histories, two very different situations. Put simply, south of you you have Mexico and south of us we have you.

But we *are* all in this together, not just as citizens of our respective 15 nation states but more importantly as inhabitants of this quickly shrinking and increasingly threatened earth. There are boundaries and borders, spiritual as well as physical, and good fences make good neighbors. But there are values beyond national ones. Nobody owns the air; we all breathe it.

## EXPLORATIONS

1. How does Margaret Atwood summarize her childhood concept of "typical American" (para. 1)? How would you summarize her present concept of "typical American"?

2. What aspects of "A View from Canada" show that it was written as a speech, to be heard rather than read by its audience? What can you tell about Atwood's intended audience?

3. What qualities does Atwood seem to consider typically Canadian? At what points do her comments about Canadians reveal her opinion of Americans?

4. Find at least three places where Atwood uses humor in "A View from Canada." In each case, what purpose(s) does her humor serve?

## CONNECTIONS

1. In paragraph 12 Atwood contrasts the Canadian and American enclaves in New Delhi, India. In what ways does the Changs' apartment in Gish Jen's "Helen in America" (p. 22) resemble each of these enclaves?

2. Compare Atwood's description of Americans in India (para. 12) with Octavio Paz's description in "Hygiene and Repression" (p. 15, para. 6). What similarities do you find?

3. "Canadians, oddly enough, *are* more international in outlook than Americans are," writes Atwood (para. 10). Do you think Ishmael Reed would agree? Cite evidence for your opinion from "What's American About America?" (p. 3).

## ELABORATIONS

1. Go through Atwood's essay and note the main points she makes about Canadians and about Americans. Rewrite "A View from Canada" as a shorter, more direct comparison-contrast essay.

2. Using Atwood's "A View from Canada," Jen's "Helen in America," Paz's "Hygiene and Repression," Carroll's "Money and Seduction" (p. 8), and Reed's "What's American About America?" as sources, write your own essay defining what is typically American.

# ES'KIA MPHAHLELE

## *Tradition and the African Writer*

Es'kia Mphahlele (pronounced m-fa-lay-lay) was born Ezekiel Mphahlele in South Africa in 1919. He grew up in the capital city of Pretoria
and received his B.A. with honors from the University of South Africa.
Although he was banned from teaching in 1952 for protesting the segre-
gationist Bantu Education Act, Mphahlele completed his master's degree and served as fiction editor for a Johannesburg magazine before
leaving the country in 1957. In Paris he became director of African
programs for the International Association for Cultural Freedom. Moving to the United States, he received his Ph.D. from the University of
Denver and taught in the English department there; he also has taught
at the University of Pennsylvania and in Kenya, Nigeria, and Zambia.
Mphahlele returned to South Africa in 1977. "There is a force I call the
tyranny of place," he has said; "the kind of unrelenting hold a place has
on a person that gives him the motivation to write and a style." Even
though his books were banned under apartheid, he taught and became
head of African Literature at the University of Witwatersrand. Mphahlele
has published story collections, works of criticism, novels, and a children's book; his essays have appeared in numerous journals. His autobiographical novel *The Wanderers* was designated Best African Novel of
1968–1969. "Tradition and the African Writer" comes from his essay
"African Literature: What Tradition?" which originally appeared in the
*Denver Quarterly*.

Covering Africa's southern tip, the Republic of South Africa is about
twice the size of Texas. Bantus (blacks) are a majority of the population,
which also includes Afrikaners (whites of Dutch descent), Asians (mostly
Indians), and Coloureds (those of mixed Khoisan and white descent).
The region's Khoisan tribes — formerly known as Bushmen and Hottentots — had been joined by Bantus from the north by the time Dutch
settlers arrived in the seventeenth century. Many of Mphahlele's works
are concerned, directly or indirectly, with the racial and political
conflicts in his homeland, which began when the British seized the Cape
of Good Hope in 1806. At that time many Dutch moved north and
founded two new republics, the Transvaal and the Orange Free State,
displacing native Khoisan and Bantu tribes. They and their white compatriots kept political control by means of apartheid, a policy of racial
separation that severely limits blacks' access to jobs, housing, income,
and influence. Conflict intensified when diamonds and gold were discovered in the late 1800s. The ensuing Anglo-Boer (British versus Dutch)
War was won by the British, who created the Union of South Africa in
1910. In 1948 apartheid became official legally enforcing racially sepa-

rate development and residential areas. In 1961, with only whites allowed to vote, South African voters withdrew their nation from the British Commonwealth. In the late 1980s, Asians and Coloureds received the right to vote (with restrictions), and laws banning interracial marriage were repealed. Today South Africa continues to reverse long-standing repressive policies and move gradually toward a more fair and representative political system (see p. 587).

It all started when Africa was shanghaied into the history of the West in the late nineteenth century. What were we coming into? — a long line of continuity going back some 9,000 years since the civilizations of the great river valleys of the Nile, the Tigris and Euphrates, the Indus, and the Hwang-ho had launched man on a long intellectual quest. We had been discovered by an aggressive Western culture which was never going to let us be. Nor could we cease following the neon lights — or has it been a will o' the wisp? Time will tell. Perhaps Hegelian historical determinism will have it that it is as it should be: How could Africa be left out of it all indefinitely?

And so here I am, an ambivalent character. But I'm nothing of the oversimplified and sensationalized Hollywood version of a man of two worlds. It is not as if I were pinned on a rock, my legs stretched in opposite directions. Education sets up conflicts but also reconciles them in degrees that depend on the subject's innate personality equipment. It seems to me a writer in an African setting must possess this equipment and must strive toward some workable reconciliation inside himself. It is an agonizing journey. It can also be humiliating to feel that one has continually to be reassessing oneself with reference to the long line of tradition he has entered — the tradition of the West. How else? I have assimilated the only education the West had to offer me. I was brought up on European history and literature and religion and made to identify with European heroes while African heroes were being discredited, except those that became Christians or signed away their land and freedom, and African gods were being smoked out. I later rejected Christianity. And yet I could not return to ancestral worship in any overt way. But this does not invalidate my ancestors for me. Deep down there inside my agnostic self, I feel a reverence for them.

The majority of writers in Africa, I venture to say, are attached in a detached manner to one indigenous religion or another. They are not involved in its ritual, but they look at it with reverence. When, in their full consciousness, they have found themselves Christian — which can often just mean baptized — they have not adopted churchianity. Because our whole education system in Africa has been mission-ridden right from the beginning, and the white minister was supposed by the government or commercial or school-board employer to know the "native," you had always to produce a testimonial signed by a white church minister when you were applying for a job. Not even black ministers could speak for you. If you wanted to go out for further studies, you knew where to find St. Peter. The black minister himself required testimonials from one of his white brethren, never from another black minister. So we called ourselves Christians; we entered "Christian" on the line against an item that asked for it on all the multiplicity of forms, just in order to save ourselves the trouble of explaining and therefore failing to go through the gates. In independent Africa, we are luckily able to trust fellow blacks who vouch for us and others. And you can almost see the Christian veneer peeling off because it has nothing to do with conscience. . . .

By far the larger part of Africa is still traditionally minded in varying degrees. The whole dialogue around tradition is an intellectual one. The parents of people of my generation, although they may be urbanized, are still close to tradition. They worry a great deal about the way in which we break loose at one point and ignore some elements of tradition. Each time an African mother sends a child to high school, it is like giving birth to him all over again. She knows she is yielding something. Dialogue between her and the child decreases and eventually stays on the level of basic essentials: our needs, our family relations, family life, which must continue more or less normally, whatever else around us may progressively be reduced to abstractions or gadgets. It is no less excruciating for the young man who stands in this kind of relationship with his parents. But he can reconcile himself to it — the very educational process that wrenches him from his moorings helps him to arrange a harmonization within himself.

The parent will often moan and complain to him about the awkward distance he has reached away from tradition. But it is never a reprimand; it is an indulgent complaint. Because, I think, the parents are always aware that this whole business of education does not of itself engage you in an activity that expressly subverts the morals of the family, the clan, or of the tribe. They are aware of the many situations around them that require an education to cope with them. The benefits of tradition are abstract, and the parents' own thinking has not been stagnant while the whole landscape around them has been changing, while the white man's government has been impinging on their way of life over several decades. And the benefits of a modern education are tangible, real.

I have always asked myself what it is in one's formal education that leads to the rupture, to the ever-widening gulf between one and one's parents and one's community. You recognize the alphabet, then words, and then you can extract meaning from many sentences in a row. With that shock of recognition, words leap into life in front of you. They set your mind on fire; longings and desires you would never have known are released and seem to whirl around in currents that explode into other currents: something like what you see in a glass flask of water that you have on a naked flame to observe the movement of heat in liquid. From then on, one must not stop. Yet it is not something one can take for granted in an African context, because to start at all is not inevitable: education is not compulsory, and the financial cost of it is immense.

In your higher education, you assimilate patterns of thought, argument, and so on from an alien culture in an alien language; they become your own. Of course you cannot help using your African setting as your field of reference; you cannot help going out of the queue of Western orientation now and again to consult those of your people who are not physically in it. You try to express their philosophy in a European language whose allegory, metaphor, and so on are alien to the spirit of that philosophy: something that can best be understood in terms of allegory and metaphor that are centered heavily on human relationships and external nature. All the same, you are in the queue, and you belong not only to an African community but also to a worldwide intellectual or worldwide economic community, or both. This is why communication becomes difficult, sometimes impossible between your people who are still not tuned into Western intellectual systems and yourself. Your mind operates in a foreign language, even while you are actually talking your mother tongue, at the moment you are engaged in your profession. You try hard to find correspondences and you realize there are only a few superficial ones: you have to try to *make* most of them. In the pure sciences, which are universally applicable, the correspondences are numerous; there is no problem.

Indigenous languages that have only recently become literary, that is, only since the church missions established presses in Africa, seem to have relied more and more heavily on the spoken word, so that gesture, facial expression, inflection of voice became vital equipment in communication. Language became almost a ritual in itself, and metaphor and symbol became a matter of art and device. Metaphor became a sacred thing if it had descended from usage in earlier times; when an elder, in a traditional court case, prefaced a proverb or aphorism or metaphor by saying, "Our elders say . . ." his audience listened with profound reverence. Notice the present tense in "our elders *say.* . . ." Because his elders would be the ancestors, who are still present with us in spirit. You can imagine what confusion prevails in a modern law court when a witness or the accused operate in metaphor and glory in the sensuousness of the spoken word quite irrelevant to the argument at hand. Ask any magistrate or prosecutor or lawyer in a differentiated Western-type society whether they find a court trial a sensuous activity, and hear what they say. Even the rhetoric that a lawyer may indulge in is primarily a thing of the brain rather than of the heart. In African languages, activities overlap a great deal, and there are no sharp dividing lines between various functions.

All that I have said so far has been an attempt to indicate the relative distances between tradition and the present — some shifting, others freezing, some thawing, others again presenting formidable barriers. And we are living in a situation in which the past and the present live side by side, because the past is not just a segment in time to think *back* upon: we can see it in living communities. We need to appreciate these distances if we are to understand what the African writer is about. He is part of the whole pattern.

# EXPLORATIONS

1. As an African writer, to what "two worlds" does Es'kia Mphahlele belong? What choices does his dual heritage force him to make?

2. Why does Mphahlele perceive education as so crucial an issue for African writers? What price do they pay for it? What happens if they refuse to pay that price?

3. "The whole dialogue around tradition is an intellectual one," writes Mphahlele (para. 4). Cite three or four passages that show him to be part of the Western intellectual tradition. What passages show that he also belongs to the African tradition, in which speakers "operate in metaphor and glory in the sensuousness of the spoken word" (para. 8)?

4. How would you summarize the thesis of Mphahlele's essay? What are his main sources of information?

# CONNECTIONS

1. How did Mphahlele's education in South Africa resemble Margaret Atwood's in Canada? (See "A View from Canada" on p. 29.) What changes does each author seem to be recommending in his or her country's approach to educating children?

2. Both Mphahlele's and Atwood's educations showed them they did not fit the profile of "writer." What were the main obstacles each one had to overcome to be a writer? What was Atwood's main advantage over Mphahlele? What was Mphahlele's main advantage over Atwood?

3. According to Mphahlele, speakers of African languages tend to rely more on metaphor and respect for ancestors than speakers of English do (para. 8). What

evidence can you find in Gish Jen's "Helen in America" (p. 22) that speakers of Chinese share this African trait?

4. "Africa was shanghaied into the history of the West," Mphahlele writes in his opening paragraph. In what respects is this also true of Latin America? Look back at Octavio Paz's "Hygiene and Repression" (p. 15). What qualities does Mphahlele value in African tradition which Paz also values in Latin American culture?

## ELABORATIONS

1. "I have always asked myself," writes Mphahlele, "what it is in one's formal education that leads to the rupture, to the ever-widening gulf between one and one's parents and one's community" (para. 6). Write a cause-and-effect essay that addresses this question, using "Tradition and the African Writer" and your own experience as sources.

2. "The benefits of tradition are abstract," writes Mphahlele. "The benefits of a modern education are tangible, real" (para. 5). What does he mean? Looking at your own role in the world as an adult, what have you gained (or do you hope to gain) from your education? From the tradition(s) in which you grew up? Write an essay classifying the abstract and tangible benefits to you of your education and heritage.

# PAUL HARRISON

## The Westernization of the World

Paul Harrison is a free-lance writer and journalist based in London. He has traveled widely in Asia, Africa, and Latin America and has written extensively about population and the environment. He has contributed frequently to the *Guardian, New Society,* and *New Scientist,* and to publications of major United Nations agencies, such as the World Health Organization, the Food and Agriculture Organization, UNICEF, and the International Labor Organization. In 1990 and 1992 he was the principal researcher for the UN Population Fund's major annual report, *The State of the World Population.* Harrison attended Manchester Grammar School and took master's degrees at Cambridge University and the London School of Economics. His interest in the Third World began in 1968 when he was lecturing in French at the University of Ife, Nigeria. Among his recent books are *The Greening of Africa* (1987) and *The Third Revolution* (1992).

"The Westernization of the World" comes from the second edition of Harrison's 1981 book *Inside the Third World,* reprinted with a revised postscript in 1987. Harrison based the book on research and travel between 1975 and 1980, visiting Sri Lanka, Upper Volta and the Ivory Coast, Colombia and Peru, Brazil, Indonesia and Singapore, India, Bangladesh, and Kenya. "In some ways it was a mad enterprise to attempt to cover so much ground," he admits. However, "The underdevelopment of countries and of human beings cannot be compartmentalized if it is to be fully grasped. It is a total situation, in which every element plays a part."

Like many commentators, Harrison refers to underdeveloped countries and their citizens collectively as the *Third World.* The term has more than one definition; typically it is applied to nations in Africa, Asia, and Latin America that are not heavily industrialized and have a low standard of living. Shiva Naipaul has noted ironically: "The exemplary Third World denizen . . . lives a hand-to-mouth existence, he is indifferent to the power struggles of the mighty ones, and he is dark-skinned." Naipaul adds, "To blandly subsume, say, Ethiopia, India, and Brazil under the one banner of Third Worldhood is as absurd and as denigrating as the old assertion that all Chinese look alike." Still, keeping in mind the dangers noted by Simone de Beauvoir of dividing humanity into "us" and "them" (see p. 329), we can use the concept of the Third World to examine, as Harrison does, certain tendencies shared by nations that are otherwise dissimilar.

> The bourgeoisie has, through its exploitation of the world market, given a cosmopolitan character to production and consumption in every country.
>
> —Karl Marx

In Singapore, Peking opera still lives, in the back streets. On Boat Quay, where great barges moor to unload rice from Thailand, raw rubber from Malaysia, or timber from Sumatra, I watched a troupe of traveling actors throw up a canvas-and-wood booth stage, paint on their white faces and lozenge eyes, and don their resplendent vermilion, ultramarine, and gold robes. Then, to raptured audiences of bent old women and little children with perfect circle faces, they enacted tales of feudal princes and magic birds and wars and tragic love affairs, sweeping their sleeves and singing in strange metallic voices.

The performance had been paid for by a local cultural society as part of a religious festival. A purple cloth temple had been erected on the quayside, painted papier-mâché sculptures were burning down like giant joss sticks, and middle-aged men were sharing out gifts to be distributed among members' families: red buckets, roast ducks, candies, and moon cakes. The son of the organizer, a fashionable young man in Italian shirt and gold-rimmed glasses, was looking on with amused benevolence. I asked him why only old people and children were watching the show.

"Young people don't like these operas," he said. "They are too old-fashioned. We would prefer to see a high-quality Western variety show, something like that."

He spoke for a whole generation. Go to almost any village in the Third World and you will find youths who scorn traditional dress and sport denims and T-shirts. Go into any bank and the tellers will be dressed as would their European counterparts; at night the manager will climb into his car and go home to watch TV in a home that would not stick out on a European or North American estate.[1] Every capital city in the world is getting to look like every other; it is Marshall McLuhan's global village, but the style is exclusively Western. And not just in consumer fashions: The mimicry extends to architecture, industrial technology, approaches to health care, education, and housing.

To the ethnocentric Westerner or the Westernized local, that may seem    5 the most natural thing in the world. That is modern life, they might think. That is the way it will all be one day. That is what development and economic growth are all about.

Yet the dispassionate observer can only be puzzled by this growing

---

[1]Housing development. — ED.

world uniformity. Surely one should expect more diversity, more indigenous styles and models of development? Why is almost everyone following virtually the same European road? The Third World's obsession with the Western way of life has perverted development and is rapidly destroying good and bad in traditional cultures, flinging the baby out with the bathwater. It is the most totally pervasive example of what historians call cultural diffusion in the history of mankind.

Its origins, of course, lie in the colonial experience. European rule was something quite different from the general run of conquests. Previous invaders more often than not settled down in their new territories, interbred, and assimilated a good deal of local culture. Not so the Europeans. Some, like the Iberians[2] or the Dutch, were not averse to cohabitation with native women: unlike the British, they seemed free of purely racial prejudice. But all the Europeans suffered from the same cultural arrogance. Perhaps it is the peculiar self-righteousness of Pauline[3] Christianity that accounts for this trait. Whatever the cause, never a doubt entered their minds that native cultures could be in any way, materially, morally, or spiritually, superior to their own, and that the supposedly benighted inhabitants of the darker continents needed enlightening.

And so there grew up, alongside political and economic imperialism, that more insidious form of control — cultural imperialism. It conquered not just the bodies but the souls of its victims, turning them into willing accomplices.

Cultural imperialism began its conquest of the Third World with the indoctrination of an elite of local collaborators. The missionary schools sought to produce converts to Christianity who would go out and proselytize among their own people, helping to eradicate traditional culture. Later the government schools aimed to turn out a class of junior bureaucrats and lower military officers who would help to exploit and repress their own people. The British were subtle about this, since they wanted the natives, even the Anglicized among them, to keep their distance. The French, and the Portuguese in Africa, explicitly aimed at the "assimilation" of gifted natives, by which was meant their metamorphosis into model Frenchmen and Lusitanians,[4] distinguishable only by the tint of their skin.

The second channel of transmission was more indirect and voluntary.    10
It worked by what sociologists call reference-group behavior, found when

---

[2]Spanish or Portuguese (i.e., from the Iberian peninsula). — ED.
[3]Relating to the writings and teachings of St. Paul. — ED.
[4]Portuguese. Lusitania was the Roman name for the part of the Iberian peninsula that is now Portugal. — ED.

someone copies the habits and life-style of a social group he wishes to belong to, or to be classed with, and abandons those of his own group. This happened in the West when the new rich of early commerce and industry aped the nobility they secretly aspired to join. Not surprisingly, the social climbers in the colonies started to mimic their conquerors. The returned slaves who carried the first wave of Westernization in West Africa[5] wore black woolen suits and starched collars in the heat of the dry season. The new officer corps of India were molded into what the Indian writer Nirad Chaudhuri has called "imitation, polo-playing English subalterns," complete with waxed mustaches and peacock chests. The elite of Indians, adding their own caste-consciousness to the class-consciousness of their rulers, became more British than the British (and still are).

There was another psychological motive for adopting Western ways, deriving from the arrogance and haughtiness of the colonialists. As the Martiniquan political philosopher, Frantz Fanon, remarked, colonial rule was an experience in racial humiliation. Practically every leader of a newly independent state could recall some experience such as being turned out of a club or manhandled on the street by whites, often of low status. The local elite were made to feel ashamed of their color and of their culture. "I begin to suffer from not being a white man," Fanon wrote, "to the degree that the white man imposes discrimination on me, makes me a colonized native, robs me of all worth, all individuality. . . . Then I will quite simply try to make myself white: that is, I will compel the white man to acknowledge that I am human." To this complex Fanon attributes the colonized natives' constant preoccupation with attracting the attention of the white man, becoming powerful like the white man, proving at all costs that blacks too can be civilized. Given the racism and culturism of the whites, this could only be done by succeeding in their terms, and by adopting their ways.

This desire to prove equality surely helps to explain why Ghana's Nkrumah built the huge stadium and triumphal arch of Black Star Square in Accra. Why the tiny native village of Ivory Coast president Houphouët-Boigny has been graced with a four-lane motorway starting and ending nowhere, a five-star hotel and ultramodern conference center. Why Sukarno transformed Indonesia's capital, Jakarta, into an exercise in gigantism, scarred with six-lane highways and neofascist monuments in

---

[5]One of many plans for solving the problem of slavery in the United States was to send freed slaves to Africa. The Republic of Liberia in West Africa was founded for this purpose in 1822. — ED.

the most hideous taste. The aim was not only to show the old imperialists, but to impress other Third World leaders in the only way everyone would recognize: the Western way.

The influence of Western life-styles spread even to those few nations who escaped the colonial yoke. By the end of the nineteenth century, the elites of the entire non-Western world were taking Europe as their reference group. The progress of the virus can be followed visibly in a room of Topkapi, the Ottoman palace in Istanbul, where a sequence of showcases display the costumes worn by each successive sultan. They begin with kaftans and turbans. Slowly elements of Western military uniform creep in, until the last sultans are decked out in brocade, epaulettes, and cocked hats.

The root of the problem with nations that were never colonized, like Turkey, China, and Japan, was probably their consciousness of Western military superiority. The beating of these three powerful nations at the hands of the West was a humiliating, traumatic experience. For China and Japan, the encounter with the advanced military technology of the industrialized nations was as terrifying as an invasion of extraterrestrials. Europe's earlier discovery of the rest of the world had delivered a mild culture shock to her ethnocentric attitudes. The Orient's contact with Europe shook nations to the foundations, calling into question the roots of their civilizations and all the assumptions and institutions on which their lives were based.

In all three nations groups of Young Turks[6] grew up, believing that their countries could successfully take on the West only if they adopted Western culture, institutions, and even clothing, for all these ingredients were somehow involved in the production of Western technology. As early as the 1840s, Chinese intellectuals were beginning to modify the ancient view that China was in all respects the greatest civilization in the world. The administrator Wei Yüan urged his countrymen to "learn the superior technology of the barbarians in order to control them." But the required changes could not be confined to the technical realm. Effectiveness in technology is the outcome of an entire social system. "Since we were knocked out by cannon balls," wrote M. Chiang, "naturally we became interested in them, thinking that by learning to make them we could strike back. From studying cannon balls we came to mechanical inventions which in turn led to political reforms, which led us again to the political philosophies of the West." The republican revolution of 1911

15

---

[6]Members of an aggressive reform group; see page 380. — Ed.

attempted to modernize China, but her subjection to the West continued until another Young Turk, Mao Zedong, applied that alternative brand of Westernization: communism, though in a unique adaptation.

The Japanese were forced to open their border to Western goods in 1853, after a couple of centuries of total isolation. They had to rethink fast in order to survive. From 1867, the Meiji rulers Westernized Japan with astonishing speed, adopting Western science, technology, and even manners: short haircuts became the rule, ballroom dancing caught on, and *moningku* with *haikara* (morning coats and high collars) were worn. The transformation was so successful that by the 1970s the Japanese were trouncing the West at its own game. But they had won their economic independence at the cost of losing their cultural autonomy.

Turkey, defeated in the First World War, her immense empire in fragments, set about transforming herself under that compulsive and ruthless Westernizer, Kemal Atatürk. The Arabic script was abolished and replaced with the Roman alphabet. Kemal's strange exploits as a hatter will probably stand as the symbol of Westernization carried to absurd lengths. His biographer, Lord Kinross, relates that while traveling in the West as a young man, the future president had smarted under Western insults and condescension about the Turkish national hat, the fez. Later, he made the wearing of the fez a criminal offense. "The people of the Turkish republic," he said in a speech launching the new policy, "must prove that they are civilized and advanced persons in their outward respect also. . . . A civilized, international dress is worthy and appropriate for our nation and we will wear it. Boots or shoes on our feet, trousers on our legs, shirt and tie, jacket and waistcoat — and, of course, to complete these, a cover with a brim on our heads. I want to make this clear. This head covering is called a hat."

## EXPLORATIONS

1. Early in his essay Paul Harrison asks the central question: "Why is almost everyone following virtually the same European road?" (para. 6). What are the characteristics of this "European road"? What are the origins of the specific examples the author cites?

2. What general cause, and what specific channels, does Harrison cite as responsible for the Third World's Westernization? What differences between Western newcomers and Third World natives seem to have most strongly affected relations between them?

3. "By the end of the nineteenth century," writes Harrison, "the elites of the entire non-Western world were taking Europe as their reference group" (para.

13). How does he explain the initial westward tilt of countries that were never colonized? What explanation does he suggest for their continuing interest in Western ways?

4. What types of evidence does Harrison present for his assumptions about Western homogeneity? Do you think his evidence justifies his conclusions? Why or why not?

## CONNECTIONS

1. In paragraph 9 Harrison mentions Christian missionary schools as one means by which "cultural imperialism began its conquest of the Third World." What specific steps or tactics in this process does Es'kia Mphahlele mention in "Tradition and the African Writer" (p. 35)?

2. What does Harrison say in paragraph 7 about the policy of the Iberian (Spanish and Portuguese) colonizers toward the native peoples they met in the New World? Look back at Octavio Paz's "Hygiene and Repression" (p. 15). How do Latin American food and attitudes toward food reflect that colonial Spanish policy?

3. In paragraph 10 Harrison discusses "reference-group behavior." What examples of this behavior can you find in Raymonde Carroll's "Money and Seduction" (p. 8)?

## ELABORATIONS

1. Harrison focuses on Westernization in non-Western countries. What explanation (if any) does he offer for the spread of a single cultural trend all over Europe and North America? On the basis of Harrison's theories, plus evidence from other selections you have read, write an essay identifying causes and effects behind the West's homogeneity.

2. It has become fairly common for childless couples and individuals in the United States to adopt babies from Third World countries. In what ways does cross-cultural adoption benefit the child, the original and adoptive parents, and the child's original and adoptive homeland? What are the drawbacks of this practice? Write an argumentative essay defending or opposing cross-cultural adoption, or a process analysis essay advising the would-be parent(s) on how to protect the interests of all involved.

# V. S. NAIPAUL

## Entering the New World

Sir V. S. (Vidiadhar Surajprasad) Naipaul was born in Trinidad of Indian descent but has lived most of his life in England. Feeling stifled on his small native island, which lies off the coast of Venezuela and constitutes half the Republic of Trinidad and Tobago, Naipaul vowed to escape. In 1950, at the age of eighteen, he left for Oxford University on a government scholarship. At twenty-one he became a broadcaster for the Caribbean Service of the British Broadcasting Company (BBC). He wrote three novels, two of which were in print by the time he was twenty-six. At twenty-nine he published what is widely considered his masterpiece, *A House for Mr. Biswas.* Since then Naipaul has lived in India, Africa, South America, and the Middle East as well as England. He has written twenty-two books, the majority nonfiction, including *In a Free State* (1971), which won England's prestigious Booker Prize, and *The Enigma of Arrival* (1987). Naipaul was knighted in 1990. He lives with his wife, Patricia Hale, whom he met at Oxford, and writes alone in a Wiltshire cottage. "Entering the New World" comes from "The Crocodiles of Yamoussoukro," a narrative about his travels in the Ivory Coast, published as part of his 1984 book *Finding the Center.*

The Ivory Coast (République de la Côte d'Ivoire) lies almost directly across the Atlantic Ocean from Trinidad, between Liberia and Ghana on Africa's Gulf of Guinea. A former French colony, it gained independence in 1960. Economic (particularly agricultural) diversification, foreign investment, and close ties to France helped make the Ivory Coast the most prosperous of tropical African nations. However, a drop in cocoa and coffee prices in the world market, and aging President Huphouët-Boigny's austere solutions, including a 25 to 40 percent income tax to pay off foreign debt, led to an economic slump and political dissent. In 1990, Huphouët-Boigny was forced to subject his thirty-year-old presidency to popular elections. Naipaul's meeting with Ebony takes place in Abidjan, then the Ivory Coast's capital city (it is now Yamoussoukro). For more information on the Ivory Coast, see page 258.

"Volta" is Upper Volta, which also became independent of France in 1960; its name was changed to Burkina Faso in 1984. Landlocked in the southwest African savannah north of the Ivory Coast, Burkina Faso has a largely agricultural economy but only 10 percent arable land; several hundred thousand of its farm workers migrate every year to the Ivory Coast and Ghana. Benin — another French colony until 1960 — lies east of the Ivory Coast beyond Ghana and Togo.

In the morning I was telephoned from the hotel lobby by a man called Ebony. He said he had heard from Busby that a writer was in Abidjan, and he had come to meet this writer. He, Ebony, was himself a poet.

I went down to see him. He was a cheerful young man of regal appearance, with the face of a Benin bronze, and he was regally attired, with a brightly patterned skullcap and a rich African tunic. He said the skullcap and tunic were from Volta. His family employed laborers from Volta and he had always, even as a child, liked their clothes.

He had been a journalist, he said, but he had given it up, because in the Ivory Coast journalism was like smoking: It could damage your health. He liked the joke; he made it twice. But he was vague about the journalism he had done. He said he was now a government servant, in the department of the environment. He had written a paper on things that might be done environmentally in the Ivory Coast. But after twelve months he had heard nothing about his paper. So now he just went to the office and from time to time he wrote poetry.

He said, "I have a theory about African administrations. But it is difficult and will take too long to tell you."

He had come to see me — and the hotel was a good way out of the town — because he was sociable; because he wanted to practice his English; and because, as a poet and intellectual, he wanted to try out his ideas. 5

I offered coffee. He offered me a cola nut, the African token of friendship. I nibbled at my grubby, purple-skinned nut: bitter. He chewed his zestfully, giving little dry spits of chewed husk to his left and right, and then at the end of his chew taking out the remainder of the husk with his fingers and placing it on the ashtray.

He asked why I had come to the Ivory Coast. I said because it was successful and French.

He said, "Charlemagne wasn't my ancestor."

I felt it had been said before, and not only by Ebony. He ran on to another idea. "The French run countries like pigsties. They believe that the sole purpose of men is to eat, to go to the toilet, and to sleep." So the French colonialists created bourgeois people. Bourgeois? "The bourgeois want peace, order. The bourgeois can fit into any political system, once they have peace. On the other hand, the British colonialists created entrepreneurs." Entrepreneurs? "Entrepreneurs want to change things." Entrepreneurs were revolutionaries.

Antithesis, balance: the beauty rather than the validity of a thought: I thought I could detect his French training. I began to examine his ideas of the bourgeois and the entrepreneur, but he didn't encourage me. He said, playfully, it was only an idea. 10

Starting on another cola nut — he had a handful in his tunic pocket — he said, "Africans live at peace with nature. Europeans want to conquer or dominate nature."

That was familiar to me. I had heard similar words from young Muslim fundamentalists in Malaysia: ecological, Western romance bouncing back like a corroborating radio signal from remote, inactive worlds. But that again was an idea Ebony didn't want to stay with.

Ebony said, "I saw white men for the first time when I was fourteen or fifteen, when I went to school. That was the first time I discovered the idea of racial superiority. African children are trained not to look elders in the eye. It is disrespectful. At school the French teachers took this to be a sign of African hypocrisy."

What was the point of this story?

Ebony said, "So I thought my French teachers inferior." 15

I felt this racial story, with its triumphant twist, had previously had a sympathetic foreign listener. And it turned out that there was a Scandinavian woman journalist who had made a great hit with Ebony. She was now in Spain and Ebony earnestly asked me — two or three times — to look her up and pass on his regards.

Ebony said, "When my father sent me to the school, do you know what he said? He said, 'Remember. I am not sending you to the school to be a white man or a Frenchman. I am sending you to enter the new world, that's all.'"

I felt that in his own eyes Ebony had done that. . . . Ebony said he had no money, no car. The salary he got from the government was less than the rent he paid. He had come to the hotel on his bicycle. But I thought he was relaxed, a whole man. He knew where he was, how he had got there, and he liked the novelty of what he saw. There was no true anxiety behind his scattered ideas. At any rate he was less anxious than a romantic or concerned outsider might have wished him to be. Ideas about Africa, words, poetry, meeting foreigners — all this was part of his relishing of life, part of his French-inspired role as intellectual, part of the new world he had happily entered.

He went away on his bicycle, and I took a taxi later to a beach restaurant at the other end of the city, beyond the industrial and port area. The lunch there, and the French style of the place, were usually worth the fare and the journey in the midday heat through the traffic and the crowds. But today it wasn't so.

It was more than a matter of an off day. The waiters, impeccable the 20 day before, were casual, vacant. There were long delays, mistakes, some of the portions were absurdly small; the bill, when it came, was wrong. Someone was missing, perhaps the French or European manager. And with him more than good service had gone: The whole restaurant idea had vanished. An elaborate organization had collapsed. The waiters — Ivorian: These jobs were lucrative — seemed to have forgotten, from one day to the next, why they were doing what they did. And their faces seemed to have altered as well. They were not waiters now, in spite of their flowered tunics. Their faces and manners radiated various degrees of tribal authority. I saw them as men of weight in the village: witch doctors, herbalists, men who perhaps put on masks and did the sacred dances. The true life was there, in the mysteries of the village. The restaurant, with its false, arbitrary ritual, was the charade: I half began to see it so.

Ebony had been told by his father: "I am not sending you to the school to become a white man. I am sending you to enter the new world."

The new world existed in the minds of other men. Remove those men, and their ideas — which after all had no finality — would disappear. Skills could be taught. What was fragile — to men whose complete, real life lay in another realm of the spirit — was faith in the new world.

## EXPLORATIONS

1. "The new world existed in the minds of other men," writes V. S. Naipaul in his closing paragraph. "Remove those men, and their ideas — which after all had no finality — would disappear." What incidents during the author's lunch at a "French" restaurant trigger this conclusion? What assumption does Naipaul make about the restaurant to explain the incidents? On what evidence does he base that assumption?

2. "Antithesis, balance," Naipaul remarks of Ebony's comparison between French and English colonialists (para. 10). Find at least two other comparisons made by Ebony. What value judgment does each comparison express? Do you agree with Naipaul that Ebony is more interested in the beauty than the validity of a statement? Why or why not?

3. What impression of Ebony does Naipaul give us in the first half of his essay? What tactics does he use to create this impression? How do you think he means our impression to change in the second half?

4. What is Ebony's view of the French influence on the Ivory Coast? What statements express his view? What is Naipaul's view of the French influence? What statements express his view?

# CONNECTIONS

1. What statements by Paul Harrison in "The Westernization of the World" (p. 41) are echoed by Naipaul and Ebony? How does Naipaul's assessment of Western influence on the Third World differ from Harrison's?

2. How would you summarize Ebony's view of the difference between French and British colonizers? How would you summarize Paul Harrison's view of this difference? In what respects do these two commentators agree and disagree?

3. Like Es'kia Mphahlele in "Tradition and the African Writer" (p. 35), Naipaul investigates the impact of a dual heritage on an African writer. What evidence in "Entering the New World" suggests that Ebony has faced the same conflict between native and European influences as Mphahlele? How does Naipaul suggest that Ebony has (or has not) resolved his dilemma?

# ELABORATIONS

1. What does Naipaul's opinion of Ebony seem to be? Does he like Ebony? Does he respect his views? How can you tell? List the comments Naipaul makes that reveal his personal response to Ebony. Then write an essay analyzing the techniques Naipaul uses to depict Ebony sympathetically or unsympathetically without directly stating his opinion.

2. Have you ever eaten in a restaurant, or patronized a store, where you unexpectedly became aware of the "real" life of someone waiting on you? Have you ever held a job, attended a class, or participated in a social function where an unplanned event shattered the group's customary identity? Write an essay using your experience to illustrate Naipaul's comments about the fragility of worlds that exist mainly in someone's mind.

# PATRICK SMITH

## *Nippon Challenge*

Patrick Smith, a former editor at the *New York Times*, has been a newspaper and magazine correspondent in Asia for eleven years. In 1985 he won an Overseas Press Club Award for his coverage of South Korea. He served as bureau chief for the *International Herald Tribune* in Hong Kong and Tokyo from 1986 to 1991. He now writes on Japan for *The New Yorker* magazine, in which "Nippon Challenge" appeared in longer form. That article was taken from Smith's book *The Nippon Challenge: Japan's Pursuit of the America's Cup* (1992), as are these biographical notes. The sailing syndicate Nippon Challenge did well in preliminary America's Cup rounds, and Japan became a semifinalist along with New Zealand, Italy, and France; but it was New Zealand that faced the United States in the big race, and the United States that won.

"Nippon Challenge" includes a good deal of historical and geographical information about Japan. For more, see page 122.

It is not very often that Westerners get to see the Japanese just as they are. The difficulty we have when we look at Japan — the layers-of-the-onion problem — can be so frustrating that we tend to raise our own screen of assumptions and expectations, or we content ourselves with images of the Japanese as they would like to be seen. If you live in Japan, you learn to value moments of clarity — times when you feel as if you'd walked into a room where someone is talking to himself and doesn't know you're there.

Over the last five years, the yachtsmen of Nippon Challenge — the sailing syndicate representing Japan in the America's Cup races off San Diego this spring — have provided just such an occasion: a moment of national revelation. Nippon Challenge is intended by its managers, sponsors, and sailors to be a display of new and unfamiliar ambitions felt by the Japanese. It is also intended to reveal Japan's capacity to fulfill those ambitions. The lavish imagery associated with competitive yachting — skippers with the sensitivity of artists, crews pitted against time and the elements — no longer adequately reflects the reality of a complex sailing campaign. Yet it holds enormous appeal for the Japanese. Because racing for the America's Cup requires them to do so many things they have never even attempted before, they see in it a chance to respond to the urgent question that is implicit in most of what we have to say to them these days: Can Japan and the Japanese change? The campaign also reminds us, though, of how easily symbols can be mistaken for substance when we look at the Japanese, because the Japanese generally do not distinguish between the two.

It is a result of their peculiar history that the Japanese, although island dwellers, are not a seafaring people. Until the seventeenth century, Japan had been well on its way to building a seaborne empire as extensive as that of Portugal, Spain, or Holland. Its ships were comparable in size, if not sophistication, to any then being constructed in the West, and its trade routes stretched to what are now Indonesia and India and to the coast of Africa. But the Tokugawa shogunate, which lasted from 1603 until 1868, changed all that. By 1640, its policy of *sakoku,* or isolation, had virtually closed the Japanese islands to the outside world. The sea became known as a perilous place, and those who lived beyond it as aggressive, barbaric people. In many rather obvious ways, this view continues to color Japan's attitudes toward the world beyond its shores.

The Japan with which we are all familiar is a trading nation of unparalleled reach, but it remains a nation of people living with their backs to the sea. One can earn a living by doing business across the ocean, but that is a matter of commercial necessity, and it directly involves few. The art and science of sailing have been largely ignored — left alone as the preserve of a few passionate pioneers. Until quite recently, official policy encouraged such neglect. In the early postwar years, all but the smallest sailboats were classified as luxury items and were taxed at a rate of 40 percent. Sailors talk about that tax today the way they might have talked about *sakoku* in another age: It meant they couldn't participate in many of the regattas held around the world each year and couldn't organize a serious regatta of their own. You understand how slowly Japan has come to recognize itself as a nation of great wealth when they tell you that the tax on sailboats was not fully removed until April 1, 1989.

There is also the nature of sailing to consider. If the sport can be said to require one quality above any other, that quality is flexibility in the face of changing circumstances: No two days on the water are ever the same. Whatever else it is, yacht racing is a test of one's ability to react to a situation that is always unpredictable. A lengthy competitive campaign — preparing for and racing for the America's Cup, for instance — means being willing to drop everything and to start anew in response to technical discoveries, altered weather conditions, or a surprise development on the part of an opponent. It requires a dedication to competing and to winning which allows nothing else to matter.

For all these reasons, sailing is not a sport for which the Japanese are particularly well conditioned. Since the Meiji Restoration opened the

modern era, 124 years ago, their way of dealing with the world has been
to prepare at home, behind closed doors, and wait to challenge opponents
at a moment when they can be quickly dominated. Their commitment
is not to flexibility but to a process. This philosophy is part of what used
to be called *wakon yosai*, meaning "Japanese spirit, Western things." I've
never seen the term used outside history books, but it was one of the
essential creeds of the Meiji years. *Wakon yosai* meant learning from
abroad how to bake bread, brew beer, or build an army, or how to write
a constitution without letting such notions as democracy and individual
choice disrupt traditional values and attitudes — the web of duties and
obligations which keeps the Japanese living in a rigidly defined hierarchy
of authority. *Wakon yosai* enabled Japan to modernize in an extraordinarily brief time — a matter of decades — and in our own age, of course,
the philosophy has been applied in industry after industry with evident
success. But it has come up short whenever creativity or ingenuity was
required. *Wakon yosai* has not, for instance, produced the kind of inner-
driven individuals needed to steer a yacht to victory.

When you look at the America's Cup in this light, it's hard to think of
anything else that so neatly confronts the Japanese with so many challenges to their way of doing things. That is what has made their America's
Cup venture so curious a phenomenon to observe. In our troubled
relations with Japan, we clamor for changes in trade regulations and
business practices, though what fundamentally separates us is differences
of psychology and method, and divergent views of what competition is
all about. You can't win the America's Cup by copying, for instance,
because the technology moves too fast. How, then, is a nation historically
reliant on learning from abroad supposed to build an America's Cup
yacht? Finding the right crew poses a similar problem. It's a plain contradiction to apply *wakon yosai* to the task of assembling a team of sailors
driven by a desire to compete.

These have been formidable problems for the Japanese. Until Nippon
Challenge, no one in Japan had even attempted to design a yacht of the
size and sophistication required by the America's Cup. As for Japanese
sailors, they've accumulated a mixed record, at best, in the few world-class
events in which they've raced. It isn't simply a question of physical
ability — although Japanese have often told me that physiology is the
main problem. The more important deficiency is that of attitude. The
Japanese do not value winning the way it is valued in the West. Instead
of passion and desire, they bring to sports a sense of *asobi*, which means
play, participation, doing one's best as a Japanese. They prefer contests
that end up with a prize for everybody. In sumo wrestling, for instance,

there is not just a winning trophy but a *kanto-sho,* a trophy for "good achievement"; a *doryoku-sho,* for "good effort"; and a *gino-sho,* for "good technique."

Since I began following Nippon Challenge, almost two years ago, the word *gambatte* has also struck me as an important key to Japanese attitudes. *Gambatte* is normally used the way "Good luck!" is used in English: You say it to someone at the start of an endeavor. But its broader meaning is "Persist, try harder, stick with it," and the implication is "Think long-term." If you don't succeed this time, there is the next time, and the time after that. *"Gambatte!"* is a familiar salutation in the corridors of corporate Japan — you hear it all the time in Tokyo. And a long-term perspective is, of course, one of the reasons for the nation's economic success. But the America's Cup isn't contested by corporations — not directly, at least. The expression that has traditionally been associated with the Cup since its beginning, in 1851, is "There is no second."

To me, the difference between *asobi* and *gambatte,* on the one hand,     10
and "There is no second," on the other, says everything you need to know about why the Japanese might well have decided to stay away from the expensive and obsessive, all-or-nothing world of the America's Cup. It's simply too much a game for the *gaijin,* the "outside people." But the very notion of the Cup as somehow off limits is what drove the syndicate's organizers forward. Nippon Challenge is as much a Japanese product of the 1980s as the fabulous art acquisitions, the corporate takeovers, and the huge property purchases in major Western cities are. It is partly an announcement to the rest of us that the long Japanese effort to catch up with the West, begun during the Meiji era, has finally succeeded. "It had to do with the times," a sailor named Taro Kimura once told me of the sailing syndicate's first days. "There was an inevitability about it. Everyone felt that now we can do this, now we can afford it — whatever it happened to be. We had wealth, but we wanted to find some other value in life besides working and producing. That was a common perception among the Japanese."

Taro Kimura has offered many such comments in the years I've known him. More than almost anyone else in the Japanese campaign, he is eager to attach some larger meaning to the enterprise. Kimura has been part of Nippon Challenge since its beginning, when it consisted of nothing more than a few middle-aged executives with a passion for yachting and a dream of competing for the sport's premier prize. Kimura, who is well traveled and speaks English flawlessly, is a noted TV anchorman; one of his many American friends once called him the Ted Koppel of Japan, and it is as good a description as any. Because he has an easy manner and a made-for-television smile, Kimura early on assumed a variety of public-relations duties, one of which was to cultivate sponsors prepared to finance the syndicate. It has been a curious exercise, he says, and he has found himself less a hard-selling impresario than a kind of house ideologue. Though Kimura's object was simply to finance a sailing syndicate, accomplishing that meant transforming Nippon Challenge — symbolically, at least — into something that it might otherwise not have become.

When Kimura began trying to bring sponsors on board, his promotional material consisted of a slightly blurred brochure made on a borrowed four-color photocopier, and a homemade video produced with footage lifted from the library at his television network. Thus armed, Kimura laid out the commercial and public-relations benefits that would accrue to corporations supporting Japan's first America's Cup challenge. As a marketing strategy, it seemed eminently sound. In mid-1987, however, this approach got Kimura nowhere. Cheap capital was abundant then, and corporate sponsorships were the rage. But the kind of friction between Japan and the United States which we now seem to take for granted was just beginning, and all that Kimura heard from business friends was "What if we win this thing? What then?"

Kimura remains proud of the way he answered that question. One evening at his home in Zushi, a seaside town an hour's train ride south of Tokyo, he decided to write an imaginary newspaper editorial. It was his idea of what the *New York Times* would publish the day after Nippon Challenge won the America's Cup. Shortly after I met Kimura, he handed me a copy of what he had written, as a kind of primer on the Japanese campaign. "This proves the Japanese aren't monsters," he said. The editorial read:

> Japan, long pushed to increase its imports, has just spent $15 million to bring home an old vase. It won't reduce the trade surplus, but it surely is more significant than $15 million worth of purchases overseas. The vase proves that the Japanese are not monsters, economic animals, but human beings like ourselves.
>
> The America's Cup is, in a sense, the world's greatest meaningless event. 15 You invest millions, but all you get back, if you win, is the old silver vase. It requires the latest technology, but it is technology that does not necessarily enrich our daily lives right away. The young people who fought in the race won't even get a medal, as in the Olympic Games. However, we in the West have pursued this race because we think man is distinguished as the only creature that can be enthusiastic about meaningless things.
>
> Japan has given us the best in television sets, Walkman stereos, and cars, but sometimes we have found it difficult to decide whether the Japanese

are really human beings. They seem to have sacrificed their individual lives to contribute to their companies. They are rational people, a people who are careful not to waste, but they seem too inhuman.

Now the Japanese have made a huge investment in the world's greatest meaningless event, and they have done so even more enthusiastically than we have. They have happily returned home with the Cup that bears no correspondence to their investment in getting it.

The meaning for us is simple: We have discovered through the America's Cup that the people upon whom much of the world's future depends are also human beings.

I've never been able to decide whether Kimura's editorial fantasy was taken up out of extreme idealism (rare in corporate Japan) or extreme cynicism (somewhat more common), but, in any case, it's obvious that he struck just the right gong. His imaginary *Times* piece has been an essential marketing device. When Kimura started his recruiting, Nippon Challenge hoped for ten official sponsors to contribute a hundred million yen each — about seven hundred thousand dollars at the time. When the syndicate arrived in San Diego, a little more than a year ago, it had thirty official sponsors, each one in for a hundred and fifty million yen; forty-three "honorary sponsors," "official suppliers," and "co-suppliers," each of which made contributions of its own; and thousands of individual supporters.

## EXPLORATIONS

1. According to Patrick Smith, what are the reasons no Japanese sailing team ever entered the America's Cup competition until recently?

2. What motives finally won support in Japan for Nippon Challenge? How does Smith's opening sentence prepare us to appreciate the Japanese motives revealed at the end of his essay?

3. What important differences does Smith identify between Japanese and Western attitudes? What are his sources of information about Japanese attitudes? About Western attitudes?

# CONNECTIONS

1. In V. S. Naipaul's "Entering the New World" (p. 48), Ebony's father tells him: "I am not sending you to the school to become a white man. I am sending you to enter the new world." Do you think the same reasoning applies to the Japanese decision to enter the America's Cup competition? Why or why not?

2. According to Paul Harrison in "The Westernization of the World" (p. 41), the Japanese "won their economic independence at the cost of losing their cultural autonomy" (para. 16). What does he mean? In what respects do Smith and Harrison agree about the Westernization of Japan? In what respects do they disagree?

3. In "Helen in America" (p. 22), Gish Jen's Chinese-born characters list "typical American" qualities (para. 39). Based on "Nippon Challenge," what qualities do you think a Japanese person would list as "typical American"?

# ELABORATIONS

1. Smith quotes a Japanese view that people in the West "think man is distinguished as the only creature that can be enthusiastic about meaningless things" (para. 15). Are we in the West enthusiastic about many meaningless things besides the America's Cup? Write an essay either supporting or opposing this view of Westerners.

2. In paragraph 2, Smith notes that the Japanese generally do not distinguish between symbols and substance. Do we make this distinction in the United States? Choose some facet of public life in this country — music, fashion, advertising, TV news, a political campaign — and analyze the relationship between symbols and substance.

# PART TWO

# THE FAMILY

*Cornerstone of Culture*

### LOOKING AT OURSELVES

Michael Novak, Norman Boucher, William R. Mattox, Marilyn
Berlin Snell, Patricia Schroeder, Angela Davis, Paula Fomby,
Richard Rodriguez, Ellen Goodman, Christopher Lasch

Rigoberta Menchú, *Birth Ceremonies* (GUATEMALA)

Louise Erdrich, *Adam* (UNITED STATES)

Liang Heng and Judith Shapiro, *Chairman Mao's Good
Little Boy* (CHINA)

Wole Soyinka, *Nigerian Childhood* (NIGERIA)

John David Morley, *Acquiring a Japanese Family* (JAPAN)

Gyanranjan, *Our Side of the Fence and Theirs* (INDIA)

Ved Mehta, *Pom's Engagement* (INDIA)

Marguerite Duras, *Home Making* (FRANCE)

Gholam-Hossein Sa'edi, *The Game Is Over* (IRAN)

ALL OVER THE WORLD, FAMILIES ARE THE MEANS BY WHICH NEW MEM-
bers of a society start learning its rules. From this introduction come the
child's earliest ideas about what is "normal" and what is "strange." Human
beings are astonishingly adaptable. Thus, as we scan different societies,
we see children — and their parents — playing a wide variety of roles.

Just as the family's structure and dynamics change from one society to
another, so does the writer's focus. What is significant about families?
Unusual? Amusing? Inspiring? Tragic? We open with *Looking at Ourselves* passages: Michael Novak on capitalism's impact on the American
family; Norman Boucher on a trip to Disney World; William R. Mattox
on fast-track families; Marilyn Berlin Snell on changing parental roles;
Patricia Schroeder on the child-care dilemma; Angela Davis on African-
American families; Paula Fomby on growing up in a gay family; Richard
Rodriguez on the extended family of Roman Catholicism; Ellen Goodman assessing the family as "social glue"; and Christopher Lasch questioning the notion of "quality time."

As we see how writers of different nationalities approach this universal
institution, we look into the heart of culture. In "Birth Ceremonies,"
Rigoberta Menchú describes the rituals with which Quiché children in
Guatemala are welcomed into the world. "Adam" is Louise Erdrich's
poignant reflection on living with a Native American son crippled by fetal
alcohol syndrome. In "Chairman Mao's Good Little Boy," Liang Heng
and Judith Shapiro recount the anguish of a Chinese family torn apart
by state-controlled parenthood. Wole Soyinka's "Nigerian Childhood"
depicts an Anglican household where British propriety is cheerfully
mixed with African magic.

Identification between self, home, and family infuses John David
Morley's "Acquiring a Japanese Family": In Japan, the word for *home* can
also mean *myself*. In Gyanranjan's short story "Our Side of the Fence and
Theirs," an Indian family watches their new neighbors for breaches of the
social code. A nonfictional Indian family prepares the oldest daughter for
marriage in Ved Mehta's autobiographical "Pom's Engagement." French
writer Marguerite Duras reminisces and speculates in "Home Making"
about family members' relationships with each other and their houses.
Finally, in Gholam-Hossein Sa'edi's chilling story "The Game Is Over,"
poverty and parental abuse spur two Iranian boys to an act that staggers
their whole village.                                                      ◇

# LOOKING AT OURSELVES

## 1

Choosing to have a family used to be uninteresting. It is, today, an act of intelligence and courage. To love family life, to see in family life the most potent moral, intellectual, and political cell in the body politic is to be marked today as a heretic.

Orthodoxy is usually enforced by an economic system. Our own system, postindustrial capitalism, plays an ambivalent role with respect to the family. On the one hand, capitalism demands hard work, competition, sacrifice, saving, and rational decision making. On the other, it stresses liberty and encourages hedonism.

Now the great corporations (as well as the universities, the political professions, the foundations, the great newspapers and publishing empires, and the film industry) diminish the moral and economic importance of the family. They demand travel and frequent change of residence. Teasing the heart with glittering entertainment and gratifying the demands of ambition, they dissolve attachments and loyalties. Husbands and wives live in isolation from each other. Children of the upwardly mobile are almost as abandoned, emotionally, as the children of the ghetto. The lives of husbands, wives, and children do not mesh, are not engaged, seem merely thrown together. There is enough money. There is too much emotional space. It is easier to leave town than to pretend that one's lives truly matter to each other. (I remember the tenth anniversary party of a foreign office of a major newsmagazine; none of its members was married to his spouse of ten years before.) At an advanced stage capitalism imparts enormous centrifugal forces to the souls of those who have most internalized its values, and these forces shear marriages and families apart. . . .

An economic order that would make the family the basic unit of social policy would touch every citizen at the nerve center of daily life. The family is the primary teacher of moral development. In the struggle and conflicts of marital life, husbands and wives learn the realism and adult practicalities of love. Through the love, stability, discipline, and laughter of parents and siblings, children learn that reality accepts them, welcomes them, invites their willingness to take risks. The family nourishes "basic trust." From this spring creativity, psychic energy, social dynamism. If infants are injured here, not all the institutions of society can put them back together.

– Michael Novak
"The Family Out of Favor"
*Harper's*, 1976

## 2

I am on the teacup ride. Officially, it is known as the Mad Tea Party, after the 1951 Disney movie version of *Alice in Wonderland*. To my left sits my wife, Kathryn, who has been talking about this, her favorite ride, since we began planning the trip to Florida. To my right is Alex, my six-year-old nephew, on whose behalf, ostensibly at least, we chose Walt Disney World as our destination. My parents are in another teacup somewhere on this whirling platform. My sister Flo, Alex's mother, is standing near the ride, her video camera at the ready. The rotational speed of each teacup is controlled by turning a metal wheel in its center, and Kathryn, Alex, and I are jointly turning ours as fast as we can. "Other way!" Kathryn cries out, and we force the wheel, and our teacup, in the other direction. We are shrieking, mostly for effect.

During our first day at Disney World we are on our best, if guarded, behavior. We're still trying to live up to the happy-family ideal. My secret hope is that Disney World, described in Steve Birnbaum's guidebook as "the most popular manmade attraction on this planet," will distract us from the irritants that are bound to arise. Here we can relinquish our troubled adulthood. Here we can be uninhibited tourists, protected from unpleasant surprises. Even the picture opportunities have been laid out for us: The best vantage points are labeled with signs that say "Kodak Photo Spot."

Here the world is flat and measures forty-three square miles. By sleeping in a Disney hotel and eating at Disney restaurants, visitors can spend days, even weeks, cocooned in make-believe. Here the myth is nourished that life can be as clean and smooth as a whitewashed picket fence, that surface and substance are one and the same. At the Magic Kingdom, Disney World's centerpiece theme park, details such as the delicate moldings crowning the buildings along Main Street, USA, and the filigree reaching skyward on the Cinderella Castle are the architectural equivalent of the magic pixie dust sprinkled about by Tinkerbell in *Peter Pan*. . . .

Kathryn, the newcomer to our clan's psycho-dramas, has become our navigator. The rest of us are putty in her hands. It is an immutable natural law that whenever my sisters, parents, and I assemble, the ability to make even the simplest decision goes up in smoke. Apart, we are opinionated, headstrong individuals, but together we induce a crippling current of irresolution in one another that confounds outsiders. When, on our third day, Kathryn returns to the hotel and tends to an hour of unfinished business, the rest of us are left high and dry amid a sea of purposeful theme-park tourists. In a daze we stare at buildings and at maps, waiting for someone to pick a direction and a ride, each of us reluctant to commit, fearing that someone will be displeased. We dread waking the sleeping beast, the bundle of suppressed grievances that each of us carries as steadfastly as the fanny packs secured to our waists. Alex, too young to comprehend any of this, finally speaks up. "Let's go to the Muppet Show!" he says, rousing us from our paralysis.

We have our closest call over lunch at Epcot Center. Assuming that we would simply eat our way around the eleven pavilions of the World Showcase, we have failed to anticipate the effect of so many choices on our Achilles' heel. Even Kathryn has trouble steering us when the decision is made to sit down somewhere and eat. In our strategy session the night before, foods were eliminated as either too familiar (Chinese), too spicy (Moroccan), or too unusual (Japanese) for one or more of us. That approach, unfortunately, has left eight countries to choose from. Fortunately, a chance conversation with a woman who claims to have dined at every pavilion leads to a recommendation and a choice: the English pub.

There are murmurs of discontent. While we wait for a table, my parents study the menu for a long time. I enter the pub, order a pint of lager, two half-pints of stout, and a Coke with cherries at the bar, then carry them outside, where Kathryn, Flo, Alex, and I sit in the sunshine with our drinks. My parents still have not joined us. After a while, Flo goes to investigate and upon returning announces, "They don't want to eat here. They said it's all fried food, and with their heart conditions they can't eat fried food."

The stout has emboldened me. I go over to the bench where my parents sit memorizing the menu. "What's wrong?" I ask, sitting beside my father.

"There's nothing here we can eat," he says.

I look at the menu over his shoulder. "What do you mean? Look, here's broiled fish, here's a vegetable plate, here's a vegetable pie. . . ."

Slowly I convince them, but it is a vaguely unsatisfying lunch. I feel the tension rising, the illusions slipping, and not until Alex has his picture taken hugging a kimono-clad Minnie Mouse at the Japan pavilion am I able to fully relax again.

And so it goes, long periods of unbridled laughter and soaring joy darkened suddenly and, it seems, randomly by a cloud of disquiet and vertigo. Only later does it occur to me what is happening: We are acting like children. We are acting like wounded, bratty children. I have heard the clichés about Walt Disney connecting you with the child within, but this, certainly, is not what he had in mind. Or is it?

One afternoon, at Disney-MGM Studios, we stop for ice cream sun-
daes (sugar is love in my family) at the '50s Prime Time Cafe, a campy
shrine to the Formica culture of the 1950s and 1960s. Here waiters and
waitresses sport period dress, and every seat has an unobstructed view of
boxy television sets playing nonstop segments from sit-coms such as "I
Love Lucy" and "The Donna Reed Show." Alex knows these programs
as reruns on cable, but Kathryn, Flo, and I were about his age when they
first appeared. They are the images of our childhood.

Seated, we read our menus and marvel at the details around us. It has
been a day of especially unruffled fun — Star Tours, The Great Movie
Ride, autographs from the Ninja Turtles. Yet when the waitress approaches our table and asks, "Have you all washed your hands?" there is
a second of uncertain silence as, off-balance, we wonder how to react to
this stern parental inquiry.

"Yes," Kathryn the Navigator replies.

"Then what color is the soap?"

Another silence. Kathryn: "Pink!"

We all chuckle over this exchange, but when the waitress leaves, I find
I am thinking about my dirty hands. Excusing myself, I go off to find the
men's room. For a few minutes I am alone, happy to be away from the
others. Tomorrow we will be leaving the world of Disney for that other
world again. But now when I look into the mirror above the sink it reveals
to me an obedient, slightly guilty, sometimes irritated, and often irritating
child. The awakened beast. How did this happen? I put my hands beneath
the soap dispenser, and a pink powder sprinkles down onto them. It has
the texture of pixie dust.

> — Norman Boucher
> "Three Generations Do Disney"
> *Boston Globe Magazine*, 1991

◇◇◇◇◇

# 3

The American family today lives in a time-pressure cooker. "On the
fast track of two-career families in the go-go society of modern life, the
most rationed commodity in the home is time," observes syndicated
columnist Suzanne Fields. Accordingly, today's family schedules are often
quite complex.

"Increasingly, family schedules are intricate applications of time-mo-
tion principles, with everything engineered to the minute and with every
piece designed to fall in the right place at the right time," says Barbara
Dafoe Whitehead, a social historian who has done extensive field research
on how families organize and manage their time. "When a shoe is lost,

or a cold car engine fails to turn over, or the baby fills his diaper just after he's been zipped into his snowsuit, or the staff meeting runs late, the whole intricate schedule can unravel and fall apart." . . .

Time pressures can be especially daunting for single parents — and especially harmful to their children. Children in single-parent homes usually receive less parental attention, affection, and supervision than other children. Not only is one parent absent from the home (and research by sociologist Frank Furstenberg shows that three-fourths of all children of divorce have contact with their fathers fewer than two days a month), but the other parent is overloaded with money making and household tasks. Indeed, [sociologist John] Robinson's data show that, on average, single mothers spend one-third less time each week than married mothers in primary child-care activities such as dressing, feeding, chauffeuring, talking, playing, or helping with homework.

Moreover, children in single-parent families often have very irregular schedules. One study found that preschool children of single mothers sleep two fewer hours a night on average than their counterparts in two-parent homes, in part because harried mothers find it difficult to maintain a consistent bedtime routine.

This lack of household order and predictable routine negatively affects child development. "I don't think we can escape the conclusion that children need structure and oftentimes the divorce household is a chaotic scene," writes psychologist John Guidubaldi.

The time deficits in single-parent households are aggravated by the devastating emotional effects of divorce on children. It is little wonder that, when compared with children in two-parent families, children in single-parent homes have lower measures of academic achievement and increased levels of depression, stress, anxiety, aggression, mental illness, substance abuse, juvenile delinquency, youth gang membership, and other physical, emotional, and behavioral problems.

— William R. Mattox
"The Parent Trap"
*Policy Review,* 1991

## 4

Prior to the Industrial Revolution, there was efficacy in gender-based roles. Men presided over the physical aspects of farming, while women's primary sphere of influence — where she reared children, wove cloth, and canned food — was the home. The roles were separate, but were equally necessary and valued equally.

It was *this* arrangement, where the work of both men and women revolved around the home, which cemented the traditional family. Contrary to popular myth, the "Father-Knows-Best" era, in which the husband left before the kids were awake and didn't come home until dark, signaled the breakup of the traditional family far more than its quintessence.

– Marilyn Berlin Snell
"On Gender Roles"
*New Perspectives Quarterly*, 1990

<><><><><>

# 5

Our society cannot decide how to treat the working woman. We have considered child care a "woman's" issue rather than what it really is: a family issue. Our ambivalence stems from two deep-rooted biases: First, we believe that people should not have children unless they can afford them; second, we feel mothers should stay at home with their young children.

Additionally, many people believe that those who "choose" to work don't deserve any assistance in their effort to balance work and family. They see the choice of working outside the home solely as a life-style decision and not as an economic issue. In fact, government statistics tell us that only one woman in ten will get through life with the option to decide whether she wants to work. The other nine will have to work.

To make progress on child care we must bury these cultural biases. Middle-class women are in the workplace because they want the same things for their families that they themselves had as children.

Modern-day economic realities have put pressures on the family that have not been levied on any other generation, and it is quite clear to me that the family unit is breaking down, in large part, because we don't give it any support. We do less than any other industrialized nation: In terms of tax breaks, we would do better raising thoroughbred dogs or horses than children.

Many people today, as in the past, fight legislation that would acknowledge the kinds of lives women really lead, for fear they will be accused of destroying the mythical family. I think we need to acknowledge the family as an economic unit and basic building block of our society and then get on with reinforcing it. . . .

For American companies, the most popular approach to helping parents care for their children has been the establishment of flexible personnel policies: such programs as flex-time, part-time work schedules, flex-place, job sharing, and flexible leave. The programs vary: Flex-time allows an employee to choose, within constraints set by the employer, the time when he or she arrives at and departs from work. In job sharing, two people share the responsibilities of one full-time job and prorate the salary and benefits.

For many corporate executives, the term *child care* conjures up an expensive on-site center with high insurance rates and complicated building codes. Yet most managers don't realize they can offer some child-care benefits that are relatively inexpensive and not burdensome. These include courses to teach parents how to find and evaluate providers; child-care resource and referral services to help parents find good child care; and salary redirection programs, under which specific amounts of money from employee paychecks are withheld, deposited into accounts to pay child-care expenses, and subtracted from the employee's taxable income.

The American women's movement has long been asking for equal rights, but its conception of equality has never had anything to do with "sameness." Pregnancy, after all, is like nothing else.

What we have always maintained is that women bring extra responsibilities to the workplace and if women are ever going to have equality, they need equal access to opportunity. If that means instituting special, compensatory policies so that women can compete on an equal footing with men, and still be able to take time out to bear children, so be it.

Take another example: The person who is confined to a wheelchair will never get the job if ramps aren't cut into the curb so that they can gain access to the office building. If they can do the job, we, as a society, need to do whatever it takes to assure that they have the opportunity to succeed.

> – Patricia Schroeder
> "From Star Wars to Child Care"
> *New Perspectives Quarterly*, 1990

◇◇◇◇◇

# 6

Much of the public debate in recent years about the breakdown of the African-American family has failed to acknowledge that the traditional nuclear family has never been the typical model of the black family. First of all, from the days of slavery to the present, both husband and wife have been compelled to work outside the home. Secondly, the predominant model in the African-American community has been the extended family, which has conferred important roles on grandmothers, grandfathers, aunts, uncles, and cousins. This expansive domestic environment has often been much healthier for the child and has functioned as a child-care system available to working parents.

The African-American family structure evolved out of the fusion of African extended-family traditions with the conditions imposed by slavery.

During this era, the father was relegated to the negligible role of providing the "seed." In most cases, the name of the father was not even acknowledged, but was subordinated to the mother's name. If, for example, the father's name was John, and the woman who bore his child was Mary, he would be called "Mary's John" — and his name would not even appear in the birth records. The slave family, as viewed by the slave owners, consisted solely of the mother and her children. This practice succeeded in annihilating the "family space" within which resistance to slavery could develop.

The slave community attempted to challenge this assault on the family by creating surrogate family members and by establishing naming practices which affirmed the place of the father, even though he was often sold away. The creativity with which African-American people improvised family connections is a cultural trait that has spanned the centuries.

Today, considering the devastating impact of crack cocaine on the black community, the family is experiencing grave problems. The majority of crack users among African-Americans are women. Yet, despite the economic obstacles to maintaining the extended family, the babies of young women addicted to crack are often reared by their grandmothers — and sometimes great-grandmothers. This is indicative of a desperate effort to maintain the integrity of the family. Even so, because the African-American family has not perfectly mirrored the middle-class family model, the assumption has often been that it is collapsing.

In attempting to make sense of the crises that currently beset the family, it is essential to address the economic roots of these problems. The seemingly inescapable impoverishment of large sectors of the African-American community has often been linked to the high rates of teenage pregnancy. In actuality, the rise in single parenthood among teenagers is more a symptom of poverty than the cause of it.

As a matter of fact, pregnancy rates among black teenagers are actually declining. The problem resides in the fact that fewer and fewer of these young women are able to marry the fathers of their babies.

In the 1950s and 1960s, and even in the early 1970s, the possibility still existed for young, black men to find jobs that permitted them to contribute to the support of their families, at least in a rudimentary fashion. The contemporary failure to consolidate two-parent families among black youths is a direct consequence of the unemployment crisis which has pushed more than one-third of our people into the ranks of unmitigated poverty.

Many young fathers cannot find work — or if they do, the job rarely pays above minimum wage. If they cannot find work, why should they marry? Young mothers face precisely the same dilemma, which means that they are frequently supported by their families — or by the welfare system. Should they marry the fathers of their children, further economic burdens result.

In the final analysis, the real issue is not whether the African-American family is in chaos, but that society has refused to assume more responsibility for the economic well-being of its members and for the care and education of our children. Quality child care must be available to the poor as well as to the wealthy, and this will only happen if the government intercedes.

– Angela Davis
"Child Care or Workfare"
*New Perspectives Quarterly*, 1990

◇◇◇◇◇◇

**7**

I grew up in the closet, waiting for my mother to come out first. When I was thirteen, she told me that she was a lesbian and confessed what I had assumed, that the woman who had lived with us for four years was her lover. I cried; when I remember it, I picture myself running away from her and down the street.

Being the child in a gay family, for me, meant telling lies. My mother asked me not to tell my friends that she was gay, comparing the embarrassment to a secret we shared about an eraser I had once stolen from a stationery store. There was little danger that I would say anything. Through high school, I constructed my social life around the fact that my mother and her lover were asleep by ten o'clock, making sure I had no guests in our house, who might see them go to bed. Should anyone actually see them disappear behind the same closed door, I was quick to invent an explanation. If my mother and Connie overheard the stories I made up, they never said anything, taking this, I suppose, as my method of defense.

Children have clear signals about what it means to be gay — where I lived, a limp wrist, a high-pitched voice, a purple polo shirt for boys, and anything leaning toward hippie fashion for girls. To be gay was to be stupid; the two words were literally synonymous. I was slow to understand that the shared bed in my house and the insults made in the cafeteria line were all supposed to be part of the same thing.

The hardest part of having a gay mother was accepting homosexuality and all its consequences before I even knew what that involved. I loved my mother and Connie, but I cringed at the mention of the gay-pride parade, and I looked at their gay friends skeptically, eager for reasons to dislike them. I never said anything, valiantly trying to support a cause I didn't even want to discuss with my friends. As long as they kept it quiet, I was content; otherwise, I hated the danger their social lives posed to mine.

In order to live peaceably, I accepted my mother's life-style a long time ago; feeling comfortable with it has come more recently. . . .

[The] constant tension between defending gays while defining myself as straight finally articulated itself when I realized that there are not simply gay couples with children; there are gay families, where everyone must deal with the prejudice surrounding homosexuality.

The fact that there is no real definition of the gay family is obvious when I try to explain Connie. To dismiss Connie as an entity existing in our house only for my mother's sake negates the impact she's had on more than half of my life. She has been a part of my decisions, she has purchased my groceries, she has entertained my ambitions. She has been far more than a roommate to me, and I love her, want to protect her, and make her happy. I know also what she means to my mother — they are wedded in everything but the legal sense.

Each person in my family has matured into what it means to be gay individually. My mother and Connie have become more involved in the gay community since I left home. Seeing them take pride in their relationship makes me more proud to talk about them, and I have met people who say "it's pretty cool" to come from such a unique family. My willingness to discuss coming from a gay family results as much from the support of friends and college teachers as it does from my unchanging belief, idealized in all families, that my mother always does the right thing.

I realize I'm lucky to have been raised by people I genuinely like, and being a woman raised by women, I've not had the problems in relating to my parents that a man might have had. However, I've heard enough jokes and insults to know that people don't really believe the gay family exists in large numbers and turns out healthy, well-balanced children. It is time for society to expand the definition of family. While everyone can agree that the usual sit-com family is increasingly atypical, there is no description of what has evolved to replace it. With a broader sense of family available to children, there would be no reason to be ashamed of any kind of love.

> – Paula Fomby
> "Why I'm Glad I Grew Up in a Gay Family"
> *Mother Jones*, 1991

◇◇◇◇◇

# 8

I went to the nine o'clock mass every Sunday with my family. At that time in my life, when I was so struck by diminished family closeness and the necessity of public life, church was a place unlike any other. It mediated between my public and private lives. I would kneel beside my brother and sisters. On one side of us would be my mother. (I could hear her whispered Spanish Hail Mary.) On the other side, my father. In the pew directly in front of us were the Van Hoyts. And in front of them were the druggist and his family. Over to the side was a lady who wore fancy dresses, a widow who prayed a crystal rosary. She was alone, as was the old man in front who cupped his face in his hands while he prayed. It was this same gesture of privacy the nuns would teach me to use, especially after Communion when I thanked God for coming into my soul. . . .

*Sister* and *Brother* were terms I used in speaking to my teachers for twelve years. *Father* was the name for the priest at church. I never confused my teachers or the priests with actual family members; in fact they were most awesome for being without families. Yet I came to use these terms with ease. They implied that a deep bond existed between my teachers and me as fellow Catholics. At the same time, however, *Sister* and *Father* were highly formal terms of address — they were titles, marks' of formality like a salute or a curtsey. (One would never have spoken to a nun without first calling her Sister.) It was possible consequently to use these terms and to feel at once a close bond, and the distance of formality. In a way, that is how I felt with all fellow Catholics in my world. We were close — somehow related — while also distanced by careful reserve.

– Richard Rodriguez
*Hunger of Memory*, 1982

# 9

They are going home for Thanksgiving, traveling through the clogged arteries of airports and highways, bearing bridge chairs and serving plates, Port-a-Cribs and pies. They are going home to rooms that resound with old arguments and interruptions, to piano benches filled with small cousins, to dining-room tables stretched out to the last leaf.

They no longer migrate over the river and through the woods straight into that Norman Rockwell poster: Freedom from Want. No, Thanksgiving isn't just a feast, but a reunion. It's no longer a celebration of food (which is plentiful in America) but of family (which is scarce).

Now families are so dispersed that it's easier to bring in the crops than the cousins. Now it's not so remarkable that we have a turkey to feed the family. It's more remarkable that there's enough family around to warrant a turkey.

For most of the year, we are a nation of individuals, all wrapped in separate cellophane packages like lamb chops in the meat department of a city supermarket. Increasingly we live with decreasing numbers. We create a new category, like Single Householder, and fill it to the top of the Census Bureau reports.

For most of the year, we are segregated along generation lines into retirement villages and singles complexes, young married subdivisions and college dormitories, all exclusive clubs whose membership is defined by age. . . .

The family — as extended as that dining-room table — may be the one social glue strong enough to withstand the centrifuge of special interests which sends us spinning away from each other. There, in the family, the Elderly Rights are also grandparents and the Children Rights are also nieces and nephews. There, the old are our parents and the young are our children. There, we care about each others' lives. There, self-interest includes concern for the future of the next generation. Because they are ours.

Our families are not just the people (if I may massacre Robert Frost) who, "when you have to go there, they have to let you in." They are the people who maintain an unreasonable interest in each other. They are the natural peacemakers in the generation war.

"Home" is the only place in society where we now connect along the ages, like discs along the spine of society. The only place where we remember that we're all related. And that's not a bad idea to go home to.

> – Ellen Goodman
> "Family: The One Social Glue"
> *Close to Home,* 1979

# 10

In the contemporary American family, all economic, educational, and authoritative functions have been stripped away: The parents work away from the home; children spend their early years in child-care centers and are later educated in schools; authority in our liberal, consumer society has pretty much been trampled underfoot by the stampede of personal gratification.

This portrait of the late-modern American family is now a mainstay of sociology. Few sociologists, however, are attentive to the profound consequences of stripping down the family to its affectional core, a process that has found its ultimate expression in the notion of "quality time." Since parents and children have so little time together, this notion is understood to mean that those precious moments should all be "good times" filled with affection.

But, as we know from Bruno Bettelheim's famous study of the Israeli kibbutz, where children were raised collectively and parents saw them only for "good time" visits, the quality-time approach to child rearing produces people who lack a capacity for introspection or the inner-direction we associate with "conscience." While those who grew up in the kibbutz were strongly peer-oriented, they were seldom capable of deciding on their own what was true or false, what was good or bad — precisely the stabilizing attributes of character . . . necessary for responsible individuals in a free society.

While institutionalization of child rearing in America has not gone as far as the kibbutz, it is already tending to produce the character traits of children raised without parents.

That is why I believe that fixing whatever is wrong with the nuclear family doesn't lie in further weakening it through a never-ending expansion of child care.

> — Christopher Lasch
> "The Crime of Quality Time"
> *New Perspectives Quarterly*, 1990

## REFLECTIONS

1. How do you think Michael Novak (p. 63) would define "family"? How would Angela Davis (p. 69) define it? How would Paula Fomby (p. 71) define it? Which definition makes the most sense to you, and why?

2. Several of the authors of *Looking at Ourselves* allude to the breakdown (or breakup) of the American family. What do they mean by this?

3. What are the most valuable functions of a family? According to the selections in *Looking at Ourselves*, what changes in our culture have impeded the family in the United States from performing those functions?

4. What are the biggest disagreements among the authors in *Looking at Ourselves* regarding recommendations for solving the problems facing the family in the United States today?

# Birth Ceremonies

The week that marked the 500th anniversary of Christopher Columbus's arrival in the New World also saw the Nobel Peace Prize awarded
to a thirty-three-year-old Central American Indian. Rigoberta Menchú is
a Mayan of Guatemala's Quiché group. She grew up poor and uneducated in the village of Chimel with her parents and ten brothers and
sisters. A migrant farm worker from the age of eight, she later became a
live-in maid in Guatemala City, where she taught herself to read and
write Spanish. Her father, an organizing member of the Peasant Unity
Committee, fought for property rights. In 1979 her sixteen-year-old
brother was kidnaped by Guatemalan soldiers, tortured for two weeks,
flayed, and burned alive with several other prisoners in front of their
families. The next year her father was killed when police stormed the
Spanish embassy his group was occupying and burned it. Soon afterward,
Menchú's mother was abducted, raped, and tortured to death by soldiers.
Menchú fled to Mexico City. There the Venezuelan writer Elisabeth
Burgos-Debray helped her create the book *Me llamo Rigoberta Menchú
y asi me nacio la conciencia* ("I am named Rigoberta Menchú and in
that way my conscience was born"), which has been translated into more
than ten languages. "Birth Ceremonies" comes from the English translation by Ann Wright, *I, Rigoberta Menchú: An Indian Woman in
Guatemala* (1984). Menchú has returned to Guatemala for visits but
currently makes Mexico the base from which she works for peace and
represents her people to the world.

The Mayan empire flourished in Mexico and Guatemala for a thousand years before Spanish conquistadors colonized the region. The Central American states declared independence from Spain in 1821; the
Republic of Guatemala was established in 1839. Although Indians are
still a majority of the country's 9.5 million population, *ladinos* (Spanish
speakers of mixed descent) are politically and economically dominant.
Guatemala's recent history has been contentious, as peasant groups rebel
against repressive regimes, and advocates of land reform vie for power
with foreign investors and their allies. Over the past thirty years, some
120,000 people have died in the struggle. In May 1993, President Jorge
Serrano Elias — a civilian elected in 1991 — was overthrown after he
dissolved the congress and suspended the constitution. As we go to press,
Latin American and European countries as well as the United States have
welcomed the new government being formed by former human rights
ombudsman Ramiro de Leon Carpio.

> Whoever may ask where we are, tell them what you know of
> us and nothing more.
>
> Learn to protect yourselves, by keeping our secret.
>
> –Popol Vuh[1]

In our community there is an elected representative, someone who is highly respected. He's not a king but someone whom the community looks up to like a father. In our village, my father and mother were the representatives. Well, then the whole community becomes the children of the woman who's elected. So a mother, on her first day of pregnancy, goes with her husband to tell these elected leaders that she's going to have a child, because the child will not only belong to them but to the whole community and must follow as far as he can our ancestors' traditions. The leaders then pledge the support of the community and say: "We will help you, we will be the child's second parents." They are known as *abuelos*, "grandparents" or "forefathers." The parents then ask the "grandparents" to help them find the child some godparents, so that if he's orphaned, he shouldn't be tempted by any of the bad habits our people sometimes fall into. So the "grandparents" and the parents choose the godparents together. It's also the custom for the pregnant mother's neighbors to visit her every day and take her little things, no matter how simple. They stay and talk to her, and she'll tell them all her problems.

Later, when she's in her seventh month, the mother introduces her baby to the natural world, as our customs tell her to. She goes out in the fields or walks over the hills. She also has to show her baby the kind of life she leads, so that if she gets up at three in the morning, does her chores and tends the animals, she does it all the more so when she's pregnant, conscious that the child is taking all this in. She talks to the child continuously from the first moment he's in her stomach, telling him how hard his life will be. It's as if the mother were a guide explaining things to a tourist. She'll say, for instance, "You must never abuse nature and you must live your life as honestly as I do." As she works in the fields, she tells her child all the little things about her work. It's a duty to her child that a mother must fulfill. And then, she also has to think of a way of hiding the baby's birth from her other children.

When her baby is born, the mother mustn't have her other children around her. The people present should be the husband, the village leaders, and the couple's parents. Three couples. The parents are often away in other places, so if they can't be there, the husband's father and the wife's mother can perhaps make up one pair. If one of the village

---

[1]Sacred book of the Quiché Indian tribe.

leaders can't come, one of them should be there to make up a couple with one of the parents. If none of the parents can come, some aunts and uncles should come to represent the family on both sides, because the child is to be part of the community. The birth of a new member is very significant for the community, as it belongs to the community, not just to the parents, and that's why three couples (but not just anybody) must be there to receive it. They explain that this child is the fruit of communal love. If the village leader is not a midwife as well, another midwife is called (it might be a grandmother) to receive the child. Our customs don't allow single women to see a birth. But it does happen in times of need. For instance, I was with my sister when she went into labor. Nobody else was at home. This was when we were being heavily persecuted. Well, I didn't exactly see, but I was there when the baby was born.

My mother was a midwife from when she was sixteen right up to her death at forty-three. She used to say that a woman hadn't the strength to push the baby out when she's lying down. So what she did with my sister was to hang a rope from the roof and pull her up, because my brother wasn't there to lift her up. My mother helped the baby out with my sister in that position. It's a scandal if an Indian woman goes to the hospital and gives birth there. None of our women would agree to that. Our ancestors would be shocked at many of the things which go on today. Family planning, for example. It's an insult to our culture and a way of swindling the people, to get money out of them.

This is part of the reserve that we've maintained to defend our customs    5 and our culture. Indians have been very careful not to disclose any details of their communities, and the community does not allow them to talk about Indian things. I too must abide by this. This is because many religious people have come among us and drawn a false impression of the Indian world. We also find a *ladino* using Indian clothes very offensive. All this has meant that we keep a lot of things to ourselves and the community doesn't like us telling its secrets. This applies to all our customs. When the Catholic Action[2] arrived, for instance, everyone started going to mass and praying, but it's not their only religion, not the only way they have of expressing themselves. Anyway, when a baby is born, he's always baptized within the community before he's taken to church. Our people have taken Catholicism as just another channel of expression, not our one and only belief. Our people do the same with other religions. The priests, monks, and nuns haven't gained the people's confidence because so many of their things contradict our own customs.

---

[2]Association created in 1945 by Monsignor Rafael Gonzalez, to try and control the Indian fraternities of the *Altiplano*.

For instance, they say, "You have too much trust in your elected leaders." But the village elects them *because* they trust them, don't they? The priests say, "The trouble is you follow those sorcerers," and speak badly of them. But for our people this is like speaking ill of their own fathers, and they lose faith in the priests. They say, "Well, they're not from here, they can't understand our world." So there's not much hope of winning our people's hearts.

To come back to the children, they aren't to know how the baby is born. He's born somewhere hidden away and only the parents know about it. They are told that a baby has arrived and that they can't see their mother for eight days. Later on, the baby's companion, the placenta, that is, has to be burned at a special time. If the baby is born at night, the placenta is burned at eight in the morning, and if he's born in the afternoon, it'll be burned at five o'clock. This is out of respect for both the baby and his companion. The placenta is not buried, because the earth is the mother and the father of the child and mustn't be abused by having the placenta buried in it. All these reasons are very important for us. Either the placenta is burned on a log and the ashes left there, or else it is put in the *temascal*. This is a stove which our people use to make vapor baths. It's a small hut made of adobe and inside this hut is another one made of stone, and when we want to have a bath, we light a fire to heat the stones, close the door, and throw water on the stones to produce steam. Well, when the woman is about four months pregnant, she starts taking these baths infused with evergreens, pure natural aromas. There are many plants the community uses for pregnant women, colds, headaches, and things like that. So the pregnant mother takes baths with plants prescribed for her by the midwife or the village leader. The fields are full of plants whose names I don't know in Spanish. Pregnant women use orange and peach leaves a lot for bathing and there's another one we call Saint Mary's leaf which they use. The mother needs these leaves and herbs to relax because she won't be able to rest while she's pregnant since our women go on working just as hard in the fields. So after work, she takes this calming bath so that she can sleep well, and the baby won't be harmed by her working hard. She's given medicines to take as well. And leaves to feed the child. I believe that in practice (even if this isn't a scientific recommendation) these leaves work very well, because many of them contain vitamins. How else would women who endure hunger and hard work give birth to healthy babies? I think that these plants have helped our people survive.

The purity with which the child comes into the world is protected for eight days. Our customs say that the newborn baby should be alone with his mother in a special place for eight days, without any of her other

children. Her only visitors are the people who bring her food. This is the
baby's period of integration into the family; he very slowly becomes a
member of it. When the child is born, they kill a sheep and there's a
little fiesta just for the family. Then the neighbors start coming to visit
and bring presents. They either bring food for the mother or something
for the baby. The mother has to taste all the food her neighbors bring to
show her appreciation for their kindness. After the eight days are over,
the family counts up how many visitors the mother had and how many
presents were received; things like eggs or food apart from what was
brought for the mother, or clothing, small animals, and wood for the fire,
or services like carrying water and chopping wood. If, during the eight
days, most of the community has called, this is very important, because
it means that this child will have a lot of responsibility toward his community when he grows up. The community takes over all the household
expenses for these eight days and the family spends nothing.

After eight days, everything has been received, and another animal is
killed as recognition that the child's right to be alone with his mother is
over. All the mother's clothes, bedclothes, and everything she used during
the birth are taken away by our elected leader and washed. She can't
wash them in the well, so no matter how far away the river is, they must
be carried and washed there. The baby's purity is washed away and he's
ready to learn the ways of humanity. The mother's bed is moved to a part
of the house which has first been washed with water and lime. Lime is
sacred. It strengthens the child's bones. I believe this really is true. It gives
a child strength to face the world. The mother has a bath in the *temascal*
and puts on clean clothes. Then the whole house is cleaned. The child
is also washed and dressed and put into the new bed. Four candles are
placed on the corners of the bed to represent the four corners of the
house and show him that this will be his home. They symbolize the
respect the child must have for his community, and the responsibility he
must feel toward it as a member of a household. The candles are lit and
give off an incense which incorporates the child into the world he must
live in. When the baby is born, his hands and feet are bound to show
him that they are sacred and must only be used to work or do whatever
nature meant them to do. They must never steal or abuse the natural
world, or show disrespect for any living thing.

After the eight days, his hands and feet are untied and he's now with
his mother in the new bed. This means he opens the doors to the other
members of the community, because neither the family or the community
know him yet. Or rather, they weren't shown the baby when he was born.
Now they can all come and kiss him. The neighbors bring another
animal, and there's a big lunch in the new baby's house for all the

community. This is to celebrate his integration "in the universe," as our parents used to say. Candles will be lit for him, and his candle becomes part of the candle of the whole community, which now has one more person, one more member. The whole community is at the ceremony, or at least, if not all of it, then some of it. Candles are lit to represent all the things which belong to the universe — earth, water, sun, and man — and the child's candle is put with them, together with incense (what we call *pom*) and lime — our sacred lime. Then the parents tell the baby of the suffering of the family he will be joining. With great feeling, they express their sorrow at bringing a child into the world to suffer. To us, suffering is our fate, and the child must be introduced to the sorrows and hardship, but he must learn that despite his suffering, he will be respectful and live through his pain. The child is then entrusted with the responsibility for his community and told to abide by its rules. After the ceremony comes the lunch, and then the neighbors go home. Now there is only the baptism to come.

When the baby is born, he's given a little bag with a garlic, a bit of lime, salt, and tobacco in it to hang round his neck. Tobacco is important because it is a sacred plant for Indians. This all means that the child can ward off all the evil things in life. For us, bad things are like spirits, which exist only in our imagination. Something bad, for instance, would be if the child were to turn out to be a gossip — not sincere, truthful, and respectful, as a child should be. It also helps him collect together and preserve all our ancestors' things. That's more or less the idea of the bag — to keep him pure. The bag is put inside the four candles as well, and this represents the promise of the child when he grows up.

When the child is forty days old, there are more speeches, more promises on his behalf, and he becomes a full member of the community. This is his baptism. All the important people of the village are invited and they speak. The parents make a commitment. They promise to teach the child to keep the secrets of our people, so that our culture and customs will be preserved. The village leaders come and offer their experience, their example, and their knowledge of our ancestors. They explain how to preserve our traditions. Then, they promise to be responsible for the child, teach him as he grows up, and see that he follows in their ways. It's also something of a criticism of humanity, and of the many people who have forsaken their traditions. They say almost a prayer, asking that our traditions again enter the spirits of those who have forsaken them. Then, they evoke the names of our ancestors, like Tecun Umán and others who form part of the ceremony, as a kind of chant. They must be remembered as heroes of the Indian peoples. And then they say, . . ."Let no landowner extinguish all this, nor any rich man wipe out

10

our customs. Let our children, be they workers or servants, respect and keep their secrets." The child is present for all of this, although he's all wrapped up and can scarcely be seen. He is told that he will eat maize,[3] and that, naturally, he is already made of maize because his mother ate it while he was forming in her stomach. He must respect the maize; even the grain of maize which has been thrown away, he must pick up. The child will multiply our race, he will replace all those who have died. From this moment, he takes on this responsibility, and is told to live as his "grandparents" have lived. The parents then reply that their child promises to accomplish all this. So, the village leaders and the parents both make promises on behalf of the child. It's his initiation into the community.

The ceremony is very important. It is also when the child is considered a child of God, our one father. We don't actually have the word God but that is what it is, because the one father is the only one we have. To reach this one father, the child must love beans, maize, the earth. The one father is the heart of the sky, that is, the sun. The sun is the father and our mother is the moon. She is a gentle mother. And she lights our way. Our people have many notions about the moon, and about the sun. They are the pillars of the universe.

When children reach ten years old, that's the moment when their parents and the village leaders talk to them again. They tell them that they will be young men and women and that one day they will be fathers and mothers. This is actually when they tell the child that he must never abuse his dignity, in the same way his ancestors never abused their dignity. It's also when they remind them that our ancestors were dishonored by the White Man, by colonization. But they don't tell them the way that it's written down in books, because the majority of Indians can't read or write, and don't even know that they have their own texts. No, they learn it through oral recommendations, the way it has been handed down through the generations. They are told that the Spaniards dishonored our ancestors' finest sons, and the most humble of them. And it is to honor these humble people that we must keep our secrets. And no one except we Indians must know. They talk a lot about our ancestors. And the ten-years ceremony is also when our children are reminded that they must respect their elders, even though this is something their parents have been telling them ever since they were little. For example, if an old person is walking along the street, children should cross over to allow him to pass by. If any of us sees an elderly person, we are obliged to bow and greet

---

[3]Corn. — ED.

him. Everyone does this, even the very youngest. We also show respect to pregnant women. Whenever we make food, we always keep some for any of our neighbors who are pregnant.

When little girls are born, the midwives pierce their ears at the same time as they tie their umbilical cords. The little bags around their necks and the thread used to tie their umbilical cord are both red. Red is very significant for us. It means heat, strength, all living things. It's linked to the sun, which for us is the channel to the one God, the heart of everything, of the universe. So red gives off heat and fire, and red things are supposed to give life to the child. At the same time, it asks him to respect living things too. There are no special clothes for the baby. We don't buy anything special beforehand but just use pieces of *corte*[4] to wrap him in.

When a male child is born, there are special celebrations, not because    15
he's male but because of all the hard work and responsibility he'll have as a man. It's not that *machismo* doesn't exist among our people, but it doesn't present a problem for the community because it's so much part of our way of life. The male child is given an extra day alone with his mother. The usual custom is to celebrate a male child by killing a sheep or some chickens. Boys are given more, they get more food because their work is harder and they have more responsibility. At the same time, he is head of the household, not in the bad sense of the word, but because he is responsible for so many things. This doesn't mean girls aren't valued. Their work is hard too and there are other things that are due to them as mothers. Girls are valued because they are part of the earth, which gives us maize, beans, plants, and everything we live on. The earth is like a mother which multiplies life. So the girl child will multiply the life of our generation and of our ancestors whom we must respect. The girl and the boy are both integrated into the community in equally important ways; the two are interrelated and compatible. Nevertheless, the community is always happier when a male child is born and the men feel much prouder. The customs, like the tying of the hands and feet, apply to both boys and girls.

Babies are breast-fed. It's much better than any other sort of food. But the important thing is the sense of community. It's something we all share. From the very first day, the baby belongs to the community, not only to the parents, and the baby must learn from all of us. . . . In fact, we behave just like bourgeois families in that, as soon as the baby is born, we're thinking of his education, of his well-being. But our people feel that the

---

[4]Multicolored material that Guatemalan women use as a skirt. It is part of their traditional costume.

baby's school must be the community itself, that he must learn to live like all the rest of us. The tying of the hands at birth also symbolizes this; that no one should accumulate things the rest of the community does not have and he must know how to share, to have open hands. The mother must teach the baby to be generous. This way of thinking comes from poverty and suffering. Each child is taught to live like the fellow members of his community.

We never eat in front of pregnant women. You can only eat in front of a pregnant woman if you can offer something as well. The fear is that, otherwise, she might abort the baby or that the baby could suffer if she didn't have enough to eat. It doesn't matter whether you know her or not. The important thing is sharing. You have to treat a pregnant woman differently from other women because she is two people. You must treat her with respect so that she recognizes it and conveys this to the baby inside her. You instinctively think she's the image of the baby about to be born. So you love her. Another reason why you must stop and talk to a pregnant woman is because she doesn't have much chance to rest or enjoy herself. She's always worried and depressed. So when she stops and chats a bit, she can relax and feel some relief.

When the baby joins the community, with him in the circle of candles — together with his little red bag — he will have his hoe, his machete, his axe, and all the tools he will need in life. These will be his playthings. A little girl will have her washing board and all the things she will need when she grows up. She must learn the things of the house, to clean, to wash, and to sew her brothers' trousers, for example. The little boy must begin to live like a man, to be responsible and learn to love the work in the fields. The learning is done as a kind of game. When the parents do anything they always explain what it means. This includes learning prayers. This is very important to our people. The mother may say a prayer at any time. Before getting up in the morning, for instance, she thanks the day which is dawning because it might be a very important one for the family. Before lighting the fire, she blesses the wood because that fire is going to cook food for the whole family. Since it's the little girl who is closest to her mother, she learns all of this. Before washing the *nixtamal*,[5] the woman blows on her hands and puts them in the *nixtamal*. She takes everything out and washes it well. She blows on her hands so that her work will bear fruit. She does it before she does the wash as well. She explains all these little details to her daughter, who learns by copying her. With the men it's the same. Before they start work

---

[5]Cauldron where the maize is cooked.

every day, whatever hour of the morning it is, they greet the sun. They remove their hats and talk to the sun before starting work. Their sons learn to do it too, taking off their little hats to talk to the sun. Naturally, each ethnic group has its own forms of expression. Other groups have different customs from ours. The meaning of their weaving patterns, for example. We realize the others are different in some things, but the one thing we have in common is our culture. Our people are mainly peasants, but there are some people who buy and sell as well. They go into this after they've worked on the land. Sometimes when they come back from working in the *finca*,[6] instead of tending a little plot of land, they'll start a shop and look for a different sort of life. But if they're used to greeting the sun every morning, they still go on doing it. And they keep all their old customs. Every part of our culture comes from the earth. Our religion comes from the maize and bean harvests which are so vital to our community. So even if a man goes to try and make some money, he never forgets his culture springs from the earth.

As we grow up we have a series of obligations. Our parents teach us to be responsible, just as they have been responsible. The eldest son is responsible for the house. Whatever the father cannot correct is up to the eldest son to correct. He is like a second father to us all and is responsible for our upbringing. The mother is the one who is responsible for keeping an account of what the family eats and what she has to buy. When a child is ill, she has to get medicine. But the father has to solve a lot of problems too. And each one of us, as we grow up, has our own small area of responsibility. This comes from the promises made for the child when he is born, and from the continuity of our customs. The child can make the promise for himself when his parents have taught him to do it. The mother, who is closest to the children, does this, or sometimes the father. They talk to their children explaining what they have to do and what our ancestors used to do. They don't impose it as a law, but just give the example of what our ancestors have always done. This is how we all learn our own small responsibilities. For example, the little girl begins by carrying water, and the little boy begins by tying up the dogs when the animals are brought into the yard at night, or by fetching a horse which has wandered off. Both girls and boys have their tasks and are told the reasons for doing them. They learn responsibility because if they don't do their little jobs well, their father has the right to scold them, or even beat them. So, they are very careful about learning to do their jobs well, but the parents are also very careful to explain exactly why the jobs have

---

[6]Plantation, estate.

to be done. The little girl understands the reasons for everything her mother does. For example, when she puts a new earthenware pot on the fire for the first time, she hits it five times with a branch, so that it knows its job is to cook and so that it lasts. When the little girl asks, "Why did you do that?" her mother says, "So that it knows what its job is and does it well." When it's her turn to cook, the little girl does as her mother does. Again this is all bound up with our commitment to maintain our customs and pass on the secrets of our ancestors. The elected fathers of the community explain to us that all these things come down to us from our grandfathers and we must conserve them. Nearly everything we do today is based on what our ancestors did. This is the main purpose of our elected leader — to embody all the values handed down from our ancestors. He is the leader of the community, a father to all our children, and he must lead an exemplary life. Above all, he has a commitment to the whole community. Everything that is done today is done in memory of those who have passed on.

## EXPLORATIONS

1. Besides recognizing biological parenthood, in what other ways do the Quiché Indians apply the concepts of mother and father?

2. What ceremonies mark the landmarks in a Quiché child's life, both before and after birth? What are the main purposes of these ceremonies?

3. What specific steps are taken by a Quiché baby's parents, and what steps are taken by others in the community, to make sure the child learns his or her responsibilities?

## CONNECTIONS

1. In *Looking at Ourselves* (p. 73), Ellen Goodman calls family the "social glue" that links Americans of different generations. According to Goodman, how does family play this role? According to Rigoberta Menchú, how does family play this role among the Quiché Indians?

2. In *Looking at Ourselves* (p. 68), Patricia Schroeder talks about the dilemma of child care in the United States. How is the need for child care met by the Quiché of Guatemala? What contrasts between American and Quiché social structures are responsible for the difference?

3. Michael Novak, in *Looking at Ourselves* (p. 63), describes values, ideas, and skills that American children can learn in the family. What values, ideas, and

skills are mentioned by Menchú as being learned by Quiché children in the family and the community?

4. What similarities exist between Menchú's account of a Quiché childhood and Richard Rodriguez's account of a Roman Catholic childhood in *Looking at Ourselves* (p. 73)?

## ELABORATIONS

1. In Quiché society, talismans are given to a child to "ward off all the evil things in life" (para. 10). What evil things are warded off in this way? What tactics are used in the United States to ward off similar (or different) evils? Write an essay describing the dangers from which our culture tries to protect children, and the methods we use to do this. One way of writing about these dangers is to classify them according to some meaningful scheme.

2. How are Quiché children taught to regard their ancestors? Write a narrative or descriptive essay about the role of ancestors in your life or in your culture.

# LOUISE ERDRICH

## *Adam*

Karen Louise Erdrich (pronounced Er-drick) was born in 1954 in Little Falls, Minnesota, the oldest of seven children. Part German, part French, and part Turtle Mountain Chippewa, she grew up near a Sioux Indian reservation in Wahpeton, North Dakota. She met Michael Dorris (see p. 569) when she entered Dartmouth College in 1972 as a member of the first class to include women. After graduation she worked on a television documentary about the Northern Plains Indians, earned her master's degree at Johns Hopkins University, worked for the Boston Indian Council, waited tables, taught, wrote, and edited. In 1981 she came back to Dartmouth as a writer in residence and married Dorris. As she describes in "Adam," she also became the mother of his three adopted children. Erdrich and Dorris since have had three more children together. They have developed an equally collaborative approach to writing: He became the agent for her first novel, *Love Medicine* (1984), which won the National Book Critics Circle Award and has been translated into over eighteen languages; now each reads and revises everything the other writes until both are satisfied with the result. *The Crown of Columbus* (1991) was their first formally coauthored novel. "Adam" comes from Erdrich's preface to Dorris's autobiographical book, *The Broken Cord* (1989), which dramatically publicized the impact of Fetal Alcohol Syndrome on their son Abel (Adam's real name) and other children, particularly Native Americans. Abel was hit by a car and died at the age of twenty-three.

The snow fell deep today. February 4, 1988, two days before Michael and I are to leave for our first trip abroad together, ten days before Saint Valentine's holiday, which we will spend in Paris, fifteen days after Adam's twentieth birthday. This is no special day, it marks no breakthrough in Adam's life or in mine, it is a day held in suspension by the depth of snow, the silence, school closing, our seclusion in the country along a steep gravel road which no cars will dare use until the town plow goes through.

It is just a day when Adam had a seizure. His grandmother called and said that she could see, from out the window, Adam lying in the snow, having a seizure. He had fallen while shoveling the mailbox clear. Michael was at the door too, but I got out first because I had on sneakers. Jumping into the snow I felt a moment of obscure gratitude to Michael for letting me go to Adam's rescue. Though unacknowledged between us, these are the times when it is easy to be a parent to Adam. His seizures are increasingly grand mal now. And yet, unless he hurts himself in the fall, there is nothing to do but be a comforting presence, make sure he's turned on his side, breathing. I ran to Adam and I held him, spoke his name, told him I was there, used my most soothing tone. When he came back to consciousness I rose, propped him against me, and we stood to shake out his sleeves and the neck of his jacket.

A lone snowmobiler passed, then circled to make sure we were all right. I suppose we made a picture that could cause mild concern. We stood, propped together, hugging and breathing hard. Adam is taller than me, and usually much stronger. I held him around the waist with both arms and looked past his shoulder. The snow was still coming, drifting through the deep-branched pines. All around us there was such purity, a wet and electric silence. The air was warm and the snow already melting in my shoes.

It is easy to give the absolute, dramatic love that a definite physical problem requires, easy to stagger back, slipping, to take off Adam's boots and make sure he gets the right amount of medicine into his system.

It is easy to be the occasional, ministering angel. But it is not easy to      5
live day in and day out with a child disabled by Fetal Alcohol Syndrome or Fetal Alcohol Effect. This set of preventable birth defects is manifested in a variety of ways, but caused solely by alcohol in an unborn baby's developing body and brain. The U.S. Surgeon General's report for 1988 warned about the hazards of drinking while pregnant, and many doctors now say that since no level of alcohol has been established as safe for the fetus, the best policy to follow for nine months, longer if a mother nurses, is complete abstinence. . . . Every woman reacts differently to alcohol, depending on age, diet, and metabolism. However, drinking at the wrong time of development can cause facial and bodily abnormalities, as well as lower intelligence, and may also impair certain types of judgment, or alter behavior. Adam suffers all the symptoms that I've mentioned, to some degree. It's a lot of fate to play with for the sake of a moment's relaxation.

I never intended to be the mother of a child with problems. Who does? But when, after a year of marriage to their father, I legally adopted Adam, Sava, and Madeline — the three children *he* had adopted, years before, as a single parent — it simply happened. I've got less than the ordinary amount of patience, and for that reason I save all my admiration for those like Ken Kramberg, Adam's teacher, and others who work day in and day out with disability. I save it for my husband, Michael, who spent months of his life teaching Adam to tie his shoes. Living with Adam touches on my occupation only in the most peripheral ways; this is the first time I've ever written about him. I've never disguised him as a fictional character or consciously drawn on our experience together. It is, in fact, painful for a writer of fiction to write about actual events in one's personal life. . . .

Although he has no concern about us as professionals, neither pride nor the slightest trace of resentment, Adam takes pleasure when, as a family, our pictures have occasionally been in the paper. He sees Michael and me primarily in the roles to which we've assigned ourselves around the house. Michael is the laundryman, I am the cook. And beyond that, most important, we are the people who respond to him. In that way, though an adult, he is at the stage of a very young child who sees the world only as an extension of his or her will. Adam is the world, at least his version of it, and he knows us only as who we are when we enter his purview.

Because of this, there are ways Adam knows us better than we know ourselves, though it would be difficult for him to describe this knowledge. He knows our limits, and I, at least, hide my limits from myself, especially when I go beyond them, especially when it comes to anger. Sometimes it seems to me that from the beginning, in living with Adam, anger has been inextricable from love, and I've been as helpless before the one as before the other.

We were married, Michael, his three children, and I, on a slightly overcast October day in 1981. Adam was thirteen, and because he had not yet gone through puberty, he was small, about the size of a ten-year-old. He was not, and is not, a charming person, but he is generous, invariably kind-hearted, and therefore lovable. He had then, and still possesses, the gift — which is also a curse, given the realities of the world — of absolute, serene trust. He took our ceremony, in which we exchanged vows, literally. At the end of it we were pronounced husband, wife, and family by the same friend, a local judge, who would later formally petition for me to become the adoptive mother of Adam, Sava, and Madeline; then still later, as we painfully came to terms with certain truths, he helped us set up a lifelong provision for Adam in our wills. As Judge Daschbach pronounced the magic words, Adam turned to me with delight and said, "Mom!" not Louise. Now it was official. I melted. That trust was not to change a whit, until I changed it.

Ten months pass. We're at the dinner table. I've eaten, so have our other children. It's a good dinner, one of their favorites. Michael's gone. Adam eats a bite then puts down his fork and sits before his plate. When I ask him to finish, he says, "But, Mom, I don't like this food."

"Yes, you do," I tell him. I'm used to a test or two from Adam when Michael is away, and these challenges are wearying, sometimes even maddening. But Adam has to know that I have the same rules as his father.

He has to know, over and over and over. And Adam *does* like the food. I made it because he gobbled it down the week before and said he liked it, and I was happy.

"You have to eat or else you'll have a seizure in the morning," I tell him. This has proved to be true time and again. I am reasonable, firm, even patient at first, although I've said the same thing many times before. This is normal, Adam's way, just a test. I tell him again to finish.

"I don't like this food," he says again.

"Adam," I say, "you have to eat or you'll have a seizure."

He stares at me. Nothing.                                                          15

Our younger children take their empty dishes to the sink. I wash them. Adam sits. Sava and Madeline go upstairs to play, and Adam sits. I check his forehead, think perhaps he's ill, but he is cool, and rather pleased with himself. He has now turned fourteen years old. But he still doesn't understand that, in addition to his medication, he must absorb so many calories every day or else he'll suffer an attack. The electricity in his brain will lash out, the impulses scattered and random.

"Eat up. I'm not kidding."

"I did," he says, the plate still full before him.

I simply point.

"I don't like this food," he says to me again.                                    20

I walk back to the cupboard. I slap a peanut butter sandwich together. He likes those. Maybe a concession on my part will satisfy him, maybe he'll eat, but when I put it on his plate he just looks at it.

I go into the next room. It is eight o'clock and I am in the middle of a book by Bruce Chatwin. There is more to life . . . but I'm responsible. I have to make him see that he's not just driving me crazy.

"Eat the sandwich . . ."

"I did." The sandwich is untouched.

"Eat the dinner . . ."                                                             25

"I don't like this food."

"Okay then. Eat half."

He won't. He sits there. In his eyes there is an expression of stubborn triumph that boils me with the suddenness of frustration, dammed and suppressed, surfacing all at once.

"EAT!" I yell at him.

Histrionics, stamping feet, loud voices, usually impress him with the        30
serious nature of our feelings much more than the use of reason. But not this time. There is no ordering, begging, or pleading that will make him eat, even for his own good. And he is thin, so thin. His face is gaunt, his ribs arch out of his sternum, his knees are big, bony, and his calves and thighs straight as sticks. I don't want him to fall, to seize, to hurt himself.

"Please . . . for me. Just do it."

He looks at me calmly.

"Just for me, okay?"

"I don't like this food."

The lid blows off. Nothing is left. If I can't help him to survive in the    35
simplest way, how can I be his mother?

"Don't eat then. And don't call me Mom!"

Then I walk away, shaken. I leave him sitting and he does not eat, and
the next morning he does have a seizure. He falls next to the aquarium,
manages to grasp the table, and as his head bobs and his mouth twists, I
hold him, wait it out. It's still two days before Michael will arrive home
and I don't believe that I can handle it and I don't know how Michael
has, but that is only a momentary surge of panic. Adam finally rights
himself. He changes his pants. He goes on with his day. He does not
connect the seizure with the lack of food: He won't. But he does connect
my words, I begin to notice. He does remember. From that night on he
starts calling me Louise, and I don't care. I'm glad of it at first, and think
it will blow over when we forgive and grow close again. After all, he
forgets most things.

But of all that I've told Adam, all the words of love, all the encourage-
ments, the orders that I gave, assurances, explanations, and instructions,
the only one he remembers with perfect, fixed comprehension, even
when I try to contradict it, even after months, is "Don't call me Mom."

Adam calls me "Mother" or "Mom" now, but it took years of patience,
of backsliding, and of self-control, it took Adam's father explaining and
me explaining and rewarding with hugs when he made me feel good, to
get back to mother and son again. It took a long trip out west, just the
two of us. It took a summer of side-by-side work. We planted thirty-five
trees and one whole garden and a flower bed. We thinned the strawberries, pruned the lilacs and forsythia. We played tic-tac-toe, then Sorry. We
lived together. And I gave up making him eat, or distanced myself enough
to put the medicine in his hand and walk away, and realize I can't protect
him.

That's why I say it takes a certain fiber I don't truly possess to live and    40
work with a person obstinate to the core, yet a victim. Constant, nagging
insults to good sense eventually wear on the steel of the soul. Logic that
flies in the face of logic can madden one. In the years I've spent with
Adam, I have learned more about my limits than I ever wanted to know.
And yet, in spite of the ridiculous arguments, the life-and-death battles
over medication and the puny and wearying orders one must give every
day, in spite of pulling gloves onto the chapped, frost-bitten hands of a

nearly grown man and knowing he will shed them, once out of sight, in the minus-thirty windchill of January, something mysterious has flourished between us, a bond of absolute simplicity, love. That is, unquestionably, the alpha and omega of our relationship, even now that Adam has graduated to a somewhat more independent life.

But as I said, that love is inextricable from anger, and in loving Adam, the anger is mostly directed elsewhere, for it is impossible to love the sweetness, the inner light, the qualities that I trust in Adam, without hating the fact that he will always be kept from fully expressing those aspects of himself because of his biological mother's drinking. He is a Fetal Alcohol Effect victim. He'll always, all his life, be a lonely person.

I drank hard in my twenties and eventually got hepatitis. I was lucky. Beyond an occasional glass of wine, I can't tolerate liquor anymore. But from those early days, I understand the urge for alcohol, its physical pull. I had formed an emotional bond with a special configuration of chemicals, and I realize to this day the attraction of the relationship and the immense difficulty in abandoning it.

Adam's mother never did let go. She died of alcohol poisoning, and I'd feel sorrier for her, if we didn't have Adam. As it is, I only hope that she died before she had a chance to produce another child with his problems. I can't help but wish, too, that during her pregnancy, if she couldn't be counseled or helped, she had been forced to abstain for those crucial nine months. On some American Indian reservations, the situation has grown so desperate that a jail internment during pregnancy has been the only answer possible in some cases. Some people . . . have taken more drastic stands and even called for the forced sterilization of women who, after having previously blunted the lives of several children like Adam, refuse to stop drinking while they're pregnant. This will outrage some women, and men, good people who believe that it is the right of individuals to put themselves in harm's way, that drinking is a choice we make, that a person's liberty to court either happiness or despair is sacrosanct. I believed this, too, and yet the poignancy and frustration of Adam's life has fed my doubts, has convinced me that some of my principles were smug, untested. After all, where is the measure of responsibility here? Where, exactly, is the demarcation between self-harm and child abuse? Gross negligence is nearly equal to intentional wrong, goes a legal maxim. Where do we draw the line?

The people who advocate forcing pregnant women to abstain from drinking come from within the communities dealing with a problem of nightmarish proportions. Still, this is very shaky ground. Once a woman decides to carry a child to term, to produce another human being, has she also the right to inflict on that person Adam's life? Because his mother drank, Adam is one of the earth's damaged. Did she have the right to take away Adam's curiosity, the right to take away the joy he could have felt at receiving a high math score, in reading a book, in wondering at the complexity and quirks of nature? Did she have the right to make him an outcast among children, to make him friendless, to make of his sexuality a problem more than a pleasure, to slit his brain, to give him violent seizures?

It seems to me, in the end, that she had no right to inflict such harm,        45
even from the depth of her own ignorance. Roman Catholicism defines two kinds of ignorance, vincible and invincible. Invincible ignorance is that state in which a person is unexposed to certain forms of knowledge. The other type of ignorance, vincible, is willed. It is a conscious turning away from truth. In either case, I don't think Adam's mother had the right to harm her, and our, son.

Knowing what I know now, I am sure that even when I drank hard, I would rather have been incarcerated for nine months and produce a normal child than bear a human being who would, for the rest of his or her life, be imprisoned by what I had done.

And for those still outraged at this position, those so sure, so secure, I say the same thing I say to those who would not allow a poor woman a safe abortion and yet have not themselves gone to adoption agencies and taken in the unplaceable children, the troubled, the unwanted:

If you don't agree with me, then please, go and sit beside the alcohol-affected while they try to learn how to add. My mother, Rita Erdrich, who works with disabled children at the Wahpeton Indian School, does this every day. Dry their frustrated tears. Fight for them in the society they don't understand. Tell them every simple thing they must know for survival, one million, two million, three million times. Hold their heads when they have unnecessary seizures and wipe the blood from their bitten lips. Force them to take medicine. Keep the damaged of the earth safe. Love them. Watch them grow up to sink into the easy mud of alcoholism. Suffer a crime they won't understand committing. Try to understand lack of remorse. As taxpayers, you are already paying for their jail terms, and footing the bills for expensive treatment and education. Be a victim yourself, beat your head against a world of brick, fail constantly. Then go back to the mother, face to face, and say again: *"It was your right."*

When I am angriest, I mentally tear into Adam's mother. When I am saddest, I wish her, exhaustedly . . . but there is nowhere to wish her worse than the probable hell of her life and death. And yet, if I ever met her, I don't know what I'd do. Perhaps we'd both be resigned before this enormous lesson. It is almost impossible to hold another person responsible for so much hurt. Even though I know our son was half-starved, tied to the bars of his crib, removed by a welfare agency, I still think it must have been "society's fault." In public, when asked to comment on Native American issues, I am defensive. Yes, I say, there are terrible problems. It takes a long, long time to heal communities beaten by waves of conquest and disease. It takes a long time for people to heal themselves. Sometimes, it seems hopeless. Yet in places, it is happening. Tribal communities, most notably the Alkali Lake Band in Canada, are coming together, rejecting alcohol, reembracing their own humanity, their own culture. These are tough people and they teach a valuable lesson: To whatever extent we can, we must take charge of our lives.

Yet, in loving Adam, we bow to fate. Few of his problems can be solved    50
or ultimately changed. So instead, Michael and I concentrate on only what we can control — our own reactions. If we can muster grace, joy, happiness in helping him confront and conquer the difficulties life presents . . . then we have received gifts. Adam has been deprived of giving so much else. . . .

Michael and I have a picture of our son. For some reason, in this photograph, taken on my grandfather's land in the Turtle Mountains of North Dakota, no defect is evident in Adam's stance or face. Although perhaps a knowing doctor could make the fetal alcohol diagnosis from his features, Adam's expression is intelligent and serene. He is smiling, his eyes are brilliant, and his brows are dark, sleek. There is no sign in this portrait that anything is lacking.

I look at this picture and think, "Here is the other Adam. The one our son would be if not for alcohol." Sometimes Michael and I imagine that we greet him, that we look into his eyes, and he into ours, for a long time and in that gaze we not only understand our son, but he also understands us. He has grown up to be a colleague, a peer, not a person who needs pity, protection, or special breaks. By the old reservation cabin where my mother was born, in front of the swirled wheat fields and woods of ancestral land, Adam stands expectantly, the full-hearted man he was meant to be. The world opens before him — so many doors, so much light. In this picture, he is ready to go forward with his life.

## EXPLORATIONS

1. For Louise Erdrich, what is the hardest part of being Adam's mother? What is the most rewarding part?

2. "This is no special day," writes Erdrich in paragraph 1. What incident in this day would make it special for most other people? What is the effect of Erdrich's saying it isn't special for her and her family?

3. How would the impact of Erdrich's essay change if she stated that Adam is a victim of Fetal Alcohol Syndrome, and defined this problem, in her opening paragraph? Where does she give such information instead?

## CONNECTIONS

1. By what steps did Erdrich's and Adam's family come into being? How do you think Erdrich would define *family*? Which selections in *Looking at Ourselves* imply a similar definition of *family*?

2. How do Erdrich and her husband deal with the problems of child care mentioned by Patricia Schroeder and others in *Looking at Ourselves*? As professional writers, what advantages and disadvantages have this couple created for themselves as parents?

3. What similarities can you find between Erdrich's family and the Quiché Indian families described in Rigoberta Menchú's "Birth Ceremonies" (p. 76)?

## ELABORATIONS

1. Choose one of the incidents Erdrich narrates in "Adam" and rewrite it from Adam's point of view. Include whatever awareness you imagine Adam has of being affected by Fetal Alcohol Syndrome.

2. In *Looking at Ourselves*, Norman Boucher (p. 64), Angela Davis (p. 69), and Paula Fomby (p. 71) write about three contrasting kinds of family. Is there such a thing as a typical American family? In "Adam," how do Adam's distinctive characteristics and needs affect his parents' responsibilities? If their son were a gifted athlete, chess player, or musician, would Erdrich's and her husband's roles change? In what ways? Use your own experience and evidence from your reading to write an essay defining *family* in terms of its functions, or classifying different kinds of family.

# LIANG HENG and
# JUDITH SHAPIRO

## Chairman Mao's
## Good Little Boy

Liang Heng was born in 1954 in Changsha, the central Chinese city where Communist Party Chairman Mao Zedong went to high school. Liang's childhood coincided with a period of violent pendulum swings in Party policy. For about eight years after establishing the People's Republic of China in 1949, Chairman Mao and his cohorts enjoyed wide popular support. Although Mao's regime modernized an ancient empire by unifying the government and improving social conditions, its methods included periodic crackdowns on ideological foes — real or imagined (see p. 22). In the mid-1950s, the Party's moves to encourage criticism boomeranged into an "Anti-Rightist" campaign against the critics. "Chairman Mao's Good Little Boy" comes from the first chapter of Liang's autobiography, *Son of the Revolution* (1983), coauthored with Judith Shapiro, which describes the chaos and fear of those years.

His family's victimization hardly dampened Liang's revolutionary loyalty, however. After the events he narrates here, Liang became one of Mao's Red Guards (working-class students opposing the "bourgeoisie" and intellectuals). The Party's goals were ambitious, its tactics drastic, and its impact often tragic: During the Great Leap Forward, launched in 1958, hundreds of millions of people were put to work on large industrial projects and over 40 million starved to death. Liang Heng almost became one of the casualties. Swept up in Mao's Confucian philosophy of saving the Chinese spirit by rejecting Western culture, politics, and technology, he went on an arduous "New Long March," during which he nearly starved and froze. He traveled to Beijing to see Mao, plunged into the "black society" of teenage dropouts scrounging for a living on the streets of Changsha, and worked on a commune. His escape route was basketball, which took him to a city job and eventually college.

Judith Shapiro was born in 1953. She met Liang while teaching American literature at Hunan Teachers' College. Their secret romance led to marriage in 1980; they coauthored two books on China after Mao before divorcing. Liang, who received a master's degree in literature from Columbia University, lives in New York and edits *The Chinese Intellectual*, a quarterly for visiting scholars and students from the People's Republic. Shapiro became a resident scholar at the Foreign Policy Research Institute in Philadelphia and an adjunct lecturer in sociology at the University of Pennsylvania. She is now the Asia program officer at the National Endowment for Democracy.

Once when I was nearly four, I decided to escape from the child-care center. The idea of waiting through another Saturday afternoon was unbearable. I would stand with the other children in the office doorway, yelling out the names of those whose relatives we spotted coming to rescue them. I would become frantic and miserable as the possibility that I had been forgotten seemed more and more real. Then at last the frail figure of my beloved Waipo, my maternal grandmother, would appear to take me away. But this week I wouldn't have to wait. I had just discovered a doorway leading from the kitchen directly onto the Changsha streets, left ajar, perhaps, by the cooks now that the bitter winter weather had passed. So, during after-lunch nap, I crawled over the green bars of my crib and stole softly out, past the sleeping rows of my fellow inmates, past Nurse Nie dozing in her chair. I crept into the coal-dark kitchen with its silent black works. Then I exploded out the door into the dazzling light of freedom.

The child-care center was hateful. You couldn't eat sweets when you wanted to, and you had to fold your hands behind your back and sing a song before the nurses would let you eat your meals. Then, if you ate too fast, they hit you over the head with a fly swatter. The songs and dances — like "Sweeping the Floor," "Working in the Factory," and "Planting Trees in the Countryside" — were fun, but I was constantly in trouble for wanting to dance the army dance when it was time for the hoeing dance or for refusing to take the part of the landlord, the wolf, or the lazybones. I also had problems with the interminable rest periods. We weren't allowed to get up even if we weren't tired, so I had nothing to do but stare at a small mole on my leg for hours at a time.

At the time, such early education was a privilege for which only the children of cadres were eligible. Although neither of my parents' ranks was high, my father's position as reporter, editor, and founding member of the Party newspaper the *Hunan Daily*, and my mother's as a promising cadre in the Changsha Public Security Bureau were enough to qualify me. My parents were deeply involved in all the excitement of working to transform China into a great Socialist country, eager to sacrifice themselves for others. They dreamed passionately of the day when they would be deemed pure and devoted enough to be accepted into the Party. It was only natural that the family come second; Father's duties at the newspaper often kept him away for several months at a time, and my mother came home only on Sundays, if at all, for she had a room in her own unit and stayed there to attend evening meetings. So at the age of three I was sent off to the child-care center for early training in Socialist thought through collective living, far from the potentially corrupting influence of family life. My departure may have been harder for my two grandmothers, of course. They had had the major responsibility for raising the three of us children; I was the last child to go, and they would miss me very much.

I had lived first with my paternal grandmother, my Nai Nai, a tall, stern, bony woman who always wore traditional black. She lived in the apartment the *Hunan Daily* had allotted to Father, two rooms on the second floor of a cadres' dormitory, spacious enough but with a shared kitchen and an outhouse some distance away. She was a pious Buddhist and a vegetarian, strict with herself and everyone else but her own grandchildren.

At ten pounds, I had been the biggest baby ever recorded at Chang-    5 sha's No. 1 Hospital, and Nai Nai had hired a series of seven wet nurses before she found one who could satisfy my appetite. She was a nineteen-year-old peasant girl from a town beyond the city whose own baby had died. Nai Nai told me later that she was the only one who had enough milk so that I could suck her breasts dry without throwing a tantrum immediately afterwards; I have always given credit to her for my unusual height — I am six-foot one. Then after she left because she had no Changsha city residence card, Nai Nai sent me to live with my maternal grandmother, my Waipo, who lived off a winding little alleyway not far away.

It was much more crowded there, since Waipo, my Uncle Yan, and his wife and their small children made three generations in a single dark room. But I liked the place for its liveliness and because I was Waipo's favorite. She gave me candies and took me everywhere with her, even to the free market to buy from the peasants who had carried in their vegetables from the suburbs. Waipo was a tiny woman with big twisted teeth and little wrinkled hands, talkative and lively and very different from Nai Nai. Her husband had died when she was young, after only two children, whereas Nai Nai's husband had given her nine before he slipped and fell on the icy road in front of the old City Gate. In the old society, a woman couldn't remarry and remain respectable, so Waipo had supported herself and her children by making shoe soles at home. She continued to do this even after Mother and Uncle Yan were grown and had jobs, and the cloth patches she used were among my first toys.

Another reason I liked living with Waipo was that Mother often preferred to go there on Sundays rather than to our own home, where Nai Nai was, because she didn't get along well with her mother-in-law. Nai Nai sometimes carried her concern for others so far that she became a busybody. She was always the first to sweep the public stairwell or volunteer to lead neighborhood hygiene movements, and she was constantly scolding Mother for not dressing us warmly enough or not buying us more milk to drink. She was so tall that she must have been imposing for Mother to deal with, and tradition demanded that Mother obey her. So although Mother was a feisty woman, she was supposed to look on silently as Nai Nai spoiled us with candy and, in later years, did my second sister's homework for her. Father was no help, because he was bound by the same filial laws as she.

In any case, Mother's ties to her new home could not have been strong ones, for she had hardly known Father before they married. Someone had introduced them as prospective mates; they had exchanged a few letters (Father was working in Guilin at the time) and decided the question soon after on the basis of their common political enthusiasm. Father was far more intellectual than she, for he had been trained by the Party as a reporter, had a wide range of literary interests, and was an accomplished poet as well as an amateur composer and conductor. Mother was capable too, of course, a strong-willed person who liked to express her opinions, and a loving mother when she had the time. Still, as I thought back on it in later years, I realized my parents were so rarely together that it was almost a marriage of convenience.

So it was Waipo's home that was my early emotional center, and it was there that I went on the fresh spring day of my flight. I had to cross a large street, but fortunately I made it from one side to the other without mishap, and ran the remaining few hundred yards to the narrow room off the little gray alley.

To my utter dismay, Waipo didn't look at all glad to see me. "Little Fatso, what are you doing here?" she cried, and with scarcely a pause grabbed my hand and pulled me the few blocks to Nai Nai's home in the *Hunan Daily* compound. From there the two old ladies half lifted, half dragged me back to my confinement, ignoring my screams and tears.

The nurses had discovered my absence. Without any show of the politeness they usually maintained before their charges' relatives, they cursed and scolded me as if they would never stop. When my grandmothers had left, they locked me up in a room with two other offenders, saying, "You are not Chairman Mao's good little boy; you haven't upheld Revolutionary discipline. You can stay in there until you think things over."

My fellow captives were as miserable as I. One had stolen some candy, and the other, having graduated proudly from wearing slit pants, had promptly soiled his new ones. Although it was certainly convenient to be able to squat down anywhere and do one's business, among us children the slit was an embarrassing symbol of immaturity. It had another drawback too: Nai Nai's blows still stung on my bottom. I looked at the unlucky boy with pity. He would now be doomed to at least another year of babyhood and easy spankings.

The nurses' words had another kind of sting for me, since I had been taught Chairman Mao was like the sun itself. At home, "Mao" had been my first word after "Mama," "Baba," and "Nai Nai," for I had been held up to the large framed picture Father had hung over the doorway and instructed in the sound. Later I had learned how to say "I love Chairman Mao" and "Long Live Chairman Mao." But it wasn't until I got to the child-care center that I really began to understand. He presided over our rest and play like a benevolent god, and I believed that apples, grapes, everything had been given to us because he loved us. When the nurses told me the next day that Chairman Mao had forgiven me, I was the happiest child in the world.

During the next year, my second at the child-care center, I learned how to write my first characters. The first word was made up of the four strokes in the Chairman's name. Next I learned to write the characters in my own name, and I discovered that I was not called "Little Fatso," as Waipo had proudly nicknamed me, but something quite different, with a political story behind it:

On the morning of May 2, 1954, the Vietnamese won a decisive victory      15 over the French at Dien Bien Phu. That very afternoon my mother gave birth to me, a ten-pound baby boy, the distant sounds of drums and cymbals an accompaniment to her labors. My father, reporting the Vietnam story for the *Hunan Daily*, thought it only natural to name me Liang Dian-jie, "Liang Good News from Dien Bien Phu." He was flushed with a double victory, for at last he had a son to carry on the family line.

It wasn't the first time he had chosen a significant name for a child. My eldest sister was born in 1949, so she joined the ranks of thousands of children named for the birth of New China with the name Liang Fang, "Liang Liberation." My second sister, born in 1952 when the Chinese armies were marching across the Yalu River to defend Korea against the Americans, was called Liang Wei-ping, "Liang Defender of Peace." As we grew up we discovered that you could often guess someone's age by his name, and that at times, if someone had been named at the height of some movement that was later discredited, a name could become an embarrassment, a burden, or even a reason for being attacked. My parents' own names reflected an earlier, less politicized time; my mother Yan Zhi-de was "Yan the Moral," and my father Liang Ying-qiu was "Liang Whose Requests Will Be Answered," although he usually went by his literary name, Liang Shan.

I came gradually to recognize all of these characters and more, for during the third year and final fourth year at the child-care center we began our study properly, writing "Chairman Mao is our Great Saving Star," "We are all Chairman Mao's good little children," "The Communist Party is like the sun," "When I am big I will be a worker" (or peasant or soldier). We also learned simple arithmetic, paper folding, and paper cutting, and were given small responsibilities, like watering the plants or cleaning the classroom.

Meanwhile, whenever I went home to Waipo's, I hoped Mother would be there, for I loved her very much despite our limited time together. But when I was about four, I began to sense there was something wrong. She would come home looking worried and she never played with me, just talked on and on with Uncle Yan in a hushed Liuyang County dialect which I couldn't understand. Finally, one Saturday afternoon it was Nai Nai who came to get me, and I was told Mother had gone away and I shouldn't go to Waipo's house anymore.

Only years later was I old enough to understand what had happened, and more than twenty years passed before anyone, including Mother herself, got the full picture. In early 1957 the "Hundred Flowers Movement" had been launched. Its official purpose was to give the Party a chance to correct its shortcomings by listening to the masses' criticisms. Father was away in the countryside reporting on something, but in the Changsha Public Security Building, meetings were held and everyone was urged to express his or her opinions freely.

Mother didn't know what to do. She really loved the Party and didn't 20 have any criticisms to make; the Party had given her a job and saved her from the most abject poverty. Still, her leaders said that everyone should participate actively in the movement, especially those who hoped someday to join the Party. Mother was already in favor; she had been given the important job of validating arrest warrants for the whole city. So, regarding it her duty to come up with something, she finally thought of three points she could make. She said that her Section Head sometimes used crude language and liked to criticize people, that he should give his housekeeper a bed to sleep on instead of making her sleep on the floor, and that sometimes when it came time to give raises, the leaders didn't listen to the masses' opinions.

But then, with utterly confusing rapidity, the "Hundred Flowers Movement" changed into the "Anti-Rightist Movement." Perhaps the Party was caught off guard by the amount of opposition and felt compelled to crack down. Or maybe, as I've heard said, the "Hundred Flowers Movement" had been a trap designed from the beginning to uncover Rightist elements. Anyway, every unit was given a quota of Rightists, and Mother's name was among those at the Public Security Bureau.

It was disastrous. When she was allowed to see her file in 1978, she found out that she had been given a Rightist's "cap" solely because of those three criticisms she had made. Perhaps her Section Head was angry at her; perhaps her unit was having trouble filling its quota. At the time she had no idea what the verdict was based on, she only knew that a terrible wrong had been done. But there was no court of appeal. Mother was sent away to the suburb of Yuan Jia Ling for labor reform. She lost her cadre's rank and her salary was cut from fifty-five to fifteen *yuan* a month. (A *yuan* is one hundred Chinese cents. . . .) My naive and trusting mother went to work as a peasant.

Just as his wife was being declared an enemy of the Party, Father was actively participating in the Anti-Rightist Movement in his own unit. Father believed in the Party with his whole heart, believed that the Party could never make a mistake or hand down a wrong verdict. It was a tortuous dilemma; Father's traditional Confucian sense of family obligation told him to support Mother while his political allegiance told him to condemn her. In the end, his commitment to the Party won out, and he denounced her. He believed that was the only course that could save the family from ruin.

I still remember the first time Mother came home for a visit. It was a rainy Sunday in late autumn, and Father and Nai Nai were both out. There were footsteps on the stairs and in the corridor, but it was almost a minute before the knock came, timidly. Liang Fang opened the door.

Mother was almost unrecognizable. She was in patched blue peasant          25
clothing, muddy up to the knees. The skin on her kind round face looked thick, leathery, and not too clean, and someone had chopped her hair off short and uneven. There was something both broader and thinner about her. "Mama!" cried Liang Fang.

Liang Wei-ping and I ran up to her too, and she was hugging us all at once, weeping, forgetting to put down her oilpaper umbrella. Then as my sisters rushed to pour tea and bring a basin of hot water for her to wash her face, she sat on the bed and held me tightly for a long time. After she had rested, she busied herself with all the housework Nai Nai couldn't do alone, sweeping, dusting, and sharpening our pencils for us, scrubbing our clothes, and cleaning the windows. She wouldn't speak of where she'd been, just asked us about our schoolwork, our health, Father's health. We were so happy. We thought Mother had come home.

She was tying bows on Liang Fang's braids when Father came back.

He was astounded to see her, and not very warm. "What are you doing here?" he demanded. "Did you ask for leave?"

Mother lowered her head at his harshness. "Of course I asked for leave," she said defensively. "I can come home once a month."

This silenced Father for a few minutes, and he paced meditatively around the room, his tall thin frame overpowering hers as Nai Nai's used to do. Then he poured out a stream of words, political words — on the meaning of the Anti-Rightist Movement, on her obligation to recognize her faults and reform herself. It was as if he had turned into a propaganda machine. I suppose he thought it was his duty to help reeducate her.

For a while she listened in silence, her head bowed, but at last she      30 protested. "All right, I'm a Rightist, it's all my fault. You don't have to say anything else, my head is bursting. I hear this kind of thing all day long, write self-criticisms every week, and now I come home and I have to hear it all over again."

"I don't think you recognize what you've done. You're just wasting your labor reform," he said.

"What makes you so sure?" Mother's face was white and defiant.

Father exploded: "Rightist element! Have some thought for your influence on the children."

It was Mother's turn to lose control. "What did I ever do wrong? The Party asked me to make suggestions, so I did. You give me one example —" But Mother stopped midsentence, for Father had struck her a ringing blow across the face.

She fell back on the bed, weeping; Father strode into the other room      35 and slammed the door. Then slowly, painfully, she picked up her dirty jacket and umbrella as we sobbed miserably. When she was halfway out the door, Father emerged and shouted after her, "Don't come back until you've reformed yourself. The children in this house need a Revolutionary mother, not a Rightist mother." When she paused and turned her tear-streaked face to him, his voice became gentler. "It doesn't matter what you say here, I won't tell anyone. But please watch what you say at the labor camp."

Despite Father's cruelty, Mother came back every month to see us. She must have missed us very much to endure Father's lectures and the inevitable fights. Sometimes she slept in Father's bed and I slept with them; she never lay still and her pillow was always wet in the morning. On other occasions the quarrel was so fierce that she left again almost as soon as she arrived. Father often warned us against her, and if we defended her he became furious, calling us ignorant children who understood nothing.

We didn't know that Father had already raised the question of divorce. He must have reasoned that all of us were doomed unless he broke off with Mother completely, for the custom in such instances was that the whole family would be considered as guilty as the single member who had committed the crime. If there were no legal separation, Father would never be allowed to join the Party, and the files that would be opened on us when we came of age for middle school would say that we came from a Rightist background. We would be branded forever as people with "questions," and it would be difficult for us to go to middle school and college, get decent jobs, or find husbands and wives. Mother's misfortune might mean the end of all of Father's dreams for himself and for his children; he must have hated her for what she had done.

Mother was a proud woman. She believed so deeply she had been wrongly accused that she told him she would divorce him only after her Rightist label was removed. Her stubbornness enraged Father, particularly because there was a secondary movement to criticize those with Rightist tendencies, and with his Rightist wife, Father was a natural target. He had to criticize Mother publicly, write reports confessing his innermost thoughts. And the pressure became even greater after what happened to Uncle Yan.

When Mother first came under attack, her older brother had been as outraged as she. He went to the Public Security Bureau to argue in her defense, and spoke for her at his own unit, the No. 1 Hospital, where he worked with the Communist Youth League. He even came to our house to urge Father to try to help her, although Father thought he was crazy to stick out his neck like that. Sure enough, Uncle Yan was punished for his family loyalties and given a Rightist "cap" of his own to wear, bringing a second black cloud to rest over Waipo's home. His experience proved that Father's sad choice had been a practical one in view of the harsh political realities; when we were old enough to understand, we could hardly blame Father for what he had done.

Nai Nai was frightened to see how easily the Rightist label could spread    40
from one member of the family to another. She had been an enthusiastic supporter of the "Get Rid of the Four Evils" hygiene movement, but where cartoons had once shown housewives sweeping away rats, flies, mosquitoes, and fleas, now they had added a fifth evil, Rightists. Nai Nai could no longer face lecturing lazy neighbors on the dangers of letting water stagnate; she could imagine what they might be saying behind her back about how she ought to get rid of that evil in her own house. When, with traditional filial deference, Father asked for her opinion on the

divorce question, she agreed with relief. The family burden was too heavy for her.

Meanwhile, Mother was working hard to rid herself of her "cap." The calluses on her hands were thicker and sharper every time she came home, and her shoulders were rough where the shoulder pole rested. Her skin toasted to a rich yellow-brown. It was a hard life for a young woman who had lived between the protection of her mother's home and her Public Security Bureau office.

The Rightists at Yuan Jia Ling were all trying to prove to the political officials in charge that they had reformed themselves and were ready to leave. There were all types of people, intellectuals, high-ranking cadres, and ordinary workers, but friendships were impossible because the best strategy for gaining the officials' confidence was to report on others. Thus everyone was always watching everyone else, and a grain of rice dropped on the floor could mean an afternoon of criticism for disrespecting the labors of the peasants. Everything was fair game, even what people said in their sleep.

The second essential strategy was to write constant Thought Reports about oneself. Few of the people in the camp felt they were really Rightists, but the only thing to do was to confess one's crimes penitently, record one's lapses, and invent things to repent. Writing these reports eventually became a kind of habit, and Mother almost believed what she was saying about herself.

The last important route to freedom was hard work. One had to add deliberately to one's misery in small ways, like going without a hat under the hot summer sun or continuing to work in the rain after everyone else had quit. Generally the Rightists did ordinary peasants' work, like digging fish-breeding ponds and planting fruit trees, but sometimes they were taken in trucks to special laboring areas to break and carry stones. Then they were put together with ordinary thieves, hoodlums, and Kuomintang (KMT)[1] spies. The people whose arrest warrants Mother had once been in charge of validating were now her equals; it was almost more than she could bear. Still, bear it she did, and all the rest of it, and after three long years, when she could carry more than a hundred pounds of rocks on her back with ease, a bored-looking official summoned her and told her she was no longer a Rightist. She could go home.

She came to the house late at night, looking like a beggar traveling 45 with her ragged belongings. But when she spoke, her voice was clear and proud. "Old Liang," she announced to Father, "I'm a person again." She

---

[1]Non-Communist political party; see page 22. — ED.

told us she had been assigned to the headlight-manufacturing plant on May First Road as an ordinary worker. Her salary would be much lower than it had been at the Public Security Bureau and the loss of her cadre status would be permanent, but she was free, a normal member of society. My sisters and I thought all the trouble was over, but that night as I lay in bed with them I heard talk not of the beginning of a new family life but of how to institute divorce proceedings.

The difficulty lay in what to do with us. We were fought over like basketballs that winter, for Mother insisted that she wanted at least one of us, preferably Liang Fang, who was already eleven and understood life better than Liang Wei-ping and I. Mother was staying at Waipo's, but she came every day to the house. When I got home from the *Hunan Daily's* Attached Primary School, she was always there, waiting.

One bitterly cold Sunday she took the three of us out to the Martyr's Park so we could talk alone. No one else was out in that weather; they were all at home huddled under their blankets or warming themselves by coal burners. We were bundled up in everything we had, and I felt as though I could have been rolled down a hill, but I was still cold. The park was desolate and beautiful, the huge monument to the dead martyrs a lonely pinnacle over the city, the pavilions gray and defenseless against the wind. We walked to the large manmade lake, the park's main attraction, and sat by the water, usually filled with rowboats but now covered with a thin layer of ice. I crawled between Mother's knees and Liang Fang and Liang Wei-ping pressed up on each side of her. She spoke to us with great emotion and tenderness.

"Your mother is an unlucky woman. When you're older, you'll understand how I've wept for all of us these three years. Now I won't be able to come see you anymore, but you can visit me at Waipo's house. Liang Fang will live with me, but I don't have enough money for all of you. . . ."

Liang Wei-ping and I were in tears, saying that we wanted to go with her too. Soon everyone was crying. Mother held us so tightly that I could hardly believe it was true that she would go away.

We stayed in the park for a long time, but when Mother noticed that my cheeks were chapped red, she took us home. She brought us to the stairwell and refused to come up. Her parting words were "Remember, Liang Fang, you'll come with me."                     50

That evening Father called us into the inner room. "Children, you're still small and there are many things you don't understand," he said sadly. "If you went with your mother, your life with her would be unhappy. Look at the way your father has to criticize himself because of her. Stay here with me and Nai Nai and we'll take care of you."

Liang Fang wouldn't listen. "Mama isn't a Rightist anymore," she said. "What difference does it make who I go with? Isn't it glorious to be a worker?"

"Your mother's political life is over," said Father with annoyance. "Her file will always have a black mark, and the Party will never trust her again. Don't you know that if you want to go to middle school you'll be asked if your parents have made any political mistakes? If you stay with me, you won't even have to mention your mother, because there will be a legal separation. But if you go with her, you might not even get to go to middle school, to say nothing of joining the Communist Youth League or the Party. And you," he said angrily, turning to me and Liang Wei-ping. "Can't you guess why you haven't been allowed to join the Young Pioneers? Isn't it because of your mother?"

Nai Nai rushed into the room to urge him to control his temper, then she turned to us. "Children, your father is good to you, he understands the situation. Don't I wish I had a good daughter-in-law? Don't I know you need a good mother? But Fate is inevitable. Stay with us, children. It's the only way."

Ultimately, the question was decided in court. Father came home one    55
afternoon looking exhausted and said, "It's settled, you'll all stay with me. Mother is coming in a little while to say good-bye."

We had dinner with her that night, and even Nai Nai's eyes were wet. No one said anything, and no one had any appetite for the fish or the tofu soup. As Nai Nai took the dishes away and washed up, Mother went through her possessions, leaving almost everything for us. Father sat smoking furiously, as he did whenever he was upset. Finally she stood up to leave.

Then the three of us broke out of our numbness and ran to her, begging her not to go, pulling her back, wrapping ourselves around her legs so she couldn't walk. Father didn't interfere; he just let her embrace us again and again and at last shake us off and close the door firmly behind herself. We ran to the balcony and called after her until her broad square figure turned the corner and she was gone.

In fact, Father had been much too optimistic, and the divorce did nothing to rid us of having a Rightist in the family. He even forbade our having the slightest contact with Mother, thinking that if we drew a clear line of separation, things might be better. But there wasn't the slightest change in our status: In the eyes of the Party, my sisters and I were the children of a Rightist and Father had a Rightist wife. Liang Fang still had to say she had a Rightist mother on her application to go to middle school, Liang Wei-ping still found "Rightist child" written on her desk in chalk when she went to class, and I was still turned down when I asked to be allowed to join the Young Pioneers.

When I first went to the Attached Primary School in the *Hunan Daily* compound at age six, my classmates had often teased me about Mother. I had always shrugged off their taunts because I did well and achieved more than enough recognition to offset a few minor slights. I remember how pleased Father was when I started to take prizes for my paintings; my drawing of a morning glory was first in the whole primary school.

But as I got older, more and more stress was placed on the three stages    60 of Revolutionary glory: the Young Pioneers, the Communist Youth League, and the Party itself. It became clear to me that success in the political arena was a prerequisite for success in anything else, and if I had the slightest ambitions for myself I had to achieve these basic signs of social recognition. Those students who had the right to wear the Pioneer's triangular red scarf received much more praise than those who didn't, no matter what their grades; and at home Father and Nai Nai were constantly asking me if my application had been approved. But it was no use. I was rejected year after year, until I found myself in a tiny minority of outsiders whose "political performances" were the very worst in the class.

One day I was given a clue to the trouble when our teacher gave us a lecture. "We all have to join forces to oppose Capitalist thought," Teacher Luo said. "Some students want to eat well and dress well from the time they are small. This is Capitalist thought. Some students are from good worker or Revolutionary cadre backgrounds; they should be careful not to be proud of themselves. And those students from families with questions — they must be more careful to draw a clear line of separation." He looked meaningfully at me and at the other boy with a Rightist in his family. And all the other students in the classroom turned to stare at us too.

In fact, after the divorce I had continued to go secretly to see my mother despite Father's warnings that doing so would harm my future. She was always overjoyed to see me, and, even during China's hard years, just after the breakup, she always found a way to give me a few *fen* (a *fen* is a Chinese cent . . .) or a roasted sweet potato. But after Teacher Luo's lecture, it really began to bother me when other students mocked me as a Rightist's son. And they became bolder in their mockery, as well. They would slap me, or kick me when I wasn't looking, and then pretend not to have done anything. Sometimes I would get into real fights, and then there were reprimands from Father and the teachers. The other Rightist's son was as lonely as I, but we never spoke much, for that might have made things even worse.

So perhaps inevitably, over the years, I came to resent my mother for making my life so miserable. I began to believe that she really had done something wrong. My father and teachers said so, and my classmates hated me for her supposed crimes. At last I no longer wished to visit her despite my loneliness, and when I saw her at a distance I didn't even call out to her. I cut her out of my life just as I had been told to do, and became solitary and self-reliant. But that was when I was much older, and many things happened before then.

## EXPLORATIONS

1. What appears to be the standard Party definition of a Rightist? Of a Revolutionary? What definition of each term was in use when Liang Heng's mother was discredited?

2. Where did the various members of Liang's family live when he was a small child? Who would have been affected, and how, if Liang's father as well as his mother had been removed from his job and sent away for rehabilitation? In what other ways did the Party use housing, work, and family ties to control behavior?

3. Look at Liang's first paragraph, particularly the last sentence. How do he and his coauthor, Judith Shapiro, notify their readers of the point of view they intend to take? Through whose eyes is Liang's childhood depicted? Through what kind of consciousness is it interpreted? What is the significance of the paragraph's last sentence?

## CONNECTIONS

1. "Chairman Mao's Good Little Boy," Louise Erdrich's "Adam" (p. 88), and Paula Fomby's selection in *Looking at Ourselves* (p. 71) all concern an estrangement between a mother and her child. In each case, how and why is the parent-child bond damaged? How and why is it (or isn't it) repaired?

2. In the United States, writes Patricia Schroeder in *Looking at Ourselves* (p. 68), "we have considered child care a 'woman's' issue rather than what it really is: a family issue." Which kind of issue is child care in Mao's China? In what ways are the goals of the Chinese child-care system different from those of the American system?

3. In *Looking at Ourselves* (p. 63), Michael Novak cites problems that the United States's capitalist economic system creates for the family. Which of these problems are also created by the Chinese Communist system? On balance, which economic system establishes a better climate for families, and how does it do so?

4. Look at Ellen Goodman's observations in *Looking at Ourselves* (p. 73). How does the Chinese family, as Liang and Shapiro depict it, serve as "social glue" among generations?

## ELABORATIONS

1. Liang and Shapiro scatter information about Liang's child-care center through the first seventeen paragraphs of this essay. List all the relevant details in those paragraphs. Then write a descriptive essay about the child-care center: For instance, where is it? What rooms and furnishings does it have? What do the children do there? What roles do adults at the center play?

2. Do parents in the United States name their children after military victories? Do they divorce each other to avoid government and public censure? Write a comparison-contrast essay about public influence on personal decisions in Mao's China and in the United States today.

# WOLE SOYINKA

## *Nigerian Childhood*

Playwright, poet, novelist, and critic Wole Soyinka won the 1986 Nobel Prize for literature. He was born Akinwande Oluwole Soyinka near Abeokuta, Nigeria, in 1934. Educated in Ibadan, Nigeria, and at Leeds University in England, he studied theater in London and had a number of plays produced there. Returning to Ibadan, Soyinka became co-editor of the literary journal *Black Orpheus* and was instrumental in the development of a Nigerian theater. His career was interrupted by two years in prison for allegedly supporting Biafra's secession from Nigeria (see p. 716). Soyinka has taught drama and comparative literature at the universities of Ibadan, Lagos, and Ife in Nigeria, and at Cambridge and Cornell universities. He holds the French title of Commander of the Legion of Honor, the traditional chieftaincy title Akogun (Warlord) of Isara, and several honorary degrees; his awards include England's prestigious John Whiting Drama Prize. His plays have appeared in theaters around the world, including Ife, London, Stratford, New York, and Chicago. "Nigerian Childhood" comes from his 1981 autobiography *Aké: The Years of Childhood*, which was followed in 1988 by *Isara: A Voyage around Essay*. He currently edits the influential Africa-based international journal *Transition*.

A pluralistic nation of many tribes (Soyinka is a Yoruba), Nigeria lies in the large curve of Africa's western coast. Its early cultures date back to at least 700 B.C. Portuguese and British slavers began arriving in the fifteenth century. In 1861 Britain seized the capital city of Lagos during an antislavery campaign and gradually extended its control over the country. Nigeria regained its independence a century later and is now a republic within the British Commonwealth. British influence remains strong; the nation's official language is English. For most of the thirty years since independence, Nigeria's governments have been military. General Ibrahim Babangida, who became president in a 1985 coup, pressed for greater national self-reliance and pledged to return the country to civilian rule in 1992, a promise he failed to keep.

"Nigerian Childhood" takes place about twenty years before the end of British rule. At that time Soyinka lived with his father, Essay, the headmaster of the Anglican Girls' School in the town of Aké; his mother, nicknamed Wild Christian; and his sister Tinu. "Bishop Ajayi Crowther" is Samuel Adjai Crowther. Enslaved in 1821, freed and educated by the British, he became the first black African bishop of the Anglican Church.

If I lay across the lawn before our house, face upwards to the sky, my head towards BishopsCourt, each spread-out leg would point to the inner compounds of Lower Parsonage. Half of the Anglican Girls' School occupied one of these lower spaces, the other half had taken over BishopsCourt. The lower area contained the school's junior classrooms, a dormitory, a small fruit garden of pawpaws, guava, some bamboo, and wild undergrowth. There were always snails to be found in the rainy season. In the other lower compound was the mission bookseller, a shriveled man with a serene wife on whose ample back we all, at one time or the other slept, or reviewed the world. His compound became a short cut to the road that led to Ibarà, Lafenwá, or Igbèin and its Grammar School over which Ransome-Kuti presided and lived with his family. The bookseller's compound contained the only well in the parsonage; in the dry season, his place was never empty. And his soil appeared to produce the only coconut trees.

BishopsCourt, of Upper Parsonage, is no more. Bishop Ajayi Crowther would sometimes emerge from the cluster of hydrangea and bougainvillea, a gnomic face with popping eyes whose formal photograph had first stared at us from the frontispiece of his life history. He had lived, the teacher said, in BishopsCourt and from that moment, he peered out from among the creeping plants whenever I passed by the house on an errand to our Great Aunt, Mrs. Lijadu. BishopsCourt had become a boarding house for the girls' school and an extra playground for us during the holidays. The Bishop sat, silently, on the bench beneath the wooden porch over the entrance, his robes twined through and through with the lengthening tendrils of the bougainvillea. I moved closer when his eyes turned to sockets. My mind wandered then to another photograph in which he wore a clerical suit with waistcoat and I wondered what he really kept at the end of the silver chain that vanished into the pocket. He grinned and said, Come nearer, I'll show you. As I moved towards the porch he drew on the chain until he had lifted out a wholly round pocket watch that gleamed of solid silver. He pressed a button and the lid opened, revealing, not the glass and the face dial but a deep cloud-filled space. Then, he winked one eye, and it fell from his face into the bowl of the watch. He snapped back the lid, nodded again and his head went bald, his teeth disappeared, and the skin pulled backward till the whitened cheekbones were exposed. Then he stood up and, tucking the watch back into the waistcoat pocket, moved a step towards me. I fled homewards.

BishopsCourt appeared sometimes to want to rival the Canon's house. It looked a houseboat despite its guard of whitewashed stones and luxuriant flowers, its wooden fretwork frontage almost wholly immersed in bougainvillea. And it was shadowed also by those omnipresent rocks from whose clefts tall, stout-boled trees miraculously grew. Clouds gathered and the rocks merged into their accustomed gray turbulence, then the trees were carried to and fro until they stayed suspended over BishopsCourt. This happened only in heavy storms. BishopsCourt, unlike the Canon's house, did not actually border the rocks or the woods. The girls' playing fields separated them and we knew that this buffer had always been there. Obviously bishops were not inclined to challenge the spirits. Only the vicars could. That Bishop Ajayi Crowther frightened me out of that compound by his strange transformations only confirmed that the Bishops, once they were dead, joined the world of spirits and ghosts. I could not see the Canon decaying like that in front of my eyes, nor the Rev. J. J. who had once occupied that house, many years before, when my mother was still like us. J. J. Ransome-Kuti had actually ordered back several ghommids[1] in his lifetime; my mother confirmed it. She was his grandniece and, before she came to live at our house, she had lived in the Rev. J. J.'s household. Her brother Sanya also lived there and he was acknowledged by all to be an òrò,[2] which made him at home in the woods, even at night. On one occasion, however, he must have gone too far.

"They had visited us before," she said, "to complain. Mind you, they wouldn't actually come into the compound, they stood far off at the edge, where the woods ended. Their leader, the one who spoke, emitted wild sparks from a head that seemed to be an entire ball of embers — no, I'm mixing up two occasions — that was the second time when he chased us home. The first time, they had merely sent an emissary. He was quite dark, short and swarthy. He came right to the backyard and stood there while he ordered us to call the Reverend.

"It was as if Uncle had been expecting the visit. He came out of the house and asked him what he wanted. We all huddled in the kitchen, peeping out."

"What was his voice like? Did he speak like an *egúngún*?"[3]

"I'm coming to it. This man, well, I suppose one should call him a man. He wasn't quite human, we could see that. Much too large a head, and he kept his eyes on the ground. So, he said he had come to report us. They didn't mind our coming to the woods, even at night, but we were to stay off any area beyond the rocks and that clump of bamboo by the stream."

---

[1]Wood spirits. — ED.
[2]A kind of tree demon.
[3]Spirit of a dead ancestor. — ED.

"Well, what did Uncle say? And you haven't said what his voice was like."

Tinu turned her elder sister's eye on me. "Let Mama finish the story."

"You want to know everything. All right, he spoke just like your father. Are you satisfied?"                                                              10

I did not believe that but I let it pass. "Go on. What did Grand Uncle do?"

"He called everyone together and wanted us to keep away from the place."

"And yet you went back!"

"Well, you know your Uncle Sanya. He was angry. For one thing the best snails are on the other side of that stream. So he continued to complain that those òrò were just being selfish, and he was going to show them who he was. Well, he did. About a week later he led us back. And he was right you know. We gathered a full basket and a half of the biggest snails you ever saw. Well, by this time we had all forgotten about the warning, there was plenty of moonlight and anyway, I've told you Sanya is an òrò himself. . . ."

"But why? He looks normal like you and us."                                      15

"You won't understand yet. Anyway, he is òrò. So with him we felt quite safe. Until suddenly this sort of light, like a ball of fire began to glow in the distance. Even while it was still far we kept hearing voices, as if a lot of people around us were grumbling the same words together. They were saying something like, 'You stubborn, stiff-necked children, we've warned you and warned you but you just won't listen. . . .'"

Wild Christian looked above our heads, frowning to recollect the better. "One can't even say, 'they.' It was only this figure of fire that I saw and he was still very distant. Yet I heard him distinctly, as if he had many mouths which were pressed against my ears. Every moment, the fireball loomed larger and larger."

"What did Uncle Sanya do? Did he fight him?"

"*Sanya wo ni yen?* He was the first to break and run. *Bo o ló o yǎ mi, o di kítìpà kítìpà!*[4] No one remembered all those fat snails. That *iwin*[5] followed us all the way to the house. Our screams had arrived long before us and the whole household was — well, you can imagine the turmoil. Uncle had already dashed down the stairs and was in the backyard. We ran past him while he went out to meet the creature. This time that *iwin* actually passed the line of the woods, he continued as if he meant to

---

[4]If you aren't moving, get out of my way!
[5]A ghommid; a wood sprite which is also believed to live in the ground.

chase us right into the house, you know, he wasn't running, just pursuing us steadily." We waited. This was it! Wild Christian mused while we remained in suspense. Then she breathed deeply and shook her head with a strange sadness.

"The period of faith is gone. There was faith among our early Chris- 20 tians, real faith, not just church-going and hymn-singing. Faith. *Igbàgbó*. And it is out of that faith that real power comes. Uncle stood there like a rock, he held out his Bible and ordered, 'Go back! Go back to that forest which is your home. Back, I said, in the name of God.' Hm. And that was it. The creature simply turned and fled, those sparks falling off faster and faster until there was just a faint glow receding into the woods." She sighed. "Of course, after prayers that evening, there was the price to be paid. Six of the best on every one's back. Sanya got twelve. And we all cut grass every day for the next week."

I could not help feeling that the fright should have sufficed as punishment. Her eyes gazing in the direction of the square house, Wild Christian nonetheless appeared to sense what was going on in my mind. She added, "Faith and — Discipline. That is what made those early believers. Psheeaw! God doesn't make them like that any more. When I think of that one who now occupies that house . . ."

Then she appeared to recall herself to our presence. "What are you both still sitting here for? Isn't it time for your evening bath? Lawanle!" "Auntie" Lawanle replied "Ma" from a distant part of the house. Before she appeared I reminded Wild Christian, "But you haven't told us why Uncle Sanya is *òrò*."

She shrugged, "He is. I saw it with my own eyes."

We both clamored, "When? When?"

She smiled, "You won't understand. But I'll tell you about it some 25 other time. Or let him tell you himself next time he is here."

"You mean you saw him turn into an *òrò*?"

Lawanle came in just then and she prepared to hand us over. "Isn't it time for these children's bath?"

I pleaded, "No, wait Auntie Lawanle," knowing it was a waste of time. She had already gripped us both, one arm each. I shouted back, "Was Bishop Crowther an *òrò*?"

Wild Christian laughed. "What next are you going to ask? Oh I see. They have taught you about him in Sunday school have they?"

"I saw him." I pulled back at the door, forcing Lawanle to stop. "I see 30 him all the time. He comes and sits under the porch of the Girls' School. I've seen him when crossing the compound to Auntie Mrs. Lijadu."

"All right," sighed Wild Christian. "Go and have your bath."

"He hides among the bougainvillea. . . ." Lawanle dragged me out of hearing.

Later that evening, she told us the rest of the story. On that occasion, Rev. J. J. was away on one of his many mission tours. He traveled a lot, on foot and on bicycle, keeping in touch with all the branches of his diocese and spreading the Word of God. There was frequent opposition but nothing deterred him. One frightening experience occurred in one of the villages in Ijebu. He had been warned not to preach on a particular day, which was the day for an *egúngún* outing, but he persisted and held a service. The *egúngún* procession passed while the service was in progress and, using his ancestral voice, called on the preacher to stop at once, disperse his people, and come out to pay obeisance. Rev. J. J. ignored him. The *egúngún* then left, taking his followers with him but, on passing the main door, he tapped on it with his wand, three times. Hardly had the last member of his procession left the church premises than the building collapsed. The walls simply fell down and the roof disintegrated. Miraculously however, the walls fell outwards while the roof supports fell among the aisles or flew outwards — anywhere but on the congregation itself. Rev. J. J. calmed the worshippers, paused in his preaching to render a thanksgiving prayer, then continued his sermon.

Perhaps this was what Wild Christian meant by Faith. And this tended to confuse things because, after all, the *egúngún* did make the church building collapse. Wild Christian made no attempt to explain how that happened, so the feat tended to be of the same order of Faith which moved mountains or enabled Wild Christian to pour ground-nut oil from a broad-rimmed bowl into an empty bottle without spilling a drop. She had the strange habit of sighing with a kind of rapture, crediting her steadiness of hand to Faith and thanking God. If however the basin slipped and she lost a drop or two, she murmured that her sins had become heavy and that she needed to pray more.

If Rev. J. J. had Faith, however, he also appeared to have Stubbornness 35 in common with our Uncle Sanya. Stubbornness was one of the earliest sins we easily recognized, and no matter how much Wild Christian tried to explain the Rev. J. J. preaching on the *egúngún*'s outing day, despite warnings, it sounded much like stubbornness. As for Uncle Sanya there was no doubt about his own case; hardly did the Rev. J. J. pedal out of sight on his pastoral duties than he was off into the woods on one pretext or the other, and making for the very areas which the *òrò* had declared out of bounds. Mushrooms and snails were the real goals, with the gathering of firewood used as the dutiful excuse.

Even Sanya had however stopped venturing into the woods at night, accepting the fact that it was far too risky; daytime and early dusk carried little danger as most wood spirits only came out at night. Mother told us that on this occasion she and Sanya had been picking mushrooms, separated by only a few clumps of bushes. She could hear his movements quite clearly, indeed, they took the precaution of staying very close together.

Suddenly, she said, she heard Sanya's voice talking animatedly with someone. After listening for some time she called out his name but he did not respond. There was no voice apart from his, yet he appeared to be chatting in friendly, excited tones with some other person. So she peeped through the bushes and there was Uncle Sanya seated on the ground chattering away to no one that she could see. She tried to penetrate the surrounding bushes with her gaze but the woods remained empty except for the two of them. And then her eyes came to rest on his basket.

It was something she had observed before, she said. It was the same, no matter how many of the children in the household went to gather snails, berries, or whatever, Sanya would spend most of the time playing and climbing rocks and trees. He would wander off by himself, leaving his basket anywhere. And yet, whenever they prepared to return home, his basket was always fuller than the others'. This time was no different. She came closer, startling our Uncle, who snapped off his chatter and pretended to be hunting snails in the undergrowth.

Mother said that she was frightened. The basket was filled to the brim, impossibly bursting. She was also discouraged, so she picked up her near empty basket and insisted that they return home at once. She led the way but after some distance, when she looked back, Sanya appeared to be trying to follow her but was being prevented, as if he was being pulled back by invisible hands. From time to time he would snatch forward his arm and snap,

"Leave me alone. Can't you see I have to go home? I said I have to    40 go."

She broke into a run and Sanya did the same. They ran all the way home.

That evening, Sanya took ill. He broke into a sweat, tossed on his mat all night, and muttered to himself. By the following day the household was thoroughly frightened. His forehead was burning to the touch and no one could get a coherent word out of him. Finally, an elderly woman, one of J. J.'s converts, turned up at the house on a routine visit. When she learnt of Sanya's condition, she nodded wisely and acted like one who knew exactly what to do. Having first found out what things he last did before his illness, she summoned my mother and questioned her. She

told her everything while the old woman kept on nodding with understanding. Then she gave instructions:

"I want a basket of *àgìdi*, containing fifty wraps. Then prepare some
*èkuru* in a large bowl. Make sure the *èkuru* stew is prepared with plenty
of locust bean and crayfish. It must smell as appetizing as possible."

The children were dispersed in various directions, some to the market
to obtain the *àgìdi*, others to begin grinding the beans for the amount of
*èkuru* which was needed to accompany fifty wraps of *àgìdi*. The children's
mouths watered, assuming at once that this was to be an appeasement
feast, a *sàarà*[6] for some offended spirits.

When all was prepared, however, the old woman took everything to          45
Sanya's sickroom, plus a pot of cold water and cups, locked the door on
him, and ordered everybody away.

"Just go about your normal business and don't go anywhere near the
room. If you want your brother to recover, do as I say. Don't attempt to
speak to him and don't peep through the keyhole."

She locked the windows too and went herself to a distant end of the
courtyard where she could monitor the movements of the children. She
dozed off soon after, however, so that mother and the other children were
able to glue their ears to the door and windows, even if they could not
see the invalid himself. Uncle Sanya sounded as if he was no longer
alone. They heard him saying things like:

"Behave yourself, there is enough for everybody. All right you take this,
have an extra wrap . . . Open your mouth . . . here . . . you don't have
to fight over that bit, here's another piece of crayfish . . . behave, I
said . . ."

And they would hear what sounded like the slapping of wrists, a scrape
of dishes on the ground, or water slopping into a cup.

When the woman judged it was time, which was well after dusk, nearly     50
six hours after Sanya was first locked up, she went and opened the door.
There was Sanya fast asleep but, this time, very peacefully. She touched
his forehead and appeared to be satisfied by the change. The household
who had crowded in with her had no interest in Sanya however. All they
could see, with astonished faces, were the scattered leaves of fifty wraps
of *àgìdi*, with the contents gone, a large empty dish which was earlier
filled with *èkuru*, and a water pot nearly empty.

No, there was no question about it, our Uncle Sanya was an *òrò*; Wild
Christian had seen and heard proofs of it many times over. His companions were obviously the more benevolent type or he would have come to

---

[6]An offering, food shared out as offering.

serious harm on more than one occasion, J. J.'s protecting Faith notwith-
standing.


## EXPLORATIONS

1. What is the relationship in Wole Soyinka's family between Anglican religious
   beliefs and traditional African magic? At what points in "Nigerian Childhood"
   do parents use each of these belief systems to control or teach children? At
   what points do the children's beliefs guide them toward "good" behavior?

2. "Stubbornness was one of the earliest sins we easily recognized," writes Soyinka in paragraph 35. What other virtues, failings, and rules of behavior have
   these children evidently been taught? Cite specific evidence for your conclusions.

3. What aspects of Soyinka's narrative make it clear that he was an adult when
   he wrote "Nigerian Childhood"? What passages indicate that he is telling his
   story from a child's rather than an adult's point of view?


## CONNECTIONS

1. "Nigerian Childhood," like Liang and Shapiro's "Chairman Mao's Good Little
   Boy" (p. 97), has two parts: a solo adventure in which the narrator sets the
   scene, followed by a longer section involving his whole family. How does the
   young Wole Soyinka's encounter with Bishop Ajayi Crowther prepare us for
   his mother's story about her brother Sanya? How would the effect of the Sanya
   story change without this introduction? How does the young Liang Heng's
   short-lived escape from the child-care center prepare us for his mother's
   ostracism as a Rightist?

2. What chores do the children perform in "Nigerian Childhood"? Do children
   play as important a socioeconomic role in this community as in the Quiché
   community described by Rigoberta Menchú in "Birth Ceremonies" (p. 76)?
   How can you tell?

3. In "Entering the New World" (p. 48), V. S. Naipaul describes the fragility of
   European rituals among Africans "whose complete, real life lay in another
   realm of the spirit." Reread the last few paragraphs of Naipaul's essay. Which
   of his ideas about the old and new worlds does "Nigerian Childhood" support,
   and which does it contradict?

4. In *Looking at Ourselves* (p. 69), Angela Davis refers to "African extended-
   family traditions." In what specific ways does Soyinka's family in "Nigerian
   Childhood" show what Davis means?

# ELABORATIONS

1. In "Tradition and the African Writer" (p. 35), Es'kia Mphahlele talks of embodying two distinct cultural histories. How has Soyinka made use of a similar dual heritage? Is Soyinka writing as "an ambivalent character . . . a man of two worlds" (Mphahlele's self-description) or as someone who has reconciled his histories? Write a comparison-contrast essay using Mphahlele and Soyinka as examples of Mphahlele's theses.

2. When you were a child, were you afraid of imaginary monsters? Have you or a friend ever had an encounter with a ghost? Write a narrative essay about an experience that most American adults would respond to with skepticism, depicting it (as Soyinka does) as a real event.

# JOHN DAVID MORLEY

## Acquiring a Japanese Family

"John David Morley was born in Singapore in 1948 and was educated at Merton College, Oxford. His first job was in Mexico, as tutor to the children of Elizabeth Taylor and Richard Burton. Then he went to Germany to work in the theater, and by the age of twenty-four had begun to develop an interest in the drama — and later the general culture — of Japan, and to teach himself the language. He went to Japan on a Japanese government scholarship, to study at the Language Research Institute of Waseda University, Tokyo. Since then he has made his home in West Germany, where he works for Japanese television as a liaison officer and interpreter, researching TV documentaries. He has translated some thirty Japanese scripts into English and German." Morley's books include *In the Labyrinth* (1986) and *The Case of Thomas N.* (1987). "Acquiring a Japanese Family" comes from his semiautobiographical novel *Pictures from the Water Trade: Adventures of a Westerner in Japan* (1985), as does most of this paragraph.

Japan is a 2,360-mile archipelago off Asia's east coast consisting of four main islands and over 3,000 smaller ones. Most of the country is hills and mountains, many of them dormant or active volcanoes. Japan has intrigued Westerners since its self-imposed isolation was ended in 1854 by U.S. Commodore Matthew C. Perry, who forced the opening of trade. Japan was then ruled by the shoguns, a series of military governors who had held power since 1192. Before the shogunate came the empire, which supposedly began in 660 B.C., and which reestablished itself in 1868 (the Meiji Restoration). Soon afterward Japan began an aggressive campaign of expansion, clashing with China, then Russia, Korea, Germany, and finally the United States. At the outset of World War II, Japan allied with Germany and the other Axis powers. Its attack on Pearl Harbor in Hawaii in 1941 led to its defeat four years later after the United States dropped the world's first nuclear bombs on Hiroshima and Nagasaki. In its postwar constitution Japan renounced the right to wage war and shifted law-making authority to the Diet, or parliament. Today Emperor Akihito is Japan's head of state in a parliamentary democracy led by a prime minister. In 1993, a series of scandals and widespread corruption ended thirty-eight years of one-party rule by the Liberal Democrats and made Morihiro Hosokawa, a descendant of warlords, Japan's youngest prime minister. The country remains ethnically homogeneous, but contact with the West has spurred enough cultural and economic change to give Japan a growth rate envied by other industrialized nations.

For more background on Japan, see "Nippon Challenge," page 53; on Japanese immigrants in the United States, see page 487.

Boon did not like the Foreign Students Hall where it had been arranged for him to live, and on the same evening he moved in he decided he would move out. . . . But the decision that he did not want to live there was one thing, finding somewhere else to stay was quite another, and this in turn would have been impossible or at least very difficult if he had not happened to meet Sugama a few days after arriving in the country.

The introduction was arranged through a mutual acquaintance, Yoshida, at the private university where Boon was taking language courses and where Sugama was employed on the administrative staff. They met one afternoon in the office of their acquaintance and inspected each other warily for ten minutes.

"Nice weather," said Boon facetiously as he shook hands with Sugama. Outside it was pouring with rain.

"Nice weather?" repeated Sugama doubtfully, glancing out of the window. "But it's raining."

It was not a good start.                                                                 5

Sugama had just moved into a new apartment. It was large enough for two, he said, and he was looking for someone to share the expenses. This straightforward information arrived laboriously, in bits and pieces, sandwiched between snippets of Sugama's personal history and vague professions of friendship, irritating to Boon, because at the time he felt they sounded merely sententious. All this passed back and forth between Sugama and Boon through the mouth of their mutual friend, as Boon understood almost no Japanese and Sugama's English, though well-intentioned, was for the most part impenetrable.

It made no odds to Boon where he lived or with whom. All he wanted was a Japanese-speaking environment in order to absorb the language as quickly as possible. He had asked for a family, but none was available.

One windy afternoon in mid-October the three of them met outside the gates of the university and set off to have a look at Sugama's new apartment. It was explained to Boon that cheap apartments in Tokyo were very hard to come by, the only reasonable accommodation available being confined to housing estates subsidized by the government. Boon wondered how a relatively prosperous bachelor like Sugama managed to qualify for government-subsidized housing. Sugama admitted that this was in fact only possible because his grandfather would also be living there. It was the first Boon had heard of the matter and he was rather taken aback.

It turned out, however, that the grandfather would "very seldom" be there — in fact, that he wouldn't live there at all. He would only be there on paper, he and his grandson constituting a "family." That was the point. "You must *say* he is there," said Sugama emphatically.

The grandfather lived a couple of hundred miles away, and although he never once during the next two years set foot in the apartment he still managed to be the bane of Boon's life. A constant stream of representatives from charities, government agencies, and old people's clubs, on average one or two a month, came knocking on the door, asking to speak to grandfather. At first grandfather was simply "not in" or had "gone for a walk," but as time passed and the flow of visitors never faltered, Boon found himself having to resort to more drastic measures. Grandfather began to make long visits to his home in the country; he had not yet returned because he didn't feel up to making the journey; his health gradually deteriorated. Finally Boon decided to have him invalided, and for a long time his condition remained "grave." On grandfather's behalf Boon received the condolences of all these visitors, and occasionally even presents.

Two years later grandfather did in fact die. Boon was thus exonerated, but in the meantime he had got to know grandfather well and had become rather fond of him. He attended his funeral with mixed feelings.

Sugama had acquired tenure of his government-subsidized apartment by a stroke of luck. He had won a ticket in a lottery. These apartments were much sought after, and in true Japanese style their distribution among hundreds of thousands of applicants was discreetly left to fate. The typical tenant was a young couple with one or two children, who would occupy the apartment for ten or fifteen years, often under conditions of bleak frugality, in order to save money to buy a house. Although the rent was not immoderate, prices generally in Tokyo were high, and it was a mystery to Boon how such people managed to live at all. Among the lottery winners there were inevitably also those people for whom the acquisition of an apartment was just a prize, an unexpected bonus, to be exploited as a financial investment. It was no problem for these nominal tenants to sublet their apartments at prices well above the going rate.

Boon had never lived on a housing estate and his first view of the tall concrete compound where over fifty thousand people lived did little to reassure him. Thousands of winner families were accommodated in about a dozen rectangular blocks, each between ten and fifteen stories high, apparently in no way different (which disappointed Boon most of all) from similar housing compounds in Birmingham or Berlin. He had naively expected Japanese concrete to be different, to have a different color, perhaps, or a more exotic shape.

But when Sugama let them into the apartment and Boon saw the interior he immediately took heart: this was unmistakably Japanese. Taking off their shoes in the tiny boxlike hall, the three of them padded reverently through the kitchen into the *tatami* rooms.

"Smell of fresh *tatami*," pronounced Sugama, wrinkling his nose.                    15

Boon was ecstatic. Over the close-woven pale gold straw matting lay a very faint greenish shimmer, sometimes perceptible and sometimes not, apparently in response to infinitesimal shifts in the texture of the falling light. The *tatami* was quite unlike a carpet or any other form of floor covering he had ever seen. It seemed to be alive, humming with colors he could sense rather than see, like a greening tree in the brief interval between winter and spring. He stepped onto it and felt the fibers recoil, sinking under the weight of his feet, slowly and softly.

"You can see green?" asked Sugama, squatting down.

"Yes indeed."

"Fresh *tatami*. Smell of grass, green color. But not for long, few weeks only."

"What exactly is it?"                                                                 20

"Yes."

Boon turned to Yoshida and repeated the question, who in turn asked Sugama and conferred with him at great length.

"*Tatami* comes from *oritatamu*, which means to fold up. So it's a kind of matting you can fold up."

"Made of straw."

"Yes."                                                                               25

"How long does it last?"

Long consultation.

"He says this is not so good quality. Last maybe four, five years."

"And then what?"

"New *tatami*. Quite expensive, you see. But very practical."                        30

The three *tatami* rooms were divided by a series of *fusuma*, sliding screens made of paper and light wood. These screens were decorated at the base with simple grass and flower motifs; a natural extension, it occurred to Boon, of the grasslike *tatami* laid out in between. Sugama explained that the *fusuma* were usually kept closed in winter, and in summer, in order to have "nice breeze," they could be removed altogether. He also showed Boon the *shoji*, a type of sliding screen similar to the *fusuma* but more simple: an open wooden grid covered on one side with semitransparent paper, primitive but rather beautiful. There was only one small section of *shoji* in the whole apartment; almost as a token, thought Boon, and he wondered why.

With the exception of a few one- and two-room apartments, every house that Boon ever visited in Japan was designed to incorporate these three common elements: *tatami*, *fusuma*, and *shoji*. In the houses of rich people the *tatami* might last longer, the *fusuma* decorations might be more costly, but the basic concept was the same. The interior design of all houses being much the same, it was not surprising to find certain similarities in the behavior and attitudes of the people who lived in them.

The most striking feature of the Japanese house was lack of privacy; the lack of individual, inviolable space. In winter, when the *fusuma* were kept closed, any sound above a whisper was clearly audible on the other side, and of course in summer they were usually removed altogether. It is impossible to live under such conditions for very long without a common household identity emerging which naturally takes precedence over individual wishes. This enforced family unity was still held up to Boon as an ideal, but in practice it was ambivalent, as much a yoke as a bond.

There was no such thing as the individual's private room, no bedroom, dining- or sitting-room as such, since in the traditional Japanese house there was no furniture determining that a room should be reserved for any particular function. A person slept in a room, for example, without thinking of it as a bedroom or as his room. In the morning his bedding would be rolled up and stored away in a cupboard; a small table known as the *kotatsu*, which could also be plugged into the mains to provide heating, was moved back into the center of the room and here the family ate, drank, worked, and relaxed for the rest of the day. Although it was becoming standard practice in modern Japan for children to have their own rooms, many middle-aged and nearly all older Japanese still lived in this way. They regarded themselves as "one flesh," their property as common to all; the *uchi* (household, home) was constituted according to a principle of indivisibility. The system of movable screens meant that the rooms could be used by all the family and for all purposes: walls were built round the *uchi*, not inside it.

Boon later discovered analogies between this concept of house and the Japanese concept of self. The Japanese carried his house around in his mouth and produced it in everyday conversation, using the word *uchi* to mean "I," the representative of my house in the world outside. His self-awareness was naturally expressed as corporate individuality, hazy about quite what that included, very clear about what it did not. . . .

The almost wearying sameness about all the homes which Boon visited, despite differences in the wealth and status of their owners, prompted a rather unexpected conclusion: the classlessness of the Japanese house. The widespread use of traditional materials, the preservation of traditional structures, even if in such contracted forms as to have become merely symbolic, suggested a consensus about the basic requirements of daily life which was very remarkable, and which presumably held implications for Japanese society as a whole. Boon's insight into that society was acquired very slowly, after he had spent a great deal of time sitting on the *tatami* mats and looking through the sliding *fusuma* doors which had struck him as no more than pleasing curiosities on his first visit to a Japanese-style home.

Sugama, Yoshida, and Boon celebrated the new partnership at a restaurant in Shinjuku, and a week later Boon moved in.

The moment he entered the apartment a woman who was unexpectedly standing in the kitchen dropped down on her knees and prostrated herself in a deep bow, her forehead almost touching the floorboards, introducing herself with the words "*Irrashaimase. Sugama de gozaimasu . . .*"

Boon was extremely startled. He wondered whether he should do the same thing and decided not, compromising with a halfhearted bow which unfortunately the woman couldn't even see, because she had her face to the ground. She explained that she was *o-kaasan*, Sugama's mother.

Sugama had a way of springing surprises — or rather, he indicated his    40 intentions so obtusely that Boon usually failed to realize what would happen until it was already in progress — and so for quite a while Boon assumed that there must have been a change in plan, that the mother had perhaps joined the household as a stand-in for the grandfather. He greeted her in fluent Japanese (he had been studying introductions for the past week) and promptly fell into unbroken silence, mitigated by the occasional appreciative nod. Boon for his part hardly understood a word of what Sugama's mother was saying but she, encouraged by the intelligible sounds he had initially produced, talked constantly for the best part of an hour, and by the time Sugama eventually arrived Boon had become resigned to the idea that his talkative mother was going to be a permanent resident.

The misunderstanding was swiftly ironed out. No, *o-kaasan* had only come up to Tokyo for a few days (from whatever angle of the compass one approached Tokyo the journey to the capital was described as an elevation) in order to help with the move.

Sugama's mother was a small, wiry woman in her late fifties. Her teeth protruded slightly; like most Japanese women, even those who had very good teeth, she covered her mouth with her hand whenever she laughed. She was a vivacious woman and laughed frequently, so one way and another, with all the cooking, cleaning, and sewing she also did during the next four days, her hands were kept continually busy. She was of slight build but very sound in lung, with the effect that when she laughed it resounded throughout her whole body, as if the laugh were more than the body could accommodate. Perhaps this laughter drew Boon's attention to a girlish quality she had about her, despite her age and a rather plain appearance. He often watched her working, and in the spare, effortless movements of a woman who has performed the same tasks so many times that not even the tiniest gesture is superfluous there was also something unexpectedly graceful.

On the far side of the *fusuma* Boon often heard them talking late into the night. Night after night she sawed away at him with her flinty, abrasive voice. In the mornings Sugama was moody, the atmosphere in the house increasingly tense. Boon was left guessing. Gradually, in the course of weeks and months, Sugama began to take him into his confidence, and in retrospect he learned what must have been the subject of those nightly conversations.

*O-kaasan's* most pressing concern was that her son, at the advanced age of twenty-eight, was still unmarried. Boon couldn't see what the fuss was about, but Sugama was slowly coming round to his mother's view, who was quite sure it was a disaster. "The wind blows hard," he announced mysteriously, apparently by way of explanation — Boon himself had to blow pretty hard to keep up with conversations on this level. He said it was up to Sugama to decide when and whether he wanted to get married. It wasn't anybody else's business. Sugama would clearly have liked to be able to agree with this facile advice and just as clearly he could not, entangled in a web of sentiment and duty of which Boon was wholly ignorant.

The promptings of filial duty which caused Sugama such heartache    45
and which to Boon were so alien demanded of Sugama a second, even more painful decision. He was the *chonan*, the eldest son, thereby inheriting the obligation not merely to provide for his aging parents but to live with them in the same house. There were two alternatives open to him. He could either bring his parents to live with him in Tokyo or he could return home to his province in the north. A house in Tokyo large enough to provide room for grandfather, parents, Sugama, and — sooner or later — a fourth-generation family was out of the question; on his present salary he would have to work for several lifetimes in order to pay for it. A one-way ticket home came a great deal cheaper, which was just as well, since the only job awaiting him at the other end would be poorly paid and with even poorer prospects. Such was the path of righteousness. . . .

*O-kaasan* had only just packed her bags and gone home when — as usual without any forewarning — Sugama turned up late one evening accompanied by an old man, his wife, and an enormous cardboard box. Boon was sitting in his pajamas eating noodles out of a saucepan when these unexpected visitors arrived. Consternation. The old lady caught sight of him and dropped her bag (very probably she had not been forewarned either), immediately prostrating herself on the floor in the deepest of deep bows, old-style obeisance with the added advantage of concealing momentary shock and embarrassment. The old man was no slouch either. Palms on the floor and fingers turned inwards he bobbed his head up and down several times in Boon's direction, apologizing profusely every time he came up for air. All this happened so quickly that the astonished Boon didn't even have the presence of mind to put down the saucepan he was holding, and he sat there in his pajamas uneasily aware that he was the most unworthy object of the visitors' attentions.

Sugama came forward rather sheepishly, stepping in cavalier fashion between the prone bodies on the kitchen floor, and explained who they were.

"My grandfather's brother — younger brother — and wife."

"Not your grandfather?" asked Boon doubtfully, always alert to the possibility of misunderstandings when Sugama ventured into English.

"No, no *not* my grandfather."                                            50

"Your *great*-uncle, then."

"Ah! Great-uncle? *Great* uncle?"

Sugama paused to digest this new word, mustering his ancient relative with pursed lips. It was clear what was passing through his mind.

Boon was still not reassured. He kept an eye on the ominous cardboard box, quite large enough to accommodate a third, perhaps enfeebled relative, and wondered what else was in store for him.

"What are they doing here?"                                               55

"Earthquake," said Sugama simply. Boon fetched his dictionary and Sugama, reverting to Japanese, sat down to explain the situation.

At about nine o'clock that evening his great-uncle had called him in his office (Sugama worked a late shift) with the startling news that a major earthquake was imminent. How did he know? His wife had told him so. How did she know? A fortune-teller she regularly visited and in whom she placed absolute confidence had seen it in his cards and crystal ball. She was terrified, and having personally experienced the Great Kanto Earthquake of 1923 in which over a hundred thousand people had died she was not taking any chances. Her fortune-teller couldn't predict exactly when the earthquake would occur, but it might be at any time within the next three days; the greatest likelihood of its occurrence was forecast for midnight on the following day. The two old people ran a little shop in the downtown area of Tokyo where many of the houses were flimsy wooden structures which tended to slump and collapse very easily, even without the encouragement of an earthquake. But their great-nephew, they heard, had just moved into a marvelous modern building that was supposed to be *earthquake-proof*. Could they come and stay for a few days? Of course, said Sugama. So without more ado they bundled their worldly goods into the largest available box and Sugama brought them over in a neighbor's truck.

As a matter of fact there had been a slight tremor the previous evening. It was Boon's first. He had been standing in the kitchen helping himself to another glass of whiskey when the floor unaccountably began to sway and a set of irreproachable stainless steel ladles, which until then had given him no cause for complaint, started rattling menacingly on the kitchen wall. Boon had replaced the whiskey and made himself a cup of tea instead.

Great-uncle and his wife knelt on the *tatami* listening to Sugama's recital, wagging their heads and smiling from time to time, as if allowing that there was something rather droll about the situation, but also wanting to be taken absolutely seriously. However, with every moment they spent in the apartment this became increasingly hard to do, for the eccentric old couple seemed to be guided by a mischievous genius — they belonged to nature's blunderers, everything they touched turned to farce. Their great-nephew had just finished his dramatic account when there was a shrill call of *ohayo!* (Good morning) from the kitchen, and all eyes turned to the neglected cardboard box.

"Oh dear! The poor thing!" crowed the old lady, getting up at once      60
and pattering over to the box. She pulled open the flap and gently lifted out a bright yellow parrot. The indignant bird rapped her knuckles a couple of times with the side of his beak and settled frostily on the tip of her finger.

Sugama, Boon, the elderly couple, and the yellow parrot housed together for the next three days. Once he had provided his relatives with a roof over their heads Sugama took no further interest in them and was unaccountably busy for as long as they stayed there, leaving the house earlier and returning later than usual. His prodigiously long working hours impressed great-uncle and worried his wife, who took to preparing nutritious cold snacks for the laboring hero before retiring for the night. Sugama did justice to these snacks with the same appetite he applied himself to his work, warding off their anxieties with careless equanimity.

"You've got to hand it to him — he certainly works hard," said great-uncle at breakfast one morning, just after Sugama had left the house.

"Ah," replied Boon noncommittally. He knew perfectly well that Sugama's overtime was not spent at the office but at mah-jongg parlors in Nakano and Takadanobaba.

In the meantime Boon was left to study the evacuees and the evacuees Boon with mutual curiosity. On the whole he had the impression that they were rather disappointed in him. At first they looked at him as if he had descended from another planet, but when it became obvious that he was not going to live up to these expectations their interest declined into an attitude of gently reproachful familiarity. For Boon did not sleep on a bed, he dispensed with bacon and egg, he knew nothing about baseball, ate rice and drank green tea with relish, and was unpardonably fond of dried cuttlefish and raw squid, foods which foreigners were commonly supposed to regard with horror and loathing. Altogether Boon was not as Boon should be, and they were rather disconcerted.

This attitude — a national prejudice, really — that foreigners and the 65 Japanese way of life must almost as a matter of principle be wholly incompatible was something Boon encountered time and again. Under the cover of courtesy, of polite considerations for differences in tastes and customs, many Japanese would gleefully reveal their own select cabinet of horrors, confronting their guest with fermented bean curd or prawns drowned in sake not as something he might care to sample but as a kind of ethnological litmus test: If he found it indigestible and swiftly turned green this would be taken by them as confirmation of their own cultural and racial singularity. With barely concealed triumph the host would commiserate with his victim, invariably remarking *Yappari, nihonjin ja nai to* . . . (Ah well, unless one is Japanese . . .). . . .

On the fateful morning great-uncle took cover under the *kotatsu* earlier than usual and sat tight for the rest of the day. His wife went about her household tasks as briskly as ever, but when there was nothing left for her to do and at last she knelt down beside great-uncle at the little table it became evident how restless she really was. From time to time she laid down her sewing, listened intently, sighed, and picked it up again. As the evening wore on and the tension began to mount, Boon couldn't resist cracking a few jokes, which great-uncle good-humoredly deflected at his wife. It was only to set her mind at rest that they had come to stay, he assured Boon. Women couldn't resist fortune-tellers, but it was just a lot of nonsense after all; and for good measure he made a few jokes himself at her expense. Boon was not deceived. Throughout the evening great-uncle helped himself to the bottle of fine old malt whiskey, originally intended as Sugama's present, much more liberally than he otherwise did and by midnight he was in true fighting spirit, his face shining with such particular splendor that his wife's attention was diverted from the impending destruction of Tokyo to the threat of great-uncle's imminent collapse.

There was no earthquake that night, but the old lady couldn't quite believe this and for two more days she sat it out in her nephew's apartment waiting for the dust to clear. Sugama was dispatched, like a kind of dove from Noah's Ark, to report on the state of the world, and it was only after he had personally confirmed that the house in downtown Tokyo was still in perfect order that she consented to their departure. Boon particularly regretted the loss of the parrot, which spoke few words of Japanese but those very frequently, thus improving his pronunciation of the language.

## EXPLORATIONS

1. According to John David Morley, what are the two meanings of the Japanese term *uchi* (paras. 34–35)?

2. How are Sugama's obligations to the older members of his family different from those of most twenty-eight-year-olds in the United States?

3. Morley describes his experiences in Japan through the eyes of the fictional character Boon. What advantages do you think Morley gains from writing in the third person rather than the first person?

4. Morley has interwoven information about Japanese customs with the story of Boon, Sugama, and his family. How would the impact of "Acquiring a Japanese Family" change if the factual sidelights (for example, on interior decoration) were omitted? What information in this narrative do you as a reader find most striking and memorable?

## CONNECTIONS

1. "Acquiring a Japanese Family," like Wole Soyinka's "Nigerian Childhood" (p. 112), depicts characters with beliefs that most people in the United States would regard as superstitious. What similarity do you notice between Morley's and Soyinka's way of handling these beliefs? How does the author's approach affect your response to his characters' superstitions?

2. Scarcity of space is a major influence on life in both Japanese and Chinese cities. In what ways do the Communist Chinese described in Liang Heng and Judith Shapiro's "Chairman Mao's Good Little Boy" (p. 97) approach this issue differently from the capitalist Japanese? What attitudes and tactics do the two cultures share? How does the family's function as "social glue" appear to differ in Japan and China?

3. What concepts of how the family functions (or should function) appear in both "Acquiring a Japanese Family" and Michael Novak's passage in *Looking at Ourselves* (p. 63)? Which of these concepts are depicted by Novak as endangered in the United States and by Morley as thriving in Japan? What factors can you identify as having influenced the family's divergence in these two cultures?

## ELABORATIONS

1. Much of the information Morley gives his readers about the Japanese family is indirect: for example, his discussion of the interior of Japanese homes and the concept of *uchi*. After carefully rereading "Acquiring a Japanese Family," write an essay describing Japanese attitudes toward the family: its social role, its influence on the individual, and the responsibilities and privileges of family members.

2. Morley writes: "The most striking feature of the Japanese house was lack of privacy; the lack of individual, inviolable space. . . . It is impossible to live under such conditions for very long without a common household identity emerging which naturally takes precedence over individual wishes. This enforced family unity was still held up to Boon as an ideal, but in practice it was ambivalent, as much a yoke as a bond" (para. 33). In your own family, in what ways did a common household identity develop as a result of living together? For instance, what habits did you pick up from other members of your family or in response to their needs? (Examples might include getting up, going to bed, eating, bathing, or watching television at certain times; preparing foods or folding laundry in certain ways; buying certain products.) Write an essay about your own *uchi*.

# GYANRANJAN

## *Our Side of the Fence and Theirs*

The son of a renowned writer, Gyanranjan was born in 1936 in
Allahabad, India, where he received his M.A. from Allahabad University.
Although he began his literary career as a poet, he published his first
short story in 1960 and was soon hailed as representing the new writing
of the sixties. "Our Side of the Fence and Theirs" is the title story from
his first collection, published in 1968 and translated from the Hindi by
Gordon C. Roadarmel. A second collection followed in 1971. Today
Gyanranjan continues to work mainly in the story form.

With a third of the area of the United States, India has three times
its population. The Indian civilization is one of the world's oldest, dating
back more than five thousand years. European traders discovered this
South Asian peninsula in the sixteenth century; by the mid-1800s the
British had wrested control from the native rajas. After World War I,
Mohandas "Mahatma" Gandhi led his people in nonviolent resistance
and civil disobedience. From independence in 1947 until 1989, India's
central family was that of its first prime minister, Jawaharlal Nehru,
whose daughter Indira Gandhi (no relation to Mohandas) succeeded
him and was in turn succeeded by her son Rajiv. The Nehru-Gandhi
dynasty ended when Rajiv Gandhi lost the November 1989 election and
was assassinated while campaigning two years later. His successors have
faced an electorate that is more assertive and more impatient, a new
divergence between state and society, increasing clashes between Hindus
and Muslims, and ongoing tensions between India and its neighbors,
particularly Pakistan.

For more background on India, see page 142.

Mukherji has been transferred and no longer lives in our neighborhood. The new people who moved in have no contact with us. They
appear to be Punjabis, but maybe not. It's hard to know anything about
them.

Ever since they arrived, I've been strangely anxious to find out about
them. For some reason I can't stand staying detached. Even on journeys
I have to get acquainted with the other travelers. Perhaps it's just my
nature. But no one at our house is indifferent to those people. We're
respectable, honorable people. Having young women in the home, we're
forced to understand everything and to be constantly aware. We're full of

curiosity, and keep forming impressions based on the activities of our new neighbors.

I'd like to invite the whole family over to our house and be able to come and go at their place. But probably they're completely unaware of my feelings. Their life is an unusual one. They spend a good part of the day sitting around on chairs set on the firm ground near the veranda of their house. Those chairs remain outside all the time, even at night. They're very careless, but the chairs have never been stolen.

On one side of our house, there's a government office and a high brick wall. Behind us is the back of a two-story apartment building and, in front, the main street. As a result, we have no real proximity with any other family. The new neighbors seem like certain people found in big cities who establish no connection with others and keep strictly to themselves. Both this city and the neighborhood are quiet and peaceful. People come and go at a leisurely pace and stroll around casually, since life has no great urgency. That's why we find our neighbors strange.

I went outside. Those people were having morning tea, at the late hour of nine. Besides the husband and wife, there's one girl who must be their daughter. One always sees these same three people, never a fourth. The daughter may not be pretty, but she's a well-mannered young woman. If she used the right makeup, she might even look pretty. I've noticed that she laughs a lot — and frequently. Her mother and father laugh also. They always look happy. What sorts of things do they talk about, and why are they always laughing? Are their lives so full of delightful circumstances which keep them laughing? Or are they insensitive to the harsh, realistic circumstances of life? Amazed, I compare my family with the neighbors.

They startle me by suddenly bursting into laughter. I'd been concentrating on the rose beds, but now my trowel stopped. Their laughter seemed unable to stop. The girl rose from the chair and stood up, handing her teacup to her mother for fear of spilling it. Instead of standing straight, she was doubled over. Something funny in the conversation, perhaps a joke, must have set off the explosion of laughter. The girl, helpless with laughter, was unaware that her dupatta[1] had slipped off one shoulder. The movement of her bosom was visible — free and unrestrained. This was too much! Her mother should have scolded her for that carelessness. What kind of person was she not to mind? But maybe, unlike me, none of them had even looked in that direction.

Daily a kind of mild compulsion grips me, and my helpless fascination

---

[1] A long, thin scarf worn over the shoulders. — ED.

about the new neighbors grows. I'm not the only one. Puppi is very curious too, and keeps praising the material of that girl's kurtas.[2] My brother's wife also glances periodically from the kitchen toward their house, and Granny even knows when the neighbors have bought water chestnuts or squash and when the stove has been lit. Nevertheless, those people don't show a scrap of interest in us.

The girl never looks in our direction, nor do her parents. It doesn't even seem intentional. So the thought of them conversing with us is remote and unimaginable. Perhaps they don't need us in their world. Maybe they consider us inferior. Or maybe they fear trouble because of our proximity. I don't know to what extent that could be true, however, since the sight of a young man in the vicinity doesn't seem to fill her parents with the fear which my father feels for Puppi at the sight of my friends.

We never hear a radio at their place, while ours blares constantly. There's bare ground in front of their house, with not even a blade of grass. Our house has a lawn, along with a vegetable garden and beds of strong-smelling flowers. Why doesn't that girl make friends with my sister and my sister-in-law? Why don't her parents mix with mine? Why don't they notice us drinking tea out of cups prettier than theirs? What they ought to do is add us to their list of acquaintances. They should be interested in everything of ours. Next to the fence, on our side, there's a big tall tamarind tree with fruit six inches long hanging from it. Girls are crazy about tamarind fruit, and yet this neighbor girl never even looks over longingly. She's never given me the satisfaction of breaking a piece of fruit off the tree.

I keep waiting. . . .                                                                    10

Our neighbors evidently have no problem that might make them want to seek our help. Perhaps the little internal problems that exist in our home and others don't exist in theirs, which is astonishing. None of the three ever appears worried. The girl's father must frown occasionally, and at times her mother must get upset, but nothing can be seen or heard from our place. Possibly the girl has some secret and private corner in her heart — some complication or emotional conflict. Maybe so, maybe not. Nothing definite can be known.

A light usually burns at night in their middle room, where Mukherji and his whole family used to sleep. Apparently even indoors they sit together and talk. They must have an endless supply of stories and material for conversation. A sigh slips from my lips. In our house the talk

---

[2]Long, loose shirts. — Ed.

deals only with the weather, mosquitoes, the birth of children, the new wives of relatives, kitchen matters, and ancient divine heroes who obliterate the present.

The fence between our houses is a barrier only in name. It's only a foot-high ridge of dirt with some berry bushes, a long stretch of dry twisted wild cactus, and some unknown shrubs with white ants clustered around the roots. In between, the ridge is broken in several places. Paths have formed, used by the fruit and vegetable sellers as well as the sweeper woman and the newspaper vendor. The postman and milkman have been using these paths for years. Despite the damage from dogs and cats coming and going and from animals grazing on the plants, the fence remains much the same as ever. Until a short time ago, Mukherji's daughter Shaila used to take this route bringing books over to me. It's such a convenient and simple fence that we can easily ride bicycles through the gaps from one side to the other without dismounting. And previously we used to pass through that way, but no longer, because our neighbors interpret a fence as something uncrossable.

They've been living here for three months. . . .

I often move my desk outdoors for study. At this time of year the outside      15
air is lovely, like ice water in an intense summer thirst. But studying there is difficult. My eyes leap the fence and my mind hovers around the neighbors' house. A young and unattached girl. Cheerful and fearless parents. If only I'd been born in that home! That's the way my mind wanders.

At times the neighbor girl sits outside all alone, doing some work or doing nothing. Occasionally she strolls over to the wall on the other side of her house. Elbows propped on the wall, she watches the street. Then she returns. Loafers from other neighborhoods come into our area a lot. Not that there's any lack of them in our neighborhood too. But she always seems innocent and free, walking with small swaying steps.

At our place, in contrast, my sister-in-law takes Puppi along even when she goes outside to get flowers for worship. She's scared outside the house and in it too. She's kept scared. A sharp eye is kept on Puppi also. One time the neighbor girl's father put his hand on his wife's shoulder in the course of conversation, and Puppi was immediately called into the house on some pretext. That scene produced an uproar at our place. Such shamelessness! Gradually people in our house have begun considering the neighbors quite dangerous.

With the passing of time, the attraction toward the neighbors has changed into dislike, though they might as well be nonexistent as far as we're concerned. In time, however, our family has made the neighbors a focal point for all the evils in the world. Our eyes cross the fence thousands of times in what has become a part of our daily routine. A new distress has crept into our minds, added to our other worries. I, too, waste a lot of time, but not a glance from there ever falls this way.

Somewhere nearby a diesel engine, finding no signal to proceed, stands shrieking. The novelty of the sound is startling. For a while all of us will talk about nothing but the diesel engine.

Yesterday those neighbors had not been home since noon. A few guests were staying at their place, but there was no hustle and bustle — just the usual carefree atmosphere. I rose and went inside. Sister-in-law was drying her hair. Then, I don't know why, she teased me slyly, connecting me with the neighbor girl. Smiling to myself, I went outdoors. Just then the girl and her mother returned, probably from the bazaar, carrying some packages. The father must have remained behind.

Both that evening and this morning people kept coming and going there. But it couldn't be considered a large number of people. Their house has the atmosphere of some ordinary festival celebration — just faintly. We were all astonished when the milkman reported that the daughter's marriage took place last night. It was some man from the other side of town. She'd had an Arya Samaj[3] wedding. My sister-in-law threw me a teasing look of sympathy, and I started laughing. I laughed openly and freely, thinking what dreamers we all are.

Now and then three or four people would arrive at their house. They'd go inside, then come out a little later and go away. They were mostly serious and restrained people. At times children gathered, shouting and running around, but otherwise there was no commotion — as though everything were taking place easily and smoothly. There was no way to know just what was happening, nor how.

At our house this has been a day of great uneasiness. After several hours, the girl emerged. She was wearing a sari, maybe for the first time. She stepped out on the veranda straightening her sari and carrying a coconut. Her swaying walk was restricted considerably by the sari and she moved forward with an eye on each step. She hadn't veiled herself in any way, nor, even with her husband walking so close to her, did she show any of the embarrassment and coquettishness of a traditional bride. Her husband looked like some friend of mine. No one was weeping and wailing. Several times the girl's mother kissed her warmly on both cheeks. The father patted her head. The girl's eyes could no longer conceal a shimmer of tears reflecting her excitement over the new life ahead.

Squirrels were darting across the fence from one corner to the other.

---

[3]A reform sect of Hinduism that stresses a return to the principles and practices found in the Vedic scriptures. — ED.

Mother expressed amazement to me over the girl's failure to cry. According to her, the girl had become hardened by her education and had no real love or attachment for her mother and father. "They're all like that these days . . . with not one tear for those who struggled and sacrificed to raise them."

I was not interested in listening to such things. I observed that Mother was enjoying the sun, shifting her position to stay in the patches of sunshine. Then Father made a pronouncement — "In the old days, girls would cry all the way to the edge of the village. Anyone who didn't was beaten and forced to cry. Otherwise her life at her husband's home could never be happy." Father feels very distressed that things are no longer like that. "The old days are passing and men's hearts have become machines, just machines!" At such times his voice grows sharp, and the wreckage of Kali Yug, this Age of Darkness, dances before his eyes.

A few small isolated fragments of cloud have appeared in the sky over our home and then passed on. The parents and relatives reached the gate and were waiting to give the girl a last farewell. The boy's party had brought a Herald car for the groom which looked like a colorful room. That colorful room glided slowly away and was gone.

Granny was the most astounded of all and kept muttering to herself. This marriage made no sense at all to her. "No fanfare, no uproar, no feasting. What's the point of such stinginess! And besides, not even asking the neighbors on such an occasion. What's happening to mankind? Good god!"

Having said good-bye to the girl, the people walked back to the house. Each carried out a chair and sat down outdoors. Ever since the girl's departure, her mother had been a little sad and subdued. A few people kept her company, probably trying to cheer her up. My friend Radhu swore that he could prove the girl was a woman of the world. I felt only the sadness of an intense loss. A sort of strange emptiness — an emptiness at being left behind and an emptiness produced by Radhu's loose talk about the girl. Absolutely unfounded! Maybe talking about a girl's misconduct provides a kind of depraved satisfaction. But perhaps in one corner of my mind, I, too, like my family, can't tolerate the behavior of the neighbors.

Night is sloughing off the cover of evening. The people who were seated around a table across the fence have risen and dispersed. As usual, a light is burning in the middle room of the neighbors' house. Their night has become peaceful and quiet as usual, and there's no way to know how they're feeling about the absence of one member of the family. At our house, though, the bazaar of neighbor-criticism is doing a heated business.

# EXPLORATIONS

1. What are the social functions of the Indian family as Gyanranjan depicts it? Based on "Our Side of the Fence and Theirs," how would you describe Indian parents' responsibilities to their children, and children's obligations to their parents?

2. Gyanranjan's narrator gives only fragmentary information about himself and his family members in terms of such standard characteristics as name, gender, age, relationship, and appearance. What can you deduce about the narrator and the other members of his household from clues in the story? What aspects of people does the narrator seem to think are more interesting and important than these "standard" characteristics?

3. How would you describe the narrator's attitude toward the family next door? Looking back through "Our Side of the Fence and Theirs," note each place where the narrator judges the other family's behavior. What sense do these judgments give you of what kind of people the next-door neighbors are? What sense do they give you of the narrator and his family in comparison?

4. The only dialogue in "Our Side of the Fence and Theirs" comes near the end of the story. Technically, *dialogue* means speech between two or more characters, such as a conversation or an argument. How do the quoted speeches in this story diverge from that definition? What role do these speeches play in the story? How would the story's impact change if Gyanranjan used true dialogue throughout?

# CONNECTIONS

1. How does the relationship of Gyanranjan's narrator to his housemates resemble that of Boon in John David Morley's "Acquiring a Japanese Family" (p. 122)? What similarities in personality do you notice between these two characters? How are their functions as point-of-view characters (that is, characters through whose eyes we view events) alike and different?

2. In "Our Side of the Fence and Theirs," as in Liang and Shapiro's "Chairman Mao's Good Little Boy" (p. 97), the pressures of respectability and conformity create problems. How does using a child narrator in each selection help the author to explore these pressures and problems?

3. What views expressed in *Looking at Ourselves* about the family's functions and values are echoed by the narrator's family in "Our Side of the Fence and Theirs"? What views expressed in *Looking at Ourselves* are embodied by the family on the other side of the fence?

## ELABORATIONS

1. "We're respectable, honorable people," declares Gyanranjan's narrator in the second paragraph. On the basis of "Our Side of the Fence and Theirs," write a definition essay describing the values, habits, attitudes, and relationships that the narrator's family apparently believes define a "respectable, honorable" Indian family.

2. With his first sentence, Gyanranjan lets us know that this is the story of someone who believes his life is shaped by events outside his control. We learn by paragraph 2 that the narrator wishes he could get to know the family next door but feels powerless to do so. Most of us have had similar experiences. Write a narrative essay about a situation in which you wanted to become better acquainted with someone but felt prevented from doing so by family or social pressure.

# VED MEHTA

## *Pom's Engagement*

Completely blind since the age of three, Ved Mehta is the author of more than a dozen books of autobiography, Indian social and political history, and interviews with international historians, philosophers, and theologians. His documentary film *Chachaji, My Poor Relation* airs periodically on public television. Mehta's family was instrumental in his success: He was sent away (briefly) to a school in Bombay when he was five and to the Arkansas State School for the Blind at age fifteen. He went on to graduate Phi Beta Kappa from Pomona College in California, received a master's degree from Harvard University, and won a scholarship at Balliol College of Oxford University. Mehta has received numerous grants and fellowships, including a MacArthur Foundation fellowship. He is currently a writer for *The New Yorker* magazine and holds the Rosenkranz Chair in Writing at Yale University. "Pom's Engagement" comes from his 1984 autobiography *The Ledge Between the Streams*.

Born in 1934, Mehta grew up in the Punjab, a large plain formed by five rivers in northwestern India and northeastern Pakistan. Here the earliest Indian civilization flourished thousands of years ago. Mussoorie is a hill station — a former British summer resort — to the east; a journey to Dehra Dun, a city in the same region, would have meant an over-500-mile round-trip from the Mehta home in Lahore.

The Indian caste system is an ancient hereditary class structure that operated to preserve the status quo. The four principal castes are the Brahman (priests and scholars), the Kshatriya (warriors and rulers), the Vaisya or Bania (farmers and merchants), and the Sudra (peasants and laborers). Below all these was the now illegal caste of Untouchables, or Panchamas, who performed the most menial tasks.

For more background on India, see page 134.

Before we moved to Lahore, Daddyji had gone to Mussoorie, a hill station in the United Provinces, without telling us why he was going out of the Punjab. Now, several months after he made that trip, he gathered us around him in the drawing room at 11 Temple Road while Mamaji mysteriously hurried Sister Pom upstairs. He started talking as if we were all very small and he were conducting one of our "dinner-table-school" discussions. He said that by right and tradition the oldest daughter had to be given in marriage first, and that the ripe age for marriage was nineteen. He said that when a girl approached that age her parents, who had to take the initiative, made many inquiries and followed many leads. They investigated each young man and his family background, his relatives, his friends, his classmates, because it was important to know what kind of family the girl would be marrying into, what kind of company she would be expected to keep. If the girl's parents decided that a particular young man was suitable, then his people also had to make their investigations, but, however favorable their findings, their decision was unpredictable, because good, well-settled boys were in great demand and could afford to be choosy. All this took a lot of time. "That's why I said nothing to you children about why I went to Mussoorie," he concluded. "I went to see a young man for Pom. She's already nineteen."

We were stunned. We have never really faced the idea that Sister Pom might get married and suddenly leave, I thought.

"We won't lose Pom, we'll get a new family member," Daddyji said, as if reading my thoughts.

Then all of us started talking at once. We wanted to know if Sister Pom had been told; if she'd agreed; whom she'd be marrying.

"Your mother has just taken Pom up to tell her," Daddyji said. "But     5 she's a good girl. She will agree." He added, "The young man in question is twenty-eight years old. He's a dentist, and so has a profession."

"Did you get a dentist because Sister Pom has bad teeth?" Usha asked. Sister Pom had always been held up to us as an example of someone who, as a child, had spurned greens and had therefore grown up with a mouthful of poor teeth.

Daddyji laughed. "I confess I didn't think of anyone's teeth when I chose the young man in question."

"What is he like?" I asked. "What are we to call him?"

"He's a little bit on the short side, but he has a happy-go-lucky nature, like Nimi's. He doesn't drink, but, unfortunately, he does smoke. His father died at an early age of a heart attack, but he has a nice mother, who will not give Pom any trouble. It seems that everyone calls him Kakaji."

We all laughed. Kakaji, or "youngster," was what very small boys were     10 called.

"That's what he must have been called when he was small, and the name stuck," Daddyji said.

In spite of myself, I pictured a boy smaller than I was and imagined him taking Sister Pom away, and then I imagined her having to keep his pocket money, to arrange his clothes in the cupboards, to comb his hair. My mouth felt dry.

"What will Kakaji call Sister Pom?" I asked.

"Pom, silly — what else?" Sister Umi said.

Mamaji and Sister Pom walked into the room. Daddyji made a place    15
for Sister Pom next to him and said, "Now, now, now, no reason to cry.
Is it to be yes?"

"Whatever you say," Sister Pom said in a small voice, between sobs.

"Pom, how can you say that? You've never seen him," Sister Umi said.

"Kakaji's uncle, Dr. Prakash Mehrotra, himself a dentist, has known
our family from his student days in Lahore," Daddyji said. "As a student
dentist, he used to be welcomed in Babuji's Shahalmi Gate house. He
would come and go as he pleased. He has known for a long time what
kind of people we are. He remembered seeing you, Pom, when we went
to Mussoorie on holiday. He said yes immediately, and his approval
seemed to be enough for Kakaji."

"You promised me you wouldn't cry again," Mamaji said to Sister Pom,
patting her on the back, and then, to Daddyji, "She's agreed."

Daddyji said much else, sometimes talking just for the sake of talking,    20
sometimes laughing at us because we were sniffling, and all the time
trying to make us believe that this was a happy occasion. First, Sister Umi
took issue with him: parents had no business arranging marriages; if she
were Pom she would run away. Then Sister Nimi: all her life she had
heard him say to us children, "Think for yourself — be independent,"
and here he was not allowing Pom to think for herself. Brother Om took
Daddyji's part: girls who didn't get married became a burden on their
parents, and Daddyji had four daughters to marry off, and would be
retiring in a few years. Sisters Nimi and Umi retorted: they hadn't gone
to college to get married off, to have some young man following them
around like a leech. Daddyji just laughed. I thought he was so wise, and
right.

"Go and bless your big sister," Mamaji said, pushing me in the
direction of Sister Pom.

"I don't want to," I said. "I don't know him."

"What'll happen to Sister Pom's room?" Usha asked. She and Ashok
didn't have rooms of their own. They slept in Mamaji's room.

"Pom's room will remain empty, so that any time she likes she can
come and stay in her room with Kakaji," Daddyji said.

The thought that a man I never met would sleep in Pom's room with    25
Sister Pom there made my heart race. A sob shook me. I ran outside.

The whole house seemed to be in an uproar. Mamaji was shouting at
Gian Chand, Gian Chand was shouting at the bearer, the bearer was
shouting at the sweeper. There were the sounds of the kitchen fire being
stoked, of the drain being washed out, of water running in bathrooms.
From behind whichever door I passed came the rustle of saris, salwars,

and kemises. The house smelled of fresh flowers, but it had a ghostly chill. I would climb to the landing of Sister Pom's room and thump down the stairs two at a time. Brother Om would shout up at me, "Stop it!" Sister Umi would shout down at me, "Don't you have anything better to do?" Sister Nimi would call to me from somewhere, "You're giving Pom a headache." I wouldn't heed any of them. As soon as I had thumped down, I would clatter to the top and thump my way down again.

Daddyji went past on the back veranda. "Who's coming with Kakaji?" I asked. Kakaji was in Lahore to buy some dental equipment, and in a few minutes he was expected for tea, to meet Sister Pom and the family.

"He's coming alone," Daddyji said, over his shoulder. "He's come from very far away." I had somehow imagined that Kakaji would come with at least as many people as we had in our family, because I had started thinking of the tea as a kind of cricket match — the elevens facing off.

I followed Daddyji into the drawing room. "Will he come alone for his wedding, too?"

"No. Then he'll come with the bridegroom's party." 30

We were joined by everyone except Mamaji and Sister Pom, who from the moment we got the news of Sister Pom's marriage had become inseparable.

Gian Chand came in, the tea things rattling on his tray.

Later, I couldn't remember exactly how Kakaji had arrived, but I remember noticing that his footfall was heavy, that his greeting was affectionate, and that his voice seemed to float up with laughter. I don't know what I'd expected, but I imagined that if I had been in his place I would have skulked in the *gulli*, and perhaps changed my mind and not entered at all.

"Better to have ventured and lost than never to have ventured at all," Daddyji was saying to Kakaji about life's battles.

"Yes, Daddyji, just so," he said, with a little laugh. I had never heard 35 anybody outside our family call my father Daddyji. It sounded odd.

Sister Pom was sent for, and she came in with Mamaji. Her footsteps were shy, and the rustle of her sari around her feet was slow, as if she felt too conscious of the noise she was making just in walking. Daddyji made some complimentary remark about the silver border on her sari, and told her to sit next to Kakaji. Kakaji and Sister Pom exchanged a few words about a family group photograph on the mantelpiece, and about her studies. There was the clink of china as Sister Pom served Kakaji tea.

"Won't you have some tea yourself?" Kakaji asked Sister Pom.

Sister Pom's sari rustled over her shoulder as she turned to Daddyji.

"Kakaji, none of my children have ever tasted tea or coffee," Daddyji said. "We consider both to be bad habits. My children have been brought up on hot milk, and lately Pom has been taking a little ghi in her milk at bedtime, for health reasons."

We all protested at Daddyji's broadcasting family matters.                    40

Kakaji tactfully turned the conversation to a visit to Mussoorie that our family was planning.

Mamaji offered him onion, potato, and cauliflower pakoras. He accepted, remarking how hot and crisp they were.

"Where will Sister Pom live?" Usha asked.

"In the summer, my practice is in Mussoorie," Kakaji said, "but in the winter it's in Dehra Dun."

It struck me for the first time that after Sister Pom got married people    45 we didn't know, people she didn't know, would become more important to her than we were.


Kakaji had left without formally committing himself. Then, four days later, when we were all sitting in the drawing room, a servant brought a letter to Mamaji. She told us that it was from Kakaji's mother, and that it asked if Sister Pom might be engaged to Kakaji. "She even wants to know if Pom can be married in April or May," Mamaji said excitedly. "How propitious! That'll be the fifth wedding in the family in those two months." Cousins Prakash and Dev, Cousin Pushpa (Bhaji Ganga Ram's adopted daughter), and Auntie Vimla were all due to be married in Lahore then.

"You still have time to change your mind," Daddyji said to Sister Pom. "What do you really think of him?"

Sister Pom wouldn't say anything.

"How do you expect her to know what her mind is when all that the two talked about was a picture and her bachelor's exam in May?" Sister Umi demanded. "Could she have fallen in love already?"

"Love, Umi, means something very different from 'falling in love,'"   50 Daddyji said. "It's not an act but a lifelong process. The best we can do as Pom's parents is to give her love every opportunity to grow."

"But doesn't your 'every opportunity' include knowing the person better than over a cup of tea, or whatever?" Sister Umi persisted.

"Yes, of course it does. But what we are discussing here is a simple matter of choice — not love," Daddyji said. "To know a person, to love a person, takes years of living together."

"Do you mean, then, that knowing a person and loving a person are the same thing?" Sister Umi asked.

"Not quite, but understanding and respect are essential to love, and that cannot come from talking together, even over a period of days or months. That can come only in good time, through years of experience.

It is only when Pom and Kakaji learn to consider each other's problems as one and the same that they will find love."

"But, Daddyji, look at the risk you're taking, the risk you're making Pom take," Sister Nimi said.

"We are trying to minimize the risk as much as we can by finding Pom a family that is like ours," Daddyji said. "Kakaji is a dentist, I am a doctor. His life and way of thinking will be similar to mine. We are from the same caste, and Kakaji's family originally came from the Punjab. They eat meat and eggs, and they take religion in their stride, and don't pray every day and go to temples, like Brahmans. Kakaji knows how I walk into a club and how I am greeted there. The atmosphere in Pom's new home will be very much the same as the atmosphere here. Now, if I were to give Pom in marriage to a Brahman he'd expect Pom to live as he did. That would really be gambling."

"Then what you're doing is perpetuating the caste system," Sister Nimi said. She was the political rebel in the family. "You seem to presuppose that a Kshatriya should marry only a Kshatriya, that a Brahman should marry only a Brahman. I would just as soon marry a shopkeeper from the Bania caste or an Untouchable, and help to break down caste barriers."

"That day might come," Daddyji said. "But you will admit, Nimi, that by doing that you'd be increasing the odds."

"But for a cause I believe in," Sister Nimi said.

"Yes, but that's a whole other issue," Daddyji said.

"Daddyji, you say that understanding and respect are necessary for love," Sister Umi said. "I don't see why you would respect a person more because you lived with him and shared his problems."

"In our society, we think of understanding and respect as coming only through sacrifice," Daddyji said.

"Then you're advocating the subservience of women," Sister Nimi said, "because it's not Kakaji who will be expected to sacrifice — it's Pom. That's not fair."

"And why do you think that Pom will learn to respect Kakaji because she sacrifices for him?" Sister Umi said, pressing her point.

"No, Umi, it is the other way around," Daddyji said. "It is Kakaji who will respect Pom because she sacrifices for him."

"But that doesn't mean that Pom will respect Kakaji," Sister Umi persisted.

"But if Kakaji is moved by Pom's sacrifices he will show more consideration for her. He will grow to love her. I know in my own case I was moved to the depths to see Shanti suffer so because she was so ill-prepared to be my wife. It took me long enough — too long, I believe — to reach that understanding, perhaps because I had broken away from the old traditions and had given in to Western influences."

"So you admit that Pom will have to suffer for years," Sister Umi said.

"Perhaps," Daddyji said. "But all that time she will be striving for ultimate happiness and love. Those are precious gifts that can only be cultivated in time."

"You haven't told us what this ultimate happiness is," Sister Umi said.  70
"I don't really understand it."

"It is a uniting of ideals and purposes, and a merging of them. This is the tradition of our society, and it is the means we have adopted to make our marriages successful and beautiful. It works because we believe in the goodness of the individuals going into the marriage and rely on the strength of the sacred bond."

"But my ideal is to be independent," Sister Nimi said. "As you say, 'Think for yourself.'"

"But often you have to choose among ideals," Daddyji said. "You may have to choose between being independent and being married."

"But aren't you struck by the fact that all the suffering is going to be on Pom's part? Shouldn't Kakaji be required to sacrifice for their happiness, too?" Sister Nimi said, reverting to the old theme.

"There has to be a start," Daddyji said. "Remember, in our tradition  75
it's her life that is joined with his; it is she who will forsake her past to build a new future with him. If both Pom and Kakaji were to be obstinate, were to compete with each other about who would sacrifice first, who would sacrifice more, what hope would there be of their ever getting on together, of their ever finding love?"

"Daddyji, you're evading the issue," Sister Nimi said. "Why shouldn't he take the initiative in this business of sacrifice?"

"He would perhaps be expected to if Pom were working, too, as in the West, and, though married, leading a whole different life from his. I suppose more than this I really can't say, and there may be some injustice in our system, at that. In the West, they go in for romantic love, which is unknown among us. I'm not sure that that method works any better than our method does."

Then Daddyji said to Sister Pom, "I have done my best. Even after you marry Kakaji, my responsibility for you will not be over. I will always be there in the background if you should need me."

"I respect your judgment, Daddyji," Sister Pom said obediently. "I'll do what you say."

Mamaji consulted Shambu Pandit. He compared the horoscopes of  80
Sister Pom and Kakaji and set the date of the marriage for the eleventh of May. . . . "That's just three days after she finishes her B.A. finals!" we cried. "When will she study? You are sacrificing her education to some silly superstition."

But Shambu Pandit would not be budged from the date. "I am only going by the horoscopes of the couple," he said. "You might as well protest to the stars."

We appealed to Daddyji, but he said that he didn't want to interfere, because such matters were up to Mamaji. That was as much as to say that Shambu Pandit's date was a settled thing.

I recall that at about that time there was an engagement ceremony. We all — Daddyji, Mamaji, Sister Pom, many of our Mehta and Mehra relatives — sat cross-legged on the floor of the front veranda around Shambu Pandit. He recited the Gayatri Mantra, the simple prayer he used to tell us to say before we went to sleep, and made a thank offering of incense and ghi to a fire in a brazier, much as Mamaji did — behind Daddyji's back — when one of us was going on a trip or had recovered from a bout of illness. Servants passed around a platter heaped up with crumbly sweet balls. I heard Kakaji's sister, Billo, saying something to Sister Pom; she had just come from Dehra Dun bearing a sari, a veil, and the engagement ring for Sister Pom, after Romesh Chachaji, one of Daddyji's brothers, had gone to Dehra Dun bearing some money, a silver platter and silver bowls, and sweetmeats for Kakaji. It was the first time that I was able to think of Kakaji both as a remote and frightening dentist who was going to take Sister Pom away and as someone ordinary like us, who had his own family. At some point, Mamaji prodded me, and I scooted forward, crab fashion, to embrace Sister Pom. I felt her hand on my neck. It had something cold and metallic on it, which sent a shiver through me. I realized that she was wearing her engagement ring, and that until then Mamaji was the only one in our family who had worn a ring.

In the evening, the women relatives closeted themselves in the drawing room with Sister Pom for the engagement singsong. I crouched outside with my ear to the door. The door pulsated with the beat of a barrel drum. The pulse in my forehead throbbed in sympathy with the beat as I caught snatches of songs about bedsheets and henna, along with explosions of laughter, the songs themselves rising and falling like the cooing of the doves that nested under the eaves of the veranda. I thought that a couple of years earlier I would have been playing somewhere outside on such an occasion, without knowing what I was missing, or been in the drawing room clapping and singing, but now I was crouching by the door like a thief, and was feeling ashamed even as I was captivated.

# EXPLORATIONS

1. What members of Pom's nuclear and extended family are involved in arranging the match between her and Kakaji?
2. What views does Pom's father express about the importance of individual happiness in a marriage? What goals does he consider more important?
3. What steps between selection of a mate and marriage are mentioned in "Pom's Engagement"? Which steps involve the bride's and groom's families, and what roles do they play?
4. Reading "Pom's Engagement" it is easy to forget that the author is blind. What sensory impressions does Ved Mehta describe where a sighted writer might focus on what he or she sees? Give at least five examples.

# CONNECTIONS

1. In what ways does Pom's family resemble the narrator's family in Gyanranjan's "Our Side of the Fence and Theirs" (p. 134)? In what ways is Pom's family more like the family on the other side of the fence?
2. In his last sentence, Ved Mehta speaks of "feeling ashamed even as I was captivated." At what point(s) in Gyanranjan's story does his narrator express similar feelings? What appear to be the reasons for these contradictory emotions?
3. Look back at Liang Heng's comments about his parents' marriage in paragraph 8 of "Chairman Mao's Good Little Boy" (p. 97). What aspects of that courtship and marriage are similar to and different from Pom Mehta's courtship and her parents' marriage?
4. In paragraph 31 Mehta writes, "Mamaji and Sister Pom . . . from the moment we got the news of Sister Pom's marriage had become inseparable." How does this mother-daughter relationship resemble the one described by Rigoberta Menchú in "Birth Ceremonies" (p. 76)?

# ELABORATIONS

1. Judging from Gyanranjan's "Our Side of the Fence and Theirs" and "Pom's Engagement," how do Indian assumptions about the subordination of the individual to the family differ from ours? Given Indian values and priorities, what are the advantages of their system of arranged marriages? What benefits might such a system have in the United States, with its high divorce rate and disintegrating nuclear family? Write an argumentative essay exploring one or more of these questions.

2. In paragraph 73 Mehta quotes Daddyji: "But often you have to choose among ideals. You may have to choose between being independent and being married." What do the authors represented in *Looking at Ourselves* have to say about the choices we make in the United States between individual freedom and the bonds of family? Write an essay contrasting the pros and cons of living alone versus living in a family.

# MARGUERITE DURAS

## Home Making

Marguerite Duras is one of France's most eminent novelists, as well as a distinguished playwright, filmmaker, and nonfiction writer. She was born Marguerite Donnadieu in 1914 in French Indochina, now Vietnam, and educated in Saigon. At age fifteen, living in poverty with her mother and brothers, Duras became involved with a twenty-seven-year-old Chinese millionaire. The affair shaped her life and work and became the subject of her book *The Lover* (1984; film, 1992), which won France's prestigious Prix Goncourt and has appeared in at least twenty-nine foreign editions. At age nineteen Duras moved to France to study law. Her first novel was published in 1943; since then, she has produced over fifty novels, plays, and films, including the screenplay for Alain Resnais's film *Hiroshima mon amour* (1960). "Home Making" comes from her 1987 book *Vie matérielle* (*Practicalities*, 1990), created by Duras and Jérôme Beaujour from conversations, and translated from the French by Barbara Bray. As Leslie Garis wrote in the *New York Times* magazine: "Considering . . . her participation in the French Resistance, her Communism and ultimate disaffection with the Party, her two marriages and many liaisons, the near-fatal cure she underwent for alcoholism in 1982, and, especially, her miraculous recovery from a five-month coma induced by complications from emphysema in 1988, it is reasonable to suggest that Marguerite Duras is a force of nature." She currently lives in Paris.

A house means a family house, a place specially meant for putting children and men in so as to restrict their waywardness and distract them from the longing for adventure and escape they've had since time began. The most difficult thing in tackling this subject is to get down to the basic and utterly manageable terms in which women see the fantastic challenge a house represents: how to provide a center for children and men at one and the same time.

The house a woman creates is a Utopia. She can't help it — can't help trying to interest her nearest and dearest not in happiness itself but in the search for it. As if the search were the point of the whole thing, not something to be rejected out of hand because it's too general. She says you must both understand and be chary of this strange preoccupation with happiness. She thinks this attitude will help the children later on. For that's what a woman, a mother wants — to teach her children to take an interest in life. She knows it's safer for them to be interested in other people's happiness than to believe in their own.

At Neauphle I often used to cook in the early afternoon. That was when no one else was there — when the others were at work, or out for a walk, or asleep in their rooms. Then I had all the ground floor of the house and the garden to myself. It was then I saw most clearly that I loved them and wished them well. I can recall the kind of silence there was after they went out. To enter that silence was like entering the sea. At once a happiness and a very precise state of abandonment to an evolving idea. A way of thinking or perhaps of not thinking — the two things are not so far apart. And also of writing.

Slowly and carefully, so as to make it last, I'd cook, those afternoons, for the people who weren't there. I'd make some soup so that it would be ready for them if they came in very hungry. If no soup was ready there wasn't anything. If nothing was ready it was because there wasn't any-thing; nobody was there. Often the ingredients were there, bought that morning, and all I had to do was prepare the vegetables, put the soup on, and write.

I thought for a long while about buying a house. I never imagined I    5
could ever own a new one. The house at Neauphle used to be a couple of farms built a little while before the Revolution. It must be just over two hundred years old. I've often thought about it. It was there in 1789 and 1870. It's where the forests of Rambouillet and Versailles meet. And in 1958 it belonged to me. I thought about it some nights till it almost hurt. I saw it lived in by the women. I saw myself as preceded by them, in the same bedrooms, the same twilights. There'd been nine generations of women before me within those walls; dozens of people gathered around the fires — children, farm workers, cow girls. All over the house there were surfaces rubbed smooth where grown-ups, children, and dogs had gone in and out of the doors.

The thing women brood on for years — it's the bed their thoughts flow along while the children are still small — is how to keep them safe from harm. They usually brood in vain.

Some women can never manage it — they can't handle their houses, they overload them, clutter them up, never create an opening toward the world outside. They can't help it, but they get it all wrong and make the house unbearable, so that the children run away as soon as they're fifteen, the same as we did. We ran away because the only adventure left to us was one all worked out by our mothers.

   Lots of women never solve the problem of disorder — of the house
being overrun by the chaos families produce. They know they'll never be
able to overcome the incredible difficulties of keeping a house in order.
Though anyhow there's nothing to be done about it. That sort of woman
simply shifts disorder from one room to another; moves it about or hides
it in cellars, disused rooms, trunks, or cupboards. Women like that have
locked doors in their own houses that they daren't open, even in front of
the family, for fear of being put to shame. Many are willing enough but
naïve — they think you can solve the problem of disorder by putting the
tidying-up off until later, not realizing their "later" doesn't exist and never
will. And that even if it did come it would be too late. They don't realize
that disorder, or in other words the accumulation of possessions, can only
be dealt with in a way that's extremely painful. Namely by parting with
them. Some families with big houses keep everything for three hundred
years — dresses, toys, and anything to do with the children, the squire,
or the mayor.
   I've thrown things away, and regretted it. Sooner or later you always
regret having thrown things away at some time or other. But if you don't
part with anything, if you try to hold back time, you can spend your whole
life tidying life up and documenting it. Women often keep gas and
electricity bills for twenty years, for no other reason than to record time
and their own virtues. The time they once had, but of which nothing
remains.

   I say it again. It bears a lot of repetition. A woman's work, from the        10
time she gets up to the time she goes to bed, is as hard as a day at war,
worse than a man's working day. Because she has to make her time-table
conform to those of other people — her own family and the various
organizations it's connected with.
   In a morning five hours long, she gets the children's breakfasts, washes
and dresses them, does the housework, makes the beds, washes and
dresses herself, does the shopping, does the cooking, lays the table. In
twenty minutes she gives the children their lunch, yelling at them the
while, then takes them back to school, does the dishes, does the washing,
and so on and so on. Maybe, at about half-past three, she gets to read the
paper for half an hour.

   From the man's point of view a woman is a good mother when she
turns this discontinuity into a silent and unobtrusive continuity.
   This silent continuity used to be regarded as life itself, not just one of
its aspects, the same as work. And now we've got to the root of the matter
or the bottom of the mine.

The silent continuity seemed so natural and lasted so long that in the end, for the people around the woman who practiced it, it no longer existed at all. To men, women's work was like the rain-bringing clouds, or the rain itself. The task involved was carried out every day as regularly as sleep. So men were happy — men in the Middle Ages, men at the time of the Revolution, and men in 1986: Everything in the garden was lovely. . . .

The mental house and the physical house.                                        15
My first school was my mother herself. How she ran her houses. How she did the work. It was she who taught me cleanliness — the thorough-going, morbid, superstitious cleanliness of a mother with three young children in Indochina in 1915.

What my mother wanted was to make sure that we, her children, whatever happened, however serious, even war — that we'd never in all our lives be caught unawares. As long as we had a house and our mother, we'd never be abandoned or swept away or taken by surprise. There could be wars, droughts, we might be cut off by floods; but we'd always have a house, a mother, and something to eat and drink. I believe that right up to the end of her life she made jam in preparation for a third war. She stockpiled sugar and pasta. Hers was a kind of gloomy arithmetic derived from a fundamental pessimism which I've inherited in its entirety. . . .

She brought us up completely unaided. She told us she'd been swindled and abandoned because our father was dead and she was defenseless. One thing she was certain of, and that was that we were all abandoned.
I have this deep desire to run a house. I've had it all my life. There's still something of it left. Even now I still have to know all the time what there is to eat in the cupboards, if there's everything that's needed in order to hold out, live, survive. I too still hanker after a sort of shipboard self-sufficiency on the voyage of life for the people I love and for my child.

I often think of the houses my mother had, the ones that went with     20
her various posts. Seven hours' trek along unmade roads from the nearest white settlement and the nearest doctor. The cupboards were always full of food and medicine — gruel, soft soap, alum, acids, vinegars, quinine, disinfectants, Emetine, Peptofer, Pulmoserum, Hepatrol, charcoal. I mean, she wasn't just my mother — she was a kind of institution. The natives used to come to her too, for treatment. A house is that too — it overflows. That was how it was with us. We were conscious of it very early on, and were very grateful to our mother for it. Home was simultaneously

her and the house — the house around her and her inside the house. And she extended beyond herself with predictions of bad weather and years of disaster. She lived through two wars — nine years of it altogether — and she expected there to be a third. I think she expected it right up to her death, just as everyone else expects the next season. I think she only read the paper for that — to try to read between the lines whether war was getting closer. I don't remember her ever saying it was getting further away.

Sometimes, when we were children, she played at war to show us what it was like. She'd get hold of a stick about the same length as a gun, put it over her shoulder, and march up and down in front of us singing *Sambre et Meuse*. Then she'd burst into tears, and we'd try to console her. Yes, my mother liked the wars of men.

I believe that always, or almost always, in all childhoods and in all the lives that follow them, the mother represents madness. Our mothers always remain the strangest, craziest people we've ever met. Lots of people say, "My mother was insane — I say it and I mean it. Insane." People laugh a lot at the memory of their mothers. I suppose it is funny.

In the house in the country, at Neauphle-le-Château, I made a list of all the things that ought to be always in the house. There were a few dozen of them. We kept the list — it's still there — because it was I who'd written it down. It still includes everything.

Here at Trouville it's different — it's only an apartment. I wouldn't think of doing such a thing for here. But at Neauphle there have always been stocks of things. Here's the list:

| | | |
|---|---|---|
| table salt | butter | lavatory paper |
| pepper | tea | light bulbs |
| sugar | flour | kitchen soap |
| coffee | eggs | Scotchbrite |
| wine | canned tomatoes | eau de Javel |
| potatoes | kitchen salt | washing powder |
| pasta | Nescafé | (hand) |
| rice | nuoc mam | Spontex |
| oil | bread | Ajax |
| vinegar | cheeses | steel wool |
| onions | yogurt | coffee filters |
| garlic | window cleaner | fuses |
| milk | | insulating tape |

The list's still there, on the wall. We haven't added anything. We    25
haven't taken to using any of the hundreds of new articles that have been
invented in the twenty years since it was written.

Outer and inner order in a house. The outer order is the visible
running of the house, and the inner order is that of the ideas, emotional
phases, and endless feelings connected with the children. A house as my
mother conceived it was in fact *for* us. I don't think she'd have done it
for a man or a lover. It's an activity that has nothing to do with men. They
can build houses, but they can't make homes. As a general rule, men
don't do anything for children. Nothing practical. They might take them
to the cinema or out for a walk. But I think that's about all. The child is
put into their arms when they get home from work — clean, changed,
ready to go to bed. Happy. That makes a mountain of difference between
men and women.

I seriously believe that to all intents and purposes the position of
women hasn't changed. The woman is still responsible for everything in
the house even if she has help, even if she's much more aware, much
more intelligent, much bolder than before. Even if she has much more
self-confidence. Even if she writes much more, a woman is just the same
as she was before in relation to men. Her main ambition is still to watch
over and look after the family. And even if she has changed socially,
everything she does is done *on top of* that change. But have men
changed? Almost not at all. Perhaps they don't shout so much. And they
talk less. Yes. I can't see anything else. They can sometimes keep quiet.
Be reduced to silence. Naturally. As a rest from the sound of their own
voice.

The woman is the home. That's where she used to be, and that's where
she is still. You might ask me, "What if a man tries to be part of the
home — will the woman let him?" I answer yes. Because then he
becomes one of the children.

Men's needs have to be met just the same as children's. And women
take the same pleasure in meeting them. Men think they're heroes —
again just like children. Men love war, hunting, fishing, motorbikes, cars,
just like children. When they're sleepy you can see it. And women like
men to be like that. We mustn't fool ourselves. We like men to be
innocent and cruel; we like hunters and warriors; we like children.

It's been going on for a long time. Ever since my son was a little boy    30
I've brought the food from the kitchen and put it on the table. And when
one course was finished and the next one was due, I'd go and fetch it

without thinking, quite happily. Lots of women do it. Just like that, like
me. They do it when the children are less than twelve years old, and they
go on doing it afterwards. With the Italians, for example, you see women
of eighty serving children of sixty. I've seen it myself in Sicily.

     With a house — might as well admit it — it's rather as if you'd been
given a boat, a yacht. And it's a very demanding job, running a house —
the building itself and its human and other contents. It's only women
who are not really quite women at all, frivolous women who have no
idea, who neglect repairs. Now I've got where I wanted to get to — the
repairs. I'd love to go into all the details, but perhaps the reader wouldn't
understand why. Anyhow, here's what I have to say. Women who wait
until there are three electric plugs that don't work, and the vacuum
cleaner is unusable, and the taps drip, before they phone the plumber or
buy some new plugs — these women have got it all wrong. As a rule it's
women who've been neglected themselves who let things go like that —
women who hope their husbands will notice and deduce that they're
making their wives unhappy. Such women don't realize men never notice
anything in a house run by their womenfolk: It's something they take for
granted, something they got used to in their childhood with the woman
who happened to be their mother. They can see very well that the plugs
don't work, but what do they say? They say: "Good heavens, the plugs
don't work," and go on with what they were doing. If the vacuum cleaner's
broken they won't even notice. They simply don't see that sort of thing.
Just like children — they don't notice anything. So women's behavior is
incomprehensible to men. If a woman omits to do something — forgets,
or gets her own back by not buying new plugs — the men just won't take
it in. Or they'll think she has reasons of her own for not buying new plugs
or not getting the vacuum cleaner mended, and it would be tactless to
ask what those reasons are. They're probably afraid they might suddenly
be confronted by the women's despair, afraid they might be overwhelmed
by despair themselves. People say men are "adapting" now. It's hard to
know what's really going on. Men try to "adapt" themselves as regards
practical things — one can accept that. But I don't really know what to
think. I have a man friend who does the cooking and the housework. His
wife doesn't do anything. She loathes housework, and doesn't know the
first thing about cooking. And so my friend brings up the children and
does the cooking; he washes the floors, does the shopping, makes the
beds, sees to all the chores. And on top of all that he works to provide
for them all. His wife wanted to be out of all the turmoil and have lovers
whenever she felt like it. So she's taken a little house next door to the
one her husband lives in with the two children, and he accepts this in
order to keep her. Because she's the mother of his children. He accepts

everything. He doesn't even suffer anymore. What can you say to that? I personally feel slightly repelled by a man with such a strong sense of duty.

I'm told men often do the rough work and that you often see them in the household section of department stores. I don't even answer that sort of thing. Rough work is fun for men. To cut down trees after a day at the office isn't work — it's a kind of game. Of course, if you tell a man of ordinary build and average strength what needs doing, he does it. Wash up a couple of plates — he does it. Do the shopping — he does it. But he has a terrible tendency to think he's a hero if he goes out and buys some potatoes. Still, never mind.

People tell me I exaggerate. They say it all the time. Do you think exaggeration is the word? You talk of idealization, say I idealize women. Perhaps. Who's to say? Women could do with being idealized a bit.

You can think what you like about what I've just said. I must sound incomprehensible to you, talking about women's work. The main thing is to talk about them and their houses and their surroundings, and the way they manage other people's good.

Men and women are different, after all. Being a mother isn't the same as being a father. Motherhood means that a woman gives her body over to her child, her children; they're on her as they might be on a hill, in a garden; they devour her, hit her, sleep on her; and she lets herself be devoured, and sometimes she sleeps because they are on her body. Nothing like that happens with fathers. . . .

There are also houses that are too well made, too well thought out, completely without surprises, devised in advance by experts. By surprise I mean the unpredictable element produced by the way a house is used. Dining rooms are large because that's where guests are entertained, but kitchens are small — and getting smaller and smaller. Yet everyone squeezes in there to eat. When one person leaves the kitchen the others have to stand up to make way. But the habit persists.

Efforts are made to break it, but it's in the kitchen that everybody congregates at the end of the day. It's warm there, and you can be with Mother and hear her talk while she gets on with the cooking. Pantries and linen rooms don't exist anymore either, yet they're really irreplaceable. Like big kitchens. And yards.

Nowadays you can't design your own house anymore. It's frowned on. "That was all very well in the past," they tell you, "but now there are experts and they can do it much better than you."

This kind of attitude is increasingly common, and I dislike it intensely.

In most modern houses there are none of the rooms you need to supplement the basics of kitchen and bedrooms. I mean rooms to keep things
in. How can you do without them, and where are you supposed to do
the ironing and the sewing and store things like nuts and apples and
cheese and machines and tools and toys and so on?

And modern houses don't have passages, either, for children to play
and run about in, and for dogs, umbrellas, coats, and satchels. And don't
forget that passages and corridors are where the young ones curl up and
go to sleep when they're tired, and where you go and collect them to put
them to bed. That's where they go when they're four years old and have
had enough of the grown-ups and their philosophy. That's where, when
they're unsure of themselves, they go and have a quiet cry.

Houses never have enough room for children, not even if they're
castles. Children don't actually look at houses, but they know them and
all their nooks and crannies better than their mothers do. They rummage
about. They snoop around. They don't consciously look at houses any
more than they look at the walls of flesh that enclose them before they
can see anything at all — but they know them. It's when they leave the
house that they look at it.

## EXPLORATIONS

1. According to Marguerite Duras, what are a mother's responsibilities to her
   family? What are a father's responsibilities to his family?

2. How does Duras's description of motherhood in paragraph 32 relate to her
   concept of a woman's involvement with her house?

3. Which of Duras's ideas about home and family are most traditional? Which
   ones are most unconventional? Which of her ideas do you disagree with?

4. What kinds of evidence does Duras use to support her generalizations in this
   essay? Do you find her evidence convincing? Why or why not?

## CONNECTIONS

1. What household responsibilities belong to women in both "Home Making"
   and Ved Mehta's "Pom's Engagement" (p. 142)? What similar roles do men
   play in these two selections?

2. In "Pom's Engagement," Daddyji tells his children that a wife must sacrifice
   and suffer for her husband. What comments by Duras suggest that she agrees?

3. Reread the selections by William R. Mattox (p. 66), Patricia Schroeder (p. 68),

and Christopher Lasch (p. 74) in *Looking at Ourselves*. How does Duras's depiction of a mother in France differ from these writers' depiction of a mother in the United States? What are the main reasons for the contrast?

## ELABORATIONS

1. In her last paragraph Duras writes: "Children don't actually look at houses, but they know them and all their nooks and crannies better than their mothers do." Write a descriptive essay about a home you lived in as a child.

2. If you could design a house for yourself and your past, present, or future family, what would it be like? Reread Duras's paragraphs 33–38; then write an essay classifying the functions you think a house should fulfill and the ways your dream house would fulfill them.

# GHOLAM-HOSSEIN SA'EDI

## *The Game Is Over*

Widely considered the leading Iranian writer of his time, Gholam-Hossein Sa'edi was born in Tabriz in 1935. He became involved in political activities while studying medicine; as a physician specializing in psychiatry, he served the poorest section of Tehran. A satirical author of plays, novels, and short stories attacking social injustice, Sa'edi was imprisoned and tortured by the shah's regime. Many of his writings were banned. He was eventually released and allowed to come to the United States but insisted on returning home. Sa'edi is one of the founders of Iran's modern drama and theater; *The Cow*, a film adapted from one of his novels, was shown at international film festivals, such as the prestigious Edinburgh Film Festival. When the Ayatollah Khomeini replaced the shah, Sa'edi was forced underground and into exile in Paris, where he died in 1985. "The Game Is Over" ("Bazi tamam shud") first appeared in the Tehran publication *Alifba* in 1973. The following translation from the Farsi, by Robert Campbell, was done for Sa'edi's American story collection *Dandil* (1981). For samples from two other translations, see page xxiii.

Sa'edi's homeland, the Islamic Republic of Iran, lies east of Iraq and west of Pakistan and Afghanistan. Iran is an expanse of large salt deserts and mountains dotted with oases and forest areas. Long known as Persia, it was conquered repeatedly over its 4,000-year history. The British and Russian empires vied for influence there in the nineteenth century; Afghanistan was severed from Iran by the British in 1857. The notorious dynasty of the shahs began in 1925 with military leader Reza Khan. He abdicated in 1941 in favor of his son. Shah Mohammad Reza Pahlavi — a U.S. ally — instituted economic and social reforms, but he also arrested thousands and executed hundreds of political opponents. Conservative Muslim protests erupted into violence in 1978. In 1979 the shah fled to Egypt, where he died the following year. Meanwhile, the exiled religious leader Ayatollah Ruhollah Khomeini returned to Iran and became president. Political turmoil, arrests, and executions continued, while mounting religious fanaticism isolated Iran from most of the rest of the world. In 1989 Khomeini sparked international riots and protests by calling on Muslims everywhere to kill the "blasphemous" British novelist Salman Rushdie (see p. 240). The death sentence remained in effect even after the Ayatollah's death several months later and during the tenure of his replacement by the more moderate President Hashemi Rafsanjani.

*I*

Hasani said it to me himself: "Let's go over to my place tonight." I'd never been to their place. He'd never been to mine. What I'm getting at is, we were always too afraid of our fathers. He was a lot more afraid than I was. But that night it was different: Hasani was mad at me. He imagined that I didn't like him anymore, that I wasn't his friend. So we went. Usually we just met each other outside. In the morning I would go to their little shack and give a long-drawn-out whistle that Hasani had taught me. When I whistled, Hasani would grab a can and come out. Instead of saying "Hi," we would fight a little. We would hit each other hard so it hurt. That's how we'd decided to behave, and whenever we met, or whenever we left each other, we would fight like that — unless we were either angry or had tricked each other.

After that we'd go running between all the little shacks and drop into Body Washer's Hollow. The city garbage trucks dumped their trash there. We'd root around in the trash. One day I might pick up some tin, and Hasani might find some glass. Now and then we'd get our hands on something better, like an empty salad oil can, a baby's bottle, a broken doll, a useful shoe, a perfectly good sugar bowl with a handle broken off, or maybe a plastic pitcher. Once I found a gold charm with a verse from the Koran on it. Like from a baby's necklace. Hasani had found a full pack of foreign cigarettes. When we got tired, we'd go to the side of the hollow where there's a big flat place: Hājji Timur's Kiln is at the far side of the terrace. They didn't use it anymore. It was ruined.

There were all these big wells on the terrace — not just two or three, but well after well after well. Once I got the idea of counting them two by two. After we counted fifty, we got tired of it and quit. Every time we went to the wells we played these games that were fun. We would lie down and crawl up to where our chests were over the wells, and then we'd make funny noises. The noises would echo in the wells and come out again. Every well was different and would answer us with a special sound. Mostly we'd just laugh into the well, and instead of laughs, we'd hear cries coming back out. We'd get scared, and we'd laugh some more, louder, but the crying just got louder too. Hasani and I would be alone, mostly. Other kids hardly ever came to the hollow. Their mamas wouldn't let them. They were scared they'd fall in a well or get hurt some other way. But Hasani and me, it wasn't just that we'd gotten bigger, or that we always came home with sackfuls of stuff. Our mamas didn't mess with us anymore. They never said anything.

That afternoon, the one before the night I went to Hasani's place, Hasani came out, and he was really low. He was wrinkling his forehead.

You could see he'd been crying a lot. He didn't feel like doing anything. His heart wasn't in it. When we went to the hollow, he just wandered around, poking at the trash with his stick. He swore at his dad some. I knew what had happened. His dad had come home from work at noon and been really mad. He had argued with his boss and been fired, and when he got home he had jumped Hasani and beat him like there was no tomorrow.

We'd heard Hasani yelling. My ma had sworn at Hasani's dad. She   5
said, "Why are you beating an innocent child?" I saw the marks the belt had left on his shoulders, and a place under one eye that had gotten swollen and turned black and blue. Every night when Hasani's dad came home, before he changed clothes or washed, he would beat Hasani. He would beat him with his fists. He'd kick him. He'd use a club, or a rope, or a belt. He swore at Hasani and beat him till he cried bloody murder; you could hear him scream all over the place.

The neighbors would go running up. They'd swear, "May I die and you die," and make him let him go. Hasani's dad would beat him every night, but my dad would only beat Ahmad and me once or twice a week. Like when he was feeling bad, or things at the shop hadn't gone well, he would take it out on us. He'd beat us till suppertime. My ma would take to crying and carrying on and saying, "You bastard! Why are you killing my children! Why are you crippling them!" My dad would turn around and start taking it out on her. She'd yell, "Children, get out, get out!" By the time we'd got out, my dad would have calmed down. He'd just sit real quiet in a corner and chew on his mustache, and he'd say, "Call the children and let's guzzle down something."

But Hasani's dad didn't bother the other kids. He just beat on Hasani, and his ma would never say, "Get out!" Because Hasani's dad would always block the door and lay into him just like that. He would hit and kick him all over. He'd grab his head and pound it on the wall.

That was the first day he'd taken it out on Hasani around noon. Hasani was really down, so I tried to cheer him up. I said to him, "Let's go up there." We got out of the hollow and went to the flat place where the wells are. We sat down beside one. No matter what I tried, he didn't say anything. He just stayed gloomy. I even lay down by the well and stuck my head in, and I made noises like a cow and a puppy, and I laughed and cried and did everything I knew how to do. But would you believe it? Hasani just sat there frowning. He kept hitting his toes with his stick. At last I whistled to him in our private code, "Hasani, what's with you?" Hasani didn't answer. I called again, "Hasani, Hasani." He turned around and said, "What?" I said, "What are you being so cross for?"

"Why should it be for anything?"

"By God, stop your frowning. What are you frowning for?"  10

"I didn't make myself start frowning. How can I quit?"

I got up and said, "Come on, get up and let's do something so you'll cheer up."

Hasani, who was still hitting his toes with his stick, said, "Like what?"

I thought a bit, but couldn't come up with anything to bring him around. I said, "Let's go to the road and watch the cars."

"What for?"  15

"Let's go and count the hearses like we did the other day. Let's see how many go by in an hour."

"As many as go by, go by. So what?"

"You want to go on top of Hājji Timur's Kiln and throw rocks?"

He said listlessly, "I don't feel like it. If you want, go by yourself and throw rocks."

I sat down on a heap of garbage. No way was he going to listen to what  20
I was saying. I said, "Better yet, get up, let's go to the square. There's lots to see."

"What's there to see?"

"We'll look at movie posters, then we'll go back of Stone Cutter's Square, and watch Sagdast the Dervish do magic tricks."

"By the time we get to the square it'll be dark."

"So we'll take a bus."

"With what money?"  25

"I've got twelve *riāls.*"

"Keep it for yourself."

"Let's go get something to eat, OK?"

"There's no point in eating anything."

I was at my wits' end. I went on looking around, and my eyes fell on  30
Shokrāi's garden. I said, "Hey, Hasani, do you want to go steal walnuts?"

"Yeah, since I haven't been beaten enough today, let's go get caught by the gardener."

A while went by. Neither of us said anything. Two men showed up from behind the kilns. They stood around and watched us for a while, and then they headed for the garden and jumped over the wall. First there were yells. Then we could hear some men in there laughing. I said to Hasani, "Why are you mad at me?"

He said, "I'm not mad at you."

We shut up again. Hasani went on hitting his toes. I said, "Cut that out. Are you going crazy?"

He said, "All right. But it doesn't hurt."  35

"Now you say something."

"I don't know anything to say."

Angrily, I shouted, "You're getting pretty sickening. Get up, let's go."

We both got up and got going. While we were walking along between the wells, I said, "Hasani!"

"What?"                                                                                    40

"Out with it. Whatever you want, whatever's on your mind, spit it out."

"I want to beat the crap out of that father of mine."

"Great. Well, go beat the crap out of him."

"I can't do it all by myself."

"Of course you can't."                                                                     45

He stopped all of a sudden and asked me, "Will you come with me so we can give him what's coming to him?"

I thought a bit. Hasani's dad hated children. You couldn't so much as look at him. He'd never say hello back to you. He'd just go by glaring. My dad would say that this bastard's crazy, a bit cracked, unsound of mind, you might say. Now how was I going to jump him? And if I didn't do it, Hasani would be mad at me. I didn't want Hasani mad at me. I was turning this over in my mind when Hasani said, "Don't you want to help me?"

"Why not? I want to. I want to a lot."

"Then why don't you answer me?"

"So how are we going to jump him?"                                                         50

"You come over to our place tonight. We each hide in a corner. When he comes after me, all of a sudden we attack and grab his legs and knock him down and wipe him out!"

"And then what?"

"And then nothing. Just he'll know what it feels like to be beaten. I'll be happy."

"OK."

So that's how we wound up at his place. It was just about sunset, the    55
time when the sky is turning gray. Hasani's dad hadn't shown up yet. Hasani's ma told us to go bring water for them. We went and got the water, and then we just waited, shifting from foot to foot. Finally we saw Hasani's dad way off. He was bent over, with a bag across his shoulder. Hasani said, "Here comes the son of a bitch." We went running off. We took a short cut and got to his shack. Hasani's ma was sitting outside cooking tomatoes over the primus. Hasani's little brother was sitting with his ma's arm around him. He was bawling. We went in the yard and set the pitcher of water by the window, then walked into the house. Hasani's ma yelled from outside, "Hey, Hasani, light the lamp."

Hasani lit the lamp. His little sister had gone to sleep in a corner of the room. I said, "What do we do now?"

"Nothing. Just sit there by the door and don't do nothing."

I sat and waited. Hasani sat on the other side of the room. There was no sign of his dad yet.

Hasani said, "Don't forget, just grab his leg."

"What are you going to do?"                                              60

"First I'll punch him in the jaw, then I'll jump him and beat him into the ground."

Fear grabbed hold of me. I didn't know how things were going to end up. I was waiting like that when we heard his dad yelling outside. He started shouting, "You filthy slut, I hadn't come yet. What are you cooking dinner for?"

Hasani's ma said, "What the hell am I supposed to do? You always want to wolf something down when it gets dark."

Hasani's dad shouted, "Are you and your whelps eating too, you slut?"

Hasani's ma cried out, "Help, people! Help! Would to God you get          65
crippled and your legs broken at the roots."

Hasani said, "You hear?"

"Hear what?"

"He's kicking my ma. The crazy pig!"

We heard Hasani's dad start yelling, "What's this little bastard doing hanging around here?"

"So where's he supposed to hang around?"                                 70

"How should I know, somewhere else, some other corner."

He came into the yard and set his bag and junk beside the door. He started coughing and spitting up phlegm. He cursed under his breath, then picked up the water jug, sloshed some water around his mouth, gulped some down and came toward the room. He took off his shoes. My heart had stopped beating. As his dad came in, Hasani looked just like a cat that's scared, half-crouching and inching back. His dad gnashed his teeth and snarled. Hasani, who was pinned up against the wall, said, "What are you going to do?" His dad said, "Nothing. What can one do with you, you snot-nosed little brat?" All of a sudden he noticed me. He looked me over from head to foot and twirled his mustache. I was terrified. I began edging back without getting up. "Glory be, what's this fat baboon doing here?" he sneered.

"He's my friend, Abdul Āghā's son."

"I don't care what piece of shit's son he is. What's he doing in my house?"

"I told him he could come."                                              75

"You mean the wretches don't have a hole of their own to crawl in?"

"Sure they have a house, a much nicer one, too."

"So how did he wind up here?"

He turned on me and yelled, "Get up, beat it, go crawl in your own shack."

Full of fear, I was getting up, when he said, "Move it!"                                80

Hasani said from the back of the room, "He's not going. He stays here."

Hasani's dad turned around and clenched his fists. He headed for Hasani. "You fruit of adultery, you've become so brazen you're standing up to your father?"

Hasani's little sister woke up with a start and ran in panic out of the room. Hasani's dad was moving in and raising his fists, when suddenly Hasani shouted, "Come on!" I charged in. As Hasani's dad brought his fists down, Hasani jumped to one side. His fists hit the wall. I lunged and grabbed his leg. Hasani got loose from his dad and grabbed the other leg. We both yanked, and Hasani's dad fell on us shouting. First a fist connected with my head, and then another fist got Hasani's. Then he hit both our heads at the same time. The two of us wriggled out from under him. Hasani, swearing under his breath, kicked his dad in the side, and we both lit out the door. The guy kept yelling, "Now I'm really going to get you bastards. You couldn't take it, so you're going after your hit man to finish me off?"

He took after us. Hasani's ma stood by the lantern wailing. She didn't know what to do. We went right past her and flew like the wind up a back path to the hollow. We heard Hasani's dad shouting, "Catch them! Catch them!"

He ran a few steps behind us, and then he stood still, swearing and          85
wailing. It had gotten dark. Nobody came after us, and nobody seemed to feel like catching us. We jumped into the hollow, panting. We took each other's hands and waited to see if Hasani's dad or anyone else would show up and grab us. I said to Hasani, "We better get out of the hollow."

"Yeah. Or you'll see the bastard coming along with a club in his hand. Then we've had it."

We climbed up out of the hollow and sat down on a little rise. While we were catching our breath, I said to Hasani, "We did a good job of getting away from him."

"It's a shame we couldn't really work him over."

"When do you want to go home?"

"Go home? The hell I want to go back home! God, he's just waiting          90
for me to go back so he can get his hands on me and really tear me to pieces."

"So what do you want to do?"

"Nothing."

"Where will you stay the night?"

"Nowhere. I've got nowhere to go."

"Come on over to our place."                                               95

"Right, fall into *your* dad's clutches. Those bastards are all alike. There's not a shred of mercy in them."

"If you don't go back tonight, what will you do tomorrow? What will you do day after tomorrow? Finally you'll have to go back."

"I'm not so sure. One of these days you'll look and see I've up and gone somewhere else."

"Like where?"

"Wherever."                                                                100

"To do what?"

"How should I know what I'll end up doing? I'll become an apprentice. I'll run errands. I'll be a porter."

"You're just a kid. Nobody will hire you."

"Why not!"

"Because you don't know how to do anything."                              105

"So I don't know a trade. I can wash and sweep in front of stores."

"Anyway you'd have to be bigger for them to hire you."

"I could still collect trash and sell it."

"Where'd you sleep nights?"

"In the ruins."                                                            110

"It's no good. A day, two days, OK. Finally you'll die of hunger or something will happen to you."

"Never! I won't die. I'll go and beg and survive."

"Right. So keep on dreaming. They'll take you and put you in the poorhouse. Have you forgotten about the kids at Asadul and Ābji-ye Rezā?"

"So what should I do?"

"I don't know. It seems to me you should go back home."                   115

We both shut up. The moon had come out, and most everywhere was brightly lit, except for the dark holes of the wells that nothing could light up. You could see lanterns here and there among the shacks. Hasani looked at them and said, "There's no going back home now. He'd peel the skin off my head."

We were quiet again and listened to the crickets. Hasani all of a sudden jumped up and said, "Listen, I've got a plan. You get up now and run like hell to the houses and start crying and carrying on and yelling and start a commotion and say Hasani's fallen in a well."

I jumped up with my heart in my throat. I cried, "You mean you want to throw yourself in a well?"

"You think I'm such a jackass that I'd go throwing myself in a well? You just say I've fallen, and then you'll see my dad pass out cold. Then you'll see him get his."

"And then?"                                                                              120

"And then nothing. I'll go and settle down somewhere."

"Then they'll go search the wells."

"They can't search all the wells. So what if they look in one or two? Finally they'll get tired and guess that I've died. Then they'll get together and cry for me, and read out of the Koran. My ma and dad will beat their heads and say nice things about me."

"Hasani, this isn't a good thing to do."

"Why isn't it?"                                                                          125

"If your dad just wastes away, or your ma dies of grief, then what will you do?"

"You're imagining things. It's not like that at all. I know them better than that. They won't waste away and they won't die of grief. When they've finally made mincemeat of themselves and beaten their heads and chests, you come quietly and let me know. I'll go running home. When they see I'm alive and I haven't fallen in the well, you don't know how happy they'll be. I think my dad will make peace and not beat me anymore."

"Well . . ."

"Well what?"

"Well, I'm afraid of your dad. I'm afraid that after I say this stuff, he'll   130 get me and kill me."

"What do you have to do with my dad? When you get to the houses, start yelling and beating your head and say, 'Hasani's fallen in the well! Hasani's fallen in the well!'"

"Then I'll have to cry. What if I can't?"

Hasani looked me up and down and said, "You're such a jackass! In the dark who'll know if you're crying or not?"

"OK. Then what will you do?"

"I'll go sit in some cranny of the kiln."                                                135

"And when you die of hunger?"

He asked me, with his voice full of surprise, "You mean you won't bring me water and bread? Huh? You really won't come?"

"Sure I'll come."

"Fine, so get going."

I was starting off when Hasani said something else. "What is it?" I   140 asked.

"Don't forget I'm hungry. Bring me some bread and water in the morning."

"OK. I'll come for sure."

"Good. So go!"

I still hadn't made my mind up to go or not. Hasani grabbed my hand and said, "First come here. I'll show you where I'll be."

We were on our way to Hājji Timur's Kiln when some dogs came at　145 us. We took care of them with rocks. Then we went around the wells and went into the last oven. Its roof had fallen in, and nobody would have believed anyone could possibly be staying in there. Hasani said to me, "I'll stay right here. OK?"

"OK."

He said, "Don't wait around. Get going. Don't forget to really really yell."

"Right. OK."

I walked around the kiln and went between the wells. Then I dropped into the hollow. A bunch of dogs were running around. They ran away when they saw me. My throat was clogged with dust. I drank a little water from the tap. I remembered that I had to run harder and to yell bloody murder.

I jumped up and rushed screaming toward the shacks. There was a　150 crowd around our place. I didn't know what was going on. You would have thought from hearing me that Hasani had really and truly fallen in a well, I raised such hell and wailed so loud. The crowd milled in my direction. I saw my dad and Hasani's dad. They seemed to lunge at me at the same time. I wailed in a tear-choked voice, "Hasani! Hasani!" Hasani's dad, standing there with a club in his hand, asked, "What happened to Hasani? Huh? What happened?"

"He fell," I wailed, "He fell! He fell!"

I started crying in earnest, tears pouring down my face.

Hasani's dad shouted, "Where did he fall? Tell me, where did Hasani fall?" I yelled, "In the well, he fell in the well!" For a minute everyone was silent, and then a strange murmuring rose up. A jumble of voices near and far shouted, "Hasani's fallen in the well! Hasani's fallen in the well!"

People lost their heads and didn't know what to do. Those who were in their houses came pouring out. Some brought lanterns. Everyone set out running toward the upper part of the hollow. I was stretched out on the ground wailing when my dad bent over me and took my hand to pull me to my feet. He said, "Get up. Come on, let's see, which well did he fall in?" We had just started running when several men surrounded me. They ran right along with my dad and me, asking over and over, "Which well? Which one did he fall in?"

We passed the hollow and got to the wells. The moon had risen higher,　155 and the holes of the wells had gotten darker and deeper. Everyone was standing around. Hasani's father swayed like a willow. He grabbed my arms and shook me, saying, "Which one? Which one?"

Before I could answer, he threw himself onto the trash heap and began wailing loudly. Two or three men went up to him. Abbās Charkhi kept trying to comfort him, saying, "Don't worry a bit. We'll have him out of there in no time. Nothing's the matter. Don't cry. Take it easy, we'll find him soon."

By the time Hasani's father had calmed down, another commotion had begun. The women came weeping. Hasani's mother was in front of them all, beating her head and clawing at her face, moaning from the bottom of her heart, "My Hasani! My Hasani! My Hasani!"

She said other things you couldn't make out. Abbās Charkhi came closer and said to me, "Listen, child. Tell us which one he fell into."

"I don't know."

Hasani's father rushed me, shouting, "Bastard! Say what really hap-  160
pened to my child!" Āghā Ghāder held him back and told him, "Get a hold of yourself. Let him say what happened." I swallowed my sobs and said, "Hasani's dad caught us and he was going to beat us up."

Hasani's father broke in: "Just tell us where he fell!"

"Hurry up and tell us!" yelled my dad.

Abbās Charkhi said, "Let him have his say, man. How did it happen?"

"We got away and came here. Hasani was way in front of me. We were both running. Hasani was afraid his dad would catch up and grab us, so he ran faster than me. I turned around and looked in back of me and saw he wasn't coming. Nobody was coming. I yelled, 'Wait, Hasani!' But he didn't wait. Just then all of a sudden he screamed and fell."

Hasani's dad said, "Where did he fall!"                                                165

I said, "I thought the earth had swallowed him up. I called and called, but he didn't answer. However much I looked, I couldn't find him."

Hasani's dad just shouted again, "Which one did he fall in!"

Abbās Charkhi said in a mean voice, "How should he know which one he fell in? Let's go find him ourselves."

Then he turned to the men and said, "Get moving. Come ahead. Be careful!"

As they set out, they stopped talking. No one cried. No one shouted.   170
Only Hasani's mother moaned softly, while the other women kept telling her, "Be calm, sister, don't fuss, they'll find him now and get him out."

Some people kept going, "Shhh." You'd think Hasani was sleeping and might wake up. They went up to several wells, and then Hasani's dad lowed like a cow, "Hasani, Hasani." He was so mean and nasty that if maybe Hasani had really fallen in a well and could get out, he would grab him and start hitting and kicking him again. Abbās Charkhi said, "Calm down a bit. Cool down and let us get on with our work."

Someone said out of the dark, "We must have rope and lanterns. We can't go into wells empty-handed."

Several people went running to the houses. A couple of lanterns were brought up. Abbās Charkhi took one of them. He stretched out by one of the wells, and held it over the hole. Everyone had made a circle around the well. Abbās, with his head in the well, said in a muffled voice, "I don't think he's fallen into this one."

So they went to the next well. This time it was Mosayyeb who stretched out flat and held the lantern over the well. He said, with his drawn-out voice like a peddler's, "Where are you, child? Where are you?"

There was no answer. They went on to the third well. Then to the   175 fourth well. Then to the fifth well. Then to the sixth. Then they split up into two groups, then into four. They brought extra lanterns, seven or eight of them, and a lot of rope. Several people started tying knots in the ropes. The more they went on with no sign of Hasani, the madder they got, and the more they would argue. After a while they called everyone to one well, I mean Abbās Charkhi called everyone, and everyone ran up to it. Abbās had gone out of his wits. He said, "I think he's here. I heard something. It's as if someone is crying in there." Everyone fell silent. Several people stretched out and stuck their heads into the well, listened, and said, "Yeah. That is it."

Hasani's dad started raising hell. He said, "Hurry up, hurry up. Get my boy out of there! Get my boy out!"

Mosayyeb said, "Who will go down?"

Ghāder said, "The well is old. It might cave in."

Hasani's father said, "By God, it won't cave in. Go on in, go in and get him out."

Everyone looked at one another. Abbās Charkhi said, "No one's man   180 enough? I'll go myself. Pass the rope and let's see."

Abbās's wife cried out from where the women were, "Not you, not you! You can't! You don't know how!"

Abbās shouted angrily, "What business is it of yours, you bitch? Shut up, I can't let the boy die in there!"

His wife shoved everyone aside, ran up and clung to Abbās, saying, "I won't let you. I won't let you. By God, I won't let you!"

Abbās slapped his wife hard and said, "Get lost, you're being impossible."

Then he shouted firmly, "Rope!" They brought rope and tied it around   185 Abbās's waist. Then they tested the knots one by one. Abbās said, "Be careful. Don't let go of me on the way down."

Several men said, "Don't worry. We'll be careful."

Abbās got ready. He grabbed one of the lanterns, bent over, and looked down the well. Then he handed the lantern to someone and said "*Bismillāh*" loudly. Everyone prayed then. Hasani's dad raised his hands to the sky and said, "O most Merciful of the merciful, O Grandfather of Hosein the Oppressed, O Grandfather of Fātemeh the Pure, O Grandfather of Khadijeh the Magnificent, bring up my child alive, bring Hasani back alive!"

Abbās was hanging there in the well with his elbows resting on the rim. He said, "Watch that rope closely. When I jerk on it, pull me up." His wife started crying behind us. My ma comforted her. Then Abbās went down. Five or six of the men held the rope. They clutched it tightly and let it go handspan by handspan. They muttered things to each other. Hasani's dad was walking around in circles, saying things like, "O God! O God!" I had completely forgotten that Hasani was at the kiln. In the bottom of my heart I was saying, "Oh, if only Hasani were in there, and Abbās wouldn't come out empty-handed, and everything would be OK!" After a while, my dad, who was holding the rope with the others, said, "Haul it up. Haul it up. Haul it up."

Rahmat said, "What for?"

"The rope is shaking. Are you blind or something?"                    190

Everyone stopped talking. They started drawing up the rope. Hasani's dad was peering over the heads of the others and waiting for Abbās to appear. Then Abbās's two hands gripped the rim of the well. He drew his elbows up the rim, hauled himself over it, and flung himself across the ground. Ghāder asked, "Wasn't he in there? Wasn't he in there?" Hasani's dad wailed and started to cry and groan. Abbās rolled over and sat up. He said, "I was suffocating."

Ghāder said, "That's all?"

"All there was in there was the carcass of a fat dog."

Mosayyeb said, "You're sure?"

"Imbecile, can't I tell Hasani from a dead dog?"                       195

He got up and took the rope off his waist. Everyone got together again and went to another well, then to a third, then to a fourth. They divided again, and then again. They would kneel over each well, calling Hasani. At that point I sneaked off and headed for the houses, slipping through the shadows and byways so that nobody would see me. I drank some water from the tap and then went behind the tin wall. I crept into our own place. No one was there. I scooped up a loaf of flatbread and a pitcher without a handle. I scurried out, and, when I got to the tap again, I drew some water. I passed the hollow, turned at the road, and reached Hājji Timur's Kiln just where Hasani was staying. I peeped in and called him softly. He didn't answer. I called him again. He didn't answer. I called him loudly. There was nothing. I was afraid. Then I said to myself, "God forbid he should mistake me for someone else." I started whistling and right away I heard Hasani's whistle over my head. He was stretched out on the platform and was watching me. I said, "Hey Hasani!"

He said, "Come up carefully."

I handed him the pitcher, got hold of the bricks of the wall, and climbed. We both crawled slowly forward and sat by the bottom of the kiln's chimney. I said, "Hadn't we decided that you would wait down there?"

He said, "I climbed up to see what was going on."

"You know what would happen if they saw you?"                    200

"No way. No one will see me."

He began to laugh. I asked, "What are you laughing for?"

He said, "I'm laughing at my old man, at all of them. Look at them, the way they're running around."

He pointed to the terrace of the wells. Some people with lanterns in their hands were going this way and that around the wells. Others seemed to be glued to one well. They weren't moving.

I said, "We've done something very bad, Hasani."                    205

"Why?"

"Your dad's killing himself. You don't know the state he's in."

"Don't worry, he won't kill himself. What's my mother doing?"

"She's beating her head and chest. She keeps crying."

"Let her."                                                          210

"You don't know how it is. Abbās went down a well, and instead of finding you, he found a fat dog's body down there."

"He's found his father's body."

We both laughed. I took out the bread, and we split it up and ate it. I wasn't thirsty, but Hasani gulped down some water. I said, "Now shouldn't we go down to them?"

He said, "For what?"

"To get the thing over with. They can't go through all those wells one    215
by one."

"It's much too soon. Let them try."

"Someone might fall in a well and die."

"Don't worry. They all have dogs' lives and nothing'll happen to them."

"This is an awful thing we've done."

He turned and looked me up and down, and said, "Isn't it an awful    220
thing they do, always going around and beating us before supper?"

"For God's sake, cut it out, Hasani. Come on, let's go back."

"I can't go."

"Why not, then?"

"Supposing I go back. What will I say?"

"Say you'd gone to Shokrāi's garden to eat walnuts."                    225

"Then they'd find out you were lying."

"I'll say, how would I know where you'd gone. I thought you'd fallen in the well."

"No. They'll know for sure and it'll be all over for us."

"By God, let it be. Come on."

"I'm not coming. I can't come."                                          230

"Then I'll go and say Hasani hasn't fallen in a well, that he's staying at Hājji Timur's Kiln."

He turned, looked at me angrily, and said, "Fine. Go and tell. From then on we'll have nothing to do with each other. You'll see me when you see the back of your ear."

"Then when do you want to go back to your house?"

"The day of mourning, when they read the Koran for me. All of a sudden I'll come in. That will feel so great!"

"Don't talk garbage. What'll be so great about it?"                      235

"It's so obvious. When everyone is beating their heads and chests, I'll just quietly saunter up, walk in real nonchalant-like, and say '*Hello!*' First everyone will be scared. They'll cringe. The women'll scream. The children will run away thinking I've come back from the next world. Then when they see, no, it's just me, I'm alive, I see, I laugh, I move my hands and feet, they'll all be happy. They'll leap in the air. They'll fall on the ground. They'll keep hugging me and kissing my face. You don't think that's any fun? Really?"

We went on staring at the people going around the wells with their lanterns. Now and then I would hear men or women shouting. I said, "So I guess I'll be going back."

"Go on, but don't let them know where I am."

I crawled down from the recess on all fours. I looked around and jumped to the ground. I passed by the roadside, dropped into the hollow, and climbed out again. Everyone had formed a circle around one well. I went running up to it too. I saw my mother pounding on her head and wailing. The men had a rope hanging down the well. I squeezed through and got to the brim. I saw Abbās saying to the other men, "Haul up! Haul up!"

Ghāder asked, "What for?"                                                240

"Are you blind or something? Can't you see it's shaking?"

Everyone fell silent and started hauling on the rope. Behind me Hasani's father was beating on his chest rhythmically. He was saying, "O

Great Khadijeh! O Prophet Mostafā! O Stranger of Strangers! O Lord of
the Martyrs!"

Then I saw my dad with his elbows on the rim of the well drawing
himself up. He had turned black from head to foot and was gasping.
Abbās said, "Lie down. Stretch out and catch your breath." Several men
got hold of my dad under the arms and stretched him out beside the
well.

## II

The next morning, no one went to work. Everyone was worn out and
went back to their shacks. They hadn't found Hasani. Abbās Charkhi said,
"It's no use. No one can search all the wells."

They had just been through the deeper wells that opened into one
another and had sewage running through them. In their black depths
weird things had been seen. Ustā Habib had run across some creature,
about as big as a cow, with four tails and a dead man's head between its
teeth, going here and there. The Sayyed had run into a bunch of naked
people covered with wool clinging to the sides of the well. When they
saw him, they dived into the sewage and disappeared. Mir Jalāl had seen
with his own eyes huge, black wings that flew around by themselves. They
said weird noises had come from the very depths, like the sounds of cats
wailing, and the laughter of women you couldn't see. Several of them
had even heard cymbals and trumpets, like they play on the Day of
Āshurā. They'd heard wailing and crying behind them.

Abbās said it was no use, it was all over, there was no way to find
Hasani. So then they went back home, tired and sleepy, and dazed.
Everyone but Hasani's dad, who kept on wandering around the shacks,
jerking his head right and left, forward and back, pounding his hands
together and saying, "Did you see what happened? Did you see how my
child has gone away? How he's died young?"

Hasani's dad wasn't wailing and crying anymore. Instead he began
worrying about pointless things, like the roofs of the houses, the dark
openings of tombs, covered barrels lined up against the walls, stains on
the gunny sacks hanging in front of the houses. Now and then he would
stop and bend over to pick some stupid thing off the ground — a scrap
of tin, or a broken glass, or a worn-out shoe. He would fiddle with it, and
then throw it away and go after something else, muttering, "Now they're
eating him. It's all over. My Hasani is finished."

I walked around him several times. It was always the same. He wouldn't see me, or he would see me and not care. After a few minutes of this, I remembered that Hasani would be hungry and waiting for me. I went to our place. Everyone was asleep. My dad had flopped over so that his muddy feet stuck out. I snitched a loaf of bread and a fistful of lump sugar that were in easy reach, and went out again. Everything was sullen and gloomy. I saw Hasani's dad standing behind a house scraping his fingernail across something on the wall. The sun was up and lighting everything. I got to the tap and drank some water. No one was around. I dropped into the hollow, and, past the upper end, I made it to Hājji Timur's Kiln. I headed for the recess, knowing Hasani was there. Hasani was sleeping. When I called him, he woke up with a start. He got scared and shouted, "Who is it? Who is it?"

"Don't worry," I said, "it's just me."

He sat up. He looked different. His eyes were sunken, and his hands   250 shook. I said, "What's up with you? Anything happened?"

"I dreamed that I fell in a well, and whatever I tried, I couldn't get out."

"It's your own fault. You were the one who wanted to keep up this game. Your dad has cracked up."

He didn't say anything. He just dragged himself outside. We both sat in the sun. I handed him the bread and the handful of sugar. He hadn't finished his water. He picked up the pitcher, gulped down some water, and splashed some over his face. As he woke up more, he asked, "How have things gone?"

"They're sure now you've died," I said.

"What did you do?"                                                       255

"I didn't do anything. I didn't say anything."

"Now what do they want to do?"

"They haven't decided on anything."

"Aren't they going to read the Koran for me?"

"I don't know. I haven't heard anything."                                260

"I think they'll do it this afternoon."

"Where do you get that?"

"Do you remember when Bibi's grandson died? They read the Koran the day after."

"If that's how it goes, this is your big day all right."

"Yeah. God, let it be today. I can't handle any more of this."           265

"God willing, this will be the day."

"You won't forget to come tell me?"

"No, why should I forget? But get yourself ready for a real beating."

"No way. I'll just make them happy."

"Go right on thinking that. You'll see."                                 270

"Want to bet?"

"What's the bet?"

"If they get sore about like why am I alive and didn't die, and they jump me and beat me up, you win, and if they're glad, I win, and you'll get a real thrashing from me."

"That's just great. I've gone through all this for you, and in return you want to beat me up?"

He laughed and said, "I'm kidding. I'll buy you an ice cream."　　275

"OK. You're on."

He tore off a piece of bread and stuffed it in his mouth. He asked, "Now what do we do?"

"Nothing," I said. "You stay in this cranny, and I go to the house to see what happens."

"If the reading is tonight, you'll let me know?"

"Sure."　　280

Hasani's reading was that afternoon, in front of the houses. Abbās had nailed a piece of black cloth on the end of a stick and had stuck it into the ground at the head of the square. Everyone was sitting outside, the women on one side, and the men on the other. People from other places had been told, and were coming in batches. From Yusof Shāh Hollow, from the tenements of Sarpich, the kilns of Shamsābād, the hovels of Shotor Khun and Mollā Ahmad Hollow. They were all strangers, and they were dressed in every color you can think of. As they would come into the square, the women would run up to Hasani's mother. She was sitting with her scratched and bloody face in front of their house. She wasn't crying anymore. She was beating her head and sometimes pounding her chest. As the women came up to her, they would begin to cry, tearing at their own faces and saying, "Dear sister, dear sister, what has befallen you, what has befallen you?"

Hasani's dad was sitting in front of our place, not sitting exactly, but sprawled across the ground, staring ahead senseless. Whoever came and understood who the dead boy's father was, went up to him and said, "*Salām*." Not hearing an answer, he would turn away and go sit down. Abbās, who was standing, bellowed, "Fātiheh!"

The men recited the Fātiheh, the Opening of the Koran. Ustā Habib went around the crowd with a pitcher, giving water to the thirsty. Two old men had come from Ghoribā Hollow with a pouch of tobacco. They were rapidly rolling cigarettes in newspaper and setting them on a tray. Bibi's oldest son Ramazān was passing the tray among the people. Everyone smoked, and everyone drank water, except Hasani's dad. He didn't do either. He just kept running his tongue over his lips, and sometimes he would spit on the ground.

An hour had gone by when a lot of people showed up running from the road. Everybody turned and looked. Abbās shouted, "The Gypsies of the Black Tents from Elders' Hollow are coming. Let's go meet them."

Several people took off. The Gypsies, panting hard, came running. A     285
lot of them were holding banners. There were several old men in worn-out clothing running in front of everyone. They beat their breasts and looked nervous. Among them was a thin *ākhond*[1] with a long neck and a small turban. The women came behind, all of them barefoot and dusty. As they got to the little square, the sounds of prayers rose up. The men and women separated. The women ran shrieking toward Hasani's ma, and the old men greeted his dad. He didn't answer. Then the *ākhond* went off to sit on the steps of our place. Esmāil  Āghā shouted, "Make prayers! Make them loud!"

Everyone offered prayers. The *ākhond* said in a hoarse, nasal voice, "Be seated, all be seated, all be seated. Be seated so that we may weep and recite the doleful story of Ghāsem son of Hasan, how he found martyrdom at Karbalā, in remembrance of this other unfortunate youth." First he read a strange prayer, and then he started reciting the story. All at once, people started crying and wailing. Everyone cried. The men cried. The women cried. Their children cried. Even I cried. Only Hasani's dad did not cry, but kept wandering here and there, running his tongue over his parched lips. The crying got louder and louder. The Gypsies rose and bared their chests. The *ākhond* rose and bared his chest. He said in a loud voice, "Now to rejoice the Lord of the Martyrs and the dear unfortunate one, we will beat our breasts."

He began reciting songs of mourning. The Gypsies began beating their breasts. The other men stood up and bared their breasts and began beating them. The women shrieked even louder, as they stood arm in arm, wailing. Suddenly I remembered: Now is the time. Now I must go tell Hasani.

No one was paying any attention to me. No one was paying any attention to anyone at all but himself or herself. I slipped away quietly. First I backed away, then I turned and ran. I wiped away my tears. When I got to the tap, I drank some water. Then I dropped into Body Washer's Hollow and climbed out. No one was around. I started running again. Running like the wind, I went around the wells and kept on. My heart was full of dread. Sweat was pouring down my face when I reached Hājji Timur's Kiln, circled around, and made my way to Hasani's niche. Hasani

---

[1]One learned in religious matters; a mullah.

was stretched out on the platform. When he saw me he stood up, stepped out, and said, "What's going on?"

"They're mourning for you," I said.

"What are they doing?"                                                              290

"People have come from everywhere and they're beating their chests for you."

He stared at me for a moment and said, "What are you crying for?"

"For you."

"You're such a jackass! You knowing I was alive and hadn't died!"

"It's all the fault of the *ākhond* the Gypsies brought along. He made        295 everybody cry."

He clapped his hands together in delight and said, "So it's time, right?"

"All right, I think it's time."

"Now we'll see who wins the bet."

"Would to God that you win."

He laughed and said, "Run, we're off!"                                            300

He broke into a run. And then so did I. We both charged ahead, but Hasani was flying like the wind. He ran so fast no one could have caught up with him. I kept shouting, "Hasani! Hasani!"

He called back, "Hoo! Hoo!"

Then, suddenly, I don't know what happened — how can I say what happened? Hasani hit his foot against a pile of rubbish, and — just like that — he fell. He fell right into a well. I thought — I mean I didn't think Hasani had fallen in a well — I thought the earth had swallowed him up. I ran up. There was no Hasani. Hasani had fallen in a well. In a huge well, bigger than all the rest of them. My tongue became tied in knots. I wanted to shout "Hasani!" but I couldn't. I had no voice. My mouth wouldn't open. No matter how hard I tried, I couldn't say "Hasani!" I sat on the heap of garbage and held my shoulders. I couldn't catch my breath. Three times I pounded my head on the garbage, and then I got up, not by myself, but it seemed like something picked me up and set me on my two feet. I started to run again. Faster than ever, faster than Hasani had run. I wished I had jumped and fallen in a well. All of a sudden, I found myself running down the road. When I reached the tap, I caught my breath, my tongue came untied and I said softly, "Hasani! Hasani! Hasani!"

As I came up to the square, the breast-beating had come to an end. Everyone was sitting quietly facing each other. Ramazān was passing out cigarettes among the men, and Ustā Habib was going here and there carrying the pitcher of water. I shrieked, "Hasani! Hasani! Hasani!" I pounded my head hard with my fists and rolled on the ground. Everyone

got up and mobbed me. Abbās, who was the first to get to me, took my
hands so I wouldn't beat myself and asked me, "What happened? What
happened?"

I shouted, "Hasani. Hasani fell in the well."                    305

I rolled over and bit the ground. First there was a murmuring, and
then a clamor. Everyone tried to calm me down. They kept saying, "OK.
OK. May God have mercy on him. Don't hit yourself anymore. Be calm."
I shouted, "Just now he fell, just now, this very minute he fell, Hasani fell
in the well!" My dad pushed the others away and came up to me, saying,
"Shut up, child. Don't make things more painful for his father and
mother."

"He fell, he fell in the well before my eyes."

"I said shut your mouth. Be silent, you little jackass."

He picked me up and gave me a hard slap on the ear. Esmāil Āghā
pulled my dad back and roared, "Don't hit him, you son of a bitch. Can't
you see he's out of his head?" He took me in his arms and said, "Calm
down, calm down."

Ustā Habib handed Esmāil Āghā a glass of water, and he poured it    310
over my face. However hard I fought to get free from the arms of Esmāil
Āghā, it was no use. Several people helped him keep me from getting
away. I was wailing loudly, "Hasani fell! He fell in the well! Hasani!
Hasani!" when Esmāil Āghā clapped a big hand over my mouth, and they
all dragged me into our own house. As I was dragged past Hasani's dad,
I looked at him and pointed at the wells with my hand. He didn't look
at me. He wasn't aware of me. He just went on staring ahead. As we went
into my house, Esmāil Āghā said, "Be still, child. Everyone knows Hasani
was your friend. You liked each other a lot. Now what can one do? This
was the will of fate."

I yelled, "He fell just now! He fell just now!"

I tried to break away and get out, but they didn't let me. My dad said,
"What do we do with him? Huh? What do we do with him?" Esmāil
Āghā said, "He's gone mad. It's best we bind his hands and feet." So then
they bound my hands and feet. I started to wail. My dad said, "What do
we do about his wailing?" Esmāil Āghā said, "We'll gag him." They
gagged me and tossed me into a corner. My dad rubbed his hands
together and said over and over, "What will I do? My God, my God, if
he stays this way, what the hell am I to do!"

Esmāil Āghā said, "Don't worry. Right now we'll go ask the *ākhond* of
the Gypsies to write out a talisman for him. Then he'll improve."

Ustā Habib said, "If he doesn't get better, we'll take him to the shrine
at Shāh 'Abdol 'Azim."

My dad moaned a long-drawn-out moan, and began walking in circles,   315
saying, "O Imam of the Age, O Imam of the Age, O Imam of the Age!"

Esmāil Āghā said, "Better we leave him alone. Perhaps he'll come
around."

They left the house and fastened the door. The sounds of the gathering's prayers rose up again, and the *ākhond* of the Gypsies read the eulogy
in his hoarse, nasal voice.


## EXPLORATIONS

1. Gholam-Hossein Sa'edi starts his story with a suggestion from Hasani, the
   significance of which becomes evident only later. What sentence in his first
   paragraph does the author use as a transition out of the present? Where and
   how does he make the transition back into the moment of Hasani's suggestion?
   What does Sa'edi accomplish by jumping around in time rather than telling
   his story in chronological order?

2. Sa'edi lets us know immediately that Hasani and the narrator have already
   been influenced by the violence in their families. What signs of this influence
   do you find in paragraph 1? Over the next few pages, what other speeches
   and actions by the story's characters reveal their attitudes toward physical and
   emotional abuse within the family?

3. What is your response to the ending of "The Game Is Over"? How would the
   story's impact be different if Hasani did show up at his own funeral? What
   tactics does Sa'edi use to make his readers curious about how Hasani's parents
   and others will react to his miraculous return? Did these tactics keep you from
   guessing the story's ending?


## CONNECTIONS

1. In paragraphs 39–41 of "Home Making" (p. 152), Marguerite Duras writes
   about places in and around a house that meet the needs of children. What
   needs of Hasani's does his house fail to meet, contributing to his tragedy?

2. What roles does religion play in "The Game Is Over" and in Gyanranjan's
   "Our Side of the Fence and Theirs" (p. 134)? What major advantages do
   Gyanranjan's characters have over Sa'edi's?

3. In *Looking at Ourselves* (p. 63), Michael Novak writes: "The lives of husbands,
   wives, and children do not mesh, are not engaged, seem merely thrown
   together." What causes does Novak identify for this problem in upwardly
   mobile America? What causes does Sa'edi identify for this problem in the
   Iranian village of "The Game Is Over"?

## ELABORATIONS

1. Imagine you are a journalist covering Hasani's tragic story for a magazine or newspaper. Based on "The Game Is Over," write an account of the boy's fate, its apparent causes, and its implications for other children like Hasani. (Your "article" may take either an expository or an argumentative form.)

2. Friction, as we all know, is part of family dynamics. Nearly every young person living with his or her parents or guardians feels tempted at some point to leave home because of a conflict. Write an essay about an experience that caused you to leave home either permanently or temporarily, or to seriously consider leaving. What do you think of your decision in retrospect? How did the experience affect you as an individual? As a family member?

# PART THREE

# LANDMARKS AND
# TURNING POINTS

## *The Struggle for Identity*

### LOOKING AT OURSELVES

Gail Sheehy, Michael Dorris, Langston Hughes, Terry Galloway,
Bernard Cooper, Alfred Kazin, James Baldwin,
Joyce Carol Oates, Malcolm X

Susan Orlean, *Quinceañera* (UNITED STATES/MEXICO)

Liliana Heker, *The Stolen Party* (ARGENTINA)

Sophronia Liu, *So Tsi-fai* (HONG KONG)

Mario Vargas Llosa, *On Sunday* (PERU)

Salman Rushdie, *The Broken Mirror* (INDIA)

Amy Tan, *Two Kinds* (UNITED STATES/CHINA)

Christopher Reynolds, *Cultural Journey to Africa*
(IVORY COAST/UNITED STATES)

Günter Grass, *After Auschwitz* (GERMANY)

Yoram Binur, *Palestinian Like Me* (ISRAEL/PALESTINE)

THE LIFELONG TASK OF FIGURING OUT WHO WE ARE PROGRESSES IN fits and starts. What traits have I inherited or learned from my family? How do my ethnic and cultural backgrounds influence who I am? What qualities are uniquely mine? We search for answers not in a mirror but amid a bombardment of events which play their own part in shaping our identity.

All change, good or bad, creates not only growth but stress. The playwright George Bernard Shaw wrote that when you learn something, it feels at first as if you've lost something. Most cultures offer rituals to ease and mark the biggest transitions: from solitude into companionship, from intimacy into loss, from childhood ignorance into adult awareness.

The *Looking at Ourselves* passages explore social landmarks in the United States. Gail Sheehy writes about the developmental phase she calls Pulling Up Roots. Michael Dorris comments on coming-of-age rites for American Indian boys. Langston Hughes reminisces about the Christian call of salvation. Terry Galloway describes coming to grips with deafness, Bernard Cooper with the realization that he is gay. Alfred Kazin recalls his Jewish boyhood in New York; James Baldwin recalls discovering racism. Joyce Carol Oates celebrates the power of reading, and Malcolm X remembers his first encounter with that power.

As we shift our focus outward, Susan Orlean describes in "Quinceañera" the Arizona version of a traditional Mexican debut for young ladies. In Liliana Heker's short story "The Stolen Party," an Argentine maid's bright, spunky daughter confronts class prejudice at a birthday celebration. "So Tsi-fai" shows Sophronia Liu still haunted by a rebellious classmate's suicide during sixth grade in Hong Kong. "On Sunday" is Mario Vargas Llosa's short story about a Peruvian teenager's dangerous plunge into rivalry with his best friend.

Salman Rushdie, an Indian writer living in England, looks at the distortions of memory in "The Broken Mirror." Amy Tan's short story "Two Kinds" depicts a battle of wills between a California daughter and her Chinese-born mother. Curiosity about their heritage spurs a group of successful African-Americans to visit the Ivory Coast in Christopher Reynolds's "Cultural Journey to Africa." In "After Auschwitz," Günter Grass confronts his political heritage as a twentieth-century German. The Israeli journalist Yoram Binur goes underground to explore a different aspect of World War II's legacy in "Palestinian Like Me."   ◇

# LOOKING AT OURSELVES

## 1

Before eighteen, the motto is loud and clear: "I have to get away from my parents." But the words are seldom connected to action. Generally still safely part of our families, even if away at school, we feel our autonomy to be subject to erosion from moment to moment.

After eighteen, we begin Pulling Up Roots in earnest. College, military service, and short-term travels are all customary vehicles our society provides for the first round trips between family and a base of one's own. In the attempt to separate our view of the world from our family's view, despite vigorous protestations to the contrary — "I know exactly what I want!" — we cast about for any beliefs we can call our own. And in the process of testing those beliefs we are often drawn to fads, preferably those most mysterious and inaccessible to our parents.

Whatever tentative memberships we try out in the world, the fear haunts us that we are really kids who cannot take care of ourselves. We cover that fear with acts of defiance and mimicked confidence. For allies to replace our parents, we turn to our contemporaries. They become conspirators. So long as their perspective meshes with our own, they are able to substitute for the sanctuary of the family. But that doesn't last very long. And the instant they diverge from the shaky ideals of "our group," they are seen as betrayers. Rebounds to the family are common between the ages of eighteen and twenty-two.

The tasks of this passage are to locate ourselves in a peer group role, a sex role, an anticipated occupation, an ideology or worldview. As a result, we gather the impetus to leave home physically and the identity to *begin* leaving home emotionally.

Even as one part of us seeks to be an individual, another part longs to restore the safety and comfort of merging with another. Thus one of the most popular myths of this passage is: We can piggyback our development by attaching to a Stronger One. But people who marry during this time often prolong financial and emotional ties to the family and relatives that impede them from becoming self-sufficient.

A stormy passage through the Pulling Up Roots years will probably facilitate the normal progression of the adult life cycle. If one doesn't have an identity crisis at this point, it will erupt during a later transition, when the penalties may be harder to bear.

– Gail Sheehy
*Passages*, 1974

◇◇◇◇◇

## 2

In most cultures, adulthood is equated with self-reliance and responsibility, yet often Americans do not achieve this status until we are in our
late twenties or early thirties — virtually the entire average lifespan of a
person in a traditional non-Western society. We tend to treat prolonged
adolescence as a warm-up for real life, as a wobbly suspension bridge
between childhood and legal maturity. Whereas a nineteenth-century
Cheyenne or Lakota teenager was expected to alter self-conception in a
split-second vision, we often meander through an analogous rite of passage for more than a decade — through high school, college, graduate
school.

Though he had never before traveled alone outside his village, the
Plains Indian male was expected at puberty to venture solo into the
wilderness. There he had to fend for and sustain himself while avoiding
the menace of unknown dangers, and there he had absolutely to remain
until something happened that would transform him. Every human being, these tribes believed, was entitled to at least one moment of personal,
enabling insight.

Anthropology proposes feasible psychological explanations for why this
flash was eventually triggered: Fear, fatigue, reliance on strange foods, the
anguish of loneliness, stress, and the expectation of ultimate success all
contributed to a state of receptivity. Every sense was quickened, altered
to perceive deep meaning, until at last the interpretation of an unusual
event — a dream, a chance encounter, or an unexpected vista — rever-
berated with metaphor. Through this unique prism, abstractly preserved
in a vivid memory or song, a boy caught foresight of both his adult
persona and of his vocation, the two inextricably entwined.

– Michael Dorris
"Life Stories"
*Antaeus*, 1989

## 3

I was saved from sin when I was going on thirteen. But not really saved.
It happened like this. There was a big revival at my Auntie Reed's church.
Every night for weeks there had been much preaching, singing, praying,
and shouting, and some very hardened sinners had been brought to
Christ, and the membership of the church had grown by leaps and
bounds. Then just before the revival ended, they held a special meeting
for children, "to bring the young lambs to the fold." My aunt spoke of it
for days ahead. That night I was escorted to the front row and placed on

the mourners' bench with all the other young sinners, who had not yet been brought to Jesus.

My aunt told me that when you were saved you saw a light, and something happened to you inside! And Jesus came into your life! And God was with you from then on! She said you could see and hear and feel Jesus in your soul. I believed her. I had heard a great many old people say the same thing and it seemed to me they ought to know. So I sat there calmly in the hot, crowded church, waiting for Jesus to come to me.

The preacher preached a wonderful rhythmical sermon, all moans and shouts and lonely cries and dire pictures of hell, and then he sang a song about the ninety and nine safe in the fold, but one little lamb was left out in the cold. Then he said: "Won't you come? Won't you come to Jesus? Young lambs, won't you come?" And he held out his arms to all us young sinners there on the mourners' bench. And the little girls cried. And some of them jumped up and went to Jesus right away. But most of us just sat there.

A great many old people came and knelt around us and prayed, old women with jet-black faces and braided hair, old men with work-gnarled hands. And the church sang a song about the lower lights are burning, some poor sinners to be saved. And the whole building rocked with prayer and song.

Still I kept waiting to *see* Jesus.

Finally all the young people had gone to the altar and were saved, but one boy and me. He was a rounder's son named Westley. Westley and I were surrounded by sisters and deacons praying. It was very hot in the church, and getting late now. Finally Westley said to me in a whisper: "God damn! I'm tired o' sitting here. Let's get up and be saved." So he got up and was saved.

Then I was left all alone on the mourners' bench. My aunt came and knelt at my knees and cried, while prayers and songs swirled all around me in the little church. The whole congregation prayed for me alone, in a mighty wail of moans and voices. And I kept waiting serenely for Jesus, waiting, waiting — but he didn't come. I wanted to see him, but nothing happened to me. Nothing! I wanted something to happen to me, but nothing happened.

I heard the songs and the minister saying: "Why don't you come? My dear child, why don't you come to Jesus? Jesus is waiting for you. He wants you. Why don't you come? Sister Reed, what is this child's name?"

"Langston," my aunt sobbed.

"Langston, why don't you come? Why don't you come and be saved? Oh, Lamb of God! Why don't you come?"

Now it was really getting late. I began to be ashamed of myself, holding everything up so long. I began to wonder what God thought about Westley, who certainly hadn't seen Jesus either, but who was now sitting proudly on the platform, swinging his knickerbockered legs and grinning down at me, surrounded by deacons and old women on their knees praying. God had not struck Westley dead for taking his name in vain or for lying in the temple. So I decided that maybe to save further trouble, I'd better lie, too, and say that Jesus had come, and get up and be saved.

So I got up.

Suddenly the whole room broke into a sea of shouting, as they saw me rise. Waves of rejoicing swept the place. Women leaped in the air. My aunt threw her arms around me. The minister took me by the hand and led me to the platform.

When things quieted down, in a hushed silence, punctuated by a few ecstatic "Amens," all the new young lambs were blessed in the name of God. Then joyous singing filled the room.

That night, for the last time in my life but one — for I was a big boy twelve years old — I cried. I cried, in bed alone, and couldn't stop. I buried my head under the quilts, but my aunt heard me. She woke up and told my uncle I was crying because the Holy Ghost had come into my life, and because I had seen Jesus. But I was really crying because I couldn't bear to tell her that I had lied, that I had deceived everybody in the church, that I hadn't seen Jesus, and that now I didn't believe there was a Jesus any more, since he didn't come to help me.

> – Langston Hughes
> "Salvation"
> *The Big Sea*, 1940

# 4

I'm something of an anomaly in the deaf world. Unlike most deaf people, who were either born deaf or went deaf in infancy, I lost my hearing in chunks over a period of twelve years. Fortunately I learned to speak before my loss grew too profound, and that ability freed me from the most severe problem facing the deaf — the terrible difficulty of making themselves understood. My opinion of deafness was just as biased as that of a person who can hear. I had never met a deaf child in my life, and I didn't know how to sign. I imagined deaf people to be like creatures from beyond: animal-like because their language was so physical, threatening because they were unable to express themselves with sophistication — that is, through speech. I *could* make myself understood, and because I had a talent for lipreading it was easy for me to pass in the wider world. And for most of my life that is exactly what I did. . . .

From the time I was twelve until I was twenty-four, the loss of my hearing was erratic. I would lose a decibel or two of sound and then my hearing would stabilize. A week or a year later there would be another slip and then I'd have to adjust all over again. I never knew when I would hit bottom. I remember going to bed one night still being able to make out the reassuring purr of the refrigerator and the late-night conversation of my parents, then waking the next morning to nothing — even my own voice was gone. These fits and starts continued until my hearing finally dropped to the last rung of amplifiable sound. I was a college student at the time, and whenever anyone asked about my hearing aid, I admitted to being only slightly hard of hearing.

My professors were frequently alarmed by my almost maniacal intensity in class. I was petrified that I'd have to ask for special privileges just to achieve marginal understanding. My pride was in flames. I became increasingly bitter and isolated. I was terrified of being marked a deaf woman, a label that made me sound dumb and cowlike, enveloped in a protective silence that denied me my complexity. I did everything I could to hide my handicap. I wore my hair long and never wore earrings, thus keeping attention away from my ears and their riders. I monopolized conversations so that I wouldn't slip up and reveal what I was or wasn't hearing; I took on a disdainful air at large parties, hoping that no one would ask me something I couldn't instantly reply to. I lied about the extent of my deafness so I could avoid the stigma of being thought "different" in a pathetic way.

It was not surprising that in my senior year I suffered a nervous collapse and spent three days in the hospital crying like a baby. When I stopped crying I knew it was time to face a few things — I had to start asking for help when I needed it because I couldn't handle my deafness alone, and I had to quit being ashamed of my handicap so I could begin to live with its consequences and discover what (if any) were its rewards.

When I began telling people that I was *really* deaf, I did so with grim determination. Some were afraid to talk to me at any length, fearing perhaps that they were talking into a void; others assumed that I was somehow an unsullied innocent and always inquired in carefully enunciated sentences: "Doooooooo youuuuuuuuu driiinnk liquor?" But most people were surprisingly sympathetic — they wanted to know the best way to be understood, they took great pains to talk directly to my face, and they didn't insult me by using only words of one syllable.

It was, in part, that gentle acceptance that made me more curious about my own deafness. Always before it had been an affliction to wrestle with as one would with angels, but when I finally accepted it as an inevitable part of my life, I relaxed enough to do some exploring. I would take off my hearing aid and go through a day, a night, an hour or two — as long as I could take it — in absolute silence. I felt as if I were indulging in a secret vice because I was perceiving the world in a new way — stripped of sound.

Of course I had always known that sound is vibration, but I didn't know, until I stopped straining to hear, how truly sound is a refinement of feeling. Conversations at parties might elude me, but I seldom fail to pick up on moods. I enjoy watching people talk. When I am too far away to read lips I try reading postures and imagining conversations. Sometimes, to everyone's horror, I respond to things better left unsaid when I'm trying to find out what's going on around me. I want to see, touch, taste, and smell everything within reach; I especially have to curb a tendency to judge things by their smell — not just potato salad but people as well — a habit that seems to some people entirely too barbaric for comfort. I am not claiming that my other senses stepped up their work to compensate for the loss, but the absence of one does allow me to concentrate on the others. Deafness has left me acutely aware of both the duplicity that language is capable of and the many expressions the body cannot hide.

Nine years ago I spent the summer at the University of Texas's experimental Shakespeare workshop at Winedale, and I went back each year for eight years, first as a student and then as a staff associate. Off and on for the last four years I have written and performed for Esther's Follies, a cabaret theater group in Austin. Some people think it's odd that, as deaf as I am, I've spent so much of my life working in the theater, but I find it to be a natural consequence of my particular circumstance. The loss of sound has enhanced my fascination with language and the way meaning is conveyed. I love to perform. Exactly the same processes occur onstage as off — except that onstage, once I've memorized the script, I know what everybody is saying as they say it. I am delighted to be so immediately in the know. It has provided a direct way to keep in touch with the rest of the world despite the imposed isolation.

— Terry Galloway
"I'm Listening as Hard as I Can"
*Texas Monthly*, 1981

# 5

Theresa Sanchez sat behind me in ninth-grade algebra. . . . She was the tallest girl in school. Her bouffant hairdo, streaked with blond, was higher than the flaccid bouffants of other girls. Her smooth skin, plucked eyebrows, and painted fingernails suggested hours of pampering, a worldly and sensual vanity that placed her within the domain of adults. Smiling dimly, steeped in daydreams, Theresa moved through the crowded halls with a languid, self-satisfied indifference to those around her. "You are merely children," her posture seemed to say. "I can't be bothered." The week Theresa hid *101 Ways to Cook Hamburger* behind her algebra book, I could stand it no longer and, after the bell rang, ventured a question.

"Because I'm having a dinner party," said Theresa. "Just a couple of intimate friends."

No fourteen-year-old I knew had ever given a dinner party, let alone used the word "intimate" in conversation. "Don't you have a mother?" I asked.

Theresa sighed a weary sigh, suffered my strange inquiry. "Don't be so naive," she said. "Everyone has a mother." She waved her hand to indicate the brick school buildings outside the window. "A higher education should have taught you that." Theresa draped an angora sweater over her shoulders, scooped her books from the graffiti-covered desk, and just as she was about to walk away, she turned and asked me, "Are you a fag?"

There wasn't the slightest hint of rancor or condescension in her voice. The tone was direct, casual. Still I was stunned, giving a sidelong glance to make sure no one had heard. "No," I said. Blurted really, with too much defensiveness, too much transparent fear in my response. Octaves lower than usual, I tried a "Why?"

Theresa shrugged. "Oh, I don't know. I have lots of friends who are fags. You remind me of them." Seeing me bristle, Theresa added, "It was just a guess." I watched her erect, angora back as she sauntered out the classroom door.

She had made an incisive and timely guess. Only days before, I'd invited Grady Rogers to my house after school to go swimming. The instant Grady shot from the pool, shaking water from his orange hair, freckled shoulders shining, my attraction to members of my own sex became a matter I could no longer suppress or rationalize. Sturdy and boisterous and gap-toothed, Grady was an inveterate backslapper, a formidable arm wrestler, a wizard at basketball. Grady was a boy at home in his body.

My body was a marvel I hadn't gotten used to; my arms and legs would sometimes act of their own accord, knocking over a glass at dinner or flinching at an oncoming pitch. I was never singled out as a sissy, but I could have been just as easily as Bobby Keagan, a gentle, intelligent, and introverted boy reviled by my classmates. And although I had always been aware of a tacit rapport with Bobby, a suspicion that I might find with him a rich friendship, I stayed away. Instead, I emulated Grady in the belief that being seen with him, being like him, would somehow vanquish my self-doubt, would make me normal by association. . . .

One day I made the mistake of asking my mother what a "fag" was. I knew exactly what Theresa had meant but hoped against hope it was not what I thought; maybe "fag" was some French word, a harmless term like "naive." My mother turned from the stove, flew at me, and grabbed me by the shoulders. "Did someone call you that?" she cried.

"Not me," I said. "Bobby Keagan."

"Oh," she said, loosening her grip. She was visibly relieved. And didn't answer. The answer was unthinkable.

In the school library, a *Webster's* unabridged dictionary lay on a wooden podium, and I padded toward it with apprehension. . . . I had decided to consult the dictionary during lunch period, when most of the students would be on the playground. I clutched my notebook, moving in such a way as to appear both studious and nonchalant, actually believing that, unless I took precautions, someone would see me and guess what I was up to. The closer I came to the podium, the more obvious, I thought, was my endeavor; I felt like the model of The Visible Man in our science class, my heart's undulations, my overwrought nerves legible through transparent skin. A couple of kids riffled through the card catalogue. The librarian, a skinny woman whose perpetual whisper and rubber-soled shoes caused her to drift through the room like a phantom, didn't seem to register my presence. Though I'd looked up dozens of words before, the pages felt strange beneath my fingers. *Homer* was the first word I saw. *Hominid. Homogenize.* I feigned interest and skirted other words before I found the word I was after. Under the heading HO·MO·SEX·U·AL was the terse definition: *adj. Pertaining to, characteristic of, or exhibiting homosexuality. –n. A homosexual person.* I read the definition again and again, hoping the words would yield more than they could. I shut the dictionary, swallowed hard, and, none the wiser, hurried away.

. . . By the following summer, however, I had overheard from my peers a confounding amount about homosexuals: They wore green on Thursday, couldn't whistle, hypnotized boys with a piercing glance. To this lore, Grady added a surefire test to ferret them out.

"A test?" I said.

"You ask a guy to look at his fingernails, and if he looks at them like this" — Grady closed his fingers into a fist and examined his nails with manly detachment — "then he's okay. But if he does this" — he held out his hands at arm's length, splayed his fingers, and coyly cocked his head — "you'd better watch out." Once he'd completed his demonstration, Grady peeled off his shirt and plunged into our pool. I dove in after. It was early June, the sky immense, glassy, placid. My father was cooking spareribs on the barbecue, an artist with a basting brush. His apron bore the caricature of a frazzled French chef. Mother curled on a chaise longue, plumes of smoke wafting from her nostrils. In a stupor of contentment she took another drag, closed her eyes, and arched her face toward the sun.

Grady dog-paddled through the deep end, spouting a fountain of chlorinated water. Despite shame and confusion, my longing for him hadn't diminished; it continued to thrive without air and light, like a luminous fish in the dregs of the sea. In the name of play, I swam up behind him, encircled his shoulders, astonished by his taut flesh. The two of us flailed, pretended to drown. Beneath the heavy press of water, Grady's orange hair wavered, a flame that couldn't be doused.

I've lived with a man for seven years. Some nights, when I'm half-asleep and the room is suffused with blue light, I reach out to touch the expanse of his back, and it seems as if my fingers sink into his skin, and I feel the pleasure a diver feels the instant he enters a body of water.

I have few regrets. But one is that I hadn't said to Theresa, "Of course I'm a fag." Maybe I'd have met her friends. Or become friends with her. Imagine the meals we might have concocted: hamburger Stroganoff, Swedish meatballs in a sweet translucent sauce, steaming slabs of Salisbury steak.

> – Bernard Cooper
> "A Clack of Tiny Sparks:
> Remembrances of a Gay Boyhood"
> *Harper's*, 1991

◇◇◇◇◇

# 6

The kitchen was the great machine that set our lives running; it whirred down a little only on Saturdays and holy days. From my mother's kitchen I gained my first picture of life as a white, overheated, starkly lit workshop redolent with Jewish cooking, crowded with women in housedresses, strewn with fashion magazines, patterns, dress material, spools of thread — and at whose center, so lashed to her machine that bolts of energy seemed to dance out of her hands and feet as she worked, my mother stamped the treadle hard against the floor, hard, hard, and silently, grimly at war, beat out the first rhythm of the world for me. . . .

Twice a year, on the anniversaries of her parents' deaths, my mother placed on top of the ice-box an ordinary kitchen glass packed with wax, the *yortsayt*, and lit the candle in it. Sitting at the kitchen table over my homework, I would look across the threshold to that mourning-glass, and sense that for my mother the distance from our kitchen to *der heym*, from life to death, was only a flame's length away. Poor as we were, it was not poverty that drove my mother so hard; it was loneliness — some endless bitter brooding over all those left behind, dead or dying or soon to die; a loneliness locked up in her kitchen that dwelt every day on the hazardousness of life and the nearness of death, but still kept struggling in the lock, trying to get us through by endless labor.

With us, life started up again only on the last shore. There seemed to be no middle ground between despair and the fury of our ambition. Whenever my mother spoke of her hopes for us, it was with such unbelievingness that the likes of us would ever come to anything, such abashed hope and readiness for pain, that I finally came to see in the flame burning on top of the ice-box death itself burning away the bones of poor Jews, burning out in us everything but courage, the blind resolution to live. In the light of that mourning-candle, there were ranged around me how many dead and dying — how many eras of pain, of exile, of dispersion, of cringing before the powers of this world!

— Alfred Kazin
*A Walker in the City*, 1951

# 7

It comes as a great shock around the age of five, six, or seven to discover that the flag to which you have pledged allegiance, along with everybody else, has not pledged allegiance to you. It comes as a great shock to see Gary Cooper killing off the Indians, and, although you are rooting for Gary Cooper, that the Indians are you.

It comes as a great shock to discover that the country which is your birthplace and to which you owe your life and identity has not, in its whole system of reality, evolved any place for you. The disaffection and the gap between people, only on the basis of their skins, begins there and accelerates throughout your whole lifetime. . . .

I remember when the ex–Attorney General Mr. Robert Kennedy said it was conceivable that in forty years in America we might have a Negro president. That sounded like a very emancipated statement to white people. They were not in Harlem when this statement was first heard. They did not hear the laughter and the bitterness and scorn with which this statement was greeted. From the point of view of the man in the Harlem barber shop, Bobby Kennedy only got here yesterday and now he is already on his way to the presidency. We were here for four hundred years and now he tells us that maybe in forty years, if you are good, we may let you become president. . . .

It is a terrible thing for an entire people to surrender to the notion that one-ninth of its population is beneath them. Until the moment comes when we, the Americans, are able to accept the fact that my ancestors are both black and white, that on that continent we are trying to forge a new identity, that we need each other, that I am not a ward of America, I am not an object of missionary charity, I am one of the people who built the country — until this moment comes there is scarcely any hope for the American dream. If the people are denied participation in it, by their very presence they will wreck it. And if that happens it is a very grave moment for the West.

> — James Baldwin
> "The American Dream and
> the American Negro"
> *The Price of the Ticket*, 1965

# 8

There are pleasures in reading so startling, so intense, they shade into pain. The realization that one's life has been irrevocably altered by . . . can it be mere words? Print on a page? The most life-rending discoveries involve what has in fact never been thought, never given form, until another's words embody them.

> — Joyce Carol Oates
> *(Woman) Writer:*
> *Occasions and Opportunities*, 1988

# 9

I had come to the Norfolk Prison Colony still going through only book-reading motions. Pretty soon, I would have quit even these motions, unless I had received the motivation that I did.

I saw that the best thing I could do was get hold of a dictionary — to study, to learn some words. I was lucky enough to reason also that I should try to improve my penmanship. It was sad. I couldn't even write in a straight line. It was both ideas together that moved me to request a dictionary along with some tablets and pencils from the Norfolk Prison Colony school.

I spent two days just riffling uncertainly through the dictionary's pages. I'd never realized so many words existed! I didn't know *which* words I needed to learn. Finally, just to start some kind of action, I began copying.

In my slow, painstaking, ragged handwriting, I copied into my tablet everything printed on that first page, down to the punctuation marks.

I believe it took me a day. Then, aloud, I read back, to myself, everything I'd written on the tablet. Over and over, aloud, to myself, I read my own handwriting.

I woke up the next morning, thinking about those words — immensely proud to realize that not only had I written so much at one time, but I'd written words that I never knew were in the world. Moreover, with a little effort, I also could remember what many of these words meant. I reviewed the words whose meanings I didn't remember. Funny thing, from the dictionary's first page right now, that "aardvark" springs to my mind. The dictionary had a picture of it, a long-tailed, long-eared, burrowing African mammal, which lives off termites caught by sticking out its tongue as an anteater does for ants.

I was so fascinated that I went on — I copied the dictionary's next page. And the same experience came when I studied that. With every succeeding page, I also learned of people and places and events from history. Actually the dictionary is like a miniature encyclopedia. Finally the dictionary's A section had filled a whole tablet — and I went on into the B's. That was the way I started copying what eventually became the entire dictionary. It went a lot faster after so much practice helped me to pick up handwriting speed. Between what I wrote in my tablet, and writing letters, during the rest of my time in prison I would guess I wrote a million words.

I suppose it was inevitable that as my word-base broadened, I could for the first time pick up a book and read and now begin to understand what the book was saying. Anyone who has read a great deal can imagine the new world that opened. Let me tell you something: From then until I left that prison, in every free moment I had, if I was not reading in the library, I was reading on my bunk. You couldn't have gotten me out of books with a wedge. Between Mr. Muhammad's teachings, my correspondence, my visitors, . . . and my reading of books, months passed without my even thinking about being imprisoned. In fact, up to then, I never had been so truly free in my life. . . .

I have often reflected upon the new vistas that reading opened to me.

I knew right there in prison that reading had changed forever the course of my life. As I see it today, the ability to read awoke inside me some long dormant craving to be mentally alive. I certainly wasn't seeking any degree, the way a college confers a status symbol upon its students. My homemade education gave me, with every additional book that I read, a little bit more sensitivity to the deafness, dumbness, and blindness that was afflicting the black race in America. Not long ago, an English writer telephoned me from London, asking questions. One was, "What's your alma mater?" I told him, "Books." You will never catch me with a free fifteen minutes in which I'm not studying something I feel might be able to help the black man.

> – Malcolm X with Alex Haley
> "Learning to Read"
> *The Autobiography of Malcolm X*, 1964

## REFLECTIONS

1. In which selection(s) in *Looking at Ourselves* does someone discover that being honest about him- or herself leads to acceptance by most other people? In which selection(s) does someone discover that being honest about him- or herself cannot lead to acceptance?

2. Michael Dorris (p. 188) describes the sudden shift from childhood to adulthood undergone by a nineteenth-century Cheyenne or Lakota teenager. What do you think would be the advantages of such an abrupt transition over the decade-long one common in modern Western society? What are the advantages of the longer transition?

3. After reading Langston Hughes's recollection about being "saved" (p. 188), look back at Michael Dorris's comments. What other explanation(s) can you suggest for the teenage transformation described by Dorris besides the ones he mentions?

4. What biblical sentence patterns can you identify in Hughes's selection? How does he use these patterns to create the mood of a prayer meeting? How does James Baldwin (p. 196) use repetition to drive home a point? How does Bernard Cooper (p. 193) use physical description to emphasize the physicality of the discovery he is making about himself?

# SUSAN ORLEAN

## *Quinceañera*

Susan Orlean was born on Halloween in 1955 in Cleveland, Ohio. After graduating from the University of Michigan she became a writer for *Willamette Week* in Portland, Oregon, then for the *Boston Phoenix*, and then for the *Boston Globe*. Her first book was a collection of essays from the *Globe* entitled *Red Sox and Bluefish: Meditations on What Makes New England New England* (1987). Orlean now lives in New York, where she writes for *The New Yorker* and is a contributing editor for *Rolling Stone*. "Quinceañera" comes from her book *Saturday Night* (1990).

Azteca Plaza, the biggest formal wear shopping center in the world, is on a skinny strip of sandy, cactus-studded Arizona real estate, a few miles east of downtown Phoenix, in a neighborhood that does not yet illustrate the vitality of the Sunbelt economy. . . . Azteca Plaza has the corner on the greater metropolitan Phoenix prom-dress trade. It also does a brisk business in the fancy ball gowns Hispanic girls wear at their *quinceañeras*, the ceremony that takes place when they are fifteen years old — *quince años* — to celebrate their passage into womanhood, commitment to Catholicism, and debut into society. In the last decade, the number of Hispanics in Phoenix has grown by 125 percent. The *quinceañera* business at Azteca Plaza has enjoyed a corresponding upswing.

Azteca Plaza is just a few blocks away from Immaculate Heart Church, a boxy stucco-colored structure that serves as a central parish for the Hispanic community in the Phoenix diocese. Immaculate Heart was built in 1928, fourteen years after it was revealed that the priests at the main basilica in Phoenix, St. Mary's, had been obliging their Mexican parishioners to hold their masses and weddings and *quinceañeras* in the basement rather than on the main floor of the church. It used to be common for certain churches to serve an ethnic group rather than a geographical area — in most American cities, there would be French, Hispanic, Polish, Irish, and German Catholic churches. The practice is rare these days, and Immaculate Heart is one of the few such ethnic parishes left in the entire country. Someone in Phoenix, recounting for me the history of Hispanic mistreatment at St. Mary's, credited the continued existence of a national parish in Phoenix to the dry Arizona desert air, which, he claimed, had preserved the unpleasant memory of bargain-basement weddings at the basilica in many Hispanics' minds. Hispanics in Phoenix now regularly attend the churches in their immediate neighborhoods, but for sentimental and historical reasons they continue to think of Immaculate Heart as the mother ship. Not coincidentally, Immaculate Heart was for years the site of most of Phoenix's many *quinceañeras* — that is, the site of the mass when the girl is blessed and is asked to affirm her dedication to the Church. The party in which she is introduced to society and celebrates her birthday is held after the mass at a hotel or hall. For a while, there were so many *quinceañeras* at Immaculate Heart that they outnumbered weddings. For that matter, there were so many *quinceañera* masses and parties that they were a standard Saturday-night social occasion in town.

In early summer I was invited to a large *quinceañera* in Phoenix at which sixteen girls were to be presented. The event was being sponsored by the girls' parents and the Vesta Club, a social organization of Hispanic college graduates. In the Southwest, constituents of this subset are sometimes known as "chubbies" — Chicano urban professionals. Chubbies give Azteca Plaza a lot of business. The girls' fathers and the sixteen young men who were going to be escorts at the *quinceañera* had rented their tuxedos from Azteca Plaza and would be picking them up on Saturday morning. The girls, of course, had gotten their gowns months before.

The traditional Mexican *quinceañera* gown is white or pink, floor length but trainless, snug on top and wide at the bottom, with a skirt shaped like a wedding bell. But like most traditions that migrate a few hundred miles from their point of origin and make it through a couple of generations in this country, *quinceañeras* have yielded somewhat to interpretation, and the gowns that the Vesta Club girls were going to wear demonstrated the effects of Americanization on taste as well as a certain American-style expansiveness in price. All of the gowns were white and full-length but otherwise they were freestyle — an array of high necks, fluted necklines, sweetheart necklines, leg-o'-mutton sleeves, cap sleeves, cascade collars, gathered bodices, beaded bodices, bustles, and sequins; one had a train and one had a flouncy peplum and a skirt that was narrow from the hip to the floor. Further Americanization has taken place with regards to scheduling. In Mexico, *quinceañeras* traditionally take place on the day the girl actually turns fifteen. In the United States, *quinceañeras* — like many important ceremonies in American life — take place on Saturday nights.

When I first mentioned to a woman I know in Phoenix that I wanted 5 to attend a *quinceañera*, that I thought they seemed like interesting ceremonies and great displays of community feeling and a good example of how ethnic tradition fits into American Saturday nights, she clucked sympathetically and said she was very sentimental about her own *quinceañera* but had become convinced that they were now going the way of many other ethnic ceremonies in this country — changed beyond recognition, marketed like theme parks, at the very least irrelevant to assimilated youngsters who would rather spend Saturday nights at keg parties than reenacting an old-world ceremony. An inevitable pattern transforms such things: Immigrants gather in their leisure time so that they can bolster one another and share their imported traditions, their children tolerate the gatherings occasionally because they have a likeable familiar ring, and then the children of *those* children deplore them because they seem corny and pointless, and finally there is a lot of discussion about how sad it is that the community doesn't get together anymore.

That is partly what has become of *quinceañeras* in Phoenix, but the real problem, ironically, is that they have been too popular for their own good. A few years ago, the bishop of Phoenix, a slight, freckle-faced man from Indiana named Thomas O'Brien, started hearing complaints from some priests about *quinceañeras*. According to the bishop, the chief complaint was that *quinceañera* masses were beginning to dominate church schedules. This would surprise no one with an eye on the city's demographics: Three-quarters of the Hispanics in Phoenix are under thirty-five years old and a significant number of them are girls — all potential subjects of a *quinceañera* mass and party. The priests complained that some girls came to their *quinceañera* mass without the faintest idea of its religious significance, never came to church otherwise, demanded a mass even if they were pregnant or using drugs or in some other way drifting outside the categories usually in good stead with the religious community, and badgered their families — some chubbies, but many not — into giving them opulent postmass parties. Some *quinceañera* parties in Phoenix were running into the high four figures and beyond. Many families could hardly afford this. In response to these concerns, Father Antonio Sotelo, the bishop's vicar for Hispanic affairs, surveyed the diocese's priests and then wrote a guidebook for *quinceañeras* similar to ones circulated recently in a few other American parishes with large Hispanic populations, advising that girls take five classes on Bible study, Hispanic history, *quinceañera* history, and modern morals, and go on a church-sponsored retreat with their parents before the event. He also recommended that *quinceañeras* be held for groups of girls rather than for individuals, in order to offset the queen-for-a-day quality that many of them had taken on, and so that the cost could be spread around.

One morning before the Vesta Club *quinceañera*, I stopped by Father Sotelo's office at Immaculate Heart. Besides being vicar for Hispanic affairs, Father Sotelo is the pastor of Immaculate Heart. His small office in the back of the church is decorated with pictures of his parishioners and dominated by a whale of a desk. Father Sotelo is short and wiry and has rumpled graying hair, an impish face, and a melodious voice. His manner of address is direct. He is known for holding and broadcasting the opinion that anyone who wears shorts and a T-shirt to church should be escorted out the door, and that the men in his congregation who walk with a sloppy, swinging, barrio-tough gait look like gorillas. Father Sotelo grew up in San Diego. His heritage is Mexican and American Indian. He says that he considered the *quinceañera* issue a simple matter of facing reality, and he doesn't mind that the requirements have discouraged many girls from having *quinceañeras*. "We knew perfectly well that most girls were only thinking about the party," he said. "It was a big dream for them. Everyone wants a fancy *quinceañera* party. Unlike an American debutante ball, *quinceañeras* are not limited to the upper class. Any girl can celebrate it. But there are spoiled brats in every class. Many of these girls were demanding that their parents spend thousands of dollars on them whether they could afford it or not. People at the lower end of the economic scale cling to tradition most fervently, so they were most determined to have a traditional *quinceañera*, and their daughters would have the most expensive dresses and parties. And when these girls would walk down the aisle with their parents at the mass, you could tell that quite often the girls and their parents couldn't stand one another. It was an empty ceremony. For what they were getting out of the church part of the *quinceañera*, they could have gone out and done the whole thing in the desert and had someone sprinkle magic pollen on their heads."

After the guidelines were circulated around the diocese, a few churches, including Immaculate Heart, set up the *quinceañera* classes and retreats. But to the enormous displeasure of parishioners who enjoyed spending Saturday nights at their friends' daughters' *quinceañeras*, and who imagined that on some Saturday night in the future their own daughters would be feted at a mass and nice reception of their own, many priests in Phoenix announced that they agreed with Father Sotelo but they lacked the time and facilities to run classes and retreats. Therefore, they declared, they would no longer perform *quinceañera* masses at all.

The one priest who took exception was Frank Peacock, the pastor of a poor church in a scruffy South Phoenix neighborhood. Father Peacock made it known that he thought the guidelines were too strict, and that they inhibited the exercise of a tradition that rightfully belonged to the people, and that as far as he was concerned, anyone in any condition or situation who wanted a *quinceañera* could come to him. "We get calls here all the time from people asking very meekly for Father Peacock's number," Father Sotelo said to me, looking exasperated. "They're not fooling anyone. I know exactly what they want."

A few weeks before I got to Phoenix, a small yucca plant on the corner    10 of Twelfth and Van Buren, about a half mile down the street from Immaculate Heart, sprouted a stem that then shriveled up into an unusual shape and was subsequently noticed by a passerby who thought it bore a striking resemblance to Our Lady of Guadeloupe. The yucca stem was never certified as a genuine miracle by church hierarchy, but for several weeks, until someone shot at it with a small-caliber handgun and then two artists took it upon themselves to cut it down with a chainsaw as the climax of a performance piece, it attracted large crowds of people who came to marvel at it and pray.

Our Lady of Guadeloupe, the vision who appeared to the Mexican-Indian Juan Diego on December 9, 1531, and who was so awe-inspiring a sight that she more or less nailed down the entire country of Mexico for the Catholic Church, has appeared in other places as unlikely as the corner of Twelfth and Van Buren. For instance, Our Lady of Guadeloupe also happens to be spray-painted on the trunk of at least one souped-up low-rider car in Phoenix, which I noticed bouncing down the street one afternoon when I was in town. Father Peacock had seen this same car and says he finds it remarkable. The day before the Vesta Club Ball, he and I had gotten together so he could show me videotapes of some of the outlaw *quinceañera* masses he had presided over at Our Lady of Fatima. Before we started the tapes, I said that Father Sotelo had pointed out that people were perfectly entitled to have *quinceañeras* that cost ten thousand dollars and celebrated fifteen-year-olds with heavy marijuana habits, but that the Church shouldn't necessarily endorse them or hold celebration masses for them. "People have a right to enjoy things that the Church doesn't endorse," Father Peacock said. "We don't endorse low-riders, do we?" He interrupted himself. "Actually, I endorse low-riders. I love them. Have you ever seen one? Oh, they can be gorgeous, really beautiful. Did you ever see the one painted with Our Lady of Guade-loupe?" . . .

Some of the people who come to Father Peacock for a *quinceañera* are poor, or are recent immigrants who are still attached to the traditional Mexican style of the ceremony and resist what they could well consider pointless time-consuming requirements or irritating Americanizations. Quite often, Father Peacock is approached by affluent Hispanics as well, who tell him they want their daughters to have their own celebrations, not *quinceañeras* with a group of other girls, and that they want to go all out with the six-tiered *quinceañera* cake and the rhinestone crown and the catered sit-down dinner for three hundred and the mariachi band and the lavish gifts from the godparents and the fifteen boy escorts and fifteen girl attendants in matching outfits who traditionally accompany the *quinceañera* girl. Father Peacock says he has given *quinceañera* masses for daughters of state senators as well as for girls whose parents are illiterate. Most of the time, he begins his address at the mass by asking for forgiveness for his failures and then says, "You have asked us to take care of a fifteenth-birthday celebration and we say no — this is one of our failures." Sometimes the people at the altar look bored or are wearing dark sunglasses and conspicuous amounts of jewelry and can't even remember the words to the Lord's Prayer when Father Peacock recites it. "That is one of my motivations," he says. "This might be the only chance I have to get that sort of person into church and try to reach them." Some of the families have experienced child abuse, sexual abuse, divorce, separation, or a combination of all four, and Father Peacock says he loves seeing such families together at the occasional happy affair like a *quinceañera*. Some of them take out loans to pay for their daughters' gowns. Father Peacock usually urges the poorer families to hold their parties at South Mountain Park, a city facility with a hall that can be used for free, but he says he can understand if they prefer a fancier place. On this point, he always says something in the homily like, "Through self-sacrifice we get our pleasure," and has said many times that he would rather that people go into hock for a traditional, ethnic, religious occasion — no matter how marginally religious it might turn out to be — than for something like a car or a boat. "A *quinceañera* costs a lot of money," he says. "But it's worth a lot of money. Anyway, I don't try to change people. I like to meet them in their own way." . . .

"Father Peacock will do anything," a young woman named Alice Coronado-Hernandez, this year's chairman of the Vesta Club *Quinceañera* Ball, said to me one afternoon. "Everyone knows that about Father Peacock, so everyone calls him." At the time, I was having lunch at a bad Mexican restaurant in a good part of Phoenix with Alice, her mother, Caroline, and Mary Jo Franco-French, a physician who helped found the Vesta *quinceañera* fifteen years ago. When she was organizing that first *quinceañera*, Mary Jo had just finished medical school and was pregnant with her daughter Laura. This year, Laura was going to be one of the girls up on the stage.

The Vesta Club is not going to be calling on Father Peacock anytime soon. "We're really happy with doing our *quinceañera* the way Father Sotelo has suggested," Caroline said. "We felt the classes and the retreat were really good for the girls. We saw what was going on with the *quinceañeras* — we saw the problem out there. Even if we could afford it, we knew it wasn't good to continue the old way."

Alice said, "It was crazy what people were spending. When I was that age, the girls were really competitive about their *quinceañeras* and about how nice they would be." Caroline nodded. "My *quinceañera* was at the first Vesta Club Ball," Alice went on. "That year, I must have been invited to *quinceañeras* for friends of mine just about every weekend, so it was a pretty regular Saturday-night activity for me. But even then I could see how some people got very extravagant about it."

"They were hocking their souls for the fancy private *quinceañera*," Caroline added. "The diocese could see that it was becoming detrimental to the economy of their parishioners."

The three of them spent some time talking about last-minute details of the Vesta *quinceañera*. After a mass at Immaculate Heart, there was going to be dinner for the four hundred and fifty guests at Camelback Inn, an elegant resort north of the city, and a short ceremony in which each girl would be presented by her father. Then the girls and their escorts would perform a *quinceañera* waltz — a complicated dance to the "Blue Danube" which the kids had practiced once a week for the last three months. "The waltz is such a beautiful tradition," Mary Jo said. "It's what we have that makes the event really special. That, and having them learn about their Hispanic heritage. The kids have worked so hard at that waltz. They've really practiced, and they've really gotten good at it."

"They *have* gotten good at it, haven't they?" Caroline said, nodding. "It's hard to believe that some of them had never danced a step before they started to learn."

The Fifteenth Annual Vesta Club *Quinceañera* Mass began at five o'clock with a procession of the sixteen girls up the center aisle of Immaculate Heart. I sat on the left side of the church, a row behind Mary Jo Franco-French and her husband, Alfred, an eye surgeon of Gallic extraction who has a large practice in Phoenix. Beside me were four cousins of Mary Jo's who had flown in from Juarez, Mexico, for the event. The day had been dry-roasting hot, and at five, the long, dusty southwestern dusk was just beginning and the light was hitting the city at a flat angle and giving everything a yellowy glow. The *quinceañera* girls in their white dresses had been standing on the sidewalk outside the church when I walked in, and each time a car drove down the street in front of the church, the updraft would blow their big skirts around. Immaculate Heart is a bulky, unadorned building with dark wooden pews, a vaulted ceiling, some stained glass, a wide altar with simple lines, and a pail hanging just outside the side door into which parishioners are advised to deposit their chewing gum. After I sat down, I noticed Father Sotelo and Bishop O'Brien seated together at the altar. The Vesta Club *quinceañera* is the only one in Phoenix at which the bishop celebrates the mass. He told me that it is the only one he attends because he liked the seriousness with which the club approached the spiritual content of the ceremony, and also because no one else having a *quinceañera* had ever invited him.

After a few minutes, the organist hit a chord and the procession began. The Vesta Club girls walked in, trailing satin and netting. The gowns were a spectacle: Each one was bright white, with different structural embellishments and complicated effects. I noticed the girl wearing the dress with the little train and the one with the narrow skirt. "Wow," whispered Carmen Gonzalez, one of Mary Jo Franco-French's cousins, who had celebrated her own *quinceañera* a few years ago at a country club in Juarez. "Pretty nice dresses. These girls look so *grown-up.*"

"The third one down is my niece Maria," the woman behind us said. "Fifteen already, but I still think of her as a baby. I think her mother's praying that Maria keeps her figure so she can wear the dress again when she gets married."

The procession took several minutes. Then the girls sat down in two rows of chairs at the altar, and the bishop made his greetings and began the mass. After a few prayers, he announced that it was time for the parents to bless their daughters individually. He turned and nodded at the dark-haired girl at the end of the row. She stood up cautiously, walked to the center of the apse and down the three steps, turned around and knelt down, partially disappearing in the folds of her dress. Her parents stood up in their pew and walked over to her, leaned down and made the sign of the cross on her forehead, kissed her, whispered something in her ear, and then returned to their seats. The girl rose up and walked back to the altar. Someone in a pew behind me sobbed lightly and then blew loudly into a handkerchief. A faulty key in the church organ stuck and started to squeal. The next girl stood up, smoothed her huge skirt, stepped down, knelt, was blessed by her parents, and returned to her seat. Laura Josefina Franco-French, a tall and elegant-looking fifteen-year-old with long dark hair and a serene expression, came forward and was blessed by Alfred and Mary Jo. Then the girl who was wearing the tight skirt stood up. We all sat forward. She walked in tiny steps across the apse, eased herself down the stairs, turned around, and then, with the agility of a high school cheerleader at the season's big game, she folded her legs beneath her and knelt without straining a seam.

There were still some golfers on the greens at Camelback Inn when the Vesta Club partygoers arrived. The ballroom wasn't ready for us to be seated, so everyone milled around the pool having drinks and talking. I wondered if the golfers were curious about what we were doing — four hundred well-dressed people, mostly adult, and sixteen girls in formal white gowns. It might have looked like a wedding, except there were too many young women in white, and it might have looked like a prom, except no one has parents at her prom. It felt mostly like a community reunion. "It's a big group, but it's a small world," said a woman in a beaded lilac gown standing beside me at the bar.

"Relatives or friends?" I asked.

"Both," she said. "About half of these people were at my daughter's    25 *quinceañera* last year." I must have looked surprised, because she started to laugh and then said, "Some of these families even knew each other in Mexico. You could say that we're just keeping the chain or circle or what have you, intact. I had my *quinceañera* longer ago than I'm happy to say. It's an old-fashioned event but I love it." She took her drink and joined a group of people nearby who were talking about an expensive shopping center just opening in Scottsdale. One of the men in the group kept sweeping his hands out and saying "Boom!" and the woman beside him would then slap his shoulder playfully and say "For godsakes, come on, Adolfo!" Alfred Franco-French III, who was escorting his sister Laura, walked past the bar and muttered that he hoped he would remember the waltz when it came time to waltz. The patio got noisier and noisier. No one was speaking Spanish. One of the girls' fathers started a conversation with me by saying, "There are plenty of bums in the world out there, sad to say," but then he got distracted by someone he hadn't seen in a while and walked away. I had driven out to Camelback with one of Laura Franco-French's school friends, and after a few minutes we ran into each other. She said she was impressed with the *quinceañera* so far. She talked about how there was usually never anything to do on Saturday nights in Phoenix, and then she talked about how favorably Laura's involvement in a formal event, in particular one that required the purchase of a really nice fancy dress, was regarded by other students at their largely non-Hispanic private school. It happened that this girl was not Hispanic and had never been to a *quinceañera* before and had also never before considered what advantages ethnicity might include. She looked across the pool where the debutantes were standing in a cluster and said, "I never thought about it one way or another. But now that I'm at one of these *quinceañeras*, I'm thinking that being Hispanic might be really cool." I walked to the far side of the pool, where I had a long view of all the people at the party, in their fresh tuxes and filmy formals; with their good haircuts and the handsome, relaxed posture common to people whose businesses are doing well and to whom life has been generous; who were standing around the glimmery pool and against the dark, lumpy outline of Camelback Mountain, holding up light-colored drinks in little crystal glasses so that they happened to catch the last bit of daylight. It was a pretty gorgeous sight.

Finally, Alice Coronado-Hernandez and Caroline Coronado sent word that the ballroom was ready. The doors of the Saguaro Room were propped open. The patio emptied as the crowd moved inside. At one end of the ballroom, a mariachi band was ready to play. Around the dance floor were fifty tables set with bunchy flower arrangements and good china. I had been seated with Alice Coronado-Hernandez and her family. At the tables, each place was set with a program printed on stiff, creamy paper; it listed the Vesta Club officers, last year's *quinceañera* debs and escorts, and this year's debs and escorts, and had formal portraits of each of the girls. This was similar in style to the program for the St. Luke's Hospital Visitors' Society Cotillion — Phoenix's premier society event — at which the girls being presented are far more likely to have names like Bickerstaff and Collins than Esparza and Alvarez. I had seen the 1988 St. Luke's program when I had dinner one night with the Franco-Frenches. Laura had been studying the program so energetically that some of the pages were fingerprinted and the binding was broken. In the time since Mexicans in Phoenix were forced to hold their masses in the basement of St. Mary's, a certain amount of social amalgamation has come to pass: Laura Franco-French, half-Mexican in heritage and at least that much in consciousness, will also be presented at St. Luke's in a few years. Similarly, there was a Whitman and a Thornton among the debutantes at the Vesta Ball. . . .

"When do they announce debutante of the year?" Alice's stepdaughter asked her. Alice drummed her fingers on the table and said, "Later." Just then, the master of ceremonies coughed into the microphone and the room got quiet. The girls lined up around the edge of the dance floor with their fathers. The mothers were stationed near them in chairs, so that they would be readily available for the father-mother waltz, which comes after the father-daughter waltz and after the special *quinceañera* waltz — a complex piece of choreography, in which the girls spin around their escorts and then weave through their arms, form little circles and then big circles and finally waltz in time around the dance floor. After all these waltzes, the mariachi band was going to play — although I had heard that for the sake of the teenagers, who appreciated their heritage but who were, after all, American kids with tastes of their own, the Mexican music was going to be alternated throughout the evening with current selections of rock 'n' roll.

The announcer cleared his throat again and said, "*Buenos noches, damas y caballeros.*" He had a sonorous, rumbling voice that thundered through the ballroom. "*Buenos noches.* We present to you this year's Vesta Club debutantes."

## EXPLORATIONS

1. How does the name of the store with which Susan Orlean opens "Quinceañera" illustrate the dual identity of the culture she is writing about?

2. What purposes was a *quinceañera* originally created to serve (para. 1)? Which of them, if any, are served by the *quinceañeras* described here? What are the current purposes of a *quinceañera* from the point of view of the Roman Catholic Church? The girl involved? Her parents? What do you think are the main reasons for the ceremony's changes in function since its origin in Mexico?

3. What sources of information does Orlean cite in this essay? What kinds of sources would you expect her to cite that she does not? How does that choice affect "Quinceañera"?

4. What role does Orlean herself play in the story she is telling? How would the essay's impact change if she did not appear in it?

## CONNECTIONS

1. Which of the tendencies of the Pulling Up Roots phase described by Gail Sheehy in *Looking at Ourselves* (p. 187) appear among the slightly younger girls in "Quinceañera?" Cite specific examples.

2. In what ways do you think a *quinceañera* might provide the same kind of transition from childhood to adulthood as the rite of passage Michael Dorris describes among the Plains Indians in *Looking at Ourselves* (p. 188)?

3. Reread Richard Rodriguez's comments on page 73 about growing up Catholic. What evidence in this essay suggests that the girls celebrating their *quinceañera* share Rodriguez's feelings, positive and negative?

## ELABORATIONS

1. Major social occasions such as proms and weddings often are exciting to look forward to, beautiful or comical to look back on, and miserable to experience. (See, for instance, Langston Hughes's conversion in *Looking at Ourselves,* p. 188.) Has this ever happened to you? Write an essay recalling an event that was supposed to be glorious (for you or a friend or family member) but in fact was either painful or ridiculous.

2. Susan Orlean in "Quinceañera" and Michael Dorris and Langston Hughes in *Looking at Ourselves* describe social rituals designed to mark a turning point in a young person's life. What are the main elements of these rituals, and what is the purpose of each one? Write an essay describing a religious or other ritual in your own life that functioned as a rite of passage, analyzing its component parts and their purposes.

# LILIANA HEKER

## The Stolen Party

Argentine writer Liliana Heker published her highly regarded first volume of short stories, *Those Who Beheld the Burning Bush*, while still in her teens. As editor in chief of the literary magazine *El Ornitorrinco* ("The platypus"), Heker kept open a national forum for writers throughout the years of Argentina's chaotic and bloody military dictatorships. In its pages she debated with the late Julio Cortázar about the proper role of a writer in a strife-torn, oppressed society: Cortázar, living in Paris, defended his role as a writer in exile, while Heker took a position similar to Nadine Gordimer's in South Africa (see p. 578): "To be heard, we must shout from within." Heker's second novel, *Zona de Clivage*, was published in 1988 and won the Buenos Aires Municipal Prize. "The Stolen Party," first published in 1982, was translated from the Spanish by Alberto Manguel for his anthology *Other Fires* (1985).

Four times the size of Texas, Argentina occupies most of South America's southern tip. When the first Spanish settlers appeared in the early 1500s, nomadic Indians roamed the pampas. By the late 1800s nearly all of them had been killed, making room for the influx of Europeans who today comprise 97 percent of the population. Argentina had won independence from Spain in 1819; by the century's end it was the most prosperous, educated, and industrialized Latin American nation. Military dictatorships and coups have dominated this century, however. Aside from General Juan Perón, elected president from 1946 to 1955 and again in 1973, most regimes have been nasty, brutish, and short-lived. Argentina's failed attempt to take the Islas Malvinas (Falkland Islands) from Great Britain in 1982 led to the first general election since Perón's, which established a democratic government in this economically beleaguered nation. Despite opposition from former military officers and some of his fellow Peronists, current President Carlos Menem's aggressive economic policies have begun to slow Argentina's runaway inflation and budget deficit.

As soon as she arrived she went straight to the kitchen to see if the monkey was there. It was: What a relief! She wouldn't have liked to admit that her mother had been right. *Monkeys at a birthday?* her mother had sneered. *Get away with you, believing any nonsense you're told!* She was cross, but not because of the monkey, the girl thought; it's just because of the party.

"I don't like you going," she told her. "It's a rich people's party."

"Rich people go to Heaven too," said the girl, who studied religion at school.

"Get away with Heaven," said the mother. "The problem with you, young lady, is that you like to fart higher than your ass."

The girl didn't approve of the way her mother spoke. She was barely      5
nine, and one of the best in her class.

"I'm going because I've been invited," she said. "And I've been invited because Luciana is my friend. So there."

"Ah yes, your friend," her mother grumbled. She paused. "Listen, Rosaura," she said at last. "That one's not your friend. You know what you are to them? The maid's daughter, that's what."

Rosaura blinked hard: she wasn't going to cry. Then she yelled: "Shut up! You know nothing about being friends!"

Every afternoon she used to go to Luciana's house and they would both finish their homework while Rosaura's mother did the cleaning. They had their tea in the kitchen and they told each other secrets. Rosaura loved everything in the big house, and she also loved the people who lived there.

"I'm going because it will be the most lovely party in the whole world,     10
Luciana told me it would. There will be a magician, and he will bring a monkey and everything."

The mother swung around to take a good look at her child, and pompously put her hands on her hips.

"Monkeys at a birthday?" she said. "Get away with you, believing any nonsense you're told!"

Rosaura was deeply offended. She thought it unfair of her mother to accuse other people of being liars simply because they were rich. Rosaura too wanted to be rich, of course. If one day she managed to live in a beautiful palace, would her mother stop loving her? She felt very sad. She wanted to go to that party more than anything else in the world.

"I'll die if I don't go," she whispered, almost without moving her lips.

And she wasn't sure whether she had been heard, but on the morning      15
of the party she discovered that her mother had starched her Christmas dress. And in the afternoon, after washing her hair, her mother rinsed it in apple vinegar so that it would be all nice and shiny. Before going out, Rosaura admired herself in the mirror, with her white dress and glossy hair, and thought she looked terribly pretty.

Señora Ines also seemed to notice. As soon as she saw her, she said:

"How lovely you look today, Rosaura."

Rosaura gave her starched skirt a slight toss with her hands and walked

into the party with a firm step. She said hello to Luciana and asked about
the monkey. Luciana put on a secretive look and whispered into Rosaura's
ear: "He's in the kitchen. But don't tell anyone, because it's a surprise."

Rosaura wanted to make sure. Carefully she entered the kitchen and
there she saw it: deep in thought, inside its cage. It looked so funny that
the girl stood there for a while, watching it, and later, every so often, she
would slip out of the party unseen and go and admire it. Rosaura was the
only one allowed into the kitchen. Señora Ines had said: "You yes, but
not the others, they're much too boisterous, they might break something."
Rosaura had never broken anything. She even managed the jug of orange
juice, carrying it from the kitchen into the dining room. She held it
carefully and didn't spill a single drop. And Señora Ines had said: "Are
you sure you can manage a jug as big as that?" Of course she could
manage. She wasn't a butterfingers, like the others. Like that blonde girl
with the bow in her hair. As soon as she saw Rosaura, the girl with the
bow had said:

"And you? Who are you?"                                                    20

"I'm a friend of Luciana," said Rosaura.

"No," said the girl with the bow, "you are not a friend of Luciana
because I'm her cousin and I know all her friends. And I don't know
you."

"So what," said Rosaura. "I come here every afternoon with my mother
and we do our homework together."

"You and your mother do your homework together?" asked the girl,
laughing.

"I and Luciana do our homework together," said Rosaura, very seri-    25
ously.

The girl with the bow shrugged her shoulders.

"That's not being friends," she said. "Do you go to school together?"

"No."

"So where do you know her from?" said the girl, getting impatient.

Rosaura remembered her mother's words perfectly. She took a deep    30
breath.

"I'm the daughter of the employee," she said.

Her mother had said very clearly: "If someone asks, you say you're the
daughter of the employee; that's all." She also told her to add: "And proud
of it." But Rosaura thought that never in her life would she dare say
something of the sort.

"What employee?" said the girl with the bow. "Employee in a shop?"

"No," said Rosaura angrily. "My mother doesn't sell anything in any
shop, so there."

"So how come she's an employee?" said the girl with the bow.         35

Just then Señora Ines arrived saying *shh shh*, and asked Rosaura if she wouldn't mind helping serve out the hotdogs, as she knew the house so much better than the others.

"See?" said Rosaura to the girl with the bow, and when no one was looking she kicked her in the shin.

Apart from the girl with the bow, all the others were delightful. The one she liked best was Luciana, with her golden birthday crown; and then the boys. Rosaura won the sack race, and nobody managed to catch her when they played tag. When they split into two teams to play charades, all the boys wanted her for their side. Rosaura felt she had never been so happy in all her life.

But the best was still to come. The best came after Luciana blew out the candles. First the cake. Señora Ines had asked her to help pass the cake around, and Rosaura had enjoyed the task immensely, because everyone called out to her, shouting "Me, me!" Rosaura remembered a story in which there was a queen who had the power of life or death over her subjects. She had always loved that, having the power of life or death. To Luciana and the boys she gave the largest pieces, and to the girl with the bow she gave a slice so thin one could see through it.

After the cake came the magician, tall and bony, with a fine red cape.   40
A true magician: he could untie handkerchiefs by blowing on them and make a chain with links that had no openings. He could guess what cards were pulled out from a pack, and the monkey was his assistant. He called the monkey "partner." "Let's see here, partner," he would say, "turn over a card." And, "Don't run away, partner: time to work now."

The final trick was wonderful. One of the children had to hold the monkey in his arms and the magician said he would make him disappear.

"What, the boy?" they all shouted.

"No, the monkey!" shouted back the magician.

Rosaura thought that this was truly the most amusing party in the whole world.

The magician asked a small fat boy to come and help, but the small   45
fat boy got frightened almost at once and dropped the monkey on the floor. The magician picked him up carefully, whispered something in his ear, and the monkey nodded almost as if he understood.

"You mustn't be so unmanly, my friend," the magician said to the fat boy.

"What's unmanly?" said the fat boy.

The magician turned around as if to look for spies.

"A sissy," said the magician. "Go sit down."

Then he stared at all the faces, one by one. Rosaura felt her heart   50
tremble.

"You, with the Spanish eyes," said the magician. And everyone saw that he was pointing at her.

She wasn't afraid. Neither holding the monkey, nor when the magician made him vanish; not even when, at the end, the magician flung his red cape over Rosaura's head and uttered a few magic words . . . and the monkey reappeared, chattering happily, in her arms. The children clapped furiously. And before Rosaura returned to her seat, the magician said:

"Thank you very much, my little countess."

She was so pleased with the compliment that a while later, when her mother came to fetch her, that was the first thing she told her.

"I helped the magician and he said to me, 'Thank you very much, my        55
little countess.'"

It was strange because up to then Rosaura had thought that she was angry with her mother. All along Rosaura had imagined that she would say to her: "See that the monkey wasn't a lie?" But instead she was so thrilled that she told her mother all about the wonderful magician.

Her mother tapped her on the head and said: "So now we're a countess!"

But one could see that she was beaming.

And now they both stood in the entrance, because a moment ago Señora Ines, smiling, had said: "Please wait here a second."

Her mother suddenly seemed worried.                                         60

"What is it?" she asked Rosaura.

"What is what?" said Rosaura. "It's nothing; she just wants to get the presents for those who are leaving, see?"

She pointed at the fat boy and at a girl with pigtails who were also waiting there, next to their mothers. And she explained about the presents. She knew, because she had been watching those who left before her. When one of the girls was about to leave, Señora Ines would give her a bracelet. When a boy left, Señora Ines gave him a yo-yo. Rosaura preferred the yo-yo because it sparkled, but she didn't mention that to her mother. Her mother might have said: "So why don't you ask for one, you blockhead?" That's what her mother was like. Rosaura didn't feel like explaining that she'd be horribly ashamed to be the odd one out. Instead she said:

"I was the best-behaved at the party."

And she said no more because Señora Ines came out into the hall with    65
two bags, one pink and one blue.

First she went up to the fat boy, gave him a yo-yo out of the blue bag, and the fat boy left with his mother. Then she went up to the girl and gave her a bracelet out of the pink bag, and the girl with the pigtails left as well.

Finally she came up to Rosaura and her mother. She had a big smile on her face and Rosaura liked that. Señora Ines looked down at her, then looked up at her mother, and then said something that made Rosaura proud:

"What a marvelous daughter you have, Herminia."

For an instant, Rosaura thought that she'd give her two presents: the bracelet and the yo-yo. Señora Ines bent down as if about to look for something. Rosaura also leaned forward, stretching out her arm. But she never completed the movement.

Señora Ines didn't look in the pink bag. Nor did she look in the blue    70 bag. Instead she rummaged in her purse. In her hand appeared two bills.

"You really and truly earned this," she said handing them over. "Thank you for all your help, my pet."

Rosaura felt her arms stiffen, stick close to her body, and then she noticed her mother's hand on her shoulder. Instinctively she pressed herself against her mother's body. That was all. Except her eyes. Rosaura's eyes had a cold, clear look that fixed itself on Señora Ines's face.

Señora Ines, motionless, stood there with her hand outstretched. As if she didn't dare draw it back. As if the slightest change might shatter an infinitely delicate balance.

## EXPLORATIONS

1. In what senses is Luciana's birthday party a stolen party?

2. What central conflict does Liliana Heker establish in her opening paragraph? What conflict does she introduce in her second paragraph? How would the story's balance change if Heker started with the second paragraph, leaving the monkey question until its chronological place?

3. At the end of "The Stolen Party," what is the intended message of Señora Ines's gift to Rosaura? What message does Rosaura draw from the gift? What changes occur in the characters' perceptions of each other, and of themselves, in the story's last two paragraphs?

4. Rosaura has a number of standards for judging people — more specifically, for measuring herself against others. For example, in paragraph 5: "The girl didn't approve of the way her mother spoke. She was barely nine, and one of the best in her class." Find at least four other points in the story when Rosaura makes a comparative judgment. How well does she fare in her own estimation? What do you learn about Rosaura as a character from these judgments?

# CONNECTIONS

1. What seem to be the goals of Luciana's mother for her daughter's birthday party? How do her goals differ from Luciana's? What seem to be the goals of the mothers in charge of the *quinceañera* in Susan Orlean's "Quinceañera" (p. 200)? How would you guess their goals differ from their daughters'?

2. In paragraphs 4–7 of "Tradition and the African Writer" (p. 35), Es'kia Mphahlele discusses "the ever-widening gulf between one and one's parents and one's community" that comes with education (para. 6). Why does Luciana's birthday party open a gulf between Rosaura and her mother? What factors mentioned by Mphahlele are likely to widen this gulf further? Which problems (and remedies) mentioned by Mphahlele are not relevant for Rosaura?

3. How is Rosaura's shock at the end of "The Stolen Party" similar to the disillusion James Baldwin describes in *Looking at Ourselves* (p. 196)? How are her experience and situation different from his?

# ELABORATIONS

1. The characters in "The Stolen Party" — particularly the two mother-daughter pairs — all have different concepts of the extent to which they control their own destinies. Write an essay classifying these concepts: Describe each mother's and daughter's sense of herself as a social actor; identify the factors she views as conferring or limiting her power, such as age, intelligence, and social class; and cite the evidence in the story that supports your conclusions.

2. Heker in "The Stolen Party," James Baldwin in *Looking at Ourselves* (p. 196), and Ved Mehta in "Pom's Engagement" (p. 142) all are concerned with the suffering that comes when youthful innocence ends. In what ways is this suffering due to the young person's ignorance? In what ways is it due to ignorance on the part of the more powerful adults whose world the young person is entering? Write an essay discussing whether and how parents can protect their children from suffering as they enter adulthood. Use evidence from Heker's, Baldwin's, and Mehta's selections to support your ideas.

# SOPHRONIA LIU

## *So Tsi-fai*

Born in Hong Kong in 1953, Sophronia Liu came to the United States to study at the age of twenty. Some of her family are still in Hong Kong; others now live in the United States, Canada, and England. Liu received a bachelor's degree in English and French, and a master's degree in English, from the University of South Dakota. She taught composition at the University of Minnesota while working toward her Ph.D. in English. She returned to Hong Kong in the fall of 1990 to do research for a program she is developing for Asian-American students. Under the program, students will travel abroad to learn about their Asian roots, and they will be encouraged to do autobiographical writing, as Liu has done. Liu's dissertation is her memoir, which she hopes to publish. "So Tsi-fai" was written in response to a class assignment and originally appeared in the Minnesota feminist publication *Hurricane Alice.*

Hong Kong, where Liu attended The Little Flower's School with So Tsi-fai, is a British Crown colony at the mouth of China's Pearl River. Its nucleus is Hong Kong Island, which Britain acquired from China in 1841. Most of the colony's 409 square miles consist of other Chinese territory held by Britain on a ninety-nine-year lease. Hong Kong's population of over five million includes fewer than 20,000 British; it absorbed more than a million Chinese refugees after Mao's Communists won the mainland in 1949. In 1985 China and Britain agreed that Hong Kong will revert to China in 1997, when the lease expires, but will be allowed to keep its social, economic, and legal system for fifty years after that. In the meantime, Hong Kong (meaning "fragrant harbor") remains a thriving capitalist port.

Voices, images, scenes from the past — twenty-three years ago, when I was in sixth grade:

"Let us bow our heads in silent prayer for the soul of So Tsi-fai. Let us pray for God's forgiveness for this boy's rash taking of his own life . . ." Sister Marie (Mung Gu-liang). My sixth-grade English teacher. Missionary nun from Paris. Principal of The Little Flower's School. Disciplinarian, perfectionist, authority figure: awesome and awful in my ten-year-old eyes.

"I don't need any supper. I have drunk enough insecticide." So Tsi-fai. My fourteen-year-old classmate. Daredevil; good-for-nothing lazybones (according to Mung Gu-liang). Bright black eyes, disheveled hair, defiant sneer, creased and greasy uniform, dirty hands, careless walk, shuffling feet. Standing in the corner for being late, for forgetting his homework, for talking in class, for using foul language. ("Shame on you! Go wash your mouth with soap!" Mung Gu-liang's sharp command. He did, and came back with a grin.) So Tsi-fai: Sticking his tongue out behind Mung Gu-liang's back, passing secret notes to his friends, kept behind after school, sent to the Principal's office for repeated offense. So Tsi-fai: incorrigible, hopeless, and without hope.

It was a Monday in late November when we heard of his death, returning to school after the weekend with our parents' signatures on our midterm reports. So Tsi-fai also showed his report to his father, we were told later. He flunked three out of the fourteen subjects: English Grammar, Arithmetic, and Chinese Dictation. He missed each one by one to three marks. That wasn't so bad. But he was a hopeless case. Overaged, stubborn, and uncooperative; a repeated offender of school rules, scourge of all teachers; who was going to give him a lenient passing grade? Besides, being a few months over the maximum age — fourteen — for sixth graders, he wasn't even allowed to sit for the Secondary School Entrance Exam.

All sixth graders in Hong Kong had to pass the SSE before they could      5 obtain a seat in secondary school. In 1964 when I took the exam, there were more than twenty thousand candidates. About seven thousand of us passed: four thousand were sent to government and subsidized schools, the other three thousand to private and grant-in-aid schools. I came in around no. 2000; I was lucky. Without the public exam, there would be no secondary school for So Tsi-fai. His future was sealed.

Looking at the report card with three red marks on it, his father was furious. So Tsi-fai was the oldest son. There were three younger children. His father was a vegetable farmer with a few plots of land in Wong Juk-hang, by the sea. His mother worked in a local factory. So Tsi-fai helped in the fields, cooked for the family, and washed his own clothes. ("Filthy, dirty boy!" gasped Mung Gu-liang. "Grime behind the ears, black rims on the fingernails, dirty collar, crumpled shirt. Why doesn't your mother iron your shirt?") Both his parents were illiterate. So Tsi-fai was their biggest hope: He made it to the sixth grade.

Who woke him up for school every morning and had breakfast waiting for him? Nobody. ("Time for school! Get up! Eat your rice!" Ma nagged and screamed. The aroma of steamed rice and Chinese sausages spread all over the house. "Drink your tea! Eat your oranges! Wash your face! And remember to wash behind your ears!") And who helped So Tsi-fai do his homework? Nobody. Did he have older brothers like mine who knew all about the arithmetic of rowing a boat against the currents or with the currents, how to count the feet of chickens and rabbits in the same cage, the present perfect continuous tense of "to live" and the future perfect tense of "to succeed"? None. Nil. So Tsi-fai was a lost cause.

I came first in both terms that year, the star pupil. So Tsi-fai was one of the last in the class: he was lazy; he didn't care. Or did he?

When his father scolded him, So Tsi-fai left the house. When he showed up again, late for supper, he announced, "I don't need any supper. I have drunk enough insecticide." Just like another one of his practical jokes. The insecticide was stored in the field for his father's vegetables. He was rushed to the hospital; dead upon arrival.

"He gulped for a last breath and was gone," an uncle told us at the funeral. "But his eyes wouldn't shut. So I said in his ear, 'You go now and rest in peace.' And I smoothed my hand over his eyelids. His face was all purple."

His face was still purple when we saw him in his coffin. Eyes shut tight, nostrils dilated and white as if fire and anger might shoot out, any minute.

In class that Monday morning, Sister Marie led us in prayer. "Let us pray that God will forgive him for his sins." We said the Lord's Prayer and the Hail Mary. We bowed our heads. I sat in my chair, frozen and dazed, thinking of the deadly chill in the morgue, the smell of disinfectant, ether, and dead flesh.

"Bang!" went a gust of wind, forcing open a leaf of the double door leading to the back balcony. "Flap, flap, flap." The door swung in the wind. We could see the treetops by the hillside rustling to and fro against a pale blue sky. An imperceptible presence had drifted in with the wind. The same careless walk and shuffling feet, the same daredevil air — except that the eyes were lusterless, dripping blood; the tongue hanging out, gasping for air. As usual, he was late. But he had come back to claim his place.

"I died a tragic death," his voice said. "I have as much right as you to be here. This is my seat." We heard him; we knew he was back.

. . . So Tsi-fai: Standing in the corner for being late, for forgetting his homework, for talking in class, for using foul language. So Tsi-fai: palm outstretched, chest sticking out, holding his breath: "Tat. Tat. Tat." Down came the teacher's wooden ruler, twenty times on each hand. Never batting an eyelash: then back to facing the wall in the corner by the door. So Tsi-fai: grimy shirt, disheveled hair, defiant sneer. So Tsi-fai. Incorrigible, hopeless, and without hope.

The girls in front gasped and shrank back in their chairs. Mung Gu-liang went to the door, held the doorknob in one hand, poked her

10

15

head out, and peered into the empty balcony. Then, with a determined jerk, she pulled the door shut. Quickly crossing herself, she returned to the teacher's desk. Her black cross swung upon the front of her gray habit as she hurried across the room. "Don't be silly!" she scolded the frightened girls in the front row.

What really happened? After all these years, my mind is still haunted by this scene. What happened to So Tsi-fai? What happened to me? What happened to all of us that year in sixth grade, when we were green and young and ready to fling our arms out for the world? All of a sudden, death claimed one of us and he was gone.

Who arbitrates between life and death? Who decides which life is worth preserving and prospering, and which to nip in its bud? How did it happen that I, at ten, turned out to be the star pupil, the lucky one, while my friend, a peasant's son, was shoveled under the heap and lost forever? How could it happen that this world would close off a young boy's life at fourteen just because he was poor, undisciplined, and lacked the training and support to pass his exams? What really happened?

Today, twenty-three years later, So Tsi-fai's ghost still haunts me. "I died a tragic death. I have as much right as you to be here. This is my seat." The voice I heard twenty-three years ago in my sixth-grade classroom follows me in my dreams. Is there anything I can do to lay it to rest?

## EXPLORATIONS

1. How do you think Sophronia Liu regarded So Tsi-fai before his death? How did her view change after his suicide? How can you tell? What other attitudes did Liu evidently reexamine and alter at that point?

2. Whom and what does Liu blame for So Tsi-fai's suicide? What preventive measures does her story suggest to protect other students from a similar fate? Judging from Liu's narrative, what changes in Hong Kong's social and educational institutions do you think would help students like So Tsi-fai?

3. Liu's first three paragraphs consist almost entirely of incomplete sentences. How does she use these sentence fragments to establish her essay's central conflict? At what points does she use complete sentences? What is their effect?

# CONNECTIONS

1. Both Liu's "So Tsi-fai" and Liliana Heker's "The Stolen Party" (p. 212) focus on young people who represent, to themselves or their families or both, ambitions higher than their present circumstances. What disadvantages do So Tsi-fai and Rosaura share? Why does Rosaura appear likely to succeed where So Tsi-fai fails?

2. Like So Tsi-fai, Sugama in John David Morley's "Acquiring a Japanese Family" (p. 122) is his parents' oldest son. What dilemma does this status create for Sugama? What dilemma does it create for So Tsi-fai?

3. Look back at Wole Soyinka's "Nigerian Childhood" (p. 112). Both Soyinka and Liu describe encounters with ghosts. What role does each ghost play in the narrative? How are their dramatic functions different? What cultural similarities do they suggest between Nigeria and Hong Kong?

# ELABORATIONS

1. What is the role of Mung Gu-liang/Sister Marie in "So Tsi-fai"? Do you think the nun would agree with Liu's assessment of what happened? How might her memory and interpretation of these events differ from Liu's? Write a narrative or argumentative version of So Tsi-fai's story from Mung Gu-liang's point of view.

2. When you were in elementary school, who were the outcasts in your class and why? If you recall one student in particular who was regarded as "different," write an essay describing him or her and narrating some of the incidents that set him or her apart. If your class consisted of two or more distinct groups, write an essay classifying these groups according to their special characteristics and their behavior toward each other. In either case, how has your attitude toward the "outcasts" changed?

# MARIO VARGAS LLOSA

## *On Sunday*

Novelist, playwright, and essayist Mario Vargas Llosa made headlines in the spring of 1990 by running for president of Peru. (He lost the close election to agronomist Alberto Fujimori.) Born in Arequipa in 1936, Vargas Llosa received his early education in Bolivia, where his grandfather was the Peruvian consul. Back home in Lima, Peru's capital, his family sent him to military school. His response was to use the school as the setting for his first novel, *La ciudad y los perros* ("The city and the dogs," 1963; published in English as *Time of the Hero*, 1966). Vargas Llosa edited two literary journals and worked as a journalist and broadcaster. Since receiving his doctorate from the University of Madrid, he has lived in Paris, London, and Barcelona and has lectured and taught throughout the West. In addition to numerous novels, plays, and stories, Vargas Llosa is the author of *Gabriel García Márquez: Historia de un deicidio* (1972) and critical studies of the French writers Gustave Flaubert, Jean-Paul Sartre, and Albert Camus. Along with Colombia's García Márquez (see p. 497), Mexico's Carlos Fuentes (see p. 303), and Argentina's Julio Cortázar, Vargas Llosa is a pillar of Latin America's literary "Boom." "On Sunday" ("Día domingo," 1959) first appeared in *Los jefes*; the following translation from the Spanish is by Alastair Reid.

Peru, an arid coastal strip north of Chile along the Pacific Ocean, was the heart of South America's ancient Inca empire. Spaniards led by Francisco Pizarro conquered the region in 1532, reducing the Indians to serfdom. Peru regained its independence almost three hundred years later as part of the general liberation movement among Spain's South American colonies, led by rebels including Simón Bolívar and the Argentine José de San Martín, who took Lima in 1821. The present population is 45 percent Indian, 37 percent mestizo (mixed Spanish and Indian), 15 percent white, and the rest black and Asian. Over 90 percent of Peruvians are Roman Catholic; Spanish and Quechua are both official languages. After a succession of civilian and military governments, a constitutional republic was established in 1980. Democracy, however, did not solve Peru's problems. Vargas Llosa was propelled into politics by his country's corrupt and bloated bureaucracy, economic problems including a nearly 3,000 percent inflation rate, and political violence, mainly by the Maoist guerrilla group Sendero Luminosa ("Shining Path"). Sendero's leader, Abimael Guzman Reynoso, was captured and sentenced to life in prison in 1992, a few months after President Fujimori seized control of the government and dissolved the National Congress.

He held his breath an instant, dug his nails into the palms of his hands, and said quickly: "I'm in love with you." He saw her redden suddenly, as if someone had slapped her cheeks, which had a smooth and pale sheen to them. Terrified, he felt confusion rising and petrifying his tongue. He wanted to run off, be done with it; in the still winter morning, he felt the surge of that inner weakness which always overcame him at decisive moments. A few moments before, among the vivid, smiling throng in the Parque Central in Miraflores, Miguel was still saying to himself: "Now. When we get to Avenida Pardo. I'll take a chance. Ah, Rubén, if you knew how I hate you!" And even earlier, in church, looking for Flora, he spotted her at the foot of a column and, elbowing his way brusquely through the jostling women, he managed to get close to her and greet her in a low voice, repeating tersely to himself, as he had done that morning, stretched on his bed watching the first light: "Nothing else for it. I must do it today, this morning. Rubén, you'll pay for this." And the previous night he had wept for the first time in many years, realizing that the wretched trap lay in wait for him. The crowd had gone on into the park and the Avenida Pardo was left empty. They walked on along the avenue, under the rubber trees with their high, dense foliage. "I have to hurry," Miguel thought, "or else I'll be in trouble." He glanced sideways, round about him. There was nobody; he could try it. Slowly he moved his left hand until it touched hers. The sudden contact told her what was happening. He longed for a miracle to happen, to put an end to that humiliation. "Tell her, tell her," he thought. She stopped, withdrawing her hand, and he felt himself abandoned and foolish. All the glowing phrases prepared passionately the night before had blown away like soap bubbles.

"Flora," he stammered, "I've waited a long time for this moment. Since I've known you, I think only of you. I'm in love for the first time, truly. I've never known a girl like you."

Once again a total blankness in his mind, emptiness. The pressure was extreme. His skin was limp and rubbery and his nails dug into the bone. Even so, he went on speaking painfully, with long pauses, overcoming his stammer, trying to describe his rash, consuming passion, till he found with relief that they had reached the first oval on the Avenida Pardo, and he fell silent. Flora lived between the second and third tree after the oval. They stopped and looked at one another. Flora by now was quite agitated, which lent a bright sheen to her eyes. In despair, Miguel told himself that she had never looked so beautiful. A blue ribbon bound her hair, and he could see where her neck rose, and her ears, two small and perfect question marks.

"Please, Miguel." Her voice was smooth, musical, steady. "I can't answer you now. Besides, my mother doesn't want me to go out with boys until I finish school."

"All mothers say that, Flora," Miguel insisted. "How will she know?    5
We'll meet when you say so, even if it's only Sundays."

"I'll give you an answer, only I have to think first," Flora said, lowering her eyes. And after a moment, she added, "Forgive me, but I have to go. It's late."

Miguel experienced a deep weariness, a feeling which spread through his whole body, relaxing it.

"You're not angry with me, Flora?" he asked, feebly.

"Don't be an idiot," she answered brightly. "I'm not angry."

"I'll wait as long as you want," said Miguel. "But we'll go on seeing    10
each other, won't we? We can go to the movies this afternoon, can't we?"

"I can't this afternoon," she said softly. "Martha's invited me to her house."

A warm flush swept violently through him and he felt himself lacerated, stunned, at the reply he had expected, which now seemed to him torture. So it was true what Melanés had whispered fiercely in his ear on Saturday afternoon. Martha would leave them alone; it was the usual trick. Later, Rubén would tell the gang how he and his brother had planned the setup, the place, and the time. In payment, Martha had claimed the privilege of spying from behind the curtain. His hands were suddenly wet with anger.

"Don't Flora. We'll go to the matinee as usual. I won't speak about this. I promise."

"No, I really can't," said Flora. "I've got to go to Martha's. She came to my house yesterday to invite me. But afterwards I'll go with her to the Parque Salazar."

Not even in those final words did he feel any hope. A moment later,    15
he was brooding on the spot where the slight blue figure had disappeared, under the majestic arch of the rubber trees of the avenue. It was possible to take on a simple adversary, but not Rubén. He remembered the names of the girls invited by Martha, one Sunday afternoon. He could do nothing now; he was beaten. Once more there arose that fantasy which always saved him in moments of frustration: Against a distant background of clouds swollen with black smoke, at the head of a company of cadets from the Naval Academy, he approached a saluting base set up in the park; distinguished people in formal dress, top hats in hand, and ladies with glittering jewels, all applauded him. Thick on the sidewalks, a crowd in which the faces of his friends and enemies stood out, watched him in awe, murmuring his name. Dressed in blue, a broad cape flowing from his shoulders, Miguel marched at the head, gazing off to the horizon. He

raised his sword; his head described a half circle in the air. There, in the center of the stand, was Flora, smiling. In one corner, ragged and ashamed, he noticed Rubén. He confined himself to a brief, contemptuous glance. He went on marching; he disappeared amid cheers.

Like steam wiped off a mirror, the image disappeared. He was in the doorway of his house, hating the whole world, hating himself. He entered and went straight up to his room. He threw himself face down on the bed. In the half-dark under his eyelids appeared the girl's face. "I love you, Flora," he said out loud — and then came the face of Rubén, with his insolent jaw and his mocking smile. The faces were side by side, coming closer. Rubén's eyes turned to mock him while his mouth approached Flora.

He jumped up from his bed. The wardrobe mirror gave him back a face both ravaged and livid. I won't allow it, he decided. He can't do that, I won't let him pull that on me.

The Avenida Pardo was still empty. Increasing his pace, he walked on till it crossed Avenida Grau; there he hesitated. He felt the cold — he had left his jacket in his room and his shirt alone was not enough to protect him from the wind which came from the sea and which combed the dense foliage of the rubber trees in a steady swish. The dreaded image of Flora and Rubén together gave him courage and he went on walking. From the door of the bar beside the Montecarlo cinema, he saw them at their usual table, occupying the corner formed by the far and left-hand walls. Francisco, Melanés, Tobías, the Scholar, they noticed him and, after a second's surprise, they turned toward Rubén, their faces wicked and excited. He recovered himself at once — in front of men he certainly knew how to behave.

"Hello," he said, approaching. "What's new?"

"Sit." The Scholar drew up a chair. "What miracle brings you here?"  20

"It's a century since you've been this way," said Francisco.

"I was keen to see you," Miguel said warmly. "I knew you'd be here. What are you so surprised about? Or am I no longer a Buzzard?" He took a seat between Melanés and Tobías. Rubén was opposite him.

"Cuncho!" called the Scholar. "Bring another glass. Not too dirty a one." When he brought the glass and the Scholar filled it with beer, Miguel toasted "To the Buzzards!" and drank it down.

"You'd have the glass as well!" said Francisco. "What a thirst!"

"I bet you went to one o'clock Mass," said Melanés, winking one eye  25
in satisfaction, as he always did when he was up to something. "Right?"

"Yes, I went," said Miguel, unperturbed. "But only to see a chick, nothing more."

He looked at Rubén with a challenge in his eyes, but Rubén paid no attention. He was drumming on the table with his fingers and, the point of his tongue between his teeth, he whistled softly "La Niña Popoff."

"Great," Melanés applauded. "Great, Don Juan. Tell us, which chick?"

"That's a secret."

"Among the Buzzards, there are no secrets," Tobías reminded him. 30 "Have you forgotten? Come on, who was it?"

"What's it to you?" said Miguel.

"A lot," said Tobías. "I have to know who you go with to know who you are."

"There you are!" said Melanés to Miguel. "One to zero."

"I'll bet I can guess who it is," said Francisco. "Can't you?"

"I know," said Tobías.                                                         35

"Me too," said Melanés. He turned to Rubén, his eyes and voice all innocence. "And you, brother, can you guess? Who is it?"

"No," said Rubén coldly. "And I couldn't care less."

"My stomach's on fire," said the Scholar. "Is nobody going to order a beer?"

Melanés drew a pathetic finger across his throat. "I have not money, darling," he said in English.

"I'll buy a bottle," Tobías announced with a grand gesture. "Who'll 40 follow me? We have to quench this moron's fire."

"Cuncho, bring a half dozen Cristals," said Miguel. Cries of enthusiasm, exclamations.

"You're a real Buzzard," Francisco affirmed.

"Crazy, crazy," added Melanés. "Yes sir, a Top Buzzard."

Cuncho brought the beers. They drank. They listened to Melanés tell dirty stories, crude, exaggerated, and lushed-up, and a bitter argument on football broke out between Tobías and Francisco. The Scholar told a story. He was coming from Lima to Miraflores on a bus. The other passengers got off at the Avenida Arequipa. At the top of Javier Prado, Tomasso got on, the one they call the White Whale, that giant albino who's still in the first grade, lives in Quebrada, get it? — pretending to be interested in the bus, he began to ask the driver questions, leaning over the seat from behind, at the same time slicing the cloth of the seat back systematically with a knife.

"He did it because I was there," the Scholar said. "He wanted to show 45 off."

"He's a mental degenerate," said Francisco. "You do things like that when you're ten. At his age it isn't funny."

"The funny thing is what happened next," laughed the Scholar. "'Listen, driver, don't you know that that monster is destroying your bus?'"

"What's that?" said the driver, braking suddenly. Ears flaming, eyes wide with fright, Tomasso the Whale forced his way out the door.

"With his knife," the Scholar said. "Imagine the state he left the seat in."

The Whale finally managed to get out of the bus. He set off at a run 50 down the Avenida Arequipa. The driver ran after him shouting: "Grab that creep!"

"He got him?" Melanés asked.

"I don't know. I got out. And I took the ignition key as a souvenir. Here it is."

He took a little silver key from his pocket and placed it on the table. The bottles were empty. Rubén looked at his watch and stood up.

"I'm off," he said. "See you."

"Don't go," said Miguel. "Today I'm rich. I invite you all to eat." 55

A shower of hands clapped him on the back; the Buzzards thanked him noisily, cheered him.

"I can't," said Rubén. "I have things to do."

"All right then, go, my boy," Tobías said. "Say hello to Martha for me."

"We'll be thinking about you, brother," said Melanés.

"No," Miguel shot out. "I'm inviting everybody or nobody. If Rubén 60 goes, it's off."

"You hear him Buzzard Rubén?" said Francisco. "You've got to stay."

"You've got to stay," said Melanés, "no question."

"I'm going," said Rubén.

"The thing is that you're drunk," said Miguel. "You're going because you're afraid of screwing up in front of us, that's all."

"How many times have I taken you home nearly passed out?" said 65 Rubén. "How many times have I helped you up the railing so your father wouldn't catch you? I can hold ten times more than you."

"You could," said Miguel. "Now it'd be difficult. Want to try?"

"With pleasure," said Rubén. "We'll meet tonight, here?"

"No. Right now." Miguel turned to the others, arms open. "Buzzards, I'm making a challenge."

Fortunately, the old formula still worked. In the midst of the noisy excitement he had provoked, he saw Rubén sit down, pale.

"Cuncho!" shouted Tobías. "The menu. And two baths of beer. A 70 Buzzard has just made a challenge."

They ordered steaks *a la chorrillana* and a dozen beers. Tobías put three bottles in front of each of the competitors. The others had the rest. They ate, scarcely speaking. Miguel drank after each mouthful and tried to show some zest, but the fear of not being able to hold the beer grew in proportion to the acid taste in his throat. They finished the six bottles just after Cuncho had taken the plates away.

"You order," said Miguel to Rubén.

"Three more each."

After the first glass of the new round, Miguel felt a buzzing in his ears. His head was spinning slowly; everything was moving.

"I need to piss," he said. "I'm going to the john." The Buzzards        75
laughed.

"Give up?" asked Rubén.

"I'm going to piss," shouted Miguel. "Have them bring more if you want."

In the lavatory, he vomited. Then he washed his face thoroughly, trying to remove every revealing sign. His watch said half past four. In spite of the overwhelming sick feeling, he felt happy. Rubén could do nothing. He went back to the others.

"*Salud!*" said Rubén, raising his glass.

He's furious, Miguel thought. But I've stopped him now.        80

"There's corpse smell," said Melanés. "Someone here's dying on us."

"I'm like new," affirmed Miguel, trying to overcome both his disgust and his sickness.

"*Salud!*" repeated Rubén.

When they had finished the last beer, his stomach felt leaden; the voices of the others reached him as a confused mixture of sounds. A hand appeared suddenly under his eyes, white and large-fingered, took him by the chin, and forced him to raise his head. Rubén's face had grown. He was comical, all tousled and angry.

"Give up, kid?"        85

Miguel pulled himself together suddenly and pushed Rubén, but before the gesture could be followed up, the Scholar intervened.

"Buzzards never fight," he said, making them sit down. "They're both drunk. It's all over. Vote."

Melanés, Francisco, and Tobías agreed, grumblingly, to declare a draw.

"I already had it won," said Rubén. "This one's incapable. Look at him."

Indeed, Miguel's eyes were glassy, his mouth hung open, and a thread        90
of saliva ran from his tongue.

"Shut up," said the Scholar. "You are no champion, as we say, at beer-swilling."

"You're not beer-drinking champion," added Melanés. "You're only the swimming champion, the scourge of the swimming pools."

"Better keep quiet," said Rubén. "Can't you see you're eaten up with envy?"

"Long live the Esther Williams of Miraflores," said Melanés.

"Over the hill already and you hardly know how to swim," said Rubén.     95
"Don't you want me to give you lessons?"

"Now we know it all, champ," said the Scholar. "You've won a swimming championship. And all the chicks are dying over you. The little champ."

"Champion of nothing," said Miguel with difficulty. "He's a phony."

"You're about to pass out," said Rubén. "Will I take you home, girl?"

"I'm not drunk," Miguel insisted. "And you're a phony."

"You're pissed off because I'm going to see Flora," said Rubén. "You're     100
dying of jealousy. Do you think I don't catch on to things?"

"Phony," said Miguel. "You won because your father is Federation President. Everybody knows that he pulled a fast one, just so you would win."

"And you most of all," said Rubén, "you can't even surf."

"You swim no better than anyone else," said Miguel. "Anybody could leave you silly."

"Anybody," said Melanés. "Even Miguel, who is a creep."

"Permit me to smile," said Rubén.     105

"We permit you," said Tobías. "That's all we need."

"You're getting at me because it's winter," said Rubén. "If it weren't, I'd challenge you all to go to the beach to see if you'd be so cocky in the water."

"You won the championship because of your father," said Miguel. "You're a phony. When you want to take me on swimming, just let me know, that's all. On the beach, in Terrazas, where you like."

"On the beach," said Rubén. "Right now."

"You're a phony," said Miguel.     110

"If you win," said Rubén, "I promise I won't see Flora. And if I win, you can go sing somewhere else."

"Who do you think you are?" stammered Miguel. "Bastard, just who do you think you are?"

"Buzzards," said Rubén, spreading his arms, "I'm offering a challenge."

"Miguel's not in shape now," said the Scholar. "Why don't you just toss for Flora?"

"You keep out of it," said Miguel. "I accept. Let's go to the beach."     115

"They're crazy," said Francisco. "I'm not going to the beach in this cold. Make a different bet."

"He's accepted," said Rubén. "Let's go."

"When a Buzzard makes a challenge, everyone holds his tongue," said Melanés. "Let's go to the beach. And if they're scared to go in, we'll throw them in ourselves."

"They're both drunk," the Scholar insisted. "The challenge doesn't stand."

"Shut up, Scholar," roared Miguel. "I'm a big boy. I don't need you to look after me."                                                                           120

"All right," said the Scholar, shrugging his shoulders. "Suit yourself, then."

They went out. Outside, a quiet grayness hung in wait for them. Miguel took deep breaths; he felt better. Francisco, Melanés, and Rubén walked ahead, Miguel and the Scholar behind. There were a few idlers on the Avenida Grau, mostly maids dressed up, out on their free day. Gray-looking men, with long lank hair, followed them and watched them greedily. They laughed, showing gold teeth. The Buzzards paid no attention. They walked with long strides, excitement slowly growing in them.

"Feeling better?" said the Scholar.

"Yes," replied Miguel. "The fresh air's done me good."

At the corner of Avenida Pardo, they turned. They walked, deployed                 125
like a squadron, in the same line, under the rubber trees of the walk, over the flagstones bulged from time to time by huge tree roots which occasionally broke through the surface like great hooks. Going down Diagonal, they passed two girls. Rubén bowed to them, very formally.

"Hello, Rubén," they sang out together.

Tobías imitated them, fluting his voice.

"Hello, Prince Rubén."

The Avenida Diagonal gave out on a short bend which forked; in one direction wound the Malecón, paved and shining; in the other, there was an incline which followed the downward slope and reached the sea. It is called the "bathers' descent" and its surface is smooth and shines from the polish of car tires and the feet of bathers from many summers.

"Let's give off some heat, champs," shouted Melanés, breaking into a                 130
run. The others followed him.

They ran against the wind and the thin fog which came up from the beach, caught up in a whirlwind of feeling. Through ears, mouth, and nostrils, the air came in, into their lungs, and a feeling of relief and clearheadedness spread through their bodies as the slope steepened and suddenly their feet obeyed only a mysterious force which seemed to come from deep in the earth. Arms whirling like propellers, a salty tang on their tongues, the Buzzards ran down in full cry to the circular platform over the bathing huts. The sea disappeared some fifty meters from the shore, in a thick cloud which seemed ready to charge against the cliffs, the high dark bulk of which spread all along the bay.

"Let's go back," said Francisco. "I'm frozen."

At the edge of the platform there was a banister stained here and there with moss. An opening in it indicated the head of the almost vertical ladder which led down to the bench. The Buzzards looked down from there at a short strip of clear water, its surface unbroken, frothing where the fog seemed to join with the foam from the waves.

"I'll leave if this one gives up," said Rubén.

"Who's talking about giving up?" retorted Miguel. "Who do you think     135
you are?"

Rubén went down the ladder three rungs at a time, unbuttoning his shirt as he did so.

"Rubén!" shouted the Scholar. "Are you crazy? Come back!"

But Miguel and the others also went down, and the Scholar followed them.

From the terrace of the long, wide building backed against the cliff, which contains the changing rooms, down to the curving edge of the sea, there is a stretch of smooth stones where, in summer, people took the sun. The small beach hummed with life then, from early morning until twilight. Now the water was well up the slope, there were no brightly colored umbrellas, no elastic girls with bronzed bodies, no melodramatic screams of children and women when a wave succeeded in splashing them before receding backward over the groaning stones and pebbles, there was not a strip of beach to be seen under the flooding current which went up as far as the dark narrow space under the columns which held up the building; and in the surge of the tide, it was difficult to make out the wooden ladders and the cement supports, hung with stalactites and seaweed.

"You can't see the surf," said Rubén. "How will we do it?"     140

They were in the left-hand gallery, the women's section; their faces were serious.

"Wait until tomorrow," said the Scholar. "At noon it will be clear. Then you can judge it."

"Now that we've come all the way, let it be now," said Melanés. "They can judge it themselves."

"All right by me," said Rubén. "You?"

"Fine," said Miguel.     145

When they had undressed, Tobías joked about the veins which spread across Miguel's smooth stomach. They went down. The wood of the steps, steadily worn for months by the water, was slippery and very smooth. Holding the iron rail so as not to fall, Miguel felt a shiver run from the soles of his feet to his brain. He figured that, in some ways, the mist and the cold were in his favor, that success would depend not so much on skill as on endurance, and Rubén's skin was already purple, risen all over in gooseflesh. One rung lower, Rubén's neat body bent forward. Tensed, he waited for the ebb and the arrival of the next wave, which came evenly, lightly, leading with a flying crest of foam. When the top of the wave was two meters from the ladder, Rubén leaped. His arms stretched like arrows, his hair streaming with the dive, his body cut the air cleanly, and fell without bending, his head not dropping, his knees straight, he entered the foam, hardly going down at all, and immediately, making use of the tide, he glided forward; his arms appeared and disappeared in a frenzy of bubbles, and his feet were leaving behind a steady, flying wake. Miguel in turn climbed down one rung and waited for the next wave. He knew that the bottom there was shallow, that he would have to dive like a board, hard and rigid, without moving, or he would scrape the stones. He closed his eyes and dived; he did not touch bottom but his body was lacerated from forehead to knees, and he stung all over as he swam with all his strength to bring back to his limbs the warmth which the water had suddenly drained away. In that stretch of sea beside the Miraflores beach, the waves and undertow meet, there are whirlpools and conflicting currents, and last summer was so far away that Miguel had forgotten how to ride the water without using force. He did not remember that you had to go limp, let go, let yourself be carried with the ebb, submitting, swimming only when a wave gets up and you are on the crest, on that shelf of water where the foam is, which runs on top of the water. He forgot that it is better to suffer with patience and a certain resistance that first contact with the sea ebbing from the beach, which tumbles the limbs and makes water stream from eyes and mouth, not to resist, to be a cork, to gulp air, nothing more, every time a wave comes in without force, or through the bottom of the wave if the breaking crest is close — to cling to a rock and wait out patiently the deafening thunder of its passing, to push out sharply and keep forging ahead, furtively, with the arms, until the next obstacle, and then to go limp, not struggling against the undertow but moving slowly and deliberately in a widening spiral and suddenly escaping, at the right moment, in a single burst. Farther out, the surface is unexpectedly calm, the movement of surf small; the water is clear and level, and at some points you can make out dark, underwater rocks.

After fighting his way through the rough water, Miguel stopped, exhausted, and gulped air. He saw Rubén not far away, looking at him. His hair fell in curls on his forehead; his teeth were bared.

"Let's go."

"Okay."

After swimming a few moments, Miguel felt the cold, which had     150
momentarily gone, surge back, and he stepped up his kick, for it was in the legs, above all in the calves, where the water had most effect, numbing them first and then stiffening them. He was swimming with his face in

the water, and every time his right arm came out of the water, he turned his head to get rid of his held breath and to breathe again, immediately dipping his forehead and chin, lightly, so as not to check his forward motion, and to make instead a prow which parted the water, the easier to slip through. At each stroke he would see Rubén with one eye, swimming smoothly on the surface, not exerting himself, scarcely raising a wash, with the ease and delicacy of a gliding gull. Miguel tried to forget Rubén and the sea and the surf (which must still have been some distance away, for the water was clear, calm, and crossed only by small, spontaneous waves). He wanted to keep in mind only Flora's face, the down on her arms which on sunny days gleamed like a small forest of gold thread, but he could not prevent the girl's face from being succeeded by another image, shrouded, dominant, thunderous, which tumbled over Flora and hid her, the image of a mountain of tormented water, not exactly the surf (they had once reached the surf, two summers ago, with its thundering waves and greenish-black foam, for out there, more or less, the rocks ended and gave way to mud, which the waves brought to the surface and stirred up with clumps of seaweed, staining the water), instead a sea on its own wracked by internal storms, in which rose up enormous waves which could have lifted up a whole ship and upset it quickly and easily, scattering passengers, lifeboats, masts, sails, buoys, sailors, bull's-eyes, and flags.

He stopped swimming, his body sinking until it was vertical. He raised his head and saw Rubén drawing away. He thought of calling to him on some pretext, of shouting for example, "Why don't we rest a moment?" but he refrained. All the cold in his body seemed to be concentrated in his calves; he felt the muscles growing numb, the skin tightening, his heartbeat accelerating. He moved his legs weakly. He was in the center of a circle of dark water, enclosed by the fog. He tried to make out the beach, or at least the shadow of the cliffs, but the fog which appeared to dissolve as he penetrated it was deceptive, and not in the least transparent. He saw only a short stretch of sea surface, blackish, green, and the shrouding clouds, flush with the water. At that point he felt fear. The memory of the beer he had drunk came back and he thought "That could have weakened me, I suppose." Suddenly it seemed that his arms and legs had disappeared. He decided to go back, but after a few strokes in the direction of the beach, he turned and swam as easily as he could. "I won't make the beach alone," he thought: "Better to be close to Rubén. If I poop out I'll tell him he's won but we'll get back." Now he was swimming carelessly, his head up, swallowing water, stiff-armed, his eyes fixed on the imperturbable shape ahead of him.

The activity and the energy relaxed his legs, and his body recovered some warmth. The distance between him and Rubén had lessened and that calmed him. Shortly after, he caught him up; flinging out an arm, he touched one of Rubén's feet. Immediately the other stopped. Rubén's eyes were very red, his mouth open.

"I think we've gone off course," said Miguel. "We seem to be swimming sideways on to the beach."

His teeth were chattering, but his voice was firm. Rubén looked all around him. Miguel watched him, tense.

"You can't see the beach any more," said Rubén.                    155

"Not for some time," said Miguel. "There's a lot of fog."

"We haven't gone off," said Rubén. "Look. There's the surf."

Actually, some waves were reaching them with a fringe of foam which dissolved and suddenly formed again. They looked at them in silence.

"Then we're close to the surf," Miguel said, finally.

"Sure. We've been swimming fast."                              160

"I've never seen so much fog."

"Are you very tired?" asked Rubén.

"Me? You're crazy. Let's go."

He immediately regretted that reply, but it was now too late. Rubén had already said, "Okay, let's go."

He had counted twenty strokes before he decided that he could not    165
go on. He was hardly moving forward; his right leg was semiparalyzed by cold, his arms felt limp and heavy. Panting, he called out, "Rubén!" The other one kept on swimming. "Rubén, Rubén!" He turned and began to swim toward the beach, or to splash, rather, in desperation; and suddenly he was praying to God to save him, he would be good in the future, he would obey his parents, he would not miss Sunday mass, and then he remembered having confessed to the Buzzards, "I go to church only to see a chick," and he was struck by the certainty that God was going to punish him by drowning him in those troubled waters which he was desperately battling, waters beneath which a terrible death was awaiting him and, beyond that, possibly Hell itself. Into his distress there suddenly swam up a phrase used occasionally by Father Alberto in his religion class, that divine mercy knows no limits, and while he flailed at the water with his arms — his legs were hanging down like lead weights — moving his lips, he prayed to God to be good to him, he was so young, and he swore that he would become a priest if saved, but a second later he corrected that quickly and promised that instead of becoming a priest he would offer up sacrifices and other things and dispense charity, and then he realized that hesitation and bargaining at so desperate a time could prove fatal, and suddenly he heard, quite close, wild shouts coming from

Rubén, and, turning his head, he saw him, some ten meters away, his face half submerged, waving an arm, pleading:

"Miguel, friend Miguel, come, I'm drowning. Don't go!"

He remained rigid a moment, puzzled, and then it was as if Rubén's desperation stifled his own, for he felt his courage and strength return, and the tightness in his legs relax.

"I have a stomach cramp," Rubén hissed out. "I can't go on, Miguel. Save me, whatever you do, don't leave me, pal."

He floated toward Rubén and was about to go to him when he remembered that drowning men always manage to hang on like leeches to their rescuers, drowning them with them, and he kept his distance, but the cries frightened him and he realized that if Rubén drowned, he would not reach the beach either, and he went back. Two meters from Rubén, a white shriveled mass which sank and then rose, he shouted: "Don't move, Rubén. I'm going to pull you by the head, but don't try to hang on to me. If you hang on we'll both drown. Rubén, you're going to keep still, pal. I'm going to pull you by the head but don't touch me." He kept a safe distance, stretching out a hand until he grasped Rubén's hair. He began to swim with his free arm, doing all he could to help himself along with his legs. Progress was slow and painful. He concentrated all his efforts and scarcely heard Rubén's steady groaning, or the sudden terrible cries of "I'm going to die; save me, Miguel!" or the retching that convulsed him. He was exhausted when he stopped. He supported Rubén with one hand, making a circular sweep on the surface with the other. He breathed deeply through his mouth. Rubén's face was twisted in pain, his lips drawn back in a strange grimace.

"Friend Rubén," gasped Miguel, "there's not far to go. Have a shot at    170
it. Answer me, Rubén. Shout. Don't stay like that."

He slapped him sharply, and Rubén opened his eyes; he moved his head weakly.

"Shout, pal," Miguel repeated. "Try to move yourself. I'm going to massage your stomach. It's not far now. Don't give up."

His hands went underwater and found the tightness of Rubén's stomach muscles, spreading over his belly. He rubbed them several times, slowly at first, and then strongly, and Rubén shouted, "I don't want to die, Miguel; save me!"

He began to swim again, this time pulling Rubén by his chin. Each time a wave caught up with them, Rubén choked, and Miguel shouted at him to spit out. And he kept swimming, not resting a moment, closing his eyes at times, in good spirits because a kind of confidence had sprung up in his heart, a warm, proud, stimulating feeling which protected him against the cold and fatigue. A stone scraped one of his feet, and he shouted aloud, and hurried. A moment later he was able to stand up, and he reached out his arms to support Rubén. Holding him against himself, feeling his head leaning on one of his shoulders, he rested a long time. Then he helped Rubén to move and loosen his shoulders, and supporting him on his forearms, he made him move his knees. He massaged his stomach until the tightness began to yield. Rubén had stopped shouting and was doing all he could to get moving again, massaging himself with his own hands.

"Better?"                                                                          175

"Yes, pal. I'm fine. Let's go."

An inexpressible joy filled them as they made their way over the stones, leaning forward against the undertow, oblivious of sea urchins. Soon they caught sight of the groins of the cliffs, the bathing house, and finally, close to the water's edge by now, the Buzzards, standing in the women's gallery, looking out.

"Listen," Rubén said.

"Yes."

"Don't say anything to them. Please don't tell them I was crying for      180
help. We've always been good friends, Miguel. Don't do that to me."

"Think I'm a creep?" said Miguel. "I won't say a thing, don't worry."

They came out shivering. They sat down on the foot of the ladder, with the Buzzards buzzing around them.

"We were ready to send out condolences to your families," said Tobías.

"You've been in over an hour," said the Scholar. "Tell us, how did it come out?"

Speaking steadily, drying his body with his shirt, Rubén explained:    185
"Nothing at all. We got to the surf and then we came back. That's how the Buzzards do things. Miguel beat me. By nothing more than a hand's reach. If it had been in a pool, of course, I'd have made him look silly."

A rain of congratulatory handclaps fell on the shoulders of Miguel, who had dressed without drying himself.

"Why, you're becoming a man," Melanés said to him.

Miguel did not reply. Smiling, he thought that that very evening he would go to the Parque Salazar. All Miraflores would know, thanks to Melanés's ready mouth, of the heroic trials he had come through and Flora would be waiting for him with shining eyes. Before him was opening a golden future.

# EXPLORATIONS

1. In the first paragraph of "On Sunday," why does Miguel think, "Ah, Rubén, if you knew how I hate you!" and "Rubén, you'll pay for this"? What has apparently been the relationship between Miguel and Flora up until now? Between Miguel and Rubén?

2. When Miguel and Rubén stagger onto the shore, why are they filled with "an inexpressible joy" (para. 177)? What has Miguel learned from his swimming contest with Rubén?

3. In what ways does the outcome of the swimming match resemble Miguel's fantasy in paragraph 15? How and why is Miguel's response in reality different from his response in fantasy?

4. What are Flora's dramatic functions in "On Sunday"? What information does Mario Vargas Llosa give us about the kind of person she is? What seem to be Miguel's and Rubén's reasons for vying for her? How much control does Flora have over her role in this drama?

# CONNECTIONS

1. What common purpose is shared by Miguel when he risks his life in the ocean and So Tsi-fai in Sophronia Liu's essay (p. 219) when he drinks insecticide? How and why are these young men's purposes different?

2. In what ways does Miguel's experience in "On Sunday" qualify as the kind of turning point described by Michael Dorris in *Looking at Ourselves* (p. 188)?

3. "Whatever tentative memberships we try out in the world, the fear haunts us that we are really kids who cannot take care of ourselves," writes Gail Sheehy in *Looking at Ourselves* (p. 187). What statements and acts in "On Sunday" are examples of Sheehy's observations?

# ELABORATIONS

1. In "On Sunday," Miguel's feelings about Flora strongly affect his feelings about Rubén, and vice versa. What do you think are the likely advantages and disadvantages of this two-way influence? Write an essay comparing and contrasting the importance of opposite-sex relationships and same-sex relationships to someone moving, like Miguel, from youth into adulthood.

2. Look closely at Vargas Llosa's long description of the swimming match between Miguel and Rubén. What passages could apply to either or both of the relationships in which Miguel is floundering? Write an essay examining the parallels between the literal sea and the sea of human drama in this story.

# SALMAN RUSHDIE

## *The Broken Mirror*

Ahmed Salman Rushdie was born in Bombay, India, in 1947. His wealthy Muslim family sent him to a British-style private school in Bombay until he was thirteen, then to Rugby, an elite private school in England. He published his first novel in 1975; his second novel, *Midnight's Children* (1979), won the prestigious Booker Prize. The book that made Rushdie famous, however, is *The Satanic Verses* (1988). Immediately banned in India, *The Satanic Verses* caused a worldwide uproar for allegedly blaspheming the Islamic religion. On February 14, 1989, the Iranian Ayatollah Khomeini issued a *fatwa*, or death sentence, offering a $1 million reward to any Muslim who assassinates Rushdie (see p. 162). Rushdie went into hiding in England and has stayed hidden ever since, guarded by Scotland Yard's Special Branch. He and his wife separated and later divorced. In 1990 he declared himself a Muslim; but Khomeini's successor, the Ayatollah Khamenei, refused to withdraw the *fatwa*, and Rushdie recanted his conversion. In 1991 the novel's Italian translator was knifed and its Japanese translator was murdered. Despite pressure from the West, Iran's President Rafsanjani and parliament have upheld the *fatwa*, and religious leader Khamenei has raised the reward to between $2 and 3 million. Rushdie's novel *The Moor's Last Sigh* is due to be published in 1994. "The Broken Mirror," written before the *fatwa*, comes from his book *Imaginary Homelands* (1991).

For information on India, see pages 134 and 142. For information on England, see page 551.

An old photograph in a cheap frame hangs on a wall of the room where I work. It's a picture dating from 1946 of a house into which, at the time of its taking, I had not yet been born. The house is rather peculiar — a three-storied gabled affair with tiled roofs and round towers in two corners, each wearing a pointy tiled hat. "The past is a foreign country," goes the famous opening sentence of L. P. Hartley's novel *The Go-Between*, "they do things differently there." But the photograph tells me to invert this idea; it reminds me that it's my present that is foreign, and that the past is home, albeit a lost home in a lost city in the mists of lost time.

A few years ago I revisited Bombay, which is my lost city, after an absence of something like half my life. Shortly after arriving, acting on an impulse, I opened the telephone directory and looked for my father's name. And, amazingly, there it was; his name, our old address, the unchanged telephone number, as if we had never gone away to the unmentionable country across the border. It was an eerie discovery. I felt as if I were being claimed, or informed that the facts of my faraway life were illusions, and that this continuity was the reality. Then I went to visit the house in the photograph and stood outside it, neither daring nor wishing to announce myself to its new owners. (I didn't want to see how they'd ruined the interior.) I was overwhelmed. The photograph had naturally been taken in black and white; and my memory, feeding on such images as this, had begun to see my childhood in the same way, monochromatically. The colors of my history had seeped out of my mind's eye; now my other two eyes were assaulted by colors, by the vividness of the red tiles, the yellow-edged green of cactus-leaves, the brilliance of bougainvillaea creeper. It is probably not too romantic to say that that was when my novel *Midnight's Children* was really born; when I realized how much I wanted to restore the past to myself, not in the faded grays of old family-album snapshots, but whole, in CinemaScope and glorious Technicolor.

Bombay is a city built by foreigners upon reclaimed land; I, who had been away so long that I almost qualified for the title, was gripped by the conviction that I, too, had a city and a history to reclaim.

It may be that writers in my position, exiles or emigrants or expatriates, are haunted by some sense of loss, some urge to reclaim, to look back, even at the risk of being mutated into pillars of salt.[1] But if we do look back, we must also do so in the knowledge — which gives rise to profound uncertainties — that our physical alienation from India almost inevitably means that we will not be capable of reclaiming precisely the thing that was lost; that we will, in short, create fictions, not actual cities or villages, but invisible ones, imaginary homelands, Indias of the mind.

Writing my book in North London, looking out through my window onto a city scene totally unlike the ones I was imagining onto paper, I was constantly plagued by this problem, until I felt obliged to face it in the text, to make clear that (in spite of my original and I suppose somewhat Proustian ambition to unlock the gates of lost time so that the past reappeared as it actually had been, unaffected by the distortions of memory) what I was actually doing was a novel of memory and about memory, so that my India was just that: "my" India, a version and no more than one version of all the hundreds of millions of possible versions. 5

---

[1]Rushdie refers to the biblical story of Lot, whose wife was turned into a pillar of salt when she disobeyed God's order not to look back as the couple fled their homeland. — ED.

I tried to make it as imaginatively true as I could, but imaginative truth is simultaneously honorable and suspect, and I knew that my India may only have been one to which I (who am no longer what I was, and who by quitting Bombay never became what perhaps I was meant to be) was, let us say, willing to admit I belonged.

This is why I made my narrator, Saleem, suspect in his narration; his mistakes are the mistakes of a fallible memory compounded by quirks of character and of circumstance, and his vision is fragmentary. It may be that when the Indian writer who writes from outside India tries to reflect that world, he is obliged to deal in broken mirrors, some of whose fragments have been irretrievably lost.

But there is a paradox here. The broken mirror may actually be as valuable as the one which is supposedly unflawed. Let me again try and explain this from my own experience. Before beginning *Midnight's Children*, I spent many months trying simply to recall as much of the Bombay of the 1950s and 1960s as I could; and not only Bombay — Kashmir, too, and Delhi and Aligarh, which, in my book, I've moved to Agra to heighten a certain joke about the Taj Mahal. I was genuinely amazed by how much came back to me. I found myself remembering what clothes people had worn on certain days, and school scenes, and whole passages of Bombay dialogue verbatim, or so it seemed; I even remembered advertisements, film posters, the neon Jeep sign on Marine Drive, toothpaste ads for Binaca and for Kolynos, and a footbridge over the local railway line which bore, on one side, the legend "Esso puts a tiger in your tank" and, on the other, the curiously contradictory admonition: "Drive like Hell and you will get there." Old songs came back to me from nowhere. . . .

I knew that I had tapped a rich seam; but the point I want to make is that of course I'm not gifted with total recall, and it was precisely the partial nature of these memories, their fragmentation, that made them so evocative for me. The shards of memory acquired greater status, greater resonance, because they were *remains*; fragmentation made trivial things seem like symbols, and the mundane acquired numinous[2] qualities. There is an obvious parallel here with archaeology. The broken pots of antiquity, from which the past can sometimes, but always provisionally, be reconstructed, are exciting to discover, even if they are pieces of the most quotidian[3] objects.

---

[2]Spiritual, supernatural, mysterious. — ED.
[3]Everyday. — ED.

It may be argued that the past is a country from which we have all emigrated, that its loss is part of our common humanity. Which seems to me self-evidently true; but I suggest that the writer who is out-of-country and even out-of-language may experience this loss in an intensified form. It is made more concrete for him by the physical fact of discontinuity, of his present being in a different place from his past, of his being "else-where." This may enable him to speak properly and concretely on a subject of universal significance and appeal.

But let me go further. The broken glass is not merely a mirror of    10
nostalgia. It is also, I believe, a useful tool with which to work in the present.

John Fowles begins *Daniel Martin* with the words: "Whole sight: or all the rest is desolation." But human beings do not perceive things whole; we are not gods but wounded creatures, cracked lenses, capable only of fractured perceptions. Partial beings, in all the senses of that phrase. Meaning is a shaky edifice we build out of scraps, dogmas, childhood injuries, newspaper articles, chance remarks, old films, small victories, people hated, people loved; perhaps it is because our sense of what is the case is constructed from such inadequate materials that we defend it so fiercely, even to the death. The Fowles position seems to me a way of succumbing to the guru-illusion. Writers are no longer sages, dispensing the wisdom of the centuries. And those of us who have been forced by cultural displacement to accept the provisional nature of all truths, all certainties, have perhaps had modernism forced upon us. We can't lay claim to Olympus, and are thus released to describe our worlds in the way in which all of us, whether writers or not, perceive it from day to day. . . .

The Indian writer, looking back at India, does so through guilt-tinted spectacles. (I am of course, once more, talking about myself.) I am speaking now of those of us who emigrated . . . and I suspect that there are times when the move seems wrong to us all, when we seem, to ourselves, post-lapsarian[4] men and women. We are Hindus who have crossed the black water; we are Muslims who eat pork. And as a result — as my use of the Christian notion of the Fall indicates — we are now partly of the West. Our identity is at once plural and partial. Sometimes we feel that we straddle two cultures; at other times, that we fall between two stools. But however ambiguous and shifting this ground may be, it is not an infertile territory for a writer to occupy. If literature is in part the business of finding new angles at which to enter reality, then once again

---

[4]After the Fall; that is, after Adam and Eve's expulsion from Paradise. — ED.

our distance, our long geographical perspective, may provide us with such
angles.

## EXPLORATIONS

1. What does the mirror represent in Salman Rushdie's essay? What does the
   broken mirror represent?
2. "We are now partly of the West" (para. 12), says Rushdie of writers who have
   emigrated from India. What references in "The Broken Mirror" show that this
   statement is true of him?
3. What does Rushdie seem to value most about the Western part of his identity?
   What does he seem to value most about the Indian part?
4. In what sense do writers in exile who look back at their past "risk . . . being
   mutated into pillars of salt" (para. 4)?

## CONNECTIONS

1. In paragraphs 16–17 of "On Sunday" (p. 227), Mario Vargas Llosa uses two
   of the same literary devices as Rushdie: mirrors and memory. How is Vargas
   Llosa's use of these devices similar to and different from Rushdie's?
2. In *Looking at Ourselves*, Terry Galloway (p. 190), Bernard Cooper (p. 193),
   and Malcolm X (p. 197) write about major changes in their lives. In each
   account we hear the voice of experience describing a younger, more ignorant
   self. Having read "The Broken Mirror," examine these three before-and-after
   self-portraits. In what sense does Rushdie's broken-mirror metaphor apply to
   each one? What advice do you think each writer would give now to his or
   her younger self?
3. Compare Rushdie's description of the expatriate Indian writer in paragraph 12
   with Es'kia Mphahlele's self-portrait in paragraph 2 of "Tradition and the
   African Writer" (p. 35). What points are made by both writers?

## ELABORATIONS

1. Reread Rushdie's essay, particularly paragraph 7. Then think back to a bygone
   place and time in your own life, and write a description of everything you
   remember about it: clothes, conversations, signs, songs, and whatever else you
   can recall. What do you notice is missing? What do you suspect is distorted?
2. In paragraph 5, Rushdie writes about creating from memory his own India,
   one that might not be literally accurate but "only . . . one to which I . . .

was . . . willing to admit I belonged." Does memory always shape history to fit us? Does it always cast the person who remembers in a starring role? Write an essay comparing and contrasting two versions of some past event — a Union and a Confederate soldier's account of a Civil War battle, for instance, or a long-ago fight in your family, or a house you lived in as a child and revisited as an adult. How does the identity of the rememberer influence what he or she recalls?

# AMY TAN

## Two Kinds

Amy Tan's parents emigrated from China to Oakland, California, shortly before she was born in 1952. Her Chinese name, An-mei, means "blessing from America." Like the mother in "Two Kinds," Tan's mother had to leave the daughters of her disastrous first marriage in China after the Red Army marched into Beijing in 1949. Tan recalls learning of her half sisters at fifteen, when her father died. At that point her mother, having lost a son as well as her husband to cancer, moved her remaining son and daughter from Santa Clara, California, to Europe for a year. Amy Tan returned to enroll in Linfield College in Oregon; she graduated from San Jose State University. She became a language-development consultant and later a business writer. "Two Kinds" comes from her book *The Joy Luck Club* (1989; film 1993), which began as three short stories and grew into a novel told in the voices of four Chinese women and their California-born daughters. The central character, Jing-mei (June) Woo, bears the closest resemblance to her creator, whose mother expected her to be not only a concert pianist but a neurosurgeon. Tan followed up *The Joy Luck Club*, which has been translated into seventeen languages, with a second successful novel, *The Kitchen God's Wife* (1991), based on her mother's harrowing experiences in China. Tan and her husband live in San Francisco.

For background on China, see pages 22 and 219.

My mother believed you could be anything you wanted to be in America. You could open a restaurant. You could work for the government and get good retirement. You could buy a house with almost no money down. You could become rich. You could become instantly famous.

"Of course you can be prodigy, too," my mother told me when I was nine. "You can be best anything. What does Auntie Lindo know? Her daughter, she is only best tricky."

America was where all my mother's hopes lay. She had come here in 1949 after losing everything in China: her mother and father, her family home, her first husband, and two daughters, twin baby girls. But she never looked back with regret. There were so many ways for things to get better.

We didn't immediately pick the right kind of prodigy. At first my mother thought I could be a Chinese Shirley Temple. We'd watch Shirley's old movies on TV as though they were training films. My mother would poke my arm and say, "*Ni kan*" — You watch. And I would see Shirley tapping her feet, or singing a sailor song, or pursing her lips into a very round O while saying, "Oh my goodness."

"*Ni kan*," said my mother as Shirley's eyes flooded with tears. "You already know how. Don't need talent for crying!"                                   5

Soon after my mother got this idea about Shirley Temple, she took me to a beauty training school in the Mission district and put me in the hands of a student who could barely hold the scissors without shaking. Instead of getting big fat curls, I emerged with an uneven mass of crinkly black fuzz. My mother dragged me off to the bathroom and tried to wet down my hair.

"You look like Negro Chinese," she lamented, as if I had done this on purpose.

The instructor of the beauty training school had to lop off these soggy clumps to make my hair even again. "Peter Pan is very popular these days," the instructor assured my mother. I now had hair the length of a boy's, with straight-across bangs that hung at a slant two inches above my eyebrows. I liked the haircut and it made me actually look forward to my future fame.

In fact, in the beginning, I was just as excited as my mother, maybe even more so. I pictured this prodigy part of me as many different images, trying each one on for size. I was a dainty ballerina girl standing by the curtains, waiting to hear the right music that would send me floating on my tiptoes. I was like the Christ child lifted out of the straw manger, crying with holy indignity. I was Cinderella stepping from her pumpkin carriage with sparkly cartoon music filling the air.

In all of my imaginings, I was filled with a sense that I would soon   10 become *perfect*. My mother and father would adore me. I would be beyond reproach. I would never feel the need to sulk for anything.

But sometimes the prodigy in me became impatient. "If you don't hurry up and get me out of here, I'm disappearing for good," it warned. "And then you'll always be nothing."

Every night after dinner, my mother and I would sit at the Formica kitchen table. She would present new tests, taking her examples from stories of amazing children she had read in *Ripley's Believe It or Not*, or *Good Housekeeping, Reader's Digest*, and a dozen other magazines she kept in a pile in our bathroom. My mother got these magazines from people whose houses she cleaned. And since she cleaned many houses each week, we had a great assortment. She would look through them all, searching for stories about remarkable children.

The first night she brought out a story about a three-year-old boy who knew the capitals of all the states and even most of the European countries. A teacher was quoted as saying the little boy could also pronounce the names of the foreign cities correctly.

"What's the capital of Finland?" my mother asked me, looking at the magazine story.

All I knew was the capital of California, because Sacramento was the    15
name of the street we lived on in Chinatown. "Nairobi!" I guessed, saying the most foreign word I could think of. She checked to see if that was possibly one way to pronounce "Helsinki" before showing me the answer.

The tests got harder — multiplying numbers in my head, finding the queen of hearts in a deck of cards, trying to stand on my head without using my hands, predicting the daily temperatures in Los Angeles, New York, and London.

One night I had to look at a page from the Bible for three minutes and then report everything I could remember. "Now Jehoshaphat had riches and honor in abundance and . . . that's all I remember, Ma," I said.

And after seeing my mother's disappointed face once again, something inside of me began to die. I hated the tests, the raised hopes and failed expectations. Before going to bed that night, I looked in the mirror above the bathroom sink and when I saw only my face staring back — and that it would always be this ordinary face — I began to cry. Such a sad, ugly girl! I made high-pitched noises like a crazed animal, trying to scratch out the face in the mirror.

And then I saw what seemed to be the prodigy side of me — because I had never seen that face before. I looked at my reflection, blinking so I could see more clearly. The girl staring back at me was angry, powerful. This girl and I were the same. I had new thoughts, willful thoughts, or rather thoughts filled with lots of won'ts. I won't let her change me, I promised myself. I won't be what I'm not.

So now on nights when my mother presented her tests, I performed    20
listlessly, my head propped on one arm. I pretended to be bored. And I was. I got so bored I started counting the bellows of the foghorns out on the bay while my mother drilled me in other areas. The sound was comforting and reminded me of the cow jumping over the moon. And the next day, I played a game with myself, seeing if my mother would give up on me before eight bellows. After a while I usually counted only

one, maybe two bellows at most. At last she was beginning to give up hope.

Two or three months had gone by without any mention of my being a prodigy again. And then one day my mother was watching "The Ed Sullivan Show" on TV. The TV was old and the sound kept shorting out. Every time my mother got halfway up from the sofa to adjust the set, the sound would go back on and Ed would be talking. As soon as she sat down, Ed would go silent again. She got up, the TV broke into loud piano music. She sat down. Silence. Up and down, back and forth, quiet and loud. It was like a stiff embraceless dance between her and the TV set. Finally she stood by the set with her hand on the sound dial.

She seemed entranced by the music, a little frenzied piano piece with this mesmerizing quality, sort of quick passages and then teasing lilting ones before it returned to the quick playful parts.

"*Ni kan,*" my mother said, calling me over with hurried hand gestures. "Look here."

I could see why my mother was fascinated by the music. It was being pounded out by a little Chinese girl, about nine years old, with a Peter Pan haircut. The girl had the sauciness of a Shirley Temple. She was proudly modest like a proper Chinese child. And she also did this fancy sweep of a curtsy, so that the fluffy skirt of her white dress cascaded slowly to the floor like the petals of a large carnation.

In spite of these warning signs, I wasn't worried. Our family had no      25 piano and we couldn't afford to buy one, let alone reams of sheet music and piano lessons. So I could be generous in my comments when my mother bad-mouthed the little girl on TV.

"Play note right, but doesn't sound good! No singing sound," complained my mother.

"What are you picking on her for?" I said carelessly.

"She's pretty good. Maybe she's not the best, but she's trying hard." I knew almost immediately I would be sorry I said that.

"Just like you," she said. "Not the best. Because you not trying." She gave a little huff as she let go of the sound dial and sat down on the sofa.

The little Chinese girl sat down also to play an encore of "Anitra's      30 Dance" by Grieg. I remember the song, because later on I had to learn how to play it.

Three days after watching "The Ed Sullivan Show," my mother told me what my schedule would be for piano lessons and piano practice. She had talked to Mr. Chong, who lived on the first floor of our apartment building. Mr. Chong was a retired piano teacher and my mother had traded housecleaning services for weekly lessons and a piano for me to practice on every day, two hours a day, from four until six.

When my mother told me this, I felt as though I had been sent to hell. I whined and then kicked my foot a little when I couldn't stand it anymore.

"Why don't you like me the way I am? I'm *not* a genius! I can't play the piano. And even if I could, I wouldn't go on TV if you paid me a million dollars!" I cried.

My mother slapped me. "Who ask you be genius?" she shouted. "Only ask you be your best. For you sake. You think I want you be genius? Hnnh! What for! Who ask you!"

"So ungrateful," I heard her mutter in Chinese. "If she had as much         35 talent as she has temper, she would be famous now."

Mr. Chong, whom I secretly nicknamed Old Chong, was very strange, always tapping his fingers to the silent music of an invisible orchestra. He looked ancient in my eyes. He had lost most of the hair on top of his head and he wore thick glasses and had eyes that always looked tired and sleepy. But he must have been younger than I thought, since he lived with his mother and was not yet married.

I met Old Lady Chong once and that was enough. She had this peculiar smell like a baby that had done something in its pants. And her fingers felt like a dead person's, like an old peach I once found in the back of the refrigerator; the skin just slid off the meat when I picked it up.

I soon found out why Old Chong had retired from teaching piano. He was deaf. "Like Beethoven!" he shouted to me. "We're both listening only in our head!" And he would start to conduct his frantic silent sonatas.

Our lessons went like this. He would open the book and point to different things, explaining their purpose: "Key! Treble! Bass! No sharps or flats! So this is C major! Listen now and play after me!"

And then he would play the C scale a few times, a simple chord, and       40 then, as if inspired by an old, unreachable itch, he gradually added more notes and running trills and a pounding bass until the music was really something quite grand.

I would play after him, the simple scale, the simple chord, and then I just played some nonsense that sounded like a cat running up and down on top of garbage cans. Old Chong smiled and applauded and then said, "Very good! But now you must learn to keep time!"

So that's how I discovered that Old Chong's eyes were too slow to keep up with the wrong notes I was playing. He went through the motions in half-time. To help me keep rhythm, he stood behind me, pushing down on my right shoulder for every beat. He balanced pennies on top of my wrists so I would keep them still as I slowly played scales and arpeggios. He had me curve my hand around an apple and keep that shape when playing chords. He marched stiffly to show me how to make each finger dance up and down, staccato like an obedient little soldier.

He taught me all these things, and that was how I also learned I could be lazy and get away with mistakes, lots of mistakes. If I hit the wrong notes because I hadn't practiced enough, I never corrected myself. I just kept playing in rhythm. And Old Chong kept conducting his own private reverie.

So maybe I never really gave myself a fair chance. I did pick up the basics pretty quickly, and I might have become a good pianist at that young age. But I was so determined not to try, not to be anybody different that I learned to play only the most ear-splitting preludes, the most discordant hymns.

Over the next year, I practiced like this, dutifully in my own way. And 45 then one day I heard my mother and her friend Lindo Jong both talking in a loud bragging tone of voice so others could hear. It was after church, and I was leaning against the brick wall wearing a dress with stiff white petticoats. Auntie Lindo's daughter, Waverly, who was about my age, was standing farther down the wall about five feet away. We had grown up together and shared all the closeness of two sisters squabbling over crayons and dolls. In other words, for the most part, we hated each other. I thought she was snotty. Waverly Jong had gained a certain amount of fame as "Chinatown's Littlest Chinese Chess Champion."

"She bring home too many trophy," lamented Auntie Lindo that Sunday. "All day she play chess. All day I have no time do nothing but dust off her winnings." She threw a scolding look at Waverly, who pretended not to see her.

"You lucky you don't have this problem," said Auntie Lindo with a sigh to my mother.

And my mother squared her shoulders and bragged: "Our problem worser than yours. If we ask Jing-mei wash dish, she hear nothing but music. It's like you can't stop this natural talent."

And right then, I was determined to put a stop to her foolish pride.

A few weeks later, Old Chong and my mother conspired to have me 50 play in a talent show which would be held in the church hall. By then, my parents had saved up enough to buy me a secondhand piano, a black Wurlitzer spinet with a scarred bench. It was the showpiece of our living room.

For the talent show, I was to play a piece called "Pleading Child" from

Schumann's *Scenes from Childhood.* It was a simple, moody piece that sounded more difficult than it was. I was supposed to memorize the whole thing, playing the repeat parts twice to make the piece sound longer. But I dawdled over it, playing a few bars and then cheating, looking up to see what notes followed, I never really listened to what I was playing. I daydreamed about being somewhere else, about being someone else.

The part I liked to practice best was the fancy curtsy: right foot out, touch the rose on the carpet with a pointed foot, sweep to the side, left leg bends, look up and smile.

My parents invited all the couples from the Joy Luck Club to witness my debut. Auntie Lindo and Uncle Tin were there. Waverly and her two older brothers had also come. The first two rows were filled with children both younger and older than I was. The littlest ones got to go first. They recited simple nursery rhymes, squawked out tunes on miniature violins, twirled Hula Hoops, pranced in pink ballet tutus, and when they bowed or curtsied, the audience would sigh in unison, "Awww," and then clap enthusiastically.

When my turn came, I was very confident. I remember my childish excitement. It was as if I knew, without a doubt, that the prodigy side of me really did exist. I had no fear whatsoever, no nervousness. I remember thinking to myself, This is it! This is it! I looked out over the audience, at my mother's blank face, my father's yawn, Auntie Lindo's stiff-lipped smile, Waverly's sulky expression. I had on a white dress layered with sheets of lace, and a pink bow in my Peter Pan haircut. As I sat down I envisioned people jumping to their feet and Ed Sullivan rushing up to introduce me to everyone on TV.

And I started to play. It was so beautiful. I was so caught up in how      55
lovely I looked that at first I didn't worry how I would sound: So it was a surprise to me when I hit the first wrong note and I realized something didn't sound quite right. And then I hit another and another followed that. A chill started at the top of my head and began to trickle down. Yet I couldn't stop playing, as though my hands were bewitched. I kept thinking my fingers would adjust themselves back, like a train switching to the right track. I played this strange jumble through two repeats, the sour notes staying with me all the way to the end.

When I stood up, I discovered my legs were shaking. Maybe I had just been nervous and the audience, like Old Chong, had seen me go through the right motions and had not heard anything wrong at all. I swept my right foot out, went down on my knee, looked up and smiled. The room was quiet, except for Old Chong, who was beaming and shouting, "Bravo! Bravo! Well done!" But then I saw my mother's face, her stricken face. The audience clapped weakly, and as I walked back to my chair, with my whole face quivering as I tried not to cry, I heard a little boy whisper loudly to his mother, "That was awful," and the mother whispered back, "Well, she certainly tried."

And now I realized how many people were in the audience, the whole world it seemed. I was aware of eyes burning into my back. I felt the shame of my mother and father as they sat stiffly throughout the rest of the show.

We could have escaped during intermission. Pride and some strange sense of honor must have anchored my parents to their chairs. And so we watched it all: the eighteen-year-old boy with a fake mustache who did a magic show and juggled flaming hoops while riding a unicycle. The breasted girl with white makeup who sang from *Madama Butterfly* and got honorable mention. And the eleven-year-old boy who won first prize playing a tricky violin song that sounded like a busy bee.

After the show, the Hsus, the Jongs, and the St. Clairs from the Joy Luck Club came up to my mother and father.

"Lots of talented kids," Auntie Lindo said vaguely, smiling broadly.      60

"That was somethin' else," said my father, and I wondered if he was referring to me in a humorous way, or whether he even remembered what I had done.

Waverly looked at me and shrugged her shoulders. "You aren't a genius like me," she said matter-of-factly. And if I hadn't felt so bad, I would have pulled her braids and punched her stomach.

But my mother's expression was what devastated me: a quiet, blank look that said she had lost everything. I felt the same way, and it seemed as if everybody were now coming up, like gawkers at the scene of an accident, to see what parts were actually missing. When we got on the bus to go home, my father was humming the busy-bee tune and my mother was silent. I kept thinking she wanted to wait until we got home before shouting at me. But when my father unlocked the door to our apartment, my mother walked in and then went to the back, into the bedroom. No accusations. No blame. And in a way, I felt disappointed. I had been waiting for her to start shouting, so I could shout back and cry and blame her for all my misery.

I assumed my talent-show fiasco meant I never had to play the piano again. But two days later, after school, my mother came out of the kitchen and saw me watching TV.

"Four clock," she reminded me as if it were any other day. I was      65
stunned, as though she were asking me to go through the talent-show torture again. I wedged myself more tightly in front of the TV.

"Turn off TV," she called from the kitchen five minutes later.

I didn't budge. And then I decided. I didn't have to do what my mother said anymore. I wasn't her slave. This wasn't China. I had listened to her before and look what happened. She was the stupid one.

She came out from the kitchen and stood in the arched entryway of the living room. "Four clock," she said once again, louder.

"I'm not going to play anymore," I said nonchalantly. "Why should I? I'm not a genius."

She walked over and stood in front of the TV. I saw her chest was     70
heaving up and down in an angry way.

"No!" I said, and I now felt stronger, as if my true self had finally emerged. So this was what had been inside me all along.

"No! I won't!" I screamed.

She yanked me by the arm, pulled me off the floor, snapped off the TV. She was frighteningly strong, half pulling, half carrying me toward the piano as I kicked the throw rugs under my feet. She lifted me up and onto the hard bench. I was sobbing by now, looking at her bitterly. Her chest was heaving even more and her mouth was open, smiling crazily as if she were pleased I was crying.

"You want me to be someone that I'm not!" I sobbed. "I'll never be the kind of daughter you want me to be!"

"Only two kinds of daughters," she shouted in Chinese. "Those who     75
are obedient and those who follow their own mind! Only one kind of daughter can live in this house. Obedient daughter!"

"Then I wish I wasn't your daughter. I wish you weren't my mother," I shouted. As I said these things I got scared. I felt like worms and toads and slimy things were crawling out of my chest, but it also felt good, as if this awful side of me had surfaced, at last.

"Too late change this," said my mother shrilly.

And I could sense her anger rising to its breaking point. I wanted to see it spill over. And that's when I remembered the babies she had lost in China, the ones we never talked about. "Then I wish I'd never been born!" I shouted. "I wish I were dead! Like them."

It was as if I had said the magic words. Alakazam! — and her face went blank, her mouth closed, her arms went slack, and she backed out of the room, stunned, as if she were blowing away like a small brown leaf, thin, brittle, lifeless.


It was not the only disappointment my mother felt in me. In the years     80
that followed, I failed her so many times, each time asserting my own will, my right to fall short of expectations. I didn't get straight As. I didn't

become class president. I didn't get into Stanford. I dropped out of college.

For unlike my mother, I did not believe I could be anything I wanted to be. I could only be me.

And for all those years, we never talked about the disaster at the recital or my terrible accusations afterward at the piano bench. All that remained unchecked, like a betrayal that was now unspeakable. So I never found a way to ask her why she had hoped for something so large that failure was inevitable.

And even worse, I never asked her what frightened me the most: Why had she given up hope?

For after our struggle at the piano, she never mentioned my playing again. The lessons stopped. The lid to the piano was closed, shutting out the dust, my misery, and her dreams.

So she surprised me. A few years ago, she offered to give me the piano,      85
for my thirtieth birthday. I had not played in all those years. I saw the offer as a sign of forgiveness, a tremendous burden removed.

"Are you sure?" I asked shyly. "I mean, won't you and Dad miss it?"

"No, this your piano," she said firmly. "Always your piano. You only one can play."

"Well, I probably can't play anymore," I said. "It's been years."

"You pick up fast," said my mother, as if she knew this was certain. "You have natural talent. You could been genius if you want to."

"No I couldn't."                                                                90

"You just not trying," said my mother. And she was neither angry nor sad. She said it as if to announce a fact that could never be disproved. "Take it," she said.

But I didn't at first. It was enough that she had offered it to me. And after that, every time I saw it in my parents' living room, standing in front of the bay windows, it made me feel proud, as if it were a shiny trophy I had won back.

Last week I sent a tuner over to my parents' apartment and had the piano reconditioned, for purely sentimental reasons. My mother had died a few months before and I had been getting things in order for my father, a little bit at a time. I put the jewelry in special silk pouches. The sweaters she had knitted in yellow, pink, bright orange — all the colors I hated — I put those in moth-proof boxes. I found some old Chinese silk dresses, the kind with little slits up the sides. I rubbed the old silk against my skin, then wrapped them in tissue and decided to take them home with me.

After I had the piano tuned, I opened the lid and touched the keys. It sounded even richer than I remembered. Really, it was a very good piano. Inside the bench were the same exercise notes with handwritten scales, the same secondhand music books with their covers held together with yellow tape.

I opened up the Schumann book to the dark little piece I had played      95
at the recital. It was on the left-hand side of the page, "Pleading Child." It looked more difficult than I remembered. I played a few bars, surprised at how easily the notes came back to me.

And for the first time, or so it seemed, I noticed the piece on the right-hand side. It was called "Perfectly Contented." I tried to play this one as well. It had a lighter melody but the same flowing rhythm and turned out to be quite easy. "Pleading Child" was shorter but slower; "Perfectly Contented" was longer but faster. And after I played them both a few times, I realized they were two halves of the same song.

## EXPLORATIONS

1. How many different meanings for the story's title can you find in "Two Kinds"?

2. What appears to be the top goal of the narrator's mother in "Two Kinds"? Which of her statements and actions show how important it is to her? What clues in the story's first three paragraphs suggest why she has fixed on this goal?

3. What is the primary goal of the narrator at the beginning of "Two Kinds"? Why has she fixed on this goal? How does her goal change as the story progresses and why?

4. Why does the narrator say that "what frightened me the most" was her mother's giving up hope (para. 83)? Why do you think her mother's offering her the piano "made me feel proud, as if it were a shiny trophy I had won back" (para. 92)?

## CONNECTIONS

1. "This wasn't China," Jing-mei Woo declares defiantly in paragraph 67. Recall Salman Rushdie's comments about an emigrant's memory being a broken mirror (p. 242). What aspects of her mother's life in China are vivid to Jing-mei? What additional aspects of her life in China apparently are vivid to Mrs. Woo?

2. What central dilemma does Jing-mei Woo, the narrator of "Two Kinds," share with Sophronia Liu's schoolmate So Tsi-fai (p. 219)? In what sense do both Jing-mei Woo and So Tsi-fai take the same way out?

3. "Two Kinds," Liu's "So Tsi-fai," and Liliana Heker's "The Stolen Party" (p. 212) show adults opposing children. What adult in each selection creates obstacles for the young main character? What strategy is tried by all three adults, and why does it fail?

4. How do Jing-mei Woo's struggles fit the pattern described by Gail Sheehy in *Looking at Ourselves* (p. 187)? Find evidence in "Two Kinds" for at least three of Sheehy's statements.

## ELABORATIONS

1. In "Tradition and the African Writer" (p. 35), Es'kia Mphahlele comments about parents: "They worry a great deal about the way in which we break loose at one point and ignore some elements of tradition." How is this true of the characters in "Two Kinds"? Reread Mphahlele's essay and Amy Tan's story. Then write a cause-and-effect essay about the problems faced by families consisting of traditional parents and nontraditional children.

2. Why do you think Tan chose the ending she did for "Two Kinds"? Write an essay examining how the narrator's final actions and conclusions (paras. 93–96) bring the story to an appropriate close.

# CHRISTOPHER REYNOLDS

## *Cultural Journey to Africa*

Christopher Reynolds was born in Fresno, California, in 1960. After graduating from Fresno State University in 1982, he became a reporter for the *San Diego Union-Tribune*. In 1990 he joined the staff of the *Los Angeles Times* as a news and features writer; since 1992 he has been the *Times*'s only travel writer. Every year he goes somewhere with a tour group in order to write about people interacting with another culture. "Cultural Journey to Africa" is his report on Culturefest 1992, a trip to the Ivory Coast, on which Reynolds was the only white person. He describes the experience as "an exercise in making myself invisible, like a sponge."

For additional information on the Ivory Coast, see page 48.

Air Afrique Flight 95 soars directly from New York to West Africa, crossing 4,300 miles of Atlantic Ocean and 500 years of excruciating history. The route brings African exchange students home from studies in the United States, carries bankers to international debt conferences, shuttles hotel magnates to far-flung properties. But Flight 95 also delivers pilgrims, and recently it brought a rare and remarkable assembly of them.

Ahneva Ahneva is a Los Angeles fashion designer. Larry Spruill is a minister and American history teacher from Mount Vernon, New York. Mary Ann Collins, raised in Los Angeles, is a Texas-based flight attendant. . . . Dexter Wansel is a composer and musical arranger from Philadelphia. They are all black Americans, a sampling of the more than 500 who were drawn to the Ivory Coast's largest city by an American-organized tour and celebration of African heritage known as Culturefest 1992. . . . The program, billed as the first of its kind, included performances, classes, and informal gatherings, all aimed at the idea of building connections between Africa and African-Americans.

From the beginning, it was complicated. Seeking roots and cultural resonance, the Americans found coconut trees and skyscrapers, trash fires and rich fabrics, French voices and Vietnamese restaurants. Taxicabs dashed around the edges of a placid lagoon while sewage collected at its edges and the fishermen silently paddled on the calm water. Beaming children scampered along filthy urban avenues. And somewhere in nearly every scene, a burden-bearing woman strode along a roadside, laundry and groceries balanced atop her head.

"It's like going to meet relatives you've never met," said Mary Ann Collins.

And like some family reunions, the occasion wasn't what everyone    5
expected. Some things happened late, some didn't happen at all, and almost nothing came off exactly as planned. But before a week was over, there were flashing blades at a tribal initiation, perplexed frowns beneath a brilliant basilica dome, and joyous choruses under the coconut fronds.

"Africa is a stretch of the imagination," wrote Gerri Anderson of Stamford, Connecticut, in her diary after eight days on the continent. "It's the final link to the souls of our ancestors, and it is a spiritual awakening."

Black Americans have been making journeys of rediscovery for generations, from the founders of Liberia in the early nineteenth century to author Alex Haley in the 1960s and 1970s. Few African-American families, however, are able to trace their roots with the specificity that Haley described in "Roots." Most have to settle for a staggering historical generality: Ten million or more slaves were shipped by Europeans to North America, South America, and the Caribbean from the fifteenth to the nineteenth centuries, and the vast majority of them came from West Africa.

So, while wildlife seekers chase the lions and elephants of Kenya to the east or Zimbabwe to the south, the African-American cultural pilgrims aim for the continent's west coast. In Gambia lies the village of Juffure, where Haley described the birth of Kunta Kinte in 1750. Off the coast of Senegal stands Goree Island, said to have served as a slave-ship loading dock for three centuries, now home to a museum. On the coast of English-speaking Ghana, visitors follow the footsteps of slaves through the 500-year-old halls of Portuguese-built Elmina Castle.

The Ivory Coast ("Côte d'Ivoire" in French), southeast of Senegal and west of Ghana, was never a regular slavers' stop. But French colonists seized control of the New Mexico–sized area in the nineteenth century and used forced labor to build a wealthy plantation economy. With rich soil, miles of beaches, and sixty ethnic groups under French domination and language, the Ivory Coast emerged as a continental crossroads. That status remains after thirty-two years of independence, and the Ivory Coast's population of 12 million is estimated to include 2.4 million migrants from other West African nations. On this ground, a black American inevitably stands among distant kin.

The Culturefest headquarters was the Hotel Ivoire, a giant complex   10
with lagoon frontage, a twenty-fourth-floor restaurant, and one of the few

ice rinks on the African continent. Owned by the government and operated by Inter-Continental Hotels, the place towers over Abidjan's most affluent neighborhood, Cocody, and for thirty years has stood as a symbol of Western wealth.

Seated on the Ivoire patio on August 17, several dozen Americans looked out upon their first African night: poolside drummers; distant city lights; a starless, smoggy sky; and a delay. They were tired and hungry, but protocol dictated that dinner wait until the arrival of the Ivorian minister of culture.

"There's an adjustment period," Selma Edwards, a New York tour operator and principal organizer of the festival, had warned. The Americans, she said, "have to adjust to what they imagined to be the reality of the country. It takes people two to three days to get mellow, because they get caught up in things going wrong."

The Americans spent time investigating Abidjan, a city with French boulevards, American billboards, and an enduring pattern of village life in its back streets. Just a few hundred yards from the Hotel Ivoire's property, in fact, an Ebrie Lagoon fishing village persists, its residents still paddling canoes and relying on their fishing nets for much of their sustenance.

But around such villages has risen one of Africa's most cosmopolitan cities. While Yamoussoukro is the nominal capital of Ivory Coast, Abidjan is the engine that runs the country. The population, which swelled during the growth of the coffee and cocoa industries in the 1960s, 1970s, and early 1980s and kept on swelling after those markets crashed in 1986, is estimated at 2.7 million.

Thousands of those residents labor in skyscrapers, navigate the busy streets of the downtown Plateau area, and indulge their appetites at restaurants and food stalls in the bustling Treichville district. Those establishments line the streets and clutter the sidewalks, with lean chicken and ungutted fish slowly blackening above street-level coals.

"It's like a vacation from racism," said Mary Beth Mitchell, a Denver gift-shop operator on her fifth trip to Africa. "The people are just black and tall and regal and beautiful."

"I don't like squalor," complained Mrs. Bernard Walker, a retired Detroit court reporter and first-time visitor. "I don't like deprivation. And the women are the slaves over here. They're doing all the hard work and carrying all the babies."

One day early in the week, Ivorian tour guide Clement Pauleroux took a busload of Americans to the working-class neighborhood of Adjame and had the driver pause at a spectacularly busy intersection.

"This," pronounced Pauleroux, "is the real Africa."

Beyond him, on a gently sloping hill, stretched an infinity of wooden    20
shacks, bright fabrics, and children in motion. Vendors offered grain sacks
and plastic buckets and coconuts and bananas. On their heads, women
carried clothespins, combs, peanuts, telephone directories, dish towels,
and tins of corned beef. The Americans, just a few moments removed
from their tidy, spacious hotel, nodded and blinked, overwhelmed.

At the Banco River, they watched hundreds of immigrants from Burkina Faso earn their living waist-deep in water, scrubbing clothes all day.

Twenty-five miles up the coast at Grand Bassam, they strolled beneath
coconut trees along white-sand beaches, lazy restaurants, and craft shops
lying nearby along the tranquil road, the Atlantic beginning at their feet.

"This is how I see Africa," said Jon Haggins, a New York fashion
designer.

Soon it was Saturday, the last full day of the trip for many.

On a morning boat tour of Ebrie Lagoon, Long Island, New York,    25
video producer Aurora Workman had ducked into a thatched hut to share
a sip of home-brewed cane liquor with a wizened patriarch. Three shots
later, she emerged with a grin, climbed back onto the boat, and fell asleep.

Lisa Robinson, Esther Grant, Deborah Womack, Dana Powell, Curtis
Brown, and Mark Q. Murray — collectively known as the Gospel Show-
case of New York — had shared a stage with the 135-voice choir of the
Church of St. Joan of Arc of Treichville.

Deborah Hyde-Jackson, the brain surgeon from Los Angeles, had
announced plans to buy Ivorian property. "I want to own a piece of
African soil," she declared.

Gerri Anderson had set aside a day for market-going, and brought
along a sweatshirt, jeans, shoes, and six bags of Avon beauty products.
When the bartering was done, she had three custom-tailored, two-piece
suits.

"The level of creativity!" said Anderson. "I have never in my life seen
so much creativity."

But that afternoon, less than twenty-four hours before the flight home,    30
an unannounced tour possibility materialized in the hotel lobby. Led by
local sources of Selma Edwards, half a dozen Americans in hired cars
rumbled off the main highway, climbed five miles of dirt road, and rolled
into a remote village on the day of a rare initiation.

This was no scene of mud huts and rural purity — one village man
of means had champagne to offer in crystal flutes — but it was traditional.
Drums pounded. At the center of a crowd, men danced and brandished
knives in hatchets. Adolescent boys danced with them, risking a slashing
to demonstrate their courage and manhood. Elders in elaborate regalia
watched.

Larry Spruill shot eight rolls of film and almost got slashed by a hatchet. Dexter Wansel strolled away from the crowd, listened to the drums, watched some canoes on the water . . . and had a moment.

"It all came together," he said later. "I found my Africa."

That night, a dozen Americans celebrated their last African night in a fashionable bar a few miles from the hotel. Many Mambas were ordered. Group pictures were taken. Aurora Workman recited Langston Hughes to an English-hungry Ivorian schoolteacher. Sanogo Abdoul-Bakary, the Ivoir-'Soir reporter, collected numbers to call on his next visit to the United States. And the singers from the Gospel Showcase of New York, bowing to repeated requests, set aside their Orangina sodas and rose to put their voices together one more time.

With coconut trees silhouetted against the sky overhead, a patio full        35
of Ivorians glancing their way, and African pop music jangling in the background, they quietly offered a brief song of praise.

"You're Easy to Love," it began. The harmonies weren't perfect, but for the moment they were close enough.

## EXPLORATIONS

1. According to Christopher Reynolds, what are the goals of the participants in Culturefest 1992? What tactics do they (and their guides) use to achieve these goals?

2. Why is Ivory Coast a good destination for this cultural journey? Why do you think a luxurious hotel in the nation's largest city was picked as the tour's headquarters?

3. At what points does Reynolds include facts about Ivory Coast's history and geography in his essay? How would the essay's impact be different if Reynolds had started it with a paragraph containing all of this background information?

## CONNECTIONS

1. The participants in Culturefest 1992, like Jing-mei Woo in "Two Kinds" (p. 246), have powerful ties to an ancestral homeland they have never seen. In what ways is this heritage a burden? In what ways is it a blessing?

2. In "The Broken Mirror" (p. 240), Salman Rushdie describes revisiting Bombay "after an absence of something like half my life" (para. 2). What resemblances do you notice between Rushdie's visit and the Americans' visit to Ivory Coast in "Cultural Journey to Africa"?

3. What Western influences does Reynolds identify in Abidjan? What Western

influences does V. S. Naipaul identify in the same city in "Entering the New World" (p. 48)? To each writer, what features of Abidjan and Ivory Coast are the most and least attractive to Western visitors? Why do you think their assessments differ?

4. In "The Westernization of the World" (p. 41), Paul Harrison writes about cultural borrowing from the West in Africa (and elsewhere). In what ways does Culturefest 1992 represent cultural borrowing in the other direction?

## ELABORATIONS

1. What parts of the world do your ancestors come from? Write an essay summarizing what you know and what you would like to know about your heritage outside the United States, and evaluating how your heritage has influenced your identity.

2. Reynolds mentions several attractions that Africa offers to Western tourists. In "The Westernization of the World," Paul Harrison describes Peking opera in Singapore (para. 1). What role do tourists play in the preservation — or re-creation — of traditional sites and customs that might otherwise disappear? Write an essay addressing this question either on a general level or with respect to a specific place you have visited, whether foreign or American.

# GÜNTER GRASS

## *After Auschwitz*

Günter Grass is not only Germany's most celebrated contemporary novelist but a poet, playwright, essayist, graphic artist, and sculptor. Born in 1927 in Danzig, Germany (now Gdansk, Poland), he worked as a farm laborer, potash miner, black marketeer, stonecutter, and jazz drummer before becoming a speechwriter for Willy Brandt, later mayor of West Berlin. As he recalls in "After Auschwitz," Grass was a member of the Hitler Youth in the 1940s and served in the Luftwaffe (air force) after being drafted into the German army. His first published book was *Vorzuege der Windhuehner* (1956; "The advantages of windfowl"), a volume of drawings and poetry. His novel *Die Blechtrommel* ("The tin drum") followed in 1959 and made him a controversial international celebrity. Grass has published dozens of other works since. Always an outspoken political prophet, he has drawn considerable criticism for his recent attacks on German policies, particularly reunification. "After Auschwitz" comes from his 1990 collection *Two States — One Nation?*

Berlin, where Günter Grass now lives, was formally reunited along with the rest of Germany in October 1990 after being divided for forty-five years. The Allies (the United States, the United Kingdom, France, and the Soviet Union) defeated the Axis powers (Germany, Italy, and Japan) and ended World War II in 1945. German Führer Adolf Hitler committed suicide a month before his Third Reich's surrender ended the Nazi (National Socialist Party) conquest of Europe and slaughter of millions of Jews and others. The Allies — recalling such horrors as Auschwitz (in Poland) and the other concentration camps in which Nazi victims were imprisoned and killed — divided Germany into four zones of control. In 1949 the American, British, and French zones together became the Federal Republic of Germany (West Germany), while the Soviet zone became the German Democratic Republic (East Germany). West Germany included West Berlin, a section of the nation's former capital islanded inside East Germany (and still joined like a Siamese twin to the East German capital, East Berlin).

In 1961 East Germany built the Berlin Wall, a massive structure of concrete, barbed wire, and guard posts, to keep East Germans from fleeing to West Berlin. The West German economy was booming, however, and efforts to emigrate continued. As the Soviet Union's grip on Eastern Europe loosened in 1989, nearby countries provided a more roundabout escape route from East to West Germany. Finally, on November 9, the East German government announced it would open (and later tear down) the Berlin Wall. Within a year Germany had become a single nation again, with Berlin as its capital. As Günter Grass predicted, reunification has created problems as well as solving them. Economic, political, religious, and other differences have sparked tension within united Germany; and massive immigration from Eastern Europe has met sometimes violent resistance.

A writer, asked to give an account of himself, which means of his work, would have to evaporate into that ironic distance in which everything shrinks if he wished to avoid discussing the time period that has marked him, shaped him, kept him immobilized in erroneous contradictions (despite various changes of scene), and made him a witness. . . .

Since I was invited by a university and am speaking specifically to students, thus finding myself face to face with the innocent curiosity of a generation that grew up under conditions entirely different from my own, let me first go back a few decades and sketch the circumstances in which I found myself in May 1945.

When I was seventeen years of age, living with a hundred thousand others in an American prison camp out under the open sky, in a foxhole, I was famished, and because of this I focused, with the cunning born of hunger, exclusively on survival — otherwise I had not a clear notion in my head. Rendered stupid by dogma and accordingly fixated on lofty goals: This was the state in which the Third Reich released me and many of my generation from our oaths of loyalty. "The flag is superior to death" was one of its life-denying certainties.

All this stupidity resulted not only from a schooling knocked full of holes by the war — when I reached fifteen, my time as Luftwaffe helper began, which I mistakenly welcomed as liberation from school — it was, rather, an overarching stupidity, one that transcended differences of class and religion, one that was nourished by German complacency. Its ideological slogans usually began with "We Germans are . . . ," "To be German means . . . ," and, finally, "A German would never . . ."

This last-quoted rule lasted even beyond the capitulation of the    5
Greater German Reich and took on the stubborn force of incorrigibility. For when I, with many of my generation — leaving aside our fathers and mothers for now — was confronted with the results of the crimes for which Germans were responsible, crimes that would be summed up in the image of *Auschwitz*, I said: Impossible. I said to myself and to others, and others said to themselves and to me: "Germans would never do a thing like that."

This self-confirming Never was even pleased to view itself as steadfast. In response to the overwhelming number of photographs showing piles of shoes here, piles of hair there, and again and again bodies piled on top of each other, captioned with numerals I could not grasp and foreign-sounding place names — Treblinka, Sobibor, Auschwitz — there was one ready answer, spoken or unspoken, but always firm, whenever American educational zeal forced us seventeen- and eighteen-year-olds to look at the documentary photos: Germans never could have done, never did do a thing like that.

Even when the Never collapsed (if not earlier, then with the Nuremberg Trials[1]), the former Reich Youth Leader Baldur von Schirach declared that we, the Hitler Youth, were free of responsibility. It took several more years before I began to realize: This will not go away; our shame cannot be repressed or come to terms with. The insistent concreteness of those photographs — the shoes, the glasses, the hair, the corpses — resisted abstraction. Even if surrounded with explanations, Auschwitz can never be grasped.

Since then, much time has passed. Certain historians have been busy digging up facts and figures to make this "unfortunate phase in German history," as they call it, a valid academic subject. Yet no matter what has been admitted to, lamented, or otherwise said out of a sense of guilt — as in this speech — the monstrous phenomenon for which the name Auschwitz stands remains beyond facts and figures, beyond the cushioning academic study, a thing inaccessible to any confession of guilt. Therefore it remains impossible to grasp, forming such a divide in human history that one is tempted to date events before and after Auschwitz.

And in retrospect a persistent question confronts the writer: How was it possible to write — after Auschwitz? Was this question posed merely to fulfill a ritual of contrition? Was the agonized self-searching of the fifties and early sixties no more than a literary exercise? And does the question even matter nowadays, when the very idea of literature is being challenged by the new media?

Back to the stupid, unwavering adolescent. Come to think of it, he 10 wasn't so stupid and unwavering. Because despite the shortness of his schooling he had had a few teachers who taught him, more in secret than openly, aesthetic values, artistic sensibility. The woman sculptor, for example, assigned to teaching as her compulsory wartime service, who noticed the schoolboy constantly drawing and slipped him exhibition catalogs from the twenties. At considerable risk, she shocked and infected

---

[1]In 1945–1946, Nazis accused of crimes during World War II were tried at Nuremberg, Germany. — Ed.

him with the work of Kirchner, Lehmbruck, Nolde, Beckmann. I clung to that. Or it clung to me. In the face of such artistic provocations the certainty of this Hitler Youth began to waver, or, rather, it did not waver but softened in one spot, and let in other kinds of egocentric certainties — the unthinking, unfocused, yet intense, bold desire to be an artist.

From the age of twelve, I could not be dissuaded from this — not by the paternal pointing to a more solid profession, not by the difficult times later on: ruins everywhere, and nothing to eat. My youthful obsession kept its vitality, survived unharmed — again, unwaveringly — the end of the war, then the first postwar years, and even the currency reform, which wrought changes all around.

And thus the choice of career was made. After an apprenticeship as a stonemason and sculptor, I went to study sculpture, first at the Academy of Art in Düsseldorf, then at the School of Fine Arts in Berlin. Yet these autobiographical data do not say much, except perhaps that my desire to become an artist showed — you might say an admirable, but I would say, in retrospect, a questionable singleness of purpose: admirable, perhaps, because the decision was made quite simply, despite my parents' reservations and without regard for material security, but still questionable and in the end not admirable at all, because my artistic development, which soon led by way of poetry to writing, again proceeded unwaveringly, not wavering even in the face of Auschwitz.

No, my path was not chosen in ignorance, for in the meantime all the horrors had been brought to light. Nevertheless my path led me blindly, with a purposeful blindness, past Auschwitz. After all, there were plenty of other signposts. Not the sort that blocked one and caused one's step to hesitate. The names of previously unknown authors lured me, seized possession of me: Döblin, Dos Passos, Trakl, Apollinaire. The art exhibitions of those years were not self-stylized displays by bored professionals; instead, they opened up vistas of new worlds — Henry Moore or Chagall in Düsseldorf, Picasso in Hamburg. And travel became possible: hitch-hiking to Italy, to see not only the Etruscans but also spare, earth-toned pictures by Morandi.

As the ruins increasingly vanished from view, and though people all around resumed weaving according to the old pattern, it was a time of radical change — and of the illusion that one could build something new on old foundations. . . .

I recall Easter marches organized to protest the atom bomb. Always 15 there, always in opposition. The obstinate horror of the seventeen-year-old who had refused to believe the atrocity stories had given way to opposition on general principle. In the meantime the real dimensions of the genocide were now demonstrated in volumes of documentation, and the anti-Semitism[2] of one's youth was exchanged for philo-Semitism,[3] and one defined oneself unquestioningly and without risk as antifascist. But I, and many of my generation, did not take the time to think through fundamental questions, questions dictated with Old Testament sternness, questions like: Can one do art after Auschwitz? Is it permissible to write poems after Auschwitz?

There was the dictum by Theodor Adorno: "To write a poem after Auschwitz is barbarous, and also undermines our understanding of why it has become impossible to write poems nowadays." Since 1951 a book by Adorno had been available — *Minima Moralia: Reflections from a Damaged Life,* where for the first time, to my knowledge, Auschwitz was seen as a great divide, an irreparable tear in the history of civilization. Yet this new categorical imperative was promptly misunderstood to be a prohibition. A prohibition like other stern prohibitions standing in the way of the thirst for change and the belief, apparently undamaged, in the future. An uncomfortable imperative, off-putting in its abstractness, and easy to circumvent.

Before people took the time to examine Adorno's remarks within the context of the reflections that preceded and followed them, and thus to realize that they were not a prohibition but a standard to be met, resistance to them had already consolidated. The abbreviated Adorno statement, that no poem should be written after Auschwitz, was refuted in a similarly abbreviated and unthinking form, as if enemies were exchanging blows. Adorno's prohibition was declared barbarous; it asked too much of human beings; it was inhumane; after all, life, no matter how damaged, had to go on.

My reaction, too, based on ignorance — on hearsay only — was to oppose it. Feeling myself in full possession of my powers, of my unique talents, I wanted to give them free rein, to prove them. Adorno's prohibition struck me as unnatural, as if someone had had the godthefatherly audacity to forbid birds to sing.

Was it defiance again or my old unwavering certainty that led me to dismiss Adorno so quickly? Didn't I know from personal experience what had horrified me and now haunted me? Why not put aside, if only for a short while, my sculpting, and impose a Lenten fast on my lyrical imagination, that greedy lodger within me?

---

[2]Hatred of Jews. — ED.
[3]Love of Jews. — ED.

Today I suspect that Adorno affected me more strongly than I could admit at the time. Something had been stirred up in me, and despite my resistance a control had been placed over me. The freedom of creativity, thought to be unlimited, a thing not won but handed to us, had come under surveillance. . . .

All of us, the young poets of the fifties — let me name Peter Rühmkorf, Hans Magnus Enzensberger, also Ingeborg Bachmann — were aware, some clearly, some vaguely, that we belonged to the Auschwitz generation — not as criminals, to be sure, but in the camp of the criminals. That in our biography, therefore, among the usual dates was written the date of the Wannsee Conference.[4] But we also knew this much: that Adorno's imperative could be refuted, if at all, only by writing.

But how? From whom should we learn? From Brecht? Benn? The early Expressionists? What tradition should we adopt, what criteria? The minute I picture myself as a young poetic talent next to the young Enzensberger and Rühmkorf, I realize that our head start — and talent is nothing but a head start — was playful, artistic, art-infatuated to the point of artificiality, and would probably have played itself out in a manner not worth mentioning if we had not had leaden shackles placed on us at the right moment. One of those shackles, which we wore even as we refused to wear it, was Theodor Adorno's imperative. I took my course from his signpost. And that course called for renouncing color; it called for gray in all gray's endless shadings.

It meant abandoning absolutes, the black and white of ideology, it meant showing belief the door and placing all one's bets on doubt, which turned everything, even the rainbow, to gray. But this imperative yielded wealth of another sort: The heartrending beauty of all the shades of gray was to be celebrated in damaged language. That meant hauling down one's flag and daubing the geraniums with ash. . . .

I read my poems and one-act plays at the meetings of Group 47, which in the person of Hans Werner Richter, regularly invited me, the beginner, from the fall of 1955 on. Many of the manuscripts read there were more outspoken than mine. Some of them attacked National Socialism, as if to make up for lost time, unambiguously, with the help of positive heroes. The lack of ambiguity made me nervous. Such belated antifascism had the sound of a required exercise, conformist in a time of abject confor-

---

[4]At the Wannsee Conference, held January 20, 1942, the National Socialists met to plan the "final solution" of the Jewish Question.

mism, hence dishonest, and positively obscene when compared with the real resistance to National Socialism, a resistance which, though doomed to failure and pathetically weak, had left real traces.

These first experiences with literature and what goes on around it   25 caused me to regress. I was seventeen again. The end of the war. The unconditional surrender. Imprisoned in foxholes. Photographs showing piles of eyeglasses, shoes, bones. My stubborn refusal to believe it. And turning the counter back even farther: fifteen, fourteen, thirteen years old. Campfires, flag drills, shooting practice with small-caliber weapons. The dull routine of school interrupted by vacations, while the news came in special bulletins. Certainly: schoolboy defiance, boredom during Hitler Youth exercises. Stupid jokes about the party bigwigs, who dodged service at the front and were mockingly called "golden pheasants." But resistance? Not a trace, not even the stirring of resistance, not even in the most fleeting thoughts. Instead, admiration for military heroes and a persistent mindless credulity that nothing could put a dent in. An embarrassment even today.

How could I think to capture resistance on paper ten years later, ascribing antifascism to myself, when "writing after Auschwitz" had shame, shame on every white page as its prerequisite? Rather, what emerged from the fifties was opposition to the scale of new false notes, to the facade-art flourishing all around, to smug gatherings of complacent Philistines — if some of them had known nothing, guessed nothing, and now presented themselves as children seduced by demonic forces, the others had always been against it, if not out loud then at least in secret.

A decade of lies that even today have market value, but a decade, too, of momentous decisions. Rearmament and the German Treaty were the key words here. Two German states were coming into being, tit for tat, each zealously trying to be the model pupil in its respective political bloc, each delighted at being fortunate to count itself among the victors. Divided, yes, but united in the perception of having survived one more time.

It was not until [1956], when I moved from Berlin to Paris, that the distance from Germany enabled me to find the language and the breath to write down in fifteen hundred pages what was necessary for me to write, in spite of and after Auschwitz. Driven by the recklessness that is specific to the profession, and by a persistent writing frenzy, I completed — without interruption, though in several versions, in Paris and then Berlin after my return in 1960 — *The Tin Drum, Cat and Mouse,* and *Dog Years.*

No writer, I would assert, will undertake a major epic without being pushed, provoked, and lured by others into that great avalanche zone. In Cologne, when I was passing through, it was Paul Schallück who gave me the push to write prose. The provocation came from the current pervasive, even official, demonization of the Nazi period — I wanted to illuminate the crime, bring it into the open — and I was lured into continuing, after relapses, by a difficult, almost inaccessible friend, Paul Celan, who understood sooner than I did that the first book, with its 730 galloping pages, did not tell the whole story, but rather that this profane epic onion had to be unpeeled layer by layer, and that I must not take a break from the peeling. . . .

Thirty years later, it is easy for me to say that later everything became      30
more difficult. Bored with itself, fame stood in the way. Friendships fell apart. Reviewers panting with specific expectations insisted that my sole subject should be Danzig, only Danzig, with its flat and hilly environs. Whenever I turned to the present, whether with *The Plebeians* or with prose again — *Local Anaesthetic* and *From the Diary of a Snail* — or if I got involved in a German election campaign, down to all the provincial details, and took an active role in politics as a citizen, their judgment was sure to fall: He should stick to Danzig and his Kashubians. Politics has brought nothing but harm to writers. Goethe knew that. And other such schoolmasterly admonitions.

But writing after Auschwitz could not and cannot be dealt with so solicitously. The past casts its hard shadows over present and future terrain — I later coined the term "pastpresentfuture" and tried out that concept in *Diary of a Snail*. Inspired by Heine's fragment, "The Rabbi of Bacharach," I wanted to describe the history of the Danzig synagogue congregation up to its liquidation — once again digging up the past — but I also had a mission in the present: The 1969 election campaign was clouded by an agreement that a former National Socialist would be acceptable as chancellor for the Great Coalition. . . .

Where can literature still find an outlet if the future has already been dated, the terrible statistical bottom line calculated? What is left to narrate if the human race's capacity for destroying itself and all other life in a multitude of ways is proven daily and practiced in computer simulations? Nothing. Yet the atomic self-annihilation, which might come at any hour, relates to Auschwitz and expands the "final solution" to global dimensions.

A writer who reaches this conclusion — and from the beginning of the eighties the renewed arms race points to such a conclusion — must either make silence his imperative, or else — and after three years of abstinence I began to work on a novel again — try to give a name to this human possibility, self-annihilation.

*The Rat*, a book in which "I dreamed I had to say good-bye," was an attempt, then, to continue the crippled project of the Enlightenment. But the Zeitgeist,[5] and with it the highly paid jabbering of a culture business mightily pleased with itself, refused to be needled. Art fairs pushing one another from the market, overdirected theatrical performances, and the gigantomania of provincial tycoons who have recently discovered art are features of the eighties. The entertaining bustle of mediocrity and its talk show hosts, who can say absolutely anything but are not allowed to pause, lest they fall into shocked silence — all this dynamic mindlessness did not begin to stumble until, beyond the pale of this doubly fortified prosperity, the peoples of Eastern and Central Europe rose up, one after the other, and gave new meaning to old-fashioned words like solidarity and freedom.

Since then something has happened. The West stands naked. The cry       35
over there, "We are the people," found no echo over here. "We are already free," people here said. "We already have everything, the only thing missing is unity." And thus a thing that yesterday raised hopes and brought Europe into focus becomes twisted into German aspirations. Once again the call is heard for "all of Germany."

. . . I want — in closing — to confront the break in civilization epito-mized by Auschwitz with the German longing for reunification. Ausch-witz speaks against every trend born of manipulation of public opinion, against the purchasing power of the West German economy — for the hard currency of Deutschmarks even unification can be acquired — and yes, even against the right to self-determination granted without hesitation to other peoples. Auschwitz speaks against all this, because one of the preconditions for the terrible thing that happened was a strong, unified Germany.

By themselves not Prussia, not Bavaria, not even Austria could have developed the methodology and the will for organized genocide, and implemented it; it had to be all of Germany. We have every reason to fear ourselves as a unit. Nothing, no sense of nationhood, however idyl-lically colored, and no assurance of late-born benevolence can modify or dispel the experience that we the criminals, with our victims, had as a unified Germany. We cannot get around Auschwitz. And no matter how greatly we want to, we should not attempt to get around it, because

---

[5]The spirit of the age. — ED.

Auschwitz belongs to us, is a permanent stigma of our history — and a positive gain! It has made possible this insight: Finally we know ourselves.

Thinking about Germany is also part of my literary work. Since the mid-sixties and into the present continuing turmoil, there have been occasions for speeches and essays. Often my necessarily cutting remarks have struck my contemporaries as excessive interference, as extraliterary meddling. That is not my concern. Rather, I am left with a sense of inadequacy after completing this thirty-five-year balance sheet. Something remains to be said that has not yet been put into words. An old story wants to be told altogether differently. Perhaps I will succeed in this task. My speech has to find its end, but there is no end to writing after Auschwitz, no such promise can be made — unless the human race gives up on itself completely.

## EXPLORATIONS

1. Auschwitz is a town in southwestern Poland. What else does the name refer to? When Günter Grass speaks of Auschwitz in this essay, what larger meaning is he invoking?

2. What was Grass's involvement with National Socialism before and during World War II? How has his involvement affected his life since the war ended?

3. What is Grass's attitude toward German reunification? What reason does he give for his position?

4. Why would you guess Grass was asked to make this speech? What appears to be his purpose in speaking?

## CONNECTIONS

1. Christopher Reynolds's "Cultural Journey to Africa" (p. 258) and Grass's "After Auschwitz" both describe efforts to reclaim a lost heritage. Whose task do you think is harder, and why?

2. In "So Tsi-fai" (p. 219), Sophronia Liu is haunted by a schoolmate's death. In "Chairman Mao's Good Little Boy" (p. 97), Liang Heng recalls his mother's ostracism. In "After Auschwitz," Grass looks back at the Third Reich. What are the similarities in these three authors' associations with the tragic injustices they are writing about? What was each author's view of the situation at the time, and what is it now?

3. Look back at Salman Rushdie's observations about being a writer in exile in "The Broken Mirror" (p. 240). Judging from Rushdie's comments, how do

you think leaving their homelands has affected Sophronia Liu's and Liang Heng's writing about the past? How has staying in Germany had a different impact on Günter Grass's writing about the past?

## ELABORATIONS

1. One of Grass's explanations for Nazi crimes is other Germans' belief that "Germans would never do a thing like that" (para. 5). What role does such a belief play in political controversies involving the United States? Investigate a recent domestic or international problem in which people have relied on their faith that Americans (or Republicans, or Christians, or elected officials, or "my child," or whoever) would never do a thing like that. Write an essay showing what impact their belief had on the situation and indicating whether or not it was valid.

2. "How was it possible to write — after Auschwitz?" asks Grass in paragraph 9. "And does the question even matter nowadays, when the very idea of literature is being challenged by the new media?" Is literary writing still essential to our culture? Write an essay defining the functions of writing and arguing for or against its continuing importance.

# YORAM BINUR

## *Palestinian Like Me*

At 33, Israeli journalist Yoram Binur was fluent in Arabic and knowledgeable about Palestine. He had lived in the Arab city of Ramallah while serving as a lieutenant in the Israeli Defense Forces' elite Parachutists' Unit in 1976. As a reporter for the Jerusalem newspaper *Kol Ha'ir*, Binur decided to make bold use of his skills. A committed Zionist, for six months he posed as an Arab laborer in Jerusalem and Tel Aviv. Living as part of a despised minority group showed him an unexpectedly dark side of these familiar cities, as he became the victim of prejudice, discrimination, and sometimes violence from his own people. Out of Binur's experiences came his book *My Enemy, My Self* (1989), from which "Palestinian Like Me" was excerpted in *New Age Journal* (May/June 1989) and reprinted in the *Utne Reader* (Sept./Oct. 1989). Yoram Binur continues to live and work in Jerusalem.

After World War I, victorious Britain and France divided up the Middle Eastern remnants of Turkey's Ottoman Empire. France was to control Syria and Lebanon, while Britain continued to dominate Egypt, Iraq, the newly created Transjordan, and Palestine (the southeastern Mediterranean coast). Their plans to make these territories independent were hampered in Palestine by the struggle for dominance between its Arab and Jewish populations. With World War II, and the Nazi slaughter of Jews, the need for an official Jewish homeland became urgent. After the war, Britain turned Palestine over to the United Nations, which in 1948 voted to create the state of Israel. The angry Arabs denied Israel's right to exist. Tensions flared in 1967 into the Six Day War, which ended with Israel not only intact but in control of the rest of Palestine, previously managed by Syria, Jordan, and Egypt (see p. 629). A new attack on Israel by Syria and Egypt in 1973 brought the United States into the picture as a mediator. An Arab summit conference the next year recognized the Palestine Liberation Organization (PLO) under Yasir Arafat as the sole legitimate representative of the Palestinian people — that is, the Arab Palestinians living in the West Bank and Gaza Strip, now occupied by Israel. Israel's refusal to negotiate with the PLO and its policy of building settlements in the occupied territories increased Arab resentment, Palestinian resistance, and Israeli reprisals. It was in that climate of hostility, repression, and terrorism that Yoram Binur launched the experiment he describes in "Palestinian Like Me." His essay continues into the *intifada*, an uprising of Palestinians inside and outside Israeli-run refugee camps against the troops whom they regard as an army of occupation (see paras. 44–45). The Israeli government treated the grass-roots violence of the intifada as a terrorist campaign. However, the hundreds of Palestinian casualties focused worldwide attention on the PLO's demand for an independent Palestinian state. In 1993 Israel and the PLO officially recognized each other's legitimacy and agreed that Israel would cede control of the Gaza Strip and the West Bank town of Jericho to the Palestinians.

For more background on Palestine and Israel, see page 629. For more background on the Arab countries, see pages 361 and 372.

In 1984, I began work as a reporter for the local weekly newspaper in Jerusalem, *Kol Ha'ir* ("The voice of the city"). I took the Arab beat, covering not only East Jerusalem but also most of the West Bank and occasionally the Gaza Strip as well. My close daily interaction with Arabs from the occupied territories considerably improved my command of spoken Arabic as well as my knowledge of Arab manners and gestures.

I first became aware of the degree to which I had absorbed Palestinian culture when I traveled to Nablus with Danny Rubinstein, a seasoned reporter from the newspaper *Davar*, to interview a relative of Abu Nidal, the notorious Palestinian terrorist leader. During our conversation, I learned that the interviewee thought I was Rubinstein's Arab guide. On other occasions, too, Arabs from the occupied territories mistook me for a compatriot.

This misapprehension, together with the fact that news items on the West Bank tended to be rather dull and routine at the time, led me to suggest to my editor a different approach to my reporting. My idea was to offer a fresh perspective on Israeli Jews' relationship with the Palestinians by posing as a Palestinian in a variety of settings and recording my feelings, as well as the reactions of people toward me.

After I'd established an identity and made my preparations, I discussed my plan with Feisal Al Husseini, one of the most important Arab leaders in the occupied territories (who had recently spent nine months under administrative detention). Husseini explained the risk I was running: if the Arabs I contacted suspected me of being an undercover agent working for the Shin Beth (the Israeli secret service, now known as Shabak), my life would be in danger. Husseini gave me a letter in which he asked that I be given all possible assistance so that I might carry out my journalistic mission without hindrance. In view of his uncontested leadership among the people of the occupied territories, the letter would serve as a sort of insurance policy. It could save my life in a tight spot — provided I had time enough to whip it out.

And so, over a period of six months, I lived more or less continuously   5 as an Arab, generally seeking to involve myself in situations that were typical for the average Palestinian living under Israeli military rule. I stayed in cities and in refugee camps. I worked in restaurants and garages. I lodged with Arab laborers. I even, in my guise as an Arab, had a relationship with a Jewish Israeli woman and volunteered on a kibbutz.

Posing as a Palestinian Arab enabled me to see the conflict in a different perspective and to experience it with a greater intensity. To state that Arabs are discriminated against in the Jewish state of Israel is hardly an earthshaking revelation. But posing as a Palestinian, I was able to understand, for the first time, what it means for a man to feel afraid and insecure inside his own home when a military patrol passes outside his window. I had heard Palestinians tell of such things many times, and I had always regarded it as an exaggerated example used to embellish their arguments against the occupation. But when I was myself gripped by that paralyzing fear, when I felt it in my guts, I grasped a dimension of their lives in a way that I never really could have as an Israeli journalist, however understanding I might be of the Palestinian situation. It wasn't a question of discovering new facts, but of discovering what it meant to *feel* the facts.

Among my first jobs was a stint as a restaurant worker at Hatuki ("The Parrot"), a small Tel Aviv pub. A family atmosphere prevailed there, but, needless to say, I wasn't really a part of the family. I was a servant. Everyone ordered me around: "I see our Arab is a little idle, so let him take out the glasses and wash them over again." Once, when Osnat, a young waitress, had some friends visiting, I overheard one of them ask about "her" Arab worker. I also clearly heard her answer: "This Arab, I swear — with just a little improvement he could be a Jew."

One night at Hatuki, all the feelings of frustration and humiliation that I was to experience as an Arab worker were brought home. The owner's sister, Michal, and her boyfriend came in the kitchen around two in the morning, when most of the customers had already gone. I was in the kitchen washing dishes. Laughing excitedly, they pushed their way into the kitchen — which had hardly enough room for one person to move around in — and squeezed themselves into a small corner between me and the refrigerator and proceeded to kiss each other passionately.

Suddenly, a sort of trembling came over me. I realized that they had not meant to put on a peep show for my enjoyment. The two of them were not the least bit concerned about what I saw or felt, even when they began practically screwing under my nose. For them I simply didn't exist. I was invisible, a nonentity! It is difficult to describe the extreme humiliation I felt. Looking back, I think it was the most degrading moment of my entire posing adventure.

I stuck with my awful job at Hatuki more out of inertia than by virtue of any strength of will. In the meantime, I moved in with a group of          10

Arabs, residents of the Israeli town of Um El Fahem. Since they were citizens of Israel, they were not living in the city illegally, and the flat was rented for them by the restaurant at which they all worked.

On my first night there, I dined with my roommates. They had brought a bag from their restaurant containing some pita bread and various salads. When we ran out of pita and were still hungry, Abu Kasem, the eldest of the group, took a few shekels out of his pocket and turned to the youngest. "Hussein," he requested, "go to the bakery and get some more pita." Hussein checked his shirt pocket to confirm that his ID card was in place and asked Kasem whether there were any police detectives about. Kasem assured him that the coast was clear, and Hussein left.

It was around seven in the evening, an hour when innocent pedestrians aren't ordinarily arrested in the streets, and I professed astonishment at their caution. "What? You have an Israeli ID, don't you?"

"What do you know?" replied Kasem. "In the West Bank, you call us 'Jews,' but for the cops here we're 100 percent Arabs, and it's bad news when they get their hands on us.

"Our land has all been appropriated by the Jews," he continued, "so there's nothing to cultivate. There aren't any factories, and there are no other jobs, so we depend completely on the Jews for work."

Hussein — who had by then returned with the pita — joined in,      15 pointing out that the Arabs from the occupied territories are not the only ones who suffer. "At the restaurant they were looking for someone educated to sit by the cash register. I brought in my cousin, who is studying computers at Tel Aviv University. When they saw he was an Arab, they said they didn't need anyone anymore, and a few days later they brought in a Jewish guy who had hardly finished elementary school."

The television set was on and the news broadcast had begun. A report of a terrorist attack on a Jewish synagogue in Istanbul was accompanied by harrowing images of the victims being taken away for burial. Just then, Hussein took a phone call. After a few seconds, he pounded violently on the table in front of him. "What do you want from me? What do you *suppose* I think about it?!" he shouted, and slammed down the receiver. A few minutes later he calmed down sufficiently to tell us what the argument had been about. "That was my Jewish girlfriend. She saw the news and called to ask me what I thought about the [Palestinian] organizations' attacking a synagogue in Istanbul and killing the Jewish worshipers. I'm fed up with having to justify myself every time something like that happens. They demand constantly that you prove you aren't a terrorist and want you to apologize for everything that happens in the world."

That was the sort of bitterness I would be exposed to throughout my project. Another such incident occurred at the small home of Abd Al

Karim Lubad, with whom I stayed for a couple of weeks while visiting Jebalya, one of the largest refugee camps in the area that was occupied by Israel in 1967. Several of my host's friends had stopped by; one of them was telling us about his experience working among the Jews:

"Once I was picking fruit on some farm near Ashkelon. We worked like donkeys from morning to evening and slept in a stinking, run-down shed in the orchard. After a week, payday came around, and that night the boss brought in some thugs armed with guns who beat us and chased us, yelling, 'You're all terrorists!' We had to get out of there, and a whole week of hard work went to hell. We didn't get a shekel."

Lubad, my host, erupted. "Those Zionists are getting money from America all the time. Like a flock of sheep, they just stand with mouths open and ask for more. And they're always talking about what Hitler did to them in Europe. I don't believe that Hitler killed the Jews, they just killed each other."

His wicked assertion made my blood boil. The young Palestinians in    20 whose company I found myself were intellectuals who knew — or should have known — the truth about the Holocaust. But because so much of their pent-up anger and frustration had resulted from their growing up in a refugee camp, it would have been hard for me to protest against the hatred they felt toward anything that even faintly smacked of Zionism.

In October 1986, I ventured to a large right-wing Israeli demonstration in support of "Jewish Underground" members who had been imprisoned for terrorist acts — bombings, shootings, murder, and more — against Palestinians living on the West Bank. The demonstration took place in the square opposite the main synagogue in Jerusalem, less than a mile away from the Arab section of the city. Most of the men were bearded and wore knitted skullcaps, a style that Israelis instantly identify with a form of religious nationalism tinged with a messianic streak. Some of the men were also armed. Many of the demonstrators were waving small replicas of the Israeli flag.

The event was a show of strength for Israel's radical right wing, and my presence there, in my Arab outfit, was an extreme form of provocation. I pushed my way through the crowd and began listening to the speeches about the "beloved sons who were not guilty of any wrongdoing." The prevailing sentiment was that to spray a college campus with bullets and to freely fling hand grenades at students did not constitute a criminal offense so long as the victims were Arabs. Nor was it considered a crime to plant bombs in the cars of public servants, or to demolish buses loaded with peaceful civilians, if those being blown to pieces were Arabs.

Suddenly a hand grabbed hold of my arm and viciously yanked me backward. Turning, I found myself confronting a very red, bearded face that was contorted with hatred. The face rapidly fired questions at me in English: "Who are you? What are you doing here? Where are you from?"

"This is a public place and it is my right to be here," I protested feebly.

Under the circumstances, I could hardly have chosen a less effective    25
argument. Some members of the crowd seemed convinced that this time they had a bona fide terrorist on their hands. Curses, kicks, and blows rained down on me. Curious newcomers, inquiring what it was all about, received this illuminating explanation: "There's an Arab here!" A voice in the mob cried out, "Get out of here! You have nothing to do with us!" I undoubtedly would have complied with this helpful suggestion if only I could have freed myself from the tight group in which I was being held. And so the hysterical shouting went on: "We've caught an Arab, call the police! Quick!"

A path opened up in the crowd as people moved aside to let a policeman through. Without wasting words, he led me away. As we left, we were joined by two of my captor's colleagues, young border policemen like himself. Together we crossed the street and headed toward a very dark and narrow alley. These cops have a devilish knack for finding — conveniently close to the commotion — the kind of dark and isolated corner that perfectly suits their purposes.

"Stand up straight!" I was ordered, and a direct punch in the stomach immediately followed. It was powerful enough to make me double up in pain — in violation of the instruction I'd just been given. A second policeman countered the effect of the blow by shoving a crooked finger under my chin, like a hook, and abruptly pulling me back to an up-right position. They announced their next decision: "All right! Now we'll take out everything he's got in his stinking pockets." All they found was a keffiyeh (the traditional Arab headdress), a bunch of keys, and a wallet.

They returned the keys and the wallet to me, but one of them wound the red keffiyeh (the color favored by many Palestinian leftists) tightly around his hand, as if underscoring the point that I wasn't going to get it back soon. "Now take out your ID."

I was released with another blow, this time to the back of my neck. I hastily drew my Israeli ID from my wallet and fearfully handed it over. I knew that this humiliating experience could continue for hours. The policeman examining my document whistled in surprise. "We've caught a big fish here! He's got a false ID. I'm taking him over to the patrol car, and you" — he turned to his subordinates — "keep very close watch from behind so he doesn't escape."

The two policemen obediently positioned themselves behind me while    30
the one in charge escorted me, steering me by the arm. "Come on, you

bastard. We're taking you to our superior now; then you're going for a ride to detention, and on the way we'll take care of you in such a way that you'll never forget it as long as you live."

The blows that were urging me to move along ceased abruptly the moment we reached the brightly lit street. I was taken to a border-police jeep that was parked across from the demonstration. A giant of an officer, well over six feet tall, accepted my ID and keffiyeh with as much satisfaction as if he'd just been presented with a firearm taken from a captured terrorist. Then he instructed me to wait a short distance from the jeep while he spoke into his walkie-talkie. He reported that an extremely suspicious ID had been found on the person of an Arab who was just apprehended at the demonstration, where he had been loitering with no apparent purpose.

Soon, the walkie-talkie barked back instructions concerning my ID: it seemed that the police computer had a file on me. The officer wasn't able to hide his frustration as he gave me the welcome news, "I'm giving you three minutes to get out of here, and don't you dare enter the area of the demonstration or you'll be arrested."

This time I had no intention of compromising. "I have a right to be at the demonstration," I insisted.

"All right," the officer conceded, "but without that red keffiyeh. If I see you with the keffiyeh, I'm arresting you on the spot." Of course, there was no legal basis for this demand, either. His job, as a policeman, was to protect me even if I went in there with a dozen keffiyehs, but I had no strength for further arguments.

I returned to the demonstration, which was about to end. The flags    35
were raised up high and the crowd began to sing "Hatikva"; they must have felt that invoking the Israeli national anthem was an appropriate gesture in support of Jewish terrorists. They stood motionless as they sang, but I couldn't remain still and moved restlessly about. Even though I was an Israeli Jew, their *tikva* ("hope") was certainly not mine.

Before one can speak of the *intifada*, as the Palestinians call the current uprising, one must first understand how the Palestinians have coped with life under the Israeli occupation up to this point. The key concept in this respect is *sumud*, which means "sticking with it," "staying put," "holding fast" to one's objectives and to the land — in a word, survival. Sumud is an attitude, a philosophy, and a way of life. It maintains that one must carry on in a normal and undisturbed fashion, as much as possible. Compared with organized civil disobedience, or passive resistance as preached by Gandhi, sumud is a more basic form of resistance growing out of the idea that merely to exist, to survive, and to remain on one's land is an act of defiance — especially when deportation is the one thing Palestinians fear most.

Although sumud is essentially passive by nature, it has a more active aspect, consisting of gestures that underscore the difference between surviving under difficult conditions and accepting them. During the course of my project, I was several times presented with examples of this active sumud. On one occasion, I met a Palestinian youth whom I shall call Abed, who told me about his version of sumud. "Despite the fact that I am a university graduate," he said, "I can't find work in my profession, so I earn my living as a construction worker."

"Where do you work?" I asked.

"In Beit El, up there." He pointed at the hill that overlooked the refugee camp. On the hillside, one could see scattered houses with the European-style, slanted red-tile roofs that are characteristic of the Jewish settlements in the West Bank. "That means you not only work for the Jewish, but you work for the worst of them, for the settlers," I said, in an admonishing tone of voice.

Abed exchanged glances with his friends — as if to ask them whether    40
to include me in their little secret — and replied, "True, we work for the settlers. The money we earn allows us to live here, to be *samidin* (practitioners of sumud), but that isn't all. For us, in this camp, sumud isn't just bringing home money and buying a sack of rice and a few bags of sugar. When I work at the settlement I take advantage of every opportunity to fight them."

"What can you do as a simple laborer?"

"Quite a bit. First of all, after I lay tiles in the bathroom or kitchen of an Israeli settler, when the tiles are all in place and the cement has already dried, I take a hammer and break a few. When we finish installing sewage pipes, and the Jewish subcontractor has checked to see that everything is all right, then I stuff a sackful of cement into the pipe. As soon as water runs through that pipe the cement gets hard as a rock, and the sewage system becomes blocked."

Two older men who were sitting at a table near ours joined in the conversation. Abu Adnan and Abu Ibrahim represented a generation of Palestinians that is haunted by the stinging defeat of 1948, at which time the Arabs either fled — leaving behind their villages and land — or were forcibly deported. But the younger generation, which is more active in resisting the occupation, owes its nationalistic education and inspiration to these elders. The elders are the ones who nurtured and sustained the Palestinian's identification with the villages of their origin. When asked where they are from, even youngsters who have never known an existence other than in the miserable shanties of a refugee camp can proudly name the place of their family's origin — which is often a village that ceased to exist long before they were born.

The intifada, which means "the shaking" (in the sense of shaking oneself free or awake), began with demonstrations in the Jebalya refugee camp on December 8, 1987, spread quickly to other camps, and continues to this day. There have been hundreds of deaths and casualties, mostly among Palestinians.

The intifada, in my opinion, can be understood as the anguished cry     45
of a minority trying to call attention to the discrimination that is being practiced against it, as much as a demand for national liberation. But Israeli officials prefer to speak of "violent disturbances of order," or just plain riots.

About three weeks after the intifada broke out, I visited the Shati refugee camp near Gaza. Shati is a miserable place to live even in ordinary times; now the chaos was unprecedented. The sewer had run over, flooding entire streets. Large garbage cans were being used as road barriers, and the sand in the alleys was covered with a black layer of burned rubber, the residue of all the tires that had blazed there over the past three months. Children, rulers of the intifada, could be found at all points along the perimeter of the camp, armed with improvised slingshots and creating an atmosphere of apocalypse and anarchy.

We went over to the Shifa hospital, which was located near the camp. There we visited, among others, Muhriz Hamuda Al Nimnin, a young victim of the recent violence. His brother, who was at his bedside, said, "If they had done it to me it would at least have made some sense, because I throw rocks and Molotov cocktails. But Muhriz is a sick person who never participated in a demonstration." He then told us as much of the story as he knew.

People in the camp had seen Muhriz being arrested by the soldiers who manned a lookout post. Eighteen days after his arrest, he was found unconscious in front of the entrance to the Shifa hospital. In addition to the usual injuries inflicted by the Israeli troops — broken arms and legs — Muhriz had been hit on the head. He was now a vegetable, incapable of speaking, unable to tell what had happened. The palms of his hands and his fingers were badly burned, as though he had been forced to grasp a red-hot metal object.

I asked Muhriz's brother if he was sure that it was the soldiers who had inflicted these injuries. He replied that there were witnesses who had seen Muhriz being beaten by soldiers when he was arrested, "but not in such a way." The brother spread out the contents of a sack that had been found next to Muhriz at the gate of the hospital. In it were the clothes that the victim had apparently worn throughout the period of his absence.

To my dismay, I discovered a damning piece of evidence among the    50
foul-smelling rags: a strip of flannel cloth of the kind used in the army
for wiping weapons clean of grime and oil. The rag was tied in the shape
of a loop the size of a man's head. Since soldiers commonly use these
strips of cloth for blindfolding suspects, the chances seemed good that
the criminal act of sadism committed against Muhriz had indeed been
carried out by members of the Israeli Defense Forces.


For twenty years the Palestinians have lived among us. During the day
we have been the employers who profited by their labor and exploited
them for all they are worth; in the afternoon we have been the police; in
the evening we have been the soldiers at the roadblock on the way home;
and at night we have been the security forces who entered their homes
and arrested them. The young Palestinians work in Tel Aviv, Jerusalem,
and other Israeli cities. They identify with the values of Israeli society at
least as much as they do with their traditional backgrounds. They get a
whiff of the democratic privileges that Israeli citizens enjoy, but they
cannot share in them. The young man who spends his work week among
a people living under democratic rule returns to his home, which is only
an hour away but which has (in effect, if not officially) been under curfew
for twenty years. Any Arab who walks in the streets at a late hour can
expect to be detained and questioned about his actions, even during
periods of relative calm. He sees and recognizes the value of freedom but
is accorded the kind of treatment that characterizes the most backward
dictatorial regimes. How can he be anything but frustrated?
    In the end, the impressions I was left with formed a depressing picture
of fear and mistrust on both sides. The Palestinians, employed as a cheap
labor force, are excluded from Israeli society, whereas Israeli Jews are
satisfied to rule without the least curiosity about how the other side lives.
My conclusion is that a continuation of Israel's military presence in the
West Bank and Gaza Strip threatens to change Israel into a place that
many people, including myself, will find unlivable. I am tired of witnessing the disastrous results of the occupation every day. And I am frightened
that many more people, on both sides, may be doomed to suffer bloodshed and destruction.

# EXPLORATIONS

1. What did Yoram Binur hope to accomplish when he started posing as an Arab? What surprises did his project bring him? How does he change from the beginning to the end of this essay?

2. What are the similarities between *sumud* (para. 36) and the *intifada* (paras. 44–45)? What are the differences?

3. What does Binur gain by reporting as a Jew and an Arab at the same time? How would the impact of his essay change if he wrote from an objective third-person viewpoint instead of a subjective first-person viewpoint?

# CONNECTIONS

1. Why does Binur's friend Abd Al Karim Lubad declare, "I don't believe that Hitler killed the Jews" (para. 19)? According to Günter Grass in "After Auschwitz" (p. 264), why did many Germans make the same assertion during and after the Holocaust?

2. In "Nippon Challenge" (p. 53), Patrick Smith writes that "symbols can be mistaken for substance when we look at the Japanese, because the Japanese generally do not distinguish between the two" (para. 2). What examples can you find in "Palestinian Like Me" of people mistaking symbols for substance, or judging inaccurately by appearance? What are the results?

3. Reread James Baldwin's comments in *Looking at Ourselves* (p. 196). How is the shocking discovery he describes similar to Binur's? In what ways is the basis of racism different in the United States and Israel?

# ELABORATIONS

1. In paragraphs 19–20, Binur recalls a Palestinian denying Hitler's slaughter of Jews during the Holocaust. Throughout his account he describes people choosing to believe their prejudices rather than the evidence. What reasons can you identify for this irrational behavior? Write a cause-and-effect essay explaining it, and, if possible, suggesting some remedies.

2. In "Tradition and the African Writer" (p. 35), Es'kia Mphahlele talks about black Africans' second-class status in their own countries. Write an essay comparing and contrasting that experience with the Palestinian's experience described by Binur.

3. Review the selections you have read in *Landmarks and Turning Points: The Struggle for Identity*, including *Looking at Ourselves*. Write an essay classifying the different ways a person (or group) clarifies his or her identity. Which ones involve discovering something about oneself? Recognizing a bond with other people? Identifying an enemy?

# PART FOUR

# WOMEN AND MEN

## *Images of the Opposite Sex*

### LOOKING AT OURSELVES

Paula Gunn Allen, Daniel Evan Weiss, Gloria Steinem,
Joe Kane, Sally Jacobs, Camille Paglia, Lawrence Wright,
Rose Weitz, Richard Goldstein, Deborah Tannen

Carlos Fuentes, *Matador and Madonna* (SPAIN/LATIN AMERICA)

Leslie Marmon Silko, *Yellow Woman* (UNITED STATES)

Nikos Kazantzakis, *The Isle of Aphrodite* (GREECE)

Simone de Beauvoir, *Woman as Other* (FRANCE)

Alberto Moravia, *The Chase* (ITALY)

Ken Bugul, *The Artist's Life in Brussels* (BELGIUM/SENEGAL)

Marjorie Shostak, *Nisa's Marriage* (BOTSWANA)

Naila Minai, *Women in Early Islam* (ARAB WORLD)

Miriam Cooke, *The Veil Does Not Prevent
Women from Working* (SAUDI ARABIA)

Yashar Kemal, *A Dirty Story* (TURKEY)

ESSENTIAL TO THE SURVIVAL OF HUMANITY IS THE BOND BETWEEN A woman and a man. Recognizing its importance, nearly every culture creates a social structure of rules, expectations, ideals, and rituals around this central relationship. Yet perhaps in no other aspect of existence is the contrast between cultures so striking. We differ not only in our courtship and marriage customs but in our basic assumptions about what love is, what constitutes a good reason for two (or more) people to marry or divorce, and even how women and men are fundamentally different.

It is this last subject — the variety of ways men and women perceive each other — on which we focus here. In *Looking at Ourselves*, Paula Gunn Allen examines female images among American Indians, and Daniel Evan Weiss compares gender images on television. Gloria Steinem notes the illogic of oppression; Joe Kane comments on rivalry over power; Sally Jacobs asks if backlash against traditional power roles means that now-adays white men can't win. Camille Paglia and Lawrence White give contrasting views on men's biological aggressiveness. Rose Weitz talks about both genders' fears of homosexuality; Richard Goldstein considers homosexual marriages. Deborah Tannen contrasts female and male communication styles.

Moving abroad, Mexican writer Carlos Fuentes describes gender images in Spain and Latin America in "Matador and Madonna." Leslie Marmon Silko's short story "Yellow Woman" shows a Laguna Pueblo woman entranced by a lover sprung from the old tribal legends. In "The Isle of Aphrodite," Greek writer Nikos Kazantzakis finds diverse female images on Cyprus, the goddess's birthplace.

To French feminist Simone de Beauvoir, conflict between the sexes arises from man's age-old habit of viewing woman as alien and therefore threatening. Alberto Moravia shows that male tendency in a different light with his short story "The Chase," in which an Italian husband gains a new appreciation for his wife's unpredictability. Ken Bugul feels alien on two levels in "The Artist's Life in Brussels" as a woman who has left a Senegalese hut for a European ménage à trois. Marjorie Shostak's "Nisa's Marriage" is a Botswana woman's recollections of becoming first a wife and then an adult.

In the Middle East, Naila Minai's "Women in Early Islam" explains how Muhammad created a religion meant to safeguard women. Miriam Cooke disputes Western images of Muslim women in "The Veil Does Not Prevent Women from Working." Sexual harassment escalates into violence in Yashar Kemal's "A Dirty Story" when neighbors in a fictional Turkish farming village turn a victim into a villain.                    ◇

# LOOKING AT OURSELVES

## 1

An American Indian woman is primarily defined by her tribal identity. In her eyes, her destiny is necessarily that of her people, and her sense of herself as a woman is first and foremost prescribed by her tribe. The definitions of woman's roles are as diverse as tribal cultures in the Americas. In some she is devalued, in others she wields considerable power. In some she is a familial/clan adjunct, in some she is as close to autonomous as her economic circumstances and psychological traits permit. But in no tribal definitions is she perceived in the same way as are women in Western industrial and postindustrial cultures.

In the West, few images of women form part of the cultural mythos, and these are largely sexually charged. Among Christians, the Madonna is the female prototype, and she is portrayed as essentially passive: her contribution is simply that of birthing. Little else is attributed to her, and she certainly possesses few of the characteristics that are attributed to mythic figures among the Indian tribes. This image is countered (rather than balanced) by the witch-goddess/whore characteristics designed to reinforce cultural beliefs about women, as well as Western adversarial and dualistic perceptions of reality.

The tribes see women variously, but they do not question the power of femininity. Sometimes they see women as fearful, sometimes peaceful, sometimes omnipotent and omniscient, but they never portray women as mindless, helpless, simple, or oppressed. And while the women in a given tribe, clan, or band may be all these things, the individual woman is provided with a variety of images of women from the interconnected supernatural, natural, and social worlds she lives in.

> – Paula Gunn Allen
> "Where I Come from Is Like This"
> *The Sacred Hoop*, 1986

## 2

### *Females and Males on Prime-Time TV*

33 percent of the characters on prime-time TV are female. 67 percent are male.

43 percent of the characters in sit-coms are female. 57 percent are male.

25 percent of the characters in action-adventure programs are female. 75 percent are male.

66 percent of the females on prime-time shows are age 18 to 35. 52 percent of the males on prime-time shows are age 35 or older.

3 percent of the female and 12 percent of the male characters on prime-time shows have gray hair.

35 percent of the female and 7 percent of the male characters on prime-time shows are blond.

19 percent of the female and 12 percent of the male characters on prime-time shows are married.

The marital status of 31 percent of the female and 58 percent of the male characters on prime-time shows is undetermined.

Female characters on prime-time shows are 10 times more likely to be wearing provocative attire than males.

18 percent of all cartoon characters with an identifiable sex are female. 82 percent are male.

> – Daniel Evan Weiss
> *The Great Divide: How Females
> and Males Really Differ*, 1991
> [Data from *Media Report to Women*,
> 1986, 1987]

## 3

Living in India made me understand that a white minority of the world has spent centuries conning us into thinking a white skin makes people superior, even though the only thing it really does is make them more subject to ultraviolet rays and wrinkles.

Reading Freud made me just as skeptical about penis envy. The power of giving birth makes "womb envy" more logical, and an organ as external and unprotected as the penis makes men very vulnerable indeed.

But listening recently to a woman describe the unexpected arrival of her menstrual period (a red stain had spread on her dress as she argued heatedly on the public stage) still made me cringe with embarrassment. That is, until she explained that, when finally informed in whispers of the obvious event, she had said to the all-male audience, "and you should be *proud* to have a menstruating woman on your stage. It's probably the first real thing that's happened to this group in years!"

Laughter. Relief. She had turned a negative into a positive. Somehow her story merged with India and Freud to make me finally understand the power of positive thinking. Whatever a "superior" group has will be used to justify its superiority, and whatever an "inferior" group has will be used to justify its plight. Black men were given poorly paid jobs because they were said to be "stronger" than white men, while all women were relegated to poorly paid jobs because they were said to be "weaker." As the little boy said when asked if he wanted to be a lawyer like his mother, "Oh no, that's women's work." Logic has nothing to do with oppression.

> – Gloria Steinem
> *Outrageous Acts and Everyday Rebellions,*
> 1984

# 4

For all the supposed enlightenment of the last decade, there is still no accepted place in our culture for the man whose mate is a more powerful figure than he is.

Women have begun to ascend — *have* ascended — into roles of power and prestige once reserved for men. No corresponding change in acceptable roles has occurred for men. . . .

Come on, admit it: When you meet an ambitious, successful woman, and the man in her life is not an achiever of equal note, you figure him for a wimp, don't you? And your judgment of him is far more severe than your judgment of her would be if the situation were reversed. If there is no new role for men in a world where women are rising, men will just be that much more reluctant to give up the roles they already have.

> – Joe Kane
> "Star Wars: How Men Are Coping
> with Female Success"
> *Ms.,* 1985

# 5

The message often comes quiet as a whisper, but it's hard to miss.

One white man got it sitting in a parents group at his son's school: "Everyone wants to know what the African-American and the Haitian and the Native American think, but no one really cares what the white man thinks. I am a known quantity. I am invisible."

Another white man got it from white women.

"They think white men are very uncool; they've heard it all before," a

Boston lawyer said. "Sometimes I think I should make it up, like I tell them I was emotionally abused. Fortunately I have my ethnicity to fall back on since I'm Jewish."

They are white men in a changing world, the only ethnic group — as they see it — that is not in vogue. Men, of course, have been the subject of jokes for as long as there have been women. But held up against an earnest PC [politically correct] morality, some white men object that they are not only the victims of sexist and racist humor but are being held singularly responsible for the travails of Western civilization.

They are.

In a world to which diversity is the password, white men are white bread. Unfeeling, undeserving, imbued with privilege from their pasty pates to their tasseled toes — or so the stereotype goes — white men are out of fashion, out of touch, and in a few cases out of a job. And while there are many who believe it's long overdue, some white men find it all a little unnerving.

"White guys can't jump, they can't dance, they can't think, they can't [expletive], they don't get it at all," said Asa Baber, author of the "Men" column in *Playboy* magazine and a self-described "embattled white man." "We are by definition healthy, wealthy, and oppressive. Almost by definition we are jerks." . . .

People who are not white men — everybody else — have little sympathy for the groaning of a group that they consider to have been uniquely privileged throughout the nation's history, and generally at someone else's expense. Despite two decades of affirmative action, it is largely white men who occupy the seats of power in American life, seats they show little inclination of vacating voluntarily. Indeed, some say the whining of white men would be amusing, if it were not so infuriating.

"Their complaints are the most egregious example of whining self-pity to come down the pike in a long, long time," said Julian Bond, civil-rights activist and a visiting professor at Williams College. "White men have had, and do have, greater opportunity and unparalleled privilege in this country. So to hear complaints from this population just doesn't wash."

White men — particularly those who complain most bitterly about the stereotype with which they feel they've been pegged — are quick to say that the discrimination they experience pales in comparison to that suffered by other groups. No one, they insist, could be more supportive of equality and fair treatment for all peoples than they are.

And yet, there is a feeling among some white men that somehow those laudable goals are being achieved largely at their expense, that they are being made to bear the burden of hundreds of years of history in which they played no part. And it is a feeling felt most forcefully by men in their twenties and thirties, men relatively early in their careers who find their aspirations tempered by a more competitive reality than they were reared to expect.

"They say 350 years ago they were in chains, or 40 years ago they were beat up or were in prison camps, and I totally sympathize with that," said a white male library worker in Southern California who asked not to be identified. "But then I realize that the cross hairs fall on me. To them, I represent all white men. But the men who did that are long dead. I'm just me."

It is the subtlest of things: There are no protest marches against white men on Main Street, no effigies of middle-aged WASP bankers being torched in front of the local savings and loan. But white men see it out there.

They see it in the "white-men-are-slime" jokes made by women comedians. In the boiling furor over college curriculum changes that target the writings of Dead White European Males as not reflecting a multicultural world. In diversity programs in corporations across the country, they feel their views are ignored, their ideas dismissed. And they see it in the jobs and promotions they do not get.

"White working-class males have been screwed," said Terry West, [a] historian in Washington. "All I want is acknowledgement of our pain, acknowledgement of the price we have paid. Acknowledgement would go a long way to healing the wounds."

As one white professional in his early thirties said: "I feel like I have to work two or three times harder than anyone else, to really kick ass to get a promotion."

Which is precisely what women and minorities and others say they've been doing for generations.

"What they're complaining about," Bond said, "is that they used to have 100 percent of the slots and now they have to share and it burns them up." . . .

That some white men resent affirmative action — believing it allows less competent workers to get jobs or rise in their stead — is yesterday's news. But as women and minorities have painstakingly carved out their own comparatively small bit of turf, some white men have lashed out. The PC moniker itself is sometimes used derisively by white men as a means of belittling social norms they find restrictive. Some have deliberately embraced white male chauvinist behaviors as personified by Andrew Dice Clay and Rush Limbaugh.

But Frederick Lynch, author of *Invisible Victims: White Males and the*

*Crisis of Affirmative Action*, says that far more often white men keep to themselves their belief that they have been wronged. Part of the reason for that, he says, is that they are white men. And part of the reason is fear.

"It's like a new kind of McCarthyism," Lynch said. "White men are scared that if they complain they'll be tagged as racist and sexist. To complain is to confirm the stereotype."

On the other hand, it could serve to magnify the apparent threat.

"However we white males feel about what is going on, we still run the country, no doubt," said Joe Feagin, sociology professor at the University of Florida. "We like to exaggerate the challenge we face, to talk about reverse discrimination, because it plays down our power. . . . People may bash us, but it's like a light rain. It doesn't really affect us."

And few things gall people who are not white men more than white men telling their children that it does affect them.

"White parents are telling their children that women and minorities are getting all the jobs, but that's just not true; they are teaching old-fashioned racism and sexism," said Roger Wilkins, a black activist and professor of history at George Mason University. "What is happening is that white men are having to compete and they're not used to that." . . .

What, finally, are embattled, beleaguered, belittled white men to do? At a time when no substratum of society seems safe without its own support group, some white men suggest — with a glance behind their back — a support group of their own. But then, maybe that's not necessary.

"White men don't need a support group because they already have one," Bond said. "It's called the United States of America."

> – Sally Jacobs
> "White Men Can't Win"
> *Boston Sunday Globe*, 1992

# 6

Rape is an outrage that cannot be tolerated in civilized society. Yet feminism, which has waged a crusade for rape to be taken more seriously, has put young women in danger by hiding the truth about sex from them. . . .

Feminism keeps saying the sexes are the same. It keeps telling women they can do anything, go anywhere, say anything, wear anything. No, they can't. Women will always be in sexual danger.

One of my male students recently slept overnight with a friend in a passageway of the Great Pyramid in Egypt. He described the moon and sand, the ancient silence and eerie echoes. I will never experience that.

I am a woman. I am not stupid enough to believe I could ever be safe there. There is a world of solitary adventure I will never have. Women have always known these somber truths. But feminism, with its pie-in-the-sky fantasies about the perfect world, keeps young women from seeing life as it is. . . .

The sexes are at war. Men must struggle for identity against the overwhelming power of their mothers. Women have menstruation to tell them they are women. Men must do or risk something to be men. Men become masculine only when other men say they are. Having sex with a woman is one way a boy becomes a man.

College men are at their hormonal peak. They have just left their mothers and are questing for their male identity. In groups, they are dangerous. A woman going to a fraternity party is walking into Testosterone Flats, full of prickly cacti and blazing guns. If she goes, she should be armed with resolute alertness. She should arrive with girlfriends and leave with them. A girl who lets herself get dead drunk at a fraternity party is a fool. A girl who goes upstairs alone with a brother at a fraternity party is an idiot. Feminists call this "blaming the victim." I call it common sense. . . .

Aggression and eroticism are deeply intertwined. Hunt, pursuit, and capture are biologically programmed into male sexuality. Generation after generation, men must be educated, refined, and ethically persuaded away from their tendency toward anarchy and brutishness. Society is not the enemy, as feminism ignorantly claims. Society is woman's protection against rape.

> – Camille Paglia
> *Sex, Art, and American*
> *Culture,* 1992

# 7

In his early studies on the origins of neurosis, Sigmund Freud came to a damning conclusion about men. So many of his patients had revealed stories about sexual experiences in infancy or childhood that Freud decided the "seduction" of children must be the root of all neurotic behavior. When his own sister began to exhibit signs of neurosis, Freud declared: "In every case the father, not excluding my own, had to be blamed as a pervert."

I consider this statement as I stroke my daughter's hair. Caroline is ten years old. Her eyes are closed, and her head is in my lap. This should be a tender, innocent scene, but we no longer live in a time when anyone believes in innocence. Blame and suspicion color the atmosphere. As a man and a father, I feel besieged and accused. I am appallingly aware of the trust I hold, in the form of my daughter's sleeping body. The line between affection and abuse is in the front of my mind. I feel like a German coming to grips with Nazi guilt. Yes, some men are perverts — but all men? Am I?

Freud later rejected his early hypothesis after his own father died. He suspected that many of the stories his patients had related were fantasized. But now there are those who say in effect that Freud was closer to the truth the first time.

"Men are pigs and they like it that way," an angry writer stated in the op-ed section of the *New York Times*. At a 1991 women's political symposium, Texas governor Ann Richards's ethics adviser, Barbara Jordan, decreed: "I believe that women have a capacity for understanding and compassion which a man structurally does not have, does not have it because he cannot have it. He's just incapable of it." At the same meeting, Houston mayor Kathy Whitmire said that men are less intelligent than women. If these female chauvinists had been speaking of any constituency other than men, they would be run out of public life. But men feel too guilty to defend themselves. . . .

Is it possible that of the two genders nature created, one is nearly perfect and the other is badly flawed? Well, yes, say the psychobiologists. Unlike women, who carry two X chromosomes, men have an X and a Y. The latter has relatively little genetic information except for the gene that makes us men. A woman who has a recessive gene on one X chromosome might have a countering dominant gene on the other. That's not true for men, who are therefore more vulnerable to biological and environmental insults, as well as more prone to certain behavioral tendencies that may be genetically predetermined. Although male hormones (called androgens) don't cause violent criminal or sexual behavior, they apparently create an inclination in that direction. A low level of arousability — that is to say, a lack of responsiveness to external stimuli — is more common in men than in women. It is reflected in the greater number of male children who die of sudden infant death syndrome and the much larger proportion of boys who are hyperactive and require far more excitement than most children to keep from becoming bored. In adults, this biological need for extra stimulation seems to be connected to higher rates of criminality. Androgens are associated with a number of other male traits (in humans as well as animals), including assertive sexual behavior, status-related aggression, spatial reasoning, territoriality, pain tolerance, tenacity, transient bonding, sensation seeking, and predatory behavior. Obviously, this list posts many of the most common female complaints about men, and yet androgens make a man a man; one can't separate maleness from characteristic male traits.

"Why have any men at all?" wrote Sally Miller Gearhart in a 1982 manifesto titled "The Future — If There Is One — Is Female." Gearhart is an advocate of ovular merging, a process that involves the mating of two eggs, which has been successfully accomplished with mice. Only female offspring are produced. I've always worried that one day women would figure out how to get along without us and they would be able to reproduce unilaterally, like sponges. It's not genocide, exactly. It's more like job attrition, the way employers cut back positions without actually firing anyone. "A 75 percent female to 25 percent male ratio could be achieved in one generation if one half of a population reproduced heterosexually and one half by ovular merging," according to Gearhart. "Such a prospect is attractive to women who feel that if they bear sons, no amount of love and care and non-sexist training will save those sons from a culture where male violence is institutionalized and revered. These women are saying, 'No more sons. We will not spend twenty years of our lives raising a potential rapist, a potential batterer, a potential Big Man.'" . . .

I'm mad at men too. I am disgusted by the rise in child-abuse cases and reported rapes. I deplore sexual harassment. I'm grateful for the ascendancy of women in business and politics, which may yet advance the humanity of those callings. I have to issue these disclaimers because I'm a man writing on the subject. But I'm also mad at being the object of slanders such as that men are incapable of compassion. Anyone looking at men today should be able to see that they are confused and full of despair. It's not just our place in society or the family that we are struggling for; we're fighting against our own natures. We didn't create the instincts that make us aggressive, that make us value action over consensus, that make us more inclined toward strength than sympathy. Nature and human history have rewarded those qualities and in turn have created the kind of people men are. Moreover, these competitive qualities have been necessary for the survival of the species, and despite the debate over masculinity, they are still valued today. . . .

Somehow men have got to find a place for themselves again in the family. We're only beginning to see some of the consequences of fatherlessness, especially where boys are concerned. My personal fear is that fatherlessness will have unanticipated political and spiritual consequences, such as a longing for authoritarianism and a further lack of attachment between the sexes. The rise in gangs seems to be connected to the absence of male role models. There is a well-established connection between children of broken homes (a term that seems quaint these days) and the likelihood of committing serious criminal offenses. In any case, children who grow up not knowing who men are pay a price as well. I'm not saying that single mothers — or single fathers — can't do a good job of raising children. But a society of children who don't understand men produces men who don't understand themselves.

I lift up Caroline and take her to bed. Nothing in the world means more to me than our love for each other. I love the difference between us, her femaleness and my maleness. It is a powerful and curious experience to see parts of myself manifested in little-girl form; she is a sort of mirror for me, across time and gender.

I'm afraid of what life has to offer her. I'm worried that the family idea is finished and that the sexes have pulled so far apart that some radical and soulless bureaucratic arrangement is in the process of replacing it. I want Caroline to find love and to experience the joy that I have in being her parent. I want her to find a man who will love her as deeply as I do, who will take care of her and nurture her and stay with her the rest of her life. But I think the chances of that happening are small.

I know that her relationships with men will depend, in large measure, on what she gets from me. That is the most important thing I can give her, a sense of being with a man, trace memories of having me tickle her and toss her in the air, of my taking her temperature when she's sick and rubbing her face with a cool cloth, of her dancing on my shoes. She will remember these things in some almost unrememberable way: They will be a part of her character; she will be the kind of person these things happened to. Therefore she will probably be more trusting of men. That may be a mistake. Who knows what kind of men she is going to meet?

But perhaps her generation will come to a different conclusion. They may decide that the sexes have something special to offer each other, and they'll be able to look at the very things that separate men and women and appreciate them, even savor them. In that case, the language they will learn to speak to each other will be that of love, not blame.

— Lawrence Wright
*Texas Monthly*, 1992

# 8

Western culture teaches that women are the weaker sex, that they cannot flourish — or perhaps even survive — without the protection of men. Women are taught that they cannot live happy and fulfilled lives without a Prince Charming, who is superior to them in all ways. In the struggle to find and keep their men, women learn to view each other as untrustworthy competitors. They subordinate the development of their own psychological, physical, and professional strengths to the task of finding male protectors who will make up for their shortcomings. In this way, Western culture keeps women from developing bonds with each other, while it maintains their dependence on men.

Lesbians throw a large wrench into the works of this cultural system. In a society that denigrates women, lesbians value women enough to spend their lives with women rather than with men. Lesbians therefore do not and cannot rely on the protection of men. Knowing that they will not have that protection, lesbians are forced to develop their own resources. The very survival of lesbians therefore suggests the potential strength of all women and their ability to transcend their traditional roles. At the same time, since lesbians do not have even the illusion of male protection that marriage provides, and since they are likely to see their fate as tied to other women rather than to individual men, lesbians may be more likely than heterosexual women to believe in the necessity of fighting for women's rights; the heavy involvement of lesbians in the feminist movement seems to support this thesis.

Lesbians also threaten the dominant cultural system by presenting, or at least appearing to present, an alternative to the typical inequality of heterosexual relationships. Partners attempting to equalize power in a heterosexual relationship must first neutralize deeply ingrained traditional sex roles. Since lesbian relationships generally contain no built-in assumption of the superiority of one partner, developing an egalitarian relationship may be easier. Lesbian relationships suggest both that a love between equals is possible and that an alternative way of obtaining such a love may exist. Regardless of the actual likelihood of achieving equality in a lesbian relationship, the threat to the system remains, as long as lesbian relationships are believed to be more egalitarian. This threat increases significantly when, as in the past few years, lesbians express pride in and satisfaction with their life-style. . . .

The sanctions against male homosexuality appear even stronger than those against lesbianism. Why might this be so? First, I would argue that anything women do is considered relatively trivial — be it housework, mothering, or lesbianism. Second, whereas lesbians threaten the status quo by refusing to accept their inferior position as women, gay males may threaten it even more by appearing to reject their privileged status as men. Prevailing cultural mythology holds that lesbians want to be males. In a paradoxical way, therefore, lesbians may be perceived as upholding "male" values. Male homosexuality, on the other hand, is regarded as a rejection of masculine values; gay males are regarded as feminized "sissies" and "queens." Thus male homosexuality, with its implied rejection of male privilege, may seem even more incomprehensible and threatening than lesbianism. Finally, research indicates that people are more fearful and intolerant of homosexuals of their own sex than of homosexuals of the opposite sex. The greater stigmatization of male than female homosexuality may therefore simply reflect the greater ability of males to enforce their prejudices.

– Rose Weitz
"What Price Independence?"
*Women: A Feminist Perspective*, 1984

◇◇◇◇◇

## 9

Despite the cultivated image of homosexuals as emotional nomads, most gay people, at some point in their lives, establish a stable, central relationship. And, despite all that Oscar Wilde has said about marriage ("It's as demoralizing as cigarettes and far more expensive"), there is nothing new about gay people holding Ceremonies of Union, holy or otherwise. . . . What is new is the public nature of these ceremonies, and the active participation of family and clergy. Not since the year 342, when homosexual marriage was outlawed in Europe (it had flourished in the Roman Empire, largely among the aristocracy; Nero married two men, one of whom was accorded the status of an empress), has an established religion performed such ceremonies. But in 1984, the Unitarian/Universalist Association voted overwhelmingly to permit its ministers to marry congregants of the same sex. Reverend Robert Wheatly has married many homosexual couples, especially of the Catholic faith, at his Unitarian church in Boston. To "sanctify a relationship satisfies a very human need," he says. "It adds a dimension of integrity and longevity." Individual Quaker meetings will perform such ceremonies, and so will individual rabbis. "If a gay couple have, despite all the prejudices, managed to build an enduring relationship, it deserves to be recognized," says Yoel Kahn of San Francisco.

– Richard Goldstein
"The Gay Family"
*The Village Voice*, 1986

◇◇◇◇◇

## 10

At the time I began working on this book, [my husband and I] had jobs in different cities. People frequently expressed sympathy by making comments like "That must be rough," and "How do you stand it?" I was inclined to accept their sympathy and say things like "We fly a lot." Sometimes I would reinforce their concern: "The worst part is having to pack and unpack all the time." But my husband reacted differently, often with irritation. He might respond by de-emphasizing the inconvenience: As academics, we had four-day weekends together, as well as long vacations throughout the year and four months in the summer. We even benefited from the intervening days of uninterrupted time for work. I once overheard him telling a dubious man that we were lucky, since studies have shown that married couples who live together spend less than half an hour a week talking to each other; he was implying that our situation had advantages.

I didn't object to the way my husband responded — everything he said was true — but I was surprised by it. I didn't understand why he reacted as he did. He explained that he sensed condescension in some expressions of concern, as if the questioner were implying, "Yours is not a real marriage; your ill-chosen profession has resulted in an unfortunate arrangement. I pity you, and look down at you from the height of complacence, since my wife and I have avoided your misfortune." It had not occurred to me that there might be an element of one-upmanship in these expressions of concern, though I could recognize it when it was pointed out. Even after I saw the point, though, I was inclined to regard my husband's response as slightly odd, a personal quirk. He frequently seemed to see others as adversaries when I didn't.

Having done the research that led to this book, I now see that my husband was simply engaging the world in a way that many men do: as an individual in a hierarchical social order in which he was either one-up or one-down. In this world, conversations are negotiations in which people try to achieve and maintain the upper hand if they can, and protect themselves from others' attempts to put them down and push them around. Life, then, is a contest, a struggle to preserve independence and avoid failure.

I, on the other hand, was approaching the world as many women do: as an individual in a network of connections. In this world, conversations are negotiations for closeness in which people try to seek and give confirmation and support, and to reach consensus. They try to protect themselves from others' attempts to push them away. Life, then, is a community, a struggle to preserve intimacy and avoid isolation. Though there are hierarchies in this world too, they are hierarchies more of friendship than of power and accomplishment.

Women are also concerned with achieving status and avoiding failure, but these are not the goals they are *focused* on all the time, and they tend to pursue them in the guise of connection. And men are also concerned with achieving involvement and avoiding isolation, but they are not *focused* on these goals, and they tend to pursue them in the guise of opposition.

> – Deborah Tannen
> *You Just Don't Understand:*
> *Women and Men in Conversation,* 1990

## REFLECTIONS

1. Look at Paula Gunn Allen's comments about American Indian women (p. 289), Rose Weitz's comments about lesbians (p. 300), and Deborah Tannen's comments about differences in women's and men's ways of approaching the world (p. 300). What common ideas about women emerge from these three contrasting viewpoints?

2. Look at Lawrence Wright's comments about men (p. 295) and Richard Goldstein's comments about gay marriages (p. 300). What stereotype is each writer arguing against? What ability do both writers believe men have that is often underestimated?

3. According to the selections in *Looking at Ourselves*, what positive traits do men tend to share? As members of society, what advantages do men have over women? What appear to be the authors' main sources of evidence for their generalizations about men?

4. According to the selections in *Looking at Ourselves*, what positive traits do women tend to share? As members of society, what advantages do women have over men? What appear to be the authors' main sources of evidence for their generalizations about women?

# CARLOS FUENTES

## *Matador and Madonna*

Carlos Fuentes acquired his international perspective in 1928, when he was born in Panama to the family of a Mexican diplomat. Thanks to his father's career, Fuentes spent his childhood in various Latin American capitals as well as Washington, D.C. He returned to Mexico to study law before doing graduate work in Geneva, Switzerland. In the early 1950s he worked for the United Nations Information Center in Mexico City and published his first book of short stories. After cofounding the *Mexican Review of Literature*, he became director of international cultural relations for Mexico's Ministry of Foreign Affairs. His first novel, *La región más transparente*, was published in 1958 (*Where the Air Is Clear*, 1960), followed four years later by the celebrated *La muerte de Artemio Cruz* (*The Death of Artemio Cruz*, 1964). Along with Mario Vargas Llosa of Peru (see p. 224) and Gabriel García Márquez of Colombia (see p. 497), among others, Fuentes triggered the eruption of Latin American literature known as "El Boom." Besides continuing to write, and teaching as a visiting writer at universities in Mexico, England, Paris, and the United States, he served as Mexico's ambassador to France from 1975 to 1977. However, his denunciation of U.S. intervention in Vietnam caused the State Department to refuse him a visa and impede his entry into the United States up through the late 1980s. Fuentes's books, particularly *El gringo viejo* (*The Old Gringo*, 1985), have won numerous international awards. "Matador and Madonna" comes from *The Buried Mirror: Reflections on Spain and the New World* (1992), which accompanied a TV miniseries he wrote and narrated on the evolution of Hispanic culture.

Latin America comprises those countries south of the United States where languages derived from Latin are spoken — Portuguese in Brazil, Spanish in the rest of South America, Central America, and Mexico. España ("Spain" in English) occupies most of the Iberian peninsula, with Portugal to its west and France to its east. Conquered by Rome around 200 B.C., the region was converted to Christianity by invading Visigoths, then to Islam by African Moors. In 1469, the kingdoms of Aragon and Castile were united by the marriage of Ferdinand II and Isabella I. Their victory over the last Moorish stronghold in Granada in 1492 extended their rule and completed Spain's return to Roman Catholicism. That same year, Cristobal Colon's discovery of America launched the wave of exploration and conquest that won Spain its vast colonial empire. Chilean poet Pablo Neruda has written: "The fierce conquistadors . . . swallowed up everything, religions, pyramids, tribes, idolatries just like the ones they brought along in their huge sacks. . . .

But words fell like pebbles out of the boots of the barbarians, out of their beards, their helmets, their horseshoes, luminous words that were left glittering here . . . our language."[1] Although Spain lost its American colonies in the 1800s, its language, religion, and descendants still pervade Latin America. Spain itself was ruled by a series of monarchs and dictators; in 1969, Generalissimo Francisco Franco's death ended his thirty-year dictatorship and allowed King Juan Carlos to become head of a constitutional monarchy.

For background on Mexico, see page 15.

The first matador was the Athenian national hero, Theseus, who slew the Minotaur.[2] His contemporary, Hercules, brought the mythology of the bull to Spain. Like Theseus, Hercules killed a fire-breathing bull in Crete. But he also traveled to Spain, there to steal the herd of red bulls belonging to the three-bodied giant, Geryon, and drive them back to Greece. Hercules had to cross the narrow strait between Africa and southern Spain to do this; therefore the name of that passage, the Pillars of Hercules. Yet the strait is more than a geographic recognition. It symbolizes both the bond and the separation inherent in one of humankind's oldest ceremonies: a ritual slaying of the sacred animal. Hercules proved his nobility by returning some of the cattle to Spain, in recognition of the hospitality he received there. The ruling king, Chrysaor, then established the ritual of sacrificing a bull to Hercules every year.

Hercules is but the symbol of the cavalcade of peoples that came to Spanish shores, beginning in the remotest antiquity. All of them shaped the body and soul not only of Spain but of her descendants in the New World. The first Iberians arrived over three thousand years ago and gave the peninsula its lasting name. They also left their own image of the bull, guarding their cattle trails, protecting a route that takes us all the way to the first great commonplace of Spain, the bullring. But a "common place" means exactly that, a meeting ground, a place of recognition, a place that we share with others. What exactly is it that meets and recognizes itself in the bullring? Well, first of all, the people themselves. Impoverished, agrarian, isolated in a rough and remote geography, in the bullring they come together for what was once a weekly ritual, the Sunday afternoon sacrifice, the pagan incline of the Christian mass. Two ceremonies united by the sense of sacrifice but differing in their time of day: mass at noon, corridas at vespers. The mass, a corrida illuminated by an

---

[1]"Lost in the City," from the book *Memoirs*, translated by Hardie St. Martin (1977).
[2]See page 322. — ED.

unambiguous sun at its zenith; the corrida, a mass of light and shadows, tinged by impending dusk.

In the *plaza de toros*, the people meet themselves and meet the symbol of nature, the bull, rushing out toward the center of the space, dangerously scared, fleeing forward, menaced but menacing, crossing the boundary between sun and shade that divides the ring like day and night, like life and death. The bull rushes out to meet the human antagonist, the matador in his suit of lights.

Who is the matador? Again, a man of the people. Bullfighting has existed since the time of Hercules and Theseus, but in its present form it was only organized around the middle of the eighteenth century. It then ceased to be a sport of heroes and aristocrats and became a popular profession. In the age of Goya, which was an age of slumming, the aristocracy delighted in aping the common people by imitating bullfighters and actresses. This gave the entertainment professions an emblematic power comparable to the one they enjoy today. Spanish bullfighters have been every bit as idolized as Elvis Presley or Frank Sinatra in our own time. Like these singers, they represent a triumph of the people.

But bullfighting is also, lest we forget it, an erotic event. Where else    5 can the male strike such provocative sexual poses except in the bullring? The effrontery of the suit of lights, its tight-hugging breeches, the flaunting of the male sexual organ, the importance given to the buttocks, the obviously seductive and self-appraising stride, the lust for blood and sensation — the bullfight authorizes this incredible arrogance and sexual exhibitionism. Its roots are deep and dark. When the young villagers learn to fight the bulls, they can do so only by night and by stealth, perhaps crossing a river naked, or a thorny field ragged, to get into the rich man's cattle ranch, there to fight the forbidden bulls, secretly, illegally, in the darkest hour. Traditionally, the young *torerillos* have been tempted toward this sort of encounter because they must fight the bull at extremely close quarters, guessing the shape of the beast, feeling its warmly aggressive body, since they cannot see it. In this way the novitiates learn to distinguish the form, the movements, and the quirks of their opponent, the bull.

So the young matador is a prince of the people, a deadly prince who can kill only because he exposes himself to death. The bullfight is an opening to the possibility of death, and it is subject to a precise set of rules. The bull is deemed to have been born fully armed, with all the gifts that nature endowed him with, like the mythological Minotaur. It is up to the matador to discover what sort of animal he has to contend with, in order to transform his meeting with him from a fact of nature into a ceremony, a ritual, a taming of the natural force. The bullfighter must first of all measure himself against the horns of the bull, see which way the bull charges, and then cross himself *against* the bull's horns. That is, he must fight the bull on the opposite horn to that with which the animal charges. This is done by the stratagem of "breaking the bull's charge," *cargar la suerte*, which is at the heart of bullfighting. It consists, simply put, of using the cape artfully to control the bull instead of letting him follow his instincts. By capework and footwork, the matador makes the bull change direction and go toward the field of battle chosen by the bullfighter; leg forward, hip bent, the matador summons the bull with the cape, bull and bullfighter moving together, achieving the perfect *pase*, the astonishing instant of a statuesque coupling, bull and fighter enlaced, entwined, giving each other the qualities of force, beauty, and risk, in an image that seems at the same time immobile and dynamic. The mythic moment is restored: man and bull are once more, as in the labyrinth of Minos, the same.

The matador is a tragic representation of man's relation to nature, the actor in a ceremony of remembrance of our violent survival at the expense of nature. We cannot refuse the exploitation of nature, because it is the condition of our survival. The men and women who painted the animals in the cave of Altamira already knew this.

Spain rips off the mask of our puritanical hypocrisy in relation to nature and transforms the memory of our origins and our survival at the expense of the natural into a ritual of bravery and artistry, perhaps even of redemption. On the Sunday of Resurrection, the bullfighting season begins at the great plaza of La Maestranza in Seville. As the cuadrilla comes out to the music of the *paso doble* honoring the Virgen de la Macarena, the circle that goes from the bullfight to the flamenco to the cult of the Virgin and back to her protected son, the bullfighter — the Iberian ring, as the modern playwright Valle Inclán would call it — closes in upon itself.

Whatever the face of the matador on this particular afternoon, one always remembers the quintessential bullfighter, Pedro Romero, as painted by Goya. The portrait depicts Romero with noble features, firm jaw, taut cheeks, a small, pressed mouth, a perfectly straight nose, fine, separated eyebrows, a clear forehead, and the hint of a widow's peak. On his temples the first silvery strands have appeared. But the center of attention is the eyes, full of competence and tenderness. He has long, delicate, strong hands, and is wearing a dark pink velvet cape, a dark blue jacket, and a colorless waistcoat, which gives the linen of the front and neck of the shirt an exceptional whiteness. The whole painting offers an extraordinary impression of serenity and masculine beauty, which one feels, and fears, the painter himself envied.

Pedro Romero was painted by Goya when the matador was forty years   10
old. Romero started modern bullfighting in the arena at Ronda. In his
lifetime, he killed 5,558 brave bulls, and he died at eighty without a single
scar on his body.

It could be argued that the virgin body of this perfect bullfighter, who
never shed his blood in the ring, is not deserving of the black tears of a
single one of Spain's virgin mothers. But Jesus Christ, the God who died
lacerated on the cross, his body wounded on hands, brow, feet, knees, the
side, does deserve this motherly pity — and Spain gives it to him in
abundance.

The original mother figures of Spain are near each other in Madrid's
Archaeological Museum. La Dama de Baza was excavated from a tomb
near Granada in 1971. Sitting on her armchair, holding a dove, her
ringed hands a symbol of maternal authority, she is dressed in flowing
robes and forever presides over the birth and the death of her people.
Interpreted as a funerary goddess, she is also entitled, by the fact that she
remained buried for twenty-four centuries, to the name of earth goddess.

But next to the mother figure, always, we find the temptress, in this
case la Dama de Elche. The dates are controversial (she could have been
created anytime between the fifth and the second century B.C.), and she
possesses equally confusing physical and symbolic traits. Although she has
come down as the prototypical work of art of Iberian Spain, . . . Greek
influence is absolutely apparent in the execution of the face: the symmetry, the realism, the sense of proportion, and the finesse of the lines. Yet
if this is a classical lady, she is also a classy barbarian act. The Greek
balance is broken by the sumptuous Oriental ornaments she is decked
out with — headdress, earrings, necklaces. Wearing, perhaps, the first
mantilla, she sports enormous disks that cover her ears like some kind of
primitive headset, which communicates to her the music of a region that
only she understands. Heaven? Earth? Hell? She seems deaf to moral
platitudes. Erotically perverse maiden, voluptuous lover, priestess: One
could cast her in any of these roles.

Her most disturbing feature, nevertheless, is that she is slightly cross-
eyed, an ageless sign of erotic secrecy. The woman stares at you with the
eyes of a basilisk. A forbidding vamp, la Dama de Elche . . . sends us
back to the elemental truth that all original earth goddesses are mysterious, two-faced, tender and demanding, mother and lover, virgin and
temptress. And they are figures of fecund impurity, like the terribly
ambiguous goddesses of the Aztec pantheon. The supreme earth mother,
Coatlicue, gave birth to a brood of gods through signs of extreme pain
and cruelty. And the Venus figure of ancient Mexico, the goddess

Tlazolteotl (the Devourer of Filth), represents both purity and impurity: She devours filth in order to cleanse the earth.

The virginal figure that has presided over the life of Spain and Spanish    15
America with such power and for so long is not a stranger to these ancient maternal symbols of both Europe and the New World. In Spain during the great Easter celebrations, and in Spanish America through a reimposed link with the pagan religions, this figure of veneration becomes a troubling, ambiguous mother too, directly linked to the original earth goddesses.

Christianity intensely enriched the previous imagery of Spain with God the father, creator of the world, and His son, Christ the redeemer, who suffered and died for us and for our salvation. But along with them came the Madonna, who gives birth and protection. Mother and son are united by compassion and mystery. The supreme mystery, of course, is that of the Immaculate Conception. Christ is born of a virgin and is therefore the object of faith. The early Christian writer Tertullian said of the faith, "It is true because it is absurd." Which means that you must believe, even if you don't understand.

All of these religious and erotic mutations of the Spanish psyche reach the heights of passion and compassion in the bond between the Virgin and her son. It is at the center of the most ravishing and troubling, sensuous and mystical of all Spanish spectacles — Holy Week in Seville. Over fifty images of the Virgin Mary are displayed in processions that move through the city from Thursday night to Saturday morning. In every neighborhood, men from the lowest to the highest rank march in brotherhoods honoring their own Virgin and doing penance for the love of Christ and his mother. Each *penitente* wears the solemn robes of his brotherhood and carries a cross or, according to the size of his sins, a short or a long candle.

During the whole year, but also from generation to generation, guilds of dyers and textile merchants, weavers of linen, and dealers in gold thread labor to make cloaks and mantles, the veils and tunics of the divine seraglio:[3] Virgen del Rocío, Señora de los Reyes, Virgen de la Macarena, Virgen de Triana. Now, in their shirtsleeves, these men carry the floating temple of their Virgin along the streets of Seville on their shoulders. They are barefoot, invisible beneath the skirts of the Virgin, protected by her billowing drapery, bearing the throne of the Mother of God.

She is, of course, the center of attention. Her face, wrapped in a cowl, is moon-colored and streaked with heavy black tears. She is crowned by

---

[3]Harem. — ED.

a sunlike tiara with razor-sharp rays and hugs dead roses to her bosom. A great triangular cape contrived with the most elaborate ornamentations of ivory and precious stones, medallions shaped like flowers and coiled like metal snakes, drapes her.

What is the meaning of this "multicolored feast," as the philosopher 20 José Ortega y Gasset called it? Is it an exercise in collective narcissism, by which Seville mounts its own spectacle and then becomes its own spectator? Or is it the way in which Andalusia deals with the cultural shock of repeated invasions — Greeks, Romans, Arabs — absorbing them all in the melting pot of religious sensuality and sacred paganism?

It is also a playful ceremony. How else to understand the cries that follow the Virgin everywhere, "Guapa, guapa," meaning beautiful, gorgeous? This playfulness is best expressed by the Gypsy song that says, "The Child Jesus is lost, his Mother is looking for him. She finds him by the side of the river, having fun with the Gypsies." . . .

The second commonplace of Spain is the *tablado flamenco*, the almost sacred stage where the Spanish temptress, Carmen, the goddess in movement, can perform.

On the *tablado*, the male singers and guitarists strum, prepare, hum, intone, while the women sit and clap. They are as nubile and thin as broomsticks, or old and paunchy yet full of fire, animating the proceedings with their clapping hands and stumping twirls. But mostly they are the beautiful *bailaoras*, dark, tall, and full-figured, their hair sometimes teased but usually combed straight back and held together by the *peineta*, the tall Spanish comb. Their bodies are swathed in frills, satins, silks, lace, complicated girdles, unimaginable underwear, stockings, shawls, knots, carnations, combs. They will never undress, but their hair is certain to come apart and spring forth like Medusa's during the dance. They raise their arms, wrote Rainer Maria Rilke, who went to see them in Ronda, "like startled serpents."

The dancing woman comes from afar. She can be found on the floors of Pompeii. The dancing girls of Cádiz were the rage of imperial Rome. Martial wrote of their "practiced writhings," while Juvenal described them as "fired by applause, sinking to the ground with quivering buttocks." Lord Byron might have seen them as "black-eyed maids of heaven," but another, less flamboyant but more moralistic English traveler of the nineteenth century said that while the dances of Spain might have been indecent, the dancers themselves were inviolably chaste. Federico García Lorca, as always, had the final word in matters Andalusian. The dancing Gypsies, he wrote, were half bronze, half dream. He saw them as women paralyzed by the moonlight, as if under a lunar spell.

And so it is, for the flamenco *dance* is but the satellite of the Gypsy   25
*song, cante jondo,* the deep song, "the river of voices," to quote García
Lorca again. The dance is the moon, revolving around the song, which
is the center of the solar system of the *cante jondo;* the sun-song goes
right to the solar plexus with its ancient, atavistic[4] magnetism. It is a
hybrid form, and it attracts into its system over five hundred different
musical types, from the Arab call to prayer to the latest tropical rumba,
transforming them all so that our deepest urge will be fulfilled: to sing
the most extreme and intimate human situations. Love, jealousy, vengeance, nostalgia, desperation, death, God, the Mother — here tragic
destiny takes over completely, and words start to lose their everyday shape,
becoming in effect a river of song, a mere verbal fountainhead of the
most inexpressible emotions. The flamenco sometimes can translate its
form of improvised song into something that resembles a cry — a cry, it
has been said, not beneath words but above them, when words are not
enough. For the soul speaks out in the *cante,* uttering its darkest, most
uncontrollable emotions.

The center of the flamenco dance and the *cante jondo* is the erotic
event, and at the center of the center is, of course, the woman once more,
the temptress, fully decked out in the swashing draperies of the Gypsy
costume, shawled, high-heeled, beribboned, swimming in frills. She provides a sharp contrast to yet another Spanish and Spanish American trait:
sexual turbulence clad in saintly longings, as exhibited by the Virgin
figures carried through the streets of Seville. That is sensuality repressed
by faith but sublimated in mystical dreams. The *cante jondo* is translated
to a religious setting, the processions, which come to a halt when a man
on a street corner or a woman on a balcony sings out the *saeta,* literally
the dart, addressed to the Virgin in a lovingly familiar way. The Virgin
gazes on, offering both power and protection. Her power comes from
love. She is intimately known. She is like a member of the family. She
is the Virgen de la Macarena, the patroness of bullfighters, crying for the
death and destiny of her sons.

*

---

[4]Having characteristics of an ancestor; throwback. — ED.

# EXPLORATIONS

1. According to Carlos Fuentes, what qualities of the matador make him a model of Hispanic manhood? What qualities does he share with Jesus Christ?

2. Why do you think Fuentes describes la Dama de Baza and la Dama de Elche before discussing the Virgin Mary?

3. What words and ideas does Fuentes use that connect the flamenco dancer and the matador? The dancer and the Madonna?

# CONNECTIONS

1. Look at the second paragraph of Paula Gunn Allen's selection in *Looking at Ourselves* (p. 289). How does Allen's characterization of the Madonna compare with Fuentes's?

2. What are the similarities between Fuentes's depiction of boys' initiation into manhood (para. 5) and Mario Vargas Llosa's depiction in "On Sunday" (p. 224)?

3. What qualities are shared by Holy Week in Seville, as Fuentes describes it (paras. 17–21), and the *quinceañera* in Phoenix, as Susan Orlean describes it in "Quinceañera" (p. 200)?

# ELABORATIONS

1. Look at the comparison Deborah Tannen makes in *Looking at Ourselves* between men's and women's typical ways of engaging the world (p. 300). Write an essay showing how Tannen's ideas apply (or do not apply) to the Spanish and Spanish-American male and female roles characterized by Fuentes in "Matador and Madonna."

2. Fuentes, like Wole Soyinka in "Nigerian Childhood" (p. 112), describes a Christianity that has been grafted onto and mixed with older religious traditions. Write an essay comparing the hybrid Christianity in Soyinka's Nigeria with that in Fuentes's Spain.

# LESLIE MARMON SILKO

## *Yellow Woman*

The novelist and poet Leslie Marmon Silko was born in Albuquerque, New Mexico, in 1948. Part Laguna Pueblo, part Mexican, and part Anglo, she grew up on the Laguna Pueblo Reservation in the shadow of Mt. Taylor, legendary home of the ka'tsina spirits that appear in Pueblo and Hopi mythology. In the matrilineal Pueblo culture, houses and land are generally owned and passed down through the women. Work and family life overlap and involve everyone. So, says Silko, "The kinds of things that cause white upper-middle-class women to flee the home for a while to escape or get away from domination and powerlessness and inferior status, *vis-à-vis* the husband, . . . they're not operating at all." Silko graduated from the University of New Mexico in 1969, the same year she wrote "Yellow Woman." After teaching at Navajo Community College in Arizona, she moved to Ketchikan, Alaska, where she would later set the title story for her collection *Storyteller* (1981). Returning to the Southwest, she taught at the University of New Mexico and at the University of Arizona, Tucson, where she has been a professor of English since 1978. Silko's stories have appeared in a variety of magazines and collections. Among her writing awards is a 1983 MacArthur Foundation Fellowship. Her highly praised novel *Ceremony* (1977), the first novel published by a Native American woman, is regarded as a landmark in American fiction. Her most recent novel is *Almanac of the Dead* (1992).

## I

My thigh clung to his with dampness, and I watched the sun rising up through the tamaracks and willows. The small brown water birds came to the river and hopped across the mud, leaving brown scratches in the alkali-white crust. They bathed in the river silently. I could hear the water, almost at our feet where the narrow fast channel bubbled and washed green ragged moss and fern leaves. I looked at him beside me, rolled in the red blanket on the white river sand. I cleaned the sand out of the cracks between my toes, squinting because the sun was above the willow trees. I looked at him for the last time, sleeping on the white river sand.

I felt hungry and followed the river south the way we had come the afternoon before, following our footprints that were already blurred by lizard tracks and bug trails. The horses were still lying down, and the black one whinnied when he saw me but he did not get up — maybe it was because the corral was made out of thick cedar branches and the horses had not yet felt the sun like I had. I tried to look beyond the pale red mesas to the pueblo. I knew it was there, even if I could not see it, on the sand rock hill above the river, the same river that moved past me now and had reflected the moon last night.

The horse felt warm underneath me. He shook his head and pawed the sand. The bay whinnied and leaned against the gate trying to follow, and I remembered him asleep on the red blanket beside the river. I slid off the horse and tied him close to the other horse. I walked north with the river again, and the white sand broke loose in footprints over footprints.

"Wake up."

He moved in the blanket and turned his face to me with his eyes still     5
closed. I knelt down to touch him.

"I'm leaving."

He smiled now, eyes still closed. "You are coming with me, remember?" He sat up now with his bare dark chest and belly in the sun.

"Where?"

"To my place."

"And will I come back?"                                                                                         10

He pulled his pants on. I walked away from him, feeling him behind me and smelling the willows.

"Yellow Woman," he said.

I turned to face him. "Who are you?" I asked.

He laughed and knelt on the low, sandy bank, washing his face in the river. "Last night you guessed my name, and you knew why I had come."

I stared past him at the shallow moving water and tried to remember     15
the night, but I could only see the moon in the water and remember his warmth around me.

"But I only said that you were him and that I was Yellow Woman — I'm not really her — I have my own name and I come from the pueblo on the other side of the mesa. Your name is Silva and you are a stranger I met by the river yesterday afternoon."

He laughed softly. "What happened yesterday has nothing to do with what you will do today, Yellow Woman."

"I know — that's what I'm saying — the old stories about the ka'tsina spirit and Yellow Woman can't mean us."

My old grandpa liked to tell those stories best. There is one about Badger and Coyote who went hunting and were gone all day, and when the sun was going down they found a house. There was a girl living there alone, and she had light hair and eyes and she told them that they could sleep with her. Coyote wanted to be with her all night so he sent Badger into a prairie-dog hole, telling him he thought he saw something in it. As soon as Badger crawled in, Coyote blocked up the entrance with rocks and hurried back to Yellow Woman.

"Come here," he said gently.                                                         20

He touched my neck and I moved close to him to feel his breathing and to hear his heart. I was wondering if Yellow Woman had known who she was — if she knew that she would become part of the stories. Maybe she'd had another name that her husband and relatives called her so that only the ka'tsina from the north and the storytellers would know her as Yellow Woman. But I didn't go on; I felt him all around me, pushing me down into the white river sand.

Yellow Woman went away with the spirit from the north and lived with him and his relatives. She was gone for a long time, but then one day she came back and she brought twin boys.

"Do you know the story?"

"What story?" He smiled and pulled me close to him as he said this. I was afraid lying there on the red blanket. All I could know was the way he felt, warm, damp, his body beside me. This is the way it happens in the stories, I was thinking, with no thought beyond the moment she meets the ka'tsina spirit and they go.

"I don't have to go. What they tell in stories was real only then, back   25 in time immemorial, like they say."

He stood up and pointed at my clothes tangled in the blanket. "Let's go," he said.

I walked beside him, breathing hard because he walked fast, his hand around my wrist. I had stopped trying to pull away from him, because his hand felt cool and the sun was high, drying the river bed into alkali. I will see someone, eventually I will see someone, and then I will be certain that he is only a man — some man from nearby — and I will be sure that I am not Yellow Woman. Because she is from out of time past and I live now and I've been to school and there are highways and pickup trucks that Yellow Woman never saw.

It was an easy ride north on horseback. I watched the change from the cottonwood trees along the river to the junipers that brushed past us in the foothills, and finally there were only piñons, and when I looked up at the rim of the mountain plateau I could see pine trees growing on the edge. Once I stopped to look down, but the pale sandstone had disappeared and the river was gone and the dark lava hills were all around. He touched my hand, not speaking, but always singing softly a mountain song and looking into my eyes.

I felt hungry and wondered what they were doing at home now — my mother, my grandmother, my husband, and the baby. Cooking breakfast, saying, "Where did she go? — maybe kidnaped," and Al going to the tribal police with the details: "She went walking along the river."

The house was made with black lava rock and red mud. It was high    30
above the spreading miles of arroyos and long mesas. I smelled a mountain smell of pitch and buck brush. I stood there beside the black horse, looking down on the small, dim country we had passed, and I shivered.

"Yellow Woman, come inside where it's warm."


## II


He lit a fire in the stove. It was an old stove with a round belly and an enamel coffeepot on top. There was only the stove, some faded Navajo blankets, and a bedroll and cardboard box. The floor was made of smooth adobe plaster, and there was one small window facing east. He pointed at the box.

"There's some potatoes and the frying pan." He sat on the floor with his arms around his knees pulling them close to his chest and he watched me fry the potatoes. I didn't mind him watching me because he was always watching me — he had been watching me since I came upon him sitting on the river bank trimming leaves from a willow twig with his knife. We ate from the pan and he wiped the grease from his fingers on his Levi's.

"Have you brought women here before?" He smiled and kept chewing, so I said, "Do you always use the same tricks?"

"What tricks?" He looked at me like he didn't understand.    35

"The story about being a ka'tsina from the mountains. The story about Yellow Woman."

Silva was silent; his face was calm.

"I don't believe it. Those stories couldn't happen now," I said.

He shook his head and said softly, "But someday they will talk about us, and they will say, 'Those two lived long ago when things like that happened.'"

He stood up and went out. I ate the rest of the potatoes and thought    40
about things — about the noise the stove was making and the sound of the mountain wind outside. I remembered yesterday and the day before, and then I went outside.

I walked past the corral to the edge where the narrow trail cut through the black rim rock. I was standing in the sky with nothing around me but the wind that came down from the blue mountain peak behind me. I could see faint mountain images in the distance miles across the vast spread of mesas and valleys and plains. I wondered who was over there to feel the mountain wind on those sheer blue edges — who walks on the pine needles in those blue mountains.

"Can you see the pueblo?" Silva was standing behind me.

I shook my head. "We're too far away."

"From here I can see the world." He stepped out on the edge. "The Navajo reservation begins over there." He pointed to the east. "The Pueblo boundaries are over here." He looked below us to the south, where the narrow trail seemed to come from. "The Texans have their ranches over there, starting with that valley, the Concho Valley. The Mexicans run some cattle over there too."

"Do you ever work for them?"                                                    45

"I steal from them," Silva answered. The sun was dropping behind us and shadows were filling the land below. I turned away from the edge that dropped forever into the valleys below.

"I'm cold," I said; "I'm going inside." I started wondering about this man who could speak the Pueblo language so well but who lived on a mountain and rustled cattle. I decided that this man Silva must be Navajo, because Pueblo men didn't do things like that.

"You must be a Navajo."

Silva shook his head gently. "Little Yellow Woman," he said, "you never give up, do you? I have told you who I am. The Navajo people know me, too." He knelt down and unrolled the bedroll and spread the extra blankets out on a piece of canvas. The sun was down, and the only light in the house came from outside — the dim orange light from sundown.

I stood there and waited for him to crawl under the blankets.          50

"What are you waiting for?" he said, and I lay down beside him. He undressed me slowly like the night before beside the river — kissing my face gently and running his hands up and down my belly and legs. He took off my pants and then he laughed.

"Why are you laughing?"

"You are breathing so hard."

I pulled away from him and turned my back to him.

He pulled me around and pinned me down with his arms and chest.      55
"You don't understand, do you, little Yellow Woman? You will do what I want."

And again he was all around me with his skin slippery against mine, and I was afraid because I understood that his strength could hurt me. I lay underneath him and I knew that he could destroy me. But later, while he slept beside me, I touched his face and I had a feeling — the kind of feeling for him that overcame me that morning along the river. I kissed him on the forehead and he reached out for me.

When I woke up in the morning he was gone. It gave me a strange feeling because for a long time I sat there on the blankets and looked around the little house for some object of his — some proof that he had been there or maybe that he was coming back. Only the blankets and the cardboard box remained. The .30–30 that had been leaning in the corner was gone, and so was the knife I had used the night before. He was gone, and I had my chance to go now. But first I had to eat, because I knew it would be a long walk home.

I found some dried apricots in the cardboard box, and I sat down on a rock at the edge of the plateau rim. There was no wind and the sun warmed me. I was surrounded by silence. I drowsed with apricots in my mouth, and I didn't believe that there were highways or railroads or cattle to steal.

When I woke up, I stared down at my feet in the black mountain dirt. Little black ants were swarming over the pine needles around my foot. They must have smelled the apricots. I thought about my family far below me. They would be wondering about me, because this had never happened to me before. The tribal police would file a report. But if old Grandpa weren't dead he would tell them what happened — he would laugh and say, "Stolen by a ka'tsina, a mountain spirit. She'll come home — they usually do." There are enough of them to handle things. My mother and grandmother will raise the baby like they raised me. Al will find someone else, and they will go on like before, except that there will be a story about the day I disappeared while I was walking along the river. Silva had come for me; he said he had. I did not decide to go. I just went. Moonflowers blossom in the sand hills before dawn, just as I followed him. That's what I was thinking as I wandered along the trail through the pine trees.

It was noon when I got back. When I saw the stone house I remembered that I had meant to go home. But that didn't seem important anymore, maybe because there were little blue flowers growing in the meadow behind the stone house and the gray squirrels were playing in the pines next to the house. The horses were standing in the corral, and there was a beef carcass hanging on the shady side of a big pine in front of the house. Flies buzzed around the clotted blood that hung from the carcass. Silva was washing his hands in a bucket full of water. He must have heard me coming because he spoke to me without turning to face me.

"I've been waiting for you."

"I went walking in the big pine trees."

I looked into the bucket full of bloody water with brown-and-white animal hairs floating in it. Silva stood there letting his hand drip, examining me intently.

"Are you coming with me?"

"Where?" I asked him.                                                                65

"To sell the meat in Marquez."

"If you're sure it's O.K."

"I wouldn't ask you if it wasn't," he answered.

He sloshed the water around in the bucket before he dumped it out and set the bucket upside down near the door. I followed him to the corral and watched him saddle the horses. Even beside the horses he looked tall, and I asked him again if he wasn't Navajo. He didn't say anything; he just shook his head and kept cinching up the saddle.

"But Navajos are tall."                                                              70

"Get on the horse," he said, "and let's go."

The last thing he did before we started down the steep trail was to grab the .30–30 from the corner. He slid the rifle into the scabbard that hung from his saddle.

"Do they ever try to catch you?" I asked.

"They don't know who I am."

"Then why did you bring the rifle?"                                                  75

"Because we are going to Marquez where the Mexicans live."

### III

The trail leveled out on a narrow ridge that was steep on both sides like an animal spine. On one side I could see where the trail went around the rocky gray hills and disappeared into the southeast where the pale sandrock mesas stood in the distance near my home. On the other side was a trail that went west, and as I looked far into the distance I thought I saw the little town. But Silva said no, that I was looking in the wrong place, that I just thought I saw houses. After that I quit looking off into the distance; it was hot and the wildflowers were closing up their deep-yellow petals. Only the waxy cactus flowers bloomed in the bright sun, and I saw every color that a cactus blossom can be; the white ones and the red ones were still buds, but the purple and the yellow were blossoms, open full and the most beautiful of all.

Silva saw him before I did. The white man was riding a big gray horse, coming up the trail toward us. He was traveling fast and the gray horse's feet sent rocks rolling off the trail into the dry tumbleweeds. Silva motioned for me to stop and we watched the white man. He didn't see us right away, but finally his horse whinnied at our horses and he stopped. He looked at us briefly before he loped the gray horse across the three hundred yards that separated us. He stopped his horse in front of Silva, and his young fat face was shadowed by the brim of his hat. He didn't look mad, but his small, pale eyes moved from the blood-soaked gunny sacks hanging from my saddle to Silva's face and then back to my face.

"Where did you get the fresh meat?" the white man asked.

"I've been hunting," Silva said, and when he shifted his weight in the    80
saddle the leather creaked.

"The hell you have, Indian. You've been rustling cattle. We've been looking for the thief for a long time."

The rancher was fat, and sweat began to soak through his white cowboy shirt and the wet cloth stuck to the thick rolls of belly fat. He almost seemed to be panting from the exertion of talking, and he smelled rancid, maybe because Silva scared him.

Silva turned to me and smiled. "Go back up the mountain, Yellow Woman."

The white man got angry when he heard Silva speak in a language he couldn't understand. "Don't try anything, Indian. Just keep riding to Marquez. We'll call the state police from there."

The rancher must have been unarmed because he was very frightened    85
and if he had a gun he would have pulled it out then. I turned my horse around and the rancher yelled, "Stop!" I looked at Silva for an instant and there was something ancient and dark — something I could feel in my stomach — in his eyes, and when I glanced at his hand I saw his finger on the trigger of .30–30 that was still in the saddle scabbard. I slapped my horse across the flank and the sacks of raw meat swung against my knees as the horse leaped up the trail. It was hard to keep my balance, and once I thought I felt the saddle slipping backward; it was because of this that I could not look back.

I didn't stop until I reached the ridge where the trail forked. The horse was breathing deep gasps and there was a dark film of sweat on its neck. I looked down in the direction I had come from, but I couldn't see the place. I waited. The wind came up and pushed warm air past me. I looked up at the sky, pale blue and full of thin clouds and fading vapor trails left by jets.

I think four shots were fired — I remember hearing four hollow explosions that reminded me of deer hunting. There could have been more shots after that, but I couldn't have heard them because my horse was running again and the loose rocks were making too much noise as they scattered around his feet.

Horses have a hard time running downhill, but I went that way instead of uphill to the mountain because I thought it was safer. I felt better with the horse running southeast past the round gray hills that were covered with cedar trees and black lava rock. When I got to the plain in the distance I could see the dark green patches of tamaracks that grew along the river; and beyond the river I could see the beginning of the pale sandrock mesas. I stopped the horse and looked back to see if anyone was coming; then I got off the horse and turned the horse around, wondering if it would go back to its corral under the pines on the mountain. It looked back at me for a moment and then plucked a mouthful of green tumbleweeds before it trotted back up the trail with its ears pointed forward, carrying its head daintily to one side to avoid stepping on the dragging reins. When the horse disappeared over the last hill, the gunny sacks full of meat were still swinging and bouncing.

## IV

I walked toward the river on a wood-hauler's road that I knew would eventually lead to the paved road. I was thinking about waiting beside the road for someone to drive by, but by the time I got to the pavement I had decided it wasn't very far to walk if I followed the river back the way Silva and I had come.

The river water tasted good, and I sat in the shade under a cluster of silvery willows. I thought about Silva, and I felt sad at leaving him; still, there was something strange about him, and I tried to figure it out all the way back home.                                                              90

I came back to the place on the river bank where he had been sitting the first time I saw him. The green willow leaves that he had trimmed from the branch were still lying there, wilted in the sand. I saw the leaves and I wanted to go back to him — to kiss him and to touch him — but the mountains were too far away now. And I told myself, because I believe it, he will come back sometime and be waiting again by the river.

I followed the path up from the river into the village. The sun was getting low, and I could smell supper cooking when I got to the screen door of my house. I could hear their voices inside — my mother was telling my grandmother how to fix the Jell-O and my husband, Al, was playing with the baby. I decided to tell them that some Navajo had kidnaped me, but I was sorry that old Grandpa wasn't alive to hear my story because it was the Yellow Woman stories he liked to tell best.

# EXPLORATIONS

1. Why does the narrator leave her home and family to go off with Silva? Why does she return at the end of the story?

2. From whose viewpoint do we get to know Silva? What are his outstanding qualities? How is our image of him different from the image expressed by the white man who appears in paragraph 78?

3. At what points in the story does the narrator state her feelings directly? In what other ways are her feelings revealed?

4. Does the narrator believe that she and Silva really are the ka'tsina and Yellow Woman? How can you tell? What are her reasons for wanting to believe this?

# CONNECTIONS

1. What characteristics of ka'tsina and Yellow Woman can you infer from the narrator's references to them? What characteristics of these mythical beings does she reveal by linking them with herself and Silva? What qualities do ka'tsina and Yellow Woman share with the Spanish images of male and female described by Carlos Fuentes in "Matador and Madonna" (p. 303)?

2. What qualities does the white man in "Yellow Woman" share with the white-man stereotype in Sally Jacobs's selection in *Looking at Ourselves* (p. 291)?

3. What similar attitudes toward mythical beings appear in "Yellow Woman" and Wole Soyinka's "Nigerian Childhood" (p. 112)? How do characters in these two selections react differently to spirits and magic? What factors do you think are responsible for the differences?

# ELABORATIONS

1. What is the role of magic in American culture? Write a definition or classification essay indicating what forms magic takes in our society, whom it affects, and how significant an influence it is.

2. What clues in "Yellow Woman" suggest that Silva may have given the narrator an excuse to make a break she had been considering for some time? Write a narrative essay about a dramatic change made by you or someone you know. Identify both the event(s) that triggered the change and the long-standing circumstances that paved the way for it.

# NIKOS KAZANTZAKIS

## *The Isle of Aphrodite*

A novelist, poet, essayist, playwright, travel writer, and translator, Nikos Kazantzakis is best known in the United States for his novel *Zorba the Greek* (1952; *Bios kai politeia tou Alexi Zorba*, 1946), which also became a motion picture (1964) and Broadway musical (1968). Kazantzakis was born into a peasant farming family on the island of Crete in 1883. In 1897 the Cretans revolted against Turkish rule, and the family fled to the Greek island of Naxos. At a monastery there Kazantzakis studied languages and Western philosophy, and he developed the Christian preoccupation with the mystery of existence that pervades his writing. In 1906 he earned a law degree from the University of Athens, published his first novella, and moved to France. He continued to travel, write, and study; later he also worked for the Greek government. Kazantzakis wrote in the spoken (demotic) form of Greek rather than the customary literary form. He was nearly excommunicated from the Greek Orthodox Church for portraying it unfavorably in his novel *The Greek Passion* (*Ho Christos xanastavronetai*, 1954). A series of controversial novels culminated with *The Last Temptation of Christ* (1960; *Ho teleftaios peirasmos*, 1955; motion picture, 1988). When Kazantzakis died from leukemia in Germany in 1957, the Church refused him a burial Mass in Greece, so he was buried where he was born, in Iraklion, Crete. "The Isle of Aphrodite" comes from his essay collection, *Journeying* (1961), translated from the Greek by Themi and Theodora Vasils.

Iraklion is named for the mythical hero Hercules, whose legendary twelve labors included mastering a Cretan bull terrorizing the court of King Minos. Minos's palace — built around 1600 B.C. — also housed the labyrinth devised by Daedalus and Icarus to hide the monstrous Minotaur. Excavated in this century, it contained lavish frescoes, pottery, jewelry, the earliest form of written Greek, and indoor plumbing. The Athenian prince Theseus overthrew Minos, bringing Crete under control of his father, King Aegeus (for whom the Aegean Sea is named). Over the next thousand years Athens became a hub of Mediterranean civilization, the birthplace of democracy, theater, and Western philosophy. Rome conquered Greece between 150 and 100 B.C. In the mid-1400s the Turks took over; and in 1827 Greece won independence. George I (Kazantzakis's employer) became king in 1863 and reigned for fifty-seven years, during which Crete and most of the other Aegean islands shifted from Turkish back to Greek control. The monarchy was replaced by a republic in 1923, followed by a series of military dictatorships, another brief monarchy, a briefer republic, and finally, in 1967, a civilian government. In 1981 Greece joined the European Community (see p. 723).

Cyprus is indeed the native land of Aphrodite. Never have I seen an island with so much fertility or breathed air so saturated with perilous sweet persuasions. In the late afternoon when the sun goes down and the gentle breeze blows in from the sea, soft languor overtakes me — drowsiness and sweetness. And when the small children spill out on the seashore, their hands filled with jasmine, and the little caïques[1] sway lightly in the sea, to right and left, my heart breaks loose and surrenders like the Pandemos Aphrodite.[2]

Here you live incessantly what elsewhere you feel only in rare moments of torpor. You feel it slowly as it penetrates deeply, like the scent of jasmine. "Thought is an effort that goes contrary to the direction of life. The lifting of the soul, the vigilance of the mind, the charge toward the heights, all are the great ancestral sins against the will of God."

The other day while I was still wandering over the mountains of Judea I could hear a contrary relentless cry coming up from the entire land. "Let the hand be severed that it may glorify the Lord. Let the leg be severed that it may dance eternally." The sand trembled and the peaks of the mountains smoldered in the heat of the sun. A harsh god, without water, without a tree, without a woman, walked by, and you could feel the bones in your skull caving in. All of life leaped through the fevered brain like a battle cry.

And now Cyprus reposes in the middle of the open sea, singing softly like a Siren,[3] soothing my troubled head after the abrasive journey through the Judean mountains beyond. We sailed across the narrow sea and in one night passed from Jehovah's camp to the bed of Aphrodite. I was going from Famagusta to Larnaca and from Larnaca to Limassol, all the while getting closer to that holy spot in the sea at Paphos,[4] that fickle, indestructible liquid element in whose foam this feminine mask of mystery was born.

I could clearly feel the two great torrents struggling within me: The 5 one pushes toward harmony, patience, and gentleness. It functions with ease, without effort, following only the natural order of things. You throw a stone up high and for a second you force it against its will; but quickly it joyfully falls again. You toss a thought in the air but the thought quickly tires, it becomes impatient in the empty air and falls back to earth and settles with the soil. The other force is, it would seem, contrary to nature.

---

[1]Small sailboats. — ED.
[2]The earthly goddess of carnal love.
[3]A mythical sea nymph who lured sailors to destruction by singing. — ED.
[4]The ancient city sacred to Aphrodite, on the western tip of Cyprus. Aphrodite's birth from sea foam is believed to have occurred at Paphos.

An unbelievable absurdity. It wants to conquer weight, abolish sleep, and, with the lash, prod the universe upward.

To which of these two forces shall I conform and say: "This is my will," and finally be able with certainty to distinguish good from evil and impose a hierarchy on virtues and passions?

These were my thoughts on the morning I set out from Limassol for Paphos. By noon we were driving through jagged, uninteresting scenery. Carob trees, low mountains, red earth. Now and then a blossoming pomegranate tree unfolded along the way and flickered like flames in the noonday whiteness. Here and there two or three olive trees swayed gently and tamed the landscape.

We passed a dry riverbed blooming with oleander. A small owl was roosting on a stone bridge on the road, motionless, half blinded, and paralyzed by the intense light. The landscape was gradually growing gentler. We drove through a village brimming with orchards — the apricots were glimmering like gold on the trees and hulking clusters of loquats shone through the dark thick leaves.

Women began emerging on their doorsteps, plump and heavily dressed. Several men in the coffeehouses turned their heads as we drove by, the others continued their card playing with a passion. A young girl carrying on her shoulder a large round jug that was painted with primitive black designs stepped out of our way, frightened, and took refuge on a large rock. But as I smiled, her face lit up as though the sun shone on it.

The automobile stopped.                                                                    10

"What's your name?" I asked the girl.

I waited for her to say "Aphrodite" but she replied:

"Maria."

"And is Paphos still far from here?"

The girl looked flustered; she didn't understand what I was saying.       15

"You mean Kouklia,[5] my boy," broke in an old woman. "You mean Kouklia, where you'll find the palace of the Mistress of the Oleanders. It's there, right behind the carob tree."

"And why do they call it Kouklia, ma'am?"

"What? Don't you know? They find dolls there, my boy; little clay women. Here, dig, and you'll find some, too. You're a lord,[6] aren't you?"

---

[5]Kouklia is the new town built on the site of old Paphos.

[6]Since [the eighteenth-century British archaeologist] Lord Elgin, the villagers, accustomed to English lords excavating their landscape, assumed all strangers interested in antiquities were English lords.

"And what do they do with these little women?"

"How should I know? Some say they're gods, others say they're devils.      20
Who can tell the difference?"

"What does religion say?"

"What can our poor religion say? Do you think it knows everything?"

The chauffeur was in a hurry so the conversation ended. We passed
the village and soon the sea stretched out to our left, again, infinite, deep
blue, foamy. And suddenly, as I turned to the right, I saw on the peak of
a low hill, far from the road, the ruins of an open, multiwindowed fortress.
I knew it was the renowned main temple of Aphrodite. I looked around
at the outlines of the mountain, the sea, the small plain where the
worshipers must have camped. I tried to isolate this enclave of the
much-beloved, full-breasted goddess and relive the vision that once existed here. But, as so often happens to me, my heart was unmoved and
unreceptive to all these fleshless fantasies.

The chauffeur stopped in front of a taverna on the road and called
out:

"*Kyria* Kalliopi!"[7]                                                    25

The small door of the taverna opened quickly and the proprietress
came out and stood on the doorstep.

I shall never forget her. Tall, full-bodied with ample buttocks, about
thirty years old, this smiling, coquettish, earthy, all-enchanting Aphrodite
filled the doorway with her presence. The chauffeur looked at her, sighed
softly, and stroked his youthful mustache.

"Come here," he called. "Are you afraid?"

She laughed and stepped down from her threshold, chuckling. I
eagerly cocked my ear to hear the conversation.

"Tomorrow I want you to make me two okas of your best *loukoumia*,"[8]   30
the chauffeur said.

"Twenty-four *grosia*,"[9] answered the woman, sobering. "Nothing less."

"Eighteen."

"Twenty-four."

The man looked at her for a moment; he sighed again.

"All right," he said. "Twenty-four? Twenty-four!"                        35

The bargaining ended. The entire landscape took on an unexpected
sweetness. This little trifling dialogue had excited my heart. The great

---

[7]*Kyria*: Mrs.; *Kalliopi* (or *Calliope*): The legendary Muse who presided over epic poetry. —
ED.

[8]A jellylike, gummy confection sprinkled with powdered sugar, known as Turkish delight.

[9]About 3 cents. — ED.

temple, all the inspiration of the renowned landscape, the memories, the historical profundity, were unable to move me, but this small human moment resurrected in a flash all of Aphrodite in me.

Thus, joyously, I set out and began the slow climb up the sacred hill.

The thyme, the daffodils, poppies, all the familiar elements one encounters on a Greek mountainside, were there. A young shepherd, goats, sheep dogs, an innocent downy newborn donkey that was frisking about, still looking at the world with surprise.

The sun was finally setting, the shadows were lengthening and touching the earth, the Star of Aphrodite was glittering, playing, and twirling in the sky as I entered the deserted temple of the "Mistress." I entered quietly, without excitement, as though I were entering my house. I sat on a rock, thinking of nothing, making no effort at thought. I was gently tired, gently happy, and settled comfortably on the rock. Gradually I began to look at some insects that were chasing each other in the air, intermittently flitting from plant to plant, and I listened to the brittle metallic sound of their wings.

Suddenly, as I was observing the insects, a mysterious fear overtook      40
me. At first I couldn't comprehend the cause, but slowly, with dread, I understood. Engrossed as I was in the insects I remembered, at first dimly, but later more vividly, a frightful sight I had seen in my adolescent years.

One afternoon as I was wandering through a dry riverbed I saw two insects mating under a plane tree leaf. They were two green, willowy, charming little "ponies of the Virgin." I approached them slowly, holding my breath. But suddenly I stopped short, stunned: the male, small and weak, was on top, struggling to consummate its sacred duty; and with horror I saw that its head was missing. The female was calmly chewing it and when she finished she slowly turned and cut off the neck and then she cut off the breast of the male who was clamped tightly over her still pulsating . . .

This terrifying scene suddenly bolted out of the ruins before me. Tonight blue lightning rips through and illumines my heart.

The full-breasted goddess lifts her veil. The breath of the unfathomable is more obvious to plants and animals than it is to man. They, faithful and naked, follow the great Cry. To them, love and death are identical. When we see them headless and chestless, struggling to defeat death by giving birth, we recognize with awe the same Cry within us. The giddiness, the certainty of death; and yet, above this is the joy, the madness in death, and the lunge for immortality . . .

It was finally dark. An old man had been watching me from the opposite hill and had come down. He was standing behind me for a long time but did not dare approach but now, as he saw me getting up, he reached out his hand.

"Sir, I've brought you an antique to buy." 45

He put a small stone in my hand; I looked at it but could not discern what it portrayed. The old man lit a match. Now I could make out the sculptured head of a woman with a war helmet. And as I kept turning the little stone around, I noticed that the upper part of the helmet portrayed the upside-down head of a warrior. I suddenly recalled Ares, and shuddered to see Aphrodite wearing the male thus, as an ornament on her head. I hastily returned the ring stone to the old man.

"Go," I said with involuntary curtness. "I don't like it."

That night I slept at a small hotel nearby. At dawn I had a dream: I was holding a rose, the blackest of roses, in my palm. And as I held it I could feel it slowly, voraciously, silently, eating away at my hand.

## EXPLORATIONS

1. What deities and what places are represented by the two opposing torrents or forces described in paragraphs 5–6? What are the differences between them? What use does Nikos Kazantzakis make of gender in this opening section?

2. What is Kazantzakis looking for on the island of Cyprus? How does he find it?

3. What is the meaning of the dream in Kazantzakis's last paragraph? How has he prepared us to interpret his dream?

4. What religion does Kazantzakis apparently belong to? Cite evidence from his essay.

## CONNECTIONS

1. What similar strategy do Kazantzakis and Leslie Marmon Silko use to begin "The Isle of Aphrodite" and "Yellow Woman" (p. 312)? How is this strategy appropriate for a piece of writing in which sex is important?

2. Which goddess in Fuentes's "Matador and Madonna" (p. 303) is most like Kazantzakis's Pandemos Aphrodite? What qualities do they share? How are they different?

3. Reread Kazantzakis's paragraphs 40–48. What does this view of relations between the sexes have in common with the view Camille Paglia expresses in *Looking at Ourselves* (p. 294)? How are Kazantzakis's and Paglia's views different?

4. Compare Kazantzakis's description of two opposing torrents in paragraph 5 with Mario Vargas Llosa's description of swimming in the sea in paragraph 146 of "On Sunday" (p. 224). When and why does Vargas Llosa favor each of Kazantzakis's two forces?

## ELABORATIONS

1. Write an essay comparing and contrasting Kazantzakis's use of Christian and pre-Christian imagery in "The Isle of Aphrodite" with Wole Soyinka's in "Nigerian Childhood" (p. 112).

2. "To which of these two forces shall I conform . . . ?" asks Kazantzakis in paragraph 6. What do you think he means? What does he decide? How can you tell? (Cite evidence from the text.) Write an essay translating Kazantzakis's metaphors into more literal language, analyzing the question he is really asking, and explaining his answer.

# SIMONE DE BEAUVOIR

## Woman as Other

Simone de Beauvoir, born in Paris in 1908, was best known for her feminist fiction and nonfiction and for her lifelong relationship with the existentialist philosopher and writer Jean-Paul Sartre. Beauvoir was twenty when she met Sartre while studying at the Sorbonne. The two never married, lived together, or viewed their liaison as exclusive, but they worked closely together and kept apartments in the same building until Sartre's death in 1980. Beauvoir's several memoirs chronicle her social and political development; her novels examine existentialist ideas and sometimes their proponents as well. *The Mandarins* (1954), based on her affair with American novelist Nelson Algren, won the prestigious Prix Goncourt. Beauvoir's most famous work is the international bestseller *The Second Sex* (1952; *Le deuxième sexe*, 1949), translated from the French by H. M. Parshley, from which "Woman as Other" is taken. A vigorous champion of antiestablishment causes, Beauvoir died in Paris in 1986.

For background on France, see page 8.

What is a woman?

To state the question is, to me, to suggest, at once, a preliminary answer. The fact that I ask it is in itself significant. A man would never get the notion of writing a book on the peculiar situation of the human male. But if I wish to define myself, I must first of all say: "I am a woman"; on this truth must be based all further discussion. A man never begins by presenting himself as an individual of a certain sex; it goes without saying that he is a man. The terms *masculine* and *feminine* are used symmetrically only as a matter of form, as on legal papers. In actuality the relation of the two sexes is not quite like that of two electrical poles, for man represents both the positive and the neutral, as is indicated by the common use of *man* to designate human beings in general; whereas woman represents only the negative, defined by limiting criteria, without reciprocity. In the midst of an abstract discussion it is vexing to hear a man say: "You think thus and so because you are a woman"; but I know that my only defense is to reply: "I think thus and so because it is true," thereby removing my subjective self from the argument. It would be out of the question to reply: "And you think the contrary because you are a man," for it is understood that the fact of being a man is no peculiarity. A man is in the right in being a man; it is the woman who is in the wrong.

It amounts to this: Just as for the ancients there was an absolute vertical with reference to which the oblique was defined, so there is an absolute human type, the masculine. Woman has ovaries, a uterus; these peculiarities imprison her in her subjectivity, circumscribe her within the limits of her own nature. It is often said that she thinks with her glands. Man superbly ignores the fact that his anatomy also includes glands, such as the testicles, and that they secrete hormones. He thinks of his body as a direct and normal connection with the world, which he believes he apprehends objectively, whereas he regards the body of woman as a hindrance, a prison, weighed down by everything peculiar to it. "The female is a female by virtue of a certain *lack* of qualities," said Aristotle; "we should regard the female nature as afflicted with a natural defectiveness." And St. Thomas for his part pronounced woman to be an "imperfect man," an "incidental" being. This is symbolized in Genesis where Eve is depicted as made from what Bossuet called "a supernumerary bone" of Adam.

Thus humanity is male and man defines woman not in herself but as relative to him; she is not regarded as an autonomous being. Michelet writes: "Woman, the relative being. . . ." And Benda is most positive in his *Rapport d'Uriel*: "The body of man makes sense in itself quite apart from that of woman, whereas the latter seems wanting in significance by itself. . . . Man can think of himself without woman. She cannot think of herself without man." And she is simply what man decrees; thus she is called "the sex," by which is meant that she appears essentially to the male as a sexual being. For him she is sex — absolute sex, no less. She is defined and differentiated with reference to man and not he with reference to her; she is the incidental, the inessential as opposed to the essential. He is the Subject, he is the Absolute — she is the Other.

The category of the *Other* is as primordial as consciousness itself. In the most primitive societies, in the most ancient mythologies, one finds the expression of a duality — that of the Self and the Other. This duality was not originally attached to the division of the sexes; it was not dependent upon any empirical facts. It is revealed in such works as that of Granet on Chinese thought and those of Dumézil on the East Indies and Rome. The feminine element was at first no more involved in such pairs as Varuna-Mitra, Uranus-Zeus, Sun-Moon, and Day-Night than it was in the contrasts between Good and Evil, lucky and unlucky auspices, right and left, God and Lucifer. Otherness is a fundamental category of human thought.

Thus it is that no group ever sets itself up as the One without at once    5
setting up the Other over against itself. If three travelers chance to occupy the same compartment, that is enough to make vaguely hostile "others"

out of all the rest of the passengers on the train. In small-town eyes all persons not belonging to the village are "strangers" and suspect; to the native of a country all who inhabit other countries are "foreigners"; Jews are "different" for the anti-Semite, Negroes are "inferior" for American racists, aborigines are "natives" for colonists, proletarians are the "lower class" for the privileged.

Lévi-Strauss, at the end of a profound work on the various forms of primitive societies, reaches the following conclusion: "Passage from the state of Nature to the state of Culture is marked by man's ability to view biological relations as a series of contrasts; duality, alternation, opposition, and symmetry, whether under definite or vague forms, constitute not so much phenomena to be explained as fundamental and immediately given data of social reality." These phenomena would be incomprehensible if in fact human society were simply a *Mitsein* or fellowship based on solidarity and friendliness. Things become clear, on the contrary, if, following Hegel, we find in consciousness itself a fundamental hostility toward every other consciousness; the subject can be posed only in being opposed — he sets himself up as the essential, as opposed to the other, the inessential, the object.

But the other consciousness, the other ego, sets up a reciprocal claim. The native traveling abroad is shocked to find himself in turn regarded as a "stranger" by the natives of neighboring countries. As a matter of fact, wars, festivals, trading, treaties, and contests among tribes, nations, and classes tend to deprive the concept *Other* of its absolute sense and to make manifest its relativity; willy-nilly, individuals and groups are forced to realize the reciprocity of their relations. How is it, then, that this reciprocity has not been recognized between the sexes, that one of the contrasting terms is set up as the sole essential, denying any relativity in regard to its correlative and defining the latter as pure otherness? Why is it that women do not dispute male sovereignty? No subject will readily volunteer to become the object, the inessential; it is not the Other who, in defining himself as the Other, establishes the One. The Other is posed as such by the One in defining himself as the One. But if the Other is not to regain the status of being the One, he must be submissive enough to accept this alien point of view. Whence comes this submission in the case of woman?

There are, to be sure, other cases in which a certain category has been able to dominate another completely for a time. Very often this privilege depends upon inequality of numbers — the majority imposes its rule upon the minority or persecutes it. But women are not a minority, like the American Negroes or the Jews; there are as many women as men on earth. Again, the two groups concerned have often been originally independent; they may have been formerly unaware of each other's existence, or perhaps they recognized each other's autonomy. But a historical event has resulted in the subjugation of the weaker by the stronger. The scattering of the Jews, the introduction of slavery into America, the conquests of imperialism are examples in point. In these cases the oppressed retained at least the memory of former days; they possessed in common a past, a tradition, sometimes a religion or a culture.

The parallel drawn by Bebel between women and the proletariat is valid in that neither ever formed a minority or a separate collective unit of mankind. And instead of a single historical event it is in both cases a historical development that explains their status as a class and accounts for the membership of *particular individuals* in that class. But proletarians have not always existed, whereas there have always been women. They are women in virtue of their anatomy and physiology. Throughout history they have always been subordinated to men, and hence their dependency is not the result of a historical event or a social change — it was not something that *occurred*. The reason why otherness in this case seems to be an absolute is in part that it lacks the contingent or incidental nature of historical facts. A condition brought about at a certain time can be abolished at some other time, as the Negroes of Haiti and others have proved; but it might seem that a natural condition is beyond the possibility of change. In truth, however, the nature of things is no more immutably given, once for all, than is historical reality. If woman seems to be the inessential which never becomes the essential, it is because she herself fails to bring about this change. Proletarians say "We"; Negroes also. Regarding themselves as subjects, they transform the bourgeois, the whites, into "others." But women do not say "We," except at some congress of feminists or similar formal demonstration; men say "women," and women use the same word in referring to themselves. They do not authentically assume a subjective attitude. The proletarians have accomplished the revolution in Russia, the Negroes in Haiti, the Indochinese are battling for it in Indochina; but the women's effort has never been anything more than a symbolic agitation. They have gained only what men have been willing to grant; they have taken nothing, they have only received.

The reason for this is that women lack concrete means for organizing      10
themselves into a unit which can stand face to face with the correlative unit. They have no past, no history, no religion of their own; and they have no such solidarity of work and interest as that of the proletariat. They are not even promiscuously herded together in the way that creates community feeling among the American Negroes, the ghetto Jews, the

workers of Saint-Denis, or the factory hands of Renault. They live dispersed among the males, attached through residence, housework, economic condition, and social standing to certain men — fathers or husbands — more firmly than they are to other women. If they belong to the bourgeoisie, they feel solidarity with men of that class, not with proletarian women; if they are white, their allegiance is to white men, not to Negro women. The proletariat can propose to massacre the ruling class, and a sufficiently fanatical Jew or Negro might dream of getting sole possession of the atomic bomb and making humanity wholly Jewish or black; but woman cannot even dream of exterminating the males. The bond that unites her to her oppressors is not comparable to any other. The division of the sexes is a biological fact, not an event in human history. Male and female stand opposed within a primordial *Mitsein*, and woman has not broken it. The couple is a fundamental unity with its two halves riveted together, and the cleavage of society along the line of sex is impossible. Here is to be found the basic trait of woman: She is the Other in a totality of which the two components are necessary to one another.

One could suppose that this reciprocity might have facilitated the liberation of woman. When Hercules sat at the feet of Omphale and helped with her spinning, his desire for her held him captive; but why did she fail to gain a lasting power? To revenge herself on Jason, Medea killed their children; and this grim legend would seem to suggest that she might have obtained a formidable influence over him through his love for his offspring. In *Lysistrata* Aristophanes gaily depicts a band of women who joined forces to gain social ends through the sexual needs of their men; but this is only a play. In the legend of the Sabine women, the latter soon abandoned their plan of remaining sterile to punish their ravishers. In truth woman has not been socially emancipated through man's need — sexual desire and the desire for offspring — which makes the male dependent for satisfaction upon the female.

Master and slave, also, are united by a reciprocal need, in this case economic, which does not liberate the slave. In the relation of master to slave the master does not make a point of the need that he has for the other; he has in his grasp the power of satisfying this need through his own action; whereas the slave, in his dependent condition, his hope and fear, is quite conscious of the need he has for his master. Even if the need is at bottom equally urgent for both, it always works in favor of the oppressor and against the oppressed. That is why the liberation of the working class, for example, has been slow.

Now, woman has always been man's dependent, if not his slave; the two sexes have never shared the world in equality. And even today woman is heavily handicapped, though her situation is beginning to change. Almost nowhere is her legal status the same as man's, and frequently it is much to her disadvantage. Even when her rights are legally recognized in the abstract, long-standing custom prevents their full expression in the mores. In the economic sphere men and women can almost be said to make up two castes; other things being equal, the former hold the better jobs, get higher wages, and have more opportunity for success than their new competitors. In industry and politics men have a great many more positions and they monopolize the most important posts. In addition to all this, they enjoy a traditional prestige that the education of children tends in every way to support, for the present enshrines the past — and in the past all history has been made by men. At the present time, when women are beginning to take part in the affairs of the world, it is still a world that belongs to men — they have no doubt of it at all and women have scarcely any. To decline to be the Other, to refuse to be a party to the deal — this would be for women to renounce all the advantages conferred upon them by their alliance with the superior caste. Man-the-sovereign will provide woman-the-liege with material protection and will undertake the moral justification of her existence; thus she can evade at once both economic risk and the metaphysical risk of a liberty in which ends and aims must be contrived without assistance. Indeed, along with the ethical urge of each individual to affirm his subjective existence, there is also the temptation to forgo liberty and become a thing. This is an inauspicious road, for he who takes it — passive, lost, ruined — becomes henceforth the creature of another's will, frustrated in his transcendence and deprived of every value. But it is an easy road; on it one avoids the strain involved in undertaking an authentic existence. When man makes of woman the *Other*, he may, then, expect her to manifest deep-seated tendencies toward complicity. Thus, woman may fail to lay claim to the status of subject because she lacks definite resources, because she feels the necessary bond that ties her to man regardless of reciprocity, and because she is often very well pleased with her role as the *Other*.

## EXPLORATIONS

1. "Woman as Other" was originally published as part of *The Second Sex* in 1949. Which, if any, of Simone de Beauvoir's observations about women's status have been invalidated since then by political and social changes? Which of the problems she mentions are live issues in our society today?

2. What emotionally loaded words, phrases, and sentences indicate that Beauvoir is presenting an argument in "Woman as Other"? Who is her intended audience? To what extent, and for what reasons, do you think she expects part or all of her audience to resist the case she is making?

3. What kinds of sources does Beauvoir cite? In what ways would her essay gain or lose impact if she included quotations from interviews with individual women and men? In what ways would it gain or lose impact if she cut all references to outside sources?

# CONNECTIONS

1. Which points made by Beauvoir in "Woman as Other" are illustrated in Kazantzakis's "The Isle of Aphrodite" (p. 322)? Give specific references from both selections.

2. What evidence in Leslie Marmon Silko's "Yellow Woman" (p. 312) shows the narrator perceiving herself as defined by or dependent on men, in the way Beauvoir describes? What evidence shows Silko's narrator holding views that contradict Beauvoir's?

3. Which of the passages in *Looking at Ourselves* show men viewing women as "Other"? Which ones show women viewing men as "Other"? What recommendations do the American authors make about overcoming the problems Beauvoir describes?

4. In paragraph 10, Beauvoir writes of women and men as "a totality of which the two components are necessary to one another." What does she see as the implications of this mutual dependence? Compare Rose Weitz's comments in *Looking at Ourselves* on homosexual men and women (p. 298). How would you expect Weitz to disagree with Beauvoir? How would you expect her to agree?

# ELABORATIONS

1. Beauvoir notes that male glands affect men's thinking as much as female glands affect women's thinking. How do the writers in *Looking at Ourselves* apply this idea? On the basis of their observations and Beauvoir's, write a cause-and-effect essay about the relationship (or absence of a relationship) between gender and attitudes.

2. "What is a woman?" asks Beauvoir in her opening paragraph. She goes on: "If I wish to define myself, I must first of all say: 'I am a woman.'" Already she is letting her readers know that her choice of *definition* as the form for her inquiry has a political as well as a rhetorical basis. That is, she is not simply

defining woman, as her opening question implies; she is examining a definition of woman imposed by men. The same tactic can be applied to any issue
in which a preexisting definition is crucial to the argument. Choose such an
issue that interests you — for instance, What is a drug? or What is military
defense? Write a definition essay exploring the issue by examining the tacit
definitions that underlie it.

# ALBERTO MORAVIA

## *The Chase*

Alberto Moravia has been called the first existentialist novelist in Italy — a forerunner of Jean-Paul Sartre and Albert Camus in France. Moravia is best known in the United States for the films that have been based on his work: Michelangelo Antonioni's *L'Avventura* (1961), Jean-Luc Godard's *Le Mépris* (*Contempt*, 1965), and Bernardo Bertolucci's *The Conformist* (1970). The film of *Conjugal Love* (1949) was directed by Moravia's wife, Dacia Maraini. Born Alberto Pincherle in Rome in 1907, Moravia had little formal schooling but was taught to read English, French, and German by governesses and earned a high school diploma. He began his first novel at age sixteen while in a sanatorium for the tuberculosis he had contracted when he was nine; he considered his long illness a major influence on his career. Moravia's novels, stories, and scripts are too numerous to list. Many of them, including his 1987 novel *The Voyeur*, are available in English. "The Chase," translated from the Italian in 1969 by Angus Davidson, is from the story collection *Command, and I Will Obey You*. Moravia also represented Italy in the European Parliament as of 1984 (see p. 723). He died in 1990.

Italy, a boot-shaped peninsula across the Mediterranean Sea from Libya, has been occupied since the Stone Age. Its political heyday was the Roman Empire, which by A.D. 180 ruled from Britain to Africa to Persia (now Iran). The Roman civilization fell to barbarian invaders in the fourth and fifth centuries but left as a legacy its capital city, alphabet, roads, laws, and arts. The United Nations Educational, Scientific, and Cultural Organization (UNESCO) estimates that half of the world's cultural heritage has come from Italy, which still houses much of the finest architecture, sculpture, painting, and other visual arts in Europe.

Italy remained politically fragmented until the 1860s, when it united under a parliament and king. In 1922 Fascist dictator Benito Mussolini took over the government, proclaiming Victor Emmanuel III emperor and subsequently joining Germany in World War II. After Fascism was overthrown in 1943, Italy declared war on Germany and Japan. Mussolini was killed in 1946, and the monarchy was voted out. Democratic postwar governments have tended to be short-lived. However, Italy was a founding member of the European Economic Community (see p. 723) and continues to have a thriving market economy. Recently the government has cracked down on the Mafia, or Cosa Nostra, the multinational criminal organization based on the Italian island of Sicily; although arrests and prosecutions proceed, some officials have been murdered by the mob and others implicated in a web of political and corporate corruption.

For more background on Italy, see page 463.

I have never been a sportsman — or, rather, I have been a sportsman only once, and that was the first and last time. I was a child, and one day, for some reason or other, I found myself together with my father, who was holding a gun in his hand, behind a bush, watching a bird that had perched on a branch not very far away. It was a large, gray bird — or perhaps it was brown — with a long — or perhaps a short — beak; I don't remember. I only remember what I felt at that moment as I looked at it. It was like watching an animal whose vitality was rendered more intense by the very fact of my watching it and of the animal's not knowing that I was watching it.

At that moment, I say, the notion of wildness entered my mind, never again to leave it: Everything is wild which is autonomous and unpredictable and does not depend upon us. Then all of a sudden there was an explosion; I could no longer see the bird and I thought it had flown away. But my father was leading the way, walking in front of me through the undergrowth. Finally he stooped down, picked up something, and put it in my hand. I was aware of something warm and soft and I lowered my eyes: There was the bird in the palm of my hand, its dangling, shattered head crowned with a plume of already-thickening blood. I burst into tears and dropped the corpse on the ground, and that was the end of my shooting experience.

I thought again of this remote episode in my life this very day after watching my wife, for the first and also the last time, as she was walking through the streets of the city. But let us take things in order.

What had my wife been like; what was she like now? She once had been, to put it briefly, "wild" — that is, entirely autonomous and unpredictable; latterly she had become "tame" — that is, predictable and dependent. For a long time she had been like the bird that, on that far-off morning in my childhood, I had seen perching on the bough; latterly, I am sorry to say, she had become like a hen about which one knows everything in advance — how it moves, how it eats, how it lays eggs, how it sleeps, and so on.

Nevertheless I would not wish anyone to think that my wife's wildness    5
consisted of an uncouth, rough, rebellious character. Apart from being extremely beautiful, she is the gentlest, politest, most discreet person in the world. Rather her wildness consisted of the air of charming unpredictability, of independence in her way of living, with which during the first years of our marriage she acted in my presence, both at home and abroad. Wildness signified intimacy, privacy, secrecy. Yes, my wife as she sat in front of her dressing table, her eyes fixed on the looking glass, passing the hairbrush with a repeated motion over her long, loose hair, was just as wild as the solitary quail hopping forward along a sun-filled

furrow or the furtive fox coming out into a clearing and stopping to look around before running on. She was wild because I, as I looked at her, could never manage to foresee when she would give a last stroke with the hairbrush and rise and come toward me; wild to such a degree that sometimes when I went into our bedroom the smell of her, floating in the air, would have something of the acrid quality of a wild beast's lair.

Gradually she became less wild, tamer. I had had a fox, a quail, in the house, as I have said; then one day I realized that I had a hen. What effect does a hen have on someone who watches it? It has the effect of being, so to speak, an automaton in the form of a bird; automatic are the brief, rapid steps with which it moves about; automatic its hard, terse pecking; automatic the glance of the round eyes in its head that nods and turns; automatic its ready crouching down under the cock; automatic the dropping of the egg wherever it may be and the cry with which it announces that the egg has been laid. Good-bye to the fox; good-bye to the quail. And her smell — this no longer brought to my mind, in any way, the innocent odor of a wild animal; rather I detected in it the chemical suavity of some ordinary French perfume.

Our flat is on the first floor of a big building in a modern quarter of the town; our windows look out on a square in which there is a small public garden, the haunt of nurses and children and dogs. One day I was standing at the window, looking in a melancholy way at the garden. My wife, shortly before, had dressed to go out; and once again, watching her, I had noticed the irrevocable and, so to speak, invisible character of her gestures and personality: something which gave one the feeling of a thing already seen and already done and which therefore evaded even the most determined observation. And now, as I stood looking at the garden and at the same time wondering why the adorable wildness of former times had so completely disappeared, suddenly my wife came into my range of vision as she walked quickly across the garden in the direction of the bus stop. I watched her and then I almost jumped for joy; in a movement she was making to pull down a fold of her narrow skirt and smooth it over her thigh with the tips of her long, sharp nails, in this movement I recognized the wildness that in the past had made me love her. It was only an instant, but in that instant I said to myself: She's become wild again because she's convinced that I am not there and am not watching her. Then I left the window and rushed out.

But I did not join her at the bus stop; I felt that I must not allow myself to be seen. Instead I hurried to my car, which was standing nearby, got in, and waited. A bus came and she got in together with some other people; the bus started off again and I began following it. Then there came back to me the memory of that one shooting expedition in which I had taken part as a child, and I saw that the bus was the undergrowth with its bushes and trees, my wife the bird perching on the bough while I, unseen, watched it living before my eyes. And the whole town, during this pursuit, became, as though by magic, a fact of nature like the countryside: the houses were hills, the streets valleys, the vehicles hedges and woods, and even the passersby on the pavements had something unpredictable and autonomous — that is, wild — about them. And in my mouth, behind my clenched teeth, there was the acrid, metallic taste of gunfire; and my eyes, usually listless and wandering, had become sharp, watchful, attentive.

These eyes were fixed intently upon the exit door when the bus came to the end of its run. A number of people got out, and then I saw my wife getting out. Once again I recognized, in the manner in which she broke free of the crowd and started off toward a neighboring street, the wildness that pleased me so much. I jumped out of the car and started following her.

She was walking in front of me, ignorant of my presence, a tall woman     10
with an elegant figure, long-legged, narrow-hipped, broad-backed, her brown hair falling on her shoulders.

Men turned around as she went past; perhaps they were aware of what I myself was now sensing with an intensity that quickened the beating of my heart and took my breath away: the unrestricted, steadily increasing, irresistible character of her mysterious wildness.

She walked hurriedly, having evidently some purpose in view, and even the fact that she had a purpose of which I was ignorant added to her wildness; I did not know where she was going, just as on that far-off morning I had not known what the bird perching on the bough was about to do. Moreover I thought the gradual, steady increase in this quality of wildness came partly from the fact that as she drew nearer to the object of this mysterious walk there was an increase in her — how shall I express it? — of biological tension, of existential excitement, of vital effervescence. Then, unexpectedly, with the suddenness of a film, her purpose was revealed.

A fair-haired young man in a leather jacket and a pair of corduroy trousers was leaning against the wall of a house in that ancient, narrow street. He was idly smoking as he looked in front of him. But as my wife passed close to him, he threw away his cigarette with a decisive gesture, took a step forward, and seized her arm. I was expecting her to rebuff him, to move away from him, but nothing happened: Evidently obeying the rules of some kind of erotic ritual, she went on walking beside the young man. Then after a few steps, with a movement that confirmed her own complicity, she put her arm around her companion's waist and he put his around her.

I understood then that this unknown man who took such liberties with my wife was also attracted by wildness. And so, instead of making a conventional appointment with her, instead of meeting in a café with a handshake, a falsely friendly and respectful welcome, he had preferred, by agreement with her, to take her by surprise — or, rather, to pretend to do so — while she was apparently taking a walk on her own account. All this I perceived by intuition, noticing that at the very moment when he stepped forward and took her arm her wildness had, so to speak, given an upward bound. It was years since I had seen my wife so alive, but alas, the source of this life could not be traced to me.

They walked on thus entwined and then, without any preliminaries,    15
just like two wild animals, they did an unexpected thing: They went into one of the dark doorways in order to kiss. I stopped and watched them from a distance, peering into the darkness of the entrance. My wife was turned away from me and was bending back with the pressure of his body, her hair hanging free. I looked at that long, thick mane of brown hair, which as she leaned back fell free of her shoulders, and I felt at that moment her vitality reached its diapason, just as happens with wild animals when they couple and their customary wildness is redoubled by the violence of love. I watched for a long time and then, since the kiss went on and on and in fact seemed to be prolonged beyond the limits of my power of endurance, I saw that I would have to intervene.

I would have to go forward, seize my wife by the arm — or actually by that hair, which hung down and conveyed so well the feeling of feminine passivity — then hurl myself with clenched fists upon the blond young man. After this encounter I would carry off my wife, weeping, mortified, ashamed, while I was raging and brokenhearted, upbraiding her and pouring scorn upon her.

But what else would this intervention amount to but the shot my father fired at that free, unknowing bird as it perched on the bough? The disorder and confusion, the mortification, the shame, that would follow would irreparably destroy the rare and precious moment of wildness that I was witnessing inside the dark doorway. It was true that this wildness was directed against me; but I had to remember that wildness, always and everywhere, is directed against everything and everybody. After the scene of my intervention it might be possible for me to regain control of my wife, but I should find her shattered and lifeless in my arms like the bird that my father placed in my hand so that I might throw it into the shooting bag.

The kiss went on and on: Well, it was a kiss of passion — that could not be denied. I waited until they finished, until they came out of the doorway, until they walked on again still linked together. Then I turned back.


# EXPLORATIONS

1. What are the functions of the long opening section of "The Chase"? What role does the narrator assign himself here in relation to the adult male world? How would the story's impact change without this section?

2. At what point(s) in "The Chase" does the narrator recall his childhood hunting incident again? How is his role different now from the first time he mentioned the incident? How does the narrator vacillate between roles at the end of the story, and what role does he finally choose for himself?

3. Reread Alberto Moravia's last sentence; then look back at his third paragraph. What do you conclude that the narrator has done, and intends to do, after the point when the story ends? In what way is he himself adopting qualities he prizes in his wife? What effects does he apparently expect this behavior to have on his marriage?


# CONNECTIONS

1. What evidence in "The Chase" confirms Simone de Beauvoir's contention in "Woman as Other" (p. 329) that men perceive women as Other? How does Moravia's narrator feel about his wife's "otherness"? What can you deduce from the story about his wife's view of their situation?

2. Like "The Chase," Leslie Marmon Silko's "Yellow Woman" (p. 312) is a first-person story about a woman who temporarily leaves her husband for another man. Which of these marriages do you think is more likely to continue successfully after the wife returns home, and why?

3. In what ways is the narrator's revelation in "The Chase" similar to the narrator's revelation in "The Isle of Aphrodite" (p. 322)?

# ELABORATIONS

1. Near the end of "The Chase" the narrator observes, "Wildness, always and everywhere, is directed against everything and everybody" (para. 17). What does he mean? Do you agree? What other aspects of life are affected by wildness as Moravia defines it? Write an essay arguing for or against Moravia's statement, or examining a specific human action (e.g., putting animals in zoos or destroying ancient forests) to which his statement applies.

2. In the first section of "The Chase," Moravia's narrator speaks as if he knows his wife as completely as a farmer knows his hens. In the second section, he discovers that he does not know her so well after all. Think of a situation in which you based your expectations about another person on an image — perhaps an idealized social role, such as mother, grandfather, friend, or fiancé. How did you come to realize that the person was not as predictable as you thought? Write a narrative essay about the incident(s) that changed your attitude.

# The Artist's Life in Brussels

Ken Bugul, a Wolof phrase meaning "the person no one wants," is the pseudonym of Marietou M'Baye of Senegal. She took it on the advice of her publisher, who feared the sexual aspects of her autobiography, *Le Baobab fou* (1984), might create scandal in predominantly Muslim Senegal. "The Artist's Life in Brussels" comes from the book's English version, *The Abandoned Baobab* (1991), translated from the French by Marjolijn de Jager. M'Baye was born in 1948 in an isolated rural Senegalese village dominated by a baobab tree. Her mother left her for a year at age five and her Muslim father ignored her; M'Baye sought consolation in her studies at a French missionary school. She welcomed a scholarship to a Belgian university in the early 1960s, hoping to find her niche in the European homeland of Senegal's colonizers. She dropped out of school within a year, however, and careened from promiscuity to drugs to prostitution. After nearly two decades in Europe she returned to Senegal; she now holds a bachelor's degree in Spanish and English from the University of Dakar. M'Baye is currently the program officer for Central and West Africa for International Planned Parenthood Federation and is based in Lomé, Togo. Since *Le Baobab fou* she has written a novel, *La Chute des nuages* (*Cloudfall*).

Senegal lies across the Atlantic Ocean from southern Mexico. Its capital, Dakar, is the westernmost point in Africa. The region has been inhabited since ancient times and is home to a variety of ethnic and linguistic groups, the largest being the Wolof (the Peul, mentioned by Ken Bugul in paragraph 51, are another). Senegal's name probably comes from the Zenaga Berbers, who established Islam here around A.D. 1000. Four hundred years later the Portuguese set up trading posts, followed in the seventeenth century by the Dutch. It was the French, however, who made Senegal a colony, exporting peanuts (the chief crop), building towns and railroads, fending off challenges from the British, and eventually consolidating all of French West Africa under a French governor. Senegal gained independence and a democratic government in 1960. In 1973 it and six other states formed the West African Economic Community.

Brussels is the capital of the Kingdom of Belgium, a constitutional monarchy whose official languages are French and Flemish (a form of Dutch). A small country between France, Germany, and the Netherlands, it has changed hands repeatedly since Julius Caesar conquered it in 50–57 B.C. After periods of French, Spanish, Austrian, and Dutch rule, among others, Belgium declared independence in 1830. By the end of the century it was building an empire of its own in Africa: King Leopold II acquired the Congo (now Zaire), and after Germany's defeat in World War I, Belgium kept control of Ruanda-Urundi, part of German East Africa. The Congo became independent Zaire in 1960; Ruanda-Urundi became two nations, Rwanda and Burundi, in 1962. Despite tension between French and Flemish speakers, Belgium has been politically stable; it was a founding member of the Benelux (Belgium-Netherlands-Luxembourg) Economic Union, the North Atlantic Treaty Organization (NATO), the European Coal and Steel Community, and the European Common Market (see p. 723).

One day, at a restaurant, I met Jean Wermer, dressed like an Arabic prince. He took an interest in me right away. Intimacy was very quickly established since he was a friend of [my friend] Leonora's. He courted me discreetly, with many a wink, as the Belgians do so well. It was winter. It was cold enough to want to throw yourself in someone's warm arms and shiver with pleasure. . . .

I spent most of my time with him. He lived alone in a house that was his studio, his living quarters, and his gallery. Jean Wermer was an artist.

The ground floor was littered with carpets, blankets from countries around the world; on the second floor was the white and spacious kitchen and the orange living room; on the third floor was the studio with its glassed-in bay window, filled with light, overlooking the Volvoendal Park. The house felt as if it stood in the middle of the park. Light, white, and green. With its skylight, the attic seemed to have two levels of windows; it was the bedroom.

Jean Wermer had been married and had three children. When I met him, he had just been divorced.

Through his children I met his ex-wife and we established a warm friendship from the first day. She was living with a Tutsi from East Africa. 5

I ended up living with Jean Wermer and left the rue de Toulouse and all that it entailed. One street's entire life.

It was the first time I'd ever lived with a man. I was discovering other people. Other walks of life. This new life seemed to suit me wonderfully well. Spring and summer ran into each other. I was becoming worldly. Invited out, entertaining, gallery openings, meeting people who emerged from another universe. It had nothing to do with anything I'd learned from my school texts. Jean Wermer and I were doing quite well together apparently. As the days went by he told me about his life.

I was feeling good.

He didn't want us to be a bourgeois couple; what did he mean? We definitely weren't following in the footsteps of our "ancestors" very well down there in the village! In order to be with it, I learned my lesson in liberalism quite thoroughly. Jean would talk and laugh with other women, go out with them, spend part of the night with them.

"Why don't you do the same?" he'd say.                                          10

I was shocked.

"I'm not tired of you," I would answer.

"It's not a question of being tired of each other, it's a question of living freely, of doing what you want to do."

"What I want to do is precisely what I am doing: staying home, reading, writing, waiting. I'm not bored; I like being here."

"That's no life!"                                                               15

"It pleases me, Jean."

"Oh no, you're not asserting yourself, you should at least recognize that."

Then I'd phone people, make new friends, have lunch and dinner out, spend my evenings with people I knew. Without conviction.

The artist's life! It was all new to me. A new way of life that seemed to suit me. But there were moments when my educational frame of reference, tradition, took the upper hand and I'd feel plagued, torn.

We had all our meals together, which was pleasant. I was so involved      20
in playing the Western game that both Jean and I were under the impression there was nothing left to clarify. The little birds in the garden, the wind that would rise over the park with all its scents of nature made me want to jump, skip, and shriek like a child without a care in the world. The days and nights were filled with discoveries and new encounters. And yet I wasn't really satisfied; deep inside myself I was still looking for the explanation of the void that bloated me.

One night, Jean Wermer went out by himself. I stayed home alone, reading, listening to music, thriving on the sweetness of those moments when solitude brings that sense of well-being. Time was passing and Jean was still not back. I was beginning to get worried, not because I thought he'd had an accident, but wondering where he was and with whom.

The ghastly anguish of waiting. I wanted to live a certain kind of life, I had to immerse myself in it, but it wasn't always easy. I had never known this before. Down in the village, men didn't deceive their women. The evenings were spent together until a man's attention was caught by someone else, quite openly, and then he married her.

The hours were creeping by. I stretched out on the couch in the orange living room, since I couldn't really sleep.

Morning came and felt exactly the same as the previous one. The same morning, rising from the park like an erotic dream. Jean Wermer was still not home. I was sleepy, I was cold, I was tired, and I was as sad as a broom standing unused in a corner on a rainy day.

At long last Jean Wermer arrived. I was glad to see him. I felt com-  25
forted, but deep in my heart a slow-growing wound was quietly bleeding. He greeted me with a quick kiss on each cheek and asked me to come down with him to the ground floor. My heart was beating loudly enough to stop me in my tracks, yet I wanted to remain calm.

We went down the steps he himself had painted a shiny black, black in this burrow of whiteness and light. Had someone died? But it seemed to me that he looked embarrassed rather than upset.

This was the first time we'd ever had a talk like this, solemn and serious. There was an aura of mysteriousness. All of which only made my discomfort greater. We weren't used to hiding things from each other in this pretend life we were living. I had a premonition of the worst.

Jean Wermer spoke:

"I thought I ought to tell you: You know, I feel good being with you; I can't really explain it all to you for it goes back to my childhood, but I like being with men."

"What's wrong with that?" I said.  30

"You don't understand; I have homosexual tendencies."

I almost collapsed on the low bed where we were sitting, side by side amidst the multicolored pillows, on the black linen spread we had chosen together. Homosexual?

"I like women, but it isn't the same thing. The relationship is different. When I'm with you I'm happy, but I need the affection, the tenderness of a man. When I'm with a man, I melt away in his embrace without going any further. For me it's the need for tenderness. If I didn't come home last night it's because I spent the night with a man."

What did he want me to answer? I knew there were homosexuals, we had them in my country. I myself had had a homosexual slave, inherited from long tradition. "Gor Djigen" they called him. It had always remained an abstract idea for me. But Jean Wermer had been married, had children, and he didn't act like the Gor Djigens.

"I have homosexual tendencies. They're just tendencies," he empha-  35
sized. "You are my beauty," which is what he called me when he didn't call me his princess.

Our life together continued in its course with its gallery openings and its sophisticated events where one was obliged to make small talk for I know not what reason, even if it meant discussing the color of toilet paper. Was this then the life of Western artists? But not every artist was a homosexual and not every homosexual was an artist. In the final analysis,

I thought Jean Wermer was looking to be homosexual. In those days, homosexuality had become part of the mores of artists and intellectuals. It was almost fashionable.

I was playing the game and even bragged about living with a homosexual. Yet all that had been so foreign to me remained foreign.

We went to gay bars, around the Grand-Place in Brussels. I went so far as to flirt with possible companions for Jean and became rapidly known in these circles, as I met new faces or the most recent faces.

I discovered the sweetness and the special attentions homosexuals pay to women. I rather liked the atmosphere. It was a new world for me, but I seemed to have become a part of it. I was always there. My compatriots seemed far away to me.

Laure had some influence on my life at the time, as did so many others    40
later. I had met her between two glasses of champagne at a retrospective at the Gallery Empain; with her hair long as the lianas of the savanna, her almost beautiful face, her eyes that laughed along with her teeth, she was as dark as a Polynesian. She embodied availability and tolerance; I went to see her very often, incessantly. Her life-style suited me. I didn't feel so out of place at her house. Was it because she had pillows made of monkey hair from Zaire? We seemed to speak the same language, listen to the same music. It was the period when the West was becoming enamored of the exotic. What made us different was that she was white, married, and rich, while I was an "unbalanced" black woman, an adventurer. Though married, she had been living with another man for more than ten years.

An artist. This was the artist's life. The life of the middle class. The artist was always a bourgeois: He could allow himself anything.

In my village, living in a *ménage à trois* was nothing new. A man could have three, four wives in the same house. But one woman with two men!

I often went to her place. I would eat there. Sometimes I would sleep there. My relationship with her was a bit ambiguous. I didn't know exactly what my feelings for her were, but in her I had found sweetness, tenderness, and a kind of guilt. But why?

Laure preoccupied herself with me in a way different from Leonora's. Laure felt bad for me, Leonora helped me. Laure gave in to anything that pleased me; she even taught me to be unpredictable with her and sometimes I imposed my fantasies on her. I was beginning to wonder whether she wasn't in love with me, if she really cared for me, or if she was just playing games with me. I had reached a point where I no longer knew where I stood at all. I discovered luxurious restaurants, luxurious weekends, luxurious people, luxurious homes. The West in its generous decline. And how well I was playing my part in it! I was the pawn whom these people needed to break free from an unacknowledged guilt. I was everywhere at once and I didn't go unnoticed because I was black, provocative, sophisticated, and quite knowledgeable about their cultures, their civilizations. This took them by surprise.

I couldn't have imagined their decadence, since all I'd been taught 45 about them, for twenty years running, was their superiority. Why then, aware of all this, did I insist on playing the game?

My encounter with a woman from Argentina in a Greek restaurant led me to drugs. It was the sort of very inexpensive restaurant where intellectuals — real or imaginary — left-wing students — real or imaginary — hippies and marginals, the Western dregs, those unconscious because of their dizzying descent into alcohol and drugs, group sex, the mixing of races and of ideas, tacitly met.

I was alone that particular evening and was sitting across from some gypsy types who had come from somewhere else. Among them was a girl with long thick hair who didn't stop looking and smiling at me. We began to talk and they gave me their address.

And so one evening I went to visit them, a question of seeing other people, as Jean Wermer wanted me to, and also of checking to what point I'd become assimilated with my new way of life.

About ten people lived in the house and a thousand others would pass through regularly. Every nationality in the world was rubbing shoulders there, but at the time it was particularly South America under the Fascist regimes: taking a Chilean in was a good thing to do.

This truly was communal living; everything was run by a philanthropic 50 patron, a high-ranking officer of the Common Market. Everyone helped with the cooking; there was a communal dining room with a huge table that could seat twenty. The ease with which I connected with them made me feel as if I'd known them forever. We ate dinner lightheartedly. Again the same story: "My country, my race, at home, you people," but not in a tormenting way. I had my repertoire, too; everywhere I went it was the same thing. The "you people" was beginning to irritate me, for I understood more and more clearly that the Gauls were not my ancestors. At the same time it was a weapon, for I was different, and sometimes I felt superior; a pointless feeling. "You have such fine hands, such fine wrists and ankles . . . what is your origin?"

The West was interested in Africa. The bookstores were overflowing with books on Africa, and every Westerner was in a position to state that the Pygmies existed, that the Maasai women shaved their heads, that the Peul were very astute. The Westerner wanted to come to terms with the black man, but he insisted on knowing who that person was in order to justify the relationship. It was very stylish to know an authentic Tutsi or a Peul.

During dessert I smoked hashish for the first time; the cigarette they called a joint went from hand to hand like a peace pipe and I began to have an attack of uncontrollable, mad laughter. I was laughing as I'd never laughed before, a laughter that knew no bounds, to the point where people felt obliged to ask me whether I was all right, my laughter seeming more like sobs.

Beforehand nobody had asked me if I'd ever smoked, since to them it was obvious that anyone who stopped in was a smoker; moreover, being foreign and black, I came from the tropical countries where the plant grew. They didn't know that we don't have the same vision of things. The West secularizes everything. In Africa, the plant has ceremonial or thera-peutic uses, which are sacred functions.

The Western women were beginning their struggle for liberation and I almost impressed them as being avant-garde.

Jean Wermer seemed to be madly in love with François, but since he       55
wasn't fully admitting his homosexuality, he refused to accept it. We had discussed it for nights on end, but I was afraid that he would think I was jealous. None of this had changed anything in our relationship as far as I was concerned. It even brought me some happiness, for now not everything was focused on me, and I found that a relief; now I could devote myself to finding the true me, my only preoccupation.

The evenings that I spent alone at the house were filled with reading, writing, or sewing until I would fall asleep. The two men would come to say good night before going to bed.

In the beginning of this new life *à trois*, Jean Wermer would sometimes not sleep with me for several nights in a row. This reminded me of when a man in the village married a new wife. In case the man was already married, he would ask permission from his first wife to spend several consecutive nights with his new, young wife before he would put the traditional rotation into practice. This would allow them to get used to each other, to enhance the feeling, to get to know each other better, to permit the man to spend the time that the woman was fertile with her, to prevent the man from being with one of his other wives while thinking of the new one.

But my new life with these two men was different. If my mother only knew! And my brothers and sisters, my friends down there in the village and at school!

Ah! had I only known the sweet realities of my race and my people!

I'd never been closed off from experience, but my former environment 60
had suggested nothing of the life I was now leading.

Summer in Belgium, my first summer in the West. François and I
found work in a potter's studio. It was interesting, dusty but fun. I discovered shapes in the pottery and my sense of touch began to be sharpened.

At night, we would take a well-deserved bath, sometimes together with
Jean Wermer, and we'd have a ball washing each other. Afterward, we
would get together in the kitchen, freshly dressed in Indian cottons, to
have bergamot or jasmine tea. Apparently, we were happy. Later at night,
dressed to kill, we would go out for dinner, very aware that we weren't
going unnoticed. We weren't dressed, we were disguised. It was the style.
At the flea market where we went every Sunday, the poor rag sellers
hadn't yet figured out what this craze was for old garb from periods gone
by. Jean Wermer and François boasted about being with me: I was the
one they needed to better pass off their homosexuality. This life of ours
didn't last long, for François and I were to shake its foundation.

It began one night when they came to say good night to me, as they
usually did. François came after Jean Wermer. That night he began to
talk about himself, his life, the one and only time he had tried to go out
with a girl, a white South African with whom he hadn't made love. He
had never made love to a woman.

He spent the night with me upstairs until early morning. He spoke of
wanting to marry me because I could understand him. We — black
women, Arab women — we were the only ones in the world with whom
he ever expected to have a chance of working things out. François wanted
either to "work things out" or to assume his homosexuality fully. But if
there was a way to work things out, he would prefer that. He wanted to
be "a man" like every other man.

The next morning at breakfast Jean Wermer showed his irritation. 65

Ah! the wrath of men where a woman is concerned. It was beyond
belief! Jean Wermer was ranting as I'd never seen him carry on before.
François hadn't expected it, nor had I; we had seemed so liberal in our
behavior.

"I let you stay with me, and this is how you treat me, how low of you,
how vile," he railed at François. "Ken Bugul is *my* woman. She is mine.
I don't want to see you anymore." It was in that tone that Jean spoke to
François, who was unnerved, not because he was being told to go but
because it was his fault that Jean was so upset. Jean Wermer was afraid
of losing François.

The morning was heavy, painful, desperate between human beings
who were wrangling with each other from within their most primitive

instincts. Ah! the convolutions of feelings, where could it all lead? I had nothing to say and said nothing. I listened to them, I watched them. They had both seemed white to me like other whites; they were turning one color, then another, sometimes with moments of terrible pallor.

Down there in the village, such scenes didn't happen and people didn't take on such colors. Why and how had I ever gotten into this situation? I felt like fleeing far from this house, far from these beings who were no longer human. And I, who used to think that everything about them was marvelous . . . the reality was so different. These people would be true savages, if the stakes of their existence were limited only to these kinds of situations.

For all that, the life didn't wholly displease me. But whom am I going    70
to tell about it?

Alone, Jean Wermer and I couldn't live together anymore. François had packed his bags and taken his Hockney drawings away with him. More and more, Jean and I were fighting; he'd even gone so far as to hit me. The house of tranquility, to which I had come looking for happiness, had crumbled.

In the beginning of the fall I moved; we had decided that it was better if I went to live somewhere else. Our life together had become unlivable. Jean Wermer was in the full swing of his homosexual tendencies. Since François's departure, he went out more and more, always alone. Sometimes he would stay away. I must have made it uncomfortable for him to satisfy his desires at home and I realized that it was his home, that he had every right to avail himself of it and to do what he wanted to do. One had a home in order to be at home. With all the laws out there, all the constraints, all the prohibitions, his home offered the refuge in which his instincts could fully bloom. "Home" was what I had missed all my life.

## EXPLORATIONS

1. How is *bourgeois* defined in this narrative (paras. 9 and 41)? What definitions of *artist* are proposed? What role does art play in the lives of these artists?

2. In paragraph 27 Ken Bugul refers to "this pretend life we were living." What does she mean? What other words and phrases in her essay show that she is not really comfortable in Jean Wermer's social circle?

3. Ken Bugul alludes to several different social groups in Brussels — for instance, *women* and *foreigners*. How many of these groups can you identify? To which ones is she an insider? To which ones is she an outsider?

4. In paragraphs 24–26 Ken Bugul uses several metaphors and similes. What do you think were her reasons for choosing this kind of language for this section of her narrative?

## CONNECTIONS

1. "The Artist's Life in Brussels" and Alberto Moravia's "The Chase" (p. 337) both concern romantic triangles. What roles do freedom and wildness play in each triangle?

2. "Ah, the wrath of men where a woman is concerned," Ken Bugul writes in paragraph 66. How do you think Simone de Beauvoir would explain this statement? Cite evidence from "Woman as Other" (p. 329).

3. "I understood more and more clearly that the Gauls were not my ancestors," writes Ken Bugul in paragraph 50. In "Entering the New World" (p. 48), the poet Ebony tells V. S. Naipaul, "Charlemagne wasn't my ancestor" (para. 8). What does each of them mean by this?

## ELABORATIONS

1. When we enter an unfamiliar situation, one tactic we use to get along is making generalizations: "Mexican trains are never on time." "The English can't cook vegetables." From such generalizations we derive expectations, and on these expectations we base our actions. As an African living in Europe for the first time, what generalizations does Ken Bugul make about the things she sees and experiences? Which ones are well founded and which are not? What actions does she base on her generalizations? Which sequences of generalization and action work out well for her, and which ones work out badly? Write an essay analyzing the role of generalization making in Ken Bugul's effort to find a niche in Brussels.

2. "I couldn't have imagined their decadence, since all I'd been taught about them, for twenty years running, was their superiority," writes Ken Bugul in paragraph 45. "Why then, aware of all this, did I insist on playing the game?" Why indeed? What factors in Ken Bugul's position do you think led her to make the choices she reports in "The Artist's Life in Brussels"? Write an essay answering her question, using her essay and other selections you have read as sources.

# MARJORIE SHOSTAK

## Nisa's Marriage

"Nisa's Marriage" comes from Marjorie Shostak's 1981 book *Nisa: The Life and Words of a !Kung Woman*, based on Shostak's two and a half years among the !Kung San of Botswana. (The ! indicates a clicking sound.) At the time she was a research assistant on the Harvard Kalahari Desert Project, having previously received a bachelor's degree in English literature from Brooklyn College. Shostak, born in 1945, now teaches anthropology at Emory University in Atlanta. Her most recent book, coauthored with S. Boyd Eaton and Melvin Konner, is *The Paleolithic Prescription: A Program of Diet and Exercise and a Design for Living*. In 1989 Shostak returned to Botswana and met up with Nisa, who was then in her mid-sixties. Shostak is currently writing a book about their visit.

In her introduction to *Nisa*, Shostak writes: "Nisa is a member of one of the last remaining traditional gatherer-hunter societies, a group calling themselves the *Zhun/twasi*, the "real people," who currently live in isolated areas of Botswana, Angola, and Namibia. . . . They are also known as the !Kung Bushmen, the !Kung San, or simply the !Kung. They are short — averaging about five feet in height — lean, muscular, and, for Africa, light-skinned. They have high cheekbones and rather Oriental-looking eyes." Population biologists call these people Khoisan, from *Khoi*, the group previously known as Hottentots, and *San*, the group known as Bushmen, who together were the original inhabitants of South Africa (see pp. 35 and 587). Botswana, Nisa's homeland, gained its name and independence in 1966 after eighty years as the British protectorate of Bechuanaland.

Shostak describes meeting Nisa, who was then close to fifty years old: "Nisa wore an old blanket loosely draped over the remnants of a faded, flower-print dress, sizes too big. . . . [She] was all activity: Constantly in motion, her face expressive, she spoke fast and was at once strong and surprisingly coquettish." In the following excerpt, the events Nisa describes took place more than thirty-five years earlier, just as she entered puberty.

The day of the wedding, everyone was there. All of Tashay's friends were sitting around, laughing and laughing. His younger brother said, "Tashay, you're too old. Get out of the way so I can marry her. Give her to me." And his nephew said, "Uncle, you're already old. Now, let *me* marry her." They were all sitting around, talking like that. They all wanted me.

I went to my mother's hut and sat there. I was wearing lots of beads and my hair was completely covered and full with ornaments.

That night there was another dance. We danced, and some people fell asleep and others kept dancing. In the early morning, Tashay and his relatives went back to their camp; we went into our huts to sleep. When morning was late in the sky, they came back. They stayed around and then his parents said, "Because we are only staying a short while — tomorrow, let's start building the marriage hut."

The next day they started. There were lots of people there — Tashay's mother, my mother, and my aunt worked on the hut; everyone else sat around, talking. Late in the day, the young men went and brought Tashay to the finished hut. They set him down beside it and stayed there with him, sitting around the fire.

I was still at my mother's hut. I heard them tell two of my friends to go and bring me to the hut. I thought, "Oohh . . . I'll run away." When they came for me, they couldn't find me. They said, "Where did Nisa go? Did she run away? It's getting dark. Doesn't she know that things may bite and kill her?" My father said, "Go tell Nisa that if this is what she's going to do, I'll hit her and she won't run away again. What made her want to run away, anyway?

I was already far off in the bush. They came looking for me. I heard them calling, "Nisa . . . Nisa . . ." I sat down at the base of a tree. Then I heard Nukha, "Nisa . . . Nisao . . . my friend . . . a hyena's out there . . . things will bite and kill you . . . come back . . . Nisa . . . Nisao . . ."

When Nukha finally saw me, I started to run. She ran after me, chasing me, and finally caught me. She called out to the others, "Hey! Nisa's here! Everyone, come! Help me! Take Nisa, she's here!"

They came and brought me back. Then they laid me down inside the hut. I cried and cried. People told me, "A man is not something that kills you; he is someone who marries you, who becomes like your father or your older brother. He kills animals and gives you things to eat. Even tomorrow, while you are crying, Tashay may kill an animal. But when he returns, he won't give you any meat; only he will eat. Beads, too. He will get beads but he won't give them to you. Why are you so afraid of your husband and what are you crying about?"

I listened and was quiet. Later, we went to sleep. Tashay lay down beside the opening of the hut, near the fire, and I lay down inside; he thought I might try and run away again. He covered himself with a blanket and slept.

While it was dark, I woke up. I sat up. I thought, "How am I going to jump over him? How can I get out and go to mother's hut to sleep beside

5

10

her?" I looked at him sleeping. Then came other thoughts, other thoughts in the middle of the night, "Eh . . . this person has just married me . . ." and I lay down again. But I kept thinking, "Why did people give me this man in marriage? The older people say he is a good person, yet . . ."

I lay there and didn't move. The rain came beating down. It fell steadily and kept falling. Finally, I slept. Much later dawn broke.

In the morning, Tashay got up and sat by the fire. I was so frightened I just lay there, waiting for him to leave. When he went to urinate, I went and sat down inside my mother's hut.

That day, all his relatives came to our new hut — his mother, his father, his brothers . . . everyone! They all came. They said, "Go tell Nisa she should come and her in-laws will put the marriage oil on her. Can you see her sitting over there? Why isn't she coming so we can put the oil on her in her new hut?"

I refused to go. They kept calling for me until finally, my older brother said, "Uhn uhn. Nisa, if you act like this, I'll hit you. Now, get up and go over there. Sit over there so they can put the oil on you."

I still refused and just sat there. My older brother grabbed a switch     15
from a nearby tree and started coming toward me. I got up. I was afraid. I followed him to where the others were sitting. Tashay's mother rubbed the oil on me and my aunt rubbed it on Tashay.

Then they left and it was just Tashay and me. . . .

That Zhun/twa, that Tashay, he really caused me pain.

Soon after we were married, he took me from my parents' village to live at his parents' village. At first my family came and lived with us, but then one day they left, left me with Tashay and his parents. That's when I started to cry. Tashay said, "Before your mother left, you weren't crying. Why didn't you tell me you wanted to go with them? We could have followed along." I said, "I was afraid of you. That's why I didn't tell you."

But I still wanted to be with my mother, so later that day, I ran away. I ran as fast as I could until I finally caught up with them. When my mother saw me she said, "Someday a hyena is going to kill this child in the bush. She's followed us. Here she is!" I walked with them back to their village and lived with them a while.

A long time passed. One day Tashay left and came to us. When I saw     20
him, I started to cry. He said, "Get up. We're going back." I said, "Why does this person keep following me? Do I own him that he follows me everywhere?" My father said, "You're crazy. A woman follows her husband when he comes for her. What are you just sitting here for?"

Tashay took me with him and I didn't really refuse. We continued to live at his village and then we all went and lived at another water hole.

By then, I knew that I was no longer living with my mother. I had left my family to follow my husband.

We lived and lived and then, one day, my heart started to throb and my head hurt; I was very sick. My father came to visit and went into a medicinal trance to try and cure me. When I was better, he left and I stayed behind.

After Tashay and I had been living together for a long time, we started to like each other with our hearts and began living nicely together. It was really only after we had lived together for a long time that he touched my genitals. By then, my breasts were already big.

We were staying in my parents' village the night he first had sex with me and I didn't really refuse. I agreed, just a little, and he lay with me. But the next morning, I was sore. I took some leaves and wound them around my waist, but I continued to feel pain. I thought, "Ooo . . . what has he done to my insides that they feel this way?"

I went over to my mother and said, "That person, last night . . .       25
I'm only a child, but last night he had sex with me. Move over and let me eat with you. We'll eat and then we'll move away. Mother . . . mother . . ."

My mother turned to my father and said, "Get up, get a switch and hit this child. She's ruining us. Get up and find something to hit her with." I thought, "What? Did I say something wrong?"

My father went to find a switch. I got up and ran to my aunt's hut. I sat there and thought, "What was so bad? How come I talked about something yet . . . is that something so terrible?"

My father said to my aunt, "Tell Nisa to come back here so I can beat her. The things this young girl talks about could crack open the insides of her ears."

My mother said, "This child, her talk is terrible. As I am now, I would stick myself with a poison arrow; but my skin itself fears and that's why I won't do it. But if she continues to talk like that, I will!"

They wanted me to like my husband and not to refuse him. My mother      30
told me that when a man sleeps with his wife, she doesn't tell; it's a private thing.

I got up and walked away from them. I was trembling, "Ehn . . . nn . . . nn . . ." I looked at my genitals and thought, "Oh, this person . . . yesterday he took me and now my genitals are ruined!" I took some water and washed my genitals, washed and washed.

Because, when my genitals first started to develop, I was afraid. I'd look at them and cry and think something was wrong with them. But people told me, "Nothing's wrong. That's what you yourself are like."

I also thought that an older person, an adult like my husband, would tear me apart, that his penis would be so big that he would hurt me. Because I hadn't known older men. I had only played sex play with little boys. Then, when Tashay did sleep with me and it hurt, that's when I refused. That's also when I told. But people didn't yell at him, they only yelled at me, and I was ashamed.

That evening, we lay down again. But this time, before he came in, I took a leather strap, held my leather apron tightly against my legs, tied the strap around my genitals, and then tied it to the hut's frame. I was afraid he'd tear me open and I didn't want him to take me again.

The two of us lay there and after a long time, he touched me. When      35
he touched my stomach, he felt the leather strap. He felt around to see what it was. He said, "What is this woman doing? Last night she lay with me so nicely when I came to her. Why has she tied her genitals up this way? What is she refusing to give me?"

He sat me up and said, "Nisa . . . Nisa . . . what happened? Why are you doing this?" I didn't answer. He said, "What are you so afraid of that you had to tie up your genitals?" I said, "Uhn, uhn. I'm not afraid of anything." He said, "No, now tell me. In the name of what you did, I'm asking you."

Then he said, "What do you think you're doing when you do something like this? When you lie down with me, a Zhun/twa like yourself, it's not as though you were lying with another, a stranger. We are both Zhun/twasi, yet you tied yourself up!"

I said, "I refuse to lie down with anyone who wants to take my genitals. Last night you had sex with me and today my insides hurt. That's why I've tied myself up and that's why you won't take me again."

He said, "Untie the strap. Do you see me as someone who kills people? Am I going to eat you? No, I'm not going to kill you, but I have married you and want to make love to you. Do you think I married you thinking I wouldn't make love to you? Did you think we would just live beside each other? Do you know any man who has married a woman and who just lives beside her without having sex with her?"

I said, "I don't care. I don't want sex. Today my insides hurt and I      40
refuse." He said, "Mm, today you will just lie there, but tomorrow, I will take you. If you refuse, I'll pry your legs open and take you by force."

He untied the strap and said, "If this is what use you put this to, I'm going to destroy it." He took his knife and cut it into small pieces. Then he put me down beside him. He didn't touch me; he knew I was afraid. Then we went to sleep.

The next day we got up, did things, and ate things. When we returned to our hut that night, we lay down again. That's when he forced himself on me. He held my legs and I struggled against him. But I knew he would have sex with me and I thought, "This isn't helping me at all. This man, if he takes me by force, he'll really hurt me. So I'll just lie here, lie still and let him look for the food he wants. But I still don't know what kind of food I have because even if he eats he won't be full."[1]

So I stopped fighting and just lay there. He did his work and that time it didn't hurt so much. Then he lay down and slept.

After that, we just lived. I began to like him and he didn't bother me again, he didn't try to have sex with me. Many months passed — those of the rainy season, those of the winter season, and those of the hot season. He just left me alone and I grew up and started to understand about things. Because before that, I hadn't really known about men. . . .

We continued to live and it was as if I was already an adult. Because,   45 beginning to menstruate makes you think about things. Only then did I bring myself to understand, only then did I begin to be a woman.

When Tashay wanted to lie with me, I no longer refused. We just had sex together, one day and then another. In the morning, I'd get up and sit beside our hut and I wouldn't tell. I'd think, "My husband is indeed my husband now. What people told me, that my husband is mine, is true."

We lived and lived, the two of us, together, and after a while I started to really like him and then, to love him. I had finally grown up and had learned how to love. I thought, "A man has sex with you. Yes, that's what a man does. I had thought that perhaps he didn't."

We lived on and I loved him and he loved me. I loved him the way a young adult knows how to love; I just *loved* him. Whenever he went away and I stayed behind, I'd miss him. I'd think, "Oh, when is my husband ever coming home? How come he's been gone so long?" I'd miss him and want him. When he'd come back my heart would be happy, "Eh, hey! My husband left and once again has come back."

We lived and when he wanted me, I didn't refuse; he just lay with me. I thought, "Why had I been so concerned about my genitals? They aren't that important, after all. So why was I refusing them?"

I thought that and gave myself to him, gave and gave. We lay with   50 each other and my breasts were very large. I was becoming a woman.

---

[1]Food and eating are universally used by the !Kung as metaphors for sex. However, they claim no knowledge or practice of oral-genital contact.

# EXPLORATIONS

1. What is Nisa's concept of a husband when she first marries Tashay? How does her concept change over the course of their marriage? What are the reasons for the changes?

2. Judging from "Nisa's Marriage," what specific rituals are part of a Zhun/twasi wedding? What is the practical or symbolic (or both) purpose of each ritual?

3. What facts can you glean about the Zhun/twasi way of life from "Nisa's Marriage"? What appears to be the group's main food source? What dangers do they fear? What images in their speech reflect these basic elements of their existence?

4. When Nisa runs home to her mother after having sex with her husband, her mother says, "As I am now, I would stick myself with a poison arrow; but my skin itself fears and that's why I won't do it. But if she continues to talk like that, I will!" (para. 29). What does she mean? How might an American mother express the same sentiments?

# CONNECTIONS

1. What African customs and concepts about marriage appear in both "Nisa's Marriage" and "The Artist's Life in Brussels" (p. 344)? What attitudes toward relations between the sexes do Nisa and Ken Bugul apparently share?

2. What attitudes toward marriage does Nisa share with Pom in Ved Mehta's "Pom's Engagement" (p. 142)?

3. By the end of her narrative, how does Nisa feel about moving from childhood to womanhood? What statements in Mario Vargas Llosa's "On Sunday" (p. 224) indicate a comparable response by Miguel? How does gender affect their feelings about adulthood?

# ELABORATIONS

1. "Nisa's Marriage" illustrates a very different approach to sexuality from that of Western cultures. List all the rules you can identify that govern marriage, sexual intercourse, and gender roles among the Zhun/twasi. What needs of the society shape its sexual rules? Write an essay comparing and contrasting social needs and sexual rules among the Zhun/twasi with those you are familiar with as an American.

2. Nisa's last sentence is: "I was becoming a woman." What does she mean? How many definitions of *woman* and *man* have you encountered in this unit? Write a classification essay listing them, explaining them, and showing how they are related.

# NAILA MINAI

## *Women in Early Islam*

Naila Minai was born in Japan and grew up in Turkey and many other countries of the Middle East. "My Turkish-Tatar grandmother was tutored at home, married a polygamous man, and has never discarded her head veil," she writes. "My mother never wore the veil, studied in schools close to home, and settled down as a housewife in a monogamous marriage. I left my family as a teenager to study in the United States and Europe, where I hitchhiked from country to country . . . eventually making a solo trip across the Sahara." Minai's flight took her to the Sorbonne in Paris and the University of California, Berkeley, where she received her degrees in literature and biology. She has worked as a UN correspondent and has continued to travel widely as a free-lance journalist. "Women in Early Islam" comes from her 1981 book, *Women in Islam.* She currently divides her time between the United States and her extended family in the Middle and Far East.

The city of Mecca, where Islam originated, lies near the Red Sea in what is now Saudi Arabia; Medina is north of Mecca. Arabia — the peninsula divided from Africa by the Red Sea and from Iran by the Persian Gulf — currently comprises Saudi Arabia, Yemen, South Yemen, Oman, the United Arab Emirates, Qatar, Kuwait (see p. 696), Bahrain, and several neutral zones. North of the Arabian Peninsula, and among the members of the Arab League, are the Islamic nations of Jordan, Syria, Lebanon, and Iraq (see p. 677). Iran to the east and Turkey to the north are also Islamic by religion but have ethnically distinct populations from Arabia (see pp. 162 and 380). Egypt, Sudan, Libya, Tunisia, Algeria, and Morocco in northern Africa belong to the Arab League as well, are predominantly Islamic, and generally are counted as Arab nations. Israel, surrounded by Islamic Arabs, is a Jewish nation (see pp. 275 and 629).

Khadija, an attractive forty-year-old Arabian widow, ran a flourishing caravan business in Mecca in the seventh century A.D., and was courted by the most eligible men of her society. But she had eyes only for an intelligent and hardworking twenty-five-year-old in her employ named Muhammad. "What does she see in a penniless ex-shepherd?" her scandalized aristocratic family whispered among themselves. Accustomed to having her way, however, Khadija proposed to Muhammad and married him. Until her death some twenty-five years later, her marriage was much more than the conventional Cinderella story in reverse, for Khadija not only bore six children while comanaging her business with her husband, but also advised and financed him in his struggle to found Islam, which grew to be one of the major religions of the world.

It was a religion that concerned itself heavily with women's rights, in a surprisingly contemporary manner. A woman was to be educated and allowed to earn and manage her income. She was to be recognized as legal heir to her father's property along with her brother. Her rights in marriage were also clearly spelled out: She was entitled to sexual satisfaction as well as economic support. Nor was divorce to consist any longer of merely throwing the wife out of the house without paying her financial compensation.

This feminist bill of rights filled an urgent need. Meccans in the seventh century were in transition from a tribal to an urban way of life. As their town grew into a cosmopolitan center of trade, kinship solidarity had deteriorated, but municipal laws had not yet been fully established to protect the citizens. Women were particularly vulnerable, their rights closely linked with the tribal way of life their people had known before renouncing nomadism to settle in Mecca around A.D. 400. In nomadic communities of the desert a woman was not equal to a man. During famine a female could be killed at birth to increase her brother's food supply. However, if she managed to reach adulthood she had a better status in the desert than in the city, largely because her labors were indispensable to her clan's survival in the harsh environment. While the men protected the encampment and engaged in trade, she looked after the herds and produced the items to be traded — meat, wool, yogurt, and cheese, all of which bought weapons and grains as well as other essentials. As a breadwinner the tribal woman enjoyed considerable political clout. Even if she did not always participate in council meetings, she made her views known. Only a fool refused to heed his womenfolk and risked antagonizing a good half of his tribe, with whom he had to live in the close confines of the camp and caravan.

If tribal discord was uncomfortable in the best of circumstances, it was catastrophic during the battles that broke out frequently among the clans over pasture and watering rights or to avenge heroes slain by the enemy. With the battlefront so close to home, a woman was needed as a nurse, cheerleader, and even soldier. She was sometimes captured and ransomed or sold into slavery. If her tribesmen could not pay her captors the required number of camels in ransom, they valiantly stormed the enemy's camp to rescue her. These were men brought up on recitations of epic poems about brave warriors who rescued fair damsels in distress. Poets and poetesses of the tribe kept chivalry alive, constantly singing praises of heroism among their people and condemning cowardliness and disloyalty. No one who wanted a respectable place in his tribe could afford to ignore the ubiquitous "Greek chorus," for life without honor was worse than death to a nomad, who could not survive as an outcast in the desert.

Marriage customs varied from tribe to tribe, but the most popular were those that tended to maintain the woman's independence, if only incidentally, by having her remain within her family circle after marriage. If the husband was a close relative, the couple set up a conjugal tent near both of their parents. A husband who was not kin merely visited her at her home. In some clans women could be married to several visiting husbands at the same time. When the wife bore a child, she simply summoned her husbands and announced which of them she believed to be the child's father. Her decision was law. Actually, it did not matter greatly who the biological father was, since children of such unions belonged to the matrilineal family and were supported by communal property administered by her brothers or maternal uncles.

Life in the desert was so hard and precarious that some of the most impoverished tribes renounced nomadism to submit to a less independent existence in towns. Muhammad's ancestors, a segment of the Kinanah tribe, were among them. They settled down at the crossroads of important caravan routes in the place which is now Mecca, and prospered as middlemen under the new name of Quraysh. Their great wealth and power undoubtedly helped their deities extend their spiritual influence far beyond Mecca's boundaries and make Kaaba, their sanctuary, the most important shrine in central Arabia. As keepers of the shrine the leading Quraysh families grew immeasurably rich, but the wealth was not equitably distributed. As survival no longer depended on communal sharing and on women's contributing equally to the family budget, Meccans became more interested in lucrative business connections than in kinship ties. Glaring socioeconomic differences — unknown among nomads — emerged. Women lost their rights and their security.

If brothers went their separate ways, their sister who continued to live with them after marriage lost her home unless one of them took her and her children under his protection. A woman could not automatically count on her brothers to assume this duty, for with the rise of individualism the patrilineal form of marriage, which had coexisted with other marital arrangements in seventh-century Mecca, was gaining popularity. A self-made man tended to prefer leaving his property to his own sons, which sharpened his interest in ensuring that his wife bore only his children. The best ways to guarantee this was to have her live under close supervision in his house. The woman thus lost her personal freedom, but the security she gained from the marital arrangement was precarious at best in the absence of protective state laws. Not only did she have to live at her in-laws' mercy, she could be thrown out of the house on her husband's whim. Khadija escaped such a fate because she was independently wealthy and belonged to one of the most powerful families of the Quraysh — a fact that must have helped her significantly to multiply her fortune.

It was against such a backdrop of urban problems that Islam was born. Even though Muhammad lived happily and comfortably with his rich wife, he continued to identify with the poor and the dispossessed of Mecca, pondering the conditions that spawned them. He himself had been orphaned in early childhood and passed on from one relative to another. Since his guardians were from the poor and neglected branch of the Quraysh, Muhammad earned his keep as a shepherd from a very early age. But he was luckier than other orphans, for he at least had a place in loving homes and eventually got a good job with Khadija's caravan, which allowed him to travel widely in the Middle East.

These journeys had a direct bearing on his spiritual growth and gave focus to his social concerns by exposing him to Christian monks and well-educated Jewish merchants. They intrigued him, for they seemed to have put into practice a monotheistic faith which a few Meccans of the educated circles were beginning to discuss. How did the Christian God inspire such diverse nationalities to worship Him alone? How did the Judaic God manage to unite widely dispersed Semitic groups under one set of laws which provided for the protection of women and children even in large cities? The astral deities that Muhammad's people inherited from their nomadic ancestors demanded offerings but gave nothing in return. After discussions with people of various faiths, Muhammad sought the ultimate solution to his community's problems in the solitude of a cave on Mount Hiraa overlooking Mecca, where he often retreated in his spare moments, with Khadija or by himself.

While meditating alone one day in the cave, Muhammad heard a       10
voice which he believed to be the angel Gabriel's. "Proclaim in the name of thy Lord and Cherisher who created, created man out of a clot of congealed blood" (Quran,[1] surah [chapter] 96, verses 1–2), it said, pointing out that there was only one God and that man must serve Him alone. When Muhammad recovered from his ecstasy, he ran back, shaken, and described his experience to his wife. Having shared his spiritual struggles, Khadija understood that her husband had received a call to serve the one God whom the Christians and the Jews also worshiped. Bewildered and confused, Muhammad went on with his daily work in the city and occasional meditations on Mount Hiraa. Again the voice commanded

---

[1]Variation of Koran, the sacred text of Islam. — ED.

him to tell his people about the one omnipotent God, who would welcome believers into heaven and cast wicked people into hell. With Khadija's repeated encouragement, Muhammad finally accepted his prophetic call and devoted the rest of his life to preaching God's word as the new religion of Islam (which means "submission [to the will of God]"). Converts to it were called Muslims ("those who submit"). They were not to be called Muhammadans, because they did not worship Muhammad, who was merely a human messenger for the one God. Though invisible and immortal, this God was named Allah after the Zeus of the old Meccan pantheon.

Numerous revelations that Muhammad received from Allah throughout his life were compiled shortly after his death into the Muslim bible, named the Quran, which formed the basis for the Shariah, or Islamic law. A supplement to it was provided by the Hadith, or Muhammad's words, which were recorded over many years as his survivors and their descendants remembered them. Despite the exotic Arabic words in which it is couched, Islam's message is similar in its essentials to the one promulgated by Judaism and Christianity, and can be summed up by the Ten Commandments. *Allah*, after all, is but the Arabic name for the God worshiped by both Jews and Christians. But the rituals differed. Muhammad required his followers to obey the commandments through the practice of five specific rituals, called the pillars of Islam. A Muslim must (1) profess faith in one God; (2) pray to Him; (3) give alms to the poor; (4) fast during Ramadan, the month in the lunar calendar during which Muhammad received his first revelation; and (5) go on a pilgrimage to Mecca at least once in his lifetime (if he can afford to do so) to pay respects to the birthplace of Islam and reinforce the spirit of fellowship with Muslims from all over the world. Although these laws preached fairness and charity among all mankind, God — through Muhammad — preferred to establish specific guidelines to protect the interests of women.

Once he had united enough people under Allah to make a viable community, Muhammad devoted an impressive number of his sermons to women's rights. In doing so, however, he did not attempt to fight the irreversible tide of urbanization. Nor did he condemn the trend toward patrimonial families, although they often abused women. Too shrewd a politician to antagonize Mecca's powerful patriarchs, he introduced a bill of rights for women which would not only ensure their protection under patriarchy but also reinforce the system itself so that it would stand as a minitribe against the rest of the world.

He did this mainly by providing for women's economic rights in marriage in such a way that they had a financial stake in the system which constantly threatened to erode their independence. Upon marriage a man had to pay his bride a dowry, which was to be her nest egg against divorce or widowhood. While married to him, she could manage the dowry and all other personal income in any way that she pleased, exclusively for her own benefit, and will them to her children and husband upon her death. In her lifetime she did not have to spend her money on herself, or her children for that matter, since only the man was responsible for supporting his family. If the woman stayed married to her husband until his death, she also inherited part of his property. While her share was less than her children's, she was assured of being supported by her sons in widowhood. By the same line of reasoning, her inheritance from her father was half that of her brother's: Her husband supported her, whereas her brother had to support his wife. The daughter's right to inherit tended to divide the patriarch's wealth, but the problem was customarily solved by having her marry a paternal first cousin. Failing that, the inheritance became a part of yet another Muslim family in the same tribe of Islam, united through faith rather than kinship. In either case, a Muslim woman with neither a paid occupation nor an inheritance enjoyed a modicum of financial independence, at the price of her submission to a patriarchal form of marriage.

But she was to be allowed to choose her own spouse, according to the Hadith: "None, not even the father or the sovereign, can lawfully contract in marriage an adult woman of sound mind without her permission, whether she be a virgin or not." This freedom was to be assured by a law that required the dowry to be paid to the bride herself. Since the parents were not to pocket it, as they often did before Islam, they were presumably above being "bought." But the brides' freedom remained largely theoretical, since most of them were barely ten years old when engaged to be married for the first time. Aysha, whom Muhammad married after Khadija's death, was only about six or seven years old when she was betrothed and about ten when she moved into her husband's house with her toys. Muhammad was not playing legal tricks on women, however. He did revoke the parents' choice of mate when their daughters complained to him about it. Although parents were to be honored and obeyed, he made it clear that the grown-up daughter was to be respected as an individual — so much so that the marriage contract could be tailored to her specific needs: The bride could impose conditions on her contract. A cooperative wife, he pointed out, was the best foundation for a stable marriage.

Though Muhammad repeatedly preached compassion and love as the most important bonds of marriage, he also gave men financial enticements to keep the family together. The husband was allowed to pay only    15 a part of the dowry upon marriage, with the balance payable upon divorce. If the dowry was large enough, the arrangement deterred the husband from throwing out his wife without substantial cause. In fact, under Islam he could no longer just throw her out. He had to pay her not only the balance of the dowry but also "maintenance on a reasonable scale" (Quran 2:241). He was also to support her through the ensuing *idda*, the three months of chastity which the Shariah asked her to observe in order to determine whether she was carrying his child. If pregnant, she was to be helped until she delivered and had nursed the infant to the point where he could be cared for by the husband's family. All of her children remained under the paternal roof. In a patriarchal society where men were not eager to support others' children or to provide employment for women, the child custody law assured children a decent home and enabled the divorcée to remarry more easily, but even an independently wealthy woman was forbidden to walk out of her husband's home with her children.

Any sexual behavior that would weaken the patriarchal system was strongly discouraged or made illegal. If the custom of taking a visiting husband was frowned upon, her taking more than one at a time was condemned as adultery, which was punishable by whipping. Although men were also forbidden to sow wild oats, they could marry up to four wives and have as many concubines as they could afford. This law may have been partly a concession by Muhammad to the widely accepted custom among wealthy urban men, but he also saw it as a way to attach surplus women to the men's households for their own protection as well as to maintain social order. Due to frequent intertribal warfare and attacks on the merchants' caravans, women always outnumbered men. The conflict became increasingly serious as Muhammad's following grew large enough to threaten the purse and the prestige of the families who amassed fortunes from pilgrims to the Kaaba. So vicious were the attacks that in A.D. 622, after Khadija died, Muhammad moved his budding Muslim community to Medina, an agricultural community without important shrines that would be threatened by Allah. Moreover, the perpetually quarreling clans of Medina welcomed Muhammad because of his reputation as a just man and a skillful arbitrator.

Muhammad succeeded brilliantly in settling the clans' differences and won a prominent place in Medina. This made Meccans even more determined to destroy him before he built up an alliance against them. Violent battles between the Muslims and the Meccans followed. Alliances and betrayals by various tribal factions during each battle engendered more battles, which decimated the Muslim community. The number of widows mounted to such catastrophic proportions after the battle fought at Uhud, near Medina, that God sent a message officially condoning polygamy: "Marry women of your choice, two, or three, or four." But He added, "If you fear that you cannot treat them equitably, marry only one" (3:3). A polygamous husband was required to distribute not only material goods but also sexual attention equally among his wives, for sexual satisfaction, according to Muhammad, was every woman's conjugal right. Besides, a sexually unsatisfied wife was believed to be a threat to her family's stability, as she was likely to seek satisfaction elsewhere.

Unmarried men and women also posed a threat to Muhammad's scheme of social order, which may be one reason why he frowned upon monasticism. Sexual instincts were natural, he reasoned, and therefore would eventually seek fulfillment in adultery[2] unless channeled into legitimate marriage. Wives and husbands were thus necessary for each other's spiritual salvation. "The curse of God be upon those women who remain unwed and say they will never marry," he said, "and a man who does not marry is none of mine."

Though the Quran abolished the ancient custom of stoning adulteresses to death and called instead for public whipping — a hundred lashes administered to male and female offenders alike — Muhammad knew that the sexual double standard would single out women as targets of slander. After a bitter personal experience, he hastened to build safety features into his antiadultery and antifornication laws.

One day Aysha was left behind inadvertently by Muhammad's caravan    20 when she stepped away to look for a necklace that she had lost. She was brought back to the caravan the following morning by a man many years younger than her middle-aged husband, which set tongues wagging. Even Ali, Muhammad's trusted cousin and son-in-law, cast doubt on her reputation. The Prophet's faith in his wife was severely shaken. Aysha was finally saved when her husband fell into a trance, which indicated that he was receiving a message from God. Relief spread over his face. God had vouched for her innocence. The "affair of the slander," as it came to be known, was closed. Four witnesses were henceforth required to condemn women of adultery, as against only two for business transactions and murder cases. Moreover, false witnesses were to be whipped publicly.

Other than false witnesses, violators of women's rights were not punished on this earth. The law would catch up with them in the next world, where they would be cast into the fire (an idea borrowed from the

---

[2]Here *adultery* refers to premarital as well as extramarital sex.

Christians). The good, on the other hand, would reside forever in a heavenly oasis with cool springs in shady palm groves where their every whim would be served by lovely dark-eyed houris. Like the Christian preachers who promised believers a heaven with pearly gates and haloed creatures floating about on white clouds, Muhammad merely presented images that would spell bliss to the common man. Though he did not specify who was going to serve the deserving women, probably for fear of offending their husbands, Muhammad guaranteed a place for them in paradise. Women had the same religious duties as men, and their souls were absolutely equal in God's eyes, with not even the responsibility for original sin weighing upon them. Islam rejects the idea of original sin altogether, claiming that every child is born pure. Nor does the Quran single out Eve as the cause of man's fall (though folklore in various parts of the Middle East does condemn her). According to the Quran, Allah tells both Adam and Eve not to eat the apple. "Then did Satan make them slip from the Garden" (2:36). Allah scolds them both equally, but promises mercy and guidance when they repent.

Muhammad's decision to rely on each man's conscience to fulfill his Islamic obligation toward women reflected a realistic approach to legislation. He seems to have recognized how far he could carry his reforms without losing his constituents' support. In a city where woman had neither economic nor political weight, men would take only so much earthly punishment for disregarding her rights. By the same token, they would not entirely give up their old prerogative of divorcing their wives for any cause without answering to a third party, or pay them more than comfortably affordable compensation. Muhammad therefore struck a compromise in his laws, but repeatedly emphasized the spirit of kindness and respect for women which was implied in them. . . .

The unspecified rights that women had enjoyed during Muhammad's time were chipped away gradually. But the meticulously detailed laws on marital and financial rights were too specific to be ignored entirely, and gave women a modicum of security and independence in the patriarchal family, which survived as a minitribe in the sprawling empire. Within the family circle women exerted considerable influence, not only on their men but also on the blossoming of Arab culture in the Middle Ages. An exceptional few followed Aysha's example and ruled the caliphs and their empire, which spread Islam to lands and peoples far beyond the Arabian peninsula.

# EXPLORATIONS

1. According to Naila Minai, what were the main responsibilities, privileges, and dangers of being female in a nomadic tribe?

2. Why did Khadija's and Muhammad's Quraysh ancestors gain by giving up their nomadic existence? In what ways did the urbanization of Mecca pave the way for a monotheistic religion? For a social code ensuring protection for women?

3. How did Muhammad's marriage to Khadija contribute to the founding of Islam? How did his marriage to Aysha contribute to the religion's rules?

4. What is the effect of Minai's opening her essay with a romantic anecdote? What elements in this first paragraph were presumably added by the author rather than drawn from source documents? How would you evaluate the balance she has struck between human interest and historical accuracy?

# CONNECTIONS

1. What rules governing sexuality and marriage among Muslims also appear among the Zhun/twasi as described in "Nisa's Marriage" (p. 354) by Marjorie Shostak? What explanations does Minai offer for these rules in Arabia that also may explain them in Botswana?

2. Alberto Moravia's "The Chase" (p. 337) defines marital success in terms of attraction between the partners. According to Minai's summary, did the Islamic code treat sexual attraction as valuable or dangerous to a marriage? Cite evidence for your answer.

3. Look back at Ved Mehta's "Pom's Engagement" (p. 142). In what ways do the Hindu concepts of male and female rights and responsibilities resemble those of Islam? What aspects of both cultures' definition of sex roles illustrate points made by Simone de Beauvoir in "Woman as Other" (p. 329)?

# ELABORATIONS

1. Minai undertook a delicate task in deciding to write about a religion and its founder. What different viewpoints toward Islam do you think she anticipated among her audience? What concessions, if any, does her writing show to Muslims? To members of other religions? Having looked at Minai's tactics for handling a sensitive subject, write an essay about the history of a social phenomenon with which you are familiar. For example, you might compare attitudes toward marriage in your parents' generation, your grandparents' generation, and your own; or you might describe changes in your church that

have resulted from social developments in the past decade. Shape your essay, as Minai does, for a potentially diverse audience.

2. When Muhammad went home after hearing God's message from the angel Gabriel, writes Minai, "Khadija understood that her husband had received a call to serve the one God" (para. 10). In our culture people who report receiving messages from God are seldom believed. Why is this true, given the centrality of such messages in our Judeo-Christian religions? Write an essay classifying or defining the role(s) of divine intervention in our history and in our contemporary culture.

# MIRIAM COOKE

## The Veil Does Not Prevent
## Women from Working

Miriam Cooke received her master's degree in Arabic and Islamic
Studies from Edinburgh University in Scotland in 1971 and her Ph.D.
in Arabic Literature from Oxford University in 1980. She has won a
number of awards and grants for her research, teaching, and writing,
including a Fulbright Research Scholarship to work in Lebanon and
Yemen. Cooke is currently a professor and the director of Asian and
African Languages and Literature at Duke University, as well as a trans-
lator, editor, and author. Her publications are too numerous to list;
among her most recent books are *War's Other Voices: Women Writers in
the Lebanese Civil War* (1988) and *Opening the Gates: A Century of
Arab Feminist Writing* (1990), which she co-edited. "The Veil Does Not
Prevent Women from Working" comes from her article "The Heart's
Direction: The Changing Images and Reality of Saudi Women" in the
March 1991 issue of *The World and I.*

The Kingdom of Saudi Arabia occupies most of the Arabian Peninsula
(see p. 361). Currently headed by King Fahd, it is a monarchy based on
the Sharia (Islamic law) as revealed in the Koran (the holy book) and the
Hadith (teachings and sayings of the prophet Muhammad). After Muhammad united the Arabs in the seventh century, his followers created
an empire stretching from Africa through the Middle East which lasted
until the Turks invaded during the sixteenth and seventeenth centuries.
It was King Ibn Saud, however, who in the early 1900s forged the union
of emirates that today bears his name. The discovery of oil in 1936
bolstered Saudi Arabia's economy and its international clout. In 1990,
when Iraq invaded Kuwait (see pp. 677 and 696), U.S. forces moved into
Saudi Arabia to protect it from possible invasion and use it as a base for
operations against Iraq.

In the wake of Saddam Hussein's invasion of Kuwait, the American
public became dramatically aware of the Saudi Arabian world its troops
were being sent to defend. In early September, the Universal Press
Syndicate distributed a page of stereotypical Arabic vocabulary, sayings,
and recipes that even the *News-Times* of Morehead City–Beaufort, North
Carolina, picked up.

And the men and women detailed to the Saudi front were provided with a hastily compiled booklet of instructions, the do's and don'ts of Saudi campaigning.

The military administration had been obliged not to neglect the human aspect of the desert. How would Saudi men and women respond to the onslaught of American military personnel, particularly to tough women soldiers driving juggernauts or laboring in the heat of the midday sun? The media assured the American public that the encounter could have unforeseen consequences. Saudi women, who do not even have the right to drive, would be empowered by the sight of — and doubtless would wish to emulate — their Western sisters. When news of Saudi women's emergency access to employment was released — and when fifty unveiled women staged a demonstration by driving family cars through the streets of Riyadh in November 1990 — the American media crowed: Even if nothing else was won in this war, a trail had been blazed for the emancipation of those silent, secluded, shrouded women. But what is consistently, even willfully, omitted from such coverage is a discussion of Saudi — as well as other Arab Muslim — women's own agency.

In a real sense, the stereotypical American image of Muslim women — anonymous black shapes gliding along high walls, sensuous odalisques reclining against the harem's soft pillows — was shaped not in America but in Europe. It was a crass image that differentiated women from men chiefly in relationship to lust. Despite the extraordinary variety of Islamic peoples, customs, traditions, and lands, Europeans and, subsequently, Americans have insisted on perceiving Muslims everywhere as one and the same. Although Britain, France, and Holland had for centuries been in contact with Islamic peoples and Muslim cultures, their objectives had been narrowly pragmatic. Government administrators paid scholars to study these new cultures as part of the colonial process. While resident in the Muslim world, these scholars studied classical Muslim languages, especially Arabic, and they translated major Islamic documents into European languages (the Koran was rendered into German as early as the sixteenth century). Some also commented extensively on the societies with which they came into contact; for example, the nineteenth-century orientalist Edward W. Lane, who wrote *The Manners and Customs of the Modern Egyptians*.

In addition to the scholars who traveled to their countries' "outposts"      5 were such painters and writers as Eugène Delacroix, Pierre Loti, and Gustave Flaubert. And it is through the works of such artists that we begin to see the emergence of a stereotype for the Muslim woman. She was cloistered and oppressed on the one hand, seductive and mysterious on the other. Hidden in her harem this odalisque was the preserve of a tyrannical ruler, but if only she could be abducted from the seraglio she would realize the Victorian fantasies of any European man. As Edward Said writes in his controversial exposé *Orientalism* (1978):

> Women are usually the creatures of a male power-fantasy. They express unlimited sensuality, they are more or less stupid, and above all they are willing. . . . The Orient was a place where one could look for sexual experience unobtainable in Europe. . . . In time "Oriental sex" was as standard a commodity as any other available in the mass culture, with the result that readers and writers could have it if they wished without necessarily going to the Orient.

Such images seem to portray all that is incomprehensible about the Muslim world — these women are silent, secluded, entirely segregated. In the American imagination, the harem, far from being a historical institution, where veiled wives eked out a miserable existence under the harsh rule of a domestic despot, is a living and exotic fantasy made reality. Unfortunately, such a stereotype is reinforced by a superficial glance at the societies of the Arabian Peninsula, where the bedouin *burqa* (the black face covering with apertures for the eyes) and the *batula* (the beaklike mask made of polished indigo-impregnated cloth that resembles leather, or even metal) further enhance the alien image of Muslim women.

As far as most Westerners are concerned, the life of the Arab woman is the life of the Muslim woman, because all live according to Islam (Copts, Maronites, and other Christians as well as Jews seem to be subsumed under this rubric). Islam is comprehensive and inescapable, reducing every possible variety to strict uniformity. These women are seen to live in a timeless sphere, where change and development are irrelevant or, worse, impossible. Islam, it is thought on the strength of media coverage, has imposed eternal stagnation on women. . . .

Shafiqa Jazzar, poet, entrepreneur, and grandmother at forty-five, was one of the first five Saudi girls to be sent abroad (to Egypt) in the late 1940s for her education, over a decade before the first girls' schools were opened in Saudi Arabia. Upon her return she married and soon thereafter embarked upon her business career. She received a commercial permit — the first Saudi woman to do so — and opened a clothes shop in her house.

Today, twenty years later, Jazzar still owns a clothes shop, but this one is in downtown Jidda and is called The Veil Does Not Prevent Women from Working. She has a number of women working for her, both here and in other projects. A major venture, presently on hold, was to be the building of a multimillion-dollar complex for women. In this center women were to manage jewelry shops, photo studios, and banquet halls and have their own conference facilities. The Islamic Bank agreed to finance the project because it was judged to be Islamic.

When asked why she wore the veil, Jazzar seemed surprised. Why not?     10
This lyrical businesswoman was adamant in asserting that one can do anything in Saudi Arabia, as long as one plays according to the rules. Indeed, it seems that the more Saudi Arabia modernizes, the more some women cling to their traditions, particularly the veil. Ramazani quotes some American-educated women who defend the veil vehemently:

> In what way is the veil a hindrance? The veil is not an issue here — it is part of our heritage, our customs, our way of life. The important thing is that women should be educated so that they have a choice of working outside the home if they want to, and so that they can take part in building our country.

Images, as always, have distorted reality. Saudi women have not been collectively banished behind screens and veils. They choose segregation even at a time when veiling is not mandatory.

Although the countries of the Arabian Peninsula never discarded the veil, other Muslim countries, such as Egypt, Lebanon, Syria, Iraq, Iran, Turkey, and Pakistan did. At some point, usually around the time of independence, the veil became a bone of contention, and it was officially rejected. However, during the past two decades, some sectors of the female population have been reveiling. Does this new veil symbolize class and status, as the old did until the twentieth-century nationalist movements? Or does it represent religious and political affiliation? Or does it, perhaps, have something to do with the current awakening of feminist consciousness in parts of the Islamic world — the realization that women, whatever their apparent gains in the workplace, have not yet approached equality, and that to truly succeed, their sexuality must be neutralized symbolically?

This new political veil, akin to a nun's habit, does not hark back to some previous traditional modest dress. It is called the *ziyy islami,* to be distinguished from the *hijab,* which is the umbrella term used for the veil whatever the local cultural variations may be. The women wearing the *ziyy islami* have made a political decision; they have proclaimed a new identity within a religious framework. The question now might be, which of these veils are the Saudi women wearing? Or are these veils, the traditional/social and the political/feminist, not necessarily mutually exclusive in the peninsula?

Veiling is a Judeo-Perso-Byzantine accretion, which had by the second century of the Muslim era come to be regarded by many as an orthodox Islamic practice. Legal jurists referred to the Koranic verse on modest attire and also that dealing with the veiling of the prophet's wives (so they might be recognized by the new converts and therefore not be molested as female infidels) as proof incontrovertible that the Koran calls for the veiling and seclusion of women. In fact, veiling was favored by men because it guaranteed possession and prestige while claiming to be the ultimate mark of respect for something that had to be protected. Protection, however, has several possible meanings: It may connote concern for the woman's safety or it may indicate anxiety about the woman's sexuality — in which case it is the men who are being protected. In either case, of primary concern is the safeguarding of honor, the man's honor. As Fatima Mernissi says, virginity does seem to be a game that men play with each other, women merely serving as "silent intermediaries."

It was only at the beginning of this century that men and women   15
intellectuals (such as the Lebanese woman Nazira Zayn al-Din and the Egyptian man Qasim Amin) interpreted the veil and seclusion as blatant sources of oppression. In 1923 Huda Sharawi, director of the newly formed Egyptian Feminist Union, upon her return from the International Women's Conference in Rome, emerged from the train in Cairo with her veil raised. Many Egyptian women were ready to follow suit. In the 1930s both Iranian and Turkish authorities declared the wearing of the veil illegal. Some older women, however, decided that staying at home for the rest of their lives was preferable to appearing "naked" in the streets.

The women fighters in the Algerian Revolution (1954–1962) finally discarded their veils and cut their hair to take part more fully in their nation's struggle. They doffed their social and religious veil, which had symbolized their distinctness from the infidel French and which they had used early in the revolution to conceal arms. However, many resumed it after the revolution. They did so because their husbands and fathers needed tangible proof that they had regained control and that virility and honor had been safeguarded. It was felt that the French had encouraged the Algerian women to dress immodestly and to flaunt their independence of Islamically sanctioned norms of behavior. Feminist literature that has come out of postindependence Algeria is full of anger and bitterness at the men's betrayal but also at the women's silence and acquiescence to oppression.

Since 1973, and certainly since 1979, young women in many Islamic countries, particularly Egypt and the West Bank, have adopted the veil or *ziyy islami*, even in the sanctity of the home. This decision is described by men with awe and admiration mingled with pride, for such a show of piety brings credit to all the family. There is, however, undoubtedly also incomprehension, disapproval, and anxiety at the threat of loss of control. These modestly clad women are venturing forth unchaperoned into the streets and into the mosques where they are organizing meetings. They meet to pray and to study the Koran and the sunna. But they also meet (in countries such as Egypt, Malaysia, and Pakistan) in consciousness-raising gatherings to organize groups of women who will go out into the community, particularly into the rural areas, to teach young and old to read the Koran.

Islamic fundamentalism, though posing a threat to female visibility, may also provide a vehicle for implementing justice. The women who seem to be under pressure to disappear into the sanctity of the home are using religiosity and its trappings to gain access to the public sphere. Carefully, and often heavily, veiling themselves, some women venture out of their anonymity and into the centers of education and religion. Most important of all in Sharia-minded Muslim countries is the teaching of the Koran (as a legal as well as religious document), so that women may learn for themselves what their sacred rights are, and may therefore know what to demand without transgressing canon.

Women are drawing boundaries between their world and that of the males, using mechanisms sanctioned by the male world. In Riyadh, Khairiya as-Saqqaf, the short story writer, has been director of the women journalists of the daily paper *Ar-Riyadh* for the past three years. At thirty-one, she has long been in print and is currently also professor of Arabic literature in King Saud University.

The women's section of *Ar-Riyadh* is a novel concept in journalism.   20 Women journalists are physically segregated from the main building of *Ar-Riyadh* while being functionally integrated. These women refuse to write a women's page or appendix, eschewing the sexual objectification of a feminine press. Women, they say, are not a priori interested in feminine issues; this interest is created and developed by a male-dominated press. They call themselves *muharrirat,* self-consciously adopting an ambiguous nomenclature, for the word means both editors and emancipators. They write about politics, literature, and economics, and their articles are published side by side with the men's. The men refer to the women's articles in the same way that they refer to articles by male colleagues. Although there is great familiarity with each other's writings, there is never any question of mixing.

Saudi women intellectuals consider themselves to be part of Arab women's literary mainstream. They quote each other's words and dedicate works to one another. It seems fitting to conclude with a poem that Fawziya Abu Khalid wrote for the Palestinian poet and intellectual Salma

Khadra Jayyusi. "A Pearl" draws Salma into a family of Saudi women, making her part of what has thus become a tradition of women's writing, while also redefining and projecting the family as a literary sisterhood.

> This pearl
> Was a gift of my grandmother
>   that great lady
>   to my mother
>   and my mother gave it to me
> And now I hand it on to you
> The three of you and this pearl
> Have one thing in common
>   simplicity and truth
> I give it with my love
>   and with the fullness of heart
>   you excel in
>
> The girls of Arabia will soon grow
>   to full stature
> They will look about and say:
>   "Salma has passed by this road"
>   and point to the place of sunrise
>   and the heart's direction.

## EXPLORATIONS

1. According to Miriam Cooke, what was the stereotypical Western image of Islamic women during the colonial era? What is the stereotypical American image of Islamic women now?

2. What official and unofficial reasons does Cooke give for the traditional veiling of Islamic women? Why did some women cast off the veil starting in the early 1900s? Why have some recently resumed it?

3. What advantages do Muslims see in segregating men and women in public places? What advantages and disadvantages do you see in this custom?

4. What assumption does Cooke set up in the first four paragraphs of her essay that she proceeds to overturn? How would the impact of her essay change if she opened it from the Saudi rather than the Western point of view?

# CONNECTIONS

1. What Arab beliefs and policies about relations between men and women appear in both "The Veil Does Not Prevent Women from Working" and Naila Minai's "Women in Early Islam" (p. 361)? What evidence of change do you notice from the creation of Islam to its present application?

2. What Islamic practices described by Cooke support Simone de Beauvoir's contention that men perceive women as Other (p. 329)? How do these practices bear out (or contradict) Beauvoir's explanation of why men hold this perception, and why women cooperate with it?

3. Alberto Moravia in "The Chase" (p. 337) depicts wildness as sexually attractive. "Wildness signified intimacy, privacy, secrecy" (para. 5). How does this idea relate to the Western and Islamic interpretations of veiling and sexual segregation noted by Cooke?

# ELABORATIONS

1. Cooke writes: "As Fatima Mernissi says, virginity does seem to be a game that men play with each other, women merely serving as 'silent intermediaries'" (para. 14). Do you agree? Why or why not? Write an argumentative essay supporting your position.

2. In Cooke's paragraph 10, the entrepreneur Shafiqa Jazzar asserts that "one can do anything in Saudi Arabia, as long as one plays according to the rules." What other factors besides playing by the rules enabled Jazzar to succeed? Would her statement be true in the United States? If so, what are the rules, who makes them, and how are they communicated? If not, what other factors affect success? Choose a goal and write a process essay in which you outline the rules one must follow to achieve it, including the fine print.

# YASHAR KEMAL

## *A Dirty Story*

Yashar Kemal, a Nobel Prize candidate, is widely considered Turkey's greatest living writer. Born in 1923 as Yashar Kemal Gokceli, he grew up among the desperately poor Anatolian peasants, whose plight became a central theme of his writing and his life. At the age of five he saw his father murdered in a mosque; after three years of secondary school he went to work in the Turkish cotton fields and factories. Kemal held a variety of jobs before his arrest in 1950 for alleged Communist propaganda (he was later acquitted). Moving to Istanbul, he dropped his surname, became a journalist, and rose to the post of Anatolian bureau chief of the daily paper *Cumhuriyet*. His 1955 novel *Ince Memed*, translated into more than fifteen languages, reached the English-speaking world in two parts: *Memed, My Hawk* (1961) and *They Burn the Thistles* (1977). Other fiction, nonfiction, and plays have followed. "A Dirty Story" comes from *Anatolian Tales* (*Butun hikayeler*, 1967) and was translated from the Turkish by the author's wife, Thilda Kemal. In the mid-sixties Kemal was a member of the central committee and a political candidate for the Turkish Workers' Party (now banned); in 1971 he was again arrested and briefly imprisoned for Communist propaganda. His recent works include *The Sea-Crossed Fisherman* (1985) and *The Birds Have Also Gone* (1987). He lives in Istanbul.

The Islamic nation of Turkey consists of a European section and an Asian section separated by water. European Turkey borders Greece and Bulgaria. Asian Turkey, or Anatolia, is many times larger; it borders Syria, Iraq, Iran, Armenia, and Georgia and includes the capital city of Ankara. Human habitation there dates back to the Stone Age, at least 7000 B.C. Istanbul, perhaps the most strategically sited city in the world, stands mostly in Europe with suburbs in Asia. Founded by Greeks as Byzantium in the seventh century B.C., it was captured after a thousand years by the Roman emperor Constantine, who made it his capital and renamed it Constantinople. In 1453 the Ottoman sultan Mehmed II swept westward from Anatolia and took the city. The Ottoman Empire, which in the sixteenth century ruled much of Europe, the Middle East, and North Africa, lasted through World War I. The Young Turk movement started a revolt in 1908, which culminated in Turkey's becoming a republic under President Kemal Ataturk in 1923. After siding with Germany in World War I, Turkey stayed neutral through most of World War II and joined the North Atlantic Treaty Organization (NATO) in 1952. As Yashar Kemal's story suggests, the economy remains agrarian, and many of the Turkish people must eke out a living under unfavorable conditions.

The three of them were sitting on the damp earth, their backs against the dung-daubed brush wall and their knees drawn up to their chests, when another man walked up and crouched beside them.

"Have you heard?" said one of them excitedly. "Broken-Nose Jabbar's done it again! You know Jabbar, the fellow who brings all those women from the mountain villages and sells them in the plain? Well, this time he's come down with a couple of real beauties. The lads of Misdik have got together and bought one of them on the spot, and now they're having fun and making her dance and all that . . . It's unbelievable! Where does the fellow find so many women? How does he get them to come with him? He's the devil's own son, he is . . ."

"Well, that's how he makes a living," commented one of the men. "Ever since I can remember, this Jabbar's been peddling women for the villagers of the Chukurova plain. Allah provides for all and sundry . . ."

"He's still got the other one," said the newcomer, "and he's ready to give her away for a hundred liras."

"He'll find a customer soon enough," put in another man whose head was hunched between his shoulders. "A good woman's worth more than a team of oxen, at least, in the Chukurova plain she is. You can always put her to the plow and, come summer, she'll bind and carry the sheaves, hoe, do anything. What's a hundred liras? Why, a woman brings in that much in one single summer. In the fields, at home, in bed. There's nothing like a woman. What's a hundred liras?"

Just then, Hollow Osman came up mumbling to himself and flopped down beside them without a word of greeting. He was a tall, broad-shouldered man with a rather shapeless potbellied body. His lips drooped foolishly and his eyes had an odd squintlike gaze.

"Hey, Osman," the man who had been talking addressed him. "Broken-Nose Jabbar's got a woman for sale again. Only a hundred liras. Tell Mistress Huru to buy her for you and have done with living alone and sleeping in barns like a dog."

Osman shrugged his shoulders doubtfully.

"Look here, man," pursued the other, "this is a chance in a million. What's a hundred liras? You've been slaving for that Huru since you dropped out of your mother's womb and she's never paid you a lira. She owes you this. And anyway she'll get back her money's worth in just one summer. A woman's good for everything, in the house, in the fields, in bed . . ."

Osman rose abruptly.

"I'll ask the Mistress," he said. "How should I know? . . ."

A couple of days later, a short, broad-hipped girl with blue beads strung into her plaited hair was seen at the door of Huru's barn in which Hollow Osman always slept. She was staring out with huge wondering eyes.

A month passed. Two months . . . And passersby grew familiar with the sight of the strange wide-eyed girl at the barn door.

One day, a small dark boy with a face the size of a hand was seen pelting through the village. He rushed up to his mother where she sat on the threshold of her hut gossiping with Seedy Doneh.

"Mother," he screeched, "I've seen them! It's the truth, I swear it is.       15
Uncle Osman's wife with . . . May my eyes drop out right here if I'm telling a lie."

Seedy Doneh turned to him sharply.

"What?" she cried. "Say it again. What's that about Fadik?"

"She was with the Agha's son. I saw them with my own eyes. He went into the barn with her. They couldn't see me where I was hiding. Then he took off his boots, you know the shiny yellow boots he wears . . . And then they lay down and . . . Let my two eyes drop out if . . ."

"I knew it!" crowed Seedy Doneh. "I knew it would turn out this way."

"Hollow Osman never had any manhood in him anyway," said the       20
child's mother. "Always under that viper-tongued Huru's petticoats . . ."

"Didn't I tell you, Ansha, the very first day she came here that this would happen?" said Doneh. "I said this girl's ready to play around. Pretending she was too bashful to speak to anyone. Ah, still waters run deep . . ."

She rose quickly and hurried off to spread the news.

"Have you heard? Just as I foretold . . . Still waters . . . The Agha's son . . . Fadik . . ."

In a trice all the neighboring women had crowded at Ansha's door, trying to squeeze the last drop of information out of the child.

"Come on, tell us," urged one of the women for perhaps the hun-       25
dredth time. "How did you see them?"

"Let my two eyes drop out right here if I'm lying," the child repeated again and again with unabated excitement. "The Agha's son came in, and then they lay down, both of them, and did things . . . I was watching through a chink in the wall. Uncle Osman's wife, you know, was crying. I can't do it, she was saying, and she was sobbing away all the time. Then the Agha's son pulled off those shiny yellow boots of his . . . Then I ran right here to tell Mother."

The news spread through the village like wildfire. People could talk about nothing else. Seedy Doneh, for one, seemed to have made it her job to leave no man or woman uninformed. As she scoured the village for new listeners, she chanced upon Osman himself.

"Haven't you heard what's come upon you?" she said, drawing him aside behind the wall of a hut. "You're disgraced, you jackass. The Agha's son has got his fingers up your wife's skirt. Try and clear your good name now if you can!"

Osman did not seem to understand.

"I don't know . . ." he murmured, shrugging his shoulders. "I'll have to ask the Mistress. What would the Agha's son want with my wife?"    30

Doneh was incensed.

"What would he want with her, blockhead?" she screamed. "Damn you, your wife's become a whore, that's what! She's turned your home into a brothel. Anyone can come in and have her." She flounced off still screaming. "I spit on you! I spit on your manhood . . ."

Osman was upset.

"What are you shouting for, woman?" he called after her. "People will think something's wrong. I have to ask the Mistress. She knows everything. How should I know?"

He started walking home, his long arms dangling at his sides as though    35 they had been hitched to his shoulders as an afterthought, his fingers sticking out wide apart as was his habit. This time he was waylaid by their next-door neighbor, Zeynep, who planted herself before him and tackled him at the top of her voice.

"Ah Osman! You'd be better off dead! Why don't you go and bury yourself? The whole village knows about it. Your wife . . . The Agha's son . . . Ah Osman, how could you have brought such a woman into your home? Where's your honor now? Disgraced . . . Ah Osman!"

He stared at her in bewilderment.

"How should I know?" he stammered, his huge hands opening out like pitchforks. "The Mistress knows all about such things. I'll go and ask her."

Zeynep turned her back on him in exasperation, her large skirt ballooning about her legs.

"Go bury yourself, Osman! I hope I see you dead after this."    40

A group of children were playing tipcat nearby. Suddenly one of them broke into a chant.

"Go bury yourself, Osman . . . See you dead, Osman . . ."

The other children joined in mechanically without interrupting their game.

Osman stared at them and turned away.

"How should I know?" he muttered. "I must go to the Mistress."    45

He found Huru sitting at her spinning wheel. Fadik was there too, squatting near the hearth and listlessly chewing mastic gum.

"Mistress," said Osman, "have you heard what Seedy Doneh's saying? She's saying I'm disgraced . . ."

Huru stepped on the pedal forcefully and brought the wheel to a stop. "What's that?" she said. "What about Seedy Doneh?"

"I don't know . . . She said Fadik . . ."                                              50

"Look here," said Huru, "you mustn't believe those lying bitches. You've got a good wife. Where would you find such a woman?"

"I don't know. Go bury yourself, they said. The children too . . ."

"Shut up," cried Huru, annoyed. "People always gossip about a beautiful woman. They go looking for the mote in their neighbor's eye without seeing the beam in their own. They'd better hold their peace because I've got a tongue in my head too . . ."

Osman smiled with relief.

"How could I know?" he said.                                                           55

Down in the villages of the Chukurova plain, a sure sign of oncoming spring is when the women are seen with their heads on one another's lap, picking the lice out of one another's hair. So it was, on one of the first warm days of the year. A balmy sun shone caressingly down on the fields and village, and not a leaf stirred. A group of women were sitting before their huts on the dusty ground, busy with the lice and wagging their tongues for all they were worth. An acrid odor of sweat hung about the group. Seedy Doneh was rummaging in the hair of a large woman who was stretched full length on the ground. She decided that she had been silent long enough.

"No," she declared suddenly, "it's not as you say, sister! He didn't force her or any such thing. She simply fell for him the minute she saw those shiny yellow boots. If you're going to believe Huru! . . . She's got to deny it, of course."

"That Huru was born with a silver spoon in her mouth," said whitehaired, toothless old Zala, wiping her bloodstained fingers on her ragged skirt. "Hollow Osman's been slaving for her like twenty men ever since she took him in, a kid the size of your hand! And all for a mere pittance of food. And now there's the woman too. Tell me, what's there left for Huru to do?"

"Ah," sighed another woman, "fortune has smiled on Huru, she has indeed! She's got two people serving her now."

"And both for nothing," old Zala reminded her.                                         60

"What it amounts to," said Seedy Doneh spitefully, "is that Huru used to have one wife and now she's got two. Osman was always a woman, and as for Fadik she's a real woman. He-he!"

"That she is, a real woman!" the others agreed.

"Huru says the Agha's son took her by force," pursued Doneh. "All right, but what about the others? What about those lining up at her door all through the night, eh? She never says no to any one of them, does she? She takes in everyone, young and old."

"The Lady Bountiful, that's what she is," said Elif. "And do you know something? Now that Fadik's here, the young men are leaving Omarja's yellow bitch in peace . . ."

"They've got somewhere better to go!" cackled the others.                    65

Omarja's dumpy wife jumped up from where she was sitting on the edge of the group.

"Now look here, Elif!" she cried. "What's all this about our yellow dog? Stop blackening people's characters, will you?"

"Well, it's no lie, is it?" Doneh challenged her. "When was that bitch ever at your door where she should be all night? No, instead, there she came trotting up a-mornings with a rope dangling from her neck!"

"Don't go slandering our dog," protested Omarja's wife. "Why, if Omarja hears this, he'll kill the poor creature. Upon my word he will!"

"Go on!" said Doneh derisively. "Don't you come telling me that          70
Omarja doesn't know his yellow bitch is the paramour of all the village youths! What about that time when Stumpy Veli caught some of them down by the river, all taking it in turns over her? Is there anyone in this village who didn't hear of that? It's no use trying to whitewash your bitch to us!"

Omarja's wife was alarmed.

"Don't, sister," she pleaded. "Omarja'll shoot the dog, that's sure . . ."

"Well, I'm not to blame for that, sister," retorted Doneh tartly. "Anyway, the bitch'll be all right now that Fadik's around. And so will Kurdish Velo's donkey . . ."

Kurdish Velo's wife began to fidget nervously.

"Not our fault," she blurted out in her broken Turkish. "We lock our          75
donkey in, but they come and break the door! Velo furious. Velo say people round here savage. He say, with an animal deadly sin! He say he kill someone. Then he complain to the Headman. Velo going sell this donkey."

"You know what I think?" interposed Seedy Doneh. "They're going to make it hot for her in this village. Yes, they'll do what they did to Esheh."

"Poor Esheh," sighed old Zala. "What a woman she was before her man got thrown into prison! She would never have come to that, but she had no one to protect her. May they rot in hell, those that forced her into it! But she is dead and gone, poor thing."

"Eh!" said Doneh. "How could she be otherwise after the youths of five villages had done with her?" She straightened up. "Look here, sister," she said to the woman whose head was on her lap, "I couldn't get through your lice in days! They say the Government's invented some medicine

for lice which they call Dee-Dee. Ah, if only we had a spoonful of that
. . . Do you know, women, that Huru keeps watch over Fadik at night?
She tells the youths when to come in and then drives them out with a
stick. Ha-ha, and she wants us to believe in Fadik's virtue . . ."

"That's because it suits her. Where will she find people who'll work
for nothing like those two?"

"Well, the lads are well provided for this year," snickered Doneh.      80
"Who knows but that Huru may hop in and help Fadik out!"

Just then, Huru loomed up from behind a hut. She was a large woman
with a sharp chin and a wrinkled face. Her graying hair was always
carefully dyed with henna.

"Whores!" she shouted at the top of her voice, as she bore down upon
them with arms akimbo. "City trollops! You get hold of a poor fellow's
wife and let your tongues go wagging away. Tell me, are you any better
than she? What do you want of this harmless mountain girl?" She
pounced on Doneh who cringed back. "As for you, you filthy shitty-assed
bitch, you'll shut your mouth or I'll start telling the truth about you and
that husband of yours who pretends he's a man. You know me, don't
you?"

Doneh blenched.

"Me, sister?" she stammered. "Me? I never . . . Other people's good
name . . ."

The women were dispersing hastily. Only Kurdish Velo's wife, unaware    85
of what was going on, continued picking lice out of her companion's hair.

"Velo says in our country women like this burnt alive. He says there
no virtue in this Chukurova. No honor . . ."

The eastern sky had only just begun to pale as, with a great hullabaloo
and calls and cries, the women and children drove the cattle out to
pasture. Before their houses, red-aproned matrons were busy at the churns
beating yogurt. The damp air smelled of spring.

Osman had long ago yoked the oxen and was waiting at Huru's door.
She appeared in the doorway.

"Osman, my lion," she said, "you're not to come back until you've      90
plowed through the whole field. The girl Aysheh will look after your
food and get you some bedding. Mind you do the sowing properly, my
child. Husneh's hard pressed this year. And there's your wife to feed too
now . . ."

Husneh was Huru's only child, whom in a moment of aberration she
had given in marriage to Ali Efendi, a low-salaried tax collector. All the
product of her land, everything Huru had, was for this daughter.

Osman did not move or say a word. He stood there in the half-light, a large black shadow near the yoked oxen whose tails were flapping their legs in slow rhythm.

Huru stepped up to him.

"What's the matter with you, Osman, my child," she said anxiously. "Is anything wrong?"

"Mistress," whispered Osman, "it's what Seedy Doneh's saying. And      95
Zeynep too . . . That my house . . . I don't know . . ."

Huru flared up.

"Shut up, you spineless dolt," she cried. "Don't you come babbling to me about the filthy inventions of those city trollops. I paid that broken-nosed thief a hundred good bank notes for the girl, didn't I? Did I ask you for as much as a lira? You listen to me. You can find fault with pure gold, but not with Fadik. Don't let me hear such nonsense from you again!"

Osman hesitated.

"I don't know . . ." he murmured, as he turned at last and drove the oxen off before him.

It was midmorning. A bright sun glowed over the sparkling fields.        100

Osman was struggling with the lean, emaciated oxen, which after plowing through only one acre had stretched themselves on the ground and simply refused to budge. Flushed and breathless, he let himself drop onto a mound and took his head in his hands. After a while, he rose and tried pulling the animals up by the tail.

"Accursed beasts," he muttered. "The Mistress says Husneh's in need this year. Get up this minute, accursed beasts!"

He pushed and heaved, but to no avail. Suddenly in a burst of fury, he flung himself on the black ox, dug his teeth into its nose, and shook it with all his might. Then he straightened up and looked about him sheepishly.

"If anyone saw me . . ." He swore as he spat out blood. "What can I do? Husneh's in need and there's Fadik to feed too. And now these heathen beasts . . . I don't know."

It was in this state of perplexity that Stumpy Veli found him when he      105
strolled over from a neighboring field.

"So the team's collapsed, eh?" he commented. "Well, it was to be expected. Look at how their ribs are sticking out. You won't be able to get anything out of them."

"I don't know," muttered Osman faintly. "Husneh's in a bad way and I got married . . ."

"And a fine mess that's landed you in," burst out Veli angrily. "You'd have been better off dead!"

"I don't know," said Osman. "The Mistress paid a hundred liras for her . . ."

Stumpy Veli took hold of his arm and made him sit down.                    110

"Look, Osman," he said, "the villagers told me to talk to you. They say you're giving the village a bad name. Ever since the Agha's son took up with your wife, all the other youths have followed suit and your house is just like a brothel now. The villagers say you've got to repudiate her. If you don't, they'll drive you both out. The honor of the whole village is at stake, and you know honor doesn't grow on trees . . ."

Osman, his head hanging down, was as still as a statue. A stray ant had caught his eye.

What's this ant doing around here at this time of day, he wondered to himself. Where can its nest be?

Veli nudged him sharply.

"Damn you, man!" he cried. "Think what'll happen if the police get     115
wind of this. She hasn't got any papers. Why, if the gendarmes once lay their hands on her, you know how it'll be. They'll play around with her for months, poor creature."

Osman started as though an electric current had been sent through his large frame.

"I haven't got any papers either," he whispered.

Veli drew nearer. Their shoulders touched. Osman's were trembling fitfully.

"Papers are the business of the Government," Veli said. "You and me, we can't understand such things. If we did, then what would we need a Government for? Now, listen to me. If the gendarmes get hold of her, we'll be the laughingstock of villages for miles around. We'll never be able to hold up our heads again in the Chukurova. You mustn't trifle with the honor of the whole village. Get rid of her before she drags you into more trouble."

"But where will I be without her?" protested Osman. "I'll die, that's    120
all. Who'll do my washing? Who'll cook bulgur pilaf for me? I'll starve to death if I have to eat gruel again every day. I just can't do without her."

"The villagers will buy you another woman," said Veli. "We'll collect the money among us. A better woman, an honorable one, and beautiful too . . . I'll go up into the mountain villages and pick one for you myself. Just you pack this one off quickly . . ."

"I don't know," said Osman. "It's the Mistress knows about these things."

Veli was exasperated.

"Damn the Mistress!" he shouted. "It's up to you, you idiot!"

Then he softened. He tried persuasion again. He talked and talked. He talked himself hoarse, but Osman sat there immovable as a rock, his mouth clamped tight. Finally Veli spat in his face and stalked off.

It was well on in the afternoon when it occurred to Osman to unyoke the team. He had not stirred since Veli's departure. As for the oxen, they had just lain there placidly chewing the cud. He managed to get them to their feet and let them wander about the field, while he walked back to the village. He made straight for the Agha's house and waited in the yard, not speaking to anyone, until he saw the Agha's son riding in, the bridle of his horse lathered with sweat.

The Agha's son was taken aback. He dismounted quickly, but Osman waylaid him.

"Listen," he pleaded, "you're the son of our all-powerful Agha. What do you want with my wife?"

The Agha's son became the color of his famous boots. He hastily pulled a five-lira note out of his pocket and thrust it into Osman's hand.

"Take this," he mumbled and hurried away.

"But you're a great big Agha's son!" cried Osman after him. "Why do you want to drive her away? What harm has she done you? You're a great big . . ."

He was crushed. He stumbled away toward Huru's house, the five-lira note still in his hand.

At the sight of Osman, Huru blew her top.

"What are you doing here, you feebleminded ass?" she shouted. "Didn't I tell you not to come back until you'd finished all the plowing? Do you want to ruin me, you idiot?"

"Wait, Mistress," stammered Osman. "Listen . . ."

"Listen, he says! Damn the fool!"

"Mistress," he pleaded, "let me explain . . ."

Huru glared at him.

"Mistress, you haven't heard. You don't know what the villagers are going to do to me. They're going to throw me out of this village. Stumpy Veli said so. He said the police . . . He said papers . . . We haven't got any papers. Fadik hasn't and I haven't either. He said the gendarmes would carry Fadik away and do things to her. He said I must repudiate her because my house is a brothel. That's what he said. I said the Mistress knows these things . . . She paid the hundred liras . . ."

Huru was dancing with fury. She rushed out into the village square and began howling at the top of her voice.

"Bastards! So she's a thorn in your flesh, this poor fellow's wife! If you want to drive whores out of this village why don't you start with your own wives and daughters? You'd better look for whores in your own homes, pimps that you are, all of you! And tell your sons to leave poor folks' women alone . . ."

Then she turned to Osman and gave him a push.

"Off you go! To the fields! No one's going to do anything to your wife. Not while I'm alive."

The villagers had gathered in the square and had heard Huru out in profound silence. As soon as she was gone, though, they started muttering among themselves.

"Who does that bitch think she is, abusing the whole village like       145
that? . . ."

The Agha, Wolf Mahmut, had heard her too.

"You just wait, Huru," he said grinding his teeth. "If you think you're going to get away with this . . ."

The night was dark, a thick damp darkness that seemed to cling to the face and hands. Huru had been waiting for some time now, concealed in the blackest shadow of the barn, when suddenly she perceived a stirring in the darkness, and a voice was calling softly at the door.

"Fadik! Open up, girl. It's me . . ."

The door creaked open and a shadow glided in. An uncontrollable       150
trembling seized Huru. She gripped her stick and flung herself on the door. It was unbolted and went crashing back against the wall. As she stood there trying to pierce the darkness, a few vague figures hustled by and made their escape. Taken by surprise, she hurled out a vitriolic oath and started groping about until she discovered Fadik crouching in a corner. She seized her by the hair and began to beat her with the stick.

"Bitch!" she hissed. "To think I was standing up for you . . ."

Fadik did not utter a sound as the blows rained down on her. At last Huru, exhausted, let go of her.

"Get up," she ordered, "and light some kindling."

Fadik raked out the dying embers and with much puffing and blowing managed to light a stick of torchwood. A pale honeyed light fell dimly over the stacked hay. There was an old pallet in one corner and a few kitchen utensils, but nothing else to show that the place was lived in.

Huru took Fadik's hand and looked at her sternly.       155

"Didn't you promise me, girl, that you'd never do it again?"

Fadik's head hung low.

"Do you know, you bitch," continued Huru, "what the villagers are going to do? They're going to kick you out of the village. Do you hear me?"

Fadik stirred a little. "Mistress, I swear I didn't go after them! They just came in spite of everything."

"Listen to me, girl," said Huru. "Do you know what happened to    160
Esheh? That's what you'll come to if you're not careful. They're like ravening wolves, these men. If you fall into their clutches, they'll tear you to shreds. To shreds, I tell you!"

"But Mistress, I swear I never did anything to — "

"You must bolt your door because they'll be after you whether you do anything or not, and their pimps of fathers will put the blame on me. It's my hundred liras they can't swallow. They're dying to see it go to pot . . . Just like Esheh you'll be. They had no one in the world, she and her man, and when Ali was thrown into jail she was left all alone. He'd lifted a sheep from the Agha's flock and bought clothes and shoes for their son. A lovely child he was, three years old . . . Ali doted on him. But there he was in jail, and that yellow-booted good-for-nothing was soon after Esheh like the plague. She kept him at arm's length for as long as she could, poor Esheh, but he got what he wanted in the end. Then he turned her over to those ravening wolves . . . They dragged her about from village to village, from mountain to mountain. Twenty, thirty good-for-nothings . . . Her child was left among strangers, the little boy she had loved so. He died . . . Those who saw her said she was like a consumptive, thin and gray, but still they wouldn't let her go, those scoundrels. Then one day the village dogs came in all smeared with blood, and an eagle was circling over the plain. So the men went to look, and they found Esheh, her body half devoured by the dogs . . . They'd made her dance naked for them . . . They'd done all sorts of things to her. Yes, they as good as killed her. That's what the police said when they came up from the town. And when Ali heard of it, he died of grief in jail. Yes, my girl, you've got Esheh's fate before you. It isn't my hundred liras that I care for, it's you. As for Osman, I can always find another woman for him. Now I've warned you. Just call me if they come again. Esheh was all alone in the world. You've got me, at least. Do you swear to do as I'm telling you?"

"I swear it, Mistress," said Fadik.

Huru was suddenly very tired.

"Well, I'm going. You'll call me, won't you?"    165

As soon as she was gone, the youths crept out of the darkness and sneaked into the barn again.

"Hey, Fadik," they whispered. "Huru was lying to you, girl. Esheh just killed herself . . ."

There was a stretch of grass in front of the Agha's house, and on one side of it dung had been heaped to the size of a small hillock. The dung steamed in the early morning sun and not a breath stirred the warm air. A cock climbed to the top of the heap. It scraped the dung, stretched its neck, and crowed triumphantly, flapping its wings.

The group of villagers squatting about on the grass silently eyed the angry Agha. Wolf Mahmut was a huge man whose shadow when he was sitting was as large as that of an average man standing up. He was never seen without a frayed, checked overcoat, the only one in the village, that he had been wearing for years now.

He was toying irritably with his metal-framed glasses when Stumpy     170
Veli, who had been sent for a while ago, made his appearance. The Agha glared at him.

"Is this the way you get things done, you fraud?" he expostulated. "So you'd have Hollow Osman eating out of your hand in no time, eh?"

Stumpy Veli seemed to shrink to half his size.

"Agha," he said, "I tried everything. I talked and talked. I told him the villagers would drive them both out. I warned him of the gendarmes. All right, he said, I'll send her away. And then he didn't . . . If you ask me, Huru's at the bottom of it all."

The others stirred. "That she is!" they agreed.

Mahmut Agha jumped up. "I'll get even with her," he growled.          175

"That, you will, Agha," they assented. "But . . ."

"We've put up with that old whore long enough," continued the Agha, sitting down again.

"Yes, Agha," said Stumpy Veli, "but, you see, she relies on her son-in-law Ali, the tax collector. They'd better stop treading on my toes, she said, or I'll have Ali strip this village bare . . ."

"He can't do anything," said the Agha. "I don't owe the Government a bean."

"But we do, Agha," interposed one of the men. "He can come here      180
and take away our blankets and rugs, whatever we have . . ."

"It's because of Huru that he hasn't fleeced this village up to now," said another. "We owe a lot of money, Agha."

"Well, what are we to do then?" cried Mahmut Agha angrily. "All our youths have left the plow and the fields and are after the woman night and day like rutting bulls. At this rate, the whole village'll starve this year."

An old man spoke up in a tremulous voice. "I'm dead, for one," he wailed. "That woman's ruined my hearth. High morning it is already. Go to the plow, my son, I beg the boy. We'll starve if you don't plow. But he won't listen. He's always after that woman. I've lost my son because of that whore. I'm too old to plow anymore. I'll starve this year. I'll go and throw myself at Huru's feet. There's nothing else to do . . ."

The Agha rose abruptly. "That Huru!" He gritted his teeth. "I'll settle her account."

He strode away.                                                              185

The villagers looked up hopefully. "Mahmut Agha'll settle her account," they muttered. "He'll find a way . . ."

The Agha heard them and swelled with pride. "Yes, Mahmut Agha'll settle her account," he repeated grimly to himself.

He stopped before a hut and called out.

"Hatije Woman! Hatije!"

A middle-aged woman rushed out wiping her hands on her apron.             190

"Mahmut Agha!" she cried. "Welcome to our home. You never visit us these days." Then she whirled back. "Get up, you damned lazybones," she shouted angrily. "It's high morning, and look who's here."

Mahmut Agha followed her inside.

"Look, Agha," she complained, pointing to her son, "it's high morning and Halil still abed!"

Startled at the sight of the Agha, Halil sprang up and drew on his black *shalvar* trousers shamefacedly, while his mother continued with her lamentations.

"Ah, Mahmut Agha, you don't know what's befallen us! You don't      195 know, may I kiss your feet, my Agha, or you wouldn't have us on your land any longer . . . Ah, Mahmut Agha! This accursed son of mine . . . I would have seen him dead and buried, yes, buried in this black earth before . . ."

"What are you cursing the lad for?" Mahmut Agha interrupted her. "Wait, just tell me first."

"Ah, Agha, if you knew! It was full day when he came home this night. And it's the same every night, the same ever since Hollow Osman's woman came to the village. He lies abed all through the livelong day. Who'll do the plowing, I ask you? We'll starve this year. Ah, Mahmut Agha, do something! Please do something . . ."

"You go outside a little, will you, Hatije," said the Agha. Then he turned to Halil, stretching out his long, wrinkled neck which had become as red as a turkey's. "Listen to me, my boy, this has got to end. You must get this whore out of our village and give her to the youths of another village, any village. She's got to go and you'll do it. It's an order. Do you hear me?"

"Why, Agha!" Halil said ingratiatingly. "Is that what's worrying you?

I'll get hold of her this very night and turn her over to Jelil from Ortakli village. You can count on me."

The Agha's spirits rose.                                                      200

"Hatije," he called out, "come in here. See how I'm getting you out of this mess? And all the village too . . . Let that Huru know who she's dealing with in the future. They call me Wolf Mahmut and I know how to put her nose out of joint."

Long before dawn, piercing shrieks startled the echoes in the village.

"Bastards! Pimps!" Huru was howling. "You won't get away with this, not on your life you won't. My hundred liras were too much for you to swallow, eh, you fiends? You were jealous of this poor fellow's wife, eh? But you just wait and see, Wolf Mahmut! I'll set the tax collector after you all in no time. I'll get even with you if I have to spend my last penny! I'll bribe the Mudir, the Kaymakam, all the officials. I'll send telegrams to Ankara, to Ismet Pasha, to the head of the Democrats. I'll have you all dragged into court, rotting away in police stations. I'll get my own back on you for Fadik's sake."

She paused to get her breath and was off again even louder than before.

Fadik had disappeared, that was the long and the short of it. Huru soon    205
found out that someone else was missing too. Huseyin's half-witted son, The Tick.

"Impossible," she said. "The Tick ravishing women? Not to save his life, he couldn't! This is just another trick of those good-for-nothings . . ."

"But really, Huru," the villagers tried to persuade her, "he was after her all the time. Don't you know he gathered white snails in the hills, threaded them into a necklace, and offered it to Fadik, and she hung it up on her wall as a keepsake? That's the plain truth, Huru."

"I don't believe it," Huru said stubbornly. "I wouldn't even if I saw them together with my own eyes . . ."

The next day it started raining, that sheer, plumb-line torrent which sets in over the Chukurova for days. The minute the bad news had reached him, Osman had abandoned his plow and had rushed back to the village. He was standing now motionless at Huru's door, the peak of his cap drooping over his eyes. His wet clothes clung to his flesh, glistening darkly, and his rawhide boots were clogged with mud.

"Come in out of the rain, Osman, do!" Huru kept urging him.              210

"I can't. I don't know . . ." was all he could say.

"Now, look here, Osman," said Huru. "She's gone, so what? Let them have that bitch. I'll find you a good woman, my Osman. Never mind the money. I'll spend twice as much on a new wife for you. Just you come in out of the rain."

Osman never moved.

"Listen, Osman. I've sent word to Ali. Come and levy the taxes at once, I said. Have no mercy on these ungrateful wretches. If you don't fleece them to their last rag, I said, you needn't count on me as a mother again. You'll see what I'm going to do to them, my Osman. You just come inside . . ."

The rain poured down straight and thick as the warp in a loom, and     215
Osman still stood there, his chin resting on his staff, like a thick tree whose branches have been lopped off.

Huru appealed to the neighbors. Two men came and pulled and pushed, but he seemed nailed to the ground. It was well in the afternoon when he stirred and began to pace the village from one end to the other, his head sunk between his shoulders and the rain streaming down his body.

"Poor fellow, he's gone mad," opined the villagers.

A few strong men finally carried him home. They undressed him and put him to bed.

Huru sat down beside him. "Look, Osman, I'll get you a new woman even if it costs me a thousand liras. You mustn't distress yourself so. Just for a woman . . ."

The next morning he was more his normal self, but no amount of     220
reasoning or pleading from Huru could induce him to go back to the field. He left the house and resumed his pacing up and down.

The villagers had really begun to feel sorry for him now.

"Alas, poor Osman!" they murmured as he passed between the huts.

Osman heard them and heaved deep, heartrending sighs. And still he roamed aimlessly round and round.

Wolf Mahmut should have known better. Why, the whole village saw with half an eye what a rascal Halil was! How could he be trusted to give up a woman once he had got her into his hands? He had indeed got Fadik out of the way, but what he had done was to shut her up in one of the empty sheep pens in the hills beyond the village, and there he had posted The Tick to guard her.

"Play around with her if you like," he had told him contemptuously.     225
"But if you let her give you the slip — " and he had seized The Tick's wrist and squeezed it until it hurt — "you're as good as dead."

Though twenty years old, The Tick was so scraggy and undersized that at first glance people would take him to be only ten. His arms and legs were as thin as matchsticks and he walked sideways like a crab. He had always had a way of clinging tenaciously to people or objects he took a fancy to, which even as a child had earned him his nickname. No one had ever called him by his real name and it looked as though his own mother had forgotten it too . . .

Halil would come every evening bringing food for Fadik and The Tick, and he would leave again just before dawn. But it was not three days before the village youths found out what was going on. After that there was a long queue every night outside the sheep pen. They would take it in turns, heedless of Fadik's tears and howls, and at daybreak, singing and firing their guns as though in a wedding procession, they would make their way back to the village.

Night was falling and Fadik began to tremble like a leaf. They would not be long now. They would come again and torture her. She was weak with fear and exhaustion. For the past two days, her gorge had risen at the very sight of food, and she lay there on the dirt floor, hardly able to move, her whole body covered with bruises and wounds.

The Tick was dozing away near the door of the pen.

Fadik tried to plead with him. "Let me go, brother," she begged. "I'll      230
die if I have to bear another night of this."

The Tick half-opened his eyes. "I can't," he replied.

"But if I die, it'll be your fault. Before God it will . . . Please let me go."

"Why should it be my fault?" said The Tick. "I didn't bring you here, did I?"

"They'll never know. You'll say you fell asleep. I'll go off and hide somewhere. I'll go back to my mother . . ."

"I can't," said The Tick. "Halil would kill me if I let you go."          235

"But I want to go to my mother," she cried desperately. "You must let me go. Please let me go . . ."

It was dark now and the sound of singing drifted up from the village.

Fadik was seized with a violent fit of trembling. "They're coming," she said. "Let me get away now, brother. Save me! If you save me, I'll be your woman. I'll do anything . . ."

But The Tick had not been nicknamed for nothing.

"They'd kill me," he said. "Why should I die because of you? And      240
Halil's promised to buy me a pair of shoes, too. I'm not going to go without shoes because of you."

Fadik broke into wild sobbing. There was no hope now.

"Oh, God," she wept, "what shall I do now? Oh, Mother, why was I ever born?"

They lined up as usual at the entrance to the pen. The first one went in and a nerve-racking scream rose from Fadik, a scream that would have moved the most hardened of hearts. But the youths were deaf to everything. In they went, one after the other, and soon Fadik's screams died down. Not even a moan came out of her.

There were traces of blood on the ground at the back of the sheep pen. Halil and the Agha's son had had a fight the night before and the Agha's son had split open Halil's head.

"The woman's mine," Halil had insisted. "I've a right to go in first."      245

"No, you haven't," the Agha's son had contended. "I'm going to be the first."

The other youths had taken sides and joined the fray which had lasted most of the night, and it was a bedraggled band that wended back to the village that night.

Bowed down with grief, Hatije Woman came weeping to the Muhtar.

"My son is dying," she cried. "He's at his last gasp, my poor Halil, and it's the Agha's son who did it, all because of that whore of Huru's. Ah, Muhtar, if my son dies what's to become of me? There he lies struggling for life, the only hope of my hearth. But I won't let the Agha get away with this. I'll go to the Government. An old woman's only prop, I'll say . . ."

The Muhtar had great difficulty in talking Hatije out of her purpose.      250

"You go back home, Hatije Woman," he said when she had calmed down a little, "and don't worry. I'll deal with this business."

He summoned the Agha and the elders, and a long discussion ensued. It would not do to hand over the woman to the police station. These rapacious gendarmes! . . . The honor of the whole village was at stake. And if they passed her on to the youths of another village, Huru was sure to find out and bring her back. She would not rest until she did.

After long deliberation, they came to a decision at last. The woman would be returned to Osman, but on one condition. He would take himself off with her to some distant place and never appear in the village again. They had no doubt that Osman, grateful to have Fadik back to himself, would accept. And that would cook Huru's goose too. She would lose both the woman and Osman. It would teach her to insult a whole village!

A couple of men went to find Osman and brought him back with them to the Muhtar's house.

"Sit down," they urged him, but he just stood there grasping his staff,      255
staring about him with bloodshot eyes. His clothes hung down torn and

crumpled and stained yellow from his lying all wet on the hay. His hair was a tangled, clotted mass and bits of straw clung to the stubble on his chin.

Wolf Mahmut took off his glasses and fidgeted with them.

"Osman, my lad," he remonstrated, "what's this state you're in? And all for a woman! Does a man let himself break down like this just for a woman? You'll die if you go on like this . . ."

"I don't know," said Osman. "I'll die . . ."

"See here, Osman," said the Agha. "We're here to help you. We'll get your woman back for you from out of those rascals' hands. Then you'll take her and go. You'll both get away from here, as far as possible. But you're not to tell Huru. She mustn't know where you are."

"You see, Osman," said Stumpy Veli, "how good the Agha's being to    260
you. Your own father wouldn't have done more."

"But you're not to tell Huru," the Agha insisted. "If you do, she'll never let you go away. And then the youths will come and take your woman away from you again. And how will you ever get yourself another woman?"

"And who'll wash your clothes then?" added Stumpy Veli. "Who'll cook your bulgur pilaf for you? You mustn't breathe a word to Huru. Just take Fadik and go off to the villages around Antep. Once there, you'll be sure to get a job on a farm. You'll be much better off than you ever were with Huru, and you'll have your woman with you too . . ."

"But how can I do that?" protested Osman. "The Mistress paid a hundred liras for Fadik."

"We'll collect that much among us," the Agha assured him. "Don't you worry about that. We'll see that Huru gets her money back. You just take the woman and go."

"I don't know," said Osman. His eyes filled with tears and he swal-    265
lowed. "The Mistress has always been so good to me . . . How can I . . . Just for a woman . . ."

"If you tell Huru, you're lost," said the Agha. "Is Huru the only mistress in the world? Aren't there other villages in this country? Take the woman and go. You'll never find another woman like Fadik. Listen, Veli'll tell you where she is and tomorrow you'll take her and go."

Osman bowed his head. He thought for a long time. Then he looked up at them.

"I won't tell her," he said at last. "Why should I want to stay here? There are other villages . . ."

Before dawn the next day, he set out for the sheep pen which Stumpy Veli had indicated.

"I don't know . . ." He hesitated at the door. "I don't know . . ." Then   270
he called out softly, "Fadik? Fadik, girl . . ."

There was no answer. Trembling with hope and fear, he stepped in,
then stopped aghast. Fadik was lying there on the dirt floor with only a
few tatters left to cover her naked body. Her huge eyes were fixed vacantly
on the branches that roofed the pen.

He stood frozen, his eyes filling with tears. Then he bent his large
body over her.

"Fadik," he whispered, "are you all right?"

Her answering moan shook him to the core. He slipped off his shirt
and helped her into it. Then he noticed The Tick who had shrunk back
into a corner, trying to make himself invisible. Osman moved on him
threateningly.

"Uncle Osman," cried The Tick shaking with fear, "I didn't do it. It   275
was Halil. He said he'd buy me a pair of shoes . . . And Fadik would have
died if I hadn't been here . . ."

Osman turned away, heaved Fadik onto his back swiftly, and threw
himself out of the pen.

The mountain peaks were pale and the sun was about to rise. A few
white clouds floated in the sky and a cool breeze caressed his face. The
earth was wet with dew.

The Tick was scurrying off toward the village.

"Brother," Osman called after him, "go to the Mistress and tell her I
thank her for all she's done for me, but I have to go. Tell her to forgive
me . . ."

He set out in the opposite direction with Fadik on his back. He walked   280
without a break until the sun was up the height of two minarets. Then
he lowered Fadik to the ground and sat down opposite her. They looked
at each other for a long while without speaking.

"Tell me," said Osman. "Where shall we go now? I don't know . . ."
Fadik moaned.

The air smelled of spring and the earth steamed under the sun.

## EXPLORATIONS

1. In what ways is "A Dirty Story" an appropriate title for Yashar Kemal's narrative? What people or factors does Kemal blame for Fadik's fate? What remedies, if any, does he recommend?

2. Reread the opening scene of "A Dirty Story" (paras. 1–11). What concept of
   women's role is presented here? Who holds this concept? How do we as

readers learn it? How would the story's impact change if Kemal had written this scene as an expository paragraph from the author's point of view?

3. According to Kemal, by what qualities are men in this culture judged as successful or unsuccessful by other men? By women? How does women's concept of their own social role differ from men's concept?

4. The third scene in "A Dirty Story" (paras. 56–86) takes place among the village women. How do they interpret the situation between Fadik, Huru, and the local youths? How do their comments about Omarja's dog and Velo's donkey suggest that the situation is not really as the women depict it? What do you think is actually going on between Fadik, the youths, Osman, and Huru at this point in the story? What other clues in this scene help you to guess what is happening?

## CONNECTIONS

1. Like Miriam Cooke's "The Veil Does Not Prevent Women from Working" (p. 372), Kemal's "A Dirty Story" examines sex roles and stereotypes in an Islamic culture. How are women's and men's social roles in upper-middle-class Saudi Arabia similar to those in the poor, rural Turkish village of Chukurova? How are they different? What factors do you think account for the differences?

2. Look again at "The Veil Does Not Prevent Women from Working." In that essay and in Kemal's short story, what role is played by government? By religion? What is Cooke's view of the Islamic customs of veiling and segregation for women? How do you think Kemal would agree and disagree?

3. In "Woman as Other" (p. 329) Simone de Beauvoir gives several reasons why women collaborate with men's perception and treatment of them as Other. What evidence of those reasons can you find in "A Dirty Story"? Why do you think the women of Chukurova show so little inclination to protect or even stand up for Fadik?

## ELABORATIONS

1. Kemal avoids editorializing in "A Dirty Story"; he follows the time-honored writers' rule of "*show* rather than *tell*." For example, woven into his narrative is a vivid description of his native Anatolia. Go through "A Dirty Story" and pick out passages about its setting. Then write an imaginary travel article for a magazine in which you describe this region of Turkey as it would appear to a Western visitor.

2. Kemal also applies a strategy of "show rather than tell" to his characters' weaknesses. How would the story's impact change if he stated their faults and mistakes explicitly? Think of a dramatic incident in your experience in which

one person or group caused harm to another without acknowledging that they were behaving badly. An example might be schoolmates bullying a weakling, an older sibling teasing a younger, or an employer or landlord discriminating on the basis of race or sex. Write a narrative essay about the incident in which you let the characters' actions speak for them, as Kemal does.

3. What factors affect sex roles? Naila Minai in "Women in Early Islam" (p. 361), Miriam Cooke, and Kemal all describe Islamic attitudes toward male and female roles. Minai and Kemal also focus on the poverty, lack of technology, and subsistence-farming economy that many Islamic communities have in common. On the basis of these three selections, write an essay examining the relation between male-female roles and such factors as economics and education.

# PART FIVE

# WORK

---

## *We Are What We Do*

### LOOKING AT OURSELVES

Linda Hasselstrom, Larry Bird, Fred Moody, Elliot Liebow,
Stephen Blackburn, Russell Baker, Anonymous, Joy Harjo,
Vladimir Nabokov, John Updike, Studs Terkel

Maya Angelou, *Mary* (UNITED STATES)

David Abram, *Making Magic* (BALI/UNITED STATES)

Le Ly Hayslip, *Rice Farming in Vietnam* (VIETNAM)

Edna O'Brien, *Sister Imelda* (IRELAND)

Primo Levi, *Uranium* (ITALY)

Tomoyuki Iwashita, *Why I Quit the Company* (JAPAN)

Raymond Bonner, *A Woman's Place* (KUWAIT)

Yoshimi Ishikawa, *Strawberry Fields* (UNITED STATES/JAPAN)

Gabriel García Márquez, *Dreams for Hire* (COLOMBIA)

We IDENTIFY OURSELVES AND RECOGNIZE EACH OTHER BY WHAT WE DO. People's work varies from plowing fields to judging disputes, from teaching children to leading armies, from feeding chickens to programming computers. For some of us, work is a burden; for some, a pleasure; and for some, a source of pride. How we feel about our work both affects and is affected by how we feel about ourselves.

*Looking at Ourselves* starts with Linda Hasselstrom comparing the physical labor of ranching with the mental labor of writing. Larry Bird recalls the hours of practice it took him to become — and to stay — a first-class basketball player. Fred Moody comments on Americans' obsessiveness about work. The drawbacks of menial jobs are considered by Elliot Liebow; Stephen Blackburn examines the economics of working for minimum wage. Russell Baker sympathizes with modern children who can't understand what Daddy does, and a clown who entertained children as Ronald McDonald tells why he quit. Joy Harjo talks about writing from a mixed heritage; Vladimir Nabokov compares the tasks of writers and readers; and John Updike sums up the challenge of being an artist. Finally, Studs Terkel presents organizer Bill Talcott's views on his work with and for other workers.

A more extended look at work around the world begins with "Mary," Maya Angelou's recollection of her first job as a maid in a white woman's kitchen in the American South. David Abram's "Making Magic" tells of an American magician's successful struggle to find a niche on the Indonesian island of Bali. Northward across the Java and South China Seas, Le Ly Hayslip describes the intimate relationship between humans, rice, and the earth that filled her childhood in "Rice Farming in Vietnam." Edna O'Brien's short story "Sister Imelda" depicts a more austere girlhood, as a sympathetic nun eases the burdens of convent school for an Irish teenager.

"Uranium" takes the Italian writer Primo Levi back to an odd adventure in customer service, part of "the decathlon of the factory chemist." A tougher corporate decathlon is described in "Why I Quit the Company" by Tomoyuki Iwashita, a former rising star in fast-track Japan. Raymond Bonner uncovered virtual slavery in Kuwait, where "A Woman's Place" in wealthy households is filled by maids imported from southern Asia. Yoshimi Ishikawa tells a happier immigrant-labor story in "Strawberry Fields," his reminiscence about coming from Japan to be a California farmer. In "Dreams for Hire," a Cuban tidal wave reconnects the Colombian writer Gabriel García Márquez with an old friend who earned her living by dreaming.                                              ◇

# LOOKING AT OURSELVES

## 1

Virtually all of my friends have at one time or another suggested that I get away from my South Dakota ranch, give up the physical labor it requires, and pursue some respectable occupation like teaching. Why, they ask, should I waste my education and strain my muscles pitching hay to cows? Neighboring ranchers say, "Isn't it too bad you wasted all that time in college when you were just going to come back here and work anyway?" Neither group understands why I laugh instead of answering.

In our admirable desire to educate ourselves, we have begun to believe that an education should keep us from *having* to work. Many ranchers still urge their children to get college educations, "so you won't have to work as hard as I did." Many nonranchers, such as urban professionals, politicians, and academics, also imply that anyone who enjoys physical labor must be too dumb to get an education.

"Education, I fear, is learning to see one thing by going blind to another," said Aldo Leopold. While writing this essay, I went out into a cold, wet wind and stacked green wood for twenty minutes. When I came back to the computer, my ears were freezing, my back hurt, my blood was racing, my heart pounding, and I was delighted to be struggling with words. When words temporarily defeat me, I can check the cows, or carry wood inside, or pile rocks around my trees. I'm often tired, but never bored. When I'm confronted with a job I detest, six other jobs I prefer can delay it another day.

The variety of work keeps me from becoming blind in the sense I believe Aldo Leopold meant, my vision narrowed until I can see only words, or only physical labor. I believe that for a human being to see, literally or figuratively, he or she must look both near and far off; in the same way, labor should be both physical and mental in order to keep all circuits healthy.

I also think not working, in the sense of avoiding physical labor, is literally killing a lot of us. We buy expensive exercise clothing and equipment to eliminate the side effects — obesity, heart disease, stress, lung cancer — of being so well educated we never use a muscle. But no amount of artificial exercise can replace real labor and the satisfactions that accompany it.

— Linda Hasselstrom
*The North American Review,* 1991

◇◇◇◇◇

## 2

I had no idea that my fascination with basketball would lead me to where I am today. I'm proud of my image because hard work has never scared me. Of course, I'm lucky that I grew to be six-nine, but I also know that there are a lot of seven-footers out there who can't play basketball at all.

I've worked hard because I *had* to. I always worried that I couldn't run and couldn't jump, so I tried to be a great shooter and passer and I learned how to box people off the boards — all things that I hoped would compensate for any shortcomings I might have. I learned how to get good position and use my body correctly. Some people are natural shooters. They pick the ball up and they automatically get great rotation. They are true "natural" athletes. Danny Ainge is one of those people.

I had great training from [high school basketball coach] Jim Jones. Some of the things he taught me have never left me. Even after I became a Celtic and I'd go back to French Lick after the season, I had the same drive to excel. One day we played for about four hours and then I stuck around, shooting for hours afterward.

As a kid, I *always* thought I was behind and I needed that extra hour to catch up. Jim Jones once told me, "No matter how many shots you take, somewhere there's a kid out there taking one more. If you dribble a million times a day, someone is dribbling a million and one." Whenever I'd get ready to call it a day, I'd think, "No. Somebody else is still practicing. Somebody — *somewhere* — is playing that extra ten or fifteen minutes and he's going to beat me someday." I'd practice some more and then I'd think, "Maybe that guy is practicing his free throws now." So I'd go to the line and practice my free throws and that would take another hour. I don't know if I practiced more than *anybody*, but I sure practiced enough. I *still* wonder if somebody — somewhere — was practicing more than me.

Practice habits were crucial to my development in basketball. I didn't play against the toughest competition in high school, but one reason I was able to do well in college was that I mastered the fundamentals. You've got to have them down before you can even *think* about playing. When I went from high school to college, I was so fundamentally sound that I fit right in with everybody else because I knew how to do all the basics.

There are many times when you're better off practicing than you are playing, but most people just don't understand that. I love to play, to scrimmage against other players. But if that's all I ever did, I wouldn't know the game of basketball as well as I do.

– Larry Bird with Bob Ryan
*Drive: The Story of My Life*, 1989

◇◇◇◇◇◇

## 3

Work now pervades our nonworking lives in unprecedented, widely accepted ways: cellular phones, answering machines, personal and portable computers. The career, for many people, has taken precedence over such time-honored human endeavors as building a strong family or seeking spiritual and philosophical truths. The person who works right up to the point of self-destruction is often accorded far more esteem than the person who seeks to lead a balanced life. Overworking is an American trait, much commented on by European observers; and it has become the hallmark of strenuous yuppies, whose chief complaint about life is "I don't have enough time."

> – Fred Moody
> "When Work Becomes an Obsession"
> (Baltimore) *City Paper*, 1988

◇◇◇◇◇◇

## 4

Menial jobs are not, by and large, the starting point of a track system which leads to even better jobs for those who are able and willing to do them. The busboy or dishwasher in a restaurant is not on a job track which, if negotiated skillfully, leads to chef or manager of the restaurant. The busboy or dishwasher who works hard becomes, simply, a hard-working busboy or dishwasher. Neither hard work nor perseverance can conceivably carry the janitor to a sit-down job in the office building he cleans up. And it is the apprentice who becomes the journeyman electrician, plumber, steamfitter, or bricklayer, not the common unskilled Negro laborer.

Thus, the job is not a stepping-stone to something better. It is a dead end. It promises to deliver no more tomorrow, next month, or next year than it does today.

Delivering little, and promising no more, the job is "no big thing." The man appears to treat the job in a cavalier fashion, working and not working as the spirit moves him, as if all that matters is the immediate satisfaction of his present appetites, the surrender to present moods, and the indulgence of whims with no thought for the cost, the consequences, the future. To the middle-class observer, this behavior reflects a "present-time orientation" — an "inability to defer gratification." It is this "present-time" orientation — as against the "future orientation" of the middle-class person — that "explains" to the outsider why Leroy chooses to spend the day at the Carry-out rather than report to work; why Richard, who was paid Friday, was drunk Saturday and Sunday and penniless Monday;

why Sweets quit his job today because the boss looked at him "funny" yesterday.

But from the inside looking out, what appears as a "present-time" orientation to the outside observer is, to the man experiencing it, as much a future orientation as that of his middle-class counterpart. The difference between the two men lies not so much in their different orientations to time as in their different orientations to future time or, more specifically, to their different futures.

> – Elliot Liebow
> *Tally's Corner: A Study of
> Negro Streetcorner Men,* 1967

◇◇◇◇◇◇

# 5

Consider the life of a full-time worker at the new $4.25 minimum wage, who will earn about $735 a month, before taxes:

• The basic financial obligations of lower income families are not significantly less than those for the middle class. In a sample of 5,000 low-income families in Kansas City (who had an average income of $580 a month), families paid 68.5 percent of their income for rent, water, gas, and electricity. That left them $180 a month for child care, groceries, clothing, transportation, medical expenses, and entertainment. About 40 percent of working, two-parent, poor American families have no medical coverage.

• Transportation for poor people can be a problem, especially in big cities. Work isn't often available in the inner cities, and bus service to the more affluent metropolitan areas can involve time-consuming transfers, waits, and shifting bus schedules, if routes exist at all.

• Child-care costs run a minimum of $50 to $60 a week per child. Thus, notes Kansas City poverty activist David Shulman, if you're making today's minimum wage, by the time you've paid your taxes and paid someone else to look after your kids, you'll be lucky to have ten bucks in return for a week of labor.

• Low-income people actually pay higher utility bills than higher income people because they're living in substandard housing that isn't energy efficient. Shulman says the poor in Kansas City pay an average $155 a month for gas, electricity, and water; the typical bill of a middle-class family in the Kansas City area is around $120.

• Sixty percent of minimum-wage workers are adults, and two-thirds are female. The "typical" minimum-wage earner is a young adult who works part time. When layoffs occur, the part-timers are the first to go.

— Stephen Blackburn
*Kansas City Pitch*, 1991

# 6

It is not surprising that modern children tend to look blank and dispirited when informed that they will someday have to "go to work and make a living." The problem is that they cannot visualize what work is in corporate America.

Not so long ago, when a parent said he was off to work, the child knew very well what was about to happen. His parent was going to make something or fix something. The parent could take his offspring to his place of business and let him watch while he repaired a buggy or built a table.

When a child asked, "What kind of work do you do, Daddy?" his father could answer in terms that a child could come to grips with. "I fix steam engines." "I make horse collars."

Well, a few fathers still fix engines and build things, but most do not. Nowadays, most fathers sit in glass buildings performing tasks that are absolutely incomprehensible to children. The answers they give when asked, "What kind of work do you do, Daddy?" are likely to be utterly mystifying to a child.

"I sell space." "I do market research." "I am a data processor." "I am in public relations." "I am a systems analyst." Such explanations must seem nonsense to a child. How can he possibly envision anyone analyzing a system or researching a market?

— Russell Baker
*Poor Russell's Almanac*, 1969

# 7

ACT: *How were you trained to be a Ronald McDonald?*

Ronald: I'd already been trained to be a clown, doing magic tricks and the like — I'm an artist, an actor. My McDonald's training lasted a year and a half. The job itself was very luxurious, touring first-class to high schools and malls like a rock star. I made $50,000 a year. But basically I was their stooge. I'd go to high schools doing magic and safety shows, thinking I was doing it for the kids when really the whole point was to create product awareness.

*ACT: Why did you go into the corporate clown business in the first place?*

*Ronald:* I was desperate. Being a clown seemed to be all there was to do back then. But the people were assholes, so I quit. I became a Burger King for a while, but it was the same shit. Being Ronald was more luxurious, but it was all a lie.

> – Anonymous
> "Confessions of a Corporate Clown,"
> *ACT: Artists for Cultural Terrorism,* 1992

# 8

I was born in Tulsa, Oklahoma. . . . When I looked around I saw my mother, only nineteen, of mixed Cherokee and French blood, who had already worked hard for her short life. And my father, a few years older, a tall, good-looking Creek man who was then working as a mechanic for American Airlines. . . . We are descended from a long line of tribal speakers and leaders from my father's side. Menawa, who led the Red Stick War against Andrew Jackson, is our great-great (and possibly another great) grandfather. I don't know much about the family on my mother's side except there were many rebels and other characters. They are all part of who I am, the root from which I write, even though I may not always name them.

I began writing around the time I was twenty-two years old. I am now thirty-four and feel that after all this time I am just beginning to learn to write. I am only now beginning to comprehend what poetry is, and what it can mean. Each time I write I am in a different and wild place, and travel toward something I do not know the name of. Each poem is a jumping-off edge and I am not safe, but I take more risks and understand better now how to take them. They do not always work, but when they do it is worth it. I could not live without writing and/or thinking about it. In fact, I don't have to think about it; it's there, some word, concept always being born or, just as easily, dying.

I walk in and out of many worlds. I used to see being born of this mixed-blood/mixed-vision a curse, and hated myself for it. It was too confusing and destructive when I saw the world through that focus. The only message I got was not belonging anywhere, not to any side. I have since decided that being familiar with more than one world, more than one vision, is a blessing, and know that I make my own choices. I also know that it is only an illusion that any of the worlds are separate.

> – Joy Harjo
> "Ordinary Spirit"
> *I Tell You Now:*
> *Autobiographical Essays*
> *by Native American Writers*, 1987

# 9

To minor authors is left the ornamentation of the commonplace: These do not bother about any reinventing of the world; they merely try to squeeze the best they can out of a given order of things, out of traditional patterns of fiction. The various combinations these minor authors are able to produce within these set limits may be quite amusing in a mild ephemeral way because minor readers like to recognize their own ideas in a pleasing disguise. But the real writer, the fellow who sends planets spinning and models a man asleep and eagerly tampers with the sleeper's rib, that kind of author has no given values at his disposal: He must create them himself. The art of writing is a very futile business if it does not imply first of all the art of seeing the world as the potentiality of fiction. The material of this world may be real enough (as far as reality goes) but does not exist at all as an accepted entirety: It is chaos, and to this chaos the author says "go!" allowing the world to flicker and to fuse. It is now recombined in its very atoms, not merely in its visible and superficial parts. The writer is the first man to map it and to name the natural objects it contains. Those berries there are edible. That speckled creature that bolted across my path might be tamed. That lake between those trees will be called Lake Opal or, more artistically, Dishwater Lake. That mist is a mountain — and that mountain must be conquered. Up a trackless slope climbs the master artist, and at the top, on a windy ridge, whom do you think he meets? The panting and happy reader, and there they spontaneously embrace and are linked forever if the book lasts forever.

> – Vladimir Nabokov
> "Good Writers and Good Readers"
> *Lectures on Literature*, 1980

## 10

An artist mediates between the world and minds; a critic merely between minds. An artist therefore must even at the price of uncouthness and alienation from the contemporary cultural scene maintain allegiance to the world and a fervent relation with it.

– John Updike
*Hugging the Shore*, 1983

## 11

My work is trying to change this country. This is the job I've chosen. When people ask me, "Why are you doing this?" it's like asking what kind of sickness you got. I don't feel sick. I think this country is sick. The daily injustices just gnaw on me a little harder than they do on other people.

I try to bring people together who are being put down by the system, left out. You try to build an organization that will give them power to make the changes. Everybody's at the bottom of the barrel at this point. Ten years ago one could say the poor people suffered and the middle class got by. That's not true anymore. . . .

I put together a fairly solid organization of Appalachian people in Pike County [Kentucky]. It's a single industry area, coal. You either work for the coal company or you don't work. Sixty percent of its people live on incomes lower than the government's guidelines for rural areas.

I was brought in to teach other organizers how to do it. I spent my first three months at it. I decided these middle-class kids from Harvard and Columbia were too busy telling everybody else what they should be doing. The only thing to do was to organize the local people. . . .

The word *organizer* has been romanticized. You get the vision of a mystical being doing magical things. An organizer is a guy who brings in new members. I don't feel I've had a good day unless I've talked with at least one new person. We have a meeting, make space for new people to come in. The organizer sits next to the new guy, so everybody has to take the new guy as an equal. You do that a couple of times and the guy's got strength enough to become part of the group.

You must listen to them and tell them again and again they are important, that they have the stuff to do the job. They don't have to shuck themselves about not being good enough, not worthy. Most people were raised to think they are not worthy. School is a process of taking beautiful kids who are filled with life and beating them into happy slavery. That's as true of a twenty-five-thousand-dollar-a-year executive as it is for the poorest.

You don't find allies on the basis of the brotherhood of man. People are tied into their immediate problems. They have a difficult time worrying about other people's. Our society is so structured that everybody is supposed to be selfish as hell and screw the other guy. Christian brotherhood is enlightened self-interest. Most sins committed on poor people are by people who've come to help them.

I came as a stranger but I came with credentials. There are people who know and trust me, who say so to the others. So what I'm saying is verifiable. It's possible to win, to take an outfit like Bethlehem Steel and lick 'em. Most people in their guts don't really believe it. Gee, it's great when all of a sudden they realize it's possible. They become alive.

Nobody believed PCCA [Pike County Citizens' Association] could stop Bethlehem from strip mining. Ten miles away was a hillside being stripped. Ten miles away is like ten million light-years away. What they wanted was a park, a place for their kids. Bethlehem said, "Go to hell. You're just a bunch of crummy Appalachians. We're not gonna give you a damn thing." If I could get that park for them, they would believe it's possible to do other things.

They really needed a victory. They had lost over and over again, day after day. So I got together twenty, thirty people I saw as leaders. I said, "Let's get that park." They said, "We can't." I said, "We can. If we let all the big wheels around the country know — the National Council of Churches and everybody start calling up, writing, and hounding Bethlehem, they'll have to give us the park." That's exactly what happened. Bethlehem thought: This is getting to be a pain in the ass. We'll give 'em the park and they'll shut up about strip mining. We haven't shut up on strip mining, but we got the park. Four thousand people from Pike County drove up and watched those bulldozers grading down that park. It was an incredible victory.

Twenty or thirty people realized we could win. Four thousand people understood there was a victory. They didn't know how it happened, but a few of 'em got curious. The twenty or thirty are now in their own communities trying to turn people on. . . .

I work all the way from two in the morning until two the next morning seven days a week. (Laughs.) I'm not a martyr. I'm one of the few people I know who was lucky in life to find out what he really wanted to do. I'm just havin' a ball, the time of my life. I feel sorry for all these people I run across all the time who aren't doing what they want to do. Their lives are hell. I think everybody ought to quit their job and do what they want to do. You've got one life. You've got, say, sixty-five years. How on earth can you blow forty-five years of that doing something you hate?

I have a wife and three children. I've managed to support them for six years doing this kind of work. We don't live fat. I have enough money to buy books and records. The kids have as good an education as anybody in this country. Their range of friends runs from millionaires in San Francisco to black prostitutes in Lexington. They're comfortable with all these people. My kids know the name of the game: living your life up to the end.

All human recorded history is about five thousand years old. How many people in all that time have made an overwhelming difference? Twenty? Thirty? Most of us spend our lives trying to achieve some things. But we're not going to make an overwhelming difference. We do the best we can. That's enough.

The problem with history is that it's written by college professors about great men. That's not what history is. History's a hell of a lot of little people getting together and deciding they want a better life for themselves and their kids.

I have a goal. I want to end my life in a home for the aged that's run by the state — organizing people to fight 'em because they're not running it right. (Laughs.)

– Bill Talcott
Studs Terkel's *Working*, 1972

## REFLECTIONS

1. According to Linda Hasselstrom (p. 406), what are the greatest rewards of her work as a rancher? According to Joy Harjo (p. 410), what are the greatest rewards of her work as a writer? How are these two women's responses to their work alike and how are they different?

2. Which kinds of work described in *Looking at Ourselves* involve working the most hours? Which ones involve the most independence? What are the pros and cons of being one's own boss?

3. What are the greatest rewards of the kinds of work mentioned by Fred Moody (p. 407)? By Elliot Liebow (p. 407)? By Russell Baker (p. 409)?

4. What factors give a person the most ability to choose what kind of work to do?

# MAYA ANGELOU

## *Mary*

Maya Angelou came to nationwide attention in 1993 when President Clinton named her Poet Laureate of the United States, asking her to compose and deliver an original poem ("On the Pulse of Morning") at his inauguration. Angelou was already known to television audiences for her performance in Alex Haley's "Roots," for which she received an Emmy Award nomination.

At the time "Mary" took place, Angelou was still going by her birth name, Marguerite Johnson. Born in St. Louis, Missouri, in 1928, by the age of sixteen she had survived rape, the breakup of her family, and unwed motherhood. (The rapist was her mother's friend Mr. Freeman, who was tried, convicted, and later found beaten to death — the sequence of events Angelou refers to in para. 21.) Support from her mother and her brother, Bailey, helped to keep her going through five years in which she never spoke. She later became a dancer, appeared in several plays (including a twenty-two-nation tour of *Porgy and Bess*), worked with the Harlem Writers' Guild, lived in Ghana, and produced a series on Africa for the Public Broadcasting System. Angelou has been awarded numerous honorary doctorates and, at the request of Martin Luther King, Jr., served as a coordinator for the Southern Christian Leadership Conference. President Ford appointed her to the Bicentennial Commission and President Carter to the Commission of International Woman's Year. The author of six books of poetry, various songs and musical scores, and several plays and screenplays, Angelou is best known for her five-volume autobiography. "Mary" comes from the first volume, *I Know Why the Caged Bird Sings* (1970), which recounts her childhood in Stamps, Arkansas. She currently lives in North Carolina, where she holds a lifetime chair in American Studies at Wake Forest University.

Recently a white woman from Texas, who would quickly describe herself as a liberal, asked me about my hometown. When I told her that in Stamps my grandmother had owned the only Negro general merchandise store since the turn of the century, she exclaimed, "Why, you were a debutante." Ridiculous and even ludicrous. But Negro girls in small Southern towns, whether poverty-stricken or just munching along on a few of life's necessities, were given as extensive and irrelevant preparations for adulthood as rich white girls shown in magazines. Admittedly the training was not the same. While white girls learned to waltz and sit gracefully with a tea cup balanced on their knees, we were lagging behind, learning the mid-Victorian values with very little money to indulge them. (Come and see Edna Lomax spending the money she made picking cotton on five balls of ecru tatting thread. Her fingers are bound to snag the work and she'll have to repeat the stitches time and time again. But she knows that when she buys the thread.)

We were required to embroider and I had trunkfuls of colorful dishtowels, pillowcases, runners, and handkerchiefs to my credit. I mastered the art of crocheting and tatting, and there was a lifetime's supply of dainty doilies that would never be used in sacheted dresser drawers. It went without saying that all girls could iron and wash, but the finer touches around the home, like setting a table with real silver, baking roasts, and cooking vegetables without meat, had to be learned elsewhere. Usually at the source of those habits. During my tenth year, a white woman's kitchen became my finishing school.

Mrs. Viola Cullinan was a plump woman who lived in a three-bedroom house somewhere behind the post office. She was singularly unattractive until she smiled, and then the lines around her eyes and mouth which made her look perpetually dirty disappeared, and her face looked like the mask of an impish elf. She usually rested her smile until late afternoon when her women friends dropped in and Miss Glory, the cook, served them cold drinks on the closed-in porch.

The exactness of her house was inhuman. This glass went here and only here. That cup had its place and it was an act of impudent rebellion to place it anywhere else. At twelve o'clock the table was set. At 12:15 Mrs. Cullinan sat down to dinner (whether her husband had arrived or not). At 12:16 Miss Glory brought out the food.

It took me a week to learn the difference between a salad plate, a bread    5
plate, and a dessert plate.

Mrs. Cullinan kept up the tradition of her wealthy parents. She was from Virginia. Miss Glory, who was a descendant of slaves that had worked for the Cullinans, told me her history. She had married beneath her (according to Miss Glory). Her husband's family hadn't had their money very long and what they had "didn't 'mount to much."

As ugly as she was, I thought privately, she was lucky to get a husband above or beneath her station. But Miss Glory wouldn't let me say a thing against her mistress. She was very patient with me, however, over the housework. She explained the dishware, silverware, and servants' bells.

The large round bowl in which soup was served wasn't a soup bowl, it was a tureen. There were goblets, sherbet glasses, ice-cream glasses, wine glasses, green glass coffee cups with matching saucers, and water glasses. I had a glass to drink from, and it sat with Miss Glory's on a separate shelf from the others. Soup spoons, gravy boat, butter knives, salad forks, and carving platter were additions to my vocabulary and in fact almost represented a new language. I was fascinated with the novelty, with the fluttering Mrs. Cullinan and her Alice-in-Wonderland house.

Her husband remains, in my memory, undefined. I lumped him with all the other white men that I had ever seen and tried not to see.

On our way home one evening, Miss Glory told me that Mrs. Cullinan couldn't have children. She said that she was too delicate-boned. It was hard to imagine bones at all under those layers of fat. Miss Glory went on to say that the doctor had taken out all her lady organs. I reasoned that a pig's organs included the lungs, heart, and liver, so if Mrs. Cullinan was walking around without those essentials, it explained why she drank alcohol out of unmarked bottles. She was keeping herself embalmed. 10

When I spoke to Bailey[1] about it, he agreed that I was right, but he also informed me that Mr. Cullinan had two daughters by a colored lady and that I knew them very well. He added that the girls were the spitting image of their father. I was unable to remember what he looked like, although I had just left him a few hours before, but I thought of the Coleman girls. They were very light-skinned and certainly didn't look very much like their mother (no one ever mentioned Mr. Coleman).

My pity for Mrs. Cullinan preceded me the next morning like the Cheshire cat's smile. Those girls, who could have been her daughters, were beautiful. They didn't have to straighten their hair. Even when they were caught in the rain, their braids still hung down straight like tamed snakes. Their mouths were pouty little cupid's bows. Mrs. Cullinan didn't know what she missed. Or maybe she did. Poor Mrs. Cullinan.

For weeks after, I arrived early, left late, and tried very hard to make up for her barrenness. If she had had her own children, she wouldn't have had to ask me to run a thousand errands from her back door to the back door of her friends. Poor old Mrs. Cullinan.

Then one evening Miss Glory told me to serve the ladies on the porch. After I set the tray down and turned toward the kitchen, one of the women asked, "What's your name, girl?" It was the speckled-faced one. Mrs. Cullinan said, "She doesn't talk much. Her name's Margaret."

"Is she dumb?" 15

"No. As I understand it, she can talk when she wants to but she's usually quiet as a little mouse. Aren't you, Margaret?"

I smiled at her. Poor thing. No organs and couldn't even pronounce my name correctly.

---

[1]The author's brother. — ED.

"She's a sweet little thing, though."

"Well, that may be, but the name's too long. I'd never bother myself. I'd call her Mary if I was you."

I fumed into the kitchen. That horrible woman would never have the    20
chance to call me Mary because if I was starving I'd never work for her.
I decided I wouldn't pee on her if her heart was on fire. Giggles drifted
in off the porch and into Miss Glory's pots. I wondered what they could
be laughing about.

Whitefolks were so strange. Could they be talking about me? Everybody knew that they stuck together better than the Negroes did. It was
possible that Mrs. Cullinan had friends in St. Louis who heard about a
girl from Stamps being in court and wrote to tell her. Maybe she knew
about Mr. Freeman.

My lunch was in my mouth a second time and I went outside and
relieved myself on the bed of four-o'clocks. Miss Glory thought I might
be coming down with something and told me to go on home, that
Momma would give me some herb tea, and she'd explain to her mistress.

I realized how foolish I was being before I reached the pond. Of course
Mrs. Cullinan didn't know. Otherwise she wouldn't have given me the
two nice dresses that Momma cut down, and she certainly wouldn't have
called me a "sweet little thing." My stomach felt fine, and I didn't
mention anything to Momma.

That evening I decided to write a poem on being white, fat, old, and
without children. It was going to be a tragic ballad. I would have to watch
her carefully to capture the essence of her loneliness and pain.

The very next day, she called me by the wrong name. Miss Glory and    25
I were washing up the lunch dishes when Mrs. Cullinan came to the
doorway. "Mary?"

Miss Glory asked, "Who?"

Mrs. Cullinan, sagging a little, knew and I knew. "I want Mary to go
down to Mrs. Randall's and take her some soup. She's not been feeling
well for a few days."

Miss Glory's face was a wonder to see. "You mean Margaret, ma'am.
Her name's Margaret."

"That's too long. She's Mary from now on. Heat that soup from last
night and put it in the china tureen and, Mary, I want you to carry it
carefully."

Every person I knew had a hellish horror of being "called out of his    30
name." It was a dangerous practice to call a Negro anything that could
be loosely construed as insulting because of the centuries of their having
been called niggers, jigs, dinges, blackbirds, crows, boots, and spooks.

Miss Glory had a fleeting second of feeling sorry for me. Then as she handed me the hot tureen she said, "Don't mind, don't pay that no mind. Sticks and stones may break your bones, but words . . . You know, I been working for her for twenty years."

She held the back door open for me. "Twenty years. I wasn't much older than you. My name used to be Hallelujah. That's what Ma named me, but my mistress give me 'Glory,' and it stuck. I likes it better too."

I was in the little path that ran behind the houses when Miss Glory shouted, "It's shorter too."

For a few seconds it was a tossup over whether I would laugh (imagine being named Hallelujah) or cry (imagine letting some white woman rename you for her convenience). My anger saved me from either outburst. I had to quit the job, but the problem was going to be how to do it. Momma wouldn't allow me to quit for just any reason.

"She's a peach. That woman is a real peach." Mrs. Randall's maid was      35
talking as she took the soup from me, and I wondered what her name used to be and what she answered to now.

For a week I looked into Mrs. Cullinan's face as she called me Mary. She ignored my coming late and leaving early. Miss Glory was a little annoyed because I had begun to leave egg yolk on the dishes and wasn't putting much heart in polishing the silver. I hoped that she would complain to our boss, but she didn't.

Then Bailey solved my dilemma. He had me describe the contents of the cupboard and the particular plates she liked best. Her favorite piece was a casserole shaped like a fish and the green glass coffee cups. I kept his instructions in mind, so on the next day when Miss Glory was hanging out clothes and I had again been told to serve the old biddies on the porch, I dropped the empty serving tray. When I heard Mrs. Cullinan scream, "Mary!" I picked up the casserole and two of the green glass cups in readiness. As she rounded the kitchen door I let them fall on the tiled floor.

I could never absolutely describe to Bailey what happened next, because each time I got to the part where she fell on the floor and screwed up her ugly face to cry, we burst out laughing. She actually wobbled around on the floor and picked up shards of the cups and cried, "Oh, Momma. Oh, dear Gawd. It's Momma's china from Virginia. Oh, Momma, I sorry."

Miss Glory came running in from the yard and the women from the porch crowded around. Miss Glory was almost as broken up as her mistress. "You mean to say she broke our Virginia dishes? What we gone do?"

Mrs. Cullinan cried louder, "That clumsy nigger. Clumsy little black      40
nigger."

Old speckled-face leaned down and asked, "Who did it, Viola? Was it Mary? Who did it?"

Everything was happening so fast I can't remember whether her action preceded her words, but I know that Mrs. Cullinan said, "Her name's Margaret, goddamn it, her name's Margaret!" And she threw a wedge of the broken plate at me. It could have been the hysteria which put her aim off, but the flying crockery caught Miss Glory right over her ear and she started screaming.

I left the front door wide open so all the neighbors could hear.

Mrs. Cullinan was right about one thing. My name wasn't Mary.


## EXPLORATIONS

1. When Maya Angelou first goes to work for Mrs. Cullinan, what is her attitude toward her employer? At what points does her attitude change, in what ways, and for what reasons?

2. What reason does Angelou give for a black person's horror of being "called out of his name" (para. 30)? Why does she find her change of name so offensive?

3. In paragraph 24, Angelou decides "to write a poem on being white, fat, old, and without children." Why do you think she wanted to do this? What personal goals does she seem to have achieved by writing about Mrs. Cullinan in her autobiography?


## CONNECTIONS

1. In what ways does young Marguerite's job match the description given by Elliot Liebow in *Looking at Ourselves* (p. 407)? What are Marguerite's sources of satisfaction in her job?

2. Look back at Simone de Beauvoir's analysis of the master-slave relationship in "Woman as Other" (pp. 333–334, paras. 12–13). Which statements by Beauvoir also apply to the mistress-servant relationship in "Mary"?

3. Reread paragraphs 19 and 20 of V. S. Naipaul's "Entering the New World" (p. 48). How does Naipaul explain the disorder he observed at the restaurant? After reading "Mary," what alternative explanation can you suggest?

# ELABORATIONS

1. How old were you when you first worked for money? What do you remember of your feelings about the job, the people involved, and having an income? Write a narrative essay about your experience as an employee.

2. In paragraph 4 Angelou describes the "inhuman" exactness of Mrs. Cullinan's house: glasses precisely placed, meals precisely scheduled. Do you know anyone who is so demanding? Is there any aspect of your life — the way you arrange your desk, a recipe you prepare, specialized clothing you put on for some activity — that is so exact? Write a descriptive or process analysis essay about your experience with exactness.

# DAVID ABRAM

## *Making Magic*

Ecologist, writer, and free-lance magician David Abram was born on Long Island, New York, in 1957. A summa cum laude graduate of Wesleyan University in Connecticut, he received his Ph.D. in philosophy from the State University of New York at Stony Brook. Abram took up magic in high school and began performing professionally during his first year at college. In 1980 he was awarded a Watson Fellowship for a year's research among tribal healers in Indonesia, Nepal, and Sri Lanka. "Making Magic" grew out of that research; it was first published in *Parabola* in August 1982 and excerpted in the January–February 1988 *Utne Reader*. Abram's articles on ecological perception and indigenous cultures have appeared in *The Ecologist, Journal of Environmental Ethics, Orion,* and *Wild Earth*. He has taught at various universities and lectured extensively on the Gaia hypothesis, which holds that the earth's atmosphere is being modulated by all of the earth's organisms acting collectively. A resident of New Mexico, Abram has an abiding interest in interspecies communication and has written a book on language and the ecology of sensory experience.

Indonesia, where the following adventures took place, is a republic comprising 13,500 islands south of the Philippines and north of Australia. Besides Bali, it includes Java, Sumatra, most of Borneo, and the western half of New Guinea. The islands' location made them attractive to European traders. First the Portuguese dominated, then the Dutch. In 1824 the British and Dutch split their holdings in the region, then known as the East Indies. The southern Dutch East Indies declared independence in 1945 as Indonesia, after being occupied by Japan through World War II. The northern British East Indies evolved into part of the Federation of Malaya, now Malaysia.

They told me I had powers.

Powers? I had been a magician for seven years, performing steadily back in the States, entertaining in clubs and restaurants throughout the country, yet I had never heard anyone mention powers. To be sure, once or twice a season I was rebuked by some spectator fresh out of Bible school for "doing the work of Satan," but the more customary refrain was: "How did you do that?" Every evening in the clubs: "How? How did *that* happen?" "C'mon, tell us — how does that work?"

"I don't know," I took to saying, mostly out of boredom, yet also because I felt there was a grain of truth in that statement, because there was some aspect of my sleight-of-hand tricks that mystified even me. It was not something I could experience when rehearsing alone, at home, or when practicing my sleights before a mirror. But when I would stand before my audience, letting my fingers run through one of their routines with some borrowed coins, and I'd see the spectators' eyes slowly widening with astonishment, well, there was something astonishing about that for me as well, although I was unable to say just what it was.

When I received a fellowship to support a year's research on the intertwining of magic and medicine in Asia, I thought I might have a chance to explore the secrets that lay hidden within my own magic, or at least to discern what mysteries my magic had in common with the magic used in traditional cultures not merely for entertainment, but for healing, fortification, and transformation. I was intending to use my skills as a Western sleight-of-hand magician to gain access to the native practitioners and their rituals — I would approach them not as an academic researcher, not as an anthropologist or sociologist, but as a magician in my own right, and in this manner would explore the relation between ritual and transformation from the inside.

As it turned out, this method worked well — at first almost too well,    5
for the potency my magic tricks took on in rural Asia brought some alarming difficulties. In the interior of Sri Lanka, where I began my quest, I was rather too open with my skills; anxious to get a sense of the local attitude toward magic, I began performing on village street corners much as I had three years earlier while journeying as a street magician through Europe. But these were different streets, much more worn and dusty than those concrete thoroughfares, reeking with smells of incense and elephants, frequented as much by gods and demons as by the human inhabitants of the island. Less than a week after I began plucking handkerchiefs from the air, "the young magician from the West" was known throughout the country. Huge crowds followed me wherever I went, and I was constantly approached by people in the grip of disease, by the blind and crippled, all asking me to cure them with my powers. What a frightful, saddening position to be in! When, like a fool, I attempted to show that my magic feats were but illusions accomplished by dexterous manipulations, I only insulted these people — clearly, to them, I was using clumsy explanations to disguise and hide my real powers. I fled Sri Lanka after only three weeks, suffering from a severe case of ethical paradox, determined to begin my work afresh in Indonesia, where I would above all keep my magic more to myself.

It was five months later — after carefully immersing myself in the

Indonesian island universe, observing and recording the patterns of culture, while slowly, inadvertently, slipping into those patterns myself —
that I first allowed myself a chance to explore the more unusual possibilities of my position. For five months I had been true to my resolve, keeping
my magic much more "up my sleeve" than I had in Sri Lanka — waiting
for just the right moment to make something impossible happen, and
performing for only a few people at a time, perhaps in a tea stall or while
sauntering past the rice paddies. In this manner I slowly and much more
surely wove my way into the animist fabric of the society. I had the sense
that I was becoming known in the region, but in a more subtle and
curious manner than before — here and there I had begun to hear stories
about a Westerner, glimpsed on the far side of the island, who actually
had access to the invisible world, to the spirits.

   Gradually I had been contacted by a number of *dukuns,* or sorcerers,
often in some clandestine manner, through a child or a friend, and asked
to visit them in their homes. The initial meetings had been strained,
sometimes frightening, for these practitioners felt their status threatened
by a stranger who could so easily produce shells from the air or make
knives vanish between his hands. And I in return felt threatened by the
resultant antagonism — I did not want these magicians to view me as
their competitor, for I knew the incredible power of the imagination and
had no wish to be the victim of any dark spells. (When I came down with
a nightmarish case of malaria, I was sure, in my delirium, that I had
brought it upon myself by offending a particular sorcerer.) As the months
unfolded, I had learned not to shy away from these tensions, but to work
with them. I had become adept at transforming the initial antagonism
into some sort of mutual respect, at times into a real sense of camaraderie.
I had lived with a sorcerer-healer in Java and traded magic with a *balian
tapakan,* or spirit medium, in Bali, both of whom were convinced that
my presence in their household enhanced their own access to the gods
and accentuated their power as healers. But that is another story.

   On a certain early monsoon day I sat in a rice stall in a small fishing
village on the coast of Bali, shielding myself from the afternoon rain.
Munching my rice, I stared out at a steamy, emerald landscape — with
the rainy season finally breaking overhead, all the Balinese greens were
beginning to leak into the air. Inside, the old woman was serving rice
across the wooden slab of a counter to two solemn fishermen; in the
corner of the hut three others were laughing and conversing in low
Balinese. The downpour outside stopped abruptly; now other sounds —
dogs fighting in the distance, someone singing.

   I stood up to pay the woman, counting out the correct number of coins
and reaching across to drop them into her hand. I opened my fingers —

the coins were not there! The woman and I looked at each other, astonished. I turned my empty hands over several times, looked on the dirt floor behind me, then reached under my rice bowl and found the coins. Feigning relief, I took them up and reached across to hand them to the bewildered woman — except that the coins were missing once again when I opened my fist. By now the men in the corner had stopped talking and the two at the counter had paused in the middle of their meal, watching as I became more and more annoyed, searching the floor and the bench without finding my money. One of the fishermen suggested that I look under my bowl again. I lifted it up, but the coins were not there. Upset, I stared at the others. One of them backed slowly into the street. I shrugged my shoulders sadly at the woman, then caught sight of the two half-filled rice bowls resting in front of the other men at the counter. I motioned hesitantly for one of the fishermen to lift up his bowl. He looked around at the others, then gingerly raised one edge of the bowl — there they were! The coins glittered on the palmwood as the fishermen began shouting at each other, incredulous. The old woman was doubled over with laughter.

The man who had uncovered the coins stared at me long and hard.    10 As the others drifted out onto the street, still shouting, this man shoved his rice aside, leaned over to me, and asked, in Indonesian, if I would be so kind as to accompany him to meet his family. Something urgent in his voice intrigued me; I nodded. He paid the old woman, who clapped me on the shoulder as we left, and led me down the street toward the beach. He turned off to the right before reaching the sand, and I followed him through the rice paddies, balancing like a tightrope-walker on one of the dikes that separate the flooded squares. To our left the village spread itself out along the shore: A young woman nursed an infant, smoke rose from cooking fires, three pigs rummaged through a pile of rags and wood. The man turned to the left between two paddies and led me through a makeshift gate into his family compound. Children were playing. He motioned me inside one of the two buildings — his brother lives in the other, he explained — where a young woman sat with a child on her lap. Before I could make a formal greeting, the fisherman pushed his wife and child out the door, slinging a blanket over the doorway and another over the window. He sat me down in the dark, offered a Javanese cigarette, lit one for himself, then sat down cross-legged on the floor next to me. He gripped my ankle as he began to explain his situation. He spoke quickly, in broken Indonesian, which was good, since I could never have followed his story had he spoken so quickly in Balinese.

Essentially what he had to say was this: that he was a poor and ignorant fisherman blessed with a loving wife and many children, and that despite his steady and enthusiastic propitiation of the local gods and ancestors, he had been unable to catch any fish for the last six months. This was especially upsetting since before that time he had been one of the most successful fishermen in the village. He said it was evident to everyone in the village that his present difficulties were the result of some left-handed magic; clearly a demon had been induced by some sorcery to take up residence in the hull of his fishing boat, and was now frightening the fish away from his nets. Furthermore, he knew that another fisherman in the village had secretly obtained a certain talisman from a priest, a magic shell that made this other man's boat fill up with fish whenever he took it out on the water. And so perhaps I, who obviously knew about such things and had some powers of my own, would be willing to work some special magic on *his* boat so that he could once again catch enough fish to feed his family.

Now, it was clear that this man was both honest and in earnest (his grip on my poor ankle had increased considerably), but I had been in this position before, and though less disconcerted by it than I had been five months earlier, I was still reluctant to play very deeply within the dream-space of a culture that was not my own. And so I explained to Gedé (one of his many names) that my magic was only good for things like making coins vanish or causing fruit to appear (I plucked a ripe banana out of the darkness, making him laugh), that my magic was useless when it came to really practical matters. Besides, I told him, I had never worked with fish, but was sure (since they could breathe underwater and all) that their own powers were even more potent than mine; if a demon was frightening them away, he or she was certainly beyond my influence. Gedé nodded in agreement, released my ankle, and changed the subject. After a few minutes he led me to the doorway and thanked me for coming.

I felt sure I had convinced him with my excuses. But perhaps I had failed to take into account the Balinese habit of self-effacement before accepting praise (*Saya bodoh,* "I am stupid," any Balinese healer will reply when told that he or she is skillful), including, apparently, the praise and respect implied in being offered a difficult task. Unaware, I walked along the beach toward the little bamboo hut I had procured for the night. As the sun sank into the land, the moon rose from the ocean, pale white, nearly full. In the distance, between the rising and the lowering, sat the great volcano, silently looming on the horizon.

That night I had difficulty falling asleep. A weird symphony of chirping crickets accompanied the chorus of frogs gurgling in unison outside my hut. Sometimes this loud music stopped all at once — leaving only the faint lapping of waves and the afternoon rain dripping off the night leaves.

Toward midnight I was awakened by a persistent tapping at the window.    15
I stumbled to my feet and lifted the thin slab of wood — there was Gedé,
grinning nervously. He hissed that we must attempt the magic now, while
the others were asleep. In an instant I understood the situation — that
Gedé was not taking no for an answer, or rather that he had taken my
refusal as an acceptance — and I found myself, oddly enough, giving in
to the challenge this time without hesitation. Wrapping a sarong around
myself, I recalled the dream from which Gedé's tapping had awakened
me: I had been back in the States, performing strange, hypnotic magic
for sea monsters in a nightclub that was actually an aquarium. Just before
waking, I had heard one monster applauding; his clapping had become
the tapping at my window. Now, looking around hastily for something to
use, I grabbed an empty Coke bottle I had tossed in the corner, then, on
an inspiration, dug in my backpack for some flashpaper I'd brought from
the States. (Flashpaper, a common tool of the stage magician, is thin
paper that has been soaked in a magnesium solution. When crumpled
and ignited, it goes up in a sudden bright flash, leaving no ashes behind — wonderful stuff.) I shoved the flashpaper into a fold in my sarong
and, gripping the Coke bottle, hurried outside where Gedé was fidgeting
anxiously. When he saw me, he turned and led the way down to the
beach.

We walked quickly along the water's edge to where the boats were
resting on the sand, their long, painted hulls gleaming in the moonglow.
As we walked, Gedé whispered to me that the fishermen don't go out
fishing on nights when the moon is full or nearly full, since the fish can
then see the nets. Only on such a night as this could we accomplish the
magic in secret, while the other fishermen slept. He stopped before a
sleek blue and white boat, somewhat longer than most of the others, and
motioned for me to help him. We lifted the bamboo outriggers and slid
the craft into the dark water. I hopped back onto the beach and scooped
my Coke bottle full of the black, volcanic sand, then waded back out and
climbed into the boat with Gedé. Really a long dugout canoe with
limbs — the two bamboo outriggers and a short, rough-hewn mast near
the bow — it rested on the swells while Gedé unrolled a white triangle
of sail and hoisted it from a beam on the mast. The breeze rose up and
the boat glided silently into the night. Overhead, the moon drifted behind
a cloud and set the whole cloud glowing. The volcano, luminous,
watched and waited.

In the Balinese universe, the volcano provides a sort of gateway to and
from the upper world, the world of the ancestors, of the gods. The sea,
meanwhile, provides passage to the lower world of demons; these destructive forces are known to reside in the black depths of the waters that

surround the island. Consequently, those islanders who live near the shore, and especially the fishermen who make their living on the water, are a highly nervous and wary bunch, and they partake even more than the average Balinese of the animistic rites and ceremonies of protection for which the island is famous. At this point in my journey I was only beginning to sense what I would later see clearly: that while the magicians of all traditional cultures are working fundamentally toward the same mystery, the magic of each culture takes its structure from the particular clues of the region, that is, from the particular powers of earth to be found only there — whether volcanoes, or wind, or ocean, or desert — for magic evolves from the land.

The wind shifted, became cooler. I moved close to where Gedé sat in the stern guiding the rudder, and asked him why it was so necessary for us to work in secret. "So other fishermen not jealous," he explained softly. He lit himself a cigarette. After some time I turned away from him and slipped a piece of flashpaper, crumpled, into the mouth of the Coke bottle. The beach was a thin silver line in the distance. I told Gedé that I thought we were out far enough for the magic to take effect, and he agreed. As I took down the sail, I wedged the rest of the flashpaper under a splinter near the top of the mast. Gedé heaved an anchor over the side, then settled back into the stern, watching me carefully.

How to improvise an exorcism? I leaned with my back against the mast, emptying my mind of thoughts, feeling the rock and sway of this tiny boat on the night waters. Small waves slapped against the hull, angrily at first, then softer, more playful, curious. Gradually something regular established itself — the swaying took on a rhythm, a steady rock and roll that grew in intensity as my body gave in to the dance. Phosphorescent algae glimmered like stars around me. The boat became a planet, and I leaned with my back against the axis of the world, a tree with roots in the ocean and branches in the sky, tilting, turning.

Without losing the rhythm, I began to move toward the rear of the          20
boat, keeping it rocking, swinging the bottle of black sand around myself in circles, from one hand to the other. When I reached Gedé I took the cigarette from his hand, puffed on it deeply once or twice, then touched the lit end to the mouth of the bottle. A white flash of fire exploded from the bottle with a "Whooshh," propelled by the pressure inside, a wild spirit lunging for air.

Gedé sat bolt upright, with his arms quivering, grasping the sides of the hull. I motioned for him to cup his hands, he did so, and I tipped the bottle down, pouring a small mound of spirit-sand onto his fingers. There were little platforms affixed symmetrically around the hull, platforms upon which Gedé, when fishing, would place his lanterns to coax the fish up from the depths. I moved around to each of them, nine in all, the cardinal points of this drifting planet, and carefully anointed each one with a mound of sand. I then sat down in the bottom of the carved-out hull and planted my hands against the wood, against the inside of that hollowed-out tree, waiting to make contact with whatever malevolent presence slumbered beneath the chiseled surface. I felt the need for a sound, for some chant to keep the rhythm, but I could think of nothing appropriate, until a bit of Jewish liturgy sprang to my lips from somewhere, perhaps from my own initiation at age thirteen. I sang softly. The planet heaved and creaked, the hollow tree rolled from side to side, the upright tree with roots in the sea swung like a pendulum against moon-edged clouds.

At some point the moon itself rolled out from a cloud pocket and the whole mood shifted — sharp shadows slid back and forth across the wood. Somewhere inside me another planet turned; I began to feel slightly sick. I stood up and began weaving from one side of the boat to the other, sweeping the mounds of sand off the platforms. When I came to the fisherman, I reached into the sky above him and produced another cigarette, already lit, from the dark. I felt a fever flushing my forehead and cheeks. I held the cigarette first to his mouth, then to my own, and we each took a puff on it. I held my breath, walked back rather dizzily, and blew a long line of smoke from the bottom to the top of the mast.

Then I touched the cigarette to the paper wedged in up among the invisible branches. A rush of flame shot into the sky. Instantly I felt better — the fever was gone, the turning stopped, the little boat rocked on the waves. I turned to Gedé and nodded. A wide grin broke across his face and he tossed the sand, still cupped in his hands, over his head into the water. We drew anchor, hoisted the sail, and tacked back to the village with Gedé singing gaily at the rudder.

I had to leave the coast the next day to begin work with a healer in the interior, but I promised Gedé I would return in a month or so to check on the results of my impromptu exorcism.

Five weeks later I returned, with mounting trepidation, to the fishing    25
village. I found Gedé waiting for me with open arms. I was introduced to his family, presented with gifts, and stuffed with food. The magic had been successful. The fishing business was thriving, as was apparent from the new gate and the new building Gedé had built to house the family kitchen. After the meal Gedé took me aside to tell me of his new ideas, projects he could accomplish if only he had a little magic help. I backed off gracefully, paid my respects, and left the village, feeling elated and strange.

I am scribbling the last words of this story at a table in the small Vermont nightclub where I have been performing magic this winter. Tonight I was doing mostly card magic, with some handkerchiefs and coin stuff thrown in for good measure. Some hours ago a woman grabbed my arm. "How?" she gasped. "How did you do that?"

"I really don't know," I told her.

I think there's something honest in that.

## EXPLORATIONS

1. What statements in David Abram's essay suggest that he regards his magic as tricks and illusions? What statements suggest that he thinks there is more to it?

2. When Abram agrees to try to remove the spell from Gedé's boat, what are his hopes and expectations? What kinds of tactics does he use?

3. What role is played by descriptive and expository passages about the narrator's Balinese surroundings (see, for instance, paras. 14 and 17)? How would the essay's impact change without such passages?

## CONNECTIONS

1. Abram, like Maya Angelou in "Mary" (p. 415), is forced into an awkward position by the demands of someone else. What tactics does each narrator use to escape? How would each dilemma come out differently if the narrator's tactics were more confrontational?

2. In Fred Moody's comments in *Looking at Ourselves* (p. 407), what factors divide people's work from their nonworking lives? What factors create this division for the fisherman Gedé? How does Gedé's concept of work — and its role in his life — differ from Moody's?

3. In "The Artist's Life in Brussels" (p. 350), Ken Bugul writes of smoking marijuana: "They didn't know that we don't have the same vision of things. The West secularizes everything. In Africa, the plant has ceremonial or therapeutic uses, which are sacred functions." At what points in "Making Magic" does a similar contrast emerge between Western and Indonesian cultures?

# ELABORATIONS

1. "Making Magic" and Christopher Reynolds's "Cultural Journey to Africa" (p. 258) both describe Americans exploring unfamiliar cultures. What similar discoveries emerge in both accounts? Write an argumentative or classification essay about what someone from the United States can learn from spending time in a less technologically oriented country.

2. Many Americans define work as what goes on in their places of employment between 9:00 A.M. and 5:00 P.M. How does this definition differ from the fisherman Gedé's? What elements of each definition appear in Abram's biographical headnote and in "Making Magic"? Write a comparison-contrast or definition essay on the roles a person's work can play in his or her life.

# LE LY HAYSLIP

## *Rice Farming in Vietnam*

As her essay suggests, Le Ly Hayslip was born a fighter. "Rice Farming in Vietnam" comes from her autobiography *When Heaven and Earth Changed Places* (1989), written with Jay Wurtz. Hayslip was betrothed at age thirteen but "ruined" for marriage when Vietcong soldiers raped her. Pregnant, she was exiled from home. In her book *Child of War, Woman of Peace* (1993) she writes: "By age fifteen I had been in battle, captured, tortured by the South Vietnamese Republicans, and had been condemned to death and raped by the Vietcong. By sixteen I was an unwed mother supporting my family on Danang's black market." In 1970, at twenty, she married a much older American who brought her and her two sons to California. He died; she remarried, had another son, and worked as a housekeeper, on a factory assembly line, and in a restaurant to support her family. In 1986, despite a Vietcong death sentence, she returned to Vietnam to see her mother and siblings. The next year she started East Meets West Foundation, a charitable relief and world peace organization. She lives in Los Angeles.

The Socialist Republic of Vietnam was unified by force in 1976, twenty-two years after being divided by a cease-fire agreement. Its recorded history began some 2,000 years ago. Settled by immigrants from China and Indonesia, Vietnam was dominated by China until France began conquering it, part by part, in the mid-1800s. Japan occupied it in the 1940s; nationalist forces rallied under the Communist guerrilla leader Ho Chi Minh. After Japan's defeat in World War II, France and China backed opposing factions and in 1954 split the country in two. Supported by North Vietnamese President Ho Chi Minh, as well as China and the Soviet Union, Vietcong guerrillas kept fighting for a single Communist nation. The United States and other Western countries sent military advisers and then troops to South Vietnam's aid, but domestic opposition ultimately led to withdrawal of U.S. forces. In 1975 North Vietnam won the war.

"Suffocate her!" the midwife told my mother when I came into the world.

I weighed only two pounds and looked just terrible — like a *meo con* kitten. My mother was forty-one when I was conceived, and so was very nervous about her ability to deliver a healthy child and survive. She sang heroic songs to her tight belly, ate sparingly, and worked extra hard during those months so that we both might be as strong as possible. When her bag of water broke, she was working in the fields in the midst of a winter storm. As she ran toward our house, warm fluid streaming down her legs, she cradled her aching belly and called to my father, "Trong — get the midwife!" — which he knew very well to do, having sired two sons and three daughters before me.

As a consequence, I came into the world very small but very tough. My mother answered the midwife, "I will bury her when she stops breathing. Now get out of here."

My mother was born in 1908 in the village of Man Quang on the Thu Bon river. In her prime, she was nearly five feet tall, which is very big for a Vietnamese woman. Her hair was beautiful, long, and black, and whenever she cut it, which was usually once each year, village women would gather around and offer money for the clippings, called *cai chang.* These they sold again to the city wig-makers. Hair-selling was an important way for village women to make money, and my mother's long, healthy hair always fetched the best prices. Just as often, though, my mother would give the clippings to relatives and so keep the product of her body in the family. I used to grab a scrap or two myself — not for wig-money, but because it was so pretty and because it was so rare to see her with her hair down. Hard labor demanded that she always wear it up. . . .

Because villagers shun anything that's odd, my family avoided me as     5 an infant and only my mother would hold me and tend to my needs. They said later it was because they did not want to become attached to anything so unlikely to stay in this world, but I think they secretly hoped I would die and so free my mother to care again for them. Who could blame them for that? After all, I was the youngest, I looked sickly, and I was a girl. Everybody wants sons and brothers, not daughters and sisters. I was just an extra mouth. It took three months of feeding that extra mouth before the baby around it grew to the size of an average newborn. . . .

When I could walk, my sister Lan (who was eight years older than I was) would take me out to play with the other children. Once, we were playing in the dusty street when people began to scream and thunder broke from a sunny sky. The ground shook as in an earthquake and giant snakes with many heads coughed loudly. Although I didn't see them, I knew they were snakes because the villagers shouted that the "devils" were coming back. I knew they had many heads because they coughed so rapidly. I knew they were giants because they were so loud. The snakes' spittle flew into the village and splattered people with blood. When the snake-monsters came, Lan grabbed me under the arms and whisked me into one of the trenches that had been dug by the road. While we lay huddled together like burrowing animals, she sang in my ear:

> French come, French come,
> Cannon shells land, go hide!
> Cannon shells sing,
> Like a song all day!

Despite the terrifying din and dirt walls crumbling around us, she sang it like a happy washing song and it slowed my racing heart. I knew I would be safe as long as she was there.

When things quieted down, we sneaked back out like frightened mice. Sometimes, after other visits, the snakes' keepers would be in the village. The keepers were giant men who smelled bad because they were big and sweaty and often had to crawl through piles of dung. Sometimes they would pick me up, make devily faces and jiggle me, and give me cookies and some dark, sticky sweet water to drink. Some of the strangers were black, but most had white faces with the black men's marks on their cheeks. Because of these fearsome marks, we called them *ma duong rach mac*, or "slash face." They had long noses, round eyes, and wore funny hats. They carried jangly packs on their backs and enough pots and pans and knives and metal fruits on their webbed belts to be mistaken for traveling merchants. They swayed and swaggered when they walked and moved not at all like the villagers, who walked like people. In every way they resembled the demons in our stories. They had long teeth, horns sticking out every which way, faces like horses or boars, and made the noise and fire of dragons. Even the friendly ones made us sick with horror.

When we had more warning that the snake-monster was coming, my mother would pack me into a small bamboo basket (I discovered that I could fit into many small things — a handy talent) and flee with our family: sister Hai, the eldest, who was engaged; sister Ba Xuan, who was four years younger than Hai; brother Bon Nghe, who was my mother's favorite; sister Lan, who took care of me often; and brother Sau Ban, who was nearest to me in age. I was called "Bay" Ly because I was sixth-born, *Bay* meaning "six" — number names made good nicknames when there were only so many given names to go around.

Sometimes we escaped to Danang and stayed with Uncle Nhu, usually    10
with just the clothes on our backs. During the journey we would camp in old bunkers and often had nothing to eat. My mother would hold us and rock us and sing the song of our plight:

> In our village today
> A big battle was fought,
> French kill and arrest the people;
> The fields and villages burn,

The people, they run to the winds:
To the north, to the south,
To Xam Ho, to Ky La.
When they run, they look back;
They see houses in flames.
They cry, Oh, my God —
Our houses are gone —
Where will we lay our heads?
In our village today,
A big battle was fought.
Old ladies and children,
Were sent straight to hell.
Our eyes fill with tears
While we watch and ask God:
Why is the enemy so cruel?

Upon returning we discovered, true to the song, that the snake-monster had breathed on many houses and left them in ashes. Once, even our own home was burned.

On that occasion, we heard the alarm and fled in the middle of the night with no time to take anything. I was especially scared because my father soon left us and I did not see him again until we returned a week later. By then, our house was a smoldering ruin. As I climbed out of my basket, I could still hear the snake-monster snorting and bellowing in the distance. We all cried when we saw the living embers of what used to be our home. My father and mother walked past the foundation and inspected the dikes that marked our land. They seemed relieved that the earth had not been wounded too badly. Magically, my father brought our heirlooms, ancestral shrine, and some of our furniture — including his tools and farm implements — out of the forest. He had stayed behind to save what he could from the devils. Without pausing for sleep, my father and mother began rebuilding our home.

Gradually, I forgot about the snake-monster and its fiery breath. My mother carried me to the fields or I stayed at home and sister Lan looked after me. Although the land remained fertile, farming was often interrupted and the whole village came close to starvation. Sometimes we had to eat banana roots, banana skins, orange peels, or whatever else we could scavenge. My father and brothers caught fish when they could, but angling is not the farmer's art. Sometimes they went into the forest and trapped jungle rats (bigger and healthier than city rats), which my mother would fry like rabbits. But this was rare. As hunters they made better fishermen.

One day when things were really bad, my father brought home some sweet potatoes, which we all knew he had stolen. Our crop had been destroyed, they did not grow wild, and he had no money to buy them. That night, we children filled our bellies while our parents ate animal fodder: pig bran and bamboo shoots. My father hated stealing, but he hated starving his children more. Only when I was older did I realize how much my parents suffered during this time. I made a child's solemn oath to be a dutiful, perfect daughter. I would stay close at hand when I grew up and help them when they were old. I would let nothing prevent me from repaying their love.

My sister Lan took this pledge as well and for a while became my guardian angel. She kept me washed when the other kids went dirty. She sewed my old clothes while my playmates ran around in rags. She kept my hair brushed and beautiful and clean. Because of her attention, I was favored by the *ma duong rach mac* whenever they came to the village. They would be nice to me while they treated the other kids like gnats. It helped me put up with them without showing the terror I really felt.

Twice a year, in May and October, we villagers prepared the land for planting. Because these months followed the winter and summer monsoons, it meant we had a variety of natural (as well as war-made) disasters to repair: from floods and high winds to plagues of grasshoppers and the wearing out of the soil itself.

Although we grew many crops around Ky La — sweet potatoes, peanuts, cinnamon, and taro — the most important by far was rice. Yet for all its long history as the staff of life in our country, rice was a fickle provider. First, the spot of ground on which the rice was thrown had to be just right for the seed to sprout. Then, it had to be protected from birds and animals who needed food as much as we did. As a child, I spent many hours with the other kids in Ky La acting like human scarecrows — making noise and waving our arms — just to keep the raven-like *se-se* birds away from our future supper.

According to legend, god did not mean for us to work so hard for our rice. My father told me the story of *ong trang bu hung*, the spirit messenger who had been entrusted by god to bring rice — the heavenly food — to earth for humans to enjoy. God gave the messenger two magic sacks. "The seeds in the first," god said, "will grow when they touch the ground and give a plentiful harvest, anywhere, with no effort. The seeds in the second sack, however, must be nurtured; but, if tended properly, will give the earth great beauty."

Of course, god meant for the first seeds to be rice, which would feed millions with little effort; and the second to be grass, which humans couldn't eat but would enjoy as a cover for bare ground. Unfortunately, the heavenly messenger got the sacks mixed up, and humans immediately paid for his error: finding that rice was hard to grow whereas grass grew easily everywhere, especially where it wasn't wanted.

When god learned of this mistake, he booted the messenger out of  20 heaven and sent him to earth as a hard-shelled beetle, to crawl on the ground forever lost in the grass to dodge the feet of the people he had so carelessly injured. This harsh karma, however, did nothing to make life easier for farmers.

When the seeds had grown into stalks, we would pull them up — *nho ma* — and replant them in the paddies — the place where the rice matured and our crop eventually would be harvested.

After the hard crust had been turned and the clods broken up with mallets to the size of gravel, we had to wet it down with water conveyed from nearby ponds or rivers. Once the field had been flooded, it was left to soak for several days, after which our buffalo-powered plows could finish the job. In order to accept the seedling rice, however, the ground had to be *bua ruong* — even softer than the richest soil we used to grow vegetables. We knew the texture was right when a handful of watery mud would ooze through our fingers like soup.

Transplanting the rice stalks from their "nursery" to the field was primarily women's work. Although we labored as fast as we could, this chore involved bending over for hours in knee-deep, muddy water. No matter how practiced we were, the constant search for a foothold in the sucking mud made the tedious work exhausting. Still, there was no other way to transplant the seedlings properly; and that sensual contact between our hands and feet, the baby rice, and the wet, receptive earth, is one of the things that preserved and heightened our connection with the land. While we worked, we sometimes sang to break the monotony and raise our spirits. One song my mother taught me went:

> We love the words *hoa binh*;
> *Hoa binh* means peace — first *hoa*, then *binh*:
> *Hoa* means "together" and *binh* means "all the same."
> When we're all together, no one is parted.
> When we're the same, no one's at war.
> Peace means no more suffering,
> *Hoa binh* means no more war.

When the planting was done, the ground had to be watered every other day and, because each parcel had supported our village for centuries, fertilized as well. Unless a family was very wealthy, it could not buy chemicals for this purpose, so we had to shovel manure from the animal pens and carry it in baskets to the fields where we would cast it evenly onto the growing plants. When animals became scarce later in the war, we sometimes had to add human waste collected from the latrines outside the village. And of course, wet, fertile ground breeds weeds and pulling them was the special task of the women and children. The first big weeding was called *lam co lua di,* followed a month later by a second "weeding party" called *lam co lua lai.* The standing water was also home for mosquitoes, leeches, snakes, and freshwater crabs and you were never too sure just what you would come up with in the next handful of weeds. It was backbreaking, unpleasant labor that ran fourteen hours a day for many days.

When the planting was over, we would sit back and turn our attention    25
to the other tasks and rewards of village life: from making clothes and mending tools to finding spouses for eligible children and honoring our ancestors in a variety of rituals.

On the fourteenth of each month (measured on our lunar calendar) and on the thirtieth and thirty-first of the month (*ram mung mot* — when the moon is full) we brought fruit, flour, and the special paper objects such as money, miniature furniture, and clothes — all manufactured for religious purposes — into the house and burned them at our family altar. My father would then bow and pray for the safety of our property and our lives. His main concern was for our health, which he addressed specifically if one of us was sick, but he never ended a prayer without a heartfelt request for the war to stop.

But planting was only part of village life. Like daylight and darkness, wakefulness and sleep, the labors and rituals of harvest defined the other half of our existence.

According to legend, human problems with rice didn't end with the forgetful beetle. When god saw that the mix-up in magic sacks had caused so much trouble on earth, he commanded the rice to "present itself for cooking" by rolling up to each home in a ball. Of course, the rice obeyed god and rolled into the first house it was supposed to serve. But the housewife, unprepared for such a sight, became frightened and hit it with a broom, scattering the rice ball into a thousand pieces. This so angered the rice that it went back outside and shouted, "See if I come back to let you cook me! Now you'll have to come out to the fields and bring me in if you want your supper!"

That was the closest any Vietnamese ever came to a free bowl of rice.

Beginning in March, and again in August, we would bring the mature    30
rice in from the fields and process it for use during the rest of the year. In March, when the ground was dry, we cut the rice very close to the soil — *cat lua* — to keep the plant alive. In August, when the ground

was wet, we cut the plant halfway up — *cat gat* — which made the job much easier.

The separation of stalk and rice was done outside in a special smooth area beside our house. Because the rice was freshly cut, it had to dry in the sun for several days. At this stage, we called it *phoi lua* — not-yet rice. The actual separation was done by our water buffalo, which walked in lazy circles over a heap of cuttings until the rice fell easily from the stalks. We gathered the stalks, tied them in bundles, and used them to fix roofs or to kindle our fires. The good, light-colored rice, called *lua chet*, was separated from the bad, dark-colored rice — *lua lep* — and taken home for further processing. The very best rice, of course, we gave back to Mother Earth. This seed rice was called *lua giong* and we put it into great jars which we filled with water. The wet rice was then packed under a haystack to keep warm. The nutrients, moisture, and heat helped the rice seeds to sprout, and after three days (during which we watered and fertilized the seedbed like a garden), we recovered the jars and cast the fertile *geo ma* seeds onto the ground we had prepared. But this was rice we would enjoy another day. The preparation of rice to eat now was our highest priority.

When the *lua chet* was dry, we stored a portion in the main part of our house, which we called *nha tren*, or top house, because my father slept there and it held our ancestral shrine. This rice was kept in bins behind a bamboo curtain which was also a hiding place for valuables, weapons and supplies, and little kids like me when soldiers came to the village.

In the back part of the house, called *nha duoi*, or lower house (because the mother and children slept there), we had an area of open floor where we would eventually conclude our labor. Once the brown rice grains were out of their shells, we shook them in wide baskets, tossing them slightly into the air so that the wind could carry off the husks. When finished, the rice was now ready to go inside where it became "floor rice" and was pounded in a bowl to crack the layer of bran that contained the sweet white kernel. When we swirled the cracked rice in a woven colander, the bran fell through the holes and was collected to feed the pigs. The broken rice that remained with the good kernels was called *tam* rice, and although it was fit to eat, it was not very good and we used it as chicken feed (when the harvest was good) or collected it and shared it with beggars when the harvest was bad.

We always blamed crop failures on ourselves — we had not worked hard enough, or, if there was no other explanation, we had failed to adequately honor our ancestors. Our solution was to pray more and

sacrifice more and eventually things always got better. Crops ruined by
soldiers were another matter. We knew prayer was useless because soldiers
were human beings, too, and the god of nature meant for them to work
out their own karma just like us.

In any event, the journey from seedling to rice bowl was long and          35
laborious and because each grain was a symbol of life, we never wasted
any of it. Good rice was considered god's gemstone — *hot ngoc troi* —
and was cared for accordingly on pain of divine punishment. Even today
a peasant seeing lightning will crouch under the table and look for lost
grains in order to escape the next bolt. And parents must never strike
children, no matter how naughty they've been, while the child is eating
rice, for that would interrupt the sacred communion between rice-eater
and rice-maker. Like my brothers and sisters, I learned quickly the advantages of chewing my dinner slowly.

When I was old enough to help, I spent every day in the rice fields
with my mother. While we worked, she taught me everything I had to
know about life. In the West, for example, people believe they must
"pursue happiness" as if it were some kind of flighty bird that is always
out of reach. In the East, we believe we are born with happiness and one
of life's important tasks, my mother told me, is to protect it. It seemed
strange to me, then, when the Catholic teachers told us that little babies
were "born in sin" and must spend their lives struggling miserably to
overcome it. How can one be happier than a little baby? They come into
the world with nothing and could not be more pleased about it. How
long must a pious rich man live to be happier than a baby?

Among the other things my mother taught me was how to be a virtuous
wife and dutiful daughter-in-law: how to bring myself to my husband as
a virgin and how to take care of the family I would have one day. I
remember once, when soldiers were in Ky La, my mother and sister mixed
red vegetable dye with water and stained the crotches of their pants. They
said it would make the soldiers think they had their periods and discourage any ideas of rape. Unfortunately, a few soldiers didn't care what stains
were on a woman's pants, but that was every girl's risk in Ky La. My
mother taught me, too, that even when soldiers weren't around, child-
bearing and menstruating women were not as clean as men or old ladies.
We had to use the side doors of temples or churches and wash our
layered, bloodstained underclothes before the sun — which bore on its
face the image of our male god — came up to be offended by our *mau
co toi* — the blood of sin. No wonder they called it the "woman's curse."

I learned from my mother, too, that a good wife needn't care too much
about her husband's wealth provided she protected what wealth he had.
Although we had no mortgage or utility bills, coming up with cash for

necessities (like material for clothes and incense for worshiping our ancestors) or luxuries (like beer for my father) was the wife's responsibility. My mother raised extra produce in her garden and sold our fattest ducks in the market. If she could afford to buy a bit of gold or jewelry, she would bury it immediately in the yard. Whatever she couldn't make, she had to buy, so she became very handy and thrifty. Whatever she bought, she saved, and on more than one occasion, I would learn, her savings meant the difference between life and death. . . .

Traditionally, farm mothers bought gold and jewelry for their children at a tender age so that girls could have a small dowry and boys could buy the tools and livestock they needed to support a family. Marriages were arranged by parents with an eye for the spouses' compatibility, security, and improvement of the family's position in the community. To choose a spouse yourself and marry only for love was considered a terrible folly — in the same category as gambling away an inheritance or accidentally setting fire to your house. This put the relationship between husbands and wives on a business-first basis: that business being survival and the preservation of the family and the link with one's ancestors. Because of this, respect between husband and wife was more common than affection, although it could grow into the kind of devout family love that characterized the strongest couples.

This focus on duty before heart often led village men to mistreat their wives. In fact, wife-beating was so common it was accepted as a necessary way for men to blow off steam and, oddly enough, keep the family together — for we believed the main reason men abandoned their families was because of bad karma: They had lost all hope of living a happy life. Like the extremes single mothers sometimes went to for survival, we accepted wife abuse without condoning it — as an unfortunate but sometimes inescapable part of life, like hard work and disease. Consequently, women seldom left a healthy husband voluntarily; too much was riding on everyone playing his or her part no matter what. If a married woman felt abused, she had only to look at an unmarried cousin or widowed sister to learn what life without a man was like. "Better to sell cheap than not sell at all!" the saying went. If my parents, for example, had wanted me to marry a bad-tempered man, I would have had to accept it — no ifs, ands, or buts. If he beat me, nobody would say anything to him about it, least of all my parents. Everyone would assume it was my fault, because keeping a husband satisfied would have been my primary duty. To run away or go to outside authorities to get a divorce would have been unthinkable — a betrayal not only of my duty to my husband, but to my parents as well. In fact, people who took it upon themselves to violate our most important customs also were expected to turn their backs

40

on their families, just as their families were expected to reject them in turn. Given our peasant society's desire for safety and tradition, such rules made perfect sense to us, no matter how illogical they seemed to outsiders. From the cradle, we Vietnamese had learned to respect all forms of authority: parental, religious, governmental. To fit in, we had to respect the rights of others. Telling us how to observe these rights was the natural role of fathers, priests, and officials, and our duty was to obey them. Because boys had to support a family and fight wars, they were forgiven many mistakes. Because girls received the benefit of their menfolk's labor and sacrifice in battle, they were expected to do nothing wrong. Fair or not, this was the basic contract that bound our village together. Before the Americans came, it seemed to work well enough.

## EXPLORATIONS

1. What is the occupation of the "snakes' keepers" Le Ly Hayslip describes in paragraph 8? What is their nationality? How do you know?

2. What do Hayslip's parents do for a living? What is the children's involvement in their work?

3. In what ways did war affect the lives of Hayslip's family? Cite specific references. Which of these impacts seem to have been intended by the warring sides? Which were unintended?

4. In paragraph 25 Hayslip mentions "the other tasks and rewards of village life" besides work. What part does recreation apparently play in this culture?

## CONNECTIONS

1. In paragraph 23 Hayslip writes: "That sensual contact between our hands and feet, the baby rice, and the wet, receptive earth, is one of the things that preserved and heightened our connection with the land." How does this statement fit with David Abram's comments in "Making Magic" (p. 422) about the role of the land in magic (para. 17)?

2. At what age and for what reasons did Maya Angelou start working in "Mary" (p. 415)? At what age and for what reasons did Hayslip start working? What were her first jobs (paras. 17 and 24)?

3. In what ways are the duties of a Vietnamese wife as described by Hayslip (paras. 37–40) similar to those of an Indian wife as described by Ved Mehta in "Pom's Engagement" (p. 142)? What information can you glean from these essays about the main functions of marriage in each of these cultures?

4. What similar techniques for teaching children are used by the Vietnamese parents in "Rice Farming in Vietnam" and the Quiché parents of Guatemala in Rigoberta Menchú's "Birth Ceremonies" (p. 76)?

## ELABORATIONS

1. "Rice Farming in Vietnam" describes a culture functioning at survival level, where every person has clear responsibilities and every task has a clear purpose. Write an essay comparing and contrasting the nature and role of work in Hayslip's village with that in American culture in general (see, for instance, Fred Moody's and Russell Baker's selections in *Looking at Ourselves*, p. 407 and p. 409), or with the nature and role of work in an American subculture you are familiar with (see, for instance, Linda Hasselstrom's and Larry Bird's selections in *Looking at Ourselves*, pp. 405 and 406).

2. What chores did your parents give you as a child? When you were small, which jobs were you eager to get big enough to do? Which ones did you soon learn to hate? Which did you enjoy? How has your perspective on chores changed in adulthood? Choose one of these aspects of work in your family and write an essay about it.

# EDNA O'BRIEN

## *Sister Imelda*

Ireland's most successful woman writer is Edna O'Brien, author of novels, stories, plays, screenplays, television scripts, poetry, and nonfiction. She was born in 1930 in County Clare in western Ireland, the fifth child of a farming family. Although their village had no library, and her parents mistrusted books, O'Brien loved writing. In 1941 she began studies at the Convent of Mercy in County Galway, where she dreamed of becoming a nun or, better, a saint. Instead she moved to Dublin and got a job as a shop assistant. While taking classes at the Pharmaceutical College, she began writing for a local newspaper. In 1950 she eloped with novelist Ernest Gebler, with whom she had two sons. After nine years of reading manuscripts part-time for a publisher, she wrote her first novel, *The Country Girls* (1960), "in a three-week spasm." That book was banned under Ireland's censorship laws for its candor about women, sex, and religion; so were her next six novels. Elsewhere, however, audiences welcomed her work. Divorced in 1967, O'Brien continued to bring up her sons and to write in London. Her films include *The Girl with Green Eyes* (1963) and *X, Y & Zee* (1972), starring Elizabeth Taylor and Michael Caine. Among her recent novels are *The High Road* (1988) and *Time and Tide* (1992). "Sister Imelda" comes from her short story collection *A Fanatic Heart* (1985).

Eire, or the Republic of Ireland, occupies all of the island west of Great Britain except for six northern counties which are part of the United Kingdom of Great Britain and Northern Ireland (see p. 624). Ireland has been inhabited since the Stone Age. Around the fourth century B.C., Celts from the European mainland established a Gaelic civilization. St. Patrick brought Christianity in A.D. 432, and monasteries became centers of learning comparable to universities. In the twelfth century the Pope gave Ireland to Henry II of England, creating a relationship that persisted even after Henry VIII broke away from the Roman Catholic Church. In 1801 the Act of Union formally established the United Kingdom of Great Britain and Ireland. Nationalist uprisings led to the proclamation of an Irish republic in 1919 and its recognition three years later as the Irish Free State, a dominion of Great Britain. (The six northern counties voted to stay with the United Kingdom; see p. 615.) In 1949 the Republic of Ireland became official and withdrew from the British Commonwealth. Gaelic (or Irish) and English remain its national languages. In 1990 Ireland inaugurated its first woman president, Mary Robinson.

For more background on Ireland, see pages 615 and 624.

Sister Imelda did not take classes on her first day back in the convent but we spotted her in the grounds after the evening Rosary. Excitement and curiosity impelled us to follow her and try to see what she looked like, but she thwarted us by walking with head bent and eyelids down. All we could be certain of was that she was tall and limber and that she prayed while she walked. No looking at nature for her, or no curiosity about seventy boarders in gaberdine coats and black shoes and stockings. We might just as well have been crows, so impervious was she to our stares and to abortive attempts at trying to say "Hello, Sister."

We had returned from our long summer holiday and we were all wretched. The convent, with its high stone wall and green iron gates enfolding us again, seemed more of a prison than ever — for after our spell in the outside world we all felt very much older and more sophisticated, and my friend Baba and I were dreaming of our final escape, which would be in a year. And so, on that damp autumn evening when I saw the chrysanthemums and saw the new nun intent on prayer I pitied her and thought how alone she must be, cut off from her friends and conversation, with only God as her intangible spouse.

The next day she came into our classroom to take geometry. Her pale, slightly long face I saw as formidable, but her eyes were different, being blue-black and full of verve. Her lips were very purple, as if she had put puce pencil on them. They were the lips of a woman who might sing in a cabaret, and unconsciously she had formed the habit of turning them inward, as if she, too, was aware of their provocativeness. She had spent the last four years — the same span that Baba and I had spent in the convent — at the university in Dublin, where she studied languages. We couldn't understand how she had resisted the temptations of the hectic world and willingly come back to this. Her spell in the outside world made her different from the other nuns; there was more bounce in her walk, more excitement in the way she tackled teaching, reminding us that it was the most important thing in the world as she uttered the phrase "Praise be the Incarnate Word." She began each day's class by reading from Cardinal Newman, who was a favorite of hers. She read how God dwelt in light unapproachable, and how with Him there was neither change nor shadow of alteration. It was amazing how her looks changed. Some days, when her eyes were flashing, she looked almost profane and made me wonder what events inside the precincts of the convent caused her to be suddenly so excited. She might have been a girl going to a dance, except for her habit.

"Hasn't she wonderful eyes," I said to Baba. That particular day they were like blackberries, large and soft and shiny.

"Something wrong in her upstairs department," Baba said, and added ⁵
that with makeup Imelda would be a cinch.

"Still, she has a vocation!" I said, and even aired the idiotic view that
I might have one. At certain moments it did seem enticing to become a
nun, to lead a life unspotted by sin, never to have to have babies, and to
wear a ring that singled one out as the Bride of Christ. But there was the
other side to it, the silence, the gravity of it, having to get up two or three
times a night to pray and, above all, never having the opportunity of
leaving the confines of the place except for the funeral of one's parents.
For us boarders it was torture, but for the nuns it was nothing short of
doom. Also, we could complain to each other, and we did, food being
the source of the greatest grumbles. Lunch was either bacon and cabbage
or a peculiar stringy meat followed by tapioca pudding; tea consisted of
bread dolloped with lard and occasionally, as a treat, fairly green rhubarb
jam, which did not have enough sugar. Through the long curtainless
windows we saw the conifer trees and a sky that was scarcely ever without
the promise of rain or a downpour.

She was a right lunatic, then, Baba said, having gone to university for
four years and willingly come back to incarceration, to poverty, chastity,
and obedience. We concocted scenes of agony in some Dublin hostel,
while a boy, or even a young man, stood beneath her bedroom window
throwing up chunks of clay or whistles or a supplication. In our version
of it he was slightly older than her, and possibly a medical student, since
medical students had a knack with women, because of studying diagrams
and skeletons. His advances, like those of a sudden storm, would intermittently rise and overwhelm her, and the memory of these sudden
flaying advances of his would haunt her until she died, and if ever she
contracted fever, these secrets would out. It was also rumored that she
possessed a fierce temper and that, while a postulant, she had hit a girl
so badly with her leather strap that the girl had to be put to bed because
of wounds. Yet another black mark against Sister Imelda was that her
brother Ambrose had been sued by a nurse for breach of promise.

That first morning when she came into our classroom and modestly
introduced herself, I had no idea how terribly she would infiltrate my life,
how in time she would be not just one of those teachers or nuns but
rather a special one, almost like a ghost who passed the boundaries of
common exchange and who crept inside one, devouring so much of one's
thoughts, so much of one's passion, invading the place that was called
one's heart. She talked in a low voice, as if she did not want her words
to go beyond the bounds of the wall, and constantly she stressed the value

of work both to enlarge the mind and to discipline the thought. One of her eyelids was red and swollen, as if she was getting a sty. I reckoned that she overmortified herself by not eating at all. I saw in her some terrible premonition of sacrifice which I would have to emulate. Then, in direct contrast, she absently held the stick of chalk between her first and second fingers, the very same as if it were a cigarette, and Baba whispered to me that she might have been a smoker when in Dublin. Sister Imelda looked down sharply at me and said what was the secret and would I like to share it, since it seemed so comical. I said, "Nothing, Sister, nothing," and her dark eyes exuded such vehemence that I prayed she would never have occasion to punish me.

November came and the tiled walls of the recreation hall oozed moisture and gloom. Most girls had sore throats and were told to suffer this inconvenience to mortify themselves in order to lend a glorious hand in that communion of spirit that linked the living with the dead. It was the month of the Suffering Souls in Purgatory, and as we heard of their twofold agony, the yearning for Christ and the ferocity of the leaping flames that burned and charred their poor limbs, we were asked to make acts of mortification. Some girls gave up jam or sweets and some gave up talking, and so in recreation time they were like dummies making signs with thumb and finger to merely say "How are you?" Baba said that saner people were locked in the lunatic asylum, which was only a mile away. We saw them in the grounds, pacing back and forth, with their mouths agape and dribble coming out of them, like melting icicles. Among our many fears was that one of those lunatics would break out and head straight for the convent and assault some of the girls.

Yet in the thick of all these dreads I found myself becoming dreadfully    10
happy. I had met Sister Imelda outside of class a few times and I felt that there was an attachment between us. Once it was in the grounds, when she did a reckless thing. She broke off a chrysanthemum and offered it to me to smell. It had no smell, or at least only something faint that suggested autumn, and feeling this to be the case herself, she said it was not a gardenia, was it? Another time we met in the chapel porch, and as she drew her shawl more tightly around her body, I felt how human she was, and prey to the cold.

In the classroom things were not so congenial between us. Geometry was my worst subject, indeed, a total mystery to me. She had not taught more than four classes when she realized this and threw a duster at me in a rage. A few girls gasped as she asked me to stand up and make a spectacle of myself. Her face had reddened, and presently she took out her handkerchief and patted the eye which was red and swollen. I not only felt a fool but felt in imminent danger of sneezing as I inhaled the smell of chalk that had fallen onto my gym frock. Suddenly she fled from the room, leaving us ten minutes free until the next class. Some girls said it was a disgrace, said I should write home and say I had been assaulted. Others welcomed the few minutes in which to gabble. All I wanted was to run after her and say that I was sorry to have caused her such distemper, because I knew dimly that it was as much to do with liking as it was with dislike. In me then there came a sort of speechless tenderness for her, and I might have known that I was stirred.

"We could get her defrocked," Baba said, and elbowed me in God's name to sit down.

That evening at Benediction I had the most overwhelming surprise. It was a particularly happy evening, with the choir nuns in full soaring form and the rows of candles like so many little ladders to the golden chalice that glittered all the more because of the beams of fitful flame. I was full of tears when I discovered a new holy picture had been put in my prayer book, and before I dared look on the back to see who had given it to me, I felt and guessed that this was no ordinary picture from an ordinary girl-friend, that this was a talisman and a peace offering from Sister Imelda. It was a pale-blue picture, so pale that it was almost gray, like the down of a pigeon, and it showed a mother looking down on the infant child. On the back, in her beautiful ornate handwriting, she had written a verse:

> Trust Him when dark doubts assail thee,
> Trust Him when thy faith is small,
> Trust Him when to simply trust Him
> Seems the hardest thing of all.

This was her atonement. To think that she had located the compartment in the chapel where I kept my prayer book and to think that she had been so naked as to write in it and give me a chance to boast about it and to show it to other girls. When I thanked her next day, she bowed but did not speak. Mostly the nuns were on silence and only permitted to talk during class.

In no time I had received another present, a little miniature prayer book with a leather cover and gold edging. The prayers were in French and the lettering so minute it was as if a tiny insect had fashioned them. Soon I was publicly known as her pet. I opened the doors for her, raised the blackboard two pegs higher (she was taller than other nuns), and handed out the exercise books which she had corrected. Now in the margins of my geometry propositions I would find "Good" or "Excellent," when in the past she used to splash "Disgraceful." Baba said it was foul to be a nun's pet and that any girl who sucked up to a nun could not be trusted.

About a month later Sister Imelda asked me to carry her books up four 15 flights of stairs to the cookery kitchen. She taught cookery to a junior class. As she walked ahead of me, I thought how supple she was and how thoroughbred, and when she paused on the landing to look out through the long curtainless window, I too paused. Down below, two women in suede boots were chatting and smoking as they moved along the street with shopping baskets. Nearby a lay nun was on her knees scrubbing the granite steps, and the cold air was full of the raw smell of Jeyes Fluid. There was a potted plant on the landing, and Sister Imelda put her fingers in the earth and went "Tch tch tch," saying it needed water. I said I would water it later on. I was happy in my prison then, happy to be near her, happy to walk behind her as she twirled her beads and bowed to the servile nun. I no longer cried for my mother, no longer counted the days on a pocket calendar until the Christmas holidays.

"Come back at five," she said as she stood on the threshold of the cookery kitchen door. The girls, all in white overalls, were arranged around the long wooden table waiting for her. It was as if every girl was in love with her. Because, as she entered, their faces broke into smiles, and in different tones of audacity they said her name. She must have liked cookery class, because she beamed and called to someone, anyone, to get up a blazing fire. Then she went across to the cast-iron stove and spat on it to test its temperature. It was hot, because her spit rose up and sizzled.

When I got back later, she was sitting on the edge of the table swaying her legs. There was something reckless about her pose, something defiant. It seemed as if any minute she would take out a cigarette case, snap it open, and then archly offer me one. The wonderful smell of baking made me realize how hungry I was, but far more so, it brought back to me my own home, my mother testing orange cakes with a knitting needle and letting me lick the line of half-baked dough down the length of the needle. I wondered if she had supplanted my mother, and I hoped not, because I had aimed to outstep my original world and take my place in a new and hallowed one.

"I bet you have a sweet tooth," she said, and then she got up, crossed the kitchen, and from under a wonderful shining silver cloche she produced two jam tarts with a crisscross design on them where the pastry was latticed over the dark jam. They were still warm.

"What will I do with them?" I asked

"Eat them, you goose," she said, and she watched me eat as if she 20 herself derived some peculiar pleasure from it, whereas I was embarrassed about the pastry crumbling and the bits of blackberry jam staining my lips. She was amused. It was one of the most awkward yet thrilling moments I had lived, and inherent in the pleasure was the terrible sense of danger. Had we been caught, she, no doubt, would have had to make massive sacrifice. I looked at her and thought how peerless and how brave, and I wondered if she felt hungry. She had a white overall over her black habit and this made her warmer and freer, and caused me to think of the happiness that would be ours, the laissez-faire if we were away from the convent in an ordinary kitchen doing something easy and customary. But we weren't. It was clear to me then that my version of pleasure was inextricable from pain, that they existed side by side and were interdependent, like the two forces of an electric current.

"Had you a friend when you were in Dublin at university?" I asked daringly.

"I shared a desk with a sister from Howth and stayed in the same hostel," she said.

But what about boys? I thought, and what of your life now and do you long to go out into the world? But could not say it.

We knew something about the nuns' routine. It was rumored that they wore itchy wool underwear, ate dry bread for breakfast, rarely had meat, cakes, or dainties, kept certain hours of strict silence with each other, as well as constant vigil on their thoughts; so that if their minds wandered to the subject of food or pleasure, they would quickly revert to thoughts of God and their eternal souls. They slept on hard beds with no sheets and hairy blankets. At four o'clock in the morning while we slept, each nun got out of bed, in her habit — which was also her death habit — and chanting, they all flocked down the wooden stairs like ravens, to fling themselves on the tiled floor of the chapel. Each nun — even the Mother Superior — flung herself in total submission, saying prayers in Latin and offering up the moment to God. Then silently back to their cells for one more hour of rest. It was not difficult to imagine Sister Imelda face downward, arms outstretched, prostrate on the tiled floor. I often heard their chanting when I wakened suddenly from a nightmare, because, although we slept in a different building, both adjoined, and if one wakened one often heard that monotonous Latin chanting, long before the birds began, long before our own bell summoned us to rise at six.

"Do you eat nice food?" I asked.                                                                         25

"Of course," she said, and smiled. She sometimes broke into an eager smile, which she did much to conceal.

"Have you ever thought of what you will be?" she asked.

I shook my head. My design changed from day to day.

She looked at her man's silver pocket watch, closed the damper of the range, and prepared to leave. She checked that all the wall cupboards were locked by running her hand over them.

"Sister," I called, gathering enough courage at last — we must have some secret, something to join us together — "what color hair have you?" 30

We never saw the nuns' hair, or their eyebrows, or ears, as all that part was covered by a stiff white wimple.

"You shouldn't ask such a thing," she said, getting pink in the face, and then she turned back and whispered, "I'll tell you on your last day here, provided your geometry has improved."

She had scarcely gone when Baba, who had been lurking behind some pillar, stuck her head in the door and said, "Christsake, save me a bit." She finished the second pastry, then went around looking in kitchen drawers. Because of everything being locked, she found only some castor sugar in a china shaker. She ate a little and threw the remainder into the dying fire, so that it flared up for a minute with a yellow spluttering flame. Baba showed her jealousy by putting it around the school that I was in the cookery kitchen every evening, gorging cakes with Sister Imelda and telling tales.

I did not speak to Sister Imelda again in private until the evening of our Christmas theatricals. She came to help us put on makeup and get into our stage clothes and fancy headgear. These clothes were kept in a trunk from one year to the next, and though sumptuous and strewn with braiding and gold, they smelled of camphor. Yet as we donned them we felt different, and as we sponged pancake makeup onto our faces, we became saucy and emphasized these new guises by adding dark pencil to the eyes and making the lips bright carmine. There was only one tube of lipstick and each girl clamored for it. The evening's entertainment was to comprise scenes from Shakespeare and laughing sketches. I had been chosen to recite Mark Antony's lament over Caesar's body, and for this I was to wear a purple toga, white knee-length socks, and patent buckle shoes. The shoes were too big and I moved in them as if in clogs. She said to take them off, to go barefoot. I realized that I was getting nervous and that in an effort to memorize my speech, the words were getting all askew and flying about in my head, like the separate pieces of a jigsaw puzzle. She sensed my panic and very slowly put her hand on my face and enjoined me to look at her. I looked into her eyes, which seemed fathomless, and saw that she was willing me to be calm and obliging me to be master of my fears, and I little knew that one day she would have to do the same as regards the swoop of my feelings for her. As we continued to stare I felt myself becoming calm and the words were restored to me in their right and fluent order. The lights were being lowered out in the recreation hall, and we knew now that all the nuns had arrived, had settled themselves down, and were eagerly awaiting this annual hotchpotch of amateur entertainment. There was that fearsome hush as the hall went dark and the few spotlights were turned on. She kissed her crucifix and I realized that she was saying a prayer for me. Then she raised her arm as if depicting the stance of a Greek goddess; walking onto the stage, I was fired by her ardor.

Baba could say that I bawled like a bloody bull, but Sister Imelda, who    35 stood in the wings, said that temporarily she had felt the streets of Rome, had seen the corpse of Caesar, as I delivered those poignant, distempered lines. When I came off stage she put her arms around me and I was encased in a shower of silent kisses. After we had taken down the decorations and put the fancy clothes back in the trunk, I gave her two half-pound boxes of chocolates — bought for me illicitly by one of the day girls — and she gave me a casket made from the insides of match boxes and covered over with gilt paint and gold dust. It was like holding moths and finding their powder adhering to the fingers.

"What will you do on Christmas Day, Sister?" I said.

"I'll pray for you," she said.

It was useless to say, "Will you have turkey?" or "Will you have plum pudding?" or "Will you loll in bed?" because I believed that Christmas Day would be as bleak and deprived as any other day in her life. Yet she was radiant as if such austerity was joyful. Maybe she was basking in some secret realization involving her and me.


On the cold snowy afternoon three weeks later when we returned from our holidays, Sister Imelda came up to the dormitory to welcome me back. All the other girls had gone down to the recreation hall to do barn dances and I could hear someone banging on the piano. I did not want to go down and clump around with sixty other girls, having nothing to look forward to, only tea and the Rosary and early bed. The beds were damp after our stay at home, and when I put my hand between the sheets, it was like feeling dew but did not have the freshness of outdoors. What depressed me further was that I had seen a mouse in one of the cupboards, seen its tail curl with terror as it slipped away into a crevice. If there was one mouse, there were God knows how many, and the cakes we hid in secret would not be safe. I was still unpacking as she came down the narrow passage between the rows of iron beds and I saw in her walk such agitation.

"Tut, tut, tut, you've curled your hair," she said, offended.                    40

Yes, the world outside was somehow declared in this perm, and for a second I remembered the scalding pain as the trickles of ammonia dribbled down my forehead and then the joy as the hairdresser said that she would make me look like Movita, a Mexican star. Now suddenly that world and those aspirations seemed trite and I wanted to take a brush and straighten my hair and revert to the dark gawky somber girl that I had been. I offered her iced queen cakes that my mother had made, but she refused them and said she could only stay a second. She lent me a notebook of hers, which she had had as a pupil, and into which she had copied favorite quotations, some religious, some not. I read at random:

> Twice or thrice had I loved thee,
> Before I knew thy face or name.
> So in a voice, so in a shapeless flame,
> Angels affect us oft . . .

"Are you well?" I asked.

She looked pale. It may have been the day, which was wretched and gray with sleet, or it may have been the white bedspreads, but she appeared to be ailing.

"I missed you," she said.

"Me too," I said.                                                                45

At home, gorging, eating trifle at all hours, even for breakfast, having little ratafias to dip in cups of tea, fitting on new shoes and silk stockings, I wished that she could be with us, enjoying the fire and the freedom.

"You know it is not proper for us to be so friendly."

"It's not wrong," I said.

I dreaded that she might decide to turn away from me, that she might stamp on our love and might suddenly draw a curtain over it, a black crepe curtain that would denote its death. I dreaded it and knew it was going to happen.

"We must not become attached," she said, and I could not say we    50 already were, no more than I could remind her of the day of the revels and the intimacy between us. Convents were dungeons and no doubt about it.

From then on she treated me as less of a favorite. She said my name sharply in class, and once she said if I must cough, could I wait until class had finished. Baba was delighted, as were the other girls, because they were glad to see me receding in her eyes. Yet I knew that the crispness was part of her love, because no matter how callously she looked at me, she would occasionally soften. Reading her notebook helped me, and I copied out her quotations into my own book, trying as accurately as possible to imitate her handwriting.

But some little time later when she came to supervise our study one evening, I got a smile from her as she sat on the rostrum looking down at us all. I continued to look up at her and by slight frowning indicated that I had a problem with my geometry. She beckoned to me lightly and I went up, bringing my copybook and the pen. Standing close to her, and also because her wimple was crooked, I saw one of her eyebrows for the first time. She saw that I noticed it and said did that satisfy my curiosity. I said not really. She said what else did I want to see, her swan's neck perhaps, and I went scarlet. I was amazed that she would say such a thing in the hearing of other girls, and then she said a worse thing, she said that G. K. Chesterton was very forgetful and had once put on his trousers backward. She expected me to laugh. I was so close to her that a rumble in her stomach seemed to be taking place in my own, and about this she also laughed. It occurred to me for one terrible moment that maybe she had decided to leave the convent, to jump over the wall. Having done the theorem for me, she marked it "100 out of 100" and then asked if I had any other problems. My eyes filled with tears, I wanted her to realize that her recent coolness had wrought havoc with my nerves and my peace of mind.

"What is it?" she said.

I could cry, or I could tremble to try to convey the emotion, but I could not tell her. As if on cue, the Mother Superior came in and saw this glaring intimacy and frowned as she approached the rostrum.

"Would you please go back to your desk," she said, "and in future kindly allow Sister Imelda to get on with her duties."

I tiptoed back and sat with head down, bursting with fear and shame. Then she looked at a tray on which the milk cups were laid, and finding one cup of milk untouched, she asked which girl had not drunk her milk.

"Me, Sister," I said, and I was called up to drink it and stand under the clock as a punishment. The milk was tepid and dusty, and I thought of cows on the fairs days at home and the farmers hitting them as they slid and slithered over the muddy streets.

For weeks I tried to see my nun in private; I even lurked outside doors where I knew she was due, only to be rebuffed again and again. I suspected the Mother Superior had warned her against making a favorite of me. But I still clung to a belief that a bond existed between us and that her coldness and even some glares which I had received, were a charade, a mask. I would wonder how she felt alone in bed and what way she slept and if she thought of me, or refusing to think of me, if she dreamed of me as I did of her. She certainly got thinner, because her nun's silver ring slipped easily and sometimes unavoidably off her marriage finger. It occurred to me that she was having a nervous breakdown.

One day in March the sun came out, the radiators were turned off, and, though there was a lashing wind, we were told that officially spring had arrived and that we could play games. We all trooped up to the games field and, to our surprise, saw that Sister Imelda was officiating that day. The daffodils in the field tossed and turned; they were a very bright shocking yellow, but they were not as fetching as the little timid snowdrops that trembled in the wind. We played rounders, and when my turn came to hit the ball with the long wooden pound, I crumbled and missed, fearing that the ball would hit me.

"Champ . . ." said Baba, jeering.                                                          60

After three such failures Sister Imelda said that if I liked I could sit and watch, and when I was sitting in the greenhouse swallowing my shame, she came in and said that I must not give way to tears, because humiliation was the greatest test of Christ's love, or indeed *any* love.

"When you are a nun you will know that," she said, and instantly I made up my mind that I would be a nun and that though we might never be free to express our feelings, we would be under the same roof, in the same cloister, in mental and spiritual conjunction all our lives.

"Is it very hard at first?" I said.

"It's awful," she said, and she slipped a little medal into my gym-frock pocket. It was warm from being in her pocket, and as I held it, I knew that once again we were near and that in fact we had never severed. Walking down from the playing field to our Sunday lunch of mutton and cabbage, everyone chattered to Sister Imelda. The girls milled around her, linking her, trying to hold her hand, counting the various keys on her bunch of keys, and asking impudent questions.

"Sister, did you ever ride a motorbicycle?"                                              65

"Sister, did you ever wear seamless stockings?"

"Sister, who's your favorite film star — male?"

"Sister, what's your favorite food?"

"Sister, if you had a wish, what would it be?"

"Sister, what do you do when you want to scratch your head?"                          70

Yes, she had ridden a motorbicycle, and she had worn silk stockings, but they were seamed. She liked bananas best, and if she had a wish, it would be to go home for a few hours to see her parents and her brother.

That afternoon as we walked through the town, the sight of closed shops with porter barrels outside and mongrel dogs did not dispel my refound ecstasy. The medal was in my pocket, and every other second I would touch it for confirmation. Baba saw a Swiss roll in a confectioner's window laid on a doily and dusted with castor sugar, and it made her cry out with hunger and rail against being in a bloody reformatory, surrounded by drips and mopes. On impulse she took her nail file out of her pocket and dashed across to the window to see if she could cut the glass. The prefect rushed up from the back of the line and asked Baba if she wanted to be locked up.

"I am anyhow," Baba said, and sawed at one of her nails, to maintain her independence and vent her spleen. Baba was the only girl who could stand up to a prefect. When she felt like it, she dropped out of a walk, sat on a stone wall, and waited until we all came back. She said that if there was one thing more boring than studying it was walking. She used to roll down her stockings and examine her calves and say that she could see varicose veins coming from this bloody daily walk. Her legs, like all our legs, were black from the dye of the stockings; we were forbidden to bathe, because baths were immoral. We washed each night in an enamel basin beside our beds. When girls splashed cold water onto their chests, they let out cries, though this was forbidden.

After the walk we wrote home. We were allowed to write home once a week; our letters were always censored. I told my mother that I had made up my mind to be a nun, and asked if she could send me bananas when a batch arrived at our local grocery shop. That evening, perhaps as I wrote to my mother on the ruled white paper, a telegram arrived which said that Sister Imelda's brother had been killed in a van while on his way home from a hurling match. The Mother Superior announced it, and asked us to pray for his soul and write letters of sympathy to Sister Imelda's parents. We all wrote identical letters, because in our first year at school we had been given specimen letters for various occasions, and we all referred back to our specimen letter of sympathy.

Next day the town hire-car drove up to the convent, and Sister Imelda,    75
accompanied by another nun, went home for the funeral. She looked as white as a sheet, with eyes swollen, and she wore a heavy knitted shawl over her shoulders. Although she came back that night (I stayed awake to hear the car), we did not see her for a whole week, except to catch a glimpse of her back, in the chapel. When she resumed class, she was peaky and distant, making no reference at all to her recent tragedy.

The day the bananas came I waited outside the door and gave her a bunch wrapped in tissue paper. Some were still a little green, and she said that Mother Superior would put them in the glasshouse to ripen. I felt that Sister Imelda would never taste them; they would be kept for a visiting priest or bishop.

"Oh, Sister, I'm sorry about your brother," I said in a burst.

"It will come to us all, sooner or later," Sister Imelda said dolefully.

I dared to touch her wrist to communicate my sadness. She went quickly, probably for fear of breaking down. At times she grew irritable and had a boil on her cheek. She missed some classes and was replaced in the cookery kitchen by a younger nun. She asked me to pray for her brother's soul and to avoid seeing her alone. Each time as she came down a corridor toward me, I was obliged to turn the other way. Now Baba or some other girl moved the blackboard two pegs higher and spread her shawl, when wet, over the radiator to dry.

I got flu and was put to bed. Sickness took the same bleak course, a         80
cup of hot senna delivered in person by the head nun, who stood there while I drank it, tea at lunchtime with thin slices of brown bread (because it was just after the war, food was still rationed, so the butter was mixed with lard and had white streaks running through it and a faintly rancid smell), hours of just lying there surveying the empty dormitory, the empty iron beds with white counterpanes on each one, and metal crucifixes laid on each white, frilled pillow slip. I knew that she would miss me and hoped that Baba would tell her where I was. I counted the number of tiles from the ceiling to the head of my bed, thought of my mother at home on the farm mixing hen food, thought of my father, losing his temper perhaps and stamping on the kitchen floor with nailed boots, and I recalled the money owing for my school fees and hoped that Sister Imelda would never get to hear of it. During the Christmas holiday I had seen a bill sent by the head nun to my father which said, "Please remit this week without fail." I hated being in bed causing extra trouble and therefore reminding the head nun of the unpaid liability. We had no clock in the dormitory, so there was no way of guessing the time, but the hours dragged.

Marigold, one of the maids, came to take off the counterpanes at five and brought with her two gifts from Sister Imelda — an orange and a pencil sharpener. I kept the orange peel in my hand, smelling it, and planning how I would thank her. Thinking of her I fell into a feverish sleep and was wakened when the girls came to bed at ten and switched on the various ceiling lights.

At Easter Sister Imelda warned me not to give her chocolates, so I got her a flashlamp instead and spare batteries. Pleased with such a useful gift (perhaps she read her letters in bed), she put her arms around me and allowed one cheek to adhere but not to make the sound of a kiss. It made up for the seven weeks of withdrawal, and as I drove down the convent drive with Baba, she waved to me, as she had promised, from the window of her cell.

In the last term at school, studying was intensive because of the examinations which loomed at the end of June. Like all the other nuns, Sister Imelda thought only of these examinations. She crammed us with knowledge, lost her temper every other day, and gritted her teeth whenever the blackboard was too greasy to take the imprint of the chalk. If ever I met her in the corridor, she asked if I knew such and such a thing, and coming down from Sunday games, she went over various questions with us. The fateful examination day arrived and we sat at single desks supervised by some strange woman from Dublin. Opening a locked trunk, she took out the pink examination papers and distributed them around. Geometry was on the fourth day. When we came out from it, Sister Imelda was in the hall with all the answers, so that we could compare our answers with hers. Then she called me aside and we went up toward the cookery kitchen and sat on the stairs while she went over the paper with me, question for question. I knew that I had three right and two wrong, but did not tell her so.

"It is black," she said then, rather suddenly. I thought she meant the dark light where we were sitting.

"It's cool, though," I said.                                                          85

Summer had come; our white skins baked under the heavy uniform, and dark violet pansies bloomed in the convent grounds. She looked well again, and her pale skin was once more unblemished.

"My hair," she whispered, "is black." And she told me how she had spent her last night before entering the convent. She had gone cycling with a boy and ridden for miles, and they'd lost their way up a mountain, and she became afraid she would be so late home that she would sleep it out the next morning. It was understood between us that I was going to enter the convent in September and that I could have a last fling, too.

Two days later we prepared to go home. There were farewells and outlandish promises, and autograph books signed, and girls trudging up the recreation hall, their cases bursting open with clothes and books. Baba scattered biscuit crumbs in the dormitory for the mice and stuffed all her prayer books under a mattress. Her father promised to collect us at four. I had arranged with Sister Imelda secretly that I would meet her in one of the summerhouses around the walks, where we would spend our last half hour together. I expected that she would tell me something of what my life as a postulant would be like. But Baba's father came an hour early. He had something urgent to do later and came at three instead. All I could do was ask Marigold to take a note to Sister Imelda.

> Remembrance is all I ask,
> But if remembrance should prove a task,
> Forget me.

I hated Baba, hated her busy father, hated the thought of my mother standing in the doorway in her good dress, welcoming me home at last. I would have become a nun that minute if I could.

I wrote to my nun that night and again the next day and then every week for a month. Her letters were censored, so I tried to convey my feelings indirectly. In one of her letters to me (they were allowed one letter a month) she said that she looked forward to seeing me in September. But by September Baba and I had left for the university in Dublin. I stopped writing to Sister Imelda then, reluctant to tell her that I no longer wished to be a nun.

In Dublin we enrolled at the college where she had surpassed herself. I saw her maiden name on a list, for having graduated with special honors, and for days was again sad and remorseful. I rushed out and bought batteries for the flashlamp I'd given her, and posted them without any note enclosed. No mention of my missing vocation, no mention of why I had stopped writing.

One Sunday about two years later, Baba and I were going out to Howth on a bus. Baba had met some businessmen who played golf there and she had done a lot of scheming to get us invited out. The bus was packed, mostly mothers with babies and children on their way to Dollymount Strand. We drove along the coast road and saw the sea, bright green and glinting in the sun, and because of the way the water was carved up into millions of little wavelets, its surface seemed like an endless heap of dark-green broken bottles. Near the shore the sand looked warm and was biscuit-colored. We never swam or sunbathed, we never did anything that was good for us. Life was geared to work and to meeting men, and yet one knew that mating could only lead to one's being a mother and hawking obstreperous children out to the seaside on Sunday. "They know not what they do" could surely be said of us.

We were very made up; even the conductor seemed to disapprove and snapped at having to give change of ten shillings. For no reason at all I thought of our makeup rituals before the school play and how innocent it was in comparison, because now our skins were smothered beneath layers of it and we never took it off at night. Thinking of the convent, I suddenly thought of Sister Imelda, and then, as if prey to a dream, I heard the rustle of serge, smelled the Jeyes Fluid and the boiled cabbage, and saw her pale shocked face in the months after her brother died. Then I looked around and saw her in earnest, and at first thought I was imagining things. But no, she had got on accompanied by another nun and they were settling themselves in the back seat nearest the door. She looked older, but she had the same aloof quality and the same eyes, and my heart began to race with a mixture of excitement and dread. At first it raced with a prodigal strength, and then it began to falter and I thought it was going to give out. My fear of her and my love came back in one fell realization. I would have gone through the window except that it was not wide enough. The thing was how to escape her. Baba gurgled with delight, stood up, and in the most flagrant way looked around to make sure it was Imelda. She recognized the other nun as one with the nickname of Johnny who taught piano lessons. Baba's first thought was revenge, as she enumerated the punishments they had meted out to us and said how nice it would be to go back and shock them and say, "Mud in your eye, Sisters," or "Get lost," or something worse. Baba could not understand why I was quaking, no more than she could understand why I began to wipe off the lipstick. Above all, I knew that I could not confront them.

"You're going to have to," Baba said.

"I can't," I said.                                                                                  95

It was not just my attire; it was the fact of my never having written and of my broken promise. Baba kept looking back and said they weren't saying a word and that children were gawking at them. It wasn't often that nuns traveled in buses, and we speculated as to where they might be going.

"They might be off to meet two fellows," Baba said, and visualized them in the golf club getting blotto and hoisting up their skirts. For me it was no laughing matter. She came up with a strategy: It was that as we approached our stop and the bus was still moving, I was to jump up and go down the aisle and pass them without even looking. She said most likely they would not notice us, as their eyes were lowered and they seemed to be praying.

"I can't run down the bus," I said. There was a matter of shaking limbs and already a terrible vertigo.

"You're going to," Baba said, and though insisting that I couldn't, I had already begun to rehearse an apology. While doing this, I kept blessing myself over and over again, and Baba kept reminding me that there was only one more stop before ours. When the dreadful moment came, I jumped up and put on my face what can only be called an apology of a smile. I followed Baba to the rear of the bus. But already they had gone. I saw the back of their two sable, identical figures with their veils being blown wildly about in the wind. They looked so cold and lost as they hurried along the pavement and I wanted to run after them. In some way I felt worse than if I had confronted them. I cannot be certain what I would have said. I knew that there is something sad and faintly distasteful about love's ending, particularly love that has never been fully realized. I might have hinted at that, but I doubt it. In our deepest moments we say the most inadequate things.

## EXPLORATIONS

1. What has Sister Imelda had to give up to be a nun? What are the rewards of her job?

2. At what points in her story does Edna O'Brien allude to what is going to happen? What is the effect of these hints?

3. What is the nature of Sister Imelda's power over the narrator and other students? What is dangerous about her power? How would the story's impact be different if the job description of its central character called for ambition and competitiveness instead of poverty, humility, and obedience?

4. Find at least four comments by the narrator's friend Baba during her year at the convent school. What is their tone? What are this character's functions in the story?

## CONNECTIONS

1. "Sister Imelda," like "Rice Farming in Vietnam" (p. 432), depicts a spartan way of life. Why do the characters in each account have few, if any, luxuries? How do they respond to their economic and social restrictions? Which restrictions would be hardest for you to put up with?

2. Being a nun entails different values from, say, being a banker. Which writers in *Looking at Ourselves* share some of Sister Imelda's values, and what values do they share? Which writers have dramatically different values from Sister Imelda?

3. On one level "Sister Imelda" is a love story, like Leslie Marmon Silko's "Yellow Woman" (p. 321). In each of these stories, what dreams, ideals, or wishes of the narrator are represented by the character she falls in love with? What vision of life does she choose instead, and why?

# ELABORATIONS

1. Imagine you are the Mother Superior at Sister Imelda's convent. Write a job description for a teacher coming in, as Sister Imelda did, from an urban university. Include the background the applicant should have, the requirements of the position, its perquisites, and other relevant information.

2. What aspects of "Sister Imelda" remind you of your own life? Write an essay about a person (such as a teacher) who inspired and encouraged you, or about a place where you have spent time (such as a summer camp) that you hated.

# PRIMO LEVI

## *Uranium*

Primo Levi is renowned for his novels, memoirs, and poetry; he also worked for much of his life as a chemist. Levi was born in Turin, Italy, in 1919. He was living in the same apartment when he died from a fall (apparently a suicide attempt) in 1987. An Italian Jew, he graduated summa cum laude from the University of Turin despite the Fascist dictator Mussolini's 1938 laws barring Jews from such institutions. Levi found a job with difficulty, and after Mussolini fell in 1943, he joined a guerrilla band in the mountains to resist the Nazi occupation of Italy. They were betrayed; Levi was captured and sent to the Auschwitz concentration camp (see p. 264). His physical toughness got him assigned to slave labor at a rubber factory instead of the gas chamber. Later his training in chemistry spurred a transfer to the factory's laboratory, where he fell sick and could not be evacuated with the other prisoners (most of whom died) when the Nazis fled a Russian liberating force. Back in Turin, Levi wrote down his memories of the camps with a scientist's objectivity. The result was his acclaimed first book, *Se questo e un uomo* (1947; *If This Is a Man*, 1959, also titled *Survival in Auschwitz*). Levi went back to work in chemistry and continued to write about Auschwitz, the Holocaust, and related issues. "Uranium" comes from his book of autobiographical sketches *Il sistema periodico* (1975; *The Periodic Table*, 1984). In 1977 he left his job; over the next decade he grew pessimistic and weary as his nightmare from Auschwitz seemed to come true: People refused to hear or think about the Jews' enormous suffering and loss during World War II.

The history of Italy, too, has been turbulent. Fragmented when the Roman Empire declined, it was reunited by the French emperor Napoleon, who declared himself King of Italy in 1805. After his fall, Austria moved in. In the 1830s, Giuseppe Mazzini organized a nationalist movement that was carried on by the Count di Cavour and then Giuseppe Garibaldi. King Victor Emmanuel II of Sardinia became king of a united Italy in 1861. After World War I, however, Benito Mussolini (*Il Duce*, "the leader") organized the Fascist Party, took the title of premier, and led a dictatorship which conquered Ethiopia and allied with Germany's new dictator, Adolf Hitler (see p. 264). Mussolini was overthrown during the war and executed afterward. A brief return to monarchy ended with voters opting for democracy. Postwar governments have been short-lived: Italy has had over fifty of them.

For more information on Italy, see page 337.

One cannot employ just anyone to do the work of customer service [CS]. It is a delicate and complex job, not much different from that of diplomats: To perform it with success you must infuse faith in the customers, and therefore it is indispensable to have faith in yourself and in the products you sell; it is therefore a salutary activity, which helps you to know yourself and strengthens your character. It is perhaps the most hygienic of the specialities that constitute the decathlon of the factory chemist: the speciality that best trains him in eloquence and improvisation, prompt reflexes, and the ability to understand and make yourself understood; besides, you get a chance to travel about Italy and the world, and it brings you into contact with all sorts of people. I must also mention another peculiar and beneficent consequence of CS: By pretending to esteem and like your fellow men, after a few years in this trade you wind up really doing so, just as someone who feigns madness for a long time actually becomes crazy.

In the majority of cases, at the first contact you have to acquire or conquer a position superior to that of your interlocutor; but conquer it quietly, graciously, without frightening him or pulling rank. He must feel you are superior, but just a little: reachable, comprehensible. Never, but never, for instance, talk chemistry with a nonchemist: This is the ABC of the trade. But the opposite danger is much more serious, that the customer outranks you: And this can easily happen, because he plays at home, that is, he puts the products you're selling him to practical use, and so he knows their virtues and defects as a wife knows her husband's, while usually you have only a painless, disinterested, often optimistic knowledge of them, acquired in the lab or during their production. The most favorable constellation is that in which you can present yourself as a benefactor, in whatever way: by convincing him that your product satisfies an old need or desire of his, perhaps overlooked; that, having taken everything into account, at the end of the year it would prove to cost less than the competition's product, which moreover, as is known, works well at first but, well, I don't really want to go into it. You can, however, assist him also in different ways (and here the imagination of the CS candidate is revealed): by solving a technical problem for him that has little or nothing to do with your business: furnishing him with an address; inviting him to dinner in a typical restaurant; showing him your city and helping him or advising him on the purchase of souvenirs for his wife or girlfriend; finding him at the last moment a ticket in the stadium for the local soccer match (that's right, we do this too). My Bologna colleague has a collection of dirty stories continually brought up to date, and reviews them diligently together with the technical bulletins before setting out on his sales trip in the cities and provinces; since he has a faulty memory, he keeps a record of which he has told to whom, because to administer the same joke twice to the same person would be a serious mistake.

All these things are learned through experience, but there are technical salesmen who seem born to it, born CS like Athena. This is not my case, and I am sadly conscious of it: When it falls to me to work in CS, at the office or traveling, I do it unwillingly, with hesitation, compunction, and little human warmth. Worse: I tend to be brusque and impatient with customers who are impatient and brusque, and to be mild and yielding with suppliers who, being in their turn CSs, prove to be just that, yielding and mild. In short, I am not a good CS, and I fear that by now it is too late for me to become one.

Tabasso had said to me, "Go to _____ and ask for Bonino, who is the head of the department. He's a fine man, already knows our products, everything has always gone well, he's no genius, we haven't called on him for three months. You will see that you won't have any technical difficulties; and if he begins to talk prices, just keep to generalities: Tell him that you'll report to us and it's not your job. . . ."

I had myself announced; they gave me a form to fill out and handed     5
me a badge to stick to my lapel, which characterized you as an outsider and immunized you against reactions of rejection on the part of the guards. They had me sit down in a waiting room; after not more than five minutes Bonino appeared and led me to his office. This is an excellent sign, and it doesn't always go like this: There are people who, coldly, make a CS wait for thirty or forty minutes even if there is an appointment, with the deliberate aim of putting him down and imposing their superior rank; it is the same goal aimed at, with more ingenious and more obscene techniques, by the baboons in the big ditch in the zoo. But the analogy is more general: All of a CS's strategies and tactics can be described in terms of sexual courtship. In both cases it's a one-to-one relationship; a courtship or negotiation among three persons would be unthinkable. In both cases one notes at the beginning a kind of dance or ritualized opening in which the buyer accepts the seller only if the latter adheres rigidly to the traditional ceremonial; if this takes place, the buyer joins the dance, and if the enjoyment is mutual, mating is attained, that is, the purchase, to the visible satisfaction of the two partners. The cases of unilateral violence are rare; not by chance are they often described in terms borrowed from the sexual sphere.

Bonino was a round little man, untidy, vaguely canine, carelessly shaved, and with a toothless smile. I introduced myself and initiated the propitiatory dance, but right off he said, "Ah yes, you're the fellow who wrote a book." I must confess my weakness: This irregular opening does not displease me, although it is not very useful to the company I represent; indeed, at this point the conversation tends to degenerate, or at least lose itself in anomalous considerations, which distract from the purpose of the visit and waste professional time.

"It's really a fine novel," Bonino continued. "I read it during my vacation, and I also got my wife to read it; but not the children, because it might frighten them." These opinions usually irritate me, but when one is in the CS role one must not be too discriminating: I thanked him urbanely and tried to bring the conversation back on the proper tracks, that is, our varnishes. Bonino put up some resistance.

"Just as you see me, I also risked finishing up like you did. They had already shut me up in the barracks courtyard, on Corso Orbassano; but at a certain point I saw him come in, you know very well who I mean, and then, while nobody saw me, I climbed the wall, threw myself down on the other side, which was a good five meters, and took off. Then I went to Val Susa with the Badogliani."[1]

I had never heard a Badogliano call the Badogliani Badogliani, I set up my defenses and, in fact, caught myself taking a deep breath, as someone does when preparing for a long immersion. It was clear that Bonino's story would be far from brief; but I remembered how many long stories I myself had inflicted on people, on those who wanted to listen and those who didn't. I remembered that it is written (Deuteronomy 10:19): "Love ye therefore the stranger: for ye were strangers in the land of Egypt," and I settled back comfortably in my chair.

Bonino was not a good storyteller: He roamed, repeated himself, made            10
long digressions, and digressions inside digressions. Besides, he had the curious bad habit of omitting the subject of some sentences and replacing it with a personal pronoun, which rendered his discourse even more nebulous. As he was speaking, I distractedly examined the room where he had received me: evidently his office for many years, because it looked neglected and untidy like him. The windows were offensively dirty, the walls were grimy with soot, the gloomy smell of stale tobacco stagnated in the air. Rusty nails were driven into the walls: some apparently useless, others holding up yellowed sheets. One of these, which could be read from my observation post, began like this: "SUBJECT: Rags. With ever greater frequency. . . ." Elsewhere you could see used razor blades, soccer pool slips, medical insurance forms, picture postcards.

---

[1]The group, after the collapse of Mussolini's government in September 1943, that supported General Badoglio, who in turn supported the King. — Trans.

". . . So then he told me that I should walk behind him, no in fact ahead of him: It was he who was behind me, a pistol pointed at me. Then the other guy arrived, his crony, who was waiting for him around the corner; and between the two of them they took me to Via Asti, you know what I mean, where there was Aloisio Smit. He would send for me every so often and say talk talk because your pals have already talked and there's no point playing the hero. . . ."

On Bonino's desk there was a horrible reproduction in a light alloy of the Leaning Tower of Pisa. There was also an ashtray made from a seashell, full of cigarette butts and cherry pits, and an alabaster penholder shaped like Vesuvius. It was a pathetic desk, not more than 0.6 square meters at a generous estimate. There is not a seasoned CS who does not know this sad science of the desk: Perhaps not at a conscious level, but in the form of a conditioned reflex, a scanty desk inexorably proclaims a lowly occupant; as for that clerk who, within eight or ten days after being hired, has not been able to conquer a desk, well, he is a lost man: He cannot count on more than a few weeks' survival, like a hermit crab without a shell. On the other hand, I have known people who at the end of their careers disposed of a surface of seven or eight square meters with a polyester gloss, obviously excessive but a proper expression in code of the extent of their power. What objects rest on the desk is not important quantitatively: There is the man who expresses his authority by maintaining on its surface the greatest disorder and the greatest accumulation of stationery; there is on the contrary the man who, more subtly, imposes his rank by a void and meticulous cleanliness: That's what Mussolini did, so they say, at Palazzo Venezia.

". . . But all these men were not aware that in my belt I had a pistol too. When they began to torture me, I pulled it out, made them all stand facing the wall, and I got out. But he . . ."

He who? I was perplexed; the story was getting more and more garbled, the clock was running, and though it is true that the customer is always right, there's also a limit to selling one's soul and to fidelity to the company's orders: Beyond this limit you make yourself ridiculous.

". . . As far as I could; a half hour, and I was already in the Rivoli section. I was walking along the road, and there what do I see landing in the fields nearby but a German plane, a Stork, the kind that can land in fifty meters. Two men get out, very polite, and ask me please which way to Switzerland. I happen to know these places and I answered right off: straight ahead, like that, to Milan and then turn left. '*Danke*,' they answer, and get back in the plane; then one of them has a second thought, rummages under his seat, gets out, and comes over to me holding some- 15 thing like a rock in his hand; he hands it to me and says, 'This is for your trouble: Take good care of it, it's uranium.' You understand, it was the end of the war, by now they felt lost, they no longer had the time to make the atomic bomb and they didn't need uranium anymore. They thought only of saving their skins and escaping to Switzerland."

There is also a limit to how much you can control your facial muscles: Bonino must have caught some sign on my face of incredulity, because he broke off in a slightly offended tone and said, "Don't you believe me?"

"Of course I believe you," I responded heroically. "But was it really uranium?"

"Absolutely; anyone could have seen that. It had an incredible weight, and when you touched it, it was hot. Besides, I still have it at home; I keep it on the terrace in a little shed, a secret, so the kids can't touch it; every so often I show it to my friends, and it's remained hot, it's hot even now." He hesitated a moment, then added, "You know what I'll do? Tomorrow I'll send you a piece so you'll be convinced, and maybe, since you're a writer, along with your stories one of these days you'll also write this one."

I thanked him, dutifully did my number, explained a certain new product, took a rather large order, said good-bye, and considered the case closed. But the next day, on my 1.2-square-meter desk, sat a small package addressed to my attention. I opened it, not without curiosity: It contained a small block of metal, about half a cigarette pack in size, actually quite heavy and with an exotic look about it. The surface was silvery white, with a light yellowish glaze; it did not seem hot, but it was not to be confused with any of the metals that a long everyday experience also outside chemistry had made familiar to me, such as copper, zinc, and aluminum. Perhaps an alloy? Or perhaps actually uranium? Metallic uranium in our parts has never been seen by anyone, and in the treatises it is described as silvery white; and a small block like that would not be permanently hot: Perhaps only a mass as big as a house can remain hot at the expense of disintegrating energy.

As soon as it was decently possible I popped into the lab, which for a     20
CS chemist is an unusual and vaguely improper thing to do. The lab is a place for the young, and returning there you feel young again, with the same longing for adventure, discovery, and the unexpected that you have at seventeen. Of course, you haven't been seventeen for some time now, and besides, your long career as a para-chemist has mortified you, rendered you atrophied, handicapped, kept you ignorant as to where reagents and equipment are stored, forgetful of everything except the fundamental reactions; but precisely for these reasons the lab revisited is a source of

joy and exerts an intense fascination, which is that of youth, of an indeterminate future pregnant with possibilities, that is, of freedom.

But the years of nonuse don't make you forget certain professional tics, a certain stereotyped behavior that marks you out as a chemist whatever the situation: probing the unknown material with your fingernail, a penknife, smelling it, feeling it with your lips whether it is "cold" or "hot," testing whether it scratches the windowpane or not, observing it under reflected light, weighing it in the palm of your hand. It is not so easy to estimate the specific weight of a material without a scale, yet after all uranium has a specific weight of 19, much more than lead, twice as much as copper: The gift given to Bonino by the Nazi aeronaut-astronauts could not be uranium. I was beginning to discern, in the little man's paranoiac tale, the echo of a tenacious and recurrent local legend of UFOs in the Val Susa, of flying saucers, carriers of omens like the comets in the Middle Ages, erratic and devoid of results like the spirits of the spiritualists.

But if it wasn't uranium, what was it? I cut off a slice of the metal with the handsaw (it was easy to saw) and offered it to the flame of the Bunsen burner: an unusual thing took place: a thread of brown smoke rose from the flame, a thread which curled into volutes. I felt, with an instant of voluptuous nostalgia, reawaken in me the reflexes of an analyst, withered by long inertia: I found a capsule of enameled porcelain, filled it with water, held it over the sooty flame, and saw form on the bottom a brown deposit which was an old acquaintance. I touched the deposit with a drop of silver nitrate solution and the black-blue color that developed confirmed for me that the metal was cadmium, the distant son of Cadmus, the sower of dragon's teeth.[2]

Where Bonino had found the cadmium was not very interesting: probably in the cadmium-plating department of his factory. More interesting but undecipherable was the origin of his story: profoundly his, his alone, since, as I found out later, he told it often and to everyone, but without substantiating it with the support of material, and with details that gradually became more colorful and less believable with the passing of the years. It was clearly impossible to get to the bottom of it; but I, tangled in the CS net of duties toward society, the company, and verisimilitude, envied in him the boundless freedom of invention of one who has broken through the barrier and is now free to build for himself the past that suits him best, to stitch around him the garments of a hero and fly like Superman across centuries, meridians, and parallels.

---

[2]The dragon's teeth planted by the mythical prince Cadmus grew into five warriors with whom he founded the new city-state of Thebes. — ED.

# EXPLORATIONS

1. How did Bonino ask Primo Levi to pay him back for his gift of "uranium"? On the basis of Levi's statements about him, do you imagine Bonino considers himself repaid? Why or why not?

2. At the time of these events, what was Levi's job? What does he consider to be his real job?

3. What clues about Bonino suggest why Levi assumes he invented his tale of being given uranium by Germans? What clues about Levi suggest why he embraces this assumption?

4. How does Levi's quotation from the Bible (para. 9) apply to his situation at that point? How does it apply to other elements in his narrative?

# CONNECTIONS

1. In what ways is Levi good at his customer service job? Why does he consider himself unsuited to it? In what ways is Sister Imelda in Edna O'Brien's story (p. 444) good at her job, and in what ways is she unsuited to it?

2. How is "Uranium" similar in structure to David Abram's "Making Magic" (p. 422)? At what point in "Making Magic" might Abram have cited the same quotation from Deuteronomy as Levi does in paragraph 9?

3. What aspects of Levi's description of his CS job (paras. 1–2) also apply to David Abram's job as a magician?

# ELABORATIONS

1. Think of a job you have done that brought you into contact with an interesting character. Using a structure similar to Levi's in "Uranium" and Abram's in "Making Magic," write a narrative essay describing the encounter.

2. "By pretending to esteem and like your fellow men, after a few years . . . you wind up really doing so, just as someone who feigns madness for a long time actually becomes crazy" (para. 1). Affection and madness are two of many conditions we can develop if we fake them long enough. Choose a literary character (such as Hamlet) or a real person (such as yourself), and write a process or cause-and-effect essay showing how that person became what at first he or she only pretended to be.

# TOMOYUKI IWASHITA

# *Why I Quit the Company*

As the following essay indicates, Tomoyuki Iwashita took a prestigious job with a Japanese corporation immediately after receiving his university degree. He now works as a journalist in Tokyo. "Why I Quit the Company" appeared in *The New Internationalist* in May 1992.

For information on Japan, see "Nippon Challenge," page 53, and the headnote on page 122.

When I tell people that I quit working for the company after only a year, most of them think I'm crazy. They can't understand why I would want to give up a prestigious and secure job. But I think I'd have been crazy to stay, and I'll try to explain why.

I started working for the company immediately after graduating from university. It's a big, well-known trading company with about 6,000 employees all over the world. There's a lot of competition to get into this and other similar companies, which promise young people a wealthy and successful future. I was set on course to be a Japanese "yuppie."

I'd been used to living independently as a student, looking after myself and organizing my own schedule. As soon as I started working all that changed. I was given a room in the company dormitory, which is like a fancy hotel, with a twenty-four-hour hot bath service and all meals laid on. Most single company employees live in a dormitory like this, and many married employees live in company apartments. The dorm system is actually a great help because living in Tokyo costs more than young people earn — but I found it stifling.

My life rapidly became reduced to a shuttle between the dorm and the office. The working day is officially eight hours, but you can never leave the office on time. I used to work from nine in the morning until eight or nine at night, and often until midnight. Drinking with colleagues after work is part of the job; you can't say no. The company building contained cafeterias, shops, a bank, a post office, a doctor's office, a barber's. . . . I never needed to leave the building. Working, drinking, sleeping, and standing on a horribly crowded commuter train for an hour and a half each way: This was my life. I spent all my time with the same colleagues; when I wasn't involved in entertaining clients on the weekend, I was expected to play golf with my colleagues. I soon lost sight of the world outside the company.

471

This isolation is part of the brainwashing process. A personnel manager     5
said: "We want excellent students who are active, clever, and tough.
Three months is enough to train them to be devoted businessmen." I
would hear my colleagues saying: "I'm not making any profit for the
company, so I'm not contributing." Very few employees claim all the
overtime pay due to them. Keeping an employee costs the company 50
million yen ($400,000) a year, or so the company claims. Many employ-
ees put the company's profits before their own mental and physical
well-being.

Overtiredness and overwork leave you little energy to analyze or criticize your situation. There are shops full of "health drinks," cocktails of
caffeine and other drugs, which will keep you going even when you're
exhausted. *Karoshi* (death from overwork) is increasingly common and is
always being discussed in the newspapers. I myself collapsed from working too hard. My boss told me: "You should control your health; it's your
own fault if you get sick." There is no paid sick leave; I used up half of
my fourteen days' annual leave because of sickness.

We had a labor union, but it seemed to have an odd relationship with
the management. A couple of times a year I was told to go home at five
o'clock. The union representatives were coming around to investigate
working hours; everyone knew in advance. If it was "discovered" that we
were all working overtime in excess of fifty hours a month our boss might
have had some problem being promoted; and our prospects would have
been affected. So we all pretended to work normal hours that day.

The company also controls its employees' private lives. Many company
employees under thirty are single. They are expected to devote all their
time to the company and become good workers; they don't have time to
find a girlfriend. The company offers scholarships to the most promising
young employees to enable them to study abroad for a year or two. But
unmarried people who are on these courses are not allowed to get married
until they have completed the course! Married employees who are sent
to train abroad have to leave their families in Japan for the first year.

In fact, the quality of married life is often determined by the husband's
work. Men who have just gotten married try to go home early for a while,
but soon have to revert to the norm of late-night work. They have little
time to spend with their wives and even on the weekend are expected to
play golf with colleagues. Fathers cannot find time to communicate with
their children and child rearing is largely left to mothers. Married men
posted abroad will often leave their family behind in Japan; they fear that
their children will fall behind in the fiercely competitive Japanese education system.

Why do people put up with this? They believe this to be a normal     10 working life or just cannot see an alternative. Many think that such personal sacrifices are necessary to keep Japan economically successful. Perhaps, saddest of all, Japan's education and socialization processes do not equip people with the intellectual and spiritual resources to question and challenge the status quo. They stamp out even the desire for a different kind of life.

However, there are some signs that things are changing. Although many new employees in my company were quickly brainwashed, many others, like myself, complained about life in the company and seriously considered leaving. But most of them were already in fetters — of debt. Pleased with themselves for getting into the company and anticipating a life of executive luxury, these new employees throw their money around. Every night they are out drinking. They buy smart clothes and take a taxi back to the dormitory after the last train has gone. They start borrowing money from the bank and soon they have a debt growing like a snowball rolling down a slope. The banks demand no security for loans; it's enough to be working for a well-known company. Some borrow as much as a year's salary in the first few months. They can't leave the company while they have such debts to pay off.

I was one of the few people in my intake of employees who didn't get into debt. I left the company dormitory after three months to share an apartment with a friend. I left the company exactly one year after I entered it. It took me a while to find a new job, but I'm working as a journalist now. My life is still busy, but it's a lot better than it was. I'm lucky because nearly all big Japanese companies are like the one I worked for, and conditions in many small companies are even worse.

It's not easy to opt out of a life-style that is generally considered to be prestigious and desirable, but more and more young people in Japan are thinking about doing it. You have to give up a lot of superficially attractive material benefits in order to preserve the quality of your life and your sanity. I don't think I was crazy to leave the company. I think I would have gone crazy if I'd stayed.

## EXPLORATIONS

1. What facts does Tomoyuki Iwashita give about the kind of company he worked for? About the nature of his work? What is the effect of his supplying so little information on those subjects?

2. According to Iwashita, what are the top goals of "Japanese yuppies"? What are their fears? What appear to be his sources of information for his concept of "yuppies"?

3. What luxuries did Iwashita's company provide for its employees that most American companies would not? What demands did the company make that most American employees would not tolerate?

## CONNECTIONS

1. What kind of relationship between employer and employee does Iwashita describe in paragraph 5? How does this compare with the relationship Primo Levi describes in paragraph 1 of "Uranium" (p. 464)?

2. Compare Iwashita's comments on work with Fred Moody's in *Looking at Ourselves* (p. 407). What are the similarities? What are the differences? How do you think Iwashita would respond to Moody's statement, "Overworking is an American trait" (p. 407)?

3. What generalizations about the Japanese does Patrick Smith make in "Nippon Challenge" (p. 53) that are supported by Iwashita?

## ELABORATIONS

1. Look back at Patrick Smith's "Nippon Challenge" and John David Morley's "Acquiring a Japanese Family" (p. 122). On the basis of those two selections and Iwashita's "Why I Quit the Company," write an essay describing what a day in the life of a young Japanese businessman might be like.

2. In paragraph 10 Iwashita writes: "Perhaps, saddest of all, Japan's education and socialization processes do not equip people with the intellectual and spiritual resources to question and challenge the status quo. They stamp out even the desire for a different kind of life." Is this the case in the United States? Write an essay arguing either that it is or that it isn't, and explaining why.

# RAYMOND BONNER

## A Woman's Place

Free-lance journalist and writer Raymond Bonner was born in Jefferson City, Missouri, in 1942. He was educated at MacMurray College and Stanford Law School and in 1968 was admitted to the California State Bar. That same year he joined the U.S. Marine Corps, where he rose to captain and was decorated for his service in the Vietnam war. Bonner's first book (coauthored) was *The Discarded Army: Veterans After Vietnam* (1972). He practiced public-interest law in Washington, D.C., then in San Francisco. In 1979 he went to Latin America as a free-lance journalist and later became a correspondent for the *New York Times*. His next two books, *Weakness and Deceit: U.S. Policy and El Salvador* (1984) and *Waltzing with a Dictator: The Marcoses and the Making of American Policy* (1988), won between them the Robert F. Kennedy, Overseas Press Club, and Sidney Hillman Foundation awards. Bonner has also been a staff writer for *The New Yorker*, where "A Woman's Place" appeared in 1992. His most recent book is *At the Hand of Man: Peril and Hope for Africa's Wildlife* (1993), written after five years in Nairobi, Kenya. He now lives in Warsaw.

Slightly smaller than New Jersey, Kuwait lies on the northwestern coast of the Persian Gulf between Saudi Arabia and Iraq. It has been ruled by the Al-Sabah dynasty since 1759; the current emir is Sheik Jaber al-Ahmad al-Sabah. He appoints a prime minister, who appoints a cabinet. Only Kuwaitis can vote, and only 28 percent of residents are Kuwaitis. The mostly Islamic emirate became a British protectorate in 1897 to avoid a Turkish takeover; it regained independence in 1961. Oil was discovered in the 1930s, and with 20 percent of known reserves, Kuwait became the world's second largest oil exporter (after Saudi Arabia). Half the profit goes to the sheik, who spends most of it on his kingdom. Kuwait sided with Iraq in its war with Iran during the 1980s; in 1987 the United States gave its protection to Kuwaiti oil tankers in the Gulf. In August 1990, two years after Iraq and Iran agreed to a cease-fire, Iraq invaded Kuwait (see "Baghdad Diary," p. 677). The United States and its allies thwarted the takeover in February 1991. The Kuwaiti emir has since pledged to hold parliamentary elections but has set no date.

For more information on Kuwait, see "Torture in Kuwait," page 696.

In a small, noisy room at the Philippine Embassy in Kuwait City one day last month, a Kuwaiti man wearing a long white robe and a white

headdress pleaded with a Philippine woman named Jenny Casanova. Her
left eye was black and blue and yellow, and she also had a large bruise
on her upper right arm and bruises on her left calf and thigh. The
woman, who was thirty years old, had been a maid in the man's house
until five days before, when she was beaten by the man's wife. After the
beating, she had escaped to the embassy. The man now wanted her to
go to the employment agency that had brought her to Kuwait, so that he
could get back the money he had paid for her; she wanted him to return
her passport — she couldn't leave the country without it — and to give
her a release, so that she could either go back to the Philippines or find
employment locally on her own. As he stormed out, having failed to
persuade her, I asked him what had happened, and he said, "She hit my
wife." And then his wife hit her, he added. He crossed the street, got into
a gold-colored Cadillac, and drove off.

The Philippine Embassy in Kuwait has become a home for battered
women and runaways, and also an unofficial employment office. Jenny
Casanova is among thousands of young Asian women who have come to
Kuwait to find work and escape poverty at home — young women who
are exploited by just about everyone and protected by almost no one. The
Kuwaiti government says that there are now 71,000 domestic servants
from Asia in the country — 30,000 from India, 25,000 from the Philippines, 11,000 from Bangladesh, and 5,000 from Sri Lanka. Some are
men, who work as drivers, cooks, or houseboys, but the large majority are
women, most of whom work as maids. Almost none of them speak Arabic,
and the language barrier frequently results in problems between employer
and employee. Many of the maids have been recruited by unscrupulous
agencies, which take their money without telling them what lies ahead,
or even, in some cases, where they are going. In Kuwait and throughout
the Persian Gulf states, these women are taken advantage of by their
employers: They are forced to work long hours for low pay, and are often
virtually imprisoned. They find that they have almost no place to go for
protection. The Kuwaiti government offers them next to nothing, and
their own embassies in Kuwait help them only grudgingly.

Jenny Casanova's story is typical. She has three daughters, all under
the age of ten. She had no job in Manila, so she sought work in Kuwait,
she says, "for the future of my children," who are still in the Philippines.
She had to pay an agency in Manila 12,000 pesos — about 500 dollars —
to find her a job, and when she got to Kuwait, in November of 1991, her
employer withheld her first two months' wages to recover part of what he
had paid a Kuwaiti recruiting agency. Her salary was 45 dinars a month —
165 dollars. The minimum wage in Kuwait is 170 dinars a month, but

domestic servants are not covered by the country's labor law, and maids are routinely paid only 30 to 45 dinars.

Casanova got up at five-thirty every morning, was allowed to sit down during the day only for meals, and worked until almost midnight. She had to do all the cooking and cleaning and take care of four children, aged fifteen, fourteen, twelve, and six. She had no day off. When I spoke with Casanova at the embassy, she told me that she had once said to her employer's wife, "'Ma'am, I want to go to church.' She said that Filipinos don't go outside."

Casanova told me that she had been beaten several times by the woman she worked for. When I asked why she hadn't fled earlier, she said that she had never been allowed to leave the house, and added, "I was afraid." Then, on the morning of October 4, the woman yelled at her for not keeping the children's shoes in the right place. Casanova tried to explain to her that the children were always moving them. The woman began beating her, with her hands, with a stick, and with a vacuum-cleaner hose. "I could not move, but she forced me to work," Casanova recalled. Later that day, the woman, thinking that Casanova would flee if she was left alone, took her along on a visit to a relative. A maid at the relative's house saw what had happened, and told Casanova to run away. "Go to the gate slowly, then run," the other maid said, and she gave Casanova a dinar. Casanova left the house and took a taxi to the embassy. There she found more than two hundred other Philippine maids who had recently fled their employers. They were — and are — encamped in an annex, their suitcases piled on a patio, their clothes spread on a wall to dry in the sun.

Kuwaitis and expatriates go to the Philippine Embassy in search of cheap labor. Most of the negotiations take place in a seedy room containing two dilapidated desks and several white plastic chairs. One day when I was there, an American woman who had lived in Kuwait for twenty-two years stood against a wall, interviewing young women. In a corner, a man and his wife were talking to a young Filipino woman wearing a T-shirt with the logo "Best Beach Club — California." In her previous job, Shirley (as she asked to be called) had been paid 50 dinars a month, for which she had worked from six in the morning until nine at night. She had had one day off during the week. She had liked the job. "She was good, she gave me a lot of time to rest," Shirley said of her former employer. That Shirley was grateful for a job that required her to work fifteen hours a day, six days a week, for 50 cents an hour says a great deal about what it is like to be a maid in Kuwait — and also, no doubt, about conditions in the Philippines. Shirley had been dismissed because she had too many boyfriends. (Most Kuwaiti employers object to a maid's having a boyfriend, because they fear that the maid's values may be passed on to their children.) Shirley went to another family, but they paid her only 40 dinars, and she had to work from five-thirty in the morning until after midnight. She fled after two weeks. She did not have a release from her former employer, and the couple interviewing her said they would call and try to arrange one. Unless a runaway maid has a release, it is virtually impossible for a new employer to get her a visa that allows her to remain in Kuwait.

Across the room, two Kuwaiti women in long black scarves and black cloaks had backed a small Philippine woman against the wall. She had been employed by one of the women for fourteen months, and now the woman and her friend were demanding that she give them 400 dinars — the fee that had been paid to a recruiting agency. A man in white robes and a white headdress approached the Kuwaiti women and spoke to them in Arabic, and, as they turned to go, one of them pointed at the former maid and said, "I want it right now!"

Shortly after they left, a couple named Richard and Mona Brook entered the annex, escorted by a diplomat from the Philippine Embassy. Brook, an accountant, is British; his wife, who teaches at a Montessori school in Kuwait City, is Egyptian. They sat in white plastic chairs by one of the desks, and soon a young Philippine maid who identified herself only as Becky appeared, with four others behind her. The four stood quietly in front of the desk while Becky negotiated. The Brooks, who have two young boys, asked if any of the four women had had experience with children, and all of them said that they had. After fifteen minutes of such interviewing, the Brooks decided they would like to hire a twenty-three-year-old named Josephine, who agreed to take the job for 40 dinars a month. She had arrived in Kuwait on December 3, 1991, and on October 5 had fled the family she worked for. She told Mrs. Brook that her employer's twenty-nine-year-old son had hit her and threatened to kill her.

Mrs. Brook left the annex and went into the embassy to call Josephine's former employer and find out whether he would release her. She returned disappointed. She had offered to pay him 300 dinars for Josephine's release, but he had said that it had cost him 500 dinars to bring her to Kuwait, and that he wouldn't release her even for that amount. Mrs. Brook tried to tell him that he wasn't going to get the maid back — that she would eventually be deported, and then he would lose everything. He wasn't persuaded. "This is Kuwait, I'm Kuwaiti, and I'm going to get her out of the embassy," he declared. "It's a matter of principle."

"Principle! His son tried to kill her and he's talking about principle!"          10
Mrs. Brook said as she reported the conversation to her husband.

On three evenings recently, I went to a police station in the Dasma
district of Kuwait City. It was a ramshackle three-story building, in which
policemen in white robes lounged about on sagging vinyl-covered
couches with the stuffing coming out. But the policemen had computers
and cellular phones, and the air-conditioning was on full blast, with the
door and the windows open. (Energy conservation is not a high priority
in Kuwait.) The Dasma police station has become a sort of informal
complaint-resolution center for runaway maids. Between five and six
o'clock many evenings, buses arrive from the embassies with maids who
have fled the homes of their employers; these days, most are from Sri
Lanka and the Philippines. With the assistance of volunteers from their
own countries, the women tell their stories to policemen. The hope is
that the police can then persuade the employer to bring the woman her
passport, a release, and maybe even money for a ticket home.
    Perhaps sixty Sri Lankan and Philippine maids were at the station each
evening I was there. I spoke with half a dozen Sri Lankans, all of whom
had been beaten by the women they worked for. A number of people in
Kuwait told me that Sri Lankan maids were probably treated worse than
Philippine maids, and that they tended to endure more before fleeing —
in part because they were less worldly and aggressive. Bader Nisa, one of
the Sri Lankans I spoke with, had a large bruise on her upper left arm
and another on her right shoulder blade; she also had bruises on her right
forearm and her right leg. She was twenty-four years old, and was from
a small village in northern Sri Lanka. "My father is sick, and there is no
one to feed the family, so I came to Kuwait to get some money," she told
me. (Many of the workers who go abroad on contracts send most of their
earnings home to their families; this money is a major revenue source for
many countries.) Nisa's family sold a small piece of land, and she borrowed from villagers, in order to raise the money to pay an agency in
Colombo. She arrived in Kuwait on September 25, and almost from the
day she was hired, she said, the woman she worked for beat her. The day
before I met her, she had been beaten so severely that she fled. She said
that while she was cleaning the bathroom the woman tried to tell her
something, but, because she didn't speak Arabic, she didn't understand.
"She took the brush and started beating me," Nisa said. "She was yelling
at me, but I didn't know what she was saying."
    A second Sri Lankan, who was eighteen years old, told me that she
had been beaten often by the woman she worked for. "Baba is a good

man," she said, referring to the husband. "Sometimes he tried to stop Madame from beating me, but she doesn't listen to him." Asked why she hadn't fled earlier, she said, "I have written to my mother about this, and she told me, 'You must stay in that house, because you are still not married.'"

On another evening at the police station, I talked to a Philippine woman who had bruises on her legs. She told me that she had been beaten not by her employer but by a woman at the agency that had brought her to Kuwait. She had been taken to the agency by the woman she worked for, with the complaint that the maid did not work hard enough. This was not an isolated occurrence, a Philippine official told me later. He said that employers often took difficult maids to the employment agencies, and that there they were "sometimes beaten, incarcerated, and not given food."

The next day, I called the agency that had brought in one of the Sri      15
Lankan maids I had interviewed. The woman who answered told me that in addition to finding employment for foreign maids the agency specialized in cleaning windows, carpets, and marble floors. I knew that a recently enacted law requires that a potential employer must have a contract with a domestic employee before the employee can be brought into Kuwait, but when I asked if I needed a contract to bring in a maid the woman at the agency said no. I asked if I would have to give the maid a day off.

"It depends on you," she said.

What about the hours?

"There is no limit, because they are housemaids. They belong to you. It is not like in Europe or America."

I decided to visit the agency that had brought Jenny Casanova to Kuwait. It was housed in a small office on the third floor of a run-down building across from a municipal parking garage, and also served as an importing firm. The woman in charge of the maid-recruiting operation gave her name as Aisha, and told me that she had come to Kuwait from the Philippines several years ago as a maid. She, too, assured me that I did not need a contract, and that the hours and days a maid worked were up to me. Aisha said that the agency's fee for a Muslim would be 300 dinars and the equivalent of three months' salary in advance; for a Christian, it would be 200 dinars and two months' salary in advance. Though Aisha called part of the fee an advance, it wasn't, really, she explained: An employer recovers the advance from the maid. "She has to work in your house for two or three months without salary — or you can deduct half her salary for four months," Aisha said.

When I asked about hiring a Philippine maid, Aisha said that that      20 would be difficult. Because of alleged abuses, she said, the Philippine government had placed tight restrictions on the freedom of young women to come to Kuwait for work. When I returned to the agency a few hours later, however, she informed me that she had seven Philippine women in Qatar who were available to come to Kuwait; she even provided me with faxes of their passports. It is almost certain, according to Philippine diplomats, that these women had gone from the Philippines to Qatar in order to circumvent the restrictions on traveling to Kuwait.

"It's a case of exploitation, and of connivance by unscrupulous agencies in the Philippines and some in Kuwait," I was told by Lamberto Marin, the labor attaché at the Philippine Embassy in Kuwait. He said that corrupt immigration officials in the Philippines were also part of the scheme: They issued visas for young women to come to Kuwait even though the women didn't have the proper documents. In other cases, the women were told that they were going to work in Kuwait as dressmakers, beauticians, or saleswomen, Marin said, but when they reached Kuwait they had to work as domestics. And in some cases the duplicity has been even more egregious. One Philippine woman told me that she had been promised work in Dubai as a secretary, at a salary of 500 dollars a month. "When we reached the airport in Dubai, a man took all our papers," she said. "There were twenty-nine of us — teachers, midwives, nurses." All twenty-nine were put on a plane to Kuwait, where their real employers were waiting for them.

Kuwaitis are surely among the most privileged and pampered people in history. With their vast oil wealth, they simply hire people to do almost all their work. Before the invasion by Iraq, on August 2, 1990, 80 percent of the labor force was non-Kuwaiti, and there were 200,000 non-Kuwaiti servants in the country. "Every family had five or six servants," a Kuwaiti journalist told me recently. Since the invasion, the Kuwaitis have decided, for security reasons, to reduce the number of foreigners in the country. Consequently, in October of 1991 the minister of the interior issued regulations limiting the number of servants a family could employ. A family of five could have only two; a family larger than that could have four. Many Kuwaitis found such restrictions too harsh, however, and within a week the law was amended to allow a family to pay an annual fee if it wanted more servants — 50 dinars for the first, 100 for the second, and so on, with no limit except the employer's willingness to pay the fees.

This year, more than two thousand Philippine maids have fled their employers and, like Jenny Casanova, have sought refuge in the embassy. Each day, ten to twenty Sri Lankan maids show up at the Sri Lankan Embassy, complaining of underpayment, overwork, beatings. While the hardships these women endure are even worse in other Gulf states than they are in Kuwait — observers have told me that being a maid in Saudi Arabia or Dubai is akin to being a slave — more attention has been focused on the problem in Kuwait, because, at least since its liberation, it has been a more open society. Kuwait has allowed into the country two fact-finding missions sent from New York by the Lawyers Committee for Human Rights, and also an investigative team from Middle East Watch and the Women's Rights Project, which are part of the New York–based Human Rights Watch. I received a journalist's visa for Kuwait in only a few days, and once I was there numerous officials cooperated openly with me; it is almost impossible for a journalist to get a visa for Saudi Arabia, say, and the government there won't for a moment entertain the notion of human-rights activists or reporters wandering around the country and talking freely to people.

The reasons for the widespread mistreatment of maids in Kuwait and elsewhere are found partly in cultural traditions and values. "First, it is because they are women, and women are mistreated generally in Kuwait," Eman al-Bedah, a Kuwaiti human-rights activist, told me. "Second, because they are maids. They are lower-class, and people exercise their power over them." Bedah, a twenty-eight-year-old telecommunications engineer, lives at home, and her mother employs two Sri Lankan maids. She allows them to attend religious services, and they may receive phone calls and have visits from friends. "Our neighbors say we are spoiling them," Bedah told me.

Much of the reporting by journalists and human-rights groups about the mistreatment of maids in Kuwait has focused on rape and sexual abuse by men, but Bedah told me that women, who are responsible for supervising the maids and have contact with them throughout the day, were guilty of most of the mistreatment. Of a woman who mistreats her maid Bedah said, "She's treating her maid the way her husband is treating her."                                                                            25

The status of women in Kuwait is marked by contradictions. Their political rights are severely circumscribed — they don't have the right to vote, for example — but the popular Western image of the veiled Arab woman, docile and subservient to her husband, doesn't apply in Kuwait. In Saudi Arabia, a woman is not allowed to drive, or to be seen in public with a man who isn't her husband, her father, a son, or a brother. In Kuwait, women drive expensive cars along freeways while talking on cellular phones. One woman I interviewed over dinner took charge of ordering the meal, even though the menu was in English and the waiter spoke English, and when the check came, she grabbed it.

Kuwait's labor code, which was adopted in 1964, was an extraordinary piece of progressive legislation for its time, and it is exceptional even today. It protects children — no one under eighteen is allowed to work at night, for instance — and provides that "a female laborer shall be granted a wage similar to that of a man if she carries out the same work." American feminists are still campaigning for a federal law like that. In Kuwait, a new mother is entitled by law to ten weeks of paid maternity leave, and after she returns to work the law gives her the right to take up to two hours off every day to go home and breast-feed her baby.

"We enjoy everything except our political rights," Dr. Moudi al-Houmoud told me one day. From 1983 to 1989, Dr. Houmoud was the dean of the School of Commerce of Kuwait University, and she still teaches there; she is also part owner of a management-consulting firm, where I met with her. In Kuwait's professional and business worlds, women do well, she said. At Kuwait University a few years ago, four of seven deans were women; the student body, of thirteen thousand, is today more than 60 percent female. At the government-financed Kuwait News Agency, the deputy editor of the English desk and the deputy editor of the Arabic desk are women. Dr. Houmoud told me that the progress of women in Kuwait, at least in comparison to other Arab countries, could be traced to the era before oil was discovered, when Kuwait was a marine economy. "Men made their money from the sea, either diving for pearls or fishing, so they were away for long periods," she said. "That left the woman to run the whole show. From that history, her character developed." She said that as early as the 1930s young Kuwaiti women were being educated at home, and by the fifties they had begun to go abroad for their education — mostly to Egypt. "These women were pioneers," Dr. Houmoud said. "They went abroad to be educated and then returned home with modern ideas." In the sixties, some Kuwaiti women publicly demonstrated against the wearing of the aba, a head-to-ankle cloak. And in the past couple of decades more and more Kuwaiti women have been going to the United States, England, and France to study, and returning home with more ideas about the rights of women.

The Gulf war brought further freedom for women. "The liberation of Kuwait has liberated Kuwaiti women," a twenty-seven-year-old Kuwaiti journalist named Khouloud al-Feeli told me. She said that the liberation of women had come about partly because during the occupation Kuwaiti women led public demonstrations against Saddam Hussein and were also active in the underground resistance. Besides, since the war Kuwait has prevented the return of some three hundred thousand Palestinians who fled during the occupation, many of whom held managerial jobs. Now these positions have to be filled, "and the best Kuwaiti man for the job is a Kuwaiti woman," Feeli said.

Despite the number of women in executive positions, a woman "can't    30
go to the top of the ladder — only three-quarters of the way," Dr. Houmoud told me. Of the hundred largest companies in Kuwait, only three
have women on their boards of directors, she said. "It's still a male-dominated society, still a man's world."

The Asian maids in Kuwait suffer from more than just being women
in a male-dominated society, however. They are foreigners in an extremely closed and xenophobic society. You aren't automatically entitled
to citizenship unless you can prove that your family was in Kuwait before
1920. That leaves tens of thousands of essentially stateless people, called
*bidun jinsiyyah* (the phrase means "without nationality") — many of
them people who were born in Kuwait and have lived their entire lives
in Kuwait, and whose fathers and grandfathers were born there, but who
are not Kuwaiti citizens. Even other Arabs are considered inferior by the
Kuwaitis, and the maids, being Asians, are at the bottom of the heap.
    "People don't see it as a problem; they don't think that many are
mistreated," Ghanim al-Najjar, one of Kuwait's most prominent human-
rights activists, told me in October. "We have a lot of maids in this
country, and abuse and mistreatment are not very common." Referring
to a recent report by Middle East Watch that is a comprehensive documentation of the problem, he said, "They don't talk about the 99 percent,
or more, of the maids who are not being raped or mistreated." As for the
failure of the Kuwaiti government to protect the maids, he said, "Whatever happens to the maids is happening inside the house, and what goes
on inside the house is personal. In Kuwait, homes are traditionally and
constitutionally sacred places." In other words, it is not the business of
the state to regulate anything that happens in the home. He also said,
"It's very hard to know what really happened. If a maid says she's been
beaten or neglected, how on earth do you prove that?"
    Some American human-rights activists speak disparagingly about Naj-
jar because of his views on the maids, but he has demonstrated a vigorous
commitment to human rights. He was a founder of the Amnesty International chapter in Kuwait in the late 1980s, at a time when the country
was far less open politically than it is today, and in 1991 he was a founder
of the Kuwaiti Association to Defend War Victims, a broad-based human-
rights organization, of which he is currently the chairman.
    Najjar is not the only Kuwaiti with human-rights credentials who
thinks that the maids' problem has been exaggerated by foreigners. "If
one thousand or two thousand are treated badly, it's not a daily practice,"
I was told by Meshari al-Osaimi, another founder of the Kuwaiti Associa-

tion to Defend War Victims. He is also the head of the Kuwait Lawyers' Association, and in Kuwait's parliamentary election on October 5 — the first since the Assembly was dissolved by the Emir in 1986 — he was elected as a member of the opposition. "I don't think it's a human-rights issue," he added. As he sees it, the solution to the maids' problem is quite simple: Amend the labor law so that it includes maids. Back in 1964, when the law was enacted, it specifically excluded domestic servants, because, Osaimi said, at that time only the royal family and the very wealthy had servants.

It would be tempting to dismiss Najjar's and Osaimi's views as reflect-    35
ing the male chauvinism of Kuwaiti society. But Dr. Houmoud also characterized the situation with the maids as a legal problem. "The maids are being treated badly because there is no law," she said. According to her and several other women I spoke with, women's-rights groups are not likely to take up the maid issue, and my questions seemed to take them by surprise. "I don't think existing groups see it as a problem — or not a big problem, at least," one woman activist explained.

The Kuwaiti government has recently enacted regulations to license the recruiting agencies, but these regulations are not likely to be enforced, Western diplomats in Kuwait say, since the agencies are owned by Kuwaitis. And even though Kuwait does have laws against assault, they have not been enforced when a maid has been attacked by her employer. Officials in the Ministry of the Interior, which has responsibility for the maids, could provide no documentation of any man's having been prosecuted for the rape of a maid, or of a woman's having been prosecuted for beating a maid; Philippine and Sri Lankan diplomats said that they were aware of no criminal prosecutions of employers for assaults on maids. It seems unlikely that the situation will change until the Kuwaitis themselves are willing to acknowledge the seriousness of the problem.

## EXPLORATIONS

1. What is the complete expression from which this essay's title comes? What expectations did this title create for you as a reader? In what sense is the title ironic?

2. What is the thesis of "A Woman's Place"? What causes does Raymond Bonner identify for the central problem he examines?

3. What kinds of evidence does Bonner use to make his case? Where does he present opposing views? How does he respond to those views?

# CONNECTIONS

1. What problems are shared by maids in Kuwait and the corporate employees in Japan described in Tomoyuki Iwashita's "Why I Quit the Company" (p. 471)? What are the differences between these two groups? Whose situation do you think is worse, and why?

2. What are the similarities between a maid's job in Kuwait and Maya Angelou's job as a maid in "Mary" (p. 415)? What advantages did Angelou have over the maids in Kuwait?

3. Reread paragraphs 26–30. What attitudes, accomplishments, and obstacles do Kuwaiti women seem to share with the Saudi Arabian women described by Miriam Cooke in "The Veil Does Not Prevent Women from Working" (p. 372)? How does Bonner's perspective on Saudi women differ from Cooke's?

4. In what ways do the observations in Bonner's paragraph 25 apply to the domestic violence in Gholam-Hossein Sa'edi's "The Game Is Over" (p. 162)?

# ELABORATIONS

1. In paragraphs 11–14 Bonner describes visiting a police station in Kuwait City. Drawing on information throughout his essay, write an imaginary argument in which a Kuwaiti employer and his or her runaway maid present their cases in turn to a police officer. Make each speaker as reasonable and sympathetic as you can.

2. Reread Simone de Beauvoir's "Woman as Other" (p. 329). Write an essay using Beauvoir's ideas to explain the problems described by Bonner in "A Woman's Place" (see his para. 31, for example), or using Bonner's information to illustrate Beauvoir's points.

# YOSHIMI ISHIKAWA

## *Strawberry Fields*

Yoshimi Ishikawa grew up on the tiny island of Oshima, south of Japan's southern tip and east of Shanghai, China. American soldiers stationed in Japan after World War II introduced him and his older brother, Anchan, to Coca-Cola, pin-ups, and dreams of the exotic world across the Pacific. In 1965 Ishikawa sailed to California to meet Anchan, now established as a farmworker. America turned out to be a land of dirt and hard labor, but over time Ishikawa learned English, and his brother managed to buy land eighty miles south of Los Angeles. "Strawberry Fields" tells of planting their first crop; it comes from Ishikawa's autobiography *Strawberry Road: A Japanese Immigrant Discovers America* (1991), translated from the Japanese by Eve Zimmerman. A best-seller in Japan, the book also has been made into a film. Ishikawa has written several other books in Japanese and is working on a historical novel. After returning to Japan from California, he received his law degree from Keio University; he contributes frequently to Japanese newspapers and magazines and lives in Tokyo.

The California Gold Rush that began in 1849 lured thousands of people to the west coast of the United States. As American entrepreneurs built mines, businesses, and towns, then farms, canneries, and railroads, they depended on cheap labor. Chinese immigrants were welcomed until their growing numbers led concerned whites to pass the Chinese Exclusion Act of 1892. A wave of immigration from Japan followed. By 1909, nearly 40,000 Japanese worked on American farms, mostly in menial jobs. Under pressure from President Theodore Roosevelt, Japan agreed to issue passports only to nonlaborers and family members of previous emigrants. In 1913 the California legislature passed the Alien Land Act: Aliens who were "ineligible for citizenship" (specifically, Asians) could not own agricultural property. Although the *issei* (first generation) generally retained their Japanese identity, the *nisei* (second generation) adapted to the surrounding culture. They began organizing to overcome job and social discrimination. But in 1941, Japan bombed the American military base at Pearl Harbor in Hawaii. On grounds of security, over a hundred thousand American residents of Japanese origin were moved from their homes to internment camps, losing their communities and property. Not until the 1980s did the U.S. government recognize this injustice and attempt to make some belated amends.

For background on Japan, see "Nippon Challenge," page 53, and the headnote on page 122.

I was attending American high school simply to improve my English for college, and I chose courses accordingly. Some days I only took two or three classes, which left plenty of time to work. In fact, it was much easier for me to work in the field than sit in classes where I couldn't understand what was going on. I half-worried that if my English improved and I got used to American life, I might turn out like Frankie Noda or the other nisei. Part of me wanted to become American as quickly as possible; the other part of me wanted to run back home.

Little by little I learned how pleasurable it was to cool off by lounging naked in the evening air after a day of hard work in the field. Physical satisfaction is usually linked with sex, but I definitely felt it after working too. Human beings are built not only with a desire to reproduce, but to work, and we can do any task if we push ourselves hard enough.

[My brother Anchan and I] had risen in the world, but we were still mere laborers. In Japan it's easy to predict how much you will make in a year of hard work. But on an American farm you can make a huge amount of money on a single harvest if the competition slips up. The few thousand yen a man gets for simple physical work in Japan can turn into hundreds of thousands of yen here.

Frank Machida had come back to America as a nisei speaking little English at the age of eighteen, leased an 800-acre field for five years, bought land, and made hundreds of thousands of dollars. But Frank had paid for his prosperity: Although wealth had been the fruit of his labors, you had only to look at his leathery face and his swollen, dirt-stained fingers to see that it had taken its toll on his body. And then there were subtle disturbances of his spirit.

I have no doubt that cruel physical labor can inflict brain damage on        5
people. The damage that preys on farm workers does not destroy them; rather it turns them back into children. When the body is maltreated, one is cleansed of a sense of shame and a regard for custom. The civilized obsession to assign "meaning" to things breaks down; man pushed to the limits of his endurance reverts to his most basic form.

Once, soon after arriving in America, I had seen my brother watering the rows in the field. Saying he was thirsty, he bent down, drank some of the muddy water, wiped his mouth with his hand, and exclaimed, "Delicious!" It startled me, but when I think back on it, my brother's life *was* the farm, and he had simply adapted to it.

Six months later I, too, found that I could drink the muddy water in the fields, and consider it delicious. A farmer can't mold the land to suit himself; rather, it transforms and creates him anew. We were the ones who had to change.

The day I discovered that Anchan was really a farmer we stood talking about our hopes for our patch of land.

"Frank has made so much on his land — we should be able to do the same," I said.

"*Yuu,* it's not that simple. We still don't know if this soil is right for strawberries."

"But they're doing fine next door, and we're just across the road."

"But this land has never been farmed. I don't know if we can grow strawberries. The only way to find out is to try. That's the way farming is in America." Anchan sounded different from usual. He scooped up some soil from the field and popped it in his mouth, his face crinkling at the taste.

"What are you doing? Are you drunk?"

"Umm, this here . . . this is OK."

My brother walked around tasting soil in every section of the field while I followed mutely. Suddenly his eyes narrowed.

"Do you know what I'm doing? I'm testing for salt. It doesn't rain much here, and the sun's very strong, so the salt never gets washed out of the soil — it just hardens on top. This spot is a little salty, so it will only produce small strawberries."

I don't know where he learned it, but my brother could test the soil just by tasting it. Next he examined some rocks and turned over the earth in different places with a shovel.

"Too many rocks, too. It's never been farmed, and it isn't flat either."

Anchan knew what he was doing. Somewhere along the way my carpenter brother had become an accomplished farmer. The land had taught him. Often I heard him say, "Learn by doing." I was impressed.

Anchan then lay down on his stomach to measure the angle of the ground. If the ground was uneven, pools would form when water was piped in and the strawberries would end up different sizes. So, my brother said, we had to till the land many times with a tractor to make it as flat as possible. This was especially important because we were completely dependent on underground water. On many of the farms around us there were ponds to hold water that was siphoned off below ground. In order to draw water from these reservoirs to irrigate, we first had to put down pipes three feet below ground.

So how did we convert our field?

First we used a tractor fitted with a big rake that dug effortlessly through two feet of soil and unearthed all the rocks. This tractor was followed by another, slowly dragging a cart. Farm workers walked on either side, picking up the rocks and throwing them into the cart; the large ones were the size of a man's head and the smaller ones the size of a fist.

After the rocks were gone, we watered the field again and again. This was done not only to wash the salt from the soil but also to make the seeds of any weeds sprout. The wind had scattered all kinds of seeds over our vacant plot. After the seeds had sprouted, we turned them over with the tractor and left them to wither and die in the sun.

When we watered the dry earth, however, all kinds of bacteria and insects flourished, so next we had to exterminate. We covered the soil with plastic and sprayed the pesticide underneath. The gas sank two feet into the earth as it blended with the water, killing off pests and their eggs.

Next we put down fertilizer a number of times. Southern California    25
soil is not of the highest quality (even weeds don't flourish here). After that, we watered the whole field again and turned the soil with the tractor. Finally, we used a bulldozer to get the earth as flat as possible, to ensure that water would spread evenly.

When all this was done, a piece of scrubby land had been transformed into a fertile field before our eyes. The black soil looked saturated with moisture. If we had planted flowers, you can bet that blossoms would have appeared in no time.

Now we began to farm. First we made rows and planted two-inch strawberry seedlings four inches apart. To do this, we needed a lot of temporary help. Strawberries in a field of hundreds of acres must be planted in no longer than two to three days if you want the fruit to ripen at the same time. This autumn we would need as many illegal Mexican workers as we had last harvesttime. The farm workers tied bags that held fifty strawberry plants in a bundle around their waists and moved silently down the rows, setting each plant in the ground.

When the planting was done, we turned on the sprinklers connected to the underground pipes. It takes hundreds of pipes to run the sprinklers, each of which covers an area about fifteen feet square. When all the sprinklers were running, a little rainbow appeared over the field. After about two months of sprinkling, the strawberry plants had taken root. Then we started to pipe water directly into the rows.

Farming means different things in Japan and America. In Japan farming means planting land that has been used before, putting down fertilizer, and eventually harvesting a crop. The outcome is fairly easy to predict. But in America you have to begin by making the land arable. No one can guess what will happen if you plant a crop in land that is being farmed for the very first time.

"Things look good so far. As long as it keeps going like this into next    30
year. I don't see any salt deposits and the strawberry plants are 100 percent

rooted," my brother said with relief in his voice, two months after we had gotten the field ready.

Early every morning my brother went out by himself and checked the roots of the strawberry plants one by one. By the time I woke up, he had finished this task and was sipping coffee. Having his own field had lifted his spirits — he nearly glowed. Every day I was back from school by three o'clock to help him.

One morning in October, when the days and evenings were much cooler, I came home to find my brother gone. I went to the adjoining field, where I found Frank, Pete, Ted, Charlie, Anchan, and the secretary in a huddle. Everyone looked tense.

"What is it?" I asked.

"*Yuu*, it's bad. The Mexicans are on strike. They didn't show up today, and González and Antonio have been missing since this morning," said my bewildered brother.

"Goddam Chicanos," swore Ted. "This is why I don't like them. Son of a bitch. This is going to screw up our schedule." 35

"*Yuu*, listen, if this were picking time, we'd be in hot water. The strawberries would rot. But it's not so bad now — we're just watering and weeding," Frank answered.

Frank's uniform was muddy. I wondered if he had been weeding since the morning. With the Mexicans protesting, the well-oiled machine of farm life had gone haywire.

"I wonder how long it's been since I weeded," Frank mused, not sounding altogether upset. All the supervisors that morning had returned to the simple tasks of the old days. In a field that held two hundred workers at harvesttime, it was a rare sight to see only four or five Japanese talking together spiritedly.

For a while anyway, all we had to do was to take care of the strawberry plants, so the farm didn't need too many hands. Frank had only hired about twenty Mexicans that month. But who would pick all the strawberries if they didn't show up next year? Our farm wasn't the only one. Bob Yamada's onion field in the next town and Imanishi-san's cauliflower field would be hit equally hard. The survival of California agriculture depended on the mood of the many Mexicans who came from all over to work for us.

"*Don worri*, it's OK. They'll be back. They're pigeons, the *Mexi-tachi*, 40 said Frank typically.

"Why are they striking now?" I asked.

"There's a Mexican leader named Cesar Chavez in central California. The strike started out on the grape farms, but for some reason it's spread this far," explained Frank.

According to him, on Mexican Independence Day of that year, September 16, the Mexicans, led by Cesar Chavez, had boycotted the grape fields of Delano, a town in central California. They were demanding a wage increase and a formal guarantee that the Immigration Bureau would grant them visas. We heard from the Japanese Americans who dropped by and the white representatives of the fertilizer company that many farms paid below minimum wage and that the worst ones would report the illegal workers on their farms to the authorities the day before payday and pocket their wages. In the face of such injustice, the pickers could do nothing. The Mexicans wanted special visas, because it was their cheap labor that kept the farms going. Their demands seemed perfectly reasonable to me, but I wondered why it had happened so suddenly. Then I remembered that the Mexican farm workers had been on the news frequently for the past month or so. Perhaps I just hadn't noticed what was obviously a big social problem, but I wasn't the only one in the dark. The supervisors themselves who had lived and worked with the Mexicans for years didn't seem to understand why they were striking.

"I didn't think the strike would get this big," said Frank.

"Frank, this is different from Chavez's strike, *I thinku jisu yea too muchi*  45
*hotto weza,* so maybe the *Mexis* don't feel like working." Frank's younger brother Pete was spouting nonsense, and Frank interrupted him. "*Yuu,* shut up, Pete. *Whato aru yuu talkingu?* If hot weather's the reason, the *Mexi-tachi neba . . .* never come to *Californi* farms," he yelled.

"Easy, Frank, easy," said Charlie, trying to calm him down. "It's hard on the Mexicans since the bracero program ended. Still, I can't believe they've all joined this strike. It's never happened before. Maybe it's going to be a hot year, you know."

The bracero program, founded by the Mexican and American governments in 1951 to send seasonal farm workers to America, had ended in 1964. After the war, America had industrialized quickly, and people had gravitated toward the cities, which resulted in a shortage of farm labor. The bracero program had been created to fill this gap, and it had succeeded, particularly in the Southwest. Its goal had been to send approximately 300,000 workers to various harvests on American farms every year.

Braceros worked hard, but in the end their low wages froze those of American farm workers, and the agricultural unions put pressure on the government to cancel the program. When it was halted, 250,000 to 350,000 Mexican workers were suddenly sent home. Panic spread through the Mexican border towns and a tidal wave of illegal immigration began. The Mexicans had returned home having tasted the riches of America; they would set out again to pursue their dreams to the north.

Many of the workers on our farm had come into the country on the bracero program and stayed on when it ended.

Of course, illegal immigration had always been a problem for the two neighbors. But it was only in the mid-sixties that the numbers of illegals started climbing into the hundreds of thousands. The situation along the border was very tense. After years of working on American farms, they had connections there and they could expect to get work from their former employers.

Because of the tense situation, the American and Mexican govern-          50
ments had put their heads together and come up with the Border Indus-
trialization Program, which was an attempt to stabilize the area. Under this program, American raw goods and capital were brought into Mexico, Mexican labor assembled a product, then it was shipped back to the States. The program had other names: *twin plants* or *maquiladora*. Nowa-days the phrase *borderless economy* is commonly used, but in 1965 *maquiladora* seemed groundbreaking. The borderless age between Mex-ico and America dates back to 1965. One can't deny that this program really suited American interests. American capital built workplaces in Mexico, and Americans profited on cheap labor. In addition, the program had a different outcome than was intended. It blurred the jurisdictions of the two governments, and a free zone emerged along the border.

Cesar Estrada Chavez was a second-generation Mexican from Arizona. Born to migrant workers, he moved from farm to farm as a child, having attended thirty schools by the time he dropped out in seventh grade. Chavez established the first union for farm workers in Delano, a town of grape farms in central California. His eloquence enthralled both the farm workers and Christian groups, and his union grew very powerful. He became even more active in 1964 after the bracero program ended, and in 1965 the pickers went on strike. One should note, however, that the Mexicans went on strike because they sympathized with the Filipino grape pickers who were demanding better working conditions.

Japanese immigrants were an important presence in California agri-culture before the war. Japanese farmers produced 11 percent of Califor-nia's fruit and 40 percent of its vegetables. When World War II broke out, Japanese Americans were sent to the camps and the Japanese farmer all but disappeared from California. Filipinos took their places.

After the war, the Japanese returned to their farms after a four-year hiatus, but they had lost too much and only a handful managed to become big farmers again. Most had to start over. . . . Men like Frank, who left the camps and rebuilt their businesses in less than five years, were rare exceptions.

The plight of the Filipinos, however, was also horrendous. As more recent immigrants, they, too, had been terribly exploited by white farmers. Cesar Chavez had stood up in solidarity with the Filipinos.

"It's a Mexican strike, but even Ramón the Filipino didn't come to work today. What's going on?" grumbled Frank.                                 55

Chavez's movement reached its peak in 1966. Nearly 300,000 Mexican and Filipino workers walked 300 miles from Delano to Sacramento, the state capital, during almost a month of protest. The damage to the fruit and vegetable crops of 1966 (especially lettuce and grapes) was tremendous. The farm workers had simply disappeared from central California, the largest farming belt of the state, and thrown California agriculture into the greatest crisis it had ever known. . . .

"America's getting all stirred up," Frank commented. "First the blacks got restless and now the Mexicans."

"*Zatso raito.* So I say don't give civil rights to the blacks and the Mexicans. Or the students. *Looku whatso happeningu to zisu kantori. Studento tachi neba studee.* All they talk about is free speech and marijuana. Remember when we were young. They always called us Japs but we never *gibu uppu.* But young people these days — *no goodo yo. Justo crazy.* Next time the Mexicans show up, we should work them harder and pay them less so they won't get even lazier," Ted ranted.

Ted's son was in Vietnam. Soon we were on that subject. "We were put in camps in the last war. No matter how much we say we're Americans, the government *neba* believe us. Even when we say we'll fight for America they don't let us out right away. So I say to my son, when America goes to war, you go too. What's this all about, these students at Berkeley draft dodging and making speeches. What about my poor son? *Rasto weeku,* I get a letter. It's a horrible war, he says, but at least we're fighting the commies. I'm telling you."

Just when I thought that the conversation had moved from the Mexican strike to the Vietnam war, Pete chimed in.                               60

"*My garu,* she's always talking about *woman ribu,*" Pete chimed in. "*Garu* should stay at *homu.* But now she comes home late at night and fights with my wife."

In my experience, all immigrant groups in America — Chinese, Italian, Irish, and Mexican — shared this belligerent conversational style. As everyone knows, Americans love to express their own opinions. Raising their voices, they pound on a table to make their point. Their behavior at the negotiating table or in the conference room comes from growing up in a jostling immigrant society where everyone is a talker.

When immigrants come to this country they survive by talking at other people, not by listening to what they have to say. Everyone they meet at work or school is a stranger, and they must make others understand who they are, by force if necessary. Otherwise, they will be doomed to live here eternally as invisible people. This is why it is so important to "sell yourself" in America. Later generations have inherited this tradition even if they were born in this country.

Moreover, when Americans enter into diplomatic or economic negotiations with other nations, they hope to find good listeners. With a good listener, an American may take his most natural role — that of the talker — and the meeting will be fruitful. The reason that economic negotiations between Japan and America have gone askew is due to the fact that Japan doesn't know how to listen correctly, and wavers in the face of an opinionated and forceful America. A nation must be mature to be a good listener, and Japan has had to take on this role too soon after a period of rapid economic growth.

Just then Jiisan drove slowly up the road in a '49 Ford that looked like an armadillo. "*Yuu-tachi*, what's with the Mexicans? They didn't come to my field today," he called out.

"Jiisan, they're on strike," my brother explained.

"Oh, really. I thought they just weren't coming. Well, it's *alrigh* if they take a break sometimes. They'll be there tomorrow. But, Frank, I wanted to ask you how your roots are doing. Some of my plants look sick; maybe I didn't water them right."

"Maybe the field wasn't flat enough so the water didn't spread evenly," said Frank sympathetically.

"Hmm. Maybe I just got some bad plants."

The old man was more talkative than usual.

"Hmm, these plants have good roots," he said, walking into our field and examining the rows.

Two days later, the strike ended and everything went back to normal.

## EXPLORATIONS

1. "A farmer can't mold the land to suit himself," writes Yoshimi Ishikawa (para. 7). What evidence in his essay confirms this statement? What evidence contradicts it?

2. Ishikawa's paragraph 7 concludes: "We were the ones who had to change." In what ways have the characters in his essay changed since they emigrated from Japan? What circumstances besides the nature of their farmland have forced them to change?

3. What part of "Strawberry Fields" describes a process? What process is explained?

# CONNECTIONS

1. In what ways is the relationship between the Japanese and the Mexicans in "Strawberry Fields" similar to the relationship between the Kuwaitis and their Asian maids in "A Woman's Place" (p. 475)? What motives and problems do the Mexican farm workers share with the Asian maids?

2. What statements in "Strawberry Fields" and in Le Ly Hayslip's "Rice Farming in Vietnam" (p. 432) show the physical love farmers have for their land? What processes appear in both essays?

3. What ideas about farming does Ishikawa share with Linda Hasselstrom in *Looking at Ourselves* (p. 405)?

4. Look at Ishikawa's statements in paragraphs 62–64 about Japanese relating to Americans. How does his assessment compare with Patrick Smith's in "Nippon Challenge" (p. 53), especially in the imaginary *New York Times* article Smith quotes?

# ELABORATIONS

1. Choose a job you have held or a skill you are good at, and write a process essay similar to Ishikawa's explaining how the work is done.

2. "Physical satisfaction is usually linked with sex, but I definitely felt it after working too," writes Ishikawa. "Human beings are built not only with a desire to reproduce, but to work" (para. 2). What activities in your life supply the kind of satisfaction he is talking about? Write an essay describing one.

# GABRIEL GARCÍA MÁRQUEZ

## *Dreams for Hire*

"It bothers me that the people of the United States have appropriated the word *America* as if *they* were the only Americans," Gabriel García Márquez told an interviewer shortly before he won the 1982 Nobel Prize for literature. A devotee of North American fiction, García Márquez was for a time prevented from entering the United States because he had worked for the Cuban news agency in New York in 1961. His old friendship with Fidel Castro, he says, is based on a shared love of literature and fish recipes. Born in the Caribbean coastal village of Aracataca, Colombia, in 1928, García Márquez grew up listening to his grandfather's tales of war and politics and his grandmother's stories of the supernatural. Out of this mix came the fictional town of Macondo, the setting for much of his fiction. García Márquez studied at the University of Bogotá in Colombia's capital; he left to be a journalist, traveling to other parts of South America, the United States, and Europe, and began writing short stories. Recognition came with his 1961 novella *El coronel no tiene quien le escriba* (*No One Writes to the Colonel*, 1968), during the flowering of Latin American literature referred to as "El Boom" (see pp. 224 and 303). But it was *Cien años de soledad* (1967; *One Hundred Years of Solitude*, 1970) that made him famous, selling more than 10 million copies in more than thirty languages. García Márquez's fusion of naturalism and fantasy has given him a central place in the genre known as magic realism. Among his other novels are *Crónica de una muerte anunciada* (1981; *Chronicle of a Death Foretold*, 1982), which won the Nobel Prize, and *General en su Laberingo* (1989; *The General in His Labyrinth*, 1990), a novel about South American liberator Simón Bolívar which sold 700,000 copies in its first two weeks. "Dreams for Hire," translated from the Spanish by Nick Caistor, appeared in the Autumn 1992 volume of *Granta*.

The Panama-Colombia border is where Central and South America meet. Colombia thus is the only South American country with both a Caribbean and a Pacific coast. Like Panama, Venezuela, and Ecuador, it was ruled by Spain as part of New Granada from the 1500s until independence in 1819. (Venezuela and Ecuador broke away ten years later; Panama followed in 1903.) The national language is Spanish, and 97 percent of Colombians are Roman Catholic. Ethnically a majority are mestizos (mixed Spanish and Indian blood). One of the continent's longest-lived democracies, Colombia continues to be plagued by economic and social problems, most notably the war between the government and the drug cartels.

For background on Cuba, see page 528.

At nine o'clock in the morning, while we were having breakfast on the terrace of the Hotel Riviera in Havana, a terrifying wave appeared out of nowhere — the day was sunny and calm — and came crashing upon us. It lifted the cars that had been passing along the sea front, as well as several others that had been parked nearby, and tossed them into the air, smashing one into the side of our hotel. It was like an explosion of dynamite, spreading panic up and down the twenty floors of our building and transforming the lobby into a pile of broken glass, where many of the hotel guests were hurled through the air like the furniture. Several were wounded in the hail of glass shards. It must have been a tidal wave of monumental size: The hotel is protected from the sea by a wall and the wide two-way avenue that passes before it, but the wave had erupted with such force that it obliterated the glass lobby.

Cuban volunteers, with the help of the local fire brigade, set to sweeping up the damage, and in less than six hours, after closing off the hotel's sea front entrance and opening up an alternative, everything was back to normal. Throughout the morning no one paid any attention to the car that had been smashed against the wall of the hotel, believing it had been among the vehicles parked along the avenue. But by the time it was eventually removed by a crane, the body of a woman was discovered inside, moored to the driving seat by her seat belt. The blow had been so great that there wasn't a bone in her body which was left unbroken. Her face was messy and unrecognizable, her ankle boots had burst at the seams, her clothes were in tatters. But there was a ring, still worn on her finger, which remained intact: It was made in the shape of a serpent and had emeralds for eyes. The police established that she was the house-keeper for the new Portuguese ambassador and his wife. In fact she had arrived with them only fifteen days before and had that morning left for the market in their new car. Her name meant nothing to me when I read about the incident in the papers, but I was intrigued by that ring, made in the shape of a serpent with emeralds for its eyes. I was, unfortunately, unable to find out on which finger the ring had been worn.

It was an essential detail: I feared that this woman might be someone I knew and whom I would never forget, even though I never learned her real name. She, too, had a ring made in the shape of a serpent, with emeralds for its eyes, but she always wore it on the first finger of her right hand, which was unusual, especially then. I had met her forty-six years ago in Vienna, eating sausages and boiled potatoes and drinking beer straight from the barrel, in a tavern frequented by Latin American students. I had arrived from Rome that morning, and I still recall that first impression made by her ample opera-singer's bosom, the drooping fox tails gathered around the collar of her coat, and that Egyptian ring made in the shape of a serpent. She spoke a rudimentary Spanish, in a breathless shopkeeper's accent, and I assumed that she must be Austrian, the only one at that long wooden table. I was wrong: she had been born in Colombia and between the wars had traveled to Austria to study music and singing. When I met her she must have been around thirty, and she had begun aging before her time. Even so, she was magical; and, also, among the most fearsome people I've ever met.

At that time — the late forties — Vienna was nothing more than an ancient imperial city that history had reduced to a remote provincial capital, located between the two irreconcilable worlds left by the Second World War, a paradise for the black market and international espionage. I couldn't imagine surroundings better suited to my fugitive compatriot, who went on eating in the students' tavern on the corner only out of nostalgia for her roots, because she had more than enough money to buy the whole place, its diners included. She never told us her real name; we always referred to her by the German tongue twister that the Latin American students in Vienna had invented for her: Frau Frida. No sooner had we been introduced than I committed the fortuitous imprudence of asking her how she came to find herself in a part of the world so distant and different from the windy heights of the Quindío region in Colombia. She replied matter-of-factly, "I hire myself out to dream."

That was her profession. She was the third of eleven children of a prosperous shopkeeper from the old region of Caldas, and by the time she learned to speak, she had established the habit of telling all her dreams before breakfast, when, she said, her powers of premonition were at their most pure. At the age of seven, she dreamt that one of her brothers had been swept away by a raging torrent. The mother, simply out of a nervous superstitiousness, refused to allow her son to do what he most enjoyed, swimming in the local gorge. But Frau Frida had already developed her own system of interpreting her prophecies.

"What the dream means," she explained, "is not that he is going to drown, but that he mustn't eat sweets."

The interpretation amounted to a terrible punishment, especially for a five-year-old boy who could not imagine life without his Sunday treats. But the mother, convinced of her daughter's divinatory powers, ensured that her injunction was adhered to. Unfortunately, following a moment's inattention, the son choked on a gob-stopper that he had been eating in secret, and it proved impossible to save him.

Frau Frida had never thought that it would be possible to earn a living from her talent until life took her by the scruff of the neck and, during a harsh Viennese winter, she rang the bell of the first house where she wanted to live, and, when asked what she could do, offered the simple reply: "I dream." After only a brief explanation, the lady of the house took her on, at a wage that was little more than pocket money, but with a decent room and three meals a day. Above all, there was a breakfast, the time when the members of the family sat down to learn their immediate destinies: the father, a sophisticated *rentier*;[1] the mother, a jolly woman with a passion for Romantic chamber music; and the two children, aged eleven and nine. All of them were religious and therefore susceptible to archaic superstitions, and they were delighted to welcome Frau Frida into their home, on the sole condition that every day she revealed the family's destiny through her dreams.

She did well, especially during the war years that followed, when reality was more sinister than any nightmare. At the breakfast table every morning, she alone decided what each member of the family was to do that day, and how it was to be done, until eventually her prognostications became the house's sole voice of authority. Her domination of the family was absolute: Even the slightest sigh was made on her orders. The father had died just prior to my stay in Vienna, and he had had the good grace to leave Frau Frida a part of his fortune, again on the condition that she continued dreaming for the family until she was unable to dream any more.

I spent a month in Vienna, living the frugal life of a student while      10 waiting for money which never arrived. The unexpected and generous visits that Frau Frida paid to our tavern were like fiestas in our otherwise penurious regime. One night, the powerful smell of beer about us, she whispered something in my ear with such conviction that I found it impossible to ignore.

"I came here specially to tell you that last night I saw you in my dreams," she said. "You must leave Vienna at once and not come back here for at least five years."

Such was her conviction that I was put, that same night, on the last train for Rome. I was so shaken that I have since come to believe that I survived a disaster I never encountered. To this day I have not set foot in Vienna again.

Before the incident in Havana I met up with Frau Frida once more, in Barcelona, in an encounter so unexpected that it seemed to me especially mysterious. It was the day that Pablo Neruda set foot on Spanish soil for the first time since the [Spanish] Civil War, during a stopover on

---

[1]Someone of independent means. — ED.

a long sea journey to Valparaiso in Chile.[2] He spent the morning with us, big game hunting in the antiquarian bookshops, buying eventually a faded book with torn covers for which he paid what must have been the equivalent of two months' salary for the Chilean consulate in Rangoon. He lumbered along like a rheumatic elephant, showing a childlike interest in the internal workings of every object he came across. The world always appeared to him as a giant clockwork toy.

I have never known anyone who approximated so closely the received idea of a Renaissance Pope — that mixture of gluttony and refinement — who even against his will, would dominate and preside over any table. Matilde, his wife, wrapped him in a bib which looked more like an apron from a barbershop than a napkin from a restaurant, but it was the only way to prevent him from being bathed in sauces. That day Neruda ate three lobsters in their entirety, dismembering them with the precision of a surgeon, while concurrently devouring everyone else's dishes with his eyes, until he was unable to resist picking from each plate, with a relish and an appetite that everyone found contagious: clams from Galicia, barnacle geese from Cantabria, prawns from Alicante, swordfish from the Costa Brava. All the while he was talking, just like the French, about other culinary delights, especially the prehistoric shellfish of Chile that were his heart's favorite. And then suddenly he stopped eating, pricked up his ears like the antennae of a lobster, and whispered to me: "There's someone behind me who keeps staring at me."

I looked over his shoulder. It was true. Behind him, three tables back, 15 a woman, unabashed in an old-fashioned felt hat and a purple scarf, was slowly chewing her food with her eyes fixed on Neruda. I recognized her at once. She was older and bigger, but it was her, with the ring made in the form of a serpent on her first finger.

She had traveled from Naples on the same boat as the Nerudas, but they had not met on board. We asked her to join us for coffee, and I invited her to talk about her dreams, if only to entertain the poet. But the poet would have none of it, declaring outright that he did not believe in the divination of dreams.

"Only poetry is clairvoyant," he said.

After lunch, and the inevitable walk along the Ramblas, I deliberately fell in with Frau Frida so that we could renew our acquaintance without the others hearing. She told me that she had sold her properties in Austria and, having retired to Porto, in Portugal, was now living in a house that she described as a fake castle perched on a cliff from where she could

[2]See p. 303.

see the whole Atlantic as far as America. It was clear, although she didn't say as much explicitly, that, from one dream to another, she had ended up in possession of the entire fortune of her once unlikely Viennese employers. Even so, I remained unimpressed, only because I had always thought that her dreams were no more than a contrivance to make ends meet. I told her as much.

She laughed her mocking laugh. "You're as shameless as ever," she said. The rest of our group had now stopped to wait for Neruda who was speaking in Chilean slang to the parrots in the bird market. When we renewed our conversation, Frau Frida had changed the subject.

"By the way," she said, "you can go back to Vienna if you like."                               20

I then realized that thirteen years had passed since we first met.

"Even if your dreams aren't true, I will never return," I told her, "just in case."

At three o'clock we parted in order to accompany Neruda to his sacred siesta, which he took at our house, following a number of solemn preparatory rituals that, for some reason, reminded me of the Japanese tea ceremony. Windows had to be opened, others closed — an exact temperature was essential — and only a certain kind of light from only a certain direction could be tolerated. And then: an absolute silence. Neruda fell asleep at once, waking ten minutes later, like children do, when we expected it least. He appeared in the living room, refreshed, the monogram of the pillow case impressed on his check.

"I dreamt of that woman who dreams," he said.

Matilde asked him to tell us about the dream.                                                 25

"I dreamt she was dreaming of me," he said.

"That sounds like Borges," I said.

He looked at me, crestfallen. "Has he already written it?"

"If he hasn't, he's bound to write it one day," I said. "It'll be one of his labyrinths."

As soon as Neruda was back on board ship at six that afternoon, he                            30
said his farewells to us, went to sit at an out-of-the-way table, and began writing verses with the same pen of green ink that he had been using to draw flowers, fish, and birds in the dedications he signed in his own books. With the first announcement to disembark, we sought out Frau Frida and found her finally on the tourist deck just as we were about to give up. She, too, had just woken from a siesta.

"I dreamt of your poet," she told us.

Astonished, I asked her to tell me about the dream.

"I dreamt he was dreaming about me," she said, and my look of disbelief confused her. "What do you expect? Sometimes among all the dreams there has to be one that bears no relation to real life."

I never saw or thought about her again until I heard about the ring made in the form of a serpent on the finger of the woman who died in the sea disaster at the Hotel Riviera. I could not resist asking the Portuguese Ambassador about it when we met up a few months later at a diplomatic reception.

The ambassador spoke of her with enthusiasm and tremendous admiration. "You can't imagine how extraordinary she was," he said. "You would have been unable to resist wanting to write a story about her." And he continued in the same spirit, on and on, with some occasional, surprising details, but without an end in sight.

"Tell me then," I said finally, interrupting him, "what exactly did she do?"

"Nothing," he replied, with a shrug of resignation. "She was a dreamer."

## EXPLORATIONS

1. In what ways do the structure, content, and style of "Dreams for Hire" make it seem more like a short story than an essay? What aspects of the piece remind us that it is a factual account?

2. What is Gabriel García Márquez's attitude toward Frau Frida's occupation? What is Frau Frida's attitude toward her occupation? Cite evidence for your answers.

3. What elements in Pablo Neruda's encounter with Frau Frida (paras. 14–17 and 23–33) suggest there is more than one reason for the tension between them? What are these reasons?

4. In what way is the last sentence of "Dreams for Hire" ambiguous? How would the narrative's impact change if the Portuguese ambassador explicitly identified his dead housekeeper as Frau Frida?

## CONNECTIONS

1. Necessity is the mother of invention, goes the old saying. How does necessity determine Frau Frida's career path? What other careers you have read about in "Work: We Are What We Do" were decided by necessity? Which ones turned out best and worst? What factors made the difference?

2. What are the similarities between Frau Frida's line of work and David Abram's in "Making Magic" (p. 422)? How do Frau Frida and Abram differ in their attitudes toward their work? What attitudes do they share, and why?

3. Look back at Octavio Paz's "Hygiene and Repression" (p. 15), especially his

first two paragraphs. What ideas in Paz's essay are illustrated by the lunch scene in "Dreams for Hire" (paras. 14–17)?

## ELABORATIONS

1. Gabriel García Márquez is one of the best writers in the world. To analyze his art is probably a task beyond the most ambitious critic; but we can learn a lot about writing by studying his craft. For instance, how does he use the literary device of a quest to create purpose, momentum, and suspense in this essay? Whose quest is it, and what is its object? What incidents begin and end it? What adventures along the way maintain our curiosity? Write an essay analyzing García Márquez's use of a quest as his central thread in "Dreams for Hire."

2. In "Hygiene and Repression," (p. 15) Octavio Paz writes: "In American society, unlike in ours, science from the very beginning has occupied a privileged place in the system of beliefs and values. The quarrel between faith and reason never took on the intensity that it assumed among Hispanic peoples" (para. 7). How do these statements apply to "Dreams for Hire"? How do they apply to Liliana Heker's "The Stolen Party" (p. 212)? To Mario Vargas Llosa's "On Sunday" (p. 224)? To Carlos Fuentes's "Matador and Madonna" (p. 303)? Write an essay exploring the quarrel between faith and reason in the Hispanic selections you have read in this book.

# PART SIX

# WE THE PEOPLE

## Individuals and Institutions

### LOOKING AT OURSELVES

*The New Yorker*, Wendell Berry, Haunani-Kay Trask, Vine
Deloria, Jr., and Clifford M. Lytle, Theodore Sizer, Toni
Morrison, Martin Luther King, Jr., Shelby Steele, Lewis H.
Lapham, Jim Whitewolf

Eduard Shevardnadze, *Life with the Party*
(FORMER SOVIET UNION)

Tim Golden, *Cubans Try to Cope with Dying Socialism* (CUBA)

Anonymous, *Evicted: A Russian Jew's Story (Again)* (RUSSIA)

Václav Havel, *Moral Politics* (CZECH REPUBLIC)

Fay Weldon, *Down the Clinical Disco* (GREAT BRITAIN)

Neil Postman, *Future Shlock* (UNITED STATES)

Michael Dorris, *House of Stone* (ZIMBABWE)

Nadine Gordimer, *Amnesty* (SOUTH AFRICA)

Nelson Mandela, *Black Man in a White Court* (SOUTH AFRICA)

OUTSIDE THE FAMILY, NEIGHBORHOOD, AND WORKPLACE, WE PARTICIpate — willingly or not — in a variety of social and political institutions. The U.S. government is one example. Its Constitution is a contract: In return for benefits such as security and order, "we the people" agree to give up some individual liberty. A challenge for every institution is striking a balance between the group interests for which it was formed and members' freedom to pursue other, sometimes competing, interests. In Part 6 we examine this balance and the impact of institutions on individuals.

*Looking at Ourselves* begins with remarks from *The New Yorker* on the news media's uneasy relationship with government. Wendell Berry questions our culture's faith in economic competition; Haunani-Kay Trask questions the United States's interpretation of Hawaii's native economy. Vine Deloria, Jr., and Clifford M. Lytle compare European-based and American Indian political structures. Theodore Sizer reports on high school. Toni Morrison suggests that slavery and its victims have cast a shadow over literature in the United States; Martin Luther King, Jr., outlines the economic basis of slavery; Shelby Steele depicts current racial tensions as a competing quest for innocence between the descendants of slaves and those of slaveholders. Lewis H. Lapham deplores the tendency among privileged Americans to lump together drugs, race, poverty, and crime. Jim Whitewolf shows drugs in a more spiritual context by describing Native Americans' ritual use of tobacco and peyote.

In "Life with the Party," former Communist leader Eduard Shevardnadze recalls the elaborate deceptions practiced by top bureaucrats in the former Soviet Union. Tim Golden describes the impact of the Soviet breakup on Fidel Castro and his people in "Cubans Try to Cope with Dying Socialism." An anonymous writer is reluctantly trying to emigrate in "Evicted: A Russian Jew's Story (Again)." Elsewhere behind the fallen Iron Curtain, Czech playwright Václav Havel tells in "Moral Politics" how his experience as a head of state has confirmed his dissident ideals.

A different kind of institution is Broadmoor, the British hospital for the criminally insane from which the narrator in Fay Weldon's short story "Down the Clinical Disco" is celebrating her release. Neil Postman's "Future Shlock" jumps from Hitler's Third Reich to Mel Brooks's "Springtime for Hitler" in a wry look at cultural erosion. "House of Stone" is Michael Dorris's frustrated response to the famine in Zimbabwe, seen by most Americans as one more competing demand for money and compassion. South African novelist Nadine Gordimer views her country's upheaval through the eyes of a black activist's girlfriend in the short story "Amnesty." South Africa's most famous activist and statesman, Nelson Mandela, speaks eloquently for himself in "Black Man in a White Court." ◇

# LOOKING AT OURSELVES

## 1

As it happens, some of the most interesting, if least publicized, confessions of this campaign year have come not from the candidates but from television journalists — specifically, Dan Rather, Tom Brokaw, Peter Jennings, Jim Lehrer, and Bernard Shaw, the anchors of the major national evening newscasts. You wouldn't know it from watching their broadcasts, but these men apparently feel considerable remorse over the job that they and their colleagues have done in covering the presidential contest. The five anchors recounted their journalistic shortcomings at a panel discussion in New York last month, which was sponsored by Harvard's Fran Shorenstein Barone Center on the Press, Politics, and Public Policy. They lamented their tendency to emphasize so-called horse-race questions, focusing on which candidate was ahead, rather than to offer substantive analyses of what the candidates stood for, and they admitted that their coverage too often favored the superficial and sensational over the important and enlightening. "It hit me in New Hampshire when I realized that the press only cared about Gennifer Flowers and the people only cared about the economy," Mr. Jennings said. Mr. Brokaw said that the media had engaged in "voyeurism for the sake of voyeurism," and Mr. Lehrer said, "We're in really serious trouble. I think we're losing our credibility." The only unrepentant note was struck by Mr. Shaw, the CNN anchor, whose conception of political reporting seems not to have changed since 1988, when he opened the final debate between George Bush and Michael Dukakis by sternly demanding to know what each candidate would do if his wife were "raped and murdered." The media were "duty bound" to report the tabloid allegations against Clinton, Mr. Shaw said now, and he added that if American voters were underinformed it was their own fault as much as it was television's.

This particular discussion didn't get much publicity (there were brief, buried stories in the *Los Angeles Times* and the *Washington Post*, and mentions on two C-Span broadcasts), but such mea culpas are becoming almost a quadrennial ritual within the news business. Every time the country holds an election, it seems, journalists end up apologizing for not living up to the promises they made four years earlier to do a better job next time. In 1984, for example, the media, and especially the television networks, happily went along with carefully orchestrated Reagan White House propaganda that passed off empty one-liners as genuine news events. Then, late in Reagan's presidency, when his aura of invincibility

unraveled amid disclosures of the Iran-Contra affair,[1] some journalists
began to criticize their previous gullibility and vowed not to be taken in
so easily during the campaign to elect Reagan's successor. Yet the coverage of the 1988 campaign, with its emphasis on Willie Horton, flag
factories, and other phony symbols, was, if anything, even emptier. In
May 1989, the [*New York*] *Times* published an article reporting that "some
television journalists . . . believe that they bear part of the responsibility
for the intellectual vacuity of the 1988 campaign." The headline asked,
"Will the Networks Succeed in Getting the Candidates to Talk Substance
in 1992?" and the article noted that key ABC News officials had begun
meeting just weeks after the 1988 election to discuss, in the words of Peter
Jennings, "how to deal with the fact that politicians and political consultants have learned so well how to manipulate us." Tim Russert, a vice-
president of NBC News, was quoted as saying that in 1992 "you'll see a
lot of movement in the direction of network selectivity in what they
cover." Yet here we are in 1992 and once again apologies are being made
for coverage that has been as simpleminded as ever — and being made,
this time, while the simpleminded coverage is still taking place.

The same thing happens when the country goes to war: The press
submits to the government after swearing that it would never be tricked
again. Whether it's the invasion of Grenada or of Panama or of the Persian
Gulf makes no noticeable difference. The military invade in secret. The
press is shocked to find itself not invited along. Eventually, the Pentagon
softens slightly, and reporters are escorted by military officials to observe
carefully selected portions of the battle area. News executives clear their
throats a few times and mumble something about the First Amendment,
but they accept the arrangement. After the fighting is over and the
president's poll numbers have soared, less flattering parts of the war story
begin to leak out. Journalists express shame and chagrin, and vow never
to betray their profession's ethics again. The military half-apologize for
getting carried away in the heat of battle, and a commission of news
executives and military officers is set up to insure free and responsible
coverage of the next war. Along comes the next war, and the military
once again invade in secret. . . .

Yet the anchors may not have been ducking responsibility so much as
being realistic about the system they are a part of. They, of all people,
recognize that money is at the root of virtually all decisions in television
news these days; it goes without saying that newscasts must enhance a

---

[1]Members of the Reagan administration illegally sold arms to the Iranian government and
used the proceeds to support the contra rebels in their fight against the Nicaraguan government. — ED.

company's competitiveness and profitability or they will not stay on the air. (Some of the same pressures confront the nominally noncommercial Public Broadcasting System, which is becoming increasingly reliant on big corporate sponsors.) Rather hinted at these constraints when he explained during the panel discussion that the reason the networks had not devoted more time to investigating campaign issues was a fear that "being serious but dull" would damage ratings.

The anchors' resigned acceptance of the status quo amounts to a confession that, for all their star power, multi-million-dollar salaries, and, in the cases of Rather and Brokaw, formal status as managing editors of their broadcasts, they feel no freer to ignore corporate imperatives than the average assembly-line worker does. But the networks may be underestimating their audience: There is more than a little evidence — some of it from the ratings themselves — that viewers are as unhappy with shallow coverage as the anchors are. They're turning to other sources for their news — phone-in interviews with the candidates, C-Span, and so on — and it will take more than confessions to get them back.

– "The Talk of the Town"
*The New Yorker*, 1992

◇-◇-◇-◇-◇

# 2

The ideal of competition always implies, and in fact requires, that any community must be divided into a class of winners and a class of losers. This division is radically different from other social divisions: that of the more able and the less able, or that of the richer and the poorer, or even that of the rulers and the ruled. These latter divisions have existed throughout history and at times, at least, have been ameliorated by social and religious ideals that instructed the strong to help the weak. As a purely economic ideal, competition does not contain or imply any such instructions. In fact, the defenders of the ideal of competition have never known what to do with or for the losers. The losers simply accumulate in human dumps, like stores of industrial waste, until they gain enough misery and strength to overpower the winners. The idea that the displaced and dispossessed "should seek retraining and get into another line of work" is, of course, utterly cynical; it is only the hand-washing practiced by officials and experts. A loser, by definition, is somebody whom nobody knows what to do with. There is no limit to the damage and the suffering implicit in this willingness that losers should exist as a normal economic cost.

The danger of the ideal of competition is that it neither proposes nor implies any limits. It proposes simply to lower costs at any cost, and to raise profits at any cost. It does not hesitate at the destruction of the life of a family or the life of a community. It pits neighbor against neighbor as readily as it pits buyer against seller. Every transaction is *meant* to involve a winner and a loser. And for this reason the human economy is pitted without limit against nature. For in the unlimited competition of neighbor and neighbor, buyer and seller, all available means must be used; none may be spared.

I will be told that indeed there are limits to economic competitiveness as now practiced — that, for instance, one is not allowed to kill one's competitor. But, leaving aside the issue of whether or not murder would be acceptable as an economic means if the stakes were high enough, it is a fact that the destruction of life is a part of the daily business of economic competition as now practiced. If one person is willing to take another's property or to accept another's ruin as a normal result of economic enterprise, then he is willing to destroy that other person's life as it is and as it desires to be. That this person's biological existence has been spared seems merely incidental; it was spared because it was not worth anything. That this person is now "free" to "seek retraining and get into another line of work" signifies only that his life as it was has been destroyed.

> — Wendell Berry
> "Economy and Pleasure"
> *What Are People For?* 1990

# 3

Burdened by a linear, progressive conception of history and by an assumption that Euro-American culture flourishes at the upper end of that progression, Westerners have told the history of Hawai'i as an inevitable if occasionally bittersweet triumph of Western ways over "primitive" Hawaiian ways. A few authors — the most sympathetic — have recorded with deep-felt sorrow the passing of our people. But in the end, we are repeatedly told, such an eclipse was for the best.

Obviously it was best for Westerners, not for our dying multitudes. This is why the historian's mission has been to justify our passing by celebrating Western dominance. [Political philosopher Frantz] Fanon would have called this missionizing, intellectual colonization. And it is clearest in the historian's insistence that pre-*haole* Hawaiian land tenure was "feudal" — a term that is now applied, without question, in every monograph, in every schoolbook, and in every tour guide description of my people's history.

From the earliest days of Western contact my people told their guests that *no one* owned the land. The land — like the air and the sea — was for all to use and share as their birthright. Our chiefs were *stewards* of the land; they could not own or privately possess the land any more than they could sell it.

But the *haole* insisted on characterizing our chiefs as feudal landlords and our people as serfs. Thus, a European term which described a European practice founded on the European concept of private property — feudalism — was imposed upon a people halfway around the world from Europe and vastly different from her in every conceivable way. More than betraying an ignorance of Hawaiian culture and history, however, this misrepresentation was malevolent in design.

By inventing feudalism in ancient Hawai'i, Western scholars quickly transformed a spiritually based, self-sufficient economic system of land use and occupancy into an oppressive, medieval European practice of divine right ownership, with the common people tied like serfs to the land. By claiming that a Pacific people lived under a European system — that the Hawaiians lived under feudalism — Westerners could then degrade a successful system of shared land use with a pejorative and inaccurate Western term. Land tenure changes instituted by Americans and in line with current Western notions of private property were then made to appear beneficial to the Hawaiians. But in practice, such changes benefited the *haole*, who alienated the people from the land, taking it for themselves.

> – Haunani-Kay Trask
> "From a Native Daughter"
> *The American Indian and
> the Problem of History*, 1987

# 4

The [North American] Europeans have had an extraordinarily difficult time in understanding the structure, substance, and procedures of the [North American] Indian manner of governing their societies. Some non-Indian observers have regarded the Indian propensity to hold land in common as the principle that distinguishes Indians from the European political traditions. Others have suggested that religious beliefs and cultural patterns have prevented Indians from organizing themselves socially or politically in a fashion familiar and acceptable to European minds. A bit of truth exists in every explanation, because the two traditions, European and North American Indian, seem to be diametrically opposed at almost every point at which they could or should be tangent and parallel.

The most profound and persistent element that distinguishes Indian ways of governing from European-American forms is the very simple fact that non-Indians have tended to write down and record all the principles and procedures that they believe essential to the formation and operation of a government. The Indians, on the other hand, benefiting from a religious, cultural, social, and economic homogeneity in their tribal societies, have not found it necessary to formalize their political institutions by describing them in a document. In addition, at least with the American experience, citizenship has been a means by which diverse peoples were brought into a relatively homogeneous social whole, and in order to ensure good citizenship, the principles of government have been taught so that newcomers to society can adapt themselves to the rules and regulations under which everyone has agreed to live. Within an Indian tribal society, on the other hand, the simple fact of being born establishes both citizenship and, as the individual grows, a homogeneity of purpose and outlook. Customs, rituals, and traditions are a natural part of life, and individuals grow into an acceptance of them, eliminating the need for formal articulation of the rules of Indian tribal society.

Violation of these customs did involve action by the community to enforce its rules. The tribe, meeting in council, discussed the violation and called upon its knowledge of precedents in community history which were factually close to the incident under consideration. Great discussions ensued as the community attempted to decide whether or not the current incident was sufficiently similar to warrant the same solution. Although tribes used precedent for making their decisions, punishment was often devised to reflect the best solution for the community at that time and was not always dependent upon following the former resolution of the problem. Because of this great flexibility, there was no need to formulate a rigid set of laws and there was little inclination to make precedents absolute in the same way that the Anglo-Saxon legal tradition found necessary.

The forms of government that Indians have experienced during their contact with the United States have been a mixture of the two traditions. Washington has considered the tribes to be political entities capable of determining their own membership and, in some cases, citizenship as well when there was a distinction between the two ideas. Self-government, consequently, has come to mean those forms of government that the federal government deems acceptable and legitimate exercises of political power and that are recognizable by the executive and legislative branches. This modern conception of self-government dates from the New Deal era, when John Collier, as Commissioner of Indian Affairs, was able to replace the existing policy of assimilation with a new program, which advocated the preservation of tribal cultures and the promotion of federally recognized governments on the reservations. It is crucial to realize at the start that these have not necessarily been the forms of government that the Indian people themselves have demanded or appreciated and are certainly not the kind of government that most Indians, given a truly free choice in the matter, would have adopted by themselves. Traditional Indians see that the task of governing themselves requires the perpetuation of customs, beliefs, and practices whose origin can be traced to precontact times. At the same time, it is important to recognize that, given the decades of erosion traditional cultures have suffered and the sparsity of viable alternatives available in the twentieth century, the present organization of tribal governments is not necessarily an unreasonable compromise between what might have been and what was possible to accept. Let us be very clear, however: Self-government is not and cannot be the same as self-determination so long as it exists at the whim of the controlling federal government.

> – Vine Deloria, Jr., and
> Clifford M. Lytle
> *The Native Within:*
> *The Past and Future*
> *of American Indian*
> *Sovereignty,* 1984

## 5

"Taking subjects" in a systematized, conveyor-belt way is what one does in high school. That this process is, in substantial respects, not related to the rhetorical purposes of education is tolerated by most people, perhaps because they do not really either believe in those ill-defined goals or, in their heart of hearts, believe that schools can or should even try to achieve them. The students are happy taking subjects. The parents are happy, because that's what they did in high school. The rituals, the most important of which is graduation, remain intact. The adolescents are supervised, safely and constructively most of the time, during the morning and afternoon hours, and they are off the labor market. That is what high school is all about.

> – Theodore Sizer
> "What High School Is"
> *Horace's Compromise: The Dilemma*
> *of the American High School,* 1984

## 6

For some time now I have been thinking about the validity or vulnerability of a certain set of assumptions conventionally accepted among literary historians and critics and circulated as "knowledge." This knowledge holds that traditional, canonical American literature is free of, uninformed and unshaped by, the 400-year-old presence of, first, Africans and then African-Americans in the United States. It assumes that this presence — which shaped the body politic, the Constitution, and the entire history of the culture — has had no significant place or consequence in the origin and development of that culture's literature. Moreover, such knowledge assumes that the characteristics of our national literature emanate from a particular "Americanness" that is separate from and unaccountable to this presence. There seems to be a more or less tacit agreement among literary scholars that, because American literature has been clearly the preserve of white male views, genius, and power, those views, genius, and power are without relationship to and removed from the overwhelming presence of black people in the United States. This agreement is made about a population that preceded every American writer of renown and was, I have come to believe, one of the most furtively radical impinging forces on the country's literature. The contemplation of this black presence is central to any understanding of our national literature and should not be permitted to hover at the margins of the literary imagination.

These speculations have led me to wonder whether the major and championed characteristics of our national literature — individualism, masculinity, social engagement versus historical isolation; acute and ambiguous moral problematics; the thematics of innocence coupled with an obsession with figurations of death and hell — are not in fact responses to a dark, abiding, signing Africanist presence.

> — Toni Morrison
> *Playing in the Dark*, 1992

⬖⬖⬖⬖⬖

# 7

For more than two hundred years before the Declaration of Independence, Africa had been raped and plundered by Britain and Europe, her native kingdoms disorganized, and her people and rulers demoralized. For a hundred years afterward, the infamous trade continued in America virtually without abatement, even after it had ceased to be legal on this continent. . . .

It is important to understand that the basis for the birth, growth, and development of slavery in America was primarily economic. By the beginning of the seventeenth century, the British Empire had established colonies all along the Atlantic seaboard from Massachusetts to the West Indies to serve as producers of raw materials for British manufacturing, a market for goods manufactured in Britain, and a source of staple cargoes for British shipping engaged in world trade. So the colonies had to provide an abundance of rice, sugar, cotton, and tobacco. In the first few years of the various settlements along the East Coast, so-called indentured servants, mostly white, were employed on plantations. But within a generation the plantation operators were demanding outright and lifetime slavery for the Africans they imported. As a function of this new economic policy, Africans were reduced to the status of property by law, and this status was enforced by the most rigid and brutal police power of the existing governments. By 1650 slavery had been legally established as a national institution.

Since the institution of slavery was so important to the economic development of America, it had a profound impact in shaping the social-political-legal structure of the nation. Land and slaves were the chief forms of private property, property was wealth, and the voice of wealth made the law and determined politics. In the service of this system, human beings were reduced to propertyless property. Black men, the creators of the wealth of the New World, were stripped of all human and civil rights. And this degradation was sanctioned and protected by institutions of government, all for one purpose: to produce commodities for sale at a profit, which in turn would be privately appropriated.

It seems to be a fact of life that human beings cannot continue to do wrong without eventually reaching out for some rationalization to clothe their acts in the garments of righteousness. And so, with the growth of slavery, men had to convince themselves that a system which was so economically profitable was morally justifiable. The attempt to give moral sanction to a profitable system gave birth to the doctrine of white supremacy.

> – Martin Luther King, Jr.
> "Racism and the White Backlash"
> *Where Do We Go from Here:*
> *Chaos or Community?* 1967

## 8

I think the racial struggle in America has always been primarily a struggle for innocence. White racism from the beginning has been a claim of white innocence and therefore of white entitlement to subjugate blacks. And in the sixties, as went innocence so went power. Blacks used the innocence that grew out of their long subjugation to seize more power, while whites lost some of their innocence and so lost a degree of

power over blacks. Both races instinctively understand that to lose innocence is to lose power (in relation to each other). To be innocent someone else must be guilty, a natural law that leads the races to forge their
innocence on each other's backs. The inferiority of the black always
makes the white man superior; the evil might of whites makes blacks
good. This pattern means that both races have a hidden investment in
racism and racial disharmony despite their good intentions to the contrary.
Power defines their relations, and power requires innocence, which, in
turn, requires racism and racial division. . . .

Historically, blacks have handled white society's presumption of innocence in two ways: They have bargained with it, granting white society
its innocence in exchange for entry into the mainstream, or they have
challenged it, holding that innocence hostage until their demand for
entry (or other concessions) was met. A bargainer says, *I already believe
you are innocent (good, fair-minded) and have faith that you will prove it.*
A challenger says, *If you are innocent, then prove it.* Bargainers *give* in
hope of receiving; challengers *withhold* until they receive. Of course,
there is risk in both approaches, but in each case the black is negotiating
his own self-interest against the presumed racial innocence of the larger
society.

>     – Shelby Steele
>     "I'm Black, You're White,
>     Who's Innocent?
>     Race and Power
>     in an Era of Blame"
>     *The Content of Our Character,* 1988

# 9

The story of the drug war plays to the prejudices of an audience only
too eager to believe the worst that can be said about people whom they
would rather not know. Because most of the killing allied with the drug
trade takes place in the inner cities, and because most of the people
arrested for selling drugs prove to be either black or Hispanic, it becomes
relatively easy for white people living in safe neighborhoods to blur the
distinction between crime and race. Few of them have ever seen an addict
or witnessed a drug deal, but the newspapers and television networks keep
showing them photographs that convey the impression of a class war, and
those among them who always worried about driving through Harlem
(for fear of being seized by gangs of armed black men) or who always
wished that they didn't feel quite so guilty about the socioeconomic
distance between East 72nd Street and West 126th Street can comfort

themselves, finally, at long last, and with a clear conscience, with the thought that poverty is another word for sin, that their BMW is a proof of their virtue, and that they or, more likely, their mothers were always right to fear the lower classes and the darker races.

As conditions in the slums deteriorate, which they inevitably must because the government subtracts money from the juvenile-justice and housing programs to finance its war on drugs, the slums come to look just the way they are supposed to look in the suburban imagination, confirming the fondest suspicions of the governing and possessing classes, justifying the further uses of force and repression. The people who pay the price for the official portrait turn out to be (wonder of wonders) not the members of the prosperous middle class — not the journalists or the academic theorists, not the politicians and government functionaries living behind hedges in Maryland and Virginia — but (mirabile dictu) the law-abiding residents of the inner cities living in the only neighborhoods that they can afford.

It is in the slums of New York that three people, on average, get killed every day — which, over the course of a year, adds up to a higher casualty rate than pertains in Gaza and the West Bank; it is in the slums that the drug trade recruits children to sell narcotics, which is not the result of indigenous villainy but of the nature of the law; it is in the slums that the drug trade has become the exemplary model of finance capitalism for children aspiring to the success of Donald Trump and Samuel Pierce; and it is in the slums that the police experiment with the practice of apartheid, obliging residents of housing projects to carry identity cards and summarily evicting the residents of apartment houses tainted by the presence of drug dealers.[1]

To the extent that the slums can be seen as the locus of the nation's wickedness (i.e., a desolate mise-en-scène not unlike the Evil Empire that Ronald Reagan found in the Soviet Union), the crimes allied with the drug traffic can be classified as somebody else's moral problem rather than one's own social or political problem. The slums become foreign, alien nations on the other side of the economic and cultural frontiers. The deliberate confusion of geography with metaphysics turns out, again to nobody's surprise, to be wonderfully convenient for the sponsors of the

---

[1]The government's own statistics indicate that the middle classes no longer recognize the drug problem as one of their own. Doing lines of cocaine hasn't been hip for at least five years, and among college and high school students, the use of drugs has declined markedly over the same period of time. In fact, the number of current cocaine users has gone down from 5.8 million in 1985 to 2.9 million in 1988. A July [1989] poll conducted by the mayor's office in Washington, D.C., showed that the white residents in town worried more about potholes than about cocaine.

war on drugs. The politicians get their names in the papers, the media have a story to tell, and the rest of us get off the hooks that otherwise might impale us on the questions of conscience or the obligation of higher taxes. In New York last week, I overheard a woman in an expensive restaurant say that she didn't understand why the government didn't arrange to put "arsenic or something" in a seized shipment of cocaine. If the government (or "the CIA or the FBI or whoever does that sort of thing") allowed the poisoned cocaine to find its way back onto the streets, then "pretty soon we'd be rid of the whole damn thing."

– Lewis H. Lapham
"A Political Opiate: The War on Drugs
Is a Folly and a Menace"
*Harper's Magazine*, 1989

◇◇◇◇◇◇

# 10

About 1896 I saw a tipi west of Anadarko. I heard that they were going to have a peyote meeting there that night. There I saw my cousin, my mother's brother's boy. His name was Carl. We went in and sat down on the south side. Then they passed around the tobacco; it was Bull Durham. At the time they were smoking, the chief was the only one to pray. The Indians there were Kiowa Apaches. . . . It was the first time I ever took part in a peyote meeting. They had peyote before this time, though.

After the smoking was over, sage was passed around. Each person would take some of it and smell it and rub himself all over with it. They did it so they would not get sickness and so they would always be strong. After the sage went around they passed the peyote around in a sack, and each one took two as it came to them and ate them. Next, the peyote chief took a bag of dried, crumbled cedar and put some in the fire. This is done because when the smoke rises up out of the fire from the cedar in it, the prayer will go out. Everyone reached out to the fire and rubbed his body with the smoke. The chief took his gourd and his staff and made a motion toward the fire four times. The drummer took his drum and drumstick and made the same motions as the chief did. Then the chief sang and the ceremony began. Each person in turn sang four songs until everyone had sung. Each one took the drum after he sang his four songs. When the chief thought it was midnight he sang one song known as the water song, *kobizi*. When he finished that song the fire chief went out after the water. He put the water right in front of the fireplace. Just after the water was brought in the peyote chief gave cedar to some member in the tipi, to pray. Then this man put the cedar into the fire. Then the tobacco was passed to the fire chief and he rolled a cigarette of corn shuck. He prayed and gave the cigarette to the drum chief. When the drum chief finished praying with this cigarette, he gave it to the peyote chief. When the chief finished praying with the cigarette, he laid it down on the floor, right in front of the representation of the moon, which is made of dirt heaped up before the fire. Then they passed the water around from the door and everyone drank. The fire chief took the water outside again. Then the drum was passed around again and the whole thing was repeated.

I sat in and watched all of this. When I ate the peyote I thought it was a wonderful thing. I felt good and listened to the songs and the prayers. They said that this was the way they prayed and that they learned it a long time ago.

When it was getting light outside and they saw morning was coming, the chief again called for water. This time he picked up a whistle that he blew four times, and then he sang the morning water song. After that the chief's wife brought in the water. Just like at midnight, they gave cedar to someone who prayed and everyone rubbed himself with the smoke. The tobacco was passed to the chief's wife and she rolled her own cigarette. Then the fire chief took a stick that is used specially for lighting the tobacco and gave her a light for her cigarette. Then she passed the cigarette around and they did the same thing as at midnight. The water went all the way around and the chief's wife was the last one to take a drink of it. She left the bucket by the fire and circled around the tipi. Then she took the bucket and went out of the tipi. When she returned with the food, they stopped singing and just continued to pass the drum on around until it got back to the chief, and then he sang four songs. The last song of the four was the final song of the night. Then the food was brought in. The chief asked someone to say a blessing for the food. After the prayer for food, the drum chief untied his drum and put his drumstick inside of it. He put the drum down in front of him. Then the chief took his gourd and staff and passed them around. Each person took the staff and held it outstretched, and shook the gourd as he said a prayer, like, "May I live to be an old man." As the gourd and staff were going around, the drum was following behind, and each one took the stick inside the drum, which had water in it, dripped the water on his hand, and smeared it on his head. As each one did this he made a wish, such as, "May I become gray-haired." Following the drum they passed around the seven rocks that were underneath the thongs which held the hide over the drum. Each one rubbed himself with the rocks and made a wish, to be strong or to keep healthy. When all of these things had returned to the chief, he put them into a satchel and smoked them over the fire four times. Then the fire chief took the satchel outside of the tipi. When the fire chief returned he circled around inside the tipi before seating himself again. Then the food, in four bowls, was passed around. After everyone had eaten, the fire chief took the bowls and went out, followed by everyone in regular order. The meeting was then over. Everyone sat on the outside and told stories, and then at noon there was a big feast, after which everyone returned home.

From that day on I liked the peyote worship and even today I go to it and enjoy it. The old people said that they hoped I would learn that it was a good thing and tell the young people, so it would always go on. I believe that it is because of going to that first meeting that I have lived to be an old man today.

> – Jim Whitewolf
> *The Life of a Kiowa Apache*, 1969

## REFLECTIONS

1. Which (if any) of the problems noted in *Looking at Ourselves* only exist in the United States? Which problems exist elsewhere in the world, and in what countries, so far as you know?

2. According to the *New Yorker* selection (p. 507), what are the worst qualities of the U.S. news media? What are the media's valuable contributions to American life?

3. What concept of land use prevailed in Hawai'i before Europeans arrived, according to Haunani-Kay Trask (p. 510)? What concept of land use prevailed among American Indian tribes, according to Vine Deloria, Jr., and Clifford M. Lytle (p. 511)?

4. What connection does Martin Luther King, Jr., make between the economics of slavery and the doctrine of white supremacy (p. 514)? How does Toni Morrison believe this connection has affected North American literature (p. 513)? In what ways do Shelby Steele's ideas about innocence apply to King's and Morrison's views (p. 515)?

# EDUARD SHEVARDNADZE

## *Life with the Party*

Eduard Shevardnadze was born in the Soviet state of Georgia in 1928. Eleven years earlier, Russia's last hereditary czar had been toppled by revolution. His successors then fell to the Bolshevik Revolution, which swept Nikolai Lenin into power. The Union of Soviet Socialist Republics (USSR, or Soviet Union), consisting of twelve member states, was formally established in 1922. (The three Baltic republics, Lithuania, Latvia, and Estonia, were freed by the revolution but reconquered by the Red Army twenty years later.) Shevardnadze was educated at the Pedagogical Institute in Kutaisi; at the age of twenty he joined the Communist Party. As he relates in the following essay, he moved quickly up the Party ladder, becoming secretary of the Komsomol Committee first for Kutaisi and then for all of Georgia. One appointment followed another, until Soviet President Chernenko died in 1985. Chernenko's successor was Shevardnadze's friend Mikhail Gorbachev, at age fifty-four the youngest man to head the Soviet Union since Joseph Stalin (1924–1953). In a surprise move, Gorbachev took the post of foreign minister away from twenty-eight-year veteran Andrey Gromyko and gave it to Shevardnadze. Gorbachev's policies of perestroika (restructuring) and glasnost (openness) included reorganizing the government, holding the first competitive elections since 1917, and facing the fact that after seventy years of communism, the Soviet economy was on the verge of collapse. Gorbachev's efforts at reform won him international respect and the 1990 Nobel Peace Prize, but by then he was losing power. Late in 1990 Shevardnadze resigned, blasting Gorbachev for shifting to the right to placate opponents. The following year, Russia created its own presidency and elected Boris Yeltsin, who had quit the Communist Party to protest the slowness of reform. A military coup attempt against Gorbachev in August 1991 was foiled largely by Yeltsin. Back in office, Gorbachev resigned as leader of the Communist Party, which was disbanded soon afterward. On Christmas Day, 1991, the Soviet Union itself was dissolved. The state of Georgia became independent not only of the Soviet Union but of the much larger state of Russia for the first time in two-and-a-half centuries. Its first attempt at electing its own leader was a failure; President Zviad Gamsakhudia was quickly deposed. In early 1992 Shevardnadze was asked to lead a provisional state council. Elections in October confirmed him in a landslide as Georgia's head of state. "Life with the Party" comes from his 1991 autobiography, *The Future Belongs to Freedom*, translated from the Russian by Catherine A. Fitzpatrick.

For more information about Russia and the Soviet Union, see page 536.

[When] I was elected Secretary of the Central Committee of the Communist Youth Union (Komsomol) of Georgia, I embarked on a new period of my life. I began to travel to Moscow and other cities more frequently. There I met my colleagues, the leaders of republic and province Komsomol organizations. The campaign to develop the country's virgin lands and forests was beginning. Trains packed with young volunteers shuttled to Kazakhstan and the Altai range. I was assigned to lead the Georgian Komsomol brigade. We lived in the Kazakh steppes for several months, tilling the virgin earth, building homes and agricultural complexes. We became acquainted with our peers from other republics. I owe much to this period of my life and retain bright memories of it. Perhaps people of my age are prone to idealize the vanished past, seeing their youth through a haze of nostalgia. But time does not distort the picture of those years or erase the remembered hardship of that life; nor do all my fellow travelers come out looking like heroes. I can clearly recall this grandiose but poorly organized "virgin land" era, the stupid decisions, and the ill-conceived strategies that canceled out many successes. We watched helplessly as equipment brought to the new territories from all over the country began to break down. Thousands of people worked themselves ragged but failed to gather in the gigantic harvest. The crops rotted in the fields, and there was no place to store grain. Billions of rubles and vast amounts of equipment and manpower were squandered.

The virgin lands campaign cost the country a great deal. Now I see that the enormous expenditures of that period could have been effective if we had used another approach to the grain problem. But that alternative was closed to us.

Still, I recall that period as good and glorious, because it gave us what I think youth needs the most: the proof that we are capable of building our lives from scratch when we have nothing, that everything we obtain comes out of our intelligence and strength.

This was also the period when I first met the people who would occupy prominent positions in the Soviet leadership. We felt ourselves to be "people of the virgin lands," tackling untouched fields with nothing but enthusiasm. "Dear Nikita Sergeyevich" promised us life under communism. The first Soviet cosmonauts were plowing the virgin territory of space. Much of what we had inherited was being subjected to review. I lived with a premonition of great changes ahead and thus kept an especially sharp eye on my contemporaries.

Among my new acquaintances was Mikhail Gorbachev, First Secretary       5
of the Stavropol Territory Komsomol Committee. We had met in Moscow at a Komsomol Central Committee plenary session. Many things had

brought us together, and we were eager to get to know each other better. We had the same peasant roots, had worked on the land at a tender age, and had the same knowledge of folk life. He was clearly also a man of learning and erudition. Geographic proximity and common concerns made for a businesslike but informal neighborliness. It's only a few hours through the Caucasus by car from Tiflis to Stavropol. Georgian shepherds drive their flocks along the way, into the mountain pastures — their shelter and safety was one of my responsibilities, and my good rapport with the regional officials helped me handle problems that were not always simple. In Gorbachev, I had a friend who was always ready to help me out, in word and deed.

But there was something else that made him stand out for me from the others. He was completely devoid of that artificial Komsomol modesty I had always found so annoying; more important, I could see that his thinking went beyond the boundaries of prescribed norms.

We saw each other often, in Moscow, Tbilisi, and in his area, and spoke to each other on the phone regularly. Gradually, unnoticed to ourselves, we opened up to each other, beginning to confide our secret thoughts.

A leap over three decades of friendship brings us to the end of the 1970s and the following scene. In a barren park on the deserted shore near the Black Sea's Cape Pitsunda, the two of us are strolling down a path between the trees. By that time, Mikhail Gorbachev was a Secretary of the CPSU[1] Central Committee and a candidate member of the Politburo, and I was First Secretary of the Georgian CP[2] Central Committee, also a candidate member of the Politburo. This "walk in the woods" was to have far-reaching consequences. We no longer held anything back.

One episode from this period will illustrate the degree and nature of the trust I had in Gorbachev.

At the beginning of the 1970s, an experiment was launched in the Abash District Center to test a new pay system for farm work, which would be tied to cost, quality, and quantity of production. If we decipher the scientific theory behind this, it was very simple: good pay for good work. The Western reader will not understand this: What's so experimental and innovative about this? It's an elementary principle of business that a worker has a vested interest in the results of his labor. Any economic activity, to be productive, must take the farmer's interest into account.

The Soviet reader will understand the code words all too well. He knows our whole economy is rigged in such a way that people often find

---

[1]Communist Party of the Soviet Union. — ED.
[2]Communist Party. — ED.

it unprofitable to work. The pay is not equal to the effort and the resulting quality. "You pretend to pay us, and we pretend to work" is the Soviet workers' folk saying, and it describes the real state of affairs.

The problem is not only that the state confiscates too much surplus value and product. It is a fundamental principle that encouraging the worker's proprietary instincts threatens the very foundations of the socialist order. If this causes the nation's economy to stagnate, that is a secondary problem. The main priority is to preserve the purity of doctrine.

In Abash District, a corn farmer who worked 400 man-days on a collective farm earned an average of 10 to 12 rubles[3] a month and 200 kilos[4] of corn a year. As a result, people stopped working, and the collective farms went broke. This occurred not in just one district, or even just in our republic. The very state that set the ideological and economic restrictions upon productive farm labor suffered enormous losses. The system was undermining itself, heading for self-destruction. It was impossible for common sense to reconcile itself to this absurdity. But it also seemed impossible to overcome it.

At this point I should decode the term *experiment*. We used it as a cover to ward off accusations that we were undermining the pillars of socialism. We told the ideological prosecutors that we were only experimenting in a limited area, and that our trials and errors would not spread. We just wanted to see how they would turn out.

But by paying the corn growers in kind — 10 percent of the grain for fulfilling the plan plus 70 percent of the excess harvest — we were able to triple grain production in the district within two years. By 1980 the average yield per hectare had increased fivefold. About 40 percent of the harvest went into family silos, but the state also began to receive far more than before.

We did not stop there. We reorganized the management of the agricultural processing complex. The peasants began to fatten their livestock with grain they themselves had produced. We abolished the ceiling of one cow per farmstead introduced under Khrushchev, and introduced a contract system whereby the collective farms provided livestock and feed to the peasants, and they fed pigs on their private plots and sold them back to the collective farm. We reduced overhead and raised the volume and quantity of sales. As a result, income rose surprisingly quickly, the population drain subsided, and new homes, roads, public cultural centers, and sports complexes went up, transforming the district.

---

[3] The equivalent of $2.50 to $3.00 in current U.S. dollars. — ED.
[4] Equal to 442 pounds. — ED.

Overall, our experiment was a successful attempt to change the relations between the peasants and the authorities and to establish new cooperative ties, with the idea of later expanding the Abash experiment through the whole republic.

In charge of agriculture at the time, Gorbachev supported our initiative. Once, having arrived to take a look at the experiment in progress, he asked to see one of the private plots.

"Let's go and see Nadareishvili," I said to Guram Mgeladze, the district Party committee secretary. He blanched. Nadareishvili was a war invalid who had fought at the front. He kept ten dairy cows at his own farmstead. By all Soviet standards, he was a *kulak*.[5]

"No, come on," I insisted. "Let Mikhail Sergeyevich see how a farmer      20 does when we get rid of excessive regulation."

We went, took a look, and had a conversation with Nadareishvili. Later Gorbachev asked me: "What do you think he is, exactly?"

"A farmer," I said. "A good manager. But if you like we can de-kulakize him. Then there won't be any farm, milk, or livestock."

Gorbachev chuckled.

"We could de-kulakize him, of course, so that your theoreticians won't get angry. But how are we going to improve rural life without this kind of *kulak*?"

One of the theoreticians, an executive at the Central Committee, had      25 said to Mgeladze:

"You've got to raise livestock productivity, but don't diverge from Marx."

I told Gorbachev this story, and he laughed. But it was a bitter joke.

We scarcely talked of anything else at our annual winter meetings. People were shackled by numerous nonsensical restrictions that prevented them from laboring with the maximum output and benefit for themselves and society. The economy was weakened at its most crucial point, the worker's standard of living. We spoke about the paradox of our having to import grain, despite the enormous tracts given over to wheat, some of the richest black-earth zones in the world. Despite the huge Soviet lumber industry we suffered constant shortages of building materials, furniture, and paper. We produced more metals and energy than anyone else, but were always on short rations.

We spoke of the many absurdities of our life and came to the conclusion that we just couldn't go on like this.

---

[5]The *kulaks* ("fists") were peasant landowners who were persecuted by starvation and exile during the period of mass collectivization. The euphemistic ideological term used at the time to describe the elimination of this class was "de-kulakization." — Trans.

In December 1979 we learned from the newspapers that Soviet troops    30
had invaded Afghanistan and hastened to meet to discuss it. We agreed
it was a fatal error that would cost the country dearly.

In those years we did not project such external questions onto the
internal situation in the Soviet Union, although it was clear to both of us
that if we did not change our foreign policy by removing the main sources
of distrust — the use of force and rigid ideology — we would never create
a zone of security around our country. However, at that time those ideas
had not crystallized for Gorbachev. The future was covered in clouds,
like the evening sky over the chilly winter sea.

Our Pitsunda talks summed up all of our thoughts. But each of us still
had a long way to travel for our ideas to become a reality. By all traditional
standards, our path was the path of success. Outwardly, at least, that was
true. From the usual viewpoint, that of the man in the street, we had
made our careers as successful Komsomol and Party functionaries. But if
we go by other standards, this was the path to discovering our political
reality, to finding out the reasons for the existing state of affairs, and to
an intense search for a way out.

## EXPLORATIONS

1. What were the nature and purposes of the Soviet Union's virgin lands campaign? In what respects was the campaign a success? In what respects was it
   a failure?

2. What was Eduard Shevardnadze's relationship to the Communist Party at the
   time he participated in the Soviet virgin lands campaign? What was his
   attitude toward the Party then? How have his relationship and attitude
   changed?

3. Why did Shevardnadze and Mikhail Gorbachev become friends? What risks
   did their friendship involve?

4. Judging from Shevardnadze's essay (see particularly paras. 10–28), what was
   the socialist concept of farming? What reasons does Shevardnadze give for its
   economic failure?

# CONNECTIONS

1. Shevardnadze criticizes Soviet economic policy: "The main priority is to preserve the purity of doctrine" (para. 12). What institutions discussed in *Looking at Ourselves* also have this problem?

2. Reread the last paragraph of "Life with the Party." What views does Shevardnadze share with Tomoyuki Iwashita in "Why I Quit the Company" (p. 471)?

3. In "Strawberry Fields" (p. 487), Yoshimi Ishikawa describes the satisfaction of physical labor (see, for example, para. 2). How does Shevardnadze explain this kind of satisfaction in his reminiscences about the virgin lands campaign (paras. 1–3)? As a worker, what advantages does Ishikawa have over Shevardnadze? What advantages does Shevardnadze have over Ishikawa?

# ELABORATIONS

1. "I can clearly recall this grandiose but poorly organized 'virgin land' era, the stupid decisions, and the ill-conceived strategies that canceled out many successes," writes Shevardnadze (para. 1). Choose a program that you participated in, or that you have heard about, that forged ahead despite serious flaws: building a doghouse, for instance, or the Stealth bomber. Write a cause-and-effect essay analyzing the program's goals, possibilities, problems, and results.

2. In paragraphs 4 and 5 Shevardnadze speaks of meeting people in his youth who would become important later on. Think of someone you know whose significance in your life has grown since you met. Write an essay describing your first encounter and comparing your expectations then with what you know now.

# TIM GOLDEN

## *Cubans Try to Cope with Dying Socialism*

Timothy N. Golden was born in 1961 in Los Angeles. After graduating magna cum laude in comparative literature with a concentration in Latin American fiction and politics, he studied French in France and taught Spanish in Mexico. In 1982 he received a grant to research U.S. policies on Latin America at the Council on Hemispheric Affairs, followed by a grant for research on Central American literature and the Nicaraguan revolution. From 1983 to 1985 he worked as a journalist for *USA Today*, United Press International (UPI), the *Los Angeles Times*, and the *Burlington* (Vermont) *Free Press*. In 1985 Golden became the *Miami Herald*'s Central America bureau chief, stationed in San Salvador and then in Rio de Janeiro. He joined the *New York Times* as a metropolitan news reporter in 1989 and has been their Mexico bureau chief since 1991. "Cubans Try to Cope with Dying Socialism" appeared in the *Times* in January 1993.

The Republic of Cuba, consisting of one large and several small islands 135 miles off Florida's southern tip, is the first Communist republic in the Western Hemisphere. Cuba became a Spanish possession in 1492, when Christopher Columbus claimed it on his first voyage to the New World. Its inhabitants at that time were Arawak Indians, who died off from enslavement, slaughter, and diseases brought by sailors and settlers. By the nineteenth century Cuba's economy centered on the sugar industry. The United States, a major trading partner and investor, became involved in the country's struggles for independence. Following the Spanish-American War, Spain freed Cuba (1899) and the United States occupied it, withdrawing its troops in 1902 but continuing to play a dominant role in the economy. Sugar, gambling, and tourism prospered but benefited only a few Cubans. In 1958 Fidel Castro and a guerrilla army, including Fidel's brother Raul and Argentine physician Ernesto "Che" Guevara, succeeded in overthrowing the government of dictator Fulgencio Batista. Allying with the Soviet Union, Castro nationalized foreign-owned businesses and instituted many Soviet-style changes. Cuba became a supporter of Communist revolution throughout the Third World, sending troops to Angola and arms and advisers to various African and Central American countries. However, as Tim Golden notes in the following essay, the breakup of the Soviet Union in 1991 (see p. 521) and the collapse of the Communist Bloc in Europe have greatly diminished Cuba's income and weakened its economy.

His island ever more an island, his scraggly beard gone gray, President Fidel Castro stands fast against the winds that have blown away most of the Communist world, along with its subsidies for Cuba and its markets for Cuban goods.

"Only socialism, only the revolution, could absorb the terrible blows that we have received," the sixty-six-year-old leader says.

Billboards and signs around the country proclaim the same faith. "Join us and you'll make it," promises one just outside Havana. On a wall not far from the Havana airport, the faded graffiti says: "We have Fidel."

As the material cost of Cuba's isolation grows, however, its mood these days is less one of heroic struggle than grim sacrifice.

In the long, concrete-block apartment buildings that the revolution   5
built and in the crumbling old Havana homes it subdivided for workers' housing, people's memories of meat have begun to fade. Pork, a Cuban favorite, cannot be obtained except on the black market, where one pound costs the average wages for nearly a week.

As a beef substitute, a television chef recommends "grapefruit steak." Carefully remove the rind, the recipe goes, season it, cover it with bread crumbs, and fry. But in search of more solid food, several Cubans said they had eaten cats.

On weekdays, the capital's still-gracious avenues have become gauntlets of blank, sullen stares. So many bus routes have been eliminated that the wait for a crosstown ride can take three hours or more. No dilapidated, Hungarian-made bus ever moves that does not spill riders from its doors.

In Trinidad, a quaint colonial town near the center of the island, a woman behind the bus station ticket window allows that the next available reserved seat to Havana is on a bus leaving in three months. But not to worry, she says, there is a waiting list.

To get people to their jobs, a million or so bicycles have been brought from China. Even on major thoroughfares, the workers riding them weave across all lanes of traffic, as though automobiles had never been a concern.

The cars are, in fact, relatively few. From ten gallons of gasoline some   10
months ago, the monthly ration for most drivers has been cut to about five gallons. In December, they got none.

High school students and boiler repairmen can explain this as easily as government economic officials: With the collapse of the Soviet Bloc and its preferential prices for barter trade with the island, Cuba's income has fallen precipitously, while the cost of imports like oil has risen sharply. In 1992, officials said, the island took delivery on about 6 million tons of oil, down from 13 million tons in 1989.

Encouraged by a new trade protocol signed with Russia in November,

Cuban officials said they expected about the same amount of oil in 1993. But in December, they extended power blackouts in Cuba's biggest cities from four hours a day to eight.

The important state offices and enterprises that earn dollars and are exempted from the outages — hotels, tourist restaurants, certain factories — flicker like candles in the night. At many intersections, the traffic lights dangle lifelessly from power lines. Television programming has been cut, and even night baseball games have become rare.

Slowly, as the island's imports have fallen by more than three-fourths, cherished social achievements of the revolution have also begun to erode. In the best hospitals, some medicines are being replaced by herbal remedies. Chalk, paper, and even milk are sometimes scarce in the schools.

In a society that prides itself on a literacy rate comparable to that of      15
industrialized nations, shipments of new books are so infrequent that a modest book fair in December drew a line nearly three city blocks long. Many newspapers and magazines have been shut down for lack of newsprint, and the Communist Party daily, *Granma*, has become precious not only for its news but as a substitute for toilet paper.

For the first time, the government has acknowledged a modicum of unemployment because of factories shut down and jobs eliminated. Of about 3.7 million state workers, they say, slightly more than 100,000 now stay at home; many more have been sent off to work in the fields. Foreign economists guess that real unemployment is considerably higher, and that close to half the work force is underemployed.

Still, in hundreds of conversations during a visit of nearly three weeks to the island, it appeared that the government had managed to maintain a substantial, if immeasurable, core of support even as it was running out of everything from antibiotics to soap and shoes.

Its health and education systems, although badly strained, continue to function. And while preserving a system of small rewards and perquisites for its partisans, the government has managed to keep an extremely tight grip on dissent.


Faith that Castro can restore Cuba to even the relative prosperity it enjoyed with annual Soviet subsidies that once ranged upward from $3 billion seemed rare even among Cubans supportive of the government. But many people said they saw their options unchanged: Tolerate the hardship or try somehow to leave.

Behind the counter of a dry goods store on Havana's southern edge, a      20
heavy-set, twenty-eight-year-old grocer looked out the other evening on

the somber customers lined up before him for a cup of oil, some sugar, a few scoops of rice.

"To put up with things," he said, "is a national custom."

Although many Cubans have grown more desperate and some more open about criticizing the government, there is almost no sign that they are any more willing to challenge its power.

"The level of disenchantment is very high," a Western diplomat said. "But the prospect of anybody doing anything about it is very low because of the danger involved." . . .

The United States, sensing a chance to succeed where it has failed for three decades, has sought to deepen the island's isolation by tightening its economic embargo. And increasingly, local inefficiency and the loss of solidarity prices from the former Soviet Bloc have receded from the official explanation for Cuba's troubles.

Two years after Castro pronounced the economic crisis "a special period in time of peace," Cubans are being told more and more of an undeclared war being waged against them by the world's last superpower. America's weapon of destruction, the radio and television news repeat, is "the Torricelli Law."   25

The law, known on the island for its chief sponsor, Representative Robert G. Torricelli, a New Jersey Democrat, prohibits foreign subsidiaries of American companies from doing business with the island, and bars foreign ships that trade there from docking at U.S. ports for six months.

But while economic analysts believe that the law will dissuade some American companies from trading with Cuba, many of them expect that it will merely inconvenience rather than threaten the Cuban government in the long run. And, in the meantime, diplomats and Cuban dissidents said that the law had given Castro a political boost by making it look as though the United States was bullying a small, geopolitically harmless country and adding to the suffering of its captive people. In a vote of the UN General Assembly on November 25, [1992,] many U.S. allies backed Cuba in a nonbinding resolution condemning the embargo.

"All the Torricelli law did was to strengthen the only argument that the government had left for maintaining its intransigent position," said Vladimiro Roca, a moderate political dissident who is the son of one of Cuba's revolutionary heroes, Blas Roca.

As ever, the central theme of official propaganda is that imperialism rather than socialism is at the source of Cuba's problems, and a sense of siege is cultivated. Despite the shortages of materials that have crippled other construction projects, the government reported that it was able this year to triple the number of "people's tunnels" to be used in the event of a U.S. attack.

Socialism, in the current formulation, is the guarantee that Cubans       30
will suffer more or less equally.

"What we have, we distribute in the most equitable way possible,"
Castro assured members of an American religious group that defied the
embargo to bring food to the island in early December. To feed and
clothe a family, however, has become an almost herculean task.

"If you have to be at work at eight, you get up before five to get the
bread," a forty-eight-year-old housewife explained.

The bread allotment, one roll per person, is served with sugary hot
water in lieu of coffee. "It does not taste very good, either, but if you don't
eat that little bread, you won't have the energy to pedal to work," she
said. The woman, the wife of a once-devout Communist Party member
grown disenchanted, looked both slightly haggard and vaguely stylish, and
the same could be said of their 1950s-style ranch house in what was once
an upper-middle-class neighborhood of Havana. The freezer contained
only a bricklike bag of tomato puree; in the refrigerator, there were a few
eggs and water.

In theory, the woman said she needed to shop only once a month for
the family's rice (five pounds per person), beans (one pound), and sugar
(four pounds), although it usually took more than one trip to find even
that.

Monthly rations of cooking oil (about two cups), soap (half a bar per       35
person), coffee (four ounces), and Chinese toothpaste, which is sometimes used as a detergent substitute, rarely seem to arrive on schedule.

Since the twelve-ounce monthly rations of chicken have dried up, the
family's butcher has sold them only four items: eggs (four per person each
week), small frozen fish, tomato puree, and a concoction of soy, gristle,
and meat remains that is euphemistically called "soy hamburger."

"If you look at the ration book and you look at what is in the stores,
you have to wonder why everyone is not dead," a diplomat said. "The
reason is that the black market is flourishing."

In some neighborhoods, the black market — known as the *bolsa*, or
"exchange" — is merely the under-the-counter sale of items that are
usually rationed over the counter but are skimmed off or otherwise
procured by the grocer. Food is often sold surreptitiously from aged
delivery trucks, and travelers returning from the countryside are often
searched for food bought from farmers. But everyone, it seems, has
"contacts."

Many Cubans have some savings in pesos. But since there is so little
to buy and demand has risen so sharply, underground prices have spiraled
upward with the black-market currency-exchange rate. With the dollar
now trading at more than forty times its official equivalency to the Cuban

peso, a $2.75 chicken can cost about the monthly minimum wage of 108 pesos, and a $10 case of beer four times that.

To overcome the obstacles to consumerism or survival is to engage in    40 the fundamental activity of Cuban life: *resolviendo,* or "resolving things."

One might "resolve" a few liters of gasoline from a relative who works at a service station. A piece of beef might be "resolved" from a pregnant friend who receives it as part of a special ration. But when one's jewelry, tennis shoes, and other effects have been sold off, one generally must hustle the currency with which to resolve.

"They have turned us all into thieves," a twenty-eight-year-old engineer complained as he hid in a dark corner at a party. The man, who seemed distraught and slightly drunk, described himself as a committed socialist. But he said he had turned to repairing appliances and doing other illicit jobs in his spare time.

"You steal a little here," he said. "You sell a little there. Nobody wants to do it, but everyone does it. We are human. We are weak. We want a pair of shoes. Good cigarettes. And I find myself doing things that are very tough."

The man referred to the young free-lance prostitutes who have become a ubiquitous nocturnal presence in Havana, hissing loudly at tourist cars and offering their companionship to foreigners for a dinner, a dress, some shampoo. "I understand those little girls," he said.

For members of the Cuban elite, there are still special privileges:    45 gasoline for cars, inconspicuous stores where they can shop for imported goods, trips abroad.

Workers who amass hundreds of hours of voluntary service in the fields or factories might still receive bicycles or motorcycles or modest vacations at the beach. But it is no longer unusual to see lieutenant colonels in the army or interior ministry riding bicycles, waiting endlessly for buses, or even hitchhiking.

From time to time, Castro betrays what seem to be flashes of pain at seeing his countrymen delivered to a poverty that differs from that of their Latin American neighbors chiefly in that it tends to come with a job, free health care, and small portions of food. But while even some Communist Party members express doubts about whether Cubans' patience might last the long years that any real economic recovery would take, their leader shows none.

"It is an epic struggle in which we find ourselves," Castro told an audience of construction workers recently. "We have had to give up many of the things in which we were involved, but what we will never give up is hope."

# EXPLORATIONS

1. According to Tim Golden, what is President Fidel Castro's attitude toward Cuba's economic plight? How can you tell? What observations in Golden's essay suggest that his attitude differs from Castro's?

2. What direct impacts do Cuban governmental policies have on people's daily lives?

3. What is *resolviendo* (paras. 40–41)? What relationship does it imply between the government and the people? How is this relationship confirmed or contradicted elsewhere in Golden's essay?

4. "Cuba's . . . mood these days is less one of heroic struggle than grim sacrifice," writes Golden (para. 4). What adjectives in his essay convey this mood? Is "grim sacrifice" the mood of individual Cubans? Cite evidence for your answer.

# CONNECTIONS

1. Golden quotes a Cuban grocer: "To put up with things is a national custom" (para. 21). What evidence in "Life with the Party" (p. 521) suggests that putting up with things also was a national custom in the Soviet Union?

2. Reread Wendell Berry's selection in *Looking at Ourselves* (p. 509). How do Berry's ideas apply to the problems in Cuba?

3. Look back at "Dreams for Hire" (p. 497). What picture does Gabriel García Márquez paint of Havana, Cuba (paras. 1–2 and 34–37)? What elements appear in both his picture and Golden's? What factors do you think are responsible for the differences between García Márquez's picture and Golden's?

# ELABORATIONS

1. What explanations does Tim Golden offer for Cuba's economic hardships? What explanations does Fidel Castro's government offer? What evidence in "Cubans Try to Cope with Dying Socialism" supports each position? Imagine you are a Cuban government spokesperson. Write an argumentative essay presenting and defending the official party line (whether or not you really agree with it).

2. Look closely at the first seven to ten paragraphs of Golden's essay. Analyze the structure he is using by making a list: What is each paragraph's purpose? Where does Golden state his thesis, and how does he support it? Choose a place you are familiar with that has deteriorated — a building, a park, a neighborhood. Use the same structure Golden uses in "Cubans Try to Cope with Dying Socialism" to write a descriptive essay focusing on the place's deterioration.

# ANONYMOUS

## *Evicted: A Russian Jew's Story (Again)*

Jews have lived in Russia for at least a thousand years, and their history there is punctuated with persecutions. In 1113 the Jewish quarter in Kiev was looted; in 1563 three hundred Jews were drowned when they refused to accept baptism. In 1667, when Russia annexed the eastern Ukraine, it expelled the Jews there. In 1762, Catherine the Great sanctioned all aliens in Russia except Jews. Although 300,000 Jews served in the army at the start of World War I, the Jewish population was blamed for Russian defeats. The Russian and Bolshevik revolutions of 1917 (see p. 521) brought a change in policy: Anti-Semitism was illegal in the new Soviet Union. At the same time, Jews were discouraged from maintaining their distinctive traditions, sometimes violently. Many Jews were assimilated; many others were deported or killed, especially during Joseph Stalin's regime in the 1930s and 1940s, and during the Nazi invasion of Russia in 1941. After World War II the Soviet Union supported the creation of Israel (see p. 275) but later allied with its Arab opponents. In the 1970s about a quarter of a million Soviet Jews were allowed to leave for Israel and the United States. Mikhail Gorbachev, who became president in 1985, increased freedom of expression for both Jews and anti-Semites and permitted another wave of Jewish emigration. With the collapse of the Soviet Union in 1991, the already shaky ideal of unity among subcultures collapsed as well, as this essay indicates.

For more background on the Soviet Union and Russia, see page 521.

A gigantic queue in front of the American Embassy. Today, the 36,124th person has been placed on the waiting list. The majority are Muscovites, but many have come from other cities — Tashkent, Kiev, Zhitomir, Vilnius, Novosibirsk, Kishinev. I, too, am standing here waiting for what everyone else is waiting for: an application to leave permanently for the United States.

Afterward, I would have liked to have gone home — I had spent six hours standing in the cold — but instead I went to the New Zealand Embassy. There, too, I registered; fortunately, I was only number 79. Numbers were supposed to be checked at 5:00 P.M. and it was only noon, so I walked through the center of Moscow, through streets that I've always loved. It was very cold, damp, and windy and I wondered: Just what has happened to you and your country that you, who were born here and have lived here for forty years, are running around in the rain in your native city looking for some way to leave forever? And why is it that nearly 40,000 of your fellow citizens are silently crowding in front of the gate of a foreign embassy?

The reason I am leaving is not because there is no meat, sugar, boots, soap, cigarettes, almost nothing in the country. And not even because the reward for any work is unimaginably small. Of course, all of that is terribly humiliating, creates bad blood, and probably even shortens our life spans. But no, that's not why I'm leaving.

I'm not fleeing; I'm being evicted. For me it's not emigration but rather evacuation. I don't feel like a rat abandoning a sinking ship so much as a dog driven away by its evil master. And all those silent people in front of the American Embassy? Somehow one doesn't see in their faces even the slightest anticipation of joy at the prospect of a heavenly life in a utopia where there are no problems with meat and soap, where the feet of each inhabitant are shod, I imagine, in no fewer than ten pairs of boots. These emigrants are anything but the dregs of society. For the most part, they are quite cultured people, and well dressed — some even have cars. What's driving them into exile? What can they be looking for there?

That's easily explained. They share one disadvantage that makes them   5 unfit to live in the country in which they were born. They are Jews. I, too, am Jewish. My passport says so. Though, in all honesty, I have always felt I was as much Russian as Jewish. Not anymore, because now I live in a country where the "Jewish Question" exists. Now I know I am a Jew, since those splendid lads of Pamyat [the right-wing, nationalist movement] have promised to squash my kind like bedbugs; because the pensioner in the adjacent house regularly recommends we scram to Israel; because when I drag a drunken woman from the street, passersby make it immediately clear to me that we alone have led the Russian people to drink. Suddenly, there is a certain "we" of which I am a part.

Perhaps — no, probably — it is regrettable, but before I was born, Jewish culture had already been lost in my family. My great-grandfather was a religious Jew; my grandfather, who fell in World War II, wrote his letters home from the front lines in Hebrew; my grandmother knew only a bit of Yiddish; my mother knows neither Hebrew nor Yiddish. To my shame, I confess that except for Sholem Aleichem — whose work belongs more to the realm of world classics than to Jewish literature specifically — I have read no Jewish authors. I learned to read at the age of four. My first reading material was Lev Tolstoy. I discovered Tsvetayeva and Akhmatova at fifteen; Pasternak and Mandelstam at nineteen; Gumilyov not until twenty-three. All of this is mine. And paintings. And music. And the landscapes. And the churches. And the villages. And it was here my grandfather fell. When the war began, he was fifty-four and had just had a serious operation. No one demanded that he go to the front. When my mother began to sob, pleading, "Papa, stay home! You're still sick and there are so many younger and healthier," he replied (I've heard it a thousand times from Mother and Grandmother), "What's the matter with you, my dear daughter! If everyone spoke and thought that way, who would defend our country?" This is our homeland. Or so I used to think. Now I think somewhat differently.

In 1987 I was walking on Gogolevski Boulevard — it was at the beginning of the era of glasnost — and I saw a group of people crowding around a newsstand reading an article with keen interest. I was curious to see what the excitement was about. The article in question was one of the first written about an organization called Pamyat. I no longer recall how it happened — maybe I accidentally said something, or perhaps it was the fault of my eloquent nose — but a lively discussion developed between them and me. My God, what horror overtook me! It was a completely new and unfamiliar horror, not a fear of violence or a fear for my own safety, but rather a fear mixed with revulsion, a fear mixed with embarrassment. Standing around me were not primitive, uncultured people. They were genuine intellectuals, people with good faces, slim hands, who spoke excellently, without restraint and with conviction. But, oh, what they were convinced of!

*Me:* What are you people talking about? Admittedly, in Russia there were pogroms, but the Russian intelligentsia were always repelled by them. They hid the Jews in their homes and protected them with icons. And today you're —

*Them:* Yes, and look at the results! This very liberalism is what has driven Russia to the edge of the present-day abyss. Give us time and we'll annihilate all of you in the name of Christ.

*Me:* Listen, I'm not your enemy. We grew up in the same country; we read the same things. Russia means Lev Tolstoy for me, too. I've just come from the Pushkin Museum — 10

*Them:* Typical! The Jews who grew up in the Russian culture are the most dangerous, because they work from the inside.

So now I am an enemy — the most dangerous enemy my country faces, it seems. My people and I must get out of here or be annihilated. I and my mother, evidently, who worked hard for fifty long years in the thankless Soviet legal system. And my Gentile husband, who, evidently, is now no longer a talented journalist but a collaborator in the Zionist conspiracy. And my son, the half-Jew, who ended his first love affair because his girlfriend didn't care a fig about Russia's destiny.

• When the thousand-year anniversary of the Russian Orthodox Church was celebrated, we didn't go, as planned, to the seat of the church in Zagorsk. Instead, we sat in our Moscow apartment behind a locked door while my husband deliberated with my juridically knowledgeable mother about whether he should fight back if they should break in. Pogroms had been announced for the anniversary day. We found obscene leaflets in our mailboxes. Apartment doors were marked with crosses.

• I come home after shopping. As I walk into my own courtyard, my path is blocked. "Hey, you Jew swine, show me what you have in your shopping bag! It's you who are consuming all our meat!" (So they've finally discovered the cause of hunger in our country.)

• At the editorial office of a progressive newspaper, two sweet women 15 of my age approach me, hissing into my face, "Leave amicably before we slaughter the lot of you!" Later, as I am walking down the corridor with a journalist friend, two employees pass and I hear a sentence fragment: " — and 24 percent of the department bosses are Jews!"

People try to console me: "Pay it no mind. You can be certain there won't be any pogroms. The government won't permit them." I believe that. The present government needs pogroms about as much as my mother and I do. But is the government strong and ubiquitous enough to prevent them?

I fear for this country. I have studied history. I know very well what can happen when a country degenerates into national hysteria. And I have no desire to be a witness, completely powerless to change anything. It is intolerable when an entity to which you were once inseparably bound rejects you as if you were some sort of foreign body. I do not fear for myself; it seems almost demeaning to be afraid of them. But I regret having to fear each day for my husband, who is accustomed to joining every street discussion about Jews. Someday he'll get a knife in his gut or a pistol butt to his head as the definitive argument from one of his opponents. I do not want my son to be asked by his fellow students what he's doing associating with that Jewish girl. I don't want to see my eighty-year-old mother killed by a criminal — reborn as a patriot — that she defended during her lifelong career as a lawyer.

I no longer want anything from this country. I no longer wish to be of use here — even after striving long and hard, and successfully, to contribute my talents to the good of my nation. When I emigrate, I shall take nothing along. I need nothing of yours. I'll have no homeland, nor do I need one, not if it doesn't need me. I want only peace and security for my family, nothing more.

Moreover, if my emigration contributes to Russia's salvation, then fine, so be it; I am prepared to sacrifice myself for the high Pamyat ideals. Who knows? When I have finally withdrawn from the Russian culture, perhaps peace, happiness, and prosperity will immediately come to Russia. Excellent! That would make me happy. Except that I don't believe it. I don't think that two people in a house will live peacefully and harmoniously simply because they've expelled a third. Hatred that rages in souls and suddenly loses its immediate object does not disappear without a trace. It will turn against those who remain.

I wish this land only good. But why don't we — no, *you* — learn a     20
lesson from these bitter truths? Why don't you see that happiness and prosperity cannot be built on the blood and tears of others? So many times in the past you have shot and driven others away and still you have not found happiness. You say you've shot the wrong people? Then try again. Maybe you'll have better luck this time. But without me. Tomorrow I'm going to the Australian Embassy.


## EXPLORATIONS

1. The anonymous author of this essay writes: "The reason I am leaving is not because there is no meat, sugar, boots, soap, cigarettes, almost nothing in the country" (para. 3). What evidence suggests that these shortages are an indirect reason she is leaving? What are the direct reasons?

2. What effects does the writer achieve with all the numbers she uses in paragraph 2?

3. "Hatred that rages in souls and suddenly loses its immediate object does not disappear without a trace. It will turn against those who remain" (para. 19). In what sense does this comment explain why the writer feels herself to be hated as a Russian Jew in the post–Cold War, post-Soviet era?

4. What appears to be the writer's chief emotion toward her fellow Russians? At what points and in what form does she express her emotion?


## CONNECTIONS

1. What is the author's response to economic shortages in Russia (para. 3)? How does her response compare with that of the Cubans interviewed and observed by Tim Golden in "Cubans Try to Cope with Dying Socialism" (p. 528)?

2. In "Evicted: A Russian Jew's Story (Again)," what is the dominant attitude of Russian non-Jews toward Jews? In Eduard Shevardnadze's "Life with the Party" (p. 521), what evidence can you find of a similar attitude? Whose attitude is it, and toward whom is it directed?

3. Which selections in *Looking at Ourselves* show people sharing this Russian writer's feeling of being pushed out of a country she helped to build?

## ELABORATIONS

1. Suppose the author of this essay, which was written as a letter to a newspaper, succeeds in emigrating to the United States. What unexpected rewards and problems will she encounter? Write a sequel to her letter a year later describing how her life has changed for the better and for the worse.

2. What groups do you identify with? Write a narrative essay recalling a time when your loyalty to one group — family, friends, religion, neighborhood, nation, or whatever — clashed with your loyalty to another. What caused the problem? What did you do about it?

# VÁCLAV HAVEL

## Moral Politics

Václav Havel's roundabout route to the Czech presidency might be a plot for one of his plays. He was born in Prague in 1936, the son of a wealthy entrepreneur. When the Communists took power in 1948, Havel's family's assets were seized. He was barred from attending college. Instead he held menial jobs, attended night school, and read and wrote whenever he could. In the late 1950s he became a stagehand for an avant-garde theater troupe and began writing plays with a political slant. *The Garden Party* (1963) was a hit in Prague, followed by *The Memorandum* (1965) a satiric look at power struggles in a state-run company. Havel came to New York in 1968 for *The Memorandum*'s U.S. opening. Three months after his return, Czechoslovakia was overrun by Soviet tanks, and his plays were banned. Although assigned to work in a brewery, Havel and his wife, Olga, managed to keep their comfortable apartment and country home.

In 1977 Havel helped create the human rights manifesto Charter 77. He was jailed briefly, then sent to prison for four years. Despite ill health, he refused to request a pardon or leave the country. He continued to write plays, which were produced in New York, and letters to his wife, which became the book *Letters to Olga* (1983). Sentenced to another prison term in February 1989, he was released four months later after a deluge of protests from fellow artists. In November his political group Civic Forum spearheaded the "velvet revolution" that toppled the Communist government. Less than a year after being a prisoner of the state, Václav Havel was unanimously elected its president. He resigned in July 1992, after the Czechs and Slovaks agreed to split the country in two, and is now president of the Czech Republic.

Czechoslovakia was part of the oft-disputed corridor between East and West, bordering Hungary, Austria, Germany, Poland, and the Ukraine. Prague, its capital, was the cultural center of Central Europe in the fourteenth century. In 1918 Bohemia and Moravia (formerly part of the Holy Roman Empire) united with Slovakia as the Republic of Czechoslovakia. Twenty years later British Prime Minister Neville Chamberlain, with the acquiescence of France, signed an agreement allowing German Führer Adolf Hitler to annex part of Czechoslovakia in return for a guarantee of peace. But World War II was not to be averted: Six months later Hitler dissolved the Czechoslovak republic and coopted Bohemia and Moravia. In 1944 Soviet leader Joseph Stalin's troops entered eastern Czechoslovakia, and in 1948 the Communists took full control of the government. Twenty years later came the famous "Prague Spring," when Slovak Alexander Dubček replaced the country's Stalinist head and pledged democratic and economic reforms. This window of hope lasted only seven months before Soviet armies and their allies once again invaded Czechoslovakia and installed a new puppet regime. Repression continued through the 1970s and 1980s, tightening at each sign of resistance, until an incident of police brutality in November 1989 sparked a popular uprising that forced the Communist government to yield power to Civic Forum. Václav Havel, the country's moral leader, became its first democratically chosen political leader in half a century. His efforts to hold Czechoslovakia together failed, however. The turmoil he describes in the following essay ended with Slovak separatists, led by Vladimir Meciar, blocking Havel's reelection in July 1992 and declaring independence. Havel resigned, and on January 1, 1993, Czechoslovakia officially divided. Meciar became prime minister of Slovakia; Havel was elected president of the Czech Republic. "Moral Politics," translated from the Czech by Paul Wilson, appeared as "Paradise Lost" in *The New York Review of Books* in April 1992 — three months before Czechoslovakia's demise.

## 1.

The return of freedom to a place that became morally unhinged has produced something that it clearly had to produce, and therefore something we might have expected. But it has turned out to be far more serious than anyone could have predicted: an enormous and blindingly visible explosion of every imaginable human vice. A wide range of questionable or at least ambivalent human tendencies, quietly encouraged over the years and, at the same time, quietly pressed to serve the daily operation of the totalitarian system, has suddenly been liberated, as it were, from its straitjacket and given free rein at last. The authoritarian regime imposed a certain order — if that is the right expression for it — on these vices (and in doing so legitimized them, in a sense). This order has now been broken down, but a new order that would limit rather than exploit these vices, an order based on a freely accepted responsibility to and for the whole of society, has not yet been built, nor could it have been, for such an order takes years to develop and cultivate.

And thus we are witnesses to a bizarre state of affairs: Society has freed itself, true, but in some ways it behaves worse than when it was in chains. Criminality has grown rapidly, and the familiar sewage that in times of historical reversal always wells up from the nether regions of the collective psyche has overflowed into the mass media, especially the gutter press. But there are other, more serious and dangerous, symptoms: hatred among nationalities, suspicion, racism, even signs of fascism; vicious demagogy, intrigue, and deliberate lying; politicking, an unrestrained, unheeding struggle for purely particular interests, a hunger for power, unadulterated ambition, fanaticism of every imaginable kind; new and unprecedented varieties of robbery, the rise of different mafias; the general lack of tolerance, understanding, taste, moderation, reason. And, of course, there is a new attraction to ideologies, as if Marxism had left behind it a great, unsettling void that had to be filled at any cost.

A look around our political scene (whose lack of civility is merely a reflection of the more general crisis of civility) should suffice: With half a year to go before the elections, almost every political activity, including debates over extremely important legislation in parliament, is taking place in the shadow of a preelection campaign, of an extravagant hunger for power and a willingness to gain the favor of a confused electorate by offering them a colorful range of attractive nonsense. Mutual accusations, denunciations, and slander among political opponents know no bounds. One politician will undermine another's work only because both belong to different political parties. Partisan considerations still visibly take precedence over unprejudiced and pragmatic attempts to arrive at a reasonable and useful solution to problems. Analysis is pushed out of the press by scandal-mongering. (Supporting the government in a good cause is considered practically shameful; kicking it in the shins, on the contrary, is praiseworthy.) Sniping at politicians who declare their support for another political group is a matter of course. Anyone can accuse anyone else of intrigue, incompetence, of having a shady past and shady intentions.

Demagogy is everywhere, and even matters as serious as the natural longing of a people for autonomy fuel power plays and stimulate deliberate lying to the public. Many members of the so-called *nomenklatura*[1] who, until very recently, were faking their concern for social justice and the working class, have cast aside their masks and, almost overnight, have openly become a class of speculators and thieves. Many a once-feared Communist is now an unscrupulous capitalist shamelessly and unequivocally laughing in the face of the same worker whose interests he once claimed to defend.

Citizens are becoming more and more clearly disgusted with all this, and their disgust is understandably directed against the democratic government that they themselves have elected. Exploiting this situation,   5

---

[1]Bureaucracy, especially the upper echelons. — ED.

many unsavory characters have been gaining popular favor with ideas such as, for instance, the need to throw the entire government into the Vltava River. Still, I am persuaded time and time again that a huge potential of goodwill is slumbering within our society.

In such a state of affairs, politicians have a duty to awaken this slumbering, or bewildered, potential to life, to offer it a direction, to ease its passage, to encourage it and give it room, or simply hope. They say a nation has the politicians it deserves. In some senses this is true: Politicians are truly a mirror of the society and a kind of embodiment of its potential. At the same time — paradoxically — the opposite is also true: Society is a mirror of its politicians. It is largely up to the politicians which social forces they choose to liberate and which they choose to suppress, whether they choose to rely on the good in each citizen, or on the bad. The former regime systematically mobilized the worst human qualities, like selfishness, envy, and hatred. This was far from merely being something we deserved: It was, at the same time, responsible for the way we became. Those who find themselves in politics therefore bear a heightened responsibility for the moral state of society, and it is their responsibility to seek out the best in that society, to develop and strengthen it.

In the 1980s, a certain Californian-Czech philosopher devoted not a little energy to a series of articles in which he subjected the "anti-political politics" of Charter 77 to crushing criticism, and, in particular, to the way I explained that notion in my essays. Trapped in his own Marxist fallacies, he believed that as a scholar he had scientifically comprehended the entire history of the world as a history of violent revolutions and vicious power struggles. The idea that the force of truth, the power of a truthful word, the strength of a free spirit, conscience, and responsibility — not armed with machine guns, with no longing for power, and no political intrigue — might actually change something was quite beyond the horizon of his understanding. Naturally, if you understand decency as merely a "superstructure" of the forces of production, then you can never understand political power in terms of decency.

Because his doctrine had taught him that the bourgeoisie would never voluntarily surrender its leading role and that it must be swept into the dustbin of history through violent revolution, this philosopher assumed there was no other way to sweep away the Communist government either. Yet it turned out to be possible. Moreover, it turned out to be the only way to do it. Not only that, it turned out to be the only way that made sense, since violence, as we know, breeds more violence. This is why most revolutions degenerate into dictatorships that devour their own children and produce new revolutionaries who prepare for new violence, unaware that they are digging their own graves and pushing society again onto the deadly merry-go-round of revolution and counterrevolution.

Communism was overthrown by life, by thought, by human dignity. Our recent history has confirmed that the Californian-Czech professor is wrong. Likewise, those who still claim today that politics is chiefly the manipulation of power and public opinion, and that morality has no place in it, are just as wrong. Political intrigue is not real politics, and although you can get away with it for a time, it does not bring much hope of lasting success. Through intrigue one may easily become prime minister, but that will be the extent of one's success: One can hardly improve the world that way.

Genuine politics, politics worthy of the name, and in any case the only    10
politics that I am willing to devote myself to, is simply serving those close to oneself: serving the community, and serving those who come after us. Its deepest roots are moral because it is a responsibility, expressed through action, to and for the whole, a responsibility that is what it is — a "higher" responsibility, which grows out of a conscious or subconscious certainty that our death ends nothing, because everything is forever being recorded and evaluated somewhere else, somewhere "above us," in what I have called "the memory of Being," an integral aspect of the secret order of the cosmos, of nature, and of life, which believers call God and to whose judgment everything is liable. Genuine conscience and genuine respon-sibility are always, in the end, explicable only as an expression of the silent assumption that we are being observed "from above," and that "up there" everything is visible, nothing is forgotten, and therefore earthly time has no power to wipe away the pangs brought on by earthly failure: Our spirit knows that it is not the only one that knows of these failures.

If there is to be a minimum chance of success, there is only one way to strive for decency, reason, responsibility, sincerity, civility, and toler-ance: and that is decently, reasonably, responsibly, sincerely, civilly, and tolerantly. I'm aware that in everyday politics this is not exactly a practical way of going about it. At the same time, however, I have one great advantage; among my many bad qualities there is one that is fortunately missing: a longing or a love for power. Not being bound by it, I am essentially freer than those who, when all is said and done, cling to their power or their position somewhat more, and this allows me to indulge in the luxury of behaving untactically.

I see the only way forward in that old, familiar injunction "to live in truth." Journalists, and in particular foreign correspondents, often ask me how the idea of "living in truth," the idea of "antipolitical politics," or the idea of politics subordinated to conscience can, in practice, be carried out. They are curious whether, finding myself in high office, I have not had to revise much of what I once wrote as an independent critic of politics and politicians. Have I not been compelled to lower my former "dissident" expectations of politics, by which they mean the standards I derived from the "dissident experience" and which are therefore scarcely applicable outside that sphere?

There may be some who won't believe me, but after more than two years as president in a land full of the kinds of problems that presidents in stable countries never even dream of, I can safely say that I have not been compelled to recant anything of what I wrote earlier, or to change my mind about anything. In fact, my opinions have been confirmed. Despite the political distress I face every day, I am still deeply convinced that politics is not essentially a disreputable business; and to the extent that it is, it is only disreputable people who make it so. I would concede, however, that it can, more than other spheres of human activity, tempt one to disreputable practices and that therefore it places higher demands on people. But it is simply not true that a politician must lie or intrigue. That is utter nonsense, very often spread about by people who — for whatever reasons — wish to discourage others from taking an interest in public affairs.

Of course in politics, as elsewhere in life, it is impossible and pointless to say everything, all at once, to just anyone. But that does not mean having to lie. What you need is tact, the proper instincts, and good taste. One surprising experience from "high politics" is this: I have discovered that good taste is more important than a postgraduate degree in political science. It is essentially a matter of form: knowing how long to speak, when to begin and when to finish, how to say something politely that your opposite number might not want to hear, how to say, always, what is most essential in a given moment, and not to speak of what is not essential or uninteresting, how to insist on your own position without offending, how to create the kind of friendly atmosphere that makes complex negotiations easier, how to keep a conversation going without prying or, on the contrary, without being aloof, how to balance serious political themes with lighter, more relaxing topics, how to plan one's journeys judiciously and how to know when it is more appropriate not to go somewhere, when to be open and when reticent, and to what degree.

But more than that, it means having a certain instinct for the time, 15 the atmosphere of the time, the mood of people, the nature of their worries, their frame of mind — these two can perhaps be more important than sociological surveys. An education in political science, law, economics, history, and culture is an invaluable asset to every politician, but I am still persuaded, again and again, that it is not the most important asset. Qualities like fellow-feeling, the ability to talk to others, insight, the capacity to grasp quickly not only problems but also human character, the ability to make contact, a sense of moderation: All these are immensely more important in politics. I am not saying, heaven forbid, that I myself am endowed with these qualities; not at all! These are merely my observations.

To sum up: If your heart is in the right place and if you have good taste, not only will you pass muster in politics, you are destined for it. If you are modest and do not lust after power, not only are you not unsuitable for politics, you belong there. The sine qua non of a politician is not the ability to lie; he need only be sensitive and know when, to whom, what, and how to say what he has to say. It is not true that a person of principle does not belong in politics; it is enough for his principles to be leavened with patience, deliberation, a sense of proportion, and an understanding of others. It is not true that only the unfeeling cynic, the vain, the brash, and the vulgar can succeed in politics; all such people, it is true, are drawn to politics, but in the end, decorum and good taste will always count for more.

My experience and observations confirm that politics as the practice of morality is possible. I do not deny, however, that it is not always easy to go that route, nor have I ever claimed the opposite.

## 2.

This is what I wrote (some months ago) when I tried to review the experience I had gained during my presidency. At that time I had no way of knowing that I would soon find that there were occasions when it was indeed difficult to go that route. Again fate played a joke on me: It punished me for my self-confident words by presenting me with an immensely difficult dilemma: What was I to do when a democratically elected parliament passed a bill which I did not consider morally proper, yet which our Constitution required me to sign?

It was a bill aimed at preventing those who had violated human rights in the past from holding offices in public administration. The public in my country find it hard to accept that in many offices they encounter the same people who were working there under the totalitarian regime. Their anger is justified and parliament's desire to purge the public administration of these people is entirely legitimate. The problem is that the relevant legislation is based on the principle of collective responsibility; it prohibits certain persons from holding certain offices solely on the basis of their membership in certain groups defined by external characteristics, without giving them the right to have their cases considered individually. This runs counter to the basic principles of democratic law. The files kept by the now-abolished secret police are made the highest, the final, the one and only criterion of eligibility. It is a necessary law, an extraordinary law, a rigorous law. Yet at the same time, from the viewpoint of fundamental human rights, it is a highly questionable law.

What was I to do in that situation?                                                    20

Basically, there were two choices. The first was to do my duty, sign the bill, thus ratifying it, and then reconcile myself to my signature being on a paper with whose contents I could not fully agree. The second alternative was to simply refuse to sign the bill. In that case it would have become effective even without my signature and I would have found myself in open conflict with our parliament, thus precipitating a political crisis and aggravating still further the rather unstable situation in my country. It would have been a typically dissident-like, a morally pure yet immensely risky act of civil disobedience. My friends were divided on the matter, some advising me to sign, others to refuse.

In the end, I decided on a third option: I signed the bill, and proposed that parliament amend it. Under the Constitution, the parliament is obliged to consider my proposal, though not, of course, to accept it. Thus it may well happen that the bill, having become law, will be valid in its present wording, with my name on it, and that a number of people will be unfairly treated as a result.[2]

I do not know whether my solution was a good one. I do not know whether I have helped or harmed my fellow citizens. History can probably be the only judge to that. But I still believe that politics, in its very essence, does not necessarily require one to behave immorally. My latest experience, however, confirms the truth of something that, until some weeks ago, I did not really appreciate — that the way of truly moral politics is not simple, or easy.

---

[2]In October 1991, President Havel addressed a letter to the Federal Assembly (parliament), in which he criticized this "lustration" law on two grounds: that it contradicted the Charter of Human Rights which had been legislated into the Czechoslovak constitution, and that in some sections it is based on the principle of collective guilt. He asked the deputies to consider the letter as his initiative for introducing amendments to the law. As of mid-March, the Federal Assembly [had] not yet debated or discussed any amendment to the law, and several of the most important political parties [had] gone on record as rejecting any notion of introducing amendments. — Trans.

## EXPLORATIONS

1. What do you think Václav Havel means when he says Czechoslovakia "became morally unhinged" (para. 1)? What do you think he means by saying
"the authoritarian regime imposed a certain order . . . on these vices" and
thus legitimized them (para. 1)?

2. How does Havel shift direction in paragraph 5? What is his essay's original
direction? What is its new one?

3. What dilemma caused Havel to write Part 2 of his essay? Do you think his
decision (para. 22) was the best way to uphold the principles he outlined in
Part 1? Why or why not?

## CONNECTIONS

1. In what ways do the statements in Havel's first two paragraphs apply to the
situation described in "Evicted: A Russian Jew's Story (Again)" (p. 536)?

2. "This is why most revolutions degenerate into dictatorships that devour their
own children and produce new revolutionaries who prepare for new violence . . ." (para. 8). What does this statement of Havel's imply for Cuba as
Tim Golden describes it in "Cubans Try to Cope with Dying Socialism"
(p. 528)?

3. Havel writes: "If you understand decency as merely a 'superstructure' of the
forces of production, then you can never understand political power in terms
of decency" (para. 7). What does he mean? What selections in *Looking at
Ourselves* express similar ideas?

## ELABORATIONS

1. Havel's opening paragraph is general rather than specific. Rewrite the paragraph using "Evicted: A Russian Jew's Story (Again)" and Eduard Shevardnadze's "Life with the Party" (p. 521) as sources, substituting actual place
names, problems, vices, and so forth for Havel's generalities.

2. Imagine that Havel's paragraphs 2–6 were written not about Czechoslovakia
but about the United States. Write an argumentative essay either affirming or
refuting his criticisms of American politics and society. (You may rephrase or
ignore his references to Marxism and the Vltava River.) Support your position
with specific examples.

# FAY WELDON

## *Down the Clinical Disco*

Fay Weldon was born Franklin Birkinshaw in 1931 in Worcestershire, England. Her family moved to New Zealand soon afterward; her father, a physician, and her mother, a writer, divorced a few years later. Weldon spent most of her youth among women, attending the Girls' High School in Christchurch, then a convent school in London, where she lived with her mother, sister, and grandmother. She received her master's degree in economics and psychology from St. Andrews University at age twenty. Weldon married a schoolmaster twenty-five years older than she, had a son, divorced, and began writing novels. For money she worked in the Foreign Office, then as a market researcher for the *Daily Mirror*, and then as an advertising copywriter. In 1960 she married Ron Weldon, with whom she has had three more sons. Her first novel was published in 1967: *The Fat Woman's Joke* (U.S. title, *And the Wife Ran Away*, 1968). Continuing to write fiction, she also branched into television scripts, plays, radio plays, and nonfiction. Weldon is best known in the United States for her novel *The Life and Loves of a She-Devil* (1983), which was made into an award-winning television serial by the British Broadcasting Company (1986) and a motion picture, *She-Devil*, starring Meryl Streep and Roseanne Barr Arnold (1989). The first woman ever to head the prestigious Booker Prize panel (1983), Weldon is currently a contributing editor for *Allure* magazine. She lives in Shepton Mallet, Somerset, and keeps a house in London. "Down the Clinical Disco" comes from her short story collection *Moon over Minneapolis* (1991).

The United Kingdom of Great Britain and Northern Ireland is a constitutional monarchy currently headed by Queen Elizabeth II and run by a prime minister and a parliament comprising the hereditary House of Lords and elected House of Commons. Slightly smaller than Oregon, it has commanded an empire that at various times included Australia and parts of Europe, North America, Asia, Africa, and Antarctica. The present United Kingdom consists of England, Scotland, and Wales on the island of Great Britain, and the six Irish counties that make up Northern Ireland (see p. 444); among its dominions are the Channel Islands, the Isle of Man, Gibraltar, the British West Indies, Bermuda, the Falklands, and several other South Atlantic islands. Geologically, Britain was part of the European continent until about 6000 B.C. The Romans conquered it in A.D. 43; after they withdrew in 410, Jutes, Angles, and Saxons raided and invaded from what are now Scandinavia and Germany. The Norman Conquest of 1066 subjugated England to France and blended its Anglo-Saxon language with French to produce English. England and France vied for power over the next several centuries, with

Scotland in and out of the fray. Henry VIII split off the Church of England from the Roman Catholic Church in 1534; his daughter Elizabeth I saw England established as a world naval power. She was succeeded by James VI of Scotland, who as James I of England united the two countries in 1603. The age of exploration and empire followed, peaking in the 1800s under Queen Victoria. In the twentieth century, independence movements have reversed British expansion. Although a victor in both world wars, Britain sustained heavy damage, and the rise of air power made its sea power less critical. The United Kingdom was a founding member of NATO and the Common Market and is a cornerstone of the European Economic Community (see p. 723).

You never know where you'll meet your own true love. I met mine down the clinical disco. That's him over there, the thin guy with the jeans, the navy jumper,[1] and the red woolly cap. He looks pretty much like anyone else, don't you think? That's hard work on his part, not to mention mine, but we got there in the end. Do you want a drink? Gin? Tonic? Fine. I'll just have an orange juice. I don't drink. Got to be careful. You never know who's watching. They're everywhere. Sorry, forget I said that. Even a joke can be paranoia. Do you like my hair? That's a golden gloss rinse. Not my style really; I have this scar down my cheek: See, if I turn to the light? A good short crop is what suits me best, always has been: I suppose I've got what you'd call a strong face. Oops, sorry, dear, didn't mean to spill your gin; it's the heels. I do my best but I can never quite manage stilettos. But it's an ill wind; anyone watching would think I'm ever so slightly tipsy, and that's normal, isn't it. It is not absolutely A-okay not to drink alcohol. On the obsessive side. *Darling, of course there are people watching.*

Let me tell you about the clinical disco while Eddie finishes his game of darts. He hates darts but darts are what men do in pubs, okay? The clinical disco is what they have once a month at Broadmoor. (Yes, that place. Broadmoor. The secure hospital for the criminally insane.) You didn't know they had women there? They do. One woman to every nine men. They often don't look all that like women when they go in but they sure as hell look like them when (and if, if, if, if, if, if) they go out.

How did I get to be in there? You really want to know? I'd been having this crummy time at home and this crummy time at work. I was pregnant and married to this guy I loved, God knows why, in retrospect, but I did,

---

[1] Sweater. — ED.

only he fancied my mother, and he got her pregnant too — while I was out at work — did you know women can get pregnant at fifty? He didn't, she didn't, I didn't — but she was! My mum said he only married me to be near her anyway and I was the one who ought to have an abortion. So I did. It went wrong and messed me up inside, so I couldn't have babies, and my mum said what did it matter, I was a lesbian anyway, just look at me. I got the scar in a road accident, in case you're wondering. And I thought what the hell, who wants a man, who wants a mother, and walked out on them. And I was working at the Royal Opera House for this man who was a real pain, and you know how these places get: The dramas and the rows and the overwork and the underpay and the show must go on though you're dropping dead. Dropping dead babies. No, I'm not crying. What do you think I am, a depressive? I'm as normal as the next person.

What I did was set fire to the office. Just an impulse. I was having these terrible pains and he made me work late. He said it was my fault Der Rosenkavalier's wig didn't fit; he said I'd made his opera house a laughingstock: The wig slipped and the *New York Times* noticed and jeered. But it wasn't my fault about the wig: Wardrobe had put the message through to props, not administration. And I sat in front of the VDU[2] — the union is against them; they cause infertility in women but what employer's going to worry about a thing like that — they'd prefer everyone childless any day — and thought about my husband and my mum, five months pregnant, and lit a cigarette. I'd given up smoking for a whole year but this business at home had made me start again. Have you ever had an abortion at five months? No? Not many have.

How's your drink? How's Eddie getting on with the darts? Started another game? That's A-okay, that's fine by me, that's normal.    5

So what were we saying, Linda? Oh yes, arson. That's what they called it. I just moved my cigarette lighter under the curtains and they went up, whoosh, and they caught some kind of soundproof ceiling infill they use these days instead of plaster. Up it all went. Whoosh again. Four hundred pounds' worth of damage. Or so they said. If you ask me, they were glad of the excuse to redecorate.

Like a fool, instead of lying and just saying it was an accident, I said I'd done it on purpose, I was glad I had, opera was a waste of public funds, and working late a waste of my life. That was before I got to court. The solicitor[3] laddie warned me off. He said arson was no laughing

---

[2]Video display unit; a computer monitor. — ED.
[3]Lawyer. — ED.

matter, they came down very hard on arson. I thought a fine, perhaps; he said no, prison. Years not months.

You know my mum didn't even come to the hearing? She had a baby girl. I thought there might be something wrong with it, my mum being so old, but there wasn't. Perhaps the father being so young made up for it.

There was a barrister chappie. He said look you've been upset, you are upset, all this business at home. The thing for you to do is plead insane; we'll get you sent to Broadmoor, it's the best place in the country for psychiatric care, they'll have you right in the head in no time. Otherwise it's Holloway, and that's all strip cells and major tranquilizers, and not so much of a short sharp shock as a long sharp shock. Years, it could be, arson.

So that's what I did, I pleaded insane, and got an indefinite sentence,     10
which meant into Broadmoor until such time as I was cured and safe to be let out into the world again. I never was unsafe. You know what one of those famous opera singers said when she heard what I'd done? "Good for Philly," she said. "Best thing that could possibly happen: the whole place razed to the ground." Only of course it wasn't razed to the ground, there was just one room already in need of redecoration slightly blackened. When did I realize I'd made a mistake? The minute I saw Broadmoor: a great black pile; the second I got into this reception room. There were three women nurses in there, standing around a bath of hot water; great hefty women, and male nurses too, and they were talking and laughing. Well, not exactly laughing, but an Inside equivalent; a sort of heavy grunting ha-ha-ha they manage, halfway between sex and hate. They didn't even look at me as I came in. I was terrified, you can imagine. One of them said "strip" over her shoulder and I just stood there not believing it. So she barked "strip" again, so I took off a cardigan and my shoes, and then one of them just ripped everything off me and pushed my legs apart and yanked out a Tampax — sorry about this, Linda — and threw it in a bin and dunked me in the bath without even seeing me. Do you know what's worse than being naked and seen by strangers, including men strangers? It's being naked and unseen, because you don't even count as a woman. Why men? In case the women patients are uncontrollable. The bath was dirty. So were the nurses. I asked for a sanitary towel but no one replied. I don't know if they were being cruel: I don't think they thought that what came out of my mouth were words. Well I was mad, wasn't I? That's why I was there. I was mad because I was a patient, I was wicked because I was a prisoner; they were sane because they were nurses and good because they could go home after work.

Linda, is that guy over there in the suit watching? No? You're sure?

They didn't go far, mind you, most of them. They lived, breathed, slept The Hospital. Whole families of nurses live in houses at the foot of the great Broadmoor wall. They intermarry. Complain about one and you find you're talking to the cousin, aunt, lover, or best friend of the complainee. You learn to shut up; you learn to smile. I was a tea bag for the whole of one day and I never stopped smiling from dawn to dusk. That's right, I was a tea bag. Nurse Kelly put a wooden frame around my shoulders and hung a piece of gauze front and back and said, "You be a tea bag all day," so I was. How we all laughed. Why did he want me to be a tea bag? It was his little joke. They get bored, you see. They look to the patients for entertainment.

Treatment? Linda, I saw one psychiatrist six times and I was there three years. The men do better. They have rehabilitation programs, Ping-Pong, carpentry, and we all get videos. Only the men get to choose the video and they always choose blue films. They have to choose them to show they're normal, and the women have to choose not to see them to show the same. You have to be normal to get out. Sister[4] in the ward fills in the report cards. She's the one who decides whether or not you're sane enough to go before the Parole Committee. The trouble is, she's not so sane herself. She's more institutionalized than the patients.

Eddie, come and join us! How was your game? You won? Better not do that too often. You don't want to be seen as an overachiever. This is Linda, I'm telling her how we met. At the clinical disco. Shall we do a little dance, just the pair of us, in the middle of everything and everyone, just to celebrate being out? No, you're right, that would be just plain mad. Eddie and I love each other, Linda, we met at the clinical disco, down Broadmoor way. Who knows, the doctor may have been wrong about me not having babies; stranger things happen. My mum ran out on my ex, leaving him to look after the baby; he came to visit me in Broadmoor once and asked me to go back to him, but I wouldn't. Sister put me back for that: A proper woman wants to go back to her husband, even though he's her little sister's father. And after he'd gone I cried. You must never cry in Broadmoor. It means you're depressed; and that's the worst madness of all. The staff all love it in there, and think you're really crazy if you don't. I guess they get kind of offended if you cry. So it's on with the lipstick and smile, smile, smile, though everyone around you is ballooning with largactyl and barking like the dogs they think they are.

I tell you something, Linda, these places are madhouses. Never, never    15

---

[4]Head nurse. — ED.

plead the balance of your mind is disturbed in court: Get a prison sentence and relax, and wait for time to pass and one day you'll be free. Once you're in a secure hospital, you may never get out at all, and they fill the women up with so many tranquilizers, you may never be fit to. The drugs give you brain damage. But I reckon I'm all right; my hands tremble a bit, and my mouth twitches sometimes, but it's not too bad. And I'm still *me*, aren't I. Eddie's fine — they don't give men so much, sometimes none at all. Only you never know what's in the tea. But you can't be seen not drinking it, because that's paranoia.

Eddie says I should sue the barrister, with his fine talk of therapy and treatment in Broadmoor, but I reckon I won't. Once you've been in you're never safe. They can pop you back inside if you cause any trouble at all, and they're the ones who decide what trouble is. So we keep our mouths shut and our noses clean, we ex-inmates of Broadmoor.

Are you sure that man's not watching? Is there something wrong with us? Eddie? You're not wearing your earring, are you? Turn your head. No, that's all right. We look just like everyone else. Don't we? Is my lipstick smudged? Christ, I hate wearing it. It makes my eyes look small.

At the clinical disco! They hold them at Broadmoor every month. Lots of the men in there are sex offenders, rapists, mass murderers, torturers, child abusers, flashers. The staff like to see how they're getting on, how they react to the opposite sex, and on the morning of the disco Sister turns up and says "you go" and "you" and "you" and of course you can't say no, no matter how scared you are. Because you're supposed to want to dance. And the male staff gee up the men — hey, look at those titties! Wouldn't you like to look up *that* skirt — and stand by looking forward to the trouble, a bit of living porno, better than a blue film any day. And they gee up the women too: Wow, there's a handsome hunk of male; and you have to act interested, because that's normal: If they think you're a lezzie you never get out. And the men have to act interested, but not too interested. Eddie and I met at the clinical disco, acting just gently interested. Eddie felt up my titties, and I rubbed myself against him and the staff watched and all of a sudden he said "Hey, I mean really," and I said "Hi," and he said "Sorry about this, keep smiling," and I said, "Ditto, what are you in for?" and he said "I got a job as a woman teacher. Six little girls framed me. But I love teaching, not little girls. There was just no job for a man," and I believed him; nobody else ever had. And I told him about my mum and my ex, and he seemed to understand. Didn't you, Eddie! That's love, you see. Love at first sight. You're just on the other person's side, and if you can find someone else like that about you, everything falls into place. We were both out in three months. It didn't matter for once if I wore lipstick, it didn't matter to him if he had to watch blue films: You stop thinking that acting sane is driving you mad: You don't have not to cry because you stop wanting to cry: The barking and howling and screeching stop worrying you; I guess when you're in love you're just happy so they have to turn you out; because your being happy shows them up. If you're happy, what does sane or insane mean, what are their lives all about? They can't bear to see it.

Linda, it's been great meeting you. Eddie and I are off home now. I've talked too much. Sorry. When we're our side of our front door I scrub off the makeup and get into jeans and he gets into drag, and we're ourselves, and we just hope no one comes knocking on the door to say, hey that's not normal, back to Broadmoor, but I reckon love's a talisman. If we hold on to that we'll be okay.

## EXPLORATIONS

1. Who is the narrator of this story? To whom is she speaking? Where does the story take place?
2. Why does the story's narrator believe she has to act normal? Who defines and enforces normality? What are the criteria?
3. What characters in "Down the Clinical Disco" behave abnormally — that is, dysfunctionally — and in what ways? What social and political institutions encourage their behavior?
4. What do you take to be Fay Weldon's central point in this story?

## CONNECTIONS

1. In "Moral Politics" (p. 542), Václav Havel writes: "I see the only way forward in that old, familiar injunction 'to live in truth'" (para. 12). What does he mean? How does his statement apply to "Down the Clinical Disco"?
2. In what ways is the narrator's dilemma in this story like that of the author of "Evicted: A Russian Jew's Story (Again)" (p. 536)? Which character do you think faces a brighter future, and why?
3. Gloria Steinem writes in *Looking at Ourselves*: "Whatever a 'superior' group has will be used to justify its superiority, and whatever an 'inferior' group has will be used to justify its plight" (p. 291). How does Weldon make a similar point in paragraph 10 of "Down the Clinical Disco"?
4. Look back at Yoram Binur's "Palestinian Like Me" (p. 275). What discovery is made both by Weldon's narrator in paragraph 10 and by Binur in paragraphs 8–9? What is each narrator's reaction to the experience?

# ELABORATIONS

1. "Down the Clinical Disco" is full of institutions and individuals that fail to carry out their assigned functions. Write a comparison-contrast essay examining these contradictions — for instance, the official purpose of the clinical disco at Broadmoor versus the role it actually plays for patients and staff. What point is conveyed by these contradictions?

2. Look closely at the techniques Weldon uses to tell her story in the form of a monologue. How does she change scenes and time frames? What is the effect of the questions at the beginning of some paragraphs? What other functions are served by the invisible character, Linda? Choose an incident in your life, such as a clash with authority, and write about it in the same monologue form Weldon uses.

# NEIL POSTMAN

## *Future Shlock*

Neil Postman has distinguished himself as a critic, writer, educator, and communications theorist since the 1960s. His early work focused on language and education; with such books as *Teaching as a Subversive Activity* (1969) and *The Soft Revolution: A Student Handbook for Turning Schools Around* (1971), both coauthored with Charles Weingartner, he became known as an advocate of radical education reform. For ten years he was editor of *Et Cetera*, the journal of general semantics. As television has played an increasingly central role in American culture, Postman has critically analyzed its impact not only on what information is available but on how we receive and understand information. His book *Amusing Ourselves to Death* (1986) explores these questions; so does "Future Shlock," which comes from his 1988 book *Conscientious Objections: Stirring Up Trouble About Language, Technology, and Education.* Postman is currently chair of the Department of Communication Arts and Sciences at New York University; he also serves on the editorial board of *The Nation* magazine. He lives in Flushing, New York.

Sometime about the middle of 1963, my colleague Charles Weingartner and I delivered in tandem an address to the National Council of Teachers of English. In that address we used the phrase *future shock* as a way of describing the social paralysis induced by rapid technological change. To my knowledge, Weingartner and I were the first people ever to use it in a public forum. Of course, neither Weingartner nor I had the brains to write a book called *Future Shock*, and all due credit must go to Alvin Toffler for having recognized a good phrase when one came along.

I mention this here not to lament lost royalties but to explain why I now feel entitled to subvert the phrase. Having been among the first to trouble the public about future shock, I may be permitted to be among the first to trouble the public about future shlock.

*Future shlock* is the name I give to a cultural condition characterized by the rapid erosion of collective intelligence. Future shlock is the aftermath of future shock. Whereas future shock results in confused, indecisive, and psychically uprooted people, future shlock produces a massive class of mediocre people.

Human intelligence is among the most fragile things in nature. It doesn't take much to distract it, suppress it, or even annihilate it. In this century, we have had some lethal examples of how easily and quickly intelligence can be defeated by any one of its several nemeses: ignorance, superstition, moral fervor, cruelty, cowardice, neglect. In the late 1920s, for example, Germany was, by any measure, the most literate, cultured nation in the world. Its legendary seats of learning attracted scholars from every corner. Its philosophers, social critics, and scientists were of the first rank; its humane traditions an inspiration to less favored nations. But by the mid-1930s — that is, in less than ten years — this cathedral of human reason had been transformed into a cesspool of barbaric irrationality. Many of the most intelligent products of German culture were forced to flee — for example, Einstein, Freud, Karl Jaspers, Thomas Mann, and Stefan Zweig. Even worse, those who remained were either forced to submit their minds to the sovereignty of primitive superstition, or — worse still — willingly did so: Konrad Lorenz, Werner Heisenberg, Martin Heidegger, Gerhardt Hauptmann. On May 10, 1933, a huge bonfire was kindled in Berlin and the books of Marcel Proust, André Gide, Émile Zola, Jack London, Upton Sinclair, and a hundred others were committed to the flames, amid shouts of idiot delight. By 1936, Joseph Paul Goebbels, Germany's minister of propaganda, was issuing a proclamation which began with the following words: "Because this year has not brought an improvement in art criticism, I forbid once and for all the continuance of art criticism in its past form, effective as of today." By 1936, there was no one left in Germany who had the brains or courage to object.

Exactly why the Germans banished intelligence is a vast and largely unanswered question. I have never been persuaded that the desperate economic depression that afflicted Germany in the 1920s adequately explains what happened. To quote Aristotle: "Men do not become tyrants in order to keep warm." Neither do they become stupid — at least not *that* stupid. But the matter need not trouble us here. I offer the German case only as the most striking example of the fragility of human intelligence. My focus here is the United States in our own time, and I wish to worry you about the rapid erosion of our own intelligence. If you are confident that such a thing cannot happen, your confidence is misplaced, I believe, but it is understandable.

After all, the United States is one of the few countries in the world founded by intellectuals — men of wide learning, of extraordinary rhetorical powers, of deep faith in reason. And although we have had our moods of anti-intellectualism, few people have been more generous in support of intelligence and learning than Americans. It was the United States that initiated the experiment in mass education that is, even today, the envy of the world. It was America's churches that laid the foundation of our admirable system of higher education; it was the Land-Grant Act of 1862 that made possible our great state universities; and it is to America that scholars and writers have fled when freedom of the intellect became impossible in their own nations. This is why the great historian of American civilization Henry Steele Commager called America "the Empire of Reason." But Commager was referring to the United States of the eighteenth and nineteenth centuries. What term he would use for America today, I cannot say. Yet he has observed, as others have, a change, a precipitous decline in our valuation of intelligence, in our uses of language, in the disciplines of logic and reason, in our capacity to attend to complexity. Perhaps he would agree with me that the Empire of Reason is, in fact, gone, and that the most apt term for America today is the Empire of Shlock.

In any case, this is what I wish to call to your notice: the frightening displacement of serious, intelligent public discourse in American culture by the imagery and triviality of what may be called show business. I do not see the decline of intelligent discourse in America leading to the barbarisms that flourished in Germany, of course. No scholars, I believe, will ever need to flee America. There will be no bonfires to burn books. And I cannot imagine any proclamations forbidding once and for all art criticism, or any other kind of criticism. But this is not a cause for complacency, let alone celebration. A culture does not have to force scholars to flee to render them impotent. A culture does not have to burn books to assure that they will not be read. And a culture does not need a minister of propaganda issuing proclamations to silence criticism. There are other ways to achieve stupidity, and it appears that, as in so many other things, there is a distinctly American way.

To explain what I am getting at, I find it helpful to refer to two films, which taken together embody the main lines of my argument. The first film is of recent vintage and is called *The Gods Must Be Crazy*. It is about a tribal people who live in the Kalahari Desert plains of southern Africa, and what happens to their culture when it is invaded by an empty Coca-Cola bottle tossed from the window of a small plane passing overhead. The bottle lands in the middle of the village and is construed by these gentle people to be a gift from the gods, for they not only have never seen a bottle before but have never seen glass either. The people are almost immediately charmed by the gift, and not only because of its novelty. The bottle, it turns out, has multiple uses, chief among them the intriguing music it makes when one blows into it.

But gradually a change takes place in the tribe. The bottle becomes an irresistible preoccupation. Looking at it, holding it, thinking of things to do with it displace other activities once thought essential. But more than this, the Coke bottle is the only thing these people have ever seen of which there is only one of its kind. And so those who do not have it try to get it from the one who does. And the one who does refuses to give it up. Jealousy, greed, and even violence enter the scene, and come very close to destroying the harmony that has characterized their culture for a thousand years. The people begin to love their bottle more than they love themselves, and are saved only when the leader of the tribe, convinced that the gods must be crazy, returns the bottle to the gods by throwing it off the top of a mountain.

The film is great fun and it is also wise, mainly because it is about a subject as relevant to people in Chicago or Los Angeles or New York as it is to those of the Kalahari Desert. It raises two questions of extreme importance to our situation: How does a culture change when new technologies are introduced to it? And is it always desirable for a culture to accommodate itself to the demands of new technologies? The leader of the Kalahari tribe is forced to confront these questions in a way that Americans have refused to do. And because his vision is not obstructed by a belief in what Americans call "technological progress," he is able with minimal discomfort to decide that the songs of the Coke bottle are not so alluring that they are worth admitting envy, egotism, and greed to a serene culture.

The second film relevant to my argument was made in 1967. It is Mel Brooks's first film, *The Producers. The Producers* is a rather raucous comedy that has at its center a painful joke: An unscrupulous theatrical producer has figured out that it is relatively easy to turn a buck by producing a play that fails. All one has to do is induce dozens of backers to invest in the play by promising them exorbitant percentages of its profits. When the play fails, there being no profits to disperse, the producer walks away with thousands of dollars that can never be claimed. Of course, the central problem he must solve is to make sure that his play is a disastrous failure. And so he hits upon an excellent idea: He will take the most tragic and grotesque story of our century — the rise of Adolf Hitler — and make it into a musical.

Because the producer is only a crook and not a fool, he assumes that the stupidity of making a musical on this theme will be immediately grasped by audiences and that they will leave the theater in dumbfounded rage. So he calls his play *Springtime for Hitler,* which is also the name of its most important song. The song begins with the words:

> Springtime for Hitler and Germany;
> Winter for Poland and France.

The melody is catchy, and when the song is sung it is accompanied   10
by a happy chorus line. (One must understand, of course, that *Springtime
for Hitler* is no spoof of Hitler, as was, for example, Charlie Chaplin's *The
Great Dictator.* The play is instead a kind of denial of Hitler in song and
dance; as if to say, it was all in fun.)

The ending of the movie is predictable. The audience loves the play
and leaves the theater humming *Springtime for Hitler.* The musical
becomes a great hit. The producer ends up in jail, his joke having turned
back on him. But Brooks's point is that the joke is on us. Although the
film was made years before a movie actor became president of the United
States, Brooks was making a kind of prophecy about that — namely, that
the producers of American culture will increasingly turn our history,
politics, religion, commerce, and education into forms of entertainment,
and that we will become as a result a trivial people, incapable of coping
with complexity, ambiguity, uncertainty, perhaps even reality. We will
become, in a phrase, a people amused into stupidity.

For those readers who are not inclined to take Mel Brooks as seriously
as I do, let me remind you that the prophecy I attribute here to Brooks
was, in fact, made many years before by a more formidable social critic
than he. I refer to Aldous Huxley, who wrote *Brave New World* at the
time that the modern monuments to intellectual stupidity were taking
shape: nazism in Germany, fascism in Italy, communism in Russia. But
Huxley was not concerned in his book with such naked and crude forms
of intellectual suicide. He saw beyond them, and mostly, I must add, he
saw America. To be more specific, he foresaw that the greatest threat to
the intelligence and humane creativity of our culture would not come
from Big Brother and ministries of propaganda, or gulags and concentration camps. He prophesied, if I may put it this way, that there is tyranny
lurking in a Coca-Cola bottle; that we could be ruined not by what we
fear and hate but by what we welcome and love, by what we construe to
be a gift from the gods.

And in case anyone missed his point in 1932, Huxley wrote *Brave New
World Revisited* twenty years later. By then, George Orwell's *1984* had
been published, and it was inevitable that Huxley would compare Orwell's book with his own. The difference, he said, is that in Orwell's book
people are controlled by inflicting pain. In *Brave New World,* they are
controlled by inflicting pleasure.

The Coke bottle that has fallen in our midst is a corporation of
dazzling technologies whose forms turn all serious public business into
a kind of *Springtime for Hitler* musical. Television is the principal instru-
ment of this disaster, in part because it is the medium Americans most
dearly love, and in part because it has become the command center of

our culture. Americans turn to television not only for their light entertainment but for their news, their weather, their politics, their religion,
their history — all of which may be said to be their serious entertainment.
The light entertainment is not the problem. The least dangerous things
on television are its junk. What I am talking about is television's preemp-
tion of our culture's most serious business. It would be merely banal to
say that television presents us with entertaining subject matter. It is quite
another thing to say that on television all subject matter is presented as
entertaining. And that is how television brings ruin to any intelligent
understanding of public affairs.

Political campaigns, for example, are now conducted largely in the      15
form of television commercials. Candidates forgo precision, complexity,
substance — in some cases, language itself — for the arts of show business: music, imagery, celebrities, theatrics. Indeed, political figures have
become so good at this, and so accustomed to it, that they do television
commercials even when they are not campaigning. . . . Even worse,
political figures appear on variety shows, soap operas, and sit-coms.
George McGovern, Ralph Nader, Ed Koch, and Jesse Jackson have all
hosted "Saturday Night Live." Henry Kissinger and former president
Gerald Ford have done cameo roles on "Dynasty." [Former Massachusetts
officials] Tip O'Neill and Governor Michael Dukakis have appeared on
"Cheers." Richard Nixon did a short stint on "Laugh-In." The late senator
from Illinois, Everett Dirksen, was on "What's My Line?," a prophetic
question if ever there was one. What *is* the line of these people? Or, more
precisely, *where* is the line that one ought to be able to draw between
politics and entertainment? I would suggest that television has annihilated
it. . . .

But politics is only one arena in which serious language has been
displaced by the arts of show business. We have all seen how religion is
packaged on television, as a kind of Las Vegas stage show, devoid of ritual,
sacrality, and tradition. Today's electronic preachers are in no way like
America's evangelicals of the past. Men like Jonathan Edwards, Charles
Finney, and George Whiteside were preachers of theological depth,
authentic learning, and great expository power. Electronic preachers such
as Jimmy Swaggart, Jim Bakker, and Jerry Falwell are merely performers
who exploit television's visual power and their own charisma for the
greater glory of themselves.

We have also seen "Sesame Street" and other educational shows in
which the demands of entertainment take precedence over the rigors of
learning. And we well know how American businessmen, working under
the assumption that potential customers require amusement rather than

facts, use music, dance, comedy, cartoons, and celebrities to sell their products.

Even our daily news, which for most Americans means television news, is packaged as a kind of show, featuring handsome news readers, exciting music, and dynamic film footage. Most especially, film footage. When there is no film footage, there is no story. Stranger still, commercials may appear anywhere in a news story — before, after, or in the middle. This reduces all events to trivialities, sources of public entertainment and little more. After all, how serious can a bombing in Lebanon be if it is shown to us prefaced by a happy United Airlines commercial and summarized by a Calvin Klein jeans commercial? Indeed, television newscasters have added to our grammar a new part of speech — what may be called the "Now . . . this" conjunction, a conjunction that does not connect two things but disconnects them. When newscasters say, "Now . . . this," they mean to indicate that what you have just heard or seen has no relevance to what you are about to hear or see. There is no murder so brutal, no political blunder so costly, no bombing so devastating that it cannot be erased from our minds by a newscaster saying, "Now . . . this." He means that you have thought long enough on the matter (let us say, for forty seconds) and you must now give your attention to a commercial. Such a situation is not "the news." It is merely a daily version of *Springtime for Hitler,* and in my opinion accounts for the fact that Americans are among the most ill-informed people in the world. To be sure, we know *of* many things; but we know *about* very little.

To provide some verification of this, I conducted a survey a few years back on the subject of the Iranian hostage crisis. I chose this subject because it was alluded to on television *every day for more than a year.* I did not ask my subjects for their opinions about the hostage situation. I am not interested in opinion polls; I am interested in knowledge polls. The questions I asked were simple and did not require deep knowledge. For example, Where is Iran? What language do the Iranians speak? Where did the Shah come from? What religion do the Iranians practice, and what are its basic tenets? What does *Ayatollah* mean? I found that almost everybody knew practically nothing about Iran. And those who did know something said they had learned it from *Newsweek* or *Time* or the *New York Times.* Television, in other words, is not the great information machine. It is the great disinformation machine. A most nerve-wracking confirmation of this came some time ago during an interview with the producer and the writer of the TV mini-series "Peter the Great." Defending the historical inaccuracies in the drama — which included a fabricated meeting between Peter and Sir Isaac Newton — the producer said that no one would watch a dry, historically faithful biography. The writer added that it is better for audiences to learn something that is untrue, if it is entertaining, than not to learn anything at all. And just to put some icing on the cake, the actor who played Peter, Maximilian Schell, remarked that he does not believe in historical truth and therefore sees no reason to pursue it.

I do not mean to say that the trivialization of American public dis-                  20
course is all accomplished on television. Rather, television is the paradigm for all our attempts at public communication. It conditions our minds to apprehend the world through fragmented pictures and forces other media to orient themselves in that direction. You know the standard question we put to people who have difficulty understanding even simple language: We ask them impatiently, "Do I have to draw a picture for you?" Well, it appears that, like it or not, our culture will draw pictures for us, will explain the world to us in pictures. As a medium for conducting public business, language has receded in importance; it has been moved to the periphery of culture and has been replaced at the center by the entertaining visual image.

Please understand that I am making no criticism of the visual arts in general. That criticism is made by God, not by me. You will remember that in His Second Commandment, God explicitly states that "Thou shalt not make unto thee any graven image, nor any likeness of anything that is in Heaven above, or that is in the earth beneath, or the waters beneath the earth." I have always felt that God was taking a rather extreme position on this, as is His way. As for myself, I am arguing from the standpoint of a symbolic relativist. Forms of communication are neither good nor bad in themselves. They become good or bad depending on their relationship to other symbols and on the functions they are made to serve within a social order. When a culture becomes overloaded with pictures; when logic and rhetoric lose their binding authority; when historical truth becomes irrelevant; when the spoken or written word is distrusted or makes demands on our attention that we are incapable of giving; when our politics, history, education, religion, public information, and commerce are expressed largely in visual imagery rather than words, then a culture is in serious jeopardy.

Neither do I make a complaint against entertainment. As an old song has it, life is not a highway strewn with flowers. The sight of a few blossoms here and there may make our journey a trifle more endurable. But in America, the least amusing people are our professional entertainers. In our present situation, our preachers, entrepreneurs, politicians, teachers, and journalists are committed to entertaining us through media that do not lend themselves to serious, complex discourse. But these producers of our culture are not to be blamed. They, like the rest of us, believe in the supremacy of technological progress. It has never occurred to us that the gods might be crazy. And even if it did, there is no mountaintop from which we can return what is dangerous to us.

We would do well to keep in mind that there are two ways in which the spirit of a culture may be degraded. In the first — the Orwellian — culture becomes a prison. This was the way of the Nazis, and it appears to be the way of the Russians.[1] In the second — the Huxleyan — culture becomes a burlesque. This appears to be the way of the Americans. What Huxley teaches is that in the Age of Advanced Technology, spiritual devastation is more likely to come from an enemy with a smiling countenance than from one whose face exudes suspicion and hate. In the Huxleyan prophecy, Big Brother does not watch us, by his choice; we watch him, by ours. When a culture becomes distracted by trivia; when political and social life are redefined as a perpetual round of entertainments; when public conversation becomes a form of baby talk; when a people become, in short, an audience and their public business a vaudeville act, then — Huxley argued — a nation finds itself at risk and culture-death is a clear possibility. I agree.

## EXPLORATIONS

1. What political developments are the context for Postman's opening description of Germany (paras. 1–2)? Where and how else does he refer to the same developments? How do these multiple references encourage us, as readers, "to take Mel Brooks as seriously as I do" (para. 12)?

2. Twice in his essay Postman uses long compound sentences consisting of clauses linked by "when" (paras. 21 and 23). In what ways do the form and placement of these sentences give impact to their content?

3. At what points does Postman address the reader directly? What is the effect of these shifts into the second person ("you")? What is the effect of his frequent use of the first person singular ("I")? The first person plural ("we")?

4. In what ways does Postman use entertainment to make his case? Is his essay a contradiction of his own argument? Why or why not?

---

[1]That is, the Soviet Union. — ED.

# CONNECTIONS

1. Neil Postman, like Fay Weldon in "Down the Clinical Disco" (p. 551), looks at institutions whose actual roles in people's lives are quite different from the roles we imagine they play. What institution is Postman's main target? What other institutions does he criticize?

2. Eduard Shevardnadze's "Life with the Party" (p. 521) and Liang Heng and Judith Shapiro's "Chairman Mao's Good Little Boy" (p. 121) both recall life under communism. What elements in these two narratives match Postman's description of the Orwellian threat to culture (paras. 12–13 and 23)?

3. What ideas in the *New Yorker* selection in *Looking at Ourselves* (p. 507) help to explain points made by Neil Postman, and vice versa?

# ELABORATIONS

1. Neil Postman makes his case by encouraging the reader to draw conclusions from evidence; sometimes he does not state his point directly. Go through "Future Shlock" and identify the thesis of each paragraph. Then write a brief essay incorporating these thesis statements into a shorter and more explicit version of Postman's argument.

2. Postman wrote "Future Shlock" during Ronald Reagan's presidency. Has the evolution of American culture since then confirmed or contradicted his diagnosis? Write an update of "Future Shlock" using more recent evidence to argue for or against Postman's position.

# MICHAEL DORRIS

## *House of Stone*

Michael Dorris, born in 1945 in Dayton, Washington, is a mixed-blood member of the Modoc tribe. His Modoc father was killed in World War II. Dorris lived for a while on a reservation in eastern Montana but grew up mostly in Louisville, Kentucky, with his mother, aunt, and grandmother. He earned his bachelor's degree at Georgetown University and his master's at Yale University. In 1971 he adopted a Native American baby named Abel who he discovered was afflicted with Fetal Alcohol Syndrome (FAS). Under the pseudonym of Adam, Abel became the central figure in Dorris's groundbreaking book on FAS, *The Broken Cord* (1989), later a television movie (see "Adam," by Louise Erdrich, p. 88). Dorris adopted another Native American son and daughter as well. In 1972 — the same year Louise Erdrich arrived as a freshman — Dartmouth College hired him to teach anthropology and chair the newly created Native American Studies department. Dorris and Erdrich renewed their friendship at a reading of her poetry several years later. He had quit writing but took it up again during a research trip to New Zealand, when they kept in touch by exchanging letters, poems, and stories. They married after he returned and have collaborated ever since on parenthood (three more daughters) and writing (short stories, novels, nonfiction, and children's books). Among his books are *Yellow Raft in Blue Water* (1987) and *Morning Girl* (1992). House of Stone originally appeared in the November/December 1992 issue of *Mother Jones*. For more information on Dorris and Erdrich, see page 88.

Zimbabwe is a landlocked country in south-central Africa, bordered by Botswana on the west (see p. 354), Zambia on the north, Mozambique on the east, and South Africa on the south (see pp. 35 and 587). It was conquered in the late 1800s by Cecil Rhodes's British South Africa Company. In 1923 its European settlers voted to become the self-governing British colony of Southern Rhodesia; in 1965 Ian Smith's white-minority government declared independence. Britain balked, insisting on a plan to turn over control eventually to the black majority. The United Nations imposed a trade embargo, but Rhodesia nevertheless proclaimed itself a republic in 1970, with a constitution limiting blacks' access to power. Internal and external tensions continued, until a new constitution was approved in 1979 which enfranchised all blacks, restructured the government, and renamed the country. In 1980 Britain recognized Zimbabwe's independence. The drought-plagued nation appealed for foreign aid in 1992 as President Robert Mugabe declared a national disaster.

During one of the famines that raked the Horn of Africa in the past ten years, there was a community in which starving human beings and starving baboons were reduced to competing directly against each other for food. Baboons are wily, agile, and hard to discourage, but the people, desperate, devised a plan. A lone female baboon was ambushed, brought back to the village, and skinned alive. Her screams echoed into the hills, and soon a ring of alarmed baboons approached the periphery of the invisible line that traditionally divided the territory of men and women from that of animals. The tortured baboon was untied and, blind with pain, she ran frantically in the direction of her home.

The sight, they say, was terrible for a person to see, and it was even worse for another baboon. Unrecognizable, the victim was the embodiment of horror: the familiar inverted to nightmare. Some baboons fled, others attacked with teeth and claws until, finally, the thing was still. But from that day forward, villagers had no rivals in their quest for the few remaining fruits and roots and grains that survived in the region. All the baboons had gone away.

Americans like me are always "discovering" grand-scale poverty and being famously shocked by the magnitude of it. Most of the time, we flirt with awareness, gulp it in sound bites from the network anchors, or register it from newspaper photographs staged to produce a maximum impact. We shudder, we recoil, we maybe even write off the occasional check or buy an overpriced ticket to a benefit, thus entertaining ourselves and doing good simultaneously. But in general, distant disasters are treated like rumors, lacking the immediacy of fear, personal danger, or entanglement. They're our problem only when we allow them time to capture our imaginations, and then, with the zeal of converts who've just received Revelation, we often become boorish and righteous. We accost our friends with dire statistics, censure their ignorance, demand their involvement. True, a few persist to make a real dent in the wall of tragedy by repeatedly crashing against it, but, for the rest of us, burnout, disappointment, and frustration are merely a matter of when. We expect results, bang for our bucks, a return on our emotional and financial investment. If we have the option of looking the other way, usually, eventually, we exercise it.

I try to explain this — and the related big business of charity appeals — to Mark Nyahada, a local Save the Children assistant field office director, when visiting Zimbabwe last July. We sit with a small, tired group at the table of a guest house deep within a government-run oasis — an agricultural station with working wells and sprinklers, a verdant dot upon the red and tan veld near the Mozambican border. A few miles to the north on an arid plateau is the starving community of Muusha, and a few miles to the southwest is the sprawling refugee camp of Tongogara, where forty-two thousand people but not a single physician are encircled by a steel fence.

"I don't understand it," Mark says, frowning. "We don't need so much,     5
but what we need, we need. Where is the help?"

I reach for the ubiquitous jar of coffee "substitute," sucrose and artificial creamer already mixed in, which, together with Coca-Cola and Orange Squash, seems to be the beverage of choice in rural Zimbabwe.

"Imagine receiving your mail in the morning," I answer. "One or two personal letters, a few bills, and then a bunch of envelopes bearing the return addresses of famous people — movie stars, ex-presidents. Inside each one is a professionally produced solicitation that tries to get you interested in a particular agenda: right to life, freedom of choice, American Indians, the election of a candidate who promises to make the country better, cancer research, kidneys, the protection of the environment. The texts are engineered by marketing experts — advertising executives with degrees in psychology — trained to grab you with an opening sentence and wring a few dollars from your conscience. Half the time you don't even unfold the paper, just toss it in the trash so you don't have to think about everything you can't change."

"How do these people know where you live?"

"Maybe a year ago you read an article about . . . AIDS," I answer. "Or you knew someone who was sick and looked for a way to show your sympathy, so you sent a contribution to support a hospice. The hospice needs money, so it sold its mailing list of donors to another charity, and they did the same thing. Soon you're on everybody's computer as being good for fifty dollars or a hundred dollars, and the machines take over. There's only one of you and a thousand deserving causes. You can drown in them. They become all the same, all wanting your attention and your spare change, like a street lined with beggars, and most people shut their eyes, close their ears, speed up, run."

The next day I ride with Mark to Tongogara, where he is supposed to     10
supervise a newly inaugurated program run cooperatively by Save the Children, the University of Zimbabwe, and a U.S. team of psychologists and social workers from Duke University. The program aims both to reunite separated family members and to care for the youngest witnesses of unspeakable violence.

"Some of these children," he tells me in his very British accent, "have seen terrible things. They've been forced to kill their parents. Made to carry ammunition across enemy lines. Seen people locked inside houses that were then set on fire."

In the late-morning torpor of the reception area, where the only sounds are the buzz of flies and the low conversation of soldiers assigned to guard duty, it's hard to imagine such atrocities — until I see the eyes of one little boy, who looks to be about ten years old. His expression is devoid of curiosity, exhausted, matching the listlessness of the elderly woman beside him.

Mark notices the direction of my gaze. "That's his grandmother," he tells me. "His mother is still somewhere in Mozambique. They hoped the father would be here, but so far we haven't been able to locate him."

Mark beckons, and the boy comes over, joins us, and, in the custom of men conversing, we squat face to face. Unmoving, the grandmother stares through us as if watching another place in another time. There are stretched holes in the lobes of her ears, from which jewelry once dangled. Mark estimates that she's no more than fifty, and yet she appears to me much older.

There's nothing childlike about this boy, nothing playful or energetic.    15
Like so many people I will meet in these camps, he has about him an air of distilled dignity, as if, stripped of every other possession, he has quietly retained possession of himself.

Speaking Shona, Mark translates the boy's story, which is, within this inhumane context, undramatic, even typical. Yes, he's gone days without eating. Yes, he and his grandmother have walked shoeless from a long distance. Yes, he's hoping to find his father, who ran away from their village some time ago to avoid execution for being the brother-in-law of the wrong person. The boy is neither rushed nor especially interested, just tired. He's never been to school, but clearly he's intelligent, a survivor. If it weren't for his size, for the absence of lines on his face, I'd think I was in the presence of a resigned, mature man.

Mark promises that he'll circulate the boy's photograph throughout the several refugee centers scattered along the frontier; he'll even forward it to his counterpart in Malawi, where more than one million Mozambicans have fled. Perhaps the lost father will see it and contact authorities. Perhaps the story will have a resolution.

The boy nods, agrees, then rejoins his grandmother. Mark and I brush off our knees and walk toward our Toyota. We're running behind a tight schedule, late for a meeting. Before I get into the car, however, I turn back for one last look. The boy is in the cradle of his grandmother's thin arms. His mouth is at her empty breast.

There are dozens of good reasons for us not to donate these days. "The economy," we complain, without being very specific. "And besides, I gave last year to [fill in the blank], and look, nothing has changed." We forgive ourselves with predictable scandals: the inflated salaries drawn by certain

CEOs of philanthropic organizations; the percentage of every dollar that goes for vague "overhead"; the imminence of closer catastrophes, where our gifts might have a more direct and monitorable impact. And then, of course, there's the suspicion that conditions are being exaggerated by those who seek to tap our sympathy. We want proof — death counts, weight-loss graphs, raw film footage — before we respond. If we give at all, it must be to the *best* place, the *neediest* victim, the *furthest* gone.

Most arrivals at Tongogara this July have been rerouted to Chambuta, a new camp Mark and I visit just beyond the dry bed of what, in a normal year, is the wide Runde River. It's on the other side of Gonarezhou National Park, where the United States is about to spend a million Zimbabwe dollars to implement an elephant preservation program, a scheme that involves the digging of borehole wells exclusively for the watering of animals.

Now full beyond capacity with 24,000 people — up from 6,000 in January — Chambuta is divided into sixteen "villages," though two of them so far lack the most rudimentary shelter. The Zimbabwean government, reeling under its own drought deprivations, has provided sufficient water and food rations, but there is no disguising the utter bleakness of the place, the stark, thorny desert, the barrenness. It is, quite literally, the end of the road.

Most of the 700 people who arrive daily, the director, Israel Choku-wenga, reports, are without clothing, confused, disoriented, sick, and always thirsty. Drought, not war, is their "presenting problem." An under-sized boy, hot with the fever of measles, lies on the ground, his head propped against a canvas pack. A tiny girl, one leg stiff and too short, lugs a can for water toward an open spigot. As she hobbles, she leaves odd footprints — the left is as it should be, the right only of flexed toes. There are flies and more flies, ever seeking the moisture that resides at the corner of a person's eyes or mouth. Many at Chambuta seem to lack the energy or the will to blink. No one even begs.

Surprisingly, life asserts itself in this desolate place. Waiting by the administration building, next to unused parking spaces demarcated in the dirt by carefully placed rocks, is an unofficial greeter. He's dressed in a knit ski cap and a tattered Hard Rock Cafe T-shirt, has advanced glaucoma in both eyes, and bears the unreadable expression of a man in the midst of a long interior monologue. Yet, equipped with a branch stretched and bent by a piece of wire, a hollow gourd for resonance, and a twig as a dancing hammer, he's making music.

Every day I spend in southeastern Zimbabwe extends the boundary of deprivation I believed human beings could endure. There is an unrelieved sense of waiting in the camps, but it's a waiting bereft of expectation, a queue so stalled that no one remembers what was supposed to be at the end. It's a waiting for the fickleness of weather, the eventuality of death, the unlikely news of civil peace, the abrupt interruption of food or drink. It hums with a passive inertia, a kind of dull concession that no individual act or thought can affect the outcome.

Bad luck has created this congestion, bad luck and the incessant meddling of foreign governments — which have lost interest in the region now that the Cold War is history. At one end of the looping line is pain, and at the other is carefree joy. At the far extreme stands that prematurely old little boy of Tongogara; a million options and possibilities away are we, am I. Thrown together by chance — at the coincident moment of time we found ourselves occupying the same place — we beheld each other, registered our similarities. For every child like him there are 100,000 more I don't happen to encounter, and for every man like me, there are millions he can't imagine, so we stare across the chasm, try to fathom the other's life.

No greater distance separates us than this: He stays, I leave. But not entirely alone. I have a daughter about his age, a shining girl whose last act before my trip was to empty her bulldog bank and send her birthday money along for me to give away. To her, on some unspoiled level, she and the boy I've just met have the obvious connection of brother and sister or potential playmates. She has not yet learned to tolerate injustice as inevitable, to become defeated in advance by the enormous odds against reaching out. For her, what's before her eyes is still visible, and the situation is a quite simple equation. They need. I have. Therefore, I give, in order to reestablish a fair balance.

Of the recent atrocities reported from the Mozambican front, one story stands out: A group of boys armed with automatic weapons appeared in a neighboring community. Swiftly they surrounded a group of local children no older than themselves and shot them. When asked why, one fourteen-year-old explained that the children of that village had been kindly treated by adults, rarely beaten, and fed daily. The attacking boys were indignant, jealous, so they evened the score. In their experience of the world, a lack of suffering was sufficient reason to die.

As Mark and I drive north on a two-lane road, past thatched-roof villages and straggling goats that seem more bone than flesh, the faces of two children — who will never meet — are superimposed and fix permanently in my imagination.

Muusha, a name given to the cluster of buildings that functions as the principal town for two precincts with a combined population of 12,000 farmers, is in the midst of its seventh and most severe winter of drought.

The conditions are brutal, dusty, too dry even for the waste of tears. If meteorological forecasts hold true, it won't rain again for another four months, and the first crop of maize won't be ready before May at the earliest.

All told, it's been a hard year in the Mutema region: The weather    30
prohibited any harvesting whatsoever last season; only five rapidly depreciating wells remain to meet the water needs of the inhabitants; the grade-school children's lunch program was eliminated, and as a result there are daily faintings and steep declines in attendance. The World Bank, anxious that the last vestiges of Zimbabwe's former inclination toward socialism be abandoned, urged the imposition of a token tuition charge for all grade levels. Equivalent to one U.S. dollar per year per child, this fee constitutes a burden to the poorest families, who, I am told, have responded by sending only boys to classes; too many of the girls resorted to prostitution in order to eat.

On the flight back to the United States, my mind races, searching for some action, some call to arms, some original and efficacious idea in response to what I've seen. I tilt between the equally useless poles of helplessness and arrogance, of throwing up my hands and of changing my life. What is the appropriate path between wanting to help, on the one hand, and knowing how to do it, on the other?

The answer, I realize, begins with empathy based at the most individual level. It's too easy to forget the picture of a crowd, no matter how miserable. We don't think of our parents, of our children, as a group, but as specific people, each with his or her own personality, perspective, and face. We must see through the burning, thirsty forest and find a tree to nurture, to water during the dry season, so that it will provide shade in a later year. We must give as if to ourselves — automatically and practically, without the demand of gratitude or closure.

To be fortunate is, in a deep moral sense, to be obliged. Confusion is no excuse; doing *something*, even if mistakes are made, will help, especially in the early stages of trouble. And even from far away, our contributions can be specifically designated, if we make the effort to inform ourselves. In Zimbabwe, for instance, $30 will send a little girl to school for a year; $140 will buy a week's worth of lunches for 400 students; $600 invested now will deepen an existing well, thus sustaining a whole community until the rains return, permitting people to stay independent rather than swelling the rolls of those forced to become internal refugees.

My final stop in Zimbabwe was the tiny settlement of Mola, far to the north, where food was very much on the mind of the village secretary for an emergency relief operation that provides a daily bowl of corn mush to children under five, pregnant women, and lactating mothers. A woman with strong arms and a sleeping toddler secured on her back, she spoke Tonga in a low voice and was all business in her negotiations with Ruben McKenzie, the local Save the Children administrator, who translated the proceedings for my benefit.

Her first proposal: A number of village women would participate in    35
this feeding program on a rotating basis, measuring out grain or weighing children for government records; they, too, should be afforded the luxury of an occasional meal, since lately some of them have passed out from hunger. Ruben should be clear, she added, that this provision would not extend to her or to members of her governing committee, who, to avoid any suspicion of profiteering, have made themselves permanently ineligible for rations.

Ruben, a handsome young man born and raised nearby, gravely explained that there was only a finite amount of food available; if more people partook, the portions would necessarily be smaller. The decision, however, was up to the secretary and her colleagues.

She nodded, one item on her agenda ticked off, and moved on. What about the agency's pull cart, she wanted to know. When it wasn't in use for this program, might she have permission to designate it for other purposes, such as transporting the sick to the airstrip? Otherwise, it would simply sit idle.

Once again Ruben confirmed her authority, and once again the woman, and the audience of recipients watching this drama for entertainment, were satisfied. There remained one final issue to be settled: Would Ruben please find out and report on his next visit what would happen to the fifty-gallon tin drum, now loaned to store water, when the rains came back? The question was posed casually, offhand even, but no one present believed for an instant that there wasn't already a specific task envisioned for this rusty object of foreign manufacture, a task that will, if humanly possible, be accomplished.

"Where does your water come from now?" I asked the woman, and was led nearly a mile down a path to the chalky expanse of what normally would have been a river bottom. Into a small hole, a scrape in the dirt, there seeped a puddle of brown water. We stood around the perimeter in silence, for the shallowness, the precariousness, was self-evident, and eventually I looked up at the secretary's face. She was frowning, thinking hard, absolutely determined to figure something out.

# EXPLORATIONS

1. What is the effect of the baboon anecdote that opens "House of Stone"? How does this anecdote relate to the rest of the essay?
2. What goal does Michael Dorris set for himself in paragraph 32? What tactics does he use to pursue his goal?
3. Identify at least three examples of comparison and contrast in this essay. What is the impact of each one?
4. What does the title "House of Stone" mean?

# CONNECTIONS

1. Which of Neil Postman's complaints about television in "Future Shlock" (p. 559) is (or are) also raised by Dorris?
2. Reread Shelby Steele's comments about innocence in *Looking at Ourselves* (p. 515). How do these comments apply to "House of Stone"?
3. Look back at Louise Erdrich's "Adam" (p. 88). What information does Erdrich give about her husband, Michael Dorris, and their family that is reflected in "House of Stone"? What further information does Dorris add here?

# ELABORATIONS

1. Michael Dorris uses a "split screen" in this essay, showing readers two different scenes at once. How does he employ stylistic techniques such as language, tense, and characters to contrast the two scenes? To unify them? Write an essay either analyzing Dorris's use of this device or utilizing it yourself to write about another subject.
2. Reread Dorris's paragraph 3. Who are "Americans like me"? Do you agree with what he says about "our" response to poverty? Write an essay arguing for or against his statements, supporting your position with evidence from your own experience.

# NADINE GORDIMER

## *Amnesty*

Born in a small gold-mining town in South Africa in 1923, Nadine Gordimer is an outspoken civil libertarian who believes that change in her country's policies is best spurred from within. Her writing — much of it focusing on the impact of apartheid on South Africans — is renowned around the world. "I think when you're born white in South Africa, you're peeling like an onion," she has said. "You're sloughing off all the conditioning that you've had since you were a child." Gordimer started writing in childhood; she was educated at a convent school and Witwatersrand University but gives most credit to her local library. Her novels, short stories, and essays have won her numerous awards and honorary degrees. She has contributed to many American magazines, including *The New Yorker*, *Harper's*, *The Atlantic Monthly*, and *The New York Review of Books*, as well as taught creative writing at Columbia University's Graduate School of the Arts. In 1978 she was elected an honorary member of the American Academy and Institute of Arts and Letters, whose citation read: "The brilliance with which she renders her varied characters has opened her country to passionate understandings which most of us have no other access to." In 1991 she became the first South African to win the Nobel Prize for literature. Gordimer currently lives with her family in Johannesburg. Her novels include *The Conservationist* (1974), *July's People* (1981), *A Sport of Nature* (1987), and *My Son's Story* (1990). "Amnesty" first appeared in the August 29, 1990, *New Yorker*.

For background on South Africa, see pages 35 and 587.

When we heard he was released I ran all over the farm and climbed through the fence to our people on the next farm to tell everybody. I only saw later I'd torn my dress on the barbed wire, and there was a scratch, with blood, on my shoulder.

He went away from this place nine years ago, signed up to work in the city with what they call a construction company — building glass walls up to the sky. For the first two years he came home for the weekend once a month and for two weeks at Christmas; that was when he asked my father for me. And he began to pay. He and I thought that in three years he would have paid enough for us to get married. But then he started wearing that T-shirt, he told us he'd joined the union, he told us about the strike, how he was one of the men who went to talk to the bosses

578

because some others had been laid off after it. He's always been good at talking, even in English — he was the best at the farm school, he used to read the newspapers the Indian wraps soap and sugar in when you buy at the store.

There was trouble at the hostel where he had a bed, and riots over paying rent in the townships, and he told me — just me, not the old ones — that wherever people were fighting against the way we are treated they were doing it for all of us, on the farms as well as in the towns, and the unions were with them, he was with them, making speeches, marching. The third year, we heard he was in prison. Instead of us getting married.

We didn't know where to find him, until he went on trial. The case was heard in a city far away. I couldn't go often to the court, because by that time I had passed my Standard 8, and I was working in the farm school, teaching the little ones. Also, my parents were short of money. Two of my brothers who had gone away to work in the city didn't send home; I suppose they lived with girlfriends and had to buy things for them. My father and other brother work here for the Boer[1] and the pay is very small; we have two goats, a few cows we're allowed to graze, and a patch of land where my mother can grow vegetables — no cash from that.

When I saw him in the court he looked beautiful, in a blue suit with a striped shirt and brown tie. All the accused — his comrades, he called them — were well dressed. The union bought the clothes so that the judge and the prosecutor would know they weren't dealing with stupid yes-baas black men who didn't know their rights. These things and everything else about the court and trial he explained to me when I was allowed to visit him in jail. Our little girl was born while the trial went on, and when I brought the baby to court the first time to show her to him, his comrades hugged him and then hugged me across the barrier of the prisoners' dock, and they had clubbed together to give me some money as a present for the baby. He chose the name for her, Inkululeko.

Then the trial was over and he got six years. He was sent to the Island.[2] We all knew about the Island. Our leaders had been there so long. But I had never seen the sea except to color it in blue at school, and I couldn't imagine a piece of earth surrounded by it. I could only think of a cake of dung dropped by the cattle, floating in a pool of rainwater they'd crossed, the water showing the sky like a looking glass, blue. I was

5

---

[1] A white man of Dutch descent (see p. 35). — ED.

[2] Robben Island, where Nelson Mandela and other South African dissidents were imprisoned (see p. 587). — ED.

ashamed only to think that. He had told me how, where he worked in the city, the glass walls showed the trees and the other buildings in the street and the colors of the cars and the clouds as the crane lifted him on a platform higher and higher through the sky to work at the top of a building.

He was allowed one letter a month. It was my letter, because his parents didn't know how to write. I used to go to them where they worked, on another farm, to ask what message they wanted to send. The mother always cried and put her hands on her head and said nothing, and the old man, who preached to us in the veld every Sunday, said, Tell my son we are praying, God will make everything all right for him. Once he wrote back, That's the trouble — our people on the farms, they're told God will decide what's good for them so that they won't find the force to do anything to change their lives.

After two years had passed, we — his parents and I — had saved up enough money to go to Cape Town to visit him. We went by train and slept on the floor at the station and asked the way, next day, to the ferry. People were kind; they all knew that if you wanted the ferry it was because you had somebody of yours on the Island.

And there it was — there was the sea. It was green *and* blue, climbing and falling, bursting white, all the way to the sky. A terrible wind was slapping it this way and that; it hid the Island, but people like us, also waiting for the ferry, pointed where the Island must be, far out in the sea that I never thought would be like it really was.

There were other boats, and ships as big as buildings which would go   10
to other places all over the world, but the ferry is only for the Island, it doesn't go anywhere else in the world, only to the Island. So everybody waiting there was waiting for the Island, there could be no mistake we were in the right place. We had sweets and biscuits, trousers, and a warm coat for him (a woman standing with us said we wouldn't be allowed to give him the clothes). And I wasn't wearing, anymore, the old beret pulled down over my head that farm girls wear — I had bought relaxer cream from the man who comes round the farms selling things out of a box on his bicycle, and my hair was combed up thick under a flowered scarf that didn't cover the gold-colored rings in my ears. His mother had her blanket tied round her waist over her dress, a farm woman, but I looked just as good as any of the city girls there. When the ferry was ready to take us, we stood all pressed together and quiet like the cattle waiting to be let through a gate. One man kept looking round with his chin moving up and down, he was counting, he must have been afraid there were too many to get on and he didn't want to be left behind. We all moved up to the policeman in charge and everyone ahead of us went

onto the boat. But when our turn came and he put out his hand for something, I didn't know what.

We didn't have a permit. We didn't know that before you come to Cape Town, before you come to the ferry for the Island, you have to have a police permit to visit a prisoner on the Island. I tried to ask him nicely. The wind blew the voice out of my mouth.

We were turned away. We saw the ferry rocking, bumping the landing where we stood, moving off, lifted and dropped by all that water, getting smaller and smaller until we didn't know if we were really seeing it or one of the birds that looked black, dipping up and down out there.

The only good thing was someone else took the sweets and biscuits along for him. He wrote and said he got them. But it wasn't a good letter. Of course not. He was cross with me: I should have found out, I should have known about the permit. He was right — I bought the train tickets, I asked where to go for the ferry, I should have known about the permit. I have passed Standard 8. There was an advice office to go to in town, the churches ran it, he wrote. But the farm is so far from town, we on the farms don't know about these things. It was as he said: Our ignorance is the way we are kept down, this ignorance must go.

We took the train back and we never went to the Island — never saw him in the three more years he was there. Not once. We couldn't find the money for the train. His father died and I had to help his mother from my pay. Because I couldn't afford to go to teacher-training college, I don't get advancement, I don't get increases. I wrote, For our people the worry is always money. When will we ever have money? Then he sent such a good letter. He said, That's what I'm on the Island for, far away from you, I'm here so that one day our people will have the things they need — land, food, the end of ignorance. There was something else — I could just read the word "power" — the prison had blacked out. All his letters were not just mine; the prison officer read them before I could.

He was coming home, after only five years! 15

That's how it seemed to me, when I heard — the five years were suddenly disappeared — nothing! — there was no whole year still to wait. I showed my — our — little girl his photo again: That's your daddy, he's coming, you're going to see him. She told the other children at school, I've got a daddy, just as she showed off about the kid goat she had at home.

We wanted him to come at once, and at the same time we wanted time to prepare. His mother lived with the family of one of his uncles; now that his father was dead there was no house of his father for him to take me to as soon as we married. If there had been time, my father would have cut poles, my mother and I would have baked bricks, cut thatch, and built a house for him and me and the child.

We were not sure what day he would arrive. We only heard on my radio his name and the names of some others who were released. Then at the Indian's store I noticed the newspaper *New Nation*, written by black people, and on the front a picture of a lot of people dancing and waving — I saw at once it was at that ferry. Some men were being carried on other men's shoulders. I couldn't see which one was him. We were waiting. The ferry had brought him from the Island, but we remembered Cape Town is a long way from us.

Then he did come. On a Saturday, no school, so I was working with my mother, hoeing and weeding round the pumpkins and mealies, with my hair, that I meant to keep nice, tied in an old *doek*.[3] A *combi* came over the veld and his comrades had brought him. I wanted to run away and wash, but he stood there stretching his legs, calling, Hey! Hey! with his comrades making a noise around him, and my mother started shrieking in the old style, Aie! Aie! and my father was clapping and stamping toward him. He held his arms open to us, this big man in town clothes, polished shoes, and all the time while he hugged me I was holding my dirty hands, full of mud, away from him behind his back. His teeth hit me hard through his lips, he grabbed at my mother and she struggled to hold the child up to him. I thought we would all fall down! Then everyone was quiet. Inkululeko hid behind my mother. He picked the child up, but she turned her head away to her shoulder. He spoke to her gently but she wouldn't speak to him. She's nearly six years old! I told her not to be a baby. She said, That's not him.

The comrades all laughed, we laughed, she ran off, and he said, She     20
has to have time to get used to me.

He has put on weight, yes; a lot. You couldn't believe it. He used to be so thin his feet looked too big for him. I used to feel his bones, but now — that night — when he lay on me he was so heavy; I didn't remember it was like that. Such a long time. It's strange to get stronger in prison; I thought he wouldn't have enough to eat and would come out weak. Everyone said, Look at him! He's a man now. He laughed and banged his fist on his chest, told them how the comrades exercised in their cells: He would run three miles a day, stepping up and down on one place on the floor of that small cell where he was kept. It used to be that after we were together at night we would whisper a long time, but

---

[3]Cloth of linen or canvas. — Ed.

now I can feel he's thinking of some things I don't know, and I can't worry him with talk. Also, I don't know what to say. To ask him what it was like, five years shut away there; or to tell him something about school, or about the child. What else has happened here? Nothing. Just waiting. Sometimes in the daytime I do try to tell him what it was like for me, here at home on the farm, five years. Teaching the little ones to sing and pray, working in my mother's vegetable garden, going to sing and pray myself on Sundays. Dancing sometimes, outside our houses, with other men when they'd been drinking (did he think of that?). He listens, he's interested, just like he's interested when people from the other farms come to visit and talk to him about little things that happened to them while he was away all that time on the Island. He smiles and nods, asks a couple of questions, and then he stands up and stretches. I see it's to show them it's enough, his mind is going back to something he was busy with before they came. And we farm people are very slow; we tell things slowly. He used to, too.

He hasn't signed on for another job. But he can't stay at home with us, either. We thought, after five years over there in the middle of that green-and-blue sea, so far away, he would rest with us a little while. The *combi* or some car comes to fetch him and he says, Don't worry, I don't know what day I'll be back. At first I asked, What week, next week? He tried to explain to me: In the Movement it's not like it was in the union, where you do your work every day and after that you are busy with meetings; in the Movement you never know where you will have to go and what is going to come up next. And the same with money. In the Movement it's not like a job, with regular pay — I know that, he doesn't have to tell me — it's like it was going to the Island, you do it for all our people, who suffer because we haven't got money, we haven't got land. Look, he said, speaking of my parents' home — my home, the home that has been waiting for him, with his child. Look at this place where the white man owns the ground and lets you squat in mud-and-tin huts here only as long as you work for him — *Baba* and your brother planting his crops and looking after his cattle, Mama cleaning his house, and you in the school without even having the chance to train properly as a teacher. The farmer owns us, he says. I had been thinking we haven't got a home because there wasn't time to build a house before he came from the Island, but we haven't got a home at all. Now I've understood that.

I'm not stupid. When the comrades come to this place in the *combi* to talk to him, I don't go away with my mother after we've brought them tea or (if she's made it for the weekend) beer. They like her beer, they talk about our culture, and there's one of them who makes a point of putting his arm around my mother, calling her the mama of all of them, the mama of Africa. Sometimes they please her very much by telling her how they used to sing on the Island, and getting her to sing an old song we all know from our grandmothers. Then they join in with their strong voices. My father doesn't like this noise traveling across the veld; he's afraid that if the Boer finds out my man is a political, from the Island, and he's holding meetings on the Boer's land, he'll tell my father to go and take his family with him. But my brother says, If the Boer asks anything, just tell him it's a prayer meeting. Then the singing is over; my mother knows she must go away into the house.

I stay, and listen. He forgets I'm there when he's talking and arguing about something I can see is important, more important than anything we could ever have to say to each other when we're alone. But now and then, when one of the other comrades is speaking, I see him look at me for a moment the way I will look over at one of my favorite children in school to encourage the child to understand. The men don't speak to me and I don't speak. When they talk about the Big Man, the Old Men, I know who these are: Our leaders are also back from prison. One of the things they talk about is organizing the people on the farms — the workers, like my father and brother, and like his father used to be. I learn what all these things are: minimum wage, limitation of working hours, the right to strike, annual leave, accident compensation, pensions, sick and even maternity leave. I am pregnant: At last I have another child inside me, but that's women's business. I told him about the child coming. He said, And this one belongs to a new country, he'll build the freedom we've fought for!

I know he wants to get married, but there's no time for that at present.  25
There was hardly time for him to make the child. He comes to sleep with me just like he comes here to eat a meal or put on clean clothes. He picks up the little girl and swings her round and there! — it's done, he's getting into the *combi*, he's already turning to his comrade that face of his that knows only what's inside his head, those eyes that move quickly as if he's chasing something you can't see. The little girl hasn't had time to get used to this man. But I know she'll be proud of him one day!

How can you tell that to a child six years old? But I tell her about the Big Man and the Old Men, our leaders, so she'll know that her father was with them on the Island, that this man is a great man, too.

On Saturday, no school, and I plant and weed with my mother. She sings, but I don't; I think. On Sunday there's no work, only prayer meetings out of the Boer's way under the trees, and beer-drinks at the mud-and-tin huts where the farmers allow us to squat on their land. I go off on my own as I used to do when I was a child, making up games and talking to myself where no one would hear me or look for me. I sit on a warm stone in the late afternoon, high up, and the whole valley is a path between the hills, leading away from my feet. It's the Boer's farm — but that's not true, it belongs to nobody. The cattle don't know that anyone says he owns it, the sheep — they are gray stones, and then they become a thick gray snake moving — don't know. Our huts and the old mulberry tree and the little brown mat of earth that my mother dug over yesterday, way down there, and, way over there, the clump of trees round the chimneys and the shiny thing that is the TV mast of the farmhouse — they are nothing on the back of this earth. It could twitch them away like a dog does a fly.

I am up with the clouds. The sun behind me is changing the colors of the sky, and the clouds are changing themselves, blowing up like bubbles. Underneath is a bar of gray, not enough to make rain. It gets longer and darker, it grows a thin snout and long body and then the end of it is a tail. There's a huge gray rat moving across the sky, eating the sky.

The child remembered the photo; when she saw him she said, That's not him. I'm sitting here where I came often when he was on the Island. I came to get away from the others, to wait alone. I'm watching the rat — it's losing its shape, eating the sky — and I'm waiting. Waiting for him to come back.

Waiting. I'm also waiting to come back home, myself.      30

## EXPLORATIONS

1. What facts do we know about the narrator of this story? When and how does Nadine Gordimer reveal basic information about her?

2. What are the narrator's chief concerns? What are the chief concerns of her fiancé? What important things do these two characters have in common? How does the contrast in their concerns affect their relationship?

3. What stylistic techniques does Gordimer use to write in the voice of a character whose age, race, and background are very different from her own?

4. What are the effects of Gordimer's choice not to name her main characters?

# CONNECTIONS

1. In "House of Stone" (p. 569) Michael Dorris writes: "My mind races, searching for some action, some call to arms, some original and efficacious idea in response to what I've seen" (para. 31). How does Gordimer's story about oppressed black South Africans reflect a similar goal?

2. What information in "Amnesty" suggests that the narrator, like the author of "Evicted: A Russian Jew's Story (Again)" (p. 536), feels ostracized in her own country? How do these two women differ in their emotional responses? How do their options and their actions differ?

3. What observations by Martin Luther King, Jr., in *Looking at Ourselves* (p. 514) apply to apartheid in South Africa as well as to slavery in America?

# ELABORATIONS

1. Unlike most accounts we read in this country, "Amnesty" depicts apartheid from the viewpoint of someone who is barely even aware of the political upheaval in South Africa. What is the significance to this story of the events and activities in which the central male character is involved? How and why is the narrator drawn into them? Go through "Amnesty" and write down every point you find that conveys its political content. Then write a cause-and-effect essay about the impact of apartheid on black South African farmers.

2. Choose someone you know fairly well who is distinctly different from you in age, race, gender, or all of these. Think about how that person would be likely to express herself or himself in writing. Then write a narrative essay from his or her point of view about an incident in which you both were involved.

# NELSON MANDELA

## *Black Man in a White Court*

In February 1990 the world celebrated Nelson Mandela's release from South African prison after twenty-seven years. Now president of the African National Congress (ANC), Mandela was born in 1918 to one of the royal families of the Transkei, the eldest son of a Tembu chief. He ran away to Johannesburg to escape an arranged tribal marriage; there he studied arts by correspondence and law at the University of Witwatersrand. With his law partner, Oliver Tambo, Mandela became active in the then illegal ANC, whose mission Tambo has described as "the African struggle against the most powerful adversary in Africa: a highly industrialized, well-armed State manned by a fanatical group of White men determined to defend their privilege and their prejudice, and aided by the complicity of American, British, West German, and Japanese investment in the most profitable system of oppression on the continent."

When an all-white referendum voted to declare South Africa a Nationalist Republic in 1961 (see p. 35), Mandela called a general strike to dramatize black opposition. He left his home, family, and office to live as a political outlaw, nicknamed "the Black Pimpernel." In 1962 he was betrayed by an informer, arrested, tried, and sentenced to three years in prison for leading the strike and for leaving the country illegally. "Black Man in a White Court" is an excerpt from his trial, reprinted in his book *No Easy Walk to Freedom* (1965). From his cell Mandela became a defendant in the notorious Rivonia Trial, accused of sabotage and conspiracy to overthrow the government by force. He and six codefendants were sentenced to life in prison.

The growing worldwide human rights movement increased international pressure on the South African government, which made such concessions as allowing Asians and Coloureds (but not blacks) to vote and repealing laws banning interracial marriage. The slow pace and limited scope of change fueled protest inside and outside South Africa, some of it violent, to the point that the government barred foreign news media from covering disruption. Popular pressure in the United States led many organizations to divest their holdings of stock in South African companies. After years of worldwide economic and political protest, President P. W. Botha was replaced by the more liberal F. W. De Klerk. Within months De Klerk met with Mandela in prison, unbanned the ANC and the Communist Party, desegregated beaches, limited detention without trial, lifted restrictions on the media, dismantled the repressive state security management system, and released seven other jailed ANC leaders before freeing Mandela. The two men began negotiating immediately for full political rights for black South Africans. In 1993 Mandela and De Klerk won the Nobel Peace Prize. The struggle is far from over: Besides opposition from conservative whites, including the neo-Nazi Afrikaner Resistance Movement (AWB), the ANC has been contending with the Zulu Inkatha, supporters of Chief Mangosuthu Buthelezi, who favor a traditional self-governing tribal structure. However, as we go to press, South Africa's first open elections are scheduled for April 1994.

For more background on South Africa, see page 35.

### *"Black Man in a White Court"*
### *First Court Statement, 1962*

Extracts from the court record of the trial of Mandela held in the Old Synagogue court, Pretoria, from October 15 to November 7, 1962. Mandela was accused on two counts, that of inciting persons to strike illegally (during the 1961 stay-at-home) and that of leaving the country without a valid passport. He conducted his own defense.

*Mandela:* Your Worship, before I plead to the charge, there are one or two points I would like to raise.

Firstly, Your Worship will recall that this matter was postponed last Monday at my request until today, to enable counsel to make the arrangements to be available here today.[1] Although counsel is now available, after consultation with him and my attorneys, I have elected to conduct my own defense. Some time during the progress of these proceedings, I hope to be able to indicate that this case is a trial of the aspirations of the African people, and because of that I thought it proper to conduct my own defense. Nevertheless, I have decided to retain the services of counsel, who will be here throughout these proceedings, and I also would like my attorney to be available in the course of these proceedings as well, but subject to that I will conduct my own defense.

The second point I would like to raise is an application which is addressed to Your Worship. Now at the outset, I want to make it perfectly clear that the remarks I am going to make are not addressed to Your Worship in his personal capacity, nor are they intended to reflect upon the integrity of the court. I hold Your Worship in high esteem and I do not for one single moment doubt your sense of fairness and justice. I must

---

[1]Mandela had applied for a remand, because the trial had two-and-a-half months previously been scheduled to take place in the Johannesburg Regional Court, where Mandela had arranged for his defense by advocate Joe Slovo. During the weekend before it opened, however, it was suddenly switched to Pretoria — and Slovo was restricted by a government banning order to the magisterial district of Johannesburg.

also mention that nothing I am going to raise in this application is intended to reflect against the prosecutor in his personal capacity.

The point I wish to raise in my argument is based not on personal considerations, but on important questions that go beyond the scope of this present trial. I might also mention that in the course of this application I am frequently going to refer to the white man and the white people. I want at once to make it clear that I am no racialist, and I detest racialism, because I regard it as a barbaric thing, whether it comes from a black man or from a white man. The terminology that I am going to employ will be compelled on me by the nature of the application I am making.

I want to apply for Your Worship's recusal[2] from this case. I challenge      5
the right of this court to hear my case on two grounds.

Firstly, I challenge it because I fear that I will not be given a fair and proper trial. Secondly, I consider myself neither legally nor morally bound to obey laws made by a parliament in which I have no representation.

In a political trial such as this one, which involves a clash of the aspirations of the African people and those of whites, the country's courts, as presently constituted, cannot be impartial and fair.

In such cases, whites are interested parties. To have a white judicial officer presiding, however high his esteem, and however strong his sense of fairness and justice, is to make whites judges in their own case.

It is improper and against the elementary principles of justice to entrust whites with cases involving the denial by them of basic human rights to the African people.

What sort of justice is this that enables the aggrieved to sit in judgment      10
over those against whom they have laid a charge?

A judiciary controlled entirely by whites and enforcing laws enacted by a white parliament in which Africans have no representation — laws which in most cases are passed in the face of unanimous opposition from Africans —

*Magistrate:* I am wondering whether I shouldn't interfere with you at this stage, Mr. Mandela. Aren't we going beyond the scope of the proceedings? After all is said and done, there is only one court today and that is the white man's court. There is no other court. What purpose does it serve you to make an application when there is only one court, as you know yourself? What court do you wish to be tried by?

*Mandela:* Well, Your Worship, firstly I would like Your Worship to bear in mind that in a series of cases our courts have laid it down that

---

[2]Withdrawal from the case on grounds of prejudice.

the right of a litigant to ask for a recusal of a judicial officer is an extremely important right, which must be given full protection by the court, as long as that right is exercised honestly. Now I honestly have apprehensions, as I am going to demonstrate just now, that this unfair discrimination throughout my life has been responsible for very grave injustices, and I am going to contend that that race discrimination which outside this court has been responsible for all my troubles, I fear in this court is going to do me the same injustice. Now Your Worship may disagree with that, but Your Worship is perfectly entitled, in fact, obliged to listen to me and because of that I feel that Your Worship —

*Magistrate:*   I would like to listen, but I would like you to give me the grounds for your application for me to recuse myself.

Mandela:   Well, these are the grounds, I am developing them, sir. If      15
Your Worship will give me time —

*Magistrate:*   I don't wish to go out of the scope of the proceedings.

*Mandela:*   — Of the scope of the application. I am within the scope of the application, because I am putting forward grounds which in my opinion are likely not to give me a fair and proper trial.

*Magistrate:*   Anyway proceed.

*Mandela:*   As Your Worship pleases. I was developing the point that a judiciary controlled entirely by whites and enforcing laws enacted by a white parliament in which we have no representation, laws which in most cases are passed in the face of unanimous opposition from Africans, cannot be regarded as an impartial tribunal in a political trial where an African stands as an accused.

The Universal Declaration of Human Rights provides that all men are      20
equal before the law, and are entitled without any discrimination to equal protection of the law. In May 1951, Dr. D. F. Malan, then prime minister, told the Union parliament that this provision of the declaration applies in this country. Similar statements have been made on numerous occasions in the past by prominent whites in this country, including judges and magistrates. But the real truth is that there is in fact no equality before the law whatsoever as far as our people are concerned, and statements to the contrary are definitely incorrect and misleading.

It is true that an African who is charged in a court of law enjoys, on the surface, the same rights and privileges as an accused who is white insofar as the conduct of this trial is concerned. He is governed by the same rules of procedure and evidence as apply to a white accused. But it would be grossly inaccurate to conclude from this fact that an African consequently enjoys equality before the law.

In its proper meaning equality before the law means the right to participate in the making of the laws by which one is governed, a constitution which guarantees democratic rights to all sections of the population, the right to approach the court for protection or relief in the case of the violation of rights guaranteed in the constitution, and the right to take part in the administration of justice as judges, magistrates, attorneys-general, law advisers, and similar positions.

In the absence of these safeguards the phrase "equality before the law," insofar as it is intended to apply to us, is meaningless and misleading. All the rights and privileges to which I have referred are monopolized by whites, and we enjoy none of them.

The white man makes all the laws, he drags us before his courts and accuses us, and he sits in judgment over us.

It is fit and proper to raise the question sharply, What is this rigid color    25
bar in the administration of justice? Why is it that in this courtroom I face a white magistrate, am confronted by a white prosecutor, and escorted into the dock by a white orderly? Can anyone honestly and seriously suggest that in this type of atmosphere the scales of justice are evenly balanced?

Why is it that no African in the history of this country has ever had the honor of being tried by his own kith and kin, by his own flesh and blood?

I will tell Your Worship why: The real purpose of this rigid color bar is to ensure that the justice dispersed by the courts should conform to the policy of the country, however much that policy might be in conflict with the norms of justice accepted in judiciaries throughout the civilized world.

I feel oppressed by the atmosphere of white domination that lurks all around in this courtroom. Somehow this atmosphere calls to mind the inhuman injustices caused to my people outside this courtroom by this same white domination.

It reminds me that I am voteless because there is a parliament in this country that is white-controlled. I am without land because the white minority has taken a lion's share of my country and forced me to occupy poverty-stricken reserves, overpopulated and overstocked. We are ravaged by starvation and disease . . .

*Magistrate:* What has that got to do with the case, Mr. Mandela?    30

*Mandela:* With the last point, sir, it hangs together, if Your Worship will give me the chance to develop it.

*Magistrate:* You have been developing it for quite a while now, and I feel you are going beyond the scope of your application.

*Mandela:* Your Worship, this to me is an extremely important ground which the court must consider.

*Magistrate:* I fully realize your position, Mr. Mandela, but you must confine yourself to the application and not go beyond it. I don't want to know about starvation. That in my view has got nothing to do with the case at the present moment.

*Mandela:* Well, Your Worship has already raised the point that here    35 in this country there is only a white court. What is the point of all this? Now if I can demonstrate to Your Worship that outside this courtroom race discrimination has been used in such a way as to deprive me of my rights, not to treat me fairly, certainly this is a relevant fact from which to infer that wherever race discrimination is practiced, this will be the same result, and this is the only reason why I am using this point.

*Magistrate:* I am afraid that I will have to interrupt you, and you will have to confine yourself to the reasons, the real reasons for asking me to recuse myself.

*Mandela:* Your Worship, the next point which I want to make is this: I raise the question, how can I be expected to believe that this same racial discrimination which has been the cause of so much injustice and suffering right through the years should now operate here to give me a fair and open trial? Is there no danger that an African accused may regard the courts not as impartial tribunals, dispensing justice without fear or favor, but as instruments used by the white man to punish those amongst us who clamor for deliverance from the fiery furnace of white rule? I have grave fears that this system of justice may enable the guilty to drag the innocent before the courts. It enables the unjust to prosecute and demand vengeance against the just. It may tend to lower the standards of fairness and justice applied in the country's courts by white judicial officers to black litigants. This is the first ground for this application: that I will not receive a fair and proper trial.

The second ground of my objection is that I consider myself neither morally nor legally obliged to obey laws made by a parliament in which I am not represented.

That the will of the people is the basis of the authority of government is a principle universally acknowledged as sacred throughout the civilized world, and constitutes the basic foundations of freedom and justice. It is understandable why citizens, who have the vote as well as the right to direct representation in the country's governing bodies, should be morally and legally bound by the laws governing the country.

It should be equally understandable why we, as Africans, should adopt    40 the attitude that we are neither morally nor legally bound to obey laws which we have not made, nor can we be expected to have confidence in courts which enforce such laws.

I am aware that in many cases of this nature in the past, South African courts have upheld the right of the African people to work for democratic changes. Some of our judicial officers have even openly criticized the policy which refuses to acknowledge that all men are born free and equal, and fearlessly condemned the denial of opportunities to our people.

But such exceptions exist in spite of, not because of, the grotesque system of justice that has been built up in this country. These exceptions furnish yet another proof that even among the country's whites there are honest men whose sense of fairness and justice revolts against the cruelty perpetrated by their own white brothers to our people.

The existence of genuine democratic values among some of the country's whites in the judiciary, however slender they may be, is welcomed by me. But I have no illusions about the significance of this fact, healthy a sign as it might be. Such honest and upright whites are few and they have certainly not succeeded in convincing the vast majority of the rest of the white population that white supremacy leads to dangers and disaster.

However, it would be a hopeless commandant who relied for his victories on the few soldiers in the enemy camp who sympathize with his cause. A competent general pins his faith on the superior striking power he commands and on the justness of his cause which he must pursue uncompromisingly to the bitter end.

I hate race discrimination most intensely and in all its manifestations. 45 I have fought it all during my life; I fight it now, and will do so until the end of my days. Even though I now happen to be tried by one whose opinion I hold in high esteem, I detest most violently the setup that surrounds me here. It makes me feel that I am a black man in a white man's court. This should not be. I should feel perfectly at ease and at home with the assurance that I am being tried by a fellow South African who does not regard me as an inferior, entitled to a special type of justice.

This is not the type of atmosphere most conducive to feelings of security and confidence in the impartiality of a court.

The court might reply to this part of my argument by assuring me that it will try my case fairly and without fear or favor, that in deciding whether or not I am guilty of the offense charged by the state, the court will not be influenced by the color of my skin or by any other improper motive.

That might well be so. But such a reply would completely miss the point of my argument.

As already indicated, my objection is not directed to Your Worship in his personal capacity, nor is it intended to reflect upon the integrity of the court. My objection is based upon the fact that our courts, as presently constituted, create grave doubts in the minds of an African accused, whether he will receive a fair and proper trial.

This doubt springs from objective facts relating to the practice of unfair 50 discrimination against the black man in the constitution of the country's courts. Such doubts cannot be allayed by mere verbal assurances from a presiding officer, however sincere such assurances might be. There is only one way, and one way only, of allaying such doubts, namely, by removing unfair discrimination in judicial appointments. This is my first difficulty.

I have yet another difficulty about similar assurances Your Worship might give. Broadly speaking, Africans and whites in this country have no common standard of fairness, morality, and ethics, and it would be very difficult to determine on my part what standard of fairness and justice Your Worship has in mind.

In their relationship with us, South African whites regard it as fair and just to pursue policies which have outraged the conscience of mankind and of honest and upright men throughout the civilized world. They suppress our aspirations, bar our way to freedom, and deny us opportunities to promote our moral and material progress, to secure ourselves from fear and want. All the good things of life are reserved for the white folk and we blacks are expected to be content to nourish our bodies with such pieces of food as drop from the tables of men with white skins. This is the white man's standard of justice and fairness. Herein lies his conception of ethics. Whatever he himself may say in his defense, the white man's moral standards in this country must be judged by the extent to which he has condemned the vast majority of its inhabitants to serfdom and inferiority.

We, on the other hand, regard the struggle against color discrimination and for the pursuit of freedom and happiness as the highest aspiration of all men. Through bitter experience, we have learned to regard the white man as a harsh and merciless type of human being whose contempt for our rights, and whose utter indifference to the promotion of our welfare, makes his assurances to us absolutely meaningless and hypocritical.

I have the hope and confidence that Your Worship will not hear this objection lightly nor regard it as frivolous. I have decided to speak frankly and honestly because the injustice I have referred to contains the seeds of an extremely dangerous situation for our country and people. I make no threat when I say that unless these wrongs are remedied without delay, we might well find that even plain talk before the country's courts is too timid a method to draw the attention of the country to our political demands.

Finally, I need only to say that the courts have said that the possibility    55
of bias and not actual bias is all that needs be proved to ground an application of this nature. In this application I have merely referred to certain objective facts, from which I submit that the possibility be inferred that I will not receive a fair and proper trial.

*Magistrate:* Mr. Prosecutor, have you anything to say?

*Prosecutor:* Very briefly, Your Worship, I just wish to point out that there are certain legal grounds upon which an accused person is entitled to apply for the recusal of a judicial officer from the case in which he is to be tried. I submit that the accused's application is not based on one of those principles, and I ask the court to reject it.

*Magistrate:* [to Mandela] Your application is dismissed. Will you now plead to your charges?

*Mandela:* I plead *not guilty* to both charges, to all the charges.


## EXPLORATIONS

1. What application is Nelson Mandela making to the court in this argument? What two grounds does he give for his application? What appears to be the true purpose of his application? Is he successful? Why or why not?

2. Does the court seriously consider Mandela's application? What statements by Mandela and by the judge are the basis for your answer?

3. In what ways does Mandela emphasize that, as a lawyer, he is part of the same elite group as the judge and prosecutor? How does his stressing that point strengthen the impact of his speech?

4. What is the effect of Mandela's referring to *Africans* and *whites* in paragraphs 8–12 and elsewhere rather than to *black South Africans* and *white South Africans*? What comments in paragraphs 2, 7, and 45 illuminate his choice of words?


## CONNECTIONS

1. The fictional political activist in Nadine Gordimer's "Amnesty" (p. 578) was released from Robben Island at the same time as Nelson Mandela and other African National Congress leaders. Now that you have read "Black Man in a White Court," reread paragraphs 25–30 of Gordimer's story. What do you interpret the story's ending to mean?

2. How do Shelby Steele's comments about innocence in *Looking at Ourselves* (p. 515) apply to the relationship between blacks and whites described by Mandela, and to Mandela's strategy in court?

3. How do Gordimer's "Amnesty" and Mandela's "Black Man in a White Court" suggest that Toni Morrison's comments about American literature (p. 513) may also apply to South African literature?

4. Reread paragraphs 5–17 of Václav Havel's "Moral Politics" (p. 542). What

statements by Havel describe Mandela's position in "Black Man in a White Court"? What statements by Mandela reflect a philosophy similar to Havel's?

## ELABORATIONS

1. Look closely at the transcript and background notes for "Black Man in a White Court." In what sense has the white South African government stacked the deck so that Mandela cannot win? How does Mandela use this stacked deck to set up a situation in which he cannot lose? Write a classification essay analyzing the various political agendas and strategies represented in this trial, and identifying winners and losers.

2. What statements about men and women in Simone de Beauvoir's "Woman as Other" (p. 329) express points made about white and black South Africans in "Black Man in a White Court"? Based on Beauvoir's discussion of the "Other," Mandela's transcript, Gordimer's "Amnesty," and the *Looking at Ourselves* selections by King, Steele, and Morrison, write an essay analyzing the causes and effects of racism.

# PART SEVEN

# VIOLENCE

## LOOKING AT OURSELVES

Ron Kovic, William Broyles, Jr., Sam Keen,
Susanne Hoeber Rudolph and Lloyd I. Rudolph, Colman McCarthy,
Rosemary L. Bray, The Associated Press, George Will,
*Mother Jones*, Joan Didion

Nell McCafferty, *Peggy Deery of Derry* (NORTHERN IRELAND)

Charles Moore, *Ireland Must Fight the IRA Too*
(GREAT BRITAIN)

David Grossman, *Israeli Arab, Israeli Jew* (ISRAEL)

Slavenka Drakulić, *Zagreb: A Letter to My Daughter*
(CROATIA/YUGOSLAVIA)

Isabel Allende, *The Los Riscos Mine* (CHILE)

Czeslaw Milosz, *American Ignorance of War* (POLAND)

Nuha Al-Radi, *Baghdad Diary* (IRAQ)

Michael Kelly, *Torture in Kuwait* (KUWAIT)

Alice Walker, *The Concord Demonstration* (UNITED STATES)

Chinua Achebe, *Civil Peace* (NIGERIA)

THE WORDS OF PATRICK HENRY, WHO HELPED TURN BRITAIN'S AMERI-can colonies into the United States, still ring true: "Gentlemen may cry, Peace peace! but there is no peace." As we near the end of the twentieth century, violence seems to be everywhere. Nations and factions are at war from South Africa to Ireland, from Cambodia to Eastern Europe. Here at home the violence we watch for entertainment on TV and movie screens occurs for real in our cities, shopping malls, places of business, homes, and even schools. Is peace possible, we ask, or is attacking each other as natural to our species as bearing children?

*Looking at Ourselves* opens with Ron Kovic's vivid memory of the day his legs were paralyzed in battle in Vietnam. William Broyles wonders why he and other veterans recall wartime with such nostalgia. Sam Keen blames men's aggressiveness on society's expectations. According to Susanne Hoeber Rudolph and Lloyd I. Rudolph, ancient feuds would not be reerupting worldwide without encouragement from public culture. Colman McCarthy examines the economic interests that foster war. The safety of her black husband from fearful whites is Rosemary L. Bray's nightly concern. Two researchers suggest that more hate crimes are motivated by thrills than fear. A nine-year-old Chicago girl teaches George Will some things about urban survival; a Los Angeles rioter explains why he looted a computer but returned it. Joan Didion reports on a young woman whose lover put her dead body out with the trash.

In Northern Ireland, a housewife and her family are sucked into the war of guns, rocks, bombs, and nerves known as the Troubles in Nell McCafferty's "Peggy Deery of Derry." British journalist Charles Moore presents a contrasting view of that conflict in "Ireland Must Fight the IRA Too." Another ethnic clash is debated by men of goodwill but opposing loyalties in David Grossman's "Israeli Arab, Israeli Jew." Slavenka Drakulić's "Zagreb: A Letter to My Daughter" laments the civil war destroying what used to be Yugoslavia.

Two friends of a "disappeared" girl challenge a Chilean general in Isabel Allende's fictional "The Los Riscos Mine." Polish writer Czeslaw Milosz reminds us in "American Ignorance of War" how lucky the United States has been in not sharing other countries' experience with violent disruption. Nuha Al-Radi's "Baghdad Diary" describes life during wartime in 1991 when the United States bombed Iraq. In "Torture in Kuwait," Michael Kelly reports some of the brutalities committed by Iraqi soldiers in Kuwait. A protest at a U.S. military base in California is the focus of Alice Walker's "The Concord Demonstration." Finally, Chinua Achebe's humorous short story "Civil Peace" shows a war-weary Nigerian family facing new challenges after the fighting stops. ◇

# LOOKING AT OURSELVES

## 1

The blood is still rolling off my flak jacket from the hole in my shoulder and there are bullets cracking into the sand all around me. I keep trying to move my legs but I cannot feel them. I try to breathe but it is difficult. I have to get out of this place, make it out of here somehow.

Someone shouts from my left now, screaming for me to get up. Again and again he screams, but I am trapped in the sand.

*Oh get me out of here, get me out of here, please someone help me! Oh help me, please help me. Oh God oh Jesus!* "Is there a corpsman?" I cry. "Can you get a corpsman?"

There is a loud crack and I hear the guy begin to sob. "They've shot my fucking finger off! Let's go, sarge! Let's get outta here!"

"I can't move," I gasp. "I can't move my legs! I can't feel anything!"

I watch him go running back to the tree line.

"Sarge, are you all right?" Someone else is calling to me now and I try to turn around. Again there is the sudden crack of a bullet and a boy's voice crying. "Oh Jesus! Oh Jesus Christ!" I hear his body fall in back of me.

I think he must be dead but I feel nothing for him, I just want to live. I feel nothing.

And now I hear another man coming up from behind, trying to save me. "Get outta here!" I scream. "Get the fuck outta here!"

A tall black man with long skinny arms and enormous hands picks me up and throws me over his shoulder as bullets begin cracking over our heads like strings of firecrackers. Again and again they crack as the sky swirls around us like a cyclone. "Motherfuckers motherfuckers!" he screams. And the rounds keep cracking and the sky and the sun on my face and my body all gone, all twisted up dangling like a puppet's, diving again and again into the sand, up and down, rolling and cursing, gasping for breath. "Goddamn goddamn motherfuckers!"

And finally I am dragged into a hole in the sand with the bottom of my body that can no longer feel twisted and bent underneath me. The black man runs from the hole without ever saying a thing. I never see his face. I will never know who he is. He is gone. And others now are in the hole helping me. They are bandaging my wounds. There is fear in their faces.

"It's all right," I say to them. "Everything is fine."

Someone has just saved my life. My rifle is gone and I don't feel like finding it or picking it up ever again. The only thing I can think of, the only thing that crosses my mind, is living. There seems to be nothing in the world more important than that.

> – Ron Kovic
> *Born on the Fourth of July,* 1976

## 2

Ask me, ask any man who has been to war about his experience, and chances are we'll say we don't want to talk about it — implying that we hated it so much, it was so terrible, that we would rather leave it buried. And it is no mystery why men hate war. War is ugly, horrible, evil, and it is reasonable for men to hate all that. But I believe that most men who have been to war would have to admit, if they are honest, that somewhere inside themselves they loved it too, loved it as much as anything that has happened to them before or since. And how do you explain that to your wife, your children, your parents, or your friends?

That's why men in their sixties and seventies sit in their dens and recreation rooms around America and know that nothing in their life will equal the day they parachuted into St.-Lô or charged the bunker on Okinawa. That's why veterans' reunions are invariably filled with boozy awkwardness, forced camaraderie ending in sadness and tears: You are together again, these are the men who were your brothers, but it's not the same, can never be the same. That's why when we returned from Vietnam we moped around, listless, not interested in anything or anyone. Something had gone out of our lives forever, and our behavior on returning was inexplicable except as the behavior of men who had lost a great — perhaps the great — love of their lives, and had no way to tell anyone about it. . . .

Alfred Kazin wrote that war is the enduring condition of twentieth-century man. He was only partly right. War is the enduring condition of man, period. Men have gone to war over everything from Helen of Troy to Jenkins's ear. Two million Frenchmen and Englishmen died in muddy trenches in World War I because a student shot an archduke. The truth is, the reasons don't matter. There is a reason for every war and a war for every reason.

For centuries men have hoped that with history would come progress, and with progress, peace. But progress has simply given man the means to make war even more horrible; no wars in our savage past can begin to match the brutality of the wars spawned in this century, in the beautifully ordered, civilized landscape of Europe, where everyone is literate and classical music plays in every village café. War is not an aberration; it is part of the family, the crazy uncle we try — in vain — to keep locked in the basement.

— William Broyles, Jr.
"Why Men Love War"
*Esquire*, 1984

## 3

Why has the gender that gave us the Sistine Chapel brought us to the edge of cosmocide? Why have the best and brightest exercised their intelligence, imagination, and energy and managed only to create a world where starvation and warfare are more common than they were in Neolithic times? Why has the history of what we dare to call "progress" been marked by an increase in the quantity of human suffering? . . .

Because men have historically been the major agents of violence, it is tempting to place the blame on our biology and to conclude that the problem lies in nature's faulty design rather than in our willfulness. But all deterministic explanations ignore the obvious: Men are systematically conditioned to endure pain, to kill, and to die in the service of the tribe, nation, or state. The male psyche is, first and foremost, the warrior psyche. Nothing shapes, informs, and molds us so much as society's demand that we become specialists in the use of power and violence, or as we euphemistically say, "defense." Historically, the major difference between men and women is that men have always been expected to be able to resort to violence when necessary. The capacity and willingness for violence has been central to our self-definition. The male psyche has not been built upon the rational "I think; therefore I am," but upon the irrational "I conquer; therefore I am."

In what has come to be the normal state of emergency of modern life, we grant the state the power to interrupt the lives of young men, to draft them into the army, and to initiate them into the ritual of violence. Clichés that pass for wisdom tell us: "The army will make a man out of you," and "Every man must have his war."

Induction into the army or, if you are one of the lucky "few," into the marines, involves the same process of systematic destruction of individuality that accompanied initiation in primitive tribes. The shaved head, the uniform, the abusive drill instructors, the physical and emotional ordeal of boot camp, are meant to destroy the individual's will and teach the dogface that the primary virtue of a man is not to think for himself but to obey his superiors, not to listen to his conscience but to follow orders. Like the rites of all warrior societies it teaches men to value what is tough and to despise what is "feminine" and tenderhearted. Nowhere so clearly as in the military do we learn the primitive maxim that the individual must sacrifice himself to the will of the group as it is represented by the authorities.

— Sam Keen
*Fire in the Belly*, 1991

## 4

On Inauguration Day, Bill Clinton told the country and the world a story about how "a generation raised in the shadows of the Cold War assumes new responsibilities in a world warmed by the sunshine of freedom but threatened still by ancient hatreds." The new president seemed to have in mind such things as ethnic cleansing and religious fundamentalism, the first a deceptive metaphor invented by extreme nationalist Serbs, the second a ubiquitous term that relieves politicians, news anchors, and policy intellectuals from thinking about the complexities of the "other." . . .

But recent news accounts that depict the violence as an outgrowth of old animosities are misleading. Hindus and Muslims in India under the Mughal emperor Akbar, the nationalistic leadership of Mahatma Gandhi, and the Congress governments of Jawaharlal Nehru have gotten along more often than they have gone for each other's throats. So did Serbs, Croats, and Muslims under Tito in Yugoslavia. Clinton and others too easily invoke "ancient hatreds" to explain what are really contemporary conflicts. The question, in other words, is not why old conflicts are flaring up anew, but rather why traditionally harmonious mosaics have been shattered. . . .

As political ideology recedes with the collapse of communism, the politics of identity and community, of religion, ethnicity, and gender have begun to occupy the space vacated by political ideology. Directly and indirectly, religion, ethnicity, and gender increasingly define what politics is about, from the standing of Muslim personal law and monuments in India to Muslim and Christian Serbs and Croats sharing sovereignty in Bosnia to the Clinton administration's effort to appoint a government that "looks like America."

Which identities become relevant for politics is not predetermined by some primordial ancientness. They are crafted in benign and malignant ways in print and electronic media, in textbooks and advertising, in India's TV megaseries and America's talk shows, in campaign strategies, in all the places and all the ways that self and other, us and them, are represented in an expanding public culture. The struggle in India . . . between quota government and Hindu nationalism reminds us that in America too the politics of interest is being overtaken by cultural politics, the politics of gender, family values, race, and sexual orientation. When TV talking heads and op-ed contributors portray "mobs" as "frenzied" and believers as "fanatic," they have given up the task of discerning the human inducements and political calculations that make politics happen. They have given up making motives visible and showing how they are trans-formed. "Ancient hatreds" function like the "evil empire." That term too was a projection on a scrim, obscuring the motives and practice that lay behind it. The doctrine of ancient hatreds may become the post–Cold War's most robust mystification, a way of having an enemy and knowing evil that deceives as it satisfies. The hatred is modern and may be closer than we think.

> – Susanne Hoeber Rudolph
> and Lloyd I. Rudolph
> "Modern Hate"
> *The New Republic,* 1993

# 5

Scenario creators in the Pentagon have come forth with a two-war strategy.

In the fantasy world of conjuring responses to predatory villains — whether it's warlords, strongmen, or "regional instability" — the United States would be poised with the weapons and troops to vanquish, say, both the Iraqi army when it acts up again in the desert and North Korea when it invades South Korea.

Even being ready for two wars is playing it close. General Colin Powell warns darkly, "The real enemy is unknown."

About the same time that Defense Secretary Les Aspin announced the two-war plan — we would be like Hulk Hogan in the ring body-slamming two monster-men at once — some arms industry executives and govern-ment officials were meeting in a Washington hotel at an exports confer-ence staged by *Defense Week* magazine. The conference title for these merchants of death was "The Markets, the Competition, and the Re-turns."

This was a moment for in-house shoptalk among executives whose industry was not only enriched by the Cold War spending spree but which also prospered as a fattened parasite. Congress allowed the Pentagon to pay for most research and development costs at the front end while picking up the cost overrun tab at the back end. That was market symmetry.

Now there's market anxiety. With the main arms buyer — the U.S. military — forced into mild economic sobriety, a frenzied push is on either to find new customers for rifles, tanks, bombs, missiles, and planes or sell more to old ones.

An official from the land systems division of General Dynamics, which is currently building tanks for Saudi Arabia and Egypt and next year for Kuwait, said that "international competition is tougher than it has ever been." An aerospace arms lobbyist predicted that "competition for world markets, including our own, will become even more intense." He told of Swiss companies selling planes to the South African military, the Swedes adopting "a more aggressive [arms] export policy," and fire-sale Russians "anxious to sell most of their weapons to all comers."

How to remain king of this mountain of gore is the challenge of the nineties.

Not that gore or any reminders of what weapons do to people is mentioned. Surrealism prevailed in the texts of the conference papers. Instead of dictators buying U.S. weapons there are "host governments" seeking "logistics support." Instead of bombs and bullets there are "complementary technologies." Instead of arms that slaughter human beings there are "interoperability benefits."

While these white-collar gunrunners strategized on how to increase profits through mass killings, another conference was in session down the corridor in the same hotel at the same time. It was here that economic sanity and political morality could be found. At this session, sponsored by the National Commission for Economic Conversion and Disarmament, and the Peace Action Education Fund, a series of speakers stated the case for alternatives to weapons exports.

They had some numbers. The United States is the world's leading arms exporter, with 57 percent of all new sales to the Third World in 1991. Of the 45 countries that had wars since 1987, only 3 were invaded by an enemy. The rest bought weapons for internal combat or civil wars. Ninety percent of those sales went to dictators.

As a counter to the arms industry's favored ethical dodge, "if-we-don't-sell-somebody-else-will," the solution was posed that instead of competing for sales against France, Britain, Russia, Sweden, Switzerland, and the other exporters, the United States ought to be cooperating with them to eliminate sales. Without that at the core of foreign policies, there is what William Hartung of the World Policy Institute at the New School called "naked economic self-interest" that "has come into the foreground as a lead argument in favor of otherwise questionable arms deals."

A global war-footing rules. Regional instability is continental instability. From 1979 to 1989, Latin American governments bought $41 billion worth of arms. War-related deaths totaled 222,000. For Africa, it was $82 billion and 2.4 million deaths. Little of that appears to bother the State Department.

It was pro-sales under Reagan and Bush, and is pro-sales under Clinton. Secretary of State Warren Christopher told a Senate subcommittee on March 25: "Where nations are buying conventional arms and they are responsible buyers, I think the United States should not be precluded from that market. We should not see that market fall into the hands of our European or Asian competitors."

And who are the responsible buyers? They're the ones with cash.

– Colman McCarthy
*Washington Post*, 1993

# 6

He phoned more than an hour ago, to say he was on his way home. But I have yet to hear the scrape of the iron gate, the rattling keys, so I worry.

Most married women fret about a tardy husband; young black women like myself worry more. For most people in New York — truth be told — the urban bogeyman is a young black man in sneakers. But we live in Central Harlem, where every young man is black and wears sneakers, so we learn to look into the eyes of young males and discern the difference between youthful bravado and the true dangers of the streets. No, I have other fears. I fear white men in police uniforms; white teenagers driving by in a car with Jersey plates; thin, panicky, middle-aged white men on the subway. Most of all, I fear that their path and my husband's path will cross one night as he makes his way home.

Bob is tall — 5'10" or so, dark, with thick hair and wire-rimmed glasses. He carries a knapsack stuffed with work from the office, old crossword puzzles, Philip Glass tapes, *Ebony Man* and *People* magazines. When it rains, he carries his good shoes in the bag and wears his Reebok sneakers. He cracks his knuckles a lot, and wears a peculiar grimace when his mind is elsewhere. He looks dear and gentle to me — but then, I have looked into those eyes for a long time.

I worry that some white person will see that grim, focused look of concentration and see the intent to victimize. I fear that some white person will look at him and see only his or her nightmare — another black man in sneakers. In fact, my husband *is* another black man in sneakers. He's also a writer, an amateur cyclist, a lousy basketball player, his parents' son, my life's companion. When I put aside the book I'm reading to peek out the window, the visions in my head are those of blind white panic at my husband's black presence, visions of a flashing gun, a gleaming knife; I see myself a sudden, horrified widow at thirty-four.

Once upon a time, I was vaguely ashamed of my paranoia about his safety in the world outside our home. After all, he is a grown man. But he is a grown black man on the streets alone, a menace to white New Yorkers — even the nice, sympathetic, liberal ones who smile at us when we're together. And I am reminded, over and over, how dangerous white people still can be, how their fears are a hazard to our health. When white people are ruled by their fears of everything black, every black woman is an addict, a whore; every black man is a rapist — even a murderer.

Charles Stuart understood this fear well enough to manipulate an entire nation. When he said a black man in Boston's Mission Hill district put a bullet through the head of his pregnant wife, who could doubt him? So a city's police force moved through the neighborhood, stopping and strip-searching black men at random, looking for the apocryphal black savage who, it turned out, existed only in Boston's collective imagination. Yet an innocent African-American man, William Bennett, was paraded before the nation for weeks, until Stuart's brother had an attack of conscience and went to the police.

The Stuart case was shameful, but it could have been worse — after all, William Bennett is still alive. When whites' fear of black people is allowed its freest reign, black people can die.

Wasn't Michael Griffith a bum out to make trouble when a teenage posse in Howard Beach chased him onto the Shore Parkway into the path of a car? Wasn't Yusef Hawkins a thug coming to beat up a white man in Bensonhurst when he was surrounded by a gang of teenagers and shot? It doesn't seem to matter that Michael Griffith was a construction worker, that Yusef Hawkins was a student looking for a used car. Someone looked at those two men and saw danger, and so they are dead. And the women who waited for them — who peeked out the front windows and listened for footsteps on the stairs — waited in vain.

So when it's ten o'clock and he's not home yet, my thoughts can't help but wander to other black men — husbands, fathers, sons, brothers — who never do make it home, and to other black women whose fingers no longer rest at a curtain's edge. Even after I hear the scrape of our iron gate, the key in the lock, even after I hear that old knapsack hit the floor of the downstairs hallway and Bob's voice calling to me, my thoughts return to them.

> – Rosemary L. Bray
> "It's Ten O'Clock and I Worry
> About Where My Husband Is"
> *Glamour*, 1990

# 7

Urban hate has many causes: growing tensions between racial and ethnic groups, increasing violence in society. But two Northeastern University researchers say most offenders are young people not yet lost to hatred. Mostly, they commit their crimes for the thrill of it. "What we are dealing with are kids who say, 'For fun, we're going to get someone who is different,'" said Jack McDevitt, associate director of the school's Center for Applied Social Research. "Simply dumping them in prison is not going to teach them that what they're doing is wrong."

McDevitt and Jack Levin, a sociologist and author of several books on prejudice, studied 169 cases filed with the Boston Police Community Disorders Unit during the past two years. McDevitt, a criminologist, also has reviewed data from eleven other cities for the FBI. His conclusion: In many cases the victims of so-called hate crimes are interchangeable. "It doesn't matter to a lot of these kids who their victim is," he said. "They are looking for someone different to attack."

The researchers classified nearly 60 percent of the cases as "thrill hate crimes" involving two or more attackers, usually teenagers. The researchers classified most remaining cases "reactive hate crimes," where someone considered an outsider is attacked for venturing into another group's area. A third classification, "mission hate crimes," is committed by dedicated ideologues like neo-Nazis. McDevitt said those crimes were rare.

Interviews with the thrill-crime offenders revealed that when the original target — a black or Asian — wasn't available, the group would seek out someone else, often homosexuals. "These are marginal kids who are not making it at home or at school," Levin said. "They want to feel okay about themselves. So the more they bash someone who is different, the more morally superior they feel."

The racial breakdown of these incidents follows demographic lines. Whites committed about 60 percent of the crimes; blacks about 25 percent. Asians, Hispanics, and homosexuals faced the greatest risk of attack in cities. "The figures are the same, both nationally and in Boston. Whites attack a variety of groups; blacks attack whites," McDevitt said. "You're seeing a rise in attacks on Asians from both groups."

Howard Ehrlich, research director for the National Institute Against Prejudice and Violence, blames an increase of such incidents on a society more tolerant of violence. "They are motivated by a kind of acceptance of violent behavior," Ehrlich said. "They pick an acceptable target, someone they think is okay to treat as a nonperson."

Levin believes antagonism has grown as various groups fight for a slice of a shrinking economic pie. "Young people no longer see the American dream as a viable resource," he said. "Whites see blacks getting special treatment; blacks see a racist behind every opportunity. This is an age of resentment."

– The Associated Press
"Thrill, Not Hate," 1993

# 8

The day Dantrell Davis died, Karen McCune wrote: "I thought my life will better than what it turned to be." That summing-up of a life was made a month ago, by a nine-year-old.

Today Karen is a forty-seven-pound miracle of resilience. She is more than a match — so far — for the pounding that cities give childhood in this era of urban regression.

The shooting of Dantrell might have elicited a "so what?" shrug of this city's broad shoulders. After all, Chicago averages a shooting every thirty-four minutes and a murder every eight hours, and the more than 13,000 shootings so far this year have killed seventeen children under fourteen. Dantrell was the third pupil at Jenner Elementary School shot dead this year. One of Dantrell's schoolmates said: "I hope that next time it won't be somebody that I know." He assumes there will be a next time, a fourth time.

Dantrell was killed by a sniper firing from a nearby high-rise as Dantrell and his mother began the forty-yard walk to Jenner from their high-rise, through the killing zone of the Cabrini-Green housing project. Today, beneath the lead-gray sky of a Chicago November, the hard wind off the lake is gusting razor-like rain horizontally and Karen is chatting in a classroom overlooking a growing puddle on the spot where Dantrell fell.

Cabrini-Green is seventy acres of appalling public policy less than a mile from Michigan Avenue's Magnificent Mile. About 7,000 people live in the thirty-one high-rises and sixty other buildings in this public housing project. More than half the residents are under age twenty. Nine percent of the residents have paying jobs.

Karen, her hair neatly braided, her white blouse and blue jumper (the voluntary school uniform that most pupils wear) immaculate, her eyes bright, and her smile dazzling, patiently tells a columnist that life's not so bad if you stay indoors. "My mommy won't allow me to go outside. I stay up in the house and read books."

She usually stays away from windows. "I be scared because my bed is by the window." But the apartment where she and some siblings live with her mother is on the seventh floor, safe from most gunfire. However, "When the Bulls won [the NBA championship], a car ran into the store [across the street from her apartment] and they were shooting up and my mommy had to duck down."

Jenner School shows its ninety years but is a wonderfully clean haven for children from a neighborhood run by armed children. For now there is a truce between the gangs, a result of a heavy police presence since Dantrell's death. The truce is a respite from the recurring need to move children into inner hallways on whichever side of the school shooting has erupted.

Karen, who even in repose has the happy can't-stop-wiggling-my-shiny-black-leather-shoes fidgets of the normal nine-year-old, nevertheless practices the prudence of the street-wise urban child: "I don't wear any Starter [a brand name] jackets because they're bad for us." Six days after Dantrell was killed, a fifteen-year-old from another school was killed evidently because he was slow to give robbers his Miami Hurricanes jacket.

Twenty years ago Jenner had 2,500 students. Today it has 630. Some of them have symptoms — short attention spans, difficulty sustaining relationships, a tendency to think only in stark opposites — often associated with survivors of a battle area. Small wonder. Shortly after Dantrell's death, Karen shared with a local newspaper reporter the sort of memory that marks childhood in this other America:

"They couldn't find my friend's mother. They looked and looked but they couldn't find her. Finally one day they found her body stuck in the sewer. It was all mushy and it stinked real bad. I'm glad Danny wasn't like that."

Her prescription for neighborhood improvement is common sense and contrary to public policy: "Take the gangbangers [gang members] out and take away all the guns." With an imperious sweep of a spindly arm in the direction of the high-rises, she decrees: "Mow down those buildings. Don't need to be high-rise. Five floors enough."

Social scientists debate the concept of a "culture of poverty," the intergenerational transmission of passivity and fatalism. There is such a culture but it has not claimed Karen. Her small face wreathed in a huge smile of serene certainty, she announces that she's going to college: "I'm not going to have no boyfriend or no husband or child when I'm fifteen or fourteen or thirteen. I'm going to wait until I get real, real big, until I'm" — she plucks a number from her imagination — "twenty-seven."

One of her best friends is a boy who wants to be a lawyer: "He uses big words, like 'interject.'" Karen says she is going to be a teacher. She already is.

— George Will
"Lessons of a Street-Wise Child"
*The Washington Post*, 1992

◇◇◇◇◇

# 9

A few days after the rioting stopped in Los Angeles and San Francisco, a man called our office to say that he wanted to return a computer he had looted from a local store, and that he had chosen *Mother Jones* for help because he liked our May/June cover story, "Race." He told managing editor David Weir his story.

When I saw white people being beaten in the street on TV, I smiled ear to ear and jumped up and down with glee, because it told me that I'm not crazy. I hate to say I did that, because I have white friends, but I've been screaming for a long time and nobody has been listening.

I grew up in South-Central Los Angeles, two miles from the epicenter. I moved to San Francisco because I didn't want to be in the gangs. I called my mother, and she asked if I got a TV. Everyone went for TVs down there. Up here, I went for a computer. I've been trying to get a computer for two years. Nowadays, if you don't have one, you can't compete. You can just end up in the streets, and I don't want that to happen to me.

I've been thinking for a long time that I'm crazy. There was one day, about a year ago, that I felt like going out and killing somebody. The denial in this country about what's really going on is so deep. For black men, we thought we were going crazy. But this event [the Los Angeles riot] convinced me I was not nuts.

I watch the news all the time, and they're going back to talking that same talk as before: "Law and order. Keep the peace." They're not putting the blame on the right people. The people rioting are not guilty. This country sacrificed these people.

I believe those jurors in the King case believed they were doing their job sincerely. They are not racists in that old way. Nowadays, everyone says this is all so senseless. But we're screaming at the tops of our lungs.

It wasn't senseless. The cause and effect were perfect. We've all been reading in the paper that all of those store owners want more cops. They are scared of the black guys who are sleeping in the doorways of their stores. And they sic the cops on us, and the cops are vicious. Is anyone amazed that they grabbed this stuff?

Personally I stopped because I was touched by Rodney King's plea. I didn't want to hurt him anymore. Look at Rodney King. Look at the black-and-white photo a year ago and the man we have now. I'm trying to make that transition. It took him a year to make it. The beating he got was a good thing for him, because it got him to a place where people care about him and are helping him. I'm trying to get to that place. But even Rodney King, in his plea, he started to say "I love everybody" but he stopped himself. He couldn't say it yet. He said he loved "people of color." I'm trying to get to that place where I can love everybody.

What I want to say is that reparations is the only way. It's the only way this country can admit its guilt with honor. It's the only answer for this particular problem. Blacks would have money and we could empower ourselves. Rebuild our own businesses.

It's all there in hip hop. Ice Cube warned you. Ice-T warned you. To the Koreans, "Give respect to the black fist or we'll burn your store to a crisp." It's not really their fault, the Koreans, we know that; but they don't have to be so rude.

The envelope was turned inside out for us, and we could see the seams. The riots straightened everything out. If the powers that be don't do something, if they don't pick up the ball and run in the right direction, there's no reason for us not to do it again. If you're not going to let us live, then nobody is going to live. Listen to me! That scares me! But I'll be there. I don't have any options.

One day my brother, when he was twenty-seven, came home wearing only boxer shorts and one sock, and he had tire tracks, car-tire tracks, across his chest. When I asked him what happened, he said he didn't know. *He didn't know what happened to him.* Later on, he was shot in the arm, and he lost the use of his arm. That's what it's like to live in South-Central. My sister was raped by nine guys. It's that desperate a situation. *That's what happens there every day.* I'm gone from there, but I carry it with me. I see white people, and they're living in a different world, man, a dreamworld.

I think I've lost the ability to cry. My lip will tremble and my eyes get hot, but no tears will fall anymore. Now they say, "We gotta have peace." That makes me mad. If they [the feds] acquit those four cops, it will take the lid off like you've never seen. They just got a warning. That's all. Rodney King is not going to stop it next time.

They look at us like we're a bunch of killers — that we're waiting for the chance to kill people. We're a bunch of people waiting for a chance to live. I stole the computer that I've been wanting. It was my chance to get it. But then I decided I don't want to get it this way.

We talk this way about whites: "You *know* the way they are. Why are they that way?" That's what we say to each other. My question for you is: What is wrong with white people? Why don't they see us?

> – Anonymous
> "Nobody Listens"
> *Mother Jones,* 1992

# 10

In April 1990, a young middle-class white woman named Laurie Sue Rosenthal, raised in an Orthodox Jewish household and at age twenty-nine still living with her parents in Jamaica, Queens, happened to die, according to the coroner's report, from the accidental toxicity of Darvocet in combination with alcohol, in an apartment at 36 East Sixty-eighth Street in Manhattan. The apartment belonged to the man she had been, according to her parents, seeing for about a year, a minor city assistant commissioner named Peter Franconeri. Peter Franconeri, who was at the time in charge of elevator and boiler inspections for the Buildings Department and married to someone else, wrapped Laurie Sue Rosenthal's body in a blanket; placed it, along with her handbag and ID, outside the building with the trash; and went to his office at 60 Hudson Street. At some point an anonymous call was made to 911. Franconeri was identified only after Laurie Sue Rosenthal's parents gave the police his beeper number, which they found in her address book. According to *Newsday,* which covered the story more extensively than the *News,* the *Post,* or the *Times,*

> Initial police reports indicated that there were no visible wounds on Rosenthal's body. But Rosenthal's mother, Ceil, said yesterday that the family was told the autopsy revealed two "unexplained bruises" on her daughter's body.
>
> Larry and Ceil Rosenthal said those findings seemed to support their suspicions that their daughter was upset because they received a call from

their daughter at 3 A.M. Thursday "saying that he had beaten her up." The family reported the conversation to police.

"I told her to get into a cab and get home," Larry Rosenthal said yesterday. "The next I heard was two detectives telling me terrible things."

"The ME [medical examiner] said the bruises did not constitute a beating but they were going to examine them further," Ceil Rosenthal said.

"There were some minor bruises," a spokeswoman for the Office of the Chief Medical Examiner told *Newsday* a few days later, but the bruises "did not in any way contribute to her death." This is worth rerunning: A young woman calls her parents at three in the morning, "distraught." She says that she has been beaten up. A few hours later, on East Sixty-eighth Street between Madison and Park avenues . . . this young middle-class white woman's body, showing bruises, gets put out with the trash.

"Everybody got upside-down because of who he was," an unidentified police officer later told Jim Dwyer of *Newsday*, referring to the man who put the young woman out with the trash. "If it had happened to anyone else, nothing would have come of it. A summons would have been issued and that would have been the end of it." In fact nothing did come of the death of Laurie Sue Rosenthal, which might have seemed a natural tabloid story but failed, on several levels, to catch the local imagination. For one thing she could not be trimmed into the role of the preferred tabloid victim, who is conventionally presented as fate's random choice (Laurie Sue Rosenthal had, for whatever reason, taken the Darvocet instead of a taxi home, her parents reported treatment for a previous Valium dependency, she could be presumed to have known over the course of a year that Franconeri was married and yet continued to see him); for another, she seemed not to have attended an expensive school or to have been employed in a glamour industry (no Ivy Grad, no Wall Street Exec), which made it hard to cast her as part of "what makes this city so vibrant and so great."

In August 1990, Peter Franconeri pled guilty to a misdemeanor, the unlawful removal of a body, and was sentenced by criminal court judge Peter Benitez to seventy-five hours of community service. This was neither surprising nor much of a story (only twenty-three lines even in *Newsday*, on page twenty-nine of the city edition), and the case's lenient resolution was for many people a kind of relief. The district attorney's office had asked for "some incarceration," the amount usually described as a "touch," but no one wanted, it was said, to crucify the guy: Peter Franconeri was somebody who knew a lot of people, understood how to live in the city, who had for example not only the apartment on East Sixty-eighth Street between Madison and Park but a house in Southampton and who also understood that putting a body outside with the trash was nothing to get upside-down about, if it was handled right.

— Joan Didion
*After Henry*, 1992


## REFLECTIONS

1. What reasons do the authors of these selections give for the continuing existence of war? Which reasons do you find most plausible?

2. What causes do Susanne Hoeber Rudolph and Lloyd I. Rudolph (p. 602) blame for clashes between ethnic groups? What comments by Rosemary L. Bray (p. 605) and the anonymous *Mother Jones* contributor (p. 610) point to the same causes? What other causes are cited in those two selections? In the Associated Press selection (p. 607)?

3. What important factor in the gang warfare described by George Will (p. 608) is not named in his essay? What actions does Will seem to be advocating? How can you tell?

4. What recommendations do the authors in *Looking at Ourselves* offer — directly or indirectly — for stopping or decreasing violence? Which authors apparently believe violence is beyond our control, and why?

# NELL McCAFFERTY

## *Peggy Deery of Derry*

Nell McCafferty was born in 1944 in Londonderry (Derry for short), the county seat of the Northern Irish county by the same name. She graduated from Queen's University in Belfast, Northern Ireland's capital city, then traveled extensively. Returning to Derry, McCafferty became active in the civil-rights movement. Later she moved to Dublin, where she participated in the women's movement and went to work for *The Irish Times*, for which she wrote for a number of years. "Peggy Deery of Derry" comes from her book "Peggy Deery: A Derry Family at War" (1988). McCafferty's first play, *The Worm in the Heart*, was produced in Dublin and London (1988; published 1990). An award-winning broadcaster as well as author and journalist, she currently lives in Dublin.

Soon after Great Britain conquered Ireland in the 1600s, Protestants from Scotland began immigrating to the island and displacing Gaelic-speaking Catholics in the northern counties known as Ulster (see p. 444). The Irish Republican Army (IRA) formed in 1919 to drive the British out. When Ireland became a dominion two years later and then a republic, Britain responded to the fears of the Ulster Protestants by keeping control of Northern Ireland. (Although the island's much larger southern section is 94 percent Catholic, the North was by now two-thirds Protestant.) Catholic resentment in Northern Ireland simmered until the 1960s, flaring in 1968–1969 into demonstrations against housing, voting, and employment discrimination. As the outlawed IRA reemerged as a militant force, Protestant paramilitary groups formed to oppose it. In 1972 Britain suspended Northern Ireland's parliament and reimposed direct rule. After thirteen more years of turmoil, including a 1981 hunger strike that left ten Republicans dead, Britain agreed over Loyalist protests to give the Republic of Ireland a voice in governing Northern Ireland. Today the Troubles continue: a passionate conflict between Protestant Loyalists, who want Northern Ireland to stay in the United Kingdom, and Catholic Republicans, who want it to merge with the Irish Republic and in the meantime seek political equality with Ulster's dominant Protestant majority.

On any given day of the week, in one of the Deery households in Derry, in Northern Ireland, a video of Owney Deery's wedding is played. The video is passed from one member of the family to another like a touchstone. It might be watched in the afternoon, or before going to bed, or before dawn, if the sister or brother cannot sleep. The wedding, in

1985, was the last occasion when Peggy Deery was filmed in the company of all of her fourteen children, all of them happy and well and looking glad to be alive.

Her eldest son Paddy, aged thirtyy, is shown in his suit, kneeling beside his mother in the chapel in Creggan, waiting for the ceremony to begin. He does not once look over his shoulder, though he is on the run. Were the police and army to venture into the area, IRA lookouts would let him know soon enough. Peggy, in a black trouser-suit, with white shirt and black string tie, pearl earrings, and a red carnation in her lapel, is clearly delighted with Paddy's company.

Owney, in formal morning suit, on his wedding day, has the looks of a young Clark Gable, complete with dimples, pencil mustache, and cleft chin. He holds the hand of his bride, Donna, as they sit in chairs before the altar watching the priest say mass. A choir of schoolchildren sings the song which the couple have chosen specially for their wedding. They sing "The Rose," with which Bette Midler had a hit record.

The video shows Peggy later, at the reception in a singing pub, dancing with her son Tony. He is far too tall for her, and she must rest her head upon his chest, as they move slowly, waltzing badly, to the music of a band which is playing "When the Evening Shadows Fall."

Michael interrupts them, making everybody laugh as he prances about                    5
in a bra, and skirt and boots. Martin and Johnny and Owney dance with their mother in turn. Her eight daughters come onto the floor, and all the guests, and they form a circle, kicking their legs up as the tempo increases. Peggy moves awkwardly, her left leg dragging, but she beams constantly.

When the band takes a break, a guest takes the microphone and sings a song which he has composed himself. He is not from Derry. He sings a lament for a dead IRA hunger-striker. His audience pays him no attention at all.

The video ends with everybody being asked what they wish for the married couple. Peggy looks into the camera and hesitates and then she says, simply and seriously, "I just hope everything goes well for them."

Owney studies this video constantly. He and Donna often talk late into the night about how their own family will turn out. They look forward to more babies. Donna says you get too much enjoyment out of children ever to complain about them. The video reassures Owney that Peggy Deery, on her best days, had no complaints about the fourteen children who danced around her.

It used to be that there was only one thing for a Catholic mother to do in Derry on a fine, wintry Sunday afternoon. On rare occasions her man would come with her, but usually she would go with another woman, a sister or sister-in-law, or once in a while, a female neighbor. The women would bring their children with them.

These Sunday afternoons spent strolling in the city cemetery were a comparative treat. The alternative for mothers was to sit at home, for the seventh day in a row, in the strict and doleful grip of a Protestant Sabbath. In Northern Ireland, on a Sunday, it used to be that everything closed down — no playgrounds, no cinemas, no pubs, no shops, nothing but the lonely toll of church bells even after the churches had closed.

The cemetery was, by contrast, a bazaar. Magnificently situated on a hill overlooking Derry, with views of the River Foyle that bisects the town, and the mountains marching toward the Republic of Ireland beyond, it afforded a sense of beauty, freedom, and reward, if not in this life, then in the next. In the cemetery, the minds and tongues of women at leisure were free to wander. The inscribed tombstones among which children played hide-and-seek were a rich source of gossip, speculation, and tribal perspective. The people of the town, which had a small population of 65,000, were intimately acquainted with each other, and with each other's seed, breed, and generation.

The launching of the civil-rights movement in Derry, in 1968, changed dramatically the nature of Sunday afternoons. The movement liberated Catholic women, albeit unintentionally. They burst out of their homes, and out of the cemetery, and spent their Sundays marching around the city, demanding freedom, just like the men and children. They joined in the chant for votes, houses, and jobs, carried banners, sat down defiantly in the roadway when the Royal Ulster Constabulary [RUC] blocked the route, helped build barricades, inhaled tear gas, broke the law for the first time in their adult lives, and agreed that there was no time to go home to make the supper.

The marches frequently deteriorated into routine set-piece battles between Derry teenagers on one hand and police and British soldiers on the other. On such Sunday afternoons, adults settled themselves into spectator positions on the hills and watched the riots.

Hardly anybody died.

In the years between 1968 and 1972, violent death in Derry was a rare and confusing occurrence, and when someone was killed one side would protest, the other would bluster, and there was a general insistence that it was not meant to happen. This was a struggle for civil rights, not a war. People were so confident of this that they continued to march on Sundays.

Peggy Deery put on her best clothes for her last march. The thirty-eight-year-old widow, mother of fourteen children, dressed herself in a black mock-leather wet-look coat, which had black fun-fur trimming at the hem, and wore black wet-look boots. She left her eldest daughter Margie, aged fourteen, in charge of the house.

The march began at the top of Derry's highest hill, where the Creggan housing estate[1] in which Peggy lived was situated. She left her home, a prefabricated one-story aluminum bungalow, and walked the short distance to the dilapidated playing field where thousands of people had gathered. She joined her nieces there, Rita and Sandra.

There was a band playing. The weather was unseasonably fine, hinting of spring. People were in good humor. The proposed route would take them on a bracing three-mile walk, downhill all the way, skirting the cemetery to plunge into Brandywell below, then back along the valley of the Bogside, and if possible, out of these Catholic ghettos into the city center.

The victories so far achieved gave a feeling of confidence on this day. The corrupt Unionist-controlled corporation had been abolished. The provincial Unionist government at Stormont had been pressured to build houses for Catholics in Derry. The Unionist minister for home affairs, William Craig, *bête noire*[2] of the Catholics and champion of the mainly Protestant police force, had been dismissed. There had been a price to pay — the internment without trial of hundreds of Catholic males — but even that ploy had rebounded. International opinion was ranged against internment, especially when it emerged that the only thing the internees had in common was the private practice of their religion or a commitment to civil rights. There was scarcely an IRA man among them.

Peggy and Rita and Sandra had a very enjoyable march. They sang all      20
the way. When the marchers moved out beyond the barricades in Rossville Street, out of the Bogside and into the bottleneck of William Street, the police and army were waiting. A huge military tanker released a jet of colored water onto their heads. The dye would help snatch-squads sort out civilians from civil-rights activists should anyone penetrate to the center of town. Stones were thrown at the troops, in retaliation. Young people pushed forward, older people tried to retreat.

In the roaring confusion, in the narrow canyon created by the houses and shops on either side of William Street, Rita chose the only escape from the crush. She climbed a lamppost, grabbed hold of the bulb, and hung on. Sandra and her aunt Peggy laughed at her. They could not persuade her to come down. They left her to take her chances while they pushed their way back through the crowd, round the corner and into Rossville Street. "I'm away on now," were Peggy's parting words to Sandra.

---

[1]Public housing development. — ED.
[2]French, "black beast"; dreaded enemy. — ED.

"I have to take a wee cake up to your granny." Peggy had brought a home-baked scone on the march, which she intended to deliver to her mother in the Bogside.

When the crowd thinned out, Rita got down off the lamppost. She did not go back toward Rossville Street. She went forward toward the troops, into the no-man's land between soldiers and rioters. The established ritual of riot procedure allowed for a cessation in hostilities if a woman wished to get through the lines. The cessation would be brief, a few seconds, and the woman would have to run quickly. On occasion, there would be no lull at all, but rioters would take care to throw stones over her head, and soldiers and police would not aim rubber bullets at her.

There was no lull this day but there was safety in the number of adults who ran forward in order to escape. So Rita ran forward and turned into Chamberlain Street. She could hear in the distance the amplified voice of Bernadette Devlin addressing the civil-rights meeting. As she ran down the street, soldiers of the First Battalion of the Parachute Regiment, Britain's crack army unit, ran after her. "There were bullets hitting off the walls, and a man was pulling me along and then I was standing in some woman's doorway. She said it was only rubber bullets, and we stood there listening, and then everything went quiet."

The soldiers had run down Rossville Street also, toward the meeting. Peggy saw them coming and she ran through the courtyard of a nearby block of flats, heading for the presumed safety of Chamberlain Street. A bullet struck her in the back of her left leg. She called out to a fleeing priest, "Father, I think I'm shot," and he called out, "Keep on running," and she did, and then she collapsed on the step of a back door of a Chamberlain Street house. As she lay on the ground a soldier with red hair came alongside. She looked up at him and said she was the mother of fourteen children. He ran on. People ran over her as she lay there. She felt their shoes strike and hurt her head. Her wounded leg felt cold. A man pulled her down an alleyway and in the front door of a house in Chamberlain Street.

It was from television newscasts that Rita got the number to phone for information on dead, injured, or missing relatives. She went with her father, hours later, to Altnagelvin Hospital, to look for Peggy. In the upper floors, people crowded outside operating rooms. A doctor confirmed the rumor that Peggy had indeed been wounded, but could give no details. Confusion abounded. Rita went to the ground floor to get cigarettes from a vending machine. "The ground floor was empty. There was nobody there. The whole place was dead quiet, no people, nothing." A man appeared, clad in a white coat and white hat. She could see his clerical collar. "He asked me if I had anybody in the hospital. I said, 'What do

25

you want to know for?' I didn't know the difference between a Protestant minister and a priest, or he might have been an army chaplain. He said his name was Father Tom O'Gara. He said the morgue was on the ground floor. He said there were thirteen dead people in there. He asked me if I would go in and see if I could identify anybody. I said no way. Then the whole McDaid family arrived. He took them to the morgue. I can hear them squealing yet."

Upstairs, doctors operated on the twenty-eight wounded.

Later that night, as Rita and her father left the hospital, they saw policemen on the ground floor. "Two of the cops were singing 'It's a Beautiful Day.' That was the first time in my life I ever cursed in front of my father."

The civil-rights movement died in Derry, on Bloody Sunday, January 30, 1972. Henceforth, when people regained the nerve to march, they marched increasingly behind the banner of Sinn Féin, political wing of the IRA.

The bullet severed the sciatic nerve on Peggy's upper thigh. Half of the buttock had been shot away. There was no sensation in her foot. It seemed as if gangrene was inevitable. Surgeons arranged to amputate her leg on Wednesday morning.

On Tuesday night Peggy's body reacted to the four pints of blood which had been hastily transfused into her on Bloody Sunday. In the consternation and chaos of mass operations there had been no time to cross-match blood samples, and she had been given Rh-positive. She was Rh-negative. Acute kidney failure threatened. "It was as serious as could be. Her life was in the balance," says her general practitioner, Dr. Donal McDermott, who was informed by the hospital of the crisis. Peggy was transferred through the night to a specialist unit in Belfast. She was jaundiced and unconscious. She spent eight weeks there. When she returned to Altnagelvin Hospital, Dr. McDermott went to see her. Peggy said to him, "I can move my big toe." He told her this was medically impossible. That a severed nerve does not grow again, and five inches of the nerve had been shot away. Nevertheless, Peggy could move her toe.

"Had she been given the right transfusion at the start, her leg would have been amputated as scheduled. She was lucky the soldiers shot so many people." Dr. McDermott has a jaundiced view of British soldiers. His son joined the IRA after Bloody Sunday and is now serving a life sentence in jail.

On the night she was shot Peggy Deery's children were looked after by Father Tom O'Gara. The twenty-five-year-old stranger, who had long hair and a guitar, walked into their home with loads of buns and chips. He made them eat and ate with them and Margie was affronted when one of the children knocked the priest's fork to the floor. She rose to get a tea-cloth but he wiped the fork on his trousers saying there was no need. Then he played his guitar and sang for them. He sang "Ebony Eyes" and "Dirty Old Town." He helped Margie wash the younger ones and put them to bed. It took Margie a while to realize that this man was not a plain-clothes British soldier, sent to keep an eye on them while their mother was, as she thought, being questioned and arrested in hospital. Father O'Gara told Margie that he had been specially seconded by his bishop to look after the Deery family.

A group of concerned priests gathered together the day after Bloody Sunday to decide on a collective response. The then bishop, Neil Farren, was not at the meeting. An elderly arch-conservative, he was bemuddled and swamped by the tide of history and he retreated into his palace demesne. The fifteen priests relived the events of the previous day, which many of them had personally witnessed. They assured themselves of two things. The soldiers were the only ones who had fired shots during the massacre, and all of the victims were unarmed. Father O'Gara mentioned that he had seen two armed members of the IRA, in the vicinity of the slaughter, about ten minutes before the soldiers swept into the Bogside. This fact was not included in the press statement which the priests then issued. They confined their description of events to the beginning, duration, and end of the soldiers' onslaught; no one who died or had been shot was a member of the IRA; no shots were fired at the soldiers; the dead and injured were unarmed.

The British Army also issued statements. All of the dead were in possession of guns or nail-bombs, and nail-bombs had been found in the pockets of their clothing. The British Information Service telegraphed embassies abroad that four of the dead were on the RUC wanted list.

A public inquiry, instituted by the British government, subsequently 35 found that none of the dead were in possession of anything other than the undigested remains of their dinners, "meat, peas, and potatoes," in the graphic words of Dr. Raymond McClean, who represented the Catholic Church at the postmortems.

Everything that the priests had said in their statement was true and everything that the British Army and British Information Service had said in theirs was untrue. Nevertheless, Father O'Gara's information, had it been divulged, would have been a propaganda godsend to the British government in the immediate aftermath of Bloody Sunday.

The relationship between the Catholic Church and its people, and the attitude of the Catholic Church to government authorities in the North, since this war began, has been delicate and fraught with ambiguity. Father O'Gara was only one of hundreds of priests who found themselves torn as the war deepened. In a document which he drew up and circulated to the clergy he outlined his view of the ministry. The document presaged the moral disarray into which Derry would eventually fall, because of the war. The Church, he wrote, did not appreciate the level or depth of people's insecurities.

> We miss the insecurities that riddle so much of their thinking. . . . These insecurities are practical needs and must determine enormously the shape into which a man's heart might be pushed and can be constrained. . . . Is it the insecurity brought by the fear of having no money to pay for family needs etc. which drives people to cheat, draw false dole, drink, and even kill? . . . I cannot answer for certain whether the people living in estates feel their lives empty. I must know more of this.

Father O'Gara knew the Deery family better than any other priest. He spent years with them, married, baptized, and counseled many of them and their relatives. He died young. Peggy continued with confidence to summon the clergy to attend all the great family rituals of birth and death and army raids and police arrests. She felt no insecurity whatsoever about her personal relationship with God.

## EXPLORATIONS

1. Look closely at the prologue about Owney Deery's wedding video (paras. 1–8). What impression does it create of Peggy Deery and her family? What later events does it foreshadow?

2. What factors appear to be responsible for the Deery family's political position? Cite specific evidence for your answer.

3. Where does Nell McCafferty first mention Protestantism? What impression does she give of it, and by what means? Where does she first mention the Republic of Ireland? What impression does she give of it, and by what means?

4. What does McCafferty tell us about the goals of Derry's civil-rights marchers? The goals of the police?

# CONNECTIONS

1. What comments by the African-American authors in *Looking at Ourselves* also could be made by the Deery family?

2. What points made by the Rudolphs in *Looking at Ourselves* (p. 602) apply to the Troubles in Northern Ireland?

3. Compare "Peggy Deery of Derry" with Nadine Gordimer's short story "Amnesty" (p. 578). What character's point of view does each selection take? How do these two writers utilize their chosen points of view similarly to comment on violence?

4. What concept of Roman Catholicism does McCafferty present in "Peggy Deery of Derry"? How is this concept similar to and different from the one Edna O'Brien presents in her short story "Sister Imelda" (p. 444)?

# ELABORATIONS

1. In "House of Stone" (p. 569), Michael Dorris notes that compassion for other people's suffering must be aroused at the individual rather than the crowd level (paras. 32–33). How does Nell McCafferty utilize this idea? What is her central argument? What details about characters and setting, and what sensory information, help her to draw readers into her essay? What use does she make of other elements, such as data, to support her position? Write an essay analyzing the writing techniques McCafferty uses in "Peggy Deery of Derry" to arouse our compassion and win our sympathy.

2. What observations by McCafferty depict marches and riots as social rather than political activities? Which characters seem to see them that way, and why? Which characters take a different view, and why? Write either a comparison-contrast essay about these two perspectives, or a pair of short narrative essays about Bloody Sunday from the viewpoints of a civil-rights activist and a police officer.

# CHARLES MOORE

## *Ireland Must Fight the IRA Too*

Charles Moore was born on Halloween in 1956. He was educated at England's prestigious Eton College and Trinity College of Cambridge University. In 1979 he joined the editorial staff of the *Daily Telegraph*. He moved to *The Spectator* from 1983 to 1990, first as an assistant editor, then as a political columnist, and finally as an editor. From 1987 to 1990 he also wrote a weekly column for the *Daily Express*. In 1990 he returned to the *Daily Telegraph* as deputy editor. Moore has co-edited two books, *The Church in Crisis* (1986) and *A Tory Seer: The Selected Journalism of T. E. Utley* (1989). He lives in London, where he is a member of the Beefsteak Club.

For information on Ireland and Northern Ireland, see pages 444 and 615.

When I flew back in to London last week the car meeting me was late. London traffic, the driver explained, had been brought to a halt because of a bomb at a railway station. Twenty-eight people had been injured. The authorities had closed all the stations, hence the gridlock.

Being British, I did not need to be told that this was the work of the Irish Republican Army. On the British mainland, such explosions are familiar occurrences. In the province of Northern Ireland, they are virtually daily, as are terrorist shootings. Scores of people are killed every year, and the numbers are rising: In 1991, ninety-seven people were killed in Britain by terrorists, more than in any year since 1982.

This year has started even worse, and as Britain embarks on a general election campaign, the IRA is preparing to do what it can to disrupt proceedings. The government is introducing emergency legislation to permit candidates, for the first time ever, to decline to put their home addresses on their nomination papers, to avoid attack.

On the whole, people in Britain accept this extraordinary state of affairs with a weary resignation. On the whole, people elsewhere give little thought to the question, but their general supposition, particularly in the United States, is that "Britain" is "occupying Ireland," that "the Irish" do not like this, and that the British should get out. So it is that Brian Dougherty, the IRA terrorist recently extradited from America, has a street named in his honor in New York. Distance lends enchantment to the view.

Unfortunately the terms of this general supposition are so vague as to     5
make it altogether misleading. The British are not "occupying Ireland."
Northern Ireland is not a colony, but a full part of the nation whose full
title is the United Kingdom of Great Britain and Northern Ireland. Most
people who live in Northern Ireland want it to remain so. Thirteen of
the seventeen Ulster seats in the House of Commons are held by Unionists, and only one by a supporter of the IRA. Unionist candidates together
receive about 60 percent of the vote in Northern Ireland. The British
troops in Northern Ireland are there with the consent of the majority, to
protect all who obey the law, just as they would protect British citizens,
were it necessary, in any other part of the kingdom.

Nor is it true to say that "the Irish" want the British out. In the first
place, the Unionist majority in Northern Ireland is not English, but Irish
(though often of Scottish descent). Harder to establish, but even more
important, is the fact that neither the government of the Republic of
Ireland, nor most of its citizens, actually want British withdrawal. To be
sure, they have a vague aspiration that Ireland will one day be united,
expressed in Articles 2 and 3 of the republic's constitution, which lay
claim to the whole island. But the people of the republic do not want to
have to cope with 1 million Ulstermen implacably opposed to Dublin
rule. Nor do they want to cope with the IRA.

It tends to be forgotten that the IRA is as committed to the overthrow
of the present Irish state as it is to driving Britain from the North: It is a
revolutionary organization that has never accepted the 1922 treaty that
partitioned the island and granted independence to the South. The IRA's
electoral support in the South is negligible. Most Irish people know that
British withdrawal would mean that Dublin would have to deal with a
civil war in the North and a wave of terrorism (at present virtually
unknown) in the South. They may not like the British and they may make
unfriendly noises about them, but they want them to stay.

Why is it, then, that the killing persists? How can it be that two
reasonably friendly democratic powers are somehow so weak that they
cannot combine to suppress the activities of a small group of fanatics? It
is not surprising that the outside world attributes to the IRA far more
legitimacy and popularity than it possesses — it seems so powerful, and
it never goes away.

Before trying to apportion the blame, it is worth recalling an interesting
fact. The IRA has been defeated in the past. From 1956 to 1962, it ran
a terrorist campaign, the same in essence, though smaller, as those it has
run since 1969. Ireland and the United Kingdom recognized a common
threat and acted together. Because the intimidation of juries made it
impossible to secure a conviction by ordinary judicial means, both coun-

tries felt justified in introducing internment — the detention of named individuals for extended periods without trial. Ireland was, if anything, more ready to act than the United Kingdom. The civil war that accompanied Irish independence, in which opponents of the partition treaty fought its supporters, taught the republic how to recognize a threat to its own existence. The terrorism petered out.

Today, matters are very different. All Dublin governments condemn     10
terrorism, but wax indignant at the idea of internment. Britain, fearing international opprobrium, dares not introduce internment alone. Besides, internment would be ineffective in such circumstances, because the wanted men could simply slip over the border to the South and live unmolested. And so the present situation continues.

Now it is obviously not very courageous of the Dublin government to act, or rather, fail to act, in this way. It benefits from international sentimentality about Ireland. One cannot imagine that if, say, Germany harbored men who crossed into France to murder people the rest of the world would put up with it for very long. But it is not surprising that Dublin behaves as it does when it is under so little pressure to do otherwise. That lack of pressure is the fault of Britain.

British policy in Northern Ireland is appallingly misguided, but not for the reasons normally touted around the world. It is based on the belief that what is needed to secure peace in the province is a moderate balance between the two camps in which London plays a role of virtuous neutrality. This balance would be achieved by some sort of power-sharing arrangement in Northern Ireland, arising from the inter-party talks that Britain tries interminably and unsuccessfully to arrange. These talks, it believes, will be assisted by bringing Dublin into some part of the process, hence the Anglo-Irish Agreement of 1985.

The result of the policy is perpetual doubt. The desire for a united Ireland is in itself as honorable as the desire for Ulster to remain part of the United Kingdom, but the one cannot be reconciled with the other. They are, by definition, opposites. All efforts to bring those two desires into governmental partnership are therefore doomed to fail, and as long as they are being made extremists will exploit the instability.

They see that Britain has no mind of its own, no unconditional determination to support the will of the majority, and is ready to juggle constitutions with the help of a foreign power. And so they take their chance to play on uncertainty. Noticing that mainland British public opinion dislikes the Ulster question and is fed up with the death of our soldiers, the terrorists believe that if they fight on they might prevail. They could, just possibly, be right. The IRA, after all, is fanatical, but it is not mad. It kills because it has at least some reasonable expectation that killing will work.

The behavior of the London government lends some credence to the     15
IRA's claim that Britain is a colonial power in Ulster. The British ministers concerned treat Ulstermen, particularly Unionists, with a patronizing contempt, and act like enlightened Westerners trying to keep order among savage tribes, confident that if things get really nasty they can take the plane out.

This is scandalous because it does not reflect reality. The reality is that terrorists are trying to overthrow democracy and the rule of law in a kingdom with the longest history of both in the world. They are having more success than any of their equivalents elsewhere in the West. They will fail only when Britain fulfills the responsibilities of a democratic government and enforces the will of the majority, integrating Ulster politics into those of the rest of the kingdom. To do that effectively, it would be greatly assisted by the unequivocal cooperation of Dublin. That is what Britain should be asking for.

## EXPLORATIONS

1. What is the effect of the anecdote that opens "Ireland Must Fight the IRA Too"? How would the essay's impact change without it?

2. According to Charles Moore, what is the dominant view of the IRA in Northern Ireland? Who holds that view, and who holds a different view?

3. According to Moore, what is the dominant view of the IRA in the Republic of Ireland? In Great Britain?

4. What is the thesis of Moore's essay? Where does he state it? What actions does he recommend?

## CONNECTIONS

1. Both Moore in "Ireland Must Fight the IRA Too" and McCafferty in "Peggy Deery of Derry" (p. 615) mention the United Kingdom's policy of internment. What facts do they agree on? What is the difference between Moore's viewpoint (paras. 9–10) and McCafferty's (para. 19)?

2. What role does religion play in Moore's analysis of the violent tension between the IRA and the government of the United Kingdom? What role does religion play in McCafferty's analysis in "Peggy Deery of Derry"?

3. What comments by the Rudolphs in *Looking at Ourselves* (p. 602) help to explain the escalating IRA violence Moore mentions in paragraph 2?

## ELABORATIONS

1. Based on "Ireland Must Fight the IRA Too" and "Peggy Deery of Derry," write an essay comparing and contrasting Charles Moore's and Nell McCafferty's positions on the IRA and the Troubles in Northern Ireland.

2. Moore writes: "On the whole, people in Britain accept this extraordinary state of affairs with a weary resignation" (para. 4). What selections in *Looking at Ourselves* suggest that a similar situation exists in the United States? Do any of Moore's recommendations for ending violence in Great Britain and Ireland apply to the United States? Using "Ireland Must Fight the IRA Too" as a model, write an essay addressing the problem of violence in this country.

# DAVID GROSSMAN

## *Israeli Arab, Israeli Jew*

Widely regarded as one of Israel's most gifted writers, David Grossman was born in Jerusalem in 1954 and graduated from Hebrew University. His first novel, *Hiyukh ha-gedi* (1983; *The Smile of the Lamb*, 1991) won the Israeli Publisher's Association Prize for best novel in 1985. Other awards have honored his children's books, second novel, two books of nonfiction, and a play. Grossman also has worked as a journalist for Kol Israel (Israeli Radio). "Israeli Arab, Israeli Jew" comes from his 1992 book *Hanochachim hanifkadim* (*Sleeping on a Wire: Conversations with Palestinians in Israel*), translated from the Hebrew by Haim Watzman.

Israel consists of roughly 8,000 square miles of land on the eastern Mediterranean coast, only a fifth of which is arable. Archaeological evidence documents a Hebrew kingdom in this region (known as Palestine) going back to about 1000 B.C., the era of the biblical House of David. Jews here always have been surrounded by Arabs: Israel currently is bounded on the north by Lebanon, on the east by Jordan, and on the southwest by Egypt. When Israel became independent in 1948, most of the Arab Palestinians living there fled or were evicted, while five Arab armies tried to destroy the new nation. By the war's end only 156,000 Arabs remained in Israel. Today there are about 900,000 — a sixth of the population. Although Israel's Declaration of Independence promises Arabs "full and equal citizenship" and "appropriate representation," discrimination is rampant. David Grossman notes that Israel has never had an Arab cabinet minister, Supreme Court justice, or director-general of a large company; only 3 out of 1,000 employees in the Ministry of Justice are Arabs; and although Arabs farm 17 percent of agricultural land, they get only 2.4 percent of the water.

For more background on Israel and Palestine, see page 275.

"You see the wall there, by the bank?" Mohammed Kiwan swings his swivel chair around and points. "There they wrote, in big letters, 'Death to the Arabs.' And next to it, 'A good Arab is a dead Arab.' And that in the heart of the fair city of Hadera, straight across from my office window. Fine, so the day they wrote it I call the Hadera[1] municipality and tell them, Hey, guys, right across from my nice little office they're hanging

---

[1]Hadera lies on Israel's northern Mediterranean coast, Um Elfahm about fifteen miles inland on the border of the disputed West Bank. — ED.

me! So please, come clean it up. Ten days passed and they didn't come
to wash it off. The graffiti pricks me in the back. When did they come?
When we brought the press into it; within a day the mayor had ordered
the graffiti cleaned up."

He is an attorney, lives in Um Elfahm, works in Hadera. At the
beginning of the 1960s he had been a teacher — "an educator," he
corrects me — and was fired because of his political activity. At the time
Kiwan was active in the Nasserist[2] nationalist movement, Al-Ard. In 1965,
after Al-Ard was outlawed, he was among the founders of Sons of the
Village, a radical Palestinian movement whose aim was to fight for an
improvement in the status of the Arabs in Israel. "We called it Abna
el-Balad, because *balad* means both 'village' and 'homeland.' It's the
unfortunate villager as opposed to the snobbish rich. It's the common
man, Voltaire's Candide. I always look for that man. Among you [Jews]
and among us. I'd like to get to the Candides among you, too. But your
communications media are blocked to us. How many times have they
interviewed an Arab on a television talk show? Despite the fact that we're
nearly 20 percent of the population and talk, God knows, just like you.
Where's equality of opportunity? We're always shouting, but no one hears.
They don't allow us to reach you. Here, two months ago I saw this guy
Jojo from Ashdod[3] on television, the one on the beach. What a wise and
simple man! What common sense and humanity! I wrote him an open
letter, for the newspaper, and called to him: 'I, Mohammed, am searching
for Jojo from Ashdod.' The paper, of course, would not print it. So I'm
still looking for those Jojos."

"It's not that complicated," I told him. "Let's drive down to see him."

It wasn't all that simple, either. Jojo Abutbul lives in Ashdod, Mohammed Kiwan in Um Elfahm. Who should go to whom? "Tell him we'll
meet halfway," Kiwan suggested. "What do you mean halfway?" Abutbul
grumbled. "I've got to be in my restaurant on the beach every day, tell
him to come here." I mediated, shuttle diplomacy by telephone, one day,
another day, until Kiwan finally gave in; after all, he wanted to talk to
Jojo, and if Jojo won't come to Mohammed, Mohammed will go to the
beach.

On a hot summer's day, at Jojo's café-restaurant, The West Coast,     5
under the palm branches spread over the roof, the two sat facing each
other. The restaurant loudspeakers played American music, the beach

---

[2]Gamal Abdel Nasser, Egypt's president from 1956 to 1970, favored Arab nationalism and
opposed Israel's existence. — ED.
[3]Mediterranean port south of Tel Aviv. — ED.

slumbered beyond. Jojo took a pack of cigarettes out of his pocket. Mohammed took out his pack. They lit their own, relaxed, and Jojo, the host, began.

"When we lived in Morocco, my mother had an Arab housemaid. She nursed me. That is, I grew up with her. I drank her milk. Let's say that when you go to sleep your life is a kind of box that you have to deposit with someone for safekeeping. That's an allegory. My mother would have had no problem handing that box, my life, over to her Arab neighbor. What I mean is that even when it was really a matter of life itself, the trust was so great that it was possible to place my life in her hands.

"So I — I don't have any preconceptions about you. An Arab is a human being. An Arab has a soul. I once talked about the pain. Fifteen get killed in the territories and they put it in small print in the newspaper. A Jew gets killed in an attack and it's on the front page! Why do they make distinctions when it comes to pain? If today I take my cigarette and put it out on Mohammed's hand, and take a cigarette and put it out on my hand, you'll measure the same force and feel exactly the same pain. Emotion. Love. Concern. Your son. These are things that weren't given to us by the Likud or the Labor Party.[4] Not by Judaism or Islam. I lost a son. I know what pain is. And that woman in Ramallah or Nablus,[5] and don't think I'm justifying in any way their stone-throwing, but he's dead. She feels the same pain I felt when my son drowned in the sea. Pain can't be divided; its force can't be measured, because of its relation to a particular person.

"So I ask you, Mohammed, where do we want to get to? Are you satisfied with your plate, your bed, your house, or are you satisfied only with my plate, my bed, my wife, and my children? On the other hand, when a Jewish guy tells me he wants security here, you know? Security has no bounds! You can put a ground-to-air missile on every square meter. Will that give you security? Tomorrow some Ahmed won't come and knife you? So where's my security and where's Mohammed's security? So that's what we have to talk about today, me and you — what are we willing to give each other? And I'm certain that if the two of us sit down and talk, we can finish off all the problems in two minutes."

Mohammed listened quietly, nodding all the while. When Jojo finished talking, he said, "First I want to tell you that I'm glad I came to meet you. We don't know each other. I saw you one time on television and I had the impression that you are a person with healthy natural

---

[4]Israel's two main political parties. — ED.
[5]Palestinian towns in the West Bank. — ED.

instincts and a love of life, and I felt that this person is really looking for a way to live together. I'm happy that the minute we met you said that we can solve all the problems straight off in two minutes. So the only question is: What work will that leave you, Grossman?"

We laughed, and drank our first cup of coffee. The beach was still    10
empty — only a few new immigrants from Russia cooking in the sun.

"Before we solve all the problems in two minutes," I said, "maybe we could clarify the most basic concepts, so that we'll know if we're talking about the same thing. What do you, Mohammed, call this country, the one Jojo calls Israel?"

"As far as I'm concerned," Mohammed said, "it's always Palestine. I don't care if Jojo calls it Israel. Jojo has the right to live here as an individual and as a nation, and my right as a Palestinian is to live in Palestine, as an individual and as a nation, with the right of self-determination for the Palestinian people. That's the basic principle, and I'm convinced Jojo will agree with me."

"I agree 100 percent," Jojo confirmed, "but you accept that this is also the Jewish state, right?"

"As far as I'm concerned, Israel can call itself whatever it wants." Mohammed smiled. "If it's just a semantic problem, I don't care. But if it means — like now — that it's a Jewish state with all the privileges and laws that discriminate in favor of the Jews, then other questions arise that I don't agree with."

Jojo stiffened. "Let's get this straight. I, as a Jew, have no country other    15
than Israel. I have to have one country that will be mine. I, Jojo Abutbul, was born Jewish. I did not decide that. I didn't have a store where I could take from whatever shelf I wanted. I was born Jewish. I deserve a place somewhere in the world to live the way I want, yes or no?"

"Ah . . . with regard to that question, you formulated it in a very difficult way."

"I did not!" Jojo cried. "That's a question from the gut, not from the head!"

"Look, Jojo," Mohammed said, getting a little more serious. "Before you came from Morocco, I was here."

"I'm not kicking you out!"

"One second, give me a second. This pretty, sparkling Ashdod of yours,    20
just for your information, even after the country was established in 1948, there were still Arabs here and in Ashkelon, and Israel expelled them in accordance with the infamous Plan D.[6] Now you're alive and you exist,

---

[6]Plan D was the first strategic plan of the IDF [Israeli Defense Force] in 1948 to occupy towns and villages populated by Arabs, in lands assigned by the UN partition to the Jewish state. — ED.

and you have this country, and I'm not challenging your right to a country, but according to what you say, 'I'm here, I don't have anywhere else to go,' ditto as regards the Palestinians — they have nowhere else to go — "

"I agree with you," Jojo cut him off. "But just a minute! I can help you with something that I don't know if you know. I say that having the Law of Return[7] only for Jews — that's racist! I'm not hiding that! But I ask you, Mohammed, you have the option of getting up tomorrow and moving to Jordan, Egypt, Syria, Lebanon — all those are Arab countries. But here I'm saying to you, in addition to all twenty-two of those countries, I'm saying to you, here I'm going to build another country for you, completely Palestinian, in Gaza and the West Bank. Wait a minute! You don't have to take your things and move there. Understand! As far as I'm concerned, you are a citizen of the State of Israel, with all your rights! But by this act that I'm making, do you accept that Israel is *my* country? You can live in it, but under my conditions, my government, my laws. And if I should want to live in your country, it will be under your laws and your government and your conditions. Can you live with that?"

"You and I, Jojo, when we're aware of those discriminatory, racist laws, and we both fight for their repeal by the legislature . . ."

Jojo: "You're not answering me! Say yes or no!"

Mohammed breathes deeply: "If you don't recognize my right to full equality here, I won't recognize your right."

"No, no, you don't understand." Jojo smiles uncomfortably. "I'm say-     25
ing this: You and I want a divorce. You've been married to me for forty-three years. I love you, you're my soul, everything. I don't want to live with you! Let's get divorced. What do you want as a dowry?"

"I'm not asking for a dowry. We really married against our wills. Not out of love. But today we're sailing on this sea in the same boat."

"And I own the sea."

"I don't agree that you own the sea!"

"But I'm the strong one! If I want, I can come today as Prime Minister Jojo and make a law — Whoever doesn't accept Israeli citizenship in the Jewish state — the *Jewish* state! — gets put in a car and taken away. Can you do anything to stop me? Nothing. Cry, scream until tomorrow!"

It's only Mohammed's mouth that is smiling at Jojo now. "First, Jojo,     30
my friend, inside, in my heart, I don't feel that you are in control and that you have power. I don't feel that I'm inferior to you. True, you now have strength and power, but I am among those who believe that power changes hands. I'm a minority under you, but you are a minority under

---

[7]The Law of Return gives every Jew the right to immigrate to Israel. — ED.

me, in the Arab Middle East. I have no feelings of inferiority with regard to you. I was born here. I have the strongest possible links with this homeland. I don't feel that I'm a guest of yours. I sometimes feel, if I may be presumptuous, that you are a guest of mine, and that I accept you because I want to be realistic. That is, the Jewish people's starting point, that they're doing me a favor when they let me live in Um Elfahm, is mistaken. Look, in Um Elfahm we had 140,000 dunams[8] of land before Israel was established, and then the Knesset[9] came and made all kinds of laws and confiscated from Israel's Arab citizens 1,200,000 dunams all at once. Today two kibbutzim and a moshav[10] sit on Um Elfahm's land. On our land! Another thing, 92 percent of Israel's land is state land. If this country really recognizes me as part of it, then I should have a proportional part of that 92 percent of the country. Do you understand why I'm shouting? Because when you tell me that you're doing me a favor by accepting me here, you have to look at things from my point of view, and then you'll begin to understand what kinds of huge concessions Palestinians are making today when they offer two states side by side. But if after the Palestinian state comes into being you come and rescind the discriminatory laws, if with regard to the Law of Return, for instance — "

"But here I'm not arguing with you," Jojo stops him. "The Law of Return has to apply to everyone."

Mohammed raises a finger. "In other words, you agree that the Arabs who were expelled from Ashdod can come back to live in Ashdod?"

"Yes! They can buy a house the way I do! I'm not giving them any privileges!"

Mohammed: "Allow me! You're saying that this country, this future country of ours, will agree that every man in the world who wants to live in it can?"

Jojo: "Suits me!"                                                                35

"Even if some miserable Kurd from Iraq or Turkey wants to live with you in Ashdod?"

"I've got no problem with that. If, if, *if.* If he promises to serve in my army, to be loyal to the *Jewish* state and not betray it. To fight together with me against whoever wants to take this country from the both of us, even to fight against Syria with me!"

"But it should be clear to you," Kiwan says, "that if there's total equality here, the country won't have its Jewish character anymore."

"Why won't it?" Jojo asks in horror. "It has to have! There'll be

---

[8]One dunam equals 1,000 square meters or about one-quarter of an acre. — ED.
[9]Israeli parliament. — ED.
[10]Jewish settlements. — ED.

maximum equality, as much as possible! But subject to this being a *Jewish* country!"

"Then it's not real equality! Then the Jews have extra rights because 40 of their Jewish birth! Then it's no longer Mohammed's country!"

"Just like in Syria there are extra rights for Arabs, as opposed to Jews!"

"Look, if you come at me with something like that" — Mohammed raised his thick, hoarse voice for the first time — "let me tell you that my counterdemand is just as purely racist — have the Palestinian state include all parts of Israel in which there are Palestinians! Give me the Galilee and the Triangle!"

"I'm ready to! I'm ready to give them to you, if — *if* you give me Nablus and Hebron, where I once lived!"

"Hey!"

"Why 'hey'? Why not? Don't you see you're talking out of both sides 45 of your mouth? Do Jews live in Hebron today? They do! Abraham lived there two thousand years ago? He did! Listen to me, Mohammed." Jojo sat back in his chair, lit two cigarettes in his mouth, pulled on both, and passed one over to Mohammed. "For years you butchered and exiled us, and for years we've butchered and exiled you. What I'm saying is this: We have two possibilities. Either we can talk nice and act bad, or talk bad and act nice. In other words, I, according to the way I see things, I prefer to get the dirt out of my mouth. Let's sit in a room and argue for twenty hours; I'll tell you you're garbage, you're crap, and you tell me the same thing, but in the end you and I get up with a clean heart, and we have no more demands, and we've divided up all the property between us, but for always! Finished!"

"I agree with you on that. But understand one thing, that the minute we repeal all the privileges Jews get here, this country will stop being a Jewish country and will become the country of the people who live in it."

"People, what people?" Jojo slaps his forehead with an open palm. "Is England a country of its people? Is Syria a country of its people? England is the country of the English, and Syria is the country of the Syrians. And you, if you live in Israel, will live in the country of the Israelis, as an Arab minority in the country of the Jews!"

Their faces are now close to each other. Their hands, waving excitedly, hit one another, and at times intertwine for a moment. Both are solidly built, with black hair and tough faces. Both look older than they are. Mohammed is about fifty, balding a bit, more careful with his words. Every so often he throws out a bit of legal jargon at Jojo in a lawyerly tone, looking at him over his glasses, putting on a tolerant and didactic expression. It drives Jojo crazy.

Jojo, thirty-eight, is in a blue undershirt and shorts. His sunglasses remain glued to his forehead even when he jumps up in indignation. He has lived on the beach since he was four years old — "Everything I know about life is from the sea." In his youth he was a violent criminal, terrorizing this beach until he won himself a place and was pacified. Ever since his appearance on television, politicians from all parties have been courting him, and he, "even though I've been Likud from my mother's womb," meets with them all, listens, gives advice — lively, heart-winning, knowing well that they all think that through him they have gained a direct linkup to "the people's voice." His face has infinite expressions, and he talks in a very loud voice, at a shout, taking control of the conversation, hyperemotional, undulating like a cat across the table from Mohammed, ambushing words and arguments. He manages the entire beach as he debates — giving advice to a young soccer player who approaches him, giving a contribution to a needy family, trading secrets with a party activist — a one-man band.

The two minutes passed. The conversation lasted close to four hours,          50
and in the process it slowly became clear to both sides how much trouble they were having bridging the gap between them. It was easy for the onlooker to realize that, despite the goodwill, their first line of defense was also their last. Jojo would never give up Israel as the Jewish state; Mohammed would never retreat from his goal of full equal rights with Jojo — that is, that Israel be "a country of its citizens" and not "the country of the Jewish people."

As this became apparent, the two of them became impatient, trying to catch hold of each other, to put it into other words, words that would circumvent an abyss. They did not want the victor in this confrontation to be familiar political differences. They wanted victory to go to those nameless things whose potency and insistence could be felt when Jojo's and Mohammed's faces came close together — that same link of expression and warmth, the mirror dialogue of mimicry, and the hidden thing that synchronized the two of them, as in a ceremonial warriors' dance. It was easy to imagine them changing roles and arguing, in an opposite state of affairs — each one making the other's points with the same fervor.

Mohammed: "The truth, Jojo: You too have suffered discrimination during your life in Israel, right?"

"Suffered?" Jojo guffaws. "I *grew up* on discrimination. I grew up on inequality. I grew up with the word *Moroccan*. I grew up with everything you've felt. Compared with the Ashkenazim,[11] I was discriminated against here, too."

---

[11]Jews of European origin or descent. — ED.

"So you are the first one who should understand the violent response of the Palestinians in the territories, and the desire of the Arabs in Israel for equality."

"No, no," Jojo rebuffed him. "Me, my whole outlook now is against violence. Ask why. Because all violence brings counterviolence. Mohammed tells me, 'You're strong in your country and weak in the Middle East.' But the Arabs are strong in the Middle East and weak in the world. The world, pal, is built like a ladder. For every strong man there's someone stronger than him, and what we're talking about is not how to be strong but how to reach an understanding. So that I can turn my back to you and sleep peacefully, and you the same. Look, Mohammed, for instance, wanted to be a lawyer. The country didn't try to trip him up, he went and learned law . . ." 55

"It certainly did try to trip me up!" Mohammed shot him down. "I'll give you a simple example. When I was studying they put me, in my second year, before exams, on house arrest, to keep me from passing the exams. I stayed at home for an entire year just for having quote unquote 'dared to protest' the injustices we spoke of before."

"But you studied and finished and became a lawyer, right? They didn't even give me the option you had! That is, between Jojo and Mohammed, Jojo was the one more discriminated against!"

"Look, Jojo. The Sephardim[12] were discriminated against and are still discriminated against. When I was in school, it hurt me to see that less than 1 percent of the students in the university were Arabs, and the same for the Sephardim!"

"Not only in the university! Also in the officer corps, and in the government!"

"It's very interesting how and why they block cooperation between the Sephardim and the Arabs here, even though, from a theoretical point of view, logic says that both of us, the underdogs, should work together. Let me remind you that here in your Ashdod the government — indirectly but deliberately — uses the Sephardim against us, and when there's an Arab attack against Israelis, it's you who go out to beat up the poor Arab laborers! You, the Sephardim! In my opinion, the response of the Sephardim, so hostile to the Arabs, derives first from them not having been given an education. They were not given a chance to study. They're a simple, unsophisticated public, and when the newspaper headlines and the radio stir them up — and that's directed very well from above — that public gets hot and blows up. Second — discrimination. You and I, Jojo, both our groups get screwed here in this country, because of the historical 60

---

[12]Jews of Mediterranean or Middle Eastern origin or descent. — EDS.

reality that the early waves of immigration were Ashkenazim, and after a period of hardship here, they became the ones who eat the cream. Then you became disadvantaged, and it's well known that the disadvantaged — it's very simple — wants to compensate himself by discriminating against others."

"I don't agree!" Jojo jumped up from his seat. "Take the most extreme anti-Arab movements we have, Kahane and the Moledet Party who want to transfer all the Arabs out of Israel, in all their hierarchies you'll hardly find a single Sephardi! The entire leadership is Ashkenazim! Americans! So tell me, how can that be? Where's your theory? Listen to me, Mohammed, don't go looking for university explanations. When it's a matter of life or death, there aren't any Ashkenazim and there aren't any Sephardim. Everyone comes together. Just as an Arab from Sudan hates me when I send my army into Lebanon, we're all against you when you butcher one of us. And precisely because you and I have the same mentality, you should understand that, and I'll explain to you: Our behavior, Mohammed, will be different from Grossman's in many ways, different from the Ashkenazi's. If he has a guest who comes in and talks to his wife, it won't bother him at all. If a guest comes and talks with my wife, he'll never enter my house again! That means with us, with you and with me, my wife, and to put it more generally, my honor, is a higher priority than my work, before everything. With the Ashkenazi, no. First his work, first advancement. With us, a guest comes to my house, even if two hours beforehand he ran over my son, the minute he comes to my house, first I welcome him in. I'll get him afterward — but that's separate. Our commitment is to honor. Our mentality all plays accompaniment to the first violin — our honor. And I, Jojo Abutbul, don't hate Arabs, but I would make a law that every Arab who throws a stone in the intifada[13] should be shot. Because for me the act of throwing a stone is not just throwing a stone. I'm not afraid of a stone!" Jojo shouts, the veins in his neck bulging. "But with me, in Morocco, who do you throw stones at? At a dog! At a snake! It insults me! I'm not his dog, not his snake! And don't forget, Mohammed, that same stone you throw at us today, we grew up with it, we remember it!"

Kiwan's face went sour. "First of all, the Israeli public — and you, I'm very sorry to say, are a part of it — doesn't understand what the intifada is. You don't understand the pathetic state of the people there, how bitterness built up to the point that — how did that writer of yours, S. Yizhar, put it — 'a nation rose up.' People had no way to remain silent

---

[13]The Palestinian uprising launched in 1987; see pp. 275–276. — ED.

any longer, so they used the stone. Not, God forbid, to insult you! They are certainly not treating you like a dog, God forbid. An Arab will also throw a stone at another Arab. It's simply the only tool he has to make the world hear him! . . .

The conversation was interrupted for a moment. One of the workers from the restaurant came up to Jojo to ask him something. He was limping a bit. Jojo introduced him to us as Uzi. "Actually," Jojo explained, "his name is Awad. I changed it to Uzi. Easier for him, easier for me." A deep, heavy glance curdled for a long moment between Mohammed Kiwan and Uzi. "He doesn't feel comfortable either when I call him Awad in front of people. Look at him, Mohammed. He lives in Gaza, and because he had good relations with Jews, your friends there put two bullets through his legs." Jojo sent the man off and resumed his flood of words. . . . "Here, in Israel, you and I will live in equality. According to the laws we make together. We are not allowed to decide to take the law into our own hands. If you or I start deciding which laws to obey, it will start today with the law about military service in the territories, tomorrow it will be the income tax law, and the day after it will be the law about how many wives I can have. You have to understand what the real meaning of democracy is. It's in your interest to understand, because you want democracy in the country you'll have someday. Democracy is that if I don't agree with the law I don't have a choice! And I want to hear from you now an answer to one question about all this — you, as a citizen here in the State of Israel: Will the Palestinian state, when it is established, satisfy you for good?"

Mohammed: "I accept that, with two of my reservations. That I have my basic rights, and then there's the last little problem that remains, my national identity."

Jojo leaned over at him suspiciously. "What's that? What did you say?"  65

Mohammed studied his fingers. "Give me recognition as a national minority. In other words, internal autonomy. In Israel. For the Arabs here."

"Oho!" Jojo erupts. "Hello, trouble! So now you've made me another problem — that you know in advance you're looking for as a problem, not a solution! Very nice! And here, from the start I've been telling you, Listen, let's the two of us bake two cakes. When it comes to how much flour, how many eggs we'll put in — about all that I'm willing to ask your advice. But the minute we've baked the two cakes, don't eat mine! And you, Mohammed, you should understand from your nature and I'm also appealing to your logic and your sense of justice — you can't take part of *mine* once I've given you yours! You got your country and flag and leadership, so leave me alone with my country and flag and leadership!" . . .

Jojo is again surging forward, and Mohammed's lips are already moving, mumbling his prepared answer, and it is already manifestly clear how
each argument lights a long wick of memories with the other, running
swiftly down the fuse of painful wounds. You can see how in each
segment of their conversation the entire conflict is reborn, from its shell
made of yesterday's newspapers back to Sarah the matriarch saying, "Cast
out this bondwoman and her son: for the son of this bondwoman shall
not be heir with my son, with Isaac."[14] And in the background — the sea,
which also, you may recall, was once assigned a role in the conflict.
"You're still not answering me about that, Mohammed, and time is
running out. Think about it now and tell me yes or no, in one sentence;
it has to be only one sentence, from the guts; you've got a problem,
Mohammed, maybe because you're a lawyer, you send it from the guts
to the brain and then to the mouth, and the whole time I've been talking
to you out of my nature. Will you, Mohammed, recognize without any
challenge my right to one Jewish state? Yes or no?"

Mohammed laughs. "Look, my dear Jojo, from the cumulative experience of the Arabs in Israel . . ."

"He's being a lawyer again."                                                            70

"Just a minute. Listen to me. After the Palestinian state is created, we'll
still have a problem with you. Our land. Our education. Our definition
as a national minority here. Our national symbols. I'm coming out of all
this, and in the most democratic way possible trying to change the
situation, trying to convince you — not violently — that my good is your
good. That we, the Arabs in Israel, will be a kind of, a canton, we
ourselves will manage the — "

"Canton?!" Jojo burst out, from the heart. "Now you've killed me! Now
you've actually created a state within a state!"

"Just a canton," Mohammed Kiwan blurted out, "a small kind of
authority . . ."

"A canton is a state within a state!" Jojo Abutbul repeated.

"Switzerland, for instance, is one country and it has cantons in it!"          75

"So you know what?" Jojo banged his fist in his hand. "I'll keep the
whole West Bank and Gaza under my control, and I'll make cantons
there! You decide what canton you want to live in!"

"I want to explain to you, Jojo, that autonomy, or a form of self-administration, call it whatever you want, does not diminish your future State
of Israel; it can even augment it and be helpful to solve all the problems
now, and not to leave any wounds under the skin, because I don't want

---

[14]From the Bible, Genesis 21:10. — ED.

to reach a situation where ten years from now, because of the country's discrimination against me, there will be an internal intifada."

"So there can be an intifada of Ethiopian Jews, too, and an intifada of Russians, and of the oppressed Moroccans, too! So we should make a Moroccan canton? Listen, Mohammed, what you're actually saying is that a man like the Transferist is right. Gandhi says, I'll transfer out the Arabs, by consent or by force, but when I finish there will be only Jews here. That way I prevent any wounds under the skin! Then there'll be one wound, one earth-shattering scream, but that will finish it off and it will be healthier for everyone! You live with all your brothers in your Palestinian state. You won't have double identities, you won't have a problem that you need ten words to explain who you are, Arab, Israeli, Palestinian, Muslim, and I won't have any problems either with citizens that threaten me constantly with an intifada."

Mohammed's face paled. "If you are such a racist and ignorant man that you think, like Gandhi, that in the twentieth century it's possible to transfer nations, then please. I think it will fail."

Jojo: "I'm against it! But now you're coming and scaring me, and not leaving me a choice!"                                                           80

"People aren't sheep to be taken to slaughter!" Mohammed shouted. "They'll oppose the transfer! There will be more bloodshed here!"

"Then 200,000 were killed and the problem was solved!" Jojo came back with a shout. "Then 400,000 were killed! But with that we've solved it for good!"

"But you already know from historical experience that that won't solve the problem! There will be a new problem!"

They pound the table furiously, shouting without listening. Two families of Russian immigrants, who might very well have arrived only a couple of days before, watch them in astonishment. They certainly have no conception how much this debate touches on them and their children. When Mohammed gets up for a moment to make a phone call, Jojo turns to me in amazement: "So there's a problem here that will never be solved! So whoever is strong will live! There's no other choice. Our leaders apparently know this problem. That's one of the things we don't know as citizens. . . . So we're back at square one with them again. We're in a round room without corners. No one can sit in his own corner; wherever you sit there's no corner. . . ." He whistles in amazement. "So it really has to be clear in the peace agreement that we solve this problem finally, and this is the last opportunity. If the PLO[15] is Mohammed's sole repre-

---

[15]Palestine Liberation Organization; see p. 275. — ED.

sentative, the PLO will have to commit itself to not having any more claims on the Galilee. We'll be sorry if that's not in the peace agreement." He rose, then sat down. "And even though I've been arguing until today that peace is the thing Israel needs most urgently, now I'll oppose it! With that kind of peace I'd rather not have it! Because then I didn't heal a wound, I only covered it up, and underneath, the wound will continue to become infected. Then my situation will be that much worse, because I've already handed over my best cards, Nablus and Hebron . . . very interesting . . . and he's honest, Mohammed, he's speaking sincerely. Someone will have to give way here, no arguing that. . . . I'm starting to understand what's happening here. . . . I've discovered a point of view that I, as an Israeli, never knew about."

Mohammed returns, sitting down heavily opposite him. Jojo turns to          85
him with a now quiet, slightly wounded voice. "I always thought that you and I were equal. You and I — part of the map. Sure there are problems, sure there isn't complete equality, but we try to attain it. You are an Israeli Arab, I don't interfere with your feelings or with your religion, and I'll try to help you as much as I can, so that your son will go to a good school, so that he has a future here like my son. I was ready to put my shoulders level with yours. *But* to reach a state where one day you'll want to set up a state within a state? I don't care what you call it — canton, self-administration, the Autonomous Region of the Galilee. I, Jojo Abutbul, would be making myself a misery that I never thought of! So Jojo Abutbul is sitting and thinking that if that's the case, maybe Gandhi and Sharon[16] really know what I didn't know and what you knew."

Mohammed's face isn't what it was before, either. With a weariness much greater than that caused by the conversation itself he says, "Linking my ideas and Gandhi's is very strange. Because if I wanted to be like Gandhi in my opinions and demands, I would have to say, 'Transfer the entire Jewish state of Israel! Abutbul will go to Morocco, the one from Russia will return to Russia, the one from Romania will return to Romania.' But what I'm trying to explain to my friend Jojo, unfortunately not with any great success — "

"No, no, you really succeeded! God help me if I understood right what I understood!"

They sat and talked for a few more minutes, repeating their indictments and marveling at one another, trying to find a crack in the round,

---

[16]Ariel Sharon (pronounced "sha-*rone*"), a vocal advocate of building Jewish settlements in the occupied territories. — Ed.

cornerless wall. Afterward Mohammed told of the classroom where his son studies, "in a four-meter-by-four-meter storage room, and in the winter, for there to be enough light, the teacher has to leave the door open."

"The country should be ashamed of itself," Jojo said. "It hurts me, it wounds my pride in my country, I won't accept it."

Mohammed continued to recount the daily hardships and harassments  90 he endured as an Arab, problems deriving from the law and an abuse whose source was deeper. He told of a Jewish boy who had come up to him on the Netanya beach when he was there with his two small children and demanded that he, Mohammed, leave "because you're polluting our beach." Jojo listened. Before they parted, in an effort to smooth over — in retrospect — the sting left by the conversation, a clumsy effort but still heartwarming in its magnanimity, Jojo tried to put the best possible face on Kiwan's demand for autonomy. "If we want Mohammed and his people to be loyal Israeli citizens," he said, "first we have to be loyal to them. That means we can't take what little remains to them: their honor, their pride, the little that a man needs in order to live. We won't think only of what we want from them, we'll also think of what they want from us. They're part of us. And if there's a Palestinian state next to the Jewish state, and Mohammed has the right to choose where to live and he decides to live here anyway, that will be to our benefit, it will bring us honor that he feels good and equal here. And when a man like Mohammed comes and says that he wants that, autonomy, his canton, he, in my opinion, doesn't really mean it. He wants security. He wants a way to defend himself. That's what he means when he asks for a canton. He actually wants a lot less than that — equality."

Mohammed Kiwan accepted the hand proffered him. It seemed to me that Jojo's moving gesture was more important to him — at that moment — than standing his ideological ground. Maybe Jojo really had understood Mohammed's intent. I don't know. "Maybe, as Jojo said with great justice," Kiwan responded, "it may well be that the ideas I raised with regard to the canton were raised as a kind of shield, as the result of the cumulative and very bitter experience of the way the government here has behaved to the Arab population. But for me the most important part of this meeting was that I met Jojo the man. I felt in a very human way Jojo's willingness to understand me, to identify with my suffering, and I leave here exhilarated, not because of what we said, but because of the sublime values of man and humanity. I always believed that every human being is, when it comes down to it, human. The stigmas, the labels Jew, Arab — this conversation proved that they are as important as an onionskin. And just for that I'm happy I came."

The two of them stood, exhausted from the conversation, and then, in an impulse of the moment, embraced.


## EXPLORATIONS

1. Why does Mohammed Kiwan want to meet "Jojo from Ashdod"? What common ground do these two men share?

2. What are the rungs in the ladder referred to by Jojo in paragraph 55?

3. What is the impact of David Grossman's choice to refer to Jojo Abutbul and Mohammed Kiwan by their first names? How would the essay's impact change if Grossman used their last names instead, or used designations such as "the restaurateur" and "the lawyer" or "the Arab" and "the Jew"?

4. Jojo often uses metaphors and analogies to make his points. What are the positive effects of this technique on the discussion? What are the negative effects?


## CONNECTIONS

1. Compare "Israeli Arab, Israeli Jew" with Nell McCafferty's "Peggy Deery of Derry" (p. 615) and Charles Moore's "Ireland Must Fight the IRA Too" (p. 624). What characteristics does the conflict in Israel share with the conflict in Northern Ireland? What are the important differences?

2. Reread Shelby Steele's comments on innocence in *Looking at Ourselves* (p. 515). How do Mohammed and Jojo each claim innocence? How and at what points do they use it in the ways Steele discusses?

3. According to Yoram Binur's "Palestinian Like Me" (p. 275), what automatic assumptions do many Israeli Jews make about the relative social status, intelligence, and competence of themselves and Israeli Arabs? What comments in "Israeli Arab, Israeli Jew" reflect the same assumption? What facts in this essay confirm or contradict that assumption?


## ELABORATIONS

1. "Israeli Arab, Israeli Jew" takes the form of a dialogue between Mohammed Kiwan and Jojo Abutbul. Go through the essay and record these two men's central and supporting arguments. Reread, too, Yoram Binur's "Palestinian Like Me." Based on the facts and opinions presented in these two selections, write a comparison-contrast or argumentative essay about the status of Arabs

in Israel. (You may want to do additional research to support points on which you or these characters have more opinion than fact.)

2. Jojo Abutbul and Mohammed Kiwan are divided not only by their ethnicity, religion, and politics but by the ways they think and express themselves. Look closely at each man's style of speaking — for instance, his use of data, imagery, comparison, and historical allusions. Write an essay comparing their styles and indicating how their rhetorical differences affect their response to each other.

# SLAVENKA DRAKULIĆ

## *Zagreb: A Letter to My Daughter*

Journalist and novelist Slavenka Drakulić was born in 1949 in Croatia, then part of Yugoslavia. The daughter of a former partisan and high-ranking Communist army officer, Drakulić never became a Party member herself. She joined a more controversial movement: feminism. Her first book, *Smrtni grijesi feminizma* (*The Deadly Sins of Feminism*, 1984), was a collection of articles on issues such as sex education in schools, media exploitation of women, and prostitution. Drakulić was a founding member of the executive committee of the first network of Eastern European women's groups and has served on the advisory boards of the Fourth International Interdisciplinary Congress of Women and *Ms.* magazine. The recipient of a Fulbright Fellowship for writers, she has been a commentator on Yugoslavia within the country and for Western publications including *The Nation* and *The New Republic*. After the breakup of the Soviet Bloc she traveled around Eastern Europe on assignment for *Ms.* in early 1990. She is now a contributing editor to *The Nation* and lives in Zagreb. "Zagreb: A Letter to My Daughter" was written on April 7, 1992, to her daughter Rujana; it appears in her book *The Balkan Express* (1993).

"I took off [from Zagreb] for London on Thursday, June 27, 1991, the day after the two secessionist republics of Slovenia and Croatia declared their independence from the rest of Yugoslavia, one year after holding their first free elections since World War II." So writes Drakulić in the introduction to her book *How We Survived Communism and Even Laughed* (1992). Yugoslavia had been created after World War I out of former provinces of the Austro-Hungarian Empire plus the state of Montenegro. Invaded by Germany in 1941, it became the Socialist Federal Republic of Yugoslavia after World War II. The partisan fighter Josip Broz, known as Marshal Tito, suppressed the violent rivalry between political and ethnic groups by executing his main competitor and running the country's Communist government until he died in 1980. For the next decade the Party leadership and presidency rotated among the heads of Yugoslavia's six member republics (Serbia, Croatia, Slovenia, Bosnia-Herzegovina, Macedonia, and Montenegro) and the two autonomous provinces within Serbia (Vojvodina and Kosovo). But with the end of the Soviet Union and its domination of Eastern Europe, the Yugoslav union began disintegrating as member republics seceded. Belgrade remained the capital of Serbian-dominated Yugoslavia, where Communists (now renamed Socialists) retained power. Zagreb became the capital of largely Roman Catholic Croatia; and Sarajevo became the capital of largely Muslim Bosnia. As we go to press, Serbia continues its campaign to bring all territory occupied by ethnic Serbs under Serbian control, typically by expelling or killing any others living there — a policy known as "ethnic cleansing." The violent civil war has spread from Croatia into Bosnia, where Muslims have been losing ground to Serbs despite the intervention of UN peacekeepers.

Zagreb, April 7, 1992

My dear R.,

This morning I went to your empty room. Its tidiness was so strange: Your usually unmade bed now covered with a blue quilt, a clean desk (with a sticker: A clean desk is a sign of a sick mind!), a chair without your T-shirts hanging from it, a carpet without at least three pairs of shoes scattered around and your two dogs Kiki and Charlie playing with a yellow rubber ball. I miss you, I miss your voice, your messages written with a lipstick on a bathroom mirror, your little notes that you leave on the table when you come in late at night and which I read with my first morning coffee.

Just today it is nine months since you left the country. Nine months is such a long time, I thought as I sat there for a moment, time for a baby to be born. What a strange thought. Or perhaps not so strange after all because you are now a grown woman and could decide to have a baby yourself. And because what was born in the past nine months was not a baby but a war — a crippled, disheartening child indeed, but we've learned to live with it by now. I knew that you would go anyway, you'd leave me, this house, your room where all of your children's toys and books remain side by side with your evening dresses and makeup. That thought comforts me. Besides, it's good for you to go away to live on your own and to escape my overmothering you, the typical fault of a single parent. *Living on her own will make her stronger, she will see the world, it is good for a young person to live abroad and Vienna is only six hours away:* I keep repeating this to myself like some kind of prayer. Except that I know that you didn't intend to leave so soon and so abruptly, not only me and your room, but your university and, more important, your friends here. You left behind so many things unfinished. You left because of the war.

It happened right after the "Slovenian war" or the attack of what was called the Yugoslav Federal Army on Slovenia on the night of June 26,

1991. It turned out to be only a prelude to the nightmare of Serbian aggression against Croatia and it seems certain that Bosnia will be next. As you know I was in London at that time, glued to a TV screen and a telephone. We both cried. "What do I do, mama?" you said on that first day of the war but I didn't know what to advise you. What does one say to one's child when the war begins? I didn't want you to panic after the army's attack on Slovenia, even if it is only a hundred miles from Zagreb. One part of me wanted to believe that it was not a real war (whatever that means) because a real war could not happen, it is too stupid, too absurd — an army attacking its own people, it might happen in some South American dictatorship, not in Europe. But there was another part of me that knew this is it and there was no way back. The signs were clear — people already killed in Plitvice and Borovo selo, and the smell of blood that evaporated from the newspaper pages filling the summer air with heaviness, with premonition.

One afternoon, Tuesday, July 2 — I remember with the clarity our memory reserves only for traumatic events — we were talking on the telephone and in the middle of our conversation you started screaming, "Mama, they are shooting next door!" I could hear the shots in a garden next to ours; I could visualize the garden and its high wall covered with roses and bunches of grapes hanging on the vine, the way the sun shone through its leaves at that particular moment of the late afternoon. And I could see you standing there, by the window overlooking it, lost and pale, trembling. You dropped the receiver and then I heard your voice, half cry and half whimper, as if you were no longer a human being but a wounded dog. I can hear it now, every sound that entered the receiver on that day, the distant sound of radio news in the background, the tram that passed by the house and the silence, that sudden silence that followed it. Then your boyfriend Andrej's frightened yet soft voice trying to calm you down. Hush, it's nothing, it's nothing he said, but it was too late because that was the moment when the war began for both of us, and we realized it.

I still think about the sound that you uttered that afternoon. I couldn't        5
recognize it as my child's voice. Because it wasn't a voice, not even a scream of utter fear. It was the sound of someone falling apart, of disintegration. I didn't recognize you because I was losing you. I sat at the end of a telephone line, my whole body weak, lifeless, collapsed. I don't think I've ever experienced such helplessness. Suddenly, an old image came back to me — of the two of us traveling on a train. You were two years old and had fallen asleep in my arms. I looked at your face, your eyelids almost transparent, half-open mouth, and forehead with tiny little drops of sweat. You looked so small and vulnerable as if anything in this world

could hurt you. I felt such an urge to protect you, like a sharp pain deep in the chest. The very same pain I felt sitting there and waiting to hear your voice again — only now I wasn't there to protect you. If only I was there, I thought, forgetting for a moment that you were grown up, you had to protect yourself, and I could only help. When Andrej came to the phone, he said it was probably a drunken soldier, nothing more. I should not worry, he said. But *worry* was not the right word. I was calm. At that moment I knew that if you didn't get out of there I'd lose you. Not from a bullet or shelling, but your mind would crack and you would enter a void where no one could reach you any longer. I know you well, I know how much you can take, and I can recognize the signs when you reach the edge. The day after, your voice still broken, different, you told me that almost all of your hair had turned gray. Ever since that day, I thank God that you are not a man, that I am the mother of a woman. To have a son in wartime is the worst curse that can befall a mother, no matter what anyone says.

You could not imagine how lonely I get sitting in your room, a kind of clutching feeling in my breast, a choking knot in my throat. Don't worry, I don't cry, I know you wouldn't like it. I just think of what this war is doing to us, breaking our lives in two, into *before* and *after*. I know that you are all right, as much as you could be living in a foreign country. The most important thing is that you are safe, that you are holding up. Living in a country at war, I try to convince myself that what happened to the two of us is nothing, we are just separated, that's all, we'd have had to face that anyway. It couldn't be compared to what other people have had to go through, loss of lives, of homes, of everything. But in suffering there are no comparisons, I cannot suffer less because someone else is suffering more, any more than I can take someone else's burden of pain. I have my own, as little as it may seem from outside. Our emotions are not based on the objective truth anyway so why should I bother with justifying my feelings? Nonetheless, I do feel guilty in another way.

There are two photos of you that I like best and, as you can imagine, I put them on the wall (yes, I know, you hate it but you have to understand that I need this): one as a girl of three dressed in jeans, with curly hair and traces of chocolate around her mouth. The other one is of a sophisticated young lady holding a cigarette (much as I disapprove of it!) taken when you were seventeen. Is it that cigarette, or rather, the way you hold it, the way you inhale and puff away the smoke, that broad gesture that reminds me of your father. I wonder what he thinks about what is going on here, sitting in Toronto. Have you heard from him recently? We married when I was eighteen and he was nineteen. I was aware that he was from a Serbian family while I was from a Croatian one, but it didn't mean anything to me, one way or the other. World War II was long over when the two of us were born, and throughout my life it seemed to me that everyone was trying to escape its shadow, to forget and just live their lives. Your father and I never even discussed the different nationality of our families. Not because it was forbidden, but because it was unimportant to the majority of our generation. It wasn't an issue. Maybe it was a consequence of the repression of the Communist regime, of the brainwashing of our education system, the plan to create an artificial "Yugoslav" nation — the fact is that in the 1980 census 1.5 million declared themselves Yugoslav, people of a nonexistent nation, and interestingly enough, they were all born after the war and approximately thirty years old. Or maybe it was just the natural course of things, I don't know. I just know that we were not interested in the past, in who killed whom and why, but in our own lives. The tragedy and the paradox of this situation now is that you will have to decide, to take his or my side, to become Croat or Serb, to take on and suffer his and my "guilt" of marrying the "wrong" nationality. In the war there is no middle position. All of a sudden, you as Croat or Serb become responsible for what all other Croats or Serbs are doing. You are reduced to a single nationality — almost sentenced to it, since nationality in the war brings a danger of getting killed just because of it. I am not talking about who is wrong or who is right in this war, the facts are known by now. I am telling you about the situation when you are forced to choose, to identify with something that has been unknown to you; a total abstraction. But you know it all. "I am from Zagreb," you said and perhaps it is the only right answer, to be a Citizen. But not now. Not here.

This war happened *nel mezzo del cammin di nostra vita*[1] so if anything, I should be old enough to try to understand where it comes from and how it started. In fact I could see it coming closer and closer with each passing year, then month, then day. One could detect the gradual return to the past long before 1989 with Milošević's invocation of Serbian nationalist feelings and hatred, first toward Albanians from Kosovo, then toward non-Serbians throughout the whole country — remember how far from us it all looked, how ready we were to deny the coming danger? There were other signs — the tallying up of war victims, justification of war criminals, the resuscitating of old national myths, the revival of religion on both the Catholic and Orthodox sides. But one could still attempt to see it as a reinterpretation of history, a necessary purge of postwar myths about the Communist revolution, if only it hadn't been

---

[1]Italian, "in the middle of the road of our life." — ED.

aimed at an entirely different purpose: at national homogenization and the growing antagonism between the nations. Long before the real war, we had a media war, Serbian and Croatian journalists attacking the political leaders from the opposite republic as well as each other as if in some kind of dress rehearsal. So I could see a spiral of hatred descending upon us, but until the first bloodshed it seemed to operate on the level of a power struggle that had nothing to do with the common people. When the first houses were burned down on Croatian territory, when neighbors of a different nationality in the mixed villages started to kill each other, then it became our war too, of your generation and mine. Not out of ideology, but for the simple reason that it changed our whole life. Yours more than mine, because men from my generation are almost too old — with their gray hair and potbellies, they'd look pretty silly in those camouflage uniforms. How many of your friends will survive? But what did *you* and your generation born in 1968 know of that past, of the hatred that is haunting us now?

After all, it was your grandfathers who fought in World War II. They had fought as Tito's Partisans, Ustashas or Chetniks.[2] Afterward, hoping for a brighter future, they rebuilt the devastated country according to Bolshevik principles, ruled by the Communist Party as the vanguard of the people. All of them lived long enough to see the Party become corrupt and repressive, but only some of them lived to see the Communist regime begin to fall apart in 1989. Yet, none of them believed that history could repeat itself. It was my generation that grew up in times of scarcity when milk and butter, meat and clothes were rationed (you know what my spine looks like because I still suffer from the consequences of rickets). Sometimes we tasted powdered milk from UNRRA packages — it was so sweet that we licked it from our palms like some special kind of sweet. Or we'd eat yellow cheddar cheese from the cans, or margarine, or "Truman's eggs," as we called powdered eggs. People moved to the cities to help build up heavy industry; we all went to schools, education was a big thing then. Married, we tried different combinations to escape living in crowded communal apartments shared by two or three families. We enrolled in the Communist Party as our fathers did, but only because it was so much easier to get jobs and promotions if you did.

In the meantime your generation of the late sixties and early seventies   10
grew up fast. You would listen to your grandaddy's war stories after family lunch on Sundays with an obvious air of boredom. You couldn't care less

---

[2]Partisan leader Marshal Tito united Croats (called Ustashas or Eustace) and Serbs (called Chetniks) under the banner of communism. — ED.

about it; everything before you were born belonged to the same category of ancient history — World War II, World War I, the Napoleonic Wars, the wars between Athens and Sparta. Sometimes you watched the old movies with Partisans and Germans and Chetniks and Ustashas, but with ironic detachment and the sophistication of someone who knows everything there is to know about Spielberg, Jarmusch, and so on. You watched us buying better cars to replace the Fiat 750, a color television, a weekend house on the Adriatic coast. We went together to Trieste or Graz to buy Nike sneakers, Levi's, Benetton pullovers, and Walkmans for you. And computers — for you too, because we were technologically illiterate. You learned languages — English, of course, was the most important — and started to travel abroad on your own and your values became more and more removed from ours: career, money, but no politics, please. Now you are back in those old movies: You have to declare your nationality despite being barely aware of the past. Maybe at the beginning it looked like a Rambo movie: Ray Bans, Uzis, bandanas tied around your heads. But too many of you have died by now for the rest to believe it is just a game. You no longer watch *Apocalypse Now,* you live it. At least you are defending your own country and I cannot but keep wondering, as I'm sure you do too, what do boys on the other side believe they are doing? For me, every death is senseless because the war itself is senseless — but if there are degrees of senselessness, their death must be the more senseless.

You were already gone when I came across an article in a local newspaper. Entitled "Will You Come to My Funeral?" it was about the younger generation and how they feel about the war. I remember an answer by Pero M., a student from Zagreb:

> Perhaps I don't understand half of what is going on, but I know that all this is happening because of the fifty or so fools who, instead of having their sick heads seen to, are getting big money and flying around in helicopters. I'm seventeen and I want a real life, I want to go to the cinema, to the beach . . . to travel freely, to work. I want to telephone my friend in Serbia and ask how he is, but I can't because all the telephone lines are cut off. I might be young and pathetic-sounding, but I don't want to get drunk like my older brother who is totally hysterical or to swallow tranquilizers like my sister. It doesn't lead anywhere. I would like to create something, but now I can't.

And then he said to the reporter interviewing him something that struck me:

> Lucky you, you are a woman, you'll only have to help the wounded. I will have to fight. Will you come to my funeral?

This is what he said in the early autumn of 1991. I could almost picture him, the streetwise kid from a Zagreb suburb, articulate, smart, probably with an earring and a T-shirt with some funny nonsense on it, hanging out in a bar with a single Coke the entire evening, talking about this or that rock group. The boy bright enough to understand that he might die and that there is nothing that he could do about it. But we — me, you, that woman reporter — we are women and women don't get drafted. They get killed, but they are not expected to fight. After all someone has to bury the dead, to mourn, and to carry on life, and it puts us in a different position in the war. At bottom, war is a man's game. Perhaps it is much easier to kill if you don't give birth. But I am reluctant to say what should follow from this: that women don't participate, or conduct or decide about wars, because they do. Not as women, but as citizens. As citizens they contribute, support, hail, exercise orders, help, and work for war — or they protest, boycott, withdraw support, lobby, and work against it. This is where our responsibility lies and we cannot be excused.

I am also not excused for what is going on in my country now. Earlier in this letter I mentioned that I felt guilty. Well, my guilt or responsibility, depending on how you define it, is in believing. It is in the political naiveté of my generation (even if '68 taught us how to think politically). We grew up in an already hypocritical atmosphere, not believing in the Communist ideology but with the regime still there to be reckoned with. As we couldn't see the end of it we conformed, believing that it was possible to change it into what we insisted on calling socialism "with a human face." Lucky Hungarians, for they suffered in 1956, lucky Czechs and Slovaks, who suffered in 1968. What happened to us, then? Under only mild repression and with a good standard of living, we in Yugoslavia didn't really suffer.

Recently an American friend asked me how it happened that the most liberal and best-off Communist country was the one that now had the war. There are analyses, no doubt, that could give more competent answers to this question. But for me, going back and remembering it all, the answer is so simple that I'm almost ashamed of it: We traded our freedom for Italian shoes. People in the West always tend to forget one key thing about Yugoslavia, that we had something that made us different from the citizens of the Eastern Bloc: We had a passport, the possibility to travel. And we had enough surplus money with no opportunity to invest in the economy (which was why everyone who could invested in building weekend houses in the mid-sixties) and no outlet but to exchange it on the black market for hard currency and then go shopping. Yes, shopping to the nearest cities in Austria or Italy. We bought everything — clothes, shoes, cosmetics, sweets, coffee, even fruit and toilet paper. I remember times when my mother who lives in a city only a short drive from Trieste would go there every week to get in stores what she couldn't get here. Millions and millions of people crossed the border every year just to savor the West and to buy something, perhaps as a mere gesture. But this freedom, a feeling that you are free to go if you want to, was very important to us. It seems to me now to have been a kind of a contract with the regime: We realize you are here forever, we don't like you at all but we'll compromise if you let us be, if you don't press too hard.

We were different then, so we are different now: It is we who have the    15
war. We didn't build a political underground of people with liberal, democratic values ready to take over the government; not because it was impossible, but on the contrary, because the repression was not hard enough to produce the need for it. If there is any excuse it is in the fact that we were deprived of the sense of future. This was the worst thing that communism did to people. What is our future now? Your future? No one asks that question and I don't like it. I am afraid this war will last and while there is a war going on even in one part of the country, there is no future. And because I am a typically selfish mother, I don't want you to be deprived of the future too. Once was enough.

Forgive me for this long, confused, and maybe pathetic letter, but I had to write it. Stay well, all my love is with you.

                                                                        Your Mother


## EXPLORATIONS

1. What mood does Slavenka Drakulić create in her opening paragraph, and by what means? How and when does the essay's mood change?

2. In paragraph 7 Drakulić writes: "We were not interested in the past, in who killed whom and why, but in our own lives." Does she regard this as good or bad? Why? How can you tell?

3. What effects does Drakulić achieve by using the form of a personal letter? How would the essay's tone change if Drakulić wrote in the third person *about* her daughter instead of in the second person *to* her?

4. At what points in her letter does Drakulić use incomplete sentences? What is their impact?

## CONNECTIONS

1. Drakulić suggests that political activism was minimal in Yugoslavia under communism because "we were deprived of the sense of future" (para. 15). What comments in "Israeli Arab, Israeli Jew" (p. 629) indicate that Mohammed's and Jojo's strong political views are linked to a sense of the future?

2. What comments about ancient hatreds by Susanne Hoeber Rudolph and Lloyd I. Rudolph in *Looking at Ourselves* (p. 602) are supported by Drakulić's letter?

3. What similarities can you identify between Drakulić's essay and Rosemary L. Bray's selection in *Looking at Ourselves* (p. 605)?

## ELABORATIONS

1. Choose a selection in this book on an issue that concerns you, such as racial discrimination or "future shlock." Write an essay in the form of a letter to your child (real or hypothetical) expressing your hopes, fears, sympathy, frustration, or all of these with regard to that issue.

2. "We traded our freedom for Italian shoes," writes Drakulić (para. 14). Are we in the West in any danger of falling into a similar trap — trading our freedom for materialistic gains? Write a comparison-contrast or cause-and-effect essay explaining why we are or are not.

## *The Los Riscos Mine*

Isabel Allende (pronounced ah-*yen*-day) was born in 1942 in Lima, Peru (see p. 224), where her father was stationed as a diplomat. The family traveled extensively: Allende discovered *The Thousand and One Nights* at age twelve in Beirut, Lebanon. Back home in Chile, she completed high school in the capital city of Santiago and got a job with the Food and Agriculture Organization (FAO) of the United Nations. Allende became a journalist when she had to fill television time for the FAO. She won a fellowship to study radio and television in Belgium; in Chile she continued to work in television and wrote plays and a magazine column. In 1970 her uncle, Dr. Salvador Allende Gossens, became president — the first Marxist-Leninist freely elected by a non-Communist country. Three years later he was ousted and killed in a U.S.-backed military coup led by Augusto Pinochet Ugarte, who ran a brutally repressive right-wing dictatorship until 1990. Isabel Allende and her family fled to Venezuela, where she switched from journalism to fiction. Her first novel, *La casa de los espiritus* (1982; *The House of the Spirits*, 1985) became an international best-seller. "The Los Riscos Mine" comes from her second novel, *De amor y de sombra* (1984; *Of Love and Shadows*, 1987, translated by Margaret Sayers Peden). Allende now lives in California, the setting for her most recent book, *The Infinite Plan* (1993). Her novels and stories have been translated into over thirty languages; some will soon appear as films.

Chile is a long strip of seacoast that runs along western South America from Peru and Bolivia to the continent's southern tip. The Andes Mountains divide it on the east from Argentina. Spain took northern Chile from the native Incas in the mid-1500s; the southern Araucanian Indians held out for another three centuries. Chile won its independence in the early 1800s under José de San Martín and Bernardo O'Higgins, who became its first dictator. A constitution adopted in 1925 brought democracy, which lasted until the overthrow of President Allende. Under a new constitution in 1980, dictator Pinochet became president for an eight-year term. At its end he was forced to hold a plebiscite which rejected his bid to stay in power. In January 1990, Pinochet finally stepped down, yielding to the election of Patricio Aylwin as the head of a seventeen-party coalition. Three months later President Aylwin charged a commission to investigate disappearances of political prisoners during Pinochet's regime.

Afterward, Irene [Beltrán] and Francisco [Leal] would ask themselves at what precise moment the course of their lives had changed, and they would point to the fateful Monday they entered the abandoned Los Riscos mine. But it may have been before that — say, the Sunday they met Evangelina Ranquileo, or the evening they promised [her mother] Digna they would help in her search for the missing girl; or possibly their roads had been mapped out from the beginning, and they had no choice but to follow them.

They drove to the mine on Francisco's motorcycle — more practical in rugged terrain than a car — carrying a few tools, a thermos of hot coffee, and the photographic equipment. They told no one the purpose of their trip; they were both obsessed with the feeling that what they were about to do was madness. Ever since they had decided to go, at night, to a place they had never been before, and open a mine without permission, they both knew such foolhardiness could cost them their lives.

They studied the map until they knew it by heart and were sure they could reach their destination without asking questions that would raise suspicions. There was no danger in the softly rolling countryside, but once they turned onto the steep mountain roads where shadows lengthen long before sunset, the landscape became wild and lonely, and echoes returned thoughts magnified by the distant cry of eagles. Uneasy, Francisco had debated the prudence of taking Irene along on an adventure whose outcome he could not foresee.

"You're not taking me anywhere. I'm the one who's taking you," she had joked, and perhaps she was right.

A rusty but still legible sign announced that the area was patrolled and    5
entry forbidden. Several threatening rows of barbed wire blocked access to the property, and for a minute Irene and Francisco were tempted to seize the pretext and retreat; immediately, however, they set aside that subterfuge and looked for a break in the network of wire that was large enough for the motorcycle to pass through. The sign and the fence further confirmed their hunch that there was something here to be discovered. Just as they had planned, night was upon them, helping to cloak their movements, by the time they reached the mine. The entrance to the mine drilled in the mountainside looked like a mouth shouting a soundless scream. Sealed with rocks, packed dirt, and masonry, it gave the impression that no one had been near it for years. Loneliness had settled in to stay, obscuring marks of a trail or any memory of life. They hid the motorcycle in some bushes and scouted the area to be sure there were no watchmen on patrol. The search calmed them somewhat since they found no trace of human life but only, some hundred meters from the mine, a miserable hut abandoned to wind and weeds. The wind had

blown off half its roof, one wall lay flat on the ground, and vegetation had invaded the interior, covering everything with a carpet of wild grasses. Such a deserted and forgotten place so near Los Riscos and the highway seemed very odd.

"I'm afraid," whispered Irene.

"So am I."

They opened the thermos and drank a long swallow of coffee, a comfort to both body and soul. They joked a little, pretending this was just a game; each tried to make the other believe that nothing bad could happen to them, that they were protected by a guardian angel. It was a clear moonlit night, and their eyes soon grew accustomed to the darkness. They took the pick and flashlight and walked toward the shaft. Neither of them had ever been inside a mine, and they imagined it as a cavern deep beneath the earth. Francisco remembered the tradition that forbade the presence of women in mines because they were thought to bring on underground disasters, but Irene mocked that superstition, determined to continue at any cost.

Francisco attacked the entrance with his pick. He had little skill when it came to physical labor; he scarcely knew how to handle the pick, and soon realized that the job would take longer than they had planned. Irene did not attempt to help him but sat on a rock, her heavy sweater pulled tightly around her, huddled against the wind blowing from the surrounding mountains. She jumped at every sound, afraid that wild animals might be circling around, or, what would be worse, that soldiers were spying on them from the darkness. At first they tried not to make any noise, but they quickly resigned themselves to the inevitable; the ring of steel against rock resounded through gorges and ravines that trapped the echo and repeated it a hundred times. If there was a patrol in the area, as the sign warned, there would be no escape. Before a half hour had passed, Francisco's fingers were stiff and his hands covered with blisters, but his efforts had opened a hole that would allow them to remove loose stones and dirt with their hands. Now Irene helped, and soon they had opened a gap wide enough to slip through.

"Ladies first," joked Francisco, motioning to the hole.                    10

As her answer, Irene handed him the flashlight and stepped back a couple of steps. Francisco thrust head and arms through the opening, shining the light inside. A rush of fetid air assaulted his nostrils. He was tempted to retreat, but he told himself he hadn't come this far to give up before he began. The beam carved a circle of light in the darkness, revealing a small chamber. It was not at all what he had imagined: It was a room excavated from the hard entrails of the mountain, opening onto two narrow tunnels blocked with debris. The wood scaffolding set there to prevent cave-ins when the ore was being mined was still in place, but the timbers had been eaten by time and were so rotten that some were in place only by the grace of a miracle and they looked as if a breath would bring them crashing down. Francisco flashed his light around the room, wanting to see what awaited him before he crawled inside. Suddenly something ran over his arm a few inches from his face. He cried out, more surprised than frightened, and the flashlight fell from his hand. Outside, Irene heard him and, fearing something horrible, grabbed him by the legs and began to pull.

"What was it?" she exclaimed, her heart in her mouth.

"Nothing, only a rat."

"Let's get out of here, I don't like this a bit!"

"Wait, I'll just take a quick look inside."  15

Francisco wriggled through the opening, carefully avoiding sharp rocks, and disappeared, swallowed by the mouth in the mountain. Irene watched the blackness envelop her friend and felt a pang of anxiety in spite of the fact that her reason told her danger lay outside the mine, not inside. If they were caught, they could expect a bullet in the head and a quick burial on the spot. People had died for far less. She remembered all the ghost stories Rosa had told her when she was a little girl: the Devil lurking in mirrors to frighten the vain; the boogeyman carrying a sack filled with kidnapped children; dogs with crocodile scales on their backs, and cloven hooves; two-headed men who crouched in the corners to catch little girls who slept with their hands beneath the sheet. Cruel stories that had caused more than one nightmare, but tales so spellbinding she could not stop listening; she would beg Rosa to tell her another, as she trembled with fright, wanting to cover her ears and squeeze her eyes shut so she could not hear them but, at the same time, avid to know every detail. Did the Devil wear clothes or was he naked? Did the boogeyman smell bad? Did pet dogs also turn into ferocious beasts? Could a two-headed man enter a room protected by a picture of the Virgin? That night, waiting at the mine entrance, Irene again experienced the mixture of fright and attraction she had felt in the long-ago days of her Nana's terrifying tales. Finally she decided to follow Francisco and, being both small and agile, she easily crawled through the hole. It took only a few seconds to get used to the darkness. The smell, though, was unbearable, like breathing a deadly poison. She took the kerchief tied around her waist and used it to cover the lower half of her face.

They walked around the cavern and examined the two passageways. The tunnel on the right seemed to be closed only with rubble and loose dirt, while the one on the left was sealed with masonry. They chose the easier and began to move rocks and scratch away the dirt at the mouth of the first tunnel. As they dug, the stench grew stronger, and often they had to go to the entry they had crawled through and lean outside to draw a breath of fresh air, which seemed to them as clean and healthful as a mountain stream.

"What exactly are we looking for?" asked Irene as her raw hands began to burn.

"I don't know," Francisco replied, and continued working in silence, for even the vibration of their voices made the rotted supports quiver.

They were nervous and apprehensive. They stole glances over their    20 shoulders, peering into the blackness behind them, imagining watching eyes, stealthy shadows, whispers from the far side of the room. They heard the old timbers creak and, between their feet, the furtive scurrying of rodents. The air was close and heavy.

Irene tugged at a large rock with all her might. She worked it back and forth, loosened it, and it rolled free at her feet: The light of the flashlight revealed a dark gaping hole. Without thinking, she thrust her hand inside and at that instant felt a terrible scream rising from the pit of her stomach; the sound filled the chamber, ricocheting against the walls as a muffled and alien echo she did not recognize as her own voice. She flung herself against Francisco, who covered her with his body and pushed her against the wall just as a beam crashed from the ceiling. For a moment that seemed eternal, they stood embraced, eyes closed, almost without breathing, and when finally silence returned and the dust raised by the collapse of the beam had settled, they were able to rescue the flashlight and make sure that their exit had not been blocked. Still holding Irene, Francisco pointed the light to the spot where the rock had rolled free, and the first discovery of that cave of horrors leaped toward them. It was a human hand — or, rather, what remained of one.

Francisco pulled Irene outside and, holding her close, forced her to breathe great gulps of the pure night air. When she was able to stand without his help, he brought the thermos and poured her coffee. She was beside herself, speechless, trembling, unable to hold the cup. Francisco held it to her lips, as he would for an invalid; he stroked her hair and tried to calm her, telling her that they had found what they had come to find; surely the body was that of Evangelina Ranquileo, and even though it was gruesome, it couldn't hurt them, it was only a dead body. Although the words had no meaning for her — she was still too shocked to recognize them as her own language — the cadence of his voice lulled her, consoling her slightly. Much later, when she was more herself, Francisco knew he must finish the job they had come to do.

"Wait here for me. I'm going back into the mine for a few minutes. Can you stay here alone?"

Irene nodded wordlessly, and, pulling up her legs like a boy, she buried her head between her knees, trying not to think, not to hear, not to see, not even to breathe, suspended in her unbearable anguish while Francisco, carrying the camera and with the kerchief tied over his face, returned to the tomb.

He pulled away rocks and brushed aside dirt until he had exposed the     25
entire body of Evangelina Ranquileo Sánchez. He recognized her by the color of her hair. She was partially covered by a poncho; she was barefoot, and was dressed in something like petticoats or a nightgown. Her body was in such an advanced state of decomposition — putrefying in a broth in which maggots were feeding, fermenting in her own desolation — that he had to call on every ounce of his strength to control his nausea and get on with his work. He was a man with a great deal of self-control; he had had professional experience with cadavers and he had a strong stomach, but he had never seen anything like this before. The despicable place, the inescapable stench, and his mounting fear — all contributed to his undoing. He could not breathe. Hurriedly, he shot several photographs, not bothering about focus or distance, hastened by the bile that rose in his throat with each flash lighting the scene. He finished as quickly as humanly possible, and fled from that sepulcher.

In the fresh air he dropped the camera and flashlight and fell to the ground on his knees, head sunk to his chest, trying to relax and conquer his retching. The stench clung to his skin like a plague, and etched on his retinas was the image of Evangelina stewing in her last consternation. Irene had to help him to his feet.

"What do we do now?"

"Close the mine, then we'll see," he said as soon as he was able to reclaim his voice from the fiery claws gripping his chest.

They piled up the stones they had removed, and closed the entrance, stunned, nervous, working with frenzy; it was as if in sealing the mine they could erase its contents from their minds and turn time back to the moment before they had known the truth; as if they could again live innocently in a radiant reality, removed from that awful discovery. Francisco took Irene by the hand and led her to the ruined hut, the only visible refuge on the hill. . . .

Father José Leal, when not working as a plumber with blowtorch or     30
monkey wrench, was kept busy with countless activities in the poor community where he had chosen to live in accordance with his incurable passion for serving his fellow man. He lived in a large, densely populated neighborhood that was invisible from the road, hidden behind walls and a row of poplar trees with naked branches stretching toward the sky — a

place where not even vegetation thrived. Behind that discreet screen lay
dirt streets and torrid heat in summer; mud and rain in winter; shacks
constructed from discarded materials; garbage; clotheslines; dogfights.
Idle men passed their hours in little groups on street corners, while
children played with bits of junk and women struggled to prevent bad
from deteriorating into worse. It was a world of deprivation and penury
in which the only consolation was solidarity. Here no one dies of hunger,
José said, in explanation of the communal stewpots, because before that
last desperate step is taken, someone holds out a helping hand. Neighbors
formed groups and contributed whatever each could scavenge for the
soup shared by all. Distant relatives moved in with those who at least had
a roof over their heads. In the soup kitchens the Church had set up for
the children, a daily ration of food was apportioned to the youngest. Even
after many years, the priest's heart still melted when he saw the freshly
bathed and combed children standing in line for their turn to enter the
shed where rows of aluminum plates of food waited on huge tables, while
their brothers and sisters, too old now to be fed by charity, loitered around,
hoping for scraps. Two or three women cooked the food the priests
obtained by means of pleas and spiritual threats. Besides serving the food,
the women watched to see that the children ate all their portions, because
many hid food and bread to take home to a family that had nothing to
put in the cooking pot but a few vegetables picked up on the rubbish
heap behind the market and a bone that more than once had been boiled
to lend a hint of flavor to the broth.

José lived in a wooden shack similar to many others, although his was
larger because it also served as an office to minister to the temporal and
spiritual needs of his disconsolate flock. Francisco, along with a lawyer
and a doctor, took his turn treating the inhabitants in their disputes,
illnesses, and depressions; all of them frequently felt totally useless, knowing there were no solutions to the mass of tragic problems confronting
their patients.

Francisco found his brother ready to go out, dressed in his workman's
overalls and carrying the heavy bag containing his plumber's tools. After
making sure that they were alone, Francisco opened his pack. While the
priest, turning paler and paler, looked at the photographs, Francisco told
him the story, beginning with Evangelina Ranquileo and her attacks of
saintliness — José had known something of this when he helped them
look for her in the morgue — and ending at the moment when the
remains in the photographs lay at their feet in the mine. Francisco
omitted nothing but the name of Irene Beltrán, in order to keep her safe
from any possible consequences.

José Leal listened to the end, then sat in an attitude of silent meditation, staring at the floor. His brother guessed that he was struggling to

gain control of his emotions. When he was young, any form of abuse, injustice, or evil had sent a searing electric current through him, blinding him with rage. His years in the priesthood and a gradual mellowing of his character had given him the strength to control these fits of anger and — with the methodical discipline of humility — to accept the world as an imperfect work where God puts souls to the test. Finally he looked up. His face was once again serene and his voice sounded calm.

"I will speak with the Cardinal," he said. . . .

Wednesday dawned as sunny as a midsummer day. The commission arrived in Los Riscos in three automobiles, headed by the Auxiliary Bishop and directed by José Leal, who, instructed by his brother, had marked the route on a map. Journalists, representatives of international organizations, and a number of attorneys were observed from a distance by the General's agents, who had kept them under surveillance since the evening before.

Irene wanted to be a part of the team from her magazine, but Francisco would not allow it. Journalists had no guarantee of safety, unlike the other members of the commission, whose positions afforded them a measure of security. If Irene and Francisco were ever connected with the discovery of the bodies, they could not hope to escape with their lives; and there was a good possibility they would be, since both . . . were known to have made inquiries about the missing girl and had maintained contact with the Ranquileo family.

The cars halted a short distance from the mine. José Leal was the first to attack the rubble at the entrance, using to advantage his bearlike strength and his familiarity with hard labor. The others followed his lead, and within a few minutes they had made an opening. From their position, the Security Corps communicated by radio to inform the General that the suspects were trespassing and opening a sealed mine in spite of posted warnings: We await instructions, General, sir; over and out. Limit yourself to observation, as I ordered you, and make no move to intervene. No matter what happens, do not get into a confrontation with those people; over and out.

The Auxiliary Bishop had decided to take the initiative, and he was the first to enter the mine. He was not an agile man, but he managed to get his legs through the opening and then, twisting like a mongoose, slipped the rest of his body inside. The stench struck him like a club, but it was not until his eyes became adjusted to the darkness and he saw the cadaver of Evangelina Ranquileo that he uttered a cry that brought the others running. He was assisted back through the entrance, helped to his feet, and led to the shade of the trees to recover his breath. Meanwhile, José Leal improvised torches from rolled newspapers, suggested that everyone cover his face with a handkerchief, and led the members of the commission, one by one, inside the sepulcher, where, half kneeling, each saw the decomposing body of the girl and the Vesuvius of piled-up bones, hair, and tattered cloth. Every stone they removed revealed new human remains. Once outside, no one was capable of speech; trembling and pale, the observers stared at one another, struggling to comprehend the enormity of what they had seen. José Leal was the only one who had the heart to close the entrance again; he was thinking of dogs that might nose among the bones, or of the possibility that the authors of those crimes, warned by the gaping hole, might spirit away the evidence — a futile precaution, since some two hundred yards away sat a parked police van equipped with European telescopes and North American infrared-ray machines that informed the Colonel of the contents of the mine almost at the same moment the Auxiliary Bishop saw them for himself. But the General's instructions are very clear: Don't interfere with the priests, wait until they take the next step to see what the shit they have in mind. After all, there's nothing there but a few unidentified bodies.

It was still early when the commission returned to the city; after swearing not to comment, they went their separate ways, planning to meet that evening to give an account of their activities to the Cardinal.

That night the lights in the Archiepiscopal Residence remained on    40
until dawn, to the discomfiture of the spies stationed in the treetops with apparatus acquired in the Far East that enabled them to see through walls in the dark. But we still don't know what they're planning, General, sir. It's past curfew now and they're still talking and drinking coffee. If you give us the word, we'll break in, search the place, and arrest everyone there. What did you say? Idiots! Try not to be such assholes!

At dawn the visitors left and the prelate bade them good-bye at the door. Only he seemed serene, for his soul was at peace and he was a stranger to fear. He went to bed for a while, and after breakfast he called the Chief Justice of the Supreme Court to ask him to receive as expeditiously as possible three of his envoys, the bearers of a letter of great importance. One hour later the envelope was in the hands of the Justice, who wished he were on the other side of the world, anywhere far away from this ticking time bomb that must inevitably explode.

To the Honorable Chief Justice,
The Supreme Court

Señor Chief Justice:

Some days ago a person communicated to a priest, in the secrecy of the confessional, that he had knowledge and proof of the existence of a number of cadavers which were to be found in a place whose location he supplied to the priest. The priest, authorized by the informant, called the aforementioned information to the attention of ecclesiastical authorities.

With the purpose of establishing the veracity of the information, yesterday, in the early hours of the morning, a commission composed of the signers of this letter, the directors of the newsmagazines *Acontecer* and *Semana*, respectively, along with officials from the Office for Human Rights, went to the location described by the informant. The site is a mine, at present abandoned, located among the foothills in the vicinity of Los Riscos.

Once at the site, and after removing the loose matter that blocked the mouth of the mine, the aforementioned individuals corroborated the existence of remains corresponding to an undetermined number of human beings. Following this verification, we cut short our inspection of the site, as our only objective was to confirm the gravity of the report received; we were not authorized to proceed further in a matter more appropriate for judicial investigation.

Nevertheless, it is our opinion that the appearance of the locale and the disposition of the remains whose existence we have established substantiate the eventual discovery of a large number of victims.

The public outcry that the aforementioned information may evoke has caused us to bring the matter directly to the attention of the highest judicial power in the land, so that the Supreme Tribunal may adopt the necessary measures for a rapid and exhaustive investigation.

With regards to Your Honor,
    we, the undersigned, remain,

                                        Very sincerely yours,

                                        Alvaro Urbaneja (Auxiliary Bishop)
                                        Jesús Valdovinos (Vicar General)
                                        Eulogio García de la Rosa (Attorney)

The Chief Justice knew the Cardinal. He recognized that this was not a skirmish and that the Cardinal was prepared to wage all-out war. He must have all the aces up his sleeve, because he was too astute to lay that pile of bones in *his* hands and challenge him to bring the forces of law to bear unless he was very sure. It required no great experience to conclude that the perpetrators of those crimes had acted with the approval of the government, and so, having no confidence in the authorities, the Church had intervened. He dried the sweat from his forehead and neck and reached for a pill for his high blood pressure and another for his heart, fearing that his moment of truth had arrived after years of juggling justice in accord with the General's instructions; after years of "losing" files and tying up the Vicariate's lawyers in bureaucratic red tape; after years of fabricating laws to fit, retroactively, recently invented crimes. Oh, why didn't I retire in time, why didn't I take my pension while it was still possible to do so with dignity, go cultivate my roses in peace and pass into history free of this burden of guilt and shame that won't let me sleep by night and that haunts me by day if I relax for so much as an instant; it's not as if I did it from personal ambition; I only meant to serve the nation, as the General himself asked me to do a few days after he assumed command; ah, but it's too late now, that damned mine is yawning at my feet like my own grave, and since the Cardinal decided to intervene, these dead cannot be silenced as so many have been; I should have retired on the day of the military coup, the day they bombed the presidential palace, jailed the ministers, dissolved the Congress, when the eyes of the world were focused on us, waiting for someone to stand up and defend the constitution; that is the day I should have gone home, claiming that I was old, that I was ill; that is what I should have done instead of placing myself at the service of the Junta, instead of undertaking the purge of my own courts of law.

The first impulse of the Chief Justice of the Supreme Court was to call the Cardinal and make him a proposition, but even as the thought occurred to him, he realized that this matter was beyond his capacity as a negotiator. He picked up the telephone, dialed the secret number, and spoke directly with the General.

A circle of iron, helmets, and boots was drawn around Los Riscos mine, but nothing had been able to prevent the rumor from spreading like a fire storm, from mouth to mouth, house to house, valley to valley, until it was known everywhere and a deep shudder had run along the spine of the nation. The soldiers held the curious at bay but did not dare block the passage of the Cardinal and his commission as they had blocked journalists and the observers from foreign countries drawn there by the atrocity of the massacre. At eight o'clock on Friday morning, personnel from the Department of Criminal Investigation, wearing masks and rubber gloves, began removal of the terrible evidence under instructions from the Supreme Court, which had in turn received its instructions from the General: Open the damned mine, get those bones out of there, and assure the people that the guilty will not go unpunished. Then we'll see — the public has a short memory. The investigators arrived in a small truck loaded with yellow plastic bags and a crew of masons to dislodge the rubble. They made orderly and accurate notations of every item: one human body, female, in an advanced state of decomposition, covered with a dark blanket; one shoe; strands of hair; bones of an inferior extremity; one scapula; one humerus; various vertebrae; a trunk with both superior extremities attached; one pair of pants; two skulls, one complete, the other lacking the mandible; a section of jawbone with metal-filled teeth; more vertebrae; pieces of ribs; a trunk with shreds of clothing; shirts and socks of various colors; a pelvic bone; and various additional bones . . . all of which filled thirty-eight bags duly sealed, numbered, and carried to the truck. It took several trips to transport the bags to the Medical Institute. The Deputy Minister counted fourteen cadavers, based on the number of heads found, but he was not unmindful of the gruesome possibility that, had they done their job more carefully, other bodies would have appeared beneath successive layers of time and earth. Someone made the macabre joke that if they dug a little deeper they would find skeletons of conquistadors, Incan mummies, and fossils of Cro-Magnon man, but no one laughed; the horror had depressed them all.

Since early that morning, people had begun to gather, coming as near    45
as possible before being stopped by the line of rifles, then standing directly behind the soldiers. First to arrive were the widows and orphans of the area, each wearing a black strip of cloth on the left arm as a sign of mourning. Later came others, almost all the country people from around Los Riscos. About noon, busloads from the outlying barrios[1] of the capital arrived. Affliction hung in the air like the forewarning of a storm, immobilizing the very birds in their flight. For many hours, the people stood beneath a pale sun that washed out the outlines and colors of the world, while bag after bag was filled. From afar they strained to recognize a shoe, a shirt, a lock of hair. Those who had the best view passed information to the others: There's another skull, this one has gray hair. It might be our friend Flores, do you remember him? Now they're closing another bag, but they're not through — they're bringing out more. They say they're going to take the remains to the morgue and that we can go there to get a closer look. And how much will that cost? I don't know, we'll have to pay something. Pay to identify your own dead? No, sir, that's something ought to be free.

All afternoon people kept coming, until they covered the hillside, listening to the sound of the shovels and picks moving the dirt, the coming and going of the truck, the traffic of police, officials, and legal advisers, the near riot of newspapermen who had been denied permission to go any closer. As the sun set, a chorus of voices was raised in a burial prayer. One person set up a tent improvised from blankets, prepared to

---

[1]In Spanish, a district; in English, a Spanish-speaking neighborhood in a city or town. — ED.

stay for an indefinite time, but the guardsmen beat him with their rifle butts and ran him off before others prepared to stay, too. That was shortly before the appearance of the Cardinal in the archdiocesan automobile; he drove through the line of soldiers, ignoring their signals to stop, descended from the vehicle, and strode purposefully to the truck, where he stood and implacably counted the bags while the Deputy Minister hastily invented explanations. When the last load of yellow plastic bags had been driven away and the police had ordered the area cleared, night had fallen and people began to walk home in the darkness, exchanging stories of their own dramas, proving that all misery has a common thread.

The next day, people from all parts of the country crowded into the offices of the Medical Institute hoping to identify their loved ones, but they were forbidden to view them by a new order: The General had said that it was one thing to disinter cadavers but quite a different matter to put them on exhibit so anyone who wanted could come take a look. What do those damn fools think this is, a sideshow? I want this matter squelched, Colonel, before I lose patience.

"And what shall we do about public opinion, the diplomats, and the press, General, sir?"

"What we always do, Colonel. You don't change your strategy in mid-battle. Take a lesson from the Roman emperors."

Hundreds of people held a sit-in in the street in front of the Vicariate,         50
displaying photographs of their missing loved ones, whispering, Where are they? Where are they? Meanwhile, a group of working priests and nuns in slacks fasted in the cathedral, adding to the total uproar. Sunday the Cardinal's pastoral letter was read from every pulpit, and for the first time in so long and dark a time people dared to turn to their neighbors and weep together. People called one another to talk about cases that multiplied until it was impossible to keep count. A procession was orga-nized to pray for the victims, and before the authorities realized what was happening, an unmanageable crowd was marching through the streets carrying banners and placards demanding liberty, bread, and justice. The march began as little trickles of people from the outlying poor barrios. Gradually the trickles flowed together, the ranks swelled and finally grew into a compact mass that surged forward chanting in unison the religious hymns and political slogans stilled for so many years that people believed they had been forgotten forever. The crowds overflowed the churches and cemeteries, the only places that until then the police had not entered with their instruments of war.

"What shall we do with this mob, General, sir?"

"What we always do, Colonel" was the reply from the depths of the bunker.

Meanwhile, television continued its usual programming of popular music, contests, lottery drawings, and light comedy and romantic films. Newspapers gave the results of the football games, and front pages showed the Commander in Chief cutting the ribbon at a bank opening. But within a few days word of the discovery in the mine and photographs of the cadavers had traveled around the world by teletype. The news services sent the story out over their wires, back to the country where it had originated and where it was impossible to contain the news of the atrocity any longer, in spite of censorship and in spite of imaginative explanations by the authorities. People saw on their screens a fatuous announcer reading the official version: The bodies were those of terrorists executed by their own henchmen; but everyone knew they were murdered political prisoners. The atrocity was discussed amid fruits and vegetables in the market, among students and teachers in the schools, among workers in the factories, and even in the closed living rooms of the bourgeoisie, where for some it was a surprise to discover that everything was not going well in the country. The timid murmur that for so many years had been hidden behind doors and closed shutters now, for the first time, came out in the street to be shouted aloud, and that lament, augmented by the countless new cases that had come to light, touched everyone.

## EXPLORATIONS

1. Who killed the people whose bodies Irene and Francisco found in the mine, and why? How and where does Isabel Allende reveal this information?

2. In what ways is the relationship between most U.S. citizens and their government different from the relationship between citizens and government in the unnamed Latin American country depicted by Allende?

3. What aspects of the General appear in "The Los Riscos Mine"? How would the story's impact change if Allende described and quoted him the same way she does her other characters?

4. What information about politics does Allende give us in her portrait of the Chief Justice of the Supreme Court (paras. 42–43)? How would the story's impact change if Allende included this information in the form of exposition instead of a character?

# CONNECTIONS

1. What are the effects of the homely details in "The Los Riscos Mine," such as the thermos of hot coffee (paras. 2, 8, and 22) and the yellow plastic bags (paras. 44 and 46)? How does Allende, like Slavenka Drakulić in "Zagreb: A Letter to My Daughter" (p. 646), use such ordinary images to dramatize violence?

2. How does the social and political role the Roman Catholic Church plays in "The Los Riscos Mine" compare with the social and political role it plays in Nell McCafferty's "Peggy Deery of Derry" (p. 615)?

3. What similarities appear in "The Los Riscos Mine" and Joan Didion's selection in *Looking at Ourselves* (p. 612)?

# ELABORATIONS

1. Throughout "The Los Riscos Mine," Irene and Francisco and the people who work with them realize they are risking their lives. Write a process essay listing the steps in the investigation of the mine, the dangers involved in each step, and the precautions taken to protect the participants.

2. Based on your reading of "The Los Riscos Mine," "Peggy Deery of Derry," and "Sister Imelda" (p. 444), write a definition or classification essay about the responsibilities of a Roman Catholic priest or nun to the people he or she serves; or, write an imaginary debate on that topic between Allende's General and Father José Leal.

# CZESLAW MILOSZ

## American Ignorance of War

Czeslaw Milosz (pronounced *ches*-law *mee*-losh) has been called Poland's greatest living poet. Ironically, his work was refused publication in
Poland from 1936 until 1980, when he won the Nobel Prize for literature.
Milosz was born in 1911 in Lithuania, a small Baltic country adjoining
Poland and controlled then by Russia. He began writing poetry and
became active in leftist politics while studying law at Lithuania's University of Vilnius. Milosz worked as a programmer for Polish National Radio
from 1935 until 1939, when Germany invaded Poland. After that he
wrote, edited, and translated for the Polish resistance in Warsaw. In 1946
he entered the diplomatic service of Poland's new Communist government and was stationed at the Polish embassy in Washington until 1950.
After a year as first secretary for cultural affairs in Paris, Milosz broke
with the Warsaw government, feeling too restricted as a writer by its
regimentation of cultural life. He now lives in Berkeley, California,
where he is a professor emeritus at the university and continues to write
both poetry and prose. "American Ignorance of War," translated from
the Polish by Jane Zielonko, comes from Milosz's first American publication, *The Captive Mind* (1953), which examines life under totalitari-
anism and explains why he defected. Written soon after World War II,
the essay appeared more than thirty-five years before the "people's democracies" of Eastern Europe (including Lithuania) began freeing themselves from Soviet domination.

Poland was annexed by the Soviet Union after being occupied by
Germany during World War II. The Poles' sense of national (and European) identity persisted, however: In the decades after the war, strict
Stalinism gradually yielded more freedom to Polish Communists and to
the Roman Catholic Church. In 1979 Pope John Paul II made a historic
visit to his Polish homeland. The next year the illegal labor union
Solidarity organized shipyard strikes and won concessions, including
legalization, most of which were reversed by the declaration of martial
law in December 1981. Fear of a Soviet crackdown kept the government
antagonistic to Solidarity and its leader, Lech Walesa, as the union
continued to press for change. Solidarity's persistence won the 1983
Nobel Peace Prize for Walesa and forced the government to agree to hold
elections. In 1990 Walesa became president, and Poland began implementing both a democratic political system and a free-market economy.
Along with rapid economic growth, however, came currency devaluation,
inflation, high unemployment, and other painful changes. In late 1993,
Poles elected an alliance including many former Communists, rebuffing
four years of free-market reforms.

"Are Americans *really* stupid?" I was asked in Warsaw. In the voice of the man who posed the question, there was despair, as well as the hope that I would contradict him. This question reveals the attitude of the average person in the people's democracies toward the West: It is despair mixed with a residue of hope.

During the last few years, the West has given these people a number of reasons to despair politically. In the case of the intellectual, other, more complicated reasons come into play. Before the countries of Central and Eastern Europe entered the sphere of the Imperium,[1] they lived through the Second World War. That war was much more devastating there than in the countries of Western Europe. It destroyed not only their economies but also a great many values which had seemed till then unshakable.

Man tends to regard the order he lives in as *natural*. The houses he passes on his way to work seem more like rocks rising out of the earth than like products of human hands. He considers the work he does in his office or factory as essential to the harmonious functioning of the world. The clothes he wears are exactly what they should be, and he laughs at the idea that he might equally well be wearing a Roman toga or medieval armor. He respects and envies a minister of state or a bank director, and regards the possession of a considerable amount of money as the main guarantee of peace and security. He cannot believe that one day a rider may appear on a street he knows well, where cats sleep and children play, and start catching passersby with his lasso. He is accustomed to satisfying those of his physiological needs which are considered private as discreetly as possible, without realizing that such a pattern of behavior is not common to all human societies. In a word, he behaves a little like Charlie Chaplin in *The Gold Rush*, bustling about in a shack poised precariously on the edge of a cliff.

His first stroll along a street littered with glass from bomb-shattered windows shakes his faith in the "naturalness" of his world. The wind scatters papers from hastily evacuated offices, papers labeled "Confidential" or "Top Secret" that evoke visions of safes, keys, conferences, couriers, and secretaries. Now the wind blows them through the street for anyone to read; yet no one does, for each man is more urgently concerned with finding a loaf of bread. Strangely enough, the world goes on even though the offices and secret files have lost all meaning. Farther down the street, he stops before a house split in half by a bomb, the privacy of people's homes — the family smells, the warmth of the beehive life, the furniture preserving the memory of loves and hatreds — cut open to

---

[1]Empire; that is, the Soviet Union. — Ed.

public view. The house itself, no longer a rock, but a scaffolding of plaster, concrete, and brick; and on the third floor, a solitary white bathtub, rain-rinsed of all recollection of those who once bathed in it. Its formerly influential and respected owners, now destitute, walk the fields in search of stray potatoes. Thus overnight money loses its value and becomes a meaningless mass of printed paper. His walk takes him past a little boy poking a stick into a heap of smoking ruins and whistling a song about the great leader who will preserve the nation against all enemies. The song remains, but the leader of yesterday is already part of an extinct past.

He finds he acquires new habits quickly. Once, had he stumbled upon          5
a corpse on the street, he would have called the police. A crowd would have gathered, and much talk and comment would have ensued. Now he knows he must avoid the dark body lying in the gutter, and refrain from asking unnecessary questions. The man who fired the gun must have had his reasons; he might well have been executing an Underground sentence.

Nor is the average European accustomed to thinking of his native city as divided into segregated living areas, but a single decree can force him to this new pattern of life and thought. Quarter A may suddenly be designated for one race; B, for a second; C, for a third. As the resettlement deadline approaches, the streets become filled with long lines of wagons, carts, wheelbarrows, and people carrying bundles, beds, chests, caldrons, and bird cages. When all the moves are effected, 2,000 people may find themselves in a building that once housed 200, but each man is at last in the proper area. Then high walls are erected around quarter C, and daily a given lot of men, women, and children are loaded into wagons that take them off to specially constructed factories where they are scientifically slaughtered and their bodies burned.

And even the rider with the lasso appears, in the form of a military van waiting at the corner of a street. A man passing that corner meets a leveled rifle, raises his hands, is pushed into the van, and from that moment is lost to his family and friends. He may be sent to a concentration camp, or he may face a firing squad, his lips sealed with plaster lest he cry out against the state; but, in any case, he serves as a warning to his fellow men. Perhaps one might escape such a fate by remaining at home. But the father of a family must go out in order to provide bread and soup for his wife and children; and every night they worry about whether or not he will return. Since these conditions last for years, everyone gradually comes to look upon the city as a jungle, and upon the fate of twentieth-century man as identical with that of a caveman living in the midst of powerful monsters.

It was once thought obvious that a man bears the same name and surname throughout his entire life; now it proves wiser for many reasons to change them and to memorize a new and fabricated biography. As a result, the records of the civilian state become completely confused. Everyone ceases to care about formalities, so that marriage, for example, comes to mean little more than living together.

Respectable citizens used to regard banditry as a crime. Today, bank robbers are heroes because the money they steal is destined for the Underground. Usually they are young boys, mothers' boys, but their appearance is deceiving. The killing of a man presents no great moral problem to them.

The nearness of death destroys shame. Men and women change as soon as they know that the date of their execution has been fixed by a fat little man with shiny boots and a riding crop. They copulate in public, on the small bit of ground surrounded by barbed wire — their last home on earth. Boys and girls in their teens, about to go off to the barricades to fight against tanks with pistols and bottles of gasoline, want to enjoy their youth and lose their respect for standards of decency.                    10

Which world is "natural"? That which existed before, or the world of war? Both are natural, if both are within the realm of one's experience. All the concepts men live by are a product of the historic formation in which they find themselves. Fluidity and constant change are the characteristics of phenomena. And man is so plastic a being that one can even conceive of the day when a thoroughly self-respecting citizen will crawl on all fours, sporting a tail of brightly colored feathers as a sign of conformity to the order he lives in.

The man of the East cannot take Americans seriously because they have never undergone the experiences that teach men how relative their judgments and thinking habits are. Their resultant lack of imagination is appalling. Because they were born and raised in a given social order and in a given system of values, they believe that any other order must be "unnatural," and that it cannot last because it is incompatible with human nature. But even they may one day know fire, hunger, and the sword. In all probability this is what will occur; for it is hard to believe that when one half of the world is living through terrible disasters, the other half can continue a nineteenth-century mode of life, learning about the distress of its distant fellow men only from movies and newspapers. Recent examples teach us that this cannot be. An inhabitant of Warsaw or Budapest once looked at newsreels of bombed Spain or burning Shanghai, but in the end he learned how these and many other catastrophes appear in actuality. He read gloomy tales of the NKVD[2] until one

---

[2]The Soviet secret police, 1935–1943. — ED.

day he found he himself had to deal with it. *If something exists in one place, it will exist everywhere.* This is the conclusion he draws from his observations, and so he has no particular faith in the momentary prosperity of America. He suspects that the years 1933–1945 in Europe[3] prefigure what will occur elsewhere. A hard school, where ignorance was punished not by bad marks but by death, has taught him to think sociologically and historically. But it has not freed him from irrational feelings. He is apt to believe in theories that foresee violent changes in the countries of the West, for he finds it unjust that they should escape the hardships he had to undergo.

## EXPLORATIONS

1. Why does Milosz's questioner wonder in the opening sentence, "Are Americans *really* stupid?" What is Milosz's answer?

2. What comments in Milosz's essay suggest why, thirty-five years later, the "people's democracies" finally rebelled against their repressive postwar governments? What comments reflect a fatalistic sense that rebellion was hopeless? What combination of events mentioned in paragraph 2 explains that sense of fatalism?

3. How would the impact of Milosz's observations change if he presented them in a historical or argumentative essay instead of in narrative form? What concepts and comments in "American Ignorance of War" struck you most forcefully, and why?

## CONNECTIONS

1. In what ways does the fictional Latin American country in "The Los Riscos Mine" (p. 656) match the war zone Milosz describes in paragraphs 4–10? Judging from these two selections (and others you have read), how does Latin America's experience of war differ from Eastern Europe's?

2. What similar images appear in "American Ignorance of War" and "Zagreb: A Letter to My Daughter" (p. 646)? What statements by Milosz apply to the situation Drakulić is writing about?

3. Which of the authors in *Looking at Ourselves* do you think would agree with Milosz's statements in paragraph 12 about American ignorance? Which authors do you think would argue that people in the United States already know "fire, hunger, and the sword"? Cite evidence for your answers.

---

[3]Hitler's takeover of Germany through World War II. — ED.

## ELABORATIONS

1. When he wrote this essay more than forty years ago, what did Milosz predict would happen in the West? What were the grounds for his prediction? How have the problems Milosz mentions produced different results from the ones he anticipated? Write a cause-and-effect essay answering these questions by doing some research and examining the course of events in Poland, or Eastern Europe in general, from World War II to the present.

2. How would your life change if the United States went to war tomorrow? Imagine your school or town under attack by a foreign power. Write a letter to a friend or family member describing, as Milosz does, what you observe around you and how you respond to it.

# NUHA AL-RADI

## *Baghdad Diary*

Nuha Al-Radi was born in Baghdad in 1941. Her father, originally an agriculturist, was in the diplomatic service, so the family's life was unusually cosmopolitan. When she was six years old they moved to India, where Al-Radi spent most of her childhood and attended high school. She studied ceramics in England and also studied at the College for Women in Beirut, Lebanon. A ceramicist for thirty years, she moved back to Baghdad in 1976 and now paints there. "Baghdad Diary" comes from the Winter 1992 issue of *Granta*; it is Al-Radi's first published work. Although not a writer, she was impelled to record the horrors of living through the bombing of her hometown.

The blitz Al-Radi describes in her diary was the United States's response to Iraq's invasion of Kuwait on August 2, 1990. As Iraqi President Saddam Hussein redefined Kuwait as the nineteenth province of his country, U.S. President George Bush built a coalition of opposition that included much of Europe and the Middle East, the Soviet Union, and Japan. On August 6, the UN Security Council outlawed trade with Iraq unless it withdrew from Kuwait by January 15, 1991. With Saudi Arabia's permission, the U.S.-dominated coalition began "Operation Desert Shield," a defensive and potentially offensive military buildup there. On January 12 the U.S. Congress approved Bush's request for authorization to use force. When the deadline passed, "Desert Shield" became "Desert Storm" as the coalition began bombing Iraq — particularly Baghdad — and Iraqi positions in Kuwait. Iraq responded by bombing Israel in the vain hope it would retaliate and prompt Arab coalition members to change sides. On February 27, 1991, Bush declared Iraq's army defeated and Kuwait liberated; and on April 6 Saddam Hussein grudgingly accepted UN peace terms.

For more information on Kuwait, see page 626; on Saudi Arabia, see page 372; on Iraq and the Persian Gulf war, see page 696.

Last week I went to the Rashid Hotel to pick up a letter which Bob Simpson had brought from Cyprus. He also sent me some packets of seeds for Italian vegetables, a tiny leak in the embargo: useful, if we ever get any water. His room was full of hacks waiting for the big moment. I told him very authoritatively that there would be no war. He said he wished he could believe me. I'm not sure why I was so positive. I should have known better; after all, I witnessed three revolutions in Iraq, the Suez War in Egypt, and most of the Lebanese civil war.

*Day One.*   I woke up at 3:00 A.M. to exploding bombs and Salvador Dali, my dog, frantically chasing around the house, barking furiously. I went out on the balcony. Salvador was already there, staring up at a sky lit by the most extraordinary firework display. The noise was beyond description. I couldn't get an answer from Ma and Needles's phone so tried Suha who answered in a hushed voice and said, Put out your lights. Suha was sitting in a shelter she had prepared under the stairs, already stashed with provisions. She'd taped up her windows and doors against nuclear fallout.

I ventured outside with Salvador to put out the garage light — we were both very nervous. Almost immediately we lost all electricity, so I need not have bothered. The phones also went dead. We are done for, I think: A modern nation cannot fight without electricity and communications. Thank heavens for our ration of Pakistani matches.

With the first bomb, Ma and Needles's windows shattered, those facing the river, and one of poor Bingo's pups was killed in the garden by flying glass — our first war casualty.

*Day Two.*   Amal and Munir also lost their windows, so they've moved in          5
here. . . . Said came by and picked us up to have lunch with Taha — kebabs and beer, delicious. Said has a good supply of petrol (which he's not prepared to share). There were no air raids, and everything seemed normal. Today, all over Baghdad, bread was thrown from government trucks to thronging crowds.

*Day Three.*   Suha and I spent the day merrily painting while the war was going on full blast outside. I wonder how we manage to feel so detached. This afternoon we saw a SAM missile explode in the sky. I caught Mundher Baig on his grandson's tricycle, his legs scrunched up under his chin, pedaling round and round his garage. He is convinced he will not see his grandchildren again.

At night there was a fire in the orchard, which I thought was from a bomb but in fact had been started by Flayih. He had been burning some dry wood near the dead core of a palm tree, trying to produce coal. It took the whole water supply from Dood's house and mine, plus the fire extinguisher from the car, to put out the fire. Now we have no water. Flayih still has no coal.

*Day Four.*   I woke to an air raid at five and went round to Zaid's house. He was there with his two aunts, both about 110 years old. One was bent double over the stove; the other never stopped chattering. Because of the constant air raids they are afraid to go upstairs to their bedrooms so they sleep in their clothes in the sitting-room. They seem oblivious to the enormity of what's happening around them and concentrate only on the immediate things; that's why, though they are so old and frail, they're so alive and entertaining. Zaid's phone still works so I tried to call Asia and Suha: no answer. Their house is on the river, directly opposite Dora refinery. There is a huge black cloud hanging over that part of Baghdad.

Mundher Baig has made a generator for his house using precious petrol. Ten of us stood gaping in wonder at this machine and the noise it made. Only four days have passed since the start of the war but already any mechanical thing seems totally alien.

Suha is experimenting with a recipe for *basturma*. The meat in our 10 freezers is thawing so it's a good thing the weather is cold.

In the evening, we cook potatoes in the fireplace. M.A.W. says you can almost taste the potato through the charcoal; admittedly they are burnt. I make a dynamite punch with aquavit, vodka, and fresh orange juice.

*Day Five.*   Munir gave me a calendar today; it's the twenty-first of January. My painting of Mundher Baig and family is nearly finished. I got my bicycle fixed. Although it's new we've been unable to inflate the tires for days. They both turn out to have punctures. I told the guy mending it that it was new, and he said they always come like this. He thought someone punctures them before they leave the factory. The bike is called Baghdad. At least it's not called Ishtar; the name of our goddess of war that already honors fridges, freezers, soap, matches, heaters, and hotels.

We are all now going to the loo in the orchard, fertilizing it and saving water. Janette, who now comes by every day, says that everyone else has gone off to the countryside because it's the best place to be during a war. Then she added that our house is like being in the country anyway. She is looking for someone to share her bed today, quite crazed; I said it wasn't uppermost in my mind right now.

Apparently people take off for the countryside with their freezers loaded on their pickup trucks and barbecue the food as it defrosts. Only Iraqis would escape from a war carrying freezers full of goodies. We've always been hoarders. Now we have to eat our hoard.

Basil is cooking up all the food from his freezer and feeding it to his 15 cats.

*Day Six.*   Got up for the regular five o'clock air raid, which finished an hour later. We went to queue for our petrol ration — twenty liters. Amal, who never remembers to wear her glasses, backed into a wall. The entire country has collapsed and disintegrated in a few days. They say that outside Baghdad everything goes on as normal. I wonder how long we can survive this kind of bombardment. Perhaps we will get water tomorrow.

*Day Seven.*  The worst has happened: We have to drink warm beer. I cleaned out the freezer and removed a ton of different kinds of bread. . . . We have to eat everything that will spoil. This means we all shit so much more, all in the garden. If we use the bathroom they say the sewage will back up on us — I have only now discovered an electric pump takes it to the sewage plant. One takes so much for granted. I wonder whether the Allies thought of these things when they planned the bombing. I fear it will be a long time until we have electricity.

Ma began making her own basturma following Suha's recipe. She stuffed the meat and spices into nylon stockings — there are no animal intestines to hand — and hung them in Dood's empty house, in posh marble surrounds. We started burning the rubbish today, clearing the orchard of dead matter. Amal insisted on wearing her high heels, even for collecting brambles.

Rumor had it that there was a difficult night ahead, the seventh, but it clouded over, so maybe God was on our side. I like the idea that some of our Scuds are decoys, probably crafty Russian training. I'd rather we didn't hit civilians but I suppose accuracy is asking too much.

We got some water today, although there wasn't enough pressure to push it up to the roof tank. Still I'm not complaining.                                    20

I finished Mundher's painting and we had a little party to celebrate its unveiling. We opened a bottle of champagne and ate *meloukhia* and a million other things. I wish that our stock of food would finish so we could eat a little less. . . .

*Day Eight.*  Silence. It's six in the morning and there's no air raid. I ate so much last night that I couldn't sleep. Depression has hit me with the realization that the whole world hates us. It is not a comforting thought. We have bitten off more than we can chew. Ma's theory is that the world now is ruled by the two smallest powers: Kuwait with its money and oil, and Israel with its power and intellect. It's an unfair world. Other countries do wrong: Look what Russia did in Afghanistan, or Turkey invading Cyprus, or Israel taking over Palestine and Lebanon. Nobody bombed them senseless. They were not even punished. Perhaps we have too much history. At least Baghdad is now on the map: I will no longer have to explain where I come from.

I had a recurrent dream before the start of the war: Americans in battle fatigues jogging down Haifa Street, lining up in the alley, kissing each other. They were led by a girl dressed in red. Then suddenly I was on my own and everything was dry as dust, and all I could see was bare earth. What bothered me was the loneliness of the dream. Am I going to be the only survivor?

*Day Nine.*   Since the war began I have been unable to read a word, not even a thriller. Ma, who usually never stops knitting, can't knit; while Suha and Amal, who have no talent for knitting, have now started. Fastidious Asam, who normally changes her clothes twice a day, now sleeps in the same clothes for two days running. She has hidden all the scissors in her house in case someone breaks in and attacks her with them. She has also wrapped her jewelry in plastic bags, boxed them, and buried them in the garden — hoping that she will remember the exact spot.

I'm trying to get M.A.W. to use his time constructively. I gave him my     25
wall clock to repair. He complained endlessly, then started to fiddle with it and got it to work. He's excellent at mending things, having an endless supply of patience for machines but almost none for life and people. He says if we defeat Israel he'll eat a spoonful of shit — sometimes it's a plateful depending on how good or bad the news. Today he says if we retain Kuwait he'll eat ten platefuls.

Basil came by and I told him to put his mind to basic agriculture. Now that we are back in the Dark Ages we have to figure out a way to haul water up from the river. People have taken to doing their washing in the Tigris, but the river is fast flowing and dangerous. The water situation is bad.

They captured an island in the Gulf that appeared suddenly at low tide: We did not even know its name.

*Day Ten.*   "Read My Lips," today is the tenth day of the war and we are still here. Where is your three-to-ten-days-swift-and-clean kill? Mind you, we are ruined. I don't think I could set foot in the West again. Maybe I'll go to India: They have a high tolerance level and will not shun us Iraqis.

Suha mended her bike today. Hers was also new and its tires were also punctured. We rode out together and caused a sensation in the streets. All very friendly. One guy on a bike sidled by and said he had a Mercedes at home. "Are we in Paris?" said another. One sour man shouted: "We don't like girls that ride bikes," and we yelled at him, "More fool you," and rode away. Nofa says I look like ET because I'm wrapped in a hundred scarves and they fly behind me; more like a witch, I'd say. Tomorrow I'll be fifty years old. I feel very depressed. Who the hell ever wanted Kuwait anyway?

M.A.W. says we can get electricity in one minute if we attach ourselves     30
to Turkey or Jordan, because we have a connected circuit. Yesterday we heard we may be getting it from Iran. But what can they connect it to if they bombed the stations?

Everyone talks endlessly about food. While eating lunch the conver- sation is about what we are having for dinner. We have cooked up all the meat we had. The *basturmas* we hung in Dood's house are beginning to stink — the whole house reeks.

Hala says she will give me a bucket of water as my birthday present.

*Day Eleven.* I had great hopes for my birthday. Lots of people were invited, and they all came and more. Drinks flowed in buckets. Someone peed on my bathroom floor (I'm sure it was that horrid Mazin who came uninvited). Fuzzle stayed the night. She said to Yasoub, "Take me out to pee," and they went out into the garden arm in arm, so romantic after all these years of marriage. There was a lovely full moon. Fuzzle later entertained us with stories about her air-raid shelter. She goes there every night with Mary, her Indian maid, from six in the evening till seven the next morning. There are three tiers of bunks; the lower one is the most coveted. Fuzzle gets very nervous when the bombing starts, and being diabetic her blood count shoots up. It was a particularly bad night and we had to take her mind off the noisy bombing outside — she was used to the quiet of the shelter and the soldiers singing to Mary. We must all have the hides of rhinos here in this house; no one seems afraid.

*Day Twelve.* We got water from the taps today. Drew endless buckets up to the tank on the roof. I filled them up below and Munir pulled them up with a rope, eighty buckets in all. Very hard work, and I got soaked in the process.

*Day Thirteen.* I'm typing by candlelight and can see very little: Maybe    35
this won't be legible tomorrow. Ma and Suha went to the souk today to buy more lanterns, and an air raid started. No one bothered to shelter or go home, but just went on with their usual business. In fact there was such a crush that Ma and Suha managed to lose each other. They were bombing the Bridge at Southgate. The shock caused all the doors of the buildings in the vicinity to blow open, and all the windows went — broken glass everywhere. Amal's shop, which is right beside the bridge, also got blown up. So now both her house and shop are destroyed. She never complains.

It was Suhub's birthday so we all met there for lunch. Driving across the Adhamiya Bridge we could see black columns of smoke rising in all directions. They are burning tires to confuse the enemy. Some confusion. Samih said that an unexploded rocket had fallen in the garden of the Rashid Hotel, and there was a mad scrabble for mementoes before the security forces sealed it off.

Are we in for a nuclear war? I must say I don't feel there is a risk of death, at least not for myself — I know that I will survive. Twenty-seven thousand bombing raids so far. Is the world mad? Do they not realize what they are doing? I think Bush is a criminal. This country is totally ruined. Who gives the Americans the license to bomb at will? I can understand Kuwait wanting to destroy us, but not the rest of the world.

The peasant's life that we now lead is very hard, and the work never stops. I get up, come downstairs, collect firewood, clean the grate, and make up the evening fire. I clean the kitchen and boil water for coffee. Suha and Amal cook the meals; Ma makes the bread and cakes. I do the soups and salads. I grow all the raw materials for it, lettuce, radishes, celery, parsley, and rocca in the orchard. Lunch is a simple snack; dinner — our one meal — is eaten between seven and eight, sometimes accompanied by bombing, other times not.

I have learned to do a lot of things in the dark, except sleep through the night. In fact, we all sleep very little; adrenalin keeps us going.

Salvador has got a new girlfriend. She is horrible. He bit Said yesterday.    40
Salvador is not a dog you can stroke.

*Day Fourteen.*   Mundher Baig died in his sleep. He had a bad heart and yesterday chased up nine floors to check the damage to our building. But he really died of sorrow: He could not comprehend why the world wanted to destroy us. He kept asking Ma yesterday why they were doing it. Somehow I knew while painting his portrait that it would never hang in his house. That was why I finished it in such a hurry, unveiling it before the paint was dry. He was not made for death, so lively and full of energy, good for laughter and for fights. We are going to miss him.

We each chose a section of Baghdad and drove around to inform friends and relatives of the funeral. I went to Mansur, crossing the Adhamiya Bridge during a full-scale air raid. Sirens were going off, rockets and bombs were falling, I was unmoved. Lubna says she saw a plane come down in Karrada; it turned out to be a cruise missile.

*Day Fifteen.*   All the water that Munir and I hauled up to the roof-tank yesterday disappeared through a leak in the downstairs toilet. A tragedy. I have lived in this house for three years and have had to change that loo twice already. It must be jinxed.

I went to help Amal clean up her shop, a mess of broken glass. The holes in Jumhuriya Bridge were neat and precise, with a lot of metal hanging underneath. The bridge was packed with people looking down through the holes. A siren was sounding but nobody moved.

*Day Sixteen.*   The women gathered in Asam's house to pay their respects    45
to Mundher Baig. Word has got round Baghdad that he has died, and

people are coming from all over, using up their hoarded petrol. He had apparently been going around Baghdad by bus, checking up on old friends and saying good-bye to them. He must have sensed his coming death.

We may be getting electricity from Qasr Shireen in Iran, but it's all rumors. Nobody knows anything. Baghdad Radio broadcasts for a few hours a day, giving us news of the battle — how many planes we have downed, how we are fighting back — propaganda to keep our spirits up. We listen to Radio Monte Carlo at eight, at night there's the BBC [British Broadcasting Corporation] or VOA [Voice of America]. Radio Austria is quite sympathetic and actually remembers that there are people living here.

The BBC says our one-day battle to take over the tiny island of Kimche was insignificant. But I thought that the Allies came into the war to protect the Saudis, where were they? I think the real issue of this war is the West's inability to accept a strong Arab nation, and a maverick one at that. Iraq is not a servile nation.

Salvador's new girlfriend crawls in through holes in the orchard fence. I keep plugging them but she finds a way in. I had to get up and shoo her away at five this morning — they were making such a racket. Howling dogs combined with the barrage in the sky was too much. The only good thing is that she exhausts Salvador enough to enable us to go to the loo in peace. Otherwise he attacks and terrorizes anyone squatting behind a tree. Amal has it the worst: He grabs at her trousers and tries to pull them off. He thinks it a wonderful game. Now she has to give him a bone every time she goes out, to distract him.

*Day Seventeen.* An awful night. Nonstop rockets and the biggest explosion ever. It was heard all over Baghdad but no one seems to know where the bomb landed. It wasn't nuclear anyway, we're still alive. I can understand the Kuwaitis hating us but what did we do to you, George Bush? I can hear it in your voice. Is it because we stood up to the United States?

Tonight we shall have music — Amal has an old crank-up Victrola    50 gramophone and M.A.W., who never throws anything away, has a lot of 78s. That we should come to this when the rest of the world has CDs.

Widad came today and showed us how to make a candle using a bottle filled with kerosene. You seal the bottle neck with a mash of dates leaving only a small section of the wick sticking out because a long wick produces columns of smoke. An advance: Our normal candles leave much to be desired; they splutter, drip, grow enormous wicks, and give off black smoke. This bottle-candle lasts for ages. Same principle as a Molotov cocktail except that they are filled with petrol.

This morning there was a huge number of dead flies on the floor. I wonder if the big explosion shocked them to death. . . .

*Day Eighteen.*   Last night M.A.W. said, "We must have continuous war. I have now got so used to eating charred food that when we finish this war we must start another." We are saving gas by cooking food in the fireplace and baking our own bread on top of an Aladdin stove. These kerosene stoves have proven their worth.

Every night I have surreal dreams. Last night it was people standing outside a third-floor window, having a conversation: a mid-air cocktail party.

The birds have had the worst beating: Their sensitive souls cannot take all this hideous noise. All the caged love-birds have died from the shock of the blasts. Birds in the wild fly upside down and do crazy somersaults. Hundreds, if not thousands, have died in the orchard. Lonely survivors fly about in a distracted fashion.

The sky is now covered with black clouds. We are still trying to confuse the enemy by burning tires. Meanwhile they use computer technology to destroy us. An astronaut on a Russian satellite said he saw huge black clouds and many fires burning across our region.

Salvador has become more used to the noise of the explosions, but an unusually loud bang still sends him chasing about distractedly. The dogs can sense an air raid before it begins; they tense up and start barking. Stray dogs in the orchard pile up against Salvador for comfort during bad air raids. He has us for his security, they have him. Some of them actually cry with fear — the most awful, pathetic sound.

It is a week since we had water. My hands and nails are disgusting. Everyone has a sooty face, and no one looks in the mirror anymore. Needles is the only one who still looks neat and clean. Raad says that in Jadiriyah they have no daylight, that the sky is permanently black from the smoke of the Dora refinery as it burns. It has been burning since the first day of the war. Poor Suha and Asia T. How are they surviving?

*Day Nineteen.* . . . There is nothing nice about war. The one thing that no one envisaged was that Baghdad was going to be bombed like this. They were supposed to be freeing Kuwait. It seems as if the whole conflict was engineered to provide an excuse to destroy our country and our army. No one will hear from us for years. Mundher Baig dead, I can't believe it.

Lubna came by today. Thieves stole his generator and the petrol Mahmoud buried in their garden. Robbery is the fashion. Generators and bicycles go for thousands. Kerosene lamps are valued like gold.

*Day Twenty.* It has now been three weeks. Forty-four thousand air raids. I have another leak in the water system. I will have to check the whole house. Bush says, we make war for peace. Such nonsense. What kind of peace is this? What kind of new world order?

*Day Twenty-one.* A week since Mundher Baig died. My hands are now so calloused they look like farmer's hands. Ma says she feels like Scarlett O'Hara in *Gone with the Wind* — though we are far from starving.

They have started targeting bridges again. Jumhuriya Bridge is in three pieces. Textile factories, flour mills, and cement plants are also being hit. What do they mean when they say they are only hitting military targets? And as for "our aim is always true"? Who will save us from these bullies? Maybe they want to destroy us so they can produce more jobs for their people in the West? Reconstruction and new military supplies will keep their economy going for years. . . .

*Day Twenty-two.* There is a sameness about the days now. I saw the Jumhuriya Bridge today; it's incredibly sad to see a bombed bridge — a murderous action, for it destroys a link. The sight affects everyone that sees it; many people cry.

Children play on streets without traffic. They have never had it so good. They call me Bicycletta and ask me how I am when I pass by. I say fine, or not, depending on my mood. We all know our neighbors; the Suleikh is like one big village. In fact, Baghdad has turned into many little villages.

65

*Day Twenty-three.* The equivalent of five Hiroshimas has already been dropped on us. We could not sleep last night because there were no air raids; we were restless. At midnight the sirens sounded and everyone promptly dropped off.

*Days Twenty-four and Twenty-five.* A sameness. Even war becomes routine.

*Day Twenty-six.* It's Monday morning, says the Voice of America. What's the difference? We had the worst night yet. The minute the all-clear sounded we went to check up on friends and relatives. . . . [We] found Adiba crying and screaming hysterically and repeating over and over again, "Please God either take my life or that of the bridge." Her house is very close to the Adhamiya Bridge which they have been trying to knock out for two days now.

Both the Martyrs' and the Suspension bridges have been hit. I feel very bitter toward the West.

*Day Twenty-seven.* Apparently the awful racket that we heard yesterday 70
was B-52 bombers. They sound horrific.

There are fat cats everywhere. Fat cats sleeping or sitting in doorways,
fat cats walking and crossing the streets with no fear of being run over.
They of all creatures seem to be totally unmoved by what is happening
around them. They have been eating to bursting point all the leftovers
from the melting freezers. Thinking of freezers reminds me of Sheikha
who returned yesterday to her house, after having spent the last three
weeks at her daughter's: Her neighbors demanded that she come back
because they couldn't stand the smell coming from her house. She put
on a face mask and emptied her giant freezer. Right on top, floating on
a sea of stagnant scummy water, was an entire sheep; and bobbing around
it were twenty-four chickens and sundry legs of lamb in various states of
decay; two dozen kubbas; sixty-eight rice patties; plus plastic bags full of
stuffed vegetables, beans and peas, three whole fishes, hunks of beef, kilos
of minced meat, loaves of bread, cakes, and pastries — everything had to
be thrown out. Sheikha's freezer was like those found in every other
well-to-do household in Baghdad. Everyone was preparing and hoarding
food in their freezers, never thinking we would lose electricity. The
bloated street animals have never had it so good.

I come back from Asam's house to find my home has been invaded
by ten more people. They all live near one of the radio stations which
today's broadcast says is going to be bombed. I have taken to calling us
*Funduq al Saadah*, "Hotel Paradiso," with every inch of the house now
occupied — people playing cards, listening to the radio, boozing. I can't
stand it for long.

*Day Twenty-eight.* . . . Why do they keep bombing the same things again
and again? Each of these bloody rockets costs a quarter-of-a-million dollars or more. Instead of feeding the hungry of the world, billions are spent
on manufacturing more and more sophisticated weapons of destruction.
Killing is the new world order. . . .

*Day Twenty-nine.* . . . A turning point in the war. They hit a shelter, the
one in Ameriya. They thought it was going to be full of a party of bigwigs,
not women and children. Whole families were wiped out. The Americans
insist that these women and children were put there deliberately. I ask
you, is that logical? One can imagine the conversation at Command
Headquarters going something like this, "Well I think the Americans will
hit the Ameriya shelter next, let's fill it full of women and children."

The garden and orchard are beginning to dry out. I use all the 75
washing-up water for the plants. I wish we could have a bit of rain.

Tonight was peaceful. Perhaps after Ameriya they will have to be more careful.

*Day Thirty.* A whole month. We are still here, ruined and going strong. Everyone was in the streets firing shots into the air today. What for? Munir said dramatically that it was an invasion. In fact, it was a salute for those who died in the shelter. I think this firing in the air can be interpreted as a sort of protest; in Mosul, they say, there was an actual demonstration.

Our big mistake was not to move out of Kuwait by January 15. That would have left the Allies in a hell of a dilemma. I wish I could see into the future, see what's in store for us.

*Day Thirty-one.* We woke up to a totally black sky and the smell of burning gasoline everywhere. A nasty, windy, sandy day. Rain, please come and feed my plants.

I had to go to the doctor — inflamed tonsils, throat, and lungs plus a blocked nose. He asked me if I smoked. Very funny. . . .

The score today: 76,000 air raids versus 67 Scuds.                                          80

*Day Thirty-two.* . . . Ma is making an orange cake in the dark, Suha hovering nearby, learning the recipe. Ma intends to bake it all night long on the dying embers; she hopes it will be like a slow oven.

We stopped burning tires after the BBC rumbled it; we have invented a new form of camouflage: eucalyptus trees. They are uprooted and made to stand upright between sandbags on bridges. I wonder which genius thought of that.

*Day Thirty-three.* I coughed all night. It rained, which was very nice. Between fits of coughing, the air-raid sirens, and the bombing I slept about half an hour. Ma's orange cake was burnt on the outside, raw on the inside, and tasted of smoke.

*Day Thirty-four.* The streets are black and shiny after the sooty rain; the puddles look like oil slicks. [Iraqi Foreign Minister] Tariq Aziz has gone to Moscow, but I don't think it will help us. Bush is fighting a dirty war and will hammer us till the bitter end, indifferent to the number of Iraqis he kills. The West has three images of Arabs: terrorists, oil-rich sheiks, and women covered in black from head to toe. I'm not even sure they know that there are ordinary human beings who live here.

Have we hit rock bottom yet?                                                                 85

Hisham came by this morning to offer his condolences for Mundher Baig's death. He was followed by Tim Llewellyn, the BBC correspondent, and the first foreigner I have seen since the war began. When I saw him at the bottom of the drive, I literally bristled. I wonder if he felt it? By the time he had walked up our drive I had overcome my hostility. After all one cannot blame individuals for the actions of governments. Otherwise we would all have to answer for the mess we are in. Tim brought faxes from Sol, Dood, and Charlie, our first contact with family and friends — a break in our isolation.

We have a new antiaircraft gun, a 16-mm or whatever, very close by. It makes a beautiful slow dull thudlike noise and adds weight to our nightly open-air concert.

At night, when the sky is covered with great big white and red flashes and our neighborhood gun is thudding away, it is almost possible to kid oneself that one is attending a Philip Glass opera with an overlay of *son et lumière.*[1]

Mr. Bush said no to the overtures of Tariq Aziz — no surprise. It doesn't serve his purpose. He's very brave. He passes judgment on us as he plays golf in Washington.

We had a super barbecue lunch today, a lovely day but quite noisy. I can't bear to hear the Voice of America going on about American children and how they are being affected by this war. Mrs. Bush, the so-called humane partner in that marriage, had the gall to comfort a group of American school kids by saying, "Don't worry, it's far away."

*Day Thirty-five.*   At about ten o'clock this morning Tim returned with a BBC retinue saying that he wanted to do a piece about us surviving *in situ.* I talked, I don't think I was very good. I didn't say any of the things I wanted to say. They filmed us drawing up buckets of water to the roof, and Najul and company camping in Dood's house with Jawdat lying sick on his mattress on the floor. I gave the crew oranges, recently picked from the orchard.

*Day Thirty-six.* . . .   My first anemones have come out from the seeds I bought last year in the United States. They are white. A sign of peace? Anyway something good from the US of A has grown here.

*Day Thirty-seven.*   Pat heard me on the BBC yesterday. I was described as an angry woman. They did not edit out the silly things I had said, like America must be jealous of us because we have culture and they don't, which must be why they have bombed our archaeological sites. But who could envy us?

M.A.W. went to have lunch with Khalil and was given his pet cockerel to eat. It gave him indigestion. Khalil had kept this cockerel for seven

---

[1]Philip Glass: A contemporary American composer. *Son et lumière*: French, "sound and light." — ED.

years. Recently it had gone crazy and killed two of their hens, before turning on the ducks. Khalil took it to the vet who advised him to cook the cockerel in a *tishreeb*. Imagine cooking a pet you have had for seven years; it's almost cannibalism.

It must have been about nine P.M. and we were all in the kitchen 95 washing up in flickering candlelight. Dinner was a delicious concoction — pasta with a vodka sauce. The pasta was the real thing, inherited from the Italian archaeologists who had rented Dood's house, not stolen Kuwaiti stuff. Suddenly there was a terrible noise and an unreal light, like a sun homing in on us through the kitchen windows. The floor was shaking so violently that we thought the house would come down on our heads. We crouched on the floor and suddenly, without our knowing how, the door had opened and all six of us were outside in the garden. An immense fireball was hovering over us, a fireball that appeared to be burning the tops of the palm trees. Suddenly this giant flaming object tilted and went roaring up into the night sky. Suha was on her knees, arms raised high, screaming, "*Ya ustad*, why here, why in the orchards among the houses?" She calls Our Leader *ustad*, teacher, a polite term considering the world is exploding around us. We later discovered from the BBC that it was a Scud missile, launched from a mobile truck; probably the one that landed in Bahrain. At the time we could not decide whether it was a plane, a missile, or a rocket. Or even whether it was coming or going.

Immediately afterward, while we were still outside, Ma took me aside and whispered hoarsely to me that this was all my fault because I'd said the Americans had no culture. Honestly. . . .

*Day Thirty-eight.* . . . It's a balmy day; spring is everywhere. It is difficult to believe that there is a war on even though we have already had two air raids this morning, planes all over the sky. Fuzzle came by and cooked us a delicious hot lentil lunch.

Apparently last night's Scud was seen and heard all over the Suleikh. Everyone thought it was directly above us. It was launched from somewhere near our bridge. How and with what does one ignite (is that the right word) a Scud? How far back does one have to stand? They seem to be horrifically inaccurate and erratic machines. . . .

*Day Thirty-nine.* Today is as ugly as yesterday was beautiful; the air is thick with smog. God knows what they are burning. It's noon and we have had five raids already. My cough will not go away. How many Hiroshimas so far? Tim Llewellyn says that the Iraqis are resigned to their fate. It's true, we are just waiting now, a few days, a few weeks. Bush and the Emir of Kuwait had a breakfast date in Kuwait on the twenty-fifth.

Well, it's the twenty-fifth today and they are not breakfasting together. Small comfort.

*Days Forty and Forty-one.* Nights and days full of noise, no sleep possi- 100
ble. For forty days and nights, a biblical figure, we have stood with our mouths open swallowing bombs. We didn't have anything to do with the Kuwaiti takeover, yet we are paying the price for it. We are living in an Indian movie, or better still we are like Peter Sellers in *The Party*, refusing to die, rising up again and again for a last gasp on the bugle. Indian movies never really end.

Tim came by to pick up the letters. He is leaving to go back to Cyprus. I was pruning the roses and taking cuttings in Najul's house. Gardening is my only relief — nothing beats plants as soothing company. When I feel aggressive I cut and prune; when I feel hopeful I plant.

*Day Forty-two.* Defeat is a terrible feeling. This morning, the forty-second day, the war stopped. They kept at us all night long, just in case we had a couple of gasps left in us. It was the worst night of bombing of the whole war. Nobody slept a wink. I think they dropped all the leftover ammunition.

They say the Americans are in Nasiriya. Will they enter Baghdad? As in my dream, will they come marching down Haifa Street?

*March 3.* The war has been over for some days. Today Schwarzkopf met with whoever we sent as representative. We agreed to everything. After all the hyperbole that they use against us, the Americans are now simply sitting in Nasiriya checking people's ID. Meanwhile our national radio continues to broadcast our victory. We fought thirty-two nations and are still here! True — until one looks at the condition that we are in.

Stories of returning soldiers are endless, even high-ranking officers are 105
walking home from the south, a total breakdown of the system. It apparently takes from a week to ten days to walk the distance from Kuwait to Baghdad, all the time dodging Allied planes; the Jaguars in particular keep trying to pick off the stragglers. Who flies Jaguars other than the Brits? And they call themselves civilized, hitting at retreating and unarmed soldiers. All the wounded who could not run away fast enough were killed. The others walk with no food or water, and collapse in heaps when they arrive at their houses.

*March 7.* We had such a storm yesterday — wind, black sky, rain, an orange-colored sandstorm, then rain again and howling wind. Two palm trees came down in Needles's orchard; they crashed right onto our fence, bringing it down. Now it's open to the wild dog packs. We have had to kill six dogs so far, and bury them in the orchard.

Sections of Baghdad already have electricity; some say we will get it tomorrow. I don't believe it. It apparently comes for a day and then goes off. I'm sure someone is trundling the same generator around to different parts of Baghdad to give everybody a taste. I have forgotten what it feels like to turn on a light switch. Rumor has it that Basra has fallen again.

*March 8.* Just returned from a yummy lunch of smoked salmon — Lubna had given me some before the war, and I stored it with Abbas, who has a generator. Took it out today and ate it at Dhafir and Mutaza's. They had electricity — and ice! Mutaza says that electricity shows up the dirt in your house, and that ever since hers came on she has been cleaning like a demented woman. I dread to think what my house is going to look like; that soot from the chimney must have left a thick film on everything. . . .

*March 12.* Many macabre funny stories. One about a taxi driver coming back from the front with a dead soldier's coffin on top of his car. He was searching for the poor bugger's parents and went into a house to ask the way — only to find his taxi and the coffin gone. There are no police to complain to. Another story is about a government truck selling gas bottles in the street. When the bottles had all been sold and the driver was ready to move off he discovered there was no petrol in the car. It had all been siphoned off. Sheikha says that the only thing the West knows about us is the fable of "The Thief of Baghdad" — perhaps they are right.

Tahsin, the grocer, told me that he had heard me talk on the BBC. 110 He asked me what it was like outside, in the United Kingdom. I could not think of much to say except that it rains so much there that your bones get wet. He thought for a minute and then said, "I guess every place has its pros and cons." A sweet man. His mother, Khairiya, a lovely smiley lady, took literacy classes and came top, but now can't read a thing, having forgotten it all. Ma and Needles's maid also had to take those classes, but after three years she was still unable to read bus numbers.

Munir crashed into some pole while on his bike and smashed his face and nose. . . .

*March 14.* What a way to raid a country — apparently we denuded Kuwait of everything plus the kitchen sink. Airplanes, buses, traffic lights, appliances, everything. Our shops are full of their goods. We know nothing about our situation.

We may have petrol by Sunday. Bush says he is worried about the mess that we are in. My, how decent of him. I must do something or go mad — perhaps build a swimming pool?

*March 16.* . . . More irises are out. It was deadly quiet during the day because the security forces were out checking for arms in houses in the Grey'at area near us. They searched Khalil and Amal's houses. They took away Khalil's typewriter even though he has permission for it. I wonder if I should hide mine. He was very upset with the officers because they fingered everything, including his wife's underwear. I asked him how he could have eaten his favorite pet cockerel. He said that he was feeling so guilty about the whole episode that he had been having disturbed dreams about it for days.

*March 17.* The stories are getting more grotesque. Kufa, Kirkuk, and Basra, bodies and bodies lie everywhere. In Kufa it seems they (who?) have pillaged the university buildings and burned papers and documents in the library — more devastation and destruction. . . . 115

*March 19.* In the coffee shops the talk is not of nationalism but of the desire for the United States to come in and take over — get it over with. Our television coverage remains the same.

*March 20.* A gang robbed Umberto's house of a thousand crates of beer which he had been storing for his company. Only his clothes and the beer were taken. Each crate of beer sells for 80 dinars. That is 80,000 dinars right there, a fortune. No one steals electrical goods anymore. Petrol, beer, and cigarettes are the popular items, although oddly they all go for the same price.

It seems we will be allowed to travel from June 1. Human rights dictate that people can travel and we must follow those guidelines. Human rights?

*March 28.* It is too depressing to write. I keep saying that it can't get worse and it does.

Met Mohammed G.'s sister today, recently fled from Kerbela. She saw horrific sights, dead bodies left on the street, relatives too frightened to remove them, bodies being eaten by dogs and cats. They have been bulldozing the area around the mosque and shrine; people were given three days to clear out of their houses. All of the old Kerbela will disappear. The whole thing is sick. 120

I have a new war: against snails. At least 10 billion snails have invaded the orchard — that is the round figure that is being bandied around for everything these days; it might as well apply to my snail count. They eat every green thing they see; they even ate my new baby magnolia, transplanted recently from Asam's garden. She says these things happen only in my garden, never hers. The dogs are on the increase again. Poor

Salvador, he has to pee so much to mark his territorial boundaries that his leg is permanently poised in midair. He is quite exhausted and probably dehydrated.

We came back walking tonight, pushing our bikes. Nearly a full moon. Naylah only found out her brother was alive when her husband in London saw him on television, a hostage in Saudi Arabia — live on CNN, as they say.

## EXPLORATIONS

1. What evidence in "Baghdad Diary" shows the author's hostility toward the West? What are the reasons for her hostility?

2. What evidence in "Baghdad Diary" shows the author's affection for the West? What are the reasons for her affection?

3. In paragraph 93 Nuha Al-Radi mentions telling the BBC that "America must be jealous of us because we have culture and they don't." What elements does her definition of *culture* evidently include, and what elements does it exclude?

4. What are the positive and negative effects of describing life during wartime in diary form rather than essay form?

## CONNECTIONS

1. What points about war are made both by Nuha Al-Radi and by Czeslaw Milosz in "American Ignorance of War" (p. 671)?

2. Reread paragraph 73 of "Baghdad Diary." What replies to the author's bitter question and comments are suggested by the writers in *Looking at Ourselves*?

3. Look back at Miriam Cooke's "The Veil Does Not Prevent Women from Working" (p. 372). Why do you think Nuha Al-Radi's bicycle ride through Baghdad "caused a sensation in the streets" (para. 29)? Whom does the "sour man" mean by *we* when he shouts, "We don't like girls that ride bikes"?

## ELABORATIONS

1. Using "Baghdad Diary" as your source, write a classification essay identifying the various ways Nuha Al-Radi and her social circle in Baghdad are influenced by Western culture, both positively (from CNN to Salvador Dali) and negatively. (You may also want to refer to Paul Harrison's "The Westernization of the World," p. 41.)

2. What time span is covered by "Baghdad Diary"? What is the author's attitude toward the West, and what is her attitude toward her own government, before the United States begins bombing Iraq? How can you tell? At what points and in what ways does each attitude change? Write a cause-and-effect essay showing how the war alters Nuha Al-Radi's sense of herself as an Iraqi and as a citizen of the world.

# MICHAEL KELLY

## *Torture in Kuwait*

Michael Kelly was born in 1957 in Washington, D.C. After majoring in history at the University of New Hampshire, he worked for the ABC television program "Good Morning America" for three years. He became a reporter on the metropolitan desk of the *Cincinnati Post*, then the Washington correspondent for the *Baltimore Sun*. In 1989 he moved to Chicago as a free-lance writer. "Torture in Kuwait" comes from his 1993 book *Martyrs' Day: Chronicle of a Small War*. The book grew out of four long trips Kelly made to the Middle East between November 1990 and November 1991 while covering events leading up to the Persian Gulf war, the war itself, and its aftermath for *The New Republic*, the *Boston Globe*, and *Gentlemen's Quarterly*. His stories in *The New Republic* won an Overseas Press Club Award and a National Magazine Award. Kelly is now a Washington correspondent for the *New York Times*; he lives in D.C. with his wife, Madelyn, a producer for "CBS Evening News."

Although Iraq lies at the northwestern end of the Persian Gulf, tiny Kuwait blocks most of its access to that key waterway. Kuwait also owns rich oil fields whose income Iraq coveted after its long and expensive war with Iran (see p. 475). Encouraged by mistrust between the United States and Iran's militant Islamic leaders, Iraqi President Saddam Hussein amassed increasing military and political power before invading Kuwait in August 1990 (see p. 677). Arab as well as Western countries wondered whether Iraq would invade Saudi Arabia next, whether the energy-hungry West would lose its access to Middle Eastern oil, and whether Iraq was building nuclear weapons, among other concerns. Heads of state debated whether economic sanctions could reverse the takeover or force was necessary. In "Torture in Kuwait," Michael Kelly documents one rumor used as an argument for a prompt military response: the Iraqi invaders' brutality to their Kuwaiti victims.

For more information on Kuwait, see page 475; on Saudi Arabia, see page 372; on Iraq and the Persian Gulf war, see page 677.

The hall at Kuwait University's school of music and drama was a place of conspicuous civilization, a big cantilevered room with blue cloth seats trimmed in gold. The walls were paneled in some rich wood, and a deep, broad stage surmounted the orchestra pit. The first discordant signs of barbarism were feathers and bones. The building was of modern design, with an exterior ramp that led several stories up to a broad concrete platform, which in turn led to the doors that opened into the top tier of the auditorium. The Iraqis had used the platform as a pen for chickens and sheep, and what the beasts had left behind made a rotting, malodorous mess underfoot.

Inside the hall a British television crew was videotaping the statement of twenty-nine-year-old Abdullah Jasman, Kuwaiti citizen, University of Pittsburgh graduate, and victim of a torture session in this unlikely setting. The crew had set their camera up on the balcony, and Jasman stood a few feet away, facing it. When I walked in, the producer in charge motioned with his finger to his lips for me to be quiet. I stopped, and the place was still and silent except for the man standing in front of the camera, talking and crying. He was a square-built black man, with strong, homely features; not the face of one for public weeping. But this sort of thing no longer surprised me. In normal life, you hardly ever see grown men cry; in war, it is a commonplace. Between the beginning of things and the end, I must have seen twenty men cry, not counting myself.

Near where the camera stood, there lay a broken rubber-handled truncheon. In a corner was a pile of academic robes, trimmed in azure and gold, sodden and reeking of wet rot and urine. Here and there the tile floor was spotted with drops of dried blood, little trails that went nowhere in particular.

"One day on the highway the Iraqis stopped us," the black man began.

"Could you just come forward a bit, Abdullah?" said the producer.   5
"Need to get you in frame properly."

He moved forward a step. The producer said, "Now, that's a good chap. Where were we, hmm?"

"I was with a group of people. They covered our eyes and roped our hands and put us in a line and walked us up here." A door cracked suddenly shut, and he jumped in a rabbity little hop.

"Oh, sorry, Abdullah," the producer said. He gestured to his Ministry of Information guide. "You there, keep that door shut." Turning back to the black man: "Now then."

"They hang us upside down. Naked, no clothes; we are not allowed to sleep or eat. They try to get us drunk, but we do not. So they started torturing us. The three days passed like years. (He was crying hard now.) Human beings can't resist. You hear people screaming next to you and then you think you are going to be next. You can't resist. What are you going to do? (Now, racking sobs) You can't sleep. You don't know, if you sleep, if you will ever wake again. . . . All the people screaming, begging, screaming."

The producer interrupted him, to prompt him toward the thing that   10
made for television. "Abdullah, could you tell us what happened to you in particular, here in this theater?" he said.

The victim pointed to the stage, on which stood a big section of steel set scaffolding. "On this stage, you can see the metal frame. They put both legs on that and they open them wide and they put a sort of wood on you that comes from one knee to another and they spread you open all the way. When you are open wide, it hurts you. It hurts you bad. They raped one of my friends here. They raped him. They were laughing. They said, 'This is what your president did to you.' I heard later he was dead."

He drifted back into hideous reverie. "You sat in these chairs, waiting to be tortured. You can't see anything. You can hear the voices loud and screaming. . . . They wanted to know where is my brother. I didn't tell them; I didn't know. . . . My family gave them five thousand Kuwait dinars and videos and a TV. . . . They let me go. . . ."

The producer gave him another little push. "And what did they do to you besides putting you on the rack, Abdullah?"

He pulled up his pants legs and showed the camera his calves, mottled with ugly deep black burn wounds. "They put electricity on you with batteries. They would put wires on your legs and your feet in water, so your whole body is electricity. They would put you with the electricity in the water twenty seconds, thirty seconds, and you would go unconscious and they would throw water on you and revive you and then do it again."

As he was finishing, he offered an observation on the nature of torture.   15 "Torture not only hurts at the time. It will hurt all your life. You get up at night and you think that you are in a torture room, not in bed. You are in a safe place, and you think that you are not safe. It is like a fingerprint for the rest of your life." He shivered when he said this, as if fevered.

The producer thanked him, and motioned for the cameraman to turn off the machine. "Well," he said, "I must say, your story is really something." The black man stood silent, with one trouser leg hiked up to the knee and tear trails streaking the dust on his face. . . .

After I left the theater, I drove to a gas station in a middle-class residential neighborhood. Gas had been largely unavailable since December 2, when the Iraqis forbade its sale to Kuwaitis, but here and there stations were getting their pumps working again, and word of where there was gas circulated around the city every day. There must have been three hundred people and a long line of cars waiting on a crew of four or five men who were working with portable pumps and generators to get the gasoline up from the underground tanks. I put my cans in line and went into the little office of the gas station to escape the heat. There was a man behind the desk who looked in charge. He said that, actually, it wasn't his gas station, but he knew his way around pumps and engines, so his neighbors had made him boss. He was a tall, skinny man, with features that were all crags and hollows. He handed me his card, which identified him, in fancy script, as Basim Eid Abhool, Assistant Electrical Engineer, Kuwait International Airport. When I gave it back to him, I noticed his fingernails, or rather the lack of them. They had been removed, and what was left was just the barest baby beginnings of new nails, little strips of cuticle as soft and fragile as the shells of the smallest shrimp. "Ah, you notice my fingers?" the man said. "Iraqis, of course."

He told his story in a matter-of-fact way, leaning his forearms on the desk, and with his hands folded so that his fingernails were tucked away. A group of men gathered around while he talked, but they were quiet, so that all you could hear was his voice and the buzzing of flies. I sat in a hard little yellow plastic chair and wrote down what he said. He spoke slowly, so it was easy to get it all verbatim.

"It was on January 19. They arrested me outside, while I was walking. They took me to a prison. They say, 'Are you in army?' I say, 'Yes, but not anymore. Now I work at airport and am an assistant engineer.' They put me in a small room and they say, 'Exactly what do you do in the army?'

"I say, 'When I am in army, I am a writer, not a soldier, and now I am not in army anyway.' 20

"They say, 'You have friends, cousins, in army?' I say, 'I don't know.' They say, 'Do you know that your president, Sheik Jaber, he is no good?'

"I say, 'I don't know.'

"They say, 'Do you know what your president do to your people?'

"I say, 'I don't know. What do he do to my people?'

"They say, "He marry two hundred women and he take all your money.' 25

"I say, 'I do not know that. Thank you for telling me.'

"They say, 'The Iraqi people have come to give freedom to people of Kuwait.'

"Then a man comes in who has no uniform. He says, 'Put him in jail.' I stay in jail until Thursday. All the time, behind me in the other room, I hear screaming. 'No, no, please, no, I don't do anything, please.' I listen. I am afraid. On the second day, they come back and they say, 'Put your hands on the table.' I put my hands on the table and they take a stick and hit my hands. They say, 'Can you feel?' I say, 'Yes.' They say, 'Good.' Then two guys take my hands and hold them and they tell me to close my eyes and they take pliers and one by one pull out all my fingers [fingernails]. Then they put them in salt water. And go away.

"You know, the first day and the second day and the third, I feel terrible. But after that I cannot feel it. My hands, my arms, my head, all feels numb. On the third day, Thursday, they take me back to the room. They take my fingers and where the nails were, they take pliers and crush. It is too much. Much too much. I faint. When I wake up, they say, 'You have Kuwait money?' I say, 'No.' They put me back in jail.

"On the fourth day, they say, 'Don't tell anybody what we do here. If you tell anybody, we will kill you.' And they let me go. I go home. My family is all gone out of Kuwait, but my friends say, 'What happen to your fingers?' I say, 'It was an electrical accident at work.' Two weeks later, I see the Iraqis who did this to me at supermarket. They are shopping. One of them says hello to me and he says, 'How are your fingers? Are they good?' I say, 'No, they are not good.' He says, 'Come back to the police station and we will make them good.' And then they laugh.

"But now — *hamdililah*[1] — I am good again."

A thin man, squatting on the floor, picking his teeth with a bit of wood, spoke up. His name was Wael Yusef al-Moutawa, twenty-three years old, an employee of the Kuwait National Petroleum Company. He said: "One day the Iraqi soldiers arrest me. I was carrying a gun because I was a resistance fighter. A Kalashnikov. They beat me, and after that, they take a rope and tie my hands behind my back and tie the rope on the ceiling and pull me up by my hands tied behind my back. They kept me hanging there. The first hour was not so bad, but then it got very bad.

"My father and mother came and they brought two thousand dinars to free me. They took the money and said to my parents, 'Soon, he will get out.'

"The next day, an Iraqi man comes to me and he says, 'You love Mr. Jaber? Okay, you watch this. This is what Mr. Jaber does to your people.' He brings in a girl twenty years old, maybe. I am staying on the wall tied up. I try not to see. The soldiers pull my head and say, 'You must see.' One soldier holds the girl hard and the other fucks her. She tries to stop them. She says, 'I am a virgin.' She says to the soldiers, 'You are a Muslim. You must be polite to me. You must be a good man. You cannot do this to me. I am a Muslim. I am your sister.'

"He says, 'I am not a Muslim.'

"She says, 'You do not believe in God?'

"He says, 'You have a God? Where is your God? There is no God. Who is Muhammad? An old man.'

"Then they rape her and I watch and I can see the blood going out. They put her on the floor of the room and do it. And then they take her out, like a sheep. It was very shameful."

---

[1] Arabic, "thank God." — Ed.

He thought about it for a minute and then he said, "I think there are no Muslims in Iraq. Not at all. Really, they are all crazy."

A smiling middle-aged man with a grocer's figure interrupted to dis-   40
agree slightly. He introduced himself as Ali Zamoon, general manager of the Kuwait National Real Estate Company. He had been educated in America and had married an American woman. He had an American sort of theory. The Iraqis were not precisely crazy, but were brainwashed, a nation of Manchurian Candidates.

"One time I was stopped by some Iraqi soldiers while I was driving my car. They asked me why I had not changed my license plates from Kuwaiti plates to Iraqi. I said I forgot to do it, or something. But they could not get over it. They could not understand how I could have failed to change the plates after Saddam had told me to do so. They said, 'How can you disobey an order from Saddam?' This made me think about it, and I realized that there was something wrong with these people. Everything they did and thought was all about Saddam. It was Saddam! Saddam! Saddam! all the time. They were like robots. They would follow this man anywhere, doing whatever, because they could not imagine disobeying him. They could not see any point to disobeying an order, even if they knew it was wrong. One day I had a talk with an Iraqi officer I had come to know a little. I asked him, 'If they tell you from Baghdad to kill me, would you kill me?' And he said, 'Yes.' I said, 'Why?' He said, 'Because if they ask me to kill you and I say no, they will kill me and then kill you anyway.'" . . .

The Iraqis I had met in Baghdad had seemed to me to be generous, likable people — this had been true even of most of the bureaucrats. I had a hard time reconciling my memory of them with the overwhelming evidence of how the Iraqis had behaved in Kuwait. At first, thinking about it, I speculated that the horror inflicted on the Kuwaitis had been largely a professional job, conducted by the torturers and executioners of the Iraqi security forces, for practical reasons. There was some truth in this. The Iraqis did have what you could fairly call a rationale for conducting a campaign of terror — that is, to subjugate a hostile, numerically overwhelming population. When the Kuwaitis resisted, the Iraqis employed the methods they had found effective, over the past twenty-five years, in quelling dissent at home: arbitrary arrest and detention, widespread torture, frequent murders, and public executions.

But the evidence was overwhelming that while the worst torture and the greatest number of executions and rapes had been committed by the security forces there had also been many instances in which ordinary soldiers and officers had committed these acts, and for no evidently logical reason. A lot of people I talked to held to the view that the Iraqis were simply, fundamentally evil. I heard this again and again: The Iraqis were not normal, they liked inflicting pain, they liked brutality and destruction, they liked killing people. The subscribers to this belief pointed to history, which they said showed the Iraqis were a bloodthirsty people, even by local standards.

It was true that the Iraqis had an exceptionally violent past. The Assyrians, sweeping out from Nineveh, in what is now north-central Iraq, to conquer everything from northern Saudi Arabia to Turkey, had set a standard of behavior remembered three thousand years later. "I built a pillar over against the city gate, and I flayed all the chief men," wrote the Assyrian king Assurnasirpal II, recalling one victorious campaign. "And I covered the pillar with their skins; some I walled up within the pillar, some I impaled upon the pillar on stakes . . . and I cut off the limbs of the officers. . . . From some, I cut off their hands and their fingers, and from others I cut off their noses, their ears . . . of many I put out their eyes. . . . Their young men and maidens I burned in the fire."

Throughout Iraq's history, violence had served as the principal means   45 of exercising political will and effecting policy. In his book *Republic of Fear*, the Iraqi political scientist Samir al-Khalil (a pseudonym) compares Saddam Hussein's reign with that of al-Hadjadj ibn Yusef al-Thaqafi, the governor of Iraq in the late seventh and early eighth centuries. Al-Hadjadj brought order to Iraq, then a chaotic, independent-minded province of the Damascus-based Umayyad dynasty, and established a bureaucracy that laid the foundations for the great Abbasid dynasty. Al-Hadjadj's inaugural speech, al-Khalil says, is known to every Iraqi schoolchild, and is regarded as a truthful depiction of the exercise of political power in Iraq:

"I see heads before me that are ripe and ready for the plucking and I am the one to pluck them, and I see blood glistening between the turbans and the beards. By God, O people of Iraq, people of discord and dissembling and evil character . . . For a long time you have lain in the lairs of error, and have made a rule of transgression. By God, I shall strip you like bark, I shall truss you like a bundle of twigs, I shall beat you like stray camels. . . ."

"The special problem of Baathi violence," writes al-Khalil, "begins with the realization that hundreds and thousands of perfectly ordinary people are implicated in it. Even Saddam Hussein's torturers and elite police units who do the dirtiest work are by and large normal. There are too many of them for it to be otherwise. From being a means to an end, violence has turned into an end in itself, into the way in which all politics (finally no politics) is experienced by the public in Iraq."

Corrupt regimes corrupt those who live under them, and in their own particular way of corruption. A regime corrupted by a lust for money creates a society sickened by greed and selfishness. A regime corrupted by a lust for violence creates a society sickened by an appetite for the true sins of the flesh, the violation and desecration and destruction of it. The young men who came from Iraq to Kuwait — some of them, by no means all — found they had the appetite to do to the Kuwaitis the terrible things that the Mukhabarat[2] did back home. And there was no one to stop them. Indeed, the masters of the evil, the professional sadists of the security forces, were among them, doing the worst of it; Ali Hassan Majid, the governor of the new nineteenth province, was known, by previous exploits among the Kurds, for his approval of the harshest measures. An astonishing and terrible thing: to be nineteen years old, a country boy, to find yourself in the richest place you had ever seen, a city filled with weak and trembling people, and to realize that you had within you terrible desires — to hurt these people, to rape a pretty girl and then throw her in the trash, to stomp a man's face under your boots — and that you had, as it were, permission to do so. It must have been blackly exciting at first, and then sickening, and by the end a descent into Conradian self-horror. All the physical signs of the occupation — the filth, the destruction, the garbage and shit even in the Iraqis' own quarters — spoke of men sinking deeper and deeper into rottenness. No wonder they had fled in the night. They must have been ashamed to think they would be caught in the place of their sins; they must have yearned to run with their backs to the awfulness, to get home to Iraq and never admit to a soul what they had done.

## EXPLORATIONS

1. What important contrast does Michael Kelly set up in paragraph 1? How would the impact of his essay's first section change without this introductory description? What is the effect of Kelly's including the British television producer's comments as well as the Kuwaiti torture victim's (paras. 2–16)?

2. What explanations do Kelly and his interviewees offer for the Iraqis' treatment of the Kuwaitis?

3. How and where in "Torture in Kuwait" does Kelly express a personal response to the incidents he reports? What tactics does he use to stir up his readers' emotions?

---

[2]Secret police. — ED.

4. In the second section of his essay, what is the effect of Kelly's describing the accidental way he got this information (para. 17)? What is the effect of his describing where and how he recorded it (para. 18)? How would the essay's impact change if Kelly excluded himself from it and reported only the Kuwaitis' testimony?

## CONNECTIONS

1. What view of Iraqis and of their invasion of Kuwait emerges from "Torture in Kuwait"? What view emerges from Nuha Al-Radi's "Baghdad Diary" (p. 677)? What factors in the writers' situations and goals account for the contrast?

2. What observations in Kelly's essay suggest that, before the Iraqi invasion, Kuwait shared the privileged ignorance Czeslaw Milosz attributes to the United States in "American Ignorance of War" (p. 671)?

3. How do Kelly's ideas about sadistic violence in paragraph 48 compare with the views expressed in the Associated Press selection in *Looking at Ourselves* (p. 607)? Do Kelly's comments offer us any help toward understanding violence in the United States? If so, how? If not, why not?

4. Look back at Gholam-Hossein Sa'edi's story "The Game Is Over" (p. 162), especially paras. 5–53. What observations in the third section of "Torture in Kuwait" (paras. 42–48) might help to explain the attitude toward violence that Sa'edi depicts in Iran?

## ELABORATIONS

1. In "House of Stone" (p. 569), Michael Dorris writes about the journalist's challenge of trying to engage readers in the problems of strangers. What tactics does Dorris use to confront this challenge? What tactics does Michael Kelly use in "Torture in Kuwait"? Write an essay comparing and contrasting the journalistic strategies in these two selections and their effectiveness; or, write an essay classifying the strategies used by Dorris, Kelly, David Grossman in "Israeli Arab, Israeli Jew" (p. 629), and Yoram Binur in "Palestinian Like Me" (p. 275).

2. Why does one individual deliberately cause harm and pain to another? Write an essay answering this question, using selections in Part Seven and elsewhere in this book as sources (for example, Gholam-Hossein Sa'edi's "The Game Is Over"; Yashar Kemal's "A Dirty Story," p. 380; Simone de Beauvoir's "Woman as Other," p. 329; and Yoram Binur's "Palestinian Like Me").

# ALICE WALKER

## *The Concord Demonstration*

Alice Malsenior Walker was born in Eatonton, Georgia, in 1944, where her parents were sharecroppers and her father was the first black man ever to vote in the United States. The youngest of eight children, she was blinded in one eye at age eight by her brother's BB gun. "Because I felt I was unpleasant to look at, filled with shame, I retreated into solitude, and read stories, and began to write poems," she recalls in her book *In Search of Our Mothers' Gardens* (1983). In high school Walker was valedictorian and senior class queen. She attended Spelman College for two years and graduated from Sarah Lawrence College in 1965. A summer in Africa supplied some material for her first book of poetry, *Once* (1968). After college Walker moved to Mississippi, where she registered black voters and met her husband, civil-rights attorney Melvyn Leventhal (they divorced in 1977). Walker worked with the Head Start children's program, as a writer in residence at Jackson State and Tougaloo colleges, and for *Ms.* magazine. She published several books of poems, stories, and nonfiction before her famous novel *The Color Purple* (1982). Besides winning the American Book Award and the 1983 Pulitzer Prize, *The Color Purple*, which has sold over 4 million copies in twenty-two languages, was made into a film by Quincy Jones and Stephen Spielberg. Walker currently lives in northern California with writer Robert Allen. Among her recent books is *Possessing the Secret of Joy* (1992).

*June 17, 1987.* Early this morning . . . I received an urgent call from "Liz" of Neighbor to Neighbor, an activist group that successfully gets out news about the wars in Central America, using U.S. media, primarily television. Two days from now there will be a program it has organized called "The Peace Oscars" — named for Archbishop Oscar Romero, who was a defender of poor people's rights in El Salvador until his assassination, by an agent of the Salvadoran government, while he administered mass in his church. At the ceremony, which will be held in the beautiful Conservatory of Flowers in Golden Gate Park in San Francisco, six of the bravest and most compassionate of human beings will be honored: people who have risked their lives to take medicine, food, clothing, and technical skills to the poor and suffering people of Central America; men and women who have been arrested many times as they exercised their opposition to the often genocidal policies of the U.S. government; people who founded the Sanctuary Movement in this country; one refugee woman from El Salvador, whose personal story of oppression, terror, escape, and commitment, told at hundreds of gatherings in the United States, radicalized the people who heard her and deepened their commitment to the struggle to end war. I am to cohost this program, and, in fact, give the Peace Oscar (a small blue ceramic bird) to the sister from El Salvador.

The urgent message from Liz, however, is that a bomb threat against the ceremony has been telephoned by a mechanical-sounding male voice that said our crime is that we do not want to fight communism. Because several of the participants and invited guests are federally appointed officials of the state of California, she tells me, there will be federal agents about, cordons of police and various SWAT teams, whose job it will be to sweep the place clean of any bombs. This often happens to movements like ours, she sighs. She tells me everyone involved will be called, in order for each to decide whether to come or stay home.

Of course I remember bomb threats, and bombs, from the sixties. I think of the children, Angela Davis's young acquaintances, blown up while in Sunday school. I think of Ralph Featherstone, a SNCC [Student Nonviolent Coordinating Committee] worker, blown up in his car. I think of the NAACP [National Association for the Advancement of Colored People] official, who, along with his wife, was blown up while in bed. When I lived in Mississippi, bombings occurred; when my husband and I moved there, the bombing/lynching of NAACP leader Vernon Dehmer was in the news. I remember the bombing of Dr. Martin Luther King's house. There is a long history of bombings in North America. This is not the first time "communism" has been used as an excuse.

I send along the message of the threat to the people I've invited. But I know I will not be deterred. I spend a few hours with my lawyer and finally draw up my overdue will and assign a durable power of attorney that will be effective through the weekend (the affair is to take place on a Friday night). It isn't fatalism, or courage; I simply can't imagine not being there to honor these amazing, but also ordinary, people. I can't imagine not being there to hug my sister from the south.

A writer, apparently, to the core (though I frequently kid myself that     5
if I never write again it's fine with me; there's so much else to do — sitting in a rocking chair watching the ocean, for instance), I find my thoughts going to my unfinished manuscripts. If anything happened to me, I wonder what my editor, John the meticulous, could make of my unfinished novel, a third typed and in a drawer, a third typed and in the computer, a third in my notebook and head.

What of this book? I realize that, as it stands, it has the rounded neatness of contemplation, and I would like to leave the reader with the uneven (I almost said ragged) edge of activity. I returned to my notes for the past week, and this is what I found:

> I am Nicaraguan; I am Salvadoran; I am Grenadian; I am Caribbean; and I am Central American.

For the past several days I have been thinking about this sentence, and wondering what I mean by it. I am also Norte Americana, an African-American, even an African-Indian-Gringo American, if I add up all the known elements of my racial composition (and include the white rapist grandfather). Perhaps this is one way that I am Nicaraguan, or Salvadoran, or Grenadian. For the people in those countries, too, are racially mixed; in their country, too, there are the reds, the blacks, the whites — and the browns.

But I think the primary reason that I feel so Central American/Caribbean is that when I look at those people — and even though I study but do not yet speak their language — I see myself. I see my family, I see my parents, I see the ancestors. When I look at Nicaraguans, at, for instance, the humble peasant woman being "interrogated" by a contra[1] carrying several guns and knives and three times her size, when I see and identify with her terror, when I look at the vulnerable faces of the nearly naked and barefoot children, when I see the suffering and pain on the faces of the men, then I am seeing a great deal of my own life.

I, too, was born poor, in an impoverished part of the world. I was born    10
on what had been a plantation in the South, in Georgia. My parents and grandparents worked hard all their lives for barely enough food and shelter to sustain them. They were sharecroppers — landless peasants — the product of whose labor was routinely stolen from them. Their parents and grandparents were enslaved. To me, Central America is one large plantation; and I see the people's struggle to be free as a slave revolt.

I can remember in my own life the days of *injusticia* that continue in so much of the world today. The days when children withered in sickness and disease (as I have withered) because there was no money to pay for their care and no concern for their health anyway, by the larger society. I myself have suffered the deprivations of poverty, so that when I look into the face of a Central American peasant, a Caribbean peasant, I see myself.

And I remember the years of fighting the white bosses of Georgia, Alabama, and Mississippi, especially, and of occasionally winning our battles for dignity and bread against them — though at a cost (so many of the people we loved were brutalized or assassinated) that still bruises

---

[1]The U.S.-backed contras fought a guerrilla war to regain control of Nicaragua's government after their right-wing military dictatorship was ousted by leftist Sandinistas. — ED.

the heart. When I see the proud though weary faces of the Sandinistas, I see our own young faces. The faces that went south in the sixties to teach black people to read and write, to go out to vote, to stand up and be counted. And to keep the eyes on the prize.

It is the same spirit. The spirit of poor people who have been ground down nearly to a fine powder of humanity and yet who stand like rocks and refuse to be blown away.

*I am Nicaraguan. I am Salvadoran. I am Grenadian, Honduran,* I chant to myself. It has almost become a mantra.[2]

*And yet,* this year I paid more in taxes than my parents and grandparents together earned all the years they worked the land of the gringos of the South. And over half of that money will go to buy weapons that will be shipped from the Concord Naval Weapons Station at Port Chicago, California, thirty miles from my home, and used against these people that I think of as myself.

These were my thoughts a few days before I was arrested for blocking one of the gates to the Concord Naval Weapons Station.

It was a hot, dusty day, June 12, 1987, and I woke up thinking of all the things I needed to bring to the demonstration: a hat, sunblock, drinking water, food, spare clothing (in case we were in jail for longer than a day), whatever medical supplies I might need. I drove to the weapons station with the three other members of my affinity group:[3] Robert, Belvie, and Paul. Belvie and I had designed beautiful turquoise-and-coral T-shirts with the name of our group (Wild Trees), a large mushroom cloud, and the words "Remember Port Chicago."

For the past ten years I have shared my life with the writer and sometimes political activist (primarily in the civil-rights movement and against the Vietnam war) Robert Allen, who all that time has been writing a book about the so-called accident at Port Chicago on July 17, 1944. What happened was that 320 men whose job it was to load the bombs being sent to use on Japan and other places in the Pacific were blown to bits (literally), along with the ships they were loading and much of the base and nearby town. Two hundred of those killed were black. Because theirs had been the job of loading the weapons onto the ships, theirs was also the job of picking up the pieces — of men and debris — left by the explosion. When asked to continue loading the bombs after this horrendous experience, most of the men said no. They were threatened, impris-

---

[2]Ritualistic incantation used in meditation.

[3]Small group formed within a larger group of demonstrators for protection and efficient action. — ED.

oned, tried for mutiny. Sentenced. Sent to jail. Released years later with dishonorable discharges.

My friend Robert has tracked down many of the surviving "mutineers" and, over the years, continued to wrestle with the implications of this event for America.

Port Chicago is now Concord. The name has been changed and the 20 old town of Port Chicago completely destroyed, razed, in fact, by the government. But the weapons remain. Rather, they remain long enough to be shipped out — to Japan (the bomb dropped on Hiroshima was shipped from here), Vietnam, Nicaragua, and now El Salvador.

A few days before the demonstration we — the organizers (The Pledge of Resistance), the news media, demonstrators-to-be, and I — stood on a hill overlooking the base. We could see the white trains — white to reflect the heat — going into bunkers built into the hillside. Inside those bunkers are some of the deadliest weapons ever devised. There is, for instance, something that sounds even worse than napalm:[4] the white phosphorous rocket. The sparks from it burn through the skin and flesh and into the bone. It can take a week for the burning to be put out. I have seen photographs of children who have lost limbs to the sparks from this rocket. I have found unbearable the suffering and questions in their eyes.

The morning of the demonstration I dress in jeans, sneakers, sunglasses, and an old felt hat, and I carry with me a sweet-faced black doll with crisp, shiny hair. I've named her Windela after a newborn niece of the same name I have not yet seen, and because I want to symbolize the connection I feel to Winnie and Nelson Mandela[5] and the common awareness that it is up to those of us who are adults to leave to all children a habitable planet.

During the previous week I have felt afraid. I have hardly been able to smile at anyone. Though I have risked arrest many times, while a student demonstrator at Spelman College, in Liberty County, Georgia, and in Mississippi as a civil-rights worker, I have been arrested only once before, during a demonstration against apartheid at University of California, Berkeley. I felt a lighthearted joy throughout that action; as I sat with other demonstrators I could not suppress smiles *and* song. I concluded that what was different this time was that I would be placing myself in such vulnerable proximity to an enormous pile of evil and death blandly passed off to motorists, who can actually see the trains and bunkers from

---

[4]A highly flammable jellylike substance used in firebombs, widely and destructively used in the Vietnam war. — ED.

[5]See p. 587. — ED.

the highway, as bucolic countryside: Cows graze placidly in the grass about the bunkers, giving them the aspect of odd kinds of barns.

Still, as I filled my backpack with a toothbrush, aspirin, and fruit, I began to take heart, the image of the children, the trees, and the animals of the planet always before me. On arrival, we went immediately to the gate to be blocked. There were a few protesters, about a hundred, already there. Across a broad yellow line, soldiers dressed in helmets and camouflage fatigues stood spread-legged holding long riot sticks. Behind them stood a row of officers in khaki from the local sheriff's department. Behind them another row of officers, presumably a SWAT team, in navy blue. The four of us walked up to face the soldiers, who were staring straight ahead. Between their row and that of the officers from the sheriff's department stood a Catholic priest, a woman in her fifties, and two old people, a man and a woman. They were all white. It was then that I made an interesting observation: Aside from myself and two members of our affinity group, there were no other people of color there. The army, represented by the soldiers standing in front of us, was much more integrated. *Merde!*[6] I thought. What does it mean, that the forces of destruction are more integrated than the forces of peace?

Almost at once a white car carrying an official of the base arrived at      25
the gate. We turned to face it, not permitting it to go through. The driver consulted with an army officer, and the car slowly pulled away. Another and another vehicle appeared. They were not admitted. Soon a woman drove up and said she needed to fill a prescription at the base; it was spontaneously agreed that she should be let through. Many of us walked behind her car to close the space behind her. Soon a man who said he had gout and was coming to see his doctor appeared. He was also let through. A woman next to me said that in anticipation of our blockade the weapons trains and trucks had been busy all night long.

We were arrested because we went through the line of soldiers — all of them mere children and obviously poor (bad skin, crooked teeth, a certain ghetto street-corner patina) — and stood with the priest and the woman in her fifties, and the two old people. The old woman, Teresa, with a wondrously wrinkled face and bright white hair (a true crone), clasped me to her thin chest. The old man, Abraham (yes), half Jewish and half American Indian, looked fixedly into the crowd behind us and sang a frail but steady version of "Amen." I felt very proud of our affinity group. Of Robert, who had joined this inner group first, of Paul, who had

---

[6]French, "shit." — ED.

promptly followed, and of Belvie, who was now smiling and talking to Teresa as if they were old friends.

A lot of things went through my mind as I was being handcuffed. Would they take my doll, whom I'd managed to stuff under one arm? No, they did not. Had my statements to the press truly reflected my feelings about weapons and war? I had been asked why I was risking arrest and I had said because I can't stand knowing that the money I pay in taxes and that my own family needs — not to mention all the other poor and sick people in this country and world — pays for weapons and the policy that maims, kills, frightens, and horribly abuses babies, children, women, men, and the old. I don't want to be a murderer, I had said.

And once, as I was being lifted into the jail van, someone yelled, "What do you have to say now, as you go off to jail?" and I made a joke that was the truth: "I'm following my tax dollars," I said.

My tax dollars. Really the crux of the matter. When will I have the courage not to pay them? I remember being audited by the IRS when my husband and I were in the civil-rights movement in Mississippi. I remember being audited here in California two years ago. It isn't so much courage that I would need, as the patience to endure the grinding malice of bureaucratic harassment. (Meanwhile, my letter to my congressman about implementation of a peace tax — a peace tax would go to build hospitals, schools, houses, and to provide food for people — has not been answered.)

My thoughts, while I was being frisked, fingerprinted, and photo-    30
graphed (I liked my mug shot) by very cordial men and women, some of whom admired my doll, turned to food. Of which, because I'd left my well-provisioned backpack in the car, I had none. As a vegetarian, which I've now been for a good three months, I get hungry frequently. I think about oranges, almonds, apples — and, yes, a well-cooked piece of chicken. As soon as I'm seated fairly comfortably in the holding area — a large gray "cattle car" from the Port Chicago explosion days — Sallie, the woman in her fifties, breaks out her stash of oranges, Swiss cheese, and Triscuits, and offers me some. I think about how hard it would be for me to engage in any kind of action now for justice and peace with the remains of murdered flesh in my body. I'm tempted to wonder about the cows who "gave" the "Swiss" cheese, but don't. I eat it with gratitude.

Apparently it is lunchtime for everyone. I look out the window of our cattle car and I see that the guards, the nurse, the people who checked us in (even the one black woman in a light-blue uniform, who asked for my autograph and said, "Oh, I'm *so* glad you're here!"), all are eating. Since this is California, they are eating thick whole-grain sandwiches fluffy with fillings, trailing juicy tomato slices, lettuce leaves, and sprouts. As we all munch, they outside and "free," me inside and "captive," I can't help a feeling of tenderness for them: The need to eat connects us. Perhaps that is why they have taken these jobs.

Though some of our demonstrators were brutalized by the police, we were not. In an effort to minimize the import of our action, the meaning of it, and to keep public anxiety about the close proximity of the nuclear weapons on the base as low as possible, they treated us, for the most part, courteously. In truth, many of them seemed bored, barely present in what they were doing. There are some demonstrators who feel it is best, as far as gaining publicity is concerned, to have at least some police brutality, but I am not one of those. The pictures of demonstrations that I like show the creativity as well as the determination of the crowd. I like costumes, slogans, effigies. I think if these things are true enough, the police can affirm them, too. The most encouraging demonstration picture I've seen recently is of a young Korean policeman, visor raised and shield lowered, smiling impishly at protesting students and giving them the victory sign. Of course, many policemen are brutal and take their position as guardians of the status quo seriously. Many of them are angry, because they feel they are poor and have to work while the demonstrators appear to be playing. I feel absolutely no anger toward the police just because they are police or toward the young men in the army. The protection of evil must be the most self-destructive job of all.

The next day, freed, my doll Windela and I address a crowd of a thousand demonstrators, two hundred of whom will later be arrested. Among other things, I read a poem about a poor Salvadoran woman whose father, husband, and sons have been killed and whose remaining small children are starving; nevertheless she is paying her taxes. Later, I stand holding Windela beside the knee-high, coiled line of razor-blade wire, on the other side of which are the same young black, white, brown, and yellow recruits. They are, at the moment, receiving much shouted information from several huge Vietnam vets, so loud and intense they frighten me — "Why do you want to go fight their stupid war for them, huh?" "Here's a body bag" — *plop* — "do you want to come back in one of those?" "I swore when I was in Nam that if I ever got out alive I'd never sit back and let kids like you go!" As I stand there, I suddenly feel a small stroking along my thigh. I look down into the large brown eyes of a small, gentle-faced olive-brown girl. She is playing shyly with Windela's foot. I hand the doll to her, and she embraces it with joy. Beside her is her mother, holding an infant. She speaks to the little girl in Spanish. I ask the mother, who appears to be in her early twenties, where she is from. She tells me she is a refugee from El Salvador, that she lives in a refugee house in San Francisco. At some point in our halting conversation in her "leetle beet" of English and my truly tongue-tied smidgen of Spanish, I ask to hold the baby, a plump, six-month-old girl, who promptly yanks off one of my earrings and then, fortunately, has trouble finding her mouth. Her mother says she is looking for a job. Can I help her? I tell her I will try. But who will hire a young mother of two small children who speaks Spanish?

I leave the doll with her daughter, Sandra, last seen sitting on the ground, oblivious to the demonstrators, the arrests, the police, and the army all around her, "being a mother." And yes, that is what motherhood more and more is like in this world. I am glad I have acted. Glad I am here, if only for her. She is the future. I want some of the best of me, of us, of this day, to go there with her.

*September 1, 1987.* Today Belvie called to tell me the news about Brian     35
Willson. He was blocking the tracks at the Concord Naval Weapons Station, along with several others, and the train ran over him, injuring his head and left ankle, and severing his right leg below the knee. He had been in a peace circle earlier in the morning with our friend Dan, whom I called immediately. Dan told me that in fact, in addition to the head injuries, which he thought very grave, and the severed right leg, Brian's left foot and ankle had been crushed, so that leg, too, below the knee, was amputated. As he talks, I feel a flush of futility that this could happen, although we've all realized it could, and, already thinking of what Brian's life will be like without the use of his legs, I can barely absorb the information Dan is giving me. Apparently the train speeded up when the demonstrators were spotted. Moments before the attack, Brian, who was preparing for a forty-day fast and sit-in on the tracks, and who had been married eight days before, had said he was willing to give his life to the struggle for peace.

Brian. White, middle-aged, wonderfully warm and expressive brown eyes (lots of light), brown hair, with some gray, a mottled beard. A really lovely and intelligent smile (how would he smile now)? — and great legs.

We met at the planning of the original blockade of the weapons station, and I had liked him right away. A week later we were together, with hundreds of others, blockading the gates. Only later did I learn he'd been an air force officer during the Vietnam war, in intelligence, no less. I could see how sick he was of war, and of the lies that protect war. He spoke very quietly but with a knowledge of what we were up against, so often missing in those who wage peace. He had the aura of someone who had seen and had enough.

I remember him telling us that if the death trains got through our blockade and over our bodies, killing or maiming us, we should realize that when their weapons reached their destinations, in Nicaragua or El Salvador, this would also be the fate of the people there. We are not more than they, he said; they are not less than we. The weapons on the trains would maim and kill children, women, and men, he said. To which I mentally added animals, trees, rivers, families, communities, cultures, friendship, love — and our own self-respect.

## EXPLORATIONS

1. What is it about Concord, California, that Alice Walker and her fellow demonstrators object to? What is the goal of their demonstration? What are their tactics for achieving their goal?

2. What damage results from the demonstration? Who causes the damage, and to whom or what?

3. At what points does Walker indicate that she is aware of being a famous writer? How does her fame affect her actions?

4. What visual images in Walker's account strike you as most and least effective, and why?

## CONNECTIONS

1. Walker writes: "The protection of evil must be the most self-destructive job of all" (para. 32). What ideas in Michael Kelly's "Torture in Kuwait" (see, e.g., para. 48) suggest why this should be true?

2. "That is what motherhood more and more is like in this world," writes Walker in paragraph 34. What does she mean? What other mothers you have read about in Part Seven match Walker's vision of motherhood, and why?

3. What does Alice Walker take with her to the demonstration (para. 17)? What do Irene Beltrán and Francisco Leal take with them to the Los Riscos Mine in Isabel Allende's story by that name (p. 656, para. 2)? In each case, what is the effect on the reader of these preparations?

4. What writers represented in *Looking at Ourselves* mention ideas similar to Walker's, and what are those ideas?

# ELABORATIONS

1. In paragraph 22 Walker writes of "the connection I feel to Winnie and Nelson Mandela." What common ideas appear in "The Concord Demonstration" and Nelson Mandela's "Black Man in a White Court" (p. 587)? Write an essay comparing and contrasting Walker's and Mandela's political beliefs, values, goals, and strategies as they appear in her account of the demonstration and his courtroom speech.

2. The story line of Walker's narrative essay is similar to that of Isabel Allende's short story "The Los Riscos Mine." What plot elements appear in both selections? Where do the two narratives diverge? What is the climax of each one? How do their differences in structure and purpose reflect political contrasts between their authors' homelands, the United States and Chile? Write an essay comparing and contrasting the goals, techniques, and (if you wish) effectiveness of "The Concord Demonstration" and "The Los Riscos Mine."

# CHINUA ACHEBE

## Civil Peace

One of the foremost contemporary African writers, Albert Chinualu-mogu Achebe was born in the Igbo (or Ibo) village of Ogidi, Nigeria, in 1930. His father was a teacher for the Church Missionary Society who screened the family from the tribal beliefs and festivities around them. Achebe attended a government-run secondary school modeled on those in England, where the Igbo storytelling tradition interwove with Dickens, Swift, and Shakespeare. By 1953, when he graduated from University College in Ibadan, Achebe had realized that "I was not on Marlowe's boat steaming up the Congo in *Heart of Darkness*. I was one of those strange beings jumping up and down on the riverbank, making horrid faces." He vowed to become a writer, shortened his name, and published several stories before going to work for the Nigerian Broadcasting Company as a producer and later director. In 1959 his first novel appeared: *Things Fall Apart*, which has sold over 2 million copies in forty-five languages. The book depicts an Igbo village in the late 1880s, just before Nigeria — a center for Portuguese and British slave traders since the 1500s — became a British colony. Achebe's next novel, *No Longer at Ease*, examines the clash between an Igbo upbringing and a Western education and life-style; it appeared in 1960, the year Nigeria became an independent entity within the British Commonwealth. Achebe turned to writing essays and poetry and joined the University of Nigeria, Nsukka, as a senior research fellow in 1966. The following year Eastern Nigeria, his tribal homeland, proclaimed itself the Republic of Biafra. Civil war followed, with casualties of over a million — including many Biafrans (mostly Igbos) who starved despite international relief efforts. In 1970 the secessionists capitulated. Achebe, who had been active on Biafra's side, began editing *Okike: An African Journal of New Writing* the next year. "Civil Peace" takes place during that postwar period; it first appeared in *Okike 2*. Since then Achebe has taught at the universities of Massachusetts and Connecticut; published essays, poetry, stories, and children's literature; and won dozens of international awards and honorary degrees. His long-awaited fifth novel, *Anthills of the Savannah*, appeared in 1987. He lives in Nsukka, where he is a professor emeritus at the university and continues to accept worldwide invitations as a visiting writer and lecturer.

For more background on Nigeria, see page 112.

Jonathan Iwegbu counted himself extraordinarily lucky. "Happy survival!" meant so much more to him than just a current fashion of greeting old friends in the first hazy days of peace. It went deep to his heart. He had come out of the war with five inestimable blessings — his head, his wife Maria's head, and the heads of three out of their four children. As a bonus he also had his old bicycle — a miracle too but naturally not to be compared to the safety of five human heads.

The bicycle had a little history of its own. One day at the height of the war it was commandeered "for urgent military action." Hard as its loss would have been to him he would still have let it go without a thought had he not had some doubts about the genuineness of the officer. It wasn't his disreputable rags, nor the toes peeping out of one blue and one brown canvas shoe, nor yet the two stars of his rank done obviously in a hurry in biro [ballpoint] that troubled Jonathan; many good and heroic soldiers looked the same or worse. It was rather a certain lack of grip and firmness in his manner. So Jonathan, suspecting he might be amenable to influence, rummaged in his raffia bag and produced the two pounds with which he had been going to buy firewood which his wife, Maria, retailed to camp officials for extra stockfish and cornmeal, and got his bicycle back. That night he buried it in the little clearing in the bush where the dead of the camp, including his own youngest son, were buried. When he dug it up again a year later after the surrender all it needed was a little palm-oil greasing. "Nothing puzzles God," he said in wonder.

He put it to immediate use as a taxi and accumulated a small pile of Biafran money ferrying camp officials and their families across the four-mile stretch to the nearest tarred road. His standard charge per trip was six pounds and those who had the money were only glad to be rid of some of it in this way. At the end of a fortnight he had made a small fortune of one hundred and fifteen pounds.

Then he made the journey to Enugu and found another miracle waiting for him. It was unbelievable. He rubbed his eyes and looked again and it was still standing there before him. But, needless to say, even that monumental blessing must be accounted also totally inferior to the five heads in the family. This newest miracle was his little house in Ogui Overside. Indeed nothing puzzles God! Only two houses away a huge concrete edifice some wealthy contractor had put up just before the war was a mountain of rubble. And here was Jonathan's little zinc house of no regrets built with mud blocks quite intact! Of course the doors and windows were missing and five sheets off the roof. But what was that? And anyhow he had returned to Enugu early enough to pick up bits of old zinc and wood and soggy sheets of cardboard lying around the neighborhood before thousands more came out of their forest holes looking for the same things. He got a destitute carpenter with one old hammer, a blunt plane, and a few bent and rusty nails in his tool bag to turn this assortment of wood, paper, and metal into door and window shutters for five Nigerian shillings or fifty Biafran pounds. He paid the pounds, and moved in with his overjoyed family carrying five heads on their shoulders.

His children picked mangoes near the military cemetery and sold          5
them to soldiers' wives for a few pennies — real pennies this time — and his wife started making breakfast akara balls for neighbors in a hurry to start life again. With his family earnings he took his bicycle to the villages around and bought fresh palm wine which he mixed generously in his rooms with the water which had recently started running again in the public tap down the road, and opened up a bar for soldiers and other lucky people with good money.

At first he went daily, then every other day, and finally once a week, to the offices of the Coal Corporation where he used to be a miner, to find out what was what. The only thing he did find out in the end was that that little house of his was even a greater blessing than he had thought. Some of his fellow ex-miners who had nowhere to return at the end of the day's waiting just slept outside the doors of the offices and cooked what meal they could scrounge together in Bournvita tins. As the weeks lengthened and still nobody could say what was what Jonathan discontinued his weekly visits altogether and faced his palm-wine bar.

But nothing puzzles God. Came the day of the windfall when after five days of endless scuffles in queues and counterqueues in the sun outside the Treasury he had twenty pounds counted into his palms as ex-gratia award for the rebel money he had turned in. It was like Christmas for him and for many others like him when the payments began. They called it (since few could manage its proper official name) *egg-rasher.*

As soon as the pound notes were placed in his palm Jonathan simply closed it tight over them and buried fist and money inside his trouser pocket. He had to be extra careful because he had seen a man a couple of days earlier collapse into near-madness in an instant before that oceanic crowd because no sooner had he got his twenty pounds than some heartless ruffian picked it off him. Though it was not right that a man in such an extremity of agony should be blamed yet many in the queues that day were able to remark quietly at the victim's carelessness, especially after he pulled out the innards of his pocket and revealed a hole in it big enough to pass a thief's head. But of course he had insisted that the money had been in the other pocket, pulling it out too to show its comparative wholeness. So one had to be careful.

Jonathan soon transferred the money to his left hand and pocket so as to leave his right free for shaking hands should the need arise, though by fixing his gaze at such an elevation as to miss all approaching human faces he made sure that the need did not arise, until he got home.

He was normally a heavy sleeper but that night he heard all the neighborhood noises die down one after another. Even the night watchman who knocked the hour on some metal somewhere in the distance had fallen silent after knocking one o'clock. That must have been the last thought in Jonathan's mind before he was finally carried away himself. He couldn't have been gone for long, though, when he was violently awakened again.

"Who is knocking?" whispered his wife lying beside him on the floor.

"I don't know," he whispered back breathlessly.

The second time the knocking came it was so loud and imperious that the rickety old door could have fallen down.

"Who is knocking?" he asked them, his voice parched and trembling.

"Na tief-man and him people," came the cool reply. "Make you hopen de door." This was followed by the heaviest knocking of all.

Maria was the first to raise the alarm, then he followed and all their children.

"Police-o! Thieves-o! Neighbors-o! Police-o! We are lost! We are dead! Neighbors, are you asleep? Wake up! Police-o!"

"You done finish?" asked the voice outside. "Make we help you small. Oya, everybody!"

"Police-o! Tief-man-so! Neighbors-o! we done loss-o! Police-o! . . ."

There were at least five other voices besides the leader's.

Jonathan and his family were now completely paralyzed by terror. Maria and the children sobbed inaudibly like lost souls. Jonathan groaned continuously.

The silence that followed the thieves' alarm vibrated horribly. Jonathan all but begged their leader to speak again and be done with it.

"My frien," said he at long last, "we don try our best for call dem but I tink say dem all done sleep-o . . . So wetin we go do now? Sometaim you wan call soja? Or you wan make we call dem for you? Soja better pass police. No be so?"

"Na so!" replied his men. Jonathan thought he heard even more voices now than before and groaned heavily. His legs were sagging under him and his throat felt like sandpaper.

"My frien, why you no de talk again. I de ask you say you wan make we call soja?"

"No."

"Awrighto. Now make we talk business. We no be bad tief. We no like for make trouble. Trouble done finish. War done finish and all the katakata wey de for inside. No Civil War again. This time na Civil Peace. No be so?"

"Na so!" answered the horrible chorus.

"What do you want from me? I am a poor man. Everything I had went with this war. Why do you come to me? You know people who have money. We . . ."

"Awright! We know say you no get plenty money. But we sef no get even anini. So derefore make you open dis window and give us one hundred pound and we go commot. Orderwise we de come for inside now to show you guitar-boy like dis . . ."

A volley of automatic fire rang through the sky. Maria and the children began to weep aloud again.

"Ah, missisi de cry again. No need for dat. We done talk say we na good tief. We just take our small money and go nwayorly. No molest. Abi we de molest?"

"At all!" sang the chorus.

"My friends," began Jonathan hoarsely. "I hear what you say and I thank you. If I had one hundred pounds . . ."

"Lookia my frien, no be play we come play for your house. If we make mistake and step for inside you no go like am-o. So derefore . . ."

"To God who made me; if you come inside and find one hundred pounds, take and shoot me and shoot my wife and children. I swear to God. The only money I have in this life is this twenty-pounds *egg-rasher* they gave me today . . ."

"OK. Time de go. Make you open dis window and bring the twenty pound. We go manage am like dat."

There were now loud murmurs of dissent among the chorus: "Na lie de man de lie; e get plenty money . . . Make we go inside and search properly well . . . Wetin be twenty pound? . . ."

"Shurrup!" rang the leader's voice like a lone shot in the sky and silenced the murmuring at once. "Are you dere? Bring the money quick!"

"I am coming," said Jonathan fumbling in the darkness with the key of the small wooden box he kept by his side on the mat.

At the first sign of light as neighbors and others assembled to commiserate with him he was already strapping his five-gallon demijohn to his bicycle carrier and his wife, sweating in the open fire, was turning over akara balls in a wide clay bowl of boiling oil. In the corner his eldest son was rinsing out dregs of yesterday's palm wine from old beer bottles.

"I count it as nothing," he told his sympathizers, his eyes on the rope he was tying. "What is *egg-rasher*? Did I depend on it last week? Or is it greater than other things that went with the war? I say, let *egg-rasher* perish in the flames! Let it go where everything else has gone. Nothing puzzles God."

## EXPLORATIONS

1. Why does Jonathan Iwegbu count himself extraordinarily lucky? What does his definition of luck say about the condition of other Biafrans? Who seems to have come out on top in this war, and who has come out on the bottom?

2. What has been the war's effect on currency? What kind of money is most plentiful in Biafra? What kind is most valuable?

3. Where does the name *egg-rasher* come from? How does Iwegbu's *egg-rasher* embody the theme of "Civil Peace"?

4. Why is "Civil Peace" an appropriate title for the story, and for the situation in Biafra when the story takes place?

## CONNECTIONS

1. Chinua Achebe, like Alice Walker (p. 705), is writing about war out of a personal sense of involvement. What is each author's attitude toward war, and what reasons can you identify for his or her attitude?

2. In paragraphs 19–31 of "Torture in Kuwait" (p. 696), a torture victim interviewed by Michael Kelly conveys the horror of his experience by understatement. At what points does Chinua Achebe use this technique in "Civil Peace"?

3. "Which world is 'natural'?" asks Czeslaw Milosz (p. 674, para. 11). "That which existed before, or the world of war?" Look closely at Milosz's examples of how war changes human perceptions, and at Achebe's examples. What changes noted in "American Ignorance of War" are illustrated in "Civil Peace"?

4. Wole Soyinka's "Nigerian Childhood" (p. 112) is a vivid example of the blend of Western and African traditions described by Es'kia Mphahlele in "Tradition and the African Writer" (p. 35). How does Achebe — also writing about Nigeria — portray that dual heritage? What items in "Civil Peace" represent native African tradition? What items represent British colonial tradition?

# ELABORATIONS

1. What does Jonathan Iwegbu mean by "Nothing puzzles God"? Write an essay explaining this expression's significance in "Civil Peace" by examining the specific contexts in which Iwegbu uses it, as well as the story as a whole.

2. Is the pen mightier than the sword? Chinua Achebe, Alice Walker, and other writers have chosen to use their professional craft and their visibility to express their views on war and other forms of violence. Choose an issue raised in Part Seven that you have strong views about. Write a narrative, argumentative, or cause-and-effect essay presenting your position.

# APPENDIX

## *The European Community (EC)*
## *The North Atlantic Treaty Organization (NATO)*

### EUROPEAN COMMUNITY

The European Community (EC) is the collective name for the older European Economic Community (Common Market), European Coal and Steel Community, and European Atomic Energy Community. The EC comprises Belgium, Denmark, France, Germany, Greece, Ireland, Italy, Luxembourg, the Netherlands, Portugal, Spain, and the United Kingdom. Some sixty nations in Africa, the Caribbean, and the Pacific are affiliated with the EC, and other nations that consider themselves part of Europe, such as Turkey and countries in the former Eastern Bloc, have indicated a desire to join. Begun as a regional economic alliance, the EC now represents a long-range plan for member nations to move toward economic and political unity. Acting cooperatively has decreased friction and red tape within Europe and increased members' political and economic clout in relation to other nations and alliances. To gain these advantages, member countries have had to yield some individual sovereignty and in several cases ally themselves with ancient rivals.

In 1944, during World War II, Belgium, the Netherlands, and Luxembourg established a customs union called Benelux. The free movement of capital and labor among member countries proved so successful that in 1952 the Benelux countries, as well as France, West Germany, and Italy, created the European Coal and Steel Community (ECSC), which lifted import and export duties for coal and steel sales between members and abolished government subsidies. In 1957 the six member nations signed the Treaty of Rome, which extended their alliance by creating the European Atomic Energy Community (Euratom) and the European Economic Community (EEC, or Common Market). The EEC's eventual goals were to abolish tariffs (achieved in 1968); to coordinate transportation systems, agricultural policies, and overall economic policies; to remove barriers to competition; and to encourage the free movement of capital and labor among member nations. In 1967 the Brussels Treaty of 1965 was implemented, merging the ECSC, Euratom, and EEC into the European Community (EC). In 1973 the United Kingdom, Denmark, and Ireland joined the EC, followed in 1981 by Greece and in 1986 by Spain and Portugal. With German reunification in 1990, East as well as West Germany became part of the EC. Meanwhile, in 1979, the first European Parliament was elected by direct vote in member countries — a revolutionary move for nations that had jealously preserved their individuality for centuries. That same year the European Monetary System was established for stable currency exchange.

The EC (although not its individual member countries) is currently governed by its own democratic institutions. A seventeen-member commission proposes policies and legislation and monitors compliance with EC decisions. A Council of Ministers from each member country enacts legislation. The 518-member European Parliament works cooperatively with these two groups. A Court of Justice adjudicates disputes. An Economic and Social Committee supplies proposals and policy advice. A Court of Auditors reviews spending.

The EC targeted 1992 as the year for "Europe without frontiers": an ambitious merger of members' economies into a single market within which people, goods, capital, and services could circulate freely. Meetings in late 1991 in the Dutch city of Maastricht provided for an economic union (including common currency and joint central bank by 1999) and collective foreign security and eventually defense policies. After nation-by-nation referenda and a few legal challenges, Germany became the final EC nation to approve the Maastricht Treaty and the European Union in October 1993. It remains unclear whether all provisions will be implemented on schedule as well as whether, when, and how European countries recently separated from the Soviet Union may become eligible for EC membership.

## NORTH ATLANTIC TREATY ORGANIZATION

The North Atlantic Treaty Organization (NATO) was created after World War II as an alliance to prevent or, if necessary, defend against future armed conflict. NATO's original members were the United States and Canada, Iceland, Norway, Denmark, the United Kingdom, Portugal, France, Belgium, the Netherlands, Luxembourg, and Italy. Since its founding in 1949, Greece, Turkey, West Germany, and Spain have also joined. NATO's members agreed to resolve disputes peacefully, to develop their resources to resist armed attack, to regard an attack on one as an attack on all, and to fight back if necessary. In 1967, after France withdrew from NATO's military affairs, the organization's headquarters was moved from Paris to Brussels. Greece withdrew in 1974 over a dispute with Turkey but rejoined in 1980. When Germany reunified in 1990, East Germany—formerly part of the Eastern Bloc's Warsaw Pact—joined West Germany as a NATO member. With the end of the Cold War and the disbanding of the Warsaw Pact, NATO's future as a mutual defense alliance has become unclear. The organization continues to thrive; indeed, several countries that used to be regarded as potential threats to members' security have indicated interest in joining: Russia, Poland, Hungary, the Czech Republic. However, whether NATO will expand further and what its role will be in the new Europe are questions not yet answered.

Joy Harjo, "Ordinary Spirit," reprinted from *I Tell You Now: Autobiographical Essays by Native American Writers*, edited by Brian Swann and Arnold Krupat. Copyright © 1987 by the University of Nebraska Press. Reprinted by permission of the University of Nebraska Press.

Paul Harrison, "The Westernization of the World," from *Inside the Third World*. Reprinted by permission of the author.

Linda Hasselstrom, excerpt from *Land Circles: Writings Collected from the Land* by Linda Hasselstrom. Copyright © 1993 by Linda Hasselstrom. Reprinted with permission of Fulcrum Publishers.

Václav Havel, "Moral Politics," originally titled "Paradise Lost," from *Summer Meditations*, trans. Paul Wilson. Copyright © 1993 by Paul Wilson. Reprinted by permission of Random House, Inc., and the author.

Le Ly Hayslip, from "When Heaven and Earth Changed Places" by Le Ly Hayslip. Copyright © 1989 by Le Ly Hayslip and Charles Jay Wurts. Used by permission of Doubleday, a division of Bantam Doubleday Dell Publishing Group, Inc.

Liliana Heker, "The Stolen Party," from *Other Fires: Short Fiction by Latin American Women* by Alberto Manguel. Translation copyright © 1986 by Alberto Manguel. Reprinted by permission of Clarkson N. Potter, Inc., a division of Crown Publishers, Inc., and the copyright holder.

Liang Heng and Judith Shapiro, "Chairman Mao's Good Little Boy," from *Son of the Revolution* by Liang Heng and Judith Shapiro. Copyright © 1983 by Liang Heng and Judith Shapiro. Reprinted by permission of Alfred A. Knopf, Inc.

Langston Hughes, "Salvation," from *The Big Sea* by Langston Hughes. Copyright © 1940 by Langston Hughes. Renewal copyright © 1968 by Arna Bontemps and George Houston Bass. Reprinted by permission of Hill & Wang, a division of Farrar, Straus & Giroux, Inc.

Yoshimi Ishikawa, from *Strawberry Road* by Yoshimi Ishikawa, translated by Eve Zimmerman. Copyright © 1991 by Yoshimi Ishikawa. Reprinted by permission of Kodanasha Publishers.

Tomoyuki Iwashita, "Why I Quit the Company." Originally appeared in the May 1992 issue of *The New Internationalist*. Copyright © 1992 by Tomoyuki Iwashita. Reprinted by permission of *The New Internationalist*.

Sally Jacobs, from "White Men Can't Win" by Sally Jacobs. Originally appeared in the November 22, 1992 issue of *The Boston Globe*. Copyright © 1992 by Sally Jacobs. Reprinted by permission of the author.

Gish Jen, from *Typical American* by Gish Jen. Copyright © 1991 by Gish Jen. Reprinted by permission of Houghton Mifflin Co. All rights reserved.

Joe Kane, from "Star Wars." *Ms.* magazine, September 1985. Reprinted by permission of the author.

Nikos Kazantzakis, "The Isle of Aphrodite," from *Journeying* by Nikos Kazantzakis. Text copyright © 1975 by Helen Kazantzakis. Translation copyright © 1975 by Themi Vasils and Theodora Vasils. Reprinted by permission of Little, Brown and Company.

Alfred Kazin, from *A Walker in the City* by Alfred Kazin. Copyright 1951 and renewed 1979 by Alfred Kazin. Reprinted by permission of Harcourt Brace & Co.

Sam Keen, from *Fire in the Belly* by Sam Keen. Copyright © 1991 by Sam Keen. Used by permission of Bantam Books, a division of Bantam Doubleday Dell Publishing Group, Inc.

Michael Kelly, "Torture in Kuwait," from *Martyrs' Day* by Michael Kelly. Copyright © 1993 by Michael Kelly. Reprinted by permission of Random House, Inc.

Yashar Kemal, "A Dirty Story," from *Anatolian Tales*. Reprinted by permission of the publisher, Collins Harvill.

Martin Luther King, Jr., excerpts from "Racism and the White Backlash," from *Where Do We Go from Here?* by Martin Luther King, Jr. Reprinted by arrangement with the heirs to the Estate of Martin Luther King, Jr., c/o Joan Daves Agency as agent for the proprietor.

Ron Kovic, excerpt from *Born on the Fourth of July* by Ron Kovic. Copyright © 1976 by Ron Kovic. Reprinted by permission of McGraw-Hill, Inc.

Lewis H. Lapham, "A Political Opiate." Copyright © 1989 by *Harper's* magazine. All rights reserved. Reprinted from the December 1989 issue by special permission.

Christopher Lasch, "The Crime of Quality Time," from the Winter 1990 edition of *New Perspectives Quarterly*. Copyright © 1990 by *New Perspectives Quarterly*. Reprinted by permission of *New Perspectives Quarterly*.

Primo Levi, "Uranium," reprinted from *The Periodic Table* by Primo Levi, trans. Raymond Rosenthal. Copyright © 1984 by Schocken Books. Reprinted by permission of Schocken Books, a division of Random House, Inc.

Elliot Liebow, from *Tally's Corner* by Elliot Liebow. Copyright © 1967 by Little, Brown and Company (Inc.). Reprinted by permission of Little, Brown and Company.

Sophronia Liu, "So Tsi-fai." Originally appeared in *Hurricane Alice*, Vol. 2, No. 4 (Fall 1986). Copyright © 1986 by Sophronia Liu. Reprinted by permission of the author.

Malcolm X, from *The Autobiography of Malcolm X* by Malcolm X, with the assistance of Alex Haley. Copyright © 1964 by Alex Haley and Malcolm X and copyright © 1965 by Alex Haley and Betty Shabazz. Reprinted by permission of Random House, Inc.

Nelson Mandela, "Black Man in a White Court" from *Mandela: No Easy Walk to Freedom.* Reprinted by permission of Heinneman Educational Books, Ltd.

William R. Mattox, from "The Parent Trap" by William R. Mattox. Originally appeared in the Winter 1991 edition of *Policy Review.* Reprinted by permission of the author.

Nell McCafferty, excerpts from "Touchstone" and "Peggy's March," from *Peggy Deery: An Irish Family at War* by Nell McCafferty. Copyright © 1988 by Nell McCafferty. Reprinted by permission of Cleis Press.

Colman McCarthy, "Kings of the Mountain of Gore." Copyright © 1993 by the Washington Post Writers Group. Reprinted by permission of the author.

Ved Mehta, reprinted from *The Ledge Between the Streams* by Ved Mehta, by permission of W. W. Norton & Company, Inc. Copyright © 1982, 1983, 1984 by Ved Mehta.

Rigoberta Menchú, "Birth Ceremonies" from *I, Rigoberta Menchú* by Rigoberta Menchú. Copyright © 1985 by Verso. Reprinted by permission.

Czeslaw Milosz, "American Ignorance of War," from *The Captive Mind* by Czeslaw Milosz, trans. J. Zielonko. Copyright 1951, 1953 by Czeslaw Milosz. Reprinted by permission of Alfred A. Knopf, Inc.

Naila Minai, "Women in Early Islam," from *Women in Islam.* Seaview Books, 1981.

Fred Moody, from "When Work Becomes an Obsession" by Fred Moody. Originally appeared in *City Paper.* Reprinted by permission.

Charles Moore, "Ireland Must Fight the IRA Too" originally appeared in the March 9, 1992 edition of the *Wall Street Journal.* Copyright © 1992 by Dow Jones & Co., Inc. Reprinted by permission of the *Wall Street Journal.* All rights reserved.

Alberto Moravia, "The Chase," from *Command and I Will Obey You* by Alberto Moravia. English translation copyright © 1967 by Gruppo Editoriale Fabbri, Bompiani, Sonzogno, Etas Spa. (Originally titled "Una cosa è una cosa" by Alberto Moravia. Reprinted with permission.

John David Morley, from *Pictures from the Water Trade: Adventures of a Westerner in Japan* by John David Morley. Copyright © 1985 by John David Morley. Used by permission of Atlantic Monthly Press.

Toni Morrison, from *Playing in the Dark* by Toni Morrison. Copyright © 1992 by Toni Morrison. Reprinted by permission of Harvard University Press, Cambridge, Massachusetts.

Es'kia Mphahlele, "African Literature: What Tradition?" retitled "Tradition and the African Writer" from *Voices in the Whirlwind and Other Essays* by Ezekiel Mphahlele. Copyright © 1972 by Ezekiel Mphahlele. Reprinted by permission of Hill & Wang, a division of Farrar, Straus & Giroux, Inc.

Vladimir Nabokov, from "Good Writers and Good Readers," from *Lectures on Literature* by Vladimir Nabokov. Copyright © 1980 by Vladimir Nabokov. Reprinted by permission of Harcourt Brace & Co.

V. S. Naipaul, from *Finding the Center: Two Narratives* by V. S. Naipaul. Copyright © 1984 by V. S. Naipaul. Reprinted by permission of Alfred A. Knopf, Inc., and Aitken, Stone & Wylie Ltd.

*The New Yorker,* from "The Talk of the Town." Originally appeared in the August 24, 1992 issue of *The New Yorker.* Copyright © 1992 by *The New Yorker.* Reprinted with permission.

"Nobody Listens" originally appeared in the Back Page section of *Mother Jones,* July/August 1992 issue. Copyright © 1992 by the Foundation for National Progress. Reprinted with permission from *Mother Jones* magazine.

Michael Novak, "The Family out of Favor," by Michael Novak. Copyright © 1976 by *Harper's* magazine. All rights reserved. Reprinted from the April issue by special permission.

*Clouds* edited by Kenneth Rosen. Copyright © 1969 by Leslie Chapman. Used by permission of Wylie, Aitken & Stone, Inc.

Theodore Sizer, "What High School Is," from *Horace's Compromise: The Dilemma of the American High School.* Copyright © 1984 by Theodore Sizer. Reprinted by permission of Houghton Mifflin. All rights reserved.

Patrick Smith, "Nippon Challenge" by Patrick Smith. Originally appeared in the April 13, 1992 issue of *The New Yorker.* Copyright © 1992 by *The New Yorker.* Reprinted with permission of the author.

Marilyn Berlin Snell, "The Purge of Nature," from the Winter 1990 edition of *New Perspectives Quarterly.* Copyright © 1990 by *New Perspectives Quarterly.* Reprinted by permission of *New Perspectives Quarterly.*

Wole Soyinka, from *Aké: The Years of Childhood* by Wole Soyinka. Copyright © 1981 by Wole Soyinka. Reprinted by permission of Random House, Inc.

Shelby Steele, from "I'm Black, You're White, Who's Innocent?" from *The Content of Our Character* by Shelby Steele. Copyright © 1988 by Shelby Steele. Reprinted by permission of HarperCollins Publishers.

Gloria Steinem, from *Outrageous Acts and Everyday Rebellions* by Gloria Steinem. Copyright © 1984 by East Toledo Productions, Inc. Reprinted by permission of Henry Holt and Company, Inc.

Amy Tan, "Two Kinds," from *The Joy Luck Club* by Amy Tan. Copyright © 1989 by Amy Tan. Reprinted by permission of The Putnam Publishing Group.

Deborah Tannen, from "Different Words, Different Worlds," from *You Just Don't Understand: Men and Women in Conversation* by Deborah Tannen. Copyright © 1990 by Deborah Tannen. Reprinted by permission of William Morrow & Company, Inc.

Studs Terkel, interview with Bill Talcott, from *Working* by Studs Terkel. Copyright © 1972, 1974 by Studs Terkel. Reprinted by permission of Pantheon Books, a division of Random House, Inc.

Excerpt from "Thrill, Not Hate: Young Offenders Can Change." Copyright © 1993 by the Associated Press. Reprinted by permission of the Associated Press.

Haunani-Kay Trask, from "From a Native Daughter," from *The American Indian and the Problem of History* by Calvin Martin. Reprinted by permission of the author.

John Updike, from *Trust Me* by John Updike. Copyright © 1987 by John Updike. Reprinted by permission of Alfred A. Knopf, Inc.

Mario Vargas Llosa, "On Sunday," from *The Cups and Other Stories.* English translation copyright © 1979 by Harper & Row Publishers, Inc. Reprinted by permission of Farrar, Straus & Giroux, Inc. and the translator.

Alice Walker, "The Concord Demonstration," from *Living by the Word* by Alice Walker. Reprinted by permission of Harcourt Brace & Co.

Daniel Evan Weiss, from "TV, Movies, and Books," from *The Great Divide: How Females and Males Really Differ* by Daniel Evan Weiss. Copyright © 1991 by Daniel Evan Weiss. Reprinted by permission of Simon & Schuster, Inc.

Rose Weitz, "What Price Independence? Social Reactions to Lesbians, Spinsters, Widows, and Nuns," from "The Women's Liberation Movement: Its Origins, Organization, Activities, and Ideas," from *Women: A Feminist Perspective,* Second Edition, Jo Freeman, ed. Copyright © 1979, 1975 by Jo Freeman. Reprinted by permission of Mayfield Publishing Company.

Fay Weldon, "Down the Clinical Disco," from *Moon over Minneapolis.* Copyright © 1991 by Fay Weldon. Reprinted by permission of Penguin USA.

Jim Whitewolf, "Peyote Meeting," from *The Life of a Kiowa Apache,* ed. and with an introduction by Charles Brant. Copyright © 1969 by Charles Brant. Reprinted by permission of Dover Publications, Inc.

George Will, "Lessons of a Street-Wise Child." Copyright © 1993 by the Washington Post Writers Group. Reprinted by permission of the author.

Lawrence Wright, from "Women and Men: Can We Get Along? Should We Even Try?" by Lawrence Wright. Originally appeared in the February 1992 edition of *Texas Monthly.* Reprinted by permission of *Texas Monthly.*

# GEOGRAPHICAL INDEX

## AFRICA

## ASIA

## CENTRAL AMERICA

# EUROPE

# THE MIDDLE EAST

# NORTH AMERICA

# SOUTH AMERICA

# INDEX OF
# AUTHORS AND TITLES

POLAND

GERMANY

CZECHOSLOVAKIA
(former)

CZECH
REP.

SLOVAKIA

CROATIA

YUGOSLAVIA
(former)

ITALY

YUGOSLAVIA
(former)

GREECE

UNITED KINGDOM
OF GREAT BRITAIN
AND
NORTHERN IRELAND

IRELAND

SEE
INSET

BELGIUM
FRANCE

SPAIN

RUSSIA

SOVIET UNION
(former)

GEORGIA

TURKEY

ISRAEL    IRAQ    IRAN

CHINA

KUWAIT

SAUDI
ARABIA

INDIA

HONG
KONG

VIET

SENEGAL

NIGERIA

IVORY
COAST

INDIAN    OCEAN

INDONE

B

ATLANTIC

OCEAN

ZIMBABWE

BOTSWANA

SOUTH
AFRICA

Shaded areas indicate countries formerly of
Czechoslovakia, the Soviet Union, and Yugoslavia that have recently gained independence. In the interest of visual clarity
and simplicity, only countries treated in the
selections are labeled on this map.

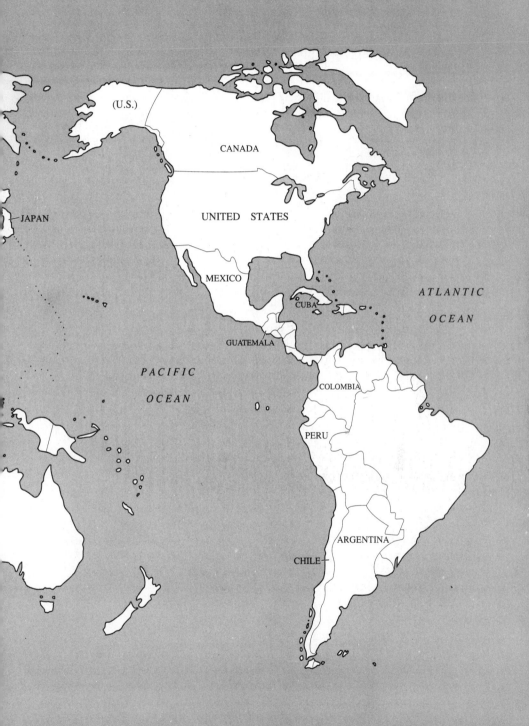

(U.S.)

CANADA

JAPAN

UNITED STATES

MEXICO

CUBA

*ATLANTIC*

*OCEAN*

GUATEMALA

COLOMBIA

*PACIFIC*

*OCEAN*

PERU

ARGENTINA

CHILE

THIRD EDITION

# OURSELVES AMONG OTHERS

*Cross-Cultural Readings for Writers*

## CAROL J. VERBURG

*Prepared by*
ALICE ADAMS *and* DAVID LUNDOW

**Resources for Teaching**

*OURSELVES AMONG OTHERS*

*CROSS-CULTURAL READINGS FOR WRITERS*

**Third Edition**

PREPARED BY

Alice Adams

Miami University of Ohio

and

David Londow

Miami - Dade Community College

BEDFORD BOOKS *of* ST. MARTIN'S PRESS • BOSTON

*For information, write:* St. Martin's Press, Inc.
175 Fifth Avenue, New York, NY 10010

*Editorial Offices:* Bedford Books *of* St. Martin's Press
29 Winchester Street, Boston, MA 02116

ISBN 0-312-08679-2

## PREFACE

We are often told that today's students are less interested in other cultures and contemporary history than past students, but the experience of instructors using previous editions of *Ourselves Among Others*, suggests otherwise. First of all, many of our students come from multicultural backgrounds within the United States or from foreign homelands. The selections in this reader provide a chance for such students to find themselves recognized for their unique contributions and the alternative points of view they can provide. Second, instructors report that students browse through this reader, finding writings of particular interest to them, and request that they be included in class assignments. Students are motivated enough by the subject matter to want to share in the shaping of class discussion and assignments. Doubtless the primary purpose of this text is to help students develop as writers, and students who are interested and involved will engage more readily both with the selections in hand and with their responses to them. Yet a further benefit of this work will become apparent as students become more aware of and better informed about other peoples and cultures. They will unconsciously absorb a great deal of geography, history, and political knowledge that should help them prepare for life in the twenty-first century.

However, many of the instructors using *Ourselves Among Others* think of themselves primarily as teachers of writing and literature. They do not necessarily have real expertise in other disciplines. Some might question whether the lack of a specialized background makes it difficult for an instructor to approach these texts. Our answer is that these essays and short stories, which have headnotes and background information provided, are very accessible. Students and instructors encounter these texts together, and they can focus on the ideas under discussion without needing to rely on additional facts. The discussions generated by these texts do not focus on "right" or "wrong" answers: Rather, the texts and the questions following then encourage readers to explore the relationships between ideas.

This manual is designed to guide instructors through the maze of new material presented in the text, providing necessary assistance in both planning and implementing the course. Used in conjunction with the text, the manual should temper the apprehension accompanying any new venture for instructors new to this reader, and it also should provide instructors, even those familiar with the earlier editions, with suggestions for ways of approaching and teaching the selections. In particular, the manual includes

An introduction, exploring teaching possibilities and providing suggestions for getting the course off the ground

Brief introductions to each unit, suggesting various combinations and subthemes and listing corresponding readings from more familiar American and European authors

Biographical notes for the authors of passages in "Looking at Ourselves"

Preface

Discussion of all Explorations and Connections questions, paying particular attention to possible student reaction to more controversial pieces

Carefully structured additional questions following the same pattern for each unit, including journal suggestions, imitation of forms, short essay assignments, research of current related topics, and further research into cultures represented in selections

Suggested syllabi, adapting the text to different types of courses

A rhetorical index, pointing out those selections that make use of particular organizing strategies

A chart of rhetorical writing assignments in the text

Additional Resources, including an index to headnote information and a concise list of reference materials to facilitate research into other cultures

A list of film, video, and audio cassette resources

Working with *Ourselves Among Others* will provide a challenge: There are always pitfalls involved when we leave familiar territory behind. But using this manual as a road map, both students and instructors should discover that, when we explore it thoroughly, the foreign territory isn't all that unfamiliar. And the people — well, now and then we see glimpses of ourselves among others.

We gratefully acknowledge the work of our predecessors, Kathleen Shine Cain (who prepared the manual for the first edition of *Ourselves Among Others*) and Marilyn Rye (who prepared the second edition manual).

# CONTENTS

Contents

# INTRODUCTION

*Ourselves Among Others* can be adapted to courses employing a number of approaches. As a thematic reader, it's well suited to an introductory writing course or a standard, reading and research oriented second-semester composition course. But its flexibility allows for use in several other types of courses as well: Instructors who focus on rhetorical analysis will find a variety of personae, tones, organizational strategies, and stylistic techniques represented in these selections. The manual includes a rhetorical index designed to assist instructors in choosing examples of various forms. The Chart of Rhetorical Assignments (p. 193) lists "Elaborations," the text's writing assignments, according to the particular rhetorical strategy the students are encouraged to use in their essays. In addition, a number of questions in the text focus precisely on style, emphasizing the profound effects realized by seemingly inconsequential choices. Several questions on Paz's "Hygiene and Repression," for example, focus on diction and imagery; a question on Carroll's essay, "Money and Seduction," focuses on tone. After answering the questions on Sophronia Liu's "So Tsi-fai," students will become aware of the use of varied sentence construction to suggest changes in the narrator's point of view. A question on Susan Orlean's "Quinceañera" will help students realize the uses of interview as a method of research. These represent only a few of the stylistic questions to be found in the text.

Those who focus on writing across the disciplines will find selections by journalists (Binur, Reynolds), anthropologists (Shostak, Minai, Carroll), political figures (Shevardnadze, Havel), and literary figures (Tan, Vargas Llosa, Rushdie), among others. For those who focus primarily on personal writing, numerous models are available (for example, Soyinka's "Nigerian Childhood," the selection from Angelou's autobiography, and Erdrich's "Adam"). The writing suggestions accompanying these and other selections offer a variety of personal essay assignments. Instructors who want to integrate "creative" literature with nonfiction will find a number of short stories (identified in the table of contents) to compare with the essays in the book.

Finally, these readings work well when used in conjunction with a longer text. For example, instructors could ask students to consider the topic of coming of age in selections by Vargas Llosa, Shostak, and the novel *Upon This Mountain* by Timothy Wangusa. Students can see how the role of women is defined in different societies according to Cooke, Beauvoir, and Duras and then examine the role of women in longer works such as *Things Fall Apart* by Chinua Achebe or *The Joys of Motherhood* by Buchi Emecheta. Other possibilities for longer texts are *Hunger of Memory* by Richard Rodriguez, *Chronicle of a Death Foretold* by Gabriel García Márquez, *I Shall Not Be Moved* by Maya Angelou, *In Good Faith* by Salman Rushdie, *Tracks* by Louise Erdrich, and *The Bluest Eye* by Toni Morrison.

*Ourselves Among Others* is also adaptable to various teaching techniques. The book suits the standard lecture-discussion quite well, especially in the discussion questions following each selection. The questions will also prove useful for instructors who opt for a collaborative classroom. Comparisons between various groups' responses, especially to "Connections" questions, should make for enlightening discussion when the class convenes as a whole.

# Introduction

Regardless of the focus or teaching approach, however, it is probably best to acknowledge the "foreignness" of this material immediately. Traditional college-age students are still at a stage when differences are perceived as threatening, and in recent years a tendency toward chauvinism has emerged in the United States. Perhaps one of the best ways to begin to chip away at prejudices and provincialism is to discuss different cultures and values represented by the class. A logical next step would be to look at other cultures' views of the United States, reexamining a familiar subject from unfamiliar viewpoints. The opening section, "The West and the World," should jolt students out of complacent views of their own society and result in some lively and emphatic responses. Also, it should allow students to broaden their horizons and become more tolerant of difference, so when they move on to subjects in the following sections they will be less judgmental and more open-minded.

Instructors can follow the introductory unit with any unit, but since students usually respond well when moving from familiar to less familiar ground, most instructors will probably choose to begin with "The Family" or "Landmarks and Turning Points." These units provide ample opportunities for students to draw on their own experience and to consider the experiences of others by comparing them with their own.

If students explore the idea of "the family" early in the course, they can use different types of writing to help them think about a familiar concept in unfamiliar cultures. Depending on the approach adopted, students may be asked to write in their journals, compose a paper, or discuss in small groups their family values and traditions. Possible topics include "Rules and Regulations for Living in the Family," "Ethnic (or Religious) Influences in the Family," "Relationships Between Members of the Family," and "Expectations Within the Family." Each of these topics is broad enough for the instructor to adapt to a particular class or for students to narrow themselves. The purpose of the assignment is threefold: One, in discussing their responses, students should discover some unusual customs among people they consider to be just like them; two, they should discover familiar customs among people they consider different; and three, after examining these customs, they should come to the conclusion that neither the similarities nor the differences mean much in the larger world. These revelations will become useful to students as they attempt to understand a wide range of customs during the semester. As they discuss the origins of family patterns, values, and relationships, as well as their benefits and liabilities, students should lose some of their suspicion of things different. After discussing their own differences, students might enjoy reading Gyanranjan's "Our Side of the Fence and Theirs" (p. 134), solely for the purpose of recognizing that we all look askance at customs that differ from our own. It's not necessary to go into a detailed analysis of the story at this point; a mere surface reading should accomplish the goal.

Once students have been introduced to the idea of differences, the course should be able to continue as the instructor wishes. Several possible syllabi, designed to adapt the text to a variety of approaches, are included at the end of the instructor's manual (p. 166).

**Part One**

**THE WEST AND THE WORLD**

## INTRODUCTION

Before looking into other cultures through the eyes of others, students first have the opportunity to look at their own culture through the eyes of others. The selections in this section do not focus on any common issue, such as family, sex roles, or work; the subject is foreignness itself. Here students will be introduced to a few of the reasons we sometimes have trouble understanding each other, as well as the reasons Western culture has become dominant in the world.

To begin working on the section, instructors may want to ask students to consider and list the views they've developed of these other cultures. These lists can then be compared with the views of the West provided in the selections. Students might also try to articulate how some of their prior prejudices or misunderstandings have been mitigated by their exposure to different cultures. These statements can be compared with the explanation of cultural differences found in the section. As they explore the selections, students will encounter some intriguing revelations about our own perceptions of others and about others' perceptions of us.

A few subthemes in the section include Western influence on other cultures (Mphahlele, Harrison, Naipaul, Smith), other cultures' perceptions of the West (Paz, Carroll, Jen, Smith, and Naipaul), and the West and the Third World (Mphahlele, Naipaul). Another important theme is the need to perceive the United States in a new light and to reconceive its cross-cultural relationships (Reed, Atwood).

Instructors may wish to consult the following familiar works in preparing related selections from *Ourselves Among Others*:

### Essays

James Baldwin, "Stranger in the Village" (*Notes of a Native Son*, Dial Press, 1955).
Alex Haley, "My Furthest-Back-Person — 'The African'" (*New York Times*, July 16, 1972).
Maxine Hong Kingston, "No Name Woman" (*The Woman Warrior*, Knopf, 1976).
George Orwell, "Shooting an Elephant" (*Shooting an Elephant and Other Essays*, Harcourt, 1950).
Richard Rodriguez, "Aria" (*American Scholar*, Winter 1981; *Hunger of Memory*, David R. Godine, 1982).

### Short Stories

Toni Cade Bambara, "The Lesson" (*Gorilla, My Love*, Random House, 1972).
Ralph Ellison, "Flying Home" (*Cross-Section*, ed. Edwin Seaver, Fischer Pub. Co., 1944).
Louise Erdrich, "American Horse" (1983; in *Imagining America*, ed. Wesley Brown and Amy Ling, Persea, 1991).

1

Franz Kafka, "The Metamorphosis" (*The Penal Colony*, Schocken, 1948).
D. H. Lawrence, "The Blind Man" (*The Complete Short Stories*, Vol. 2, Penguin, 1976).
Flannery O'Connor, "The Displaced Person" (*Complete Stories*, Farrar, Straus, 1971).
Frank O'Connor, "Guests of the Nation" (*Collected Stories*, Knopf, 1981).
Philip Roth, "Conversion of the Jews" (*Goodbye, Columbus*, Houghton Mifflin, 1959).


**ISHMAEL REED, What's American About America? (p. 3)**

**Explorations**

1. This essay demands that many students readjust their image of how American culture has evolved. Many of the ethnic foods they eat, like pizza, have become "as American as apple pie." The idea of a melting pot, which students are familiar with, implies that ethnic groups are assimilated into the dominant culture the way pizza has been assimilated into American cuisine. Americans assume that foreign traditions will contribute to and become part of the mainstream culture. However, most students have probably never eaten bouillabaisse and will need to know that it is a highly seasoned fish stew from the French Mediterranean. Several kinds of fish and shellfish are cooked so that their flavors remain distinct when they are served together. This culinary metaphor suggests that the United States consists of many colorful traditions and ethnic groups that do not become assimilated into a homogeneous and bland culture, as the term melting pot suggests. In a "cultural bouillabaisse," cultural traditions remain distinct. Also, the use of an untranslated term demands that readers respect the distinctive cultural identity of the dish, which, unlike pizza, has not become assimilated into American cuisine. Students may end by discussing the extent to which a food like pizza does retain its ethnic identity.

2. Reed's main purpose is not to prove the existence of the bias in favor of "Western civilization," but to attack the assumption on which it is based. "Western civilization," Reed argues, is not a monolith, but is the result of the meeting of many cultures. Reed offers five examples from various media to support his assumption that U.S. educators, art critics, and writers favor the monolithic model of Western civilization, but he does not cite sources. He does not name the famous novelist who says "Western civilization was the greatest achievement of mankind" (9). He does not cite the schoolbooks that idealize the Puritans (10), nor does he name the "the president of a distinguished university," the television network, or the schoolteacher who promote the idea that Western civilization is superior (13, 14). When students realize that Reed has not cited concrete sources in support of one of his major claims, they are likely to feel that his argument loses some of its credibility. Reed's strategy, however, is to convince the reader that the notion that Western culture is superior is ubiquitous among the "nation's present educational and cultural elect." He implies that anyone who watches television or reads the newspaper has encountered the bias in favor of Western civilization. However, he is more careful to cite sources to support his main point, that Western civilization is a "cultural bouillabaisse." He begins his essay with a dated quote from the *New York Times*, and although he doesn't name all his sources thereafter, he uses dates and place names to give concreteness to his argument.

3. Reed emphasizes that the term "Western civilization" has been used in a misleading way to suggest the European roots of our culture. He uses numerous examples (6–8) to show the many non-Western cultures that have helped to shape "Western" traditions. His thesis is that Americans need to abandon the idea that American society is heir only to the traditions of a white European cultural elite (the Puritans, 10) because it denies the multicultural nature of contemporary society and the influence of other ethnic traditions in shaping American culture. The habit of elevating one cultural tradition above the others leads to a devaluation of other cultural traditions and to cultural imperialism. Reed directs his criticism to "the nation's present educational and cultural elect" (6), formed by those like the schoolteacher (14) and the university president and the television producer (13) who see America as the product of European culture. He recommends that they learn to see America as a place where the world's cultures meet, thrive, and contribute richly to contemporary society (15).

## Connections

1. To begin a discussion of this question, you might ask students to add to Harrison's examples illustrating the spread of Western culture. The worldwide craze for blue jeans and rock 'n' roll music and the spread of McDonald's to Moscow are some obvious additions. As Harrison contends, the technological advances promised by Westernization are almost impossible for developing countries to resist (in spite of the environmental and political hazards that accompany them). Survival as a country is at stake. And a country cannot adopt Western technology without adopting other Western institutions and ideas, which replace their traditional counterparts. Whereas Harrison argues that the Westernization of the world promotes global cultural uniformity, Reed seems to describe a future in which diverse cultures can coexist without threatening or transforming one another. Although Harrison and Reed might disagree about how cultures interact, they would probably agree that it is not possible for cultures to exist in isolation. The idea of a "pure" culture, unaffected by outside influences, is foreign to both Harrison and Reed.

2. For many students, Morrison's piece will offer a perspective on American literature and culture they have never considered before. Morrison contends that American literature (and, by analogy, mainstream American culture) was essentially formed by the philosophies, institutions, and ideologies that made slavery possible in the United States. Although Africans and African-Americans do not receive much attention in the literature that constitutes the American canon, according to Morrison, without the influence of people of African heritage, American literature and culture would be entirely different. On the issue of Euro-American culture, Reed cites the example of a Yale professor who was condemned for his view that African cultures had influenced the development of American cultures. This example suggests that he would agree with Morrison that Americans are unwilling to confront the fact that American culture has always been based on multicultural interaction. However, Reed and Morrison differ in that Morrison's strategy is to point out the influence of Africans and African-Americans on canonical Euro-American literature, while Reed is more concerned with deconstructing the basic idea that there is such a thing as "monolithic" Euro-American culture (6).

## RAYMONDE CARROLL, Money and Seduction (p. 8)

### Explorations

1.  Carroll's thesis is that the American attitude toward money and the French attitude toward sexual conquest function in similar fashions, since each suggests the measure of an individual's success in the respective society. Both are metaphors for success, and they allow for the crossing of class boundaries. While Carroll includes references to books, the main source of information cited appears to be conversations with French and American friends or acquaintances (para. 1). Sometimes she refers to specific individuals, such as the French woman with the American brother-in-law. More often, Carroll refers to a larger group of respondents, as if to emphasize the uniformity of the response. Thus she writes of "many French informants" (2) or "many Americans" (3). Some students will recognize that, since Carroll is using evidence that is not verifiable, any observer similarly positioned between the cultures could readily refute or support her thesis using Carroll's own rules of evidence. However, her thesis depends on logic, as well as evidence. The specific ways in which French and American cultures measure personal success may be less important to Carroll's thesis than the general idea that cultures use metaphors (such as money or seduction) to express and measure movement up or down the class hierarchy.

2.  In her last paragraph, Carroll writes that "the greatest attraction of cultural analysis . . . is the possibility of replacing a dull exchange of invectives with an exploration that is . . . fascinating" (20). In her essay she shows that the French and the Americans have misunderstood each other's behavior, a misunderstanding that has led to derogatory remarks about foreign cultural practices. Carroll believes that instead of rejecting cultures on the grounds of difference, people should explore foreign cultures to find resemblances to their own. By "inviting" people to proceed in this fashion, Carroll encourages them to take a positive attitude toward foreign cultures and pays them the compliment of assuming they can arrive at analyses similar to her own. Her noncritical approach prevents readers from defending their own prejudices and identifying with only one of the cultural attitudes under discussion.

3.  Students may bring their own concept of American Playboys to this question, yielding a definition more sexually oriented than Carroll's and thus closer to her definition of French playboys. The essay contrasts not only American and French playboys' behavior, but attitudes toward them in the societies they live in. The American playboy is described as one who "squanders an inherited fortune" (8). The author makes no comment about the American playboy's sexual habits but implies that his spending habits do not help him realize his potential (8). He has "wasted the 'opportunities' offered by . . . parents or by society" (8). In contrast, being a French playboy involves hard work, for "Seduction is an art which is learned and perfected" (16). Like all art, it requires "intelligence," "expertise," and "talent" (18). Thus the French playboy is admired for his achievement, not censored for immoral behavior. An American playboy might underestimate or not appreciate how hard the French playboy must work. The French playboy might think the American playboy buys his successes, obtaining only easy victories.

**Connections**

1.  Carroll's focus is not on "social realities" but on "cultural premises." (para. 9). She uses qualifiers to hint that, in reality, class mobility in the United States is more restricted than the "cultural premise" would suggest: "[money] is *supposed* to be accessible to all"; "The highest social class is, in principle, open to everyone" (9). However, since she wishes to generalize about American culture, she does not go further in discussing the ways in which race and cultural diversity in the United States affect the social reality of class. As a result, she seems to side with the melting-pot view of American society rather than with the "cultural bouillabaisse" view Ishmael Reed proposed. Although she gives a diverse list of the many symbolic meanings of money in the United States (7), she refers to "Americans" as though every American was in a position to consider money as an abstract concept. She claims that "money has become a common denominator" (9) and refers to "the essentially idealistic significance of money in American culture" (10).

2.  According to Ishmael Reed, racial and ethnic differences provide the context for the formation of cultural subgroups in the United States. Students may need help to understand how class differences intersect with racial and ethnic differences. Because many middle-class students hold the view, expressed by Carroll, that monetary success depends solely on individual effort (9), it may be hard for them initially to recognize the confluence of race and class inequalities in our society. Once they do, the notion that money is "the only true class equalizer" in the United States will be called into doubt. Reed's essay contains a historical example of Western European culture in the United States that suggests why money, rather than seduction, would become the primary measure of success here. He recalls that the Puritans are idealized as "industrious, responsible" creators of the work ethic, but that they were also repressive and intolerant. The art of seduction, in a Puritan society, would be considered at best a waste of time and at worst a sign of immorality.

## OCTAVIO PAZ (Ok-TAH-vee-oh PAHS), Hygiene and Repression (p. 15)

**Explorations**

1.  Most students have probably encountered the word hygiene in contexts suggesting that good hygiene is a positive goal. Therefore, Paz's use of the word in a negative sense may be unexpected and confusing. Paz defines hygiene as an American obsession with cleanliness stemming from a desire to remain morally separate, untouched, and pure. He terms the American concern with the purity of food a "maniacal preoccupation" that also expresses itself as a desire for racial and cultural purity (para. 1). In paragraph 6, Paz uses the example of the fear of contagion and germs experienced by Americans traveling abroad. He compares the American fear of physical contagion with the Brahman fear of moral contamination, showing that scientific and religious conditioning can result in similar behavior and that scientific values can mask moral values. Students who have traveled abroad might consider whether they were concerned with the cleanliness of conditions. Nearer to home, they might consider the advertisements promoting cleaning agents from toothpaste to detergents that suggest that cleanliness is the basis of a healthful and moral life.

2. By his constant references to "Americans," as if all Americans belong in one category, Paz suggests that American culture is uniform and America is a melting pot. Yet since he compares the culture to the cuisine, he obviously believes that this melting pot produces a homogeneous mixture not by combining distinct flavors but by excluding any different flavors or cultures. He first characterizes American cuisine as "simple" and "nourishing" (1), but his later comparison of it with other cuisines suggests that it is without interesting nuances (3), indulges infantile longings in preferences for milk and milkshakes (2), and lacks spice or passion (4). Americans eat to be healthy and able to work, not to find pleasure in their food (5). American cuisine is compared to the "virtuous discourse" of the "Founding Fathers," a watercolor painting, and a pastel drawing of delicate shades (1).

3. Paz uses religious terms throughout his essay, and it may be difficult for students unfamiliar with these terms to grasp the analogies he sets up. For example, some of the terms used are "transubstantiation" (1), "communion" (1), "devil" (2), "apostolic" (2), and "Eucharist" (3). By drawing an analogy between eating and religious experiences, he suggests that eating has important symbolic, as well as practical functions, such as the experience of communion between elements on the plate and persons at the table. Paz is preparing the reader for his comparison of the American dread of physical contagion with the Brahman fear of moral contamination, stressing their similar origins. Because most students consider science and religion as separate categories, they will need to discuss and understand the idea of taboo before understanding the relationship between purity and isolation in both scientific and religious contexts.

4. Students might approach this essay by considering their dinner of the night before or the types of meals usually served in their homes. They should be encouraged to discuss whether Paz's descriptions of American eating habits are accurate or speak to a conceptualization of American cuisine. Some students may resent his overly simplified description of American eating habits, especially if they are familiar with the diversity of American cuisines. They might discuss Paz's distinction between "ideas and social values" and "more or less secret realities" (5) in order to understand why he does not discuss other ethnic groups. Paz himself seems to enjoy suggesting that the puritanical repressiveness of American eating habits condemns Americans to bland cuisine and a diminished sense of sin. His humor, like the Mexican cuisine he describes (3), makes contradictory and unexpected associations. For example, if a milkshake is a sign of "pregenital pleasures" (2) and can be associated with milk, home, and mother, it also can be associated with "orgies" of sugar (2). Paz implies that Americans unknowingly express moral attitudes through their food habits, but he quite consciously describes food choices in moral and religious terms. The humor here derives from his playfulness in using language, for he is not amused by his discoveries. Using a Freudian framework, Paz traces the evolution of the rationalism and plain cuisine of the Founding Fathers into a "maniacal preoccupation" with purity (1). Paz shows that Americans are not following the principles of "temperance, moderation, [and] reserve" (6); their actions are governed by "obsession" and "dread." The conclusions he reaches after comparing the attitudes of several cultures toward food lead to labels many Americans may resent hearing applied to themselves: uncommunicative, unsocial, superstitious, and, by implication, racist (7). Thus, the tactic of drawing unfavorable comparisons should generate an emotional response from readers.

## Connections

1.  Raymonde Carroll says that Americans display "disgust" for French people who boast about their sexual achievements, and she contends that Americans consider sex a subject suitable only to "uncivilized" settings such as locker rooms (para. 14). The French, according to Carroll, consider this evidence of a sexual puritanism among Americans. Paz describes a similar view of American attitudes toward food. He says that "Yankee food, impregnated with Puritanism, is based on exclusions." American food, Paz argues, reflects a culture-wide concern for racial, religious, and sexual purity (1). Food, like work and sports in the United States, is supposed to be turned to productive ends (5), not enjoyed simply for the pleasure of it.

2.  Reed's essay is full of descriptions that suggest the need to replace the idea of a traditional American cuisine and culture with the idea of a variety of ethnic cuisines and cultural traditions. Instead of roasts, carrots, and potatoes, Reed mentions pizza, Italian ices, and knishes. He sees Vietnamese grocery stores, Islamic mosques, and paintings with African mythological imagery in fast-food restaurants. He discusses the influence of the Puritans, yet he also mentions the contributions of Native Americans to American culture. Reed rejects the idea of a monolithic, Eurocentric American culture and encourages others to do the same.

3.  Both Reed and Paz refer to the historic influence of the Puritans in the development of American culture and attitudes. Reed suggests that the Puritans' inhuman treatment of those not part of the ruling elite, such as children, Indians, and servants from Barbados, reflected their distrust of difference (11). Paz sees the same attitude of the Puritans in "Yankee food, impregnated with Puritanism" (1). Reed writes that the other side of the Puritan legacy of hard work is "the strange and paranoid attitudes of that society toward those different from the elect" (12). Paz states that "the maniacal preoccupation with the purity and origin of food products has its counterpart in racism and exclusivism" (1).

## GISH JEN, Helen in America (p. 22)

## Explorations

1.  Helen considers her life in China perfect for several reasons. Students may have trouble understanding why the fact that Helen had a twin sister who died was a lucky beginning, or why her "touch-and-go start" on life turned out to be a blessing (para. 1). Girls are usually considered of less value than boys in China, but Helen became precious in part because her parents had suffered the loss of her sister and because they came close to losing Helen herself. However, many students will remember receiving special attention when they were sick during childhood, and those memories will make it easier to understand why Helen would consider her childhood illnesses a boon. Once in the United States, Helen tries to recreate her life in China by maintaining the same stillness she enjoyed there and by refusing to become involved in American cultures (2, 3). She refuses to eat American food and often goes hungry, which she hopes will make her sick again (3). She remains healthy, however, and eventually finds herself becoming interested in her new home. She gives up her isolation, even agreeing to marry, an idea that had horrified her in China.

7

2. The story about the man who took his house apart and rebuilt it elsewhere suggests the Changs' efforts to reproduce certain aspects of their life in China in their new life in the United States, including Ralph's marriage to Helen, who resembles the Changs' younger sister. In the story Ralph tells, the house the man rebuilds has the same leak as the first and is still too small — flaws that, when applied to the Changs, may mean that their efforts to live as they did in China may not be the best solution to the challenges of living in a new culture. However, Theresa speculates that maybe the man rebuilt his house because he was used to it, even with all its flaws (13). The Changs have done their best to bring over the values of their own culture, but even so they are not always comfortable in their new country (especially when they have to move into an apartment that has many more flaws than their house in China).

3. This should be an easy question for students to think through once they understand that sometimes the Changs are seeing their own characteristics reflected in the Americans around them. Helen complains of "'typical American just-want-to-be-the-center-of-things,'" a desire she has always felt herself (39). Some of their derogatory remarks ("'typical American don't-know-how-to-get-along'" and "'typical American just-dumb'") reflect their own anxieties about getting along in the United States and mastering the English language.

4. The main sources of the Changs' information about American life are the newspaper, popular magazines, the radio, and their neighbors. These are all rich sources of information, but much of what they see and read is incomprehensible to them until they read a newspaper article about how Americans have degenerated since World War II (41). After reading the article the Changs are pleased to find that Americans agree with their perceptions of the degeneracy of American life. They think they have found rational support for their need to maintain some distance from American culture, because too much contact would cause them to become "wild" (39) and deteriorate like the Americans. The evidence they gather for their hypothesis is drawn from contact with their super, neighbors, and shopkeepers, as well as from tabloid articles about bizarre occurrences, such as the animal trainer biting off his wife's ear (41). Therefore, their sources are either unreliable or merely anecdotal, feeding their tendency to generalize about "typical American" defects.

## Connections

1. Examining Octavio Paz's essay in conjunction with "Helen in America" will illuminate some of the ironies involved in trying to identify traits that are "typical" of any nationality or race. Paz's critique of Americans focusses on what he views as their characteristic lack of tolerance. He writes that Americans demand the "extirpation or separation of what is alien, different, ambiguous, impure" (para 8). Paz is primarily interested in any behavior that tends to support this view of the typical American; therefore, he discusses primarily "traditional" American cuisine, which he contends "is like watercolor painting or pastels" (1) and the behaviors of American travelers abroad, where they evince a boundless "dread of contagion"(6). This "dread" of moral and physical infection leads to the characteristic American intolerance of whatever is foreign. The Changs, by contrast, are most interested in American behaviors when they seem to provide evidence that Americans are foolish, immoral, or incomprehensible. They discover "typical" American characteristics such as an overblown sense of self-importance, the tendency to use brute

force, and an inability to cooperate. Denigrating Americans helps them to diffuse the tensions of being foreigners in a sometimes hostile environment, but it also demonstrates the tendency Paz claimed was typically American: the tendency to condemn things and people who are foreign.

2. Most students will realize that the Changs' value economy, as their choice to live in a run-down apartment as a money-saving measure shows (26). They also value hard work, exemplified in Ralph's assertion that Pete is "fooling himself" in thinking he could become a doctor or engineer without putting in years of hard work and sacrifice (31–33). Carroll says that for Americans, "to earn money, a lot of money, and to spend it, is to give the most concrete, the most visible sign that one has not wasted the 'opportunities' offered by one's parents or by society . . ." (8). Reviewing this statement may help students consider differences between the Changs' view of money and the "American" view. The Changs share with Americans a commitment to the work ethic, but they would not agree that using money as a "visible sign" of success is a virtue. Similarly, according to Carroll, seduction is a visible measure of success for the French, and it is likely the Changs would consider bragging about sexual exploits to be just as offensive as flaunting wealth.

3. The Changs enjoy certain aspects of American culture, including American print media and radio (5), but when Helen first arrives, she depends on trips to New York's Chinatown to give her a feeling of being at home. There, also, she can buy Chinese food. Other influences, such as the presence of black people in the poor apartment building the Changs move to, are harder for them to accept. But the cultural eclecticism the Changs' encounter helps them to feel that "everything . . . was going to be okay" (45).

## MARGARET ATWOOD, A View from Canada (p. 29)

### Explorations

1. Margaret Atwood sums up her youthful view of Americans when she recalls her shock at realizing her country "was owned by the kind of people who carried tin boats across portages and didn't burn their garbage" (para. 4). Earlier still, she sums up her attitude this way: "Americans were wimps who had a lot of money but did not know what they were doing" (1). Students may come up with a variety of examples from the text that reveal Atwood's current view of the "typical American." Atwood describes the United States as an isolationist nation (10, 11) and points out that Americans always try to take their American lifestyle with them when they travel internationally (12). Perhaps the most telling statement Atwood makes is that "Americans experience themselves, individually, as small toads in the biggest and most powerful puddle in the world" (13). She recognizes that Americans experience "a sense of power [that] comes from identifying with the puddle." At the same time, her image suggests that the size and power of their own country make Americans feel small and swallowed up by it.

2. Students will need help identifying the subtle indications that "A View from Canada" was written as a speech: the conversational and often jocular tone, frequent use of short phrases, and departures from formal diction ("hamburgers, cokes, and rock music surrounded you" (12)), are not obtrusive. However, it is obvious in paragraph 14 that

Atwood is giving a speech, and that her audience is American, when she says, "south of you you have Mexico and south of us we have you" (15).

3. Atwood begins to indicate a problem with Canadian self-image when she comments on the lingering effects of British colonialism, for instance the fact that British history was taught in schools in preference to Canadian history (2-3). After the war, Americans bought into the place left vacant by the British, leaving the Canadians feeling that "they'd sold their birthright for a mess" (4). However, Atwood points out the positive aspects of the Canadian outlook (although with some irony) when she writes that "Canada, having somehow become an expert at compromise, was the mediator" between Britain and the United States. Canadians are far more interested in international relations than are Americans (10). According to Atwood, unlike Americans, Canadians realize they are not isolated from the world at large (11, 12). But they also think of their country as "a small sinking Titanic squashed between two icebergs" (11), a comment Atwood supports with the example of the Canadian politician who said that Canada walks in the footstep of the United States (13).

4. Students will be able to locate many places where Atwood uses humor, but it is important to point out that Atwood's humor can be ironic, with a serious and often barbed comment buried in it. The vision, in the first paragraph, of American ineptitude exemplified in Atwood's portrait of Americans portaging a metal boat ("Typically American, we thought, as they ricocheted off another tree") offers not only a view of Americans as slapstick incompetents, but also suggests that Canadians underestimated the ability of Americans to colonize Canada with money and cultural influence. Atwood recalls the sharp-edged humor of her first example in paragraph 4, when she says Canadians woke up in the sixties to realize their country was owned by incompetents. Lighter uses of humor include Atwood's wry comments on her own history: "I know it's hard to believe in view of my youthful appearance, but when I was child there was no television" (5); "By this time I wanted to be a writer, and you can see it would be a dilemma . . . how could one be a writer and somehow manage to avoid having to become British and dead?" (7).

## Connections

1. In Gish Jen's "Helen in America," Theresa contemplates the run-down apartment the Changs share and comments, "We're not the kind of people who live like this" (para. 26). The soft, crumbling plaster and the crack in the wall indicate the Changs' lack of protection against the world outside. Unlike the Americans, who in Atwood's view "enter the outside world the way they landed on the moon, with their . . . protective spacesuits firmly in place" (12) the Changs must deal with the world directly. Nevertheless, as the story Ralph tells about the man who moves his house suggests (10), the Changs have brought their own culture and attitudes with them. When they, like Atwood, make fun of the "typical American," they are setting up walls between themselves and American cultural influences.

2. Octavio Paz writes that when he was in India, he "witnessed the obsession of Americans with hygiene" (6). They feared germs from food, water, people, and the air. Similarly, Atwood writes that Americans in New Delhi lived behind walls, insisted on eating American food, and seemed to have "their own oxygen tanks of American air strapped to their backs" (12). Paz points out that American isolationism abroad indicates a preoccupation with purity (6) that is not shared with people from other nations.

3. Because they are more used to considering themselves "Americans" than as "United States citizens," students may not realize the implications of Ishmael Reed's use of the term "North American" when he is discussing the United States (as when he says that the surrealists, "in their map of North America" made "Alaska dwarf . . . the lower forty-eight states in size" (7). Reed makes no mention of the Canadian provinces that also compose North America. All of Reed's examples of American prejudices come from the United States. In his conclusion, Reed blatantly subsumes Canada into the United States, saying the nations are "unique in the world" in that many world cultures converge in them. Atwood would disagree with Reed's tendency to assume Canada and the United States are the same, but she generalizes about Americans in such a way that the multicultural composition of the United States is suppressed.

## ES'KIA MPHAHLELE (Em-fa-LAY-lay), Tradition and the African Writer (p. 35)

### Explorations

1. Belonging to both the Western and the African worlds forces Mphahlele and his fellow artists to choose between their present, represented by Westernization, and the past, represented by African tradition. In attempting to reconcile the two, the artists must balance several opposing influences: Christianity versus traditional African religions; fact-oriented Western education versus the more spiritual knowledge of family and tribe; traditional tribal philosophy versus the European language used to articulate it; reverence for the artifact versus the creative process; and the local African community versus the larger, predominantly Western, surrounding world. Specifically, the artists choose whether to adopt Western ways, gaining power in the larger world at the risk of losing African understanding, friends, and kinship ties.

2. African writers will need education to succeed in the world beyond the community, and that education will in turn open up still newer worlds to them. But it also opens up a gulf between writers and African tradition. Writers must attempt to reconcile the education with the traditions or risk losing their moorings. Education provides new viewpoints, new subject matter, and many other sources of enrichment for writers. However, it may alienate them from the viewpoints and subject matter to which they feel closest and about which they can write most successfully. To reject education is to cut themselves off from the larger world in an attempt (not necessarily successful) to preserve the smaller one.

3. Mphahlele's first indication of his Western heritage is found in the first paragraph, when he refers to "Hegelian historical determinism." Among other illustrations of Western influence are his ability to understand the influence of his European education (para. 2), his discussion of parent-child relationships (4), and his essay's diction throughout. His African heritage is more evident, illustrated by his understanding of the value of the creative process (6) and his acknowledgment of the spirit of his ancestors (8).

4. In his essay, Mphahlele uses the word *tradition* in two ways. He says his education has taught him to use the tradition of the West as a point of reference for himself (2), yet he notes that this tradition has been superimposed upon a stronger indigenous African

11

religion and civilization (3). His thesis is that the education of the African writer places him between these two traditions and alienates him from the majority of Africans, who remain closer to the traditions of their ancestors (4). African parents desire the benefits that an education can confer, but they despair over their children's shift in allegiance. Mphahlele takes a more positive attitude toward the dual allegiances and feels that African writers can successfully reconcile, or "harmonize," the two traditions (4). Since Mphahlele doesn't quote any outside sources, he seems to generalize from his own experience (2). He includes himself in his observations by using the pronouns we (3) and you (6) when explaining the situation of African writers.

## Connections

1.  Like Margaret Atwood, Es'kia Mphahlele received an education that disparaged the history and religions of his continent. Mphahlele writes, "I was brought up on European history and literature and religion and made to identify with European heroes . . ." (para. 2). Atwood recalls that in school she was introduced primarily to British literature (7) and European and American history (8). It will be a challenge for students to deduce what changes in education Mphahlele and Atwood might recommend. Atwood might recommend developing a curriculum that emphasizes Canada's role as an international mediator (11, 12) as a way of inducing Canadians to feel less powerless (13). Mphahlele might recommend different tactics. He writes that most parents recognize that "the benefits of a modern education are tangible, real" (5), but he seems to regret the "ever widening gulf between one and one's parents and one's community" that a modern, or western, education produces (6). Some students will say that the educational system would be improved, and the gulf between generations could be reduced, if schools could incorporate more African history and literature into the curriculum. But Mphahlele has a different way of approaching the problem of what to do with the "ambivalent character" he has become as a result of his western education (2). In his conclusion, Mphahlele writes that "we need to appreciate these distances" between African traditions and the westernized modern world. This strategy, of appreciating cultural and historical differences rather than ignoring them or trying to obliterate them, would create an educational system that would better prepare the African writer to take part in "the whole pattern" (9).

2.  Both Atwood and Mphahlele grew up far from the European culture that defined *writer* in their countries. The obstacles Atwood faced included the general sense among Canadians that their history and cultures are uninteresting (9) and the fact that her education taught her to regard British literature as the only literature of merit (7). She also had to contend with the complications of gender, as suggested in her comment that she finds it hard to accept it as a compliment when men tell her she thinks like a man (1). Fortunately, her education allowed her to read British women writers, helping her to realize she did not have to identify herself with men in order to write (7). Mphahlele's main obstacle may have been the "humiliating" sense of having to continually reassess himself "with reference to . . . the tradition of the West" (2). The effort to reconcile Western influences and African traditions is "agonizing" (2). His reference only to male figures of cultural authority (3, 8) suggest that his most obvious advantage over Atwood is his gender, while her most obvious advantage over him is her European descent, which exempts her from the racial bias Mphahlele describes (3). On the other hand, Mphahlele is backed up by a long African tradition of cultural expression that he feels is as important

to his writing as the Western influences. Atwood, as a citizen of a nation with a relatively short history, has no long tradition of Canadian writing to draw on. Unlike Africans, Canadians cannot look back to a point in history when their ancestors were not a part of western culture. But Atwood makes this lack of an established tradition a strength; she is forging the literary traditions future Canadian writers will build on.

3. Respect for tradition and an appreciation of metaphor are as important to Gish Jen's "Helen in America" as they are to Mphahlele's "Tradition and the African Writer." In Jen's story, the Changs' household, especially the marriage between Ralph and his sister Theresa's best friend Helen, is arranged according to a pattern their parents would approve (10). The Changs express the appropriateness of their arrangements by evoking two metaphors. Ralph implies a comparison between their household and that of a man who "took his house apart, and moved it, and then rebuilt it, just the way it was" (10), and Helen reminds Ralph and Theresa of the saying that a wife's ankle is tied to her husband's from the time she is born (20, 21). Each of these metaphors is a way of affirming their solidarity and showing respect for Chinese tradition.

4. Both Africa and Latin America were colonized by Western Europeans who imposed their own religious and educational traditions upon the indigenous culture, although the colonizations occurred during different historic periods. Yet the resultant culture described by Paz seems able to reconcile disparate elements or opposites. Paz enjoys the sensuous nature of Mexican food, which denies the Puritan heritage of separation and subordination of foreign elements. Unlike the American cuisine, which is "based on . . . exclusions," the Mexican cuisine reflects a "fondness for dark, passionate stews . . . , for thick and sumptuous red, green, and yellow sauces (1). Mphahlele finds a similar sensuousness in language. The indigenous African languages (unlike the "unaffected sentences of virtuous discourse" described by Paz (1) influence modern witnesses to "operate in metaphor and glory in the sensuousness of the spoken word" (8).

## PAUL HARRISON, The Westernization of the World (p. 41)

### Explorations

1. The "European road" Harrison mentions is characterized by a worship of technology (especially military), a preoccupation with highways and large buildings, an infatuation with Western dress, and a rejection of traditional culture (note the opening anecdote). His examples, ranging from the bank manager's television (para. 4) to the Ivory Coast's four-lane highway going nowhere and Jakarta's "neo-fascist monuments" (12), are all traceable to a desire to impress others in the Third World with one's own successful adoption of Western ways.

2. That the general cause of the Third World's Westernization is European colonization should be readily apparent to all students. But recognizing the three specific channels through which Westernization was realized will take careful reading. Some students may point immediately to the political, economic, and cultural imperialism mentioned in paragraph 6, failing to realize that the article doesn't discuss political and economic

factors. Cultural imperialism itself is the subject of the selection, and the channels are identified in paragraphs 9, 10, and 11 as the "indoctrination [by the colonial powers] of an elite of local collaborators"; the existence in the native population of "reference-group behavior," or imitation of the behavior of the elite group; and the practice of racial humiliation "deriving from the arrogance and haughtiness of the colonialists." Harrison cites self-righteous Pauline Christianity, cultural arrogance, racial prejudice, and the possession of power as the critical factors in the colonialist attitude and a total lack of the same among the natives as the reasons for the success of Westernization. The natives had no sense of their own value with which to fend off the assault of European influence.

3.  Harrison cites "consciousness of Western military superiority" (14) as the primary force behind Westernization of noncolonial nations. The overwhelming desire to compete militarily with the European powers resulted in far-reaching social, economic, and political changes in these societies. Also important, according to Harrison, is the pervading racial prejudice of the West, leading some of the "Young Turks" who gained power in the noncolonial societies to further emulate European culture. Now that they've cast their lot with the West, a return to their own traditions would be extremely difficult. His observation that "contact with Europe shook nations to the foundations, calling into question the roots of their civilizations and all the assumptions and institutions on which their lives were based" (14) makes it quite clear that there is no turning back once Western culture has been embraced. Students may also point out his observation on the cultural price Japan has paid to become one of the leading industrial nations (16).

4.  Harrison supports his ideas with diverse and substantial evidence, including his own direct observations and also those of a range of other writers. For instance, he cites such Third World intellectuals as Fanon on racial humiliation and Chiang on the influence of military technology on society as a whole. Students can identify the types of information Harrison relies on by looking at the similarities he cites among British, French, Dutch, Iberian, and Portuguese colonies. The native "aristocracy" in all the colonies, he contends, exhibit similar proclivities, among them styles of Western dress, designs of cities and buildings, construction of highways, and mimicry of behavior. Although much of his evidence is superficial (dress, architecture, social behavior), these aspects reflect cultural values. In this sense then his evidence is sound.

## Connections

1.  In calling Africa "mission-ridden" (para. 3), Mphahlele indicates his opinion of Christianity's role in his culture. The missions set up a power structure in which a native was unable to get a job without a testimonial from a white minister. Even the black ministers were unable to rely on one another for testimonials; references had to be from a white person. Christianity also "smoked out" all the ancient African gods (2). Mphahlele describes the steps Africans follow when being drawn into this new power structure. First the African is baptized, a process that may turn him into a Christian in little more than name but that qualifies him for attending a mission school (3). At school the young African learns to elevate the tradition of the West and to downplay his own. Parents may fear that a separation between themselves and their children will result from education, but their fundamental attitude encourages their children to acquire and benefit from a modern education. The attitude helps young Africans take the important step of "harmonization," of reconciling the difficulty of communicating with their parents with the exhilaration of

14

assimilating foreign patterns of thought (4). At this point the Africans are not completely assimilated into Western culture but are somewhat distanced from their own. For example, they may still feel "reverence" for an indigenous religion, but they no longer practice its ritual (2).

2.  The Spanish are included among the Iberian conquerors discussed by Harrison in paragraph 7. He contrasts them with the British, noting that the Iberians were free from racial prejudice, which meant that, unlike the British, they intermingled with the native population, living with native women and fathering interracial children. Paz establishes that the same attitude toward "mingling" dominates Latin American cuisine and culture when he draws an analogy between gastronomy and the erotic, where "it's desire that sets substances, bodies, and sensations in motion . . . that rules their conjunction, commingling, and transmutation" (3). According to Paz, Mexican cuisine, composed of opposites which shock the taste (3), is "dark, passionate, . . . thick, . . . sumptuous," colorful, and not based on the principles of separation and exclusion (1).

3.  In paragraph 10 Harrison discusses reference-group behavior when he explains that the Africans copied the customs and habits of their conquerors. The desire to mimic created a subaltern ruling class of a native elite that adopted Western ways in place of their own traditions. Carroll's essay also gives several examples of individuals conforming to the values of a more dominant group, although the groups in her essay are formed from the indigenous culture. Thus, American men may conform to the atmosphere of the locker room, behaving quite differently than they would elsewhere, where frank discussion of their sexual exploits would be unacceptable (14). More important, Carroll notes that the symbolism of money changes quite radically depending on the group discussing it. The self-made person who discusses his wealth is encouraging others to follow his example. Since he represents a different life-style and economic status, which encourage others to emulate him, he functions very much like the reference groups in Africa or India that encourage the formation of an elite (10).

## V. S. NAIPAUL (NYE-paul), Entering the New World (p. 48)

### Explorations

1.  The attitude of the waiters, the poor service, and the inaccurate bill all indicate to Naipaul that the problem is "more than a matter of an off day" (para. 20). He assumes that the French or European owner or manager is no longer with the restaurant. How does he reach this conclusion? He has determined, after listening to Ebony's imitation of the French intellectual, that Westernization is merely an idea. Ebony is unable to support any of his pronouncements, leading Naipaul to the belief that they are all borrowed. Thus when he sees what's happening in the restaurant, he imagines that the place itself was just an idea. He sees in the waiters' faces "various degrees of tribal authority" and concludes that "the true life was there, in the mysteries of the village." Now that the people who conceived the idea of the restaurant are gone, the place itself, "with its false, arbitrary ritual, was [a] charade" (20).

2. Naipaul's observation that Ebony is concerned with "antithesis, balance" will need some attention before students go on to interpret Ebony's comparisons between Africans, the French, and the British. Naipaul's observation suggests that Ebony has an aesthetic appreciation for an argument that balances itself by evoking antitheses. Thus Ebony argues that the French create the bourgeois (who want peace), but the English create entrepreneurs (who want change) (9). He produces a similarly symmetrical argument when he says that "Africans live at peace with nature. Europeans want to conquer or dominate nature" (11). Throughout his conversation with Ebony, Naipaul seems skeptical of Ebony's seriousness as a thinker. Naipaul says that Ebony's ideas are "scattered" and that he is not as anxious about the fate of Africa as he should be (18). Under the influence of Naipaul's skepticism, many students will agree that Ebony is more interested in the beauty than the validity of an idea. But some may realize that Ebony may evoke "antitheses" as a way of establishing distance between himself and western influences. Ebony's story about his French education, when he considers the differences in nonverbal communication that led the French to consider the Africans hypocritical (13), provides him with a way to distance himself from the French colonial influence. The point of the story, Ebony maintains, is that he considered his French teachers "inferior" (15). By opposing the European to the African cultures, Ebony can draw whatever he can use from the Western tradition while still remaining allied with African perspectives.

3. In the first half of the essay Naipaul almost seems to be poking fun at Ebony. He characterizes the man as a child trying to impress an adult. A number of Naipaul's comments create this impression, among them "I felt it had been said before" (9), "Antithesis, balance: the beauty rather than the validity of a thought" (10), and "I felt this racial story, with its triumphant twist, had previously had a sympathetic foreign listener" (16). But after Ebony leaves and Naipaul visits the restaurant, he seems to realize that the fault isn't Ebony's. He, along with all his fellow citizens, has been sold a bill of goods; there is no substance to the "idea" of the new world. When the French departed, the Africans were left to create their own "new world" out of the changes that colonialism had brought about in their nation.

4. Ebony's view of the French influence on the Ivory Coast can be gleaned from three comments. In paragraph 8, Ebony points out that "Charlemagne wasn't my ancestor," suggesting that the French had no business imposing their history and culture on the Ivory Coast. In the next paragraph, Ebony goes on to talk about how badly the French governed their colonies. Somewhat later, commenting on his education under the French, Ebony implies that the French failed to understand African culture and that this failure lost them the respect of the Africans. Naipaul's view of the French is filtered partly through his observations of Ebony. His perception of the effects of Ebony's French educaton does not reflect well either on the French or on Ebony, who according to Naipaul appreciates "the beauty rather than the validity of a thought (10)." Later Naipaul comments that Ebony's ideas are merely "part of his relishing of life, part of his French-inspired role as intellectual. . . ." (18). However, Naipaul also credits the French with creating and maintaining order in the restaurant: "Someone was missing, perhaps the French or European manager. And with him more than good service had gone: The whole restaurant idea had vanished" (20). Students may infer that Naipaul is implying the French have played a similar organizing role in the Ivory Coast as a whole.

**Connections**

1.  Harrison says that the French colonialists had aimed for "'assimilation' of gifted natives" through "indoctrination of an elite of local collaborators" (para. 9). Both Naipaul and Ebony acknowledge this — Naipaul by observing the French influence in Ebony's expressions and Ebony himself (albeit unwittingly) by deciding, "as a poet and intellectual . . . to try out his ideas" (5). But Naipaul's assessment of European influence does not seem quite as harsh as Harrison's: The latter chronicles over a century of economic, social, and political undermining of African traditions, whereas the former focuses almost exclusively on the intellectual influence. In acknowledging the vacuousness of the French contribution to African culture, Naipaul's tone at the end seems wistful; Harrison's, in an outright condemnation of colonialism, is biting.

2.  While Ebony distinguishes between the French and the British, he ends by placing them in the same category of "European" in opposition to the category of "African." According to him, the French create a "bourgeois people" content to live life routinely, uncommitted to change, desirous of peace and stability. Ebony sees a striking difference in the British, whom he terms "entrepreneurs . . . dedicated to radical change" (9). This attitude most closely reflects his own, which embraces the opportunity to enter a "new" or changed world and makes it appear that he has more respect for the British. Furthermore, his conscious attitude toward the French is one of contempt, so one could assume that he values any differences from the French. His conclusion about the inferiority of the French teachers is meant to sum up his various condemnations of French influence. Yet, of course, in many ways he displays the influence of these teachers in his attempts to assume the "French-inspired role as intellectual" (18). Harrison's view would provide a means for evaluating Ebony's experience. Although Harrison does not specifically discuss the French, he does see two experiences of colonization. The British held themselves apart from the natives, with the result that the natives who imitated the British, like the Indians, rejected their own culture. The French appear to be more like the Iberians, who interacted with the native culture. Harrison and Ebony would agree that the French were less separated from native cultures, but they would disagree about the extent of French influence upon Ebony. Harrison would see Ebony as assuming European values, not able to sustain his categorization of European versus African. Ebony would not admit to the extent of French culture's influence upon him, but Harrison would argue that, although Ebony does not abandon or denigrate his own culture, he has become Westernized.

3.  Ebony's Volta costume and his habit of chewing a cola nut (and offering one as a sign of friendship) indicate African influences. But his compulsion to engage in "intellectual" sparring with another writer, as well as his conviction that he is living in the "new world" (even if that world involves a salary that's less than his monthly rent), reflects his fascination with Western influences. His refusal to offer any support for his convictions suggests that the cultural conflicts remain unresolved, but he does not see this as a problem. Instead, his lack of "true anxiety behind his scattered ideas," his "relishing of life," and his sense of being "relaxed, a whole man" (18) all point toward a contentedness alien to Mphahlele's artists.

17

**PATRICK SMITH, Nippon Challenge (p. 53)**

**Explorations**

1.  Smith cites three reasons for the failure of Japan to enter a sailing team in the America's Cup competition. The first is historical: The isolationist policies of the Tokugawa shogunate in the seventeenth century prevented sea trade (para. 3). The second reason is economics. Until 1989, sailboats were considered a luxury and were so heavily taxed that few could own them (4). The last reason has to do with what Smith implies is the national personality of the Japanese. He says they lack the flexibility and swift responses necessary to be competitive sailors (5).

2.  Smith quotes Japanese sailor Taro Kimura, who said that the Japanese "had wealth, but we wanted to find some other value in life besides working and producing" (10). This is the motive that finally won support for the Nippon Challenge. In his mock editorial, Kimura appealed to the desire of the Japanese to prove to the West that they are more than "economic animals" by investing "in the world's greatest meaningless event" (14–17). In his opening sentence, Smith prepares us to appreciate Kimura's comments by suggesting that Westerners rarely have a chance to see the Japanese as they really are — not, in other words, as merely "economic animals," but as people.

3.  Before talking about the differences Smith identifies between Japanese and Western attitudes, it may be a good idea to have students talk about their own impressions of Japanese business and culture. This will help them recognize the stereotypes they have been exposed to. Smith identifies a difference in how the Japanese and Westerners approach competition. Westerners, Smith says, value the ability to adapt quickly, and they always aim for the top: the America's Cup "requires a dedication . . . to winning which allows nothing else to matter" (5). The Japanese, on the other hand, disdain the philosophy of individualism that permeates Western society, aiming instead to prepare well ahead of time, perfect a process, and honor tradition. Their philosophy of *wakon yosai*, meaning "Japanese spirit, Western things, . . . has not... produced the kind of inner-driven individuals needed to steer a yacht to victory" (6). Smith says the Japanese tend to copy, and improve on, Western technology rather than invent their own (7). Their philosophy of sports is not individualistic either; they value "play, participation, doing one's best as a Japanese" over winning. Smith's source for the Japanese philosophy of progress and competition comes from Japanese history books (6). He gives examples of these philosophies in action from sumo wrestling (8) and corporate life (9). His sources for information on Western attitudes come primarily from the America's Cup competition itself and personal experience as a Westerner. He says that since 1851, when the competition began, its slogan has been "There is no second" (9). The America's Cup demands individuals who are "willing to drop everything and start anew in response to technical discoveries, altered weather conditions, or a surprise development on the part of an opponent" (5); these are, according to Smith, preeminently a Western ability.

**Connections**

1.  Students may be divided on the question of whether the Japanese decision to enter the America's Cup competition represents a desire to become more like Westerners or just to "enter the new world." The essay supports both positions. The philosophy of

modernization that brought the Japanese into the industrial age, according to Smith, is one of "Japanese spirit, Western things" (5), suggesting that the Japanese sought to master Western technologies without absorbing the Western philosophy of individualism. They would enter the new world, in that they would join in international trade and bring home certain kinds of technological knowledge, but they would not become like the "white man." However, Kimura's editorial, quoted near the end of the essay, suggests that, with their entry into the competition, the Japanese were seeking to prove that they, like Westerners, are able to invest themselves in an enterprise that emphasizes competition over cooperation and pure sport over productive work.

2. Paul Harrison's comments in "The Westernization of the World" about Japan's loss of cultural autonomy suggest that Japan was transformed by haircuts, ballroom dancing, and Western clothes (16). Harrison and Smith would agree that Japan successfully integrated Western technology into its culture, and that this transformation helped Japan achieve economic independence. However, Smith's view of Japanese culture takes into account more than the superficial signs of Western influence. He examines Japanese philosophies of life and work to reveal how they have managed to retain significant aspects of their traditional culture while enjoying the economic benefits of Westernization. However, the efforts of the Japanese to compete for the America's Cup is a sign that they are changing in more significant ways (2). The sailing competition "requires them to do so many things they have never even attempted before," including overcoming geographical and cultural isolation and adopting a Western sense of individualism and innovation.

3. In responding to this question, students may want to rely on Smith's commentary about the differences between Japanese and American perspectives on culture and competition, but they will be able to learn more about what qualities a Japanese person would consider "typical American" by rereading Kimura's mock *New York Times* editorial. Kimura describes the America's Cup as "the world's greatest meaningless event," suggesting that Americans like to show off their wealth by sinking millions of dollars into an enterprise that produces nothing but an "old vase" (15). Westerners, unlike the Japanese, are not only wasteful but self-centered, in that they consider themselves to be fully human, while the Japanese are just "economic animals" (14).

## ADDITIONAL QUESTIONS AND ASSIGNMENTS

1. In a journal entry or a collection of informal notes, discuss the perceptions that people in other cultures have of the West, particularly the United States. Consider such issues as materialism, views of government, the concept of freedom, and any other issues you find relevant. As you look over your notes, try to discover similarities and differences among others' perceptions and our own. Can you identify any reasons for the differences?

2. Interview someone who has come to the United States from another country, preferably a non-Western one. As you gather information, focus on the individual's response to our concepts of government, individual freedom, and rights and responsibilities, as well as the individual's perception of our culture as compared with his or her own. As you write an account of the interview, try to intersperse your own observations on the cultural differences with those of your subject.

3.  Write a newspaper column in which you describe your reaction on finding yourself in the midst of a different culture. Even if you've never visited another country, you may recall different customs in other parts of the United States, in the city or the country, in a large university or a small college, or even in the home of a different family. Try to find one image to use as a focal point, then analyze the reasons you had trouble adjusting to the different environment.

4.  Several writers in this section attempt to generalize about American culture by focusing on a particular aspect of it. Raymonde Carroll zeroes in on the significance of money in order to generalize about the American psyche. Octavio Paz analyzes the American mind by examining conventional American cuisine. Patrick Smith focuses on American sports competitiveness as a way of defining what differentiates Americans from the Japanese. Ishmael Reed's essay, by contrast, uses personal anecdotes and examples from television and other media to demonstrate that American culture is too diverse to allow for generalizations about a collective American mind. Research a single aspect of contemporary American culture (fashion, movies, art, television, architecture, cuisine, dance) in popular magazines and newspapers, searching for evidence of the diversity of American cultures. Using Reed's strategy as a model, write an analytical essay about a certain aspect of culture in which you discuss the difficulties of generalizing about American culture and the American mind.

5.  Conduct further research into one of the cultures represented in this section, focusing specifically on its perception of Western culture. It would be wise to choose a culture about which information is readily available — the "Arab World," Mexico, the Soviet Union, Japan, and Africa are likely candidates. If the selection is an excerpt from a larger work, look first at that work. You can find other sources by consulting the headnotes for other selections from that culture (if there are any) and a general encyclopedia, as well as journals devoted to the study of that culture. Narrow your topic to something manageable — such as Western influence on industry, architecture, government, or sex roles; views of Western philosophy; or rejection of Western influence — and write an expository paper in which you objectively describe the culture's encounters with and reactions to Western influences.

# Part Two

## THE FAMILY:
## CORNERSTONE OF CULTURE

### INTRODUCTION

A problem that may arise in discussing any of the selections in this book is a propensity to revert to stereotyping, especially when it comes to Communist or Middle Eastern cultures. In this section, the most difficult piece to deal with objectively will be Sa'edi's "The Game Is Over": Students may need to be reminded of the overwhelming poverty and isolation of Hasani's village. But if class discussion can emphasize the profound effect of economic and geographic forces on a given society, not only will students understand Sa'edi more fully, they will be more likely to appreciate the problems faced by Adam in Erdrich's piece and others in this section as well.

A number of possible approaches to teaching this section present themselves. Among the topics explored are methods of child rearing (Soyinka, Menchú, Erdrich, Duras, and Sa'edi), the role of the family in promoting cultural values (Heng and Shapiro, Morley, Duras, Gyanranjan, and Menchú), the concept of extended family (Menchú, Gyanranjan, Morley, and Soyinka), and the various relationships among family members (all selections). The glimpses of familiar family situations provided in *Looking at Ourselves* should ease students into the section. Many will recognize the issues raised by Novak, Schroeder, Fomby, and Davis. Students' writing about their own family experiences can be used as the foundation for discussion of selections within the unit. If the students highlight first the differences and then the similarities among their own accounts, they'll be better prepared to deal with the various images of family life awaiting them in their reading. This method might be extended to the readings themselves. Students will be confident in their ability to locate differences in family life between these cultures and their own, but they may be surprised at how quickly they compile a list of similarities. From Liang Heng's feeling caught in the middle of a conflict between his parents, through Wild Christian's use of religion to keep the children in line, to Hasani's desire to make his parents suffer, students will find many points of convergence.

Instructors may wish to consult the following familiar works in preparing related selections from *Ourselves Among Others*:

### Essays

Laura Cunningham, "The Girls' Room" (*New York Times*, September 10, 1981; *Sleeping Arrangements*, Knopf, 1989).
Joan Didion, "On Going Home" (*Slouching Towards Bethlehem*, Farrar, Straus, 1968).
Jane Howard, "Families" (*Families*, Simon and Schuster, 1978).
Maxine Hong Kingston, "No Name Woman" (*The Woman Warrior*, Knopf, 1976).
Adrienne Rich, "The Anger of a Child" (*Of Woman Born*, Norton, 1976).

Richard Rodriguez, "Aria" (*American Scholar*, Winter 1981; *Hunger of Memory*, David R. Godine, 1982).

Arlene Skolnick, "The Paradox of Perfection" (*Wilson Quarterly*, Summer 1980).

Alice Walker, "In Search of Our Mothers' Gardens" (*In Search of Our Mothers' Gardens*, Harcourt, 1983).

E. B. White, "Once More to the Lake" (1941; *Essays of E. B. White*, Harpers, 1977).

John Edgar Wideman, "Our Time" (*Brothers and Keepers*, Henry Holt, 1984).

## Short Stories

Rick De Marinis, "Gent" (*Best American Short Stories 1984*, ed. John Updike, Houghton Mifflin, 1984).

Andre Dubus, "A Father's Story" (*Selected Stories of Andre Dubus*, David R. Godine, 1988).

William Faulkner, "The Bear" (*Go Down, Moses*, Random House, 1942).

D. H. Lawrence, "A Rocking Horse Winner" (*Complete Short Stories*, Vol. 3, Penguin, 1962).

Flannery O'Connor, "Everything That Rises Must Converge" (*Complete Stories*, Farrar, Straus, 1971).

Frank O'Connor, "My Oedipus Complex" (*Collected Stories*, Knopf, 1981).

Tillie Olsen, "I Stand Here Ironing" (*Tell Me A Riddle*, Delacorte, 1961).

John Updike, "Still of Some Use" (*Trust Me*, Knopf, 1987).

## BIOGRAPHICAL NOTES ON LOOKING AT OURSELVES

1.  A conservative Roman Catholic educator, columnist, and political activist, Michael Novak is the author of *A Theology for Radical Politics* (1969), *The Joy of Sports: End Zones, Bases, Baskets, Balls, and the Consecration of the American Spirit* (1976), *Free Persons and the Common Good* (1988), *This Hemisphere of Liberty: A Philosophy for the Americas (1990)*, and *The Spirit of Democratic Capitalism* (1991).

2.  Born in 1951 in Nashua, New Hampshire, Norman Boucher has held jobs as a factory worker, groundskeeper, teacher, and editor. For the past 15 years, he has been primarily a writer whose journalism, essays, and reviews have appeared in many newspapers and magazines, including the *Boston Globe Magazine* and *SELF* magazine.

3.  William R. Mattox, Jr. is a policy analyst who focuses on work and family issues for the Family Research Council in Washington, D.C.

4.  Marilyn Berlin Snell is the Managing Editor of *New Perspectives Quarterly*.

5.  Patricia Schroeder, an attorney, has been a member of the House of Representatives for Colorado since 1972 and serves as the Chairman of the Select Committee on Children, Youth, and Families.

6.  Angela Davis, a professor at San Francisco State University, has long been an activist on behalf of the African-American community. She is the author of *If They Come in the Morning: Voices of Resistance* (1971), *Women, Race, and Class* (1983), *Violence Against Women and the Ongoing Challenge to Racism* (1987), *Angela Davis: An Autobiography* (1988), and *Women, Culture, and Politics* (1989).

7.  Paula Fomby writes for *Mother Jones*, among other publications.

8.    Richard Rodriguez, a well-known opponent of bilingual education and affirmative action and a former college teacher, is the author of *Hunger of Memory* (1982) and *Days of Obligation: An Argument with My Mexican Father* (1992).

9.    A Pulitzer Prize-winning columnist for the *Boston Globe*, Ellen Goodman has had several collections of her columns published, including *Close to Home* (1979), *At Large* (1981), *Keeping in Touch* (1985), and *Making Sense* (1989).

10.   Christopher Lasch, a professor of history at the University of Rochester, is the author of *Haven in a Heartless World: The Family Besieged* (1979), *The Culture of Narcissism* (1983), *The Minimal Self: Psychic Survival in Troubled Times* (1985), and *The True and Only Heaven: Progress and its Critics* (1991).

## Reflections

1.    Neither Michael Novak nor Paula Fomby offer specific definitions of the family, but their reasons for not providing a definition are very different. In his discussion of the potential breakdown of the family under capitalism, Novak assumes a nuclear family model. His family contains middle-class husband, wife, and children, and he does not take into account racial or cultural differences. Paula Fomby also does not provide a specific definition, but that is because she knows that the traditional American family model often fails to reflect American families accurately. Fomby explains that there is no definition of the gay family, although she knows they exist because she grew up in one. At the end of the excerpt, Fomby asserts, "It's time for society to expand the definition of family" so that children will be able to be proud of whatever family they come from. Angela Davis, speaking of the tradition of the African-American family in the United States, also notes that the nuclear family model usually does not apply. Instead, Davis describes an extended-family model, in which grandmothers, grandfathers, aunts, and uncles, are integral to the family. Davis traces this family form back to its roots in the slave era and suggests both the strength and flexibility of the African-American family when she writes, "The creativity with which African-American people improvised family connections is a cultural trait that has spanned the centuries" (para. 3). As students discuss which definition of family makes the most sense to them, they should consider how their own backgrounds affect their preference for a certain definition of "family."

2.    Many students will begin to address this question by expressing the assumption that the breakdown of the American family means the loss of working-class and middle-class nuclear families (this is, father, mother, and their biological children) as a result of divorce, economic pressures, and working mothers. This view of American families has become almost commonplace, and it is reflected in several pieces in *Looking at Ourselves*. Michael Novak's piece focuses on middle- and upper-middle-class families that are vulnerable to economic forces that "shear marriages and families apart." William Mattox sees single parenting as indicative of the breakdown of American families. Marilyn Berlin Snell says that the "traditional" family broke up when fathers started leaving home every day to go to work, and Patricia Schroeder says that the family is "breaking down . . . because we don't give it any support." Angela Davis, speaking of African-American families, contends that they are not "breaking down" as some have said, because throughout American history they never matched the white model of the nuclear family. Davis's piece may provide the best point of view for considering the significance of writers' assertions that the American family is "breaking down." In Davis's view, extended

23

families, in which grandmothers raise grandchildren, are not a sign of a family "breaking down," but instead are a sign of the strength and flexibility of families. Novak, Mattox, Schroeder, and Snell all speak of families collapsing, rather than considering the efforts people make to adapt their family structures and daily routines to economic and social pressures — efforts that may be the sign of a strong family, rather than a family on the verge of collapse.

3.  Students should be able to collect a long and diverse list of the most valuable functions of family, aside from those mentioned in the pieces included in *Looking at Ourselves*. Michael Novak writes that "the family is the primary teacher of moral development" and is the source of an individual's "creativity, psychic energy, social dynamism." Capitalism, and the individualism and greed capitalism breeds, have prevented families from fulfilling their functions. William Mattox says that two-parent families provide "structure" and that households headed by single mothers fail to do this. He claims that children reared by single mothers are vulnerable to a startlingly comprehensive list of emotional and intellectual deficits, including depression, aggression, mental illness, and gang membership. Patricia Schroeder, more sympathetic to women's efforts to work and raise their families, writes that the family functions as the "basic building block of our society," but that governmental spending on defense, coupled with a widespread lack of regard for the financial needs of families, prevents families from functioning as healthy, strong social units. Davis writes that the extended African-American family "has functioned as a child-care system available to working parents," but that increasing poverty and drug use, caused by the social and economic pressures of racism, make it hard for families to continue functioning. Ellen Goodman writes that the family is "the one social glue strong enough to withstand the centrifuge of special interests." She sees the emphasis on individuality, and especially segregation according to age, as potential obstacles to family connections. And Christopher Lasch, who seems to consider the family as a child-care unit, sees the introduction of group childcare as a menace to the integrity of the individual and the family. Throughout these selections, the family's primary function is defined as raising children. Threats to that function come from the outside, in the form of economic or social pressures, and from the inside, in the form of working mothers, absent fathers, and an emphasis on individuality.

4.  Several major disagreements emerge among writers on issues such as childcare and family structure. Christopher Lasch and William Mattox (on the one hand) and Angela Davis and Patricia Schroeder (on the other) are diametrically opposed on the issue of how to manage childcare in the American family. Lasch contends that placing children in childcare may cause them to become incapable "of deciding on their own what [is] good or bad." Although he does not recommend that mothers begin to stay home with children, this is one of the most likely results of decreasing the amount of time children spend in childcare. Single mothers are among those who work while raising children; William Mattox blames them for children's emotional and physical problems and implies that only the two-parent family can resolve the problem. Patricia Schroeder, by contrast, argues that the realities of women's lives demand that they work, and that the government and corporations can and should support their efforts to raise families by helping them with childcare. Angela Davis argues that "society has refused to assume more responsibility for the economic well-being of its members and for the care and education of our children." Some of the problems facing families could be solved, she contends, by making good childcare available to everyone.

24

## RIGOBERTA MENCHÚ, Birth Ceremonies (p. 76)

### Explorations:

1.  Among the Quiché Indians, the parent-child relationship serves as a model for relationships between leaders and community members. The man and woman elected as leaders bear parental responsibility for the entire community and become grandparents to every child born (para. 1). Thinking of the community as an extended family has several advantages for the Quiché. Because they live under harsh conditions as a marginalized group in Guatemala, the Quiché need to maintain close connections with each other, offering each other material and emotional sustenance. The Quiché religion is also based on a parent-child model, in which the sun is father and the moon is mother to the people (12). The ceremonies that introduce the newborn child to family and community integrate him or her "in the universe." The emphasis on parent-child relationships in Quiché society and religion helps to remind people of their close connections with their ancestors, encouraging group solidarity and a deep commitment to traditional values and customs important for physical and psychological survival.

2.  Each ceremony for the Quiché child marks an important milestone in her or his progress as a member of the community. Before the baby's birth, the mother and father together inform community leaders that a child is on the way so that leaders can prepare to accept the child into the community (1). Each child is born in the presence of carefully selected couples representing both family and community and is introduced to family and friends with ceremonies and celebrations. For eight days following the birth, the child is left alone with his mother while neighbors bring gifts (7). These gifts, and the feasting and celebration that follow, solidify the child's position as a community member. Other customs, including tying a bag of talismans around the baby's neck, binding the baby's hands and feet, and lighting candles at the four corners of his or her bed, symbolize important aspects of Quiché life that the child will eventually be expected to understand and respect (10, 8). The care with which children are inducted as community members impresses on everyone the need for mutual support if the Quiche are to survive as a culturally intact group.

3.  The child's education about future responsibilities begins before birth, when the mother introduces her unborn child to the natural world and to the culture by talking to her or him about Quiché life (2). When the child is eight days old, a ceremony introduces him or her to the community and the parents tell the child about the family's suffering to symbolically prepare him or her to live a hard life with dignity (9). At a large gathering forty days after a child is born, parents and community leaders promise to teach the child to follow Quiché traditions and keep the community's secrets safe from outsiders (11). They voice the expectation that the child will grow up to live as his or her ancestors did and will one day become a parent to help multiply the race. When the child reaches the age of ten, parents and village leaders again reinforce traditional values by talking to the child formally about the necessity of honoring ancestors and carrying out responsibilities toward the community (13). Throughout childhood, boys and girls are introduced to gender-specific responsibilities; girls are taught to care for the family and prepare to become mothers, and boys are prepared for their future responsibilities as heads of the family.

## Connections

1.  Ellen Goodman invokes an American holiday, Thanksgiving, as a celebration of intergenerational family ties. Family, she says, is the only social institution that may help us to withstand the pressures that categorize each generation as a "special interest group," a tendency that dissolves connections among family members. According to Rigoberta Menchú, the family in Quiché society plays a similar role, but students will need to recognize that the pressures that might pull the Quiché apart are very different from those that affect the middle-class American family Ellen Goodman analyzes. Many of the birth customs Menchú discusses are ways of reinforcing family and community ties to help the Quiché ensure survival and resist oppression and appropriation by the dominant culture. The American family in Goodman's analysis is part of the dominant culture; family unity is threatened not by oppression or material want, but by an emphasis on individualism that segregates family members from one another.

2.  In Quiché society, children are integrated into the life of the community, so that no arrangements for formal childcare need be made. Each child belongs not only to his or her parents, but to the community as a whole. Children are not segregated in schools during the day, but are educated at home and in the neighborhood. Even as small children, they work alongside their parents. Although the Quiché solution to the problems of childcare may seem attractive, it would not work in the United States, where most parents must work outside the home. Although the middle-class working mother Pat Schroeder refers to is usually considered to have primary responsibility for childcare, she cannot emulate the Quiché mother and have her children work alongside her. Furthermore, her "community" has no responsibility to provide childcare, and women are expected to give up gainful employment so that they can stay at home to care for children. According to Schroeder, the government's refusal to take some responsibility for childcare pays homage to a "mythical family" in which the mother wants to stay home and can afford to do so, but in reality the lack of government support for childcare tends to pull families apart.

3.  Both Novak and Menchú emphasize the importance of the family in teaching values to children. Novak says the family in American culture has a diminishing importance, as post-industrial capitalism promotes liberty and hedonism, values that tend to dissolve emotional bonds between parents and children. Under more ideal conditions, Novak maintains, the family would be the primary social and economic unit, and American children would learn "basic trust." Novak's ideal American family seems to have much in common with the Quiché family Menchú describes. According to Menchú, the primary values children learn in Quiché society are to respect traditions and help support the life of the community through hard work and deep involvement in community affairs. Children are taught to be proud of their family and their people's history and to resist the efforts of outsiders to lure them away from their own culture and religion. One of the problems students may encounter in responding to this question is that, while Menchú's discussion deals with a relatively small and distinct community, Novak's comments on the "American family" may invite generalizations that ignore economic and cultural difference among American families. For instance, it will be important for students to recall that the family Novak is concerned with is "upwardly mobile," and that, as Pat Schroeder points out, in reality many American children live in poverty.

4.  Most students will recognize that Rodriguez's and Menchú's accounts of childhood have in common a model of relationships between adults and children. The model is based on the children's familial respect for adults, but it is also based on the children's integration into the life of the community. Both these aspects of childhood might seem unusual to many U.S. students. Menchú discusses how tribal government draws on models of parent-child relationships; the elected leaders, for instance, are regarded as the community's mother and father (see Explorations #1 above). In Rodriguez's account, he recalls that the Catholic priest was called Father, and that the use of familial terms for nuns and priests "implied that a deep bond existed between my teachers and me as fellow Catholics." The sense of extended family, and a tightly knit community in which members share a common world view and spirituality, are factors that influence both Rodriguez's and Menchú's accounts of childhood.

## LOUISE ERDRICH (Er-drick), Adam (p. 88)

### Explorations

1.  For Louise Erdrich, perhaps the hardest part of mothering Adam is achieving enough patience to deal with the day-to-day struggle of living with a child who has Fetal Alcohol Syndrome. She mentions this problem early on (paras. 5, 6), but its full impact becomes most clear when Erdrich relates her conflict with Adam over his refusal to eat dinner (10-37). Nevertheless, Erdrich appreciates the rewards of mothering Adam, including the ease with which he initially accepted her as his mother (10). But the deeper rewards have to do with gaining self-knowledge. Erdrich writes, "In the years I've spent with Adam, I have learned more about my limits than I ever wanted to know," but the pain of that knowledge is offset by the "bond of absolute simplicity, love" that has developed between her and Adam.

2.  Most students will understand the poignancy of Erdrich's statement that a day when Adam has a seizure is "no special day" in her family. Erdrich's attitude is one of patience and resignation. Her calm, nurturing treatment of Adam after he falls shows first of all how much she cares, but it also shows how common this event is. The grand mal seizure would be an acute crisis in a family less accustomed to dealing with a major disability, but for Erdrich it is an unremarkable incident.

3.  Some students may find the opening paragraphs of Erdrich's essay as confusing as they are intriguing. Until paragraph 5, when Erdrich defines Adam's disability, students will wonder about Adam's seizure and Erdrich's calm response. Erdrich's explanation of Fetal Alcohol Syndrome will take care of any confusion, but to help students think about the choices Erdrich has made about style and organization, it may be helpful to ask them to discuss the shift in Erdrich's tone as she begins to define Fetal Alcohol Syndrome. In paragraph 5, Erdrich gives facts about the syndrome and states her opinion of women who drink while pregnant: "It's a lot of fate to play with for the sake of a moment's relaxation." If Erdrich had begun with this paragraph, her tone would have sounded merely judgmental, since her readers would not have understood that Fetal Alcohol Syndrome has a daily impact on her life and her adopted child's life.

27

## Connections

1.  In describing how her family came into being, Erdrich says, "it simply happened" (para. 6), but in fact it was a deliberate process. Her husband, Michael, had adopted Adam and two other children while he was single; Erdrich accepted them into her life along with their father, and she adopted the children a year after she and Michael married. Erdrich doesn't define "family" directly, but many students will understand that it is unlikely she would define it according to the nuclear model of two parents biologically related to their children. In *Looking at Ourselves*, Paula Fomby asserts, "It's time for society to expand the definition of family" so that children will be able to be proud of whatever family they come from. Fomby is concerned with gay families, but her comments would apply equally well to the nontraditional family that Erdrich has helped to create. Angela Davis, in her discussion of African-American families, also refutes the idea that the nuclear family model is superior. Instead, Davis describes an extended-family model, in which grandmothers, grandfathers, aunts, and uncles are integral to the family. This model would probably appeal to Erdrich, because she recognizes that the problems that face the Native American community can best be dealt with by emphasizing tribal values (50).

2.  Patricia Schroeder mentions that one of the major problems of childcare is that legislation fails to acknowledge or support the realities of family life in the United States. Although nine out of ten women must work (2), the United States does "less than any other industrialized nation: In terms of tax breaks, we would do better raising thoroughbred dogs or horses than children" (4). Erdrich would probably agree with Schroeder's assessment of the problems of childcare, and she might also argue that the lack of government support for the real needs of women and children contributes to the erosion of family and community in some Native American communities. Erdrich mentions the dedication of Adam's teacher (6), and says she and Michael have provided for Adam's care in their wills (10), but for the most part they seem to have dealt with child-care problems by sharing responsibilities between themselves.

3.  It will be a challenge for students to identify the similarities between Erdrich's middle-class Native American family and Rigoberta Menchú's description of Quiché Indian families. A good beginning would be to consider how both Erdrich and Menchú discuss the need for an extended family structure and community involvement in bearing and raising children. Menchú says that children belong not just to the parents but to the entire community (1), an idea Erdrich would agree with because she believes women have a responsibility, not only to their own children but also to the community at large, to have pregnancies free of alcohol (44–49). In Menchú's description of the treatment of pregnant women in the Quiché tribe, she gives many examples of the ways in which the community functions as a large and caring family. Community members monitor the health and nutrition of the pregnant woman, taking responsibility for her welfare: "You must treat her with respect so that she recognizes it and conveys this to the baby inside her" (17).

**LIANG HENG and JUDITH SHAPIRO, Chairman Mao's Good Little Boy (p. 97)**

## Explorations

1.  There seems to be no positive definition of Rightist in Mao's China of the 1950s; rather the term refers to anyone who questions the Revolution. The standard definition refers to capitalist tendencies, but the application of the title seems to have little to do with that ideology. A *revolutionary*, unlike a Rightist, conforms to the Revolution unquestioningly. (Some students may recognize the paradox in this interpretation of the term.) The events in this selection suggest that at the time Liang's mother was discredited, the truest test of the revolutionary was his or her denunciation of enemies of the Revolution.

2.  Liang's parents either live in dormitories or travel, so the children live with their grandparents. His parents view the Revolution as more important than raising their children. When Liang's mother is disgraced, the children are moved from the maternal to the paternal grandmother's home (really her son's dormitory apartment). Had the father been disgraced, he would have lost the apartment, which was allocated to him as an employee of the *Hunan Daily*. Had this happened, both his mother and his children would have been homeless. By exercising such control over family life, and by providing favored workers with housing, the Party is able to ensure loyalty to the state. The work environment is used in much the same way. When Liang's mother is disgraced, one of her worst punishments is to lose her job and salary. The intrusion into every aspect of an individual's life tightens government control over the individual while discouraging loyalties to anything other than the government, even to family, thus preventing the spread of ideas that might interfere with the Revolution.

3.  The absence of understanding and judgment exhibited in the first paragraph indicates that it is being told from the point of view of the child himself. Students may need a bit of encouragement to notice that when he talks of his fear that Waipo has forgotten him, Liang makes no comment on the irrationality of that fear. He also refrains from characterizing the foolishness of his escape. All we see is the experience as it appears to the child. But while limited, his consciousness rebels naturally against the constraints of the child-care center and the society it mimics. In the last sentence we see the value Liang places on freedom; words like "exploded" and "dazzling" raise the experience to a heroic level. The implication is that even a young child can recognize the abuses of human dignity suffered by those subjected to such a regime.

## Connections

1.  The contexts and outcomes of the estrangements between mother and child are very different in Heng and Shapiro's "Chairman Mao's Good Little Boy," Erdrich's "Adam," and Fomby's selection in *Looking at Ourselves*. The estrangement between Liang and his mother is by far the harshest and longest. Liang's father, family, government, and school system all work to keep Liang and his mother apart. She tries hard to keep contact with her children and to work her way back into the good graces of the Party (paras. 24, 36, 41), but she cannot overcome the effect on her children of hearing their mother constantly condemned. Liang implies that he and his mother eventually had a reconciliation, because he is able to write much of the story from her perspective (19, 20) and because,

as a mature man, he understands that she was unjustly accused and lived an agonizingly isolated life as a result (22). In Erdrich's "Adam," the estrangement between mother and child has to do with the pressures of living with Adam's disability. The specific event that causes Erdrich to tell Adam "Don't call me Mom" is a battle over food (11–37). It takes years to fully mend the rift between them (40). Adam's disability makes it difficult for him to relate to others, but Erdrich's day-to-day care of Adam does much to overcome the distance between them. Paula Fomby's relationship with her gay mother was ambivalent, but not truly estranged. Fomby writes, "In order to live peaceably, I accepted my mother's lifestyle a long time ago; feeling comfortable with it has come more recently" (5). Fomby "grew up in the closet" (1), which made her feel isolated and overly protective of her family, but with maturity she realized that there were many benefits to being raised in a gay family.

2. In the United States, group childcare, especially if it is funded by the government, has sometimes been seen as a step toward communism. For instance, Richard Nixon vetoed the Comprehensive Child Development Act of 1971, which would have provided federal funds for childcare. He argued that it sided with a "communal approach" to childrearing over a "family-centered approach." Issues of childcare have as much to do with national political goals as with families and communities. The goal of the child-care system in China was to produce children who would serve the government obediently; Liang writes that he was "sent off to the child-care center for early training in Socialist thought through collective living, far from the potentially corrupting influence of family life" (3). Pat Schroeder argues that in the United States the family is "an economic unit and basic building block of our society" (5). Affordable, adequate childcare is one essential way of reinforcing the family and preparing children for school, but few would argue that group childcare in the United States is specifically intended to indoctrinate children, either into communism (as Nixon argued) or capitalism.

3. Novak believes that the capitalist system places an emphasis on money and success that makes people neglect their family bonds and look outside the family for emotional satisfaction. Yet Liang and Shapiro's description of a Communist society shows some of the same problems, although in China people do not suffer from "too much emotional space" or a surplus of material goods. In fact, economic scarcity and the desire to succeed, which means obtaining rank in the Communist Party, make people willing to promote Party over family loyalty. Students could argue that many of the members of Liang's family remain close. He has strong attachments to his grandmothers; his maternal uncle defends his mother; and early on he sticks up for his mother as well. But the political stigma faced by the family destroys it as a nuclear group when the mother becomes an outcast. Comparing Liang's family with their own, most students will undoubtedly prefer the system with which they are familiar. While Novak paints a devastating picture of American family life, most students will find it limited to an economically affluent class to which they may not belong. Liang and Shapiro's narrative of Chinese family life pertains to the largest population group. Therefore, "on balance," most students will choose the American system as providing the better climate for families, since family members here are never asked to repudiate their relatives in order to succeed.

4. Liang and Shapiro show that the family in China is composed of several generations and that they interact on a daily basis. While this "social glue" may derive from the traditional arrangement whereby brides moved in with their husbands' families, the great shortage

of housing space in modern China reinforces the necessity of the arrangement. Three generations of Liang's family live together in his grandmother Nai Nai's house. His grandmother Waipo raises him before he goes to day care, and his maternal uncle, along with his wife and three small children, still lives with her. And when Liang's father thinks about divorcing his wife, even though he is a grown man, he consults his mother (40).

## WOLE SOYINKA (Woe-lay Shoy-ING-ka), Nigerian Childhood (p. 112)

### Explorations

1. The integration of Anglicanism and traditional magic will probably serve as a source of amusement for students. The characters seem to find no contradiction in weaving magic throughout the fabric of the religion they have been taught. In fact, the combination seems to work wonders as far as keeping children in line is concerned: Wild Christian's story of the encounter with the wood sprites is a case in point. Her lament that faith and discipline are no longer valued follows her account of the children's failure to obey the oro's orders to stay away from his place in the woods. Reverend J. J., an Anglican minister, respects the wood sprites, and when the children are chased out of the woods after disobeying the order, he whips them (after, of course, invoking the power of the Christian God to keep off the sprites). Uncle Sanya is punished too, for his stubbornness — one of the greatest of sins. Even the children themselves respond to the twin traditions: They abandon their evening visits to the woods after the incident with the wood sprites. Students may need some guidance in recognizing the essential similarity of the religion and the tradition, namely, that both depend on faith in a power greater than that of any human.

2. The stories of Reverend J. J. emphasize the need for faith (his stand against the wood sprites), perseverance (his refusal to give up preaching despite the egungun's warning), and respect for tradition (his following the old woman's orders when Sanya was ill). An interesting sideline is the narrator's confusion between perseverance and stubbornness: Try as he might, he cannot keep from characterizing Reverend J. J.'s perseverance in the face of warnings as something fearfully close to the "sin" of stubbornness.

3. Although it is sometimes difficult for students to recognize subtle changes in point of view, a close look at the selection will reveal that even though Soyinka speaks in the voice of an adult, he sees things with the eyes of a child. His grasp of history, as well as his ability to articulate his conflicting responses to his mother's stories (the sense that the children's fright was punishment enough for their foray into the woods, the feeling that Reverend J. J.'s perseverance was really stubbornness) are indications that we're hearing this story from an adult. But Bishop Crowther's apparition is definitely the experience of a child: The fact that the author never questions its authenticity allows us to perceive the experience as the child does. His matter-of-fact accounts of his mother's stories reinforce the sense that these are the observations of a child. Even when Lawanle pulls him away for his bath, we feel the reluctance of the child. More perceptive students will also point to Soyinka's mature vocabulary and style as evidence of an adult voice recounting these experiences from the point of view of a child.

31

## Connections

1.  Many students will be confused initially by young Soyinka's encounters with Bishop Ajayi Crowther. Soyinka describes the Bishop not as a dream image or fantasy, but as a figure who is as real as the bougainvillea from which he emerges. Students may find it easier to accept the interweaving of fantasy and reality in this passage (and, later, in Wild Christian's stories) if they are given a term for the technique: magic realism, an approach that gives imagination and fantasy the same authority usually accorded to supposedly solid, external reality. The story with which Soyinka opens his narrative is extremely important because it creates the context for his mother's story about Uncle Sanya. Soyinka knows from his own encounters with the Bishop that he should take Wild Christian's story seriously, and his respect for her story signals the reader to follow suit. Liang Heng's story about his abortive escape from the child-care center also helps to create a context for his mother's story of her ostracism at the hands of her community and family. Liang's attempt to escape the center, and the fact that Waipo forces him to return, suggests how thoroughly politicized the family is. The same revolutionary loyalty (and fear of retaliation) that motivates Waipo also causes Liang's father to denounce his supposedly Rightist wife and approve of her exile.

2.  Children in "Nigerian Childhood" seem to have few responsibilities. Even their gathering of firewood, snails, mushrooms, and berries is partly a game (paras. 1, 14, 35, 38). Rigoberta Menchú describes significant responsibilities for children in the Quiché community, including, for girls, cleaning, mending, and washing, and, for boys, working in the fields. Yoruban children, as Soyinka describes them, have more freedom to play and are not asked to contribute as much work to the family and community.

3.  At the end of his essay Naipaul suggests that Western ways and ideas are overlaid upon a much more vibrant and deep-seated indigenous African tradition. When the Westerners themselves disappear, the order they have created barely sustains itself. Thus Naipaul sees a dichotomy: the "real life . . . in another realm of the spirit," which stems from the traditional values versus the "false, arbitrary ritual" of forms that mimic Western ways and standards. In Soyinka's story, perhaps because it is narrated from a child's point of view, no suggestion of such a dichotomy exists. Instead, Soyinka's story shows how perfectly the traditions of American religion and African magic have become intertwined. Wild Christian's story demonstrates the intense faith of the Reverend J. J. and the miracles worked on behalf of the Christian as well as the continuing existence and powers of the African spirit world. The structures of English life — the church and the boarding school — continue to flourish without the English presence, and Wild Christian looks back to earlier days to lament the loss of the intensity of the early converts' faith, not of her forefathers' religion. Unlike Ebony, she does not try to disassociate herself from the English colonizers. Like Ebony, she has been influenced by both traditions; however, while he denies this influence even as he displays it, Wild Christian has remained unaware of a need to analyze her relationship to a Western tradition.

4.  How students view Soyinka's extended family will depend to some extent on the structure of their own families. Those who have had grandparents, cousins, or informally adopted family members living with them will identify with the African tradition. The specific evidence in "Nigerian Childhood" that Soyinka's family was part of an extended-family tradition is Wild Christian's and Sanya's upbringing in their grand uncle's home and the presence of "Auntie" Lawanle as a nanny in Wild Christian's home. Soyinka's

use of quotations around "Auntie" suggests that Lawanle is not a blood relative, but an adopted family member (22). Soyinka does not feel a need to explain the extended family structures in these families, because they are a common feature of African life, as they are in some African-American households.

## JOHN DAVID MORLEY, Acquiring a Japanese Family (p. 122)

### Explorations

1. Few American students have had the experience of living with the almost complete lack of privacy Boon encounters while living with Sugama, so they will be able to sympathize with Boon's perplexity as he considers how differently he will have to live in a house without firm inside walls. In order to understand the "corporate" concept that defines Japanese family relationships, Morley analyzes the term uchi, which means both "household" and "I." The term suggests the inseparability of self, home, and family; "I" does not mean an individual, but "the representative of my house in the world outside" (para. 35).

2. Responses to this question may vary with students' ethnic backgrounds. Some may recognize the respect accorded adults in the Japanese family, as well as the patronizing attitude that accompanies that respect. (Note Sugama's amusement at his aunt's and uncle's fears.) These students may also understand the older adults' treatment of their young adult relatives: It seems that in Japan, your parents can always tell you what to do, regardless of your age or accomplishments. Those unfamiliar with this relationship will probably find vast differences between the obligations of a young adult Japanese and his or her American counterpart. Whereas the young Japanese are responsible for their parents' welfare, most Americans view themselves as responsible only to themselves and their children. (An interesting discussion may ensue if you ask students which situation they feel is better or more compassionate.)

3. The first-person narrator often makes for a more limited perspective; Morley achieves a broader view of the meeting of cultures by writing through a third-person narrator. Boon's introduction to the apartment reveals him to be a foreigner: He is awed by the open spaces and especially by the concept of family indivisibility that leads to such construction. He must accustom himself to the apparent "classlessness" (36) of most Japanese homes. Perhaps more striking, however, are Boon's comic reaction to meeting Sugama's mother and his overtly Western advice to Sugama that the latter's plans for marriage are nobody else's business. In contrast, Boon's choice of living quarters, his increasing facility with the language, and his preference for Japanese food make him less foreign. By showing all this through Boon's eyes, Morley is able to remain distant. Both he and the reader can judge Boon's reactions and behavior objectively.

4. This question provides a wonderful opportunity to discuss the importance of apparent "sidelights" to the story as a whole. Without the descriptions of the house or the story of the earthquake, we would have to rely on exposition for information about Japanese

notions of family, home, respect for elders, reliance on what Westerners would consider superstition, perceptions of foreigners. The list goes on. Responses to the second part of the question may again underscore the different backgrounds of students; if it does, discussion should be quite lively.

## Connections

1. Skeptical students will be surprised that both Morley and Soyinka approach their characters' superstitions in a matter-of-fact way. Sugama tells the story of his great-aunt's faith in her fortune-teller's prediction without ridicule. Morley describes Sugama's relatives and their superstitions with the bemused humor that is characteristic of the entire essay. He notes, for instance that "everything they touched turned to farce" (para. 59), but he describes his initial meetings with Sugama and his mother with similar humor. Soyinka treats his characters' superstitions and their encounters with spirits with a similar respect, but more importantly, Wild Christian has specific reasons for telling her children uncanny tales. She wants to teach her children to respect religion, a motive evident in her story about how J. J. Ransome-Kuti was able to send the *iwin* away because he had a power that comes from faith and discipline (20, 21). To help students talk about their own responses to the superstitions Morley and Soyinka describe, it may be helpful to ask students to talk about superstitions they, or their relatives or friends, believe in. Some of the superstitions they describe will serve purposes similar to those evident in Morley and Soyinka's narrative: to help in dealing with real fears (of earthquakes or strangers, for instance), or to give a feeling of having control over events.

2. Although the problem may be similar, students should recognize at once a few essential differences between the Chinese and Japanese handling of overcrowding: For one thing, the lottery used to award apartments would be anathema to the Chinese, who see it as the duty of the state to house all its citizens. Furthermore, the Chinese would scoff at the apparent ineptitude of the Japanese civil servants, who swallow Sugama's increasingly preposterous explanations of his grandfather's absence. Such behavior, looked upon by Japanese (and Westerners) as inventive if a bit underhanded, would be viewed as a serious crime against the people in China. Yet students should recognize some similarities as well: Both cultures share a healthy respect for the institution of the family (as long as it doesn't interfere with the state in China) and the responsibility of each family member to the others; the multiple uses of each room and the lack of private bedrooms underscore the solidarity of the family. Both cultures also view individual goals and accomplishments in light of the larger good (in China the state, in Japan the family). Although they both foster the concept of family as "social glue," in China the strength of the family is a means to achieve the ultimate goal, the good of the state. In Japan, the family appears to be an end in itself.

3. In both pieces the concept of the family as bastion against the onslaughts of a hostile world is upheld. Novak, of course, laments the undermining of this concept in the United States, whereas Morley reveals that it thrives in Japan (Sugama's response to his aunt and uncle's fear is a case in point). Novak sees the corporate influence, with its constant push for success and its insensitivity to the need for roots, as the culprit in the assault on the American family. That same capitalist concentration on advancement presents Sugama with his dilemma of whether to marry and return to his home or to remain single and successful in the city. But Japan's culture was not built on capitalism or the concept of

free enterprise; students may be surprised to observe a country in which the prevalent economic system is rooted in an entirely different philosophy from the cultural traditions. This cultural base seems to be the force that keeps capitalism from disrupting family life in Japan the way it has in the United States.

## GYANRANJAN (Gee-ahn-ran-jan), Our Side of the Fence and Theirs (p. 134)

### Explorations

1.  It may be difficult for students to appreciate the protective role of the parents, especially the father, with regard to daughters. They can see no real danger confronting the girls in the family; nevertheless, the narrator is appalled by his neighbors' lack of concern for their daughter's safety. According to the story, parents must protect their children, especially the girls, from real or imagined harm and must provide for their future protection by selecting suitable husbands for them. Equally difficult for today's students to appreciate will be the notion of absolute obedience to parents. In the India of this story, children uphold tradition, never questioning their parents. The entire family, it seems, must act (in private as well as in public) according to long-standing rules of appropriate behavior.

2.  It's easy to miss, upon first reading the story, that this is an extended family of adults. The narrator is apparently a high-school or college student (his naïveté makes it difficult to tell), and his brother and sister-in-law, as well as his grandmother, live with the family. Instead of concentrating on standard characteristics, the narrator is fascinated with how people relate to one another — he's astounded when he sees the family next door laughing together, for example. He becomes more and more interested in what makes people happy.

3.  His fascination with the family is readily apparent, but students may initially miss the evidence of what psychologists call an attraction-aversion response. Some of his judgments involve calling their life-style "unusual" and "careless" in paragraph 3, and "strange" in paragraph 4, criticizing the mother and daughter for failing to notice that the latter's dupatta had fallen from her shoulder, exposing part of her breast in paragraph 6; and commenting on their lack of curiosity about the narrator's family in paragraph 8; among others. Yet all the while that he is criticizing their behavior, we sense his longing to be like them. They are easygoing and self-sufficient, never caring about what others think — they're probably quite Westernized. And the narrator, in comparing his family with theirs, implicitly condemns his family's rigid adherence to tradition, musing at one point, "If only I'd been born in that home!" (15).

4.  It's important for students to realize that by taking the dialogue out of context, and simply reporting bits of it as he recounts his narrative of the wedding, the narrator creates the effect of hearing a series of speeches pronouncing judgment on the family next door. Previously, we've been privy only to the narrator's thoughts; his failure to include dialogue until this point preserves the filter through which we see the neighbors. The technique also enhances his increasing feeling of isolation. By using dialogue at the end, he allows us to see where his attitudes come from. More important, however, he creates

an image of solidarity in his family — something he sorely needs now that the primary object of his attraction-aversion has gone. Gyanranjan leaves us with quite a powerful image, as the lone critic joins the "bazaar of neighbor-criticism . . . doing a heated business."

## Connections

1. Both Boon and Gyanranjan's narrator place themselves in the position of observers, separating themselves from the views of those around them. Boon is clearly "the American" to Sugama's aunt and uncle, even though he disappoints their expectations. He is an outsider who seeks to understand and adapt himself to a new culture. Gyanranjan's narrator separates himself from his family's values by casting longing glances into the neighbors' yard and imagining what his life would be like if he lived in that happier, more lenient environment. Boon never draws any contrasts, but Gyanranjan's narrator is constantly comparing the rituals of the neighboring household with those of his own and passing judgment. Even after he has learned the neighbor's religion, which seems to temper his enthusiasm for growing up in their household, his final remark passes a harsh judgment on his own family, contrasting their critical gossip with the other household's silence.

2. Focusing on a child narrator allows both Gyanranjan and Liang to look from a fresh viewpoint at family and social pressures to conform. Their child narrators don't fully understand the demands of conformity, and they share their questioning and doubts with the reader. In the first paragraph of "Our Side of the Fence and Theirs," the narrator believes that his family is "respectable, honorable" because of the way they protect their daughters and honor traditional customs. Therefore, the neighbors who do things differently are not to be trusted. But in the same paragraph, he also describes himself as curious about strangers. He has not altogether adopted the prejudices of his elders. He observes the neighbors' daughter laughing without restraint with a mixture of disapproval and fascination (para. 6). Later he recalls how any free show of affection between men and women is considered shameful in his family (12), but nevertheless he is attracted to the freedom and easy affection the neighbor family display for each other. At one point, he thinks, "If only I'd been born in that home!" (15). In Liang and Shapiro's "Chairman Mao's Good Little Boy," Liang learns about the pressures of conformity at the age of three, when he is punished for escaping from the child-care center and reprimanded by the nurses: "you haven't upheld Revolutionary discipline" (11). Liang's youthful innocence and incomprehension about why he is in disgrace helps the authors explore the far more complex problems that beset his mother when she is labelled a rightist and expelled from her job, family, and community, since she is as blameless as her son.

3. Students should immediately recognize the similarity between Novak's plea for a stronger commitment to family and the narrator's fear of anything that seems to shake family traditions. The idea that strongly defined gender roles are essential to family is represented in the selection by Marilyn Berlin Snell; a similar idea is reflected in the sense of danger felt by the narrator's family about the apparent freedom of the women in the neighboring family. Ironically, although the neighbor family seems relatively Westernized, it's difficult to find much similarity between their views and those in *Looking at Ourselves*. There may be some sympathy between them and Fomby, however, who finds

that her family evokes the same kind of anxiety that the narrator experiences in regard to his alien neighbors. Students might enjoy thinking about Goodman's definition of family — "the people who maintain an unreasonable interest in each other," in light of the narrator's "unreasonable" interest in his neighbors.

## VED MEHTA (MAY-tah), Pom's Engagement (p. 142)

### Explorations

1. It is primarily Daddyji who is responsible for arranging for Pom's engagement to Kakaji. Daddyji says a girl's *parents* investigate prospective grooms and make the selection, but Daddyji alone makes the journey to talk with Kakaji's family, and it is Kakaji's uncle who has the power to accept or refuse the engagement. Both Kakaji and Pom have some power over whether they will marry each other, but both accept their elders' choices (paras. 17, 79).

2. Most American students will find the idea of an arranged marriage disturbing. In order to help them understand Daddyji's views, it would be helpful to begin with his comments in paragraph 77 on Western marriages. He admits that there is some injustice in the Indian system, but he also notes that the Western method of marrying for romantic love probably doesn't work any better. Daddyji's views of marriage come out during his conversation with two of his daughters, Umi and Nimi, who express the feminist view that both men and women should have the right think for themselves and contribute equally to a marriage. Daddyji argues that although Pom may have to suffer for years and make many sacrifices while she tries to get used to living with and serving her husband and his family (69), this will ultimately bring her the greatest happiness, which he describes as "a uniting of ideals and purposes" between husband and wife (71).

3. The process involved in bringing about the marriage of Pom and Kakaji is very different from courtship processes in American cultures. It might be useful to have students make a step-by-step comparison between courtship in their own culture and the one Mehta describes. The process in "Pom's Engagement" begins with Daddyji's investigation of Kakaji and Kakaji's family (1); then he visits the prospective groom and discusses with them the possibility of a marriage. Only months later, when Kakaji and his family have expressed serious interest, do Daddyji and Mamaji tell Pom and her siblings of her impending engagement. There follows a brief meeting between Pom and Kakaji under her parents' watchful eyes (36–45) and a letter from his family making a formal offer of marriage (46). Mamaji then consults an astrologer to set the wedding date (80). Once this is arranged, an engagement ceremony, with prayers, songs, food, an engagement ring for Pom, and an exchange of gifts, formalizes the engagement.

4. The blind child focuses on the sounds and smells of the house when preparations are being made for Kakaji's arrival, and on the sound of the prospective husband's footfall and voice: "His footfall was heavy . . . his greeting was affectionate, and . . . his voice seemed to float up with laughter" (33). He also notices keenly the sound of Pom entering the room and later of tea being served. One of the most profound impressions is made

37

by Pom's hand, newly adorned with her engagement ring, on his neck: "It had something cold and metallic on it, which sent a shiver through me" (83). Like these, most of the other sensory impressions in the narrative involve sound and touch.

## Connections

1. As in the narrator's family in "Our Side of the Fence and Theirs," there are generational differences in Pom's family. The older members of the family are more ready to accept traditional values and customs, especially about sex roles and marriage; the younger members still respect their elders' opinions, but they are more open to new and different ways of running a family. For instance, both Gyanranjan's narrator and two of Mehta's sisters, Umi and Nimi, are intrigued by the idea of women having greater freedom and autonomy. In "Our Side of the Fence and Theirs," the narrator notices with a mixture of approval and surprise how easily the neighbor girl relates to her parents. She goes through with her simple wedding without weeping or any display of unwillingness, which suggests that she is independent of her parents and may have had some power to decide who and when she would marry. Pom's family resembles the family on the other side of the fence in that there is open communication between parents and children. Umi and Nimi disagree with their father. Rather than being shocked or angry, he discusses his own views of marriage frankly and admits the old traditions are not entirely equitable in terms of class and sex (paras. 57, 58, 77).

2. The mix of emotions Ved Mehta felt when he listened from outside the drawing room to the women's engagement singsong suggests that he realizes he is growing up and is becoming more aware of the differences between the roles of men and women. He realizes that a few years before, he might have been outside playing, or would have been invited into the room, but now that he is barred because he is a growing boy, he is at once captivated by the women and ashamed of his interest. The narrator in Gyanranjan's essay experiences a similar sense of shame and captivation in relation to the girl who lives on the other side of the fence (7). At several points he shows this mix of emotions, as when he realizes that he is probably the only one who has noticed the "movement of her bosom . . . free and unrestrained" (6). When his sister-in-law teases him about his interest in the neighbor girl, he is pleased and embarrassed (20), but by the end of the essay he is wavering between defending the girl's respectability and agreeing that she has behaved badly (28).

3. Like Pom and Kakaji, Liang's parents do not marry for romance, but because of the similarities in their backgrounds and values. They hardly know each other when they marry, but they agree about politics, and they are prepared to obey the traditions of filial loyalty (7, 8). In "Pom's Engagement," Daddyji argues that the match between Pom and Kakaji will work because Kakaji's "way of life and thinking will be similar to mine. We are of the same caste. . . . The atmosphere in Pom's new home will be very much the same as the atmosphere here" (56).

4. Birth and marriage customs in the Quiché tribe are very different from the Hindu customs Mehta describes, but to some degree they have the same purpose: to help young women accept traditions and assume their assigned roles as wives and mothers. The closeness between Pom and her mother intensifies when Pom becomes engaged because her mother is helping her through the process of taking on women's responsibilities. In

Menchú's "Birth Ceremonies," the closeness between mother and daughter serves a similar purpose. Menchú describes how a woman teaches her daughter to perform women's tasks. The mother explains everything she does, including how to say prayers, light the fire, and cook the meals. Menchú writes, "She explains all these little details to her daughter, who learns by copying her" (18). Only by spending much time observing and helping her mother can she learn to follow in her footsteps. This method of instruction, according to Menchú, "is all bound up with our commitment to maintain our customs and pass on the secrets of our ancestors" (19).

## MARGUERITE DURAS (Durah), Home Making (p. 161)

### Explorations

1. Duras sums up a mother's basic identity in this way: "The woman is the home" (para. 28). Once students understand Duras's basic assumption, developing a list of mothers' responsibilities is an easy matter. According to Duras, no matter what a woman does professionally or socially, she "is still responsible for everything in the house" (24). The mother, like the home, provides a "center" for men and children (1). She feeds them, tries to keep them safe (5), and accommodates her schedule to theirs (10). She is responsible not only for the literal running of the home, but also for keeping her family's "ideas, emotional phases, and endless feelings" in order (26). In the same paragraph, Duras says that men build houses rather than make them. Men are good for amusing children, but not for taking care of them, because the men themselves are just like the children (28, 29). Duras reports that she feels "slightly repelled" by a man she knows who does housework and cares for the children (31). In Duras's opinion, this man and his wife have disrupted the proper distribution of responsibility for the home.

2. Duras's description of motherhood reinforces her statement in paragraph 28 that a woman is the home. Earlier in the essay, Duras says that men consider a woman a good mother when her work is "like the rain-bringing clouds" (14). In paragraph 35, Duras describes the mother as part of the environment (she is a hill, a garden, something to eat, something to sleep on). In her portrayal of her own mother, Duras says that "home was simultaneously her and the house — the house around her and her inside the house" (20). Motherhood means sacrificing some part of one's individuality; a good mother "lets herself be devoured" by her family's needs (35).

3. Most students will be able to identify as traditional Duras's idea that women are primarily responsible for running the home and caring for the children. Less conventional, perhaps, is her contention that men are unnecessary to the home (see, for instance, Duras's description in paragraphs 16–18 of how her mother coped with raising her children single-handed). How students respond to Duras's ideas about home and family will depend on their own upbringing and family relationships. In order to help students understand the background for their opinions, it would be good to have them talk about the distribution of responsibilities in their own families.

4.  Duras's evidence is entirely subjective. She draws on her own experience of mothering, her memories of her own mother, and her observations of others to support the generalizations she makes about mothers and homemaking. She often makes statements of faith, as in paragraph 22, where she says she believes mothers represent madness, and in paragraph 27, where she says she seriously believes women's position hasn't changed. Duras also admits she may be "idealizing" mothers (33). As students discuss whether her evidence is convincing, it may be helpful to ask them to consider Duras's essay first as an exploration of her own personal philosophy of homemaking and mothering, and then decide whether her subjective observations and interpretations are convincing on a general level.

## Connections

1.  In both "Pom's Engagement" and "Home Making," women are responsible for day-to-day housekeeping and childcare. There are, however, important differences in how Duras and Mehta approach women's role in the family. Duras writes about women's responsibilities as someone who herself carries them out. For instance, it is clear from her account of buying a house that she identifies strongly with the nine generations of women who once lived in and ran the house that now belongs to her (para. 5). She writes of them, and of her mother and herself, as women who belong to the home, but are independent of the men they care for. Ved Mehta's description of women's responsibilities, on the other hand, comes from his father's point of view. Daddyji says that in their Hindu tradition, Pom's life will be joined with her husband's: "it is she who will forsake her past to build a new future with him" (75). Duras, speaking from the point of view of a woman and a Westerner, would not agree that a woman's life should be dependent on her husband's. Students may have some difficulty identifying similarities in men's roles in "Home Making" and "Pom's Engagement." Although the mother in both Duras's and Mehta's essay is responsible for practical arrangements and decisions, the father in Mehta's essay holds much more authority in the home than Duras believes men really have.

2.  In Ved Mehta's essay, Sister Umi accuses her father of "advocating the subservience of women" when he says that a woman should sacrifice her own interests in order to gain her husband's respect (62–65). Duras also argues that women sacrifice for their families; for instance, see her comments in paragraphs 10 and 11 about how women fit their schedules to their families' needs, as well as her comment that "a woman gives her body over to her child" (35). But she is not arguing that women should subordinate themselves to men. In fact, she writes that her mother sacrificed to make a home for her children, but that she never would have done that for a man (26).

3.  In *Looking at Ourselves*, William Mattox writes that children "in single-parent homes usually receive less parental attention, affection, and supervision than other children," factors that he believes lead to significant developmental problems. Patricia Schroeder agrees that women, especially those who are single parents, face major problems in trying to balance earning a living and running a home. Christopher Lasch, although he doesn't address the question of mothers' roles directly, argues against childcare, a stance that suggests he believes women should be back in the home rather than in the work force.

Both Mattox and Lasch imply that single mothers and working mothers are to blame for being unable to meet the needs of their children, but Schroeder blames the government for failing to support women's efforts to work and raise their children. Duras's depiction of a mother in France differs in that she has nothing to say about women who work outside the home. Her own working life as a writer is integrated into her housework, as is suggested in her statement that "all I had to do was prepare the vegetables, put the soup on, and write" (4).

## GHOLAM-HOSSEIN SA'EDI (Goo-lam-hoo-sane Sah-EE-dee), The Game Is Over (p. 162)

### Explorations

1. Students may have some difficulty recognizing the transition, because the entire piece is told in the past tense. But with a little encouragement, they should sense the shift to specific past in "But that night it was different." In paragraph 4 we return to the moment of Hasani's suggestion with "That afternoon, the one before the night I went to Hasani's place, Hasani came out, and he was really low." By intertwining present observations with the past incident, Sa'edi is able to verify some of the story. The boys' traditional greeting by fighting, their fear of their fathers, their forays to the wells — all of this is exposition that is essential for the reader to understand if the tale is to achieve its full impact. If told in chronological order, the tale would suffer first from a long and tedious expository beginning before the action begins and, second, from frequent interruptions at key points, destroying momentum.

2. When the narrator tells us that he and Hasani fear their fathers, and that they greet each other by fighting, hitting each other "hard so it hurt" (para. 1), we begin to sense the violence in their lives. Students should notice a number of other instances in which Sa'edi states or implies that these children live in a world characterized by family abuse. In paragraph 6, for example, the narrator comments in a matter-of-fact tone that "Hasani's dad would beat him every night, but my dad would only beat Ahmad and me once or twice a week." When the boys are at the wells, Hasani takes to hitting his toes with a stick, and when they reach home, they hear Hasani's mother and father calling each other vile names. The parents, in fact, treat each other with contempt. All of this, while it angers the boys, is considered by them to be simply the way things are.

3. Sa'edi has the narrator initially worrying about how Hasani's parents will react (126), what they'll do to him (the narrator) when he tells them that Hasani has fallen into a well (130), what will happen to Hasani while he's hiding out (136), and later worrying about how to effect the return (213–38). The suspense seems to center on whether Hasani will be welcomed back with caresses and tears or another beating, so the ending should be a surprise to all but the most perceptive readers. Some students may be shocked or dismayed by the story's ending, wishing that Hasani had made his triumphant return to the town. But it's difficult to imagine the impact of such an ending: This isn't Hannibal,

41

Missouri, and a joyous reunion seems out of the question for these people. A beating, though, would be anticlimactic. This question may present instructors with the opportunity to discuss consistency in a story, as well as the demands of the art itself. The ending is really the only way that both consistency and artistic integrity can be maintained.

## Connections

1. In Marguerite Duras's essay "Home Making," the primary benefit children derive from the home is a sense of emotional and physical security. She writes of her own childhood: "As long as we had a house and our mother, we'd never be abandoned or swept away or taken by surprise" (para. 17). Hasani's house provides no sense of security; it is, in fact, a dangerous place. For Hasani, home is the antithesis of what Duras describes. Mothers, in Duras's estimation, are identified with the home. Hasani's mother is too beaten down to protect her son from his father's beatings, so it is as if he had no home at all. In part, what Hasani seeks when he tries to trick his family into thinking him dead is a more secure place in his own home. He wants them to recognize him as a valued member of the family, worthy of love and protection. Hasani imagines that his family will great him with joy, and his father will not beat him when he returns from the dead (265–269). His desperate attempt to gain his family's attention demonstrates how completely his home had failed to meet his basic needs.

2. In both stories religious values provide a subdued background to the actions and thoughts of the protagonists. Although religious ideas are not overtly referred to by the characters in "Our Side of the Fence and Theirs," religion is quietly integrated into the fabric of everyday life. For example, the narrator notes that his "sister-in-law takes Puppi along even when she goes outside to get flowers for worship" (17), a statement that implies that the family is governed by traditional and religious principles. Hasani's father also appears to be a believer, although no religious principles contain his daily violence. However, in his grief he calls to an Islamic saint to restore his child (187). In "The Game Is Over," the characters turn to religion only in moments of despair or as a last resort. The characters expect their religion to work miracles, to restore the lost Hasani or the "sanity" of the narrator at the end of the story. Perhaps the harsh economic circumstances of Hasani's village accustom its inhabitants to hardship so they seek relief only in the most desperate circumstances. The characters in Gyanranjan's story live under more stable circumstances: They are not abused, completely poverty stricken, or without time for some amenities, including daily religious rituals.

3. The irony in this observation should not be lost on students. Whereas Novak cites capitalism and the desire for success as causes for the disintegration of the family, Sa'edi cites the opposite, poverty. In one case the family suffers because there are too many goods available, too many goals for individual members to strive for. In the other the lack of goods, of realistic goals, provides for a despair that undermines Iranian family life every bit as much as materialism does American life.

ADDITIONAL QUESTIONS AND ASSIGNMENTS

1.  In a journal entry or a collection of informal notes, discuss the images of children presented in three or four of these selections. Consider such issues as the rights of children, their responsibilities to their parents, parents' responsibility to protect their children, children's need for the attention and love of a caretaker, their need for independence, and any other issues you find relevant. As you look over your notes, try to discover similarities and differences among the cultures represented. Can you come to any general conclusion about the image of children in a given culture?

2.  Interview someone who grew up in a family setting different from your own. As you gather information, consider the kinds of information you're interested in eliciting — do you want to know about sibling relationships? Responsibilities of children to parents? Influence of religious or social values on the family? Roles of males and females in the family? As you write the interview, decide what information is best summarized in your own voice and what is best delivered by your subject in his or her own words.

3.  Write your own version of "Our Side of the Fence and Theirs," using one of the more popular television families (from any era) as the neighbors. You may want to begin by listing the distinctive characteristics of a family like the Cleavers, the Cartwrights, the Bunkers, the Ewings, the Simpsons, the Seavers, or the Huxtables and comparing them with the characteristics of a "real-life" family. Then imagine yourself watching them for several weeks. Record what you see, using the same kind of commentary as that provided by Gyanranjan's narrator. Remember that you'll be characterizing yourself as much as your subject family.

4.  The issue of children with two working parents is currently receiving a good deal of attention in the media. Some reports focus on the responsibility of the state to provide adequate childcare, some explore the effects of day care on the child, and some investigate the impact of working mothers on society as a whole. Research one of these topics (or choose your own related topic) by consulting magazine and newspaper articles on the subject as well as the opinions of experts found in books and interviews. Write a paper in which you present two opposing interpretations of the issue you've chosen, maintaining neutrality yourself.

5.  Conduct further research into one of the cultures represented in this section, focusing specifically on the role of the family. It would be wise to choose a culture about which information is readily available — China, France, Japan, and India are likely candidates. If the selection is an excerpt from a larger work, look first at that work. You can find other sources by consulting the headnotes for other selections from that culture (if there are any) and a general encyclopedia, as well as journals devoted to the study of that culture. Narrow your topic to something manageable — such as religious influences on the family, the place of children in the family, the role of the extended family, or the responsibility of the family to the state — and write an expository paper in which you elaborate on the view of family presented by the original selection.

**Part Three**

## LANDMARKS AND TURNING POINTS:
## THE STRUGGLE FOR IDENTITY

### INTRODUCTION

The range of cultures covered in this section, from the Hispanic community in Phoenix, Arizona, to the mixed African and Western influences in Abidjan, Ivory Coast, may leave students reeling, but the unifying theme should be eminently familiar to them. Heker, Liu, Orlean, and Tan all relate the experiences of girls on the journey to maturity; Rushdie, Grass, Binur, and Vargas Llosa represent the male experience. Other possible divisions within the unit include the awakening of social and political consciousness (Heker, Liu, Grass, and Binur), the shattering of comforting childhood illusions (Heker, Tan, Liu, and Grass), roles dictated by social class and race (Binur, Grass, Heker, and Liu) and by sex (Vargas Llosa, Tan, and Orlean), and the role of violence as a catalyst for personal growth (Liu, Vargas Llosa, Grass, and Binur).

Students may find the unit more accessible if they first discuss the various rituals involved with turning points in their own culture. They will be able to compare their own rites of initiation with those represented in Orlean, Vargas Llosa, and Grass. Some may identify with the scenes of alienation in selections by Hughes, Cooper, and Baldwin in *Looking at Ourselves*. They will probably have strong responses to the brutality represented in Grass, Binur, and Liu. They may find similarities in their own lives to the complexities and trials of growing up represented in pieces by Vargas Llosa, Tan, and Grass.

Instructors may wish to consult the following familiar works in preparing related selections from *Ourselves Among Others*:

### Essays

Maya Angelou, "Graduation" (*I Know Why the Caged Bird Sings*, Random House, 1970).
Nancy Mairs, "On Being Raised by a Daughter" (*Plaintext*, University of Arizona Press, 1986).
George Orwell, "Shooting an Elephant" (*Shooting an Elephant*, Harcourt, 1950).
Lillian Smith, "When I was a Child" (*Killers of the Dream*, Norton, 1949).
Alice Walker, "Beauty: When the Other Dancer is the Self" (*In Search of Our Mothers' Gardens*, Harcourt, 1983).
Alice Walker, "Brothers and Sisters" (*In Search of Our Mothers's Gardens*, Harcourt, 1983).

### Short Stories

Chinua Achebe, "Marriage is a Private Affair" (*Girls at War*, Doubleday, 1972).
Toni Cade Bambera, "The Lesson" (*Gorilla, My Love*, Random House, 1972).

Dorothy Canfield, "Sex Education" (*Four-Square*, Harcourt, 1945).

Kate Chopin, "The Story of an Hour" (published as "The Dreams of an Hour," *Vogue*, April 19, 1894); *The Awakening and Selected Stories*, Penguin, 1983.

Ralph Ellison, "Battle Royal" (*Invisible Man*, Random House, 1952).

Louise Erdrich, "The World's Greatest Fisherman" (*Love Medicine*, Holt, Rinehart, 1984).

William Faulkner, "The Bear" (*Go Down, Moses*, Random House, 1942).

Doris Lessing, "A Sunrise on the Veldt" (*African Stories*, Simon and Schuster, 1981).

Doris Lessing, "Through the Tunnel" (*The Habit of Loving*, 1955).

Jeanne Schinto, "Caddies' Day" (*Shadow Bands*, Ontario Review Press, 1988).

John Updike, "A & P" (*New Yorker*, July 22, 1961; *Pigeon Feathers*, Knopf, 1962).


## BIOGRAPHICAL NOTES ON LOOKING AT OURSELVES

1. A contributing writer for many magazines, Gail Sheehy has written a novel, *Lovesounds* (1970), and several studies of contemporary American and global life, including *Hustling* (1973), *Pathfinders* (1981), *Character: America's Search for Leadership* (1988), *The Man Who Changed the World: The Lives of Mikhail S. Gorbachev* (1991), and *Silent Passage: Menopause* (1992). The excerpt in *Looking at Ourselves* is taken from Sheehy's *Passages: Predictable Crises of Adult Life* (1974).

2. Michael Dorris, an anthropologist and writer, was the founder and chairman of the Department of Native American Studies at Dartmouth. He is the author of a memoir, *The Broken Cord: A Family's Ongoing Struggle with Fetal Alcohol Syndrome* (1989), and of the novels *A Yellow Raft in Blue Water* (1987) and, with Louise Erdrich, *The Crown of Columbus* (1991).

3. Poet, novelist, and short story writer Langston Hughes has been called the father of the Harlem Renaissance literary movement of the 1920s and 1930s. His "Negro Artist and the Racial Mountain" (1926) was the manifesto of the revival. His autobiographies *The Big Sea* (1940) and *I Wonder as I Wander* (1956) chronicle his worldwide travels during which he was a merchant seaman, waiter, English teacher, and Parisian bohemian.

4. Terry Galloway is the author of two plays, *Heart of a Dog*, which won the Village award in New York, and *A Hamlet in Berlin*; she has also coauthored a public television program for deaf children and published a book of poems, *Buncha Crocs in Search of Snac* (1980).

5. Bernard Cooper lives in Los Angeles and is the author of *Maps to Anywhere* (1990), a collection of autobiographical essays and poems.

6. Alfred Kazin is a prominent literary critic and memoirist whose critical works include *On Native Grounds* (1942) and *Bright Book of Life: American Novelists and Storytellers from Hemingway to Mailer* (1980). He is perhaps best known for his autobiographical trilogy: *A Walker in the City* (1969), *New York Jew* (1978), and *Starting Out in the Thirties* (1989).

7. James Baldwin was widely regarded as one of the preeminent black writers of his time. He is perhaps best known for his novels *Go Tell It on the Mountain* (1953), about the black church, and *Giovanni's Room* (1956), dealing with homosexuality, and for the essays collected in *Notes of a Native Son* (1955) and *Nobody Knows My Name: More Notes of a Native Son* (1961). His searing polemic *The Fire Next Time* appeared in 1963. He died in the south of France in 1989.

8. Joyce Carol Oates, a professor of English at Princeton University, is one of the most versatile, prolific, and acclaimed writers in contemporary America. Among her many works are the novels *them* (National Book Award 1970), *Expensive People* (1982), and *Black Water* (1992) (based on the Chappaquiddick incident); the essay collections *On Boxing* (1989) and *American Appetites* (1990); and the short story collection *Where Are You Going, Where Have You Been: Stories of Young America* (1974). She has also written gothic romances and horror stories and edited the *Oxford Book of American Short Stories* (1992).

9. Malcolm X, born Malcolm Little in 1925, became a Black Muslim in jail and, after his release, advocated black separatism until he was assassinated in 1965. His *Autobiography of Malcolm X* (coauthored with Alex Haley) appeared that same year.

**Reflections**

1. Issues of honesty are important in selections by Terry Galloway, Bernard Cooper, and Langston Hughes. Students who have difficulty in identifying with the childhood experiences of a deaf woman, a gay man, or an African-American will be better able to engage with this question if they have the opportunity to discuss the relationship between personal honesty and social acceptance in their own lives. Terry Galloway learned that it was better for her to be honest about her deafness after she suffered isolation and severe emotional stress while trying to keep her deafness a secret. She lied about her deafness in college in order to "avoid the stigma of being thought different," a motivation that was also important to Cooper and Hughes. She found it easier to gain acceptance when, as a result of facing up to the hard realities of functioning as a deaf person in a hearing world, she decided to begin to tell people of her hearing disability. Bernard Cooper faced a somewhat similar dilemma when, as a boy, he began to realize that he was gay. He lies to a potential friend, Theresa Sanchez, and his mother about his orientation, in part because he has not yet fully grasped what it means. He also lies because he fears — rightly, in relation to his mother and another boy he has befriended — that he will be rejected if he tells the truth. As an adult, Cooper reflects on this time of his life and regrets not admitting to Theresa, the one person he might have trusted with the truth, that he was gay. Whereas Cooper's situation did not involve any clear solutions to the problem of when and with whom to be honest, Langston Hughes's piece recounts an incident when being honest could not have led to acceptance. His initial refusal to claim that he had seen Jesus during a prayer meeting was an effort to represent himself honestly to his friends and family, but as time goes on and he sees that they will not accept him as he is, he finally gives in to their demands and pretends that he too has seen Jesus. However, he is left feeling bitterly alone and isolated, effects he suffers not only because he was unable to be honest, but also because he has lost faith in his aunt and their religion.

2. Students' responses to this question will depend on their personal perceptions, combined with how their unique cultural and ethnic backgrounds affect their feelings about assuming the rights and responsibilities of adulthood. Some students, recalling how impatient they were to take on the privileges of adulthood, will feel that an abrupt transition to adulthood, marked by a single event in which they could "prove" their maturity, would have been a vast improvement over a long adolescence. Others may argue that the length of time young people in the United States spend in school without taking on major responsibilities is a tremendous waste of talent. Adolescence is often

considered a long-term identity crisis in which one is no longer a child but still has not achieved adulthood; a ritual that would help resolve the crisis and situate the young person as a full adult would be welcome to many. A longer transition might appeal more to middle-class and wealthy students, whose family resources allow them more leisure to attend school, enjoy extra-curricular activities, and explore possible careers. The advantages of a longer transition might be a more complete academic education, more time to enjoy the relative freedom of a youth unencumbered by an adult work load, and more time to learn how to handle family and community responsibilities.

3. Along with considering connections between Langston Hughes's account of being "saved" in the church and Michael Dorris's description of Native American initiation rites, it will be a good idea to have students consider the different purposes of the rituals Hughes and Dorris relate. For both, one purpose is to initiate membership in a social and spiritual group. For Hughes, it is membership in the ranks of those "saved" by Jesus; for Dorris, it is membership in the ranks of adults who have faced the physical and spiritual challenges of entering the wilderness alone. However, the revival Hughes attends emphasizes the authority of the Christian god over the young people who are his "lambs." Dorris, by contrast, describes an initiation that is intended to prove the independence and individual courage of young men and to introduce them to their adult selves. Dorris writes that the insights the initiate gained may have been induced by exhaustion, hunger, or other stresses, but he affirms that the experience was ultimately a positive one. Hughes, on the other hand, must face spiritual disillusionment and the disappointment of not having experienced the transformation his aunt expected of him. The other young people at the revival, either by the force of their own convictions or because of social pressures, "went to Jesus" without resistance. It may be that for some initiates undergoing the wilderness ritual Dorris describes, a sudden transformation was achieved for similar reasons: because of pressures to conform to the expectations of family and community, along with a desire to be accepted as an adult.

4. Hughes employs biblical phrases and the repetitive, rhythmic style of revival preachers to evoke the mood of the prayer meeting. He describes the songs and sermon, and quotes the preacher imploring the children: "'Won't you come? Won't you come to Jesus? Young lambs, won't you come?'" The congregation prays "in a mighty wail of moans and voices," and when all the children had arisen, "Then joyous singing filled the room." Hughes contrasts these lyrical and biblical passages with a more conversational style that suggests the inauthenticity of the religious experience for him. He begins the piece, for instance, by saying, "I was saved from sin when I was going on thirteen. But not really saved." Hughes employs a similarly conversational style whenever he describes his inner reactions to the meeting, as when he finally gets up after deciding "that maybe to save further trouble, I'd better lie. . . ." Baldwin uses repetition for a different effect. His opening paragraph repeats the phrase, "it comes as a great shock" in order to emphasize the severity and permanence of the trauma a young black child experiences when she or he discovers that, because of racism, the mainstream culture will attempt to situate her or him as "other" — and as inferior. Later in the piece, Baldwin uses repetition to imply that the damage is felt not only by the individual child, but also by the nation as a whole. He writes, "It is a terrible thing for an entire people to surrender to the notion that one-ninth of its population is beneath them," and re-emphasizes this point in his last sentence by repeating the sentence structure: "it is a very grave moment. . . ." Cooper employs a very different style to describe his experience of growing up gay. His piece begins with

47

a physical description of Theresa Sanchez that suggests the narrator's keen sense of sensual detail. Later in the piece, with his description of Grady's body and behavior, the personal significance of his acute awareness of bodies becomes clear, because this passage describes his awakening awareness of his homosexuality. His awareness of bodies also has a defensive function; he writes that he emulated Grady's behavior and was not, therefore, "singled out as a sissy." The need for defenses is even more apparent in his description of his body as "The Visible Man in our science class." Cooper completes his essay with a sensual moment he enjoys as an adult with his lover, a passage that affirms that he has come to terms with his body and his sexuality.

### SUSAN ORLEAN, Quinceañera (p. 200)

### Explorations

1. Students may have some trouble understanding how Azteca Plaza, the formal-wear shopping center where parents shop for the gowns their fifteen-year-old daughters will wear to their quinceañeras, represents the dual nature of the Hispanic culture in Phoenix. They may find it easier if they begin by considering the dual meanings of "plaza." A plaza is a traditional outdoor marketplace and central meeting place, but it also denotes a modern shopping center. The Aztec culture thrived in Mexico until Cortés arrived in the sixteenth century. Invoking the Aztecs for a formal-wear shop may be taken as an indication of the place of quinceañeras in traditional Mexican culture. Azteca Plaza, like the Hispanic culture Orlean describes, represents a mixture of traditional Mexican and contemporary Hispanic influences.

2. Quinceañeras were originally meant to mark a girl's initiation into womanhood and society, and to affirm her commitment to the Catholic church (para. 1). Students will find plenty of evidence that quinceañeras still serve as a social debut. Whether the event is held for an individual girl or for groups of girls, it brings the community together to recognize the girls' passage from childhood to young womanhood. But some members of the Hispanic community are concerned that quinceañeras no longer serve as a meaningful religious rite. One of Orlean's informants tells her that the ethnic and religious significance of the quinceañera is irrelevent to today's young people (5). Father Sotelo tells Orlean that the quinceañera has become an empty ceremony (8). Some girls seemed to regard the event as an opportunity simply to be the center of attention at a fancy party, and some parents seemed to consider that it was their duty to go into debt to sponsor the most opulent party possible. Father Sotelo believes that the event should be primarily a religious celebration; hence his unwillingness to give masses for girls who are not religious or obedient to church doctrine. Father Peacock, on the other hand, believes that the church should work to meet people on their own terms (12) and to help them come together to celebrate family and community in any way they choose. Students will be able to come up with many reasons for the changes that have taken place in the ceremony since its Mexican origins. Most of these reasons may have to do with the impact of Anglo culture, which could be viewed as a threat to traditional values. The new deemphasis on the religious aspects of the event, the modern gowns the girls wear, the mix of Mexican

music with rock 'n' roll (27), and the emphasis on spending extravagantly to impress others, are all changes that might be put down to the negative influence of Anglo values.

3.  Orlean's selection of sources is so broad that most students will have trouble thinking of other sources she might have included. She observes firsthand Azteca Plaza, the Vesta Club quinceañeras mass, and the country club party that follows. She interviews adult community members who are involved in planning quinceañeras and two priests, Father Peacock and Father Sotelo, who have very different opinions of the meaning of the quinceañera celebration. She consults Father Sotelo's guidebook (7), written for girls who want to celebrate the mass, and she watches videotapes of quinceañera masses with Father Peacock (10). There are three sources, however, she does not cite directly. She has not consulted the elderly, who might have participated in quinceañeras in the early twentieth century and would, therefore, have a better grasp of some of the changes that have taken place. Nor does she speak with Mexican nationals, who would be able to provide a unique commentary on the ethnic significance of the celebration. And lastly, she does not include interviews with any of the sixteen girls who are taking part in the quinceañera she attends. This last omission is especially curious since the event is for them.

4.  Orlean is present as an interested observer rather than as a participant in the stories she tells. If she were closely involved, her story would dominate the essay and limit its scope. In the role she plays, Orlean is able to gather together stories from numerous informants and give a multifaceted presentation of events and opinions. Orlean's own opinions come through in the choices she makes about what scenes to include. For instance, late in the essay Orlean records a significant exchange between a girl and her mother at the quinceañera party. The girl asks when the "debutante of the year" will be announced, and her stepmother replies curtly, "Later" (27). It is a small moment, one among many Orlean might have chosen to include, but it suggests that Orlean believes that quinceañeras can be competitive and a source of parent-child tension. If Orlean were not present in the stories she tells, such a moment could not be recorded. Her essay would be a dry composite of the history and current customs related to the quinceañeras, rather than the lively piece it is.

## Connections

1.  The fifteen-year-old girls who have quinceañeras are in some senses very much connected to their families, as their participation in a traditional Hispanic celebration indicates. But like the young teenagers Sheehy discusses, these girls are also trying to redefine the celebration — and their relationship to their families — by modifying it to better suit their needs and desires. Although the original intent of the quinceañeras was to formalize a girl's "passage into womanhood" and "commitment to Catholicism," as well as her personal social debut (para. 1), for many, the emphasis is now on the last objective. Father Sotelo, for instance, complained about the "queen-for-a-day" attitude of many girls (6). In addition, for some girls, planning the quinceañera is an opportunity to exert their individuality through conflicts with family (7). Their refusal of the traditional religious meaning, and their desire to include rock 'n' roll along with traditional Mexican music (27), suggest that they are working at differentiating themselves from their families.

49

2.  It will be important for students to appreciate the historical, ethnic, and sex differences between the Native American male initiation rites Dorris describes and the quinceañera celebration. Young Plains Indian men were expected to challenge themselves physically and spiritually in order to become men. It was a private rite of passage, marking not only an external change in how an initiate would fit into his community, but also an internal change in which he would discover a personal vision and vocation. The quinceañera celebration also has a spiritual component. The emphasis, however, is not on a personal spiritual vision, but on a public affirmation of a girl's commitment to the Catholic Church (1). It is not a private ritual, and although mild physical challenges are involved (negotiating the intricate waltz, for instance), the fifteen-year-old Hispanic girl is not expected to endure privation or fend for her life. However, the two very different initiation rituals do have in common the idea that a single event can mark a profound change in how a young person relates to his or her community. Both are meant to celebrate the beginning of adulthood.

3.  Rodriguez mentions that he was "struck by diminished family closeness and the necessity of public life," and that the Catholic Church served a mediating role between his private and public lives (1). Attending mass made him feel connected to other Catholics, whether or not he wanted the connection. The girls who celebrate quinceañeras in Orlean's essay might express some of the same ambivalence about the role of the church in their lives. Father Sotelo reports that some girls expected to have a mass said for them even though they were never in church and disobeyed the church's doctrines (6), a problem that suggests some girls were not willing to establish the close connection to the church Rodriguez recalls. Father Sotelo complained that "when these girls would walk down the aisle with their parents at the mass, you could tell that quite often the girls and their parents couldn't stand one another"(7). Rodriguez recalls that he felt distanced from his family, due to generational, educational, and cultural differences. But the church served at least to bring him and his family together for the purpose of worship. Father Peacock mentions a similar purpose for the quinceañera mass. Some families, "have experienced child abuse, sexual abuse, divorce . . . [Father Peacock] loves seeing such families together at the occasional happy affair like a quinceañera " (12).

## LILIANA HEKER (HEH-kur), The Stolen Party (p. 212)

### Explorations

1.  A few students will recognize that the "theft" of the party happens in two ways. Ines steals the party from Rosaura by demonstrating that the girl was invited not as a guest, but as a servant. Rosaura, at least from Ines' point of view, steals the party by stepping outside her prescribed role and insisting on being treated as a guest. Most students, however, will be so thoroughly in sympathy with Rosaura's perspective that the dual meaning of the title will go unnoticed. The fact that the party has been "stolen" from Rosaura only becomes clear at the end, when the thing she most values, a sense of belonging and respect, is taken from her.

2.  Some students may be surprised to find two central conflicts in the same story; the two in this story are defined clearly enough, however, that students should be able to identify

them readily. By introducing the mother-daughter conflict in the first paragraph, Heker sees to it that the reader is taken in, as is Rosaura, by the seeming importance of this conflict. She sees herself and her friend as allies against the intolerance of her mother. Unlike Rosaura, however, the reader senses the legitimacy of the conflict between rich and poor introduced in the second paragraph. By constructing the story this way, Heker diverts the reader's attention from the primary conflict, clouding the issues and preventing a premature anticipation of the ending. While the reader knows that Rosaura's mother is probably right in questioning the invitation, the child's perception is so appealing that the reader willfully suspends skepticism and hopes, with Rosaura, to prove the mother wrong.

3.  While Señora Ines's ignorance and class bias allow her to think she's being generous in giving Rosaura money rather than a trinket, the child recognizes the insult for what it is and immediately presses close to her true ally, her mother. Rosaura's refusal to take the bills, as well as her stare, reveal to Ines that she has erred; however, she is paralyzed, unable to withdraw the offer but incapable of making any other gesture. Both characters realize at this point that they've been involved in a charade, and that realization makes any further pretense impossible.

4.  Among the possible responses to this question are Rosaura's certainty that her mother knows nothing about friendship (para. 8), her criticism of her mother's intolerance of rich people (13), her sense of superiority to the other children in the careful handling of dishes (19), her perception of power in being chosen to distribute the cake (39) and to hold the monkey (52), and her misinterpretation of Señora Ines's comment that she is a "marvelous daughter" (68). In each case she's attempting to repress any sense of inferiority to the rich children and to reinforce her own sense of importance. And she is indeed an accomplished child — she is an achiever in school and is interesting enough to intrigue her rich friend. But regardless of the legitimacy of her pride, her naïveté blinds her to the perceptions of society. She fails to recognize the fact that to Señora Ines her accomplishments are no more meaningful than the antics of the monkey; she may be clever, but she's still the maid's daughter.

## Connections

1.  Luciana's mother gives her a fancy birthday party that will impress the parents of the children who attend and reinforce her social position. The inclusion of Rosaura, who gracefully helps to keep things running smoothly, is part of her effort to bring off a perfect party. Luciana, like Rosaura, is too young and naïve to understand how the party might be an occasion to reinforce class divisions by displaying wealth. She only wants to enjoy herself and to be sure her guests, including Rosaura, enjoy the party too. The different goals of mother and daughter are in some ways analogous to the different goals of mothers and daughters in Susan Orlean's "Quinceañera." Quinceañeras are opportunities to impress friends and relatives with a extravagant show of clothes, money, music, and food. While the daughters enjoy receiving the attention and gifts, the mothers may use the occasion to be recognized for their social and organizational talents.

2.  Rosaura's friendship with Luciana demonstrates that she is between two worlds: the working-class world of her mother, where education and social etiquette are considered luxuries, and the upper-class world of her mother's employer. When Rosaura attends Luciana's party, she shows she is ready to take a step further into Luciana's world. She

can only do that by distancing herself from her mother's world. In spite of Ines's gesture, which is an attempt to put Rosaura squarely back in the disadvantaged place Rosaura's mother holds, Rosaura may eventually be able to use her education to move into the middle class. Mphahlele writes that when an African mother sends her son to high school, "dialogue between her and the child decreases and eventually stays on the level of basic essentials" (para. 4). A similar gulf is opening up between Rosaura and her mother as Rosaura's education progresses. However, Rosaura's mother is proud of her accomplishments and helps her prepare for the party even though she knows it will create distance between them. Less relevant to Rosaura's situation are Mphahlele's comments about the African writer's relationship to tradition (5). Rosaura would not be leaving behind her traditional cultural roots if she succeeds in moving up the socioeconomic hierarchy. The distance between her mother and her has not been opened up because of the intrusion of what Mphahlele calls an "alien" language and culture (7). Instead, it is due to the class differences that will separate them as Rosaura gains an education and enters the middle class within her own culture.

3.   It may be difficult for students to appreciate the differences in the problems with racism Baldwin is addressing and the more class-based problems Rosaura confronts. Baldwin mentions the shock an African-American child feels when he is forced to realize that, although he has given his loyalty to the United States and adopted its values, the United States has not "evolved any place" for him (1). Although the exclusion Baldwin notices has serious economic consequences, it is based on skin color (1). At the end of "The Stolen Party," Rosaura, too, is shocked to discover that she has not been accepted as the equal of the other children. However, unlike the African-American child, Rosaura is excluded because of her class status.

## SOPHRONIA LIU (Loo), So Tsi-fai (p. 219)

### Explorations

1.   In her description of So Tsi-fai in paragraph 3, Liu seems to echo the teacher's feelings: All she can see are dirty clothes, the sneering grin, the shuffling gait. But after his suicide, as she remembers him the reasons for his behavior become clear. She intersperses her own account of his hardships with the scorn and criticism of the teacher, revealing the frustration that So Tsi-fai faced daily. The ghost that comes to claim his rightful place is the product of Liu's own mind, born of her guilt. As she ponders those events during the next twenty years, she begins to question the fickleness of fate, wondering why she was chosen to be successful while he was doomed to failure.

2.   Paragraphs 6, 7, and 8 make it quite clear that Liu blames fate in the larger sense but the social system in particular for So Tsi-fai's death. When we hear Sister Marie's criticisms after we've read about the responsibilities heaped on the boy, we cannot help condemning an educational system that ignores the student's life outside the classroom. Liu seems to suggest that a more compassionate approach to education is needed, one that looks into the problems students may face out of school and attempts to help students rather than simply condemning them. (It might be interesting to compare students' sympathy with So Tsi-fai with their response to "problem students" in American

classrooms. Are we as willing to sympathize with the real person who's disrupting our classroom as we are with the character we know only from the printed page?)

3. This question should provide quite a jolt for those students who have been told that sentence fragments are among the great crimes against humanity. Regardless, exploring this question will prove enlightening. The musing effect that Liu achieves by using fragments in her first three paragraphs suggests the uncertainty — even the desperation — of the sixth-grader confronted with the suicide of a peer. The questioning, the incompleteness of the thoughts is reflected in the sentence structure. When she begins paragraph 4 with the standard "It was a Monday in late November," the reader sits back, ready to hear the story behind the questions.

## Connections

1. The similarities are numerous: Both children suffer the consequences of poverty and lower-class status in their superficial rejection by those more privileged than they. Both accept the power of authority figures either to lift them from their present state or to condemn them to a life of insignificance. So Tsi-fai is condemned by his teacher's judgment of him as "incorrigible" (para. 3); Rosaura feels exalted by her preferential treatment at the party — until the devastating revelation that Señora Ines has been using her as a maid. Rosaura's eyes, however, reveal her strength. The cold stare she levels at Señora Ines in the end suggests that she will not only survive but also will overcome the handicaps of poverty. She does not despair as does So Tsi-fai, in part because she can rely on the strength of her mother, who stands ready to protect her. In addition, her poverty and its demands are not as harsh as his. As a result, we can expect Rosaura to prevail.

2. As eldest sons, both So Tsi-fai and Sugama are expected to take on major responsibility for the welfare of the families, especially to provide for their parents and younger siblings. Sugama, a young professional in Tokyo, will be expected to live with his parents and grandfather. His dilemma is that he cannot live with and support his parents in Tokyo, since it would be too expensive for them all to live there (45). Instead, if he plans to honor his familial obligation, he will have to give up his city job and go home to take a dead-end job. So Tsi-fai's family differs from Sugama's in that they are extremely poor, making it even harder for So Tsi-fai to fulfill family obligations. As the oldest son, So Tsi-fai has had no older siblings to care for him, but he "helped in the fields, cooked for the family, and washed his own clothes" (6). With so many responsibilities, he has little time to give to studies. This is the dilemma So Tsi-fai faces: If he devoted himself to doing well in school, he would not be able to contribute to his family's immediate needs. But because he had so little support for his schooling from teachers and parents (4, 7) and because he gave his time to responsibilities in the home, he has failed in school — which means that he will be unable to fulfill his parents' expectation that he help them more substantially in the future.

3. Although the roles played by the ghosts in the two narratives are quite different, their acceptance suggests an acknowledgment of supernatural forces, probably stemming from ancient traditions. In "Nigerian Childhood" (p. 112) the ghost serves as instructor to children, reinforcing traditional values. In "So Tsi-fai" the message is the opposite: The ghost assails the status quo, condemning a tradition that contributes to the suicide of a young boy. The dramatic roles of the two ghosts differ as well: Whereas Soyinka's ghost

is a component of legend, an integral part of his heritage, Liu's ghost arises from guilt, a personification of values and ideas, and comes from within to condemn the behavior of society. Thus Liu's ghost can be viewed in two ways: If her ghost is considered less literal than Soyinka's, more of a literary technique, then perhaps it is less frightening. Conversely, if her ghost is considered to be rooted in the hearts of Liu and her classmates, then it is more frightening than Soyinka's — you can't run home to escape the ghost from within.

## MARIO VARGAS LLOSA (YOH-sa), On Sunday (p. 224)

### Explorations

1. Some students may be reluctant to extrapolate, having been warned in the past to stick to the story. But if they're encouraged to imagine relationships and situations that are consistent with the characters and themes in the story, they should be able to handle this question. Miguel has apparently been loving Flora "pure and chaste from afar" until this point. He clearly suspects that Rubén too has been with her; perhaps his rival has even told Flora of his (Miguel's) love for her. The key word here is rival: Until this situation presented itself, Miguel and Rubén had been friends, members of the same gang. Now love and competition for the same young woman have turned Miguel's comradely feeling for Rubén into enmity.

2. Students may be a bit confused by this ending, failing to understand fully the implications of the contest. Miguel and Rubén have obviously shared an accomplishment by undergoing their ordeal, but they have also settled their rivalry. What Miguel and Rubén seem to realize is that their rivalry over Flora need not undermine the bond between them nor the bright future promised by their youth, strength, and support for each other.

A less appealing but probably accurate interpretation might emphasize that the unspoken agreement between the two is that Flora (or any woman, for that matter) is simply not worth the fight. The bond between men is far stronger than the attraction of women. (Some students may find this interpretation particularly unsavory, but it is consistent with the view of women in the story.)

3. Many students will be able to identify with Miguel's fantasy of personal victory and the humiliation of his rival Rubén, although the specifics of the fantasy (a military parade) may seem foreign to them. Miguel's fantasy arises out of his suspicion that he is less of a man than Rubén. Whereas the fantasy can only temporarily help him deal with those fears, saving his friend from drowning dispels Miguel's apprehensions about his manhood. In Miguel's fantasy, Rubén is publicly shamed and Miguel is glorified. But in reality, when he has the opportunity to shame Rubén by revealing his rival's physical weakness and fear, Miguel chooses to allow Rubén to keep his dignity. In this way, he can feel better about himself and renew his friendship with Rubén.

4. This question should precipitate some lively discussion. In a traditional composition class, most of the men and many of the women will fail even to notice that Flora is merely a prize to be fought for. Some students, upon recognizing this, may not find this view

54

of women disquieting. Regardless, a close reading of the story should reveal to all students that while Flora shows some compassion for Miguel, she also lies about meeting Rubén. Beyond that, we get very little sense of a personality. Both young men seem more interested in winning her than in understanding her. For her part, Flora seems little more than a pawn: It seems not to matter at all what she does or how she acts; Miguel and Rubén will still spar. The quest itself wholly ignores Flora's wishes. The role that Flora plays is dictated by the rules governing male-female behavior in her society. Under those rules the female's role is a passive one.

## Connections

1. In entering the swimming match, Miguel behaves in a self-destructive and life-threatening fashion. This foolish act, along with his drinking to excess in the bar and his taunting of Rubén, shows that he has not yet gained enough maturity to behave responsibly. However, the disaster that might have occurred did not; Miguel still can believe that "Before him was opening a golden future" (para. 188). So Tsi-fai, like Miguel, behaves self-destructively in order to get attention, but in every other way their situations are very different. If So Tsi-fai had survived, he could not have looked forward to a "golden future." Miguel's actions are thoughtless, but he experiences none of the deep despair that causes So Tsi-fai to seek actively to destroy himself. Miguel is an accepted member of a community; he has every reason to think he will be able to have good friendships and even "win" a girl. So Tsi-fai is an outsider to others of his own generation, and he tries to be responsible for his family in ways that even an older and more able person would find hard.

2. Miguel's experience during the swimming match with Rubén gives him new insights similar to those described by Michael Dorris in his discussion of the initiation of young males in Plains Indian tribes. The personal, spiritual turning point Dorris describes takes place as a result of "Fear, fatigue, reliance on strange foods, the anguish of loneliness, stress, and the expectation of ultimate success . . ." (3). Miguel experiences many of these psychologically transformative pressures when he finds himself floundering at sea. However, when he decides to save Rubén, he ceases to call on God to save him and begins to act capably. He reacts with authority during a real emergency, wins Rubén's grudging admiration, and is recognized upon his return as having "becom[e] a man" (187). This accords with the goals for the Plains Indian initiation, which for a young man included a "foresight of . . . his adult persona" (3).

3. Students should find a number of familiar scenes in this story: Miguel's awkwardness in his meeting with Flora, his insistence on drinking despite his fear that he won't be able to hold the beer, his bold plunge into the sea followed by his "certainty that God was going to punish him by drowning him," and the resulting comic bargaining with God for his life (165). Students' ability to identify with such attempts to be adult, countered by feelings of inadequacy, should help them to grasp some of the implications of Miguel's epiphany.

55

## SALMAN RUSHDIE, The Broken Mirror (p. 240)

### Explorations

1.  Students may be better able to explore the dual meaning of the mirror if they first consider how Rushdie compares the old black-and-white photograph of his father's home with the house he sees when he visits it. His vision of his past, like the photograph, is apparently stable and fixed. When he sees the house in person, he is "assaulted by colors," and the vividness of his new vision forces him to consider how partial — how "monochromatic" — his former vision of his childhood had been (para. 2). In paragraph 6, Rushdie mentions that the narrator for his book *Midnight's Children* has a "fallible memory . . . and his vision is fragmentary." He generalizes from the narrator to expatriated Indian writers, asserting that they cannot reflect an intact vision of India because they are working with "broken mirrors, some of whose fragments have been irretrievably lost" (6). This is, however, a valuable way of viewing the past and of viewing India. Rushdie argues, in regard to his own partial memories of images from India, that "fragmentation made trivial things seem like symbols, and the mundane acquired numinous qualities" (8).

2.  Reflecting on his childhood in India and his later life in the West, Rushdie feels that "it's my present that is foreign, and that the past is home" (1). Nevertheless his Western influences affect his vision of India and his childhood. He makes reference in the first paragraph to British writer L. P. Hartley while he is exploring the idea of a foreign present and later refers to John Fowles, another British writer, on the topic of whole versus partial vision (11). He wrote *Midnight's Children* in North London, a fact that caused him to consider how his life in the West has changed his vision of India (5). Western influences affect his memories of India in more direct ways as well; Rushdie recalls seeing as a child billboards and ads for Western products (7). Rushdie makes two biblical references, the first when he alludes to Lot's wife in paragraph four and the second in the conclusion, when he addresses the issue of Western influences directly, by calling up an image of the expatriated Indian writer as "fallen" — an image that derives from Christianity (12).

3.  Although Rushdie distinguishes between the Western and Indian parts of his identity in historical terms, as when he writes that "the past is a foreign country" (1), his strongest statements about expatriate Indian writers have to do with the mix of cultures they represent: "Our identity is both plural and partial" (12). He considers his "ambiguous and shifting" position between cultures potentially productive. Rushdie wants to reclaim his Indian past (2, 3), but he also realizes that his life in the West has given him a perspective on India that is unique and unavailable to those who remained in India. He uses his knowledge of Western culture, and his memories of Indian culture, to reject the "guru-illusion" that "writers are . . . sages, dispensing the wisdom of the centuries"(11).

4.  Students may need help interpreting Rushdie's reference to Lot's wife when he writes that writers in exile who look back "risk . . . being mutated into pillars of salt"(4). Like Lot's wife, Rushdie implies, expatriate Indian writers have failed to keep their eyes on the present and future; by looking back at a doomed past instead of forward to a living future, they can become static and unable to progress. If they are "haunted" by the past, writers in exile will not be able to recognize that they are creating "imaginary homelands," not reclaiming the literal India.

**Connections**

1. Students may have trouble with this question until they have considered some of the basic differences between Rushdie's and Vargas Llosa's writing. Rushdie's essay elaborates on a complex of ideas about the fiction writer's process and the functions of memory. "On Sunday," on the other hand, is a narrative. Whereas Rushdie uses the device of the broken mirror to describe the problems and advantages for the expatriate writer of partial memory, Vargas Llosa uses the figure of the mirror to reveal something about his main character Miguel. In paragraph 16, Miguel's vivid fantasy of his victorious march at the Naval Academy parade vanishes "like steam wiped off a mirror," replaced by an equally vivid fantasy of his rival with the girl Miguel wants. The device of the mirror in this sequence functions to show us Miguel's youthful, overactive imagination and his fears of being humiliated. In the same instant, he recalls having told Flora that he loved her — a memory that, in view of his unhappy fantasy, now makes him feel angry and ashamed. In the next paragraph, Miguel sees an image of himself in the mirror: "a face both ravaged and livid." The device of the mirror, reflecting both his fantasies and himself, demonstrates how Miguel has allowed fantasy and reality to become mixed. In this sense Vargas Llosa and Rushdie use the devices of mirror and memory in similar ways; both are concerned with how memory and fiction — or fantasy — work together to influence a person's psychological state.

2. Rushdie's broken-mirror metaphor describes both the richness and the partial nature of the memory of former places and former selves. Terry Galloway describes a breakdown she underwent when she had trouble facing the ways in which her deafness would affect her life. As a result of the breakdown, however, she developed some skills she could use to help her create a new and happier life. Therefore, her memory of herself before the breakdown, and before she became completely deaf, is influenced by her current situation. As hard as her early life was, it is now evident to the mature Galloway that her young self had every reason to be confident that she would learn to cope well with her disability. At the end of his reflections on his early problems confronting his homosexuality, Bernard Cooper uses an image from earlier in the piece to form a contrast and a connection between his adult self and himself as a boy. The adult Cooper touches his lover's back and feels "the pleasure a diver feels the instant he enters a body of water." As a boy, he swam with his best friend and felt — but couldn't allow himself to admit — pleasure and desire. Cooper concludes by saying that his only regret is that he hadn't been able to admit his homosexuality when he was a boy, a regret that simultaneously indicates his current acceptance of himself and affirms that his young self had every reason to believe that he would one day be able to value himself as a gay man. Malcolm X suggests a mirror analogy when he writes that he "often reflected upon the new vistas" that learning to read offered him. What he sees reflected in his own past is a man with a "long dormant craving to be mentally alive," but this realization about his former self is only possible because he can look back from the point of view of a self-educated man.

3. It is interesting that both Rushdie and Mphahlele use the image of a man with his legs spread to suggest their dual position between their cultures of origin and the Western world. Mphahlele says in paragraph 2, "It is not as if I were pinned on a rock, my legs stretched in opposite directions." Rushdie claims that expatriate Indian writers sometimes "feel that we straddle two cultures; at other times, that we fall between two stools" (12). Although Rushdie and Mphahlele appear to disagree about whether Western educations

57

create psychological rifts for writers, in fact both agree that there are significant advantages for writers who "straddle two cultures." Rushdie claims that since literature provides one way to "enter reality," the expatriate writer is in an especially good position since his dualism allows him to see from new angles. Mphahlele writes that a Western education creates conflicts for the writer, but that depending on his "innate personality equipment," the writer must "strive toward some workable reconciliation inside himself" (2). Both Rushdie and Mphahlele, then, see that the conflicts felt by a writer between cultures also provide opportunities for a new and stronger understanding of the self and the world.

**AMY TAN, Two Kinds (p. 246)**

**Explorations**

1.  Students will find it easy to come up with several meanings for the story's title. One of the most obvious meanings is revealed late in the story, when Jing-mei's mother shouts "Only two kinds of daughters. . . . Those who are obedient and those who follow their own mind!" (para. 75). The mother's denial that Jing-mei could be obedient in some ways and independent in others reflects the all-or-nothing thinking that affects every aspect of her relationship with Jing-mei. The mother believes that one is either a genius or "not trying." Initially, Jing-mei accepts her mother's view and thinks that she "would soon become perfect" (10). At times Jing-mei views herself as divided into two kinds — the prodigy and the failure. This interpretation of "two kinds" is reinforced by the contrast between Jing-mei and Waverly, who tells Jing-mei, "You aren't a genius like me" (62). But Jing-mei has already had a moment when she sees herself as "angry, powerful" (19). She realizes that the "prodigy side" of her is someone who can resist her mother. This doesn't resolve the conflicts embedded in the idea that there are "two kinds of daughters," but it is an important step toward integrating herself. Only much later, as an adult, can Jing-mei resolve the conflicts she and her mother battled over. In the closing paragraph, Jing-mei returns to the idea of "two kinds" when she looks back at "Pleading Child," the music she tried to play at the recital, and sees that opposite it is another piece, "Perfectly Contented." She recognizes that "they were two halves of the same song," a realization that helps her put to rest the conflicts between her mother and herself.

2.  The top goal of Jing-mei Woo's mother is to make her daughter become a prodigy. Most of her actions during the story show that her life focuses on this goal. She constantly watches television or combs magazines for stories about prodigies to see which possibilities are open to her daughter (4, 12). She drills Jing-mei every evening. Finally, she exchanges cleaning chores for piano lessons and scrapes together money to buy a secondhand piano. Although students may find the mother a domineering and repellent figure, understanding her motivations will help them see the issue of meeting parental expectations from alternate points of view. The mother sees America as a magical place where anyone can be whatever she wants to be: rich, famous, a prodigy (1, 2). From her point of view, she is asking her daughter to achieve a very reasonable goal that will help Jing-mei experience a happier life than she herself has known.

3. After only one reading, students will probably interpret this story as an example of mother-daughter or parent-child conflict. However, thoughtful students who reread it will notice that the narrator herself has different feelings about being a child prodigy. Because she often shares her mother's feelings, abandoning them only after she feels incapable of meeting her mother's expectations, the conflict between Jing-mei and her mother could be interpreted as an externalization of Jing-mei's own inner struggle. At first she "is just as excited as [her] mother, maybe even more so" (9). Her parents will adore her (10). But she also is anxious that the prodigy in her will disappear (11) and she will turn out to be an ordinary person. Her failure to succeed at her mother's examinations confirms her sense of being ordinary and makes her lose faith in the possibility of becoming a genius. At that point, she says, "something inside of me began to die" (18).

4. As long as her mother retains her faith in Jing-mei's ability to become a prodigy, Jing-mei does not completely give up hope for her own success. But her mother's abandonment of hope confirms Jing-mei's inability to escape being ordinary. Furthermore, the mother is so constantly hopeful, so convinced that "there were so many ways for things to get better" (3), that the loss of this faith implies she has been defeated. By offering the piano back to her daughter, she makes Jing-mei feel that she can never completely lose faith in her.

## Connections

1. Rushdie uses the device of the broken mirror to convey the quality of the emigrant's memory, which he believes achieves a partial view of former places and former selves. The emigrant's memory mixes reality and fiction to create "imaginary homelands." Early in "Two Kinds," the narrator Jing-mei recalls her mother's life in China, where she had lost her entire family and her home (para. 3). This tragic part of her mother's history is significant to Jing-mei in part because it means that she, Jing-mei, will be expected to fulfill "all my mother's hopes." This is, of course, far too big a burden for Jing-mei to carry. The mother's selective vision allows her to see America only as a place to become "anything you wanted to be," which demonstrates that she is seeing the present, as well as her past, reflected in a "broken mirror" that gives back only a partial image. Jing-mei uses the little she knows about her mother's former life to separate herself from her mother. She tells herself, "I wasn't her slave. This wasn't China" (67). And, most painfully, she recalls the children her mother lost in China and uses this to further distance herself from her mother. After telling her "I wish you weren't my mother," Jing-mei shouts, "I wish I were dead! Like them" (78).

2. Like So Tsi-fai, Jing-mei Woo cannot realistically meet her parents' expectations. Jing-mei's mother is unrealistic in her belief that her daughter already possesses the answers to the grueling nightly quizzes (12–20) or that just working hard produces a prodigy (28). The concept of talent does not exist for her. Like Jing-mei Woo, So Tsi-fai is his family's "biggest hope" (6). His education might liberate him from a life of poverty and toil. Listing the conditions that make her feel that he could not succeed in escaping his condition, Liu describes him as "poor, undisciplined, and lack[ing] the training and support to pass his exams" (18). Both Jing-mei Woo and So Tsi-fai appear to be lazy and rebellious but behave this way to provide excuses for failure. So Tsi-fai commits suicide by drinking insecticide (9); Jing-mei Woo figuratively destroys herself by a humiliating display of her lack of achievement (54–56).

3. Jing-mei Woo's mother in "Two Kinds," Sister Marie in "So Tsi-fai," and Rosaura's mother in "The Stolen Party" try to change the outlook of the central character in each story. They belittle the children's inability to accept their adult point of view and try, through disparaging comments, to reduce them to obedience. Although Rosaura's mother seems the most sympathetic to the feelings of her child, wanting to spare her humiliation at the hands of outsiders, Herminia sneers at Rosaura's belief in the monkey (1) and criticizes her for thinking too highly of herself (4). Sister Marie, having no sympathy for So Tsi-fai, constantly criticizes him, calling him lazy and good for nothing. She exercises her authority by standing him in the corner and making him report to the principal's office, yet can't make him change his behavior (3). Jing-mei Woo's mother also criticizes her daughter, convinced she is not trying (28). Like Sister Marie, she does not hesitate to react with physical punishment (33) in an equally vain attempt to control the situation. Students can see that explanations for the adults' failure would vary from culture to culture. In our culture, we would probably feel that people respond better to positive incentives.

4. Students will easily pick out points of comparison between the two, for Jing-mei Woo seems to fit Sheehy's description of an adolescent who seeks and fears autonomy. Just as described by Sheehy, Jing-mei covers her fear of failure "with acts of defiance and mimicked confidence." She has "thoughts filled with lots of won'ts" (19), and her whole piano performance mimics the behavior of the girl on "The Ed Sullivan Show." Like the adolescent Sheehy describes who pretends to know what she wants, Jing-mei has made up her mind to assert her own identity, vowing "I won't let her change me" (19). But she still feels very much a part of her family, sharing the shame she inflicts on them (56). Jing-mei can consciously reject her mother, trying to hurt her by saying she wishes she wasn't her daughter, but this statement also scares her, since she is not ready to break all of her family ties (75).

## CHRISTOPHER REYNOLDS, Cultural Journey to Africa (p. 258)

### Explorations

1. This will be an easy question for most students because Reynolds begins his essay by defining Culturefest and its purposes. Culturefest 1992 was designed to establish cultural connections between African-Americans and the continent of Africa. Reynolds follows several African-Americans at Culturefest as they seek "roots and cultural resonances," (para. 2) and he quotes one participant who defines Africa as "the final link to the souls of our ancestors" (5). Their search for that link is complicated, since they find Abidjan a rich, chaotic mix of contemporary western and African influences (2). Students will also readily find information about the tactics participants use to discover connections between Africa and themselves. The Americans search through Abidjan (12), take a tour of working-class areas (17-20), try to get to know local people (24), and attend an initiation (29-32). One woman decides to buy property on the Ivory Coast (26), and another successfully barters at the market (27).

2. Perhaps the best reason for choosing the Ivory Coast as the site for Culturefest is its position as a "continental crossroads" where sixty ethnic groups and over 2 million

migrants from other West African countries have made their homes. "On this ground," Reynolds says, "a black American inevitably stands among distant kin" (8). In discussing the question of why a luxurious, Western-style hotel was chosen as the tour's headquarters, students who have also read Atwood's "A View from Canada" or Octavio Paz's "Hygiene and Repression," both in this volume, will recall that, unlike travelers from some other nations, people from the United States are often uncomfortable unless they feel they have brought their own culture and environment with them. One of the tour organizers comments that Americans need "an adjustment period" when they arrive (11), but it may be that the tour organizers realized that they would attract more participants if the Americans knew they would be staying in a modern hotel with all the amenities (9).

3. Reynolds does not go into the history and geography of the Ivory Coast until after he has introduced Culturefest and some of its American participants (1–6). He offers more background information on Abidjan and its economy in paragraphs 9 and 14. Most students will easily see that if Reynolds had discussed the "facts" first, readers would have been lost and unable to understand why this background information would be significant or interesting. In analyzing the rhetorical impact of Reynolds's organizational choices, it will also be important to point out that Reynolds is economical in his use of history and geography, selecting only those facts that contribute to the purpose of his essay, which is to follow the cultural journey of African-Americans as they seek a link to the Africa their ancestors left on slave ships.

## Connections

1. To help students get into the spirit of this question, it may be helpful to begin by asking them to reflect on their own immigrant heritage. Most students will be able to identify one or more homelands from which their ancestors came. Jing-mei Woo has powerful connections to China because of her mother's history, but even those students who no longer have immediate ties to a far-away homeland may be able to comment on how their ancestors' origins in (for instance) Asia, Europe, or Africa have contributed to their own identity and sense of kinship. Ironically, Jing-mei Woo experiences her ancestral homeland, China, as something that separates her and her mother. The memory of the children and other family her mother lost before she left China (paras. 3, 78) is a burden Jing-mei carries, because she feels that she can never be as good or as worthy as those her mother loved in China. Some of those who joined Culturefest 92 expressed the benefits of re-establishing ties to Africa: "cultural resonance" (2), spiritual awakening (5), sense of kinship (4), and a more tangible connection to history (6).

2. Unlike those who came to the Ivory Coast for Culturefest, Rushdie has memories of Bombay from his own childhood. However, he wants to "restore the past to myself . . . in CinemaScope and glorious Technicolor" (2). Rushdie readjusts his vision to accommodate the differences between his expectations of reality and what he actually finds in Bombay; similarly the African-Americans who went to Africa have to adjust their expectations — sometimes drastically — in order to comprehend the realities of Abidjan (11). Rushdie describes Bombay as "a city built by foreigners upon reclaimed land" (3); Abidjan also shows the effects of Western and Asian influences (2), a factor that some African-American visitors found disorienting initially. Rushdie, however, affirms the validity of "imaginary homelands," (4) which arise because physical alienation from his

nation of origin sets him free to construct "'my' India" (5). Similarly, one of the African Americans who visited the Ivory Coast later realized that "I found my Africa" (32).

3. Western, African, and other cultural influences overlap in Reynolds's depiction of Abidjan, beginning in paragraph 3 with the mention of skyscrapers, taxis, urban streets, and French restaurants intermingled with coconut trees, fishermen, and a woman bearing her laundry on her head. Later in the essay, Reynolds again demonstrates how Western and African influences intermingle when he mentions the French boulevards and American billboards amid "an enduring pattern of village life" (12). But perhaps the most important Western influence is the Hotel Ivoire, where the American participants in Culturefest stay. They venture out to investigate the African landscape and sample its culture, but at night they return to a familiar environment. Similarly, V. S. Naipaul begins his essay, "Entering the New World," by recounting his meeting in an Abidjan hotel with Ebony, and he ends his essay with a scene at a French restaurant in another part of the city. Like Reynolds, Naipaul sees Western and African cultural influences as interwoven, but for Naipaul it is Ebony himself who brings the two cultures together. In Naipaul's eyes, the mix of cultural influences in Ebony has produced uneasy results. Ebony has entered the "new world," but Naipaul does not believe Ebony takes seriously the effects of the Western influence on the Ivory Coast (18). By the end of the essay Naipaul is beginning to doubt that the "new world" has really made an impact: "Remove those men [the Europeans], and their ideas — which after all had no finality — would disappear" (22).

Students should have few problems locating the features Western visitors might find most and least attractive about Abidjan, because Reynolds has summed them up in the comments of two African-American Culturefest participants. One says that her visit to the Ivory Coast is "like a vacation from racism" (15), but in the next paragraph another woman lists the problems: squalor, deprivation, and the oppression of women. Naipaul conveys his opinions of the Ivory Coast through his observations of Ebony, whom he finds to be sociable (5) and "relaxed, a whole man" (18), even as he is irritated by Ebony's apparent intellectual dilettantism (10, 18). The more difficult problem, for most students, will be interpreting the differences in Reynolds's and Naipaul's assessments. One way to approach this question is to consider the differences in how Reynolds and Naipaul represent themselves in their essays. Reynolds says nothing about his own experience in Abidjan and does not give his opinions directly. He uses quotes from others, conveying their sense of the attractions and problems of the Ivory Coast. Naipaul, on the other hand, is a participant in the events he describes, and his emotions and opinions are apparent throughout "Entering the New World." Another way to approach this problem is to have students consider the cultural differences between the writers. Naipaul was originally from Trinidad but now lives in England. His focus is on European influences and their effects on African culture. Reynolds takes an American perspective, seeing the Ivory Coast through the eyes of people whose ancestors were once slaves in the United States and who now want to regain a sense of connection to African culture.

4. In "The Westernization of the World," Paul Harrison writes that China, Japan, and Turkey began to study and even embrace Western culture and technology as a way of dealing with the threat of Western military power and obtaining some of the benefits of industrialization (14, 15), but he also argues that the adoption of Western culture in many nations is producing "world uniformity" (6). In Reynolds's essay, Culturefest 1992 also represents a form of cultural borrowing, but the motivations and the results are very

different. The African-American visitors to the Ivory Coast are not seeking to draw power from a dominant but alien culture by adopting its ways; many are looking for general connections to their ancestors, who were enslaved by one of the most powerful Western powers, the United States. Their "borrowing" from African culture is not a movement toward "world uniformity," but an attempt to understand and appreciate the highly diverse mixture of cultures in Ivory Coast.

## GÜNTER GRASS (Grahss), After Auschwitz (p. 264)

### Explorations

1. Most students will know that Auschwitz was one of the concentration camps where the Germans interned about 4 million people, most of whom were Jews. Many Jews were exterminated at Auschwitz by phenol injections, gas, and other means. For these reasons, Auschwitz has come to symbolize the appalling crimes of the Holocaust as a whole. Günter Grass calls up vivid images of the horror of Auschwitz when he describes photographs of dead bodies and piles of hair and shoes he was forced to view in an American prison camp (para. 6). The personal meaning that Auschwitz has for Grass arises from his confrontation with the realities of what occurred there. He thinks of Auschwitz as a "monstrous phenomenon" that goes "beyond facts and figures, beyond the cushioning academic study, a thing inaccessible . . ." (8). For Grass, Auschwitz marks the beginning of his adulthood, the point in his own life when he had to rid himself of the illusions of his youth (7) and begin to consider the social and political responsibilities of himself as a writer (9).

2. Students will be better able to discuss Grass's involvement with National Socialism if they first understand that "National Socialism" is synonymous with "Nazi" (the German acronym for the party). Its main goal was to establish Aryans as a "master race" under the leadership of the Führer, who would purify the "race" by exterminating Jews and Communists, among others. As a boy, Grass was a member of the Hitler Youth (7) and recalls "campfires, flag drills, shooting practice with small-caliber weapons (25). By the time World War II began, he had been "rendered stupid by dogma" (3) — a reference to the ideologies of National Socialism. He marks the Nuremburg trials as symbolic of his disillusionment with the party (7), but his artistic impulses had already caused him, earlier in his life, to doubt his commitment to the Hitler Youth (10). After World War II, Grass rejected National Socialism completely: "the anti-Semitism of one's youth was exchanged for philo-Semitism, and one defined oneself unquestioningly and without risk as antifascist" (15). National Socialism became identified with Auschwitz, which strongly influenced the development of Grass's literary and artistic career. He agreed with Theodor Adorno that it was an "irreparable tear in the history of civilization" (16), and he considered himself to be implicated in the crimes that the Nazis committed (22). In many of his books, Grass promoted the "demonization of the Nazi period" (29), and he became involved in politics (30).

3.  Grass asserts that efforts to reunify Germany took impetus from a general desire among people in Eastern and Central Europe for the economic and political advantages that "solidarity and freedom" would bring (36). But he believes that this general hope for European unity was "twisted into German aspirations. Once again the call is heard for 'all of Germany'" (37). Grass opposed reunification because Auschwitz would not have been possible without "a strong, unified Germany" (38).

4.  Students should be able to come up with multiple responses to this question, but they should begin by considering the occasion and audience for Grass's speech. In paragraph 2, Grass identifies his audience as students. He is speaking at a Frankfurt university. Grass describes his audience as "innocent" because they did not grow up under an active Nazi influence as Grass did. Grass considers himself a "witness" (1) to the Nazi era, and in that role he is able to give Germany's young people a vivid and firsthand account of what it was like to go through a conversion from the Aryan supremacist ideologies of National Socialism to his mature, solidly antifascist stance. The university evidently invited Grass as a famous writer to talk about his professional and personal development. They may also have asked him to speak because "those who do not learn from history are condemned to repeat it." Concerned about the possibility of a resurgence of Nazi sympathies in a unified Germany, the West German university may have invited Grass because he could speak out against the Nazis from the unique position of someone who once accepted Nazi ideology unquestioningly. Grass represents the process by which he was converted as a process of maturing. It was as an embarrassingly credulous boy that he was indoctrinated (25); as he became a man, he learned to recognize the truth and reject the propaganda he was force-fed as a member of the Hitler Youth. This perspective might appeal to university students who are themselves in the process of becoming adults and learning to recognize and accept the harsher realities of their own history.

## Connections

1.  One way to approach a discussion of the basic differences between Grass's efforts to reclaim a lost heritage and the efforts of African-Americans to seek their roots in Africa is to ask students to compare the different ways that racism is relevant to Grass and African-Americans. African-Americans — even the middle-to-upper class people who could afford the trip to Africa — cope on a daily basis with the economic, psychological, and social effects of racism directed against them. Grass, on the other hand, has not been on the receiving end of racism. Instead, in his youth he was a member of the National Socialist Party, which is founded on racist principles. Grass suffers guilt and embarrassment over his personal involvement (para. 25), and he lives with the knowledge that he belonged to a party that inflicted terrible harm on Jews and other groups. Some students may think that his task is the harder one, since he has spent his life seeking to keep alive a history that makes him feel ashamed. Others may think African-Americans have the harder task, since they are reaching back into a history and a homeland that was stolen from them when their ancestors were enslaved. Most will never be able to retrieve their personal heritage. Ultimately, it will be less important for students to debate the question of whose task is harder than to consider how the unique social and historical circumstances of Grass and African-Americans influence their efforts to reclaim a lost heritage.

2.  Sophronia Liu, Liang Heng, and Günter Grass all look back with a certain amount of guilt and regret at the tragic injustices they were associated with as children. Grass declares that he and other poets of his generation "belonged to the Auschwitz generation — not as criminals, to be sure, but in the camp of the criminals" (21). As an adult he has not renounced that sense of responsibility, but he has turned it to positive use, actively seeking to prevent National Socialism from rising to power again. Liang Heng suffered personally as a result of his mother's ostracism and the family conflicts that arose over her misfortune. In the last paragraph, Liang recalls that "over the years, I came to resent my mother for making my life so miserable. . . . I cut her out of my life just as I had been told to do." But as an adult, Liang understands that his mother was not responsible for what happened. He realizes, for instance, that she made every effort to mother her children in spite of her husband's abuse of her and her own difficult circumstances (36). Sophronia Liu felt deeply the impact of So Tsi-fai's death when she was in school, but as an adult she still confronts the ghost of So Tsi-fai (19) and asks herself "Is there anything I can do to lay it to rest?" In writing about his life and death from a sympathetic perspective, and refusing to write him off as unworthy of support and respect, Liu is taking an important step toward letting go of her own sense that she was, somehow, implicated in the tragedy.

3.  Among the revealing comments Rushdie makes about expatriate writers is that they "are haunted by some sense of loss, some urge to reclaim, to look back, even at the risk of being mutated into pillars of salt" (4). In the case of Sophronia Liu and Liang Heng, leaving their homelands may have left them with a sense of being haunted by the past (see Connections #2, above), but it has also given them enough distance to explore their memories from a clearer perspective than they might have had if they had stayed. Spending much of his life in the West has given Liang a more detached, but also more comprehensive, view of the political circumstances that caused his mother to be exiled. Similarly, Sophronia Liu uses the perspective gained in the process of maturing and coming to the United States for graduate school to reassess the tragedy that "close[ed] off a young boy's life at fourteen just because he was poor, undisciplined, and lacked the training and support to pass his exams" (18). Günter Grass's situation is very different from Liang's and Liu's, since he stayed in his homeland. Like Liang and Liu, Grass lost his youthful innocence because he was confronted with unthinkable injustices. Grass may have been, in fact, more in danger of being "haunted by a sense of loss" than Liu or Liang, since he continued to live amid the memories of Nazi Germany and has devoted so much of his artistic and political life to interpreting that era and its aftereffects.

## Yoram Binur (Bee-NOOR), Palestinian Like Me (p. 275)

### Explorations

1.  Binur began his impersonation in the hope of bringing a "fresh perspective" to his journalism (para. 3) but soon learned that when his perspective changed, he reevaluated what he already knew. As he puts it, "It wasn't a question of discovering new facts, but of discovering what it meant to *feel* the facts" (6). Suddenly he learns that Arab fear of

military patrols is not just an exaggeration (6); he becomes an "invisible" man (8, 9). By the end of the essay, he has developed a sympathy for the Palestinians and accepts that the Israelis mistreat them. Yet he does not conclude by pointing a finger or affixing blame. Instead, he uses his picture of the fear and mistrust on both sides to argue that continued Israeli occupation will lead only to an oppressive society and more bloodshed (52).

2. This essay presents a picture of the Israelis radically different from the one most people in the United States have encountered. Depending on the composition of the class, responses could include anger, disbelief, and a sense of vindication. To prevent students from limiting discussion to an emotional debate on the virtues of Jews versus Arabs, they might be asked to examine the feelings of Jews and Arabs in any given situation. (Their reactions are rarely based only on the situation at hand.) Binur concludes that Jews rule "without the least curiosity about how the other side lives" (52). If students can remain curious, without immediately taking sides, they may better understand how nationalism and religious and cultural differences contribute to the explosive situation in Israel. For instance, *sumud* and *intifada* would be defined quite differently by Jews and Arabs, depending whether these acts are viewed as threat or resistance. According to Binur, *sumud* is the most basic form of Arab resistance, based on the idea that to exist and not to be driven from one's land "is an act of defiance" (36). *Sumud* uses surreptitious actions to express hostility toward the Jews. For example, the Israeli government has housing erected on occupied lands as a symbol that they will never be returned to Palestinians. Palestinian workers build the houses, then damage them in a symbolic action (42). The *intifada* is a movement of anti-Israeli demonstrations in the Palestinian refugee camps. Binur presents the Arab view when he calls the *intifada* "the anguished cry of a minority trying to call attention to the discrimination that is being practiced against it." According to Binur, the Israelis see the *intifada* as riots (45).

3. Since Binur reports as a Jew disguised as an Arab, readers would not expect him to have a pro-Arab bias. If he corroborates Palestinians' statement of their position in Israeli society, he cannot be accused of exaggerating or fomenting discontent in support of a political cause. His evaluation is more devastating because his heritage and culture have trained him to reject this point of view. Had he written from a third-person point of view his essay would have been far less convincing. Binur had an intellectual awareness of the facts of Palestinians' lives, but he could not feel what those facts meant (6). By writing in the first person, he makes his readers share his experiences so that they can reach a new awareness of what it means to be a Palestinian in Israel.

## Connections

1. Binur is angry when he hears Abd Al Karim deny that Hitler killed the Jews, but he remembers that his Palestinian friends grew up in refugee camps, where they endured unrelenting violence and privation at the hands of Israeli Jews. Through his examples of his own and Muhriz's beatings by Israeli soldiers and policemen, Binur makes clear that what the Palestinians endure under Israeli rule has left them no room for understanding or tolerance. The German denial that the Holocaust took place has very different motivations. According to Günter Grass, when the facts about Auschwitz came out, many Germans said to each other, "Germans would never do a thing like that" (para. 5). They denied German responsibility because the Holocaust overturned the Germans' view of themselves as just and compassionate.

2.  The relationship between "symbol" and "substance" in Binur's essay is complex because Binur conceals the "substance" of his Jewish identity behind the "symbols" that differentiate Palestinians from Jews. Binur uses his knowledge of the Arabic language and the Palestinian culture as a mask in order to pass as a Palestinian. In a sense, Binur himself begins to mistake symbols for substance when, in the course of his undercover research, he internalizes "that paralyzing fear" that Palestinians live with daily (6). His ability to identify with Palestinians, and indeed his entire project, depends upon the tendency of people to judge identities by superficial evidence such as clothing. For instance, radical Jewish right-wingers — marked by beards and skullcaps — accost him at their demonstration because he is dressed in Arab clothes (22). They misidentify him as an alien because of the symbolic content of his apparel. Police discover the keffiyeh and take it as a further proof of his Palestinian identity; in fact, they are skeptical about the authenticity of his Israeli I.D. because they are misled by the symbols of his Palestinian identity (29). On the basis of these symbols, Binur is harrassed, beaten, and denied his civil rights. Another manifestation of the misinterpretation of symbols is suggested in Binur's account of the demonstrators' singing the Israeli national anthem. When Binur writes that they raise Israeli flags and sing the anthem as a "gesture in support of Jewish terrorists" (35), he indicates that he believes they are mistaking the symbol for the substance of patriotism.

3.  Students should easily be able to see the parallel between the shocking discoveries Baldwin and Binur make about the social and economic privations of minorities. Both recognize that the minority is exploited by the dominant group. In his Palestinian identity, Binur works in restaurants and garages (5); even Arabs with professional degrees are forced to do manual labor (37). Palestinians have to be able to "prove" their right to be on the streets at any given moment, as when Hussein checks to make sure he has his Israeli I.D. before going out to buy pita bread (11). What Baldwin discovers is similar to the displacement exemplified in the harrassment of Palestinians by the Israeli police; Baldwin writes, "It comes as a great shock . . . to discover that the flag to which you have pledged allegiance, along with everybody else, has not pledged allegiance to you" (1). Similarly, Binur writes that young Palestinians "get a whiff of the democratic privileges that Israeli citizens enjoy, but they cannot share in them" (51). One of the most basic differences in the kinds of racism Baldwin and Binur describe is demonstrated in Binur's ability to pose as an Arab. Binur, once he learns the language and something about the culture, can "pass" into Palestinian communities. The color-based racism Baldwin describes does not permit this kind of contact. Israeli racism has a religious and nationalist basis that American racism does not demonstrate.

## ADDITIONAL QUESTIONS AND ASSIGNMENTS

1.  In a journal entry or a collection of informal notes, refer to two or three of these selections to discuss initiation rituals as they apply to women. Consider such issues as perceptions of women's ability to assume responsibility, rules governing their behavior, support (or lack of it) from other women, and their obligations toward men. As you look over your notes, try to discover similarities and differences among the cultures represented. Can you come to any general conclusion about the image of women in a given culture?

2.  Many of the selections in Part 3 deal with how individuals break with the traditions and expectations of their culture as way of defining a new self or marking their entry into a new stage of maturity. Günter Grass's break with the National Socialist Party comes at a time when he is mature enough to face the harsh realities of nazism. As part of his process of maturing, he realizes that he cannot conform to the ideologies of the party. Yoram Binur discovers he can no longer conform to conventional Jewish attitudes about the Jewish-Palestinian conflict after he lives as a Palestinian. As a result, he redefines his Jewish identity. In a personal essay, discuss what role issues of conformity have played in your process of maturing. Using Grass, Binur, Tan, or Vargas-Llosa as a model, consider at what points in your life issues of conformity and nonconformity to conventional attitudes and beliefs have become important to your self-definition.

3.  One of the laments heard frequently today is that children are growing up too fast. Statistics reveal that problems with sexuality and substance abuse that used to be found in high schools now plague junior highs and middle schools. Parents complain that everything from rock videos to advertising encourages children to imitate adults. Using magazines and newspapers from the 1950s or the 1960s and from the present, compile information on what young people were wearing, doing, listening to, and buying. Organize the information into a paper in which you compare the attitudes and life-styles of young people in the two periods, focusing on two or three of the categories you've set up (for example, clothing, musical tastes, recreation). Emphasize in your paper the positive and negative features of the experience of young people in each period.

4.  Conduct further research into one of the cultures represented in this section, focusing specifically on the emergence from childhood to adulthood. It would be wise to choose a culture about which information is readily available — Germany, Argentina, China, and India are likely candidates. If the selection is an excerpt from a larger work, look first at that work. You can find other sources by consulting the headnotes for other selections from that culture (if there are any) and a general encyclopedia, as well as journals devoted to the study of that culture. Narrow your topic to something manageable — such as a particular rite of passage, the influences of religion on the culture's rites of passage, or the differences in rites depending on class or sex — and write an expository paper in which you elaborate on the culture's treatment of initiation from childhood to adulthood.

## Part Four

## WOMEN AND MEN:
## IMAGES OF THE OPPOSITE SEX

### INTRODUCTION

Given the backlash against feminism in recent years and the discomfort some college-age students feel about discussing gender issues, teaching this section may require a bit more energy than others. But the rewards will be well worth the effort. One of the more interesting characteristics of the section may serve as a useful introduction to the selections. The subtitle, "Images of the Opposite Sex," suggests that we don't always perceive men and women in realistic terms, choosing instead to affix labels to them. Among the excerpts in *Looking at Ourselves*, students will find references to "the madonna" as a "female prototype" (Allen); "Dead White European Males" (Jacobs); "female chauvinists" (Wright); and "the weaker sex" (Weitz). A class discussion of various contemporary terms for men and women may prove enlightening, easing the way into more complex analyses of related images in other cultures.

Among the selections themselves the story by Kemal may cause difficulties. It presents the same problem of stereotyping as does Sa'edi's in Part Two. The tendency to view Middle-Eastern women as victims and perpetuators of sex-based oppression can be countered, however, by assigning Cooke's selection before Kemal's. Her comparison of western perceptions of veiling with Islamic women's own perceptions should help balance stereotypes students may develop when they read about the abhorrent behavior exhibited by the villagers of Chukurova.

Within the section there are several possible subthemes, among them romantic visions of relationships (Silko, Kazantzakis, and Moravia), the role of women in Islam (Minai, Cooke, and Kemal), European versus Islamic views of sexuality (the preceding, as well as Fuentes, Bugul, Kazantzakis, Beauvoir, and Moravia), and state-controlled sexuality (Minai and Cooke).

Instructors may wish to consult the following familiar works in preparing related selections from *Ourselves Among Others*:

### Essays

Judy Brady, "I Want a Wife" (*Ms. Magazine*, Dec. 1971).
Annie Dillard, "The Deer at Providencia" (*Teaching a Stone to Talk*, Harper, 1982).
Gretel Ehrlich, "About Men" (*The Solace of Open Spaces*, Viking, 1985).
Barbara Lawrence, "Four-Letter Words Can Hurt You" (New York Times, Oct. 27, 1973).
S. J. Perelman, "The Machismo Mystique" (*Vinegar Puss*, Simon and Schuster, 1975).
Katherine Anne Porter, "The Necessary Enemy" (*Collected Essays and Occasional Writings of Katherine Anne Porter*, Delacorte, 1970).

Scott Russell Sanders, "The Men We Carry in Our Minds" (*The Paradise of Bombs*, University of Georgia Press, 1987).

Susan Sontag, "Beauty: How Will It Change Next" (*Vogue*, May 1975).

Deborah Tannen, "Different Words, Different Worlds" (*You Just Don't Understand*, Morrow, 1990).

Paul Theroux, "On Being a Man" (*Sunrise With Seamonsters*, Houghton Mifflin, 1985).

James Thurber, "Courtship Through the Ages" (*My World — And Welcome to It*, Harcourt, 1942).

## Short Stories

Margaret Atwood, "Rape Fantasies" (*Dancing Girls*, McClelland and Stewart, 1977).

Kay Boyle, "The Astronomer's Wife" (*Life Being the Best*, New Directions, 1988).

John Cheever, "The Country Husband" (*The Stories of John Cheever*, Knopf, 1978).

William Faulkner, "A Rose for Emily" (*Collected Stories of William Faulkner*, Random House, 1950).

James Joyce, "The Dead" (*Dubliners*, Viking, 1982).

D. H. Lawrence, "The Horse Dealer's Daughter" (*Complete Short Stories*, Penguin, 1976).

D. H. Lawrence, "Tickets, Please" (*Complete Short Stories*, Penguin, 1976).

Doris Lessing, "A Woman on a Roof" (*A Man and Two Women*, Simon and Schuster, 1963).

Alice Munro, "Meneseteung" (*Friends of My Youth*, Knopf, 1990).

Katherine Anne Porter, "Rope" (*Flowering Judas*, Harcourt, 1930).

Eudora Welty, "Petrified Man" (*The Collected Stories of Eudora Welty*, Harcourt, 1980).

## BIOGRAPHICAL NOTES ON LOOKING AT OURSELVES

1. Paula Gunn Allen, professor of English and American Indian Literature at the University of California, Los Angeles, is of Laguna-Pueblo-Sioux-Lebanese descent. She has written a novel *The Woman Who Owned the Shadows* (1983), a book of poems *Skins and Bones* (1988), a collection of essays *The Sacred Hoop: Recovering the Feminine in American Indian Tradition* (1986), and edited *Spider Woman's Granddaughters: Traditional Tales and Contemporary Writing by Native American Women* (1989) and *Grandmother of the Light: A Medicine Woman's Sourcebook* (1991).

2. Daniel Evan Weiss is the author of *The Great Divide: How Females and Males Really Differ* (1991).

3. The founder of *Ms.* magazine, Gloria Steinem is the author of a biography of Marilyn Monroe, *Marilyn* (1986), a collection of essays, *Outrageous Acts and Everyday Rebellions* (1983), and the controversial *Revolution from Within: A Book of Self-Esteem* (1992).

4. Joe Kane is a free-lance writer living in San Francisco.

5. Sally Jacobs writes for the *Boston Globe*.

6. Camille Paglia teaches humanities at the University of the Arts in Philadelphia. She is the author of *Sexual Personae: Art and Decadence from Nefertiti to Emily Dickinson* (1990) and *Sex, Art, and American Culture* (1992).

7.  Lawrence Wright has taught at the American University of Cairo and been a staff writer for the *Race Relations Reporter*. He is the author of *In the New World: Growing Up with America from the Sixties to the Eighties* (1987) and *Peace Report* (1991).

8.  A professor of sociology at Arizona State University, Rose Weitz is the author of *Labor Pains: Modern Midwives and Home Birth* (1988) and *Life with AIDS* (1991).

9.  Richard Goldstein, arts editor for the *Village Voice*, writes frequently about sexual politics. He is the author of *The Poetry of Rock* (a collection of rock lyrics) (1969) and more recently, *Reporting the Counterculture* (1989) and *Superstars and Screwballs: 100 Years of Brooklyn Baseball* (1992).

10. A professor of linguistics at Georgetown Univeristy, Deborah Tannen has written both scholarly works (*Conversational Style*, 1984; *Talking Voice*, 1989) and popular books (*That's Not What I Meant*, 1986; *You Just Don't Understand: Women and Men in Conversation*, 1990).

## Reflections

1.  Two common ideas emerge in these three pieces. The first is the importance of personal and social relationships in defining women's identities. Paula Gunn Allen writes that for an American Indian woman, "her sense of herself as a woman is first and foremost prescribed by her tribe." Rose Weitz implies that among lesbians, involvement in the feminist movement and the possibility of establishing egalitarian love relationships suggests a greater sense of connectedness than is possible for heterosexual women who are involved in hierarchical relationships. And Deborah Tannen, defining the differences between her and her husband's world view, writes that she approaches "the world as many woman do: as an individual in a network of connections." Unlike Weitz, Tannen sees the tendency to relate hierarchically in personal and social situations as a matter of gender rather than sexual orientation. The second common idea is developed in Allen's and Weitz's pieces. Both writers posit a contrast between Christian (or Western) images of "woman" and realities of women's lives. Allen remarks that the "female prototype" in the Christian world is "essentially passive;" women are portrayed as "mindless, helpless, simple, or oppressed." In American Indian cultures, by contrast, women are viewed "variously . . . as fearful, sometimes peaceful, sometimes omnipotent or omnis-cient. . . ." Weitz also points to the passivity and weakness inherent in images of women in Western culture and contrasts those images to the realities of lesbians' lives, since lesbians use their strengths to survive without "even the illusion of male protection that marriage provides." Weitz writes that the ability of lesbians to live without men "suggests the potential strength of all women" and implies that they can rise above stereotypical views of women as "the weaker sex."

2.  Richard Goldstein, writing about the history of male homosexual marriage, describes the common "image of homosexuals as emotional nomads." His piece attempts to balance that stereotype by offering evidence of attempts to establish long-term, publicly acknowledged relationships between male partners. By implication, Goldstein's descrip-tion of the image of gay men as incapable of emotional commitment and sensitivity extends to heterosexual men as well, a stereotype Wright addresses in his piece about his relationship with his daughter. Wright sums up the stereotyped view of men with a quote from Barbara Jordan, who said that "women have a capacity for understanding and

71

compassion which a man structurally does not have. . . ." Both Wright and Goldstein believe that the stereotypes of men are not accurate; that the campaign to legalize male-to-male marriage (Goldstein) and the efforts of men to nurture children (Wright) are evidence of men's attempts to achieve emotional intimacy in stable relationships.

3.  Lawrence Wright ascribes the positive traits (and negative traits) of being male to genes and hormones. He writes that men are naturally more assertive sexually, tolerate pain well, are tenacious, and adept at spatial reasoning. He goes on to say that "nature and human history have rewarded" men's strength and ability to act. Many of the pieces in *Looking At Ourselves* suggest that being a man entails many privileges, including greater representation in the media (Weiss), "greater opportunity and unparalleled privilege" in comparison with all women and men of color (Julian Bond, quoted by Jacobs), and far greater freedom to experience "solitary adventure" (Paglia). Most writers seem to depend for the most part on what they believe are obvious or commonplace truisms about being a white male in western society. Wright bases some of his ideas on interpretations of scientific evidence about the effects of androgens, and Weiss simply offers the facts of gender-differentiated representation on television. Paglia relies on personal opinion and anecdote. Jacobs uses interviews with both men and women to back up her generalizations about the advantages of being white and male.

4.  Students will be able to elaborate on their responses to Question #1 as they consider the positive qualities of women and the advantages of being female. Allen, Weitz, and Tannen make the case that women are able to function well as members of families and communities because they value connectedness and see themselves as situated within networks of relationships rather than in hierarchies. Although he is critical of some feminists, Lawrence Wright makes some positive generalizations about women, saying they have brought "humanity" into business and politics and they have a greater ability to survive physically because of their genetic makeup. Gloria Steinem and Sally Jacobs imply that all women, because they deal with gender oppression, are more sensitive to the ways in which other people are oppressed.

## CARLOS FUENTES (Fwen-tays), Matador & Madonna (p. 303)

### Explorations

1.  Students may tend to differentiate between the qualities that make the figure of the matador a model of Hispanic manhood and those qualities that make him Christlike, but Fuentes implies early in his essay that they share qualities. In paragraph 4, Fuentes asks, "Who is the matador?" and immediately responds, "a man of the people." The bullfight is a popular phenomenon. The matador, like Christ, represents a sacrifice made for the common people rather than the aristocracy (paras. 2, 4). In that sense he unites the qualities associated with Jesus Christ and the gentler qualities that are associated with Hispanic manhood, such as courage, grace, and self-sacrifice. Fuentes goes on to describe the sexual energy of the matador and the blood lust of the ritual bullfight (5) — qualities not associated with Christ — but in the next paragraph he again connects the qualities of Hispanic masculinity with Christ, declaring that the matador is "a prince

of the people" and the bullfight "an opening to the possibility of death." In paragraph 9, Fuentes makes the connection more explicit, describing Goya's painting of matador Pedro Romero and associating "the virgin body of this perfect bullfighter" with the wounded and dying Jesus Christ.

2. Both la Dama de Baza and la Dama de Elche are pre-Christian Spanish mother figures (10, 11), making them antecedents to the Virgin Mary, the figure in whom their qualities were later embodied. La Dama de Baza is an earth goddess, a figure of "maternal authority" (10), while la Dama de Elche is an erotically powerful figure (11). However, the quality Fuentes most wants to highlight in the pre-Christian earth goddesses is their ambiguity — they are all "mysterious, two-faced, tender and demanding, mother and lover . . ." (12). The Virgin Mary inherited these qualities from her precursors (13). Fuentes sees this ability to adapt, to blend the pagan and the Christian, as inherently "Andalusian" (Andalusia is a region of Spain).

3. As students read this essay, they may become confused about what Fuentes is trying to accomplish by drawing connections among such disparate cultural and religious expressions as flamenco dancing, the bullfight, Jesus Christ, the Virgin Mary, and pre-Christian mother figures. In paragraph 8, Fuentes intimates his purpose when he describes as a "circle" the confluence of events on the Sunday of Resurrection, which inaugurates the season of bullfighting, prominently features flamenco dancing, and celebrates the Virgin Mary and Jesus Christ. Fuentes makes these connections conceptually, on the basis of the shared sense of redemption and resurrection, but he also makes them apparent in his use of certain words and images. The flamenco dancer is "inviolately chaste" (22) like the "virgin body" (9) of the matador. Both, nevertheless, appear in finery that emphasizes their sexual presence; the dancers' "bodies are swathed in frills, satins, silks, lace, complicated girdles, unimaginable underwear" (21) and the matador presents himself dressed in the "effrontery of the suit of lights, its tight-hugging breeches, the flaunting of the male sexual organ . . ." (5). The flamenco dancer embodies also the qualities of the Virgin Mary, being both "chaste" and erotically charged. In paragraph 24, Fuentes makes the analogy between the flamenco dancer and the Virgin explicit, writing that the dancer is "sexual turbulence clad in saintly longings, as exhibited by the Virgin figures carried through the streets of Seville."

## Connections

1. Students will be immediately able to identify the similarities between Fuentes's and Paula Gunn Allen's description of the madonna. Allen mentions the sexually charged quality of Western images of women, and she cites the madonna as the Christian (i.e., Western) "female prototype." She also emphasizes the passivity of the madonna, a quality immediately apparent in Fuentes's description of the sumptuously dressed effigies of the Virgin Mary men carry through Seville during the Easter week celebration (paras. 15–17). However, whereas Allen sees the madonna as representing a limited power of birth, Fuentes sees in her maternity a greater range of meanings and powers. These meanings are most apparent in Fuentes's description of the pre-Christian mother/temptress figures from whom the Virgin Mary inherited many of her qualities. The madonna is associated with birth and death (10); she actively demands loyalty and obedience (10, 12) and is a sexually powerful figure (12). The differences between Allen's and Fuentes's characterization of the madonna is due in part to their cultural differences. Allen attaches

greater value to mythic Native American female figures because her purpose is to resist the assimilation of those figures into the madonna. As a figure that represents the dominant Western European culture, the madonna, in Allen's view, personifies the repression of strong powers associated with female figures in some traditional Native American tribes.

2.  In order to help students evaluate the cross-cultural connections and differences among male initiation customs, discussion might begin with students describing the ways in which the young men in their communities "prove" their masculinity. It is unlikely that American boys fight bulls in the dark, as Fuentes says Spanish villagers do, or compete to see whose body and spirit will give out first swimming out to sea, as Miguel and Rubén do in "On Sunday," but chances are many students will recognize in American male initiation customs the quality these feats share: bravado, competitiveness, and disregard for personal safety. Fuentes describes how amateur bullfighters partake of the "incredible arrogance" of the bullfighter by stealing into rich men's fields to fight the bulls at night, when neither the bulls nor the toreros can see their opponents well. In "On Sunday," the drunken Miguel and Rubén goad each other into a swimming contest on a cold night when they cannot see the surf or judge direction.

3.  Both the *quinceañera* and Holy Week celebrate an ideal, Christian femininity. Orlean describes the basic events of the quinceañera as an affirmation of a girl's commitment to the Catholic Church and her introduction into society — emphasizing the significance of the quinceañera as both a religious and a social initiation for girls (2). The girls are dressed up for the occasion in expensive gowns for which their parents sometimes go into debt (12). The Holy Week custom of dressing effigies of the Mother of God in finery such as "A great triangular cape contrived with the most elaborate ornamentations of ivory and precious stones . . ." (17) also presents an image of ideal, virginal femininity exalted by opulent clothes and a public celebration.

## LESLIE MARMON SILKO, Yellow Woman (p. 312)

### Explorations

1.  The difficulty for students in this story lies in understanding the reason the narrator, a married woman, decides to follow a stranger to his home. Students may be too easily satisfied with believing she is coerced by his strength, which he demonstrates when he holds her wrist and says, "Let's go" (para. 26). However, students should not discount her uncertainty that he may be a character from the mythical world, an idea that possesses power over the narrator. She does not dismiss the tales of her culture as mere stories, as students may do. She hopes to meet someone along the way — a mythical character who would not reveal himself to anyone but her. Silva presents himself as a mythical figure, reinforcing her tendency to believe. Later, when they both meet the rancher, the nonmythical world intrudes. Suspicion that Silva murders the rancher, coupled with her fear of his strength, outweighs her desire for him, and she decides to return home.

2.  Silva is presented through the eyes of the narrator, whose only title here is "Yellow Woman," a reference suggesting that Silko, too, may view her as a character in a myth.

The narrator sees Silva as physically strong, acquainted with the stories of his culture, and adept at the traditional skills of riding and hunting. She fears his strength yet finds him sexually attractive (56). Later on she finds him "strange" (90), a term that applies equally well to mythical figures and social misfits. The rancher considers Silva a thief and rightly fears for his own life (81, 85).

3. At several points the narrator directly states her feelings about Silva. In paragraph 56 she says she is afraid of him and also mentions a desire to kiss him. At the story's end she states she is sad to leave him (90) and wants to go back and kiss him (91). She conveys her feeling indirectly on other occasions. Her heavy breathing in paragraph 52 reveals her sexual excitement. In paragraph 88 she states, "I went that way because I thought it was safer." Since it was not safer for the horse, she must be talking about her own safety and implying her desire to flee from Silva and the violent encounter.

4. At the end of the story, as she returns to the ordinary world of her home and family, the narrator has almost buried the mythic identity of "Yellow Woman." Silva is no longer present to address her by this name; her family will call her by "another name" (21). She decides to tell her family the realistic story, knowing that only her grandfather would believe in the "Yellow Woman" story. However, even as she confronts the mundane aspects of the "real" world — her mother and grandmother discussing Jell-O, the smell of cooking, her husband Al — she still believes in the mythic truth of her story. The time she spent with Silva will remain for her a rich mix of myth and everyday reality, bringing her closer to her Laguna heritage.

## Connections

1. References to Yellow Woman and the ka'tsina appear throughout Silko's story, and students will be able to draw a variety of meanings from them. Silva first calls the narrator "Yellow Woman" in paragraph 12, playfully refusing to give in to her more prosaic view of their encounter. Later, she asks if he always uses the same tricks to lure women to his house (34). Judging from these comments, the ka'tsina is a trickster who uses his wit to get what he wants. Silva also seems to have the power to captivate. He uses song (28), sex, and the old stories to entice her to stay with him. But his seduction is interlaced with coercion (55, 56), making him a complex and disturbing representation of the ka'tsina. Yellow Woman is also a fluid figure, appearing in stories as a desirable and desiring sexual being (19), as being settled in her own home (19) and ready to run away with a man (22). Both live out of time; as the narrator feels herself drawn further into the myth, she has to make an the effort to remember the reality of "yesterday and the day before" (40). Silva displays much of the "incredible arrogance" and sexual powers shown by the matador Fuentes describes (5). Like the torerillos in Fuentes' essay who illegally fight rich men's bulls by night (5), Silva takes advantage of the rich when he steals and butchers their cattle (44–46). The narrator, by contrast, plays a passive role. Even when Silva leaves her alone in the cabin, she doesn't go, mesmerized by the myth of Yellow Woman and her desire for him. Yellow Woman, like the Spanish mother figures (including the Virgin Mary) Fuentes describes (10–12), displays a certain passivity, sexual fascination, and a generous nature (19).

2. Jacobs describes the stereotype of white men as "imbued with privilege" and "out of touch" with the rest of the world (7). She quotes Playboy columnist Asa Baber, who says that white men are defined as "healthy, wealthy, and oppressive" (8). Jacobs herself

points out that white men are indeed still occupying most positions of power (9) in our society. However, the main point of Jacobs's piece is that white men are afraid of all the "others," who they believe are trying to usurp their power (15). The white rancher in Silko's story is fat, suggesting wealth and the greedy consumption of resources. He invokes the law (84) and tries to assert the symbolic power of his race over the Indian, whom he looks down on for being a thief. The Indian feels no respect for the white man's law. He is well armed and confronts the rancher fearlessly, epitomizing the threat feared by the white men in Jacob's piece who worry that those who are not like them will appropriate their privileges.

3. Both Yellow Woman and Soyinka accept the idea that mythical and physical worlds coexist. But Yellow Woman looks positively on the appearance of a "mythical" figure. She would prefer Silva to be a ka'tsina spirit; she worries that he may be a real, and perhaps dangerous, man. In Soyinka's story, spirits appear as part of the child's daily life, but he fears them and sees them as dangerous. The different reactions most logically result from the attitudes handed down by each narrator's family. Yellow Woman's grandfather loved the stories he told. Also the tales told within Silko's story do not show that human beings are threatened by mythical ones. However, Soyinka's family has a great fear of the spirit world and warn the children to keep away from the place the spirits inhabit. Soyinka's mother later relates the harm spirits can cause when not obeyed.

## NIKOS KAZANTZAKIS (Kah-zahn-zah-kis), The Isle of Aphrodite (p. 322)

### Explorations

1. This question will help students clarify Kazantzakis's premises, which might be difficult for some students to identify, given his lyrical style of writing. In paragraph 4, Kazantzakis describes passing "from Jehovah's camp to the bed of Aphrodite," a phrase that explicitly identifies the deities involved and suggests their differences. Jehovah, the Judean god, is in Kazantzakis's representation harsh and demanding, while Aphrodite, Greek goddess of love, is earthy and ready to be pleased with humanity. The journey through the Judean mountains — Jehovah's camp — was "abrasive," while the destination, Aphrodite's bed, is inviting. He defines the water over which he makes the final leg of this journey as giving rise to the "feminine" mystery of Aphrodite, suggesting the gender differences between the two deities and their relation to the natural world (para. 4). The "feminine" force associated with Aphrodite is natural and inevitable; he equates it with gravity and the tendency of things and people to return to the earth (5). The force he associates with Jehovah is opposed to the feminine; it is "contrary to nature," urging people to overcome human nature and rise above earthly concerns.

2. All through "The Isle of Aphrodite," Kazantzakis is looking for evidence of the goddess. He sees her reflected in the face of Maria, from whom he seeks directions to one of the holy places associated with Aphrodite. Kazantzakis also identifies the proprietor of a tavern as an "earthy, all-enchanting Aphrodite" (27), but soon he seeks a more personal experience of the goddess. As he approaches the temple, he finds that Aphrodite has been "resurrected" within him and feels that when he enters the temple he is coming

home (39). Thus, although he identifies Aphrodite as his "mistress," in a sense he becomes the goddess.

3. Students will be able to build on their responses to the previous questions as a way of discerning the meaning to Kazantzakis's dream. He associates Aphrodite with the earth, and therefore with mortality; Jehovah is a god concerned only with the afterlife, but Aphrodite inhabits the earth and, as he comes closer to her temple, seems to inhabit the narrator as well. The memory of the headless male insect being eaten by the female reinforces the idea of his vulnerability and mortality; the image of the warrior's head on the ring stone (46) once again reminds him of this disturbing memory. The dream in the last paragraph contains the image of a rose, a symbol of love and therefore, also a symbol of Aphrodite. It is a black rose, associated with death, an image that recalls associations Kazantzakis has made throughout the essay between the inevitable forces of the earth (gravity and mortality) and the promises and demands of love (the goddess Aphrodite).

4. There is evidence in the first three paragraphs that Kazantzakis belongs to a Christian religion. He mentions "sin" and uses biblical phrases such as "the will of God" (2) and "glorify the Lord" (3). In paragraph 21, he asks a woman whether "religion" can identify the clay models of women found at Kouklia as either gods or devils. This question suggests that he is accustomed to seeking explanations from religious sources. However, Kazantzakis does not have complete faith in conventional religion, as his search for Aphrodite implies. When the woman he questions replies that their "poor religion" cannot explain the female gods, Kazantzakis does not refute her criticism. As he hovers between the two forces, the Judaic and the pagan, Kazantzakis continues to think in terms of the Judaic traditions. In paragraph 6, Kazantzakis wonders what his free will (a Christian concept) will lead him to do; he wants to distinguish between good and evil, and he continues to be concerned with establishing hierarchies of "virtues and passions."

## Connections

1. Both Silko and Kazantzakis begin their pieces with a moment in which the narrator is overwhelmed by the sense of being in a dream. Kazantzakis writes that "drowsiness and sweetness" overtook him and so he felt ready to let go and allow his heart to break loose (para. 1). Silko begins her story with the moment of her awakening at dawn and imagining that she is leaving Silva. She stays, however, and gives into the myth of Yellow Woman he enacts with her. She realizes that she has "no thought beyond the moment" (24) and only because of this can she give in to her own desires. The dreamlike openings of both Silko's and Kazantzakis's pieces creates an atmosphere of abandonment of the self and of everyday reality, allowing the narrators to be sexually aware and open.

2. In "Matador and Madonna," Fuentes describes la Dama de Baza, a pre-Christian earth goddess, as a figure of "maternal authority" (10). La Dama de Elche, on the other hand, is an erotically powerful figure (11). Either goddess might be compared to Kazantzakis's Pandemos Aphrodite, because both embody qualities similar to Aphrodite's. Fuentes describes them as "mysterious, two-faced, tender and demanding, mother and lover . . ." (12), while Kazantzakis describes Aphrodite, when she "lifts her veil" to him, as "unfathomable." He implies that her demands cannot be understood by human beings any more than by animals; she, like the pre-Christian goddesses Fuentes describes, is "two-faced" in that she represents both birth and death (43).

3. Both Paglia and Kazantzakis subscribe to the view that the sexes are in opposition to each other. Paglia says simply that "the sexes are at war," and Kazantzakis describes two opposing forces, one that pulls us toward earth (the feminine) and one that pulls us upward (the masculine) (5). Furthermore, Paglia describes male psychological development as a matter of overcoming "the overwhelming power of their mothers," a view confirmed in Kazantzakis's piece by his fear of being eaten alive by the feminine force represented by Aphrodite. However, Paglia identifies male sexuality as aggressive, while Kazantzakis identifies Aphrodite, a symbol of feminine sexuality, as voracious and demanding (41–43).

4. When the boys run to the beach, their feet obey "only a mysterious force which [seems] to come from deep in the earth" (Llosa, 131). But when Miguel dives into the water, he abides by the second of the two forces Kazantzakis describes; he strives to "conquer weight" (Kazantzakis, 5) and the limitations of his body. Llosa writes that Miguel had "forgotten how to ride the water without using force" and at first cannot let go and allow the waves to carry him out. In a sense, Llosa favors the first of Kazantzakis's "torrents," which is associated with giving in to natural forces. If Miguel was able to give in to the force of the water, he would be better able to stay afloat. Instead he fights it, allying himself with the second of the "torrents" Kazantzakis describes, which is associated with a struggle to leave the earth behind.

## SIMONE de BEAUVOIR (See-MONE deh BOW-vwar), Woman as Other (p. 329)

### Explorations

1. Students should find it interesting to note the many changes in attitudes since Beauvoir wrote her essay. Many will be unaware of the extent to which the position of modern women has changed from that of women of even twenty-five years ago, let alone those who were contemporaries of Beauvoir. Her plea for women to dispute male sovereignty was considered radical when she wrote it; now it's seen as a relatively moderate position. Similarly, her call to women "to refuse to be a party to the deal . . . to renounce all the advantages conferred upon them by their alliance with the superior caste" (para. 13) is now a standard of middle-class feminism. But students may also be surprised to see how many current issues have been the subjects of long-standing debate. While inroads have certainly been made, the resurgence of fundamentalism in the United States, coupled with the Catholic Church's vigorous denouncement of abortion and artificial birth control, has kept the issue of a woman's control over her body alive. Recent reports also suggest that while white, middle-class women in the job market are better off than they were ten years ago, they still earn substantially less than men for similar jobs. Thus the professional status of women has yet to be established. Furthermore, such recent developments as surrogate motherhood raise new questions about a woman's legal rights.

2. Students are sure to find many loaded expressions in the selection. A few of them are "woman represents only the negative" and "A man is in the right in being a man; it is the woman who is in the wrong" (2); the litany of antifeminists, beginning with Aristotle (2–

4); the comparison between women and Jews, blacks, and the proletariat (5, 8, 9); the analogy of the master-slave relationship (12); and the use of the term *castes* (13). Beauvoir's references, as well as her language and style, suggest that she is writing for an intellectual audience that may not accept her views. That she expects men to be reluctant to relinquish their power and women their comfort is clear in her frequent references to the collaboration of women in their own oppression.

3. It might be helpful for students to review their responses to the previous question before exploring this one. Audience is important here; although interviews allow us to identify with the subject more readily, and are normally more entertaining, they don't carry the same weight as references to classical scholars, respected authors, and renowned philosophers. Beauvoir is stating an intellectual case here; thus if she included interviews or eliminated references, she could be dismissed by her audience as a single voice arguing a case that may have a few current supporters but lacks broad, long-term merit.

## Connections

1. Kazantzakis would probably agree with Beauvoir's model of woman as Other, a model that implies that the existence of men needs no explanation or justification (para. 2), but that the existence of women must be explained and accounted for. Beauvoir recalls that "it is often said she [woman] thinks with her glands" (2) and that woman are associated with sex (3). Kazantzakis's representation of Aphrodite strongly associates her with nature, the physical body, and sexuality, as is suggested in his description of a woman he compares with Aphrodite. He describes her as "earthy" and "full-bodied with ample buttocks" (27). Throughout his essay, Kazantzakis uses images of women to help him understand his own fears and desires better, rather than considering women as subjects in their own right. This strategy accords with Beauvoir's contention that, from the point of view of men, "woman" exists only in relation to men (3).

2. In "Yellow Woman," the narrator moves between two worlds, that of her home with her husband and family, and that of the myths of the ka'tsina spirit and Yellow Woman. The narrator allows Silva to define her as "Yellow Woman," since he calls her by this name and she willingly plays the role of the woman who leaves her home and follows the orders of the ka'tsina spirit. Silva articulates her relationship to him when he tells her "You will do what I want" (55). This statement and the many commands he issues make their relationship resemble the master-slave relationship defined by Beauvoir. Still, the narrator does not seem to be entirely under Silva's control. Women in this story do not appear as the completely passive beings Beauvoir describes. The narrator has no qualms about leaving either her husband or Silva when she finds it convenient, showing she is not a possession of either. She is self-sufficient enough to arrive home on her own. Furthermore, the narrator would probably reject Beauvoir's reading of her situation. By identifying her story with the archetypal one, the narrator acquires in her own eyes some of the myth's power. She does not try to define herself against a male figure, but in terms of her culture, which places her in opposition to the white culture of the rancher.

3. Sally Jacobs quotes white men who view not only white women, but all people who differ from them, as Other. This oppositional thinking comes through in the first few paragraphs, where men discuss how women and minorities no longer care what white men think. Lawrence Wright opposes himself to "female chauvinists" who denigrate men (4). Camille Paglia maintains that young women have been misled by feminism to believe

that men and women are the same (1). She says, "The sexes are at war" (4) and puts the responsibility on women to protect themselves from naturally aggressive males (5). Gloria Steinem's story implies the discomfort men feel in the presence of female sexuality. Some may place Steinem in both categories, because the woman in her story clearly feels that the men she's in front of haven't experienced anything real in ages. Deborah Tannen differentiates her "connected" way of dealing with the world from her husband's "one-up or one-down" method. The recommendations are diverse: Steinem suggests positive thinking; Lawrence Wright believes that being a loving father to his daughter may help her to appreciate the differences between men and women; Rose Weitz, more radically, argues that lesbians, in allying themselves with other women, overturn the system that defines the hierarchy of sex-based power.

4.  The opening of Weitz's observation almost seems to summarize and paraphrase Beauvoir's interpretation of the division of power in the traditional male-female relationship and women's tendency to view each other as rivals rather than allies. Beauvoir argues for a realignment of power, for she implies that men and women need to exist in a complementary relationship. Weitz makes no such assumption about the necessity of male-female relationships. She argues that the "deeply ingrained traditional sex roles" make it unlikely that power will shift in heterosexual relationships. Weitz sees lesbian and gay relationships as possible, and indeed preferable, alternatives. She argues that when both partners are of the same sex, neither partner is assumed to be superior and egalitarian relationships are possible. When Beauvoir wrote her essay, she did not believe that a woman could feel more allegiance to another woman than to a man.

## ALBERTO MORAVIA (Mo-RAH-vee-ya), The Chase (p. 337)

### Explorations

1.  This selection provides an excellent example of the use of seemingly irrelevant material to establish the groundwork for the story itself. In the long opening section, Moravia introduces his narrator's love for wildness, as well as his conclusion that males destroy the very thing they profess to love. Without this section readers would have less of a sense of the narrator's celebration of life. His actions at the end of the story would seem incomprehensible.

2.  As he watches his wife board the bus in paragraph 8, the narrator recalls the hunting incident, and he does so again in paragraph 17 as he realizes that he can't confront her. In his present position he is like his father was at the hunt: He has the power to destroy the wild creature — and he is well aware of what comes of shooting a wild bird. He first thinks that he has no choice, that nature's mandate is to kill, but then he realizes what would result if he were to confront his wife and her lover. Ultimately he chooses the role of life giver rather than taker. In doing this he preserves a sense of power, but he also avoids the consequences he recalls from the hunting incident.

3.  It can be dangerous to ask students to extrapolate; too often they rely on their own experience and desires, rather than on the evidence in the story, to create sequels. If this question is handled carefully, however, the exercise will be valuable. A close reading of

the last sentence and the third paragraph make it quite clear that the narrator will never again follow his wife. He's giving in to her "wildness" in much the same way she is, refusing either to tame or to be tamed. He probably thinks that his knowledge will bring new vitality to his marriage.

## Connections

1.  That the narrator compares his wife to a wild bird is clear evidence of his perception of woman as Other. He is enthralled by her unpredictability and laments his newfound ability to understand her and predict her behavior. He wants his wife to be Other; he finds this quality highly erotic. He sees his wife's otherness in terms of power, which he possesses. (His decision to withhold his knowledge of her affair gives him tremendous power over her.) His wife would probably share his perception; when she senses the predictability of their marriage and the resultant waning of eroticism, she seeks eroticism elsewhere. Also, the manner of the meeting between her and her lover accentuates her desire to be perceived as wild and untamed.

2.  The key to this comparison probably lies more in the attitudes of the men about their marriages, even though the women are the partners who have temporarily left their husbands. Silko's narrator is attracted to Silva, but like the original Yellow Woman, will return home after her escapade. Indeed, in the myth Yellow Woman is rescued by her husband, who desires her return. Their marriage defines them as a continuing unit. The husband of the narrator in Silko's story may be upset by his wife's absence, but after hearing her explanation that she was kidnapped by a Navajo, he will not resent her departure and will welcome her back. The wife in "The Chase" is only temporarily unfaithful, but her husband cannot be satisfied with her unless she manifests wildness. Yet this quality depends on the narrator's seeing her actions as unpredictable, a situation unlikely to result in the context of a marriage which renders her behavior quite familiar. Therefore, students will probably conclude that the marriage in the Silko story shows more promise of continuing successfully.

3.  Both Moravia's and Kazantzakis's narrators are pursuing a feminine being; in both cases, the revelations they make at the end of the pursuit are disturbing and unanticipated. The narrator's revelation in "The Chase" has to do with the independence and unpredictability of his wife, who is not at all as "domesticated" as he believed her to be before he follows her to her assignation with another man. He accepts this revelation in part because it excites him to realize that his wife is still a passionate woman and he does not have the power to deprive her of her "wildness." The goddess Aphrodite that Kazantzakis pursues in his essay is similar to Moravia's representation of the narrator's wife as a mysterious, dangerous entity who is the essence of feminine unpredictability. The wife's wildness, however, is no more personal than Aphrodite's. Moravia writes that "wildness, always and everywhere, is directed against everything and everybody" (17). It is, therefore, a destructive force, although it makes her more desirable in the narrator's eyes.

344–353 (Text pages)

## KEN BUGUL (Boo-gull), The Artist's Life in Brussels (p. 353)

### Explorations

1. The most important element in Ken Bugul's definition of "bourgeois" is the idea that middle-class people lead a life of privilege. She learns from Jean how to be "liberal," but she is always observing "the artist's life" from the position of a partial outsider (para. 19). Ken Bugul finds the privileged life of Westerners "decadent" (45). She defines the life of the artist as "bourgeois" (41). For the most part, the "artists" Ken Bugul comes into contact with attend gallery openings, make small talk, and are more concerned with fashionable lifestyles than with the production of art (36). The economically privileged life of the middle class allows Jean to pursue at least the appearance of an artist's life, but it also allows him the freedom to leave behind tradition and experiment with unconventional relationships.

2. Students will be able to build on their discussion of Explorations #1 in responding to this question. The fact that Jean and Ken Bugul have never before had a serious talk (27) suggests the superficial nature of the life they are leading. Their life together is too fragile and lacking in trust to allow for serious explorations of their inner lives, so Jean's attempts to live out his homosexuality with Ken Bugul's cooperation and understanding is doomed. Ken Bugul's discomfort with the bohemian life and with Jean's homosexuality comes through, however, when she says that "all that had been so foreign to me remained foreign" (37). Many of her comments reveal discomfort and disillusionment. Soon, she recalls, "I had reached a point where I no longer knew where I stood at all. . . . I was the pawn whom these people needed to break free from an unacknowledged guilt" (44). Having smoked hashish for the first time, Ken Bugul begins to laugh, but it seems more like sobs (52). At last, after Jean explodes over François's interest in Ken Bugul, she feels that "these beings" are "no longer human" (69).

3. Ken Bugul's references to diverse social groups abound; she spends a good deal of time among gays and artists (38, 39). Western feminists receive a brief mention (54). She describes a restaurant where intellectuals, left-wing students, and hippies meet (46) and a party where she encounters people of many different nationalities living communally (48–50). Ken Bugul feels comfortable socializing with homosexual men, and she identifies in some ways with women like Laure, with whom she speaks "the same language" (40). But for the most part, Ken Bugul feels herself an outsider to Western culture. She says that her "compatriots seemed far away to me" (39), and she continues to think of Westerners in general as "them" (45).

4. In the first simile Ken Bugul uses in this section, the morning after she has waited all night for Jean dawns "like an erotic dream" (24), but she compares herself to an unused broom on a rainy day. It is significant that she compares herself to a homely, domestic tool; she feels neglected, like part of the furniture of Jean's home. The erotic dream, by contrast, belongs to the outside world, the world Jean moves in. In the next paragraph, Ken Bugul uses the metaphor of a bleeding wound to describe her heart. The shift from simile to metaphor, along with the vividness of the image, suggests that she is moving toward a more deeply felt expression of her unhappiness. In the following paragraph, she observes the steps Jean has painted black, and then she asks, "Had someone died?" The implication is that it is she, with her heart an open wound, whose death Jean's arrival has brought about.

82

## Connections

1. Moravia defines as wild anything that "is autonomous and unpredictable and does not depend upon us" (para. 2). Near the end of "The Chase," after he observes his wife kissing another man, he elaborates: "wildness, always and everywhere, is directed against everything and everybody" (17). Ken Bugul notices that Jean and François behave savagely when their triangle becomes more complicated with François's interest in Ken Bugul; her autonomy and unpredictability sharpen Jean's possessive interest, and the men are "wrangling with each other from within their most primitive instincts" (68). The wildness that comes out in each case is primitive, heedless, and potentially destructive, but it is also a quality that allows their deepest desires and fears to be expressed openly.

2. In Beauvoir's terms, Ken Bugul is very much the "Other" to Jean and François's "One." She is "the one they needed to better pass off their homosexuality" (62); she is, by the men's definition, a person who is significant not in her own right, but in relation to them and their needs. Jean's anger is not directed at Ken Bugul, because Jean cannot imagine that Ken Bugul has what Beauvoir terms an "authentic existence" (13). According to the philosophy of gender Beauvoir describes, authenticity belongs only to men, who are capable of self-determination. For this reason, Jean holds François, but not Ken Bugul, responsible for the night he and Ken Bugul spend together.

3. Both Senegal and the Ivory Coast gained independence from France in 1960. Ken Bugul's statement that she is not descended from the Gauls (the Roman name for the French) is the equivalent of Ebony's statement that Charlemagne is not his ancestor. Naipaul's rejoinder that he'd heard it said before is well supported by Ken Bugul's restatement of the idea. Both Ebony and Ken Bugul seek to define themselves as independent of French colonial influences that have distanced them from their own cultures. Both are also attracted by Western cultures, however, and both have received an education that has allowed them to enter the "new world."

## MARJORIE SHOSTAK, Nisa's Marriage (p. 354)

### Explorations

1. In response to Nisa's running away from her marriage, people tell her that a husband "becomes like your father or your older brother" (para. 8). At first, far from seeming like a member of her family, Tashay seems like someone who is trying to steal her away from her family. She asks her father, "Do I own [Tashay] that he follows me everywhere?" (20) But her father is quick to correct her, telling her that a woman follows her husband. Nisa refers to Tashay as "that person" and "this man," reinforcing the sense that he is a stranger. But eventually, after she begins to mature sexually and gets used to Tashay, she finds that she loves him and misses him when he goes away (48).

2. The beads and ornaments adorning her, the dancing and music, the ceremonial oil, the building of the hut, all the rituals of marriage are designed to signal the transition from child to woman. Bedecking the bride signals the change that is to come over her; the dancing signifies joy; the building of the hut symbolizes the creation of a new family unit.

The anointing with oil solemnizes the union of two people. (Students may wish to continue discussion of this question by considering the symbolic significance of the wedding rituals in their own culture.)

3. That the tribe relies on hunting can be seen in the community's informing Nisa that Tashay will not let her eat the meat of the animals he kills if she keeps crying (8). They are apparently a peaceful people whose main enemies are not other people but rather the animals around them (note that Nisa is frequently warned of the dangers of running away into the forest). The hunting-meat metaphor appears in Nisa's mother's lament that she will stick herself with a poison arrow (29) and in Nisa's comparing herself as a sexual being to food (43).

4. Students should enjoy this question: Nisa's mother is echoing the age-old lament of mothers: "You frustrate and shame me so, I could kill myself," adding that the only thing preventing her from doing so is the weakness of the flesh. There should be quite a variety of responses to the second part of the question, including the threat of getting on a plane or a train, of jumping off a bridge, of driving over a cliff.

## Connections

1. The differences between customs and concepts of marriage in "Nisa's Marriage" and "The Artist's Life in Brussels" may strike students more strongly than their similarities. Ken Bugul recalls village life, but she has imbibed Western culture and is living a life far away from the village and its customs. She remembers best the customs about polygamy (paras. 22, 42, 57), which she found straightforward and respectful of all parties. Nisa, on the other hand, mentions nothing about polygamous marriages. In both Ken Bugul's and Nisa's descriptions of the customs of the people of their original cultures, however, there is the sense that marriage is an orderly process that supports the social organization of the community and reinforces connections between and among families. Ken Bugul, having left her village, has a hard time accepting the disorganized and selfish way Jean approaches love relationships. Ken Bugul's knowledge and acceptance of polygamy has partially prepared her for Jean's spending time with other women, and she tries to see his homosexual relationships in the same light, but it remains foreign to her (38).

2. Although Pom acquiesces to her parents' wishes, her silence, tears, and lack of enthusiasm suggest that she shares Nisa's fear and reluctance. Pom cries only at the announcement, however, whereas Nisa not only cries often but also runs away from her husband every chance she gets. Their ultimate compliance never seems to be in question; in each case all the unwritten laws of the society demand that they obey their parents. They simply have no alternatives.

3. By the end of her narrative, we see Nisa's acceptance of her adult role; she shows love for and pride in her husband, mentioning how she misses him when he is away. In "On Sunday" Miguel ultimately accepts his newfound maturity when he admits to feelings of "confidence" and "good spirits" as a result of saving Rubén (174) and when he looks to the future at the end of the story. Both believe that they have finally made that split between themselves and their parents (in Miguel's case, of course, this is only implied). Gender differences dictate the adult roles each is permitted to assume; Nisa's early efforts at independent action (refusing the marriage) were defeated, so she learns to find satisfaction through her relationship with her husband. Because of his sex, Miguel

encounters no familial opposition to his efforts to establish independence as an aspect of his adulthood.

## NAILA MINAI (Mee-Nye), Women in Early Islam (p. 361)

### Explorations

1. Students will probably be surprised to discover the range of responsibilities shouldered by women in what is considered a backward age. Women in the tribes looked after the herds and engaged in commerce by both producing and trading items of value. They were allowed the privilege of airing their views, enjoyed the power inherent in a matriarchal society allowing polygamy for women, and in general were valued and protected. Their only real risk was of being kidnapped for ransom.

2. The entire tribe gained stability, an easier life, and increased power and wealth. These changes, however, meant that women were no longer needed as they had been; thus they came to be valued less. They were not protected, and they lost their right to polygamy while men retained theirs. A monotheistic religion became the primary means of uniting previously separate tribes, and a social code protecting women and children was gradually established, because the previous incentives for protecting them had been eliminated with the abandonment of nomadic existence.

3. Khadija's wealth and position provided the support Muhammad needed to found his religion. She contributed to the social code of Islam by acquainting her husband with the needs of younger, less powerful women. When he married the young Aysha he began to appreciate the rights of girls, and the scandal concerning her journey with the young man convinced him of a woman's need for protection against false claims of adultery, resulting in the requirement of four witnesses before the charge could be leveled.

4. Some students may encounter difficulty in distinguishing between fictitious and factual elements in an anecdote like this; they may be prone to consider everything they read as fact. This question will allow them to explore the reasons behind and the benefits of embellishment. In opening her essay this way, Minai humanizes the story, allowing the reader to identify with a figure otherwise considered too lofty for human concerns. Her accounts of the family's response to the marriage, the courtship of the couple, and Khadija's infatuation with the young employee are probably fabrications. But she hasn't gone too far; all these elements are plausible, none alters the known facts, and more important all serve the *truth* of the story.

### Connections

1. Minai reports that under Islamic law, a woman could not be married without her permission, but that it occurred in practice, since many brides were still children when they were betrothed (para. 14). This is the case with Nisa, whose parents offer her no choice but to marry Tashay. She is given to him before she starts menstruating, and before she understands the responsibilities of marriage. Minai offers one reason that early marriage for women was considered desirable among the early Muslims when she says

that Muhammad believed that sexual instincts were natural for both men and women, but they would lead to adultery unless they were fully satisfied within marriage (18). Added to this is the role of marriage in supporting the patriarchal system (16). Nisa's early marriage, and the fact that she was given no choice but to marry Tashay, suggest that similar reasons might prevail among the Zhun/twasi. However, Shostak's book about Nisa describes how Nisa later went on to take a number of lovers, apparently a common practice among Zhun/twasi, whose hunter and gatherer economy cause them to move around a great deal. Thus Nisa's experience is in some ways closer to the marital system in the nomadic tribes before the birth of Islam. Minai describes how a woman might have several husbands, and have children by any of them, but maintained primary loyalty to her birth family (5). Nisa's father tells her she must follow her husband (20), and eventually Nisa does so willingly, but nevertheless she achieves a sexual and economic autonomy that would be difficult to attain for women living under the Islamic laws Minai describes.

2.  Students may be surprised by the author's thesis that the implementation of the Islamic code actually conferred upon women an improved position, which gave them "a modicum of security and independence in the patriarchal family" (23). Minai's analysis suggests that the successful continuation of marriages depended more on the desire to maximize the economic benefits than on sexual desire. While the Islamic code did recognize the fact of sexual desire on the part of both the male and the female, the disparate treatment of women suggests that their sexuality could be threatening unless harnessed to the institution of marriage. The Koran advises men to marry only as many women as they can satisfy sexually (17), implying that an unsatisfied woman would seek satisfaction outside her marriage. Thus her sexuality could threaten the family's stability and a male's clearly established line of descent. Both men and women were to be punished equally for adultery, but women still seemed to be singled out more frequently, although Minai attributes this fact to ingrained social prejudices and not the Islamic code. Still, while four witnesses are necessary to establish a woman's adultery, the conditions for establishing male guilt are not discussed. The author suggests this situation rarely occurs, perhaps because men can structure polygamous experience into their marriages. Although the attitudes toward women's sexuality in these two readings are very different, both Moravia's narrator and the Islamic code suggest that marriage defuses women's sexuality.

3.  In patriarchal societies such as these, women are seen as subservient to men. Thus even if the existing rules are designed to protect women, they are made by men according to their view of women's role in society. A woman's responsibilities include maintaining the home and becoming a part of her husband's family. If we consider Beauvoir's assessment of male-female relationships, we see both cultures as supporting her view. In each case women are seen as lesser creatures than men, as incomplete beings to be cared for rather than independent beings able to act on their own initiative. Each society uses the male as the norm and thus relegates women to the status of Other.

**Miriam Cooke, The Veil Does Not Prevent Women from Working (p. 372)**

**Explorations**

1. The Western image of Islamic women during the European colonial period was a variation of Victorian images of women in general. Islamic women embodied the contradiction of being "cloistered and oppressed" and "seductive and mysterious" (para. 5). The stereotypic American image of the veiled Islamic woman has changed little; Cooke describes the image as one of "anonymous black shapes gliding along high walls, sensuous odalisques reclining against the harem's soft pillows" (4). Such an image, Cooke suggests through a discussion of Edward Said's essay "Orientalism," is the product of male erotic and chivalric fantasies, and has little to do with the reality of women's lives (5, 6).

2. Cooke counters the assumption that the veiling of women is due to sexual oppression by arguing that the veil may signify "class and status . . . religious and political affiliation . . . [or] the current awakening of feminist consciousness. . . ." (12.) She further suggests that the traditional reasons for veiling — class status and social standing — are not necessarily in conflict with contemporary, political/feminist reasons (13). Aside from religious reasons, the veil was important to men because it signified ownership of women and served as a form of protection, either of the woman herself, or of men from women's sexuality (14). Early in the twentieth century, Islamic intellectuals interpreted veiling and seclusion as forms of sexual oppression (15), and some countries banned veiling. Some women have resumed wearing the veil in the last two decades, both as a way of declaring their faith and as a way of gaining some freedom to go into the streets (17, 18).

3. Students will be able to begin to respond to this question by referring to their responses to Explorations #2. Some of the advantages in veiling and in segregating men and women in Islamic countries have to do with women negotiating for rights and freedoms — without betraying their Islamic faith — that allow them to embark on otherwise unavailable professional opportunities. Cooke mentions the women's section of the Riyadh newspaper, where women are segregated physically but are "functionally integrated," not necessarily writing solely on "women's issues" (20). Most students of western backgrounds will only be able to see advantages in segregation and veiling if they are able to respect the religious devotion of women in Islamic countries and if they believe that women can build a satisfying and productive life under these circumstances.

4. Cooke's reasons for opening her essay with a discussion of Western stereotypes regarding Islamic women are significant because of the audience her essay addresses (a Western one) and the point she is trying to make (that Westerners are ignorant of the complex reasons for the segregation and veiling of women in Islamic countries). Part of her strategy for overturning Western stereotypes is to open her essay with an ironic account of American concerns about — and hopes for — the encounter between oppressed Islamic women and "liberated" American women serving in the armed forces. She implies that the expected sexual revolution could not materialize following such an encounter because of Islamic women's "own agency" — their social perspective and religious commitment — that would dictate their behaviors far more powerfully than seeing "tough women soldiers driving juggernauts" (3). If she opened her essay from the Saudi perspective, she would have had to pass up the opportunity of drawing in her Western readers with an anecdote that plays upon their biases and stereotypical images

of Islamic women. She sets up an implicit comparison between the fantasies of the West and the realities of the East, a comparison she exploits throughout her essay.

## Connections

1. According to Minai, at its inception Islam represented an extensive reform of women's rights under the law. It provided for women's education and ability to manage personal finances. Women could inherit property and were legally entitled to sexual satisfaction in marriage; divorce was regulated to protect women (para. 2). Muhammad did, however, support patriarchy (12). His laws tended to reinforce male privilege while giving women greater rights than they had previously enjoyed. But the laws were not always put into practice. For instance, a woman cannot be married without her permission, but many brides are still children when the decision about their marriage is made (14).

2. Many students will focus on veiling as the most obvious Islamic practice that supports Beauvoir's contention that men view women as Other. The veil marks women as "Other" simply because men are not required to wear it; the veil is a sign of women's different social and sexual position. In spite of her insistence that women are willing to be veiled and secluded, Cooke admits that the practice originally had to do with men's fear of women's sexuality (14). Simone de Beauvoir wrote that in the eyes of men, woman "is sex — absolute sex, no less" (4). The practice of veiling and seclusion also served men's desire to protect women as their "property" (14). Similarly, Beauvoir associates women's economic "dependence" on men with a master-slave relationship (13) — in other words, a relationship based on the ownership of the "Other" by the "One." Further, Beauvoir writes that women have found it necessary to cooperate in those practices that reinforce sex-based inequalities because refusal to cooperate made it hard to survive: "To decline to be the Other, to refuse to be a party to the deal — this would be for women to renounce all the advantages conferred upon them by their alliance with the superior caste" (13). Islamic women are attempting to use the veil as a way to gain greater personal freedom and more political clout (see Explorations #1 and #2, above), but their desire to retain the advantages of being defined as men's property also tends to reinforce the patriarchal system that inhibits their full participation (16).

3. Students will be able to build on discussions of Beauvoir's concept of Woman-as-Other (see Connections #2, above) in order to consider the significance of associating wildness with women's sexuality. The veil prevents men from viewing women's bodies and faces directly, leaving men free to create fantasies about the sexuality of women in which women are figured as "Other." Cooke contends that the early European view of veiled Islamic women "was a crass image that differentiated women from men chiefly in relationship to lust" (4). Rendered mysterious because of the veil, Islamic women were imagined to embody the elements of "wildness" that Moravia appreciates in his wife: "intimacy, privacy, secrecy." At the same time, however, veiling had come to represent the sexual and social oppression of Islamic women, in that "Islam, it is thought . . . has imposed eternal stagnation on women" (7). Therefore, to the Western mind veiling represents two opposing ideas: the wildness and sexual mystery of women and their oppressively domesticated lives. Both these ideas are also expressed in Moravia's story through the image of the wife, who seems to be "stagnant" and thoroughly predictable, but who becomes in her husband's eyes "wild" and unpredictable. This dual image of

women is also reflected in the original Islamic motivations for veiling women, which were to enforce their domestication and to conceal their sexuality (14, 16).

## YASHAR KEMAL (Keh-MAL), A Dirty Story (p. 380)

### Explorations

1. A fruitful way of approaching this question might be to ask students what they think of when they hear the term *dirty story*. The common response will be something like "a story about sex." If they then attempt to explain the title of this story, they'll be in for a surprise. It's not the sex itself that makes this a dirty story; in fact, any compassionate reader will find the sexual practices of the town boys repellent. The realization may come slowly, but students should be able to determine that it's the town itself that is dirty. Kemal blames the entire town for Fadik's tragedy: The pettiness of the villagers, their lust for gossip, their attitudes toward women, and their jealousy of Huru — all these factors contribute to a general poverty of spirit fostered by economic poverty in the town. Implicit in the story is a condemnation not only of the social attitudes of the townspeople but also of the economic conditions that give rise to such mean spiritedness as well. It is not surprising that Kemal offers no simple remedies for these problems; he seems to recommend greater tolerance and compassion as the only hope — and there is a ray of hope, however dim, in the final image of Osman carrying Fadik away from her tormentors as the earth renews itself in spring.

2. This scene reveals a classic perception of women as chattel, commodities to be used for work or pleasure. That the discussion among the men reveals no maliciousness toward women in general should be emphasized; they never even consider the plight of the women involved, any more than they would consider the feelings of animals or insects. It is essential that we believe this if we are to accept the horror that emerges in the rest of the story. Thus the attitude must be articulated by the people themselves; if the author provided it for us as an explanation of their subsequent behavior, readers would have a difficult time giving credence to it.

3. That men see strength and domination of women as vital to success should be clear to most students. How women view men is less clear, although much of their behavior indicates that they too respect a strong, domineering man. Their deference to males regardless of age or relationship is revealed in Hatije's inability to control her son's behavior. Women's views of themselves are more complicated. They expect a man to dominate, and they're quite willing to ignore Fadik's humanity. They apparently neither feel empathy toward nor express any solidarity with the victim. It seems that they have adopted the view found in the Swat Valley, namely that Fadik is at fault for the boys' lust. Their behavior is a phenomenon common to oppressed groups: In the interest of self-preservation, they try to separate themselves from members of their group who are currently being persecuted. (Perceptive students might make the connection between Fadik's predicament and that of the rape victim characterized as a seductress. If we acknowledge our solidarity with the victim, then we have to face the fact that we too are at risk.) Probably the only clear difference between men's views of women and their own

89

self-image lies in this paradox: Men see all women as seductresses, while women see only those unfortunate enough to have been exploited in that light.

4. The women's lust for gossip is evident in their interpretation of the situation. The child has clearly described a rape, commenting that "Uncle Osman's wife . . . was sobbing away all the time" (para. 26), but the women immediately (and gleefully) inform Osman that his wife has turned his home into a brothel and that "anyone can come in and have her" (32). The utter absurdity of their implication that the animals are also at fault for the boys' playing with them makes clear the women's refusal to place the blame where it belongs. At this point Fadik is being exploited, Osman is confused and helpless, and Huru is trying to convince him of the truth, namely that the rumor is based on jealousy of her power and Fadik's beauty. That there is probably no truth to the rumor is clear from the child's story and from the women's jealous tirades against Huru. The truth instead comes out in their story of Esheh, the last woman to have been subjected to the brutality of the young men in the village. Now that she is dead they can sympathize with her, but they obviously offered her no protection during her ordeal.

## Connections

1. Kemal's fictional account seems to be consistent with Cooke's observation that men are expected to dominate. Saudi women are veiled in part because they are perceived by men to be dangerously seductive. In each community we also see women circumventing their assigned roles — in Saudi Arabia by using religious laws and the custom of veiling to gain access to social and professional opportunities previously denied women and in Chukurova by using gossip to control men's actions subtly. Most students will recognize that Western women would object strongly to the characterization of women as weak, sex-driven commodities, but they may need to be reminded that evidence in "A Dirty Story" and "The Veil Does Not Prevent Women From Working" reveals that women accept their role, acting out rebellions within the constraints of the role itself. In both pieces, male honor is perceived to be dependent on women's chastity, and women are held responsible for the sexual behavior of men. The class differences evident in Kemal's and Cooke's pieces may account for the contrast in how each portrays sex role divisions. In Kemal's story, poverty, an agrarian economy, lack of education, and cultural isolation prevent men from being compassionate and women from unifying to stop the abuse; on the other hand, as Cooke's essay demonstrates, middle-class Saudi women enjoy the benefits of education, a small amount of economic freedom, and some professional opportunities.

2. In each case the government and religion clearly regulate the sexual and social behavior of women. Cooke describes how governments have either banned or required women to wear the veil, based on the (male-dominated) government and religion in power at any given time (para. 11). The delegation of legal power to the local agha in Kemal's story allows such offenses as the sale of women, gang rape, and slander against women to go unpunished. The only talk of government occurs when the women are speculating about a cure for lice and when Osman worries about the police getting hold of Fadik. It is significant that he worries less about the legal ramifications than about what fate will befall her in the hands of the gendarmes. Religion does little more to protect women. In Chukurova, the villagers, in part at least because they are so poor, seem to have no time for religion. In Saudi Arabia, middle-class women cooperate with religious and legal

restrictions as a way of gaining whatever protection and opportunities the system will allow them. Cooke, although an outsider, seeks to understand the advantages of veiling. Kemal suggests that while the misogyny behind veiling is misguided (because it is men, not women, whose sexual appetites are to be feared), veiling's central purpose — protecting women — is well-founded. Given Kemal's unsympathetic depiction of both Huru (witch) and Fadik (victim), as well as of the village women, some may argue that he'd prefer the protection of veiling to the "woman-as-beast" system.

3. Recalling Beauvoir's explanation of why women collaborate with men's treatment of them should help students to understand how the women of Chukurova behave. Beauvoir emphasizes that women are unable to unite because they have no shared history or identity and thus opt for the few benefits that accrue from a discriminatory system. This is precisely what the women in "A Dirty Story" do. With the exception of the wealthy Huru (who, by the way, keeps the villagers in line by threatening to notify her tax-collecter nephew), women in the village have no real power to resist men. If they support Fadik, then they must condemn the boys. But because their protection depends upon men, they decline to antagonize the boys. Another reason for their compliance suggests the Catch-22 situation outlined in Explorations #3: If they stand by Fadik, then they must declare solidarity with a woman denounced as a whore. Because tradition contends that all women are latent whores, they must collaborate (in denouncing the woman who has been raped) with the very custom that stigmatizes them in order to keep from being associated with the fallen woman. They are in a no-win situation.

## ADDITIONAL QUESTIONS AND ASSIGNMENTS

1. In a journal entry or a collection of informal notes, discuss the images of the opposite sex (male students write about female images and vice versa) presented in selections representing two or three different cultures. Consider such issues as rights, responsibilities, innate characteristics, fantasy images, and power. As you look over your notes, try to discover similarities and differences among the cultures represented. Then compare notes with students of the opposite sex. Can you come to any general conclusion about the way we view those considered Other? (If you have answered Question 1 under *Additional Questions* in Part Three, you may wish to compare your responses to that question and this one.)

2. Interview someone who engaged in a courtship ritual different from your own; in other words, talk to someone at least a generation older or younger than you or from a foreign country. Compile a list of the details of the ritual, paying close attention to the characterization of sex roles, the outside forces that interfered with the couple, and the particular joys offered by the ritual. As you write up the interview, try to provide your reader with enough detail of setting and dialogue from your subject to create a vivid impression.

3. Create your own myth to characterize your fantasy mate. Using Silko (and perhaps Moravia) as a guide, list the characteristics you find intriguing in members of the opposite sex. Then write a story in which those characteristics become embodied in a mythic figure. Your story should include both high and low points and should leave the reader with a definite impression of your ultimate response to this Other.

91

4.  One of the most interesting phenomena in the recent assault on pornography has been the alliance of feminists with right-wing members of the "moral majority." From congressional hearings on the subject matter of rock music to scientific studies of men's reactions to violent pornography, much has been said and written about pornography's insidious contribution to the degradation of women. Considering the statement implicit in Kemal's story — that inherent danger lurks in seemingly harmless attitudes (in this case viewing women as sex objects) — explore some of the articles in magazines and newspapers over the past ten years that examine pornography's effect on the treatment of women. Using this material as evidence, write a persuasive paper in which you argue either that pornography is harmful or that it is not.

5.  Conduct further research into one of the cultures represented in this section, focusing specifically on sex roles. It would be wise to choose a culture about which information is readily available — Western Europe, the Islamic Middle East, or a particular culture in Africa are likely candidates. If the selection is an excerpt from a larger work, look first at that work. You can find other sources by consulting the headnotes for other selections from that culture (if there are any) and a general encyclopedia, as well as journals devoted to the study of that culture. Narrow your topic to something manageable — such as the evolution of sex roles over time, the influence of religion on sex roles, the role of government in determining or perpetuating certain sex roles or courtship rituals in the culture — and write an expository paper in which you elaborate on the images of men and women presented by the original selection.

# Part Five

## WORK:
## WE ARE WHAT WE DO

### INTRODUCTION

Students should thoroughly enjoy all the selections in this section. They are readily accessible and will surely evoke laughter, pity, excitement, surprise, and anger. A college classroom is the perfect setting for a discussion of work. While some students may not have clear career goals in mind, most at least recognize their desire for something beyond a dead-end job. A profitable way to introduce the section is to compare students' own goals with those set by their parents. In *Looking at Ourselves*, Baker offers some thoughts on the abstract nature of many current job descriptions and how they affect children's career ambitions and relationships with parents. In Liebow's and Terkel's pieces we see the vast gulf between those who view their work as inconsequential and those who view themselves as moving forces in social change. A discussion of their own ambitions will provide students with a focal point from which to assess the various ambitions and frustrations they'll encounter in the main selections.

Among possible subthemes in this chapter are "men's work" versus "women's work" (O'Brien, Hayslip, Angelou, and Bonner), the dignity of one's profession (Abram, Angelou, Levi, and Iwashita), and exploitation of workers (Hayslip, Angelou, Iwashita, Ishikawa, and Bonner).

Instructors may wish to consult the following familiar works in preparing related selections from *Ourselves Among Others*:

### Essays

John R. Coleman, "Blue-Collar Journal" (*Blue-Collar Journal*, Collier, 1974).
Patrick Fenton, "Confessions of a Working Stiff" (*New York Magazine*, 1973).
Erich Fromm, "Work in an Alienated Society" (*The Sane Society*, Henry Holt, 1955).
Ellen Goodman, "The Company Man" (*Close to Home*, Simon and Schuster, 1979).
Jan Halvorsen, "How It Feels to Be Out of Work" (*Newsweek*, 1975).
Malcolm X, "The Shoeshine Boy" (*The Autobiography of Malcolm X*, Random House, 1965).
George Orwell, "Hotel Kitchens" (*Down and Out in Paris and London*, Harcourt, Brace, 1933).
Gloria Steinem, "The Importance of Work" (*Outrageous Acts and Everyday Rebellions*, Holt, Rinehart, 1983).
Lewis Thomas, "Nurses" (*The Youngest Science*, Viking, 1983).
Seymour Wishman, "A Lawyer's Guilty Secret" (*Newsweek*, Nov. 9, 1981).
Virginia Woolf, "Professions for Women" (*Death of a Moth*, Harcourt, 1942).

## Short Stories

Rick De Marinis, "The Flowers of Boredom" (*Antioch Review*, Winter 1988; *The Coming Triumph of the Free World*, Viking, 1988).

Arthur Conan Doyle, "A Scandal in Bohemia" (*The Adventures of Sherlock Holmes*, Schocken, 1976).

William Faulkner, "Barn Burning" (*Collected Stories of William Faulkner*, Random House, 1950).

Nathaniel Hawthorne, "The Birthmark" (*Mosses from an Old Manse*, Wiley and Putnam, 1846).

James Joyce, "Counterparts" (*Dubliners*, B. W. Huebsch, 1916).

Herman Melville, "Bartleby, the Scrivener" (*Piazza Tales*, Dix and Edwards, 1856).

Eudora Welty, "The Whistle" (*Collected Stories of Eudora Welty*, Harcourt, 1980).

## BIOGRAPHICAL NOTES ON *LOOKING AT OURSELVES*

1. Linda Hasselstrom has written both poetry (*Roadkill*, 1987; *Caught by One Wing*, 1990) and nonfiction (*Windbreak: A Woman Rancher on the Northern Plains*, 1987). The excerpt in *Looking at Ourselves* is taken from *Last Circle: Writings Collected From the Land* (1991).

2. Six-foot-nine Larry Bird is a nationally known basketball player whose honors include three years as the NBA's Most Valuable Player. After graduation from Indiana State in 1979, Bird went on to play thirteen seasons as a forward with the Boston Celtics. He retired in 1992.

3 Fred Moody is a free-lance journalist who contributes to the *Baltimore City Paper*.

4. Sociologist Elliot Liebow has been a director of the National Institute of Mental Health. This selection is taken from his book *Tally's Corner: A Study of Negro Streetcorner Men* (1967).

5. Stephen Blackburn is a free-lance reporter. His article originally appeared in the alternative weekly *Kansas City Pitch* in February 1991.

6. Russell Baker, Pulitzer Prize-winning columnist for the *New York Times Magazine*, has published *The Good Times* (1989) and several collections of his wry essays. His memoir *Growing Up* was a best-seller in 1983.

7. The interview with the former Ronald McDonald clown was conducted at the Sixth Annual Vegetarian Food Fair in Toronto. It was published in *ACT: Artists for Cultural Terrorism*.

8. A member of the Creek Tribe, Joy Harjo is a professor of English at the University of New Mexico. In addition to being a screenwriter and musician, she has published several collections of poetry, most recently *She Had Some Horses* (1983) and *In Mad Love and War* (1990).

9. Vladimir Nabokov was a Russian-born author of postmodern novels in both Russian and English. He achieved fame with *Lolita* (1955).

10. John Updike, whose minutely observed sketches of American life are often associated with the *New Yorker*, is perhaps best known for short story collections such as *Pigeon Feathers* (1962); novels such as *The Centaur* (National Book Award 1963) and the Rabbit tetralogy: *Rabbit Run* (1960); *Rabbit Redux* (1971); *Rabbit is Rich* (Pulitzer Prize 1982); *Rabbit at Rest* (Pulitzer Prize 1991); and several volumes of art and literary criticism.

11. Studs Terkel interviewed political organizer Bill Talcott in *Working* (1972). Terkel's other popular "oral histories" include *Hard Times: An Oral History of the Great Depression* (1970), and *The Great Divide: Second Thoughts on the American Dream* (1988). He won a Pulitzer Prize for *The Good War: An Oral History of World War Two* (1984).

## Reflections

1. Linda Hasselstrom is most pleased about the variety of work in her life. She says she is "often tired, but never bored" by the combination of running a ranch and being a writer. She believes that having a wide range of work keeps the mind from becoming too rigid: the benefits of working the ranch are specifically that it counteracts the effects of an otherwise sedentary lifestyle, which Hasselstrom believes "is literally killing a lot of us." Physical labor provides a challenge to the body that keeps us healthy. Joy Harjo begins her piece by mentioning that her mother "had already worked hard for her short life," a comment that suggests Harjo not only honors her mother's hard work but also realizes that the challenges of hard physical labor can be as wearing as they may be health-giving. Harjo, like Hasselstrom, values taking a risk, but Harjo focuses on the challenges of writing poetry rather than on physical challenges. She implies, however, that writing poetry is not sedentary, but very active: "Each poem is a jumping-off edge. . . ." Both women value the breadth of vision a varied life brings; Harjo writes that she has decided that "more than one vision . . . is a blessing"; Hasselstrom writes that a person "must look both near and far off" in order to be intellectually healthy.

2. Because college students are often thinking seriously about career decisions, they should be able to engage in a spirited debate about the advantages and disadvantages of "being one's own boss." Although many students will have worked at menial jobs such as those mentioned by Elliot Liebow, few will be able to identify with the sense of having no future that many workers struggle with. However, they will realize that most menial jobs involve long hours, poor pay, and little room for independent decision-making. Many of those whose pieces appear in *Looking At Ourselves* are writers, including Vladimir Nabokov, Linda Hasselstrom, John Updike, and Joy Harjo. All of them suggest that being a writer brings a great deal of independence. Updike's comment about the role of artist in society implies that her or his task is to ignore the dictates of literary culture and see the world in a unique way; Nabokov writes of the author as a man who must create his own values. Both Hasselstrom and Harjo, however, represent their writing as more connected to their own history and their other interests. This suggests another kind of independence, in that their work is tailored to fit in with the rest of their lives. For many, it is more often the case that one's personal life has to be tailored to fit one's work. For instance, Bill Talcott,

the labor organizer, is exceptionally dedicated to his work. He says — exaggerating only slightly — that he works 24 hours a day, and he travels a great deal. He also has a family, but chances are his family life has had to be adjusted to his long hours. Students may want to discuss why some people are attracted to an all-consuming career and others are more interested in work that doesn't distract from other interests.

3.  Most students will have a hard time coming up with significant advantages to the kind of work mentioned by Elliot Liebow. He writes about low-paying, menial work that "promises to deliver no more tomorrow . . . than it does today." They may be able to see a certain freedom in having no commitment to a job, but this will probably be offset because Liebow emphasizes that that "freedom" comes from lacking a future. Fred Moody also writes negatively about work, but his topic is the yuppie mentality that prizes hard work over family or spirituality. Students will be able to see that the advantages of working that hard at a career are mainly material. Moody mentions technological toys that bring work into one's personal life and remarks that many people admire those who work "right up to the point of self-destruction." Russell Baker, like Moody, writes about corporate work, placing it in a negative light since this kind of work is beyond the understanding of most children. However, many students may believe that the complexities involved in being a "systems analyst" would make the work more interesting than being a person who "makes horse collars," though the latter would be more easily comprehended by one's children.

4.  Elliot Liebow probably offers the most significant comment on which factors affect one's ability to choose what kind of work to do. He writes that "it is the apprentice who becomes the journeyman electrician . . . not the common unskilled Negro laborer." The class and race into which one is born are probably the most important factors in determining what work one will do. This fact will surprise students who have been raised to believe that personal ability is a far more important factor than class background or race. The class issue is implicit in pieces by Fred Moody and Russell Baker, who write about forms of work most easily available to those who come from middle class backgrounds and who have college educations. The class discussion about this question may help prepare students to consider how race and class determine the working lives represented in the essays in this section.

## MAYA ANGELOU (Mye-uh AHN-zhuh-lo), Mary (p. 415)

### Explorations

1.  The innocent, but misplaced, sympathy of the young Angelou for her imperious employer makes readers appreciate the girl's kind and gentle nature. During her employment she grows from a naïve girl into a person of accurate moral judgment. Her final retaliation wins readers' admiration since it is motivated by principle and not a mean disposition. After her arrival, Angelou refers to her employer at least three times as "poor" Mrs. Cullinan (paras. 12, 13, 17) because she pities her lack of children. She works hard to compensate for Mrs. Cullinan's unhappiness (13). Her pity is replaced by anger when

Mrs. Cullinan, acting on her friend's suggestion, decides to call Angelou "Mary" to suit her convenience. Rather than stay and compromise, Angelou decides to get fired (34). Mrs. Cullinan's final reaction to Angelou marks Angelou's moment of triumph since Mrs. Cullinan reaffirms her maid's true identity by using her given name twice (42).

2.  Angelou writes that any black she knew would find being "called out of his name" an insult (30). Like other blacks, Angelou could interpret the casual arrogance of her employer as a racial slur. Her employer, fastidious about the disposition of her belongings, feels no compulsion to recognize the personal identity of her maid. After Glory recounts that she has been renamed, Angelou wonders about the former and present names of Mrs. Randall's maid. Angelou decides not to tolerate being stripped of her individuality.

3.  Angelou recounts her experiences as a maid with a sly humor, which shows she no longer holds her early innocent view of her employer. Many observations in the story demonstrate both the young girl's naïveté and the mature Angelou's merciless mockery. The young Angelou ostensibly decides to write her poem out of pity and sympathy for her employer. However, by writing about Mrs. Cullinan in her autobiography, Angelou shows how little Mrs. Cullinan deserved any sympathy. The literal description of her employer as "white, fat, old" (24) emphasizes her unappealing appearance. Students can find many examples of irony that make Mrs. Cullinan an object of ridicule, including her efforts to "embalm" herself (10) and her inability to claim the Coleman girls as daughters (11, 12). By including these incidents in her autobiography, Angelou recounts an important turning point in her life, demonstrates the false superiority of her employer, and proves that the best revenge is writing well.

## Connections

1.  Elliot Liebow defines a menial job as one that poses no interesting challenges and offers no opportunities for advancement. Marguerite's job certainly matches Liebow's description, but she is young enough to feel she has something to learn from it, even if all she can learn is how to differentiate dishes. Initially, Marguerite is "fascinated with the novelty" of her new surroundings and duties. She also feels sorry for Mrs. Cullinan, and tries to be good to her (paras. 12, 13) out of pity and a sense of her own worth. This is the most tangible satisfaction of the job; Mrs. Cullinan is so clearly ineffectual (her "barrenness" symbolizes the general futility of her life) that Marguerite cannot help but notice how much more productive she is than her employer. Not until Mrs. Cullinan insults her by calling her "Mary" does Marguerite begin to approach her job with the disregard Liebow describes. Marguerite possesses the "future orientation" Liebow mentions, and she recognizes that if she stays with this job she will end up like Glory, "letting some white woman rename you for her convenience" (34).

2.  It will be important for students to understand that Beauvoir's discussion of the master-slave relationship need not be taken literally; she uses the master-slave relationship as a metaphor to describe relationships between the working class and the bourgeoisie. Beauvoir's main point is that the master-slave relationship is reciprocal; that is, each party is dependent on the other. However, the relationship "always works in favor of the oppressor" (12). In "Mary," Mrs. Cullinan is dependent on Glory and Marguerite, as Marguerite realizes most fully when she reflects on how Mrs. Cullinan needs her "to run a thousand errands" (13). Glory, also, seems to have acquiesced to the master-slave

relationship, even to the point of identifying her own interests with those of Mrs. Cullinan (39). Marguerite, however, has not bought into this mutual dependency, and her resistance is demonstrated in her readiness to leave the job when Mrs. Cullinan tries to take away her dignity by renaming her Mary.

3. Naipaul suggests that without the French manager present, the native employees are incapable of running the restaurant in an orderly fashion. But Angelou suggests that employees do not always share their employers' values and may quite consciously reject them. Naipaul reacts in a way that might be expected of a Westerner who feels superior to the inhabitants of the Third World country he visits. Yet perhaps "the whole restaurant idea" (20) has vanished because it is not part of the waiters' cultural heritage. The waiters may attach little importance to their lucrative jobs and the structure that supports them. They, too, may see the restaurant as a "charade" (20).

## DAVID ABRAM, Making Magic (p. 422)

### Explorations

1. Because we live in a culture that relegates magic to the realm of entertainment, students may be unfamiliar with the great respect and fear accorded magicians in other cultures. Although this essay clearly conveys the role of the magician in other cultures, students will most likely miss the connection between the magician and an underlying ecological balance that ensures the success of the ceremony. They may also find Abram's lack of skepticism hard to accept. Abram consistently refuses to limit the power of his magic to his knowledge of how the tricks are accomplished. Even though he characterizes his own magic as "sleight-of-hand tricks," he does not reduce it to tricks alone. Some unknown aspect of his performance mystifies him as well as his audience (para. 3). This attitude explains his ability to entertain the suggestion in the opening sentence that he may have real powers. Most important, his understanding of the magic used to change Gedé's luck, although it employs tricks, places him in contact with "the particular powers of earth to be found only there" (17). His sense of this contact and his later matter-of-fact acceptance of his magic's success (24) convince readers that Abram takes his experience seriously and does not dismiss the successful results as coincidences.

2. When first approached by Gedé, Abram produces explanations to convince him that his magic would not be powerful enough to accomplish the desired end. Approached a second time, later in the night, Abram leaves "without hesitation" (15). He now seems to be looking forward to the "challenge" of the experience, as if he thinks a chance exists that his magic will work. Students may puzzle about this dramatic change in his attitude. However, Abram plants a clue that helps to explain it. He says at first that he is "reluctant to play very deeply within the dream-space of a culture" not his own (12). When Gedé arrives at his door, Abram has entered this dream-space, quite literally, since he has dreamed of entertaining sea monsters. Although he gathers up some props, the flashpaper and a Coke bottle, ritualistically anoints the boat with sand, and mutters a prayer, his most meaningful "tactic" is making contact with "the particular powers of earth

to be found only there" (17). Paragraph 19 describes the moment Abram attunes himself to his surroundings, finding a harmonious spot within the system. He uses his magic to develop an ecological relationship with the universe.

3.  Abram uses the descriptive and expository passages about his Balinese environment to create an atmosphere that makes his use of magic ritual a natural and inevitable response. While it might be unusual for an American to react this way, Abram comes very close to identifying with the sensibility of a Balinese, who would share Gedé's view of the way to proceed. He unconsciously adopts this role by making a self-effacing refusal of Gedé's first offer, entering a symbolic vision of the sea universe, and even dressing, Balinese fashion, in a sarong (15). The description of Abram on the boat places him in the physical world of the Balinese fishermen, ready to accept and adapt to their code of behavior (17).

## Connections

1.  Abram's situation is, of course, very different from Marguerite's. As a black worker in a white household, Marguerite must cope with the demands and eccentricities of her employer. Their relationship is heavily influenced by racism and classism, and Marguerite's tactics for dealing with Mrs. Cullinan's insistence on calling her "Mary" reflect the complexities of her difficult social and economic position. Marguerite might have coped with the situation as Glory does, by accepting the indignity of being "called out of her name" (para. 30), but instead she begins by using passive resistance. She arrives late, leaves early and makes little effort to do a good job, hoping she will get fired (36). But when this does not work, she tries a more direct strategy, deliberately breaking Mrs. Cullinan's most valued china.

2.  Moody divides life into categories of time for work, family life, and spiritual meditation. His lament that technological innovation has allowed the workplace to invade the home suggests a belief that work should be left at the office. Gedé's story presents a different concept of life, one that integrates all activities. Although his boat and home are separate places, the fishing village he lives in is next to the sea. More important, for Gedé, spiritual belief governs every aspect of his life, including his work. His finding fish or returning home without them depends on his ability to satisfy powerful forces. For the Balinese, success in work depends on propitiation of ancestors, magic talismans, and exorcism of demons (11).

3.  Students will be able to build on their responses to Explorations #3 to help them analyze the contrast Abram sets up between Western and Indonesian culture. His experience in Sri Lanka, where people followed him hoping he would cure them and solve their problems (5) and in Bali, where Gedé demonstrates literal faith in Abram's magic, suggest the contrast between the Western view of magic as illusion and the Indonesian view of magic as a part of everyday reality. Abram suggests, however, that the contrast can be resolved. When he comes down with malaria, Abram suspects he has been cursed by another sorcerer (7). More significantly, Abram's sympathy for Gedé's predicament and his willingness to go along with the ritual exorcism demonstrate that he does not find the Balinese vision entirely foreign. Thus, although Abram draws a contrast between the

422–431 (Text pages)

West and Indonesian views like the one Bugul draws between Western and African perspectives, he does not present the view that the differences are irreconcilable. Instead, by adapting his behavior to Gedé's need, Abram begins to accept the Balinese vision of the universe.


## LE LY HAYSLIP, Rice Farming in Vietnam (p. 432)

### Explorations

1. The "snakes' keepers" are French soldiers, as is evident from the children's song following paragraph 6, which begins "French come, French come . . ."

2. Hayslip begins to discuss the specifics of her family's livelihood in paragraph 15, when she mentions the difficulties of a farmer's life during war. When the weather and the war permit, Hayslip's family and the other villagers plant a variety of crops (para. 17), but rice is their staple. The children were often involved in the growing process, acting as scarecrows (19), helping women transplant rice to the field (23), and weeding (24).

3. It should be immediately apparent to students that the war affects every part of the villager's lives. Often they have to flee their village (9, 10) and return to find homes burned and crops destroyed. The war disrupts farming (13, 16, 34). Women and girls are vulnerable to rape by soldiers (37). Hayslip first mentions the war when she describes her earliest memories of learning to walk and playing with other children; the "snake-monsters" that interrupt the children's play become a integral part of her life from that moment and as much a part of her cultural mythology as the legends about how god gave rice to the people (18–20). From the point of view of Hayslip as a child, it is difficult to sort out which effects of the war were intended and which were unintentional. She mentions that sometimes they were warned that the "snake-monster" was coming (9), but it is unclear if they were deliberately given some time to save themselves and a few of their belongings or if villagers were so vigilant that they could predict attacks. She also mentions that when crops were destroyed by soldiers, the farmers assumed that the soldiers had their own "karma" to work out, suggesting that whether or not the destruction was intentional, they held the soldiers responsible for the effects of war.

4. All the forms of recreation Hayslip mentions give the farmers a break from their work and the war, but their "recreations" are productive activities that, in various ways, promote social and familial stability or provide goods for the family. The rituals with which they honor their ancestors are occasions for praying for the family's welfare. Marriage has little to do with romance (39), so making arrangements for marriages is more a matter of doing business than celebrating love. Making clothes and tools are forms of work that seem like recreation because they offer a break from the rice fields. Even the legends they tell and the songs they sing relate to the work of planting and harvesting rice (18–20, 29).

## Connections

1. Abram's discussion of the Balinese universe and Hayslip's description of planting rice demonstrate a relationship between people and the land that most Western students will find unfamiliar. Rather than basing the relationship on the idea that land should be dominated by people, the relationship Abram and Hayslip describe is based on cooperation and respect for the land, which possesses significant power to reward or punish people. The Balinese participate in "ceremonies of protection," designed to protect people from nature's destructive powers. Similarly, the ritual exorcism Abram performs for Gedé is not intended to give Gedé control over nature, but to persuade the gods to restore his ability to catch fish. Hayslip's description of planting rice emphasizes the contact between the farmers' hands and feet and the land; they must learn to cope with the mud and the monotony of planting in order to induce the land to feed them. She describes the earth as "receptive," suggesting that it wants to yield a good harvest. In the same way, when Hayslip recounts god's gift of rice, she writes that he wanted to make the work of rice farming easy, but that a mix-up thwarted his plans (paras. 18, 19).

2. Maya Angelou started working outside her home when she was ten years old, but she writes that by that time, African-American girls were already doing basic work such as ironing and washing (2). Angelou writes with irony about how becoming domestic workers in the homes of whites was the "finishing school" for African-American girls. That these jobs were taken very seriously is suggested in her comments about needing to find an excuse for quitting that would satisfy her mother (34). The circumstances for Hayslip were similar in some ways, in that she had to work in order to contribute to the family's welfare and to prepare for the many responsibilities women take on in her culture. However, she does not work for outsiders; instead, all her work takes place within the context of her family's business. Her first jobs were scaring away birds from the crops (17) and pulling weeds in the rice fields (24).

3. Ved Mehta's father emphasizes the idea that women should make sacrifices in order to be good wives and in order to gain the respect and love of their husbands (65–67). Although it is important to find a husband for Pom who is from a cultural, class, and religious background similar to hers, Daddyji says that "it's her life that is joined with his; it is she who will forsake her past to build a new future with him" (75). Similarly, in the Vietnamese farming culture Hayslip grew up in, parents arranging marriages for their children considered compatibility, but they were most concerned with the impact of the marriage on the family's social and economic circumstances. Like Daddyji, the Vietnamese farmers considered it extremely unwise to marry for love. Hayslip recalls that "keeping a husband satisfied" was a wife's most important duty (40), and the necessity of also being a "dutiful daughter-in-law" suggests that Vietnamese peasant women, like many Indian women, are expected to move in with their husbands and serve their parents-in-law.

4. Methods for teaching girls how to take care of the family home and teaching boys how to work for the family are very similar in Hayslip's description of her girlhood and in Menchú's writing about birth ceremonies and childrearing in Quiché society. Menchú writes that the little girl spends so much time with her mother that she learns from her how to take care of the family, while little boys "must begin to live like a man" (18). For all children, education consists of working alongside parents and taking on responsibilities that, in many U.S. communities, would be considered too adult for children to be

101

able to handle. Similarly, Hayslip recalls working in the rice fields alongside her mother (34) and learning from her everything she would need to know about running a home and raising a family (37,38). Boys, like their counterparts in Quiché culture, were expected to live like men. In both cultures, boys were more likely to be favored and forgiven. The most significant circumstance that contributes to the similarities in teaching methods in the Vietnamese and Quiché communities is that both are based on an agrarian economy in which all family members need to be involved in the work.

## EDNA O'BRIEN, Sister Imelda (p. 444)

### Explorations

1. Most students will be more aware of the things Sister Imelda has had to give up than of the rewards of her job, since they will be more likely to identify with the point of view of the students in the convent school. The narrator wants to ask Sister Imelda about boys, about the color of her hidden hair, and whether she misses being in the outside world (para. 23) In paragraph 24, O'Brien describes what the girls know about the nuns' daily routine; the litany of privations includes bad food, uncomfortable clothes, waking early for prayers, silence, and self-censorship. Although she admits that these things are difficult to adjust to (64), Sister Imelda most regrets having had to give up visits with her family (71). However, she is devoted to, and excited by, teaching (3). She values the security of convent life and the possibilities for spiritual pursuits, but she has trouble accepting the limited chances for emotional intimacy, a lack that is suggested in her relationship with the narrator. Although O'Brien does not consider it directly, details such as Sister Imelda's gifts to the narrator of religious pictures and spiritual advice (14, 44) suggest that her relationship with God is active and rewarding.

2. O'Brien begins to forecast the development of an enticing but ominous intimacy between the narrator and Sister Imelda in paragraph 8, when the narrator recalls that at first she "had no idea how terribly [Sister Imelda] would infiltrate my life." Later in the same paragraph, she elaborates: "I saw in her some premonition of sacrifice which I would have to emulate." She has begun to identify with the nun, and this initiates two conflicts, one regarding her growing love for Sister Imelda, and the other regarding the question of whether she has a "vocation" to become a nun herself. In fact the two conflicts are inseparable, because it is the narrator's desire to be near to Sister Imelda, and to be like her, that spurs her fruitless decision to enter the convent. Students will feel the effect of these hints differently, depending on their religious background and their interpretations of the narrator's "crush" on Sister Imelda, but most will feel the tension and foreboding inherent in O'Brien's phrasing when she writes that she felt Sister Imelda "invading" her heart (8) and that she became "dreadfully happy" (10). O'Brien provides a future context for these hints when she has the narrator say that at the time she "had no idea" of the effect Sister Imelda would have on her life. Thus the narrator is reflecting back on her own ignorance and naïveté from a position of greater maturity and wisdom. In that sense, the hints she provides forecast the process of maturation she will undergo as a result of her relationship with Sister Imelda.

3.    The power that Sister Imelda is able to wield over her students is apparent throughout the piece. The girls are fascinated by the differences between Sister Imelda and the other nuns, as is suggested in the effect she has on her cooking students, all of whom, from the narrator's perspective, seem to be in love with her (16), and in their sense of freedom about asking questions about her life (65–70). She has differentiated herself from the other nuns by seeming to be a human being, with problems and desires, as well as being a nun. This comprises a large part of her power, since she seems to her students an oasis of humanity in an otherwise dreary and impersonal school. However, she has a passionate temper, a trait that gives her even greater power, but that also makes her seem dangerous. The possibility of violence is suggested in the rumor that circulates among the girls of Sister Imelda's having beaten a student (7) and the narrator's prayer that Sister Imelda would not ever have to punish her (8). The violence of Sister Imelda's temper is shown directly in her anger at the narrator when the latter does poorly in geometry class (11), an incident that makes the sense of danger that she exudes seem all the more real. However, Sister Imelda is perhaps most dangerous because of her ability to manipulate the narrator's emotions, not only in her moments of anger, but when she apologizes by giving presents (13, 14) and when she takes risks in order to be more intimate with her (20, 44, 52, 87). Because she embodies both earthly authority as a teacher and spiritual authority as a nun, Sister Imelda's acts carry more weight than an ordinary person's. Moreover, her sacrifices for her faith make her seem heroic. Had Sister Imelda been an ambitious, competitive character rather than humble and self-sacrificing, she would have been much less sympathetic. She wouldn't have been as accessible, nor as romantic, and her connection with the students, especially the narrator, would never have developed, leaving us essentially without a story.

4.    Students will find Baba's wry comments sprinkled throughout "Sister Imelda." Wherever she enters the narrative, Baba serves as a foil for the narrator's romanticism and spiritual longings. When the narrator comments on Sister Imelda's beautiful eyes, Baba replies that Sister Imelda has "Something wrong in her upstairs department" (5). When the narrator receives gifts from Sister Imelda, Baba says it's "foul to be a nun's pet," a comment that demonstrates not only her antagonism toward the narrator's involvement with Sister Imelda, but also her jealousy of their relationship (14). Baba sees clearly the line that separates the nuns from the students, and her comments suggest she sometimes views the narrator as a traitor to her own peer group and to Baba personally. While Sister Imelda kisses and praises the narrator for her performance in the Christmas play, Baba tells her she "bawled like a bloody bull" (35). As the narrator begins to become obsessed with Sister Imelda, Baba's comments become increasingly acerbic. However, Baba also serves to help keep the narrative grounded in the realities of convent-school life; since the narrator views events through the lens of her love for Sister Imelda, her narrative needs Baba's barbed words to help the reader realize how impossible are the obstacles of age, sex, and religious devotion that divide the narrator from the object of her affections.

## Connections

1.    The most important difference in the asceticism of convent life in "Sister Imelda" and the farmers' lives in "Rice Farming in Vietnam" is that the nuns have chosen to live without luxuries, while the farmers often do without even the necessities of living, such as an adequate diet (para. 13), because of a war over which they have no control. The nuns,

on the other hand, accept an austere and reclusive life as a way of developing their spirituality. The narrator, noticing a sty on Sister Imelda's eye, wonders if she has "overmortified herself" by refusing to eat (8). Their periods of silence outside the classroom, inadequate diet, interrupted sleep, and seclusion from friends and family are all privations that the nuns believe better prepare them to serve god. In "Rice Farming in Vietnam," on the other hand, the farmers and their families struggle to stay alive, to feed and house themselves and their families. The war continually brings destruction to their village, and they are unable to prepare for it or completely stave off its effects. When the "snake-monsters" arrive, they flee, often without a change of clothes or any food (10), and later arrive back in the village to find their homes burned to the ground (12). However, the farmers, like the nuns, show their strength by enduring hardships and by placing no importance on the luxuries they lack. They keep their families together, continue to farm, and keep their culture alive in the form of myths and prayers (26, 39).

2. Students will better appreciate Sister Imelda's unique values when they compare her attitude toward work with those represented in *Looking at Ourselves*. For instance, Elliot Liebow's piece on the plight of the unskilled African-American laborer, who never has a chance at a job worth persevering for, highlights the difference between Sister Imelda and other workers. She is not alienated from work; instead, she is entirely devoted to her work, in the sense that the convent and its school comprises almost her entire life. She has no private life; even when she goes home for her brother's funeral, another nun goes with her. Sister Imelda's work ethic validates some of the values represented negatively in Fred Moody's piece, "When Work Becomes an Obsession." Although she is seeking what Moody calls "spiritual and philosophical truths," she also seems to take her devotion to her calling so seriously that she deprives herself of rest and food. She does not seem to achieve the "balanced life" Moody advocates. Students may be able to see an analogy between Sister Imelda and the labor organizer who speaks in Studs Terkel's piece from *Working*. His job involves creating a community, a "brotherhood," of workers who will be better able to have a good life and fair working conditions if they band together. Although the purposes of convent life are different, the need to belong wholeheartedly to a group of people with the same interests is represented in "Sister Imelda" as well as the Terkel piece. Another analogy is possible between "Sister Imelda" and Linda Hasselstrom's piece about ranching in South Dakota. Hasselstrom's friends wonder why she would want the simple and hard life of a rancher when she has a college degree that could help her get a well-paying job. In "Sister Imelda," Baba wonders why Sister Imelda spent four years at a university only to come back to "poverty, chastity, and obedience" (7). Hasseltrom lives the life she does because she wants to achieve variety and balance between simple physical labor and intellectual effort, a goal that Sister Imelda might be sympathetic with, although her own goals involve devoting herself to the narrow life of the convent.

3. Students may have some difficulty in discussing "Sister Imelda" as a love story because it describes a relationship between a grown woman and a young girl, but the full impact of the story can only be appreciated when the romantic nature of the narrator's feelings for the nun is acknowledged. The narrator finds in Sister Imelda a woman she wants to emulate, as indicated in her fleeting desire to become a nun (6, 62), and she values her as a mother figure as well (17), but mixed in with these desires and wishes is a new sense

of how special she is in Sister Imelda's eyes. Sister Imelda enjoys the narrator's adoration, but she also makes the narrator feel that she is a valued person. The narrator wants to take her "place in a new and hallowed" world, and her relationship with Sister Imelda seems to offer her a way to enter that world. In "Yellow Woman," the narrator seeks through Silva a similar validation of herself as a special person separate from her life in her own family and community. Silva seems to embody the Native American myths the narrator feels herself to be a part of. But both women ultimately reject the people they fall in love with in order to choose the more ordinary route; Yellow Woman returns home to her family and leaves the mythic world behind, and the narrator in "Sister Imelda" does not return to the convent to be a nun. Instead, she chooses the more conventional route Baba urges her to take. She reports that "life was geared to work and to meeting men" even though she realized that marriage and motherhood had little to offer her (92).

## PRIMO LEVI, Uranium (p. 463)

### Explorations

1. Bonino wants Primo Levi to write down the story of Bonino's "escape," and sends him the "uranium" to convince him that the story is credible. Most students will find it easy to see the difference between the way Bonino wanted Levi to write the story and the story as Levi tells it in this piece. Bonino hoped to be taken seriously; the story as he wanted it told would have centered on his own heroism and would have been full of unlikely adventures. The frame that Levi sets up for Bonino's story makes it clear that the story is not credible and that Levi only listened to it because his job requires him to behave diplomatically with customers. The story as Levi conveys it is a sad example of self-aggrandizement and simple-mindedness, but Bonino is so naïve that Levi's ironic retelling might not have made any impression. If so, then he might consider himself well repaid by Levi's story.

2. Levi describes his job in the opening paragraphs. At the time the story took place, he was working as a customer service representative for a chemical company. His primary duties involved arranging for customers to order products from the company. In his "real job," Levi is a storyteller. Students will be able to pick up from Bonino's comments on Levi's novel that Levi is a popular writer of novels, and the fact that Levi used an incident from his customer service job in his writing suggests that Levi's "real job" is that of writer.

3. Both the manner in which Bonino tells his story and some of the events he relates suggest that he has invented it. Levi is wary as soon as he hears Bonino mention the Badogliano (para. 9). He knows that someone who had actually been with the Badogliano would not have used that label. From that moment, Levi assumes that Bonino has nothing to offer but a long-winded story. Bonino's story-telling style, which is full of digressions and vague references, also causes doubts (10). At one point, Bonino describes himself walking behind a guard and then quickly corrects himself (11), suggesting that he is unable to get his own story straight. Bonino's references to Levi's experience in the Holocaust, when he says that Levi's book might be too disturbing for children (7) and

105

then says that he (Bonino) "risked finishing up like you did" (8), imply that Levi has reason to know if Bonino's account of his own adventures had no truth. Levi's testing of the "uranium" at the end of story confirms that his assumption was correct, that the "little man's paranoic tale" was entirely invented (21).

4. In spite of his skepticism and his ironic approach to Bonino's story, Levi writes early on in the piece that his job in customer service had forced him to pretend to "esteem and like" others for so long that he had actually begun to do so. His irritation with Bonino's story is mingled with tolerance and even interest, since as a writer he is curious about how and why Bonino created his fictional history. The biblical quotation indicates that, although Bonino is alien to Levi, Levi will put up with the story patiently because he recalls that he too has sometimes told stories to people who didn't want to hear them. Bonino and Levi continue to be "strangers," however, in the sense that Levi doesn't want to hear Bonino's story because it is badly told and untrue, whereas people sometimes didn't want to hear Levi's stories because they are compellingly told and disturbingly realistic.

## Connections

1. Both Sister Imelda and Primo Levi are as much (or more) interested in people and personal relationships than in their official duties. This has advantages for both. Sister Imelda inspires respect and, in the case of the narrator, a kind of love that makes students more attentive to her teaching and more open to her religious views. That Sister Imelda has an unusually positive effect on her students is evident when she enters the classroom to teach cooking and, the narrator reports, "It was as if every girl was in love with her . . . as she entered, their faces broke into smiles" (para. 16). However, on occasion Sister Imelda's passionate nature prevents her from doing well, as when she becomes angry and storms out of the classroom (11). In addition, her close involvement with the narrator suggests that she has trouble keeping a professional distance, a fault that could have a detrimental effect on her students. Primo Levi, like Sister Imelda, is interested in people. This in itself makes him good at his job, but Levi also demonstrates that he understands the hierarchical "game" that he must play with customers (2). However, when Levi assesses his own abilities as a customer service representative, he reports that he performs the job with "compunction and little human warmth" (3), attitudes that make it difficult for him to play the game of winning over the customers.

2. Like "Making Magic," "Uranium" begins with the narrator's assessment of his own abilities. Abram sees himself as a "sleight-of-hand magician" (4) who can use his limited abilities to gain access to people who would otherwise have little to do with him. Similarly, Levi tries to convey an illusion of competence and enthusiasm in order to sell his company's products. At the center of each writer's piece is a visit to someone who is a stranger, whose views are in many ways foreign to the narrator. Gedé and Bonino both expect the writers to do them an unusual service: Gedé wants Abram to make real magic and help him catch fish again, and Bonino expects Levi to believe in and, he hopes, publish his incredible story. Both writers come away from these experiences feeling simultaneously disillusioned and satisfied with their encounters. Students will be able to locate several places in "Making Magic" where Abram might have cited the same biblical quotation as Levi: when he is being followed in Sri Lanka by sick and troubled people who want him to perform curative magic; when he visits the Balinese sorcerers who "felt

their status threatened by a stranger" (7); and when Gedé comes to his hut to insist he perform magic (15), Abram might well have considered the wisdom of respecting people even when they and their customs seem particularly alien.

3.  Levi writes that a good customer service representative is able to "infuse faith in the customer" and give the impression of being "superior" without being condescending (1, 2). The ability to create a context of trust and inattention on the part of the customer is similar to Abram's approach to performing magic. He recalls that when he sees the eyes of people in the audience "slowly widening with astonishment" he almost begins to believe in his own magic. In the same way, Levi writes that creating an atmosphere of trust with a customer has the effect of giving the representative faith in himself (1).

## TOMOYUKI IWASHITA (Toe-moe-yoo-ki Ee-wuh-SHEE-tuh), Why I Quit the Company (p. 471)

### Explorations

1.  Tomoyuki Iwashita gives little information about the company he worked for and virtually no information about what he did for the company. In the second paragraph, he identifies the company as "a big, well-known trading company," but having made this brief comment, Iwashita turns to the issue that is important to his essay: the effect of company indoctrination on the lives of employees. Initially, many students may be at a loss about how to respond to the last part of the question, but once they understand that Iwashita is more interested in portraying the social and psychological effects of company life than in discussing Japanese business, they will find it easier to analyze the effects of Iwashita's omissions. One effect of giving little specific information about the company is that it seems to take on some of the qualities of Big Brother in George Orwell's *1984*, in that the company seems to be able to take over many aspects of employee's lives and command their complete devotion, without having to justify its own existence or explain the reasons for the demands it places on employees.

2.  It should be immediately apparent to many students that "Japanese yuppies" share with their Western counterparts a strong drive to succeed in corporate life — even to the point of being willing to give up their social and family lives out of loyalty to the company's interests (paras. 5, 8, 9). They tend to try to live a luxurious lifestyle, even to the point of going into debt to achieve it (11). However, unlike the stereotype of the American yuppie, Japanese corporate employees focus on the needs and interests of the company and the Japanese economy, rather than on individual achievement and satisfaction (10). They fear failing to justify the financial investment the company claims it has made on their behalf (5), and tend to overwork in an effort to keep up with the company's expectations. Iwashita has lived the life of a yuppie in corporate Japan. His sources of information for his concept of yuppies are firsthand, drawn from his own experiences and observations on the life-styles of his friends and colleagues in the company.

3.  Japanese companies provide conveniences, and some luxuries, that American employees never receive. The dorm system, with housekeeping and meals taken care of, is completely unknown in the United States (3). However, many students will be quick to

point out that American employees can expect to receive sick leave as a part of their benefits package, but Japanese companies do not offer these benefits. Although many American employees can expect to put in long hours if their goal is to become an executive, they will probably not be expected to give the same level of dedication. Employees of Japanese corporations essentially do all their living within the company, living in company dormitories (3), depending on the company for many goods and services (4), and giving up their leisure time to entertain clients and socialize with other employees (4). Many employees do not marry until the company approves of it (8), and Iwashita writes that even the quality of family life is determined by the needs of the company (9).

## Connections

1. In paragraph 5, Iwashita discusses the isolation that the company tries to impose on its employees. The effect of this isolation is to create a relationship between employer and employee that is based on control and obedience. Iwashita discusses how the company needs only three months to train its new employees. They arrive as individuals who are "active, clever, and tough," but they will not be really useful to the company until they are "brainwashed" to be devoted to the company. Employees who have gone through this process often express the fear that they are not contributing enough; they have lost some of the self-confidence they arrived with and have adopted the attitude that the company's interests are more important than "their own mental and physical wellbeing." The employer-employee relationship suggested in Primo Levi's "Uranium" is very different. The company Levi works for does not seem to expect subservience. He describes a working life with a great deal of independence and variety. Levi writes that a customer service representative must have faith in the products he sells; the emphasis is not on unquestioning loyalty to the company, but on knowing the worth of the product. Levi also stresses the benefits for the individual of customer service work. He writes that selling "helps you to know yourself and strengthens your character." The development of the individual is not a goal in Japanese companies, which, according to Iwashita's perspective, prefer obedience and teamwork in their employees.

2. Fred Moody's account of the American work ethic accords strongly with Iwashita's comments about corporate life in Japan. Moody's beginning statement, that work has infiltrated all other aspects of American workers' lives, suggests parallels to Iwashita's description in paragraph 4 of how the working day in Japanese corporations is extended into the evenings and weekend and his comments in paragraph 8 about how the company controls its employee's private lives. After discussing Connections #1 above, however, students may be better able to analyze the differences in the work ethic Moody and Iwashita describe. Like Levi, Moody implies that the individual makes a commitment to his or her own career, not to any particular company. Moody does not say that employees of American companies have been brainwashed, as Iwashita says of Japanese employees (5). Instead, he implies that they are motivated by some of the same qualities that new employees in Japanese companies possess when they are first hired: initiative, intelligence, and strength. While Japanese employees are required to moderate these qualities to become integrated into the company, their American counterparts work on their own behalf. Many students will deduce, however, that although American and Japanese workers are motivated differently, the effect is the same: Overworking is a trait businesspeople in both countries share.

108

3.  Smith makes several generalizations about Japanese business practices and psychology that are supported by Iwashita's account of his life in a Japanese corporation. Perhaps the most significant of Smith's generalizations is that the Japanese do not favor individual choice because it might weaken the sense of obligation "which keeps the Japanese living in a rigidly defined hierarchy of authority" (6). Iwashita notes that employees of the company he worked for worried about their obligations, especially whether they were contributing enough to the company's profits (5). When Iwashita collapsed from overwork, his supervisor put the blame on Iwashita; the idea that the employee alone is responsible for work-related health problems has sometimes led to an employee's death — a phenomenon that underscores employees' commitment to the company's interests (6). Iwashita comments on the company's demand that employees become integrated into the company, committing themselves to it for life (4); in a similar vein, Smith notes that one of the maxims corporate employees offer to each other is *Gambatte*, or "Think long term" (9), suggesting that persistence is considered the key to success. Overall, Smith's perspective on Japanese business seems more positive than Iwashita's, probably because he is a Westerner, an outsider who does not live fully within the system as Iwashita does.

**RAYMOND BONNER, A Woman's Place (p. 475)**

**Explorations**

1.  The title of Bonner's essay comes from the expression "A woman's place is in the home." Students' expectations about "A Woman's Place" will vary according to their backgrounds and their ideas about women's roles, but few will identify with the Kuwaiti perspective on domestic labor. Only a few American students will have grown up in homes where maids were employed. Those who have had family members or friends employed as domestic workers will recognize that the plight of the Asian maids in Kuwait is in many respects worse than it is for domestic workers in the United States. Bonner includes information about the "liberation" of Kuwaiti women (para. 29), who legally can expect to earn the same wage as men and receive paid maternity leave (27), rights which, as Bonner points out, women in the United States are still struggling to achieve. Many Kuwaiti women are stepping out of their "place" in the home to run businesses (28), but their greater determination to win rights for themselves has not been extended to include women outside their cultural and economic group. Asian maids are still stuck in the home, but ironically they are most out of "place" when they are fulfilling traditional feminine jobs in the homes of privileged Kuwaitis.

2.  Because Bonner devotes so much of his essay to examples and narratives that illustrate the predicament of the Asian maid and little to defining the problem directly, students may be able to come up with several differing statements of his thesis. After reading his analysis in paragraph 24, some may say that his thesis is that conflicts between traditional values and modern lifestyles created a society in which abuses like those inflicted on the maids can occur. Others may identify gender, class, or cultural conflicts as the basic

problems that underlie the exploitation of poor, foreign, female workers (24, 32). In fact, however, Bonner's essay demonstrates how these conflicts have worked together to create a social system with a built-in potential for the exploitation of these workers, who lack legal rights and protections because they are foreigners (32), because they are women (28), and because they are poor. One of the most succinct statements of the Kuwaiti perspective on Asian maids comes from an agency representative who tells Bonner that he can have his housemaids work any number of hours because "they belong to you" (18). Their system of domestic employment amounts to slavery.

3. Bonner relies primarily on anecdotal evidence to support his argument about the exploitation of Asian maids in Kuwait. His essay begins with the example of a maid who fled the house where she was employed after she was beaten by her employer. To a Western reader, unacquainted with human rights issues in Arab countries, this example might seem extreme, but Bonner piles example on example, some even more extreme than the case with which he opens the essay. He creates an image of a nation of wealthy households marred by violence and abuse of domestic workers. Bonner did firsthand research (he went to the embassies (1) and police stations (11) where maids had taken refuge, and he posed as a potential employer when he visited agencies (19)), used testimony taken directly from the women who had fled the houses where they were employed, and talked with Kuwaiti women about their social and professional status. He also cites a few statistics about the numbers of foreign workers and domestic workers in Kuwait (22) and how many Asian maids have taken refuge at embassies (23), but the lack of interest among Kuwaitis about the fate of foreign workers suggests that no one has taken the trouble to document abuses. For this reason, and because his technique helps to put a human face on the problem, Bonner chose to rely heavily on anecdotal evidence gleaned during interviews.

## Connections

1. Students will be able to discuss the differences and the similarities between the situation of the Asian maids in Kuwait and the corporate employees in Japan by considering the social and economic context in which each group is attempting to deal with its labor problems. The Japanese workers are in their own country, near their friends and family. They still have civil rights and are making a relatively good living. They have some employment options open to them if they decide to leave the company. The Asian maids in Kuwait have none of these advantages. Most have no friends in Kuwait, do not speak the language, and have virtually no opportunities to improve their lot either by staying in a particular job or by attempting to leave it. In spite of these clear differences, there are some significant similarities in their situations. Both groups of workers have limited freedom of movement and little free time. Bonner, for instance, cites the case of Jenny Casanova, who worked eighteen-hour days and received no day off (para. 4). Similarly, Iwashita recalls that his life in the company "rapidly became reduced to a shuttle between the dorm and the office" (2) and that many employees became exhausted from overwork (6). The dorm system imposed by many companies on unmarried employees is somewhat similar to the situation of the maids, who also have no choice about where they reside, and whose personal lives are rigidly controlled by their employers (4–6).

2.  Aside from the similarity in the kind of work, a comparison between Mary's job and the situation of Asian maids in Kuwait can best be made by considering the moment when Mrs. Cullinan decides to call Marguerite "Mary". Mrs. Cullinan believes it is her privilege to call black domestic workers by any name she likes. In the act of naming her, Mrs. Cullinan is drawing on a long tradition dating from the slave era. Asian maids in Kuwait have their identities erased as well. Having left their native land and language behind, they are employed by people who regard them as virtual slaves (18). In both Marguerite's situation and that of Jenny Casanova (Bonner, 1), racial, cultural, and economic inequalities produce a situation in which the employer attempts to deprive the worker of dignity, but Marguerite has a somewhat better situation than Casanova, because she is not physically abused, has her family nearby, speaks the same language as her employer, and can end her employment by using her intelligence.

3.  Both Kuwaiti and Saudi women have made some progress in employment and entrepreneurship while maintaining their fidelity to traditional values. Cooke mentions the success of Shafiqa Jazzar, who began with a dress shop in her home and now owns a store (8, 9), and describes the women's section of a Riyadh newspaper, where Saudi women accept the veil and physical segregation but refuse to pursue "feminine" stories. Bonner cites similar success for women journalists in Kuwait. He mentions that two editors at the Kuwait News Agency are women (28). In contrast to Saudis, women journalists in Kuwait are not segregated from men. In both Saudi Arabia and Kuwait, there has been a degree of government support for women's employment outside the home. Kuwait adopted a labor code that guaranteed equal pay for equal work (27), and women in Saudi Arabia are receiving business permits (8) and support for their business ventures from the Islamic Bank (9). Bonner compares the status of Saudi and Kuwaiti women in paragraph 26, where he says that Saudis are disadvantaged in that they are not permitted to drive or move about alone in public. Cooke, however, is convinced that wearing the veil and other seemingly restrictive customs are no hindrance to Saudis, who go out unchaperoned (but veiled) and participate freely in religious meetings and educational opportunities (17, 18).

4.  Perhaps the first things students will notice about the representations of violence in Sa'edi's story and Bonner's essay is that violence is portrayed as an accepted part of everyday life, passed on through generations and learned through imitation. In the poor Iranian community Sa'edi describes, the narrator and his friend Hasani treat each other in the same way they are treated by their parents. They hit each other as soon as they meet (1), and suggest a beating as the stake in a bet (273, 274). Writing of the abuse of Asian maids in middle-class Kuwaiti households, Bonner quotes Eman al-Bedah, who asserts that Kuwaiti women mistreat their maids as Kuwaiti husbands mistreat their wives. Similarly, the boys in "The Game Is Over" have learned to communicate with each other through violence because their parents, especially their fathers, set the example by beating their children and their wives regularly. The acceptance of violence as a principle of living is so thoroughly rooted in the boys that when Hasani wants a sign that his parents love and value him, he stages a deception that relies on a violent act — his own death. Some Kuwaitis have a similar perspective in that they are so used to certain kinds of domestic violence that they do not see the physical abuse of maids as a problem.

111

**YOSHIMI ISHIKAWA (Yoe-SHEE-me Ee-shee-KA-wuh), Strawberry Fields (p. 487)**

**Explorations**

1.  Before interpreting Yoshimi Ishikawa's comments about farmers being unable to mold the land, students will need to consider the context. Ishikawa describes how he and his brother learned to drink irrigation water (paras. 6, 7); later, he writes that the land had taught his brother to be a farmer (19). Anchan tastes the soil to find out if it will be good for growing strawberries, but the land is so unpredictable (12) that he can't make any assumptions about it. Ishikawa states the premise behind this comment directly when he writes that the land "transforms and creates" the farmer (7). The fact that they drink, and even enjoy, muddy irrigation water means that they are literally taking the land into themselves, but it also serves as a metaphor for the necessity of the farmer's learning about, and adapting to, the land.

    However, the goal of their adapting to the land is to tame it as much as possible. They "begin by making the land arable" (29). In the process, they adapt the land to their own needs. The success of Frank, who made good money farming, attests to the farmers' ability to mold the land — to some degree at least — to their own purposes (4), but Frank has also been molded by the land, for his hard work over many years has damaged his body and spirit (4).

2.  It may be difficult for students to extrapolate from Ishikawa's essay how these characters were before they emigrated, but students will be able to draw inferences from Ishikawa's discussion of the differences in American and Japanese farming. Ishikawa stresses the predictability of farming in Japan. He mentions that farmers there knew how much they could make in a year (3), that the land had always been used before, and that the process of farming varied little (29). His emphasis on predictability may be taken as a cultural, as well as an agricultural, observation; Ishikawa and his brother knew what to expect from Japan, but the United States is much less predictable. Frank is perhaps the most outstanding example of the changes that a Japanese might undergo in the United States. Having his land taken from him, being sent to an internment camp, and rebuilding his farm after his release are all experiences that attest to the unpredictability of life in the West.

    Ishikawa also expresses his concern about change when he writes that he is worried he might become like the nisei, who are too deeply influenced by Western mores. He is troubled by the possibility of becoming acculturated and notes that immigrants change the way they communicate, becoming belligerent and less willing to listen, in an effort to make themselves visible (63). The farmers have also been affected by ethnic and international politics in their area, factors that make their experience in the United States drastically different from what it would be in their own more isolated island nation. Ishikawa has become knowledgeable about border politics and the ways in which ethnic differences among the Mexicans, Anglos, Filipinos, and Japanese affect the agricultural economy. In Japan, where ethnic and national differences are at a minimum, the problems he and his brother have learned to cope with do not exist.

3.  Students should find it easy to respond to this question. Ishikawa clearly delineates the process sections of his essay, dividing the process into two parts: 1) preparing the land and 2) planting strawberries. He announces the first part of the process with a question:

"So how did we convert our field?" (21). He describes raking, removing rocks (22), watering and weeding (23), exterminating pests (24), and fertilizing (25). Ishikawa signals the shift to the next part of the process in paragraph 27: "Now, we began to farm." He describes planting, irrigating (28), and the long process of waiting and checking on whether the strawberry plants had taken root (31, 32). Ishikawa completes the process section of the essay while this period of waiting is continuing (32).

## Connections

1.  Students will be quick to see that the relationships between the Japanese and Mexicans on one hand and Kuwaitis and Asians on the other are similar in that both are based on racial and cultural differences. In Ishikawa's essay, Pete says that the Mexicans don't want to work because it's hot (para. 45), a prejudicial comment that builds on his idea that Japanese are hardworking people and Mexicans are lazy. The Mexican workers are mistreated in that they are often paid below minimum wage — or not at all — and work under poor conditions (44). Similarly, Asian maids in Kuwait are paid little and work extremely hard (6, 19). Raymond Bonner writes that Asian maids in Kuwait "are foreigners in an extemely closed and xenophobic society" (31). Asians in Kuwait "are at the bottom of the heap." In both cases, an economically dominant group abuses its power, and it can do so because the exploited group is composed of foreigners who have virtually no civil rights and no family or friends in the area. Also similar in Bonner's and Ishikawa's essays is the dominant group's willful ignorance of the workers' plight. Ishikawa recalls that he had not been paying attention to media reports of the workers' strike and that even those who had employed Mexicans for years couldn't understand the workers' motives for going on strike. Bonner quotes a Kuwaiti human-rights activist who denies that Asian maids are exploited economically or abused physically (32), and Kuwaiti feminist groups do not recognize the working conditions of maids as a problem (35). The Japanese and Kuwaitis view foreign workers only in light of how they will contribute to their own interests; they are uninterested even in the basic needs of the workers.

    It is important for students to consider some of the differences in the employer-employee relationships Ishikawa and Bonner describe, especially the role that gender plays in both cases. Bonner points out that Asian maids are vulnerable to being exploited and abused not only because they are foreigners, but because they are women (24). Their plight remains hidden because they are scattered and hidden in homes, have no opportunity to form a union, and therefore cannot develop a sense of solidarity. The Mexican workers, however, became visible under the leadership of Cesar Chavez and were able to form a union that helped them work toward achieving better working conditions.

2.  Hayslip and Ishikawa write of a sensual relationship between the farmer and the earth. Hayslip recalls "that sensual contact between our hands and feet, the baby rice, and the wet, receptive earth" as a phenomenon that reaffirmed farmers' connection to the land (23). Ishikawa remembers seeing his brother drink muddy irrigation water and pronounce it "delicious" (6). Later on, after he, too, has learned to enjoy irrigation water, he decides that this demonstrates that the land "transforms and creates" the farmer (7). In both "Strawberry Fields" and "Rice Farming in Vietnam," the authors describe a process of preparing the land and then planting the crop. Student will be able to refer to their responses to Explorations #3 in order to compare Ishikawa's description of the process

with Hayslip's. Hayslip goes further than Ishikawa in her process description. She relates the steps in preparing the land for planting rice in paragraph 22, and then goes on to describe planting, fertilizing, and weeding (23, 24). Then she goes further, taking the process all the way through harvesting, preparing for the next planting, and preparing rice to be stored for eating (30–33).

3.  Among the ideas Ishikawa and Hasselstrom share is the idea that higher education and work on the land go hand in hand. Hasselstrom writes that many people believe "that anyone who enjoys physical labor must be too dumb to get an education." Ishikawa writes that human beings are born with a desire to work (1); his insightful reflections on the intellectual challenges of farming, along with the fact that he was attending school in order to improve his English for college during the time of which he writes, suggest that he and Hasselstrom are in agreement that the hard physical labor of farming contributes to, rather than detracts from, intellectual effort.

4.  Ishikawa both fears and hopes that he will become Americanized if he continues to study its language and culture (1). He notices the differences between American competition, which involves the possibility of vast personal losses and gains, and Japanese competition, which is extremely predictable (4). Kimura's editorial also takes note of the extravagance of American competition, where $15 million can easily be spent on a meaningless contest. The Japanese, by contrast, work hard and consistently to build "the best in television sets, Walkman stereos, and cars," but in order to be taken seriously by Americans, they will have to be willing to engage in a kind of extreme financial risk-taking that is foreign to the Japanese.

## GABRIEL GARCÍA MÁRQUEZ (Gah-bree-EL Gar-SEE-ah MAR-kez), Dreams for Hire (p. 497)

### Explorations

1.  "Dreams for Hire" partakes of some elements of the short story and some elements of the essay. Márquez offers little exposition, leaping right into the first scene of his narrative, the tidal wave that smashes into the hotel. Márquez returns to this scene at the conclusion of the piece. Thus the structure of "Dreams for Hire" is similar to a framed story, in which a central narrative is contained within, and contextualized by, another narrative displaced from it in time and space. In addition, Márquez's narrative has elements of suspense ordinarily associated with fiction, especially the mystery. Is it really Frau Frida who died? What is the significance of the serpent-shaped ring? Márquez describes his characters in detail, using their conversation to advance arguments about the association of dreams and poetry, as when Neruda expounds his opinion of dream divination in paragraphs 16 and 17. But he also pays attention to character development; his portrait of Neruda includes the poet's physical appearance (13), his eating habits, his relationship with his wife, and his propensity to dominate others, as in the "inevitable walk along the Ramblas" (18) and the "sacred siesta" (23). These are elements of character development missing in most conventional essays.

The aspects of "Dreams for Hire" that remind us Márquez is writing factually are the writer's physical presence at the real events he describes and his representation of Neruda, a famous poet.

2. Students will quickly be able to identify Márquez's ambivalence about Frau Frida's occupation in his comments to her during their walk along the Ramblas. He tells her that "her dreams were no more than a contrivance," but he still refuses to return to Vienna because he is worried about the unidentified disaster Frau Frida dreamed he would undergo there (17, 22). Frau Frida takes her dreams in a matter-of-fact way, telling Márquez that no danger awaits him in Vienna anymore. She does not create drama around her dreams and doesn't always take them seriously, as when she tells him that not all dreams represent "real life" (33). The irony of her doubting herself — because her dream about Neruda is true — is compounded by her death. Frau Frida foretold disasters for others, but it is possible she was not able to perceive the reality of her dreams when they related to her own life.

3. Márquez describes Frau Frida as "magical," but "fearsome" (3). Neruda, like Frau Frida, dominates his audience with his substantial physical presence and his ability to command attention. He even displays a clairvoyant power like hers when he says to Márquez, "There's someone behind me who keeps staring at me" (14). The elements of character they share suggest the possibility of competition between them — a possibility expressed directly by Neruda when he says, "Only poetry is clairvoyant" (17). The limits of the poet's "clairvoyance" is suggested in his misinterpretation of his dream as his own new idea (hence his disappointment in paragraph 28 when Márquez points out that the idea has probably already been taken up by another Latin American literary giant, Jorges Luis Borges). Similarly, the limits of Frau Frida's clairvoyance are established when she believes her dream about Neruda is unrelated to reality.

4. Most students will have little doubt that the ambassador's dead housekeeper was Frau Frida. The unusual ring found on the body is suggestive, but the ambassador's comment that Márquez would have been unable to resist writing a story about her (35) is even more conclusive, because Márquez did go on to write "Dreams for Hire." The ambassador's comment that "she was a dreamer" does not confirm her identity, but it does reinforce Márquez's representation of her as a mysterious, powerful woman whose identity was prone to change. Frau Frida was not her real name, and Márquez apparently never learned what her real name was (4).

## Connections

1. Responses to this question will depend on how individual students define "necessity" in relation to job choice. It was a "harsh Viennese winter" that originally drove Frau Frida to sell her skill as a dreamer (para. 8). The practical necessity of obtaining food and housing is also a compelling reason to choose a particular job in Le Ly Hayslip's "Rice Farming in Vietnam," Primo Levi's "Uranium," and Raymond Bonner's "A Woman's Place." In Hayslip's piece, villagers farm because they must feed themselves. They raise their staple diet themselves. In Primo Levi's "Uranium," the author takes a job in private industry as a salesperson in order to supplement his irregular income. And in "A Woman's Place," young Asian women come to Kuwait to be maids because they have so few employment opportunities in their own nations. But practical necessity may be

115

complemented by other kinds of necessity. Some students may view a vocation as a kind of necessity; if so, Frau Frida's vocation is similar to David Abram's in "Making Magic" and Sister Imelda's in Edna O'Brien's piece, in that she is pulled toward her profession as much because of an innate talent as by conscious choice.

2. Students will be able to build on their responses to Connections #1 when considering the similarities between Frau Frida's and David Abram's work. Both are able to use their unusual talent to give other people a greater sense of control over their own lives. Through the use of illusion, Abram helps a fisherman regain his confidence in his ability to catch enough fish to feed his family. And Frau Frida builds an entire career on her ability to interpret her own dreams as a way of forecasting the future for others. Abram discovers the significance of his talent when he realizes that, in a way, he really does have "powers" he himself can't understand (27). Frau Frida, although she is matter-of-fact about her extraordinary talent and not offended by Márquez's skepticism (19), nevertheless takes her dreams seriously and is charismatic enough to persuade others to take them seriously as well.

3. Depending on their background, some students may have found disagreeable the image of Neruda wrapped up in a bib, eating a huge amount of rich food, and carelessly sampling from everyone else's plate (14). Octavio Paz describes American cuisine as more concerned with health than pleasure or desire (3, 4), but its primary attribute is the concern with "exclusions" (1). By contrast, Paz suggests that European and Latin American cuisines are endowed with "passion," color, and spices (1, 2), a tolerance for "ambiguity and ambivalence" (3), desire, and pleasure (3, 4). In "Dreams for Hire," Márquez's depiction of Neruda's extravagant relish of his meal illustrates Paz's ideas about the relationship to food enjoyed by Latin Americans. Lunch for Neruda is not a matter of restoring health, but of luxuriating in food because of the pleasure it offers.

## ADDITIONAL QUESTIONS AND ASSIGNMENTS

1. In a journal entry or a collection of informal notes, discuss the role of workers presented in selections representing two or three cultures, with particular reference to oppression. Consider such issues as the employer-employee relationship; the role played by government, ideology, or both; and the existence (or absence) of a clearly defined working class. As you look over your notes, try to discover similarities and differences among the cultures represented. Then consider how you would describe the role of workers in the United States. Can you reach any conclusions about the differences between cultures?

2. Interview someone whose job you find particularly intriguing. Try to formulate questions that will elicit information about the person's reasons for choosing the job, the training he or she underwent, the person's perception of the importance of the job, his or her self-image with respect to the job, and the particular kind of satisfaction he or she gleans from it. As you write up the interview, try to integrate your own commentary with your subject's words.

3. Write a narrative about a character who makes a living from performing unconventional work, such as faith healing, palm reading, or astrology. Marquez' story or Abram's essay will serve as effective models. The character might be a con man or woman who manages to persuade credulous people to pay his or her way through life. Or he or she might genuinely have a unique and irreplaceable talent. In your characterization, consider what personality traits and what kind of personal history are necessary to this character's work and to what extent the work they do is dependent on the character's belief in his or her own "magic" abilities.

4. Many young women in the United States today are facing difficult decisions regarding balancing a career and family. Explore the issue of working mothers by consulting articles that have appeared in magazines and newspapers over the past several years. Look specifically for pieces that enumerate the problems faced by these women when it comes to running the home, caring for the children, and advancing on the job. Using this material as your evidence, write a classification paper in which you categorize the various problems faced by working mothers. Or write a process analysis in which you inform young women of the methods they might use to deal with the problems inherent in combining motherhood with a career.

5. Conduct further research into one of the cultures represented in this unit, focusing specifically on the country's work force. It would be wise to choose a culture about which information is readily available — the United States, Ireland, Japan, and Italy are likely candidates. If the selection is an excerpt from a larger work, look first at that work. You can find other sources by consulting the headnotes for other selections from that culture and a general encyclopedia, as well as journals devoted to the study of that culture. Narrow your primary focus to something manageable, such as the distribution of wealth in the culture, the economic philosophy, the existence or absence of a class system, or the major employment opportunities for citizens, and write a persuasive paper in which you either applaud or condemn the culture's treatment of workers.

## Part Six

## WE THE PEOPLE
## INDIVIDUALS AND INSTITUTIONS

### INTRODUCTION

Although students should find all the selections in this section fascinating, they may exhibit some discomfort with the blurring of ideological lines in many. Accustomed to defining political good versus evil in terms of Western democracy versus communism, some students may resist the negative images of America's contribution to the plight of the poor in other nations, of Israelis as oppressors, and of the South African government; equally disquieting may be the positive attitude toward reconciliation of differences between Western democracies and Communist states expressed in the essays by Havel and Shevardnadze. Precisely because of these unsettling portrayals, however, this section is one of the most important in the text. It provides a marvelous tool for encouraging students to explore political systems before judging them, to resist easy stereotypes, and to recognize similarities among seemingly disparate cultures.

To prepare students for the kind of questioning they'll need to exhibit throughout the section, instructors may want to begin by asking them to articulate their perceptions of how government acts for and against the people. The selections in *Looking at Ourselves* will be a help here: Vine Deloria, Jr., Clifford M. Lytle, and Haunani-Kay Trask all call attention to shortcomings in the U.S. system. Lapham and Berry don't look at the U.S. government per se, but they examine disturbing aspects of life in this country. Lapham traces connections between the official war on drugs and a pervasive racism and classism in U.S. society. Berry indicts our tendency to believe our lives are governed solely by economic laws; Sizer critiques American secondary schools for failing to educate and functioning simply as a way to keep young people off the labor market; and the *New Yorker* piece examines the responsibility of television news anchors for the trivialization of political campaigns. Toni Morrison and Martin Luther King provide commentary on racial issues in the United States; their pieces offer a valuable comparison with stories and essays that deal with racism and ethnocentrism in other nations, such as Nelson Mandela's "Black Man in a White Court," the anonymous writer's "Evicted: A Russian Jew's Story (Again)," and Nadine Gordimer's "Amnesty." The overview offered by these short pieces should provide a relatively easy way to introduce the kind of healthy skepticism students will encounter in the main selections. As they work their way through the section, they may need to be reminded occasionally that the purpose of exploring other cultures is simply to learn about them and to recognize the good and the evil in each government in order to become better able to judge our relationship with our own government.

Among possible subthemes in the section are the individual as victim of a political system (Mandela, Anonymous, Weldon, and Gordimer), views of Communist societies (Havel, Golden, and Shevardnadze), government as its own worst enemy (Golden, Shevardnadze, and Havel), problems resulting from changes in political conditions (Havel, Golden, and Anonymous), and the role of identity politics in the formation of nations (Mandela, Gordimer, Anonymous).

Instructors may wish to consult the following familiar works in preparing related selections from *Ourselves Among Others*:

## Essays

Martin Luther King, Jr., "Letter from Birmingham Jail" (*Why We Can't Wait*, Harper, 1963).
Walter Lippmann, "The Indispensable Opposition" (*Atlantic Monthly*, Aug. 1939).
George Orwell, "A Hanging" (*Shooting an Elephant*, Harcourt, 1950).
Jonathan Swift, "A Modest Proposal" (1729).
Henry David Thoreau, "On Resistance to Civil Disobedience" (1849).
Barbara Tuchman, "An Inquiry into the Persistence of Unwisdom in Government" (*Esquire*, May 1980; *The March of Folly*, Ch. 1, Knopf, 1984).

## Short Stories

Nadine Gordimer, "Some Monday for Sure" (*Not for Publication*, Viking, 1965).
Shirley Jackson, "The Lottery" (*The Lottery*, Farrar, Straus, 1949).
Ursula K. LeGuin, "The Ones Who Walk Away from Omelas" (*The Winds's Twelve Quarters*, Harper, 1975).
Thomas Mann, "Mario and the Magician" (*Stories of Three Decades*, Knopf, 1964).
Herman Melville, "Billy Budd, Sailor" (1891).

## BIOGRAPHICAL NOTES ON *LOOKING AT OURSELVES*

1. Wendell Berry, farmer and college professor at the University of Kentucky, has presented his agrarian, environmental philosophy eloquently in several volumes of essays (*Standing by Words*, 1983; *The Unsettling of America: Culture and Agriculture*, rev. ed. 1986; *The Hidden Wound*, 1989; *What Are People For?*, 1990), novels (*The Memory of Old Jack*, 1975), and poetry (*Collected Poems*, 1985).

2. Haunani-Kay Trask is a professor of Hawaiian Studies and Director of the Center for Hawaiian Studies at the University of Hawaii at Manoa. In 1986 she published *Eros and Power: Promise of Feminist Theory*. She is interested in the political and cultural struggles of native Islanders.

3. Vine Deloria, Jr., a Standing Rock Sioux attorney and professor of political science, has served as executive director of the National Congress of American Indians. Among his

powerfully argued works are *Custer Died for Your Sins: An Indian Manifesto* (1969), *We Talk You Listen* (1970), and *Behind the Trail of Broken Treaties* (1974).

4. Theodore Sizer is on the faculty of the School of Education at Brown University. His incisive analyses of American secondary schools are contained in *Horace's Compromise: The Dilemma of the American High School* (1984) and *Horace's School: Redesigning the American High School* (1992).

5. Winner of the 1993 Nobel Prize for literature, Toni Morrison's widely acclaimed novels include *The Bluest Eye* (1970), *Sula* (1973), *Song of Solomon* (1977), *Tar Baby* (1981), *Beloved* (Pulitizer Prize 1988), and *Jazz* (1992). She also gave a series of lectures at Harvard University published as *Playing in the Dark: Whiteness and the Literary Imagination* (1992). Most recently she edited a collection of essays on the Anita Hill-Clarence Thomas Controversy: *Race-ing Justice, En-gendering Power* (1992).

6. Martin Luther King, Jr., as head of the Southern Christian Leadership Conference, led a series of nonviolent protests and sit-ins against racial discrimination in the 1950s and 1960s that culminated in passage of the Civil Rights Act of 1964. Among his most memorable utterances were the "I Have a Dream" speech delivered in Washington, D.C., in 1963 and the "Letter from Birmingham Jail" published in *Why We Can't Wait* (1963). In 1964 he was awarded the Nobel Peace Prize. He was assassinated in 1968.

7. Shelby Steele teaches English at San Jose State University. In 1990 he published a much discussed collection of essays, *The Content of Our Character: A New Vision of Race in America.*

8. Editor of *Harper's* magazine, Lewis H. Lapham has written *Money and Class* (1987), *Imperial Masquerade* (1990), and *What's Going On Here?* (1991).

9. Jim Whitewolf, a Kiowa Apache, was born in Oklahoma around 1878. In 1949–50, Whitewolf told his story to ethnographer Charles Brant, whose record is the source for the included selection. Brant notes that Whitewolf "remained the steadfast, devoted member of the Native American Church which he had been throughout his lifetime." Whitewolf died in the mid-1950s.

## Reflections

1. This is a question that will allow students to share their general knowledge of world affairs with each other. Responses will vary a great deal depending on how much world history students know and how much international news they have encountered in the media Certainly many will realize that the manipulation of political events by the media discussed in the New Yorker selection is not a phenomenon peculiar to the United States; some will also realize that the struggle for African-American civil rights described by Martin Luther King, Jr., takes place within a society deeply influenced by white racist sentiments that also impel events in South Africa. Wendell Berry's concern that Americans are overly devoted to the idea of competition may also be familiar to students who have read about the Japanese enthusiasm for economic competition.

2. The *New Yorker* piece mentions many shortcomings of the television news. Many of the most telling criticisms come from the anchors, who said their medium focused on which candidate was ahead in the polls rather than what candidates stood for and that television news tended to privilege gossip and sensationalism over substantive news. They are also guilty of gullibility. Politicians have been able to direct the media's attention away from real news to non-issues, such as empty campaign symbols during the 1988 election campaign. The military as well has been able to mislead the media, deliberately concealing information and allowing reporters to see only carefully chosen battle sites. The *New Yorker* selection has little to say about what contributions the visual media make to American life, but it does contend that, because the media reflect the social system at large, they cannot be held solely responsible for the vacuity of substantive coverage. Further, there is a suggestion at the end of the piece that the public cares enough about the content of news programs to turn to other media in search of better coverage, a tendency that may spur television news to make changes in its practices.

3. According to Haunani-Kay Trask, Hawaiians before the arrival of the *haole* did not see their leaders as owners of the land, but as "stewards" of the land. Everyone, then, had the right to use the land, but no one could sell it. According to Vine Deloria, Jr., and Clifford M. Lytle, a similar concept of people's relationship to the land prevailed among American Indian tribes, in that they "held land in common."

4. Martin Luther King, Jr., sees the impetus for slavery as "primarily economic." Therefore, slavery heavily influenced the development of the unique social, political, and legal systems in the United States. White supremacy was literally founded on the practice of treating other human beings as property and depriving them of all rights, but white supremacy also required that the practice of slavery be rationalized — among whites — as morally just. Toni Morrison uses a similar argument in relation to the study of canonized American literature, which, in her view, has elided the important influence of "the four-hundred-year-old presence" of Africans and African-Americans on the evolution of the nation and its literature. Shelby Steele makes a valuable contribution to the arguments advanced by King and Morrison when he theorizes that white supremacy had to be justified, in the minds of whites, by an assumption of "innocence" that qualified them to subjugate black people. The loss of that sense of "innocence" — a loss brought about by the acknowledgement of the role of slavery in forming American social and legal systems and by the realization that black people have contributed directly and indirectly to American literature — also brings about a loss of power that could lead, under the best circumstances, to the end of white supremacy.

## EDUARD SHEVARDNADZE, Life with the Party (p. 521)

### Explorations

1. The virgin lands campaign was designed to develop wilderness for agriculture, largely through the labor of young volunteers in the Communist Youth Union. For Shevardnadze, the campaign was a success in that it gave him and other young people a sense that they

could accomplish great things (para. 3), but it was badly planned and badly organized, factors that "canceled out many successes." In particular, they had trouble with equipment and grain storage, which made it extremely difficult to bring the grain in once they had — successfully — grown it in the fields.

2. Shevardnadze recalls being elected Secretary of the Central Committee of Komsomol, an honor that reveals his early commitment to the Communist Party and its ideals. He felt positively about Nikita Khrushchev (4) and identified with the spirit of the Soviet cosmonauts. Later in life — in part, of course, because of his experiences with the virgin lands campaign — Shevardnadze became more skeptical about the ability of communism to create an economic system that would keep people productive. By the 1970s, Shevardnadze was still active and powerful in the Communist Party, serving as First Secretary of the Georgian CP Central Committee. But his attitude had changed; now he would try to get around the party ideologues who insisted on purity of doctrine over economic productivity (12). He currently presides over a non-Communist government.

3. Shevardnadze writes that he and Gorbachev shared "the same peasant roots, had worked on the land at a tender age, and had the same knowledge of folk life" (5). They were peers and compatriots, observing the progress and problems of the Soviet Union throughout their lives. The main risk involved in their friendship was, ironically, the need to be able to trust each other. Gorbachev could have brought Shevardnadze's career to an end after viewing his farm "experiment," which involved a modified capitalist approach to increasing productivity. Instead he recognized the effectiveness of Shevardnadze's ideas.

4. Judging from the virgin lands campaign and Shevardnadze's discussion of socialist farming, Soviet farming involved large-scale operations that were labor intensive, but involved few personal rewards for those who worked hardest. The Soviet workers' saying, "You pretend to pay us, and we pretend to work," suggests the difficulties that go along with expecting people to work for things they will not feel the benefit of in their own lives (11). Shevardnadze recalls that "a corn farmer who worked 400 man-days on a collective farm earned an average of 10-12 rubles a month and 200 kilos of corn a year" (13). This was not enough incentive to keep farmers in the fields. As a result, the Soviet Union suffered economic losses, because it was relying on its workers to produce enough to keep it solvent.

## Connections

1. Students will find a number of selections in *Looking at Ourselves* that portray institutions suffering from an obsession with "purity of doctrine." Among them, Martin Luther King, Jr., discusses how the American economy has been taken as an explainer and justifer of any action that seems to support capitalist ideologies. Wendell Berry criticizes the "ideal of competition" on which capitalism is founded, because competition can destroy familial and community relationships. King, analyzing the justifications for slavery in the United States, writes that "the attempt to give moral sanction to a profitable system gave birth to the doctrine of white supremacy." As long as slavery supported the capitalist project — as long as it was profitable — it could be justified as a valid expression of capitalism.

2. Iwashita contends that the company he worked for absorbed the lives of its employees, depriving them of any chance of independent thinking. He writes that the company controls the private, as well as professional, lives of employees (para. 8), and he found

that he could no longer believe that the relative security of life in the company was worth giving up his freedom of thought which was necessary for him if he was to "preserve the quality of [his] life and [his] sanity" (13). Shevardnadze, having lived much of his life devoted to the Communist Party, realizes that most people would think he and Gorbachev were eminently successful. But according to his own standards of success, Shevardnadze had to make "an intense search for a way out" of traditional party expectations.

3. As students discuss the relative advantages and disadvantages of Shevardnadze's work on the land as opposed to Ishikawa's, they may find themselves debating the relative merits of capitalism and communism. There is little doubt, especially in view of Shevardnadze's criticism of his own system, whose work on the land students will feel has the most advantages. Shevardnadze recalls feeling exhilarated by his farm work as a young man in the virgin lands campaign, but the poor management of that project left him skeptical about the efficacy of socialist farming. Ishikawa, by contrast, also has the experience of living very close to the land, but he and his brother — because they are farming on U.S. soil — will reap the benefits of their own labor. Instead of receiving the equivalent of 10 rubles a month, no matter how much they produce, they will take in as much profit as they produce. A few students may note that while Ishikawa's and his brother's initiative benefited only themselves, Shevardnadze's was recognized by the Party bureaucracy as potentially valuable to the larger system, so that from farming he has reaped an illustrious career.

## TIM GOLDEN, Cubans Try to Cope with Dying Socialism (p. 528)

### Explorations

1. Tim Golden's attitude about Cuba's economic woes is clear from the title of his essay: Cuba's economic system is dying; socialism cannot survive. And in paragraph 14, Golden writes that the achievements of the revolution are eroding. Castro, however, continues to believe that socialism will survive. In paragraph 2, he is quoted as saying that only a socialist revolution could survive the economic attacks on Cuba — a reference to U.S. policies that restrict trade and isolate Cuba economically. At the end of the essay, Golden inserts another Castro quote that suggests Castro will never give up the revolution. Castro says that although many sacrifices will have to be made, "what we will never give up is hope." Golden implies that Castro's insistence on the validity of socialism for Cuba is part of Cuba's problem; he asserts that the people of Cuba doubt they can endure for the "long years that any real economic recovery would take" (para. 7).

2. Students may need to differentiate the various causes of the Cubans' hardships while they discuss the effects of Cuba's policies on the daily lives of its citizens. Golden implies that a large part of the responsibility resides with Castro, although U.S. anti-Cuba policies and the demise of the Soviet Union have contributed much to Cuba's economic woes. Castro rations gasoline at a miniscule five gallons per month and bus service has been cut, making it very difficult for citizens to get across town. Government policies also decree

123

that food and electricity will be rationed (12, 38), but the rations are so small that citizens are forced into black-market trading (38).

3. "Resolviendo" is an illegal system of bartering in which whoever has access to a certain resource (either through legal ownership or through stealing) can use it to trade for items she or he needs. The system implies that Cubans are betraying the revolution by engaging in private enterprise and that they are therefore in opposition to socialism. However, as one Cuban maintains, "Nobody wants to do it, but everybody does it" (43). He implies that citizens feel guilty about trading illegally, but the dire economic situation drives them to look out for their own interests first. The government, on the other hand, maintains that it distributes all goods equally (31), but special privileges are still available to "members of the Cuban elite" who can shop at stores ordinary citizens don't even know exist (45). Both the government and Cuban citizens, then, are not living up to the ideals they publicly agree on.

4. Golden conveys the grim mood of many Cubans in paragraph 7, where he describes the "gauntlets of blank, sullen stares" of people waiting for buses that rarely arrive. The buses themselves are "dilapidated." When Golden describes a Cuban woman who used to enjoy a middle-class lifestyle and now has almost nothing to eat, he uses words such as "haggard" and — significantly — "disenchanted." The "disenchantment" of some Cubans suggests that their mood is impatient and even angry as well as "grim." Although Golden admits that a "substantial . . . core of support" remains for Castro's government (17), many see two options: endure the sacrifice or leave (18). An unidentified Western diplomat reports that people are afraid of what will happen to them if they speak out (23), but some have become more openly critical (22). A man who says he feels bad about engaging in "resolviendo" also blames the goverment for having "turned us all into thieves," a comment that suggests Cubans' tolerance for sacrifice is growing thin.

## Connections

1. Shevardnadze suggests the depth of the Soviet problem with productivity in the first paragraph of his essay, where he writes that all the money and human effort that had gone into cultivating "virgin lands" were wasted when crops rotted in the fields for lack of enough people to bring in the harvest and lack of storage for the grain. The effect of living with immense efforts and immense failures of the kind Shevardnadze describes was similar in the Soviet Union and Cuba; many people became resigned to doing without basic necessities. The Soviet workers' saying, "You pretend to pay us, and we pretend to work," also suggests their resignation about putting up with bad conditions (11). Finally, Shevardnadze states simply, "We . . . were always on short rations," indicating that doing without was as much a "national custom" in the Soviet Union as it is in Cuba.

2. Wendell Berry is writing about the negative personal and communal effects of economic competition under capitalism. However, socialism could also become the target of his attack, because socialism, like capitalism, upholds economic laws as primary shapers of reality. Berry complains that we allow the economic ideal of competition to determine our lives. He would like to believe that other laws guide us, but Golden's essay on Cuba proves that economics really is a kind of "last word" on what people are able to accomplish and how much pleasure they can take in living. Strapped for even the most

basic necessities, Cubans might argue that economic laws are indeed the ultimate laws. Although he never comments directly on socialism, Berry implies that for the losers in the capitalist system, competition will lead to the same probems Cubans are enduring.

3.  Havana as Márquez portrays it at the beginning of his story is subject to wild, destructive natural forces. A tidal wave "of monumental size" damages the Hotel Riviera. This is clearly an aberration, however, in what is otherwise depicted as a pleasant, comfortable environment for visitors. While nature is destructive, the Cuban people behave in an orderly and productive way. Volunteers quickly clean up the debris and help the hotel get back to business. Márquez pays no attention to the difficult economic and political issues that plague Cuba; his portrayal is of a modern, attractive seaside city in a well-ordered state.

## ANONYMOUS, Evicted: A Russian Jew's Story (Again) (p. 536)

### Explorations

1.  The shortages are indirectly related to the author's reasons for leaving Russia, since she provides evidence that other Russians are ready to blame Jews for food shortages (para. 14) and the lack of jobs (15). The shortages, she writes, "create bad blood" (3). However, she is correct in saying that she is not leaving because of shortages; it is anti-Semitism, expressed through intimidation, threats of violence, and discrimination, that is driving her out of Russia.

2.  The most startling figure the author quotes in paragraph 2 is that almost 40,000 Jews were trying to get out of Russia as of the day the author added her name to the waiting list. The entire passage is full of figures, however. She reports spending six hours waiting out in the cold to enter the American Embassy; she was number 79 on the New Zealand list; she would need to return at 5 PM; and she has lived in Russia for forty years. One effect of using all these figures is to foster a sense of reality and precision, depicting the author as a rational, practical person. This characterization, combined with the weight of the figures as data, helps the reader appreciate her frustration, both with the trauma of leaving her homeland, and with the necessity of waiting in long lines in order to have a chance to leave. Most of all, she conveys the near universality of her recent experience; clearly many other Russian Jews share her concern about rising anti-Semitism.

3.  Most students will recall that for many Americans, communism and the Soviet Union served during the Cold War as the ultimate object of hatred and fear. Similarly, Russians were encouraged to identify American capitalists as the enemy. But in a post–Cold War world, the old enemies have largely disappeared. Russians lost the "immediate object" of their hatred when the Soviet Union came to an end but — according to the author's idea — they did not lose their propensity to hate. Russian Jews are different enough from other Russians to be chosen as a new enemy. The author's main point, however, is that the exodus of Jews from Russia will leave other Russians with the same problem: hatred that needs an object. She suggests they will turn it on some other group that can be singled out as different.

4.  The author seems both angry and exasperated with other Russians. She says of one group discussing Jews on the street that they "were genuine intellectuals, people with good faces" (7) but that they use the irrational rhetoric of anti-Semitism to justify their "conviction" that Jews are responsible for all the problems of Russia. Her exasperation takes the form of sarcasm at several points in her essay, as when she refers to the "splendid lads of Pamyat" who want to exterminate Jews. Later she uses the same method to express her anger, when she says that "perhaps peace, happiness, and prosperity will immediately come to Russia" when the Jews are gone (19). This is, of course, precisely the opposite of what she believes will happen. In contrast to her sarcastic response to the irrational convictions of other Russians about Jews, the author's writing is straightforward and serious when she says that "happiness and prosperity cannot be built on the blood and tears of others" (20).

## Connections

1.  The economic conditions the author describes in paragraph 3 are very similar to the conditions of Cubans today. She writes that there is virtually no way to buy basic necessities and that "the reward for any work is unimaginably small." She finds that these privations lead to feelings of humiliation and alienation and may even shorten people's lives. The man that Golden interviews at a party says that he and his fellow Cubans "are weak" and that he finds himself "doing things that are very tough" (para. 43). He compares himself to prostitutes who exchange sex for "a dinner, a dress, some shampoo" (44). The feelings he describes are similar to those the author of "Evicted" notices in Russians: a sense of personal humiliation, of having failed and being alienated from the ideals of the revolution.

2.  Students may refer back to Explorations #1 and #3 to find evidence of Russian non-Jews' attitudes toward Russian Jews. Many non-Jews blame Jews for the economic woes of post–Cold War Russia, and believe that by eradicating the Jewish population — through banishment or by killing Jews — they will become prosperous. Shevardnadze describes a similar attitude among rigid socialists toward "kulaks," peasant landowners who were persecuted and driven off their farms when land was being collectivized (20–24). The systematic process of "de-kulakization" had official support, while efforts to drive Russian Jews from their homeland are not officially sanctioned by the Russian government (16). However, the process is similar in that a group is identified as being a threat to the prosperity of the dominant Russian group and is persecuted and driven away.

3.  Students will be able to come up with several pertinent examples of people in other nations sharing the author's sense of being "evicted" from her own land. Haunani-Kay Trask writes of how the *baole* took land away from Hawaiians by instituting changes in economics — specifically, introducing patterns of private land ownership — that "alienated the people from the land." Vine Deloria, Jr, and Clifford M. Lytle discuss "the decades of erosion" of traditional American Indian cultures and the imposition on tribes of European forms of government — a process that also involved great loss of tribal land. Martin Luther King, Jr., writes that "Africa had been raped and plundered by Britain and Europe, her native kingdoms disorganized" for hundreds of years before the U.S. slave

trade robbed Africans of their freedom, land, and cultural heritage. And Toni Morrison contends that the Africans who helped to build the United States have been left out of its canonized literature; each of these writers describes a phenomenon of disenfranchisement and exile that the Russian writer of "Evicted" could sympathize with.

## VÁCLAV HAVEL (VAHT-slahv HAH-vul), Moral Politics (p. 542)

### Explorations

1. Many students will have no trouble identifying communism as the force that caused Czechoslovakia to become "morally unhinged." They will follow Havel's implicit reasoning, which is that people under an authoritarian regime have few opportunities to develop a personal moral sense, since they will not be rewarded and may be severely punished for acting on any principle that runs counter to the regime's goals. When he writes that "the authoritarian regime imposed a certain order" on human vices, he suggests that this repression had the positive effect of limiting people's opportunities to behave badly. However, Havel also implies that these human vices are natural and, therefore, not caused by communism — only encouraged by it. Students may be more divided over the question of whether human beings are naturally full of vices that may be encouraged under an authoritarian regime and discouraged, presumably, under democracy.

2. Havel maintains his focus on morality in Czechoslovakian politics in paragraph 5 and beyond, but in the last sentence of the paragraph he ceases to pile up examples of human greed and corruption and writes that he is convinced that "a huge potential of goodwill" still exists within the Czechoslovakian people. He shifts from decrying his country's present state to considering the nature of politics and the responsibilities of both leaders and citizens. In paragraph 6, he implies again that Czech communism was responsible for people's "selfishness, envy, and hatred," but this time he offers hope that politicians devoted to the principles of democracy will be able to awaken the people's moral sense.

3. Havel's dilemma regarding the passage of a law that would deprive certain groups of people of opportunities for public service on the bases of their associations under the former totalitarian government forced him to reconsider his belief that simply sticking to principles of moral democracy would help him lead his people into "the way of truly moral politics" (23). Some students may agree with Havel that he has to give in when he knows that taking a rigid stance will not benefit anyone materially. Out of respect for the democratically elected parliament and so that he can try to influence the parliament to change the law in the future, Havel signed the bill. Other students will feel that Havel should have set a highly visible example of moral politics; not signing the bill would not have benefited anyone immediately, but his demonstrated devotion to principle might have influenced others to follow his lead.

## Connections

1. In "Evicted: A Russian Jew's Story (Again)," the anonymous writer confronts an upsurge in anti-Semitism following the demise of the Soviet Union. It could easily be argued that the release of human vices, such as "selfishness, envy, and hatred," that Havel notices in Czechoslovakia following the end of communism there (para. 6) is also at work in Russia, where people lived under an oppressive regime that influenced their morality in ways that benefited the government. If we follow Havel's reasoning, then, it is up to the contemporary Russian leaders to discourage the envy, fear, and hatred that fuels anti-Semitism and to encourage a respect for basic human rights.

2. Havel's basic point is that a government brought into power by violent overthrow can maintain itself only by oppressive means and will eventually die amid the same kind of violence that brought it into power. If he is correct, then Castro's government in Cuba will follow the pattern he describes. However, there is little evidence in Tim Golden's piece on Cuba that Castro's government is about to go down in a violent overthrow. Golden implies, rather, that economic hardship is killing the socialist government, which can no longer feed its people (37). Golden found that many people still support Castro, and he mentions no evidence that "new revolutionaries" are on the verge of bringing about his downfall.

3. Havel's argument is that pure Marxist philosophy fails to take human values into account. Decency, from that perspective, would be defined as any conduct that promoted production. To Havel, in contrast, decency is a moral choice that is essential to effective political power. Students will find related ideas developed in several selections in *Looking At Ourselves*. The *New Yorker* selection suggests that the mass media during election campaigns in the United States base their choices of what to cover on pressure from advertisers, directly or through consumers, more than on a commitment to honest, responsive reporting. Wendell Berry decries our tendency to devote ourselves to the ideal of economic competition, our willingness "to take another's property or to accept another's ruin as a normal result of economic enterprise. Martin Luther King, Jr., describes the "degradation" of black men when, under slavery, their humanity was ignored so that they could be treated as "commodities for sale at a profit."

## FAY WELDON, Down the Clinical Disco (p. 551)

### Explorations

1. In paragraph 2, the narrator reveals that she is a former inmate of Broadmoor, a mental institution for the criminally insane, where she was committed after setting fire to her office. Her monologue is directed at a woman named Linda she met at a pub (para. 6), who may be identified with the reader. The story begins with the pronoun "You," suggesting that the reader and Linda are being addressed directly by the narrator.

2. Some students may see the narrator as an obviously paranoid woman who believes people are continuously monitoring her behavior, even during an evening at the pub. In paragraph 1, for instance, she says, "of course there are people watching." Others may

see her as a victim of the mental health system that placed her in the position of being assessed constantly, to the point that she was forced into paranoia as a natural response to having had her smallest gesture watched and judged while she was in the institution. In paragraph 13, the narrator says that "Sister," a nurse, decided who had become "normal" enough to go up for parole and who would remain. Psychiatric professionals and judges seem to have the power to decide what constitutes normal behavior. The criteria the narrator perceives at work are narrow and maddeningly contradictory. For instance, in the first paragraph she says she doesn't drink because she has "to be careful. You never know who's watching." Later in the same paragraph, she says that "it is not absolutely A-okay not to drink alcohol." Many of the criteria she believes are applied in judging who is "normal" have to do with sexual behavior and sexual orientation. She says that women who go into Broadmoor not looking like women do look like women when they leave. Men have to pretend to want to watch heterosexual "blue movies" to prove their manhood, but women can't want to watch because it would suggest a perverted sexuality.

3.  The narrator suggests that "abnormal" behavior can more easily be observed in the nurses at Broadmoor than in the inmates. She says of "Sister" that "she's not so sane herself. She's more institutionalized than the patients" (13). The point is made graphically in a scene when she arrives at Broadmoor and is sadistically treated during a bath by a group of men and women who "were sane because they were nurses and good because they could go home after work" (10). A similar madness is evident in a nurse's game in which the narrator is made to be a tea bag for an entire day. The institutional setting, the narrator implies, is itself insane; the medical personnel who run institutions and the lawyers who send people to the institution are just as mad — or more so — than those they commit.

4.  Students should be able to come up with several different central points for Weldon's story. Some will focus on the end of the story, where the narrator says that "when you're in love you're just happy so they have to turn you out" (18). The statement implies that happiness and love give people the strength to face up to and to see beyond the efforts of society to oppress them. Others may see in the story's end a central statement regarding the problems with using "normality" as a criteria for sanity. The narrator and Eddie can be more themselves when they go home — but being themselves means they drop the pretense of socially and medically defined sanity, as Eddie gets into drag and the narrator rubs off her lipstick and dons jeans. In spite of their "abnormal" behavior, however, the narrator and Eddie are more sane and certainly more harmless than those who imprisoned them. Some students may see Weldon's story simply as a vivid depiction of a paranoid mind or of the abuses of the criminal justice system and psychiatry.

## Connections

1.  Václav Havel contends that politicians can, and should, act "decently, reasonably, responsibly, sincerely, civilly, and tolerantly" (para. 11). That, in his estimation is what would allow him, and other politicians, to "live in truth." He means that his actions should be strictly in line with his stated principles, and that any other course leads to corruption and disorder. Students may find it a challenge to apply Havel's statements about the responsibilities of politicians to the experience of the narrator in "Down the Clinical Disco." As an inmate of Broadmoor, she found it impossible to "live in truth" because her eventual release depended on her behaving in ways the medical staff approved of.

Some students may realize that her experience in Broadmoor has something in common with the experience of living under a totalitarian regime, which deprives people of the power to make their own decisions and perhaps live in accordance with their own sense of what is right.

2. Both women face difficult futures, including the possibility of violence against them and the loss of their civil rights. The narrator of "Down the Clinical Disco" says that "They can pop you back inside if you cause any trouble at all, and they're the ones who decide what trouble is" (17). Her sense that she has lost control over her own future is demoralizing and may keep her perpetually in the state she is in now: fearful to the point of paranoia, convinced she is being watched, trying to decide what "normal" behavior is so that she and Eddie will not draw attention to themselves. In effect, she has never left the institution. The anonymous writer of "Evicted: A Russian Jew's Story (Again)" also faces prejudice, a loss of her civil rights, and possibly physical violence. She has not, however, internalized the ideologies that work to oppress her. She is attempting to leave the country where she no longer feels welcome, and there is a chance that she will find a freer existence elsewhere. For these reasons, she probably has a brighter future than the narrator of "Down the Clinical Disco."

3. Weldon has her narrator justify her crime by rationalizing it: The Opera needed to be burned down (7); it was not damaged badly; the office she burned needed redecorating anyway (10). Given what is in her view the minor — even benign — nature of her crime, the narrator conveys the impression that the punishment she receives, beginning with the degrading bath, is far more criminal than the act that brought her into Broadmoor. This sense of her own innocence, and of the culpability of those who imprison her, are all she has. She also recognizes that the staff justify their "superiority" on the basis of their profession and their relative freedom: "They were sane because they were nurses and good because they could go home after work."

4. Weldon's narrator sums up the effect of her initial, traumatic bath in Broadmoor by saying that "even worse than being naked and seen by strangers" is "being naked and unseen, because you don't even count as a woman" (10). Binur makes a similar observation when he recalls being present while a Jewish man and woman, thinking he is Palestinian, almost have sex in front of him. He writes, "For them I simply didn't exist. I was invisible, a nonentity!" (8). For Binur, this moment marked the worst humiliation he experienced while posing as a Palestinian. Weldon's narrator and Binur have something in common that made them likely victims for this kind of humiliation, in that both had been deprived of basic human rights, such as the freedom of self-determination, on the basis of their identities.

## NEIL POSTMAN, Future Shlock (p. 559)

### Explorations

1. Even students who are not well versed in European history will probably recognize that Postman is referring to the rise of nazism in Germany during the 1920s and 1930s, when art, philosophy, and science were considered worthwhile only when they promoted the

interests of the party and were stamped out whenever they appeared to open the door to dissidence and tolerance of ethnic, political, and religious differences. At the end of paragraph 2, Postman proposes to "worry" the reader with the idea that what happened to culture in Nazi Germany could happen in the United States — though in a different way. Later in the essay, Postman says that although a "decline of intelligent discourse" is taking place in America, intellectuals will not be driven out as they were in Germany (para. 4). Instead, they will simply be ignored. At the end of his essay, Postman returns to the theme of nazism, again differentiating culture under nazism (culture as prison) and in contemporary America (culture as burlesque). Postman's discussion of Mel Brooks's film *The Producers* encourages the reader to believe that the film predicts that Americans will become a "trivial people . . . a people amused into stupidity" (11). Because *The Producers* is built on the theme of nazism, with which Postman opens his essay, his discussion of the film reinforces his point that Americans will accept anything — even *Springtime for Hitler*— as long as it is entertaining. This is a point students may want to debate.

2.   Both compound sentences appear toward the end of Postman's essay, where he is attempting to create a sense that the evidence for his view of the death of American culture is overwhelming. His use of *when* suggests a potential condition that sometimes happens in human history and could happen in the United States in the future. However, his repetition of *when* to introduce descriptions he has already applied or implied about American culture builds a sense of accumulating probability that this undesirable condition already exists in the United States, or is in the process of happening.

3.   Postman first addresses the reader as "you" in paragraph 2, when he says he wants to "worry you about the rapid erosion of our own intelligence." The effect of speaking directly to his readers is to suggest that his argument is important to them personally. Even before the reader becomes "you," however, Postman has established an "us" in the same paragraph. The effect of creating such a collective is to suggest that we all are affected by, and are responsible for, the death of intelligence. Readers who agree with Postman's position will accept this use of "we," while readers who are waiting to be persuaded may be drawn into agreement by it. Postman's frequent use of "I" suggests his personal commitment and personal sense of responsibility for making "us" aware of the problems he describes. Some students may note that Postman sometimes uses "we" when he is really writing about his own views, as in his assertion "we have also seen 'Sesame Street' and other educational shows in which the demands of entertainment take precedence . . ." (17).

4.   Although Postman uses a traditional format for his argument, his language and many of his rhetorical techniques have more in common with the entertainment-dominated media he criticizes than with academic style. His essay appeals fairly openly to readers' emotions along with their reason. Students will identify Postman's use of humor as his most obvious entertainment technique. His tone throughout is ironic; examples include the title "Future Shlock" and comments such as, "There are other ways to achieve stupidity, and it appears that, as in so many other things, there is a distinctly American way" (4). He also relies frequently on humorous exaggeration, as when he says that "the Germans banished intelligence" (2) and that the Empire of Reason has given way to the

Empire of Shlock (3). Postman's informal diction is another technique more common in entertainment than in academic writing. He addresses readers directly, using first and second person as well as the third; his position is openly subjective ("I wish to call to your notice"; "I cannot imagine" (5)) rather than purely objective. His evidence, too, comes from popular sources, such as films (5, 8) and television shows (15–19), as well as from academic sources such as Aristotle (2) and Henry Steele Commager (3). This choice of sources clearly suits Postman's topic, and his argument is logically constructed rather than fragmented like the television news programs he decries; however, students may differ as to whether his efforts to enlighten his audience are weakened or strengthened by his efforts to entertain them.

## Connections

1. This question should spark debate among students about what roles entertainment technologies play in the lives of Americans. Postman's main target is television, and because most students will have grown up with television as a continuous presence, they should have strong opinions about whether it is bringing about the death of intelligence and high culture in America. Since many "institutions" in the United States find their way into the electronic media, Postman moves his critique from television to politics, religion (para. 16), education, and business (17).

2. In paragraph 23, Postman describes Orwellian culture as a prison in which, by direct action taken to suppress dissidence, cultural growth is halted and intellect dies. Eduard Shevardnadze argues that the "fundamental principle" of socialism denies "proprietary instincts" in the worker (12). Adhering too closely to "the purity of doctrine" not only destroys the nation economically, but also negates all innovation. It no longer pays to work, and it no longer pays to think. In "Chairman Mao's Good Little Boy," the effects of living according to strict Communist doctrine is demonstrated in the experience of Liang's mother after she is condemned as a Rightist. She is required to assume blame for "thought crimes" she has not committed (30), and even her husband, thoroughly absorbed in Communist doctrine, demands that she "recognize her faults and reform herself" (29).

3. The *New Yorker* selection presents two contrary positions: Economic pressures encourage television newscasts to favor "the superficial and sensational over the important and enlightening," yet the source of these economic pressures — the viewers — "are as unhappy with shallow coverage as the anchors are." Postman's essay suggests a resolution for this apparent contradiction in the nature of television: As a predominantly visual medium, "it conditions our minds to apprehend the world through fragmented pictures" (20). *The New Yorker* reports that journalists who vowed after the 1984 presidential campaign to resist "empty one-liners" found themselves in 1988 emphasizing "Willie Horton, flag factories, and other phony symbols." Their dilemma may owe less to "gullibility" or "voyeurism for the sake of voyeurism" (Tom Brokaw) than to Postman's idea that "on television all subject matter is presented as entertaining" (14). On the other hand, the admissions by Peter Jennings that "politicians and political consultants have learned so well to manipulate us" and by Dan Rather that the networks fear "being serious but dull" may help to explain what Postman describes as "the frightening displacement of serious, intelligent public discourse in American culture by the imagery and triviality of what may be called show business" (3).

## MICHAEL DORRIS, House of Stone (p. 569)

### Explorations

1.  In paragraph 3, Dorris says that Westerners become aware of poverty "from newspaper photographs staged to produce a maximum impact." A shocking image calls people's attention to a problem — at least momentarily — and they are more ready to give. Dorris's opening anecdote works in the same way. Most readers will be shocked and horrified at the mental image of a screaming, skinned baboon, and they may realize that Dorris is correct when he says that the villagers' plan to rid themselves of baboons as competitors is evidence of their desperation. It is, as well, an anecdote that refutes the common perception that people who are desperately poor and hungry cannot act on their own. The villagers' plan is horrifying, but effective. Dorris's impression of the ability and willingness of the poor to work for the improvement of their condition is strongly evident in the example of the secretary near the end of the essay, in which a woman manages to disperse scarce commodities fairly, tries to gain access to tools her people could use to improve their lives, and shows herself to be "absolutely determined to figure something out" (para. 39).

2.  In paragraph 31, Dorris is trying to think of new, and more effective, ways to act. He sets himself the goal of finding an original approach to getting help for the poor and hungry people of Zimbabwe. His strategies begin with "empathy," which requires that those who suffer be recognized as human beings with individual lives (32). He says that the fortunate — Westerners — should not use confusion or doubts about where money given to charity actually goes as an excuse for not contributing (33). Anything will help, he writes, and anyway the contributor can have some control if she or he becomes informed.

3.  Students will have little trouble identifying the contrasts Dorris sets up between people who share his own position of privilege and people who are starving. In paragraph 25, Dorris posits a "looping line;" at one end is pain and at the other "carefree joy." Dorris's use of the phrase "looping line" suggests a continuum and a connection between those who are economically privileged and those who are not. He continues with a similar strategy, envisioning a starving boy he has met at one end of the continuum and himself — and us — at the other. Although they "stare across the chasm" that separates them, Dorris finds that they are similar, perhaps because they have the same basic needs, although those needs are met on only the privileged end of the continuum. Dorris continues to develop the comparison and contrast he has created, discussing his own daughter, an implicit contrast with the starving boy. Nevertheless, in his daughter's eyes they "have the obvious connection of a brother and sister or potential playmates" (26). And finally, Dorris stages another implicit contrast, this time between his daughter, willing to give her own money to help others, and a group of impoverished children who shot other children who they considered to be too well off. The only difference between his daughter and these children is how much food and security they have.

4.  Students may have different ideas about the meaning of Dorris's title, especially considering that he doesn't define it himself. The title might be considered a play on the phrase "heart of stone," suggesting that Westerners who refuse to give so that others can eat are imprisoned in their own unwillingness to perceive and empathize with another's plight.

## Connections

1. Postman writes that the weaving together of advertising and news on television "reduces all events to trivialities . . . how serious can a bombing in Lebanon be if it is . . . prefaced by a happy United Airlines commercial . . . ?" (para. 18). According to Postman, when, from the point of view of the television newscaster, the audience has spent long enough thinking about some disaster, the anchor simply moves on to a commercial and the news item is effectively wiped from the consciousness of the viewer. Dorris seems to be in agreement with Postman. He writes that we become aware of "grand-scale poverty" in "sound bites from the network anchors," but that the knowledge fails to make a deep impression (3). Dorris concludes, "If we have the option of looking the other way, usually, eventually, we exercise it."

2. Shelby Steele contends that the privileged usually attempt to justify their dominance through a process of rationalization; they reason that they are wealthy because they have worked hard and behaved responsibly; the poor and oppressed, by contrast, are in distress because of their own shortcomings. Thus the privileged are convinced of their "innocence" of cruelty. Dorris refuses the rationalizations that would permit him to assert his own "innocence;" instead, he goes to Zimbabwe and looks poverty in the face. Having seen for himself, Dorris could not claim ignorance as an excuse for not helping. His essay is designed to take away the reader's sense of his or her own "innocence" or ignorance. Once having listened to Dorris's description of his tour of the famine-ravaged land, the reader cannot claim that she or he has no idea of what is occurring, or has no idea how to help. Steele argues that when the sense of innocence disappears, so does some of the power of the dominant group. Knowledge, in that sense, does not always equate with power, because once the privileged have understood the plight of others, they cannot feel good about turning away.

3. Erdrich, in her introduction to Dorris's book, reveals that Dorris adopted three children before she met him, among them Adam, who suffers the effects of fetal alcohol syndrome. Erdrich writes of Dorris that he "spent months of his life teaching Adam to tie his shoes" (6). He does laundry (8) and writes books. Erdrich characterizes Dorris as a patient, dedicated parent and a social activist. She has more to say about Dorris and their family than Dorris does in "House of Stone," but some of the personal qualities she notices come through in his essay. For instance, in his discussion of the ways in which poverty affect children, Dorris evokes his daughter, "a shining girl whose last act" before Dorris left on his trip was to give him money for the poor. The boundaries between social action and family life are irrelevant for Dorris. Erdrich writes that his book about Adam "was a journey from the world of professional objectivity to a confusing realm where boundaries could no longer be so easily drawn" (7).

## NADINE GORDIMER, Amnesty (p. 578)

### Explorations

1. The facts Nadine Gordimer offers about the narrator are few, but essential to understanding her situation. The narrator is poor (para. 14) and has always lived on her family's farm (10). She has had almost no chance to see the world outside her community, as is apparent when she says that she has never seen the sea (6). But she has been educated and now teaches children (4). She is a mother (5). Gordimer reveals these facts at the points where they become important to the narrator's relationship with her politically active lover. For instance, her revelations about the limitations of her knowledge of the world occur in the context of trying to imagine his location on the island prison (6), and her mentions of her daughter take place in the context of his trial (5) and his return (19).

2. The narrator is chiefly concerned with maintaining the hope of having a home and family. In that sense, her differences from her lover are drawn along lines of traditional gender differences. As a man, he is concerned with the affairs of the world and she with the home. These differences are apparent throughout, but are especially apparent in her anecdote about the meetings her husband sponsors on her family's farm. Her mother serves beer and then departs before the men's political conversation gets underway (23), but the narrator stays to listen. She does not, however, participate in the discussion; instead, she is treated like a favored student (24). She accepts that the men's discussions are "more important than anything we could ever say to each other" (24), a comment that simultaneously affirms her support of her lover and underlines the unbridgeable gap between them. She says that there is no time to get married (25) and no possibility of having a home (19), but there is some resentment in her comment that "he comes to sleep with me just like he comes here to eat a meal or put on clean clothes" (25). Further, she is strong-minded enough to disagree with his thinking. He says that "the farmer owns" them, and that is why they cannot have a home. She recognizes their oppression under the white Boers, but she also realizes that the farm — and therefore the people — doesn't really belong to the Boer (27), and she clings to the distant possibility that she might be able to "come back home."

3. Gordimer's style in "Amnesty" is primarily conversational. Her narrator, as a teacher, is literate and intellectually adept. This identity makes it possible for Gordimer to sympathize with her narrator, even though the narrator's vocabulary, stylistic repertory, expertise as a writer, and breadth of experience are much more limited than the author's. "Amnesty" reads like an excerpt from the narrator's own journal, as though it is told directly from the narrator's own mind. This close connection between the writer and her narrator's voice makes it easier to accept that Gordimer, a white South African, can represent the point of view of a narrator whose age, race, background, and class are very different from her own.

4. The narrator has so strong an identity in "Amnesty" that students may not even realize that she does not name herself. Like Ralph Ellison's *Invisible Man*, Gordimer's decision not to name her character has several effects. First, the anonymity of the narrator emphasizes that white racism attempts to erase the humanity and identity of black people. Second, although her voice is clearly that of an individual with a personal history and unique opinions, the fact that she is not named suggests that she represents her

people. Although an individual, she speaks for the experience of many. Finally, it is not only the narrator who is not named; no other characters have names, either. Even the leaders (including Nelson Mandela) are designated only as "the Big Man" and "the Old Men." Their namelessness has the effect of suggesting that her lover and his comrades are still in danger from whites, who would track them down and harrass or imprison them if they could identify them.

## Connections

1.  How students respond to this question depends on whether they recognize Gordimer's story, like Dorris's essay, as a form of activism designed to work against specific injustices the writer perceives. Alternatively, students may read this question as pertaining to the narrator and her lover, both of whom, in their own ways, are "searching for some action . . . some original and efficacious idea" that will help them deal with, and find solutions to, the injustices that deplete their lives. The narrative serves as a record of the development of the narrator's political consciousness, a development she shares with the reader, who may then be moved to act as well. In that sense, the narrator and the writer are closely connected; "Amnesty" is Gordimer's attempt to call her readers to action in opposition to apartheid.

2.  When, at the end of her story, the narrator says that she is "waiting to come back home," she expresses a sense of her own homelessness that the anonymous writer of "Evicted: A Russian Jew's Story (Again)" also expresses. It is significant that neither woman identifies herself by name, a strategy that emphasizes their lack of security and lack of identity in their homeland. However, their situations differ in that the writer of "Evicted: A Russian Jew's Story (Again)" is actively trying to leave Russia and has some expectation of finding a better life elsewhere. The narrator of "Amnesty" is poor and lacks the means to leave South Africa; however, she seems committed to staying, expressing the sense that she belongs to the land (para. 27).

3.  Martin Luther King, Jr., observes that slavery, a form of racial oppression that has much in common with South African apartheid, "had a profound impact in shaping the social-political-legal structure of the nation." If legal and political structures in the United States were built on slavery and if the economy of the nation was built on the labor of enslaved African-Americans, something similar happened in South Africa, where the government, the justice system, and the system of land allocation were constructed along rigid lines of racial separatism. King writes that in the United States, racist whites rationalized their domination of African-Americans by reasoning that a system that worked to their own economic advantage must also be "morally justifiable." Similarly, the Boer in Gordimer's story who believes he owns the land and the Africans who live on the land could only maintain his position by convincing himself that his domination is morally justified.

## NELSON MANDELA, Black Man in a White Court (p. 587)

### Explorations

1.  Mandela is applying for the recusal of the white magistrate who is presiding over Mandela's case (para. 5). He wants the magistrate to excuse himself from hearing the case because, Mandela argues, an African cannot get a fair trial in a white court (6, 8) and because, as an African, Mandela does not consider himself subject to the laws his people had no part in making (6). It is the white court's racism that is Mandela's main focus; he says that he "fears that this system of justice may enable the guilty to drag the innocent before the courts." Mandela's reasonable manner and eloquence serve another purpose, however. Mandela does not believe that there is a chance he will win his own case, but he is making a larger case for his people. In paragraph 28, he says that the atmosphere of oppression he senses in the courtroom "calls to mind the inhuman injustices caused to my people outside this courtroom by this same white domination." After Mandela's articulate and passionate speech, the judge's only response is to dismiss the application (58) — a move that essentially proves both of Mandela's arguments. If Mandela's real purpose had been to win his own case, then he was not successful. But because he had a larger purpose in mind — to speak out against systematic white racism — he was successful.

2.  Building on their discussion of Explorations #1, students should realize that neither Mandela nor the court believes that Mandela's application has any chance of being approved. Mandela is elaborating on the starvation and disease his people are experiencing when the magistrate interrupts his speech to say that Mandela is "going beyond the scope" of his application (32). The magistrate goes on to say that he doesn't "want to know about starvation" (34), and he demands that Mandela stick to the "real reasons" for his application (36). The "real reasons," from the magistrate's perspective, are those that stay within the bounds of the immediate proceeding. But his attempts to define the case according to the needs and expectations of the white court are unsuccessful, and Mandela manages to make the case he is most interested in: that his people are without land, the vote, health care, or food (29).

3.  From the first words he speaks, Mandela shows that he fully grasps not only the legal but also the social and political implications of the court proceedings. His style and choice of words are similar to — although more eloquent than — the white men who are about to try him. He uses the conventions of legal discourse in paragraphs 4–6, for instance, in stating the purpose of his application and giving the grounds for it. Further, he asserts his equality directly by saying that he has decided to speak for himself rather than depend upon counsel. Only by speaking the language of the court can Mandela hope to speak at all. As a spokesperson for his people, Mandela uses his own educational and professional equality with the white men who accuse him to support his argument that all Africans should have the same rights and privileges as whites.

4.  Most students will recognize that "African" is a term that indicates that Mandela's people are the native inhabitants of the land whites now rule. By refusing to call whites "Africans," Mandela suggests that white men are trespassers on land that belongs to Africans. In paragraph 2, Mandela says, "this case is a trial of the aspirations of the African

people," and in paragraph 7, he describes the court case as a political one that represents "a clash of the aspirations of the African people and those of whites." In paragraph 45, Mandela describes himself as "a black man in a white man's court." He would like to believe that he was "being tried by a fellow South African," but as his comments on the racism of the court and his choice of the terms "African" and "white" suggest, he knows that the court will not acknowledge his entitlement as a South African to an impartial trial.

## Connections

1.  Because Gordimer's story focuses on the experience of a woman waiting for the man she loves, rather than on the experience of the political prisoner himself, students may want to consider how gender differences affect their readings of the story and the transcript of Mandela's court case. While her lover's activism takes him away from her, she tries to keep alive the idea, if not the full reality, of home and family. Nevertheless she is politically aware. She suggests that she, too, is a prisoner when she says that she is "also waiting to come back home" (para. 30). Further, when she says that "It's the Boer's farm — but that's not true, it belongs to nobody" (27), the narrator makes a point similar to Mandela's when he designates black people as "Africans." Both imply that black people belong to the African land and that the white man is trespassing on ground that does not belong to him. Throughout "Amnesty," it is apparent that the narrator is as affected by white racism as is her imprisoned lover. Mandela's contention that the "aspirations of the African people" (2) are on trial and that they have been denied "basic human rights" (9) shows that he recognizes his own experience of white racism to be representative of the plight of all other Africans; similarly, the narrator of "Amnesty" recognizes that while white racism rules in South Africa, she will not be able to "come home" any more than will her lover.

2.  A law court is by definition an arena for what Shelby Steele calls "a struggle for innocence." In the court where Nelson Mandela presents his case, representatives for both black and white South Africans claim innocence as Steele describes. The judge speaks for his fellow whites, who assert ownership over land and power and therefore claim to be victimized in this case by Mandela's breaking of a law made by whites for their protection. The judge's position matches Steele's statement, "White racism [is] a claim of white innocence and therefore of white entitlement to subjugate blacks." Mandela pleads innocent to the charges and claims innocence on a larger scale, using (as Steele puts it) "the innocence that grew out of . . . long subjugation to seize more power." Verbally Mandela responds to the judge as what Steele describes as a bargainer: *"I already believe you are innocent (good, fair-minded) and have faith that you will prove it."* His tacit position, however, is that of a challenger: *"If you are innocent, then prove it."*

3.  Toni Morrison argues that the study of canonized American literature has ignored the important influence of "the four-hundred-year-old presence" of Africans and African-Americans on the evolution of the nation and its literature. Mandela's indictment of the racist system of justice in South Africa, a system in which the civil rights of Africans are universally denied, suggests that he, like Morrison, sees a national history in which the dominant white group attempts to oppress black people and ignores their contributions to the formation of the nation. Nadine Gordimer, a white South African writer, takes up an unusual perspective in "Amnesty" when she attempts to consider the world from the

perspective of a black South African woman. The story is her attempt to recover a form of experience that the literature of her country rarely pays attention to.

4. Several of Václav Havel's statements describe Mandela's position in his courtroom presentation, including: "Politicians have a duty to awaken this slumbering, or bewildered, potential [for goodwill] to life" (6); "The idea that the force of truth, the power of a truthful word, the strength of a free spirit, conscience, and responsibility . . . might actually change something . . . " (7); "Genuine politics . . . is simply serving those close to oneself: serving the community, and serving those who come after us" (10). Mandela's statements focus more specifically on the issues of his case, but some display a similar philosophy to Havel's: "That the will of the people is the basis of the authority of government is a principal universally acknowledged as sacred throughout the civilized world and constitutes the basic foundations of freedom and justice" (39); "We . . . regard the struggle against color discrimination and for the pursuit of freedom and happiness as the highest aspiration of all men" (53).

## ADDITIONAL QUESTIONS AND ASSIGNMENTS

1. In a journal entry or a collection of informal notes, discuss governments' responsibilities to citizens as depicted in three or four of these selections, paying particular attention to ideology. Consider such issues as the state's responsibility to protect the rights of individuals, its role in providing economic and social stability, its demands on citizens, and any other issues you find relevant. As you look over your notes, try to discover similarities and differences among the cultures represented. Can you come to any conclusion about the role of ideology in the relationship between the state and the individual?

2. Using Golden and Shevardnadze as models, interview several people who espouse a particular political view and observe their organizations in action. You may use representatives of major parties (especially during an election), but you may also want to consider "special interest" groups (for example, proponents or opponents of U.S. policy toward a particular country, proponents of tax reform, opponents of nuclear power and/or weapons, or members of any organized political group, such as Greenpeace, Amnesty International, or Right to Life). As you gather information, consider the kinds of information you're interested in eliciting. Do you want to know about the group's perception of its role in politics? Its reasons for holding a particular view? Its tactics for accomplishing its goals? Its perception of opponents? As you write your description of the group, try to intersperse your own observation of their activities with members' responses to your questions.

3. Using Weldon as a model, write a narrative about an encounter with a U.S. government agency. Choose something with which you are familiar, for example, the state registry of motor vehicles, the city clerk's office, the county courthouse, or the Internal Revenue Service. In your account emphasize the effect of bureaucratic impersonality on the dignity of the individual as well as on the speed (or lack thereof) with which the system functions.

You might use particular people as illustrations of the government's response to the individual. Let the nature of your subject dictate the tone of your narrative; you need not be serious.

4. The issue of U.S. intervention in Central America has been the subject of heated debate for the past several years. Research the various opinions on American interests in El Salvador, Nicaragua (before and after the 1990 elections), or elsewhere in Central America by consulting magazine and newspaper articles on the subject as well as the opinions of experts found in books and interviews. As you read, try to place the opinions into categories, such as economic, ideological, balance-of-power, and humanitarian arguments. Write a paper in which you classify the arguments according to the categories you've established. Your purpose will not be to advocate any one position but rather to inform your readers of the reasons behind the opinions they encounter.

5. Conduct further research into one of the cultures represented in this section, focusing specifically on the culture's economy. It would be wise to choose a culture about which information is readily available — Cuba, Russia, Great Britain, and South Africa are likely candidates. If the selection is an excerpt from a larger work, look first at that work. You can find other sources by consulting the headnotes for other selections from that culture (if there are any) and a general encyclopedia, as well as journals devoted to the study of that culture. Narrow your topic to something manageable — such as the effect of ideology on the economic system, the culture's financial dependence on the world market, the role played by economics in internal politics, or the effect of economic forces on the individual — and write a cause-and-effect analysis in which you outline the relation between economic forces and some other facet of the culture.

# Part Seven

## VIOLENCE

### INTRODUCTION

This section should provide a rather startling contrast to the currently popular image of war and violence presented in *Rambo* and *Terminator* and their many clones. Having no experience of war on their own soil, most American students will likely find the selections unsettling and provocative. In order to minimize any tendency to focus merely on the sensationalist aspect of the material, instructors may want to begin by exploring the images of war presented on television and in films. Most students will acknowledge the highly unrealistic quality of the *Rambo* image, no matter how they might secretly revel in its potency. In fact, if asked to separate the realistic from the sensational in such portrayals, they should begin to get a sense of what this section is about.

The comments in *Looking at Ourselves* will certainly help — Kovic's disturbing narrative of his battlefield injuries can become a focal point from which to view the remaining perspectives. Kovic's rejection of the warrior mentality belies Broyles's analysis of wartime nostalgia and Sam Keen's smug assumption that the "warrior psyche" is an integral part of the male mind. Together, these pieces should generate a good deal of thoughtful discussion, although it's doubtful that this discussion will result in any firm conclusions, except perhaps the rather facile one that we must end all war. Rudolph and Rudolph problematize the issue of how ethnic differences contribute to war; their more complex analysis should help students rethink their initial opinions about motives for war. The discussion will generate more questions than it answers, preparing students to approach the major selections with the critical eye necessary to sort out opposing views of the causes of war, the conduct of it, its consequences to soldiers and citizenry, and its justification (if there is such a thing).

There are a number of possible subthemes in the section, among them the effects of war and civil violence on domestic life (Milosz, McCafferty, Drakulić, Al-Radi, and Achebe) or specifically on women (McCafferty, Drakulić, Allende, Al-Radi, Walker), the question of a just war (Milosz, McCafferty, Moore, Walker), the uses of torture (Allende, Kelly), and the cost of war to the country that wages it (Moore, Drakulić, Al-Radi, and Achebe).

Students might be particularly affected by Czeslaw Milosz's analysis of American ignorance of war. He is speaking directly to *us*, attempting to jolt us into a realization of the fragility of our comfortable existence. Viewed in relation to the passages in *Looking at Ourselves*, Milosz's selection should ensure that students see themselves in the characters portrayed in this section. A close perspective is essential if this section is to open their minds to the complex realities of civil violence and war. The narratives of those whose lives are touched by violence (Grossman, Drakulić, Allende, Al-Radi, Kelly, Walker) remind us that we are not discussing an abstract theme. In each work we are presented with an ultimatum and forced to confront what is certainly the most pressing reality of our times.

Instructors may wish to consult the following familiar works in preparing related selections from *Ourselves Among Others*:

## Essays

Bruce Catton, "Grant and Lee: A Study in Contrasts" (*The American Story*, ed. Earl Miers, Broadcast Music, 1956; Catton, *This Hallowed Ground*, Doubleday, 1956).

Martha Gellhorn, "The Besieged City" (*Face of War*, Atlantic Monthly Press, 1988).

Martha Gellhorn, "Last Words on Vietnam, 1987" (*Face of War*, Atlantic Monthly Press, 1988).

Abraham Lincoln, "The Gettysburg Address" (1863).

William Manchester, "Okinawa: The Bloodiest Battle" (*New York Times*, June 14, 1987; Best *American Essays* 1988, ed. Annie Dillard, Ticknor and Fields, 1988).

Carl Sagan, "The Nuclear Winter" (*Parade*, 1983).

## Short Stories

Margaret Drabble, "The Gifts of War" (Winter's Tales 16, St. Martin's; *Women and Fiction*, ed. Susan Cahill, Mentor, 1975).

Ambrose Bierce, "Chickamauga" (*In the Midst of Life*, 1892; rep. Chatto and Windus, 1964).

Ambrose Bierce, "Occurrence at Owl Creek Bridge" (*In the Midst of Life*, 1892; rep. Chatto and Windus, 1964).

Stephen Crane, "An Episode of War" (*Stories and Tales*, Vintage, 1955).

Graham Greene, "The Destructors" (*Collected Stories*, Viking, 1973).

Mark Helprin, "North Light" (*Ellis Island*, Delacorte, 1981).

William Dean Howells, "Editha" (*Between the Dark and the Daylight*, Harpers, 1907).

Tim O'Brien, "The Things They Carried" (*Esquire*, Aug. 1986; *The Things They Carried*, Houghton, 1990).

Frank O'Connor, "Guests of the Nation" (*Collected Stories*, Knopf, 1981).

Luigi Pirandello, "War" (*The Medal*, Dutton, 1939).

William Trevor, "Lost Ground" (*New Yorker*, Feb. 24, 1992).

## BIOGRAPHICAL NOTES ON *LOOKING AT OURSELVES*

1. Ron Kovic, born on July 4, 1946, was 19 when he was wounded in action in Vietnam and paralyzed from the chest down. His memoir *Born on the Fourth of July* (1976) was made into a popular movie starring Tom Cruise.

2. William Broyles, Jr., is the founding editor of *Texas Monthly* and a past editor of *Newsweek*.

3. Sam Keen, a professor of religious studies, produced a PBS series with Bill Moyers in 1987 that became the book *Faces of the Enemy: Reflections of the Hostile Imagination* (1988).

His most recent works include *To a Dancing God: Notes of a Spiritual Traveler* (1990) and *Fire in the Belly: On Being a Man* (1991).

4.  Susanne Hoeber Rudolph and Lloyd I. Rudolph are both professors of political science at the University of Chicago. They have collaborated on *The Modernity of Tradition* (1984) and *In Pursuit of Lakshmi: The Political Economy of the Indian State* (1987).

5.  Colman McCarthy is a *Washington Post* columnist.

6.  Rosemary L. Bray lives in Central Harlem and is an editor for the *New York Times Book Review*.

7.  George F. Will, a leading neo-conservative spokesman, has taught political science at Michigan State and at the University of Toronto and is a syndicated columnist and political commentator for the *Washington Post, Newsweek,* and ABC television. His columns have been collected in such volumes as *The Pursuit of Virtue and Other Tory Notions* (1982) and *The Pursuit of Happiness and Other Sobering Thoughts* (1979). He has also written on baseball (*Men at Work,* 1990) and in favor of term limits for congressmen (*The Wedge,* 1992). He won a Pulitzer Prize in 1977.

8.  Joan Didion, the widely admired prose stylist, has published several volumes of essays and reportage, including *Slouching Towards Bethlehem* (1968), *The White Album* (1979), *Salvador* (1983), *Miami* (1987), and *After Henry* (1992).

## Reflections

1.  Students may find it most illuminating to compare Ron Kovic's disturbing firsthand account of being wounded in the Vietnam war with William Broyles's and Sam Keen's more distanced reflections on the meaning—and value—of war for men. Kovic's and Broyles's pieces, especially, form an ironic contrast. For many men, Broyles implies, war is a "great" love because it represents the pinnacle of experience. For that reason, "War is not an aberration;" it is an inevitable part of men's lives. Kovic's account, by contrast, is stark and immediate. He writes that "The only thing I can think of, the only thing that crosses my mind, is living." Kovic cannot, at that moment, give reasons for the continuing existence of war. The only comment on war implied in this excerpt is that it is senselessly and brutally violent. Sam Keen asks why men have created "a world where starvation and warfare" are becoming a way of life. He responds to his own question by denying that male biology is at the root of men's predilection for war. Instead, he writes that "men are systematically conditioned . . . to kill, and to die" for their nation. The need to conquer has been built into the male psyche, he says, and that is why we have war. Students may want to take this question further than Keen or Broyles do, by discussing why some men find war a fulfilling experience, and how the desire for it came to be an integral part of the "male psyche." The selections by Susanne Hoeber Rudolph and Lloyd I. Rudolph and by Colman McCarthy identify additional contributing factors to war's continuing existence: the "doctrine of ancient hatred" promulgated by various communications media see (see Reflections #2), and competition among arms producers to sell weapons (McCarthy).

2.  Susanne Hoeber Rudolph and Lloyd I. Rudolph point to "identity politics" as they are "crafted . . . in print and electronic media," political campaigns, and education as a contemporary cause of ethnic strife. The Rudolphs contend that political positions based

on gender, race, or religion invite a simplistic treatment by the media, in which there is little or no examination of the complex motives for ethnic conflict. Rosemary Bray writes from a personal perspective, situating herself as a wife worried about her husband's safety. Her rhetorical strategies differ from the Rudolphs', but her piece takes a similar stance. She writes that she knows her husband is at risk on the streets because he is black and therefore a target for fearful and unreasoning whites. Identity politics (the tendency to establish loyalties and a sense of self along lines of racial difference) — again fostered by media oversimplification — contributes to his vulnerability and to racial antagonism in general. Bray cites three specific cases in which racial violence received wide — and biased — media coverage. The anonymous *Mother Jones* writer ascribes racial violence to media-encouraged identity politics when he writes of his initial glee at watching white people on the streets of Los Angeles being beaten on TV during the riots following the first Rodney King verdict. A later television appearance by King was aimed at cooling tempers; however, even King couldn't bring himself to say he loved "everybody." His loyalties, like those of the writer, are determined in part by identity politics: He must side with those who are most like him and who share his perspective. The Associated Press piece addresses identity politics in relation to a related phenomenon, hate crimes. The piece quotes a criminologist who claims that most offenders seek out anyone who is different from them; they attack the "other" as a way of validating themselves. Jack Levin, a sociologist, sees identity politics as contributing to the "resentment" people feel in the contemporary world about not being able to take part in "the American Dream" of economic security.

3. George Will fails to mention the racial aspects of gang warfare and the effects of white racism on the community. Cabrini–Green is a project inhabited largely by African-Americans who are poor (Will does mention that only 9 percent of the residents are gainfully employed). Some students may interpret Will's failure to mention race as an indication of his fair-mindedness. It may appear that, by ignoring race, Will is making an anti-racist gesture. However, such a strategy may in fact promote racism, since it also means Will can ignore the causal relationship between white racism and crime and violence in the African-American community. Will uses Karen—a young and innocent resident of Cabrini–Green—as an advocate for his ideas for what to do about gang violence. He writes that Karen shows "common sense" when she says, "Take the gangbangers out and take away all the guns . . . . Mow down those buildings." Neither Will nor Karen is prepared to say how to go about "taking the gangbangers out" or what the 7,000 residents of Cabrini–Green would do for housing if the high-rises were "mown down."

4. Students will be able to use their discussion of George Will's recommendations regarding Cabrini–Green as a springboard for considering how other writers approach the problem of how to decrease violence. Ron Kovic implies that teaching people to consider life as an ultimate and inviolable value is one way of decreasing the violence associated with war. William Broyles, in his last paragraph, states that "progress has simply given man the means to make war even more horrible" and that there is nothing anyone can do to change this. Sam Keen, without addressing the issue explicitly, implies that violence is an inevitable part of our lives when he writes that, for men, "violence has been central to our self-definition." The Rudolphs, by contrast, suggest that the media encourage ethnic violence by refusing to analyze the complex motives associated with it. By implication, greater attention to these matters by the media could have a positive effect

on ethnic violence. Neither the Associated Press piece nor Rosemary Bray's essay offers solutions to the problem of white-on-black violence, but the anonymous writer of "Nobody Listens" suggests that violence could decrease if whites would wake up and begin to listen to black people, who have been "screaming for a long time."

## NELL McCAFFERTY, Peggy Deery of Derry (p. 615)

### Explorations

1. The impression created in McCafferty's prologue is that the Deery family is a closely knit Catholic family. Woven into McCafferty's depiction of Peggy Deery and her family, however, is the impression that the family is threatened by civil strife. In the first paragraph, McCafferty mentions that family members have a hard time sleeping and that the wedding video shows Peggy the last time she was with all her children when all were "looking glad to be alive." Her son Paddy is on the run (para. 2) and Peggy herself cannot dance well because of a problem with her left leg (5). A guest sings a song for an IRA hunger-striker. Although everyone ignores the singer, Peggy's bad leg, and the possibility of police arresting Paddy, McCafferty's inclusion of these unhappy reminders of the Irish Troubles foreshadows the events that threaten the Deery family and others like them: the wounding of Peggy on Bloody Sunday, the imprisonment of those who belong to the IRA (31), and the ambiguous position of the Catholic Church in relation to the civil-rights movement (33, 37).

2. The Deery family's political position apparently arises from their religious loyalties and (by implication) their socioeconomic status. In Northern Ireland, to be Roman Catholic is almost inevitably to side with the Republicans against the Protestant Loyalists. The Deerys' activism undoubtedly was encouraged as well by their limited resources and their observations of the hard lives of others. Peggy Deery, a widow, had fourteen children, which would put a financial strain even on a middle-class family. But the Deerys live in a "prefabricated one-story aluminum bungalow" (17) in a poor housing development. Peggy's best clothes include a mock-leather coat trimmed with "fun fur" (16). Father O'Gara, who knew the Deerys and other families like them, speculated that being unable to meet basic practical needs made people insecure and might cause them to "cheat, draw false dole, drink, and even kill" (38).

3. McCafferty first mentions Protestantism in paragraph 10, where she describes how the "strict and doleful grip of a Protestant Sabbath" restricted Catholic women who would have liked to be able to shop or go to the pub on their only free day. With this depiction of Protestantism as a grim and oppressive institution, McCafferty sets up a contrast with the enthusiastic celebration of the Catholic wedding, where dancing and drinking are not only permitted but expected. Even the Sunday trips to the Catholic cemetery are full of play and socializing. From the cemetery, they can see "the mountains marching toward the Republic of Ireland beyond," which represents to them "beauty, freedom, and reward" (11). In the next paragraph, McCafferty carries on the image of "marching" she first associates with the Republic. She writes that the civil-rights movement brought people out of the cemetery and into the streets to march. Thus, while the Protestant

Church represents everything that oppresses the poor Catholic community, the Republic of Ireland is an inspiration to them to fight for their civil rights.

4.    McCafferty says relatively little about the goals of either side in Northern Ireland's civil-rights movement. She notes that the movement brought women as well as men and children out to march "demanding freedom" and joining "the chant for votes, houses, and jobs" (12). Their victories, as of 1972, included better housing and the defeat of a Unionist politician who supported the Protestant police. The ostensible goal of the police appears to be to keep order — to control rioters in order to prevent property damage and bodily injury. However, their unnecessarily violent tactics on Bloody Sunday suggest that their real goal was to obliterate or severely damage the civil-rights movement. Because McCafferty wrote this narrative for an Irish audience familiar with the goals of both sides, her purpose here is more to win sympathy than to inform.

**Connections**

1.    Rosemary Bray, in her selection in *Looking At Ourselves*, writes about waiting for her husband to come home and worrying that he would become the victim of white violence. She and Peggy Deery have something in common, in that Peggy Deery had similar worries about her son Paddy. In the prologue to McCafferty's essay, she mentions that Paddy is pursued by police for his involvement in the civil-rights movement. Neither Bray's husband nor Peggy's son is safe on the streets; they are both vulnerable to attack because of their backgrounds—Bray because he is black, and Paddy Deery because he is Catholic. The Associated Press piece describes the biased thinking of those who identify an Other and strike out as a way of affirming their own superiority. In the United States, for many whites, African-Americans are in the position of the Other. Peggy Deery, as a victim of police violence that could be described as a hate crime, is also in a position of being an Other in relation to the mostly Protestant police and British army. Similarly, the child in George Will's piece who comments that he hopes "that next time it won't be somebody I know" who dies from gang violence, has much in common with the Irish Catholics, whose relatives and friends are daily harrassed, arrested, and killed in conflicts with the army and with police.

2.    The Rudolphs focus on the contemporary rise of "politics of identity" to explain civil violence. They write that religion and ethnicity are among the aspects of identity that have become politicized in Eastern European conflicts. The politics of identity are also important to the Irish Troubles because they are based on religious differences between Catholics and Protestants and on cultural and nationalist differences between the British and Irish. The Rudolphs also point out that there is no need to identify these conflicts as "ancient hatreds" for which no resolution is possible; rather, they are the result of contemporary events and injustices — encouraged by simplistic and sensational media coverage — that could be resolved if everyone involved would realize the limitations of identity politics.

3.    In both "Peggy Deery of Derry" and "Amnesty," the authors look at social and political conflicts from the point of view of women whose lives have been blighted by a government's injustices. Peggy Deery took a much more activist role than does the anonymous narrator of "Amnesty," in that she marches for her own civil-rights, but both women are politically conscious and aware of the sacrifices they have had to make. In addition, both women worry about the men in their lives who place their own lives in

jeopardy because of their political activism; a conflict between their political convictions and personal lives is apparent in both. Gordimer and McCafferty both use their narrator's love and fear for those close to them to dramatize the anguish of living with poverty and oppression.

4.  In both "Peggy Deery of Derry" and "Sister Imelda," representatives of the Catholic Church are deeply involved in the lives of parishioners. Father Tom cares for the Deery family personally. He delivers not only spiritual comfort and guidance, but also practical help, as when he brings food to Deery's children and helps put them to bed (32). Sister Imelda, as a nun, is not permitted to have an involvement with her students as close as that of Tom with his parishioners, but she is expected to keep close watch over their intellectual and spiritual growth. Her passion for her vocation, like Father Tom's, suggests that the Catholic Church does not function as an abstract religious entity, but as an organization deeply integrated into the lives of Catholics.

## CHARLES MOORE, Ireland Must Fight the IRA Too (p. 624)

### Explorations

1.  Moore's initial anecdote makes the point that British citizens have been exposed to IRA terrorism for so many years that it has become an integral, and almost familiar, part of life. The anecdote lends a more human face to the statistic Moore offers in the second paragraph: Ninety-seven British people died as a result of terrorism in Britain in 1991.

2.  According to Moore, a fair assessment of the view of the IRA in Northern Ireland can be derived from the fact that only one of the seventeen Ulster seats in the House of Commons is held by a supporter of the IRA (para. 5). The "dominant view" implied by this, and by the fact that a majority of people in Northern Ireland vote for Unionists, is a lack of support for the IRA in Northern Ireland. Moore contends that the IRA has far more support outside of Ireland (in the United States, for instance) than within Ireland (8). Moore does not identify nor discuss IRA supporters within Northern Ireland.

3.  In paragraph 7, Moore asserts that in the Republic of Ireland, most people are glad the British are occupying the North and there is virtually no support for the IRA. They fear that without the British in place, there would be civil war in the north and that IRA terrorism would reach the south. By never stating a British view of the IRA beyond "weary resignation" (4), Moore implies the British offer little or no support to the IRA; but his references to IRA terrorism in Britain suggest a more active opposition.

4.  The thesis of Moore's essay is that with present conditions and policies there is no chance of resolution—there can be neither a united Ireland, nor a final acceptance that Northern Ireland is a part of Britain (13). Since Moore is not in favor of a united Ireland, he recommends that Britain integrate "Ulster politics into those of the rest of the kingdom" (16). And Dublin should cooperate fully in order to bring about the resolution Moore promotes.

147

## Connections

1. Moore and McCafferty agree only on the definition of internment and that it happened in the 1960s. Moore describes it as "the detention of named individuals for extended periods without trial" (para. 9). He says that both the United Kingdom and the Republic of Ireland thought internment for IRA terrorists was justified to "prevent intimidation of juries" — a view he apparently shares. McCafferty, in contrast, refers to internment as a "ploy" against which "international opinion was ranged" (19). She says that "hundreds of Catholic males" were held, that most of them shared a "commitment to civil rights," and that few fo them were associated witht the IRA.

2. Students' discussion of Connections #1 should lead effectively to a consideration of the differences in McCafferty's and Moore's treatment of the role of religion in the violent acts of the IRA and the response of Britain. Moore, in fact, ignores the role of religion and writes as though there are no pertinent religious differences among the combatants. For McCafferty, the conflict between Catholics and Protestants is a central issue, as is evident in her opening to the main section of her essay, where she discusses how Catholics have been oppressed by Protestants, and in her continual identification of the civil-rights movement as a Catholic effort.

3. The Rudolphs argue that the increasing tendency to employ "politics of identity" that are "crafted in benign and malignant ways in print and electronic media" promotes violence based on differences in religion and ethnicity. Moore, in his second paragraph, describes how it has become common knowledge that IRA violence has escalated in recent years, a fact he explains in part because of the international response to the IRA, which tends to see the organization as a true representative of the will of the Irish people. Moore attempts to discredit the idea that "identity politics"—pitting the Irish and British against each other—is an accurate way of viewing the situation.


## DAVID GROSSMAN, Israeli Arab, Israeli Jew (p. 629)

### Explorations

1. The Israeli Palestinian Mohammed Kiwan, looking for a bridge between his country's Palestinians and Jews, believes he can build that bridge with a "common man" like Jojo Abutbul, a Jew who expressed views similar to Kiwan's on television. Both men feel that much of the conflict is fostered at the institutional level, by the government and media, and are hopeful that "if the two of us sit down and talk, we can finish off all the problems in two minutes." Both Kiwan as a Palestinian and Abutbul as a Morocccan have experienced prejudice and view themselves to some degree as outsiders in Israel. Their ability to understand each other's point of view is limited, however, because Abutbul enjoys the civil privileges of being Jewish and wants Israel to be solely a Jewish nation (para. 21).

2.	The ladder Abutbul refers to is a hierarchy of influence and power based on "strength." Students may disagree about what constitutes "strength" in Abutbul's mind. He could be referring to military might, or economic resources, or even diplomatic influence. The most important thing in Abutbul's formulation is the idea that power at every level, from local to global, exists as a hierarchy in which "for every strong man there's someone stronger. . . ."

3.	Early on in the essay, Grossman refers to Mohammed Kiwan as "Kiwan." Only after Grossman makes a joke in which Kiwan becomes Mohammed going to the mountain that refuses to come to him does Grossman refer to both men by their first names (4). Students may realize immediately that Grossman uses this strategy to emphasize that these are common men (see Explorations #1) meeting as equals. He reinforces this impression by describing them collectively: "Both are solidly built, with black hair and tough faces" (48). He writes that he could "imagine them changing roles and arguing . . . each one making the other's points . . . " (51). If Grossman had referred to each man by his last name or his profession, his effort to establish their common ground would have failed. From the outside, their differences are more obvious than their similarities. The Palestinian Kiwan, a lawyer, is better educated than the Jewish Abutbul, a restauranteur who "manages the entire beach" (49). Using last names, professions, or ethnic designations would have undermined Grossman's attempts to portray them as men with intimate connections and equally intimate conflicts, weakening readers' ability to empathize with them.

4.	Students will be able to come up with many examples of Abutbul's use of metaphors and analogies. Some seem apt, others seem misdirected or confusing. In general, the technique makes abstract ideas more concrete and vivid, but it also distorts them, as the parallel between substance and symbol is never exact. Abutbul first uses "allegory"—and calls attention to it—in paragraph 6, where he compares his life when he was a sleeping child to a "box" that was "deposited" with the Arab housemaid who cared for him. This "allegory," in his estimation, describes the "trust" between Arabs and Jews, but significantly, the Arab in his "allegory" is a housemaid in an inferior social and economic position. In paragraph 15, Abutbul implies that since he didn't buy his Jewish identity at a store—did not, in other words, choose to be Jewish—he deserves a nation. Kiwan, of course, could have made the same point about being born Palestinian, but Abutbul thinks that Palestinians would feel at home in any other Arab nation. Perhaps the most uncomfortable analogy Abutbul draws appears in paragraph 25, where he describes his relationship to Kiwan—and the relationship of Jewish Israelis and Palestinians—as a marriage: "I love you, you're my soul, everything. I don't want to live with you!" He offers a "dowry" if the Palestinian will leave. This analogy, with its implications of a gender hierarchy in which the Palestinian is the unwanted wife of the Jew, seems particularly inflammatory between two men who consider wives as private possessions who symbolize their masculine honor (61). However, the expression of intimacy that slips out ("you're my soul") suggests that Abutbul realizes that the fate of the Jews and Palestinians are closely linked.

## Connections

1.	The most basic comparison that students might make between the Troubles in Ireland and the conflicts between Palestinians and Jews in Israel is that the strife arises from religious and nationalist differences. Like Abutbul, who believes that Palestinians need to accept the sovereignty of the Jewish state, Charles Moore in Britain believes that the citizens of Northern Ireland should (and, for the most part, already do) accept that their proper place is in the British state (paras. 5, 6). McCafferty emphasizes religious differences far more than Moore does; her portrayal of the experiences of Catholics fighting for civil rights in Northern Ireland has much in common with Kiwan's estimation of the plight of Palestinians in Israel. Kiwan says that his people in the intifadah "had no way to remain silent any longer, so they used the stone. . . . It's simply the only tool he has to make the world hear him!" (62). Some Catholics in Northern Ireland, including Peggy Deery, might be able to understand the frustration and sense of having been silenced that would drive Palestinians to "use the stone." One important difference between the Isreali and Irish conflicts is historical: Jews and Arabs have jointly occupied the region known as Palestine for thousands of years, with open conflict erupting when the United Nations created the separate Jewish state of Israel there in 1948. The influx of Scots and Britons into the northern part of Ireland began after England solidified its control of Ireland in the 1600s and was actively opposed from the start, most violently by the IRA in this century and particularly since Great Britain made its partition of Ireland official in 1992.

2.   Shelby Steele writes, "To be innocent someone else must be guilty, a natural law that leads the races to forge their innocence on each other's backs." Both Kiwan and Abutbul attempt to do this, Abutbul by claiming he has also been discriminated against (see Explorations #1) and Kiwan by magnanimously saying that he hated seeing Sephardim discriminated against (58–60). Steele says that blacks have reacted to whites' assumption of their own innocence either by bargaining or by challenging. Kiwan uses both strategies with Abutbul, beginning by bargaining. He says that it's all right with him if Abutbul thinks of his nation as Israel as long as it is all right for Kiwan to identify his nation—on the same land—as Palestine (12–14). Later, after Abutbul boasts that Prime Minister Jojo will exile Palestinians who don't accept Israeli sovereignty (29), Kiwan ceases bargaining and challenges Abutbul on the question of who has and will have power, saying that Abutbul is a guest on his land (30).

3.   Yoram Binur experienced humiliation when he posed as a Palestinian because of the assumptions Jews made about his competence, worth, and even personhood. He recalls comments from Jews about the idleness of Arabs and their inferiority relative to Jews (7). He remembers a worse humiliation, when a Jewish man and woman almost have sex in front of him because "for them I simply didn't exist" (9). Binur recalls an anecdote about a college student, a Palestinian who was passed over for a job that was later given to an uneducated Jew (15). Another Palestinian tells a story about his Jewish girlfriend, who is ready to believe he is a terrorist (16). The assumption that Arabs are idle, incompetent, violent, and—most significantly—less than human, is also apparent in the exchange between Kiwan and Abutbul. Abutbul feels it necessary to state that he believes "An Arab is a human being. An Arab has a soul" (7). His unsolicited statement suggests that some Jews do not believe that Arabs are human beings. Nevertheless he implies that Arabs tend to be violent, as when he wonders whether Kiwan wants "my plate, my bed, my wife, and my children . . ." (8). He relates the worry of "some Jewish guy" that "some Ahmed [will] come and knife you." Kiwan, sensitive to Abutbul's implications that Jewish people are inherently stronger, says that he has "no feelings of inferiority" about Abutbul; and indeed, Abutbul seems to have feelings of inferiority with regard to Kiwan, in evidence

when he complains about Kiwan's education and when he bursts out that Arab violence insults him: "I'm not his dog, not his snake!" (61).

## SLAVENKA DRAKULIĆ, (Druh-kool-itch) Zagreb: A Letter to My Daughter (p. 646)

### Explorations

1. Slavenka Drakulić's first paragraph establishes a mood of sad nostalgia and loneliness. She describes her daughter's empty room and the emblems of innocence and youth that once marked it as belonging to a much-loved child. Later in the essay, her attempts to recall her daughter's presence by evoking concrete memories give way to a more powerful realization of loss: "I didn't recognize you because I was losing you" (para. 5). But immediately, she attempts to mitigate the loss with another concrete memory, of a train trip they took together when "R" was two years old. Drakulić continues to feel her loneliness deeply (6), but her mood changes to one of thoughtful reflection, tinged with anger about the chasm war has created between men and women (12), her daughter's generation and hers (10).

2. When Drakulić looks back on her own, and her husband's, focus on their lives (7), she realizes that they should have been paying attention to the world. Instead, they continued to disassociate themselves from the "spiral of hatred descending upon us" (8)—repeating a cycle of denial also apparent in her father's generation, who never "believed that history could repeat itself" (9). Her regret also shows when she writes about her daughter's generation and its unwillingness to look at the past or learn from it (10). As her discussion of the young man who spoke on television of his lack of a future (11, 12) indicates, she realizes that the young want to live their own lives rather than feel they must spend their lives—and perhaps give up their lives—making up for the mistakes of their parents and grandparents. Yet her own generation's having taken a similar attitude is partly responsible for her daughter's now having to grapple with issues of ethnic identity and conflict.

3. Drakulić's second-person address allows the reader to feel the mother-daughter intimacy that, to some degree, connects Drakulić and "R" across the emotional and physical distance between them. She describes the choking loneliness she feels sitting in her daughter's room (6), and reminds her daughter of how well she remembers little details about her, such as her dislike of her mother's tears and her habit of leaving messages in lipstick on the bathroom mirror. She also knows her daughter's limits; she tells her daughter that if she had stayed in her own war-torn country, "your mind would [have] crack[ed] and you would [have] enter[ed] a void where no one could reach you any longer" (5). If Drakulić had used the third-person, addressing the reader rather than her daughter, much of the pathos and sense of intimacy would have been lost. Drakulić seems to want to put a human face on the conflicts between Serbs and Croats—a conflict that traps her daughter in between loyalties to her divorced parents (7). The deep concern of the mother for her daughter is more likely to capture the reader's sympathies than the more distanced approach of a third-person essay. Finally, because the essay is written

151

in the form of a personal letter, the physical distance between mother and daughter is all the more obvious.

4.   Drakulić uses incomplete sentences at several points in her letter. Overall, they are evidence of the informal, personal nature of her writing; she feels no need to attend to the formal rules of grammar in an intimate letter to her daughter. Futhermore, her incomplete sentences have the effect of stream-of-consciousness, in which thought builds upon thought through an associative process. In the second paragraph, Drakulić elaborates the metaphor of a birth to explore connections between her daughter's new maturity and the war; she uses incomplete sentences beginning with "Or" and "And" to build the analogy. Toward the end of paragraph 8, she uses fragments to a similar effect, quickly building a series of connected thoughts regarding the differences among generations. The stream-of-consciousness style is not always apparent in the fragments, however. Drakulić ends paragraph 7 with two concise fragments in response to the idea that her daughter could refuse to take sides in the Croatian/Serbian conflict: "But not now. Not here." Here, her use of fragments seems more decisive and clipped than when she is trying to connect a series of complex thoughts.

## Connections

1.   In "Israeli Arab, Israeli Jew," Abutbul points to the future when he says to Kiwan, "So I ask you, Mohammed, where do we want to get to?" (para. 8). Their argument throughout is peppered with references to potential actions and consequences, showing that—in contrast to the Yugoslav Communists cited by Drakulić—they are confident of having power over their future. They debate whether the Jews can or should—force the Arabs entirely out of Israel (29). They argue about getting a "divorce" (25, 26) and what that would mean for their future. Abutbul suggests that Kiwan has the option of "getting up tomorrow and moving to Jordan, Egypt, Syria, Lebanon" but he offers to build "another country for you" to end the strife between Arabs and Jews in Israel. Similarly, Kiwan talks about what will happen when Palestine is a nation of its own (30) and questions Abutbul about his idea of the future: "You're saying that this country, this future country of ours, will agree that every man in the world who wants to live in it can?" (34). Perhaps most telling is Jojo's "I'll try to help you as much as I can, so that your son . . . has a future here like my son" (85). Although the two men do not arrive at an agreement, their willingess to argue and their enthusiastic questioning about possible futures suggest that they have a better chance of understanding each other than the Serbs and Croats.

2.   The Rudolphs describe the term "ethnic cleansing" as an invention of Serbian nationalists. The term implies that the conflicts between Serbs and Croats are of ancient origin and that only by a process of "cleansing"—complete separation—can their conflicts be managed. The Rudolphs refute the idea that no one has responsibility for resolving the problem; the belief that nothing can be done because the Serbs and Croats are only perpetuating an ancient, irremediable, mutual hatred only has the effect of contributing to its continuation. By focusing on the immediate conflict, the Rudolphs suggest that something can be done now. Drakulić's letter to her daughter supports their views because, in her consideration of the evolution of the conflict over the last three generations, Drakulić cites changes, lulls and squalls, in the Serbian/Croation conflict. Drakulić, a Croat, married a Serb at a time when the difference was considered unimportant (7). Drakulić explains this as an effect of growing up in Communist

Yugoslavia, which she describes as "an artificial nation." Now, "there is no middle position" (7). Her daughter will have to choose between her parents, but there was a time when she didn't have to. The Rudolphs argue that there could be a time in the future when the conflict would be reduced and she wouldn't have to choose.

3. Rosemary Bray writes about her worries for her African-American husband, who is, because of his race, especially vulnerable to violence on the street. While she waits for him to come home, she considers the possibility that he will be the victim of random, fear-inspired violence and that she will be left alone. During the phone conversation between Drakulić and her daughter, Drakulić hears shots and her daughter's terrified response. "[T]hat was the moment when the war began for both of us" (4). It is also the moment when she first realizes her own helplessness (5) to help her daughter deal with the violence that surrounds her and threatens not only her body, but also her mind. Drakulić is separated from her daughter because of the war; she is, in a sense, alone as Bray feared she would be left alone. Drakulić writes that her separation from her daughter is much less terrible than the things that have happened to others, but nevertheless she feels the loss strongly.

## ISABEL ALLENDE (Ah-YEN-day), The Los Riscos Mine (p. 656)

### Explorations

1. Allende makes it clear near the end of her essay that the public recognizes that the bodies belonged to victims of the government. She writes that when the news finally appeared on television, people heard the official lies and knew the bodies were those of "murdered political prisoners" (para. 54). But the identities of the perpetrators and victims are apparent at several points earlier in the piece. Even in the opening narrative, the posted warnings, barbed wire, and Irene's fear of being discovered by soldiers (5, 9) suggest that the government is trying to hide something in the mine; when the Chief Justice says to himself, "It required no great experience to conclude that the perpetrators of those crimes had acted with the approval of the government," it is apparent that the government has been using him to cover up their crimes against citizens (42). Finally, the continued interest of the General and the readiness of his troops to interfere with the investigation suggest that the government is responsible for the deaths of the people whose bodies are discovered in Los Riscos.

2. Students' responses to this question will vary a great deal depending on their background and political beliefs. Most will agree with the premise of the question, which is that in the United States, political dissidents enjoy the same freedoms as those who agree with the dominant political philosophy. Students will realize that few U.S citizens live with the same kind of fear of the government as the citizens of the country Allende depicts. However, some students may mention the harrassment of communists during the McCarthy era in the United States, the murder of civil-rights workers during the 1960s, or instances of police brutality as evidence that U.S. citizens are not completely free to disagree with their government's policies.

3. The General appears only as a voice. In paragraph 35 he is represented by his "agents," who are spying on the investigative commission. The General gives orders from some safe and unnamed location; by means of high technologies imported from the United States (39) and "the Far East" (40), he monitors the movements of the Cardinal and the Commission. The General orders the Chief Justice to "juggle justice" and has the power to bring about the death of any citizen (42); he appears, in fact, almost as omnipotent as he is ubiquitous. If Allende treated him as she does other characters, rather than as a disembodied but powerful presence, he would seem a less impersonal and amoral force.

4. The Chief Justice clearly feels himself caught between two formidable powers, the Catholic Church and the General. When he receives the Cardinal's letter, the Chief Justice "wished he were on the other side of the world" (41) because his response to the letter will place him in a bad position either with its sender or with the General. The Chief Justice seems to have abdicated his own sense of right and wrong; after years of betraying moral principles in the service of his government, he no longer has a sense of his own responsibility for seeing justice done. If Allende had included this information in the form of exposition rather than as character description, it would have been much harder for her to convey the psychological effects of the Chief Justice's complicity with the corrupt government. Writing in his voice, she follows his distorted thought processes, revealing much more about the personal price of political dishonesty than simple exposition would have.

## Connections

1. Allende's use of homely details helps readers understand the events at the Los Riscos mine in a very different way than they would if they read about the discovery of the bodies in the newspaper or heard about it on the news. She conveys the horror of the discovery by showing how people reacted when they encountered the bodies. The details she offers give the story a feeling of reality it would otherwise lack. Drakulić uses homely details in a slightly different way, because in her letter the mention of the contents of her daughter's room in the opening paragraphs is intended to imply her personal involvement in the violence she reports. Allende, although she uses everyday details to emphasize the reality of violence, remains in the background. The events she describes happened not to her, in her own home, but to others.

2. McCafferty portrays a Catholic priest, Father Tom O'Gara, who is in many respects similar to José Leal, the priest who, in Allende's "The Los Riscos Mine," brings representatives of the Catholic Church in to investigate the discovery of the bodies of murdered political prisoners in the mine. Father O'Gara is also deeply concerned for the lives of his parishioners, as is apparent in his close attention to the welfare of Peggy Derry's family (para. 32), and the Catholic Church in both Allende's and McCafferty's pieces becomes involved in conflicts between governments and citizens. The Catholic priests in McCafferty's essay issue a statement following Bloody Sunday in support of the civil-rights marchers (33), and in Allende's account, the commission of Catholic priests initiates the investigation of Los Riscos Mine. In both cases, priests represent the interests of their parishioners rather than abiding by either the law or the interests of the government.

3. The most compelling similarity students may perceive between "The Los Riscos Mine" and Joan Didion's piece is the writers' unusual interest in violent events that most people

would choose to ignore. The woman whose body was, in Didion's words, "put out with the trash" was the victim of violence committed by a man who had enough power to get away with—perhaps—murder; because of his privileged economic class and her uninteresting history, he was not held accountable for his actions. Allende indicts a government for a similarly cavalier disregard for the human rights of its citizens, portraying characters who bring to light an incident that, but for their attention, would probably have gone unnoticed by most people.

## CZESLAW MILOSZ (CHESS-law MEE-losh), American Ignorance of War (p. 671)

### Explorations

1. This question may meet with some resistance; it's far from pleasant to be reminded that one's comfort and security might be blown to oblivion in an instant. And yet there's very little that can be done to soften the impact, because it's precisely this resistance that breeds the attitudes described as "stupid" by Milosz's questioner. He can't understand why Americans look on their way of life as "natural" and all others as "unnatural." He knows that the social order can be destroyed in an instant, that what was once considered natural and ordinary can suddenly become meaningless. Milosz's answer to the question is no, Americans are not stupid, just ignorant, and his reason is that Americans have never experienced war on their own soil. Even those Americans who have served in wars have always enjoyed the knowledge that a safe, sane home still existed for them to return to.

2. Milosz gives no specific reasons, but the entire state of affairs he describes may be seen as the ultimate debasement of human beings who finally decide they have little to lose in rebellion. Even under the worst of conditions, a rebellion, which Milosz refers to as the "Underground," existed. Most of the atrocities he describes are based on World War II experiences, but his statement that Central Europeans have learned "to think sociologically and historically" (para. 12) may be interpreted to suggest that they could imagine the repressions of the Soviet state re-creating the situation they had survived earlier. Then resistance might seem a logical course of action. By contrast, his comments indicating how quickly human beings adapt to unfavorable situations would suggest an unwillingness to risk confrontation. Milosz writes that "man is so plastic a being that one can even conceive of the day when a thoroughly self-respecting citizen will . . . [sport] a tail of brightly colored feathers as a sign of conformity to the order he lives in" (11). His fatalism results from having lived under two regimes that made "the fate of twentieth-century man . . . identical with that of a caveman living in the midst of powerful monsters" (7). The repetition of the experience (2) suggests that such conditions are not "unnatural" and could recur ad infinitum.

3. After coming to grips with their emotional responses to the first two questions, students should have no trouble answering this one. If presented with a historical or argumentative essay, we would be able to intellectualize the situation, distancing ourselves from the consequences of the argument. Instead we are forced to come to terms with a "gut" reaction to destruction. It's probably significant that in this case, even though they would normally prefer a personal rather than an intellectual account, most students would

probably feel much more comfortable with an impersonal essay. As students report on the most forceful concepts and comments, they will begin to appreciate the value and impact of the emotional versus the rational appeal.

## Connections

1. The desire of many to avoid seeing, and therefore having to deal with, the deaths of citizens at the hands of the government is apparent in both Allende and Milosz. Milosz writes about avoiding a body in the street and refusing to consider the government's culpability (para. 5); similarly, the bodies in the Los Riscos Mine remained there for so long in part because no one wanted to face the consequences of searching for them. The political activists whose bodies turned up in the Los Riscos Mine are similar to the man whom Milosz says is "pushed into a van, and from that moment is lost to his family and friends" (7). Among the differences students may notice in Allende's and Milosz's depiction of countries torn apart by governments that treat their citizens like enemies is the ethnic basis of oppression in Milosz's description of Eastern Europe. He relates how people were divided up and made to live in certain areas according to their ethnic or religious identity (6) and change their names to avoid being identified (8); in Allende's story, by contrast, the people are represented as sharing an ethnic identity that allows them to trust each other.

2. Drakulić writes that when the war broke out between Serbs and Croats, she realized the difference between knowing war can happen and having it become a part of your life: "You no longer watch *Apocalypse Now*, you live it" (10). Milosz describes the isolation of Americans from an immediate experience of war as the difference that makes it impossible for "the man of the East" to "take Americans seriously" (12). The immediacy of war, and its effects on perception, occupy the attention of both Milosz and Drakulić. Milosz writes that the experience of war teaches people that "fluidity and constant change are the characteristics of phenomena" (11). Drakulić's letter illustrates that idea, as she describes how her understanding of the history of the Serbian/Croatian conflict changed over time (7, 8).

3. Students will be able to find an indirect response to Milosz's comments about American ignorance in almost every selection in *Looking At Ourselves*. Ron Kovic's piece about his devastating war wounds points to the limitations of Milosz's contentions: Living American men have known war intimately, in World War II, in Korea, and in Vietnam. Americans have not, however, had a war on their own soil. William Broyles's contention that war is the "great love" of men's lives seems irrational from the perspective of Milosz's essay, although Broyles's statement that we cannot prevent war no matter how hard we try to avoid it seems to support Milosz's statement that "if something exist in one place, it will exist everywhere" (12). The Rudolphs' piece contends that Americans have a very superficial understanding of the problems in Eastern Europe (and at home) based on simplistic treatment of complex issues in the media. Rosemary Bray's piece about her daily fears for her husband also refutes Milosz's contention that Americans are ignorant of the kind of violence war brings to a nation; she describes a race war that is never brought to an end. This impression is deepened in the piece by the anonymous black man in Mother Jones, where he relates his reactions to the riots in Los Angeles following the original Rodney King verdict. Many residents of Los Angeles had firsthand experience of civil violence on their own streets during the riots.

## NUHA AL-RADI (Ahl-RAH-dee), Baghdad Diary (p. 677)

### Explorations

1. Many students will be sensitive to Nuha Al-Radi's hostility toward the West. They will notice especially her many disparaging references to George Bush (paras. 28, 37, 49, 61, 89, 90), which suggest that Bush symbolized the "evil" West for Iraqis much as Saddam Hussein symbolized the "barbarous" Middle East for Americans. The fact that the Allies are in the process of bombing Baghdad during the time she is writing is the most immediate and powerful reason for her hostility. Al-Radi is aware that Iraqi radio is more propaganda than real news, but she seems to accept the official version of war, in which the West and especially George Bush figure as a group of immensely powerful bullies beating up on a small nation full of innocent citizens (46). Al-Radi says that "the whole world hates us" (22); the sense of being a cohesive group of underdogs with the world against them helps Al-Radi cope with the magnitude of the country's devastation (60).

2. Al-Radi makes many references to Western movies that suggest that she enjoys Western popular culture, even if she despises the Allies in general and George Bush in particular. She and her friends have seen *E.T.* (29), *Gone with the Wind* (62), and *The Party* (100); all her comments on the movies imply that she is able to identify with the Western characters they portray. Her dog is named after a Western artist; she prizes seeds for Italian vegetables (1), European radio broadcasts (46), and anemones bought in the United States (92). She clearly values her internationalism, which seems to be a badge of socioeconomic status. However, in paragraph 28, Al-Radi makes an ambiguous comment. Although she had visited the United States recently, she doesn't think she "could set foot in the West again." She thinks she might go to India, where "they have a high tolerance and will not shun us Iraqis." Evidently she did not entirely hate the West before the war; now, however, it is unclear whether she would not visit the West because she would not expect to be welcomed there, or because she would not want to visit it out of loyalty to her own people.

3. The class discussion of Explorations #2 should lead naturally to a consideration of Al-Radi's definition of culture. Her statement concludes that American jealousy "must be why they have bombed our archealogical sites." Here culture means a long history and its artifacts. Her constant naming of friends, familiy and neighbors reinforces the implication that for Al-Radi, culture means having a well-established place in the world — in her case, as an Iraqi, a place that goes back thousands of years. But her statement is apparently made in anger rather than in earnest. Later, she calls her comment "silly." Throughout her diary, it is clear that she loves food, gardening, celebrations, music, and movies and that her enjoyment of these everyday aspects of culture include Western influences.

4. The two main effects of writing in diary form are the sense of immediacy—events and emotional responses are recorded as they happened or very soon thereafter—and a high degree of everyday details. Among the advantages of Al-Radi's approach are the probability that readers will experience these events as closer in time and space than they would if Al-Radi had written a reflective essay. Potentially, this could make the emotional impact and sense of suspense greater. The writer, like her reader, does not know what will happen next; she cannot, therefore, anticipate either for herself or for readers how the war will affect her and her friends. Although this method raises the level of suspense

and perhaps the emotional involvement of the reader, it also risks losing the impact of the war in a wealth of relatively inconsequential everyday details. It is clear from her many references to food, for instance, that Al-Radi is very concerned about where meals will come from as the war continues, but readers may be less interested in detailed accounts of what is eaten when than in the writer's overall concern about supplies. In a reflective essay, written after the war and after she had the time to find out more about what happened to others, Al-Radi could have placed her personal experience within a wider context without, perhaps, losing much of the emotional impact of her diary.

## Connections

1. Czeslaw Milosz writes that "all the concepts men live by are a product of the historic formation in which they find themselves" (para. 11). The life that felt natural before the war is replaced by a radically different life that can come to feel just as "natural" simply because it is "within the realm of one's experience." Al-Radi notices a similar phenomenon in her friends. M. A. W., for instance, says, "We must have continuous war . . . when we finish this war we must start another" (53). The comment is ironically intended, but it indicates just how "fluid" — in Milosz's term — people are. Al-Radi and her friends quickly grow used to the war. Her record for the twenty-fourth and twenty-fifth days reads, "A sameness. Even war becomes routine" (67). Likewise, behaviors that before the war would have been considered immoral or at least unusual are normalized under wartime conditions. One of her friends reacts to the war by "looking for someone to share her bed today" (13). Milosz writes that people no longer regard "banditry as a crime" (9), and Al-Radi offers several examples of thievery that neither she, nor others, regard as anything to become upset about (109).

2. Al-Radi wonders "Why do they keep bombing the same things again and again?", a question that most Americans would have no better answer to than Al-Radi does. The incomprehension apparent in her comments about how the billions spent on weaponry could be used to feed the hungry is, likewise, something Al-Radi shares with many Westerners. But William Broyles, in *Looking at Ourselves*, offers an indirect explanation when he writes that no matter how much men hate war, they are drawn to it as the most exhilarating experience of their lives. Sam Keen asks a question akin to Al-Radi's: "Why have the best and brightest exercised their intelligence . . . only to create a world where starvation and warfare are more common than they were in neolithic times?" But he answers his own question by simply saying that violence is "central" to men's self-concept. Both these writers would agree with the distinction implicit in Al-Radi's questions and comments that it is particularly Westerners who ignore the real and immediate needs of the world in pursuit of domination; they would say that men as a gender are unable to give much energy to helping the starving of the world because they are too deeply involved in experiencing their manhood through violence.

3. Iraq, like many nations in the Middle East, draws very clear lines of difference in regard to gender roles. Miriam Cooke's "The Veil Does Not Prevent Women from Working" focuses on the lives of women in Saudi Arabia, not Iraq, but it is likely that the same general understanding of gender differences applies to both Islamic cultures. However, Al-Radi is apparently a woman on her own, who maintains her own home and does not live in the shadow of any man. She has a wide circle of friends and seems very capable of caring for herself and for them. Her bicycle ride offended some, but she does not feel

shamed by their response. The man who shouts "We don't like girls that ride bikes" is speaking for the men who agree with traditional notions that women's place is in the home; he may have both religious and social motives in badgering her.

## MICHAEL KELLY, Torture in Kuwait (p. 696)

### Explorations

1. In his first paragraph, Kelly contrasts the former beauty and "conspicuous civilization" apparent in Kuwait University's School of Music with the barbaric and violent purposes to which Iraq had put the building. This contrast, situated at the opening of the essay, emphasizes the envy and hatred that motivated the Iraqis to torture Kuwaitis and defile and destroy property. The British television producer, epitomizing the civilized British gentleman, seems unaffected by the horror of Jasman's story of his surroundings. He patronizes Jasman, not only by failing to empathize with his trauma, but also calling him "a good chap" and calling him by his first name. The effect of this is that Jasman seems to be in a position of being exploited twice — once by Iraqi torturers, who injured him apparently just because they had the opportunity — and again by British television, which wants to take advantage of the sensational aspects of Jasman's story but has no apparent interest in helping him.

2. Students should be able to locate several different explanations for the extreme and apparently irrational violence of Iraqi soldiers. Perhaps the most telling "explanation" is offered by a torture victim who finds the search for reasons futile. He says simply, "Really, they are all crazy" (para. 39). In the following paragraph, a Kuwaiti with American ties says that Iraqis are "brainwashed" by Saddam Hussein to the point that they are unable to think for themselves. Kelly himself speculates that Iraq found torture and purposeless destruction an effective way "to subjugate a hostile, numerically overwhelming population" (42). Some of these Kelly interviews maintain that the Iraqis are essentially evil (43); in support of the contention that Iraqis enjoy violence, Kelly quotes a speech by an early medieval Iraqi leader and memorized by school children, in which violence and bloodshed are glorified (45, 46). Kelly concludes that the corruption of the Hussein regime inevitably corrupted all those who acted in its interests (48).

3. Kelly first introduces a personal response when he writes that he is used to seeing men cry during war; during this war he has "seen twenty men cry, not counting myself" (2). He hardly needs to offer his own personal responses, however, to stir readers' emotions. His account of Jasman's television appearance vividly portrays the lasting horror of a man's suffering at the hands of Iraqi soldiers. Kelly shows Jasman at the end of his appearance, when the television crew is finished with him, "with one trouser leg hiked up to the knee and tear trails streaking the dust on his face," an image that strongly conveys the disintegration and shock Jasman is feeling. Kelly quotes his interviewees often, letting their own words heighten the emotional impact of his story. Jasman tells of being electrocuted (14); an electrical engineer describes having his fingernails pulled out (28–30); an employee of a petroleum company recalls being hung on a wall and made

to watch the rape of a woman (34–38). By letting his interviewees tell their own stories much of the time, Kelly reduces his role as mediator between the interviewees and the reader.

4.  Kelly comes upon the electrical engineer, who is still suffering the physical effects of his torture, by accident when he stops at a gas station. By emphasizing the accidental nature of their encounter, Kelly implies that the experience of torture is widespread. He needn't seek out victims; they are everywhere, and they are eager to talk about what happened to them. The electrical engineer cooperates very willingly, even slowing down his delivery so that Kelly, sitting on a "hard little yellow plastic chair" in the office of the gas station, can record his account word for word. Kelly's representation of his own presence is important because it portrays him as a wide-open listener, ready at a moment's notice to hear and record the words of his interviewees without judgment or interruption. The effects of depicting his own presence is that Kelly sets up a narrative and creates a visual impression, pulling the reader into the scene along with him and making it harder for the reader to remain emotionally detached.

## Connections

1.  Students will be able to refer back to their discussion of Explorations #2 as they consider the contrast between Kelly's and Al-Radi's portrayal of Iraqis. Kelly does say that the Iraqis he met in Baghdad—Al-Radi's home city—were "generous, likable people," a description that seems to fit Al-Radi herself and that accords with her depiction of her friends and neighbors. He cannot understand the difference between those he met in Baghdad and the savage Iraqis he heard about, and saw evidence of, in Kuwait. In part the contrast can be explained by the national identities of the writers: Al-Radi, as an Iraqi, has a more sympathetic view of her own people than does Kelly. Both write about Iraqi soldiers coming home across the desert. Al-Radi, however, writes empathetically of the soldiers walking "with no food or water" and being gunned down by Allied planes. Kelly writes that "they had fled in the night . . . ashamed to think they would be caught in the place of their sins" (para. 48). But in part the difference can be attributed to the fact that Al-Radi has no way of knowing what Iraqi soldiers did in Kuwait; her information is filtered through the government and has been edited to exclude anything that might suggest the violent excesses of the Iraqi military.

2.  Since Kelly is interviewing only people whose entire lives have been turned upside down by the Iraqi invasion of Kuwait, there is little direct evidence of the "privileged ignorance" of war they enjoyed before the invasion. Settings such as the hall at Kuwait University's school of music and drama make it clear that life of comfortable ignorance existed. Kelly quotes other indirect evidence: One witness's idea that the Iraqis cannot be Muslims if they are capable of terrible violence shows that he has little personal acquaintance with the history of war in the Middle East. Similarly, it came as a surprising revelation to another witness that Iraqis "would follow [Saddam Hussein] anywhere, doing whatever" (41).

3.  The Associated Press piece contends that those who commit hate crimes in the United States are looking to harm those who are different from them in some way; it actually matters very little what race or religion the victim is, as long as he or she is different.

People who commit such crimes are usually looking for a thrill, rather than having any particular political motive in mind. Kelly asserts that soldiers in Kuwait were mostly young and malleable; they saw their leaders committing terrible violence and learned that no one would stop them or punish them if they, too, beat and tortured Kuwaitis (who fit the description of the "appropriate" victim for a hate crime because they are of a different nationality and culture than Iraqis). Students may be divided on the question of whether Kelly's discussion of Iraqi war crimes will help us understand violence in the United States. Some will be unable to imagine that their own people could be as cruelly inhuman as the Iraqis, but others may be able to cite instances of American cruelties in war or at home that suggest that violence is an international problem rather than a symptom of the "evil" of Iraqis in particular.

4. An unquestioning acceptance of violence as an integral part of everyday living is apparent in Sa'edi's "The Game Is Over." In paragraph 6, the narrator writes that "Hasani's dad would beat him every night, but my dad would only beat Ahmad and me once or twice a week." There is also a feeling that no one should escape the violence; this attitude seems to perpetuate violence through generations. Hasani says he'll be happy when his father learns "what it feels like to be beaten," not realizing that his father too was probably beaten regularly when he was a child. An Iraqi political scientist quoted in the third section of Kelly's essay observes that the history of Iraq is filled with violence (45) and that the tendency to commit violence cannot be considered a mark of abnormality among Iraqis, because so many engage in it (47). Both writers, then, depict violence as an ordinary and accepted, if negative, aspect of life.

## ALICE WALKER, The Concord Demonstration (p. 705)

### Explorations

1. Alice Walker and other demonstrators object to the current use of Concord, California, as a weapons depot. Walker reinforces her objections by citing the history of the site during World War II, when 320 soldiers, most of whom were black, were blown up when the bombs they were loading exploded. Soldiers who thereafter refused to load bombs were imprisoned and dishonorably discharged (para. 18). The goal of the demonstration in which Walker participates is to draw the public's attention to Concord and drum up support for closing it down. The demonstration is peaceful, designed primarily to emphasize the commitment of demonstrators to nonviolence. Their tactics include carrying banners, staging rallies, and blocking the arrival and exit of weapons from the site.

2. The military and its interests are not damaged in any way by the demonstrations, although its intended image as a protector of the American people may have been damaged when a train carrying weapons ran over demonstrators, seriously wounding Brian Willson (35). The demonstrators, then, are the only ones who suffer real damage as a result of the demonstration.

3. Walker implies in paragraph 27 the significance of her fame to the cause she is promoting. She wonders if her "statements to the press truly reflected my feelings about weapons

and war." Later, a police officer asks for her autograph (31) and after Walker is released, she addresses a crowd of a thousand demonstrators (33). Walker uses her fame and the media access it gives her to speak out against military weapons; her presence lends credibility to the demonstration, even as it draws more media attention.

4. Walker offers so many vivid images that there should be a great deal of variety in students' responses. Some may focus on Abraham, the old man who sings "Amen" (26), or the Vietnam veterans who offer their angry support to the cause (33), or Brian Willson, the demonstrator who "was willing to give his life to the struggle for peace" and, for all practical purposes, ended up making that sacrifice. The Windela doll that Walker carries may strike some students as an unusual and memorable symbol for the peace demonstration; others may be most affected by the image of the bomb explosion with which Walker opens her journal.

## Connections

1. Kelly writes that "Corrupt regimes corrupt those who live under them . . . . The young men who came from Iraq to Kuwait . . . found they had the appetite to do to the Kuwaitis the terrible things that the Mukhabarat did back home" (para. 48). He and Walker would agree that the soldiers' actions in support of an evil cause infects them and destroys their moral principles and  individual sense of responsibility.

2. Walker, observing a little girl playing mother to the Windela doll while the demonstration goes on around her, reflects that mothers try to create moments of peace and love for their children, even though the outside world is full of violence. To some degree, McCafferty's portrait of Peggy Deery supports Walker's view of the role of mothers. Deery, a mother many times over, tries to create a sense of unity in hard times by celebrating with her children, and even dancing on her bad leg, during a son's wedding; more importantly, her involvement in the civil-rights movement is an effort to fight for a better and more peaceful future for her children. Slavenka Drakulić poignantly expresses her desire to protect her daughter, both as a child and as a woman (5); she feels it to be her responsibility to create a clear, serene space for her child, and her inability to accomplish that because of the war makes her feel helpless.

3. Walker takes a hat, sunblock, food, and other items that are intended to help her be comfortable during the demonstration and the arrest that will follow. Similarly, Irene and Francisco carry the tools they will need and a thermos of hot coffee. Walker and Irene and Francisco are embarking on risky ventures in which they could be hurt, both emotionally and physically. The small items they take along for comfort remind the reader that they are vulnerable human beings, frightened and having very little to rely on except their own intelligence and courage.

4. Among the writers in *Looking at Ourselves* who deal with issues and ideas similar to Walker's are Ron Kovic and the Rudolphs. Kovic demonstrates, in his graphic account of how he suffered devastating injuries during the Vietnam war, that dealing with war as an abstract principle, and assuming that there is such a thing as a good or just war, cannot lead to peace. From Kovic's perspective, only throwing down weapons and

refusing to fight can lead to peace. The Rudolphs also argue against abstractions, though from a different perspective. Their attack on identity politics is based on the idea that identifying certain groups as "natural" enemies actually ignores contemporary causes of ethnic conflict and prevents people from dealing with the concrete, but complex, issues at stake in civil war.

## CHINUA ACHEBE (CHIN-oo-ah Ah-CHEE-bee), Civil Peace (p. 716)

### Explorations

1. Iwegbu considers himself lucky for a number of reasons: First, he, his wife, and three of their four children survived the war, second, his bicycle is still where he buried it, and third, his house is still standing. It is clear that the death toll in the war was significant; his elation over having a house and a bicycle indicates that material losses were great as well. There is an implication that the Nigerian government came out on top, but more important is the fact that the peasants were certainly the losers.

2. Currency now has become meaningless. Biafran rebel money, while plentiful, is worth little. What people want is Nigerian egg-rasher.

3. The term is a phonetic equivalent for ex gratia, or Nigerian money offered in return for turning in rebel scrip. Iwegbu gets money as he got war, for no apparent reason, and it withdraws just as arbitrarily, leaving him glad that no worse harm was done. Nothing has been gained — economic and political strife continue, but with survival as the object, not victory.

4. The term civil peace, so close to civil war, blurs the distinction between the two.

### Connections

1. In "Civil Peace," Jonathan Iwegbu's repeated exclamation that "nothing puzzles God!" (paras. 2, 4, 7) suggests that war is a mystery incomprehensible to humans, but somehow comprehensible to God. Part of that mystery is that the end of the war does not mean the end of violence. It means that a different kind of struggle for survival has begun, a struggle against the poverty brought on by the war. The attitudes expressed in Alice Walker's account of the Concord demonstration are very different. As a peace activist, Walker does not have the idea that war is inevitable. Far from being resigned to the negative effects of war on the postwar society, Walker insists that action can help stop violence.

2. Iwegbu's tendency to understate is most evident in his ability to count himself lucky rather than unfortunate – to shrug off the violence against himself and his family, as well as the loss of the "egg rasher" at the end of the story. "I count it as nothing," he tells his neighbors, because it is no greater a loss than he and many others have suffered during the war (41). Like the torture victim speaking in "Torture in Kuwait," Iwegbu is able to recognize that worse things have happened to others. His sense of perspective amid violence and disorder leads him to understatement.

3.    Colonial influence is seen in the use of currency, the entrepreneurship exhibited by Iwegbu, the presence of the shell of the tall building, the coal company, Iwegbu's use of the bicycle, and the reliance on police for order. African influences appear in Iwegbu's refrain, "Nothing puzzles God," implying that supernatural elements are at work in his good fortune, his resilience in the face of disaster, his compromise with the thief, and his philosophical approach to the loss of his money. All suggest traditions that have been rerouted but not fundamentally changed by the materialistic influences of Britain.

## ADDITIONAL QUESTIONS AND ASSIGNMENTS

1.    In a journal entry or a collection of informal notes, discuss the concept of a noble cause as depicted in three or four of these selections. Consider such issues as the conflict between loyalty to a cause and loyalty to human beings, the individual's understanding of the cause (or lack thereof), the history of the conflict surrounding the cause, and any other issues you find relevant. As you look over your notes, try to discover similarities and differences among the cultures represented. Is it possible for individuals to identify so strongly with a cause that they consider their goals synonymous with the goals of the cause? Is any cause worth dying for? In short, can you come to any conclusion about the role played by a people's commitment to a cause in wartime or in civil conflict?

2.    Using ideas about American involvement in international conflict expressed in the Milosz, Al-Radi, or Walker selections as a springboard, investigate U.S. intervention in conflicts around the world. As you do your research, consider the kinds of information you're interested in discovering. You may want to investigate dissident groups, or groups that promote U.S. involvement abroad, and analyze their role in discouraging or advocating U.S. involvement in international conflicts. What tactics do these groups use for accomplishing their goals? How do people on opposing sides of the issue define patriotism? As you write a description of the group, try to intersperse your own observations and analysis of their activities with the group's own perceptions.

3.    Write your own version of "Civil Peace," in which you present a fictional view of what life would be like in your community after an event that changed "normal" life forever. It might be easier to imagine a change precipitated by some sort of natural disaster, because so few of us have any experience — of our own or someone close to us — of war on our soil. Describe life without such modern conveniences as the electronic media, currency, motorized transportation, and mass-produced food and clothing. Create a family who, like the Iwegbus, must devise a means for economic survival. You need not include an incident similar to the visit by the thieves, but you should try to emphasize the absolute lack of any recognizable foundation on which to rebuild "normal" society. (If the situation seems too incomprehensible, you may want to start by simply recalling our helplessness when we lose electricity for more than a few hours. Then consider what it would be like if we couldn't expect power to be restored in the foreseeable future.)

4.  The issue of nuclear war has been the subject of media attention for the past ten years — two television films in particular, "The Day After" (United States) and "Threads" (Great Britain), have explored the aftermath of a nuclear war. Research various responses to these films in magazines and newspapers, and view them if possible. (Both are available on videocassette.) Considering Milosz's statements about American ignorance of war, write a paper in which you discuss the differences between the two films, focusing specifically on the realism of "Threads," produced in a country that felt the full effect of Hitler's air force in World War II, as opposed to the sentimentality of "The Day After," produced in a country that hasn't experienced battle on its own soil since the Civil War. While your discussion will inevitably compare the two films, it should also analyze the causes of the differences between them, and consider the changes in our attitudes and fears about nuclear war in the aftermath of the demolition of the Berlin Wall and the dissolution of the Soviet Union.

5.  Conduct further research into one of the cultures represented in this section, focusing specifically on the experience of war. It would be wise to choose a culture about which information is readily available — Latin America, Israel, Iraq, and Ireland are likely candidates. If the selection is an excerpt from a larger work, look first at that work. You can find other sources by consulting the headnotes for other selections from that culture and a general encyclopedia, as well as journals devoted to the study of that culture. Narrow your topic to something manageable, such as the causes of a particular war or civil conflict, its effects on the populace, the ideologies represented, or the characteristics of the combatants on either side, and write a comparison-contrast paper in which you analyze the perspectives of the two sides involved.

# SUGGESTED SYLLABI

This is a basic course description, with options for adaptation to different teaching approaches and thematic considerations. The format of the syllabus is necessarily general, making it more flexible with regard to the needs of individual instructors. Each syllabus includes four short papers and one research paper. The arrangement allows for increasing or decreasing the number of papers to satisfy instructors' wishes or departmental requirements. (It is assumed, however, that each paper will go through several drafts, ensuring a significant amount of student writing.)

## BASIC COURSE DESCRIPTION

This syllabus is designed for a lecture-discussion course focusing on reading, writing, and research. In general, the paper assignments move from personal narrative to causal analysis or persuasion involving outside sources. The thematic emphasis is on recognizing how we define ourselves, beginning with an exploration of what it means to belong to one particular culture among others and then moving to more specific roles within a family, to a recognition of ourselves as we come of age and go to work, and finally to an understanding of the conflicts and ideologies shaping us and our culture. This syllabus can be adapted to a collaborative approach simply by charging students with the responsibility for interpreting selections. Individual groups can prepare different selections and present their interpretations to the class for general discussion. Similarly, papers can be worked through a number of drafts by using peer evaluation. Research projects may be conducted individually, using peer evaluation groups for revision advice, or collaboratively, with several students composing one paper.

### Weeks 1–4

*Readings*: "The West and the World"

*Writing*: Analyses of causes for misunderstandings among different cultures (using Carroll, Paz, Jen, Naipaul, and outside sources), *or* persuasive essay arguing for increased efforts at understanding other cultures (using Reed, Harrison, and Mphahlele).

*Discussion*: Emphasis in readings on obstacles to dialogue between cultures and overcoming misconceptions about other cultures.

### Weeks 5–6

*Readings*: "The Family": *Looking at Ourselves*, Gyanranjan

*Writing*: Short essay describing family traditions (using any one of the readings as a model)

*Discussion*: Different traditions, different types of families, reactions to Gyanranjan.

**Weeks 7–9**

*Readings*: "The Family"

*Writing*: Personal narrative on family memory (see Liang and Shapiro, Mehta, Soyinka).

*Discussion*: Authors' personal reminiscences; effect of subjective point of view.

**Weeks 10–12**

*Readings*: "Landmarks and Turning Points"

*Writing*: Comparison of initiation rites in diverse cultures (for instance, Orlean, Vargas Llosa, Grass), *or* comparison of male rites (for example, Grass, Vargas Llosa) with female rites (for example, Mehta, Orlean).

*Discussion*: personal and cultural functions of coming-of-age rituals; differences in initiation experiences for males and females.

**Weeks 13–15**

*Readings*: "Work"

*Writing*: Definition of meaning of work to people in different classes and cultures (for instance, Abram, Angelou, Bonner), *or* classification of workers by identification with particular jobs (for example, García Márquez, Angelou, Ishikawa).

*Discussion*: Reactions of authors to their jobs, focusing on effects of class, race, and culture on the relationship of workers to their jobs.


**VARIATION I**

Instructors wishing to alter readings from semester to semester may do so by changing the general theme of the course. For example, the class might explore the relationships between the individual and others, keeping the first, second, and third sections of the basic syllabus and substituting the following for the fourth and fifth sections:

**Weeks 10–12**

*Readings*: "Women and Men"

*Writing*: Comparison of Western or Judeo-Christian images of males and females with those of other cultures (for example, Fuentes, Moravia, Cooke), *or* definition of male or female, based on several selections (for instance, Kazantzakis, Silko, Beauvoir). This might be done as a parody.

*Discussion*: Focus on how stereotypes and inaccurate perceptions reinforce traditional sex roles; contrast with writers' attempts to represent new and different points of view on meanings of "female" and "male."

Suggested Syllabi

**Weeks 13–15**

*Readings:* "We the People: Individuals and Institutions"

*Writing:* Comparison of benefits and liabilities of a given form of government (using Havel, Golden, Anonymous), or definition of oppression (based on Gordimer, Mandela, Weldon).

*Discussion:* Focus on similarities among different ideologies. With this syllabus, the focus in Sections 1, 2, and 3 would shift from personal identity to relationships between individuals and others, including the state. This syllabus presents a greater challenge to students than the first, because it involves an assessment of the individual's responsibilities to nations and their ideologies and institutions.


## VARIATION 2

Instructors may wish to undertake a narrower study of the individual and others, moving from relationships within a family directly to relationships between the individual and the state. Using this arrangement, the first four sections of the syllabus would remain the same, with the following substitution for the fifth section:

**Weeks 13–15**

*Readings:* "Violence"

*Writing:* Comparison or classification of methods of resistance to oppression (for example, McCafferty, Grossman, Allende, Walker).

*Discussion:* Highlight different approaches to war and violence. With this syllabus, the focus in the first four sections would shift from relatively neutral analysis to assessment of moral responsibility of individuals and governments, clashes between personal and ideological loyalties, and justifications for violence. This is the most challenging syllabus of those offered, because it involves examination of value judgements.

# RHETORICAL INDEX

Among the selections listed here are models of specific rhetorical strategies (for example, the essay by Raymonde Carroll uses comparison and contrast and the essay by Ishmael Reed uses example or illustration as primary strategies). Also listed are selections that employ several different strategies.

## Analogy

Raymonde Carroll, "Money and Seduction"
Octavio Paz, "Hygiene and Repression"
Salman Rushdie, "The Broken Mirror"
Nikos Kazantzakis, "The Isle of Aphrodite"
Alberto Moravia, "The Chase"

## Argument and Persuasion

Ishmael Reed, "What's American About America?"
Paul Harrison, "The Westernization of the World"
Patrick Smith, "Nippon Challenge"
Louise Erdrich, "Adam"
Marguerite Duras, "Home Making"
Günter Grass, "After Auschwitz"
Miriam Cooke, "The Veil Does Not Prevent Women from Working"
Václav Havel, "Moral Politics"
Nelson Mandela, "Black Man in a White Court"
Michael Dorris, "House of Stone"
Charles Moore, "Ireland Must Fight the IRA Too"
Michael Kelly, "Torture in Kuwait"
Alice Walker, "The Concord Demonstration"
Czeslaw Milosz, "American Ignorance of War"

## Cause and Effect

Es'kia Mphahlele, "Tradition and the African Writer"
Paul Harrison, "The Westernization of the World"
Yoram Binur, "Palestinian Like Me"
Eduard Shevardnadze, "Life with the Party"
Tim Golden, "Cubans Try to Cope with Dying Socialism"
Anonymous, "Evicted: A Russian Jew's Story (Again)"
Václav Havel, "Moral Politics"
Charles Moore, "Ireland Must Fight the IRA Too"
Slavenka Drakulić, "Zagreb: A Letter to My Daughter"

Rhetorical Index

## Classification

Gish Jen, "Helen in America"
Susan Orlean, "Quinceañera"
Amy Tan, "Two Kinds"
Slavenka Drakulić, "Zagreb: A Letter to My Daughter"

## Comparison and Contrast

Raymonde Carroll, "Money and Seduction"
Octavio Paz, "Hygiene and Repression"
Gish Jen, "Helen in America"
Margaret Atwood, "A View from Canada"
Patrick Smith, "Nippon Challenge"
John David Morley, "Acquiring a Japanese Family"
Gyanranjan, "Our Side of the Fence and Theirs"
Salman Rushdie, "The Broken Mirror"
Naila Minai, "Women in Early Islam"
David Grossman, "Israeli Arab, Israeli Jew"

## Definition

Ishmael Reed, "What's American About America?"
Gish Jen, "Helen in America"
Louise Erdrich, "Adam"
Marguerite Duras, "Home Making"
Susan Orlean, "Quinceañera"
Amy Tan, "Two Kinds"
Carlos Fuentes, "Matador and Madonna"
Alberto Moravia, "The Chase"
Miriam Cooke, "The Veil Does Not Prevent Women from Working"
Tomoyuki Iwashita, "Why I Quit the Company"

## Description

Margaret Atwood, "A View from Canada"
Rigoberta Menchú, "Birth Ceremonies"
Wole Soyinka, "Nigerian Childhood"
Gyanranjan, "Our Side of the Fence and Theirs"
Marguerite Duras, "Home Making "
Susan Orlean, "Quinceañera"
Salman Rushdie, "The Broken Mirror"
Tomoyuki Iwashita, "Why I Quit the Company"
Michael Dorris, "House of Stone"
Nuha Al-Radi, "Baghdad Diary"

**Example and Illustration**

Ishmael Reed, "What's American About America?"
Raymonde Carroll, "Money and Seduction"
Octavio Paz, "Hygiene and Repression"
Rigoberta Menchú, "Birth Ceremonies"
Marguerite Duras, "Home Making"
Salman Rushdie, "The Broken Mirror"
Christopher Reynolds, "Cultural Journey to Africa"
Carlos Fuentes, "Matador and Madonna"
Alice Walker, "The Concord Demonstration"

**Exposition**

Gish Jen, "Helen in America"
Paul Harrison, "The Westernization of the World"
Louise Erdrich, "Adam"
Salman Rushdie, "The Broken Mirror"
Miriam Cooke, "The Veil Does Not Prevent Women from Working"
Nell McCafferty, "Peggy Deery of Derry"
Slavenka Drakulić, "Zagreb: A Letter to My Daughter"
Isabel Allende, "The Los Riscos Mine"

**Interview**

V. S. Naipaul, "Entering the New World"
Patrick Smith, "Nippon Challenge"
Rigoberta Menchú, "Birth Ceremonies"
Susan Orlean, "Quinceañera"
Amy Tan, "Two Kinds"
Marjorie Shostak, "Nisa's Marriage"
Miriam Cooke, "The Veil Does Not Prevent Women from Working"
Raymond Bonner, "A Woman's Place"
David Grossman, "Israeli Arab, Israeli Jew"
Michael Kelly, "Torture in Kuwait"
Czeslaw Milosz, "American Ignorance of War"

**Irony**

Gish Jen, "Helen in America"
Margaret Atwood, "A View from Canada"
V. S. Naipaul, "Entering the New World"
John David Morley, "Acquiring a Japanese Family"
Alberto Moravia, "The Chase"
David Abram, "Making Magic"
Gabriel García Márquez, "Dreams for Hire"
Fay Weldon, "Down the Clinical Disco"
Václav Havel, "Moral Politics"
Nuha Al-Radi, "Baghdad Diary"

171

172

# CHART OF RHETORICAL WRITING ASSIGNMENTS

NOTE: "Elaborations" or writing assignments asking students to write an essay in a particular rhetorical form or using resources are listed below. The number following the author's name refers to the corresponding "Elaborations" question for the selection.

(For the Index of Authors and Titles, see text pp. 735–738.)

| Analogy | Argument and Persuasion | Cause and Effect |
|---|---|---|
| Vargas Llosa 2 | Achebe 2 | Achebe 2 |
| | Abram 1 | Al-Radi 2 |
| | Bonner 1 | Beauvoir 1 |
| | Cooke 1 | Binur 1 |
| | Dorris 2 | Bugul 2 |
| | Golden 1 | Drakulić 2 |
| | Grass 2 | Gordimer 1 |
| | Grossman 1 | Grass 1 |
| | Harrison 2 | Harrison 1 |
| | Havel 2 | Heker 2 |
| | Heker 2 | Kelly 2 |
| | Iwashita 2 | Kemal 3 |
| | Liu 1 | Levi 2 |
| | Mehta 1 | Mandela 2 |
| | Moore 2 | Milosz 1 |
| | Moravia 1 | Mphahlele 1 |
| | Postman 2 | Reynolds 1 |
| | Sa'edi 1 | Sa'edi 1 |
| | Smith 1 | Shevardnadze 1 |
| | | Silko 2 |
| | | Tan 1 |

| Classification | Comparison and Contrast | Definition |
|---|---|---|
| Abram 1 | Abram 2 | Abram 2 |
| Allende 2 | Atwood 1 | Achebe 1 |
| Al-Radi 1 | Binur 2 | Allende 2 |
| Binur 3 | Dorris 1 | Atwood 2 |
| Carroll 1 | Drakulić 2 | Beauvoir 2 |
| Duras 2 | Fuentes 1, 2 | Carroll 1 |
| Erdrich 2 | Grossman 1, 2 | Erdrich 2 |
| Heker 1 | Hayslip 1, 2 | García Márquez 1, 2 |
| Jen 2 | Jen 2 | Gordimer 2 |
| Kelly 1 | Kazantzakis 1 | Grass 2 |
| Liu 2 | Kelly 1 | Gyanranjan 1 |
| Mandela 1 | Liang/Shapiro 2 | Havel 1 |
| Menchú 1 | McCafferty 2 | Minai 2 |
| Minai 2 | Mandela 1 | Naipaul 2 |
| Mphahlele 2 | Mehta 2 | Paz 1 |
| Paz 1 | Minai 1 | Reed 2 |
| Reed 2 | Moore 1 | Silko 1 |
| Shostak 2 | Orlean 2 | |
| Silko 1 | Paz 2 | |
| | Reed 1 | |
| | Rushdie 2 | |
| | Shevardnadze 2 | |
| | Shostak 1 | |
| | Soyinka 1 | |
| | Vargas Llosa 1, 2 | |
| | Walker 1, 2 | |
| | Weldon 1 | |

| Description | Division/Analysis | Example and Illustration |
|---|---|---|
| Angelou 2 | Achebe 1 | Bonner 2 |
| Duras 1 | Bonner 2 | Havel 1 |
| García Márquez 1 | Bugul 1 | Morley 2 |
| Golden 2 | Carroll 1, 2 | Naipaul 2 |
| Gyanranjan 1 | Dorris 1 | |
| Havel 2 | García Márquez 1, 2 | |
| Heker 1 | Havel 1 | |
| Ishikawa 2 | Kazantzakis 2 | |
| Iwashita 1 | McCafferty 1 | |

| Description | Division/Analysis | Narration |
|---|---|---|
| Jen 1 | Naipaul 1 | Achebe 2 |
| Kemal 1 | Orlean 2 | Angelou 1 |
| Liang/Shapiro 1 | Reynolds 2 | Erdrich 1 |
| Liu 2 | Shevardnadze 1 | "Evicted" 2 |
| Menchú 2 | Smith 2 | Gordimer 2 |
| Milosz 2 | Silko 1 | Gyanranjan 2 |
| Minai 1 | Tan 2 | Kemal 2 |
| Morley 1 | Vargas Llosa 2 | Levi 1 |
| O'Brien 2 | | Liu 1, 2 |
| Orlean 1 | | McCafferty 2 |
| Paz 1, 2 | | Menchú 2 |
| Rushdie 1 | | Moravia 2 |
| Shevardnadze 2 | | Orlean 2 |
| | | Silko 2 |
| | | Soyinka 2 |

| Process Analysis | Using Sources | Other |
|---|---|---|
| Allende 1 | Bonner 2 | Allende 2 |
| Angelou 2 | Bugul 2 | (imaginary debate) |
| Cooke 2 | García Márquez 2 | Bonner 1 |
| Harrison 2 | Havel 1 | (imaginary dialogue) |
| Ishikawa 1 | Kelly 2 | Drakulić 1 (letter to a |
| Levi 2 | Mandela 2 | child) |
| | | "Evicted" 1 (letter to the |
| | | editor) |
| | | Kemal 1 (imaginary |
| | | travel article) |
| | | Milosz 2 (letter) |
| | | O'Brien 1 (job descrip- |
| | | tion) |
| | | Postman 1 (summary) |
| | | Weldon 2 (monologue) |

175

# ADDITIONAL RESOURCES

## INDEX TO HEADNOTE INFORMATION

The following index is keyed to the headnotes in the third edition of *Ourselves Among Others* and locates specific geographical, historical, and political information about countries found in the headnotes.

ARABIA: geography, distinction between Arab and Islamic countries (p. 361); geography, current monarchy based on Islamic law, general history of the Arabs, discovery of oil, in Gulf War (p. 372)

ARGENTINA: geography, general history, population, twentieth-century governments including Perón's democracy, Falkland Islands War, current President Carlos Menem's economic policies (p. 212)

BALI: see Indonesia

BELGIUM: geography, general history, African empire, political stability (p. 344)

BOTSWANA: racial makeup and description of Zhun/twasi and !Kung San peoples, independence from British rule (p. 354)

CANADA: geography, general history, tension between Canada's English and French heritages (p. 29)

CHILE: geography, Spanish conquest, independence, dictatorship under Pinochet, current seventeen party coalition (p. 656)

CHINA: Chairman Mao's regime, Cultural Revolution, current situation under Deng Xiaoping (p. 22); 1950s government repression, youth movements, Red Guards described, the Great Leap Forward (p. 97)

COLOMBIA: geography, Spanish rule, nineteenth-century independence, population (p. 497)

CZECH REPUBLIC: geography, annexation of Czechoslovakia before World War II, Communist rule, "Prague Spring," uprising and democratic elections, President Václav Havel, division of Czechoslovakia into Slovakia and the Czech Republic (p. 542)

CROATIA: see Yugoslavia

CUBA: geography, general history, struggles for independence, policies of Fidel Castro (p. 528)

FRANCE: French Revolution, nineteenth and twentieth-century political regimes, colonial empire, contemporary history and role in Europe (p. 8)

GERMANY: World War II history, postwar division into East and West, history of Berlin wall including dismantling, problems created by reunification (p. 264)

GEORGIA: independence from the Soviet Union and Russia, recent elections (p. 521)

GREAT BRITAIN: structure of government, geography of empire, history of relationship with Europe and empire, current role in international organizations (p. 551)

GUATEMALA: The Mayan empire, Republic of Guatemala established, ethnic makeup, political struggles between peasant groups and repressive regimes, new government founded by Ramiro de Leon (p. 76)

GREECE: Iraklion, Minos's Palace, Crete, general history, independence, recent governments (p. 322)

HONG KONG: geography, population, contemporary history, British influence, reversion to China in 1997 (p. 219)

INDIA: population, general history including European colonization and trade, twentieth-century, political leadership, Gandhi and 1947 independence, current political climate, clash between Hindus and Muslims and with neighbors especially Pakistan (p. 134); Punjab region, caste system (p. 142)

INDONESIA: geography, European dominance of, independence establishment of Malaysia (p. 422)

IRAN: geography, general history, British and Russian influences on, loss of Afghanistan, dynasty of Shahs, Khomeini's rule, Khomeini's death threats against Salman Rushdie (p. 162)

IRAQ: invasion of Kuwait, events of 1991 Gulf War especially bombing of Baghdad (p. 677)

IRELAND: geography, general history, the Act of Union, nationalist uprisings, Republic of Ireland recognized, first woman president (p. 444), Irish Republican Army, the Troubles (p. 615)

ISRAEL: geography, general history, independence, the Arab minority, discrimination against Arabs (p. 629); Middle East in World War I and II, establishment of by United Nations, Arab-Jewish conflict, Six-Day War, Palestine Liberation Organization, intifada and retaliation (p. 275)

ITALY: geography, general history, nineteenth and twentieth-century political struggles, cultural contribution, involvement in World War II, current political stability, population demographics (p. 337); turbulent history, Benito Mussolini and World War II, short-lived postwar governments (p. 463)

IVORY COAST: geography, French colonization of, independence, economic history, Burkina Faso (formerly Upper Volta) and Benin identified (p. 48)

JAPAN: geography, general history, nineteenth-century arrival of Perry, expansion policy and World War II, current form of government, population (p. 122)

KUWAIT: geography, Al-Sabah dynasty, as British protectorate, independence, oil exports, sided with Iraq in Iraq/Iran war in 1980s, Iraqi invasion of and U.S. involvement (p. 475); geography, oil fields, Iraqi invasion (p. 696)

MEXICO: general history, Cortés and Spanish explorers (1500s), independence, current economy, contemporary art and literature (p. 15)

NIGERIA: geography, population, general history, nineteenth-century British control of and current influence on, changing political climate, women's expanded role, Bishop Crowther (p. 112); British colonization of, independent commonwealth, civil war in Republic of Biafra (p. 716)

NORTHERN IRELAND: general history, founding of IRA, history of Protestant-Catholic conflict, current political climate (p. 615)

PALESTINE: see Israel

PERU: geography, Spanish colonization of, nineteenth-century independence, population, current government, economic and political problems including guerrilla group Sendero Luminosa (p. 224)

POLAND: date of German invasion of, Czeslaw Milosz's break with Communist government, post–World War II domination by Soviet Union, Solidarity Union's fight for independence, Walesa's Nobel Peace Prize, current democratic political system, economic changes (p. 671)

RUSSIA: history of Soviet Union, perestroika, glasnost, Yeltsin, independence (p. 521); history of Jewish persecution, relationship with Israel, effects of Soviet Union's collapse on Russian Jews (p. 536)

SAUDI ARABIA: geography, structure of government, general history, importance of oil, role in Gulf war (p. 372)

SENEGAL: geography, the Wolof and the diverse ethnic makeup, general history, French colonization of, independence, the West African Economic Community (p. 344)

SOUTH AFRICA: geography, racial makeup, apartheid defined, nineteenth-century founding by Dutch, Anglo-Boer War, history of apartheid, 1961 withdrawal from British Commonwealth (p. 35); mission of the African National Congress, worldwide economic and political pressures, current political climate (p. 587)

Additional Resources

SOVIET UNION (former): establishment, perestroika and glasnost, disbanding of Communist Party, dissolution of, independence of Russia and Georgia (p. 521)
SPAIN: geography, general history including Cristobal Colon's (Christopher Columbus's) discovery of America, American colonies, Spanish influence on Latin America (p. 303)
TURKEY: geography, general history of European and Asian Turkey and of Ottoman Empire, history of Istanbul, Young Turk movement, founding of republic, membership in NATO, economic conditions (p. 380)
UNITED KINGDOM: see Great Britain, Northern Ireland
UNITED STATES: ethnic makeup, population trends (p. 3); Pueblo Culture (p. 312); California Gold Rush, Chinese and Japanese immigrants, the Alien Land Act of California, Japanese internment camps during World War II (p. 497)
VIETNAM: forced unification in 1976, general history, French, Japanese, and Chinese control of, North Vietnamese President Ho Chi Minh and Vietcong guerrillas' war for a single Communist nation, U.S. and Western involvement with South Vietnam (p. 432)
YUGOSLAVIA (former): general history, establishment of Tito's Communist government, secession of member republics, disintegration of, current civil war including Serbian policy of "ethnic cleansing" (p. 646)
ZIMBABWE: geography, British colonization of, independence, tensions between black majority and white minority, drought (p. 569)

## BIBLIOGRAPHY

The following sources may be useful for further exploration of literary, biographical, and historical topics and for study of particular countries and regions.

### Almanacs, Series, Yearbooks

*Britannica Book of the Year.* Chicago: Encyclopedia Britannica, 1938–.
*Contemporary Authors.* Detroit: Gale, 1962–. An up-to-date biographical source on international authors in many subject areas.
*Contemporary Literary Criticism.* Detroit: Gale, 1973.
*Current Biography.* New York: Wilson, 1940. Biographical sketches of people in the news, published monthly (except December) and annually in a cumulative volume.
*Demographic Yearbook 1990.* 42nd ed. New York: United Nations, 1989.
*Europa World Year Book.* 2 vols. Detroit: Gale, 1993. Detailed information on every country in the world.
*Facts on File Yearbook.* New York: Facts on File, 1941–. Weekly summaries of news events in *Facts on File: A Weekly World News Digest,* indexed every two weeks, are published cumulatively in this annual volume.
*Information Please Almanac.* Boston: Houghton Mifflin, 1992. Detailed information on countries of the world.
*Political Handbook of the World.* New York: McGraw Hill, 1975–. Formerly *Political Handbook and Atlas of the World* (1927-1974), contains information on governments, parties, terminology, and so on.
*Statesman's Year-Book 1992–1993.* 129th rev. and updated ed. Ed. Brian Hunter. New York: St. Martin's, 1992. Detailed economic data on all the world's countries.
*Statistical Yearbook,* No. 38. New York: United Nations, 1991.
*The Universal Almanac 1993.* Ed. John W. Wright. New York: Andrews, 1992.
*The World Almanac and Book of Facts.* New York: Newspaper Enterprise Assoc., 1868–. Factual material on current and historical topics; contains chronology of previous year's events.

## Atlases

*Hammond Standard World Atlas.* Maplewood, NJ: Hammond, 1983.
*National Geographic Atlas of the World.* 6th ed. Washington, D.C.: Nat. Geographic Soc., 1990.
*Oxford Economic Atlas of the World.* 4th ed. Oxford: Oxford UP, 1972.
*The Prentice-Hall Great International Atlas.* Englewood Cliffs, N.J.: Prentice, 1981.
*Rand McNally New Cosmopolitan World Atlas.* New Census ed. Chicago: Rand, 1984.
Shepherd, William. *Historical Atlas.* New York: Barnes, 1964. Includes maps for world history
    from 1450 B.C. to the 1960s.
*The Times Atlas of the World.* 9th Comprehensive ed. New York: Random House, 1992.

## Dictionaries and Gazetteers

*Columbia Dictionary of Modern European Literature.* 2nd ed. Gen. eds. Jean-Albert Bede and
    William B. Edgerton. New York: Columbia UP, 1980.
*Dictionary of Geography.* rev ed. Ed. W. G. Moore. New York: Penguin, 1950.
*Dictionary of Islam.* 2 vols. Ed. Thomas P. Hughes. New York: Gordon, 1980.
*Facts on File Dictionary of Religion.* Ed. John R. Hinnells. New York: Facts on File, 1984.
Lacqueur, Walter. *A Dictionary of Politics.* Rev. ed. New York: Macmillan, 1974. Defines terms,
    provides historical, geographical, biographical information.
*The Times Index-Gazetteer of the World.* London: Times, 1965. Still useful.
*Webster's New Geographical Dictionary* Rev. ed. Springfield, Ill. Merriam, 1984.
*World Facts in Brief.* New York: Rand, 1986. A handy inexpensive student reference.

## Specialized Encyclopedias

*Encyclopedia of Latin American History.* rev ed. Ed. Michael R. Martin and Gabriel H. Lovett.
    1968. Westport, Conn: Greenwood, 1981.
*Encyclopedia of World Literature in the 20th Century.* 2nd ed. 5 vols. New York: Unger, 1981–
    1993.
*Harper Encyclopedia of the Modern World.* New York: Harper, 1970. Coverage from 1760
    through the 1960s.
*The International Geographic Encyclopedia and Atlas.* Boston: Houghton, 1979.
*McGraw-Hill Encyclopedia of World Biography.* 12 vols. New York: McGraw, 1973. Contains
    approximately 5,000 biographical entries on world figures.
*The New Illustrated Encyclopedia of World History.* Ed. William L. Langer. 2 vols. New York:
    Abrams, 1975. Arranged chronologically, comprehensively covers from prehistory to
    space exploration.
*New Nations: A Student Handbook.* Ed. David N. Rowe. New York: Shoe String, 1968.
*The Penguin Companion to World Literature.* 4 vols. New York: McGraw, 1969–1971. Separate
    volumes for American; English, classical, Oriental, and African; and European literature.

## Time Line

Grun, Bernard. *The Timetables of History.* 3rd rev. ed. New York: Touchstone, Simon, 1991. This
    edition is based on Werner Stein's *Kulturfahrplan.* The categories are History and
    Politics; Literature and Theater; Religion, Philosophy, and Learning; Science, Technol-
    ogy, and Growth; and Daily Life.

# FILM, VIDEO, AND AUDIOCASSETTE RESOURCES

After a section of general resources, the following list is organized according to the units in *Ourselves Among Others*, Third Edition. Within each section, the entries are organized alphabetically by title (or by author in cases where this information provides a more helpful reference.). A number of entries might be useful for more than one unit. For these entries, the full annotation is provided in what seems to be the most appropriate unit. The entry is then listed in other appropriate units with a cross-reference to the listing with complete information.

The Directory of Distributors at the end of the list of resources can help you locate these films, videos, and audiocassettes if you cannot find them in your own library or local video rental store.

## General

*Americas in Transition.* (1982) "Provides a concise, fast-paced introduction to the underlying causes of unrest in Latin America. Examines the roots of this unrest through a close look at Latin America's history of military dictatorships, attempts at democracy, communist influences, and the role of U.S. involvement." Icarus Films. 3/4-inch video. 29 minutes.

*The Bear's Embrace.* See "We the People."

*Be It Remembered.* Documentary, hosted by Eli Wallach, about immigrants past and present. 50 minutes.

*The Cummington Story.* (1945) "The true story of a family of immigrants settling in a small New England town. The participants re-create their own roles. Shows the difficulty of cultural assimilation." United World Films, Inc. 16 mm. 17 minutes.

*The Family Krishnappa.* See "The Family"

*The First 50 Years: Reflections on U.S.-Soviet Relations.* See "The West and the World."

*Global Village.* (1984) "India hurtles into the modern age, but what about its agrarian economy?" PBS: Nova. 3/4-inch video. 50 minutes.

*Immigration.* (1974) "Traces the influx into this country . . . shows the contributions made by new citizens as well as the resistance of some of the country's original population. . . . The Order of the Star-Spangled Banner (or Know-Nothings), the Immigration Restriction League, and the Ku Klux Klan are examined in their temporal context." McGraw Hill. 16 mm. 25 minutes.

*Israel and the Arab States.* (1981) "This program from the "Twentieth-Century History" series explores the establishment of the State of Israel and the resulting Arab disputes over the territory which have continued to the present day." Films, Inc. Beta, 1/2-inch video, 3/4-inch video. 20 minutes.

*Japan Reaches for the 21st Century.* See "The West and the World."

*Latin America, An Overview.* (1982) "Examines the people, cultures, religions, and geography which bind the peoples of South America, Central America, and the Caribbean into the area known as Latin America." Vladimir Bibic Productions. 16 mm. 25 minutes.

*Legacies.* See "Violence."

*A Legacy of Lifestyles.* See "The West and the World."

*Mao and the Cultural Revolution.* See "The Family."

*Mother Theresa.* (1987) Profile of the friend of the poor. PBS. 80 minutes.

*The Nature of a Continent.* (1986) (Africa) "Ali A. Mazrui hosts this overview of Africa, geographically and historically." PBS: The Africans. 1/2-inch video. 50 minutes.
*Planting Seeds for Peace.* See "Landmarks and Turning Points."
*The Rise of Asian-Americans.* PBS: Currents. 25 minutes.
*The Shadow of the West.* (1987) Part of the series "The Arabs, a Living History." Portland State Univ. Continuing Education. 1/2-inch video. 50 minutes.
*Tools of Exploitation.* See "The West and the World."

## The West and The World

Achebe, Chinua, reads *Arrow of God.* See "Violence."
*The Asianization of America.* PBS: Currents. 25 minutes.
Atwood, Margaret. (1983) "Margaret Atwood talks about a wide variety of issues pertinent to Atwood's Canadian nationalism, feminism, themes of her individual novels and short stories." American Audio Prose Library. Sound cassette. 55 minutes.
Atwood, Margaret. *Once in August.* (1988) "An intimate view of one of Canada's most elusive literary figures." Wombat Productions (NY). 1/2-inch video. 58 minutes.
Atwood, Margaret. *The Author Reads Excerpts from* Bodily Harm *and Talks About Politics.* (1986) American Audio Prose Library. Sound cassette. 30 minutes.
Atwood, Margaret. *Surfacing.* (1984) "A young woman and her companions set out to look for her lost father in the hostile wilderness of northern Canada." Media Home Entertainment (Los Angeles). 1/2-inch video. 90 minutes.
*Bali: The Mask of Rangda.* See "Work."
*Be It Remembered.* See "General."
*Bridging the Culture Gap.* See "Work."
*The Canadian Federation.* (1980) "A succinct overview of the people, politics, and government of Canada, combining interviews with documentary footage." National Film Board of Canada. Beta, VHS, 3/4-inch video. 31 minutes.
*China: A New Look.* (1988) "A look at what life is like in the world's most populous country." International Film Foundation. Beta, VHS, 3/4-inch video. 25 minutes.
*City of Refuge.* (1980) "Depicts the successful resettlement of refugees in a small midwestern town. Su Thao, the first Hmong refugee to settle in Iowa, is pictured with his family playing, working, and worshipping with the citizens of Pela, Iowa." Beta, 3/4-inch video, 1/2-inch video, 16 mm. 29 minutes.
*Crossing Borders: The Story of the Women's International League for Peace and Freedom.* (1988) "A fine assemblage of stills, newsreel footage, headlines, and period songs provides a rich historical backdrop for the group's concerns and activities." Film Project for Women's History and Future. 16 mm, 1/2-inch video. 32 minutes.
*The Cummington Story.* See "General."
*Dim Sum: A Little Bit of Heart.* See "The Family."
*The First 50 Years: Reflections on U.S.-Soviet Relations.* (1985) "A comprehensive guide to relations between the two powers since the establishment of diplomatic ties (1933) to the [mid-eighties]. Traces the up-and-down relationship through the eyes of former U.S. Ambassadors. . . . Rare archival footage . . . a concise synopsis of this critical area of international relations." Cafficus Corp. 3/4-inch video. 58 minutes.
Fuentes, Carlos. *Distant Relations.* See "Women and Men."
*Global Village.* See "General."
*The Gods Must Be Crazy.* (1980) "Peaceful primitive Bushmen of Botswana caught up in 'civilized' man's violence." Playhouse Video. Beta, VHS. 110 minutes.
*Immigration.* See "General."

*Italian Family.* (1975) "On the shores of Lake Bracciano, about thirty miles from Rome, the Giorgetti family carries on the age old traditions of Italian rural life." Britannica Films. Beta, VHS, 3/4-inch video. 30 minutes.

*Japan 2000.* (1989) "A look at some of the things that the Japanese do to make their products inexpensive and of high quality." Great Plains National Instructional Television Library. Beta, VHS, 3/4-inch video. 2 programs, 30 minutes each.

*Japan: The Nation Family.* See "The Family."

*Japan Reaches for the 21st Century.* (1986) "This documentary examines the history and current social structure of Japan, and predicts changes in Japanese society likely to occur as a result of its rapidly growing high technology industries and economy." International Motion Picture Co. 1/2-inch video. 58 minutes.

*The Japan They Don't Talk About.* See "Work."

*Japan at Work.* See "Work."

*Japanese Women.* See "Women and Men."

*Latin America, An Overview.* See "General."

*A Legacy of Lifestyles.* (1986) "Modern Africa has been shaped by indigenous, Islamic, and Western influences." PBS: The Africans. 1/2-inch video. 50 minutes.

*Mexican Tapes: El Gringo; El Ranch Grande; La Lucha; Winner's Circle.* "Four videos explore the lives of Mexicans living as illegal aliens in Southern California." Facets Multimedia. Beta, VHS. 60 minutes each.

The Mexican Way of Life. (1988) "Diversity of Mexican culture is thoroughly explored." AIMS Media, Inc. Beta, VHS, 3/4-inch video. 23 minutes.

*Miles from the Border.* (1987) "Twenty years after emigration from rural Mexico to southern California, Manuela and Ben Aparico, who arrived in their teens and now work as school counselors with other young newcomers, share their experiences of dislocation . . . and the pressures to succeed in an ethically divided community." New Day Films (New York). 1/2-inch video. 15 minutes.

Mphahlele, Es'kia. *Alex La Guma Discusses the Life and Work of Es'kia Mphahlele.* (1966) Transcription Feature Service (London). Sound cassette, no. 2 on side 2. 19 minutes.

Mphahlele, Es'kia. *Es'kia Mphahlele Chairs a Discussion on West African Writing with African Authors Kofi Awoonor and John Pepper Clark.* (1962) Transcription Feature Service (London). Sound cassette, no. 1 on side 2. 39 minutes.

Mphahlele, Es'kia. *The Author Interviewed by Cosmo Pieterse.* (1968) "The author discusses his writing and the influence of traditional oral literature on modern African writing." Transcription Feature Service (London). Sound cassette, no. 1 on side 2. 44 minutes.

Mphahlele, Es'kia. *Lecture on Black Writing.* (1976) Cornell Univ. Africana Studies and Research Center. Sound cassette. 90 minutes.

*The Nature of a Continent.* See "General."

Paz, Octavio. *Focus on Octavio Paz: The Great Mexican Poet Talks About His Life and Work.* (1971) The Center for Cassette Studies. Sound cassette. 28 minutes.

Reed, Ishmael. *Big Ego.* (1978) Giorni Poetry Systems Records (New York). 2 sound discs.

Reed, Ishmael. *Flight to Canada.* (1977) New Letters on Air (Kansas City, Mo.). Sound cassette. 29 minutes.

Reed, Ishmael. *Ishmael Reed.* "Reed reads poetry and talks about his battle with some black women writers and his opposition to being labeled a Black writer." American Audio Prose. 1 cassette. 30 minutes.

Reed, Ishmael. *The Poet Reading His Poetry.* (1976) Cornell Univ. Sound cassette. 65 minutes.

*The Rise of Asian-Americans.* See "General."

*The Shadow of the West.* See "General."

*Tools of Exploitation.* (1986) "The history of imperialism — how Africa's natural and human resources were stolen." PBS: The Africans. 1/2-inch video. 50 minutes.

*Zimbabwe.* See "We the People."

## The Family: Cornerstone of Culture

*After Solidarity: Three Polish Families in America. (1987)* "Depicts the assimilation trials and tribulations of three Polish families in America. . . . Children are the quickest to adjust, followed by the husbands and then the wives." Filmmakers Library. 1/2-inch video. 58 minutes.

*Argument About a Marriage.* (1966) "Documents a conflict between two groups of Bushmen in the Kalahari Desert over the legitimization of a marriage. The entire conflict is shown with the Bushmen voices and a few subtitles." National Geographic Society. 16 mm. 18 minutes.

*Caring.* (1984) The urban Chinese family: a case study in the industrial city of Harbin. PBS: The Heart of the Dragon. Beta, 3/4-inch video. 50 minutes.

*China: A New Look.* See "The West and the World."

*China in Revolution.* See "We the People."

*Dadi's Family.* (1979) "Portrait of the women of an extended family in northern India focuses on Dadi, the grandmother, and her ability to maintain a family unit threatened not only by social and economic change but also by internal pressures within the family." PBS Video. 16 mm, 1/2-inch video. 59 minutes.

*Dim Sum: A Little Bit of Heart.* (1985) "Intergenerational differences in a Chinese-American family." Pacific Arts Video. 80 minutes.

Dorris, Michael. *Born Drunk: Fetal Alcohol Syndrome.* "A series of reports on a defect that's 100 percent preventable." National Public Radio. 1 audiocassette. 45 minutes.

Erdrich, Louise. *Reading and Interview.* (1986) "Erdrich and her husband and collaborator, Michael Dorris, talk about how they work out of a unified vision based on their backgrounds as mixed blood natives. She reads from *Love Medicine and Beet Queen.*" American Audio Prose. 2 cassettes.

*Families: Will They Survive?* (1981) "Examines the importance of the family unit in various cultures. Studies the extended and nuclear families that have existed throughout human history and how each is faring today." Avatar Learning, Inc. 16 mm. 23 minutes.

*The Family Krishnappa.* (1976) "A realistic documentation of one day in the life of a typical rural family and its village in Southern India. Household tasks . . . farming . . . education . . . religion . . . and social customs are also dealt with." Benchmark Films, Inc. 16 mm. 18 minutes.

*The Gods Must Be Crazy.* See "The West and the World."

*The Good Earth.* (edited) (1943) "Pearl S. Buck's story of a Chinese family depicting family life, customs, and the sociological struggle in poverty-ridden China." Films, Inc. 16 mm. 42 minutes.

*Guatemala: Roads of Silence.* (1988) "This documentary examines Indian life in Guatemala's internal refugee camp where military repression and widescale human rights violations are a daily occurrence." Cinema Guild. Beta, VHS, 3/4-inch video. 59 minutes.

*Hong Kong: A Family Portrait.* See "Landmarks and Turning Points"

*Iran: A Revolution Betrayed* (1984) "The events which led up to the Iranian revolution and its aftermath, leaving a trail of political and religious unrest." Films, Inc. Beta, VHS, 3/4-inch video. 60 minutes.

*Iran: A Righteous Republic* (1989) "The effects of the Gulf War on Iran are considered." Landmark Films, Inc. Beta, VHS, 3/4-inch video. 48 minutes.

Film, Video, and Audiocassette

*Iran: The Other Story* (1989) "An examination of the political left in Iran, the fleeting movements
   which over the years have opposed the government's right fundamentalism." Cinema
   Guild. VHS. 52 minutes.
*Iran and Iraq: Background to the War.* See "Violence."
*Israel— The Promise of the Jewish People.* (1988) "Explores the relationship between the Jewish
   people and their country, through interviews with Russian refuseniks, Arabs and Jews
   who live side by side, soldiers, . . . and children." Etz Chaim Fdn. 1/2-inch video. 60
   minutes.
*Italian Family.* See "The West and the World."
*Japan 2000.* See "The West and the World."
*Japan: The Nation Family.* (1980) "Examines how the Japanese have developed their technology
   to an unimagined extent. Part of a PBS series." Wombat Productions. Beta, VHS, 3/4-
   inch video. 51 minutes.
*Japan Reaches for the 21st Century.* See "The West and the World."
*Japan at Work.* See "Work."
*Japanese Women.* See "Women and Men."
*Mao and the Cultural Revolution.: China Scholar John King Fairbank Examines Mao's Cultural
   Revolution.* (1972) Center for Cassette Studies. Sound cassette. 23 minutes.
*Marrying.* See "Women and Men."
Mehta, Ved. *Chachaji: My Poor Relation.* (1978) "An intense film about the daily struggle for
   survival in . . . India. Ved Mehta seeks to illuminate an entire people by telling us the story
   of one man's fierce will to survive." 16 mm. 58 minutes.
Mehta, Ved. *Daddyji.* (1989) Read by David Case. Books on Tape (Newport Beach). 5 sound
   cassettes.
*Middle East Series: Family Matters.* (1984) "Shows how the family is central in Middle Eastern
   society and politics. Details the historical and environmental patterns of extended family
   development and cultural norms found in the Middle East." Encyclopedia Britannica
   Educational Corp. 1/2-inch video and teacher's guide. 25 minutes.
*Nigeria: Africa in Miniature.* (1966) "Describes locations, provinces, topography, cities, and
   rivers of Nigeria." AIMS Media, Inc. Beta, VHS, 3/4-inch video. 16 minutes.
*Nigeria— Problems of Nation Building.* (1968) "Survey of Nigeria: its geography, economy, and
   people, stressing tribalism and nationalism." Atlantis Productions. Beta, VHS, 21 minutes.
*Rana.* See "Landmarks and Turning Points."
*The Three Grandmothers.* "A glimpse into the lives of three grandmothers living in widely
   differing parts of the world: an African village in Nigeria, a hill city in Brazil, and a rural
   community in Manitoba." National Film Board of Canada. 16 mm. 28 minutes.

## Landmarks and Turning Points: The Struggle for Identity

*Argentina's Jews: Days of Awe.* (1990) "Jews came to Argentina and founded the agricultural
   community of Moiseville. This video provides a history of Argentine Jews and their
   current battles with anti-Semitism, assimilation, and loss of Jewish identity." Ergo Media.
   VHS. 55 minutes.
*Hong Kong: A Family Portrait* (1979) "Provides a look at Hong Kong, a city concerned with
   family, luck, gambling, and survival." Live Home Video. 3/4-inch video. 59 minutes.
*Hong Kong: Living on Borrowed Time.* (1984) "Examines Hong Kong's inhabitants and
   international markets." Journal Films. Beta, VHS, 3/4-inch video. 28 minutes.
*Mexican Tapes.* See "The West and the World."
*The Mexican Way of Life.* See "The West and the World."

Oates, Joyce Carol. *The Author Reads from* Angel of Light *and Discusses Violence, Slavery, Revenge, Grotesques, and the American Novel.* (1980) In Our Time Arts Media (New York). Sound Cassette. 30 minutes.

*Peru: Inca Heritage.* (1970) "Explores contemporary life of the Peruvian Indians and the remains of the Incan culture." AIMS Media. Beta, VHS, 3/4-inch video. 17 minutes.

*Planting Seeds for Peace.* (1989) "Focuses on the relationships among four Israeli, Arab, Jewish, and Palestinian teenagers who come together in the U.S. to share their cultures, their personal lives, break down stereotypes, and present their views to U.S. Teens." Educational Film & Video Project. 1/2-inch video. 23 minutes.

*Rana.* (1977) "Follows the everyday activities of a young Moslem college student in Old Delhi. Points out the restrictions of her religion and includes interviews with her family." Wombat Productions (New York). 16 mm, 1/2-inch video. 19 minutes.

Tan, Amy. *The Joy Luck Club.* (1989) The author reads her novel. Dove Books on Tape. 2 sound cassettes.

Vargas Llosa, Mario, with John King. (1984) "Vargas Llosa discusses his works, including *War of the End of the World.*"Institute of Contemporary Arts: The Roland Collection. 1/2-inch video. 48 minutes.

Vargas Llosa, Mario. *La Ciudad y los Perros.* (1987) In Spanish with English subtitles. Media Home Entertainment. 1/2-inch video.

## Women and Men: Images of the Opposite Sex

*Argument About a Marriage.* See "The Family."

Beauvoir, Simone de. (1960) One of the founders of the women's liberation movement is interviewed by Studs Terkel. "Discusses Beauvoir's book *The Second Sex*and goes deeply into her philosophy of commitment to causes." Center for Cassette Studies. Sound cassette. 29 minutes.

Beauvoir, Simone de. (1982) "The author . . . discusses politics, feminism, aging, and death. . . . Helps bring the written works of the author alive." Interama Video Classics. 1/2-inch video.

Beauvoir, Simone de. *A Sound Portrait of Simone de Beauvoir.* (1980) "Dramatizes Simone de Beauvoir's life and ideas as a pioneer feminist." NPR: A Question of Place: Sound Portraits of Twentieth Century Humanists. NPR, Education Services, Washington, D.C. Sound cassette and summary sheet. 60 minutes.

Beauvoir, Simone de. "Pioneer feminist speaks out." PBS: Vive la France! 52 minutes.

*Crossing Borders: The Story of The Women's International League for Peace and Freedom.* See "The West and the World."

*Faces of Women.* (1985) "Feminism, economics, and tradition in modern-day Africa." New Yorker Films Video. 1/2-inch video. 105 minutes.

Fuentes, Carlos. *Distant Relations.* Read by Carlos Fuentes. "Fuentes talks about how the New World corrupts the Old in his novel and reads from *Distant Relations.*" American Audio Prose. 1 audiocassette. 30 minutes.

*Germans and Their Men.* (1990) "A feminist-oriented look at men in German government and what is being done to improve the lot of women." Women Making Movies. VHS. 96 minutes.

*India Cabaret.* (1987) "A group of Indian strippers, who meet with difficulty because their stance as single women is not socially acceptable, is followed through daily routine." Filmmakers' Library. 16 mm, 1/2-inch video. 60 minutes.

*Islam, The Veil and the Future.* (1980) Marriage and divorce, voting and dress for Moslem women. PBS Video. 1/2-inch video. 29 minutes.

*Japanese Women.* (1987) "The status of women in modern-day Japan is examined in this insightful film." National Film Board of Canada. Beta, VHS, 3/4-inch video. 53 minutes.

*Latin America, An Overview.* See "General."

*Marrying.* (1984) "A rural wedding, followed by a look at the changing role of women in Chinese society.: PBS: The Heart of the Dragon. Beta, 3/4-inch video. 50 minutes.

Moravia, Alberto. (1976) "Profile/interview with Moravia about his writing, his social concerns, views on fascism and Italy, accompanied by dramatic readings from his novels." Facets Multimedia. Beta, 1/2-inch video. 55 minutes.

Moravia, Alberto. *The Conformist.* (1986) English version. Paramount Home Video. 1/2-inch video. 108 minutes.

Moravia, Alberto. *Two Women.* (1987) "A shopkeeper and her daughter flee Rome during World War II, and upon their return are brutally attacked by marauding soldiers. They are left traumatized, and must fight to restore dignity and value to their lives." Embassy Home Entertainment. 1/2-inch video. 99 minutes.

*Mother Ireland.* See "Violence."

*No Longer Silent.* (1987) "Gives an overview of degrading and cruel treatment of women in India. The women are organizing workshops and resource centers to help them become aware of the help that is available." National Film Board of Canada; International Film Bureau. 16 mm, 1/2-inch video. 57 minutes.

*Rape/Crisis.* (1983) Docudrama about sexual violence. PBS: Independent Focus Retrospective. Beta, 3/4-inch video. 87 minutes.

*Rape Is a Social Disease.* (1975) "The interrelationship of women's image and rape is depicted through classical art and modern advertising. Structural sexual roles indirectly indicate how violence against women is accepted in our society." Women in Focus. 3/4-inch video, special order formats. 28 minutes.

*Rape: The Savage Crime.* (1975) The procedures that follow when a woman reports a rape are examined. . . . The impersonal and often hostile attitudes displayed by police officers and medical examiners . . . recent police reforms, such as special rape units, that have been created to deal with the problem." The Center for Humanities. 1/2-inch video. 27 minutes.

*Saudi Arabia Today.* (1987) "Introduces viewers to the people, land, politics, and customs of this Middle-Eastern country." Modern Talking Picture Service. 3/4-inch video. 28 minutes.

*The Saudis.* (1980) "Politics and business in Saudia Arabia." Phoenix/BFA. Beta, VHS, 3/4-inch video. 49 minutes.

*A Sense of Honor.* (1984) "Condemns modern stereotypes of Arabic women and offers information on the lifestyle, beliefs, customs, and social situations of fundamentalist Islamic women." BBC Films, Inc. 1/2-inch video. 55 minutes.

*The Shadow of the West.* See "General."

Silko, Leslie Marmon. *Leslie Marmon Silko.* "Silko reads from her epic novel *Almanac of the Dead* and talks about a return to tribal values in the Americas." New Letters. 1 audiocassette. 29 minutes.

Silko, Leslie Marmon. *Running on the Edge of the Rainbow: Laguna Stories and Poems.* (1981) "Leslie Marmon Silko talks about the nature of Laguna storytelling, its functions, and more of the problems she has faced using Laguna stories in her own work." Univ. of Arizona. 1/2-inch video and transcript. 28 minutes.

*Taking Back the Night.* (1981) "This program provides a comprehensive look at the problem of violence against women." Washington Univ. in St. Louis. 3/4-inch video. 20 minutes.

*A Veiled Revolution.* (1982) "In 1932, revolutionary Egyptian women were the first to publicly cast off the veil. Wearing western dress, they demanded rights for women, the vote, and equal education. Yet today, old feminists look on with dismay as their granddaughters reject western dress, putting the veil back on again." Icarus Films NY. 1/2-inch video. 27 minutes.

*Women of the Toubou.* (1974) "The Toubou of the Sahara are a happy and cheerful people of grace, elegance, and dignity. Toubou women are treated as equals by the men, they share every aspect of life." Phoenix BFA Films & Video, Inc. 16 mm. 25 minutes.

*Women Under Siege* (1982). "Rashadiyah . . . had become the setting for a camp housing 14,000 Palestinian refugees. . . . Women play a crucial role . . . as mothers, teachers, political organizers, farm laborers, and fighters." Companion film to *A Veiled Revolution.* Icarus Films NY. 1/2-inch video. 26 minutes.

## Work: We Are What We Do

Angelou, Maya. (1979) "Angelou reads some of her poetry and talks about herself and her accomplishments as a writer." Tapes for Readers (Washington, D.C.). Sound cassette.

Angelou, Maya. (1986) The author reads *I Know Why the Caged Bird Sings* (abridged). Random House Audio Books. 2 sound cassettes. 179 minutes.

Angelou, Maya. *Black Women in the Women's Movement.* (1980) "Social activist Angela Davis, writer Maya Angelou, and other Black women discuss the role of the Black women in the women's movement." NPR (Washington, D.C.). Sound cassette. 29 minutes.

Angelou, Maya. *Making Magic in the World.* (1988) "Presents a trip from the Deep South to the heart of Africa and back again." New Dimensions Foundation. 1 cassette. 60 minutes.

Angelou, Maya. *Of Life and Poetry.* (1978) Encyclopaedia Americana/CBS News Audio Resource Library. Sound cassette.

Angelou, Maya. *Our Sheroes and Heroes.* (1983) "Angelou talks about her first friendship with a white woman, her sense of religion, . . . and the difference between white and black women." Pacifica Radio Archive (Los Angeles). Sound cassette. 34 minutes.

Angelou, Maya. (1974) "Angelou discusses her life in such places as Arkansas, San Francisco, Ghana, and Israel." Center for Cassette Studies. Sound cassette. 27 minutes.

*Bali: The Mask of Rangda.* (1974) "Authentic picture of a culture as yet untouched by the West." Hartley Film Foundation. Beta, VHS, 3/4-inch video. 30 minutes.

*Brazil.* (1985). "Vivid but sobering view of a world where the work ethic has replaced all else." MCA Home Video. 1/2-inch video. 131 minutes.

*Bridging the Culture Gap.* (1983) "Presents some of the cultural differences Americans must be attuned to and accept, in order to function effectively socially and in business overseas." Copeland Griggs (San Francisco). 1/2-inch video and guide. 28 minutes.

*Japan 2000.* See "The West and the World."

*Japan: The Nation Family.* See "The Family."

*Japan Reaches for the 21st Century.* See "The West and the World."

*The Japan They Don't Talk About.* (1986) "The lives of Japanese workers are depicted. Contrary to the belief that Japan is thriving and equal opportunities exist in the work force, this film presents the 70 percent of Japanese workers who are paid low wages for long hours under poor conditions." NBC International Films. 1/2-inch video. 52 minutes.

*Japan at Work.* (1989) "Three case studies illustrate how efficient and hard working the average Japanese worker is." Journal Films. Beta, VHS, 3/4-inch video, 30 minutes.

*Japanese Women.* See "Women and Men."

Film, Video, and Audiocassette

*Kottar: Model for Development.* (1979) "In southern India, fishermen, weavers, and other craftspeople have joined in cooperative ventures to increase their incomes and improve their lives. Kottar, the prototype for an entire network of production and marketing cooperation, is documented in several distinct segments." Catholic Relief Services. 16 mm. 18 minutes.

García Márquez, Gabriel. *Magic and Reality.* (1982) "Presents a literary history of García Márquez, through conversations with the author, his friends, and his critics. . . . Explores the history of Colombia." Films for the Humanities (Princeton, N.J.). 16 mm, 1/2-inch video. 60 minutes.

García Márquez, Gabriel. *Magic and Reality.* (1984) "Delves into the world of . . . García Márquez — where historical riots and levitating grandmothers appear to be equally real (or unreal). Shot on the Colombian coast in Aracataca, the Banana Zone, Cienaga, and Barranquilla . . . the film features the author himself and the people of whom he writes." 1/2-inch video. 60 minutes.

García Márquez, Gabriel. "The Solitude of Latin America." In *Faces, Mirrors, Masks: Twentieth-Century Latin American Fiction.* (1984) NPR (Washington, D. C.). Sound cassette. 30 minutes.

*No Longer Silent.* See "Women and Men."

*Two Factories: Japanese and American.* (1974) "A documentary comparing and contrasting the environment of two electronic firms: Sylvania in Batavia, New York, and Matsushita in Osaka, Japan. The film examines similarities and differences in needs, employees, and management." Beta, 3/4-inch video. 22 minutes.

Updike, John. *The Author in Conversation with Claire Tomalin.* (1986) "Updike discusses his life and works." The Roland Collection. 1/2-inch video. 52 minutes.

Updike, John. *What Makes Rabbit Run?: A Profile of John Updike.* "Documents the life and work of John Updike. Shows Updike on a promotional tour for his novel *Rabbit Is Rich;* at his childhood home, at the offices of *The New Yorker,* where he was a staff member in the fifties; and at home with his family." Barr Films. 16 mm, 1/2-inch video. 57 minutes.

*Vietnam: After the Fire.* (1988) "An award-winning, two part documentary which examines the Vietnam conflict." Cinema Guild. Beta, VHS, 3/4-inch video. 53 minutes.

*Vietnam Reconsidered.* (1988) Thomas Vallely, a state representative from Massachusetts, returned to Vietnam in August 1985, 16 years after he left as a Marine. This film documents his attempt to understand his past and present." Northern Lights Productions. Beta, VHS, 3/4-inch video. 15 minutes.

*Vietnam Under Communism.* (1989) "Examines what is going on in Vietnam now almost 20 years after the war ended." PBS Video. Beta, VHS, 3/4-inch video. 60 minutes.

*Village Man, City Man.* (1975) "Shows the life of a young mill worker in an industrial section of Delhi and follows him on a return visit to his village. Changes and continuities in his life are documented through conversations with his friends at the mill . . . and by observing his work. The film suggests that Western models of change and modernization do not necessarily apply to the Indian context." Univ. of Wisconsin. 16 mm. 40 minutes.

## We the People: Individuals and Institutions

*Americas in Transition.* See "General."

*The Bear's Embrace.* "Shows how the decade of rule by Nikita Khrushchev thrust the Soviet Union into a critical position of international leadership. . . . Covers his movement within the Communist Party in the Ukraine, through the Stalin era, his ascension to Party Secretary, his rise to full leadership, and his final collapse and removal." Learning Corporation of America. 16 mm. 24 minutes.

*Brazil: No Time for Tears*. See "Violence."

*Chile: Hasta Caundo?* See "Violence."

*China in Revolution*. (1989) "Recounts the thirty eight years between 1911 and 1949, during which China was transformed from a centuries-old empire into the world's largest Communist state." Coronet Multimedia. Two 1/2-inch videos. 58 minutes each.

*Crossing Borders: The Story of The Women's International League for Peace and Freedom*. See "The West and the World."

*Cuba: Angry Exiles*. (1984) "History of hostility between U.S. and Cuba." Journal Films. Beta, VHS, 3/4-inch video. 14 minutes.

*Cuba: In the Shadow of Doubt*. (1986) "Examines the origins of Castro's revolution and the current state of Cuban society, including the contrasts between its socialism and the political repression faced by the average person." Filmmakers' Library. VHS, 3/4-inch video. 58 minutes.

*Czechoslovakia in Chains*. (1983) "Examines 1968 Russian military coup of Czechoslovakia." King Features Entertainment. Beta, VHS, 3/4-inch video. 15 minutes.

*Germans and Their Men*. See "Women and Men."

Gordimer, Nadine. *City Lovers, Country Lovers: The Gordimer Stories*. (1984) MGM/UA Home Video. 1/2-inch video. 121 minutes.

Gordimer, Nadine. *The Author Reads "A City of the Dead," "A City of the Living," and "The Territary."* (1986) Spoken Arts. Sound cassette. 58 minutes.

*Guns, Drugs, and the CIA*. (1988) "Investigates the CIA and its use of drug money to finance covert activities. Concentrates on drug trafficking activities from the Vietnam War to the Contra affair." PBS Video (Alexandria, Va.). 1/2-inch video. 58 minutes.

Mandela, Nelson. *Nelson and Winnie Mandela: South African Leaders Against Apartheid*. "Profiles Nelson and Winnie Mandela. The Mandelas' history since Nelson's imprisonment [but before his release] is revealed through interviews with Winnie, as well as with other friends who have shared the couple's fight against apartheid." NPR (Washington, D.C.). Sound cassette. 29 minutes.

Mandela, Nelson. *Mandela*. (1987) "Traces the life of Nelson Mandela through the founding of the African National Congress, his marriage to Winnie, and his trial and imprisonment for treason." HBO Video (New York). 1/2-inch video. 135 minutes.

Mandela, Nelson. *Mandela in America*. (1990) "An insider's view of the most memorable moments of Nelson Mandela's trip and his message on the continuing struggle against apartheid." Globalvision (New York, NY). VHS, 3/4-inch video. 90 minutes.

Mandela, Nelson. *Part of My Soul Went with Him: Dramatic Readings Based on Journals and Letters of Winnie and Nelson Mandela*. (1985) Norton Publishers (New York). Sound cassette. 60 minutes.

Mao and the Cultural Revolution. See "The Family"

*Missing. (1984)* "Based on an actual event, the story involves the search by a wife and father for a young American writer and filmmaker who has disappeared during a South American military coup." MCA Video. 1/2-inch video. 122 minutes.

Moravia, Alberto. *The Conformist*. See "Women and Men."

*Nigeria — Problems of Nation Building*. See "The Family."

*Planting Seeds for Peace*. See "Landmarks and Turning Points."

*Poland*. See "Violence."

*Poland: A Year of Solidarity*. See "Violence."

*Return from Silence: China's Revolutionary Writers*. (1983) "Interviews with five writers are intercut with old photographs, archival footage, and scenes of performances of the writers' major works. A compelling and enlightening look at recent Chinese history." 1/2-inch video. 58 minutes.

*Russia: Off the Record.* (1988) "American television crews talk to typical Soviet citizens about how their life really is." Journal Films. Beta, VHS, 3/4-inch video. 58 minutes.

*South Africa Belongs to Us.* (1980) "Interviews with five women living under apartheid. . . . Includes brief interviews with Winnie Mandela and other women involved in the anti-apartheid movement." California Newsreel. 1/2-inch video. 35 minutes.

*South Africa: The Solution.* (1989) "Historical factors are given to show why South Africa is in the state it is today. A view is also given of how it might look in the future." Journal Films. Beta, VHS, 3/4-inch video. 38 minutes.

*South Africa Today: A Question of Power.* (1988) "Two South African newspaper editors, one black, one white, talk about the problems their country faces." Journal Films. Beta, VHS, 3/4-inch video. 55 minutes.

*Spear of the Nation: The Story of the African National Congress.* (1986) California Newsreel (San Francisco). 1/2-inch video. 55 minutes.

*Stalin: Man and Image.* (1979) "Documents Stalin's rise to supreme power in the Soviet Union from the pre-revolutionary period through the late 1930's. Focuses on Stalin's use of image to expand his power." Learning Corporation of America. 16 mm. 24 minutes.

*Stand Your Ground.* "The South African group Juluka's response to human rights abuses in that country." Warner Bros. (251551-1).

*Tools of Exploitation.* See "The West and the World."

*Witness to Apartheid.* "A look at how racism and police violence affect children." PBS: Intercom. 1/2-inch video. 50 minutes.

Women Under Siege. See "Women and Men."

*Zimbabwe.* (1988) "Interviews with Robert Mugabe, Joshua Nkomo, Ian Smith, and others trace the history of Zimbabwe through the European search for gold and minerals to the overthrow of white minority rule in the 1970s." Cinema Guild. Beta, VHS, 3/4-inch video. 30 minutes.

*Zimbabwe: The New Struggle.* (1985) "The current political, social, and economic development of the newly independent nation of Zimbabwe is explored." Icarus Films. 3/4-inch video. 58 minutes.

## Violence

*48 Hours on Crack Street.* (1986) A presentation of CBS News (New York). 1/2-inch video. 120 minutes.

Achebe, Chinua. "Achebe discusses the impact of colonialism on his culture and relates that he began his own writing in reaction to certain stereotypes in western literature." Transcription Feature Service (London). Sound cassette. 30 minutes.

Achebe, Chinua. Interviewed by Jack Ludwis. (1968) "Discussion of the Nigerian-Biafran war, and the involvement of . . . writers in the conflict." Transcription Feature Service (London). Sound cassette, no. 2 on side 2. 34 minutes.

Achebe, Chinua. Interviewed by Robert Serumaga. (1967) "The author discusses his childhood, and the political situation reflected in his novels *Things Fall Apart, A Man of the People, and Arrow of God.*" Transcription Feature Service (London). Sound cassette, no. 1 on side 1. 22 minutes.

Achebe, Chinua, reads *Arrow of God.* (1988) "Achebe reading excerpts from two works: *Arrow of God*, a tale of the colonial and missionary encroachment upon traditional Ibo culture, and *Anthills of the Savannah*, a novel about the making of a dictator in contemporary Africa." American Audio Prose Library. Sound cassette. 88 minutes.

*All Our Lives.* (1986) "Women who were radicals during the Spanish Civil War discuss their activities and experiences as social reformers. Members of the Confederación Nacional de Trabajo, they had occupations ranging from journalism to nursing and technology." In Spanish with English subtitles. The Media Project, Cinema Guild. 1/2-inch video. 54 minutes.

*Americas in Transition.* See "General."

*Apocalypse Now.* (1979) Based on Conrad's *Heart of Darkness,* among the first convincing renderings of the Vietnam experience. Paramount Home Video. Beta, VHS. 150 minutes.

*Beyond War: A New Way of Thinking.* (1983) "Uses brief statements edited from . . . interviews to explore the reasons why war has become obsolete as a means of resolving conflict. . . . The possibility of new ways to relate to other nations, other cultures, other peoples are expressed by many of those interviewed." 16 mm, 1/2-inch video.

*Brazil: No Time for Tears.* (1971) "Nine recently released Brazilian political prisoners recount their ordeals under torture." Tricontinental Film Center. 16 mm. 40 minutes.

*Chickamauga.* (1968) "Adaptation of Ambrose Bierce's story which creates a symbolic world of the horrors of war as a little boy wanders away from home, reaches a battlefield, plays soldier among the dead and dying, and returns to find his house burned and his family slain." Educational Films, Inc. 16 mm.

*Chile: By Reason or By Force.* (1983) "The ten year anniversary of the military overthrow of Salvador Allende's Popular Unity coaltion government is documented." Cinema Guild. Beta, VHS, 3/4-inch video. 60 minutes.

*Chile: Hasta Caundo?* (1986) "Oscar nominated, documents the political repression in Chile under General Augusto Pinochet's brutal dictatorship." Filmmakers' Library, Inc. VHS, 3/4-inch video. 57 minutes.

*Chile: I Don't Take Your Name in Vain.* (1984) "The 'National Days of Protest,' which challenged the military dictatorship in Chile during 1985, are chronicled." Icarus Films. 3/4-inch video. 55 minutes.

*China in Revolution.* See "We the People."

*The Deer Hunter.* (1978) "The effect of the Vietnam war on the lives of several Pennsylvania steelworkers." MCA Home Video. Beta, VHS. 183 minutes.

*Gaza Ghetto.* (1984) "The Gaza Strip's half-million Palestinians live in the Israel-occupied territory most neglected by the outside world. This film investigates Israeli policy toward the area and interviews Israeli officials. The reality of life for the people . . . is brought into focus by the film's portrayal of the daily life of one family." Icarus Films (New York). 1/2-inch video. 82 minutes.

*Guernica — Pablo Picasso.* (1953) "The horror and ugliness of war and inhumanity are passionately depicted in Picasso's painting *Guernica.* Shows an understanding and empathy necessary to render one of the great artistic achievements of the 20th century." 16 mm. 15 minutes.

*The Hooded Men.* (1986) "This documentary describes methods of torture used on political prisoners in a number of countries." CBC Enterprises. 1/2-inch video. 56 minutes.

*The Hundred Years War.* (1983) "Focuses on the lives of individual Palestinians in Israel and on the Gush Emunim movement among Israeli settlers." Icarus Films (New York). Two 1/2-inch videos. 98 minutes each.

*Iran: A Righteous Republic.* See "The Family."

*Irish News, British Stories.* (1989) "Examines the way the political situation of Northern Ireland is portrayed on British television." Faction Films. 1/2-inch video.

*Israel — The Promise of the Jewish People.* See "The Family."

Film, Video, and Audiocassette

*Israel and the Arab States.* See "General."

*Israel: The Golan and Sinai Question.* (1984) "Explores the history of Golan and Sinai, their strategic values, and their roles in the Middle East Peace Plan." Journal Films. Beta. VHS, 3/4-inch video. 19 minutes.

*Israel: The Other Reality.* "Israel's Arabs and Jews try to explain why the hatred between these two races continues after thousands of years." Wombat Productions. Beta, VHS, 3/4-inch video. 58 minutes.

*Israel vs. the PLO.* (1990) "Examines how the invasion of Lebanon radically changed the character of the country." MPI Home Video. VHS. 60 minutes.

*Israel's Shattered Dreams.* (1988) "1988 Cable's Best Documentary." MPI Home Video. VHS. 173 minutes.

*The Killing Fields.* (1984) Adapted from the story "The Death and Life of Dith Pran" by Sydney Schanberg, about "a journalist who covered the war in Cambodia . . . and Dith, the translator and aide, who is exiled to Cambodian labor camps where millions have died." Warner Home Video. 1/2-inch video. 142 minutes.

*Latin America, An Overview.* See "General"

*Legacies.* (1983) "Shows the violence and destruction that have asssailed the peopleof Vietnam, Laos, and Cambodia, even since the withdrawal of U.S. troops. Discusses the change in Chinese and American relations and the lack of formal diplomatic relations of the United States with Vietnam." Films Inc. (Chicago). 1/2-inch video.

Miloz, Czeslaw. *Fire.* (1987) "The author reads selections from *Unattainable Earth* and other works. Some selections are in English and Polish." Watershed Fdn. Washington, D.C.). Sound cassette.

*Missing.* See "We the People."

Moravia, Alberto. *Two Women.* See "Women and Men."

*Mother Ireland.* (1989) "Examines the centuries-old imagery which has portrayed Ireland as a woman and discusses the social function of these stereotypes of Irish womanhood, and their relationship to the nationalist struggle and Irish women today." Celtic Production (NY). 1/2-inch video. 52 minutes.

*Nigeria: Africa in Miniature.* See "The Family."

*Nigeria — Problems of Nation Building.* See "The Family."

*No Neutral Ground.* (1983) "The fate of two of Vietnam's weaker neighbors was decided as the south disintegrated. The U.S. extension of the war into Laos and Cambodia to stop attacks and supplies from across those borders hurt those countries more that it hurt the object of the attack." Films Inc. (Chicago). 1/2-inch video.

*Northern Ireland, Past and Present.* (1986) "Giovanni Costigan lectures on the religious and political struggle in Northern Ireland.: Bellingham, Wash. 1/2-inch video. 53 minutes.

*Palestinians.* (1983) "Palestinian men and women of various ages describe how they feel as refugees in foreign countries. They describe the problems of scattered families and the lack of understanding by outsiders." Martha Stuart Communications. 1/2-inch video. 29 minutes.

"Planting Seeds for Peace." See "Landmarks and Turning Points."

*Poland, A European Country.* See "We the People."

*Poland.* (1988) "The story of vigorous people who have struggled a long time to maintain their independence." Journal Films. Beta, VHS, 3/4-inch video. 26 minutes.

*Poland: A Year of Solidarity.* (1984) "Charts history of the Solidarity movement." Journal Films. Beta, VHS, 3/4-inch video, 25 minutes.

*South Africa Belongs to Us.* See "We the People."

*Street Drugs and Medicine Chests.* (1986) "Recovering addicts tell their stories and debunk some commonly held myths about drugs. All the addicts are white and middle-class." PBS Video (Alexandria, Va.). 1/2-inch video. 18 minutes.

*The Struggles for Poland.* (1988) "Documents the history of Poland in the 20th century through the use of archival films, newsreels, stills, interviews, and readings from novels and poems." Companion book also issued: *The Struggles for Poland* by Neal Ascherson. PBS Video (Alexandria, Va.). 1/2-inch video, 9 cassettes, 58 minutes each.

*Tiananmen Square: A Blow by Blow Account.* (1989) SUNY Albany Audiovisual Center. 1/2-inch video.

*Tiananmen Square Incident.* (1989) "Commentary on the Tiananmen Square incident by one of the student leaders." Univ. of Iowa Audiovisual Center. 1/2-inch video. 35 minutes.

*To Live for Ireland* and *At the Edge of the Union.* "Different strategies in the Irish struggle." PBS: Intercom. 80 minutes.

*Torture in the Eighties.* (1984) "About Amnesty International's investigations of and campaign to stop torture around the world." Amnesty International. 1/2-inch video. 13 minutes.

*Tragedy at Tiananmen: The Untold Story.* (1989). "Various news reporters give firsthand accounts of the massacre of student protesters in Tiananmen Square in 1989." Coronet Multimedia. 1/2-inch video. 48 minutes.

*Vietnam: After the Fire.* See "Work."

*Vietnam: Images of War.* (1978) "A film montage of scenes which made headline news coverage during the 15 years of the Vietnam War. . . . Contains graphic scenes of war; pre-screening recommended." Journal Films. Beta, 1/2-inch video, 3/4-inch video. 26 minutes.

*Vietnam Reconsidered.* See "Work."

*Vietnam Under Communism.* See "Work."

*Vietnam: The War at Home.* (1978) "Featuring a wide array of news and interview footage, this acclaimed documentary examines the effects of the Vietnam political ambiguities on the home front, concentrating on student activities at the University of Wisconsin. Nominated for Best Documentary Oscar." MPI Home Video. Beta, 1/2-inch video. 100 minutes.

*Vietnam War Story II.* (1988) Three short, made-for-TV war stories set in Vietnam: "An Old Ghost Walks the Earth," "R & R," and "The Fragging." HBO Home Video. 1/2-inch video. Closed captioned. 90 minutes.

*Vietnamese & American Veterans.* (1984) "Two American veterans and two South Vietnamese veterans discuss the war from their own points of view." Univ. of California, Santa Barbara. Beta, 1/2-inch video, 3/4-inch video. 30 minutes.

Walker, Alice, *"Nineteen Fifty-Five".* (1981) Read by Alice Walker. "A story about the exploitation of black musicians by the white rock 'n' roll industry." American Audio Prose. 1 cassette. 36 minutes.

# DIRECTORY OF AUDIOVISUAL DISTRIBUTORS

AIMS Media
6901 Woodley Ave.
Van Nuys, CA 91406-4878
(818) 785-4111
1-800-367-2467

American Audio Prose Library
P.O. Box 842
1015 E. Broadway
Suite 284
Columbia, MO 65205
1-800-447-2275

Amnesty International
Publications
322 8th Avenue
New York, NY 10001
(212) 807-8400

Atlantis Productions
1252 La Granada Drive
Thousand Oaks, CA 91360
(805) 495-2790

Avatar Learning, Inc.
760 La Cienega Blvd.
Los Angeles, CA 90069

Barr Films, Inc.
P.O. Box 7878
Irwindale, CA 91706
(818) 338-7878
1-800-234-7879

BBC Films, Inc.
Video Distribution Center
P.O. Box 644
Paramus, NJ 07652
(212) 239-0530

Benchmark Films, Inc.
145 Scarborough Rd.
Blaircliff Manor
New York, NY 10510

Books on Tape
729 Farad
Costa Mesa, CA 92627
(714) 548-5525

Britannica Films
310 South Michigan Avenue
Chicago, IL 60604
(312) 347-7958

CBS Video Library
1211 Avenue of the Americas
New York, NY 10036
(212) 975-3454

California Newsreel
149 Ninth St., Rm. 420
San Francisco, CA 94103

Canadian Film-Makers' Distribution
Center
67A Portland St.
Toronto M5V 2M9
CANADA
(416) 593-1808

Catholic Relief Services
1011 First Ave.
New York, NY 10022

Celtic Productions
164 E. 33rd St.
New York, NY
(212) 689-4853

The Center for Humanities
Communications Park
Box 1000
Mount Kisco, NY 10549
1-800-431-1242

Cinema Guild
The Media Project
1697 Broadway, Rm. 802
New York, NY 10019
(212) 246-5522

Copeland Griggs Productions, Inc.
302 23rd Ave., Suite 10
San Francisco, CA 94121
(415) 668-4200

Cornell University
Audio-Visual Resources Center
8 Research Pk.
Ithaca, NY 14850
(607) 255-2091

Coronet, The Multimedia Co.
108 Wilmot Rd.
Deerfield, IL 60015
1-800-621-2131

Dove Books on Tape
12711 Ventura Blvd., Suite 250
Studio City, CA 91604
(818) 762-6662
1-800-345-9945

Educational Film and Video Project
5332 College Ave., Suite 101
Oakland, CA 94618
(415) 655-9050

Educational Films, Inc.
5547 N. Ravenwood
Chicago, IL 60640-1199

Embassy Home Entertainment
1901 Avenue of the Stars
Los Angeles, CA 90067
(213) 460-7200

Encyclopaedia Britannica
Educational Corp.
425 N. Michigan Ave.
Chicago, IL 60611
1-800-558-6968

Ergo Media
P.O. Box 2037
Teaneck, NJ 07666
(201) 692-0404

Facets Multimedia
1517 W. Fullerton Ave.
Chicago, IL 60614
1-800-331-6197

Filmmakers' Library
133 E. 58th St.
New York, NY 10022
(212) 355-6545

Films for the Humanities
P.O. Box 2053
Princeton, NJ 08543
(609) 452-1128
1-800-257-5126

Films, Inc.
5547 N. Ravenswood Ave.
Chicago, IL 60640-1199
(312) 878-2600, ext. 44
1-800-323-4222, ext. 44

Flower Films
10341 San Pablo Avenue
El Cerrito, CA 94530

Giorni Poetry Systems Records
P.O. Box 295
North Greece, NY 14515
(716) 392-2871

Great Plains National Instructional
Television Library
University of Nebraska at Lincoln
P.O. Box 80669
Lincoln, NE 68501-0669
(402) 472-2007
1-800-228-4630

HBO Video
1370 Avenue of the Americas
New York, NY 10019
(212) 977-8990
1-800-648-7650

Hartley Film Foundation
Rock Road
Cos Cob, CT 06807
(203) 869-1818

Icarus Films
153 Waverly Pl., 6th Floor
New York, NY 10014
(212) 727-1711

International Film Bureau
332 S. Michigan Ave.
Chicago, IL 60604
(312) 427-4545

International Film Foundation, Inc.
155 West 72nd Street
New York, New York 10023
(212) 580-1111

Journal Films
930 Pitner Ave.
Evanston, IL 60202
1-800-323-5448

King Features Entertainment
235 E. 45th St.
New York, NY 10017
(212) 682-5600
1-800-223-7383

Learning Corporation of America
108 Wilmot Rd.
Deerfield, IL 60015-9990
(312) 940-1260
1-800-621-2131

Live Home Video
15400 Sherman Way
Suite 500
Van Nuys, CA 91406
(818) 908-0303

MCA Home Video
70 Universal City Plaza
Universal City, CA 91608
(818) 777-4300

MGM/UA Home Video
10,000 W. Washington Blvd.
Culver City, CA 90232-2728
(213) 280-6000

MPI Home Video
15825 Rob Roy Dr.
Oak Forest, IL 60452
(312) 687-7881

Martha Stuart Communications, Inc.
147 W. 22nd St.
New York, NY 10011
(212) 255-2718

McGraw Hill
P.O. Box 674
Via De La Valle,
Del Mar, CA 92014

Media Home Entertainment
5730 Buckingham Pkwy.
Culver City, CA 90230
(213) 216-7900
1-800-421-4509

Modern Talking Picture Service
5000 Park Street North
St. Petersburg, FL 33709
(813) 541-7571
1-800-243-6877 (to order)

National Film Board of Canada
1251 Avenue of the Americas, 16th Floor
New York, NY 10020-1173
(212) 586-5131

National Geographic Society
17 and M St. NW
Washington, D.C. 20036

National Public Radio
Audio Services
2025 M St., NW
Washington, DC 20036
(202) 822-2000

New Day Films
1221 W. 27th St.
Room 902
New York, NY 10001
(212) 645-8210

New Dimensions Foundations
P.O. Box 410510
San Francisco, CA 94141
(415) 563-8899

New Letters on Air
5216 Rockhill
Kansas City, MO 64110

New Yorker Films Video
16 W. 61st St.
New York, NY 10023
(212) 247-6110

Northern Lights Productions
276 Newbury Street
Boston, MA 02116
(617) 267-0391

W. W. Norton Publishers
Trade Sales Department
500 Fifth Avenue
New York, NY 10110
(212) 790-4314

PBS Video
1320 Braddock Pl.
Alexandria, VA 22314
(703) 739-5380

Paramount Home Video
5555 Melrose Ave.
Los Angeles, CA 90038
(213) 956-5000

Phoenix Films/American Film Institute
468 Park Ave. South
New York, NY 10016
(212) 684-5910
1-800-221-1274

Playhouse Video
1211 Avenue of the Americas
New York, NY 10036
(212) 819-3238

Portland State University
Continuing Education Program
P.O. Box 1491
Portland, OR 97207-1491
(503) 725-4891

Random House Audio Books
201 East 50th St.
New York, NY 10022
(212) 872-8235
1-800-638-6460

The Roland Collection
3120 Pawtucket Rd.
Northbrook, IL 60062
(708) 291-2230

Sony Video Communications
Tape Production Department
700 W. Artesia Blvd.
Compton, CA 90220
(213) 537-4300, ext. 331

Spoken Arts
310 North Avenue
New Rochelle, NY 10801
(914) 636-5482
1-800-537-3617

Tapes for Readers
5078 Fulton Street, NW
Washington, DC 20016
(202) 362-4585

United World Films, Inc.
221 Park Avenue S.
New York, NY 10003

University of Arizona Video Campus
Harvill Bldg., No. 76
Box 4
Tuscon, AZ 85721
(602) 621-1735 or -5143

University of California, Santa Barbara
Instructional Department
Santa Barbara, CA 93106
(805) 961-3518

University of Iowa Audiovisual Center
C–215 Seashore Hall
University of Iowa
Iowa City, IA 52242
(319) 335-2539

University of Wisconsin
University Extension
1327 University Ave.
P.O. Box 2093
Madison, WI 53701

Vestron Video
1010 Washington Blvd.
Box 10382
Stamford, CT 06901
(203) 978-5400

Vladimir Bibic Productions
3490 E. Foothill Blvd.
Pasadena, CA 91107

Warner Home Video
4000 Warner Blvd.
Burbank, CA 91522
(818) 954-6000

Washington University
Learning Resources Video Center
George W. Brown School of Social Work
Campus Box 1196
St. Louis, MO 63130
(314) 889-6612 or -6683

Watershed Foundation
6925 Willow St., NW, Suite 201
Washington, DC 20012
(202) 722-9105

Wombat Productions
Division of Cortech, Inc.
250 W. 57th St., Suite 916
New York, NY 10019
(212) 315-2502

Women in Focus
849 Beatty St.
Vancouver, BC V6B 2M6
CANADA
(604) 872-2250

Women Make Movies
225 Lafayette Street
Suite 212
New York, NY 10012
(212) 925-0606

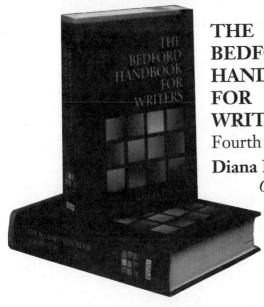

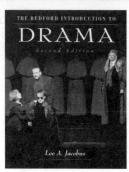
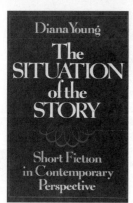

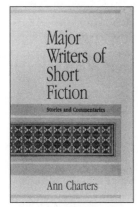
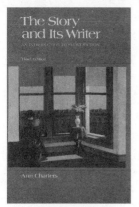

Bedford Books *of* St. Martin's Press